Toronto and the Australian National University and a regular presenter
of BBC Radio ... s include
The Mitrokhi... breaking
studies on the ... ory.

From M·I·V· wishing you
Mankinds Immortal Victory
in the New Year · 1918

DIEU ET MON DROIT

THE HIDDEN HAND

MI5's self-image at the end of 1917 on a Christmas/New Year card designed by
its deputy head, Eric Holt-Wilson, and drawn by the leading illustrator, Byam
Shaw. MI5, in the guise of a masked Britannia, impales the loathsome figure
of Subversion with her monogrammed trident before he can stab the British
fighting man in the back and prevent him achieving 'Mankind's Immortal
Victory' – MIV (MI5 in pseudo-roman form).

(*opposite*) The Security Service's all-seeing eye with a slightly unorthodox interwar
Latin motto intended to mean 'Security is the reward of unceasing vigilance.'

CHRISTOPHER ANDREW

The Defence of the Realm

The Authorized History of MI5

PENGUIN BOOKS

PENGUIN BOOKS

Published by the Penguin Group
Penguin Books Ltd, 80 Strand, London WC2R ORL, England
Penguin Group (USA), Inc., 375 Hudson Street, New York, New York 10014, USA
Penguin Group (Canada), 90 Eglinton Avenue East, Suite 700, Toronto, Ontario, Canada M4P 2Y3
(a division of Pearson Penguin Canada Inc.)
Penguin Ireland, 25 St Stephen's Green, Dublin 2, Ireland
(a division of Penguin Books Ltd)
Penguin Group (Australia), 250 Camberwell Road, Camberwell, Victoria 3124, Australia
(a division of Pearson Australia Group Pty Ltd)
Penguin Books India Pvt Ltd, 11 Community Centre, Panchsheel Park,
New Delhi – 110 017, India
Penguin Group (NZ), 67 Apollo Drive, Rosedale, North Shore 0632, New Zealand
(a division of Pearson New Zealand Ltd)
Penguin Books (South Africa) (Pty) Ltd, 24 Sturdee Avenue, Rosebank, Johannesburg 2196, South Africa

Penguin Books Ltd, Registered Offices: 80 Strand, London WC2R ORL, England

www.penguin.com

First published by Allen Lane 2009
Published with updated material in Penguin Books 2010
1

Set in 10.13/13.8 pt Sabon
Typeset by TexTech International
Printed in Great Britain by Clays Ltd, St Ives plc

A CIP catalogue record for this book is available from the British Library

ISBN: 978-0-141-02330-4

www.greenpenguin.co.uk

Penguin Books is committed to a sustainable future
for our business, our readers and our planet.
The book in your hands is made from paper
certified by the Forest Stewardship Council.

Contents

List of Illustrations   viii
Foreword by the Director General of the Security Service   xv
Preface   xix
Acknowledgements   xxii

Section A
The German Threat, 1909–1919

Introduction: The Origins of the Secret Service Bureau   3

1 'Spies of the Kaiser': Counter-Espionage before the First World War   29

2 The First World War: Part 1 – The Failure of German Espionage   53

3 The First World War: Part 2 – The Rise of Counter-Subversion   84

Section B
Between the Wars

Introduction: MI5 and its Staff – Survival and Revival   113

1 The Red Menace in the 1920s   139

2 The Red Menace in the 1930s   160

3 British Fascism and the Nazi Threat   186

Section C
The Second World War

Introduction: The Security Service and its Wartime Staff: 'From Prison to Palace'   217

1 Deception   241

  2 Soviet Penetration and the Communist Party   263
  3 Victory   283

Section D
The Early Cold War

Introduction: The Security Service and its Staff in the Early
  Cold War   319
  1 Counter-Espionage and Soviet Penetration: Igor Gouzenko
     and Kim Philby   339
  2 Zionist Extremists and Counter-Terrorism   350
  3 VENONA and the Special Relationships with the United
     States and Australia   365
  4 Vetting, Atom Spies and Protective Security   380
  5 The Communist Party of Great Britain, the Trade
     Unions and the Labour Party   400
  6 The Hunt for the 'Magnificent Five'   420
  7 The End of Empire: Part 1   442
  8 The End of Empire: Part 2   462
  9 The Macmillan Government: Spy Scandals and the Profumo
     Affair   483
 10 FLUENCY: Paranoid Tendencies   503
 11 The Wilson Government 1964–1970: Security, Subversion
     and 'Wiggery-Pokery'   522

Section E
The Later Cold War

Introduction: The Security Service and its Staff in the Later
  Cold War   547
  1 Operation FOOT and Counter-Espionage in the 1970s   565
  2 The Heath Government and Subversion   587
  3 Counter-Terrorism and Protective Security in the Early 1970s   600
  4 The 'Wilson Plot'   627
  5 Counter-Terrorism and Protective Security in the
     Later 1970s   644
  6 The Callaghan Government and Subversion   656
  7 The Thatcher Government and Subversion   670

8 Counter-Terrorism and Protective Security in the Early 1980s   683
9 Counter-Espionage in the Last Decade of the Cold War   706
10 Counter-Terrorism and Protective Security in the
   Later 1980s   734
11 The Origins of the Security Service Act   753

Section F
After the Cold War

1 The Transformation of the Security Service   771
2 Holy Terror   799
3 After 9/11   813

Conclusion: The First Hundred Years of the Security Service   841

Appendix 1: Directors and Director Generals, 1909–2009   863
Appendix 2: Security Service Strength, 1909–2009   864
Appendix 3: Nomenclature and Responsibilities of Security
   Service Branches/Divisions, 1914–1994   865

Notes   875
Bibliography   1003
Index   1019

List of Illustrations

Plates

1 Vernon Kell (Hulton Deutsch Collection/Orbis)

2 Major (later Brigadier General) James Edmonds (National Army Museum)

3 William Le Queux with his publisher (Frederic G. Hodsoll/National Portrait Gallery, London)

4 William Melville (By kind permission of Andrew Cook)

5 Gustav Steinhauer (in disguise) (Steinhauer, *The Kaiser's Master Spy: The Story as Told by Himself*, John Lane/The Bodley Head Ltd, 1930)

6 Winston Churchill, Sidney Street Siege, 1911 (Hulton Archive/Getty Images)

7 William Hinchley Cooke in German military uniform (Service Archives)

8 MI9 Chemical Branch staff testing for secret writing (KV 1/73)

9 Carl Lody (*Queer People* by Basil Thompson, Hodder & Stoughton Ltd, 1922)

10 Karl Müller (Popperfoto/Getty Images)

11 Maldwyn Haldane with Registry staff, 1918 (Service Archives)

12 Vernon Kell with heads of branches, 1918 (Service Archives)

13 Staff celebrating the Armistice on the roof of Waterloo House, 1918 (Service Archives)

14 Letter from Vernon Kell to staff on Armistice Day (Service Archives)

15 Maxwell Knight (Norman Parkinson Archive)

16 Jane Archer, 1924 (family archives)

17 Percy Glading, 1942 (© Metropolitan Police Authority 2009)

18 Melita Norwood, 1938 (Service Archives)

19 Melita Norwood, 1999 (Tony Harris/PA Archive/Press Association Images)

20 Message to Melita Norwood from her wartime controller, 1999 (by kind permission of David Burke)

21 Christopher Draper with Adolf Hitler, 1932 (*The Mad Major* by Christopher Draper, Air Review Ltd, 1962)

22 Christopher Draper flying under Westminster Bridge (*The Mad Major* by Christopher Draper, Air Review Ltd, 1962)

23 Wolfgang zu Putlitz's passport in the name of William Putter, 1938 (Service Archives)

24 Jona 'Klop' Ustinov, 1920 (Service Archives)

25 Dick White, *c.* 1939 (Service Archives)

26 Staff relaxing at Wormwood Scrubs, 1940 (Service Archives)

27 Wormwood Scrubs office, November 1939 (Mary Evans Picture Library/Illustrated London News)

28 Vernon Kell at Wormwood Scrubs, 1940 (Service Archives)

29 Folkert van Koutrik, *c.* 1940 (Service Archives)

30 Anthony Blunt in military uniform, 1940 (Service Archives)

31 Surveillance photograph of John Gollan, 1942 (Service Archives)

32 Camp 020 (Imperial War Museum HU66759)

33 Robin 'Tin-eye' Stephens (Service Archives)

34 J. C. Masterman (Service Archives)

35 Thomas Argyll 'Tar' Robertson (Service Archives)

36 Juan Pujol (GARBO) with MBE, 1984 (© Solo Syndication/Associated Newspapers Ltd)

37 Tomás 'Tommy' Harris (Service Archives)

38 Mary Sherer (Service Archives)

39 Nathalie 'Lily' Sergueiev (TREASURE) with her Abwehr case officer, Major Emil Kliemann, Lisbon, March 1944 (TNA KV 2/466)

40 Nathalie 'Lily' Sergueiev's dog, Babs (TNA KV 2/466)

41 Guy Liddell with his brother, David Liddell (Service Archives)

42 Victor Rothschild, *c.* 1940 (Service Archives)

43 German bomb hidden in a crate of onions, February 1944 (KV 4/23)

44 Klaus Fuchs (Service Archives)

45 'Jim' Skardon and Henry Arnold (Service Archives)

46 Sir John Shaw (Copyright unknown, courtesy of Harry S. Truman Library)

47 Aden, 1963 (Former member of staff, private collection)

48 Roger Hollis (Service Archives)

49 Jomo Kenyatta at Lancaster House, 1963 (PA/PA Archive/Press Association Images)

50 Gordon Lonsdale (Service Archives)

51 Harry Houghton and Ethel Gee, 1960 (Service Archives)

52 Charles Elwell, 1960 (Service Archives)

53 Evgeni Ivanov, 1961 (Service Archives)

54 The Soviet service attachés' address written in lipstick (Service Archives)

55 Evgeni Ivanov sketched by Stephen Ward (Camera Press, London)

56 Milicent Bagot with CBE, 1967 (family archives)

57 Bert Ramelson and Lawrence Daly, 1969 (Service Archives)

58 Betty Reid, 1972 (Service Archives)

59 An MI5 observation post, c. 1970 (Service Archives)

60 Oleg Lyalin, 1971 (Service Archives)

61 Soviet intelligence officers leaving the UK after Operation FOOT, 1971 (© Mirrorpix)

62 Registry staff carrying out 'look-ups' in the card index, c. 1970 (Service Archives)

63 Patrick Walker and Stephen Lander, 1984 (former member of staff, private collection)

64 Cricket score card, 23 June 1984 (Service Archives)

65 Oleg Gordievsky, 1982 (Service Archives)

66 Mr and Mrs Arkadi Guk (© Solo Syndication/Associated Newspapers Ltd)

67 Václav Jelínek, Czech illegal known as Erwin Van Haarlem, 1988 (Service Archives)

68 Van Haarlem's kitchen at the time of his arrest, 2 April 1988 (© Metropolitan Police Authority 2009)

69 PIRA mortar attack on Downing Street, February 1991 (© Metropolitan Police Authority 2009)

70 Donal Gannon and Gerard Hanratty, Operation AIRLINES, 1996 (Service Archives)

71 Siobhan O'Hanlon, Gibraltar, February 1988 (Service Archives)

72 Ceremonial Guard, Gibraltar (Service Archives)

73 Moinul Abedin, Operation LARGE, 2000 (Service Archives)

74 Omar Khyam and Mohammed Momin Khawaja, Operation CREVICE, 2004 (Service Archives)

75 Dhiren Barot, Operation RHYME, 2004 (© Metropolitan Police Authority 2009)

76 Muktah Said Ibrahim and Ramzi Mohammed, Operation HAT, July 2005 (Solo Syndication/Associated Newspaper Ltd)

77 Yassin Hassan Omar, Operation HAT, July 2005 (© Metropolitan Police Authority)

78 Ramzi Mohammed and Yassin Omar at a training camp, Cumbria, 2004 (© Metropolitan Police Authority 2009)

79 Bilal Abdulla purchasing a gas canister, 2007 (© Metropolitan Police Authority 2009)

80 Gas canister in failed bomb attack, London, 2007 (© Metropolitan Police Authority 2009)

81 Operational training (Service Archives)

82 Jonathan Evans in the Intelligence Operations Centre, 2009 (Service Archives)

With thanks to the Metropolitan Police for supplying pictures 17, 68, 69, 75, 77, 78, 79 and 80.

Integrated Illustrations

Frontispiece: 'The Hidden Hand', New Year card, 1918 (Service Archives)

Title page: The Security Service's all-seeing eye (Service Archives)

xviii Cartoon, *Spectator*, 29 November 1986 (© Michael Heath. Courtesy of the British Cartoon Archive, University of Kent)

xxiv MI5 Headquarters, 1909–2009 (all photographs from Service Archives except for 1 and 3, courtesy of the City of Westminster Archives)

16 German espionage in Essex, 1908 (The *Graphic*, 15 July 1908)

22 Memorandum recording Vernon Kell's appointment to the Secret Service Bureau, 1909 (TNA WO 106/6292)

24 Vernon Kell's letter of acceptance, 1909 (TNA WO 106/6292)

57 William Hinchley Cooke's War Office Pass, 1914 (Service Archives)

57 William Hinchley Cooke's Alien Registration Certificate, 1917 (Service Archives)

60   Maldwyn Haldane and Registry staff (Joseph Sassoon, Service Archives)

62   'Miss Thinks She is Right' (P. W. Marsh, Service Archives)

62   'The Lost File' (By kind permission of R. H. Gladstone)

64   'The Latest Recruits'.(By kind permission of R. H. Gladstone)

114, 115   Invitation to the March 1919 MI5 Victory celebrations and 'Hush-Hush' Revue, 1919 (By kind permission of R. H. Gladstone)

141   Liberty and Security, New Year card, 1920 (India Office Library MSS Eur. E. 267/10b © The British Library Board. All Rights Reserved)

165   Extract from the *Red Signal* and DPP memo, 1933 (TNA KV4/435)

169   Arnold Deutsch (Service Archives)

173   Extract from CUSS minute book (Service Archives)

233   Letter referring to staff at Keble College, 1941 (By kind permission of the Warden and Fellows of Keble College, Oxford)

243   'Susan Barton's' letter to 'Dorothy' (Dick) White, 1939 (Service Archives)

271   The Official Secrets Act signed by Guy Burgess (Service Archives)

290, 291   Extract from a Report to the Prime Minister on Activities of Security Service, 1943 (Service Archives)

295   GARBO's fictitious network of agents (Service Archives)

301–3   Notes on the code used by TREASURE (TNA KV 2/464)

303   Diagram of the code used by TREASURE (TNA KV 2/464)

306   German map with false location of Allied forces in the UK, 15 May 1944 (US National Archives)

307   Map with actual deployment of Allied forces in the UK, 15 May 1944 (US National Archives)

356   Press article, Betty Knouth, *Daily Express*, 25 August 1948 (© Express Newspapers Syndication)

414   Handwritten list of Labour MPs with alleged links to the Communist Party, 1961 (Service Archives)

437   Cartoon by Jon [William John Philpin Jones], *Daily Mail*, 2 July 1963 (© Solo Syndication/Associated Newspapers Ltd. Courtesy of the British Cartoon Archive, University of Kent)

505   Cartoon, *Sunday Telegraph*, 14 July 1963 (© John Jensen. Courtesy of the British Cartoon Archive, University of Kent)

562   MI5 recruitment advertisement, *Guardian*, 1988 (Service Archives)

564 Cartoon by Bernard Cookson, *Sun*, 29 April 1987 (© NI Syndication. Courtesy of the British Cartoon Archive, University of Kent)

568 Lyalin's map showing possible deployment of a Soviet sabotage group in the UK (Service Archives)

572 Cartoon by Bernard Cookson, *Evening News*, 1 October 1971 (© Solo Syndication/Associated Newspapers Ltd. Courtesy of the British Cartoon Archive, University of Kent)

573 Identified hostile intelligence personnel in London, 1967–1988 (Service Archives)

721 Cartoon by John Kent, *Daily Mail*, 23 April 1984 (© Solo Syndication/Associated Newspapers Ltd. Courtesy of the British Cartoon Archive, University of Kent)

729 Václav Jelínek's (Van Haarlem's) coded radio message, 1988 (Service Archives)

742 A4 surveillance map, Gibraltar, 1988 (Service Archives)

764 Cartoon, *Independent*, 26 November 1986 (© Nicholas Garland. Courtesy of the British Cartoon Archive, University of Kent)

792 MI5 recruitment advertisement, *Guardian*, 2002–3 (Service at Archives)

857 MI5 recruitment literature, 'Great assumptions about a career MI5', 2002–3 (Service Archives)

Every effort has been made to contact copyright holders. The author and publishers will gladly make good in future editions any errors or omissions brought to their attention.

Foreword by the Director General of the Security Service

I am very pleased to have the opportunity to write a foreword for Christopher Andrew's authorized history of the Security Service. Stephen Lander, Director General of the Service between 1996 and 2002, recognized that a history of the Security Service would be an appropriate way to mark our centenary in 2009 and he began the project of which this book is the outcome. Both his successor, Eliza Manningham-Buller, and I have been closely involved in its development. We decided very early on that, to generate the public understanding and support that is vital to the Service's continued success, we needed to commission an 'open' history for publication rather than a 'closed' one for internal consumption. It was also important for the book to be written by an independent historian, who could make objective judgements on the successes and failures of the Service in its first hundred years. We have been fortunate in having, in Professor Christopher Andrew, an author with an exceptional understanding of the intelligence world, a great capacity to research and identify key material from the very large volumes available in our files and the confidence to draw his own conclusions. I would like to thank him for the professionalism and dedication he has shown throughout the project.

The Security Service is, of course, an organization much of whose work must remain secret. This is to protect those who share information with us and ensure that they and others will have the confidence to do so in the future, and to prevent those who seek to harm this country and its people from gaining information which might help them carry out their plans. Writing a history for publication which covers the work of the Service up to the present day is, therefore, a considerable challenge and one which I do not believe that any other major intelligence or security service anywhere in the world has attempted. But for me, and for the previous DGs who have been involved in this project, it is a challenge worth attempting. The Security Service of 2009 is a much more open organization than that of 1909 or even 1980, when I first applied to join. This reflects the expectations of society at large that public institutions should be properly accountable. It also reflects the changing nature of the threats we face. For much of the first eighty years of its existence, the Security Service was concerned with various forms of foreign state espionage. This was, and remains, a vital area of our work, but in the last twenty years terrorism has become the most significant threat with which we deal. The direct impact of terrorism on the life of the average resident of the UK is much greater than that of espionage or some of the other threats with which the Service has dealt. It is therefore important that we as a Service are as open and transparent as possible, within the constraints of what the law allows, because that openness, by supporting public confidence in us, helps us do our job of protecting national security. In the last twenty years we have begun publicly to acknowledge the identity of the Director General of the Service; we have moved to a system of recruitment of staff through open advertising; we have established a public website; and we have instituted a programme of releasing some of our older records to The National Archives. These and other developments are a reflection of a commitment to being as open as we can about what we do, of which this History is the most recent and in many ways the most ambitious demonstration.

Striking the balance in the text between openness and the protection of national security has been a complex and demanding exercise requiring many hours of detailed discussion between Professor Andrew and members of the Service, and an extensive clearance process involving other departments and agencies. The History as published includes some information that is embarrassing or uncomfortable to the Service. Information has only been omitted if its disclosure would damage national security or, in a small number of cases, if its publication would be inappropriate for wider public interest reasons. Inevitably, more material damaging to national security has been omitted from the more modern parts of the book. Given the sensitivity of the judgements concerning omissions on national security grounds, the principles which have governed our approach to the text are given in some detail on the Service's website at www.mi5.gov.uk/output/centenary-history-policy-on-disclosure.html. In particular, we have ensured that everything included in the text is both consistent with the Government's policy on 'Neither Confirm nor Deny' (NCND) and at the same time necessary to meet our aims in publishing Professor Andrew's work. The consequence of this clearance process is that there is nothing in the book which could prejudice national security.

The judgements and conclusions drawn by Professor Andrew in the History are his own, not those of the Security Service or the Government as a whole. Giving Professor Andrew the independence to reach his own conclusions, however well or badly they reflected on the Service, was a key element of the project. In writing the History, Professor Andrew has drawn not only on Security Service records but also on a host of other material available to him. It should not, therefore, be assumed that his conclusions are based solely on material in our records which is unavailable to the public. This book is not an 'official' history within the terms of the Government programme of research and publication of Official Histories on a variety of subjects relating to government activity.

I hope that you will enjoy the History and that you will consider as I do that it provides a striking new insight into an important element in our national life over the last century and into the work of the many dedicated members of the Service whose contribution has been, and to a large degree will remain, unsung.

Jonathan Evans

'This is my first visit to MI5.'
Michael Heath's depiction (after Escher) of the mysterious public image of MI5 in
the later years of the Cold War (*Spectator*, 29 November 1986).

Preface

For most of its history the Security Service (MI5) has seemed to outsiders a deeply mysterious organization. Successive governments intended it to be so. The Service, like the rest of the intelligence community, was to stay as far from public view as possible. The historian Sir Michael Howard declared in 1985: 'So far as official government policy is concerned, the British security and intelligence services do not exist. Enemy agents are found under gooseberry bushes and intelligence is brought by the storks.' The past as well as present of the Security Service remained officially taboo. Even at the end of the Cold War, staff could scarcely have imagined that the Service would mark its hundredth birthday in 2009 by publishing this Centenary History.

The first century of the Security Service falls into six distinct periods (identified in the Contents) which reflect its changing priorities. For eighty years, the Service set out to 'defend the realm' against, alternately, Germany and Russia – and their supporters inside the United Kingdom. Before and during the two world wars, MI5's chief priority was to counter German intelligence operations. For most of the interwar years and the whole of the Cold War, by contrast, the Service's main concerns were what it saw as the linked threats of Soviet espionage and Communist subversion. Though MI5 comprehensively defeated the British operations of both Kaiser Wilhelm II's and Adolf Hitler's intelligence services, it found Soviet intelligence a more difficult opponent. Not until the mass expulsion of KGB and GRU (military intelligence) personnel from London in 1971 did the Security Service gain the upper hand.

MI5's deputy head proudly declared on its twenty-fifth anniversary in 1934: 'Our Security Service is more than national; it is Imperial.' During the quarter-century after the Second World War, its officers and many other staff could expect to spend a quarter to a third of their careers in the Empire and Commonwealth. The Service's overseas role adds another dimension to our understanding of British decolonization. Until the beginning of the 'Troubles' in 1969, the Service knew far less about Northern

Ireland than about Anglophone Africa. It also had little experience of counter-terrorism. As late as 1974 only 7½ per cent of the Service's resources were devoted to counter-terrorist operations against both the IRA and international terrorist groups, whose emergence as a security threat nearly coincided with the start of the Troubles. Until 1992 the lead intelligence role in Britain against the IRA belonged not to the Service but to the Special Branch of the Metropolitan Police.

The end of the Cold War and the disintegration of the Soviet Union transformed Security Service priorities. For the first time in its history the Service became primarily a counter-terrorist agency. Since then it has faced two serious terrorist offensives: from the IRA, which posed a more dangerous threat to mainland Britain for much of the 1990s than ever before, and from Islamist terrorists, who during the first decade of the twenty-first century emerged as an even greater threat. In 2007 thirty 'active' terrorist plots were being investigated, more than at any previous point in British history.

The transformation of Security Service priorities was accompanied by a dramatic change in its public image. The Service began to realize in the closing years of the Cold War that, as British society became more open and less deferential, levels of secrecy which went beyond its operational needs damaged public confidence and bred conspiracy theories. For the first time, the recent history of the Security Service had become front-page news. The episodes which received most publicity, however, were entirely fictitious as well as damaging to its public reputation: the non-existent career of Sir Roger Hollis (Director General from 1956 to 1965) as a Soviet agent and the Service's equally non-existent conspiracy to overthrow the Labour Prime Minister Harold Wilson.

In 1989 the Security Service Act placed the Service on a statutory footing for the first time in its history. Three years later, Stella Rimington became both the first DG whose appointment was publicly announced and the first female British intelligence chief. Rimington believed that one of the achievements of her term as DG was 'the demystification of the Service and the creation of a more informed public and media perception'. Demystification was encouraged by the establishment in 1994 of an oversight committee of parliamentarians, the Intelligence and Security Committee, which produced annual published reports on the intelligence agencies. Some of the simplistic headlines which had greeted Rimington's appointment in 1992 (among them 'MOTHER OF TWO GETS TOUGH WITH TERRORISTS') were no longer imaginable by the time she retired in 1996. A year later the Service began advertising publicly for new recruits.

There remain strict limits to 'the demystification of the Service'. Its commitment to preserving the secrecy of current operations, as well as to concealing the identities of staff and agents, has changed little over the past century. By contrast, the Service has become much less secretive about its past record. Since 1997 it has released to the National Archives over 4,000 files on its first half-century, which have given rise to a growing volume of innovative historical research.

In 2002 the Service advertised for a part-time official historian to write its Centenary History and interviewed a series of applicants. I was fortunate to be selected and began work at its Thames House headquarters in 2003. Since then I have been given virtually unrestricted access to the Service's twentieth-century files as well as to the more limited number of twenty-first-century records I have asked to see. No other of the world's leading intelligence agencies has given similar access to a historian appointed from outside. A significant minority of the files I have seen contain material on intelligence sources and methods which it was clear from the outset could not be published. I thought it important, however, to read these files in order to try to ensure that conclusions in *The Defence of the Realm* based on documents which can be quoted are not contradicted by files whose contents remain classified. Like previous official historians in Britain, I was given an assurance at the outset (which has been fully honoured) that no attempt would be made to change any of the judgements I arrived at.

Clearance of this volume has, unsurprisingly, been a protracted process. There is an inevitable tension between the needs of national security and the wishes of historians. My advocacy of the case for clearance on matters which I judge important has, as colleagues in the Security Service can confirm, not lacked vigour. The issues involved are sometimes difficult. There is much, mostly classified, evidence to support the view of the Security Service that retaining the confidence of current agents makes it necessary to conceal the identities of most of their predecessors as well as their own. The Service has, however, broken important new ground by making it possible for me to bring this history up to the present.

The most difficult part of the clearance process has concerned the requirements of other government departments. One significant excision as a result of these requirements in Chapter E4 is, I believe, hard to justify. This and other issues relating to the level of secrecy about past intelligence operations required by the current needs of national security would, in my view, merit consideration by the Intelligence and Security Committee (though that, of course, is a matter for the Committee to decide).

Acknowledgements

The sheer size of the Security Service Archive is both thrilling and intimidating. Almost 400,000 paper files survive, many of them multi-volume. Finding a path through this immense archive would have been impossible without two wonderful part-time research teams: the first, at MI5 headquarters, composed of one current and two retired members of the Security Service (who cannot, alas, be named); the second at Cambridge University, where I have been assisted by two academic colleagues, Dr Peter Martland and Dr Calder Walton. It has been a joy to work with them all.

Three successive DGs have provided indispensable support for the Centenary History: Sir Stephen Lander, whose idea it was, Baroness Manningham-Buller and Jonathan Evans. The History Team are very grateful also to the members of the Service who have made helpful comments on draft chapters and my talks on MI5 history, to the many retired members on whose memories we have drawn, and to those who have provided managerial, secretarial, computer and other support. Though current and retired members of the Service (except for DGs) cannot be named, our thanks go to them all.

Throughout the writing of this book I have benefited from the intellectual stimulation provided by the Cambridge University Intelligence Seminar, which brings together a remarkable group of postgraduates from around the world expert at identifying the role of intelligence in a variety of fields which more senior scholars have overlooked. I have learned much from them; their theses on topics related to the history of the Security Service are cited in the Notes and Bibliography. I am also grateful to Dr Tony Craig of the Intelligence Seminar for his research for the Centenary History in the National Archives. The debt I owe to the Cambridge history undergraduates I have the good fortune to teach is exemplified by Pete Gallagher's ground-breaking 2009 final-year dissertation which I cite three times.

Among my academic colleagues in the historical profession, I owe particular thanks to Dr Nicholas Hiley, who combines an unrivalled knowledge of open-source material on the early history of modern British intelligence agencies with enviable expertise on British political cartoons.

Both I and the Centenary History have been remarkably fortunate in our editor at Penguin, Stuart Proffitt, in our copyeditor, Peter James, and in the Service's literary agent, Bill Hamilton – all leaders in their fields. At Cambridge Jane Martin and Kate Williams of Corpus Christi College have helped me with friendly efficiency to organize my academic and administrative responsibilities in ways which enabled me to find time to complete this History.

Throughout this exciting and demanding project my wife Jenny, our children, their spouses/partners and our grandchildren have, as always, been my greatest inspiration.

A note on the paperback edition

I have taken the opportunity of this paperback edition to correct various points of detail and remedy a significant omission which have been kindly pointed out to me by attentive readers of the hardback. I have also been able to update substantially the recent history of counter-terrorism in ways which, for legal and other reasons, were impossible at the time of hardback publication.

Christopher Andrew, 2010

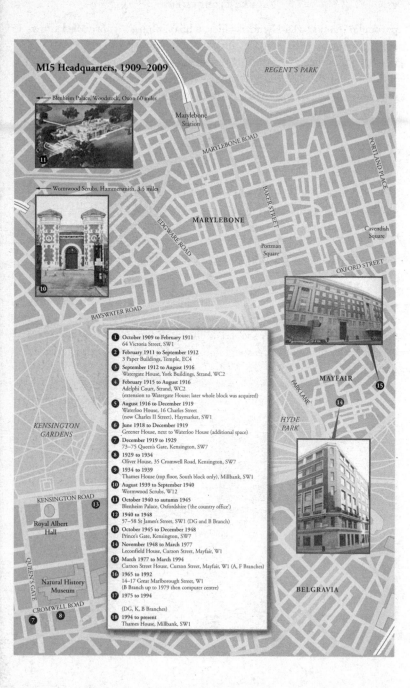

MI5 Headquarters, 1909–2009

← Blenheim Palace, Woodstock, Oxon 60 miles

← Wormwood Scrubs, Hammersmith, 3.5 miles

1. October 1909 to February 1911
   64 Victoria Street, SW1
2. February 1911 to September 1912
   3 Paper Buildings, Temple, EC4
3. September 1912 to August 1916
   Watergate House, York Buildings, Strand, WC2
4. February 1915 to August 1916
   Adelphi Court, Strand, WC2
   (extension to Watergate House; later whole block was acquired)
5. August 1916 to December 1919
   Waterloo House, 16 Charles Street
   (now Charles II Street), Haymarket, SW1
6. June 1918 to December 1919
   Greener House, next to Waterloo House (additional space)
7. December 1919 to 1929
   73–75 Queen's Gate, Kensington, SW7
8. 1929 to 1934
   Oliver House, 35 Cromwell Road, Kensington, SW7
9. 1934 to 1939
   Thames House (top floor, South block only), Millbank, SW1
10. August 1939 to September 1940
    Wormwood Scrubs, W12
11. October 1940 to autumn 1945
    Blenheim Palace, Oxfordshire ('the country office')
12. 1940 to 1948
    57–58 St James's Street, SW1 (DG and B Branch)
13. October 1945 to December 1948
    Prince's Gate, Kensington, SW7
14. November 1948 to March 1977
    Leconfield House, Curzon Street, Mayfair, W1
15. March 1977 to March 1994
    Curzon Street House, Curzon Street, Mayfair, W1 (A, F Branches)
16. 1965 to 1992
    14–17 Great Marlborough Street, W1
    (B Branch up to 1979 then computer centre)
17. 1975 to 1994
    (DG, K, B Branches)
18. 1994 to present
    Thames House, Millbank, SW1

Section A
The German Threat, 1909–1919

Introduction

The Origins of the Secret Service Bureau

The Security Service (MI5) and the Secret Intelligence Service (SIS or MI6) began operations in October 1909 as a single organization, the Secret Service Bureau, based in premises rented by a private detective, retired Chief Inspector Edward 'Tricky' Drew, at 64 Victoria Street, London SW1, opposite the Army and Navy Stores.[1] The Bureau was staffed initially by only two officers, the fifty-year-old Commander Mansfield Cumming RN and an army captain fourteen years his junior, Vernon Kell, who met for the first time on 4 October when, according to Cumming's diary, they 'had a yarn over the future and agreed to work together for the success of the cause'.[2] Cumming and Kell later parted company to become the first heads of, respectively, SIS and MI5. For several months, however, they were based in the same room, struggling, with minimal resources, 'to deal both with espionage in this country and with our foreign agents abroad'.[3]

The Secret Service Bureau owed its foundation to the recommendations of a sub-committee of the Committee of Imperial Defence, the chief defence planning council of the realm, which had been instructed in March 1909 by the Liberal government of Herbert Asquith to consider 'the nature and extent of foreign espionage that is at present taking place within this country and the danger to which it may expose us'.[4] It reported on 24 July: 'The evidence which was produced left no doubt in the minds of the subcommittee that an extensive system of German espionage exists in this country and that we have no organisation for keeping in touch with that espionage and for accurately determining its extent or objectives.'[5] Most continental high commands would have been surprised to discover that British intelligence was in such an enfeebled state. There was a widespread myth that, ever since the days when a secret service run by Queen Elizabeth I's Secretary of State, Sir Francis Walsingham, had successfully uncovered a number of Catholic plots, British intelligence, like the British Empire, had grown steadily in size and influence, spreading its tentacles across the globe.

The myth was encouraged by Edwardian spy novelists. The most prolific and successful of them, William Le Queux, allegedly Queen Alexandra's favourite novelist, assured his readers: 'The British Secret Service, although never so prominently before the public as those unscrupulous *agents provocateurs* of France and Russia, is nevertheless equally active. It works in silence and secrecy, yet many are its successful counterplots against the machinations of England's enemies.'[6] Le Queux (pronounced 'Kew') was a Walter Mitty figure who fantasized that he had played a personal part in some of these successes. In *Secrets of the Foreign Office* published in 1903, Le Queux, thinly disguised as Duckworth Drew,[7] 'secret agent in the employ of the Foreign Office, and, next to his Majesty's Secretary of State for Foreign Affairs, one of the most powerful and important pillars of England's supremacy', quickly gets the better of the long-serving French Foreign Minister, Théophile Delcassé (equally thinly disguised as Monsieur Delanne). Delcassé, alias Delanne, 'admitted that he longed to smoke one of my excellent light-coloured Corona Superbos'. But there was more to Drew's cigars than met the Minister's inattentive eye: 'To this day Monsieur le Ministre is in ignorance that that particular Corona had been carefully prepared by me with a solution of *cocculus indicus . . .*' Outwitted by the cunningly prepared Corona, the disoriented Delanne revealed the secrets Drew (sometimes considered an Edwardian prototype of James Bond) had come to collect.[8] Such fantasies found a ready market. Like Thomas Hardy and H. G. Wells, both vastly superior writers, Le Queux was paid the top rate of 12 guineas per thousand words and published far more than either.[9]

At the opposite extreme of literary merit from Le Queux, Rudyard Kipling gave an equally optimistic assessment of British successes in the intelligence duel with Russia on India's North-West Frontier. In *Kim* (probably the finest of all spy novels, though it transcends the world of espionage), unseen but ubiquitous agents of the British Raj play 'the Great Game that never ceases day and night throughout India'. And they do so with a subtlety quite beyond the capacity of Tsarist Russia, 'the dread Power of the North', and its French ally, whose emissaries are 'smitten helpless'.[10] So far as the War Office were concerned, the myth of a far-flung intelligence network, whether promulgated by Kipling or by lesser literary talents, had the incidental advantage of avoiding public revelation of British intelligence weakness. 'The only consolation', they concluded in 1907, 'is that every foreign government implicitly believes that we already have a thoroughly organised and efficient European Secret Service.'[11]

All that Britain actually had were small and underfunded military and naval intelligence departments, both with little capacity to collect secret intelligence, and the Metropolitan Police Special Branch (MPSB), founded in 1883 to counter the threat to the capital from Fenian (Irish Republican) terrorism, which had moved on to small-scale investigation of other terrorist and subversive threats but had minimal expertise in counter-espionage.[12] The three agencies had little influence in Whitehall. Spenser Wilkinson, first Chichele Professor of War at Oxford University, compared the War Office's use of their Intelligence Department (ID) during the Boer War (1899–1902) to a man who 'kept a small brain for occasional use in his waistcoat pocket and ran his head by clockwork'.[13] Although the 1903 Royal Commission on the War in South Africa concluded that the ID had been 'undermanned for the work of preparation for a great war',[14] once the war was over the pressure for intelligence reform and more resources declined.

Within the Directorate of Military Operations at the War Office, however, two diminutive departments, MO2 and MO3, were established in 1903 with responsibility for, respectively, foreign intelligence and counter-espionage. MO3 was the direct predecessor of MI5. Superintendent William Melville, who had been head of the Met's Special Branch for the previous decade, was recruited to carry out secret investigations for both MO2 and MO3, later becoming chief detective of the Security Service during its first eight years. Since he qualified for a police pension of £240 and received an additional £400 from the War Office, the terms were financially attractive. Melville's appointment was not publicly announced. Officially, he simply retired from the Special Branch. *The Times* reported that Scotland Yard had lost the services of 'the most celebrated detective of the day'.[15] The award of the MVO (Member of the Royal Victorian Order) to Melville on his official retirement in 1903 also recognized his role in overseeing, with very limited resources, the security of Queen Victoria, King Edward VII and other members of the Royal Family both at home and during their continental travels at a time when European heads of state were more regularly threatened with assassination by revolutionary and anarchist groups than at any time before or since. Those assassinated on the continent included a Russian tsar, a French president, an empress of Austria-Hungary, a king of Italy, prime ministers of Spain and Russia, but no British royal or minister. Among foreign royals whose security Melville helped to protect during visits to Britain was Kaiser Wilhelm II, who presented him at various times with a gold watch and chain, a ring and a cigarette case.[16]

The fact that early Security Service records date Melville's employment from 1903, six years before MI5 was founded, is evidence that his work for it after 1909 was seen at the time as a continuation and extension of his earlier War Office investigations. During his investigations for both the War Office and the Secret Service Bureau, Melville operated from an office at 25 Victoria Street, Westminster, using the alias 'W. Morgan, General Agent'.[17] Melville was well acquainted with Gustav Steinhauer, who became head in 1901 of the British section of the German Admiralty's newly founded intelligence service, the Nachrichten-Abteilung, usually known as 'N'. Former Kriminalkommissar of the Berlin police, Steinhauer, who grandly termed himself the 'Kaiser's spy', had trained as a private detective at the Pinkerton Agency in Chicago and spoke English fluently with an American accent.[18] He accompanied the Kaiser to England in 1901 as his personal bodyguard when Wilhelm II came to pay his last respects to his dying grandmother, Queen Victoria, and later to attend her funeral. A detective inspector in the MPSB described Steinhauer as 'a handsome soldierly figure who had seen more courts than camps'. Steinhauer remembered Melville as 'a silent, reserved man, never given to talking wildly', who entertained him to dinner with cigars and 'one or two bottles of wine' at Simpson's Grand Cigar Divan in the Strand. The presence of so much European royalty at Queen Victoria's funeral inevitably led to fears of assassination attempts. Steinhauer later gave a melodramatic account of how he had accompanied Melville in a hunt for three homicidal Russian nihilists, who made their escape after allegedly killing a female informant of the Special Branch. Melville told the Kaiser he had been impressed by Steinhauer's intelligence expertise. 'Yes, Steinhauer is a splendid fellow!' replied the Kaiser.[19]

In the spring of 1904 Melville sent his assistant, Herbert Dale Long, on the first of several missions to Germany on behalf of MO2 under commercial cover, probably to inquire into German naval construction.[20] A fragmentary file on Melville's early work for MO3 (renamed MO5 in 1907) suggests that his early priorities in Britain (particularly during the Russo-Japanese War of 1904–5) were to monitor the operations not of German intelligence but of the Okhrana, the Tsarist intelligence and security service. One of the documents in Melville's file (received from a Colonel Dawson) dramatically describes the Okhrana chief, Pyotr Rachkovsky, as 'Head of all the [Russian] secret service police in the whole world, & the most important man in Russia. Commander of the Legion of Honour in France, and has agents throughout the whole world.' When stationed in the West, Rachkovsky lived in much greater opulence than his Soviet successors. Melville reported on 25 November 1904:

I know him personally, having frequently met him in London and he often called upon me in Scotland Yard when I introduced him to some of my superiors . . . When in London, Ratchkowsky always had some of his officers with him and invariably had a suite of rooms at the Savoy Hotel. I was told that he lived in a similar style in Paris, and know that he did so at Copenhagen.[21]

Melville was probably aware that Rachkovsky and other Russian foreign intelligence officers were responsible for a series of explosions and agent-provocateur operations on the continent designed to discredit Russian revolutionary émigrés. He is unlikely to have known, however, that Rachkovsky was probably also responsible for the fabrication of the infamous anti-Semitic forgery *The Protocols of the Elders of Zion*, which purports to describe a Jewish plot for world domination.[22] Between the wars, the *Protocols*, much praised by Hitler in *Mein Kampf*, emerged as one of the central texts in Nazi anti-Semitism, as well as later appearing on numerous early twenty-first-century Islamist websites.

From 1905 to 1907, Melville concentrated increasingly on German rather than Russian espionage. Reports of suspicious behaviour by German residents and visitors convinced him that German spies were reconnoitring invasion routes in England for the German army. In 1906 he believed that he had identified a group of spies in Epping:

I mentioned to the Superintendent of Police at Epping that the Germans might be spies; he laughed at the idea as being ridiculous, adding, 'Spies! What could they spy here?' Argument was useless. The fact remains that undoubtedly they were spies, and their business, I should say, was to become thoroughly conversant with the routes from the sea coast to London, and thus to be able to guide a German army landed in this country.[23]

There can be little doubt that the Epping Superintendent's scepticism was fully justified. In other parts of the country, when making his inquiries about German spies, Melville also found the local police 'absolutely useless'.[24] He was not, however, to be deterred by the scepticism of the police from approaching the Home Office:

Owing to the almost continuous enquiries on the Eastern coast re suspected Germans, alleged staff rides by Germans, etc, from 1905 to 1907 I submitted reports outlining a scheme of surveillance on all suspected foreigners around the country. In them I suggested the utilisation of the Police, the Postal authorities and the Coast Guard Service.

Unsurprisingly, the Home Office failed to respond to Melville's proposals.[25]

By the time Major (later Brigadier General Sir) James Edmonds became head of MO5 late in 1907, 'its activities had been allowed to die down'. Save for Melville, Edmonds's staff consisted only of another major whose main preoccupation was cultivating a parliamentary constituency which three years later elected him as its Conservative MP. Apart from Melville's reports, MO5 files when Edmonds took over 'contained only papers relating to the South African [Boer] War and some scraps about France and Russia – nothing whatever about Germany'.[26] Germany, however, was Edmonds's main preoccupation. He seems to have been influenced by both Melville's alarmist reports and the international tension generated by British–German naval rivalry. The Entente Cordiale of 1904, followed by the Triple Entente of 1907, had resolved Britain's differences with France and Russia, both of which were to become wartime allies. The main threat to British security now came from the expanding German High Seas Fleet. The security of Victorian Britain had depended on Britannia's ability to rule the waves with a navy which was by far the largest in the world. But, with the launching of the new British battleship *Dreadnought* in 1906, Anglo-German naval rivalry took a new and dangerous turn. By its size and firepower the *Dreadnought* threatened to make all other battleships obsolete. With ten 12-inch guns, each with a range of over 8 miles, it was more than a match for any two of its predecessors. Overnight, the existing Grand Fleet of the Royal Navy, like every other navy in the world, seemed out of date. It was feared that the German High Seas Fleet, which also began building the dreadnought class of battleship, might soon catch up with the Grand Fleet and threaten the naval supremacy on which British security depended.

Fear of the threat from the growing High Seas Fleet encouraged the myth that it was to be used for a surprise invasion of England. William Le Queux quickly assumed the role of alarmist-in-chief. His best-seller *The Invasion of 1910*, published in 1906, described how German spies were already hard at work in England, preparing the way for the invaders. It sold a million copies and was published in twenty-seven languages, including German. Melville gave Le Queux much of the credit for 'waking up the public'.[27] At London clubs and dinner parties, Le Queux was, by his own immodest account, 'hailed as the man-who-dared-to-tell-the-truth'. Success on so heady a scale launched him further into a fantasy career as secret agent and spy-catcher extraordinary. He became a member of a 'new voluntary Secret Service Department': 'Half-a-dozen patriotic men in secret banded themselves together. Each, paying his own expenses, set to work gathering information in Germany and elsewhere that might be useful to our country in case of need.'[28]

The Invasion of 1910 was serialized several months ahead of book publication in Britain's first mass-circulation newspaper, the *Daily Mail*. The *Mail*'s proprietor, Lord Northcliffe (soon to become owner of *The Times* as well), was convinced that the invasion scare was well suited to the average Briton's liking for 'a good hate'. Germany was one of Northcliffe's own pet hates and was to figure prominently in the paranoia of his final years. (His last two wills, written shortly before his death in 1922, complained that he had been 'poisoned by the Germans by ice cream'.) Northcliffe, however, found much to criticize in the original route selected by Le Queux for the German army, which included too many villages where the market for the *Daily Mail* was small. So in the interests of circulation the German invasion route was changed to allow the Hun to terrorize every major town in England from Sheffield to Chelmsford. Special maps were published each day in the *Daily Mail* to show which district the Germans would be invading next morning. The serial added 80,000 to the *Mail*'s circulation.[29] Le Queux later complained of the 'many imitators who obtained much kudos and made much money' by jumping on the bandwagon of invasion scares.[30] Not all, however, were imitators. His most successful rival, E. Phillips Oppenheim, embarked independently on his own 'crusade against German militarism', made enough money from it to give up the family leather business and began a full-time career as one of Britain's most prolific popular novelists.[31]

By the autumn of 1907 a press campaign backed by the ageing military hero Field Marshal Lord Roberts VC (who had collaborated with Le Queux in working out the German invasion route), and some of the Conservative front bench, had persuaded the Liberal government to appoint a sub-committee of the Committee of Imperial Defence to consider the invasion threat. The membership of the sub-committee bears witness to the importance of its task. The chair was taken by Asquith, then Chancellor of the Exchequer but soon to become prime minister. With him sat four senior ministers (the Lord President, the Foreign Secretary, the Secretary for War and the First Lord of the Admiralty) and an impressive array of service chiefs. They met sixteen times between November 1907 and July 1908, completing their report on 22 October 1908. The result of their deliberations was to demolish most of the arguments of the invasion theorists and show surprise attack to be impossible. The sub-committee's conclusions, however, failed to carry conviction with most of those whose arguments it had demolished. During summer naval exercises a small force of invaders managed to elude the fleet and scramble ashore in the north of Scotland. With the Admiralty maintaining an embarrassed silence, the alleged numbers of the invaders multiplied alarmingly. Reginald McKenna, the First Lord of the Admiralty, was forced to deny a report that 70,000 invaders had landed at Wick. His critics remained sceptical. The *Daily Mail* claimed that during an invasion exercise, despite using two charabancs and a steam engine, the Territorial Army had taken three hours to reach the threatened coastline.[32]

Fear of the invading Hun was further fuelled in the autumn of 1908 by reports that Germany was secretly stepping up dreadnought construction. Though inaccurate, the reports were confirmed by the British naval attaché in Berlin and the consul in Danzig.[33] The cabinet dispute which ensued began in acrimony and ended in farce. 'In the end,' wrote Winston Churchill, 'a curious and characteristic solution was reached. The Admiralty had demanded 6 ships: the economists offered 4: and we finally compromised on 8.' This remarkable decision was the result of outside pressure. The Tory Opposition, the Tory press, the Navy League and other patriotic pressure groups worked themselves into a frenzy as they denounced government hesitation in the face of the German naval menace. 'We are not yet prepared to turn the face of every portrait of Nelson to the wall,' thundered the *Daily Telegraph*, 'and to make in time of peace the most shameful surrender recorded in the whole of our history.' Assailed by the vociferous demand 'We want eight, and we won't wait!', the Liberal cabinet surrendered to it.[34]

By 1907 Major (later Major General Sir) William Thwaites, head of the German section at the War Office, was convinced that there was 'much truth' in newspaper reports that German intelligence officers were at work in every county. The Director of Military Operations, Major General (later Lieutenant General Sir) John Spencer Ewart, also believed that Germany was pouring 'hosts of agents and spies' into Britain.[35] Edmonds, the head of MO5, agreed. German friends had told him of requests by the German Admiralty to report on the movement of British warships, work in dockyards and arsenals, aeroplane development and the building of munitions factories.[36] Late in 1907 he began keeping a record of reports of alleged German espionage 'which on inquiry appeared to offer some justification for suspicion'. Not a single case was reported to the War Office by the police. All the reports came from members of the public, many of them influenced by alarmist press reports. As Edmonds acknowledged, 'it is only since certain newspapers have directed attention to the subject that many cases have come to notice.' MO5 lacked the resources to check adequately the reports it received.[37]

Though Edmonds, Melville, Thwaites, Ewart and others at the War Office were too uncritical of alarmist reports from press and public of spies and invasion plans, they had much better grounds for believing that there was a major German espionage offensive against Britain than most historians have been willing to recognize.[38] Edmonds was arguably the leading army intellectual of his generation as well as a gifted linguist with a largely self-taught reading knowledge of many languages as well as fluency in German. After education as a day boy at King's College School, Wimbledon, he passed first into the Royal Military Academy with the best marks the examiners could remember. He also passed out first, winning a number of prizes including the sword for the best gentleman cadet, and was gazetted to the Royal Engineers, where his brilliance earned him the nickname 'Archimedes'. He later passed first once again into Staff College. In 1899 he was posted to the War Office Intelligence Department (ID), and after three years in South Africa from 1901 to 1904 returned to the ID. By the time he became head of MO5, Edmonds was an experienced intelligence officer.[39]

As a nine-year-old child living in France at the end of the Franco-Prussian War of 1870–71, Edmonds had witnessed at first hand the occupying forces of the newly united Germany. He spent much of his life thereafter studying the German army.[40] Edmonds shared with others at the War Office the belief that the Franco-Prussian War, the last between major European powers, provided important insights into likely German strategy in the next war. Germany's rapid, crushing victory in 1870–71, he believed, was due partly to the effectiveness of its intelligence services and to the ineffectiveness of French counter-espionage. The head of German field intelligence, General Lewal, had established an effective network of agents who helped to guide the invading Prusso-German regiments into France. Some of these agents were 'mobile agents', loyal German citizens (*Reichsangehörige*) in France who worked as waiters, barbers and language teachers, and sent whatever military information they could acquire back to Berlin. German intelligence in 1870 was known to have had a collecting agent in Lyons, who telegraphed all intelligence reports to Geneva, whence they were forwarded on to Germany.[41] MO5 also concluded that, in the years preceding the Franco-Prussian War, German intelligence made use of German army reservists living in France as well as the German consular service.[42] It studied German military publications such as the *Militärwochenblatt*, which included articles on the need to establish sabotage agents in enemy countries before the mobilization of troops.[43] The official German Field Manual (*Felddienstordnung*) of 1894, of which MO5 obtained a copy, 'stated without reticence the necessity of espionage, and ordered the use of spies in every command'.[44]

During the 1890s, initially as the result of exchanging intelligence on Russia, Edmonds established friendly relations with several German military intelligence officers. Though his main contact was succeeded in 1900 by an officer of 'anti-English proclivities', other informants told him – correctly – that in 1901 German intelligence had set up a new department to target Britain.[45] Neither Edmonds nor anyone else in the War Office, however, realized that the department was purely naval and had no involvement with Sektion IIIb, military intelligence. It was therefore assumed that Germany had begun to develop a military espionage network in Britain similar to its successful network in France before the Franco-Prussian War. Though MO5 was aware that German naval intelligence was at work in Britain, it mistook some of the operations of the Nachrichten-Abteilung ('N'), founded in 1901, for those of the military Sektion IIIb. The 'N' network in Britain, directed by Melville's old acquaintance Gustav Steinhauer, included both 'reporters' (*Berichterstatter*), who passed information on the Royal Navy back to Berlin during peacetime, and 'confidential agents' (*Vertrauensmänner*), who were to be mobilized after the outbreak of war. Though Steinhauer's recruitment methods, which usually involved letters by him to German citizens living in Britain written under an alias from a cover address in Potsdam and asking for their services, were somewhat hit-and-miss, the 'Kaiser's spy' also developed a more sophisticated system of 'intermediaries' (*Mittelsmänner*) to act as cut-outs between him and his agents in Britain. After the outbreak of war, a 'war intelligence system' (*Kriegsnachrichtenwesen*) was to be introduced, using agents travelling to Britain under false identities to conduct specific missions. Steinhauer, however, was left largely to his own devices with little active tasking by the German Admiralty.[46]

Edmonds's willingness to believe that German intelligence was actively engaged in the military reconnaissance of Britain, as well as collecting naval intelligence, was strengthened by mirror-imaging – his knowledge that the British army was secretly carrying out detailed reconnaissance on the continent. In 1907 the War Office ordered a secret survey of the area in which the British Expeditionary Force (BEF) was expected to be deployed in time of war. By 1908 the survey was so detailed that it included information on the population of villages and the locations of post offices, pipe water supply, bicycle shops and railway sidings.[47] Convinced that there must be similar German military reconnaissance in Britain, Edmonds was therefore predisposed to believe reports of spies working for Sektion IIIb. In his later career as official historian of the First World War, his meticulous (if sometimes ponderous) use of both British and German

military records was to earn him an honorary DLitt from Oxford University.[48] The same level of critical judgement, however, was sometimes woefully lacking in his assessment of pre-war German espionage. Despite his
reputation as the army's leading intellectual, Edmonds had what Kell later
called a 'cranky' side, which helps to explain why, despite his gifts, he
never rose above the rank of honorary brigadier general.[49]

Edmonds later attributed what he believed to be his success in uncovering
the scale of German espionage in Britain, military as well as naval, to two
remarkable 'pieces of luck', whose improbability he failed to grasp. One
of his friends, F. T. Jane (the founder of the naval and military annuals
which bear his name), who was 'on the lookout for spies', found a suspicious German in Portsmouth, drove him to Woburn and, to teach him a
lesson, claimed to have 'deposited him in the Duke of Bedford's animal
park'. Immediately following this exploit, Jane received a series of letters
about other suspected spies which he passed on to the War Office.
Edmonds's second apparent stroke of 'luck' was a flood of correspondence
to William Le Queux from readers of his books and newspaper serials,
convinced that they had seen suspicious-looking aliens on 'early morning
walks and drives', correcting maps, showing 'curiosity about railway
bridges' and making 'enquiries about gas and water supply'. During 1908
Edmonds got in touch with 'the most promising' of Le Queux's and Jane's
correspondents and made further inquiries. In February 1909 he concluded
in an alarmist memorandum:

Day in, day out, the ceaseless work of getting information and throwing dust in the
eyes of others goes on, and the final result of it all, as far as we are concerned, is
this: that a German General landing a force in East Anglia would know more about
the country than any British General, more about each town than its own British
Mayor, and would have his information so methodically arranged that he could, in
a few minutes, give you the answer to any question you asked him about any town,
village or position in that area.[50]

Le Queux's own fantasies scaled new heights in 1909 with the publi-
cation of another best-seller, *Spies of the Kaiser: Plotting the Downfall of
England*, which claimed that England was awash with 'a vast army of
German spies':

I have no desire to create undue alarm. I am an Englishman and, I hope, a patriot.
What I have written in this present volume in the form of fiction is based upon
serious facts within my own personal knowledge . . . During the last twelve months,
aided by a well-known detective officer, I have made personal inquiry into the

presence and work of these spies, an inquiry which has entailed a great amount of travelling, much watchfulness, and often considerable discomfort.

In the last chapter of the book, the heroes, John 'Jack' Jacox and his friend Ray Raymond, almost pay with their lives for their fearless investigations. In December 1908 they are presented with Christmas crackers by a group of apparently good-natured Germans, but are alerted just in time by a detective-inspector to the Germans' real intentions:

'They intended to wreak upon both of you a terrible revenge for your recent exposures of the German system of espionage in England and your constant prosecution of these spies.'

'Revenge?' [Jacox] gasped. 'What revenge?'

'Well,' replied the detective-inspector, 'both these [crackers] contain powerful bombs, and had you pulled either of them you'd both have been blown to atoms. That was their dastardly intention.'[51]

Edmonds was well aware that this and other episodes in *Spies of the Kaiser* had been produced by Le Queux 'out of his imagination', and probably regarded the claim that the book was 'based upon serious facts within [Le Queux's] own personal knowledge' as the kind of artistic licence indulged in by writers of popular thrillers. But he took seriously the 'dozens of letters telling . . . of the suspicious behaviour of Germans' sent to Le Queux by excitable readers of *Spies of the Kaiser*. Edmonds also continued to take Le Queux himself seriously. In his unpublished reminiscences written many years later after Le Queux's death, Edmonds refers to him as his 'friend'.[52] Le Queux was more plausible in person than in print. He appears to have persuaded Edmonds, as he persuaded Sir Robert Gower MP, who wrote the foreword to his official biography, that his 'interest was directed solely to the welfare of his country'.[53]

R. B. Haldane, the Secretary of State for War in the Asquith government, was at first bemused by the extraordinary reports of German espionage which Edmonds presented to him. Unlike Edmonds, Haldane remained anxious to build bridges to Berlin. After the outbreak of war he was to be hounded from office for his alleged pro-German sympathies. His initial reaction, when confronted with Edmonds's evidence, was to conclude that the alleged spies were really 'the apparatus of the white slave traffic'.[54] Some of Edmonds's evidence, for example that concerning suspicious Germans with photographic equipment in Epping 'occasionally visited by women from London for weekends',[55] did indeed lend itself to this interpretation. Edmonds, however, 'persisted', though – as he admitted later – 'I was very nearly thrown out of my job for my pains.' Finally, Haldane yielded to Edmonds's persistence and allowed himself to be convinced of the spy menace. 'What turned the scale', in Edmonds's view, was a letter from the Mayor of Canterbury, Francis Bennett-Goldney (soon to become Conservative MP for Canterbury), who reported that he 'had found two Germans wandering in his park, had talked to them and invited them in to dinner'. After dinner, the two men had revealed to a stunned Bennett-Goldney the sinister purpose of their apparently harmless excursions: 'Their tongues loosened by port, they told him they were reconnoitring the country for an advance on London from the ports of Folkestone, Dover, Ramsgate and Margate.' Even when recounting this remarkable episode many years later, Edmonds seemed unaware of its unusual irony.[56] Germans and Britons had reversed their national stereotypes. Two fun-loving German tourists had played a British practical joke on their British host who had reacted with the incomprehension commonly associated by the British with the humourless Hun.

At a deeper level Haldane's readiness to believe such remarkable tales of German espionage reflected his enormous respect for the ability and professionalism of the German General Staff. He impressed on Vernon Kell 'the excellence and precision of their planning',[57] and considered them fully capable of creating a dangerous and extensive spy network in Britain. In March 1909 Haldane set up, with cabinet approval, a high-powered sub-committee of the Committee of Imperial Defence to consider 'the nature and extent of the foreign espionage that is at present taking place within this country and the danger to which it may expose us'. The chair was taken by Haldane himself.[58]

Edmonds told the first meeting of the sub-committee on 30 March of a rapid rise in 'cases of alleged German espionage' reported to the War Office by the public. Five cases had been reported in 1907, forty-seven in 1908 and twenty-four in the first three months of 1909. Edmonds gave some particulars of thirty of these cases. Following Haldane's advice to 'lay stress on the anarchist (demolitions) motive', Edmonds emphasized the 'aggressive' nature of German espionage, claiming that it aimed not merely at intelligence-gathering but also at preparing the destruction of docks, bridges, ammunition stores, railways and telegraph lines 'on or before the outbreak of war'.[59] There was, however, nothing personally eccentric in the belief held by Haldane and Edmonds that German agents would be used for sabotage. In the decade before 1914 the influential *Journal of the Royal United Services Institution*, which was read widely throughout the British armed forces, included several articles on the possibility of a German

German Espionage in Essex

PHOTOGRAPHING THE SITE OF THE SECRET MAGAZINE
AS SEEN BY A RESIDENT OF EPPING

THE HOUSE, NOW TO LET, OCCUPIED
BY THE PARTY OF THREE. THEY
WOULD GO OFF WITH CYCLES & CAM-
ERAS SOMETIMES TOGETHER, OFTEN ALONE

HORSES FODDER, &c.
THE HARMLESS FOREIGN
GENTLEMAN WHO PHOTOGRAPHED
PICTURESQUE BARNS, ETC., & WHO COLLEC-
ED MUCH USEFUL INFORMATION WITH
A GLASS OF MILK

A FAVOURITE EVENING RENDEZVOUS. YE OLD THATCHED HOUSE HOTEL
WHERE THEY CHAFFED AND AMUSED THE FREQUENTERS

The full story of these three Germans, who left the neighbourhood at the end of June, after a residence of six months, is told on the opposite page

How the Military Spies Who Have Been Staying at Epping Conducted their Operations

DRAWN BY D. MACPHERSON, FROM MATERIALS GATHERED ON THE SPOT

Spy scares in the Edwardian media: the *Graphic* uncovers a non-existent
lair of German spies in Essex in 1908.

invasion of Britain, and sabotage operations being conducted in Britain prior to mobilization.[60]

When presenting the evidence of German espionage to the Committee of Imperial Defence sub-committee in 1909, Edmonds acknowledged, 'We have . . . no regular system or organisation to detect and report suspicious cases, and are entirely dependent on casual information.' Counter-espionage at the Admiralty was in an even sorrier state. Captain R. C. Temple of the Naval Intelligence Department told the sub-committee that his department, which did little more than collate information on foreign navies, was unable to carry out any 'investigations into espionage' at all, and therefore passed on reports that came its way to Colonel Edmonds. In presenting his evidence to the sub-committee Edmonds 'laid great stress on the fact that none of these cases were reported by the police authorities, and that he was indebted for information regarding them to private individuals'.[61] He seems, at the very least, to have been insufficiently surprised by the failure of the police to detect a single suspicious German as well as insufficiently sceptical of the information supplied by 'private individuals'.

An unknown number of the reports of suspicious Germans presented by Edmonds to the sub-committee had been investigated by Melville. Among them was a report of Germans taking photographs in the West Hartlepool area who Melville was convinced were spies.[62] Shortly before the first meeting of the sub-committee, Melville sent his assistant, Herbert Dale Long, to investigate German spies said to be living in East Anglia. In his reports Long referred to the Germans by the codename 'tariff reformers' or 'tr'. (The issue of tariff reform had split the Conservative government in the years before 1906 and was still a live issue in Liberal Free Trade Britain.)[63] The same acronym, also used by Edmonds, was later employed (capitalized as 'TR') by the first Chief of SIS, Mansfield Cumming, who sometimes referred to Germany as 'Tiaria'.[64] On 23 March 1909, a week before the first meeting of the sub-committee, Long reported that the alleged German agents at various East Anglian locations had disappeared by the time he arrived:

[I] have failed to discover tr agents at any of these places and I believe it can be taken for granted that none are residing there at the present time.

There can be little doubt, however, that the party's [German intelligence] emis-saries here worked the district; the proprietor of the Ship Hotel at 'Reedham' – H. Carter – vigorously denounces the conduct of two agents who he observed were particularly active making notes and drawings in favour of the movement last summer.[65]

The evidence of German espionage presented by Edmonds to the sub-committee now appears flimsy. His first twelve cases concerned 'alleged reconnaissance work by Germans'. In half these cases the suspicious persons were not even clearly identified as Germans. The most farcical 'reconnaissance' report seems to have come, appropriately, from Le Queux (though, like other informants, he is not identified by name and is referred to only as a 'well-known author'):

Informant, while motoring last summer in an unfrequented lane between Portsmouth and Chichester, nearly ran over a cyclist who was looking at a map and making notes. The man swore in German, and on informant getting out of his car to apologize, explained in fair English, in the course of conversation, that he was studying at Oxford for the Church, and swore in German to ease his conscience. He was obviously a foreigner.[66]

Edmonds's second category of evidence consisted of twelve cases of 'Germans whose conduct has been reported as giving rise to suspicion'. There was at least one real German spy on the list. German archives confirm that Paul Brodtmann, managing director of the Continental Tyre Company in London, had been recruited by the Nachrichten-Abteilung in 1903 to report on British battleships at Southampton and had also sent several reports to the German military attaché in London.[67] Another possibly authentic spy on Edmonds's list was Herr Sandmann, who had taken photographs inside the Portland defences which were published in the German periodical *Die Woche*. If Sandmann was a spy, however, his liking for publicity raises some doubt about his competence. Edmonds's third and final category of evidence consisted of six 'houses reported to be occupied by a succession of Germans which it is desirable to watch'. Once again Le Queux ('a well-known author') seems to have supplied one of the examples: 'A series of Germans come and go at 173, Powerscourt Road, North End, Portsmouth. They receive many registered letters from Germany.'[68] From such mostly insubstantial evidence Edmonds deduced the existence of an 'extensive' German espionage network in Britain directed, he believed, from a special office in Brussels. 'The use of motors', he believed, 'has facilitated espionage, as it enables agents to live at a distance from the scene of their operations, where their presence excites no suspicion.'[69]

At least one member of the sub-committee, Lord Esher, was less than impressed with Edmonds and described him in his journal as 'a silly witness from the WO': 'Spy catchers get espionage on the brain. Rats are everywhere – behind every arras.'[70] Probably to test the limits of Edmonds's credulity,

Esher asked him whether he 'felt any apprehensions regarding the large number of German waiters in this country'. Edmonds remained calm. He 'did not think that we need have any apprehensions regarding the majority of these waiters'.[71] Esher's initial scepticism gradually waned as the War Office revealed the extent of its concern. Whatever doubts remained on the sub-committee were successfully dispelled by the chairman. Haldane had a reputation for having not espionage but German culture on the brain. John Morley, the Secretary of State for India, complained that he 'wearies his Cabinet colleagues by long harangues on the contribution of Germany to culture'.[72] Thus when Haldane told the sub-committee that it was 'quite clear that a great deal of reconnaissance work is being conducted by Germans in this country', some of it probably to 'enable important demolitions and destruction to be carried out in this country on or before the outbreak of war', his views conveyed unusual conviction.[73]

Haldane told the second meeting of the sub-committee on 20 April that he had just returned from a visit to Germany. Though he did not think the German government had a definite invasion plan, there was little doubt that 'the German General Staff is collecting information systematically in Great Britain'. Ways must therefore be found 'to prevent them in time of war or strained relations from availing themselves of the information they had collected, by injuring our defences, stores, or internal communications'. On Haldane's proposal, it was agreed that five members of the sub-committee – Sir Charles Hardinge, PUS (permanent under secretary) at the Foreign Office, Sir George Murray, PUS at the Treasury, Sir Edward Henry, Commissioner of the Met, Major General Ewart and Rear Admiral A. E. Bethell, Director of Naval Intelligence (DNI) – should meet to consider 'how a secret service bureau could be established'.[74]

Haldane brought before the third and final meeting of the sub-committee on 12 July the most remarkable piece of bogus intelligence it had yet considered. Within the last week, said Haldane, the War Office had received a document from abroad 'which threw some light on what was going on':

This document had been obtained from a French commercial traveller, who was proceeding from Hamburg to Spa. He travelled in the same compartment as a German whose travelling-bag was similar to his own. The German, on leaving the train, took the wrong bag, and on finding out this the commercial traveller opened the bag left behind, and found that it contained detailed plans connected with a scheme for the invasion of England. He copied out as much of these plans as he was able during the short time that elapsed before he was asked to give up the bag, concerning the loss of which the real owner had telegraphed to the railway authorities where the train next halted.

Haldane had at first rightly regarded the plans as forged, possibly planted by the French to provide a stimulus for Anglo-French staff talks to prepare for war with Germany. Generals Ewart and Murray (Directors, respectively, of Military Operations and Military Training) persuaded him otherwise. The plans, in their view:

showed great knowledge of the vulnerable points in this country, and revealed the fact that, as we had already suspected, there were certain places in this country where German agents are stationed, whose duty it would be to take certain action on the outbreak of war, or during the time of strained relations preceding that outbreak.[75]

Some years later Edmonds acknowledged that the plans were, in retrospect, an obvious forgery, though he concluded somewhat bizarrely that they were probably planted by the Germans rather than the French.[76] At the time, however, no doubts were expressed by the sub-committee, which agreed unanimously that 'an extensive system of German espionage exists in this country'. The sub-committee also approved a report on the establishment and funding of a Secret Service Bureau prepared for the meeting by five of its members. The Bureau was 'to deal both with espionage in this country and with our own foreign agents abroad, and to serve as a screen between the Admiralty and the War Office on the one hand and those employed on secret service, or who have information they wish to sell to the British Government, on the other'.[77]

The report approved by the sub-committee on the establishment of the Secret Service Bureau was considered 'of so secret a nature' that only a single copy was made and handed over for safekeeping to the Director of Military Operations.[78] Once established, the Bureau remained so secret that its existence was known only to a small group of senior Whitehall officials and ministers, who never mentioned it to the uninitiated. More than half a century later, the main biographers of Asquith and his ministers seem still to have been unaware of its existence and make no mention of it. Even the nine-volume official biography of Winston Churchill, who was the main supporter of the Secret Service Bureau in the Asquith cabinet, contains no reference to it. One of the few outside the small circle of ministers and mandarins who knew of the founding of the Bureau was Le Queux, who had probably been told by Edmonds. When the *Manchester Guardian* accused him of propagating the 'German spy myth', Le Queux replied indignantly on the letters page on 4 January 1910:

The authorities in London must have been considerably amused by your assurances that German spies do not exist among us, for it may be news to you to know that so intolerable and marked has the presence of [these] gentry become that a special Government Department has recently been formed for the purpose of watching their movements.[79]

Most of the evidence of 'an extensive system of German espionage' which led to the foundation of the Secret Service Bureau was flimsy and some of it (such as the bogus German invasion plan considered at the final meeting of the sub-committee) rather absurd. Since there was no German military intelligence network in Britain at the time, the evidence of its operations considered by the sub-committee was necessarily mistaken (with the possible exception of a few private intelligence-gathering initiatives by German citizens and occasional cases of reports to the German military attaché in London by informants not working for military intelligence).[80] The case for establishing the Bureau was none the less a strong one. A German naval espionage network concentrating on naval targets *was* operating in Britain and, until the establishment of the Bureau, there was, to quote the sub-committee report, 'no organisation for keeping in touch with that espionage and for accurately determining its extent or objectives'. The continuing naval arms race between Britain and Germany, a persistent cause of tension between the two countries until the First World War, made such an organization an obvious priority. The successes achieved by the Nachrichten-Abteilung before the outbreak of war, even after the founding of the Secret Service Bureau, were sufficient to indicate that, if naval espionage in Britain had been allowed a free rein, it might well have provided the German Admiralty with a major flow of classified information on its leading rival. A well-developed German naval intelligence network would also have been able to report on the despatch of the British Expeditionary Force to the continent in August 1914.

The Secret Service Bureau got off to a confused start. The sub-committee decided that 'two ex-naval and military officers should be appointed [to the Bureau] having special qualifications', but did not seek to apportion work between the two. Nor did it say whether the army or the naval officer should head the Bureau, though whoever became head would have to be 'free from other work and able to devote his whole attention to Secret Service problems'.[81] The officers selected by the War Office and the Admiralty were Captain Vernon Kell and Commander Mansfield Cumming RN.[82]

The thirty-six-year-old Kell had been born while his mother was on a seaside holiday at Yarmouth and liked to describe himself in family circles

Memorandum
Formation of a S.S. Bureau

1. A meeting was held in Sir E. Henry's room at Scotland Yard on Thursday the 26th Augt to consider the arrangements to be made in order to give effect to the recommendations of the Sub-Committee regarding the establishment of a secret service bureau. The following were present:- Sir E. Henry, Major-General Ewart, Colonel J. E. Edmonds, Lieut-Col G.M.W. Macdonogh, & Captain Temple representing the D.N.I.

2. Sir E. Henry recommended that Mr Edward Drew, late Chief Inspector Criminal Investigation Dept, as a suitable private detective, under cover of whose name the bureau should be conducted. Mr Drew explained that he proposed setting up in business as a private detective & that he had the option of leasing suitable offices at 64 Victoria Street S.W.

3. It is proposed that the bureau should be started as soon as possession can be obtained of the offices, ie early in October.

4. As war office representative it is proposed to appoint Captain V.G. Kell South Staffordshire Regt, who proposes to retire. Captain Kell is an exceptionally good linguist & is qualified in French, German, Russian & Chinese

5. It is understood that the Admiralty will over

nominate Commander Mansfield G. Smith Cumming, who is now in charge of the Southampton Boom Defence & who possesses special qualifications for the appointment

D.M.O spoke to Sir Charles Harding on 14/9/09 & he concurred in the above arrangements

Extracts of the record of a meeting at Scotland Yard to implement the recommendation of the sub-committee of the Committee of Imperial Defence to nominate Kell and Cumming to the Secret Service Bureau, which was intended to start work in early October 1909.

as a 'Yarmouth Bloater' (kipper). His oddly chosen nickname was mislead-ing. Kell's father was an army officer who had distinguished himself in the Zulu Wars and other conflicts at the outposts of Empire, while his mother (later divorced) was the daughter of a Polish count with a string of exiled relatives scattered across Western Europe. Kell had a private education and a cosmopolitan upbringing, travelled widely on the continent to visit friends and relatives, and – according to an unpublished biography by his widow – learned five foreign languages in the process. After Sandhurst, he joined his father's regiment, the South Staffordshire, 'determined to strike out on his own and make use of his languages'. Having qualified with ease as an army interpreter in French and German, Kell left in 1898 for Moscow to learn Russian. Two years later he set out for Shanghai with his new wife Constance to learn Chinese and witnessed the anti-Western Boxer Rebellion at first hand. As Kell's widow later recalled, 'We were constantly hearing of how the Boxers were succeeding with alarming swiftness to poison the minds of the villagers and townsmen.'[83] Kell was the most accomplished linguist ever to head a British intelligence agency.

On his return to London from China in 1902, Kell was employed as a German intelligence analyst at the War Office. Probably because of the paucity of intelligence, he found the work 'not particularly interesting'.[84] His opportunity to make his mark came soon after the outbreak of the Russo-Japanese War in 1904 when the officer in charge of the Far Eastern section was found to have confused Kowloon (the city) with Kaoling (Indian corn), and to have made other embarrassing errors. Edmonds was chosen to replace him and selected Kell as his deputy and 'right-hand man'. In 1909 it was Edmonds as head of MO5 who proposed Kell (then assistant secretary of the Committee of Imperial Defence) for the Secret Service Bureau.[85] The recent claim that, by the time Kell joined the Bureau, he was 'a dyed-in-the-wool Germanophobe'[86] is clearly contradicted by the Kells' decision in 1907 to employ a German governess for their children.[87] Though, like many in the War Office, Kell wrongly believed that Britain was being targeted by German military, as well as naval, intelligence, no evidence has come to light to indicate that, like the more excitable Edmonds, he was in contact with William Le Queux.[88] In the interests of secrecy, Kell had to be removed from the active list before joining the Secret Service Bureau. He was thus taking a significant gamble in accepting the new job. As his wife wrote later: 'There was the risk that should he fail to carry it through it would leave him with his career wrecked and bring about the dismal prospect of having to provide for his family with no adequate means of doing it. But he was young and an optimist – why should he fail?'[89]

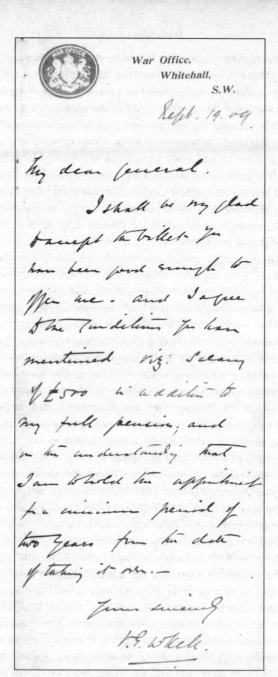

War Office,
Whitehall,
S.W.

Sept. 19. 09

My dear General.

I shall be very glad to accept the billet you have been good enough to offer me. And I agree to the conditions you have mentioned viz: Salary of £500 in addition to my full pension; and on the understanding that I am to hold the appointment for a minimum period of two years from the date of taking it over. —

Yours sincerely

V.G. Kell.

Letter from Kell to the Director of Military Operations, Major General (later Lieutenant General Sir) John Spencer Ewart, accepting the 'billet' offered him in the Secret Service Bureau.

As well as being fourteen years older than Kell, Cumming was also more extrovert. Major (later Major General Sir) Walter Kirke of MO 5, who saw Cumming almost daily during the two years before the war, found him 'the cheeriest fellow I've ever met, full of the most amusing yarns'. But, on first acquaintance, Cumming could also be intimidating. The writer Compton Mackenzie, who worked for him during the First World War, recalled how he would stare at newcomers through a gold-rimmed monocle. Peacetime secret service work, Cumming told him, was 'capital sport'.[90] There was one major similarity between the careers of Kell and Cumming. Kell had moved into desk jobs because of sometimes severe asthma. Cumming was forced to retire from active service in the navy because of illness. In 1898 he returned to the active retired list and was put in charge of the Southampton boom defences. In August 1909 he received an unexpected letter from the Director of Naval Intelligence, Rear Admiral Bethell: 'Boom defence must be getting a bit stale with you . . . You may therefore perhaps like a new billet. If so I have something good I can offer you . . .' The 'new billet' was with the Secret Service Bureau.[91]

The Admiralty and the War Office had failed to agree on what Cumming's and Kell's roles would be. Bethell initially told Cumming that he would 'have charge of all the Agents employed by him and by the W[ar] D[epart-ment]' and would have a junior colleague. By the time the Secret Service Bureau began work, however, the junior colleague, Kell, thanks to the support of the War Office, looked as if he might have the upper hand. Cumming, as he admitted in his diary after another meeting with Bethell, was 'disappointed to find that I was not to be Chief of the whole Bureau'. He was even more disappointed when Colonel George Macdonogh, who had succeeded Edmonds as head of MO 5, wrote to tell him on 10 October that he proposed to hand all War Office matters over to Kell and that he should work directly to Kell. 'The letter', wrote Cumming, 'made me very uncomfortable as I could not help feeling that under the circumstances, it was a distinct rebuff.'[92] As Cumming's biographer, Alan Judd, puts it, 'The War Office thought it controlled the Bureau, the Admiralty thought it controlled Cumming, while the Foreign Office, which paid for it, did not at this stage want too much to do with it.'[93] On 21 October Kell and Cumming agreed on a division of responsibilities which presaged their future roles as the first heads of MI 5 and SIS. Cumming wrote in his diary: '[At a] meeting with K[ell] and Macdonogh, duties assigned; K[ell] gets Home work, both naval and military (espionage and counter-espionage) and I get Foreign, naval and military, K[ell] gets M[elville] and D[ale Long] and their office, and I was to have nothing to do with them.' Kell and Cumming, however, remained in the same office only until the end of the year, with Macdonogh forwarding Cumming his monthly salary of £41 13s 8d via Kell.[94]

During these early months, Kell, as he later reported, spent most of his time 'going through the previous history of counter-espionage as shown in the War Office files, and in getting acquainted with the various aspects of the work'.[95] Melville ('M'), assisted by Dale Long ('L'), investigated a number of localities where reports of alleged German espionage had reached the War Office.[96] Despite the agreement by Cumming and Kell on dividing the Bureau's work, the relationship between them remained tense. By 1 November Cumming was close to despair:

Cannot do any work in office. Been here five weeks, not yet signed my name. Absolutely cut off from everyone while there, as cannot give my address or [be] telephoned to under my own name. Have been consistently left out of it since I started. K[ell] has done more in one day than I have in the whole time . . .

The system has been organised by the Military, who have just had control of our destinies long enough to take away all the work I could do, hand over by far the most difficult part of the work (for which their own man is obviously better suited) and take away all the facilities for doing it.

I am firmly convinced that K[ell] will oust me altogether before long. He will have quantities of work to show, while I shall have nothing. It will transpire that I am not a linguist, and he will then be given the whole job with a subordinate, while I am retired – more or less discredited.[97]

Cumming's morale improved somewhat after the DNI, Rear Admiral Bethell, assured him 'That I need not do anything to justify my appointment. I must wait patiently for work to come. That I need not sit idle in the Office but could go about and learn.'[98]

Though Cumming was somewhat reassured and intelligence leads began to reach him in early November,[99] he remained suspicious of Kell's intentions. On 26 November Cumming went to complain to Bethell that Kell was trying to interfere in his arrangements for meeting an agent, and was adamant that he, not Cumming, should pay him. Bethell sided with Cumming, insisting that he was in sole charge of all foreign work and that he – not Kell – was to pay agents. At another meeting on 30 November, Bethell also claimed that the War Office now realized they had made a mistake in dividing the Bureau's work in two and allowing Cumming to take charge of the more important part.[100]

The early Secret Service Bureau was also plagued by lack of money, as is shown by a letter from Macdonogh on 28 February 1910:

My Dear Kell,

We are and shall be very hard up until the end of this month. Will you therefore please cut down your expenses to a minimum and not incur any travelling expenses without previous reference and then only in cases that will not wait till April.

Yours sincerely
M[acdonogh][101]

At the end of 1909 Cumming had set up a separate HQ in a flat in Ashley Gardens, near Vauxhall Bridge Road, for which, because of the exiguous Bureau budget, he had to pay himself (along with the telephone). There, he later reported to Bethell, he was able to 'interview anyone . . . without the risk of my conversation being overheard'. He now also had as much work as he could handle.[102]

Kell too was looking for new premises. Cumming noted in his diary on 17 March 1910:

Called on K[ell] at his request handed over my small safe and the keys to my desk to his Clerk . . . He asked me if I should object to his coming next door, but I told him that I thought it would interfere with my privacy in my own flat and I begged he would not go forward with any such scheme. I would rather he were not in this immediate neighbourhood at all.[103]

Friction with Kell continued. Cumming listed a number of grievances in his diary on 23 March 1910. Kell had recently interviewed a Miss Yonger, who had offered to provide information, and attempted to conceal her name from Cumming 'although her information is entirely in my department'.

Secondly, K[ell] told me that he had made the acquaintance of the editor of the Standard and through him, that of a man named 'Half Term', who had supplied him with some information, and for whom he had got a retainer of £50 per year. I was expressly forbidden to approach the Editors of any paper.

Cumming also complained that Kell's department was both larger and better funded than his own – doubtless due in large measure to Kell's long association with the War Office.[104] A diary entry for 5 April records further irritation. Cumming had been telephoned by Kell 'who wanted me to come round for something "urgent". When I got there, it was only to ask me about some particular paper that had been ordered under rather curious circumstances, which I undertook to do.' Kell also produced a letter he had received from a woman in Germany offering information but refused to supply her address on the grounds that she would communicate only with him. Cumming discovered next day that the information concerned an alleged (but no doubt non-existent) German arms cache in Britain.[105]

Relations improved once the complete separation of what had now become the home and foreign departments of the Secret Service Bureau was fully recognized. On 28 April 1910 Cumming recorded in his diary: 'Kell agreed that our work was totally different and that our connection was only one of name, and that it would be better for both of us if we should work separately.'[106] At a meeting in Bethell's room at the Admiralty also attended by top brass from the War Office on 9 May, three days after the death of King Edward VII, with Whitehall in deep mourning, Macdonogh began by acknowledging that the two departments had little in common and that the respective duties of Kell and Cumming needed to be properly defined. The meeting confirmed Kell's responsibility for all work in the United Kingdom and Cumming's for all work abroad. The meeting also agreed that, though the work of Kell's department was suf-ficiently 'above board' for its existence to be acknowledged, Cumming's department could not be officially avowed.[107]

That distinction between an avowable (if unpublicized) MI5 and an unavowable SIS was to be maintained until 1992 when the existence of SIS was officially acknowledged for the first time. Following the separation of the two services in 1910, proposals for their reunion, or at least for their being housed once again in the same building, continued to resurface intermittently in Whitehall for more than eighty years. None succeeded.

I

'Spies of the Kaiser': Counter-Espionage before the First World War

Kell's section of the Secret Service Bureau, usually known to those aware of its existence as the Counter-Espionage Bureau[1] or Special Intelligence Bureau[2] (and also, within the War Office, as MO5(g)), was run on a shoestring. Its resources before the First World War were well below the minimum which any modern security service would think necessary in order to function at all. Kell did not acquire a clerk until March 1910, and the first officer recruit did not join the Bureau until January 1911. Even at the outbreak of war in August 1914, Kell's staff[3] consisted only of six officers,[4] Melville and two assistant detectives,[5] six clerical staff[6] and a caretaker.[7] Kell had by then taken the title of director.

With such minimal resources, the key to Kell's initial counter-espionage strategy was to gain the assistance of chief constables around the country. That, in turn, required the support of the Home Secretary. It was Kell's good fortune that the Home Secretary for most of 1910 and 1911 was Winston Churchill, who in the course of a long career showed greater enthusiasm for, and understanding of, intelligence than any other British politician of his generation. His adventures during the Boer War had included cycling in disguise through Johannesburg to carry out reconnaissance work behind enemy lines. Churchill later acknowledged that, had he been caught, 'No court martial that ever sat in Europe would have had much difficulty in disposing of such a case.' He would have been shot as a spy.[8] As home secretary Churchill also played an important part in the development of Kell's Bureau. General Ewart, the Director of Military Operations, wrote to him in April 1910, commending Kell as 'in every way most discreet and reliable':

This officer, who is attached to my Intelligence Department, is employed by me in making enquiries regarding the many alleged instances of Foreign Espionage and other suspicious incidents which are frequently brought to our notice. The nature of his work makes it desirable that, with your permission, he should be brought into private communication with the Chief Constables of counties, and, if you could see your way to give him some general letter of introduction, which he could produce when necessary it would help us very materially.

Churchill minuted: 'Let all facilities be accorded to Captain Kell.'[9] Next day his private secretary provided Kell with a letter of introduction to the chief constables of England and Wales which concluded: 'Mr Churchill desires me to say that he will be obliged if you will give Captain Kell the necessary facilities for his work.'[10] In June Kell obtained a similar introduction from the Scottish Office to chief constables in Scotland.[11] During the summer of 1910 he made personal contact with thirty-three English and seven Scottish chief constables, all of whom 'expressed themselves most willing to assist me in every way'.[12] The Aliens Sub-Committee of the Committee of Imperial Defence (founded in March 1910), chaired by Churchill, approved the preparation by Kell of a secret register of aliens from probable enemy powers (chiefly Germany) based on information supplied by local police forces.[13]

Kell was well aware that the German *Meldewesen* system, which made registration of all foreigners compulsory and placed restrictions on their movements and activities,[14] would be unacceptable in Britain and therefore fell back on secret registration. On the 'Return of Aliens' form devised by Kell in October 1910, chief constables were also asked to report 'Any specific acts of espionage on the part of the persons reported on; or other circumstances of an unusual nature'.[15] Even with the assistance of chief constables around the country, Kell's inadequate resources initially allowed him and Melville to do little more than investigate reports of alleged German espionage which had already reached the War Office. Kell's first progress report, submitted in March 1910, shows that he had been influenced by Melville's belief, based on earlier investigations for MO5,[16] that German espionage in Britain was linked to plans for a German invasion. Kell concluded that the 'Rusper case' and the 'Frant case' provided 'strong supplementary and confirmatory evidence to the existence in this country of an organised system of a German espionage'. The first case involved 'suspicious' German activities in the Sussex village of Rusper:

It is hardly necessary to draw attention to the fact that the knowledge of the country lying on and between the North and South Downs, including as it does the important heights of Hindhead, Box Hill, and the Towers of Holmbush, Rusper Church and Lyne House, would be of greatest value to an invading force advancing from the direction of the coast-line lying between Dover and Portsmouth, as also an intimate acquaintance with the Railway Lines leading to the Guildford, Dorking and Tunbridge junctions from the Coast.

The 'Frant case' concerned a Sussex poultry farm which was suspected by locals of being a rendezvous for German agents. Kell cited the report of 'our investigator' (probably Melville's assistant, Herbert Dale Long), who claimed 'considerable experience of all classes of Germans' and concluded that two newcomers at the poultry farm were German officers travelling incognito.

Kell arrived at two main conclusions based on the first six months of his Bureau's work:

(a) The Bureau has justified its institution
(b) The experience gained has proved that it is essential to the effective working of the Counter-espionage Section of the Bureau that all information coming within its province should be sent to and exclusively dealt with by the Bureau.

Kell also praised the co-operation of chief constables as essential to the work of the Bureau and called for strengthening of the ineffective 1889 Official Secrets Act which made it difficult to prosecute espionage cases.[17]

With the gift of hindsight, it may seem surprising that Kell's first progress report did not inspire greater scepticism. The Rusper and Frant cases did not in reality provide the strong evidence of 'an organised system of a German espionage' which Kell claimed they did. Kell, however, was preaching to the converted. Like the sub-committee of the Committee of Imperial Defence, whose recommendations had led to the founding of the Secret Service Bureau six months earlier, the readers of Kell's report in the War Office and Admiralty had 'no doubt . . . that an extensive system of German espionage exists in this country'.[18] Though significant German naval intelligence operations were being targeted against Britain, Kell's woefully under-resourced Bureau as yet lacked the means to discover them. The Bureau's investigations in the summer of 1910 produced no evidence of espionage more significant than those in his first progress report. Melville reported in June that he was on the track of 'a suspicious German', claiming to be a commercial traveller, 'who periodically visits all the German waiters round Dover and Folkestone, and also, it is believed, all along the coast'.[19] In July a Colonel R. G. Williams informed Kell that two Germans had been discovered 'signalling to each other by lamps by night' near the Sevenoaks Tunnel. Kell immediately contacted the Chief Constable of Kent, who reported that the lamps appeared to have been used by campers rather than German spies.[20]

Some of the mistaken reports of German military espionage in Britain sent to Kell came from apparently very well-informed sources. Among them was Colonel Frederic Trench, a well-known military writer whose appointment as British military attaché in Berlin in 1906 had been enthusiastically received by the Kaiser, who was a personal friend. With the Kaiser's approval, Trench had served in South-West Africa alongside German forces and had numerous friends and contacts in the German army. While in Berlin, Trench became convinced that Germany was planning a surprise attack on Britain: 'When Germany comes to the conclusion that her navy is strong enough, or the British fleet sufficiently scattered or otherwise occupied, for there to be a reasonable prospect of success . . . the first move will be made without any warning whatever . . .' Trench also believed that preparation of the invasion plans was being assisted by German spies in Britain, and some of his reports were passed to Kell.[21]

There was, in reality, clearer evidence of British espionage in Germany than of German espionage in Britain. In August 1910 Lieutenant Vivien Brandon of the Admiralty Hydrographic Department and Captain R. M. Trench of the Royal Marines (not to be confused with Colonel Trench) were arrested while on a mission assigned them by British naval intelligence to reconnoitre German North Sea coastal defences at Borkum and elsewhere. Both men showed their inexperience not merely by keeping large amounts of incriminating documents in their possession but also by their behaviour during cross-examination. Counsel for the prosecution acknowledged that it was only as a result of Trench's evidence at the trial that they knew he had entered the Borkum fortifications at all.[22] On 30 August Kell was summoned to the Admiralty for a meeting with Bethell, the DNI, Sir Graham Greene, Secretary of the Admiralty (its senior civilian official), Cumming and other senior naval officers, and asked if he 'could get up a "counter-blast" to the Borkum affair' – in other words, expose some German spies at work in Britain. Kell 'feared not'.[23]

On 5 September, however, Kell received a telegram from Portsmouth, informing him that Lieutenant Siegfried Helm of the 21st Nassau Pioneer Battalion had been arrested for suspected espionage.[24] Helm had travelled to Britain ostensibly to learn English, and had written beforehand to a Miss Wodehouse, the friend of a fellow officer, who helped find him lodgings near her home in the Portsmouth area. Wodehouse discovered that, as well as enjoying the company of a 'lovely lady friend', Helm was also making sketches of forts and military installations, and reported him to the local barracks.[25] Though the First Lord of the Admiralty, Reginald

McKenna, wanted to avoid pre-trial publicity, Kell thought 'it was an excellent thing that the arrest should become known as soon as possible as it might have a soothing effect across the water' – that is, help to deter other German spies. News of Helm's arrest was published by the *Daily Express*. No mention of Kell's role in this or any subsequent counter-espionage case appeared in the press. On 6 September, having received 'all necessary evidence and documents', including Helm's pocket book, Kell caught the train to Portsmouth to take charge of the investigation. Miss Wodehouse persuaded Kell that 'she had deliberately egged Lieut. Helm on to make love to her to gain his confidence as she suspected from the outset that he was spying.'[26]

Though described by *The Times* as 'a soldierly figure' when he appeared in court at the committal hearing on 20 September, Helm seems to have stepped straight from the pages of *Punch*. He had what his defence counsel called 'a mania for writing things in his pocket book' and a stereotypical Teutonic thoroughness in doing so, noting down exact details of his bedroom furniture and the precise distance between the chest of drawers and his bed. His drawings of forts and military installations were less impressive. Kell's later deputy, Eric Holt-Wilson, dismissed them as 'rather futile sketches of the obsolete Portsmouth land defences'. Helm said he had made the drawings of the forts not by covert reconnaissance but by looking through a large public telescope on Portsmouth's South Parade. After his arrest he wrote Wodehouse a pained but determinedly cheerful letter: 'It is a dreadful thing, but they have taken me as a spy! It was all for my own study. The officers here are very kind to me. So comfortable a time I never had!' When Helm discovered that Wodehouse had given evidence against him, he changed his tune: 'I came as a true friend and you were my enemy. The Holy Bible said right, that a wife is as false as a serpent!!' Though pleading guilty at his trial, Helm was merely bound over and discharged, with a cordial if condescending farewell from Mr Justice Bankes:

I trust that when you leave this country you will leave it with a feeling that, although we may be vigilant, and perhaps, from your point of view, too vigilant, yet ... we are just and merciful, not only to those who are subjects of this realm, but also to those who, like yourself, seek the hospitality of our shores.[27]

In Germany as well as Britain, espionage by serving officers was still regarded as indicating their patriotism and treated with some leniency. The evidence of systematic espionage was much stronger in the case of Brandon's and Trench's reconnaissance of German North Sea coastal defences than in the case of Helm, and both were sentenced to four years' imprisonment. Their trial ended, however, in a remarkably amicable, almost surreal, atmosphere. According to *The Times* correspondent:

When it was all over, they remained for some minutes chatting with counsel and others and shaking hands with acquaintances such as the Juge d'Instruction who conducted the preliminary hearing ... They were very gay and perfectly satisfied with the result of the trial.

Brandon and Trench were to serve their sentence in a fortress where they would be 'allowed to provide their own comforts and to enjoy the society of the officers, students and others, all men of education and good social position, who share the Governor's hospitality in the fortress'. 'There are no irksome regulations,' concluded *The Times* report, 'and it will not be difficult for them to obtain leave to make excursions in the town.'[28]

Since Helm was a serving army officer, his trial appeared to provide confirmation that Germany was engaged in military as well as naval espionage in Britain. German archives, however, now reveal what Kell could not have known at the time, though he might perhaps have suspected it, that Helm had been acting on his own initiative rather than on instructions.[29] After the trial was over Kell had hoped to discover more about what lay behind Helm's bungling espionage. In the train back to London he sat, unrecognized, in the same compartment as Helm and his father. To Kell's disappointment, they 'did not speak very much'.[30]

Only four days later an apparently promising lead to a more serious espionage case came from Major (later Major General Sir) William Thwaites, head of the German section at the War Office (and later Director of Military Intelligence) and a strong supporter of Kell's Bureau.[31] Thwaites reported that for the past month six Germans had been dining regularly at Terriani's restaurant, opposite Harrods: 'They appeared to be very secretive and it was suggested that they were engaged in S[ecret] S[ervice].' Kell dined in the restaurant with Melville. Also present was Captain Stanley Clarke, an army officer who had returned to Britain after eleven years' service in India and was shortly to become Kell's assistant. 'But', noted Kell in his diary, 'no Germans turned up.'[32] As with most warnings of suspicious Germans over the previous few years, the report was almost certainly a false alarm.[33]

Like Melville, Kell continued to believe that German espionage was linked to German invasion plans. In his second progress report, in October 1910, he envisaged the possibility (never apparently implemented) of 'the earmarking (and training??) of our own spies in the Coast Counties, to act behind the enemy's lines in case of invasion'.[34] At the first annual review of the Bureau's work, held in the War Office on 15 November, it was agreed to ask the Foreign Office for the funding for Kell to employ an assistant at a salary of £400 per annum (in addition, it was expected, to an army pension).[35] Kell had already earmarked Stanley Clarke, who formally began work on 1 January 1911.[36] One of Clarke's first tasks was to help Kell move from his Victoria Street office to larger (and less expensive) chambers at 3 Paper Buildings in the Temple, where they had to make their own arrangement for water and electricity supply. Soon after the move (complicated by three-weeks' sick leave by Kell) was complete on 20 February, Clarke embarked on a three-week walking tour of the Essex and Suffolk coast,[37] presumably in a vain attempt to find intelligence leads on espionage related to (non-existent) German invasion plans.

Having investigated a series of leads which, save for the somewhat farcical Helm case, had so far yielded no solid evidence of German espionage, Kell was by now rightly concerned about the low quality of the intelligence reaching him. On 3 March he had 'a long interview with M[elville] at his office and impressed upon him the necessity of being more energetic in the future': 'I expected him to think out new schemes for getting hold of intelligence.'[38] In his third report Kell wrote that, though the quality of Melville's work and his tact when making inquiries had been excellent, 'The work that he has done for me during the last eighteen months has not been of an arduous nature, and is nothing compared to the comprehensive work he was originally intended for when he was first employed.' Because of his age (Melville was now in his sixties)[39] and seniority, he could 'hardly be expected to perform such work as the shadowing by night and day, a duty which in any case is quite impossible for one man alone'.

Hitherto I have had to depend, to a great extent, on such assistance in detective work as the Metropolitan and County Police have been able to afford me, but the County Police in particular have very few plain-clothes men at their disposal, and moreover some of the Chief Constables themselves have acknowledged that however excellent their men's work may be as regards crime, they have not got all the necessary degree of tact to carry out such delicate enquiries . . .

Mr Melville has on occasions been able to enlist the services of one or two ex-police officers of his acquaintance, but who naturally were not always available when their services were required. Moreover the system of employing odd men for our kind of work is obviously undesirable, besides being very costly. It is very difficult to get private detectives to work for less than a guinea a day, plus all out-of-pocket expenses. I therefore beg to request that sanction may be given for me to engage the services of two detectives.[40]

A former Met policeman, John Regan, joined Kell's Bureau as assistant to Melville on 7 June, but Kell had to wait over a year for the second detective he had asked for.[41] He did, however, obtain funding for a 'marine assistant', Lieutenant (later Commander) B. J. Ohlson RNR,[42] who began work on 19 May with responsibility for 'the collection of information in ports along the East Coast', beginning in the Port of London.[43] Over the next month Ohlson enlisted the support of skippers of six merchant vessels plying between London and the continent who, Kell reported, 'are discreet and willing to keep their eyes open and report any useful information that comes to their notice'.[44]

In August 1911, Stanley Clarke had a remarkable stroke of luck which transformed Kell's investigations of the Nachrichten-Abteilung's British operations. Clarke found himself in the same railway carriage as Francis Holstein, the German-born proprietor of the Peacock Hotel, Trinity, Leith, who was discussing with a friend a letter he had just received from Germany asking for information about British public opinion and preparations for war. Further inquiries revealed that Holstein had received two similar letters in the previous year, both signed, like the latest one, 'F. Reimers, Brauerstrasse, Potsdam'. 'Reimers' was discovered to be an alias used by Gustav Steinhauer.[45] Extraordinary though the coincidence of the overheard conversation may appear, Steinhauer's insecure habit of sending unsolicited letters requesting information from Germans resident in Britain[46] meant that it was only a matter of time before one of the letters was revealed by its recipient. On a number of occasions German agents in Britain complained about the danger that they might be exposed to as a result of poor security, but Steinhauer brushed their complaints aside.[47] The German naval attaché in London reported to the DNI in Berlin in 1912 that recruiting Germans living in Britain as agents was 'much more complicated than imagined in Berlin': 'The Germans of middle age (only gentlemen between the age of 35 and 50 are suitable, as the younger gentlemen do not have steady jobs and change their employer far too often and without prior notice) loathe this kind of work more and more, it being hostile to England.'[48] Like Holstein, a majority of those who received Steinhauer's letters had no intention of responding to his ill-conceived intelligence cold-calling.

Churchill added a major weapon to Kell's armoury by greatly simplifying the interception of suspects' correspondence. Hitherto individual warrants signed by the Home Secretary had been required for every letter opened.

The Post Office had always held that it was very undesirable to shake public confidence in the security of the post. The Secretary to the Post Office had even argued in a paper submitted to the . . . Subcommittee on Foreign Espionage in 1909 that it appeared very doubtful whether any useful results would follow from the examination of correspondence in the case of spies as it was improbable that any letters of importance would be received or despatched by a spy without the use of devices for concealment.[49]

Had the Post Office view prevailed, Kell would have been deprived of what soon became his main counter-espionage tool. Churchill, however, overrode it, greatly extending the Home Office Warrant (HOW) system and introducing the signing of 'general warrants authorising the examination of all the correspondence of particular people upon a list to which additions were continually being made'. He was greatly impressed by the evidence of German espionage which resulted from the warrants which he signed. After clearing his desk at the Home Office in November 1911 on becoming first lord of the Admiralty, he wrote to the Foreign Secretary, Sir Edward Grey:

Capt Kell of the War Office secret service has given me the enclosed bundle of reports, which resulted from the action taken by him in conjunction with Chief Constables during my tenure at the Home Office. Although there is a lot of 'stuff' mixed up with them, they are well worth looking through because they show that we are the subject of a minute and scientific study by the German military and naval authorities, and that no other nation in the world pays us such attention. Will you show them to Lloyd George [Chancellor of the Exchequer] when he dines with you tomorrow night? I should add that Kell is thoroughly trustworthy and competent, and that of course the names and addresses of almost all the persons referred to are known. The information is of course secret. A good deal more is known through the warrants I signed as Home Secretary for the inspection of correspondence.[50]

Beginning in September 1911, Kell kept a carefully compiled, cross-referenced index of the intercepted letters between Steinhauer and his agents in Britain. An in-house MI5 history written in 1921 noted that though the original letters had been destroyed, a surviving index to them contained 1,189 entries for the period from 1911 to 1914. During the three years before the outbreak of war, Kell's Bureau thus received, on average, more than one intercepted letter a day from Steinhauer and his British network.[51] Among the most important early discoveries from the intercepts was Steinhauer's insecure use of intermediaries for communications with his agents. By obtaining HOWs on the intermediaries ('postmen'), Kell was thus able to penetrate much of the network. Probably the most active 'postman' was Karl Ernst, who owned a barber's shop near Pentonville Prison and regularly cut the hair of the chaplain and prison officers.[52] As well as handling correspondence, Ernst was also used intermittently by Steinhauer to approach disgruntled seamen who, it was hoped, might be persuaded to provide information on the Royal Navy. Some of his other inquiries were more humdrum. Ernst was asked to obtain a *Daily Express* article on Steinhauer entitled 'German Spy Bureau. Chief Organizer and How He Works. A Man of Mystery. Victims Made to Order'.[53] On at least one occasion intelligence from the 'letter checks' almost led to Steinhauer's capture. In December 1911 intercepted correspondence revealed that a German officer was travelling through Britain. By the time sufficient evidence had been assembled to justify his arrest, however, he had left the country. Another intercepted letter in February 1912 revealed that the itinerant officer had been Steinhauer himself.[54]

The first case investigated by Kell of a spy working for Steinhauer which led to prosecution was that of Dr Max Schultz, the first doctor of philosophy ever to be jailed for espionage in Britain. Despite convictions in Germany for embezzlement, he was used by 'N' to gather intelligence on the Royal Navy at Portsmouth. The flamboyant Schultz had little notion of undercover operations, setting himself up on a houseboat in Portsmouth, flying the German flag from the stern and throwing parties at which he attempted (unsuccessfully) to turn the conversation to naval matters. Though he quickly aroused suspicion, he acquired no useful information. On one occasion, while engaged in gun practice, he shot his housekeeper, Miss Sturgeon, in the arm. When Miss Sturgeon sued for damages, Schultz consulted a local solicitor, Hugh Duff, whom he also asked to collect military and naval information for a 'German newspaper'. Duff and one of his friends, Edward Tarren, agreed to do so but secretly informed the police. Kell then took charge of the case and provided bogus information for Duff and Tarren to supply to Schultz. By 17 August there was enough evidence for a warrant to be issued for Schultz's arrest. The proceedings during Schultz's trial were, at times, a match for his own personal eccentricity. He was tried in the name of Dr Phil Max Schultz, the authorities failing to realize that 'Phil' on statements signed by Schultz referred not to a given name but to his doctorate of philosophy. Lord Chief Justice Alverstone told Schultz before sentencing him to twenty-one months in jail that it was 'a sad thing to think that you, a man of education, should be capable of coming over here posing as a gentleman', attempting to obtain improper information: 'I am thankful to know that the relations between the two countries are most friendly and amicable, and no one would repudiate and condemn the practices of which you have been guilty more strongly than all the leading men in Germany.'[55]

While the case against Schultz was proceeding, the law was being changed. The 1889 Official Secrets Act had been condemned as inadequate by the 1909 espionage sub-committee, by Kell in his progress reports, and by the Committee of Imperial Defence. The Helm case lent further weight to their arguments. The magistrates' court had thrown out the charge of felony alleging intention to communicate 'certain sketches and plans . . . to a foreign State – to wit the Empire of Germany' and committed Helm for trial only on a lesser charge. Under the 1889 Act it was necessary to prove intent to obtain information illegally. This, claimed Viscount Haldane, at the House of Lords' second reading of a new Official Secrets Bill in July 1911, created intolerable problems in preventing espionage: 'Not many months ago we found in the middle of the fortifications at Dover an intelligent stranger, who explained his presence by saying that he was there to hear the singing of the birds. He gave the explanation rather hastily, because it was mid-winter.'[56]

The new Bill making it illegal to obtain or communicate any information useful to an enemy as well as to approach or enter a 'prohibited place' 'for any purpose prejudicial to the safety or interests of the State' placed the onus on the accused to show that his actions were innocently intended. The Bill was introduced in the Commons, after passing all its stages in the Lords, on 17 August. Placing the onus of proof on the accused was not entirely without legal precedent; it applied in a roughly similar way to the crime of 'loitering with intent' under the 1871 Prevention of Crimes Act.[57] But the Attorney General, Sir Rufus Isaacs, was stretching a point when he assured the Commons on 18 August that, by comparison with the 1889 Official Secrets Act, 'there is nothing novel in the principle of the Bill which the House is being asked to accept now.' The Liberal MP Sir Alpheus Morton immediately retorted: 'It upsets Magna Carta altogether.' None the less Colonel 'Jack' Seely, the Under Secretary for War, was able to exploit the sense of urgency created by the fear in the summer of 1911 that a crisis caused by German gunboat diplomacy (the sending of the SMS *Panther* to the Moroccan port of Agadir) might erupt into European war. He succeeded in pushing the Bill through all its Commons stages in the scarcely precedented space of less than an hour.[58] Kell noted in his next progress report that the new Act 'greatly facilitated' his work.[59]

The first German agent prosecuted after the passing of the 1911 Official Secrets Act was Heinrich Grosse, who was successfully convicted at the

Winchester Assizes in February 1912. Like Schultz, Grosse had a criminal background which failed to deter the Nachrichten-Abteilung from recruiting him. Indeed his past ingenuity as a criminal may actually have been seen as a positive indication of his aptitude for espionage. He was sent to Portsmouth to inquire into local naval fortifications, submarines, guns and mine-laying cruisers. Posing as a modern languages teacher and using the name 'Captain Hugh Grant', Grosse employed a naval pensioner, William Salter, to make inquiries into the coal stocks in Portsmouth. Salter immediately told the dockyard police, who in turn informed Kell. Though Grosse was an indifferent spy, Kell dealt with the case efficiently. A letter check, as well as revealing details of Grosse's espionage, also identified two of the intermediaries employed by Steinhauer to maintain contact with agents in Britain. Building on his experience of supplying bogus information to Duff during the Schultz case, Kell supplied more elaborate disinformation to Salter which Grosse passed on to Berlin. Grosse's case officer was sufficiently pleased with the disinformation to forward a more detailed list of inquiries on wireless telegraphy, range-finding, naval guns and coal supplies. Grosse was, however, told that his report about 'a floating conning-tower' (apparently one of Kell's less plausible inventions) was 'surely imaginary'. This, like the remainder of Grosse's correspondence, was duly intercepted. Finally, Kell ordered a police raid on Grosse's lodgings to obtain the incriminating evidence required for a successful prosecution. While in prison, Grosse received one further letter (also intercepted) from a representative of the Nachrichten-Abteilung, promising him 'a sum of money' which could be used either for his defence or to assist him on his release, with the implication that the latter might be the more prudent course. The judge at Grosse's trial, Mr (later Lord) Justice Darling, who tried a number of official secrets cases, found several opportunities amid the bizarre evidence produced in court for displays of his celebrated judicial wit, each greeted by sycophantic courtroom laughter. Like Lord Chief Justice Alverstone in the Schultz trial, Darling disliked the whole idea of intelligence-gathering. He concluded, when sentencing Grosse to three years' penal servitude: 'We desire to live on terms of amity with every neighbouring nation and the practice of spying can but tend to inflame hostile feelings . . . Spying upon one another gives rise to such ill-feeling that if it could be stamped out it should be.'[60]

The next German spy brought to trial, Armgaard Karl Graves, displayed once again the Nachrichten-Abteilung's penchant for recruiting criminals whose operational skills could, it believed, be adapted to intelligence-gathering. Like Schultz and Grosse, Graves was an adventurer who drifted into espionage. Unlike his predecessors, however, he was a successful confidence trickster who added both 'N' and MO5(g) to his list of victims. Steinhauer later claimed (though there is no corroboration for the claim) that Graves was never 'his spy', but had been employed against his recommendations by his superiors at the German Admiralty. In 1911, having returned to Germany after a period in Australia, Graves persuaded the Nachrichten-Abteilung to finance a Scottish intelligence mission. Following his arrival in Scotland in early 1912, he set himself up as a locum doctor in Leith on bogus Australian qualifications. The fact that Graves was a fantasist as well as a confidence trickster makes it difficult to assess his own highly coloured account of his operations in Scotland. He later claimed that, having discovered he had aroused suspicion, he decided to try 'a right royal bluff' by calling at Glasgow police headquarters and demanding to see the Chief Constable:

Presently I was shown into the chief's room, and was received by a typical Scottish gentleman. I opened fire in this way: 'Have you any reason to believe that I am a German spy?'

I saw that it had knocked him off his pins.

'Why, no,' he said, startled, 'I don't know anything about it at all.'

'It's not by your orders then that I am followed?'

'Certainly not,' he replied.[61]

If Graves was not already under surveillance, it was not long before he was. Kell's Bureau had identified him as a spy through the interception of his correspondence, and Kell moved to Glasgow to take personal charge of the investigation. Graves was arrested at Kell's request on 14 April after intercepts indicated he might be about to return to Germany.[62]

The well-publicized Schultz, Grosse and Graves prosecutions must surely have assisted Kell's campaign to gain War Office approval to recruit more staff for his diminutive Bureau. On 1 April 1912 he was allowed to recruit an additional officer, Captain (later Major) Reginald Drake (predictably nicknamed 'Duck'), who, like Kell, had begun his career in a Staffordshire regiment.[63] Drake listed a remarkable range of outdoor and sporting pursuits: 'Recreations: Hunting, Shooting, Beagling, Skiing, Golf, Cricket, Hockey, Polo, Otter-hunting, Swimming, Tennis, Lawn Tennis, Racquets, Squash Racquets'.[64] According to an enthusiastic later assessment of him by Kell's wife, Drake was 'a most able man and most successful sleuth, small hope for anyone who fell into his net'.[65] He was probably selected by Kell partly because he spoke German (in addition to French, in which he had a first-class interpreter's qualification, and Dutch).[66] When Stanley

Clarke left the Bureau late in 1912 to become deputy chief constable of Kent,[67] Drake succeeded him as Kell's chief counter-espionage investigator. In September 1912 Kell moved from the Temple to new headquarters a few hundred yards away on the third floor of Watergate House, York Buildings, Adelphi. Correspondence was forwarded from a cover address, Kelly's Letter Bureau ('Kelly' was one of Kell's aliases), in Shaftesbury Avenue.[68]

In December 1912, in place of Clarke, Kell recruited Captain (later Brigadier Sir) Eric Holt-Wilson, an Old Harrovian instructor in military engineering at Woolwich Royal Military Academy. Like Drake, Holt-Wilson was a formidable all-round sportsman, a 'champion revolver shot' (to quote his own description) and later president of the Ski Club of Great Britain. He was also, according to Lady Kell's unpublished memoirs, 'a man of almost genius for intricate organisation' and 'an intensely loyal and devoted friend'. Holt-Wilson became Kell's deputy during the war and remained in that position until he resigned after Kell was sacked in 1940.[69] He owed his nickname 'Holy Willy' to the fact that he was the son of a rector and a devout Anglican. Holt-Wilson's deep patriotism also had a quasi-religious dimension; he wrote in his diary that 'all my life and all my strength were given to the finest cause on this earth – the ennoblement of all mankind by the example of the British race.'[70] Like other pre-war recruits, Holt-Wilson took a career gamble in retiring from the army to join a bureau whose future was far from guaranteed. Before signing on, he wrote to ask Kell for:

a brief guarantee of employment in writing which will hold me up in case anything unforeseen should befall you and a generation arose 'which knew not Joseph' [a biblical analogy]. I hope you don't consider this over cautious on my part – but it is a big throw, to hurl one's commission into the fire and trust to luck for the next move.[71]

Late in 1912 Kell took a major new initiative. During the Schultz and Grosse cases he had, in effect, briefly used Duff and Salter as double agents by successfully channelling through them information and disinformation to German intelligence. Graves offered Kell a remarkable, but risky, opportunity to recruit him as a full-time double agent. On the day after his conviction Graves announced that he was willing to reveal the operations of German intelligence in Britain – but only to 'an accredited and well informed Secret Service official of the War Office'. On 9 and 10 September, using the alias 'Mr W. Robinson', Kell met him in Barlinnie Prison, Glasgow. Graves produced a plausible mixture of accurate information, including names of some senior Nachrichten-Abteilung personnel, and fabrications, such as his claim that he had been instructed to prepare for the sabotage of the Forth Railway Bridge and identify non-German 'undesirable persons to carry out terrorist attacks'. Wrongly convinced that Germany was engaged in military as well as naval espionage in Britain, Kell also took seriously Graves's assertion that German intelligence had divided the whole of England into twenty-four districts, each under the supervision of a German intelligence officer. Graves further claimed that Germany had twenty-nine 'principal agents' in Britain and one in Ireland, each with his own identifying number (Graves being '27'). Kell arranged for Graves's transfer from Barlinnie to Brixton and for his secret release on 18 December 1912. He then accepted employment by Kell's Bureau under the cover name 'Snell' or 'Schnell' at £2 per week for an initial period of six months. An interwar MI5 assessment of the Graves case, though not passing judgement on Kell himself (unsurprisingly, since he remained director), criticized MO5 (by which it meant MO5(g), Kell's Bureau) for having been so impressed by the information supplied by Graves and by his obvious ability that they 'shut their eyes to his extraordinarily bad character'.[72]

Graves did not, however, deceive the former Met sergeant Henry Fitzgerald, who joined the Bureau as a detective on 1 November 1912.[73] Fitzgerald was deputed to accompany Graves on a tour of what he claimed were German spy haunts. Though Fitzgerald's reports do not survive, an interwar MI5 summary of them notes that he 'repeatedly drew attention to the barrenness of the results obtained and reported that Schnell [Graves] was trying to draw him with regard to the personality of W. Robinson'. In short, Fitzgerald 'saw through him and reported on him somewhat ironically'. Graves's next stratagem was to claim that at German intelligence headquarters in Berlin there was a book containing 'the name, description, instructions, code, place and dates of employment of every German agent in this country'. Kell agreed to finance a trip by Graves to Berlin in late January 1913 to obtain a copy of the book.[74] Once in Berlin, Graves wired for more money, which Kell duly supplied. Graves next made contact from a liner bound for New York to report that he was shadowing a senior German intelligence officer on board, who had a copy of the secret book. On 18 March, however, a cable from the consul general in New York reported that 'Snell' 'had just left hospital after a murderous assault' and had lost all the reports he had written.[75] Kell responded to two further requests for money from Graves while he was in New York but, having finally grown suspicious, did not reply to a third. When questions were asked in the Commons about Graves's earlier release from prison, MPs were incorrectly informed that he had been freed because of poor health. In 1914 Graves caused further embarrassment to both Kell's Bureau and the Nachrichten-Abteilung by publishing newspaper articles and a book about his exploits as a secret agent.[76]

The eccentric behaviour of the first four spies to be convicted after the foundation of the Secret Service Bureau – Helm, Schultz, Grosse and Graves – makes it easy to underestimate the actual, and still more the potential, threat from German naval espionage. The final cases which came to court before the outbreak of war make clear that the threat was real. The spy trial of Karl Hentschel and George Parrott in January 1913 was the most sensational so far. Hentschel, a former German merchant seaman, was another in the series of criminal adventurers (though with a less well-developed fantasy world than Graves) who were recruited by 'N'. In 1908 he was sent to Britain, where he established himself as a language teacher first in Devonport, then in Sheerness. Many of his students were Royal Navy personnel, from whom he attempted to extract information. Hentschel married an English wife, Patricia Riley, and befriended the chief gunner on HMS Agamemnon, George Parrott. According to Steinhauer, 'Hentschel then did something that even the most unscrupulous of spies would hesitate to do,' and encouraged his wife to have an affair with Parrott. The liaison soon started to pay espionage dividends. Parrott smuggled from HMS Agamemnon four volumes of a classified Royal Navy report on gunnery progress. Kell's Bureau later established that in 1910–11 Parrott had supplied 'N' with a total of twenty-three classified naval manuals.[77]

In the spring of 1911, however, Hentschel broke contact with Parrott, apparently after quarrelling over Parrott's affair with his wife and their respective shares of the money from Berlin. Hentschel was first detected by the Counter-Espionage Bureau as a result of intercepted correspondence to his wife late in 1911 while he was spending several months in Australia.[78] The first evidence of Parrott's continuing contact with German intelligence also emerged from intercepts at almost the same time,[79] though it was several more months before the Bureau discovered his earlier connection with Hentschel.[80] Though Melville had earlier been reluctant to shadow suspects personally,[81] in July 1912 he shadowed Parrott on a ferry to Ostend, where he met a man who was 'evidently a German . . . Age about 35 to 40. Height 5ft 9 inches – hair and moustache medium dark. Dress light tweed jacket suit and straw hat. Typical German walk and style.' Steinhauer later claimed that he had simultaneously been shadowing

Melville but did not warn Parrott, perhaps for fear of making him reluctant to continue working as a German agent.[82] Parrott was arrested on his return to England, but, because of unwillingness to use the intercept evidence in court, he was dismissed from the Royal Navy rather than put on trial.[83]

Two other would-be naval spies detected by letter checks during 1912 were also not put on trial in order not to reveal intercept evidence in court. In February Frederick Ireland, a twenty-year-old stoker on HMS *Foxhound*, was persuaded by a German uncle, Otto Kruger,[84] working as a Nachrichten-Abteilung agent, to offer his services to Steinhauer. The Security Service summary of the case notes that 'Owing to the undesirability of producing certain evidence [Ireland] was dismissed the Navy without trial.'[85] On 23 March 1912 a letter was intercepted in the post addressed to 'Head, Intelligence Department, War Office, Germany', signed 'Walter J. Devlin'. 'Devlin', who offered his services as an agent, claimed to have served for seven and a half years in the Royal Navy and still to have access to various ships and naval barracks. He asked that his offer be acknowledged by placing a small ad in the *Daily Mirror*, reading, 'Your Services will be useful, Devonport' and giving an address for correspondence. The Counter-Espionage Bureau placed the small ad and, using the alias 'A. Pfeiffer', began corresponding with Devlin, who after a month gave his real name, John Hattrick, and his address in Plymouth. At a meeting with Pfeiffer on 16 May, Hattrick, who was a naval deserter, wrote out and signed an agreement undertaking to find out naval and military information as required by the German government. Next day, while inside Devonport dockyard, he was arrested on a charge of attempting to communicate information to a foreign power. He was later released (as had doubtless been intended from the outset) but warned that the case would go ahead if he had any further involvement in espionage.[86]

Parrott's intercepted correspondence revealed that, unlike Ireland and Hattrick, he remained in touch with German intelligence after he had been caught red-handed.[87] On 18 October he travelled to Hamburg to meet his case officer, 'Richard', who handed him the then considerable sum of £500. While there, Parrott was extensively debriefed by gunnery, torpedo, naval engineering and intelligence experts, and agreed to continue work as an agent. He was arrested on his return home, found guilty in January 1913 of breaking the Official Secrets Act and sentenced by Mr Justice Darling to four years' hard labour. Darling told Parrott he had been 'entrapped by a woman', and promised to try 'to procure some remission' if Parrott revealed all he knew to 'the authorities'.[88]

Parrott's recruiter, Karl Hentschel, and his wife, meanwhile, had disappeared to Australia, but, after their marriage (perhaps unsurprisingly) broke up, they returned separately to Britain in September 1913. On his return Hentschel offered to provide information about German intelligence on condition of immunity from prosecution and paid employment by the British secret service. Melville interviewed Hentschel and paid him £100 for his information.[89] Soon afterwards, having tried and failed to mend his marriage, Hentschel presented himself at Chatham police station, announced that he was a German spy and asked to be arrested. The Chatham police declined his request, but the following day Hentschel tried again at the Old Jewry police station in the City of London. 'I wish to give myself up for being a German spy,' Hentschel declared. 'You may think I am mad, but that is not so. I have had trouble with my wife; and have decided in consequence to confess what I have been doing since I have been in England.' This time he was questioned, arrested and brought before the Westminster police court on a charge of conspiracy with ex-Gunner Parrott 'to disclose naval secrets'. Hentschel's protestations of guilt caused Kell some embarrassment. It was acknowledged in court that Kell's organization (identified only as a department unconnected with the police 'especially charged to deal with matters of that kind') had paid Hentschel for 'confidential information' incriminating Parrott and had promised him immunity from prosecution provided he kept his own role secret. However, counsel for the Crown suggested disingenuously that, being a foreigner, the defendant might not have understood that 'if he made any communication in an open or public manner avowing his own participation in crime', his immunity from prosecution would lapse. The Attorney General had therefore thought it right to offer no evidence and allow the charges to be withdrawn. But Hentschel was warned in no uncertain manner not to cause Kell any future embarrassment: 'If the defendant should, under any circumstances whatever, henceforth make any open or public repetition of his own complicity in crime the authorities would hold themselves perfectly free to prosecute.'[90]

The last two German spies convicted before the war were, in very different ways, as unreliable as their predecessors. The first was Wilhelm Klauer, alias Klare. Klauer had arrived in England as a kitchen porter in 1902 but, after a period as a dentist's assistant, set himself up as a dentist in Portsmouth, where he supplemented his meagre fees from pulling teeth by living off the immoral earnings of his prostitute wife. Late in 1912 Klauer wrote to the German Admiralty offering to supply naval intelligence. Steinhauer was sent to visit Klauer and, by his own account, came to the accurate conclusion that he was a fraud who believed, probably from reading Le Queux's novels, that vast sums were to be made from espionage. Against Steinhauer's recommendation, the German Admiralty decided none the less to see if Klauer could obtain a secret report book on torpedo trials. Klauer had so little idea how to lay hands on the book that he sought the help of a German-Jewish hairdresser and chiropodist, Levi Rosenthal. Klauer told Rosenthal that it would be worth £100 to have the report book 'long enough for it to go to Germany and back'. And that, he said, was only the beginning; there were 'hundreds' more pounds where the first hundred came from. Without telling Klauer, Rosenthal went to the police. From then on he acted under control, eventually introducing Klauer to a dockyard official who supplied him with a confidential document, thus providing evidence for prosecution. In March 1913 Klauer was sentenced to five years' hard labour amid applause from a crowded courtroom.[91]

The last German spy convicted before the outbreak of war was also probably the most successful. Frederick Adolphus Schroeder, alias Gould, had been born in Germany of an English mother and German father, and after service in the German army had settled in England. Following the failure of various business ventures, he began dabbling in part-time espionage early in the twentieth century. By 1906 he was on the books of the Nachrichten-Abteilung as an 'observer' (*Beobachter*) of Sheerness and Chatham.[92] His most productive period, however, began in 1908 when he became licensee of the Queen Charlotte public house in Rochester, frequented by naval personnel from Chatham. In Steinhauer's professional opinion, Schroeder:

was not a man whom anyone would take for a spy. Had you met him in the street you would have turned round to look at him and said to yourself: 'What a fine-looking fellow!' Broad-shouldered, bearded, nature – plus twelve years in the German Army – had given him a big, athletic frame and a pleasant, cheery manner.[93]

In May 1912, on Steinhauer's recommendation, Schroeder was given a formal contract by 'N' and a regular salary of £15 a month. The two men became close friends. One undated letter from Steinhauer (probably among those intercepted by Kell's Bureau) concludes: 'You are always welcome to us. My children are always asking when Uncle Gould is coming.' From June 1912, Schroeder sent regular fortnightly reports to Berlin, mostly via Wilhelm Kronauer, one of 'N's' forwarding agents on whom Kell had obtained a Home Office Warrant. Just as he began sending the reports, Melville's assistant detective, John Regan, disguised as a sailor, succeeded in befriending Schroeder, who, he reported, talked freely (if inaccurately) about how German money was being used to foment a British revolution. It appears to have taken more than a year for the Bureau to discover that, as well as submitting written reports to Steinhauer, Schroeder and his common-law wife, Maud Sloman, also travelled regularly to the continent to meet Steinhauer and other 'N' officers.[94] In February 1914, however, an intercept revealed that Sloman was about to leave for Brussels with a gunnery drill book, charts of Bergen and Spithead, and plans of cruisers. Mrs Gould (as Sloman styled herself) was arrested on 22 February as she was on the point of boarding the Ostend boat train at Charing Cross Station, and found in possession of classified documents.[95] Schroeder was arrested on the same day and many more documents were found in his attic. Steinhauer's 'blood ran cold' when he learned of their discovery. According to Steinhauer, Schroeder had provided 'more information on naval matters than all other spies put together'. Among the classified documents referred to at his trial were 'important matters relating to engines, engine-room and engine arrangements of battleships'. In April 1914 Schroeder was sentenced to six years' hard labour.[96]

By December 1913 the Counter-Espionage Bureau's secret Register of Aliens was almost complete except for London (where about half the aliens lived), and Kell wrote to the Home Office 'to express our gratitude to the Chief Constables and their Superintendents for the excellent work they have done for us during the last three years' and to request that their local registers 'be kept under constant current revision'.[97] Kell's original plan to use police forces around the country to compile a secret register of all aliens from probable enemy powers (chiefly Germany) had proved difficult to complete because of the scale of the exercise and the limited resources of both Bureau and police. The Home Office had also insisted that no alien was to be asked any question 'of an inquisitorial nature'.[98] The results of the National Census of 1911, however, made it possible to complete a more limited and focused Register of Aliens. During 1913 the Census returns were used to record the particulars of all male aliens aged eighteen and above of eight nationalities (in particular Germans and Austrians) living in areas which would be closed to aliens in wartime. Information on aliens taken from the Census was then circulated for checking to chief constables, who were also asked to take note of those on the Register in their areas.[99]

Kell's Registry entered the aliens information received from the 1911 Census and chief constables on what were known as 'Special Cards': the beginning of MI5's card index. The Registry was among the most up to date of its era. In preference to the long-established ledger-based systems,

Kell was one of the first to adopt what was then the cutting edge of data management, the Roneo carding system.[100] Each alien was allocated a Roneo card with serial number and basic information: name, nationality, date of birth, family particulars, address (home and business), place in the household (whether householder, lodger or servant), trade or occupation, and details of any employers. Any additional information was written on the back of the card. Cards were updated when further information arrived from chief constables. Colour-coding and symbols were added to the cards to enable speedy identification of the level of threat each alien was believed to pose. A yellow wafer-seal indicated a possible suspect, subject to periodic reports from chief constables; a red wafer-seal identified those on a 'Special War List' of high-risk enemy aliens, subject to special regular reports from chief constables and to surveillance after the outbreak of war. If, in addition to the red seal, the card was marked with a cross (X), the alien was to be searched on the outbreak of war; if with two crosses (XX) he was on a wartime arrest list sent to chief constables. A small hole punched in a yellow seal indicated that the alien was no longer on the suspect list; a hole in a red seal meant removal from the Special War List.[101]

A majority of the German spies detected by the Counter-Espionage Bureau in the few years before the First World War did not come to trial. Those caught *in flagrante* while procuring classified information were prosecuted under the 1911 Official Secrets Act. Rather than arrest most other identified members of Steinhauer's network, in particular Karl Ernst and the 'postmen', Kell tried to maintain up-to-date information on their whereabouts and monitored their correspondence in order both to trace their contacts and to be in a position to cripple German espionage in Britain at the outbreak of war.[102] Premature arrests risked revealing to the Nachrichten-Abteilung the extent of his knowledge of the existing agent network and leading it to set up a new and more secure network which would be more difficult to penetrate. For that reason Kell also preferred to warn off 'N's' British sources rather than bring them to trial. He complained in August 1912:

Owing to the fact that it is impossible in this country to hold trials for espionage and kindred offences in camera (as is the custom in continental countries) it was considered contrary to the interests of the State to bring these men to trial, which would have entailed a disclosure of the identity of our informants and other confidential matters.[103]

The most important of these 'confidential matters' was that, thanks to Churchill's change in the HOW system, letter checks were far more frequent than before and had compromised much of Steinhauer's network. Doubtless to Kell's dismay, some of the contents of intercepted letters were used as evidence in the trials of Schultz and Graves.[104] *The Times* report on the Gould trial referred to a number of letters signed 'St' (though not to the fact that Gould's papers included a signed photograph of their author, Gustav Steinhauer). On 27 March a warrant was taken out for Steinhauer's arrest under the Official Secrets Act on a charge of having procured Gould to obtain information which might be useful to an enemy.[105] Though Steinhauer later claimed that he had known his letters were being read,[106] the arrests of his agents on the outbreak of war demonstrate that he was unaware of the scale of the interception of his correspondence with them. During the July Crisis which followed the assassination of the heir to the Austro-Hungarian throne, Archduke Franz Ferdinand, on 28 June 1914 and precipitated the First World War, Steinhauer made a last, daring visit to Britain to contact some of his agents. Kell knew from intercepted correspondence that a jute salesman using the name 'Fritsches' (previously identified as a probable alias of Steinhauer's) was travelling in Britain, but he lacked the resources to mount close surveillance of all the likely points on Steinhauer's route, and he escaped undetected.[107] Steinhauer later boasted of how, disguised as a gentleman fisherman rather than a jute salesman, he travelled as far north as Kirkwall.[108]

On 29 July, six days before Britain entered the First World War, Kell's Bureau began sending chief constables 'warning letters' with lists of suspected German agents and dossiers on those to be arrested.[109] During the final days of peace Kell remained in his office at Watergate House twenty-four hours a day, sleeping surrounded by telephones, and – according to Constance Kell's unpublished memoirs – ready to order the arrest of twenty-two identified German spies as soon as war was declared.[110] But for the co-operation established by Kell with chief constables since 1910 the rounding up of the core of Steinhauer's agent network would have been impossible. Never before in British history had plans been prepared for such a large number of preferably simultaneous arrests of enemy agents at diverse locations. With a total staff of only seventeen (including the caretaker) on the eve of war, Kell depended on local police forces for much of the investigation and surveillance which preceded the arrests as well as for the arrests themselves. Nowadays hundreds of Security Service staff and police officers would be required for such a large operation. Kell, however, had neither the staff nor the modern communications systems required to remain in close and constant touch with all the police forces involved. Unsurprisingly, six police forces took independent initiatives.

The Portsmouth police jumped the gun by arresting one of those on Kell's list (Alberto Rosso, alias 'Rodriguez') on 3 August, the day before Britain went to war. On or soon after 4 August other local police forces arrested seven additional suspects they had identified (apparently on flimsy evidence) whose arrest had not been ordered by Kell.[111]

Kell's original arrest list no longer survives, but was later reconstructed by the interwar Registry from MI5 files.[112] Following the premature arrest of Rosso on 3 August, nine further arrests ordered by Kell were made on the 4th, five on the 5th and five more over the next week. The final arrests were made on 15 and 16 August, bringing the total to twenty-two.[113] The total included one suspect who was not on the original arrest list: the previously unidentified husband of a female German agent, Lina Heine, who was discovered in her company when she was arrested.[114] One spy on the original arrest list, Walter Rimann, a German-language teacher in Hull, was later discovered to have taken the ferry to Zeebrugge on 1 August and never returned to Britain. His intercepted correspondence over the previous two years had revealed recurrent nervousness about his own security, following revelations about Steinhauer's British operations during espionage trials.[115]

Though the identification of the twenty-two German agents arrested in August 1914 on Kell's instructions owed much to police investigations,[116] the key role usually belonged to Kell's Bureau. At least seventeen (probably more) of the twenty-two had been subject to letter checks under HOWs obtained by Kell which provided the most reliable method of monitoring their contacts with the Nachrichten-Abteilung.[117] In the run-up to war Kell's Bureau had also begun to influence government policy, helping to draft legislation 'to prevent persons communicating with the enemy' and restrict the movement of aliens, which was rushed through parliament after the outbreak of war.[118]

The twenty men and two women arrested represented espionage threats of very different orders of magnitude. All, however, with the possible exception of Lina Heine's husband, had been in contact with German intelligence and thus clearly represented potential wartime espionage risks. The Nachrichten-Abteilung had no doubt that its British operations had been struck a devastating blow. Gustav Steinhauer later acknowledged that at the outbreak of war there had been 'a wholesale round-up of our secret service agents in England'.[119] The Kaiser, he recalled, was beside himself with fury when told the news of the arrests:

Apparently unable to believe his ears, [he] raved and stormed for the better part of two hours about the incompetence of his so-called intelligence officers, bellowing:

'Am I surrounded by dolts? Why was I not told? Who is responsible?' and more in the same vein.[120]

Steinhauer is scarcely likely to have fabricated such a devastating denunciation of his own incompetence.

In the less than five years since the founding of the Secret Service Bureau, Kell had transformed British counter-espionage. He had begun by chasing phantoms. Few, if any, of the first cases his Counter-Espionage Bureau examined involved real spies. By 1912, however, the Bureau was fully focused on actual German espionage. The cases of Parrott and Schroeder, among others, demonstrate that, if unchecked, the Nachrichten-Abteilung might well have collected an impressive amount of intelligence on the strengths and weaknesses of the Royal Navy. The expanded HOW system for authorizing letter checks and the data-management system of the Registry laid the foundations for MI5's future development. The small scale of the Bureau's resources made its achievements the more remarkable. Its staff were fewer in number than the spies whose arrest it ordered in August 1914.

Research in German archives demonstrates that Kell's Bureau did not succeed in identifying all the German agents present in Britain at the outbreak of war. It seems, however, to have rounded up all those that mattered. There is no evidence that in the critical early weeks of the war any worthwhile intelligence reached Germany from Britain. Holt-Wilson later recalled:

A German Order came into our hands early in the war which disclosed the fact that as late as the 21st August (i.e. 17 days after war was declared), the German Military Commanders were still ignorant of the despatch or movements of our main Expeditionary Force, although this had been more or less common knowledge to thousands in this country.[121]

There was, of course, much that Kell's small Bureau had not discovered about German intelligence work during its first five years. Its central error was to believe that German military as well as naval intelligence was operating in Britain. In reality, before the outbreak of war German military intelligence (Sektion IIIb) concentrated exclusively on Russia and France; indeed, intelligence from its agents in Russia helped to alert the Prussian General Staff to Russian mobilization at the end of July 1914.[122] Kell's belief that Sektion IIIb was also targeting Britain was not, however, a foolish mistake for a young intelligence agency. The head of Sektion IIIb, Lieutenant Colonel Walter Nicolai, later revealed that, though 'Time had not sufficed to extend this organisation to England, this was, indeed, to have been the next step in the organisation of our I[intelligence] S[ervice].'[123]

2

The First World War

Part 1: The Failure of German Espionage

War with Germany raised British spy mania to unprecedented heights. On 4 August 1914, the day that Britain went to war, Basil Thomson, Assistant Commissioner at Scotland Yard in charge of the Criminal Investigation Department (CID), whose responsibilities also included the 114-man Metropolitan Police Special Branch (MPSB),[1] was informed that secret saboteurs had blown up a culvert near Aldershot and a railway bridge in Kent. An inspection next day found both to be intact. Spy mania, wrote Thomson later, 'assumed a virulent epidemic form accompanied by delusions which defied treatment': 'It attacked all classes indiscriminately and seemed even to find its most fruitful soil in sober, stolid, and otherwise truthful people.' Reports flooded in of German agents planning mayhem and communicating with the enemy by a variety of improbable means. All were false alarms.[2]

The Home Secretary, Reginald McKenna, sought to calm public fears on 5 August by announcing to the Commons that twenty-one spies and suspected spies had been arrested 'all over the country' in the past twenty-four hours, 'chiefly in important military or naval centres'.[3] In his anxiety to reduce spy mania, however, McKenna had jumped the gun. Seven of the German agent network identified by Kell had still to be arrested.[4] New legislation gave the government unprecedented powers to deal with aliens and suspected spies. The Aliens Restriction Act, drafted by the Home Office in consultation with Kell and Holt-Wilson,[5] in readiness for war, was rushed through parliament on 5 August and gave the government carte blanche 'to impose restrictions on aliens and make such provisions as appear necessary or expedient for carrying such restrictions into effect'. The Defence of the Realm Act (DORA), also drafted in consultation with Kell and Holt-Wilson,[6] which became law three days later, gave the government powers close to martial law:

i to prevent persons communicating with the enemy or obtaining information
   for that purpose or any purpose calculated to jeopardise the success of the
   operations of any of His Majesty's Forces or to assist the enemy; and

ii to secure the safety of any means of communications, or of railways, docks or
   harbours.

Enemy aliens were required to register with the police and forbidden to
live in a large number of 'prohibited areas' without police permits.[7] Kell
and the other army officers on the retired list in his Bureau were mobilized
for war service as general staff officers (GSOs).[8] The Special Intelligence
Bureau (SIB), as it continued to style itself, was integrated into the War
Office as MO5(g) and its responsibilities extended to include 'military
policy in connection with civil population including aliens' and the 'administration of the Defence of the Realm Regulations in so far as they concern
the M[ilitary] O[perations] Directorate'.[9] Its role, however, was kept secret.
MO5(g) policy, approved by Whitehall, was to conceal 'the very existence
of a British Contre-Espionage Bureau'.[10]

The new wartime legislation did little in the short term to calm spy
fever. When McKenna made a further attempt to allay public anxieties on
9 October by claiming that pre-war spies had obtained 'little valuable
information' and that the whole German spy network had in all probability
been 'crushed at the outbreak of the war', The Times was 'more than a
little incredulous': 'It does not square with what we know of the German
spy system . . . In their eager absorption of the baser side of militarism, the
Germans seem to have almost converted themselves into a race of spies.'[11]
Security Service files still contain a small sample of the letters forwarded
to it by the War and Home Offices from correspondents as deluded as
those who had contributed to the spy scares of Edwardian England. An
army officer, based in London, reported, inter alia, that 'Haldane is the
first and foremost spy. His houses should be raided, as he has got a wireless
set behind the cupboard in one of his bedrooms.' Other correspondents
claimed that German coalminers in the Kent coalfields had dug a series of
tunnels which were to be used for wartime sabotage. According to a
correspondent from East Ham, one of the tunnels passed under Canterbury
Cathedral.[12]

The spy scares which followed the outbreak of war gave William Le
Queux a new lease of life. He was, he declared, 'not affected by that disease
known as spy mania' and was full of praise for the 'unremitting efforts' of
Kell's Bureau, which he referred to as 'a certain nameless department,
known only by a code number'. Le Queux fraudulently claimed to be

'intimate with its workings': 'I know its splendid staff, its untiring and painstaking efforts, its thoroughness, its patriotism, and the astuteness of its head director, who is one of the finest Englishmen of my acquaintance.' But he now considered the scale of the spy menace altogether beyond the capacity of Kell's 'nameless department': 'The serious truth is that German espionage and treasonable propaganda have, during past years, been allowed by a slothful military administration to take root so deeply that the authorities today find themselves powerless to eradicate its pernicious growth.'[13]

Milder forms of spy fever were common even among those who escaped the wilder fantasies of Le Queux and his readers. They were strengthened by the sinking of three British cruisers by U-boats in the North Sea on 22 September. Admiral Lord Charles Beresford, MP for Portsmouth and former Commander in Chief of the Channel Fleet, told a recruiting drive on 2 October: 'Three cruisers were lost by information given from this country to the German Admiralty. The British people should insist that the Home Office prevent the British Army and Navy being stabbed in the back by assassins in the shape of spies. All alien enemies should be locked up!' Soon afterwards he claimed in a letter to the press: 'Numbers of men have been caught red-handed signalling etc. and have been discharged through not enough evidence.' Requests to Beresford from the Director of Public Prosecutions for evidence to support his claims brought only confused and choleric replies. The Attorney General, Sir John Simon, however, was inclined to believe Beresford's explanation for the sinking of the cruisers. He wrote privately on 26 October:

Experience has shown that the German Navy is extraordinarily well informed of our movements, and though I have the greatest detestation of spy mania, I do not think it is open to doubt that there are a number of unidentified persons in this country, who have been making treacherous communications, and who were not known to us at the beginning of the war.[14]

MO5(g)'s growing responsibilities, combined with serious concern within and beyond Whitehall at the threat from German espionage, led to a steady expansion in its staff which continued throughout the war. By the end of 1914, MO5(g)'s staff had more than doubled in the four months since the outbreak of war (from seventeen to forty), but was still far too small to deal with the rapid increase in its work. An intensive recruitment campaign produced 227 new recruits in the following year.[15] Many officer recruits were men who had been wounded on the Western Front or other theatres of war, and been declared unfit for active service. A wartime cartoon shows a new recruit telling a visiting general: 'Oh, they knocked a piece out of my skull, so they sent me to the Intelligence Dept.'[16] Some recovered sufficiently to return to the Front. In 1915, to cope with increasing numbers, MO5(g) acquired rooms in Adelphi Court, a block of flats next to its HQ at Watergate House, York Buildings, Adelphi. Later, the whole block was acquired.

The most remarkable of MO5(g)'s early wartime recruits was the twenty-year-old William Edward Hinchley Cooke, the bilingual son of a German mother and British father, who had been to school in Dresden before becoming a student at Leipzig University. Early in 1914 he had also begun working as a clerk at the British legation in Dresden and, after being expelled with the rest of the legation at the outbreak of war, was strongly recommended to Kell by the minister, A. C. Grant Duff: 'He is entirely British in sentiment and the fact that he speaks English with a foreign accent must not be allowed to militate against him.'[17] Hinchley Cooke joined MO5(g) on 21 August and went on to become one of the few Security Service officers to serve in both world wars. In an attempt to counter the suspicion provoked by his German accent, Kell felt it necessary to write on Hinchley Cooke's War Office pass: 'He is an Englishman.' Hinchley Cooke's first assignment was to liaise with Basil Thomson at Scotland Yard, 'examining and reporting on the papers of enemy subjects, for which', Kell believed, 'his unique knowledge of German rendered him specially fitted'. Hinchley Cooke's skill in interpreting cryptic allusions in the correspondence and papers of espionage suspects, as well as an alertness to the use of secret inks before testing for them became routine, made him, in Kell's view, 'largely responsible for the arrest of several German spies'.[18]

Another early wartime recruit to MO5(g) was a fifty-two-year-old Cambridge-educated barrister at the Inner Temple, Walter Moresby, son of Admiral John Moresby, who lived near the Kells' home in Weybridge, Surrey, and joined in October 1914 as the Security Service's first legal adviser. His appointment reflected Kell's need for an experienced lawyer to advise on the increasingly complex wartime Defence Regulations as well as the high-profile prosecutions of German spies.[19] The unpublished memoirs of Kell's wife Constance describe the Moresbys as 'our cousins': 'We saw much of them and they became great friends.'[20]

On 1 October Kell divided MO5(g) into three branches:

MO5(g)A: 'Investigation of espionage and cases of suspected persons'
MO5(g)B: 'Co-ordination of general policy of Government Departments

One of Kell's first wartime recruits: William Edward Hinchley Cooke, son of a German mother and British father. (i) Hinchley Cooke's War Office pass, certifying that 'He is an Englishman' (despite his German accent). (ii) Bogus Alien Enemy Certificate of Registration card used by Hinchley Cooke when posing as the German Wilhelm Eduard Koch.

in dealing with aliens. Questions arising out of the Defence of the Realm Regulations and the Aliens Restriction Act'

MO5(g)C: 'Records, personnel, administration and port [immigration] control'[21]

As before the war, MO5(g)'s main investigative resources were its Registry and letter checks. Increased wartime responsibilities for 'suspected persons', aliens and immigration control at ports led to a steady expansion in its records. By the spring of 1917 MI5's Central Registry contained 250,000 cards and 27,000 personal files on its chief suspects kept up to date by 130 women clerks. Major (later Colonel Sir) Claude Dansey, then responsible for liaison with the United States, told American military intelligence that the Registry's filing system was 'our great standby and cornerstone': 'We have brought it to a point where every department in the government comes to us for information.' So did security services in the Empire and Allied countries.[22]

The Central Registry quickly developed standardized classifications for its suspects. First on each card in its index came the 'civil classification': BS, AS, NS or ES (British, Allied, Neutral or Enemy Subject). Then followed the 'general military (special intelligence) classification' along a mildly comic, but easily memorized, six-point scale:

AA 'Absolutely Anglicised' or 'Absolutely Allied' – undoubtedly friendly.
A 'Anglicised' or 'Allied' – friendly.
AB 'Anglo-Boche' – doubtful, but probably friendly.
BA 'Boche-Anglo' – doubtful, but probably hostile.
B 'Boche' – hostile.
BB 'Bad Boche' – undoubtedly hostile.[23]

Finally came an alphabetical series of 'Special Intelligence Black List (SI/BL) subclassifications', also designed to be committed to memory:

A 'Antecedents' in a civil, police, or judicial sense so bad that patriotism may not be the dominant factor, and sympathies not incorruptible.
B 'Banished' during the war from, or forbidden to enter, one or more of the Allied States.
C 'Courier', letter carrier, intermediary or auxiliary to enemy agents.
D 'Detained', interned or prevented from leaving an Allied State for S.I. reasons.

E   'Espion.' Enemy spy or agent engaged in active mischief (not
    necessarily confined to espionage).
F   'False' or irregular papers of identity or credential.
G   'Guarded', suspected, under special surveillance and not yet
    otherwise classified.
H   'Hawker', hostile by reason of trade or commerce with or for the
    enemy.
I   'Instigator' of hostile, pacifist, seditious or dangerous propaganda.
J   'Junction' wanted. The person, or information concerning him,
    wanted urgently by S.I. or an Allied S.I. Service.
K   'Kaiser's' man. Enemy officer or official or ex-officer or official.[24]

On the foundation of the Bureau Central Interallié in Paris in September
1915 to act as an intelligence clearing house for Allied services, Categories
A to I were adopted by the Bureau.[25]

The officer in charge of the Registry and of administration as a whole
was Lieutenant Colonel Maldwyn Makgill Haldane, variously nicknamed
'Muldoon' and 'Marmaduke', nephew of the former Secretary for War, Viscount Haldane, who in April 1914 became MO5(g)'s first graduate recruit.
Before being commissioned as second lieutenant in the Royal Scots in 1899,
Haldane had studied at University College London, Jesus College, Cambridge, and the University of Göttingen. Like many of Kell's officers, he was
a good linguist, competent in French, German and Hindustani, and listed an
impressive range of outdoor and sporting pursuits: trout fishing, rowing,
rugby, walking, poultry farming and gardening. Less typically, he also
declared an interest in 'ethnology, history, palaeontology and biology'.[26]
A satirical wartime cartoon shows him, dressed in Royal Scots tunic with
tartan trews, towering over an appreciative group of Registry staff.

Because of the expansion of the Registry and its clerical staff, by the end
of 1914 a majority of MO5(g) staff were female. According to a post-war
'Report on Women's Work':

The qualifications which M.I.5 required in its women clerks and secretaries were
intelligence, diligence and, above all, reticence. From the earliest days therefore,
M.I.5 sought its clerks in the ranks of educated women, who should naturally be
supposed to have inherited a code of honour, that is to say the women staff of M.I.5
consisted of gentlewomen who had enjoyed a good school, and in some cases a
University education.[27]

Though MI5 did not recruit men direct from university until well after the
Second World War, it sought female recruits from Oxford and London

A probably satirical cartoon by the wartime MI5 officer Joseph Sassoon depicts
Lieutenant Colonel Maldwyn Haldane, head of Registry and administration,
dressed in Royal Scots tunic with tartan trews, towering over an apparently
adoring group of Registry minions.

Universities in the First World War. Initially most women recruits were
personally recommended by existing members of staff. When, because of
the rapid wartime expansion, this method was unable to generate enough
recruits, the Service approached the heads of Cheltenham Ladies College
and other leading girls' public schools, of St Hugh's and Somerville Colleges
at Oxford University, and of Royal Holloway at London.[28] MO5(g) thus
had a higher proportion of upper-class female recruits than any other
wartime British government department or agency. Its women staff also
came, on average, from higher up the social scale than the men. Women
played a more important role in the Security Service than in any other
wartime government department.

From November 1914 the Registry was staffed solely by women and a
new 'lady superintendent', Lily Steuart, placed at its head.[29] During the
early months of the war, as a post-war report acknowledged, the Registry
was 'almost overwhelmed' by 'the tidal wave of documents' which

descended on it.[30] When Hilda Cribb (who in 1920 was to become controller of women staff) began work in the Registry on 2 February 1915 she found unfiled papers stacked on top of the filing cabinets.[31] The pressures of wartime work, exacerbated by MO5(g)'s seriously inadequate resources, probably explain why fifteen of the female clerical staff who joined between October 1914 and February 1915 left after periods ranging from a few days to two months. Among them was Miss Steuart.[32]

Steuart's successor as lady superintendent on 20 February, Edith Annie Lomax, proved to be one of the ablest administrators in Service history, later becoming the first female member of staff to be honoured with an MBE (subsequently upgraded to OBE).[33] Miss Lomax brought with her as her assistant the also formidable Elsie Lydia Harrison (subsequently Mrs Akehurst), who later succeeded her as controller, and was also awarded an MBE. Hilda Cribb noticed an immediate difference. As well as securing more recruits and accommodation, Lomax made a series of simple improvements to work practices. When she arrived, for example, card cabinets were so close together that only two staff could use them simultaneously. By spacing them out, she enabled more people to work on them. 'The hubbub', Cribb recalled, 'was incessant . . .'[34] In 1915 it was decided not to recruit women aged over forty; within a year the limit was lowered to thirty 'on account of the very considerable strain that was thrown on the brains of the workers'. Some exceptions, however, were made, such as the recruitment of two women with PhDs to write reports (and later in-house histories).[35] A sense of humour in Registry recruits was considered 'essential to enable some of the impossible things demanded to be accepted with equanimity'.[36] The anonymous post-war report on 'Women's Work', almost certainly by a female author, concluded that though most women demonstrated the stereotypically female virtues of intuition and attention to detail, a minority 'displayed the more masculine qualities of power of organization and decision and broad methods of work, and . . . did invaluable service for the Department'.[37] The author probably had Miss Lomax chiefly in mind. In 1917, Miss Lomax was promoted to the new post of controller of women's staff; her former deputy, Miss Harrison, succeeded her as superintendent of the Registry.[38]

Secretaries, like Registry staff, were female. The privileged education and upbringing of many of the secretaries made them more likely to stand up for their own points of view than most of those from humbler backgrounds. Among those who took wry amusement in observing some of the bright young secretaries politely outsmart older MO5(g) officers was probably its best-educated male recruit, Percy Marsh, a former scholar

(i) 'Miss Thinks She is Right'

Percy Marsh's drawing shows a youthful secretary querying a point with a somewhat bemused middle-aged officer. The privileged education and upbringing of many MI5 secretaries made them more likely to stand up for their own points of view than most of those from humbler backgrounds.

(ii) A cartoon of December 1915 by H. S. Gladstone, illustrating the sometimes flirtatious wartime MI5 gender relations.

of Wadham College, Oxford with first-class honours in classics, who had spent his pre-war career in the Indian Civil Service.[39] Marsh also had some talent as an artist. Among his drawings of wartime life in the Service was one entitled 'Miss Thinks She is Right', which shows a youthful secretary querying a point with a middle-aged officer of somewhat befuddled appearance.[40] There were numerous cases of such secretaries taking over, usually temporarily, the jobs of officers. Miss A. W. Masterton, secretary to the head of C (later H) Branch, Haldane, took over from him, at first temporarily, then permanently, the running of MO5(g)'s accounts, including much financial planning. The 'Report on Women's Work' concluded that this was 'the only example at this date of a woman managing the finances of a Government office'.[41] By the standards of the time, gender relations were sometimes slightly flirtatious. A wartime cartoon by the Old Etonian Cambridge graduate Captain Hugh Gladstone, entitled 'The Lost File', shows an attractive young member of the Registry telling a male officer, 'We've looked everywhere, but we can't find any BAULZ in the Registry.'[42] Harmless (not to say feeble) though the joke now appears, at the time it could not have appeared in print or been repeated in polite mixed company.

The main basis for MO5(g)'s counter-espionage operations, apart from its much expanded Registry, was greatly extended interception of letters and cables. MO5 had drawn up detailed pre-war plans for cable censorship, earmarking officers and clerks for war service under the chief cable censor, Colonel A. G. Churchill. No such preparations, however, had been made for postal censorship.[43] In September 1914 MO5 began to realize the importance of intercepting correspondence to neutral countries as a way of preventing information reaching the enemy. But the handful of MO5 staff sent to the Mount Pleasant sorting offices in Clerkenwell found the sheer volume of mail too much for them. When Colonel G. K. Cockerill visited the sorting offices shortly after taking over as head of MO5 in October, he discovered piles of opened letters awaiting examination and heaps of mailbags which had still to be opened. In November the newly appointed Director of Naval Intelligence, Captain (later Admiral Sir) Reginald 'Blinker' Hall, received alarmist reports that, due to problems at Mount Pleasant, messages to the enemy were getting through the censorship 'in some abundance'. Hall took the reports at face value, hurried round to MO5 and insisted 'that *all* foreign mails are opened and that no secret message gets through'. Cockerill replied that the cabinet was unhappy even with the existing level of censorship but agreed to allow censors chosen by Hall to make their own inspection of the mails for a two-month trial period. Hall persuaded the First Lord of the Admiralty, Winston Churchill,

The latest recruits.

A cartoon of November 1915 by H. S. Gladstone, highlighting the importance of letter interception to MI5's wartime operations.

to provide £1,600 to fund his new 'show' but was 'purposely vague' about what the money was for. His friend Lieutenant Colonel Freddie Browning (later Cumming's deputy) agreed to run Hall's 'little private censorship' and found him volunteers from the National Service League to act as censors.

Three weeks later, Browning told Hall that a censorship form had been accidentally left in a letter addressed to an MP whom he considered the 'ruddiest of rascals'. The outraged MP protested to Reginald McKenna, who summoned Hall and Cockerill to his room at the Home Office. They found the Home Secretary standing sternly in front of the fireplace. Was it true, demanded McKenna, that Hall had dared, without his authority, to tamper with the Royal Mail? 'Quite true, Mr Home Secretary,' replied Hall. The penalty for that, said the Home Secretary, was two years in jail. His mood softened as Cockerill argued that, under wartime censorship regulations, he had felt entitled to use what temporary help he could to prevent information reaching the enemy.[44] By the end of the year the number of postal censors had grown from the original one to 170. In April 1915 the censors were formally reconstituted as a new department of the War Office, MO9 (later MI9) under a retired diplomat. By the Armistice their numbers had increased to 4,861 (three-quarters of them women).[45]

As before the war, letter checks were crucial to MO5(g)'s wartime counter-espionage successes. The original mission of the first wartime agent despatched to Britain by the Nachrichten-Abteilung ('N'), Carl Lody, was to gather intelligence on Royal Navy losses in what the German Admiralty wrongly expected to be an imminent battle between its own High Seas Fleet and the British Grand Fleet.[46] Lody was a German naval reserve officer, who spoke excellent English with an American accent. After the interception of his correspondence to an address in Stockholm which was known to be used by 'N', Lody was arrested on 2 October while on his way to Queenstown, the main British naval base in Ireland.[47] Kell's head of counter-espionage, Reginald Drake, asked for Lody's trial to be held in camera but was overruled, apparently because of the belief in Whitehall that a public court-martial would advertise the success of the authorities in dealing with the threat from German espionage.[48] Had Lody been tried in camera, Drake planned to implement 'an ingenious method for conveying false information to the enemy which depended on their not knowing which of their agents had been caught'.[49] As was to happen in the Second World War, the first wartime espionage case might thus have led to the development of a 'Double-Cross System' to feed disinformation to the enemy.[50] The government's insistence, against MO5(g)'s wishes, on public trials and courts-martial for captured spies, however, made a First World War Double-Cross System impossible, though, as the war progressed, there were some more limited opportunities for deception.

At the end of October 1914, a public court martial at the Westminster Guildhall sentenced Lody to death by firing squad at the Tower of London – the first execution at the Tower for one and a half centuries. 'There was', wrote Thomson later, 'some difference of opinion as to whether it was sound policy to execute spies and to begin with a patriotic spy like Lody.' According to his wife, Kell regarded him as a 'really fine man' and 'felt it deeply that so brave a man should have to pay the death penalty'. The bravery with which Lody met his end strengthened his feelings of remorse. Lody wrote to the officer commanding Wellington Barracks:

Sir, I feel it my duty as a German Officer to express my sincere thanks and appreciation towards the staff of Officers and men who were in charge of my person during my confinement. Their kind and considered treatment has called my highest esteem and admiration as regards good-fellowship even towards the Enemy, and if may be permitted I would thank you for make this known to them.

I am, sir, with profound respect,

Carl Hans Lody, Senior Lieutenant, Imperial German Naval Res. II.D

On the morning of his execution, Lody said to the Assistant Provost Marshal, 'I suppose you will not shake hands with a spy?' The officer replied, 'No, but I will shake hands with a brave man.'[51] A German destroyer in the Second World War was named in Lody's honour.

By comparison with counter-espionage, Kell initially regarded counter-subversion as a low priority. Until 1916 pacifism and labour unrest seemed to MO5(g) to pose little threat to the British war effort. In August 1914 the Trades Union Congress announced an industrial truce for the duration of the war and Labour leaders joined their social superiors on recruiting platforms. Kell and his wife attended a public meeting in 1915 at which the veteran strike-leader Ben Tillett joined forces with the Duke of Rutland to appeal for warm clothing for the troops. 'Never shall I forget', wrote Constance Kell in a somewhat patronizing passage in her memoirs, 'the picture of Ben Tillett, very short of stature, and the Duke, very long indeed, standing together side by side, one with an amused expression, the other looking down benevolently . . .' 'Can you picture those men', Tillett asked his audience, 'with nothing but their bare bodies to oppose to the guns of the enemy?' Constance Kell found that 'a telling phrase'.[52]

Though six of the forty Labour MPs (including the future prime minister Ramsay MacDonald) opposed the war, Arthur Henderson, the wartime leader of the parliamentary Party, joined the coalition government formed by Asquith in May 1915. Early opposition to the war centred instead on the small Independent Labour Party (ILP). Kell obtained an HOW to begin a 'check' on the correspondence of the Stop-the-War Committee, founded by C. H. Norman, one of the most militant ILP leaders. The results were reassuring. According to a report submitted to Kell in July 1915, letters to the Committee were few and declining in number:

No letter has been seen which would appear to indicate that the writer has anti-British sentiments or that the Committee is in any way inspired or assisted from enemy sources . . . It appears therefore that the members of the Committee are obtaining very small results from their propaganda and the harm they are causing at the present time is practically negligable [sic].[53]

The most active period for German espionage in Britain was the first winter of the war.[54] German agents were no longer confined to those sent by the naval Nachrichten-Abteilung. After the outbreak of war, Sektion IIIb, German military intelligence, also began to target Britain, though its main priorities remained France and Russia. From early November 1914 Sektion IIIb's principal base for operations against Britain was a 'war intelligence centre' (the Kriegsnachrichtenstelle) in occupied Antwerp, which ran a 'spy school' for agents despatched to France and Britain.[55] Early in 1915 a Belgian refugee in Holland wrote to the War Office giving a name (Frans Leibacher) and an address in Rotterdam used by the Antwerp Kriegsnachrichtenstelle for correspondence with its agents in Britain.[56] Interception of letters using the address began on 30 January, and led to three arrests within the next month. The first to be caught was the German-born Anton Küpferle, who had lived in the United States and claimed to be a naturalized American but was believed by MO 5(g) to have served in the German army. Küpferle arrived in England from America in February 1915 and sent three intercepted letters to the Kriegsnachrichten-stelle Rotterdam address which, when the censorship flat iron was heated and run over them, revealed, written in secret ink (which he was the first German spy to use) what MO 5(g) considered 'information of military and naval importance'. Küpferle simplified MO 5(g)'s task by including his real name in the letters and the fact that he was staying at the Wilton Hotel, London, where he was arrested on 19 February.[57]

Küpferle inspired none of the sympathy extended to Lody, striking his interrogators as 'a typical German non-commissioned officer, stiff, abrupt, and uncouth'. In the middle of his trial at the Old Bailey he was found hanging by a silk handkerchief from the ventilator in his cell. By his body was a message written on a slate:

I can say that I have had a fair trial in the U. Kingdom, but I am unable to stand the strain any longer and take the law in my own hand. I fought many battles and death is only a saviour for me ... What I done I have done for my country. I shall express my thanks, and may the Lord bless you all.

The originals of Küpferle's correspondence do not survive, but, according to Basil Thomson, an intercepted letter written by him to another German agent showed less charity towards his captors. In it he welcomed the use of poison gas against British soldiers and the 'stupefying death' it would cause. This letter, Thomson believed, showed that Küpferle, unlike Lody, was a typical Hun with 'the true Prussian mentality'.[58] Most subsequent captured spies, whether or not they were of German nationality, also inspired little sympathy. Kell regarded most of these later spies as 'men ready to do any dirty work merely for gain' rather than patriots like Lody.[59]

While the Küpferle correspondence was being investigated by MO 5(g) in February 1915, four other letters were intercepted en route to the same Rotterdam address used by the Antwerp Kriegsnachrichtenstelle, also containing military and naval intelligence reports written in invisible ink between the lines of the letters. Inquiries identified the writer of one of the letters, posted in Deptford and signed 'Hahn' in secret ink, as John Hahn, a naturalized German-born baker living in Deptford High Street, who was arrested on 24 February. Next day his wife told Scotland Yard that she believed that a Russian named Karl Müller was involved in her husband's activities, and provided his address. Müller was arrested on 25 February, six weeks after his arrival in England. Though he had a Russian passport, MO 5(g) concluded, correctly, that he was German.[60]

The Antwerp Kriegsnachrichtenstelle was unaware of Müller's arrest and carried on sending messages to him, thus giving MO5(g)'s head of counter-espionage, Reginald Drake, the opportunity to attempt a variant of the deception which the publicity given to Lody's trial and execution had prevented in the previous year. With the help of the bilingual Hinchley Cooke, Drake sent fabricated reports from Müller, usually written in secret ink, to the Antwerp Kriegsnachrichtenstelle, which responded by sending money and requests for further information.[61] Until the end of May 1915 the fabrications were taken seriously by the Kriegsnachrichtenstelle. During April 1915 reports on a steamer allegedly leaving Bristol loaded with twenty heavy guns, the stationing of eight divisions of volunteers at Aldershot and large-scale embarkations of soldiers from Dartmouth were all rated 'credible'. An entirely fictitious report of 30 April on British preparations for an amphibious attack on Schleswig was, remarkably, rated 'reliable, confirmed by other reports'. The Kriegsnachrichtenstelle was particularly impressed by Müller's claim to have a reliable source in the Admiralty. It regarded as 'credible' a fabricated report from Müller received on 10 May, which it believed was probably based on the Admiralty source, that large numbers of troops had been assembled on the Humber and Firth of Forth which might be intended for the (non-existent) Schleswig operation or another theatre away from the Western Front. Three days later another fabricated report that Müller had personally travelled to Hull and Leith and seen large numbers of soldiers ready for embarkation was assessed as 'reliable'. On 30 May however, the Antwerp Kriegsnachrichtenstelle showed the first signs of suspicion, classifying Müller's most recent reports as 'less credible of late', probably because his claim that 80,000 additional British troops had just been sent to France was contradicted by other intelligence.[62]

German intelligence had failed to notice articles which had been appearing in *The Times* since 10 April, following the lifting of an earlier press embargo, on Müller's arrest and forthcoming trial. MO5(g)'s deception, however, began to unravel on 5 June when the Kriegsnachrichtenstelle noticed a *Times* report that Müller had been sentenced to death and his accomplice John Hahn to seven years' penal servitude.[63] Before his execution at the Tower on 22 June, Müller is reported to have shaken hands with the firing squad.[64] Drake and Hinchley Cooke, however, continued to send fabricated communications in Müller's name to Antwerp. According to a later account by the Kriegsnachrichtenstelle:

We knew without any doubt whatsoever that one of our agents [Müller] in the UK had been arrested and shot. A short time later we received a request from this 'dead agent' asking for money as he was absolutely skint. A week later he wrote again complaining bitterly that we had left him in the lurch and also sent a report that didn't contain very much. The report was a good copy of the agent's style but we immediately became suspicious that the British intelligence service should take the trouble to write reports to us in compensation for the fact that our man had suffered the ultimate fate. We gave the appearance of going along with the wishes of our dead colleague and sent him money whilst urging him on to be diligent in his work. The British were truly diligent in supplying us with the information they wanted us to have.[65]

German intelligence seems not to have realized, however, that *all* Müller's reports since the end of February had been bogus. Hinchley Cooke later recalled that MO5(g)'s attempt to continue the deception was finally abandoned when the Kriegsnachrichtenstelle summoned Müller back to Rotterdam to receive further instructions. The money sent from Antwerp to Müller enabled MO5(g) to buy a much needed second car, a two-seater Morris which was promptly christened the 'Müller'.[66] Maurice (later Lord) Hankey, secretary of the Committee of Imperial Defence, who in December 1916 became Britain's first (and so far longest-serving) cabinet secretary, later recalled, while carrying out a review of British intelligence in 1940: 'During the last war I myself was driving an automobile bought by the MI5 and lived on a salary paid by the Germans for . . . imaginary services.' He also recalled that MO5(g) had 'troubles with the Treasury' over its unauthorized expenditure of German money.[67] According to Hinchley Cooke, 'the Treasury sent a full-dress letter to the Army Council pointing out the irregular use of funds which should have been paid into the Exchequer.'[68]

The Müller deception anticipated in some respects the Double-Cross System, MI5's greatest success in the Second World War. Kell's inability to keep the arrest and trial of German spies secret, however, meant that the deception was bound to be short lived. The government was too anxious to prove to a sometimes sceptical public that it was catching German spies to suppress news of its triumphs. Even had the Müller deception continued for longer, however, its success would have been limited. Unlike the turned German agents of the Second World War, Müller was executed and therefore unable to add personal credibility to the disinformation sent to German intelligence in his name. The Double-Cross System also depended not on one individual but on a series of turned German agents as well as on the co-operation of the whole intelligence community to provide a mixture of information and disinformation capable of both impressing and deceiving the enemy for the remainder of the war. Unlike MI5 in the Second

World War, MO5(g) lacked the regular flow of SIGINT (signals intelligence) which enabled it to monitor the impact of the deception.[69]

The discovery by German intelligence of the Müller deception made it difficult for MO5(g) to attempt a similar deception without arousing German suspicions. In the summer of 1915, however, before it realized that its deception had been detected, Kell had one further opportunity. Early in May the postal censors had discovered in a mailbag from Denmark a letter addressed to Berlin which had been wrongly included in the London post. The letter was from one Robert Rosenthal in Copenhagen to 'Franz Kulbe' at an address in Berlin which MO5(g) knew to be used by German naval intelligence. It also knew that 'Franz Kulbe' was an alias employed by Captain von Prieger of the German Admiralty. Though the letter purported to be a business communication, the Censorship flat-iron revealed writing in secret ink which disclosed that he was about to leave for England disguised as a travelling salesman of cigar lighters. When Rosenthal was arrested in Newcastle, travelling on a US passport, no incriminating evidence was found on him. But when confronted with his intercepted letter to Berlin, he admitted he was German and had been sent by Prieger to spy on the Royal Navy. Though he denied he had sent Prieger information of any value, he also admitted that he had been on two previous wartime espionage missions. Like some of the German spies sent to Britain before the war, Rosenthal had a criminal record, having been imprisoned for forgery in Germany and subsequently spending five years in the United States.[70]

After Rosenthal's confession he quickly offered to become a double agent and, to prove his willingness to do so, provided information on secret inks, secret codes and the methods of passport forgery employed by German intelligence.[71] Kell rejected the offer, probably influenced by memories of the pre-war Graves case, when his first double agent (who, like Rosenthal, had a criminal record) had successfully deceived him. As the Müller deception shows, Kell thought it safer for MO5(g) to impersonate a dead German agent than to turn a living one. Rosenthal tried desperately to save his life by claiming that his loyalties were to the United States, not to Germany: 'I indeed have never cared for any German, never liked Germans, always wanted to be a real Yankee.'[72] He went to the scaffold at Wandsworth military prison on 15 July, pleading for his life and, according to an officially authorized account, 'gave unutterable disgust to the authorities by his lack of common courage'. The commandant called him a 'cur'.[73]

The use of invisible ink by German spies prompted Kell to make his first move into forensic science by seeking the assistance in 1915 of

Henry Vincent Aird Briscoe, an inorganic chemist at Imperial College, London. He and his laboratory devised a series of techniques for the detection of invisible ink in letters and the increasingly sophisticated chemicals used in secret writing.[74]

During interrogation Rosenthal had revealed that, instead of recruiting German nationals as spies, German intelligence intended to make more use of agents from neutral countries disguised, like himself, as commercial travellers. Kell responded by ordering detailed censorship of letters and cables from Britain to neutral countries. This 'super-censorship', as it was known in MO5(g), revealed a telegram dated 25 May sent from Southampton by a Dutchman Haicke Janssen, posing as a travelling cigar salesman, to Dierks & Co. in The Hague (an address already known to be used by German intelligence), ordering 4,000 Sumatra cigars 'mark A.G.K.', which MO5(g)'s existing knowledge of German codes enabled it to identify as a reference to four *Alte Grosse Kreuzer* (old-model large cruisers), which inquiry showed were indeed docked at Southampton. A further reference to 4,000 of a brand of Sumatra Havanas was thought to refer to four torpedo boats, also present in Southampton Harbour. A request from Kell to the Chief Censor for copies of all other cables sent to Dierks & Co. revealed two more sent from Edinburgh by another purported Dutch cigar salesman, Willem Roos.[75]

Though later to become essential to Security Service operations, intelligence liaison during the First World War was limited by the determination of the French and British armed forces to prevent intrusion by their allies into their own spheres of operations. French intelligence, however, made a major contribution to the Janssen case.[76] On 15 June Colonel Cartier, the head of French military SIGINT, handed to Major (later Major General Sir) Walter Kirke, an intelligence officer at British GHQ in France, decrypted German telegrams giving some details of agents in British ports. One of the decrypts clearly identified Janssen, then – like Roos – under arrest, and Kirke noted with satisfaction that 'it should ensure his being shot'. Cartier travelled to London soon afterwards for discussions with Kell.[77]

After Janssen and Roos had been sentenced to death on 16 July, both tried, like Rosenthal, to save their lives by offering to change sides. Janssen claimed that his sympathies had really been with Britain all the time and provided intelligence on the German espionage network in Holland which assisted the discovery of subsequent German agents. Roos feigned madness in a further attempt to avoid execution. Both were shot by firing squad in the Tower of London on 30 July. Kell seems never to have contemplated using either as a double agent. His wife's judgement probably reflected his own: 'It was all done for money and therefore Janssen and Roos were despicable men ready to do any dirty work merely for gain.'[78]

While Janssen and Roos were awaiting trial, the head of Cumming's Rotterdam station, Richard Tinsley (codenamed 'T'), a tough former naval officer and shipping manager described by one of his staff as 'a combination of sea captain and prize fighter',[79] reported that Josef Marks, a German agent travelling on a US passport, was shortly to leave for England. Marks was arrested on his arrival at Tilbury on 18 July, admitted he had been sent to gather intelligence on munitions production and revealed the codes he had been told to use, but claimed that he had been put under heavy pressure to undertake the mission. On 28 September he was sentenced by court martial to five years' penal servitude.[80] Intelligence from 'T' led to the detection of four other German agents in 1915[81] and one in 1916.[82]

The high point of MO5(g)'s counter-espionage operations came in June 1915, when seven German spies were rounded up in little more than a fortnight.[83] Thereafter, German intelligence operations in Britain were drastically scaled down. German archives show that the number of agents in Britain declined from twenty-two in January 1915 to only four at the end of the year.[84] For the remainder of the war Germany relied largely on brief visits by bogus commercial travellers from neutral countries who carried as much information as possible in their heads rather than on paper. They had little success. Kell's Bureau (renamed MI5 in January 1916) concluded that most had neither the aptitude nor the training required for successful espionage. The last to be executed was Ludovico Hurwitz y Zender, a Peruvian of Scandinavian descent who aroused the suspicions of the censors by sending bogus orders for large quantities of Norwegian sardines at the wrong season, and was shot in the Tower on 11 April 1916.[85]

Shortly after Hurwitz y Zender's execution, MI5 recruited its most successful double agent of the war, an American in Holland codenamed COMO, described in what remains of his file as 'working in Holland as a German Agent, but double-crossing for us'. In May 1916 COMO was sent to Britain by the Kriegsnachrichtenstelle to look up agents who had been out of contact for some time. He reported to MI5 that the first of those he contacted, Fritz Haas, was 'harmless and probably never an agent, if so unknowingly'. In July COMO was sent on a second mission to obtain intelligence on Canadian troops in England and when they were likely to be sent to France, as well as details of British naval losses at the battle of Jutland. According to an MI5 note:

We gave 'COMO' information about our Canadian Divisions – their numbers and positions, etc – at places not obviously incorrect, and gave particulars of their numbers etc, as would make them plausible. Also, fictitious information of Naval, Industrial and Political situation, most convincingly written. Also sent information regarding the effects of the Zeppelin raids on London.

In September, on MI5 instructions, COMO sent further disinformation on the military situation in England and likely movements on the Western Front. He told the Germans that the British were planning an attack on the Belgian coast on the 15th. COMO continued to pass on at irregular intervals details of the intelligence missions entrusted to him by the Kriegs-nachrichtenstelle, and MI5 continued to channel disinformation through him. According to a post-war summary, COMO 'was always quite honest and trustworthy and did some v[ery] valuable work for us, at the same time holding the German's [sic] confidence'. War Office nervousness, however, prevented the development of a full-blown Double-Cross System. On at least one occasion, the Director of Military Intelligence described the questions put to COMO by the Kriegsnachrichtenstelle as 'extremely dangerous', and instructed that 'no answers could be given'.[86]

The final attempts by German intelligence to establish a significant agent network in Britain were based on the recruitment of Americans. On 3 June 1916 Tinsley in Rotterdam supplied MI5 with a cover address in The Hague used by German intelligence, which Kell immediately ordered to be put under censorship.[87] This was reckoned by MI5 to be 'one of "T"'s best efforts',[88] since it led to the discovery of an 'important gang' of spies run from New York by Karl Wünnenberg, a German naval reserve officer, and the journalist Albert Sander.[89] To strengthen their cover in New York, Wünnenberg and Sander had no contact with German officials in the United States and were run by the Antwerp Kriegsnachrichtenstelle. They succeeded in recruiting six US journalists to work as agents, paying each up to $1,000 in advance and promised another $125 per week.[90] The large sums offered are an indication of how short of agents in Britain the Kriegsnachrichtenstelle had become.

On 29 September 1916 the censors opened a letter written from England a week before by one of the US journalists recruited by German intelligence in New York, George Vaux Bacon, to the German intelligence address in The Hague identified by Tinsley. There was a further delay before Major Carter of MI5 examined the letter on 9 October, by which time Bacon had been in Holland for over a fortnight and realized his letter had been delayed by censorship. Bacon's suspicions were further aroused when he was approached, 'somewhat clumsily' in MI5's view, by one of Tinsley's agents. Though MI5 believed that Bacon 'suspected that the British authorities were on his tracks', he none the less returned to Britain on an espionage mission early in November. MI5 noted that he had a 'loose' (promiscuous) lifestyle, but 'nothing suspicious' was found in his possession on his arrival and he managed to 'elude his watchers' while visiting naval bases in Ireland. On 9 December 1916 Bacon was interviewed at Scotland Yard, not with the expectation of persuading him to confess to espionage but in the hope that he could be 'frightened out of the country'. However, this time enough incriminating material was found in his possession for him to be kept in custody. In addition to equipment for secret writing, 'two of his socks were found to produce invisible ink when soaked in water'.[91]

Two days later, MI5 received what it considered 'information of the utmost importance' in the Bacon case from an American journalist, Roslyn Whytock, who became the second wartime German agent recruited for espionage in Britain to operate as a double agent.[92] Whytock had a colourful background. Before the war he had been both a newspaper editor in St Louis, Missouri, and a captain in the Missouri National Guard, but had to resign his commission after an affair with a local fashion model, Mrs Irma Jones, whose husband cited him as co-respondent when obtaining a divorce. Whytock appears to have possessed exceptional social skills. According to an 'exclusive' interview in the New York Times with Mrs Whytock, who also sued for divorce, Mrs Jones's husband came to St Louis 'for the purpose of killing Whytock, but the Captain talked him out of it, and they became chums in a few days'.[93]

Early in November 1916 Whytock reported to the MI5 Military Control Office in New York that the German agent Albert Sander was trying to recruit him to work as a spy in England. At the Control Office's request, Whytock pretended to accept Sander's offer but revealed all he knew to MI5 once he reached England, including the codes and secret inks used by the 'gang of American spies' and the identity of 'a disreputable US journalist', Charles Hastings, with whom Sander had told him to collaborate. Whytock explained that, probably in an attempt to improve security and outwit the censors, Sander had given instructions for his journalist agents to work in pairs. One was to collect intelligence in England, then transmit it by letters in invisible ink to his partner in Holland, who would pass it on to the Kriegsnachrichtenstelle.[94] There Whytock's role seems to have ended. No attempt appears to have been made by Kell, as it would have been in the Second World War, to continue to use him as a long-term double agent. Whytock's experience of working for MI5 was, however, later put to good use. After the United States entered the war in April 1917, he became a captain in the US Army Intelligence Service in New York.[95]

Influenced no doubt by Whytock's revelations about the 'gang of American spies', Bacon was persuaded on 9 February 1917 to make what MI5 considered 'a full confession' about his recruitment by Wünnenberg and Sander. At a court martial in the Guildhall on 4 March Bacon was sentenced to be shot by a firing squad at the Tower.[96] Washington, however, persuaded the British authorities to commute the sentence to one of life imprisonment and send Bacon to the United States to give evidence against his German spymasters. Late in March a New York court sentenced Wünnenberg and Sander to two years' penal servitude in a federal penitentiary. Judge Van Vleet himself sentenced Bacon to one year's penal servitude, but lamented that 'he disliked it very much to send such a bright young man to the penitentiary.'[97]

In the early months of 1917, as part of a policy to expose the operations of German intelligence in the United States, the DNI, Blinker Hall, with the approval of the First Lord of the Admiralty, Arthur Balfour, set out to shock Americans by publicizing the 'Zimmermann telegram' (decrypted by British codebreakers), which expressed secret German support, if the United States entered the war, for the Mexican reconquest of 'lost territory in Texas, New Mexico and Arizona'. Balfour said later that the moment when he handed over the decrypted telegram to the US ambassador in London was 'the most dramatic in all my life'.[98] President Woodrow Wilson's celebrated speech to a joint session of Congress on 2 April calling for a declaration of war on Germany cited both its intelligence operations in the US and the Zimmermann telegram as evidence that 'Germany's irresponsible government . . . is running amok':

One of the things that has served to convince us that the Prussian autocracy was not and could never be our friend is that from the very outset of the present war it has filled our unsuspecting communities and even our offices of government with spies and set criminal intrigues everywhere afoot . . .[99]

Though Wilson doubtless had chiefly in mind German sabotage operations (discussed below), the sentencing only a week earlier of Wünnenberg and Sander, and the evidence of their corruption of 'such a bright young man' as Bacon, served as a recent reminder of the German spies at work in the heart of New York.

Surviving MI5 archives contain details of sixty-five German agents who were arrested and convicted or imprisoned under the Aliens Restriction Act during the First World War.[100] German archives indicate that a total of at least 120 agents were sent to Britain at some point between 1914 and 1918.[101] Some (perhaps a majority) of the unarrested agents appear to have been 'reconnaissance agents' visiting British ports, whose access to intelligence was limited to what they could observe themselves.[102] A probably significant minority also broke contact with German intelligence after arriving in Britain. MO5(g) counter-espionage successes and the execution of convicted spies persuaded an unknown number to follow the example of Walter Rimann in 1914[103] and flee the country, or else to give up espionage. On at least two occasions the double agent COMO was asked by the Antwerp Kriegsnachrichtenstelle to track down German agents who had broken contact. He reported to MI5 in October 1916 that:

The Germans had lost track of about 20 of their agents whom they had sent to England, and could not understand what had happened to them. COMO said he satisfied their curiosity by saying they had gone across to America after receiving their £20 from the Germans, and said [the Germans] should not pay them until they had completed the work they had been sent to England to do.[104]

Though some active wartime German spies were not detected by MO5(g), no convincing evidence has yet emerged to show that any sent back significant intelligence.[105]

MI5's post-war assessment of its counter-espionage operations concluded:

If there is any single standard by which to measure the success of the Bureau, it is the level attained by the wages paid to the enemy's agents; and in the case of Great Britain, we know that, whereas at the outbreak of war £10 to £25 a month was the normal figure, it rose rapidly to £50 in 1915, to £100 about June 1916 and, by the beginning of 1918, to £150 a month. In the last year or so before the Armistice, a good spy could get practically what he chose to ask for.[106]

MI5 attributed much of its success in dealing with German espionage to good preventive security (later called 'protective security') which had turned Britain into a hard target:

It is apparently a paradox, but it is none the less true, and a most important truth, that the efficiency of a counter espionage service is not to be measured chiefly by the number of spies caught by it. For such a service, even if it catches no spies at all, may in fact perform the most admirable work by hampering the enemy's intelligence service, and causing it to lose money, labour, and, most precious of all, time, in overcoming the obstacles placed in its way. One must bear in mind the immense and rapid success of the Prussians in a campaign like that against Austria in 1866, when the Austrians had no C.E service, and when therefore spies all over Bohemia were able to report every movement of the Austrian troops, in order to fully realise the value of organisations like those of the censorship, the port controls and the other preventive machinery put in place by the S[pecial] I[ntelligence] B[ureau].[107]

One measure of the success of protective security was the lack of German sabotage in Britain. At the outbreak of war, it was entirely reasonable for Kell and Whitehall to take the threat of sabotage very seriously. General Staffs throughout Europe, as well as some leading military writers, had predicted that modern warfare would involve civilians acting as sabotage agents.[108] Kell shared those fears. As research in German archives confirms, Kell's fears were well founded. The German military intelligence department, run by Lieutenant Colonel Walter Nicolai, established a special department (Sektion P) to perform sabotage operations in Allied countries (*Agitat-Werke*) and prevent delivery to the Allies of essential supplies from the United States. Sektion P placed explosives, often disguised as coal briquettes, on several transatlantic ships in North American ports.[109] None, however, was successfully placed on ships in British ports.

Sektion P's most notorious act of sabotage was at a depot in Black Tom Pier, New Jersey, which contained over 2 million pounds of ammunition destined for a Russian offensive on the Eastern Front. On the evening of 30 July 1916 the depot was blown up, killing four people and causing $14 million worth of damage. The explosion was so powerful that the shockwaves could be felt as far as 90 miles away. An official American inquiry into the explosion after the war implicated several former members of the German intelligence services.[110] Had security in Britain been as ineffective as in the United States, German sabotage would probably have been on at least the same scale.[111] The fact that there seems to have been no attempted Sektion P operation in Britain remotely similar to the Black Tom attack owes at least something to the 'physical security' measures organized by Holt-Wilson, with central and local government authorities, which established prohibited zones around sensitive locations, such as munitions dumps, throughout Britain.[112]

In August 1915, one year after the outbreak of war, there was a major expansion of protective security. A new Port Control section (E Branch) was founded to control civilian passenger traffic to and from the UK, in collaboration with Military Permit Offices in London, Paris, Rome and New York.[113] The Military Permit Offices abroad worked closely with British consular and MO5(g) officials in issuing entry visas and monitoring British citizens abroad. Military control officers (MCOs) from MO5(g) at designated wartime British ports of entry and frontier stations in the Empire worked with aliens officers and police, and had the power to refuse entry of those considered undesirables.[114] Among those MI5 officers who questioned foreign travellers at British ports was Hinchley Cooke. The MCO at Falmouth, Major Rowland Money, reported to Kell in October 1916 that Hinchley Cooke, still only twenty-two, was 'very keen on port work. His languages have been most useful as we have a number of German women in transit through Falmouth.'[115] While questioning the German women and others Hinchley Cooke seems to have posed as a German named Wilhelm Eduard Koch, who they must have assumed had changed sides.[116] His skill in interrogation led to a number of operations over the next two years in which he also posed as a German. Hinchley Cooke's record of service contains a number of photographs of him in German army uniform as well as a 1917 Metropolitan Police Alien Enemy Certificate of Registration card in the name of Wilhelm Eduard Koch, which used the same photograph as his War Office identity document.

The main contribution of MI5 Port Control was to protective security. As the capture of the German sabotage agent Hans Boehm on landing in England in January 1917 demonstrated,[117] Britain was a hard target. The most novel as well as the most sinister form of wartime sabotage attempted by Sektion P was biological warfare. At least one of its scientists in 1916 devised a scheme to start a plague epidemic in Britain, either by infecting rats or, more improbably, by dropping plague bacilli cultures from Zeppelins over ports. The Prusso-German General Staff, however, vetoed bacteriological warfare against humans as totally contrary to international law (the Hague Laws of Warfare). No such restrictions applied to animals. The German General Staff considered that the contamination of horses, cattle and other livestock was an attack on 'military supplies', which was permissible under the Hague Laws. This was highly significant considering the important – and nowadays often underrated – role performed by horses and other livestock in the First World War. In April 1915 Sektion P sent Dr Anton Dilger, a US citizen of German parents and Heidelberg-trained physician, to the United States. At a laboratory in Washington DC, Dilger produced cultures of *bacillus anthracis* and *pseudomonas mallei*, the causative agents of anthrax and glanders. A few months after Dilger's arrival in Washington, the cultures were administered to horses and mules awaiting export to Europe in holding pens at docks in New York, Baltimore, Newport News and Norfolk, Virginia.[118] The US programme ended in the autumn of 1916, after Dilger's return to Germany. There is some evidence to suggest that Sektion P then attempted to spread anthrax and glanders to Britain as well. On 30 March 1917 MI5 and the Special Branch circulated an intelligence warning to other government departments concerning evidence that German agents were attempting to infect horses and mules in Britain with anthrax and glanders. Four outbreaks of anthrax on the Isle of Man a month later were almost certainly the result of German biological warfare.[119] But for protective security there would probably have been many more outbreaks. The last German sabotage agent to reach Britain in the course of the war was Alfred Hagn, arrested in May 1917 with the help of intelligence leads from the Norwegian security service.[120] After the death sentence (later commuted) was passed on Hagn in August, there were no further trials of German agents for the remainder of the war.

A post-war report on preventive security concluded, with a degree of overstatement, that MI5 could claim to have made 'some difference, great or small, to the life of almost every inhabitant of the United Kingdom':

[MI5] moved from being an organisation employing a few people before the war, investigating a few hundred individual suspects; to being a large body employing hundreds of people, conducting thousands and thousands of investigations, putting forward methods of control that affected every person either travelling or sending correspondence to or from foreign countries.[121]

During the war MI5 checked the background credentials of approximately 75,000 individuals against their records in the Registry, many in connection with visa applications and travel permits.[122] The best-known espionage suspect detected by MO5(g)'s Port Control was the striptease dancer and courtesan Margaretha Geertruida Zelle, alias Mata Hari. Zelle was a fantasist who, in place of her conventional Dutch bourgeois origins, invented an exotic upbringing as a dancer in a Hindu temple on the banks of the River Ganges. The audiences from Parisian high society who attended her performances were thus able to persuade themselves that they were participating not in the vulgar excitement of the can-can at the Moulin Rouge but in the sacred mysteries of the Orient.[123] According to a report in her MI5 file, the introduction of a large snake into her act, combined with her own 'scanty drapery and sinuous movements', caused particular excitement among German and Austrian audiences. In December 1915 Zelle was stopped by Ports Police at Folkestone attempting to board a boat for France, and was questioned by Captain Stephen Dillon of E Branch, who described Zelle as 'handsome, bold . . . well and fashionably dressed' in an outfit with 'raccoon fur trimming and hat to match': 'Although she had good answers to every question, she impressed me very unfavourably, but after having her very carefully searched and finding nothing, I considered I hadn't enough grounds to refuse her embarkation.'

Zelle subsequently made her way to The Hague, where, according to reports passed to MI5, she was paid by the German embassy and 'suspected of having been to France on important mission for the Germans'.[124] In November 1916, Zelle had her second brush with British intelligence. She was removed by Ports Police from a steamer which called at Falmouth en route to Holland, and taken, with her ten travelling trunks, to be questioned in London by Basil Thomson and MI5. 'Time', in Thomson's view, 'had a little dimmed the charms of which we had heard so much.' Once again, it was decided after questioning Zelle that there was insufficient evidence to justify her arrest.[125] In February 1917, however, she was arrested in Paris. Shortly afterwards, French military intelligence reported to MI5 that she had confessed to working for the Germans.[126] On 15 October Zelle was shot at dawn by firing squad at the Château de Vincennes, refusing a blindfold and blowing a kiss to her executioners just before they opened fire.[127] In November MI5's liaison officer at the French War Ministry, Lieutenant Colonel Hercules Pakenham, was allowed to read her file, which contained the transcript of a confession in which she admitted to receiving 5,000 francs per mission from German intelligence to collect Allied secrets. Pakenham reported to MI5 Head Office, however, that 'she never made a full confession.' Though Zelle admitted to passing the Germans 'general information of every kind procurable', none of the examples noted in Pakenham's report amounted to espionage.[128] MI5's earlier doubts about the strength of the case against Zelle, based on her two interrogations in Britain, were probably well founded. Zelle fantasized about espionage in much the same way that she had earlier fantasized about being a Hindu temple dancer. In the intervals between her sexual liaisons with officers of several nations, she offered her services to both French and German intelligence but does not seem to have provided significant intelligence to either.

The most extreme form of protective security in both world wars was the internment of aliens. The Aliens Restriction Act had given the government carte blanche to 'impose restrictions on aliens' and DORA Regulation 14B empowered the authorities to detain persons of enemy origin whenever 'expedient for securing the public safety or the defence of the realm'. Enemy aliens were required to register with the police and forbidden to live in a large number of 'prohibited areas' without permits from the police. The government claimed early in 1915 that 'Every single alien enemy in this country is known and is at this present moment under constant police surveillance.' For the popular press and probably for most of the public, surveillance was not enough. Spy mania and indignation at German war crimes (most but not all of them mythical) fuelled protests against government reluctance to intern more than a small minority of enemy aliens. In May 1915, somewhat against his better judgement, Asquith gave way to public pressure. McKenna reluctantly concluded that anti-alien feeling ran so high that male enemy aliens might well be safer if interned. Henceforth the government adopted, though it did not always enforce, the principle that all enemy aliens should be interned unless they could prove themselves to be harmless. Ultimately at least 32,000 (mostly men of military age) were interned, at least 20,000 (mostly women, children and non-combatant men) repatriated, and the remainder subjected to numerous restrictions.[129]

MO5(g)'s leadership supported a hardline policy on internment.[130] Its policy was informed by ethnocentric prejudice as well as by the needs of preventive security. Holt-Wilson regarded all 'persons of German blood' as security risks – despite the presence in MO5(g) of the half-German Hinchley Cooke.[131] He told the Aliens Sub-committee of the Committee of Imperial Defence in June 1915:

The patriotism and discipline inherited with their blood which lifts some men beyond the fear of death will also inspire Germans gladly to risk and suffer any penalty, and to disregard all laws of honour or humanity, that they may contribute but a trifling service to their fatherland at the cost of their enemy.

Those of German blood who had spent much of their lives in Britain were even more dangerous than recent arrivals: 'Long residence in Britain adds greatly to the mischief to be apprehended from an alien enemy.' The longer they had been in Britain, the greater their capacity to damage the war effort.[132] MO5(g) had some reason to suspect that German intelligence had long-term 'sleepers' in Britain. Karl Ernst, the 'Kaiser's postman', who played a key role in Steinhauer's communications with his agents, was well integrated into British life and was discovered after his arrest in August 1914 to have British nationality.[133] Frederick Adolphus Schroeder, alias Gould, probably Steinhauer's most successful pre-war spy, had an English mother, spoke perfect English and established himself in the quintessentially English profession of publican. But, though MO5(g)'s fears of unidentified German sleepers were reasonable, they turned out to be misplaced. The most striking characteristic of the German spies detected after the first year of the war is that most were not German.[134]

The first two years of the war saw the beginning of a rivalry between

Kell and Assistant Commissioner Basil Thomson of the Met, which was to have a significant effect on MI5's immediate post-war history. Thomson, son of the late Archbishop of York, had a remarkably colourful career. After Eton, he dropped out of Oxford University and entered the Colonial Service. He later recalled: 'My first native friends were cannibals, but I learned very quickly that the warrior who had eaten his man as a quasi-religious act was a far more estimable person than the town-bred, mission-educated native.' He went on to become prime minister of Tonga (at the age of only twenty-eight), private tutor to the Crown Prince of Siam and governor of Dartmoor Prison.[135] Once at Scotland Yard in 1913, he threw himself energetically into counter-espionage work, revelling in the publicity which resulted from it. Kell approved of the popular misconception of the Special Branch's role. As Holt-Wilson wrote later: 'We welcome the unshakeable belief of the public that "Scotland Yard" is responsible for dealing with spies. It is a valuable camouflage.'[136]

As a secret organization MI5 could not publicly claim credit for its part in the capture of German spies. The more flamboyant Thomson, already well used to publicizing his achievements, could and did. In the process he earned the collective enmity of most of MI5. Reginald Drake, head of counter-espionage in MI5 until 1917, wrote later to Blinker Hall: 'As you know B.T. did not know of the existence, name or activity of any convicted spy until I told him; but being the dirty dog he was he twisted the facts to claim that he alone did it.'[137] There was, inevitably, some overlap in the activities of MI5 and the Special Branch which added further to the rivalry between them. Eddie Bell, who was responsible for intelligence liaison at the US embassy, wrote after the war that when the embassy wished to make inquiries about people claiming American citizenship arrested on suspicion of being German spies 'it became almost a question of flipping a coin to decide whether application for information should be made to Scotland Yard, the Home Office or MI5.' Blinker Hall had much greater sympathy for the flamboyant Thomson than for the retiring Kell. Bell reported 'considerable jealousy between the Intelligence Department of the War Office and the Admiralty, the latter affecting to despise the former, particularly MI5, whom they always described as shortsighted and timorous . . .'.[138] While Thomson enjoyed the limelight, Kell shunned it. His only known publication is a letter to a newspaper on the behaviour of the lapwing.[139]

In the later stages of the war, Thomson was to emerge as the most formidable rival encountered by Kell in his thirty-one years as director. In the power struggle which ensued, Kell's Bureau became a victim of its own successes. Had German espionage remained a serious apparent threat throughout the war or Germany succeeded in launching a major sabotage campaign in Britain, Kell would have found it much easier to retain the lead domestic intelligence role. But during the second half of the war, with government now more concerned with subversion than with espionage, it was easier for Thomson than for Kell to gain the ear of ministers.

3

The First World War

Part 2: The Rise of Counter-Subversion

On 3 January 1916, as part of a War Office reorganization, Kell's Bureau became MI5: the name by which it has been best known ever since. Its three main branches were F (preventive intelligence), G (investigations) and H (secretariat, Registry and administration). Holt-Wilson, the head of F Branch, was also put in charge of Branches A (aliens), E (port and frontier control) and, later in the year, D (imperial and overseas, including Irish, intelligence).[1] Recruitment was even more rapid than in 1915: there were 423 recruits in 1916, another 366 in 1917 and 484 in 1918. There was a substantial turnover of staff, with about 700 leaving in the course of the war.[2] The turnover was greatest among the Registry and secretarial staff – an indication of the demanding and stressful nature of their work.[3] A minority were required to work even at Christmas. A caricature by Hugh Gladstone, drawn on Christmas Day 1916, shows a group of Registry staff seated around a large Christmas pudding.[4] By the Armistice MI5's card index had grown to about a million names.[5] The Black List of key suspects filled twenty-one volumes containing 13,524 names.[6]

Change in Registry (section H2) working practices owed much to the staff themselves. According to one enthusiastic account:

All the members of the staff in H-2 being intelligent people are treated as such; they are invited to make any suggestions which occur to them for the improvement of the machinery of the office and they are made to feel that they have an important and personal share in the work. So much is this the case that many of the important improvements that have been from time to time adopted, have been suggested by members of the staff.[7]

Those able to stand the pace of wartime life in MI5 later looked back fondly at its camaraderie. As one inexperienced poet wrote in the programme for the Service's end-of-war 'Hush-Hush' Revue:

We'll think of when we had the 'flu,
The days we had to 'muddle through',
And all the work we used to do
  To snare the wily Hun

Of days when strafes were in the air
And worried secretaries would tear
Great handfuls of their flowing hair
  And swear at everyone.

We'll think with something like regret
Of all the jolly friends we met;
The jokes that we remember yet
  Will once again revive.

Here's to the book that's just begun
May it recall to everyone
The jokes and laughter and the fun
  We had in M.I.5.

The steady growth in wartime staff meant that by the summer of 1916 MI5 had outgrown its accommodation in Watergate House and the neighbouring Adelphi Court, and moved to larger headquarters in Waterloo House, 16 Charles Street, Haymarket. Waterloo House contained a canteen which was big enough to double as a social club. Staff were also allowed on to the roof which, as one later recalled, provided both 'a breath of fresh air and . . . a view of Nelson's column'.[8] As expansion continued, additional premises were taken at Cork Street in April 1917, and at Greener House, next to Waterloo House, in June 1918. Protective security at MI5's wartime headquarters was, by later standards, casual. In 1918 MI5's second car, the 'Müller', purchased with funds sent by German intelligence to its agent Karl Müller, was stolen from outside the front door of Waterloo House.[9]

By the end of the war, MI5 had a total staff of 844.[10] At its London headquarters there were 84 officers (some civilian but a majority with army rank), 291 female Registry and secretarial staff, 15 male clerks, 77 'subordinate staff' and 23 police. One of the greatest changes in the course of the war was that by the Armistice over 40 per cent of staff were stationed outside London at home ports, permit offices and missions in Allied countries: 255 Ports Police (who, in an era before air travel, monitored all arrivals to and departures from the UK), 49 officers, 34 female and 7 male clerks, 9 subordinate staff.[11]

With the decline of German espionage in Britain, MI5's main priority during 1916 moved from counter-espionage to counter-subversion. It was entirely reasonable for MI5 to expect German intelligence to engage in a major campaign of subversion to try to undermine the British war effort. From the beginning of the war the Prusso-German General Staff developed a strategy of 'fomenting revolution' (*Revolutionierungspolitik*), which it sought to implement by sponsoring subversive movements in Allied countries. As Thomas Boghardt has noted: 'German agents financed French pacifists, American labour organisations and Indian nationalists. They supported Russian revolutionaries, Muslim *jihadists* and Irish republicans.'[12] The fact that, though MI5 and Whitehall failed to realize it at the time, German intelligence made no serious attempt at subversion in mainland Britain reflected not any lack of desire to damage the British war effort but the belief, particularly after the main German agents during the first year of the war had been arrested, that Britain was a harder target than its main Allies.

At the outbreak of war Berlin believed that the most effective way to subvert the United Kingdom was by assisting Irish Republican attempts to end British rule. Its main hopes were pinned on the Irish exile Sir Roger Casement, formerly a distinguished member of the British consular service, who sought German support for an Irish rebellion. The most important British informant on Casement's activities in the early months of the war was his bisexual Norwegian-American manservant and lover, Adler Christensen, who accompanied him on a journey from the United States to Oslo (then Christiania) in October 1914, en route to Germany. On his arrival in Oslo, Christensen made secret contact with the British minister, Mansfeldt de Carbonnel Findlay, and gave him copies of several incriminating documents Casement was carrying with him, including a ciphered letter of introduction from the German ambassador in Washington, Count Johann Heinrich von Bernstorff, to the German Chancellor, Theobald von Bethmann-Hollweg. The Foreign Secretary, Sir Edward Grey, found Christensen's information so important that he sent copies of Findlay's report to the Prime Minister, Herbert Asquith, the Secretary of State for War, Field Marshal Earl Kitchener, the First Lord of the Admiralty, Winston Churchill, and the Chief Secretary for Ireland, Augustine Birrell.[13]

Casement's rudimentary attempts to outwit British postal censorship were remarkably naive. On 7 December 1914 he posted a letter in Rotterdam to Alice Stopford Green in London for onward transmission to the chief of staff of the Irish Volunteers, Eoin MacNeill. As a well-known Irish nationalist, Mrs Green was an obvious target for postal censorship, as was all mail from neutral Netherlands (which included items originating in Germany). Casement's short, unsigned covering letter was full of thinly concealed references to German support for the liberation of the 'four green fields' (easily identifiable as the four provinces of Ireland) from the 'stranger' (Britain). Though this primitive level of concealment would in any case have been unlikely to deceive the censor, it was rendered pointless by the unambiguous language used by Casement in the accompanying letter to MacNeill:

I am in Berlin and if Ireland will do her duty, rest assured Germany will do hers towards us, our cause and our whole future ... Once our people[,] clergy and Volunteers know that Germany, if victorious, will do her best to aid us in our efforts to achieve an independent Ireland, every man at home must stand for Germany and Irish Freedom ... Tell all to trust the Germans – and to trust me.

Casement's letter was unsigned. 'You know who writes this,' he told MacNeill. So did MO5(g).[14]

The most important intelligence in tracking German support for Casement came from the Admiralty SIGINT unit, Room 40. Between the outbreak of war and the eve of the Easter Rising in 1916, Room 40 decrypted at least thirty-two cables exchanged between the German embassy in Washington and the Foreign Ministry in Berlin dealing with German support for Irish nationalists. The first was a telegram from the German ambassador in Washington, Bernstorff, to Berlin on 27 September 1914, reporting a meeting with Casement to discuss raising an Irish Brigade from among prisoners of war captured by the Germans (though the date at which the telegram was decrypted remains uncertain).[15] The most important decrypts were those which revealed that German arms for the Easter Rising were to be landed in Tralee Bay in the spring of 1916 and that Casement was following by U-boat. The steamer *Aud*, carrying German munitions, was duly intercepted by HMS *Bluebell* on 21 April 1916, ordered to proceed to Queenstown and scuttled by its German crew just as it arrived. After his arrest Casement was jointly interrogated at Scotland Yard by Thomson, Captain Reginald 'Blinker' Hall, the DNI, and MI5's main Irish expert, the Old Harrovian Major (later Lieutenant Colonel) Frank Hall (no relation to the DNI), a landowner from County Down.[16] The many conspiracy theorists attracted by the Casement affair have surprisingly failed to notice that before the war Frank Hall had been military secretary of the Ulster Volunteer Force and a gun-runner himself.[17] Like most officer recruits to MI5, his main recreations were outdoor pursuits, in his case shooting and yachting. As well as having a strong dislike of Irish nationalism, Hall had a keen sense of imperial pride, claiming when he joined MI5 in December 1914 to have visited 'every Imperial defended port N. of the Equator except Sierra Leone'.[18] Churchill later noted that Kell was 'not specially acquainted with Irish matters' and relied on Hall's expertise.[19]

Casement claimed that during the interrogation at Scotland Yard he asked to be allowed to appeal publicly for the Easter Rising in Ireland to be called off in order to 'stop useless bloodshed'. His interrogators refused, possibly in the hope that the Rising would go ahead and force the government to crush what they saw as a German conspiracy with Irish nationalists. According to Casement, he was told by Blinker Hall, 'It is better that a cankering sore like this should be cut out.'[20] Though the formal transcript of the interrogation finished before these comments were made, a note in Home Office files confirms Casement's version of events:

Casement begged to be allowed to communicate with the leaders to try and stop the rising but he was not allowed. On Easter Sunday at Scotland Yard he implored again to be allowed to communicate or send a message. But they refused, saying, 'It[']s a festering sore, it[']s much better it should come to a head.'[21]

Even if Casement had been allowed to issue an appeal to 'stop useless bloodshed', however, it is unlikely he would have deterred the seven-man military council of the Irish Republican Brotherhood from going ahead with the Easter Rising.[22]

Despite the polite tone of Casement's interrogators, it is clear that they despised him. One example of this contempt is their reaction to a moving poem written by Casement in prison, dated 5 July 1916, just under a month before his execution, while waiting to be received into the Catholic Church, which was preserved in MI5 files:

> Weep not that you no longer feel the tide
> High breasting sun and storm that bore along
> Your youth on currents of perpetual song;
> For in these mid-sea waters, still and wide,
> A Sleepless purpose the great Deep doth hide:
> Here spring the mighty fountains, pure and strong,
> That bear sweet change of breath to city throng,
> Who, had the sea no breeze, would soon have died.
> So, though the Sun shines not in such a blue,
> Nor have the stars the meaning youth devised,
> The heavens are nigher, and a light shines through
> The brightness that nor sun nor stars sufficed,

And on this lonely waste we find it true

Lost youth and love, nor lost, are hid with Christ.

After reading the poem, Frank Hall wrote scornfully to Basil Thomson, 'Is this working up a plea for insanity think you?!!'

While Lody had been respected as a patriot, Casement, despite his self-sacrificial bravery in the cause of Irish independence, was despised as a traitor who had tried by underhand methods to persuade Irish soldiers fighting for King and Country to desert to the enemy. Casement's interrogators had read, and doubtless been infuriated by, the evidence (preserved in MI5 files) of wounded Irish POWs repatriated from Germany during 1915, who described Casement's efforts to recruit them to an Irish Brigade. According to Private Joseph Mahony:

In Feb. 1915 Sir Roger Casement made us a speech [at Limburg POW camp] asking us to join an Irish Brigade, that this was 'our chance of striking a blow for our country'. He was booed out of the camp . . . After that further efforts were made to induce us to join by cutting off our rations, the bread ration was cut in half for about two months.[23]

Reports such as this help to explain why British intelligence chiefs were both so determined to ensure that Casement did not escape the gallows and so ready to blacken his name.

A further reason for their contempt for Casement may have been homophobia (a prejudice then common to both British intelligence and Irish nationalists). Christensen had told Findlay in October 1914 that Casement was homosexual. Sir Edward Grey reported to some of his cabinet colleagues that Casement and Christensen had 'unnatural relations'.[24] The relations appeared all the more 'unnatural' because of Christensen's admission that they began when he was a seaman aged only fifteen or sixteen and Casement was British consul in Brazil. According to Christensen, Casement followed him into a lavatory in a Montevideo hotel where they had sex.[25] Casement's 'Black Diaries', which were discovered while he was being interrogated at Scotland Yard and record in graphic detail his numerous sexual encounters with male lovers and prostitutes as well as his obsession with '*huge*', '*enormous*' genitalia,[26] reinforced the contempt of his interrogators. Though recent forensic examination has established their authenticity beyond reasonable doubt,[27] the suggestion that they were forged by British intelligence has always been deeply implausible. Neither MI5 nor any other British intelligence agency had the capacity to produce a forgery on the scale and of the complexity that would have been required.

Even the KGB, whose disinformation department, Service A, made far more use of forgery than any Western intelligence agency, never fabricated a handwritten document of comparable length.[28]

The relatively harmonious collaboration in London before Casement's trial between Frank Hall of MI5, Captain Hall and Basil Thomson contrasted with the confusion of British intelligence organization in Ireland itself. Military intelligence work was poorly co-ordinated with that of the police. Within the police the lack of co-ordination between the detective unit of the Dublin Municipal Police and the Special Crimes Branch of the Royal Irish Constabulary (RIC) added to the confusion. As the Inspector General of the RIC complained in 1916, it made little sense 'to have Dublin under the supervision of one secret service special crimes system and the remainder of the country under another'. There was no clearly defined role for MI5. Thomson concluded a month after Casement's execution: 'There is certainly a danger that from lack of coordination the Irish Government may be the last Department to receive information of grave moment to the peace of Ireland.' Until the end of the war, military and police intelligence was chiefly directed against the wrong target, concentrating on tracking down comparatively minor German intrigues rather than on following the much more important development of Irish nationalism. GHQ Ireland was later to regret that 'the opportunity was not taken to create an intelligence branch of trained brains working together to examine the military possibilities of the Sinn Fein movement',[29] which by 1917 was campaigning for the establishment of an Irish republic.

Germany's wartime subversion strategy against Britain had an imperial as well as an Irish dimension. Almost from the outbreak of war, while the British used the term 'Great War', the Germans spoke of 'World War' (*Weltkrieg*).[30] Both the German government and the Prusso-German General Staff were well aware that the Empire was crucial to the British war effort, mobilizing three million men, half of them in the Indian army. The greatest potential threat from German subversion thus came in India, the only part of the Empire with which MI5 was already in contact at the outbreak of war, communicating with the Director of Criminal Intelligence in Delhi through his London representative, Major John Wallinger.[31] Before the war, the main responsibility for dealing with Indian 'seditionists' in Britain fell to the Special Branch rather than Kell's Bureau.[32] In the summer of 1914, however, the Director of Criminal Intelligence complained that 'for some time past the information given by Scotland Yard about the doings of Indian agitators in England had been rather meagre' because 'the officers in Scotland Yard were so fully occupied with the Suffragette movement that they had very little to devote to Indians.'[33]

In September 1914 the German Chancellor, Theobald von Bethmann-Hollweg, told his Foreign Ministry: 'England appears determined to wage war until the bitter end . . . Thus one of our main tasks is gradually to wear England down through unrest in India and Egypt . . .'[34] A newly created Intelligence Bureau for the East, attached to the German Foreign Ministry, was given the task of working out how to do so. It began by setting up an Indian Committee in Berlin, led by the academic and lawyer Virendranath Chattopadhyaya, who had become a revolutionary while studying at the Middle Temple in London.[35] Berlin's hopes of stirring up disaffection among Britain's Muslim subjects were greatly encouraged when the Ottoman Empire entered the war on Germany's side on 5 November 1914. The Ottoman government issued fatwas calling on all Muslims to wage jihad against the Allies: among them the Muslims who made up one-third of the Indian army.[36] Censorship of a sample of the correspondence of the 138,000 Indian troops who fought on the Western Front in 1915 provided welcome reassurance for the Indian government and the wartime interdepartmental Whitehall committee on Indian 'revolutionary' activity. It revealed no significant support either for Indian 'revolutionaries' or for pan-Islamism, though one censor reported a worrying trend among Indian soldiers to write poetry, which he considered 'an ominous sign of mental disquietude'.[37]

Kell's main Indian expert early in the war was Robert Nathan, who, after qualifying as a barrister, had spent twenty-six years in the Indian civil service, becoming vice chancellor of Calcutta University, but had been forced to return to England because of ill health early in 1914.[38] He joined MO5(g) on 4 November 1914,[39] serving with Kell as one of the Bureau's representatives on the wartime interdepartmental Whitehall committee on Indian 'revolutionary' activity.[40] Nathan also worked closely with Basil Thomson, who praised his collaboration in all the Indian cases which came his way at Scotland Yard. Indeed Nathan was the only MI5 officer whose assistance Thomson acknowledged in his memoirs. Contrary to the impression given in the memoirs, Nathan was the more influential of the two; Thomson did not sit on the interdepartmental committee.[41]

Intercepted correspondence indicated that Indian revolutionaries in 1915 were planning an assassination campaign in England, France and Italy. Though the campaign did not materialize, Nathan had good reason to take it seriously.[42] The last political assassination in Britain had been the killing in London of Sir William Curzon Wyllie, the political aide-de-camp of the

Secretary of State for India, by an Indian student, Madan Lal Dhingra, in the summer of 1909. Even Winston Churchill, despite his hostility to Indian nationalism, had seen Dhingra as a romantic hero, calling his last words before execution 'the finest ever made in the name of patriotism'.[43] It was reasonable to expect that the First World War would produce other Dhingras. In the summer of 1915 the Indian Department of Criminal Intelligence (DCI) reported that, according to information from 'a trust-worthy source', the Indian nationalist Dr Abdul Hafiz and other German agents in Switzerland were plotting to assassinate Italian government ministers. Though Hafiz was expelled from Switzerland, reports of assassination plots continued. On 29 November Nathan sent a request through the Foreign Office to the Italian government for all Indians arriving from Switzerland to be stopped at the border and, if possible, deported to England.[44]

In October 1915 an Indian 'revolutionary', Harish Chandra, confessed during interrogation by Nathan and Thomson that he had been working for the Indian Committee in Berlin, seeking to subvert the loyalty of Indian POWs, and revealed German attempts to persuade the Amir of Afghanistan to join in a Muslim jihad against the British Raj. Nathan and Thomson succeeded in persuading Chandra to work as a double agent. In October 1915, they also recruited another Indian, Thakur Jessrajsinghji Sessodia, whose involvement in assassination plots had been discovered from his intercepted correspondence. Both Chandra and Sessodia proved to be reliable double agents. Their intelligence, some of which was corroborated by other sources, increasingly exposed the unrealistic nature of German plots to stir up Indian unrest. The interdepartmental committee in White-hall concluded in the course of 1916 that the best plan was to continue to monitor the development of the plots and encourage the Germans to waste money and resources on them.[45]

In the spring of 1916 Nathan left to head an office established in North America by the DCI to track down Indian revolutionaries.[46] His office provided the US authorities with much of the evidence used at two major trials of members of the Indian Ghadr ('Revolt') Party, charged with conspiracy to aid the Germans by plotting revolution in India. The first trial, in Chicago, ended with the conviction of three Ghadr militants in October 1917. The second trial, in San Francisco, reached a dramatic climax in April 1918 when one of the accused, Ram Singh, shot the Ghadr Party leader, Ram Chandra Peshawari, dead in the middle of the courtroom.[47] Basil Thomson commented:

In the Western [US] States such incidents do not disturb the presence of mind of Assize Court officials: the deputy-sheriff whipped an automatic from his pocket, and from his elevated place at the back of the court, aiming above and between the intervening heads, shot the murderer dead.[48]

One of Nathan's assistants wrote delightedly: 'I think the whole case is a great triumph and has done a lot to help us in this country. It has shown to the public the utter rottenness of the Ghadr Party . . . More than this, it has been a very successful piece of propaganda work.'[49] Veterans of the Indian army, police and civil service continued to make up a significant minority of MI5 personnel. Of the twenty-seven officers in G Branch (investigations) early in 1917, eight had served in India.[50]

The Indian National Congress seems to have attracted no significant wartime attention from either MI5 or any other section of the British intelligence community, because it had no German connection and posed no threat of violent opposition to British rule. Before the First World War, Congress was a middle-class debating society which met briefly each December, then lapsed into inactivity for another year. There was nothing in 1914 to suggest that it would emerge from the war as a mass movement which would become the focus of resistance to the British Raj. The man who brought about this transformation was M. K. 'Mahatma' Gandhi, an English-educated barrister of the Inner Temple who, more than any other man, set in motion the process which, a generation later, began the downfall of the British Empire. When Gandhi returned to India in 1915 from South Africa, where he developed the technique of *satyagraha*, or passive resistance, which he was later to use against the Raj, the DCI assessed him as 'neither an anarchist nor a revolutionary' but 'a troublesome agitator whose enthusiasm has led him frequently to overstep the limits of the South African laws relating to Asiatics'.[51]

In the course of the war MI5 extended its involvement in imperial intelligence from India to the Empire and Commonwealth as a whole. In August 1915, with the support of the Colonial Office, it began an attempt to 'secure rapid and direct exchange of information' between its own headquarters and colonial administrations. A year later, according to a post-war report, it was in touch with 'the authorities responsible for counter espionage in almost every one of the colonies'. In the autumn of 1916 the section of G Branch responsible for co-ordinating overseas intelligence became a new D Branch, headed by Frank Hall,[52] which was also responsible for 'Special Intelligence Missions' in Allied countries, notably in Rome and Washington DC. According to a post-war report on

D Branch, couched in unrealistically grandiloquent terms, 'particulars were obtained of German activities in all parts of the world, from Peru to the Dutch East Indies and the Islands of the Pacific, and a watch was kept on German propaganda through missionaries or otherwise on every continent.'[53] Henceforth MI5 saw its role as 'more than national': 'it is Imperial.'[54]

Subversion in mainland Britain first became a serious concern for MI5 in 1916. 'It was not until 1916', wrote Thomson later, 'that the Pacifist became active.'[55] The immediate cause of the pacifist revival was the introduction of conscription for men of 'military age' (between eighteen and forty-one), first for unmarried men in February 1916, then for married men two months later. Within MI5 the lead role in investigating the anti-conscription movement was taken by Major Victor Ferguson of G Branch, who had joined on the outbreak of war and had a combination of skills characteristic of a number of MI5 officers. He listed hunting, shooting ('some big game') and fishing as his chief recreations (followed by motoring, skiing, cricket and 'formerly football'). As well as following outdoor pursuits, he was an Oxford graduate with, again like many of his colleagues, a gift for foreign languages. Ferguson had translator's qualifications in German, Russian and French (the languages of the main foreign revolutionaries and subversives who attracted MI5's attention), in addition to having some competence in Spanish, Dutch and Arabic.[56] In June 1916, by agreement with G Branch, Special Branch officers raided the London headquarters of the No-Conscription Fellowship and removed its records and papers, as well as three-quarters of a ton of printed material. They seized a further 1½ tons of documents next day from the National Council Against Conscription (NCAC). This vast mass of paper was then examined by MI5 officers with a view to bringing prosecutions under the Defence of the Realm Act.[57] Ferguson sent a sample of the material seized to the Legal Adviser at the Home Office.[58] The real aim of the NCAC, he believed, was 'to work up feeling, especially in the workshops, against measures necessary for the successful prosecution of the war':

Whatever their policy may have been originally, and it is not denied that it was, to commence with, quite legal, there is not the least doubt that it has been divorced from its original purpose and has become a dangerous weapon whereby the loyalty of the people is being prostituted and the discipline of the army interfered with . . . If they are not for the success of our country it is not unreasonable if they are classed as pro-German. That, at any rate, is what the mass of the public consider them; and the public is substantially right.[59]

Between June 1916 and October 1917 MI5 investigated 5,246 individuals 'suspected of pacifism, anti-militarism etc.'.[60] Little came of the protest against conscription. About 7,000 conscientious objectors agreed to non-combatant service, usually with field ambulances; another 3,000 were sent to labour camps run by the Home Office; 1,500 'absolutists' who refused all compulsory service were called up and then imprisoned for refusing to obey orders.[61] These figures paled into statistical insignificance by comparison with the numbers of conscripts. By the end of 1916 conscription had increased the size of the armed services from 2½ million to 3½ million. During 1917–18 their size stabilized at between 4 and 4½ million – one in two of men of 'military age'.[62]

MI5's first contact with Communism (which after the Bolshevik Revolution was to dominate its counter-subversion operations for over seventy years) arose from its investigation, begun in 1915, of the Communist Club at 107 Charlotte Street, London, whose members included a number of Russian revolutionary exiles, among them two future Soviet foreign ministers, Georgi Chicherin and Maksim Litvinov.[63] In December 1915 Chicherin was briefly imprisoned while an unsuccessful attempt was made to assemble evidence for a successful prosecution.[64] Kell reported to the Home Office that the Russians in the Club were 'a desperate and very dangerous crowd'. Some, he believed, were 'closely connected with the Houndsditch murders' before the war.[65] The chief murder suspect in the Communist Club was the Latvian Bolshevik Yakov Peters, who after the Revolution became a bloodthirsty deputy head of the Cheka, the forerunner of the KGB. In December 1910 he seems to have been involved with a gang of violent Latvian revolutionaries who had been disturbed by a police patrol while robbing a Houndsditch jeweller to fund their cause. The revolutionaries shot three police officers dead and seriously wounded two others. Though the gang scattered, several members were arrested over the next few weeks. Among them was Peters, who was acquitted at his trial – after being ably defended by, ironically, William Melville's barrister son James (later a Labour solicitor general).[66]

During 1916 G1 (which investigated suspected espionage cases) discovered links between the Communist Club and the Diamond Reign public house, which, it reported, was 'a meeting place for bitterly hostile British citizens of German birth'. G1 reached the alarmist conclusion that the Communist Club 'fomented' the strike wave at Clydeside munitions factories in the early spring of 1916.[67] Though there is little doubt about the Club's support for 'Red Clydeside', it is unlikely to have had a significant influence on the strikes. There were, however, widespread suspicions in

Whitehall that subversive forces were at work. Christopher Addison, Parliamentary Under Secretary to the Minister of Munitions, David Lloyd George, suspected 'a systematic and sinister plan' to sabotage 'production of the most important munitions of war in the Clyde district' in order to frustrate the great offensive planned on the Western Front in the summer of 1916. His suspicions were fuelled by ill-founded reports of German machinations from a small Clydeside intelligence service secretly organized by Sir Lynden Macassey KC, chairman of the Clyde Dilution Commissioners (who dealt with the 'dilution' of skilled by unskilled labour). Addison, who was soon to succeed Lloyd George as Minister of Munitions, wrote in his diary after receiving Macassey's reports:

He has traced direct payments from Germany to three workers and also discovered that ... the man who is financing the Clyde workers ... has a daughter married in Germany, a son married to a German and his chief business is in Germany. He is evidently on the track of a very successful revelation.[68]

Macassey's reports prompted the Ministry of Munitions to found an intelligence service of its own (later known as PMS2). In February 1916 Kell provided the Ministry with a 'nucleus' of MI5 officers under Colonel Frank Labouchere to monitor aliens and labour unrest. Labouchere, who had been educated at Charterhouse and Geneva University, combined, like Kell, Ferguson and other MI5 officers, a liking for outdoor pursuits (chief among them fly-fishing and stalking) with an aptitude for languages. As well as German (the language most relevant to his investigation of possible enemy-financed subversion), he spoke French, Dutch and Persian.[69] To Macassey's extreme annoyance, his own intelligence service, of which he was inordinately proud, was taken over by Labouchere.[70]

Addison later wrote in his memoirs, 'There never was any evidence' of German involvement in the labour troubles.[71] At the time, however, there was indeed evidence, even if it later turned out to be unreliable. On 16 September Cumming sent Kell a report on intelligence from Berlin: 'Last week Persian Bank and other Banks completed arrangements for export of 800,000 marks in foreign currency to various centres outside Germany. It is reported that of the above sum about 250,000 marks are destined for labour agitation in England.'[72] Even if Cumming's intelligence was correct, it is almost certain that the money never reached England. Addison, however, was dissatisfied with PMS2's investigations into labour unrest and in December 1916, in a clear snub to Kell, asked Basil Thomson 'to undertake the whole of the intelligence service on labour matters for the whole country'. Thomson agreed, drafted twelve sergeants from the

CID into the Ministry, and was given an annual budget of £8,000 a year to run the new intelligence system. In April 1917, the administrative staff of the out-of-favour PMS2 were formally 'reabsorbed' by MI5.[73] Kell, however, made clear that he did not want back officers who had been 'concerned with labour unrest and strikes',[74] and Labouchere did not return to MI5.[75]

For much of 1916 police reports on both the Communist Club and the German-born habitués of the Diamond Reign public house tended to be reassuring. MI5 regarded the reports as seriously misleading and blamed them on corruption in the Met: 'The Germans were confident they could bribe the police . . .' In November 1916, as a result of G1 investigations, the Communist Club was raided and twenty-two of its members of various nationalities recommended for internment. The Home Secretary agreed to the internment of seventeen.[76] By this time MI5 had its own informant in the Club. Kell was deeply disturbed by what he and other sources revealed. The purpose of the Club, he reported in January 1917, was 'the hampering by all possible means (e.g. by anti-recruiting propaganda, fomentation of strikes etc) of the Execution of the War in the present crisis'. Kell was also deeply concerned by the activities of Chicherin's Russian Political Prisoners and Exiles Relief Committee:

Perhaps the greatest immediate danger arises from the instigation of enmity to the British Government on the part of the thousands of immigrants and refugees from Russia (and their offspring) now in this country . . . That the active enmity thus engendered may be cunningly manipulated at some opportune time by Germany very considerably adds to the danger of the moment.[77]

By the time he wrote these memoranda, Kell seems to have been under considerable strain, his asthma worsened by stress and long hours in the office. Like Cumming, he was still hard at work on Christmas Day 1916. In the course of that day Kell called on Cumming for 'a long yarn', and tried to persuade him to send a liaison officer to MI5. With his own staff already overstretched, Cumming was not persuaded.[78] Kell must also have been frustrated by his failure in January 1917 to persuade the Home Secretary to intern Chicherin, who, he reported, 'has openly expressed anti-British sentiments, and has freely associated on intimate terms with Germans and pro-Germans'.[79]

Early in 1917, Kell's worsening asthma forced him to give up the family's much loved country home at Weybridge in Surrey, whose large garden contained 400 rose trees and a grass tennis court, and move to a house at Campden Hill in London, closer to his office. The move, on a snowy day, did not go well. The last furniture van, which also contained the maids and what Constance Kell called the 'livestock' – 'our beloved Scottie dog, the cat and the parrot' – skidded off the road into a shop window and 'slung the parrot cage through it, the screeching bird adding to the confusion'.[80] Soon afterwards, Kell was forced to take sick leave.[81] His dismay at having temporarily to give up his role as MI5 director no doubt explains why this and two later periods of sick leave are, unusually, not noted in his record of service. During his first sick leave early in 1917 he seems to have suspected the head of G Branch (investigations), Reginald 'Duck' Drake, the longest-serving officer in MI5 (apart from Kell), of plotting to replace him. Though actual details of the quarrel do not survive, Kell said later that he became 'convinced that [Drake] was not playing the game'.[82] In March Drake left for GHQ in France, where he was responsible for gathering intelligence behind the German lines.[83]

The spring of 1917 saw major crises on both the Eastern and Western Fronts. The shockwaves from the Russian Revolution which overthrew the Tsar in March 1917 (in the Russian calendar, the 'February Revolution') created fears in the Lloyd George government, which had taken power three months earlier, that revolutionary agitators were out to undermine the British war effort. These fears were strengthened when the MPs and the National Council of the ILP acclaimed 'the magnificent achievement of the Russian people' as a step towards 'the coming of peace, based not on the dominance of militarists and diplomats, but on democracy and justice'.[84] For an assessment of the threat, the War Cabinet turned first to Basil Thomson rather than to Kell. At a Home Office conference on 5 April Thomson found 'a good deal of ignorant alarmism, especially among the generals present', and was instructed to prepare intelligence reports on 'the growth of anarchist and socialist movements and their influence on the strike'.[85]

Though the United States entered the war on 6 April, it was over a year before its forces arrived in sufficient numbers to help turn the tide of war on the Western Front. In the spring of 1917 the French Commander in Chief, General Robert Nivelle, produced a plan for a lightning offensive to win a quick victory which seduced not merely the French cabinet but, more surprisingly, Lloyd George, who was usually sceptical of the claims of generals. Ignoring the lessons of the deadlock of the past two years of trench warfare, Nivelle rashly promised a victory which would be 'certain, swift and small in cost': 'One and a half million Frenchmen cannot fail.' The offensive began in April and continued for three weeks but did not achieve a breakthrough and was followed by full-scale mutiny.[86]

Faced with the threatened collapse of the French as well as the Russian will to fight on, some ministers feared that the British war effort was also under threat. Lord Milner, next to Lloyd George the most influential voice in the War Cabinet, wrote to the Prime Minister on 1 June 1917: 'I fear the time is very near at hand when we shall have to take some strong steps to stop the "rot" in this country, unless we wish to "follow Russia" into impotence and dissolution.' But the 'rot' continued. Two days later the ILP and the smaller Marxist British Socialist Party (BSP) convened a conference at Leeds to honour the Russian Revolution. The conference endorsed the demand by the Russian provisional government for 'peace without annexations or indemnities', told the British government to demand the same, and called for British workers' and soldiers' councils on the Soviet model.[87] MI5 had been intercepting BSP correspondence for the past two years, reporting in October 1916 that the Party and its general secretary, Albert Edward Inkpin, were 'violently pro-German'.[88] Victor Ferguson, who led MI5 investigations of anti-war movements, noted the following information on Inkpin given him by a former leading member of the BSP, Victor Fisher, who had turned against Inkpin because of his opposition to the war: '?German blood. Has a brother (Christian name unknown) and both are violently pro-German. Funds from German sources may possibly filter through him. Very clever. His influence succeeded in carrying over [BSP] Executive to pro-Germanism . . .'[89] It is highly unlikely that Inkpin did receive money from German sources. Rather than being pro-German, he was passionately anti-war.[90] Inkpin had not been called up for military service, on the grounds that his leadership of a political party was work in the 'national interest'. MI5 had originally approved of the decision on the grounds that it deprived Inkpin of the opportunity to spread sedition in the armed forces. In the aftermath of the Bolshevik Revolution, Kell changed his mind and tried unsuccessfully to have Inkpin's exemption from conscription removed.[91] Inkpin went on to become first general secretary of the Communist Party of Great Britain (CPGB) in 1920; together with Lenin, Trotsky and other Communist leaders, he was elected one of the presidents of the Communist International (Comintern).[92]

The most successful German subversion operation of the war was to transport Lenin back to Petrograd ('like a plague bacillus', said Churchill) in a 'sealed' train from exile in Switzerland in the spring of 1917. Lenin's 'revolutionary defeatism' was tantamount to acceptance of German victory. Cumming passed on to MI5 a report from an agent in Berne that the Germans had required Lenin to give a guarantee that all his fellow revolutionaries on the train were 'partisans of an immediate peace'.[93]

The detailed regulations, covering such issues as smoking and the use of lavatories, which Lenin imposed upon his fellow travellers, gave an early indication of the authoritarian one-party state which he was later to create in Russia.[94] On 3 April (16 April by the Western calendar) Lenin arrived to a theatrical reception in Petrograd, though the band, presumably because it had brought the wrong music, played the French national anthem instead of the 'Internationale'. Next day a German representative in Stockholm cabled Berlin: 'Lenin's entry into Russia successful. He is working exactly as we wish.'[95] Lenin dismissed any suggestion that he should have turned down the offer of German help as 'silly bourgeois prejudices': 'If the German capitalists are so stupid as to take us over to Russia, that's their funeral.' Rumours inevitably circulated, however, that he was a German spy and they were unreliably confirmed by a Russian officer who claimed to have been told so by his German captors when a prisoner of war. On 6 July the Justice Ministry of the Russian Provisional Government ordered Lenin's arrest on a charge of high treason. Lenin was forced to shave off his beard, disguise himself as a worker and take temporary refuge in Finland.[96] 'We understand', noted Major Claude Dansey of E Branch in August, 'that the Russian General Staff have proof now of Lenin's guilt.'[97]

Given the priority which Germany gave to assisting the Bolsheviks to undermine the Russian war effort, it was reasonable – though, as it later turned out, mistaken – for MI5 to believe that it was also assisting the Bolsheviks' British sympathizers. Russian 'proof' that Lenin was in the pay of the Germans encouraged the belief that German money was also subsidizing British Bolshevism. The most dangerous Bolshevik in Britain, MI5 believed, was Georgi Chicherin, a committed supporter of Lenin's 'revolutionary defeatism'. Having pressed unsuccessfully for his internment in January 1917, MI5 did so successfully in August on the grounds:

(1) That he is of hostile associations by reason of his associations with Germans and pro-Germans at the Communist Club ...

(2) That having regard to his anti-ally and pro-German activities and sentiments, he is a danger to the public safety and the defence of the Realm[98]

In his unsuccessful appeal against internment, Chicherin made one potentially embarrassing charge. Claiming that he had been mandated by the Russian Provisional Government to investigate relations between the Tsarist Okhrana and Scotland Yard, he accused the British government of preventing his inquiry in order to conceal 'dark doings' of the Okhrana.[99] There were indeed potential embarrassments to be uncovered – not least the past dealings between MI5's chief detective William Melville (who retired a few months later and died early in the following year) and the unscrupulous Okhrana chief, Pyotr Rachkovsky.[100]

The growing evidence from France that Germany was financing opposition to the war strengthened fears that it was doing so in Britain. On 15 May Raoul Duval, a director of the left-wing newspaper *Bonnet Rouge*, notorious for its defeatism, was caught returning from Switzerland with a large cheque from a German banker. He was later found guilty of treason and executed. In August the editor of the *Bonnet Rouge*, Miguel Almereyda, committed suicide in prison. Georges Clemenceau, soon to become French prime minister, claimed that the refusal of the Interior Minister, Louis Malvy, to prosecute Almereyda and other defeatists had led to the army mutinies. Malvy was later found guilty of 'culpable negligence in the discharge of his duties' and sentenced to five years' exile. The former radical Prime Minister Joseph Caillaux, who had given financial support to the *Bonnet Rouge* before the war, was also arrested. The British ambassador reported that Clemenceau hoped he would be shot. (In a post-war trial he was found guilty of treason 'with extenuating circumstances'.)[101]

Though it later emerged that Clemenceau and his supporters had greatly exaggerated the extent of German-financed subversion, at the time many British observers took it at face value. On 3 October Sir Edward Carson, Minister without Portfolio in Lloyd George's War Cabinet, declared it a 'fact' that German money had been 'promoting industrial trouble' in Russia, France, Italy, Spain, the United States, Argentina, Chile – 'in fact wherever conditions were suitable for their interference'. Carson's claims were taken seriously by his colleagues. At the War Cabinet on 4 October: 'It was pointed out . . . that the only really efficient system of propaganda at present existing in this country was that organised by the pacifists, who had large sums of money at their disposal and who were conducting their campaign with great vigour.' The cabinet minutes record no challenge to this preposterous allegation.[102] The War Cabinet discussed the question of German finance for pacifism again at its meeting on 19 October. The minutes reveal, once again, extravagant conspiracy theories, this time that 'anti-war propaganda was being financed by wealthy men, who were looking forward to making money by opening up trade with Germany after the war'. This claim too appears to have gone unchallenged. The War Cabinet decided that the Home Office (in other words Thomson rather than Kell) should 'undertake the coordination and control of the investigation of all pacifist propaganda and of the wider subjects connected therewith', and report back.[103] Thomson groaned inwardly at the news. While he considered ministers too alarmist, he was conscious that failure to give their alarms due – or rather undue – weight might be interpreted as complacency in the face of subversion. He wrote in his diary on 22 October:

The War Cabinet . . . are not disposed to take soothing syrup in these matters. Being persuaded that German money is supporting [pacifist and revolutionary] societies they want to be assured that the police are doing something. I feel certain that there is no German money, their expenditure being covered by the subscriptions they receive from cranks.[104]

Thomson's report contrived to show a prudent awareness of the dangers of German-financed subversion, while none the less arriving at a reassuring conclusion. German money, he informed ministers, had been neither widely nor effectively deployed. Except for the ILP, pacifist organizations had been 'financially in low water for some time'; the Union of Democratic Control (UDC) was 'not a revolutionary body' and had little appeal outside 'the intellectual classes'; the British Soviets were 'moribund'; the BSP, though 'very noisy', did not 'carry very much weight' and had to be bailed out by the ILP; the shop stewards were 'generally . . . in favour of continuing the war'. Boredom, concluded Thomson, did more than Germany to encourage pacifist propaganda. The working classes (particularly young, unmarried men with money in their pockets) missed 'the relaxations to which they were accustomed before the war, owing to the curtailment of horseracing, football and other amusements, and to the reduction of hours when public houses are kept open'.[105]

News of the Bolshevik Revolution in Russia, however, revived the War Cabinet's anxieties. Following the triumph of subversion in Russia, their fears of subversion in Britain scaled new heights. The Foreign Office claimed on 12 November, five days after the Revolution, that Bolshevism had been 'fastened on and poisoned by the Germans for their own purposes' to undermine the Russian war effort: 'It is not yet possible to say which of the Bolshevik leaders have taken German money; some undoubtedly have, while others are honest fanatics.'[106] Some ministers inevitably feared that British subversives had taken German money too. The Home Secretary, Sir George Cave, suspected that German-financed subversion had been more widespread than Thomson had suggested, and ordered 'further investigations' by a joint committee of MI5 and Special Branch officers, including an examination of the records of pacifist and revolutionary societies seized in police raids to trace the source of their income.[107] No evidence of German funding for British pacifists and revolutionaries emerged from investigations by either MI5 or the Special Branch. Thomson's dismissive comments on the No-Conscription Fellowship, circulated to the War

Cabinet on 13 December, were typical of his contemptuous attitude to pacifists in general: 'The documents disclose no evidence of Enemy influence or financial support. The Fellowship is conducted in an unbusinesslike way by cranks, and its influence outside the circle of Conscientious Objectors seems to be small.'[108]

Kell took the threat of Soviet subversion more seriously. The MI5 New Year card for 1918, personally designed by Kell's deputy Holt-Wilson and drawn in the Pre-Raphaelite manner by the leading illustrator Byam Shaw, shows the loathsome, hirsute figure of Subversion, smoke billowing from its nostrils, crawling on all fours towards a British fighting man, clad in the garb of a Roman soldier and oblivious of the danger to his rear, his eyes fixed firmly on the vision on the horizon of 'Dieu et Mon Droit' and victory in 1918. Just in time MI5, depicted as a masked Britannia, impales Subversion with a trident marked with her secret monogram before it can stab the British warrior in the back. In January 1918 Kell began an investigation into possible Soviet subversion in munitions factories, urging that chief constables should:

report to us any change of attitude on the part of Russians [working] on Munitions, which would be denoted by: pacifist or anti-war propaganda, a disinclination to continue to help in the production of Munitions, or any active tendency towards holding up supplies, either by restriction of out-put, or destruction of out-put or factories.[109]

Despite its fears of Soviet subversion, MI5 seems to have made no attempt to assess the broader significance of the Bolshevik Revolution and its likely impact outside Russia.[110] The immediate impact of the Revolution on the British labour movement appears, in retrospect, surprisingly slight, arousing much less support than the overthrow of the Tsar eight months before. While the small BSP supported the Bolsheviks, most ILP leaders did not. The leading Labour journalist H. N. Brailsford in the *Herald* denounced the Revolution as 'reckless and uncalculating folly'.[111]

While interned in Brixton Prison, Georgi Chicherin discovered from the newspapers that Leon Trotsky, the Russian Commissar for Foreign Affairs, had appointed him Soviet representative in London. He telegraphed Trotsky from prison to accept.[112] In January 1918 Chicherin and another imprisoned Russian revolutionary were allowed to return to Russia in exchange for the release of Britons detained by the Bolsheviks. A friend who saw Chicherin off on the boat train at Waterloo reported that, 'as the train steamed out of the station, the "International" was sung in Russian and cheers were given for the Russian Revolution.'[113] In February 1918

Chicherin was a member of the Bolshevik delegation that concluded the peace of Brest-Litovsk which conceded to Germany huge territorial gains in the east (all lost later when it was defeated in the west). Lenin insisted that the Bolsheviks had no other option open to them but a humiliating peace: 'If you are not inclined to crawl on your belly through the mud, then you are not a revolutionary but a chatterbox.'[114] Both the peace of Brest-Litovsk and the beginning of the last great German offensive on the Western Front in March undermined British opposition to the war. Brest-Litovsk seemed evidence of the Bolsheviks' German sympathies, and Field Marshal Sir Douglas Haig's 'Back to the Wall' message to his troops on the Western Front, when it looked as if the Germans might achieve a breakthrough, was widely supported on the Home Front. Thomson declared himself taken aback by the strength of the popular reaction against pacifism due chiefly – according to all his informants – to 'the critical position of the relations of the working class who are fighting in Flanders'.[115]

During the final year of the war the main expansion of MI5 activities was the continued growth of the Ports Police (325 strong by the Armistice),[116] who were now on the lookout for Bolshevik as well as German sympathizers, the establishment of a Rome station and a substantial increase in its presence in the United States. The opening of MI5's Rome station, the British Military Mission, on 1 January 1918 was a consequence of the battle of Caporetto two months earlier when Austrian and German forces achieved what threatened to become a major breakthrough on the Italian front, which had to be shored up with six Anglo-French divisions. The head of mission, Sir Samuel Hoare MP, a baronet and future foreign secretary, was the only serving MP ever to become an MI5 officer.[117] For most of the past two years Hoare had worked for MI1c, Cumming's wartime foreign intelligence service, serving before the February Revolution as its head of station in Petrograd, where he had sent back to Cumming the first grisly details to reach the West of the assassination of Rasputin, the charismatic but dissolute monk who had won the confidence of the Tsarina. Hoare had an exaggerated view of the role of pro-German 'Dark Forces', including Rasputin, in undermining the Russian war effort,[118] and spent much of his time in Rome seeking to identify and counter similar subversion in Italy. He sent Kell a series of reports (at least some of them copied to Cumming) on the divisions within the Vatican between supporters and opponents of the Allies, denouncing the papal nuncio in Munich, Eugenio Pacelli, as 'a convinced pro-German'; in 1939 Pacelli was to become Pope Pius XII. Hoare's counter-subversion operations included bribing pro-Allied journalists, among them the former socialist Benito

Mussolini, who in 1919 was to found the Fascist movement. Hoare paid Mussolini the then considerable sum of £100 a week.[119]

During 1918 thirty MI5 staff, fourteen of them officers, were posted to its Washington and New York stations.[120] Liaison in Washington had begun immediately after the United States entered the war in April 1917 when Claude Dansey arrived to give detailed briefings to US military intelligence. Dansey plainly impressed his audience. After one of his lectures, Major General Joseph Kuhn, president of the US Army War College in Washington, emphasized 'how excellent the British service is'.[121] In August 1917. Dansey left MI5 for SIS, where he spent the rest of his career, rising to become assistant chief. In January 1918 Lieutenant Colonel Hercules Pakenham, late of the Royal Irish Rifles and an experienced foreign liaison officer, became head of MI5's Washington office.[122] An Old Etonian and former ADC to the Governors General of Canada and India,[123] Pakenham also had long American family connections; one of his ancestors not only lost the battle of New Orleans during the War of 1812, but managed to do so after the peace treaty ending the war had been signed. The arrival of US forces on the Western Front further increased the importance of American liaison. In August, because of the substantial numbers of US citizens passing through British ports and the large German-American community which had earlier opposed US entry into the war, MI5 opened an 'American suspect index', which was shared with the Director of Military Intelligence in Washington and no other ally.[124] From August onwards, a surviving MI5 visitors' book shows a small but steady stream of US intelligence officers calling at its London headquarters.[125]

On 1 March 1918 Major Norman Thwaites, previously deputy to Cumming's US head of station, Sir William Wiseman, became head of the MI5 office in New York.[126] Thwaites had been partly educated in Germany and spoke fluent German. While working in pre-war New York as private secretary to the prominent journalist Joseph Pulitzer (later founder of the Pulitzer Prizes), he had become well connected in the German-American community.[127] Before the US entry into the war, Thwaites had managed to purloin and copy a photograph of the German ambassador in Washington, Count von Bernstorff, with his arms round two women in bathing suits. Thwaites exposed Bernstorff to public ridicule by using his press contacts to arrange for its publication. The Russian ambassador kept a copy on his mantelpiece.[128] Like Hoare, Thwaites remained in touch with MI1c while working for MI5. Both collaborated closely with the New York police, the Bureau of Investigation (later FBI), US Customs, military and naval intelligence. MI1c reported that the refusal of any of the US security and intelligence agencies in New York to employ German-Americans gave Thwaites's role particular importance: 'For months Major Thwaites has been the only intelligence officer in New York who was able to read and speak German. He has spent many nights at Police headquarters, etc examining captured enemy documents.'[129] Among the US military intelligence officers in New York with whom Thwaites probably dealt (though firm evidence is lacking) was the former British double agent Captain Roslyn Whytock.[130] Thwaites's expanding operations were probably responsible for persuading Wiseman that Kell was planning to take over the New York MI1c station.[131]

Within Britain the security problem which most concerned the government during the last summer of the war was a strike by the London police. On 30 August 10,000 of the 19,000 Metropolitan Police officers failed to report for duty, demanding both the recognition of their union and an immediate rise in pay. Lloyd George was so shaken that he later claimed that Britain 'was nearer to Bolshevism that day than at any other time since'. Kell was on sick leave when the strike occurred, and no record of his assessment of the strike seems to have survived. Thomson, however, took a less alarmist view than Lloyd George. 'No strike would have taken place,' he believed, if the pay rise promised as soon as the strike began had been announced beforehand. The pay rise was sufficient to persuade the police to return to work without their union being recognized.[132] Though the strike was quickly settled, it left Thomson with a lingering unease about the willingness of the police to deal with Bolshevik-inspired unrest. The Met was to go on strike again in the following year.

The turning of the tide in favour of the Allies on the Western Front in the summer of 1918 removed the last fears of serious wartime subversion. The British victory at Amiens on 8 August was, said the German commander General Erich von Ludendorff, 'the blackest day for the German army in the history of the war'. It was the British army, stiffened by strong divisions from Canada and Australia, which bore the brunt of the fighting in the victorious final stages of the war. In the three months between Amiens and the Armistice the British army took 188,700 prisoners of war and captured 2,840 guns – almost as many as the other Allies combined.[133] As victory came in sight pacifism disappeared from view. Working-class morale all over the country, wrote Thomson on 21 October, three weeks before the Armistice, was 'probably at its highest point' since the war began.[134]

Thomson was already canvassing support for a post-war intelligence organization headed by himself to monitor peacetime subversion. He was encouraged in his ambitions by naval intelligence. Both Blinker Hall and his assistant, Claud Serocold, were on friendly terms with Thomson but disliked Kell as 'short-sighted and timorous'.[135] Thomson also enjoyed more powerful support than Kell within the government. His most committed supporter was Walter Long, Secretary of State for the Colonies. On 14 October Long sent Thomson 'unofficially and as a friend' an eccentric memorandum 'on the question of our Secret Service'. 'There is in this country', wrote Long, 'a very strong Bolshevik Agency which succeeds, owing to the want of efficient Secret Service and prompt action, in causing great domestic trouble.' Long admitted that he might be 'unduly suspicious' but argued strongly that the strikes in the police, on the railway and on the Clyde were all due to 'German intrigue and German money'. During the police strike, wrote Long, 'I have undoubted information that we escaped really by the skin of our teeth from a disaster of terrible dimensions in London.' He added: 'I believe an efficient Secret Service is the only way in which to cope with the Bolshevik, Syndicalist, and the German spy. I am satisfied that these three are still actively pursuing their infernal practices.'[136]

Privately Thomson did not take seriously Long's fears of a vast German-financed subversive conspiracy, but he was anxious not to lose Long's support. He therefore agreed with Long on the existence of 'a strong Bolshevik agency in this country, which is growing' – but added reassuringly that he knew 'the principal persons concerned in it and to some extent the source of their funds'. Thomson went on to endorse enthusiastically Long's call for a co-ordinated domestic intelligence system. He predicted that the main opposition would come from MI5, which wished to preserve a peacetime monopoly of counter-espionage – in Thomson's view 'a very essential part of Home Intelligence, the experience of the War having shown that Contra-Espionage goes far beyond the business of detecting foreign spies, since their enemy intrigue ramifies in every direction'. With Blinker Hall's and Serocold's support Thomson put the case for a civilian head of the entire intelligence community, which he intended to be himself. He supported a scheme proposed by Hall and Serocold to help finance peacetime intelligence through a secret War Loan investment of about a million pounds managed by trustees: 'It is very doubtful whether parliament will continue to vote an adequate sum for Secret Services after the War, more especially if a Labour Government comes into power . . .'[137] Long supported Thomson's proposal and forwarded it to the Prime Minister.[138] Over the next few months he bombarded Lloyd George with messages about the reorganization of intelligence. 'Unless prompt steps are taken,' he wrote on 18 November, 'I am informed we shall find the Secret Service seriously crippled just when we shall need it most.'[139]

Kell's sick leave in the final months of the war and lack of powerful backers in Whitehall left him ill equipped to compete with Thomson for the post-war control of British domestic intelligence. A surviving letter from Kell to his deputy Holt-Wilson sent from Northumberland on 7 September 1918 reveals, despite the hospitality of the Duke of Northumberland, a rather lonely and bored director whose concerns are limited to personal and office matters, with no reference to the dramatic developments on the Western Front, which appeared daily on the front pages of the newspapers, or the debate under way in Whitehall on post-war intelligence reorganization which would have a major effect on the future of MI5:

I am much fitter and have had a good rest here – But no fishing – low water and fish not taking anyhow. John [Kell's son] caught a small trout today fooling on a lake . . .

My wife has become very keen on fishing – although it has been fallow. I wish she could have come up to Morpeth with me as the Duke's fishing might be good for her.

. . . My 2 months [leave] are up on 1st Oct, but as I did 5 days work in Dubl[in] and Edinboro, I may, if the weather keeps fairly decent, add those 5 days on and return to London on Friday 4th October and look in on 5th – and start work on Sunday. But if the weather breaks I shall return earlier – and you will see me walk in any day! Looking much the better for wear. If there is any fellow who badly wants a week's leave send him along here as I am all alone and beastly dull in the evenings. I can offer him a most comfortable hotel and good food and lovely air. I am longing to be back with you.[140]

While Kell was recuperating in Northumberland, Thomson was lobbying in London for a post-war intelligence system in which he would have the leading role.

In January 1919 the War Cabinet set up a Secret Service Committee to review the performance of the intelligence agencies and how best to co-ordinate their work. The chairman was Lord Curzon, who was in charge of the Foreign Office while Balfour was at the Paris peace conference and was to succeed him as foreign secretary in June. As viceroy of India at the beginning of the century Curzon had become involved in the Great Game on the North-Western Frontier, and viewed the Bolsheviks' designs on India with even greater suspicion than those of their Tsarist forebears. Like Long and Churchill, who also served on the Secret Service Committee, he attached great importance to intelligence reports on the advance of the Red Menace. Curzon described Thomson as 'an invaluable sleuth hound'. The Secret Service Committee under his chairmanship met intermittently for two years, overseeing the reorganization on a peacetime footing of the greatly expanded intelligence services which emerged from the First World War. The Committee rejected Thomson's ambitious proposal for a single civilian head of the whole intelligence community. But it did approve an earlier proposal by Long for a 'Civil Secret Service' to monitor subversion. Its first report in February 1919 recommended Thomson's appointment as head of a new Directorate of Intelligence under the Home Office.[141] Like Kell, Thomson was knighted later in the year.

His new office, which he assumed on May Day 1919, formally confirmed him as the chief watchdog of subversion and left him in control of the Special Branch. Eddie Bell, who was responsible for intelligence liaison at the US embassy in London, told Washington in May 1919 that the coming man in British domestic intelligence was not Kell but Thomson, who was 'already well in the saddle and going strong': 'it is going to be very important to us in future to have a good liaison with him.'[142]

Section B
Between the Wars

Introduction

MI5 and its Staff: Survival and Revival

On 24 March 1919 MI5 celebrated victory in the Great War with the 'first (and last) performance' of the 'Hush-Hush' Revue, followed by a dinner-dance. The invitation card showed a female secretary dressed in male officer's tunic with very short skirt and high heels, carrying a notepad marked 'MI5'. The programme for the evening made attendance subject to 'the following conditions':

(a) That you give up all election eggs, dead cats and similar missiles at the door. These will be devoted to the starving Bolsheviks' Relief Fund (Food Committee)

(b) That you refrain from snoring, shooting and strong language

The Revue, a 'Sententious Stunt' by MI5's 'Barmy Breezies', began with a sketch featuring Captain Fond O'Fluff and Miss Dickie Bird, which continued the mildly flirtatious theme of the invitation. The hit musical *Chou Chin Chow*, then playing at the Haymarket Theatre opposite MI5's Charles Street headquarters, inspired a number of pseudo-Chinese jokes. Helen Johnson of the Registry later recalled that MI5 officers' windows 'apparently . . . looked directly into the Chorus Girls' changing rooms!'[1] A wartime MI5 cartoon shows the disappointment caused when an attractive female silhouette glimpsed by male officers through a Haymarket window turns out to be a tailor's dummy.

The Revue also drew some of its inspiration from the traditions of the regimental concert party. A majority of MI5 officers were already familiar from their military careers with the concert-party tradition of poking fun at those in authority. The commanding officer, regimental sergeant major, medical officer and chaplain, among others, were expected to show the capacity to laugh at themselves, and were liable to be offended if no mockery was directed towards them. Thus it was in MI5. Among the targets for gentle mockery in the 'Hush-Hush' Revue was Kell himself, whose wife Constance later recalled:

Invitation to the March 1919 MI5 Victory celebration dinner-dance and
programme for the 'Hush-Hush' Revue.

It was a clever take-off of all the bosses of the various sections, rather merciless in
some cases, but all of it taken in very good part and most amusing. K[ell] was very
convincingly caricatured and he was delighted with the thrusts at him, for they had
got him walking with his familiar stoop and with all his tricks of manner. The show
was followed by a really good dance, and the whole thing was voted a great success.[2]

Despite the good humour of the evening, the success of the Revue and
MI5's collective pride in its contribution to victory, the spring of 1919 was
a worrying time for Kell and for many others in MI5. The Director had

The Barmy Breezies

present their

Sententious Stunt

entitled

HUSH-HUSH

for the first (and probably the last) time by the mistaken kindness

of

Colonel V. G. W. KELL, C.B.,

aided and abetted by the Management

of the

CRIPPLEGATE INSTITUTE,

- - Golden Lane, Barbican, E.C. - -

at **20.00** *on the* 24th *MARCH*, 1919.

You are invited to attend on the following conditions :—

> (a) That you give up all election eggs, dead cats, and similar missiles at the door. These will be devoted to the starving Bolsheviks' Relief Fund (Food Committee).
>
> (b) That you refrain from snoring, shooting, and strong language.
>
> (c) That you will wait till supper is announced before beginning.
>
> (d) That you will inform the Committee whether you intend to come or not.

(Letters should be addressed to Miss Dalton, 16, Charles Street, S.W. 1. Anonymous or unstamped replies will be returned unopened.)

already lost the power struggle with Basil Thomson and now had to face the prospect of having to dismiss many of his staff. Probably unknown to most staff, Kell was fighting for the survival of MI5. He continued to do so at intervals for the next six years. The first report of the Secret Service Committee in February 1919 had paid tribute to the quality of British wartime intelligence – 'equal, if not superior, to that obtained by any other country engaged in the War' – but criticized the weakness of co-ordination between the agencies.[3] The Director of Military Intelligence, Major General Sir William Thwaites, with the support of Blinker Hall's successor as

DNI, Captain Hugh Sinclair (later chief of SIS), and the Director of Air Operations and Intelligence, Brigadier General R. M. Groves, proposed to Lord Hardinge of Penshurst, PUS at the Foreign Office, the merger of MI5 and SIS in the interests both 'of economy and of efficiency'.[4] Cumming, like Kell, was appalled at the idea of merger, which he denounced as 'utterly unworkable'.[5]

On 7 April Kell attended a meeting at the Admiralty, chaired by Lord Hardinge. Others present included Mansfield Cumming, Thwaites and the DNI. Though the proposal to combine MI5 and SIS was not mentioned, all were warned, as they had doubtless expected, of probable Treasury demands to cut the intelligence budget:

Colonel Kell said that it had occurred to him that Parliamentary opposition to the Secret Service vote* would be greatly reduced if he were to take the Labour Members into our confidence to the extent of showing some of the most prominent of them a little of the work which had been done during the War. He could easily let them see many parts of his work which were not really very secret, but which were impressive as showing good results. He thought that this would help, not only to make them interested in the continuance of the work, but would also tend to dispel the feeling which appeared to be prevalent in many quarters that Secret Service funds were used to spy upon Labour in this country.

Though the meeting agreed that Kell's proposal 'merited serious consideration', there is no evidence that it was followed up. Kell also complained that 'totally inaccurate stories were constantly being circulated' about MI5's wartime work, 'and he thought it would be a good thing to publish an accurate record now or later.'[6]

Basil Thomson, an accomplished self-publicist, beat Kell to it. On 24 April, a week before he became head of the new Directorate of Intelligence, a flattering article in the right-wing *Morning Post* reported that his new 'Special Branch' would operate 'on the lines of Continental Secret Services and will ultimately have agents throughout the United Kingdom, in the colonies, and in many parts of the world outside the British Empire'. Wildly exaggerated though the claim turned out to be, it probably accurately reflected Thomson's immense ambitions. The *Daily Mail* next day was equally flattering:

After 50 years as a sub-department of Scotland Yard the 'Special Branch' which looks after Kings and visiting potentates, Cabinet Ministers, and suffragettes, spies

---

* The Secret Service Vote (increasingly referred to as the 'Secret Vote'), which fluctuated greatly in size, had been used to finance intelligence and other secret activities since the eighteenth century.

and anarchists, has been given a home of its own and is placed under the special charge of an assistant commissioner of police, Mr Basil Thomson, who has an unrivalled knowledge of all these.

To Scotland House Mr Thomson has taken his special staff and his office furniture, including a very inviting leather armchair in which every spy of note sat at one time or another during the war.[7]

The implication that Thomson rather than Kell had taken the lead role in wartime counter-espionage must have caused particular offence in MI5.

MI5's budget was cut by almost two-thirds – from £100,000 in the last year of the war to £35,000 in the first year of peace.[8] In December 1919 the slimmed down Service moved from Charles Street to smaller and cheaper premises at 73–75 Queen's Gate, where it remained for most of the 1920s before moving to Oliver House in Cromwell Road.

By May 1920 Service staff had shrunk from 844 at the time of the Armistice to 151,[9] with further serious cuts to come. Kell, meanwhile, was still having to fight for the survival of MI5 as an independent agency, distinct from both SIS and Thomson's Directorate. The papers of Kell's deputy, Holt-Wilson, contain a document from 1920 (probably drafted by Holt-Wilson himself) setting out MI5's case for its continued existence. At this stage Soviet espionage (unlike Soviet subversion) was not yet identified as a significant threat. The main, rather exaggerated, emphasis was placed on the threat from the revival of German espionage and the new threats from Britain's wartime allies, France and Japan. All these, it was claimed, made MI5 'decidedly more necessary even than before the war': 'It may be pointed out that the total annual cost of the organization on a satisfactory basis would not exceed the actual running expenses of five Mark V tanks on a test run of 1000 miles!'[10] The document ended with a scathing attack on both Thomson and the Directorate of Intelligence:

Despite statements to the contrary in the press and elsewhere, Sir Basil Thomson's organization has never actually *detected* a case of espionage, but has merely arrested and questioned spies at the request of MI5, when the latter organization, which had detected them, considered that the time for arrest had arrived. The Army Council are in favour of entrusting the work to an experienced, tried and successful organization rather than to one which has yet to win its spurs.

Sir Basil Thomson's existing higher staff consists mainly of ex-officers of MI5 not considered sufficiently able for retention by that Department. The Army Council are not satisfied with their ability to perform the necessary duties under Sir Basil Thomson's direction, and they are satisfied that detective officers alone, without direction from above, are unfitted for the work.[11]

Holt-Wilson's contemptuous dismissal of the quality of Thomson's 'higher staff' was doubtless prompted by deep animosity towards Thomson himself and resentment towards those who had jumped ship from MI5. But, despite the inadequacies of its head, there was at least a handful of officers in the Directorate of Intelligence of undoubted ability. Among them was Captain Hugh Miller, a wartime member of MI5 who late in the war had also worked part-time for Cumming. Miller had an MA with first-class honours in English literature and a second class in modern languages from Edinburgh University, where he won two gold medals. In the decade before the First World War he worked as lecturer in English successively at the universities of Grenoble, Dijon, the Sorbonne, Cairo and Aberdeen, before joining the Royal Scots on the outbreak of war.[12] His record of service contains high praise for his abilities before his transfer to Thomson's Directorate in March 1920.[13] In 1931 Miller was to return to MI5, together with his Scotland Yard colleague Guy Liddell, who, though not previously a member of MI5, went on to become one of the Security Service's most distinguished deputy director generals (DDGs).[14]

MI5's most influential supporter in its struggle to defend its budget during 1920 was the Secretary of State for War and Air, Winston Churchill, who emerged from the war with even greater enthusiasm for intelligence than before and a deep concern about Communist subversion. Though Churchill still favoured combining Thomson's, Kell's and Cumming's agencies, he believed 'it cannot be brought about in a hurry.' In the meantime it was essential not to cripple them by budget cuts:

With the world in its present condition of extreme unrest and changing friendships and antagonisms, and with our greatly reduced and weak military forces, it is more than ever vital to us to have good and timely information. The building up of Secret Service organisations is very slow. Five or ten years are required to create a good system. It can be swept away by a stroke of a pen. It would in my judgment be an act of the utmost imprudence at the present time.[15]

In March 1920 Churchill circulated to the cabinet a memorandum drafted by the General Staff protesting against the extent of proposed cuts in the intelligence budget (in MI5's case to only £10,000 in 1921), which he hoped would receive 'earnest and early consideration'. After putting the case for SIS, the memorandum turned to MI5:

It was due entirely to the work of this organization that the whole of Germany's pre-war espionage system in this country was discovered and nursed, ready to be smashed, as in fact it was, on 3rd August 1914.

... During the war it was the means, not only of detecting and bringing to trial some 30 spies and of placing under proper control (under Regulation 14B) some hundreds of dangerous individuals, but also of furnishing information to the Secret Services of the United States of America and our Allies, which enabled them to arrest many other enemy agents operating within their territories. It was also responsible for the initiation, from time to time, of effective anti-spy legislation, and it was undoubtedly due mainly to the special Counter-Sabotage scheme which it operated, and which proved effective up to the Armistice, that no single case of sabotage, definitely known to be due to enemy action, occurred in this country during the war.

Because of inflation, the proposal to reduce the MI5 budget to only £10,000 would leave it, in real terms, with less money than before the war:

... Moreover, counter-espionage is no longer a question of steaming open a letter and reading its contents. The vast improvement in methods of collecting and transmitting information (e.g. the development of wireless telegraphy, aircraft and abstruse secret inks, photography, &c) has added very greatly to the difficulty of detecting espionage, and inter alia, it has been found necessary to add to the staff of MI5 a chemical section.[16]

The drive for economies in the intelligence budget, however, continued. In 1921 a Secret Service Committee of senior officials, chaired by Sir Warren Fisher, PUS at the Treasury, was instructed to make recommendations 'for reducing expenditure and avoiding over-lapping'. Its report, issued in July, concentrated most of its fire on Sir Basil Thomson's Directorate of Intelligence which it criticized for overspending, duplicating the work of other agencies and producing misleading reports. The Foreign Office complained that in the previous year Thomson had despatched a fifteen-man troupe to Poland 'merely to photograph one or two streets and a few villages with peasants, etc' for an anti-Bolshevik film. General Sir William Horwood, the Commissioner of the Metropolitan Police, seized the opportunity to send Lloyd George a lengthy memorandum denouncing 'the independence of the Special Branch' under Thomson as 'a standing menace to the good discipline of the force', and the Directorate of Intelligence as both wasteful and inefficient. Horwood insisted on a reorganization which would place Thomson and the Special Branch firmly under his control. Though Thomson refused, his intelligence career swiftly came to an ignominious end. He was, in his own words, 'kicked out by the P.M.'. His subsequent career had about it an air of black comedy. Thomson took to writing volumes of reminiscences and detective stories with titles such as *Mr Pepper, Investigator*. In 1925 he was found guilty of committing an act in violation of public decency in Hyde Park with a Miss Thelma de Lava. Thomson's supporters hinted darkly that he had been framed either by his enemies in the Met or by subversives.[17]

With Thomson's dismissal, the Directorate of Intelligence disappeared. Horwood successfully resisted a proposal that Kell, while remaining director of MI5, should also become director of intelligence with modified responsibilities. The Secret Service Committee was initially sceptical of the need to preserve MI5 at all but eventually concluded that, because of increasing espionage by a number of powers and the threat of Bolshevik subversion in the army and navy, MI5 should continue, on a reduced scale, to have responsibility for counter-espionage and for counter-subversion in the armed forces.[18]

Following Cumming's death in June 1923 (shortly before he was due to retire), MI5 faced a new threat to its independence from the ambitious new 'C' (Chief of SIS), Rear Admiral (later Sir) Hugh 'Quex' Sinclair, a far more flamboyant figure than Kell with a reputation for both decisive leadership and a lifestyle as a bon vivant. He derived his nickname from Sir Arthur Pinero's play *The Gay Lord Quex*. Like his namesake, playfully described as 'the wickedest man in London', Sinclair had a stormy private life during his naval career. In 1920, embarrassingly soon after becoming naval aide to the King, he was divorced. Unlike Cumming, Sinclair ceased to wear naval uniform once he became 'C'. Instead he found a bowler hat which some thought a size too small for him and, in the words of an admirer, 'rammed it as firmly as possible on his head'. While keen to maintain operational secrecy, Sinclair was a conspicuous figure to many London taxi drivers, driving round the capital in a large, ancient, open Lancia. Diplomats knew that he was visiting the Foreign Office when they saw his Lancia parked outside the ambassadors' entrance off Horse Guards.[19] Kell was driven more sedately to work each morning by his chauffeur Maclean in a car which, for reasons his staff found difficult to fathom, flew a small pennant with the picture of a tortoise (not an image likely to have appealed to Sinclair).[20]

Sinclair quickly gained overall control of the codebreakers of the Government Code and Cypher School (GC&CS), the peacetime successors of the wartime SIGINT units at the Admiralty and War Office.[21] He then turned his attention to MI5. In 1925 Sinclair told Fisher's reconvened Secret Service Committee that 'the whole organisation of British Secret Service ... was fundamentally wrong': 'All the different branches ought to be placed under one head and in one building in the neighbourhood of Whitehall, and to be made responsible to one Department of State, which ought to be the Foreign Office.' Sinclair implied, though he did not say so explicitly, that the 'one head' should be himself. He told the Secret Service Committee that it was 'impossible to draw the line' between espionage and counter-espionage, since both were concerned with either foreign intelligence or foreign intelligence agencies. Entrusting these two complementary activities to different services inevitably 'led to overlapping' between them. He was also critical of the management of MI5, which, he claimed, 'contained several vested interests due to the length of time during which certain officers had served the department' – a thinly disguised reference to Kell and his deputy, Eric Holt-Wilson. Sinclair claimed that 'with proper reorganisation' at MI5 a total staff of only five 'would probably suffice'. Horwood, the Commissioner of the Met, supported much of Sinclair's argument: 'Now that the war was over, MI5 as a separate entity was not necessary at all, and their duties should be taken over by SIS. In fact, he would agree to a combination of SIS and MI5 with the addition of either Captain Miller or Captain Liddell.' Ironically, six years later, Miller and Liddell, the two main counter-subversion experts at Scotland Yard, were to join MI5.

Apparently unaware of the evidence given by Sinclair and Horwood, Kell claimed that 'his liaison with C and Scotland Yard were excellent'. Aware, however, that MI5's survival was at stake, he put the emphasis on its unique responsibility for 'what might be described as home security':

He was responsible for the safety of the armed forces of the Crown in this country, both in respect of foreign espionage and communist interference.

. . . There was no overlapping between MI5 and Scotland Yard. The latter were not in a position to carry out the work which he did with the armed forces. He had free and direct access to all naval and military and air commands. He could see anyone he wished and give advice as to the action to be taken to deal with matters within his purview.

The Committee agreed that, if it were starting a British secret service from scratch, 'we should not adopt the existing system as our model.' After months of discussion, however, it recommended no substantial change. Impressed though the Committee was with Sinclair, his proposals were simply too radical:

We admit the vast potentialities inherent in the position of the chief of a combined secret service, but the danger there lies, we think, not so much in the use to which a good chief would put his powers, but in the difficulty of ensuring a succession of officers capable of filling such a post, and in the harm which might be done in it by a man who, after appointment, turned out to be incompetent.[22]

By 1925, though MI5 had fought off merger or extinction, it had only thirty-five staff,[23] about 4 per cent of its strength at the time of the Armistice. Since 1922 the much reduced Registry had been run by one of MI5's most remarkable wartime recruits, Kathleen 'Jane' Sissmore, who was also made controller of women staff. She had been recruited as an eighteen-year-old clerk in 1916 and rose rapidly through the ranks. The headmistress of Princess Helen's College, Ealing, where Sissmore had been head girl, described her as 'a strong character, very straight, well principled, industrious'. In her spare time, she trained as a barrister, gaining first-class examination results, and was called to the Bar in 1924.[24] Largely because of lack of resources, the Registry filing system was no longer state of the art. Though the Roneo card system had helped to give the pre-war Service an up-to-date data-management system, it fell behind between the wars[25] – with serious consequences when war broke out in 1939.[26] Kell's slender resources and diminished responsibilities were reflected in the small number of HOWs it was operating to assist its investigations: only twenty-five in June 1925, down to twenty-three a year later.[27]

Kell told the Secret Service Committee in 1925 that, because of his diminished resources, 'he had no "agents" in the accepted sense of the word, but only informants, though he might employ an agent for a specific purpose, if necessary[,] in which case he would consult Scotland Yard about him, if he were in doubt as to his character, or he might even borrow a man from Scotland Yard.'[28] One MI5 officer, Captain (later Major) Herbert 'Con' Boddington, had, however, succeeded in joining the Communist Party of Great Britain (CPGB) in 1923 on Kell's instructions. On entering MI5 in 1922 at the age of thirty, despite being wounded in the war, Boddington had listed as his recreations 'All outdoor games. Principally boxing, rowing and running.' Unusually for an MI5 recruit, however, he had added: 'Can act. Have played light comedian [sic] both at home and abroad.' Boddington also claimed 'literary experience', which included writing stories for silent films.[29] At least some of these skills were probably of assistance in passing himself off as a Communist.

Kell's search for informants to compensate for his post-war lack of an agent network led him to co-operate with Sir George Makgill, a businessman with ultra-conservative views and a deep-seated dislike of trade unions. At the end of the war, with the support of a group of like-minded industrialists, Makgill set up a private Industrial Intelligence Bureau (IIB), financed by the Federation of British Industries and the Coal Owners' and Shipowners' Associations, to acquire intelligence on industrial unrest arising from subversion by Communists, anarchists, the Irish Republican

Army (IRA) and others. From an early stage Makgill was in contact with Kell, who claimed that he had helped Makgill found 'an organisation of a secret nature somewhat on Masonic lines' – probably a reference to the IIB. (Unlike Kell, Makgill and his son Donald were both prominent Free-masons.)[30] Before joining MI5, Boddington had worked for the IIB and remained in touch with, notably, Makgill's agent, 'Jim Finney', who, like Boddington, succeeded in joining the CPGB.[31]

The IIB's most talented member was, almost certainly, Maxwell Knight, a youthful, self-taught agent-runner who later joined the Security Service. Born in 1900, Knight had become a naval cadet in 1915, serving as a midshipman in the Royal Naval Reserve during the last year of the war.[32] For several years after the war, he worked as a teacher in a preparatory school and as a freelance journalist.[33] To those unaware of his intelligence work, Knight came across as a gregarious eccentric who did not mind 'being considered a bit mad'. 'In a world where we are all tending to get more and more alike,' he believed, 'a few unusual people give a little colour to life!' Knight's most obvious eccentricity was a passion for exotic pets which he claimed went back to a picnic lunch at the age of eight when he found a lizard and hid it from his parents in his box camera. For the remainder of his life he preferred 'queer or unusual pets', ranging from grass-snakes to gorillas. Visitors to his home might, as one of them recalled, 'find him nursing a bush-baby, feeding a giant toad, raising young cuckoos or engaging in masculine repartee with a vastly experienced grey parrot'. For several years Knight also had a pet bear named Bessie who, unsurpris-ingly, 'excited a great deal of attention and admiration' when he took her, sometimes accompanied by a bulldog or a baboon, for walks near his Chelsea home.[34] 'High on the list of subjects which those who prefer to indulge in observations out of doors should embrace', wrote Knight, 'is the fascinating and essential one of the senses of animals.'[35] Some of Knight's self-taught intelligence tradecraft derived from his study of animal behaviour.

According to a later account by Knight:

In 1924 at the request of the late Sir George Makgill Bt who was then running agents on behalf of Sir Vernon Kell I joined the first of the Fascist Movements in this country – The British Fascisti. I remained with this organisation until 1930 when it more or less became ineffectual. My association with this body was at all times for the purposes of obtaining information for HM Government and also for the purposes of finding likely people who might be used by this department for the same purposes.[36]

Knight's political views in the mid-1920s had more in common with those of the British Fascisti, renamed the British Fascists (BF) in 1924, than he was later willing to acknowledge. Like a majority of the BF, however, his views were those of die-hard conservatives rather than the radical right. A young MI5 officer who served under him after the Second World War later recalled that Knight 'had no time for democracy and believed the country should be ruled by the social élite'.[37] That social elite included the Duke of Northumberland, who had provided hospitality for Kell during his convalescence in the last summer of the war[38] and went on to become one of the founders of the Fascisti.[39] In 1924 Knight became assistant chief of staff as well as director of intelligence of the BF, then about 100,000 strong; his Fascist connections in the 1920s later assisted his successful penetration of the more extreme British Union of Fascists and the Right Club during the 1930s. The first of his three wives, Miss G. E. A. Poole, whom he married in 1925, was the director of the BF Women's Units.[40] In the mid-1920s, on Knight's instructions, six British Fascists posing as Communists succeeded in joining the Party to work as penetration agents for Makgill's IIB. Knight's most important recruit while working for the British Fascists, a Communist student, continued to work for him (and later for MI5) for over thirty years.[41]

Knight claimed in a report in 1933, two years after he had joined MI5, that the early British Fascist groups were 'fundamentally constitutional': 'It can be confidently said that at no time between 1923–1927 was there any intention on the part of the British Fascisti to act in any unconstitutional manner, nor to usurp the functions of the properly constituted authorities.'[42] Admiration for Benito Mussolini's supposed achievements in Italy during the 1920s had nothing like the significance that it acquired in the 1930s. Winston Churchill called Mussolini 'the saviour of his country'. Sir Austen Chamberlain, Foreign Secretary in the Conservative governments of 1924 to 1929, felt 'confident that he is a patriot and a sincere man'. Even Ramsay MacDonald, Britain's first Labour prime minister, sent Mussolini friendly letters even while he was destroying the Italian Socialist Party. Mussolini made much of his friendship with British statesmen and their wives. In 1925 he ordered one and a half million postcards showing himself in conversation with Lady Chamberlain, and distributed them all over Italy.[43] Though Knight's early enthusiasm for Mussolini's victory over Italian Bolshevism was widely shared by mainstream conservatives, however, he had a number of more extreme Fascist acquaintances, if not friends, during the 1920s whose opinions must later have embarrassed him. He was recommended to Desmond Morton of SIS, later Churchill's intelligence adviser, by the right-wing anti-Semitic conspiracy theorist Mrs Nesta Webster.[44]

Lacking his own directly controlled agent network, Kell kept a reserve list of former members of MI5 for use in emergencies.[45] In order to keep in touch with retirees and other former MI5 officers Kell founded the IP (Intelligence and Police) dining club, which continued to meet until the Second World War.[46] During the General Strike, called by the TUC on 3 May 1926 'in defence of miners' wages and hours', the War Office department MI(B), which was given a major role in both intelligence co-ordination and intelligence collection during the strike, consisted entirely of (mostly retired) MI5 officers under Kell's deputy Holt-Wilson. The return of the retirees gave MI5 once again, though only temporarily, the resources to run agents. Five agents were sent by MI(B) to investigate reports of Communist subversion in and around the Aldershot military base, and reported, after visiting local pubs: 'In most cases, when political arguments were started the soldiers finished their beer and left at once.' The 'ordinary working men and labourers' in Aldershot, as well as the soldiers, 'seemed to be perfectly loyal'.[47]

One of the most resourceful agents employed by MI(B) succeeded in penetrating the offices of the *Daily Herald*, which was then jointly controlled by the TUC and the Labour Party.[48] He pushed his way into the offices through 'a gang of say 100 men', knocked on a door bearing a sign 'Committee meeting', and was allowed in by 'two stalwarts'. Inside he found '18 men sitting on chairs lined round the wall. Hoping not to be identified as an intruder, the agent asked a 'darkish fellow', who was taking minutes, if his name was Blackadder. 'No,' he replied, 'Blackadder has gone up to the Central Committee.' As the agent turned to go, the 'darkish fellow' stood up and demanded, 'Who are you?'

I said, 'Alright comrade, I am P.B. correspondent of the I.I.' He said, 'You will find Williams next door; go to see him. He may give you some news.'

It is uncertain what, if anything, a 'P.B. correspondent' was and whether the 'I.I.' news corporation actually existed. On his way out the agent saw Williams's wife and asked her, 'Have you any news?' 'Well the men are solid to a man,' she replied. 'They will not go back unless they are taken back in their old places.'[49] In reality the TUC quickly realized that it could not win. The General Strike was called off after ten days, and Kell wrote proudly to MI5 staff: 'I desire to thank all Officers and their Staffs, also the Ladies of the Office, for their splendid work and co-operation during the General Strike. The manner in which all hands have put their shoulders to the wheel shows that the ancient war-traditions of M.I.5 remained unimpaired.'[50]

Despite the success with which former members of the Service on Kell's reserve list had been reintegrated during the General Strike, the fortunes of MI5 were at a low ebb. Lack of resources led at the end of 1926 to the loss of one of MI5's ablest officers, Major (later Sir) Joseph Ball, the head of B Branch, which during the post-war cutbacks had taken over responsibility for investigations. Ball had joined MI5 in July 1915 after a decade at Scotland Yard, dealing mainly with aliens. He was also a barrister, having passed top of the Bar final exams, and spent much of the war questioning prisoners, internees, suspects and aliens.[51] Ball's decision to leave MI5 at the end of 1926 seems to have been related to dissatisfaction over pay and prospects. He had complained in 1925 that his pay and pension would both have been higher had he remained at New Scotland Yard.[52] In March 1927 the Conservative Party chairman, J. C. C. (later Viscount) Davidson, recruited Ball to help run 'a little intelligence service of our own', distinct from the main Central Office organization:

We had agents in certain key centres and we also had agents actually in the Labour Party Headquarters, with the result that we got their reports on political feeling in the country as well as our own. We also got advance 'pulls' of their literature. This we arranged with Odhams Press, who did most of the Labour Party printing, with the result that we frequently received copies of their leaflets and pamphlets before they reached Transport House [the Labour HQ]. This was of enormous value to us because we were able to study the Labour Party policy in advance, and in the case of leaflets we could produce a reply to appear simultaneously with their production.[53]

In 1930 Ball was appointed first director of the new Conservative Research Department, becoming a confidant of the future Party leader Neville Chamberlain.[54]

An in-house history of MI5 later concluded that midway between the wars: 'The pay was small and the prospects such as to make no appeal except to a small number of officers with private incomes. The work itself was light and no one in authority in the War Office or elsewhere was closely interested.'[55] With slender resources and little influence in Whitehall, MI5 made only modest strides in strengthening protective security (later defined as 'all aspects of security that exist for the protection of classified information viz. personnel, physical, documentary, communications and technical security').[56] The first recorded interdepartmental protective-security committee meeting took place on 29 July 1926 under Kell's chairmanship. It was convened as the result of two burglaries in the Cabinet Office, at least one with the apparent aim of purloining classified documents. The meeting's notions of protective security were limited to recommending elementary security measures such as improved control of access to government buildings and the provision of steel cupboards for housing classified documents. There was no further interdepartmental discussion of protective security until 1938.[57] Even in MI5 headquarters, protective security was primitive by today's standards. One former employee later recalled that when she joined the Service from Scotland Yard in 1931:

Security was almost non-existent. No one was vetted on joining. In most cases staff were recruited on the basis of knowing someone already employed, though in my case I came in through St James' Secretarial College which had a good reputation as it supplied Buckingham Palace with secretarial staff. No passes were issued and no one was on the door to let us in. The only instruction we were given on joining was that no one, not even our own families, should be told where we worked or for whom.[58]

In 1929 MI5 had only thirteen officers (including Kell and Holt-Wilson)[59] and two Branches (also known as Divisions):* A, which was responsible for administration, personnel, records and 'precautionary measures' (later known as protective security); and B, which conducted 'investigations and inquiries'. A Branch was headed by Major William A. Phillips, who had joined MI5 in 1917 after being wounded on the Western Front and was awarded an OBE for his work as military control officer for ten ports in the English Channel. Despite his injuries, he continued to list his recreations as shooting, fishing and 'field sports in general'.[60] According to an obituary after his death in 1933 at the age of only forty-seven, 'His natural urbanity and capacity for making new and retaining old friendships in all circles peculiarly fitted him for his special duties.'[61] Two of Phillips's four section heads in A Branch were women (though neither had officer rank): Miss Mary Dicker, who ran the Registry as well as being controller of women staff, some of whom later remembered her as 'very nice, rather beautiful' and formidable;[62] and Miss A. W. Masterton, who in the First World War had become the first female controller of finance in any government department.[63]

The head of B Branch was the forty-three-year-old Oswald A. 'Jasper' Harker, who had spent the first fourteen years of his career in the Indian

---

* Within MI5 'branch' and 'division' were often used interchangeably. In internal administrative documents 'branch' predominated until 1931, 'division' from 1931 to 1940, 'branch' in 1941–2 and 'division' from 1943 to 1950. From 1953 onwards the accepted term was 'branch'.

police, rising to become deputy commissioner at Bombay, before being invalided home in 1919, probably after a tropical illness. One of the attractions for Kell in taking on Harker, initially on loan from the India Office in 1920, at a time of heavy cutbacks, was that, until Harker formally resigned from the Indian police in 1923, he did not require a salary from MI5. On joining MI5 Harker gave his recreations as big-game hunting, riding and fishing.[64] Secretarial staff and the Registry tended to find him an intimidating figure. One later recalled Harker as 'a fearsome character',[65] another as 'rank conscious',[66] a third as 'good looking but not clever'.[67] The six officers in Harker's B Division included Jane Sissmore, formerly head of the Registry and MI5's first woman officer. In 1929 she was responsible for Soviet intelligence and the only female staff member with an MBE.[68] Sissmore later proved a formidable interrogator.[69]

Though B Division still lacked an agent-running section, Harker had a three-man Observation section (B4), responsible for shadowing suspects and making 'confidential' inquiries.[70] Its head, John Ottaway MBE, had joined MI5 in 1920 after twenty-nine years in the City of London Police (eleven as detective superintendent). The recreations listed by Ottaway on joining indicated that he came from lower down the social scale than most other officers: cricket and tennis rather than hunting and field sports.[71] Admiral Sinclair had told the Secret Service Committee in 1925 that Kell's inability to run directly more than 'informants' obliged SIS to run agents inside the United Kingdom as well as abroad. In December 1929 Desmond Morton recruited Maxwell Knight and his agents to work for SIS. He reported to Sinclair:

[Knight] makes an excellent impression, is clearly perfectly honest, and at need prepared to do anything, but is at the same time not wild. When required by his previous masters, he and two friends burgled, three nights running, the premises of the local committee of the Communist Party in Scotland, the branch of the Labour Research Department there and the Y[oung] C[ommunist] L[eague] HQ.

With Sinclair's approval, Morton despatched Knight around Britain to investigate Communist and other subversive organizations,[72] chiefly to uncover their links with Comintern. Morton reported that 'with every passing month [Knight] got his agents nearer to the target area.'[73]

Doubtless aware that MI5, as well as the Special Branch, would believe that SIS was trespassing on its territory, Morton advised Sinclair that Kell and William Phillips should not be informed about Knight's investigations. By the summer of 1930, however, both the Special Branch and MI5 had discovered what SIS was up to. Colonel J. F. C. Carter of SS1 (the Special

Branch section which dealt with Communist subversion) told Morton that he had Knight 'under observation'; Knight noticed the surveillance and suspected that Carter, a wartime MI5 officer ('recreations: polo, big game shooting') had also told Phillips: 'Colonel C[arter] then attempted to frighten M[axwell] K[night] off doing this work for Major Morton or anybody else, by suggesting that he could make his life and that of his agents a misery.' The Secret Service Committee was revived in April 1931 to 'discuss the difficulties that had arisen in the inter-relation between C's organisation and Scotland Yard'.[74]

Scotland Yard's position, however, had been fatally compromised by MI5's dramatic discovery that the Special Branch had itself been penetrated by Soviet intelligence. Though there were no prosecutions, two officers were dismissed from Scotland Yard in 1929 after a disciplinary board of inquiry.[75] At a meeting of the Secret Service Committee on 22 June 1931, Sir John Anderson, PUS at the Home Office, proposed that SS1 and its responsibilities should be transferred to Kell:

MI5 was already responsible for counter espionage not only for the fighting services but for all government departments, and . . . this was a logical extension of its duties. There would thus be only two organisations dealing with secret service work, C covering foreign countries, and MI5 the Empire.[76]

The proposal was accepted. It was agreed that SIS should confine itself to operations at least 3 miles away from British territory, and that the domestic agencies should operate only within this limit. On 15 October the lead role in countering Communist 'subversion' was also moved from the Special Branch to MI5 (henceforth officially known as the Security Service), which acquired Scotland Yard's leading experts on subversion. Scotland Yard had defined subversion somewhat more broadly than MI5 and the integration of the two sets of files therefore took some time. The head of A Branch, William Phillips, noted that a number of the categories in SS1 files were not of interest to the Security Service. Some of those in the SS1 files were, in his view, mere 'Hot Air Merchants'. He also disagreed with keeping files on Scottish nationalists who, in his view, were currently 'a perfectly sound constitutional movement, aiming at a strictly limited autonomy, similar to Northern Ireland'. Nor did Phillips think it legitimate to open files, as Scotland Yard had done, on atheists, unemployed marchers, mutinous members of the merchant navy, pacifists or policemen who had received adverse reports.[77]

If the Prime Minister, Ramsay MacDonald, was informed of the change to the Security Service's role in October 1931, he must have been told informally since there is no written record of a briefing in any Whitehall file.[78] The Security Service ceased to be a section of the War Office and acquired an enhanced but ill-defined status within Whitehall as an inter-departmental intelligence service working for the Home, Foreign, Dominion and Colonial Offices, the service departments, the Committee of Imperial Defence, the Attorney General, the Director of Public Prosecutions and chief officers of police at home and throughout the Empire.[79] For at least two years there was some confusion about the 1931 reorganization, stemming partly from the fact that the Security Service was still also known by its old title, MI5, thus appearing to imply that it was still a department of military intelligence (MI). Holt-Wilson noted in 1933 that the War Office Directorate of Military Intelligence was 'only aware in a vague way' of what had happened two years earlier, and that even MI5 had no accurate written record of the changes. He therefore drew up a memorandum 'to make it clear that the Security Service was no longer in any sense a part of the Directorate of Military Intelligence'.[80]

The transfer of SS1 from Scotland Yard brought the Security Service a small but important influx of able staff. The two most senior were Captains Hugh Miller and Guy Liddell. Despite his earlier career as an MI5 officer,[81] Miller made less of an impression than Liddell. To younger staff in particular, he seemed an old-fashioned figure. Margot Huggins, who transferred from Scotland Yard at the same time, later recalled that 'He always worked standing up at one of those Dickensian wooden desks with the lift up lid. Not government issue, of course.'[82] Miller died after an accident in 1934. His obituary in *The Times* described him as 'one of Nature's own gentlemen'. Though within a small circle of devoted friends he revealed 'a never-failing and keen sense of humour', 'Captain Miller avoided society, and devoted his spare time to gardening and to the care of his valuable collection of Japanese prints.'[83]

Guy Liddell, who was Miller's executor as well as a distant relative of Alice Liddell, the model for Lewis Carroll's *Alice in Wonderland*, became deputy head of B Branch (counter-espionage and counter-subversion) under Harker (whom he succeeded as its wartime head). Before the First World War, Liddell had studied in France and Germany, and was fluent in both languages. But for the war, in which he won the Military Cross, he might well have become a professional cellist, and he remained a keen cello player throughout his life,[84] arranging musical evenings at his flat in Sloane Street. Liddell was much more popular with staff than the sometimes irascible Harker, never raising his voice or losing his temper. His secretary for many years both at Scotland Yard and at the Security Service later remembered him as a kind, avuncular, 'rather dumpy', 'most unsoldierly' figure, despite his MC (of which he never spoke), with an astute mind and good sense of humour.[85] Even Kim Philby later recalled Liddell with affection as 'an ideal senior officer for a young man to learn from':

He would murmur his thoughts aloud, as if groping his way towards the facts of a case, his face creased in a comfortable, innocent smile. But behind the façade of laziness, his subtle and reflective mind played over a storehouse of photographic memories.[86]

But Liddell's private life was scarred by an increasingly unhappy marriage to the Honourable Calypso Baring, daughter of the Irish peer Lord Revelstoke, whom he had married in 1926. Had he been a less patient man, his colleague Dick White said later, 'he must surely have strangled Calypso'. Calypso eventually left for California with their four children; the marriage was dissolved in 1943.[87]

Liddell was quick to recognize the talent of the Service's Soviet expert, Jane Sissmore, whom he regarded as having 'a rather privileged position as a court jester'.[88] A colleague later recalled:

Jane Siss[more] was a lively soul. One never knew what she would do next. I remember her in my room once, knocking on the door of Liddell's inner sanctum and when told to come in dropping to her knees and shuffling in with hands pressed together in prayer to grant whatever request she had.[89]

Sissmore's successor as the Security Service's most influential woman in the 1940s and 1950s was to be the redoubtable Milicent Bagot, a classics graduate from Lady Margaret Hall, Oxford, who joined the Service from Scotland Yard as a twenty-four-year-old secretary in 1931 at the same time as Miller and Liddell (and is believed to be the model for John le Carré's character Connie). Like Sissmore, Bagot was to become the Service's leading expert in Soviet Communism and its allies, gradually acquiring an encyclopaedic knowledge which impressed even J. Edgar Hoover. Unlike Sissmore, Bagot was never in danger of being described as a 'court jester'. She was a powerful personality who did not suffer fools or the ignorant gladly; some found her intimidating. Her main recreation was music; she habitually left the office promptly on Tuesdays to sing in a choir.[90]

With SIS now prohibited from running agents inside the United Kingdom, Maxwell Knight gave up his work for SIS and transferred to the Security Service in October 1931 at the same time as SS1 was transferred from Scotland Yard. His network, known as 'M Section', which he ran initially from a flat in Sloane Street,[91] gave the Service an agent-running capacity which was crucial to its penetration of CPGB headquarters and, from 1933, of the British Union of Fascists. Knight later moved to a flat in Dolphin Square rented in the name of his second wife, Lois Coplestone, whom he married in 1937.[92] In December 1933 Kell sent what Knight described as a 'most handsome bonus' with a 'very encouraging message'. Knight replied:

I should like you to know how very happy I am working for the show, and also how very much I appreciate the marvellous way in which my small efforts are backed up by all concerned ... I am heart and soul in the work (without I hope being a fanatic) and it is grand to be doing something which is really of use & which is so very pleasant at the same time.[93]

Knight, however, remained something of a law unto himself. He was probably the last Security Service officer who, as one who served under him later recalled, 'would burgle premises without authority and recruit whomsoever he wished. But to his agents he was an almost mystical figure.'[94]

The most noticeable change in working conditions for most members of MI5 immediately after it became the Security Service was a pay cut, in line with the sweeping economies forced on Ramsay MacDonald's National Government late in 1931 by the Great Depression. By 1934, however, Service salaries had been restored to their previous levels.[95] Salaries (on which no income tax was charged until after the Second World War) were paid in cash. Officers were paid in what one member of the Registry remembers as 'lovely, crisp white fivers'. Female staff 'all queued up for our buff envelopes at the end of each month outside the office of a rather terrifying lady, Miss Di[ck]er [Lady Superintendent], and her equally terrifying assistant, Miss Constant, who wore a monocle.'[96] Despite the intimidating nature of pay-day, most surviving recollections of life in the Service before the Second World War are positive. According to Catherine Morgan-Smith who joined the Service in 1933, retiring thirty years later as the last lady superintendent:

We were a small closely-knit group, friends among ourselves, keenly interested in our work and proud of it. Best of all, the courtesy and kindness engendered by Sir Vernon and 'Holy Willy' [Holt-Wilson] penetrated all levels of the Service and made it a happy place to work in.

    ... At Christmas Sir Vernon would sometimes take a part of the Office staff to the circus ... At other times you might get a rather awe-inspiring invitation to dine with the Kells at Evelyn Gardens [in Chelsea, to which they had moved from Campden Hill]. When this happened to me Sir Vernon always gave me half-a-crown for a taxi home and I always took the bus and saved the half-crown which was good money in those days.[97]

One former member of staff was interviewed in 1937 for a job at MI5, first by Miss Dicker, then by Kell ('a nice man'): 'As far as I remember he only asked me two questions. Where I had been to school and did I play any games? Wycombe Abbey and Lacrosse satisfied him and he said "You'll do" and I was in.'[98] Kell's criteria, however, were not limited to family background, school and sports. As in the earliest years of MI5 recruitment, he placed a premium on foreign-language skills.[99]

Kell's management style was low key and paternalist. According to a former member of staff:

Working in the Office then was like being in a family firm, one felt secure ... Sir Vernon Kell was a small quiet man rarely seen by us. He kept an eye on our behaviour though. When a young Officer, T. A. Robertson [later in charge of the wartime double agents], joined us in the early thirties he was told that he must not socialise with the girls. The Colonel [Kell] did not approve of familiarity between officers and staff. The officers were always known by their rank and surname and, of course, they called us Miss So-and-so. I worked for twelve years for Captain Liddell before he succumbed to the wartime habit of Christian names all round. In fact, the girls knew each other only by surname. I did not know the Christian names of most of my colleagues for years.[100]

Chief among those who broke the rule not to 'socialise with the girls' was Eric Holt-Wilson. On 10 September 1931 he sent an application form for a job in MI5 to a Miss Audrey Stirling, telling her: 'I shall be pleased personally to endorse your application, and to try to secure you any suitable vacancy ...'[101] Holt-Wilson, then a fifty-six-year-old widower, set out to woo the impressionable Stirling, who was over thirty years younger, as well as to recruit her. Among the qualities which he drew immodestly to her attention was his bravery in the face of danger: 'You must remember that I have often, so often, in my life been down the steps and gazed into the dark River of Death – face to face – does the thought frighten you my darling?' Their love, Holy Willy assured Miss Stirling, was divinely blessed.[102] They married not long afterwards. Overblown though Holt-Wilson's romantic rhetoric was, the marriage was happy. In 1933 Audrey became Lady Holt-Wilson, when her husband was knighted in the King's Birthday Honours List. She told Sir Eric on his retirement in 1940 that he was 'my brave, wise, brilliant, belovedest darling'.[103]

From 1934 there was a modest increase in Service staff. MI5's share of the Secret Vote, most of which was for salaries, rose from £25,000 in 1935–6 to £50,000 for 1938 and £93,000 for 1939–40.[104] In the same year the Security Service moved from Cromwell Road to Thames House on Millbank, still a relatively new building. Sixty years later most of Thames House became the Security Service headquarters. In 1934, however, the Service occupied only the seventh floor and shared the lifts with commercial tenants of the building.[105] At the end of 1938 the Security Service's two branches were increased to four. A Branch continued to be responsible for administration and the Registry. B Branch dealt with counter-espionage and counter-subversion; Knight's 'M Section' was incorporated into the Branch as B1F.* A newly created C Branch vetted candidates for some sensitive posts in Whitehall and foreign-born candidates for commissions in the armed forces, but it had only one officer and no means of enforcing its decisions. D Branch, also newly established, oversaw protective security in munitions and aircraft factories, arsenals and dockyards, with a vaguer responsibility for railways and electricity supply. Its three officers were too few, however, to have much impact. For some years Handley Page, a major military aircraft manufacturer, had a German chief designer. All efforts to dislodge him were ignored until he was interned during the Second World War.[106] The total number of Service officers increased from twenty-six in January 1938 to thirty a year later and thirty-six in July 1939. Secretarial and Registry staff grew from eighty-six in January 1938 to 103 in January 1939 and 133 in July 1939.[107]

The growing number of Security Service investigations, combined with greater use of the telephone by suspects, often speaking in foreign languages, put increasing strain on the General Post Office resources for operating HOWs. Frederick Booth, who was employed by MI5 on 'special censorship' at the GPO, later recalled:

In 1934 the 'checks' on telephone lines were increasing rapidly and the only method of recording the conversation was by handwriting. The results were not accurate or useful and the written returns showed increasingly the remark 'Conversation in a foreign language – not understood.' Complaints were received and the matter was referred to the G.P.O. Engineering Department, but no solution was obtained.

Through an intermediary Booth began negotiations with the Dictaphone Company, which eventually provided a system for recording telephone

---

* MI5's use of upper or lower case in the titles of branch sections (for example B1F or B1f) was inconsistent. Administrative documents tended to use lower case in the 1920s, both upper and lower case for much of the 1930s, and upper case from 1941 onwards.

conversations. He was congratulated personally by both Kell and the GPO Director General, Sir Thomas Gardner.[108]

The clear division of responsibility established between the Security Service and SIS in 1931 improved the working relations between them. As part of the 1931 reorganization, SIS established a new Section V (counter-intelligence) under Valentine Vivian (later deputy chief of SIS), which liaised with MI5. According to a later internal MI5 history, the liaison worked well until the outbreak of the Second World War, due largely to 'the goodwill and readiness for give and take between the officers concerned at all levels' in both Services.[109] From 1934 Section V shared with the Security Service decrypted Comintern radio messages which provided details of Moscow's policy directives and secret subsidies to the British Communist Party.[110]

Among the Security Service recruits in the few years before the Second World War were two future DGs, Dick White and Roger Hollis, neither of whom had the military background common to most Service officers. White also went on to become chief of SIS. After graduating in history from Christ Church, Oxford, where he won the Gladstone Memorial Exhibition and an athletics Blue, he had spent two years at American universities before becoming a sixth-form teacher at Whitgift School. White had attracted the attention of Malcolm Cumming who, before joining the Security Service in 1934, had met White while both were involved in running a British public school tour of Australia and New Zealand. Cumming, who had been educated at Eton and Sandhurst ('recreations: riding, hunting, point-to-point racing'), told Harker that during the tour he had formed a 'profound respect' for White's 'ability and judgement'. Though White was likely to go to the top of the teaching profession, '. . . I happen to know he often wishes that his work was of a nature that could bring him into closer touch with current world affairs, which really form his natural interest.'[111] Harker wrote to Kell in August 1935:

Re Dick White. I am sorry to have to worry you on your holiday but I have seen this young man and I think he is what we want . . . At first appearance, his manner is a little shy and diffident, but once you get over that, I think you will agree that he is a young man both of character and very wide travel experience for one so young.

The fact that Harker contacted Kell during his summer holiday indicates how closely the Director personally supervised recruitment. Harker assured Kell that White fully understood 'that nothing is definite in any sense unless and until you have seen him and approved of him as a suitable candidate'.[112] After being accepted by Kell, White spent several months in Munich and Berlin improving his German and building up an impressive range of

German contacts before formally beginning work in the Security Service in January 1936.[113]

Roger Hollis joined the Security Service in June 1938, two and a half years after White. He came from a prominent Anglican family; both his father and elder brother were bishops. Hollis left Worcester College, Oxford, without taking his degree to begin a business career in the Far East. In 1937 he was advised to return to Britain for health reasons, and contacted the Security Service to say that he had been told there was a vacancy for 'someone with a practical knowledge of the Far East'.[114] Hollis struck his initial Service interviewer as 'A rather nice quiet young man, whose only qualifications were a knowledge of the northern Chinese language and Chinese and Japanese commercial industry. ?Might perhaps be given a job.'[115] Kell decided to recruit him.

By the time Hollis joined the Service, White had already demonstrated one quality which Kell conspicuously lacked – the ability to form close and friendly relationships with senior Whitehall officials. Malcolm Cumming had noted when recommending White: 'I know from personal experience of the remarkably successful way in which Dick White dealt with Dominion Premiers and representatives of Government Departments, and that he was afterwards congratulated by the authorities upon his work.'[116] Once in the Security Service, White quickly impressed the PUS at the Foreign Office, Sir Robert Vansittart, finding him 'eager, sometimes over-eager' to be briefed on the intelligence the Service was obtaining from within the German embassy.[117]

Despite White's contacts with Vansittart, the Security Service during the 1930s was a more introverted agency than SIS. Kell was still a less influential figure within Whitehall than the far more clubbable Quex Sinclair, Chief of SIS. Sinclair's surviving papers from the 1930s consist largely of elaborate menu cards from private dinners, some hosted by himself, at the Savoy and other exclusive locations. He treasured notes from appreciative guests such as Admiral Percy Noble, who thanked him for 'the best dinner I have eaten in years', and Admiral Bromley, who complimented him enthusiastically on his 'excellent' wines. 'C' could count on the support of the three most influential civil servants of the 1930s: Vansittart at the Foreign Office, Sir Maurice Hankey, cabinet secretary from 1916 to 1938, and Sir Warren Fisher, PUS at the Treasury and head of the civil service from 1919 to 1939. Together Vansittart, Hankey and Fisher composed the Secret Service Committee which had at least the notional responsibility for overseeing the intelligence services. When Sinclair fell ill in March 1939, well before it was clear that his illness would prove fatal, Fisher (who had, admittedly, a sometimes effusive epistolary style) wrote him an extraordinarily affectionate letter which began 'Hugh dear' and ended 'Bless you, with love, Warren'.[118] It is impossible to imagine Kell receiving a letter from Fisher which began 'Vernon dear'.

Despite Kell's low profile in Whitehall, there were signs during the 1930s that the Security Service was broadening its international horizons. With the rise of Hitler it attached greater importance to international liaison, especially with France.[119] It also showed a growing sense of its imperial role – unsurprisingly for a service in which a high proportion of officers had served in India or elsewhere in the Empire. During the 1920s the Service's most active imperial liaison had been with the Delhi Intelligence Bureau (DIB or IB), whose diminutive London office, Indian Political Intelligence (IPI), was situated inside MI5's headquarters. Among the chief topics on which MI5 exchanged intelligence with Delhi through the IPI were the secret CPGB couriers to India on which it had HOWs. The first, travelling to India in 1925 under the alias 'R. Cochrane', was Percy Glading (later jailed for spying in Britain for Soviet intelligence).[120] Glading was followed in 1926 by George Allison (alias 'Donald Campbell'), who was jailed in India in January 1927 for travelling on a forged passport.[121] Next came Philip Spratt,[122] one of the leading defendants accused of involvement in a Soviet-led plot to overthrow British rule during the long-drawn-out 'Meerut Conspiracy' trial which opened in 1929.

Despite the interchange of intelligence with Delhi during the 1920s, MI5 lacked the resources to maintain and develop the imperial connections it had created in the First World War. The tribulations of the first significant interwar MI5 mission to the Empire (or at least the first of which record survives), to assist in the Meerut Conspiracy trial in 1929, are evidence of the lack thus far of a direct working relationship between MI5 and DIB officers. The mission, headed by Holt-Wilson, included Frederick Booth, in charge of 'special censorship' at the GPO, and H. Burgess, head of the department which photographed intercepted correspondence. Holt-Wilson seems to have been well looked after in Delhi. Not so Booth and Burgess in Meerut. In November 1929 Burgess sent Holt-Wilson a despairing letter, reporting that he had been told by a representative of the DIB (then headed by the future director general Sir David Petrie) that the paperwork for funding the MI5 mission was 'so confused and inaccurate that he thought it better not to pay over anything, but to refer the matter back to Delhi'. 'No doubt', Burgess concluded, 'you will fully perceive the comedy and tragedy of the situation.'[123]

In February 1930, with the confusion apparently largely resolved,

Holt-Wilson left Delhi for what seems to have been the most extensive official tour yet undertaken by a senior Security Service officer, visiting Calcutta, Colombo, Singapore, Hong Kong, Shanghai, Kobe, Yokohama, Honolulu, San Francisco, Victoria, Toronto, Ottawa, Montreal and New York, before returning to Southampton at the start of May.[124] In 1933, following the conclusion of the Meerut trial, in which all the main defendants were found guilty (though their sentences were reduced on appeal), Holt-Wilson returned to India to confer with the Delhi Intelligence Bureau on matters of imperial security.[125] A year later he proudly proclaimed:

Our Security Service is more than national; it is Imperial. We have official agencies cooperating with us, under the direct instructions of the Dominions and Colonial Offices and the supervision of local Governors, and their chiefs of police, for enforcing security laws in every British Community overseas.

These all act under our guidance for security duties. It is our duty to advise them, when necessary, on all security measures necessary for defence and civil purposes; and to exchange information regarding the movement within the Empire of individuals who are likely to be hostile to its interests from a security point of view.[126]

Holt-Wilson's claim was essentially aspirational. With less than a hundred staff (only a quarter of whom were officers), the Service was simply too small to provide security supervision and guidance for an empire which covered a quarter of the globe. In the final years of peace, however, to counter the threat from the Rome–Berlin Axis and Comintern operations, the Security Service began posting permanent liaison officers to some British overseas territories. In 1937 MI5 established its first permanent defence security officer (DSO) abroad, in Cairo, followed in 1938 by DSOs in Palestine and Gibraltar.[127] These three DSOs formed the basis of Security Intelligence Middle East (SIME), the inter-service MI5 liaison organization operating throughout the Middle East, officially under GHQ command. The first Cairo DSO, Robert Maunsell, became the first head of SIME. British wartime strategic deception was to originate not in the European theatre of conflict but in the Middle East.[128] In the spring of 1938 Holt-Wilson went on another imperial tour with four weeks in Singapore and shorter stops in Malta, Aden, Port Said, Colombo, Bombay and Hong Kong.[129] By the outbreak of war, MI5 had DSOs in Aden, Singapore and Hong Kong, each with a small staff seconded by the local military command.[130] In the Second World War and the early Cold War the Security Service was to build the imperial security network to which Holt-Wilson had aspired in 1934.

I

The Red Menace in the 1920s

No Bolshevik had ever imagined that revolution in Russia could be other than part of a world (or at least European) revolutionary movement. The crumbling of the great empires of Central Europe during the final months of the First World War raised Lenin's hopes to fever pitch. He wrote on 1 October 1918: 'The international revolution has come so close within the course of one week that we may count on its outbreak during the next few days . . .'[1] It is easy now to dismiss such confident predictions of revolution sweeping across Europe as hopelessly optimistic, as indeed they proved to be. At the time, however, they were taken seriously by some of the Bolsheviks' opponents as well as by their supporters. 'Bolshevism', wrote President Woodrow Wilson soon after he arrived in Europe for the post-war peace negotiations, 'is moving steadily westward, has overwhelmed Poland, and is poisoning Germany.'[2]

Western leaders saw Bolshevism seeping out of Russia, threatening religion, tradition, every tie that held their societies together. In Germany and Austria soviets of workers and soldiers were already seizing power in the cities and towns. Their own soldiers and sailors mutinied. Paris, Lyon, Brussels, Glasgow, San Francisco, even sleepy Winnipeg on the Canadian prairies had general strikes. Were these isolated outbreaks or flames from a vast underground fire?[3]

The founding of the Moscow-dominated Communist International (Comintern) in March 1919 was intended to fan the flames. 'The whole of Europe', wrote Lloyd George, 'is filled with the spirit of revolution.' Soviet republics were declared in Hungary on 21 March and in Bavaria on 7 April. Grigori Zinoviev, the president of Comintern, forecast that 'within a year all Europe will be communist.' But the Bolsheviks were forced to stand helplessly by as the Bavarian Soviet was crushed after less than a month and again as the Hungarian Soviet Republic was overthrown in August.[4] Despite these reverses, hopes and fears that Bolshevik rule would spread westward from its Russian base (consolidated during the Civil War of 1918–20) lingered for several years.

In post-war Britain Soviet subversion was initially seen as a greater threat than Soviet espionage. Until 1931 the responsibility for dealing with civilian 'revolutionary movements' belonged to Thomson's Directorate of Intelligence and, after its demise, to the Special Branch. Kell was obliged to tell chief constables in 1925 that MI5 was 'only concerned with Communism as it affects the Armed Forces of the Crown'. 'Civil' subversion was Thomson's responsibility.[5] MI5's New Year card for 1920 showed the attractive figure of 'Liberty and Security' in diaphanous gown, holding aloft the torch of freedom and standing on a pedestal erected by the heroic efforts of British fighting and working men (stage right). But 'Liberty and Security' is menaced by an assortment of subversives (stage left): a defeated Hun in pumpernickel helmet (by now a reminder of past dangers rather than a present menace), the rebel Irish (a much smaller threat on the mainland than in Ireland) and Bolshevik revolutionaries. The main threat comes from the Bolsheviks, who are shown attempting to undermine the foundations of 'Liberty and Security'. Kell draws an appropriate moral from the initials MIV (V = the roman numeral 5): 'Malevolence Imposes Vigilance'. Lying full length at the bottom of MI5's New Year card, keeping watch on the subversives, however, is a note-taking policeman, not an MI5 officer.

MI5's first post-war investigation of possible subversion within the armed forces arose from the clumsily handled demobilization of the largest army in British history. The failure at the outset to adopt the simple principle 'First in, first out' bred a sense of injustice which erupted in mutinies at army camps in Calais and Folkestone. MI5 reports linking some of the troubles with pro-Soviet agitators led the War Office to circulate in February 1919 a 'secret and urgent' questionnaire to the commanding officers of all British military installations asking for information 'without fail' each week on the political sentiments of their forces 'with a view to the establishment of an efficient intelligence service whereby the Army Council can keep its finger on the pulse of the troops'. COs were asked, *inter alia*, whether any 'soldiers' councils' on the Soviet model had been formed; whether troops would 'respond to orders for assistance to preserve the public peace' and 'assist in strike breaking'; and whether they would 'parade for draft to overseas, especially to Russia'. The questionnaire, however, backfired. A copy was published in the socialist *Daily Herald* and produced, according to Thomson, 'great resentment against the Government'.[6] The attempt to distinguish between civil and military sub-

MI5's New Year card for 1920.

version, combined with the decision to make different agencies responsible for dealing with them, was a recipe for organizational confusion. As the Secret Service Committee belatedly acknowledged in 1925:

A Communist, working in naval or military circles at Portsmouth or Aldershot, may spend his Sundays making revolutionary speeches in Hyde Park. The former of these occupations is a matter for research by MI5; his week-end relaxations bring him into the preserve of the Special Branch.[7]

The Second Comintern Congress, which met in Moscow in the summer of 1920, established 'twenty-one conditions' for membership, mostly drafted by Lenin, imposing something approximating to military discipline on the infant CPGB as on all other member parties. Labour leaders had good reason to describe the CPGB as 'intellectual slaves of Moscow'. But the servitude was freely, even joyously, entered into. A critical British delegate wrote after his return from the Comintern Congress: 'It is fairly evident that to many Communists Russia is not a country to learn from, but a sacrosanct Holy of Holies to grovel before . . .' The 'twenty-one conditions' required total and unconditional support of Soviet Russia by illegal as well as legal means, including 'systematic propaganda and agitation in the armed forces and the organisation of Communist cells in every military unit. This work by Communists will for the most part have to be conducted illegally.' The Soviet-dominated executive committee of Comintern took care at regular intervals to spell out to member parties what was expected of them.[8]

Kell viewed Comintern's commitment to military subversion with peculiar horror. During the war DORA Regulation 42 had made 'any act calculated or likely to cause mutiny, sedition or disaffection among any of His Majesty's forces' punishable by life imprisonment (or death if the act was intended to assist an enemy). To Kell's dismay the Commons rejected an attempt to embody this draconian legislation in the 1919 Army Act on the sensible grounds that it would tend to stifle legitimate criticism of the peacetime armed forces. He denounced the lack of legislation specifically directed against civilian attempts to stir up 'disaffection in the services' as 'a serious gap in our national armour'. The gap was not filled until 1934.[9] In 1920 and again in 1921 MI5 investigated about ninety-five cases of 'suspected communism' in the armed forces (of which about sixty were in the army).[10]

Kell claimed that MI5's responsibility for military counter-subversion required it to keep track of civilian pro-Bolshevik movements, since it was these which were attempting to subvert the armed forces. Between the wars more MI5 resources were devoted to the surveillance and investigation of the CPGB than of any other target. MI5 followed the formation of the British Communist Party in 1920 with as close attention as its declining resources allowed, and studied the product of HOWs on its most influential leaders: among them Harry Pollitt,[11] David Ramsey,[12] Robert 'Robby' Robson,[13] John Campbell[14] and Robert 'Bob' Stewart.[15] MI5 also monitored known Communist front organizations in Britain, such as the National Minority Movement in the trade unions, as well as organizations with Communist affiliations, including Collet's Book Shop in London.[16] In October 1920 the US military attaché reported to Washington the 'considerable irritation' felt by Sir Basil Thomson at MI5's encroachment on what he regarded as his territory.[17] The deputy military attaché added in December:

Officially the British MI5 is only concerned with civilian activities as they affect the army, but in reality and especially recently, they have concerned themselves in general with revolutionary and Bolshevik agents, using the Suspect List, built up during the war and since added to, as a basis for operations.[18]

At the end of the war, the 'Defence Black List' compiled by the Registry contained 13,500 names. Retitled the 'Precautionary Index', it grew to 25,250 names by 1925, and provided 'a central register of persons potentially dangerous to National Defence' in the form of a card catalogue. The index was divided into twelve categories ranging from 'persons connected with foreign secret service' to 'persons of foreign blood or connection in British Government civil service'. Within each category names were also 'grouped by races'. According to Kell's deputy, Holt-Wilson: 'It is not the nationality by place of birth, or by law, but nationality by blood, by racial interests, and by sympathy and friendship that is taken as the deciding factor in all classifications of possible enemy agents and dangerous persons.' Kell believed that the British people regarded 'with pity and contempt a decent British subject who wilfully becomes naturalised as the subject of a foreign State, and are equally sorry for any of our women folk who marry a foreigner'. He was also suspicious of British subjects who had one foreign parent: 'We had enough trouble in the late war with half-hearted hybrids who asked not to be sent to the front to kill their relatives . . .'[19] Kell's crude prejudices about 'hybrids' are difficult to reconcile with his warm appreciation of William Hinchley Cooke, the son of a British father and German mother, whom he had recommended successfully for an OBE.[20] Though the Precautionary Index remained with MI5, Thomson had more resources than Kell for investigating British Communism. As Major William Phillips, later head of A Branch, acknowledged: 'Whatever grounds for complaint we may have had against Sir Basil Thomson, I think I am right in saying that failure to exchange all useful information was not one. On the whole we probably got from him more than we wanted.'[21]

Some of the most valuable intelligence on Soviet subversion came from the new British SIGINT agency, GC&CS. Though wartime British codebreakers had considered Tsarist diplomatic ciphers too complex to decrypt,[22] for a decade after the Bolshevik Revolution Soviet ciphers were less sophisticated. The attack on them was led by the head of the Russian section at GC&CS, Ernst Fetterlein, an early Soviet defector who had been one of the leading cryptanalysts in Tsarist Russia. He was a bespectacled, rather solitary man of grizzled appearance whose social contact with most of his colleagues went little beyond saying 'Good morning' in a thick Russian accent. The great American cryptographer William Friedman, who met Fetterlein at the end of the war, was struck by the large ruby ring on the index finger of his right hand: 'When I showed interest in this unusual gem, he told me that the ring had been presented to him as a token of recognition and thanks for his cryptanalytic successes while in the service of Czar Nicholas, the last of the line.' Fetterlein's successes in Russia had included decrypting British diplomatic traffic.[23] For much of the 1920s he had similar success in decrypting Soviet traffic in Britain.

During the ten months of Anglo-Soviet trade negotiations which began in London in May 1920, SIGINT was the Lloyd George government's most important intelligence source. For Moscow concluding the agreement, which represented the first *de facto* recognition by a major power of the Soviet regime, was of great importance. GC&CS's ability to decrypt most of the wireless messages between Moscow and its Trade Delegation in London provided an extraordinary insight into Soviet policy.[24] Record survives of only one decrypt being sent to Lloyd George while he was wartime prime minister. From May 1920, however, because he took personal charge of negotiations with the Soviet Trade Delegation, Lloyd George received a constant flow of Soviet decrypts; between June and September he received a direct delivery from GC&CS.[25] Among the decrypts was a blunt warning from Lenin to the Soviet negotiators: 'That swine Lloyd George has no scruples or shame in the way he deceives. Don't believe a word he says and gull him three times as much.'

Though Lloyd George took such insults in his stride, the Foreign Secretary, Lord Curzon, and other cabinet hardliners called for the Trade Delegation to be expelled because of their subversive activities. In addition to the evidence in the intercepts of the Trade Delegation's secret contacts with British Communists and Soviet funding for the CPGB and the socialist *Daily Herald*, Thomson's Directorate reported a stream of Russian and Comintern couriers bringing funds, propaganda and exhortation to Bolshevik sympathizers in Britain. Some of the couriers used unusual methods to smuggle former Tsarist jewels into Britain. One of the directors of the *Daily Herald*, Francis Meynell, later described how, on one occasion, he brought two strings of pearls from Copenhagen in a jar of Danish butter and, on another, he posted a large box of chocolate creams, each containing a diamond or a pearl, to the then pro-Bolshevik British philosopher Cyril Joad. Thomson reported to the cabinet that 'Jew dealers from all parts of Europe' were flocking to London to purchase the precious stones being smuggled into London by the Trade Delegation and individual couriers.

Curzon was convinced that, thanks to Soviet-financed subversion, 'the revolutionary virus is spreading with dangerous rapidity among the classes with whose leaders they [the Trade Delegation] are in daily contact.' Lloyd George, who now had a much more realistic grasp of the slender prospects for a British revolution, continued the trade negotiations. Following the signing of the Anglo-Russian Trade Agreement on 16 March 1921, the Soviet trade mission in London became a permanent presence; a British trade mission in Moscow opened in August. Though formal diplomatic relations did not follow for another three years, Soviet Russia had taken the first step to acceptance by the international community.[26]

MI5 had no formal responsibility for investigating the activities of the Trade Delegation. It already had an extensive file, however, on the Delegation's Secretary and official translator, Nikolai Klishko, who was in reality the first Soviet intelligence resident (head of station) in London. As a political refugee from Tsarist Russia in pre-war Britain, Klishko had been employed as a technical translator by the armaments firm Vickers, and had been suspected by Scotland Yard of arms smuggling to Russian revolutionaries.[27] A Vickers manager reported at the time of the Bolshevik Revolution that Klishko was 'very friendly with the notorious Lenin' and had 'the most extreme Leninite views'.[28] The head of the Russian section (G4), Captain Maurice Bray, one of MI5's Russian speakers ('recreations: shooting and golf'), concluded in July 1918 that Klishko was the 'most dangerous Bolshevik here'.[29] He was interned in August and subsequently deported, before returning to London in May 1920 with the Russian Trade Delegation. Once back in London he was kept under inadequate surveillance. It was only in the later 1920s that MI5 discovered that he had taken part in setting up a spy-ring headed by the pro-Bolshevik foreign editor of the *Daily Herald*, William Norman Ewer.[30]

The Soviet intelligence which MI5 received from SIS in the early 1920s was of variable quality.[31] In February 1921 the SIS head of station in the Estonian capital Reval (now Tallinn) reported that an agent codenamed 'BP11', 'whose reliability has been proved on many occasions', had successfully penetrated the Reval office of Maksim Litvinov, Soviet Deputy Commissar for Foreign Affairs, and gained access to its code department. During the next few months 'BP11' provided over 200 'summaries and paraphrases' of radio messages allegedly exchanged between Litvinov in Reval, Soviet leaders in Moscow and the Trade Delegation in London. The most sensational intercepts were those which reported Soviet aid (mostly channelled via the Trade Delegation) to Sinn Fein 'germ cells' in Ireland. The term 'germ cell', SIS explained, was 'used by the Bolsheviks to denote the small Communist groups which they insinuate into unions and movements of any character suitable to their purpose'. Some of the messages, which referred to military matters such as arms supplies to the Sinn Fein 'germ cells', were of direct interest to MI5.[32] In April, however, GC&CS exposed the Reval intercepts as fraudulent. It had, it reported, detected no radio traffic between Reval and Moscow, 'presumably because there is a landline', and the numbering system on the authentic intercepts it was decrypting between Reval and London bore 'no relation' to those obtained by SIS.[33] Two years later, a further forged intercept, which once again deceived the SIS station in Reval, was to cause a political sensation and persuade many on the left that British intelligence and Conservative Central Office were conspiring together to keep Labour out of power.

On 22 January 1924 James Ramsay MacDonald, illegitimate son of a Highland ploughman and a Lossiemouth mother, became Britain's first Labour prime minister at the head of a minority government dependent on Liberal support. King George V, whose hands he kissed on taking office, wrote in his diary, 'Today 23 years ago dear Grandmama [Queen Victoria] died. I wonder what she would have thought of a Labour Government!'[34] MacDonald may not have known that during the war MI5 had considered recommending his prosecution for making seditious speeches but had decided not to do so.[35] Kell was well aware, however, of Labour suspicions of MI5.[36] MacDonald, who combined the post of foreign secretary with that of prime minister, quickly made clear that he was sceptical of the intelligence he received on Soviet and Communist subversion. When shown a report on subversive activities by the head of the Special Branch, Sir Wyndham Childs, on 24 January, he commented facetiously:

it might be made at once attractive and indeed entertaining if its survey were extended to cover not only communistic activities but also other political activities of an extreme tendency. For instance a little knowledge in regard to the Fascist movement in this country . . . or possibly some information as to the source of the 'Morning Post' funds might give an exhilarating flavour to the document and by enlarging its scope convert it into a complete and finished work of art.[37]

Childs was not amused. MacDonald declined to circulate Childs's weekly reports to the cabinet, as his Conservative predecessor, Stanley Baldwin, had done. Kell as well as Childs must have been further disturbed when, on 2 February, the Labour government became the first in the West to give the Soviet regime *de jure* recognition. The Foreign Office was so nervous of MacDonald's likely response to the Soviet and other diplomatic decrypts produced by GC&CS that it delayed several months before showing any to him.[38]

MacDonald's government turned out, however, to be far less radical than Whitehall had feared. The Prime Minister, wrote Hankey, 'affects to regard me as a reactionary, and I retaliate by treating him as a visionary, but this is all more or less banter. I continue as Secretary of the Cabinet as of yore.'[39] For MI5 the most reassuring figure in the government was the Home Secretary, 'Uncle' Arthur Henderson, who had served in the War Cabinet from 1916 to 1917 and stoutly defended the Special Branch in the Commons against attacks by his own backbenchers.[40] To MI5's relief Henderson continued to authorize Home Office Warrants on the correspondence of leading Communists. (Curiously, until 1937 it was not thought necessary to seek HOWs for telephone calls.)[41] Among the Communists of most direct interest to MI5 during the life of the first Labour government was the CPGB's first Scottish organizer, Robert 'Bob' Stewart, who had spent most of his time as a wartime conscript in prison, being court-martialled four times for offences which included declaring, after the February Revolution, that he would not use his gun against Germans. Early in 1923 Stewart began working at Comintern HQ in Moscow, where he met all the main Soviet leaders, including Lenin, whose funeral he attended in 1924. He headed the Party's secret organization and was involved in passing information on the British armed forces to the Russians. According to an SIS report forwarded to MI5 on 2 July, Zinoviev, the Comintern president, had promised Stewart £3,000 a month for 'agit-prop' (agitation-propaganda) work in the armed forces.[42]

The MacDonald government as a whole began to take a more friendly view of domestic intelligence-gathering as a result of its early experience in grappling with labour unrest. MacDonald's very first cabinet meeting on 23 January had to discuss how to safeguard food, milk and coal supplies during a train drivers' strike. Over the next two months strikes, first of the dockers, then of London tramway workers, led to government plans to use the Emergency Powers Act, which had been violently denounced by Labour when it had been introduced by Lloyd George.[43] On 15 April the cabinet appointed a five-man Committee on Industrial Unrest to inquire into the recent strike wave 'with a view to ascertaining whether any appreciable percentage of the unfortunate aspects of these strikes was due to Communist activity'. Much of the evidence considered by the Committee came from intelligence supplied by the Special Branch, SIS and MI5. It included intercepted letters from British Communists, Comintern and the Red International of Labour Unions (RILU), minutes of the CPGB

Politburo and other Party committees, and reports from informers within the Communist Party and the trade unions. The Committee concluded that the CPGB regularly received both finance and instructions from Comintern and that Communists within the union movement similarly received finance and instructions from the RILU. There was also evidence of Communist involvement (with Comintern and RILU encouragement) in the recent strike wave. An intercepted 'secret circular' of 18 February revealed that Harry Pollitt of the CPGB's Central Industrial Committee (and later the Party's general secretary) had instructed district Party committees that 'anything coming to you from the British Bureau of the R.I.L.U. is to be acted upon in the same way as a Party communication.' Willie Gallacher, later Britain's longest-serving Communist MP, told his wife in an intercepted letter of 30 January that he had spent the whole of the previous day preparing reports on the strikes for Comintern. An intercepted letter from the Communist provisional secretary of the London Transport Workers Solidarity Committee, declared: 'We must be prepared to sabotage.'[44]

The Industrial Unrest Committee concluded that, while the Communists had done their best to aggravate the recent strikes, they had played only a minor part in starting them. Despite 'substantial assistance' from Comintern, the CPGB was 'constantly in great financial difficulties'. Though the Party was 'extremely active', its membership had fallen from a peak of 4,000–5,000 two years earlier. The Committee was, however, concerned by the evidence of 'systematic instructions and plans ... issued by the Communist Party' aimed at penetrating and taking over the unions. It believed that 'responsible Trade Union leaders' should be shown this secret evidence 'informally and confidentially'.[45] On 15 May the report of the Industrial Unrest Committee was approved by the cabinet, which in effect thus sanctioned the interception of Communist and Comintern communications, accepted the authenticity of the intercepts, and decided 'in favour of some form of publicity' for the intelligence derived from them.[46]

Britain's first Labour government lasted little more than nine months. No longer able to count on Liberal support, MacDonald called an election in October 1924. It was sadly ironic that Labour's election campaign should be disrupted by another intercepted Comintern communication, which became known as the 'Zinoviev letter'. This time, however, the intercept was a fabrication. As in 1921, the flow of authentic intercepted correspondence and diplomatic decrypts in 1924 was polluted by forgeries – though on a much smaller scale. Like the bogus intercepts of 1921, the Zinoviev letter came from the SIS Reval station, which appears to have been deceived once again by anti-Bolshevik White Russian forgers. Allegedly despatched by Zinoviev and two other members of the Comintern Executive Committee on 15 September 1924, the letter instructed the CPGB leadership to put pressure on their sympathizers in the Labour Party, to 'strain every nerve' for the ratification of the recent treaty concluded by MacDonald's government with the Soviet Union, to intensify 'agitation-propaganda work in the armed forces', and generally to prepare for the coming of the British revolution. On 9 October SIS forwarded copies to the Foreign Office, MI5, Scotland Yard and the service ministries, together with an ill-founded assurance that 'the authenticity is undoubted'.[47] The unauthorized publication of the letter in the Conservative *Daily Mail* on 25 October in the final week of the election campaign turned it into what MacDonald called a 'political bomb', which those responsible intended to sabotage Labour's prospects of victory by suggesting that it was susceptible to Communist pressure.

The call in the Zinoviev letter for the CPGB to engage in 'agitation-propaganda work in the armed forces' placed it squarely within MI5's sphere of action. Like others familiar with Comintern communications and Soviet intercepts, Kell was not surprised by the letter's contents, believing it 'contained nothing new or different from the [known] intentions and propaganda of the USSR'.[48] He had seen similar statements in authentic intercepted correspondence from Comintern to the CPGB and the National Minority Movement (the Communist-led trade union organization),[49] and is likely – at least initially – to have had no difficulty in accepting SIS's assurance that the Zinoviev letter was genuine. The assurance, however, should never have been given. Outrageously, Desmond Morton of SIS told Sir Eyre Crowe, PUS at the Foreign Office, that one of Sir George Makgill's agents, 'Jim Finney',[50] who had penetrated the CPGB, had reported that a recent meeting of the Party Central Committee had considered a letter from Moscow whose instructions corresponded to those in the Zinoviev letter. On the basis of that information, Crowe had told MacDonald that he had heard on 'absolutely reliable authority' that the letter had been discussed by the Party leadership. In reality, 'Finney's' report of a discussion by the CPGB Executive made no mention of any letter from Moscow. MI5's own sources failed to corroborate SIS's claim that the letter had been received and discussed by the CPGB leadership – unsurprisingly, since the letter had never in fact been sent.[51]

MI5 had little to do with the official handling of the Zinoviev letter, apart from distributing copies to army commands on 22 October 1924, no doubt to alert them to its call for subversion in the armed forces.[52] The possible unofficial role of a few MI5 officers past and present in publicizing the Zinoviev letter with the aim of ensuring Labour's defeat at the polls remains a murky area on which surviving Security Service archives shed little light. Other sources, however, provide some clues. A wartime MI5 officer, Donald Im Thurn ('recreations: golf, football, cricket, hockey, fencing'), who had served in MI5 from December 1917 to June 1919, made strenuous attempts to ensure the publication of the Zinoviev letter and may well have alerted the *Mail* and Conservative Central Office to its existence. Im Thurn later claimed implausibly to have obtained a copy of the letter from a business friend with Communist contacts who subsequently had to flee to 'a place of safety' because his life was in danger.[53] This unlikely tale was probably invented to avoid compromising his intelligence contacts. After Im Thurn left the Service for the City in 1919, he continued to lunch regularly in the grill-room of the Hyde Park Hotel with Major William Alexander of B Branch (an Oxford graduate who had qualified as a barrister before the First World War). Im Thurn was also well acquainted with the Chief of SIS, Admiral Quex Sinclair. Though he was not shown the actual text of the Zinoviev letter before publication, one or more of his intelligence contacts briefed him on its contents. Alexander appears to have informed Im Thurn on 21 October that the text was about to be circulated to army commands. Suspicion also attaches to the role of the head of B Branch, Joseph Ball.[54] Conservative Central Office, with which Ball had close contacts, probably had a copy of the Zinoviev letter by 22 October, three days before publication. Ball's subsequent lack of scruples in using intelligence for party-political advantage while at Central Office in the later 1920s[55] strongly suggests, but does not prove, that he was willing to do so during the election campaign of October 1924. But Ball was not alone. Others involved in the publication of the Zinoviev letter probably included the former DNI, Admiral Blinker Hall, and Lieutenant Colonel Freddie Browning, Cumming's former deputy and a friend of both Hall and the editor of the *Mail*.[56] Hall and Browning, like Im Thurn, Alexander, Sinclair and Ball, were part of a deeply conservative, strongly patriotic establishment network who were accustomed to sharing state secrets between themselves: 'Feeling themselves part of a special and closed community, they exchanged confidences secure in the knowledge, as they thought, that they were protected by that community from indiscretion.'[57]

Those who conspired together in October 1924 convinced themselves that they were acting in the national interest – to remove from power a government whose susceptibility to Soviet and pro-Soviet pressure made it a threat to national security. Though the Zinoviev letter was not the main cause of the Tory election landslide on 29 October, many politicians on both left and right believed that it was.[58] Lord Beaverbrook, owner of the *Daily Express* and *Evening Standard*, told his rival Lord Rothermere, proprietor of the *Daily Mail*, that the *Mail*'s 'Red Letter' campaign had won the election for the Conservatives. Rothermere immodestly agreed that he had won a hundred seats.[59] Labour leaders were inclined to agree. They felt they had been tricked out of office. And their suspicions seemed to be confirmed when they discovered the part played by Conservative Central Office in the publication of the letter.

As prime minister, Ramsay MacDonald preferred to keep the intelligence agencies quite literally at arm's length. It is unlikely that he ever knowingly met any officer from either MI5 or SIS. When he finally decided to question the head of the SIS political section, Major Malcolm 'Woolly' Woollcombe, about the Zinoviev letter in the aftermath of his election defeat before the formation of the second Baldwin Conservative government, MacDonald could not bring himself to conduct a face-to-face interview. Instead, Woollcombe was placed in a room adjoining MacDonald's at the Foreign Office while the PUS, Sir Eyre Crowe, positioned himself in the doorway between the two. The Prime Minister then addressed his questions to Woollcombe via Crowe, who reported the answers to MacDonald. At no point during these bizarre proceedings did Woollcombe catch sight of the Prime Minister.[60]

On 17 November 'C', Admiral Sinclair, submitted to a cabinet committee of inquiry chaired by Austen Chamberlain, Foreign Secretary in Baldwin's incoming Conservative government, a document probably drafted by the SIS officer Desmond Morton which detailed 'five very good reasons' – all since shown to be 'misleading, if not downright false' – why the letter was genuine. On 19 November the committee declared itself 'unanimously of opinion that there was no doubt as to authenticity of the letter'. Since the beginning of the month, however, reports had been arriving from SIS stations that the letter was a forgery, probably originating in the Baltic states. On 27 November Morton informed MI5 that 'we are firmly convinced that this actual thing is a forgery.' Probably motivated chiefly by a desire to protect SIS's reputation, however, neither Sinclair nor Morton admitted as much to the Foreign Office.[61] A series of other undetected forgeries which appeared to provide corroboration subsequently strengthened their belief that it was genuine after all. On 16 December SIS circulated a fabricated set of Sovnarkom (Soviet government) minutes in which Chicherin was quoted as saying, 'The original of the [Zinoviev] letter upon its receipt by the British Communist Party was destroyed by Comrade

Inkpin [the Party secretary general].'[62] On 9 January 1925 Morton made the extraordinary claim to the Special Branch (and probably to MI5): 'We now know the identity of every individual who handled [the letter] from the day the first person saw Zinoviev's copy to the day it reached us. With the exception of Zinoviev himself, they were all our agents.'[63] Probably by now, certainly later, Con Boddington, the only MI5 officer who was also an undercover member of the Communist Party, knew that Morton's claim that the CPGB Central Committee had discussed a document corresponding to the Zinoviev letter was false. Boddington knew 'Jim Finney',[64] whom Morton gave as the source for this claim; he also knew that 'Finney' had made no such report.[65]

Soon after Labour's election defeat in October 1924, MI5 began the long process of unravelling the first major Soviet espionage network to be detected in Britain. Its eventual success was due to a mixture of operational skill in deploying its slender resources and to the sometimes amateurish tradecraft of the network. The case started with a remarkably simple lead. An advertisement in the *Daily Herald* on 21 November 1924 announced: 'Secret Service – Labour Group carrying out investigation would be glad to receive information and details from anyone who has ever had any association with any Secret Service Department or operation – Write in first instance Box 573, Daily Herald.' Correctly suspecting a Soviet or Comintern attempt to infiltrate British intelligence, Jasper Harker, head of B Branch, arranged for an agent, 'D', to offer his services to Box 573 in the hope of penetrating the 'Labour Group'. 'D' received a reply signed 'Q.X.' (later identified as William Norman Ewer, the foreign editor of the *Daily Herald*) but, though a meeting was arranged, 'Q.X.' did not appear. The head of MI5's three-man Observation section, John Ottaway, who had been sent by Harker to keep the rendezvous for the meeting under surveillance, reported that while 'D' waited for 'Q.X.', he was kept under observation by a man he codenamed 'A' (later discovered to be a former police officer, Walter Dale, working for Ewer's network).[66] Next day 'Q.X.' contacted 'D', offered 'sincere apologies' for failing to turn up, and arranged another meeting at which he questioned 'D' about the working of the secret service and its use of agents inside the labour movement. He also revealed plans for the labour movement to set up a secret service of its own to defend itself against that of the government. Following 'D's' meeting with 'Q.X.', MI5 obtained an HOW to intercept the correspondence of Box 573 at the *Daily Herald*.[67]

On 4 February 1925, following another meeting between 'D' and a representative of the 'Labour Group' (probably Ewer, once again), Ottaway succeeded in following 'A' (Walter Dale) to the Moorgate offices of the All-Russian Co-operative Society (ARCOS), whose ostensible purpose was to promote trade between Britain and Russia but which was also used as a front for Soviet intelligence operations. From ARCOS, still tailed by Ottaway, Dale moved on to Outer Temple, 222–225 Strand, which contained, among other offices, those of the Federated Press of America (FPA). The FPA's London office, opened in 1923 and run by Ewer, had little connection with its notional American parent company, and served mainly to provide journalistic cover for espionage. Tapping the FPA telephone line produced 'immediate results', revealing calls to ARCOS, to prominent Communists and to at least one suspected Soviet intelligence operative.[68] The HOW on postal correspondence discovered regular packets from Paris addressed to 'Kenneth Milton' (a cover name for Ewer) containing 'copies of despatches and telegrams from French ministers in various foreign capitals to the Quai D'Orsay [and] reports on the French political and financial situation'.[69] MI5 discovered the provenance of the packets when one of the reports sent to 'Milton' from Paris appeared almost verbatim in the *Daily Herald* on 8 May 1925 in an article by its Paris correspondent, George Slocombe, who was also manager of the FPA Paris office.[70]

The incomplete evidence which survives suggests that from 1925 to 1927 MI5 and SIS collaborated in operations against Ewer and his network, with MI5 in charge of letter and telephone checks, as well as some physical surveillance in London, and SIS watching their movements abroad. Sinclair later reported that the operations conclusively established 'that the group, of which the head and financial controller was undoubtedly Ewer, were conducting Secret Service activities on behalf of, and with money supplied by, the Soviet Government and the Communist Party of Great Britain . . .'[71] Intercepted correspondence revealed that Ewer was paying Slocombe about $1,000 per month to pay his informants – a clear indication of the importance attached to his intelligence. (Moscow's annual secret subsidy to the CPGB was $20,000.)[72] Slocombe's correspondence also showed that he was in contact with a Paris address identified by the Sûreté, the French national police, as used by Soviet intelligence.[73] At the insistence of Sinclair, MI5 agreed not to reveal the operation to the Special Branch[74] – despite the fact that the activities of Ewer and the London office of the FPA were of obvious interest to it. That decision, though of dubious propriety, turned out to be a fortunate one since the investigation eventually revealed that the Special Branch was Ewer's most successful penetration.

MI5 and SIS operations against the Ewer network were disrupted during 1927 by what became known as the ARCOS raid. On 31 March Sinclair passed to Kell information from a disaffected former ARCOS employee that the front organization had photocopied a classified Signals Training manual from the Aldershot military base. Probably with the example of the Zinoviev letter still fresh in their minds, Kell and Harker spent the next six months checking the reliability of SIS's information, conducting inquiries at Aldershot and interviewing both the disaffected ARCOS employee and another SIS source in ARCOS, who was described by Morton as 'a British subject of undoubted loyalty'. Once convinced that ARCOS had indeed copied the classified manual, they drew up a report on the case for the Director of Public Prosecutions. At 11 a.m. on 11 May the DPP confirmed to Kell that the possession by ARCOS of the Signals Training document was an offence under the Official Secrets Act. Kell's subsequent difficulties in gaining approval for a raid on ARCOS premises shows how much less well connected he was in Whitehall than Sinclair: during the remainder of the morning of 11 May Kell tried and failed to secure appointments with, successively, the PUS at the Home Office, the Directors of Military Operations and of Military Intelligence and the Chief of the Imperial General Staff.[75] On his way back to the office from lunch, however, Kell had a chance encounter with the Secretary of State for War, Sir Laming Worthington-Evans, who agreed to see him at 5.15 p.m. Worthington-Evans in turn referred Kell to the rabidly anti-Soviet Home Secretary, William Joynson-Hicks, who immediately took a note prepared by the Director to the Prime Minister, Stanley Baldwin. Baldwin gave his permission to raid ARCOS in order to procure evidence of a breach of the Official Secrets Act.[76]

The raid on ARCOS headquarters, which the body shared with the Soviet Trade Delegation, at 4.30 p.m. on 12 May was poorly prepared and badly co-ordinated. The uniformed police, Special Branch and intelligence officers who took part in the raid were uncertain of their respective roles, and no one seemed sure who was in charge. Neither the Signals Training manual nor any other major evidence of Soviet espionage was discovered.[77] After the raid, the Soviet chargé d'affaires informed Moscow in a telegram decrypted by GC&CS that there had been no 'very secret material at the Trade Delegation'. A month earlier, with the possibility of a police raid in mind (though he doubted that the Special Branch would enter the embassy itself) he had advised Moscow in another decrypted telegram 'to suspend for a time the forwarding by post of documents of friends, "neighbours" [probably a reference to the CPGB and Soviet intelligence officers] and so

forth from London to Moscow and vice versa'.[78] A later MI5 report
concluded that the ARCOS raid had disrupted existing Soviet espionage
operations in Britain.[79] The government response to the outcome of the
raid, however, was to cause even more serious disruption to British intelligence collection.

The Baldwin cabinet found itself in a quandary when it met to discuss
Anglo-Soviet relations on 23 May. Under pressure from a vociferous backbench Conservative campaign against Soviet subversion, strongly supported by Churchill and some other ministers, the government had already
decided to break off diplomatic relations with Moscow and had hoped to
use documents seized in the ARCOS raid to justify its decision. A cabinet
committee concluded, however, that the ARCOS haul did not even prove
'the complicity of the Soviet Diplomatic Mission' in the 'propagandist
activities' of the Trade Delegation. Still lacking usable evidence of espionage, the cabinet concluded that it must at least give public proof that the
Soviet legation had breached the normal rules of diplomatic behaviour.
The only proof available was the telegrams exchanged between the legation
and Moscow decrypted by GC&CS. These were, as the cabinet minutes
euphemistically observed, 'secret documents of a class which it is not usual
to quote in published documents'.[80] To make its charges against the Russian
legation stick, the cabinet decided to follow the undiplomatic example of
Lord Curzon's outraged protest to Moscow in 1923 (the 'Curzon ulti-
matum') and quote intercepted Soviet telegrams. The first public reference
to the intercepts was made by the Prime Minister on 24 May in a Commons
statement on the ARCOS raid. Baldwin read out four Russian telegrams
which had, he drily observed, 'come into the possession of His Majesty's
Government'. An Opposition MP challenged Baldwin to say how the
government had obtained the telegrams, but there was uproar (or, as
Hansard put it, 'interruption') before he could finish his question. The
Speaker intervened and deferred further discussion until the debate two
days later on the decision to end diplomatic relations with the Soviet
Union.[81]

The debate, on 26 May, developed into an orgy of governmental indiscretion about secret intelligence for which there is no parallel in modern
parliamentary history. Both the Foreign Secretary, Austen Chamberlain,
and the Home Secretary, Joynson-Hicks ('Jix'), followed Baldwin's bad
example by quoting intercepted Russian telegrams. Chamberlain also
quoted intercepted Comintern communications in an attempt to show that
'the Zinoviev letter was not the only or the last' such document. Jix became
quite carried away while accusing the Soviet Trade Delegation of running

'one of the most complete and one of the most nefarious spy systems that it has ever been my lot to meet'. 'I happen to have in my possession', he boasted, 'not merely the names but the addresses of most of those spies.'[82] On the day of the debate Chamberlain informed the Russian chargé d'affaires of the decision to break off diplomatic relations because of Moscow's 'anti-British espionage and propaganda'. The Foreign Secretary gave his message an unusually personal point by quoting an intercepted telegram to Moscow on 1 April from the chargé d'affaires himself 'in which you request material to enable you to support a political campaign against His Majesty's Government'.[83] Baldwin's government was able to prove its charge of Soviet dabbling in British politics. But the documents seized in the ARCOS raid and the intercepted telegrams published in a government White Paper contained only a few cryptic allusions to espionage.[84] The government contrived in the end to have the worst of both worlds. It failed to produce public evidence to support Jix's dramatic charges of 'one of the most nefarious spy systems that it has ever been my lot to meet', yet at the same time compromised its most valuable Soviet intelligence source. Moscow responded to the publication of the intercepts by adopting the virtually unbreakable 'one-time pad'* for diplomatic and intelligence traffic. Between 1927 and the end of the Second World War GC&CS was able to decrypt almost no high-grade Soviet communications (though it had some success with Comintern messages).[85] Alastair Denniston, the operational head of GC&CS, wrote bitterly that Baldwin's government had 'found it necessary to compromise our work beyond question'.[86]

Following the ARCOS raid in May 1927, MI5 noted that Ewer's intelligence activities were winding down. A year later Harker, the head of B Branch, concluded that 'the organisation known as the FPA has now definitely broken up'. Intelligence on one of its members, Albert Allen, suggested that he 'may have quarrelled with his former employers, a fact which might be disclosed from his correspondence, and should this be discovered, it is obvious that we might be able, by careful approach, to get valuable information from him'. Allen, whose real name was Arthur Lakey, was a former Special Branch sergeant who had been dismissed after the police strike of 1919. On 25 June 1928 he was approached by John Ottaway of the Observation section who introduced himself as 'G. Stewart of the Anti-Communist Union' and claimed that the Union had sent him to ask Allen about his involvement with the FPA. Allen agreed to provide

---

* A one-time pad is an encryption system which uses once only a randomly generated private key known only to the sender and receiver of the message.

information on the FPA, ARCOS and other Russian 'intrigues'. Ottaway reported after the meeting that, as Harker had suspected, Allen's 'late masters evidently have let him down, and he seems embittered in consequence.' As evidence of the importance of the information he could provide, he revealed that he knew of leaks from both the Foreign Office and the Special Branch.[87]

In July 1928 Harker decided to meet Allen himself, introducing himself as someone who 'came from Colonel Kell':

I very quickly found ... that we were on quite good terms, and, by treating him rather as my opposite number, found that he was quite ready to talk up to a point. He is, I think, a man who is extraordinarily pleased with himself, and considers work which he did for some eight years for the Underground Organisation known as the FPA was admirably carried out, and has not received quite that recognition from its paymasters that Allen considers it deserves.

When Allen proved reluctant to identify his former boss, claiming to have been 'very fond of him', Harker wrote the initials 'W.N.E.' (William Norman Ewer) on a piece of paper, and asked Allen, 'That was your late boss, wasn't he?' Allen replied, 'Yes, "Trilby", "Trilby" is a good fellow and damned smart.'[88] 'Trilby', as Harker knew, was Ewer's nickname, acquired because of his youthful habit of going barefoot, like the heroine of George du Maurier's popular late-Victorian novel *Trilby*. Eventually Harker talked Allen down to a payment of £75 per meeting, and the information began to flow. Allen revealed that Ewer was paying £20 a week to sources in Scotland Yard for 'inside information' which included the names of those individuals placed under surveillance or who were to be questioned on arrival at British ports – intelligence of great importance to the running of Soviet agent operations:

Ewer was in the habit of dictating every week or ten days a list of addresses on which it was known that H.O.W.s had been taken out. These lists were typed in triplicate, one copy was sent to Chesham House [the Soviet legation], one copy was submitted through Chesham House direct to Moscow, and the third copy was sent to some individual in the C.P.G.B.

According to Allen, 'Any move that S[cotland] Y[ard] was about to make against the Communist Party or any of its personnel was nearly always known well in advance to Ewer who actually warned the persons concerned of proposed activities of the Police.' The Party and the Soviet legation were caught off guard by the ARCOS raid only because on this occasion security was so tight that the police officers in charge were initially told they were raiding government dockyards. Harker asked Allen why, despite his inside information, he was unaware that MI5 had obtained HOWs on both him and Ewer. Allen replied – correctly – that MI5 had obviously not told Scotland Yard.[89]

Shadowing other members of Ewer's network led Ottaway's Observation team to Walter Dale, who had first been observed (though his identity was then unknown) keeping under surveillance the rendezvous originally chosen for the first meeting between 'D' and Ewer. Dale in turn unwittingly led investigators to his main contacts in the Special Branch, the Dutch-born Inspector Hubertus van Ginhoven and Sergeant Charles Jane. After Dale's arrest, the discovery of his diary revealed further details of the operation of Ewer's network. It confirmed that Allen had operated for some time as the 'cut-out' between Ewer and the Special Branch officers.[90] The diary also gave details of Dale's other duties, among them the observation of British intelligence officers; surveillance of expatriate Russians; provision of lists of prominent individuals of possible interest to the Russians; and counter-surveillance for Russian agents, including Ewer and FPA employees. For the five years covered by the diary Dale and others maintained 'unremitting surveillance' on the locations and some employees of British intelligence agencies, including SIS and GC&CS, which included noting officers' licence-plate numbers and trailing them to their homes. Allen's information and Dale's diary led MI5 to conclude:

It became abundantly clear that for the past ten years, any information regarding subversive organisation and individuals supplied to Scotland Yard by SIS or MI5, which had become the subject of Special Branch enquiry, would have to be regarded as having been betrayed to Ewer's group.[91]

Ewer went to live abroad in 1928.[92] Inspector Ginhoven and Sergeant Jane were dismissed from the Special Branch after a disciplinary board of inquiry in May 1929.[93] At the time of Ginhoven's and Jane's dismissal, MI5 had a total of only thirteen officers.[94] Its resolution of the Ewer case with such slender resources was a considerable achievement.

Despite the risk that a trial would reveal intelligence techniques, SIS and probably MI5 were uneasy at the decision of the Attorney General not to prosecute Ewer, Ginhoven, Jane or any of their associates.[95] Within MI5, the decision not to prosecute was believed to have been taken on political grounds. According to a later diary entry by Guy Liddell, 'The general belief is that it was thought to be bad politics to have a show-down which might lead to the cry: "Another Zinoviev letter!" '[96] Because 1929 was election year, 'it was felt generally that another Zinoviev letter incident should be avoided.'[97] A trial would have provoked heated political contro-versy over the role of John 'Jack' Hayes, a former police officer and organizer of the 1919 police strike who had been elected as a Labour MP in 1923 and was re-elected in 1929. Trial evidence would have revealed that Hayes had run a detective service for Ewer and introduced him to both Allen and Ginhoven. He went on to become a parliamentary private secretary in the first MacDonald government of 1924, and in June 1929 attained ministerial office in the second MacDonald government as vice chamberlain for the Royal Household.[98] MI5 was doubtless right to believe that, if Ginhoven and Jane had been prosecuted, the references to Hayes during their trial would have revived the political passions aroused five years earlier by the Zinoviev letter.

Despite the fact that the Ewer case did not lead to prosecution, it marked a turning point in MI5 history. The discovery that the Special Branch had been penetrated by Soviet intelligence helped to prompt transfer from it to MI5 in 1931 of responsibility for countering civil as well as military Communist subversion.[99]

2

The Red Menace in the 1930s

Midway between the wars, Comintern was visibly cross with the CPGB. British Communist leaders, it complained, showed inadequate enthusiasm for denouncing the heresies of the non-Stalinist left. A prominent Comintern bureaucrat protested in 1929:

How does it happen that all the fundamental problems of the Communist International fail to stir our fraternal British party? ... All these problems have the appearance of being forcibly injected into the activities of the British Communist Party ... In the British party there is a sort of special system which may be characterised thus: the party is a society of great friends.

At the end of 1929 Comintern ousted the 'great friends' from office and imposed a new leadership on the submissive CPGB. At Moscow's insistence, Harry Pollitt, the new general secretary, abandoned all attempt to reach an accommodation with the 'class enemies' of the Labour Party. During 1930 the CPGB dutifully, if absurdly, denounced Ramsay Mac-Donald's second Labour government as 'social-Fascist', though the Communist National Minority Movement in the trade unions continued to be publicly accused by Moscow of 'right opportunist errors'. CPGB membership more than doubled from 2,550 at the end of 1930 to over 6,000 a year later – though as a result of the onset of the Depression and mass unemployment rather than of the policies imposed by Comintern. The Party failed, however, to make significant political capital from the resignation of the Labour government in August 1931, the split in the Labour Party and the formation of a coalition National Government with Ramsay Mac-Donald remaining as prime minister and denounced as a traitor by many of his former colleagues. The CPGB's political weakness was vividly demonstrated at the general election in October when its twenty-six candidates won a total of only 75,000 votes and not a single seat (in stark contrast to the 14 million votes cast for the National Government and the 6.5 million for the 'social-Fascist' Labour opposition).[1]

Despite the CPGB's dismal electoral performance, the Security Service remained concerned about the corrosive long-term consequences of Communist propaganda in the armed forces. During 1929 it investigated eighty-two cases of soldiers suspected of various forms of Communist activity. Of these, forty-six soldiers were 'cleared', five cases were dropped, sixteen were 'still under investigation' at the end of the year, and fifteen men were discharged (one fewer than in 1928). MI5 reported, however, that towards the end of 1929 there was an 'intensification' of both open propaganda and underground subversion. It traced much of this 'intensification' to secret instructions sent by Comintern's executive committee to the CPGB on 11 October 1929 urging it to set up cells within the armed services aimed at collecting secret information, agitating against commanding officers and distributing anti-militarist propaganda. 'That espionage, as well as propaganda, is one of the dangers against which we have to guard', MI5 reported, 'cannot be too strongly emphasised.'[2] In 1929 the French Communist Party (PCF) set up a network of 'worker correspondents' who were asked to send information from military units and the arms industry to the Party newspaper, *L'Humanité*, which forwarded it to Moscow. This open invitation to espionage led to the imprisonment of much of the PCF leadership. In July 1930, however, Comintern invited other Parties to follow the example of the PCF.[3]

Comintern's preoccupation with Western armed forces reflected Stalin's insistence that the Soviet Union faced 'the threat of a new imperialist war'. Both the OGPU (forerunner of the KGB) and the military Fourth Section (later the GRU) were actively involved in operations to counter the supposed menace of imperialist aggression. Within the OGPU, the euphemistically named Administration for Special Tasks, headed by the experienced assassin Yakov 'Yasha' Serebryansky, was given responsibility for assassinations, sabotage and terrorist operations abroad. Serebryansky later became a serious embarrassment for Soviet foreign intelligence which sought to distance itself from the bloodletting of the 1930s and portray itself – implausibly – as victim rather than perpetrator of Stalin's Terror. As late as 1993, a history based on material supplied by the post-Soviet foreign intelligence service, the SVR, claimed that Serebryansky was 'not a regular member of State Security', but 'only brought in for special jobs'. KGB files show that, on the contrary, he was a senior OGPU officer whose Administration for Special Tasks grew into an elite service, over 200-strong. Long-term preparations for sabotage behind enemy lines in time of war, part of Serebryansky's original remit, were overtaken by the increasingly homicidal hunt for 'enemies of the people' who had taken refuge abroad. Since Paris was the main centre during the 1930s of both the White Guards, the remnants of the White Armies defeated in the Russian Civil War, and the followers of the great heretic Leon Trotsky, it became Serebryansky's principal theatre of operations. A number of his officers were awarded the Order of the Red Banner for successful assassinations.[4]

MI5 had no means of knowing that the assassinations on the continent would not also take place in Britain. Its main concern, however, was Comintern-inspired subversion within the British armed forces. MI5 reported early in 1930 that 'Communist efforts to tamper with H.M. Forces has [sic] increased and is still increasing':

It is not suggested that as yet any serious harm has been done to the loyalty and discipline of the Forces generally, but in the case of certain of the more technical units, there is no doubt that this long continued and subtle propaganda is beginning to have a certain effect on both discipline and morale, which, if allowed to spread unchecked, will in the long run prove disastrous to the Forces as a whole.[5]

MI5's warnings against the dangers of subversion gained greatly in credibility after mutiny among seamen of the Atlantic Fleet at the Invergordon naval base in September 1931. The mutiny was a spontaneous protest by the lower deck against incompetently planned and unfairly distributed wage cuts. Trouble was quickly ended by reducing the cuts. The seamen themselves regarded their action as a strike; the only violent protest was a beer mug thrown at an officer in a canteen. Though short lived, the unrest in the Royal Navy caused a greater official stir than any other disturbance within the armed forces since demobilization after the First World War, briefly raising the spectre of the Russian and German naval mutinies of 1917 and 1918 which had helped to topple both Tsar and Kaiser. The impact of the exaggerated reports of mutiny in the Atlantic Fleet was heightened by the fact that they occurred in the midst of a major financial crisis at a critical moment in the life of the first National Government. The fears of foreign bankers that the government had lost its grip were strengthened by the mutiny, and the flight from the pound was, as Hankey, the cabinet secretary, complained, 'immensely stimulated'. On 17 September £10 million in gold was withdrawn from the Bank of England. Next day the figure rose to £18 million and the government was forced to make a hitherto unthinkable breach with financial orthodoxy and abandon the Gold Standard.[6]

On 21 September 1931, the day that the Bill ending the Gold Standard was rushed through all its stages in parliament, the cabinet heard an alarmist report on the progress of the mutiny, based largely on intelligence supplied by the Naval Intelligence Department and MI5. The report was treated with extraordinary secrecy, excluded from the normal cabinet minutes, and summarized in a top-secret (then 'most secret') note which was then placed in a sealed envelope to be opened only by Hankey, his deputy or their successors. The cabinet was warned that:

the situation was extremely serious. There was a complete organization on the lower deck to resist the pay cuts, and the petty officers were now affected . . . The intention now was for the crews to walk out of the ships on Tuesday morning [22 September] . . . The marines afloat were implicated and . . . the marines at the home ports were not to be trusted.

It is now clear that there were no plans for a further mutiny on the 22nd. But the inflated estimates of naval unrest inevitably magnified fears of Communist subversion. The cabinet was told that 'The Communists were active in the ports and had sent some of the best agents there.'[7]

The CPGB had indeed hurriedly sent agents to the home ports, but their attempts to stir up trouble were sometimes comically inept. On 23 September Able Seaman Bateman, whose ship had arrived in Portsmouth from Invergordon, was approached in a fish and chip shop by Stephen 'Shorty' Hutchings, a Communist militant posing as a journalist. Hutchings insisted on paying for Bateman's fish and chips, told him he wanted a story on Invergordon and arranged to meet him for drinks on the following day in a local hotel. Bateman turned up on the 24th, accompanied by Naval Telegraphist Stephen Bousfield who subsequently reported the meeting to the police and was interviewed by MI5.[8] According to Bousfield, in the course of four hours' steady drinking Hutchings revealed that he was a member of Comintern and 'wanted sailors to come out on strike'. When Bateman and Bousfield demanded money to promote a strike, Hutchings said he would have to consult 'his superiors in London'. If they agreed, he would telegraph Bousfield: 'Mother ill. Come at once. Walter.'

After receiving the expected telegram from 'Walter', Bousfield travelled to London and met a *Daily Worker* journalist, William Shepherd, at a house in Hampstead. Bousfield agreed to draft a pamphlet calling for further strikes in the Royal Navy. In return, Shepherd promised to pay Mrs Bousfield two pounds a week for the next year and make a further payment to Bateman. It was agreed that Bousfield would deliver the pamphlet for printing to a man with a yellow handkerchief in his breast pocket whom he would meet in a Portsmouth pub. The two men duly met and the pamphlet was handed over in the lavatory at Portsmouth railway station. The man with the yellow handkerchief, who was immediately arrested, turned out to be George Allison, a senior Communist who had been jailed five years earlier for travelling to India on a false passport and was currently acting general secretary of the National Minority Movement. In November Allison was sentenced to three years in jail and Shepherd to twenty months.[9]

Hutchings escaped trial by fleeing to Russia where, his intercepted correspondence revealed, he was soon complaining of miserable living conditions and separation from his family in England. Jane Sissmore, the Service's main Soviet expert, hoped that if Hutchings could be persuaded to stand trial and 'give all the information he could about the case and the methods of the C.P. generally with regard to their underground work against the Navy, it would be possible to ensure that he received a light sentence':

If we could be sure that Hutchings would play, I think it would be a most effective blow to the Communist Party here and a great deterrent to further activities of the kind in which Hutchings was engaged.

To date, Communists who overstep the law have always the assurance that they will be looked after in Moscow if they have to fly this country. Hutchings' account of his privations in Moscow may serve to dispel the illusion which the Communist Party has so carefully built up.[10]

Hutchings, however, remained in Moscow.[11]

The exaggerated fears of naval subversion provoked by Invergordon produced an extensive purge of naval personnel. Almost a thousand were discharged.[12] On 16 November the Lords Commissioners of the Admiralty formally congratulated the Security Service on its 'excellent work' in the aftermath of the Invergordon mutiny: 'My Lords realise that [the Security Service] was not organised to deal with unrest in such circumstances or on so extensive a scale and they desire to convey . . . an expression of their high appreciation.' The Admiralty paid particular tribute to the investigations carried out at Plymouth by Captain Con Boddington, Harker's 'assistant for special inquiries'.[13] Few details of Boddington's operations survive.[14]

In the aftermath of Invergordon both MI5 and the service ministries viewed with peculiar horror the crude tracts prepared by the CPGB for distribution to the armed forces. Their basic message was summed up in the *Soldier's Voice* call to class war in May 1932: 'Let us use the knowledge of arms which they give us, when the opportunity presents itself, to overthrow their rule, and in unity with our fellow workers, to establish free socialist Britain.'[15] The young Bristol Communist Douglas Hyde, later news editor of the *Daily Worker*, recalled how bundles of *Soldier's Voice* were 'smuggled down from London' to be dropped by night over the wall of the local barracks: 'Since the risks were high, volunteers were called for, who then drew lots. I volunteered but drew a blank. The unlucky one that night was caught in the act and disappeared into the neighbouring jail for eighteen months.'[16] The Security Service read *Soldier's Voice* more attentively than the Bristol soldiers.[17]

Early in 1933 new 'information of the highest importance', probably from one of Knight's agents in the CPGB,[18] threw 'a flood of fresh light' on Comintern plans for 'seducing the Armed Forces of the Crown from their allegiance'.[19] The Security Service was able to use this information to strengthen its hitherto ineffective campaign, begun after the First World War, for new legislation to discourage subversion in the armed forces.[20] On 18 October the cabinet considered the first draft of an Incitement to Disaffection Bill together with a memorandum signed by the Home Secretary and the service ministers:

The primary object of the Bill was to provide a summary method of dealing with attempts to seduce members of His Majesty's Forces from their duty and allegiance,

The Red Signal

NO. 10. THE ORGAN OF THE LOWER DECK.

LONG LIVE THE SPIRIT OF INVERGORDON!

Let's start the preparations **now**, comrades, and let the slogan ring out **PREPARE FOR A NEW INVERGORDON.**

THE "RED SIGNAL" NO.10.

The D.P.P. considers that this pamphlet contains Incitement to Mutiny and is prepared to prosucute anyone found distributing it to members of H.M.Forces. He drew particular attention to the last sentence, which, in itself, is Incitement to Mutiny.

Extract from the *Red Signal*, a Communist tract distributed to naval ratings in September 1933 which the DPP considered an incitement to mutiny.

the second main object being to empower Justices of the Peace to grant search warrants where they are satisfied that there is reasonable ground for suspecting that an offence under the Bill has been committed.[21]

The Bill made its first appearance in the Commons on 10 April 1934. At the second reading six days later the Liberal Isaac Foot (father of the future Labour leader Michael Foot) asked 'what evidence there is that a single soldier has been influenced in his allegiance or that a single sailor has done more than deride these wonderful papers, "The Soldier's Voice" and "The Red Signal" . . .'. None was produced. The National Government's huge parliamentary majority ensured none the less that the Bill became law before the year's end. To the surprise of both its opponents and its supporters, it led to only one prosecution before the Second World War.[22]

The most serious subversive threat in time of war was sabotage. MI5 and the Special Branch jointly reported in 1930:

It is an indisputable fact that the British Communist Party, under instructions from Moscow, is endeavouring by every means possible, to make such preparations that, in the event of war being declared by this country or in the event of a general mobilisation for war against Russia, chosen members of the Party should carry out previously arranged plans of sabotage. Definite orders have been issued from Moscow to the Communist Party of Great Britain that, in the event of a declaration of war, workers must be able to frustrate the campaign by general disorganisation.

The main focus of MI5 concerns about preparations for sabotage was the Soviet trading organization Russian Oil Products (ROP), which had been established as a British limited-liability company in 1924. MI5 noted in the following year that all its shareholders were Russian nationals. Among prominent Party members in contact with ROP was Willie Gallacher. MI5 and the Special Branch calculated in 1930 that ROP had almost a thousand employees, about one-third of whom were members of the CPGB, and had built up a network of thirty-three offices, depots and installations across the UK.[23] Holt-Wilson reported to the Committee of Imperial Defence that parts of the ROP network were located dangerously close to what was later called Britain's Critical National Infrastructure (CNI), especially fuel-storage depots.[24] If war broke out with the Soviet Union, MI5 believed there was a danger that ROP lorry tankers would be driven to British fuel or munitions depots and detonated. In 1934 the Home Office agreed to a Security Service proposal that, in an 'emergency' or international crisis, the movements of the tankers should be made subject to police regulation. Because of the additional danger that ROP ship tankers could be detonated in British ports, port authorities were asked to keep them under close supervision.[25]

Security Service investigations into ROP extended to counter-espionage as well as protective security.[26] The priority given by Soviet intelligence to the use of ROP as a front for scientific and technological intelligence operations is indicated by the amount of money spent on it. A combined MI5 and Special Branch analysis of ROP finances in 1930 calculated that it was run at a loss of £370,000 to £390,000 per annum.[27] The Security Service reported in 1932 that 'one of the principal comrades who acts as liaison between ROP and the Party' was Percy Glading,[28] later convicted of espionage at the Woolwich Arsenal.[29] ROP provided a sophisticated front for the increasing Soviet scientific and technological intelligence operations of the 1930s: among them probably the first Russian use in Britain of the 'false flag' technique, where a recruiter working for one agency claims to represent another. In September 1932 an employee of the ROP Bristol branch was discovered to be posing (under the alias 'Olsen') as a Romanian journalist reporting on the British oil industry, in an attempt to obtain commercial secrets from employees of the Shell Mex Company in London.[30] The Security Service obtained an HOW on 'Olsen's' address, which revealed that his real name was Joseph Volkovich Volodarsky. In November 1932 he pleaded guilty to a charge of attempting to bribe a Shell employee and was fined £50.[31] In 1933 Volodarsky left Britain for North America, where he helped to provide false identity documents for the Soviet illegal* Willy Brandes before his posting to London.[32]

Potentially the most important suspected Soviet spy investigated by the Security Service during the early 1930s was the distinguished Russian physicist and future Nobel laureate Pyotr Kapitsa, who in 1924 had come to work at the world-famous Cavendish Laboratory at Cambridge University and was elected a fellow of Trinity College. The Security Service had good reason to be suspicious of Kapitsa. Its surveillance of ARCOS, whose activities provided cover for Soviet espionage, revealed that Kapitsa was in contact with it; SIS reported that ARCOS had provided funding for his research. An informant in Trinity College also revealed that Kapitsa was in close contact with the leading Cambridge Communist Maurice Dobb,[33] later the Trinity undergraduate Kim Philby's economics supervisor and an important influence on him. It was to Dobb that Kim Philby turned on his last day in Cambridge for advice on how best to devote his life to the

---

* Illegals were deep-cover intelligence officers or agents operating under false name and nationality.

Communist cause.[34] In 1931 the Security Service obtained an HOW on Kapitsa's correspondence. In the same year, Guy Liddell had a secret meeting with an informant in the Cavendish Laboratory who, perhaps prompted partly by professional jealousy, claimed that Kapitsa was a Soviet spy.[35] Kapitsa's contact with the Communist Andrew Rothstein, who was then involved in recruiting agents to supply scientific and technological espionage, also seemed suspicious. In June 1934 an intercepted telegram from Moscow revealed that Rothstein had been instructed to obtain information from Kapitsa on his 'new plant for the dilution of helium'. A month later a Security Service report on Kapitsa noted that the Soviet ambassador, Ivan Maisky, and members of his staff were 'making mysterious motor-car drives to Cambridge and other neighbouring towns'.[36]

Though there were reasonable grounds at the time for suspicion by the Security Service, it now seems highly unlikely that Kapitsa was engaged in espionage in the Cavendish Laboratory. His willingness to talk about his own research and discuss that of his colleagues was an accepted part of Western scientific culture whose absence, despite his support for the Soviet regime, he bemoaned in Russia. The main purpose of the contacts with him by the Soviet embassy in London in the summer of 1934 was probably to persuade him to visit Moscow. When Kapitsa did so in the autumn, he was deeply dismayed to be prevented from returning to the Cavendish. It was another two years before he was able to resume the research he had been carrying out at Cambridge in low-temperature physics and magnetism.[37]

The Security Service was entirely unaware that, at the very moment when its understandable but unfounded suspicions of Kapitsa reached their peak in the summer of 1934, the most successful agent-recruitment campaign ever conducted by Soviet intelligence in Britain was just beginning, with Cambridge University as its main target. In June 1934 Kim Philby, who had graduated from Trinity College in the previous year with the conviction that 'my life must be devoted to Communism', had his first meeting with his Soviet controller. He spent most of the year after graduation in Vienna working for the Communist-backed International Workers Relief Organization and acting as a courier for the underground Austrian Communist Party. While in Vienna he met and married a young Communist divorcee, Litzi (or 'Lizzy', as Philby called her) Friedmann, after a brief but passionate love affair which included his first experience of making love in the snow ('actually quite warm, once you got used to it', he later recalled). In May 1934, they returned to live in London.[38] Not until almost thirty years later, on the eve of defecting to Moscow, did Philby at last admit how he had been recruited:

The photograph in MI5 files from which Philby later discovered the real name of the charismatic recruiter of the Cambridge Five and other Soviet agents, Dr Arnold Deutsch. Deutsch's attention to his own personal security was sometimes slipshod: but for his recall from Britain late in 1937 he might well have been caught by MI5.

... Lizzy came home one evening and told me that she had arranged for me to meet a 'man of decisive importance'. I questioned her about it but she would give me no details. The rendezvous took place in Regents Park. The man described himself as Otto. I discovered much later from a photograph in MI5 files that the name he went by was Arnold Deutsch. I think that he was of Czech origin; about 5ft 7in, stout, with blue eyes and light curly hair. Though a convinced Communist, he had a strong humanistic streak. He hated London, adored Paris, and spoke of it with deeply loving affection. He was a man of considerable cultural background.

Otto spoke at great length, arguing that a person with my family background and possibilities could do far more for Communism than the run-of-the-mill Party member or sympathiser ... I accepted. His first instructions were that both Lizzy and I should break off as quickly as possible all personal contact with our Communist friends.[39]

Philby became the first of the 'Cambridge Five', the ablest group of British agents ever recruited by a foreign intelligence service.

Deutsch, whose role as a Soviet intelligence officer was not discovered by the Security Service until 1940,[40] well after he had left England for the last time, had an even more outstanding academic record than any of the

Cambridge Five. Though, as Philby recalled, he was of Czech origin, his parents had moved to Austria when he was a child. At Vienna University he had progressed in only five years from undergraduate entry to the degree of PhD with distinction. Deutsch's description of himself in university documents throughout his student career as an observant Jew (*mosaisch*) was probably designed to conceal his membership of the Communist Party. Though his doctorate was in chemistry, he had also taken courses in psychology and philosophy. After being awarded the PhD, he had, remarkably, combined secret work for Comintern and the OGPU with open collaboration with the German Communist psychologist and sexologist Wilhelm Reich, who was then engaged in an attempt to synthesize the work of Marx and Freud and later earned a probably undeserved reputation as 'the prophet of the better orgasm'. Deutsch publicly assisted Reich in the 'sex-pol' (sexual politics) movement, which ran clinics designed to bring birth control and sexual enlightenment to Viennese workers, and founded a small publishing house, Münster Verlag (Dr Arnold Deutsch), to publish Reich's work and sex-pol literature. At the time when he moved to London in April 1934, Deutsch was under surveillance by the 'anti-pornography' section of the Vienna police.[41] Even if, during Deutsch's period in England, the Security Service had known of his earlier involvement with Reich and the sex-pol movement, it would probably have regarded his unusual career as improbable cover for a Soviet spy.

Deutsch had the lead role in recruiting the Cambridge Five.[42] The key to his success, apart from his flair as an agent-runner, was his new recruitment strategy, endorsed by the Centre (Soviet intelligence headquarters), based on the cultivation of young radical high-fliers from leading universities before they entered the corridors of power:

Given that the Communist movement in these universities is on a mass scale and that there is a constant turnover of students, it follows that individual Communists whom we pluck out of the Party will pass unnoticed, both by the Party itself and by the outside world. People forget about them. And if at some time they do remember that they were once Communists, this will be put down to a passing fancy of youth, especially as those concerned are scions of the bourgeoisie. It is up to us to give the individual recruit a new [non-Communist] political personality.

Since the universities of Oxford and Cambridge provided a disproportionate number of Whitehall's highest fliers, it was plainly logical to target Oxbridge rather than the less ancient redbrick English universities. The decision to begin the new recruitment in Cambridge rather than Oxford was due largely to chance: the fact that Philby, the first potential recruit to come to Deutsch's attention, whom he codenamed SÖHNCHEN ('Sonny'), was a Cambridge graduate.[43]

Half a century later, after his defection to Moscow, Philby still remembered his first meeting with Deutsch as 'amazing':

He was a marvellous man. Simply marvellous. I felt that immediately. And [the feeling] never left me ... The first thing you noticed about him were his eyes. He looked at you as if nothing more important in life than you and talking to you existed at that moment ... And he had a marvellous sense of humour.[44]

Though Deutsch had trained in Moscow as an OGPU illegal with the alias 'Stefan Lange',[45] he used his real name and nationality with the immigration authorities when arriving in England, probably so that he could use his cousin Oscar Deutsch, the millionaire owner of the Odeon cinema chain, as a referee.[46] (Though the name of the chain was derived from the Greek *odeion* (concert hall), the spelling was adapted to form an acronym for 'Oscar Deutsch Entertains Our Nation'.) Arnold Deutsch's Home Office file does not survive,[47] but it is clear that there was nothing on file to attract suspicion to him from the immigration authorities. Apart from the backing of his millionaire cousin, he was academically very well qualified for postgraduate work at London University which provided ideal cover for his intelligence work as well as giving him first-hand experience of British university life. From October 1934 to January 1936, he took (but did not complete) the Psychology Diploma course at University College London, which would have qualified him to move on to a PhD.[48] Though the name of his postgraduate supervisor is not recorded,[49] later Security Service investigations suggest that it may well have been the controversial head of the Psychology Department at London University, Professor Cyril Burt (later knighted), whom Deutsch used as a referee.[50]

Deutsch's initial reports to the Centre on Philby, who he believed needed 'constant encouragement', reflected his interest in psychology as well as his intelligence training:

SÖHNCHEN comes from a peculiar family. His father [currently adviser to King Ibn Saud of Saudi Arabia] is considered at present to be the most distinguished expert on the Arab world ... He is an ambitious tyrant and wanted to make a great man out of his son. He repressed all his son's desires. That is why SÖHNCHEN is a very timid and irresolute person. He has a bit of a stammer and this increases his diffidence ... However, he handles our money very carefully. He enjoys great love and respect for his seriousness and honesty. He was ready, without questioning, to do anything for us and has shown all his seriousness and diligence working for us.[51]

Deutsch asked Philby to recommend some of his Cambridge contemporaries. His first two nominations were Donald Maclean, who had just graduated from Trinity Hall with first-class honours in modern languages, and Guy Burgess of Trinity College, who was working on a history PhD thesis which he was never to complete. By the end of 1934, with Philby's help, Deutsch had recruited both, telling them – like Philby – to distance themselves from Communist friends. Burgess did so with characteristic flamboyance, becoming personal assistant in the following year to the right-wing Conservative MP Captain 'Jack' Macnamara, with whom he went on 'fact-finding' missions to Nazi Germany which, according to Burgess, were largely devoted to sexual escapades with gay members of the Hitler Youth.[52]

At the very moment when the recruitment of the Cambridge Five was beginning, the Security Service was actively investigating Pyotr Kapitsa. Identifying Cambridge's most militant student Communists at the same time would not have been difficult had the Service realized they were being targeted by Soviet intelligence. A generation later, after Philby, Maclean and Burgess had all defected to Moscow, the Service obtained, by means unknown, the minute book for the period 1928 to 1935 of Cambridge's main student Communist organization, the Cambridge University Socialist Society (CUSS), which usually met in Trinity College.[53] The minutes record that Maclean, the son of a former Liberal minister, was elected a committee member during his first year at Trinity Hall in 1931 and later put in charge of CUSS publicity at a meeting when 'Members created a precedent in Cambridge by singing the Internationale and other songs vociferously.' Philby was elected treasurer of the Society in 1932.[54] He reported in March 1933, three months before graduating, that 'the financial position of the Society was very insecure and that a deficit was in prospect owing to the fact that very few fresh members had joined in the present term.' He remained in active contact with CUSS after graduation. A committee meeting in March 1934 considered 'a ... letter from H. A. R. Philby appealing for support' for persecuted Austrian workers. It was agreed that a collection would be taken, and Guy Burgess was one of two CUSS militants put in charge of managing a fund to respond to Philby's appeal.[55] The Security Service, however, carried out no serious investigation into CUSS. Given the Service's small size and limited resources, it is perhaps understandable that student Communist groups should have been considered too low a priority to merit active investigation.

The first of the Cambridge Five to penetrate the 'bourgeois apparatus' was Maclean, who entered the Foreign Office in 1935. Burgess's main role

3. Austria.

The Secretary read a further letter from M.A.R. Philby appealing for support. The organisation of the fund was further discussed. Maitre + Burgess were to be instructed to work through Com. Peps. A collection was to be taken at next Midday meeting if possible.

Extract from the Communist-dominated Cambridge University Socialist Society's minute book for 1934, which MI5 acquired in 1972. Had the minutes been obtained before the War, Philby would probably have had much greater difficulty in entering SIS.

in his early years as a Soviet agent was as a talent-spotter. Early in 1937, by then a BBC producer, he arranged the first meeting between Deutsch and Anthony Blunt, French linguist, art historian and Fellow of Trinity College, Cambridge. Blunt in turn identified as a likely recruit his former pupil John Cairncross, a passionate Scottish Marxist nicknamed 'The Fiery Cross' by the *Trinity Magazine*, who in 1936 had graduated from Trinity with first-class honours in modern languages and come top in the Foreign Office entrance examination. Deutsch met Cairncross in May 1937 and reported to Moscow that he 'was very happy that we had established contact with him and was ready to start working for us at once'. KGB files credit Deutsch with the recruitment of twenty agents during his time in Britain. The most successful, however, were the Cambridge Five: Philby, Maclean, Burgess, Blunt and Cairncross. The Security Service had no suspicions about any of them until 1951. (After the release of the enormously popular Western *The Magnificent Seven* in 1960, some in the Centre referred to them as the 'Magnificent Five'.) All were committed ideological spies inspired by the myth-image of Stalin's Russia as a worker-peasant state with social justice for all rather than by the reality of a brutal dictatorship with the largest peacetime gulag in European history. Deutsch shared the same visionary faith as his Cambridge recruits in the future of a human race freed from the exploitation and alienation of the capitalist system. His message of liberation had all the greater appeal for the Five because it had a sexual as well as a political dimension. All were rebels against the strict sexual mores as well as the antiquated class system of interwar Britain. Burgess and Blunt were gay and Maclean bisexual at a time when homosexual relations, even between consenting adults, were illegal. Cairncross, like Philby a committed heterosexual, later wrote a history of polygamy which prompted his friend Graham Greene to comment: 'Here at last is a book which will appeal strongly to all polygamists.'[56]

The successes of Soviet agent penetration during the 1930s were made possible by Whitehall's still primitive grasp of protective security. Moscow had vastly more intelligence about British policy than the British intelligence community had about the Soviet Union's. Until the Second World War the Foreign Office had no security officer let alone a security department. Hence the relative ease with which the OGPU/NKVD* recruited FO cipher clerks in the early 1930s. The Centre believed that the first of the cipher clerks to be recruited, Ernest Oldham, was discovered by MI5 or the Foreign Office and assassinated in 1933. In reality, Oldham committed suicide and his treachery was not discovered until the Second World War. Captain John King, the most productive of the FO cipher-clerk recruits, also went undiscovered until the outbreak of war. Donald Maclean quickly established himself as a high-flyer with, according to the Foreign Office Personnel Department, 'plenty of brains and keenness', as well as being 'nice-looking', and provided Moscow with a regular flow of classified diplomatic documents. John Cairncross gained access to what he called 'a wealth of valuable information on the progress of the Civil War in Spain' before moving on to the Treasury in 1938. MI5 had little if any ability to improve the woeful state of Foreign Office security. When the FO discovered in 1937 that classified documents were haemorrhaging from the Rome embassy (as they had been doing for more than a decade), it sought help not from MI5 (as it would have done during the Cold War) but from SIS, despite the fact that SIS disclaimed any expertise in embassy security. Even when Major Valentine Vivian of SIS Section V identified the current culprit as a Chancery servant, Secondo Constantini, the ambassador refused to believe it and invited Constantini and his wife to the coronation of King George VI in May 1937 as a reward for his long and supposedly faithful service.[57]

So far as the Soviet Union was concerned, throughout the 1930s the FO was, without realizing it, often practising open diplomacy. In 1935 alone, over a hundred of the diplomatic documents purloined from the Rome embassy were considered sufficiently important to be 'sent to Comrade

---

* The first Soviet intelligence agency, the Cheka, founded six weeks after the Bolshevik Revolution, subsequently became the GPU (1922), OGPU (1923), NKVD (1934), NKGB (February 1941), NKVD again (July 1941), NKGB again (1943), MGB (1946), MVD (1953) and finally the KGB (1954). For further details, see Andrew and Mitrokhin, *Mitrokhin Archive*, p. xi.

Stalin': among them the FO records of talks between the Foreign Secretary, Sir John Simon, the junior Foreign Office Minister Anthony Eden (who became foreign secretary at the end of the year) and Hitler in Berlin; between Eden and Maksim Litvinov, Soviet Commissar for Foreign Affairs, in Moscow; between Eden and Eduard Beneš, the Czechoslovak Foreign Minister, in Prague; and between Eden and Mussolini in Rome.[58] The versions shown to Stalin, however, were doctored in order to conform to Stalin's conspiratorial worldview and remove material likely to offend him. A striking omission from the Foreign Office documents shown to Stalin in 1935 was Eden's account of talks with him in Moscow. The Centre lacked the nerve to pass on Eden's view of Stalin as 'a man of strong oriental traits of character with unshakable assurance and control whose courtesy in no way hid from us an implacable ruthlessness'.[59]

No British intelligence agency during the 1930s had access to any Soviet diplomatic documents which began to compare in importance to the British documents obtained by the Centre. Since 1927 GC&CS had had little success with most Soviet diplomatic and intelligence traffic. Early in 1930, however, naval and military intercept stations began picking up what the head of GC&CS, Alastair Denniston, described as 'a mass of unusual and unknown transmissions, all in cipher except for "operators' chat"'. Analysis of the transmissions revealed that they were messages exchanged between Comintern in Moscow and a worldwide network of clandestine radio stations.[60] The operation, codenamed MASK, to identify, locate and decrypt the Comintern messages was led by Lieutenant Colonel John Tiltman, a brilliant mathematician who had been offered but turned down a place at Oxford University at the age of only thirteen. Tiltman arrived at GC&CS in 1929 from India, where he had headed a SIGINT unit which had intercepted a variety of Soviet traffic. At the beginning of Operation MASK, two Metropolitan Police intercept operators, Harold Kenworthy and Leslie Lambert, set out to track down the Comintern radio transmitter in London by driving round the capital at night, when the transmitter was active (sometimes for only a few minutes), with direction-finding equipment in a van supplied by SIS. As Kenworthy later recalled:

Some exciting moments were experienced – particularly on one occasion, after going round a neighbourhood for some time a police car stopped us. On being asked: 'What have you got in that parcel?' – the parcel being a short-wave set – Mr Lambert said: 'I don't want to tell you.'

Thereafter Kenworthy and Lambert had to produce a special pass in order to avoid being mistaken for burglars. It took them several months to track down the Comintern transmitter to a house in Wimbledon.[61] An MI5 surveillance operation identified the owner of the house as a known CPGB member named Stephen James Wheeton, and revealed that he had regular meetings with another Party militant, Alice Holland, to whom he passed Comintern messages.[62] In April 1935 Wheeton was replaced as radio operator by another Communist named William Morrison.[63] Operation MASK continued until October 1937, when Morrison left to fight in the Spanish Civil War,[64] after which no further messages were picked up.[65]

During 1933, if not earlier, Tiltman's attack on the Comintern ciphers achieved 'complete success'.[66] On 31 January 1934 SIS forwarded to MI5 MASK decrypts for the period 22 April 1931 to 9 January 1934.[67] The decrypts provided further evidence of Soviet-inspired subversion in the navy and docks. Comintern had instructed the CPGB in May 1931:

In view of growing danger of war and preparation intervention against USSR winning over of seamen and harbour workers to our side become[s] of special importance. Political Commission direct you strengthen your work amongst seamen and harbour workers, strengthen and develop work revolutionary trades union and trades union opposition.[68]

From February 1934 to January 1937 GC&CS was able to supply current MASK intercepts of Comintern traffic to SIS Section V, which forwarded them to the Security Service.[69] The decrypts revealed the identities of a number of previously unknown secret members of the CPGB, as well as details of Comintern couriers and British Communists studying in Moscow. Among the students at the Lenin School identified in the MASK decrypts was Jomo Kenyatta, who a generation later became the first leader of independent Kenya.[70] Analysis of the decrypts showed that some of the messages to the CPGB leader Harry Pollitt used his real name, while others, relating to secret activities, used a cover name.[71] The intercepts also provided details of Moscow's secret subsidies to the CPGB and the Communist *Daily Worker*.[72] Ivan Maisky, who had arrived in London as Soviet ambassador in 1932, three years after the resumption of diplomatic relations, was informed by the Foreign Office that the subsidies were closely monitored. Partly because of the CPGB's political weakness, 'Moscow gold' caused far less outrage in Whitehall than a decade earlier. Sir John Simon, Foreign Secretary in the National Government of 1931–5, told Maisky that Soviet subsidies were 'a waste of money': 'He thought it his duty to repeat in a very friendly but very emphatic fashion his conviction that the game was not worth the candle from the Soviet Government's point of view, and that from his own it was a petty and pointless irritant.'[73]

MASK intelligence was supplemented by SIS agents in Comintern, in particular a walk-in to the SIS Berlin station, Johannes Heinrich de Graaf ('Jonny X'), a German Communist recruited by Soviet military intelligence who had been involved in the organization of the Comintern illegal network in Britain.[74] Much of the Comintern traffic, even when decrypted, turned out to be obscurely phrased. Both Comintern and the CPGB sometimes had difficulty in understanding the radio messages exchanged between them and had to ask for clarification. The Security Service and Section V of SIS, which collaborated on MASK, lacked sufficient staff to make a detailed analysis of much of it. There were simply far too many decrypts to process.[75]

Surviving MASK decrypts provide no insight into the problem of dockyard sabotage which was one of the Security Service's main concerns in the mid-1930s. Between 1933 and 1936 there were six quite serious cases of sabotage to ships' machinery (five in Devonport and one at Sheerness) which prompted a detailed investigation by the Security Service of Communist activity in royal dockyards and naval ordnance works. Investigations led by Con Boddington[76] identified as the likely ringleader John Salisbury, a Communist shipwright, who had been 'reliably reported' to have urged the Plymouth Communist Party in December 1931 'to damage as much machinery as they could. He described this as "sabotage" and said it would prevent war and would stop men from taking up arms.'[77] Following a Security Service recommendation for Salisbury's dismissal, a meeting in the room of the Director of Naval Intelligence at the Admiralty on 8 January 1936, attended by Kell, Harker and Boddington, recommended that Salisbury should be interrogated by the Admiral Superintendent of Devonport Dockyard, assisted by Boddington.[78] Salisbury was dismissed on 1 February.[79]

Salisbury's dismissal caused little protest. Local officials of the Transport and General Workers Union (TGWU) were told in confidence some of the case against him. Ernest Bevin, the TGWU general secretary (and future foreign secretary), who had already had a number of bitter disputes with Communists, said privately that 'nobody would attempt to defend Salisbury.' In October 1936 Kell recommended eight more dismissals: four from Devonport, one from Sheerness and three from the Naval Ordnance Works in Sheffield. His recommendations were considered by a three-man committee headed by Sir Archibald Carter, permanent under secretary at the Admiralty. In addition to studying Security Service reports on the eight men concerned and photographs of their intercepted correspondence, the Carter Committee also heard oral evidence from Kell and from Boddington, who impressed them 'by his fair-minded attitude'. The Committee believed it 'impossible, largely owing to the inability to disclose secret sources of information, to produce proof to satisfy a court of law'. But they concluded that in the case of the Devonport workers Francis Carne, Alfred Durston, Henry Lovejoy and Edward Trebilcock:

It is certain, beyond any reasonable doubt . . . that all four men have been actively engaged in dangerous subversive propaganda, and not merely in the doctrinaire preaching of Communism as a political creed.

There is also very strong suspicion, though not amounting to certainty, that they were intimately connected with acts of sabotage.

None of the four has been very active since the dismissal of Salisbury, but there is good reason for believing that they have received orders from above . . . We recommend that they should all be discharged.

The Committee also approved the dismissal of Henry Law, a shipwright at Sheerness, who 'apart from other considerable activities . . . took an active part in attempting to get the public to refuse cooperation in the experimental "black-out" at Sheerness in 1935'. Carter and his colleagues concluded that MI5 had not produced 'sufficiently definite evidence' to justify the dismissal of the Sheffield Ordnance workers: 'They are, however, suspicious characters, and a closer watch will be kept upon them.' On this occasion local trade union officials were not consulted and the five dismissals produced a flood of union protests. Bevin, acting both as chairman of the TUC and general secretary of the TGWU, wrote to the Prime Minister, Stanley Baldwin, calling for an independent tribunal. At a private meeting in the House of Commons, Baldwin took at least some of the wind out of Bevin's sails. When Bevin argued that in the case of Alfred Durston 'there appeared to have been a miscarriage of justice,' Baldwin read out to him compromising extracts from Durston's intercepted letters.[80]

Outside the armed services, ports and the defence industry, the Security Service believed that Communist subversion was of declining significance. During the Popular Front era of the mid-1930s, when Moscow favoured participation by Western Communist Parties in anti-Fascist fronts, agents in the CPGB and MASK intercepts provided reassuring evidence of Comintern attempts to persuade the CPGB to moderate its propaganda in the interests of anti-Fascist unity. The Special Branch reported in 1935, for example, after Comintern had sent instructions to tone down attacks on the Royal Family:

The leading members of the Communist Party in London are not at all pleased with these instructions, and they propose taking up the matter with the Communist

International. It is to be emphasised that the recent increase in the sales of the 'Daily Worker' and other communist literature is definitely attributed to MARO's anti-royalist cartoons, and the satirical articles by various writers about the King [George V] and other members of the Royal Family, which have now become a common feature.[81]

The Security Service's most valuable penetration agent in the CPGB was Olga Gray ('Miss "X" '), the twenty-five-year-old daughter of a *Daily Mail* night editor in Manchester recruited by Maxwell Knight as a long-term penetration agent in 1931. Gray was a classic example of Knight's maxim that, when seeking to penetrate any subversive body, the initial approach 'should if humanly possible always be made by the body to the agent, not the agent to the body'. On Knight's instructions, Gray, who was a highly competent secretary, came to London in the autumn of 1931 and made herself available for work in Communist organizations without ever applying for jobs in them. Initially she did not even join the CPGB but simply attended meetings of Comintern front organizations. After doing part-time voluntary typing for the Friends of the Soviet Union, she was asked to do secretarial work for the League Against Imperialism and the Anti-War Movement, where she got to know both Harry Pollitt, the CPGB general secretary, and Percy Glading, an officer of the League who was later found guilty of espionage for the Soviet Union. Only then did Gray join the CPGB. 'She had attained that very enviable position', Knight wrote, 'where an agent becomes a piece of furniture, so to speak: that is, when persons visiting an office do not consciously notice whether the agent is there or not.'[82]

In 1934 Pollitt asked Gray if she would undertake a 'special mission', 'carrying messages from here [Britain] to other countries'. The invitation was repeated by Glading. Gray did not reply immediately. Knight noted approvingly, 'With very becoming self-restraint, Miss "X" did not appear too keen.' She eventually agreed, however, to act as a courier to Indian Communist leaders, taking with her money, instructions and a questionnaire. But her travel arrangements were so incompetently planned that, as Knight noted, without his assistance she might never have reached India:

They were proposing to send her to India during the monsoon period – a time of the year when normal people do not choose to travel to India; they proposed that she should stay there for a matter of only a few weeks, another unusual circumstance; and the Party shewed themselves so out-of-touch with general social matters, that they did not realise that an unaccompanied young English woman travelling to India without some very good reason stood a risk of being turned back when she arrived to India as a suspected prostitute. Our department was faced with a peculiar situation whereby Miss 'X' had to be assisted to devise a cover-story which would meet the requirements necessary, without making it appear to the Party that she had received any expert advice. This was no easy task but eventually a rather thin story of a sea-trip under doctor's orders, combined with an invitation from a relative in India met the case.

Gray found it a gruelling trip. On her return, Knight wrote later: 'As may be readily understood, she was tired, suffering from some nervous strain; and rather disposed to feel that she had done enough. Her health suffered something of a break-down, and she retired from the scene.' Gray still had the confidence, however, of Pollitt and Glading; following a period of convalescence, she was asked to become Pollitt's personal secretary at CPGB headquarters. After a few months working for Pollitt in 1935, she found the strain of her double life too much and told Knight she wanted 'to drop my connection with the Communist Party and return to ordinary life'. Knight did not try to dissuade her, but she agreed, at his request, to keep in touch with Glading and other Party officials. Over lunch with Gray in February 1937, Glading asked her to lease a flat in her name but at the Party's expense and make it available for occasional private meetings for Glading and his associates. Though the lease would be in her name, all expenses would be covered by 'the Party'. 'To be quite frank', wrote Knight later, 'Miss "X" was none too keen to be drawn again into the Party's activities,' but he persuaded her to do so and, with his help, she found a suitable flat in Holland Road. Knight correctly deduced that this time Gray was being asked to assist with espionage.[83]

In April 1937 Glading visited the Holland Road flat with a 'Mr. Peters'. 'Nothing was discussed in front of me', Gray told Knight, 'and I gathered they had merely come so that "Mr. Peters" could meet me. He was obviously a foreigner, but I cannot say what nationality.' 'Peters', she reported, had a distinctive appearance: 6 feet 4 inches tall, with a moustache, 'shiny grey complexion' and gold fillings in his front teeth. Gray also picked up from Glading some details of his career. 'Peters' had been chaplain to an Austrian regiment during the First World War before being taken prisoner by the Russians and joining the Bolsheviks.[84] Gray reported that Glading was also working with another man, who was short and 'rather bumptious in manner': 'Glading dislikes him personally but he has to tolerate him for business reasons.' Three years later the NKVD defector Walter Krivitsky identified 'Peters' and his shorter colleague as Teodor Maly and Arnold Deutsch.[85] It was another quarter of a century, however, before Deutsch was discovered to be the chief recruiter of the Cambridge Five and Maly was identified as one of their controllers.[86]

Deutsch's and Maly's operations in 1937 included running a spy-ring inside the Woolwich Arsenal, where Glading had been employed until his dismissal nine years earlier. As Gray discovered, the flat she had leased was mainly intended as a place to photograph 'very secret' documents 'borrowed' from contacts inside the Arsenal. On 18 October two further Soviet illegals, introduced to Gray as Mr and Mrs 'Stevens', arrived at the flat to test the photographic equipment, which was to be used by Mrs 'Stevens'. Gray reported to Knight that the couple were 'clearly foreigners', that Mrs 'Stevens' spoke to her husband in French, and that she was 'by no means an expert photographer and . . . decidedly nervous about her ability to use the apparatus effectively with only a small amount of practice'. Gray was able to note some of the document titles and serial numbers visible on the photographs, thus making it possible to identify some of the classified material on defence technology smuggled out of the Woolwich Arsenal. After one photographic session Mrs 'Stevens' was followed by Security Service watchers from Holland Road to Hyde Park Corner, where she was seen meeting her husband and a man later identified as George Whomack, a gun examiner at the Woolwich Arsenal.[87] Soon afterwards Glading told Gray that Mr and Mrs 'Stevens' had returned to Moscow because their daughter was ill, but that Mr 'Stevens' was expected to return after Christmas. In the meantime Glading took over the photography.

'Stevens' failed to return to England. In hindsight, the Security Service no doubt wished that it had asked the Special Branch to move in earlier and arrest the couple before they left the country, rather than waiting until it had gathered more evidence about the spy-ring inside the Woolwich Arsenal. Mr 'Stevens' was later identified as the NKVD illegal Willy Brandes, an Eastern European with several aliases who travelled on a Canadian passport.[88] In Brandes's absence Glading felt he had been left in the lurch. On 20 January 1938 he complained to Gray that he had 'stuff parked all over London' and, because of 'Russian dilatoriness', was afraid he would have to borrow money to pay those looking after it. Glading told Gray to 'get the flat ready for something important' and said next day that there was 'urgent photography to be done'. On 21 January, according to a later case summary, Gray 'rang up and stated that Glading had just left her flat and was proceeding to Charing Cross station where at 8.15 p.m. he was to meet a man from whom he would receive the material to be photographed'.[89] Glading was arrested by the Special Branch at Charing Cross Station in the act of receiving classified documents from Albert

Williams, a hitherto unidentified spy at Woolwich Arsenal, who was also arrested. Soon afterwards, the Special Branch arrested two of Glading's other contacts in the Arsenal, George Whomack and Charles Munday. Evidence at their trial at the Old Bailey included a mass of incriminating documents and photographic material found at the homes of both Glading and Williams. In March Glading was given six years' imprisonment, Williams four and Whomack three: all light sentences by the later standards of espionage trials. Munday was acquitted. Olga Gray was congratulated by the judge for her 'extraordinary courage' and 'great service to her country'. After the trial she was invited to lunch at the Ritz by an unidentified colonel (probably Harker), who thanked her and presented her with a £500 cheque. Soon afterwards she left to start a new life in Canada under a new name. In old age she told an interviewer that she felt she had been 'dumped' and looked back nostalgically on the days when she had worked for Knight and 'the adrenalin really flowed'.[90]

With only twenty-six officers at the beginning of 1938, it is unsurprising that the Security Service failed to follow up systematically all the clues generated by the Woolwich Arsenal case. One such clue was a diary entry by Glading for 13 January 1936 which included a list of six names: among them Sirner (also transliterated as 'Sirness') and Steadman. Valentine Vivian, head of SIS counter-intelligence, whose help was sought by the Security Service, identified the two names as a reference to Melita 'Letty' Norwood, née Sirnis, a secretary in the British Non-Ferrous Metals Research Association (BNFMRA).[91] This information was independently confirmed by one of Maxwell Knight's agents in the CPGB, codenamed M2, who reported that Sirnis also used the name Steadman (her suffragette mother's maiden name):

This girl is rather a mysterious character. She is a member of the Hendon Communist Party. She is also a member of the Cricklewood branch of the Association of Women Clerks and Secretaries. She is quite an active person in her trade union but a certain amount of mystery seems to surround her actual Communist Party activities. She has a husband about whom nothing is known except that he looks rather like Charlie Chaplin ... Lettie also has a sister [Gertrude, also a Communist] who is very like her. They are both tall, fair, quite nice looking, and of a rather superior type.[92]

In April 1938 M2 supplied a 'rough sketch' (in fact a good likeness) of Melita Norwood and reported that she was 'of a type definitely suitable for underground activity ... it is also certain that she is doing some especially important Party work': 'Lettie has recently told her [Communist]

Party colleagues in the Association of Women Clerks & Secretaries that she will not be able to undertake any open Party work for some little time.'[93]

Melita Norwood had first come to the attention of the Security Service in 1933 when HOWs on a Communist militant and the Anti-War Council had revealed anti-war letters written by her, which began 'Dear Comrade' and ended 'Yours fraternally'.[94] The Service, however, had no idea that Norwood was recruited as a Soviet agent in 1937. After the Woolwich Arsenal case the NKVD put her 'on ice' for a few months, fearing she had been compromised by her contact with Glading, but, when no action was taken against her, resumed contact with her in May 1938.[95] M2's reports that Norwood was an active Communist engaged in 'especially important' secret work were not treated by the leadership of B Branch with the seriousness they deserved – a lapse which was all the more surprising since Olga Gray had just strikingly demonstrated how effective an agent a good secretary could be. Like Gray, Norwood was good at maintaining her cover. Her boss, G. L. Bailey, assistant director (later director) of BNFMRA, subsequently called her 'the perfect secretary' with a strong 'sense of honour and duty'. Though well aware that Norwood was an enthusiastic socialist and a 'staunch supporter of the "under-dog"', he was 'convinced that she is not a Communist'.[96] Had M2's reports been followed by further investigation, Norwood's career as a spy might well have been nipped in the bud. Instead she became the Soviet Union's longest-serving British agent, supplying Moscow at the end of the war with some of the secrets of the British atomic-bomb project.[97]

Save for Glading and the Woolwich Arsenal spy-ring, most of the Soviet agent network recruited in the mid-1930s survived intact. The network was, paradoxically, saved from more serious damage by Stalin's Terror, which was at its peak in the Soviet Union in 1937 with, at the very least, a third of a million executions and the largest peacetime concentration camps in European history. After Trotskyists, the largest number of alleged 'enemies of the people' to be pursued abroad by the NKVD came from the ranks of its own foreign intelligence service. In the course of 1937 all the Soviet intelligence personnel who had taken part in the Woolwich Arsenal case were recalled to Moscow and were thus out of Britain when the arrests took place in January 1938.

In the paranoid atmosphere of the Terror, Teodor Maly's religious background made him an obvious suspect. He accepted the order to return to Moscow in June 1937 with an idealistic fatalism, telling a colleague, 'I know that as a former priest I haven't got a chance. But I've decided to go there so that nobody can say: "That priest might have been a real spy after all."' Arnold Deutsch's Jewish origins and unorthodox early career made him too an obvious suspect. He seems to have been saved by the Centre's mistaken belief that he had been betrayed by another alleged traitor in the NKVD and was thus a victim rather than an accomplice of the 'enemies of the people'. Deutsch was recalled to Moscow in November 1937.[98] The recall of the Brandes couple in the same month was probably also related to the paranoia of the Terror rather than to the alleged illness of their daughter.

Had Deutsch remained in Britain, it is quite likely that he, like Mr and Mrs Brandes, would have been identified and followed by the Security Service's Observation section. Though an inspirational recruiter and agent-runner, Deutsch took some unusual risks and seemed unconcerned that some of his agents were well aware that their friends had also been recruited. The flight to Moscow of two of the Cambridge Five, Donald Maclean and Guy Burgess, in 1951 thus helped to compromise the other three.[99] Deutsch showed a similar disregard for security early in 1936 by taking up residence in Lawn Road Flats, Hampstead, where a number of other tenants also had links with Soviet intelligence.[100] In June 1937 Deutsch reported to a more senior NKVD officer that one of his agents, Edith Tudor-Hart, had lost a diary with important operational information which threatened to compromise his agent network.[101] The blame, however, may well have attached to Deutsch himself. When later questioned by a Security Service officer in Vienna, Deutsch's widow 'replied without hesitation that her husband had once lost a notebook with addresses in it. He was worried about it and thought that he had left it in a taxi.'[102] Had Deutsch not been recalled from Britain, his sometimes lackadaisical tradecraft might well have led to his identification by the Security Service. And had the Service's Observation section followed him either to Lawn Road Flats or to a meeting with one of his agents, his whole network might have begun to crumble.

Following the recall of their illegal case officers during 1937, the Five sometimes struggled over the next two years to remain in contact with the Centre but did not lose their commitment. In April 1938 the Centre handed over the running of its main British agents to the new head of the legal residency, Grigori Grafpen, who, unlike the illegals, was protected by diplomatic cover.[103] In December, however, Grafpen, like many other NKVD officers around the world, fell victim to the paranoia of the Terror, was recalled to Moscow and later despatched to the gulag. The only remaining NKVD officer in London, Anatoli Gorsky, was poorly briefed even about the residency's most important agents.[104]

Kell confidently declared at a liaison meeting with the Deuxième Bureau, France's pre-war foreign intelligence service, in January 1939 that '[Soviet] activity in England is non-existent, in terms of both intelligence and political subversion.'[105] Though close to the truth so far as the operations of the legal residency in the Soviet embassy at Kensington Palace Gardens were concerned, it was none the less the most woefully misjudged assessment of the threat from Soviet espionage that Kell had ever produced. Donald Maclean, thus far the most productive of the Cambridge Five, was four months into his first foreign posting at the Paris embassy, in the early stages of a diplomatic career which some thought might take him to the top of his profession. In December 1938 Guy Burgess reported to the Centre, probably via Paris, that he had joined Section D of SIS, founded earlier in the year to devise dirty tricks ranging from sabotage to psychological warfare. He thus became the first foreign agent to become a member of a twentieth-century British intelligence agency.[106] Despite its travails, the future for Soviet espionage in Britain at the outbreak of war was brighter than it had ever been before.

3

British Fascism and the Nazi Threat

In the aftermath of the First World War, the newly established German Weimar Republic ranked much lower in MI5's priorities than Soviet Russia and the Communist International. With an army limited by the Versailles Treaty to 100,000 men, a demilitarized Rhineland, chronic political instability and raging inflation, Weimar posed no current threat to British security. Versailles also forbade Germany to engage in espionage. The main interwar German intelligence agency, the Abwehr ('defence'), was founded in 1920 as a counter-espionage service. Since other countries continued to spy on Germany, the Abwehr reasonably regarded the prohibition on German espionage, which it later disregarded during the Nazi era, as hypocritical.[1] In Britain there were regular denunciations in the Commons during the 1920s of the activities of foreign, mostly Soviet, intelligence services, but successive governments upheld the convention (not abandoned until 1992) that there should be no mention whatever of SIS. In 1927 Arthur Ponsonby, former junior Foreign Office minister during the first MacDonald government, attacked 'the hypocrisy which pretends that we are so pure': 'The Secret Service [SIS] is supposed to be something we do not talk about in this House ... I do not see why I should not talk about it. It is about time we did say something about the Secret Service.'[2] Such parliamentary outbursts were very rare.

Though German espionage posed little threat after the First World War, MI5 had little doubt that, in any future war, it would play a major role. In the early 1920s the former head of the military Nachrichtendienst, Walter Nicolai, publicly defended the wartime achievements of German intelligence, arguing – like many other extremists in the Weimar Republic – that Germany had been 'betrayed' but not defeated in 1918.[3] He continued to insist that Germany's recovery as a great power would require it to defy Versailles and set up a strong peacetime intelligence service, which would be vital in time of war.[4] MI5's thinking on German intelligence was also strongly influenced by captured German war documents and interviews with POWs, which formed the basis for a remarkable report in 1922 by Kell's deputy, Holt-Wilson. The experience of 'total' war from 1914 to 1918, argued Holt-Wilson, had shown that for the first time states were able to mobilize all their resources against their enemies. In peacetime also authoritarian states would henceforth be able to deploy a much wider range of covert resources to undermine their opponents.[5]

There is still no detailed history of the illicit resumption of German espionage under the Weimar Republic.[6] Despite its chronic lack of resources in the 1920s, MI5 did, however, discover some of the subterfuges used by Weimar to circumvent the ban on foreign intelligence-gathering. Elements of the disbanded intelligence services of the Kaiser's Germany – the military Nachrichtendienst and the naval Nachrichten-Abteilung – were subsumed into official German commercial organizations, notably the Deutsche Überseedienst (German Overseas Service), where they continued to function as unofficial espionage agencies.[7] MI5's main leads to German espionage in the 1920s and early 1930s seem to have come from SIS. By 1922 SIS had a source in the Deutsche Überseedienst, codenamed A.14, who claimed to be responsible for paying its agents. A.14 stated that eighty-three full-time German 'organizing agents' were operating in Britain in 1922, with 188 part-time agents. He provided details of nine of the most important agents in Britain, some of whom were identified by MI5.[8] However, in 1923 SIS assessed A.14 as unreliable, 'self-glorifying' and suffering from 'acute megalomania', and broke contact with him.[9] A few years later SIS achieved a far more successful penetration of the Deutsche Überseedienst by recruiting a translator and administrative assistant who, it told MI5, was one of its 'most trusted employees'. In 1927 the agent provided SIS with a list of more than seventy individuals involved with German espionage in Britain.[10] MI5 informed SIS, probably with some pride, that over half the seventy names on the list were already known to it.[11] Unfortunately, MI5 records on subsequent surveillance of the Überseedienst espionage network do not survive. In 1931 SIS recruited another 'extremely well placed source' (about whose identity it gave few clues to the Security Service) who supplied copies of questionnaires detailing German naval and military intelligence requirements on scientific and technical developments in British defence industry: among them aircraft construction; river mines; listening apparatus; echo sound engineering; anti-aircraft armaments; torpedoes; and the Vickers cemented steel works.[12] MI5 failed, however, to identify the German naval intelligence network, the innocuously named Etappe Dienst (Zone Service), which operated in Britain and around the world during the 1920s and the 1930s, using members of

German steamship companies and other businesses to collect a wide range of intelligence (with, at least in Britain, probably only moderate success).[13] Like Germany's wartime agents, those detected between the wars were not high-flyers and did not begin to compare in quality with the best of those recruited by Soviet intelligence.

Until 1933, MI5 paid 'practically no attention' to Nazism – nor did Whitehall expect that it should.[14] The rise to power of the forty-three-year-old fanatic Adolf Hitler as chancellor of a coalition government on 30 January 1933 (in retrospect one of the turning points of modern history) rang few alarm bells either in the Security Service or in most of Whitehall. Next day *The Times* commented: 'That Herr Hitler, who leads the strongest party in the Reichstag and obtained almost one third of the more than 35 million votes in the last election, should be given the chance of showing that he is something more than an orator and an agitator was always desirable . . .'[15] The Hitler regime first showed itself in its true colours after the burning of the Reichstag on 27 February by a former Dutch Communist, Marinus van der Lubbe. Though van der Lubbe almost certainly acted alone, the entire Nazi leadership and many others convinced themselves that the fire had been intended as the signal for a Communist insurrection. Hermann Göring, then Prussian Interior Minister and police chief, issued a press statement claiming that documents seized during a police raid on German Communist Party (KPD) headquarters a few days earlier contained plans (which were never published) for attacks on public buildings and the assassination of leading politicians. An emergency decree 'For the Protection of People and State' suspended indefinitely the personal liberties enshrined in the Weimar constitution, among them freedom of speech, of association and of the press. A brutal round-up followed of Communists, Social Democrats, trade unionists and left-wing intellectuals, who were dragged into the cellars of local SA and SS units, brutally beaten and sometimes tortured. An election victory on 5 March gave Hitler and his nationalist allies the majority he needed (once Communist deputies had been excluded) to establish his dictatorship. Hitler's biographer Ian Kershaw concludes that, within Germany, 'The violence and repression were widely popular.'[16]

Even in Britain, except on the left, protests at Nazi brutality were relatively muted. *The Times* leader-writer commented on 22 March: 'However much foreign friends of the country may deplore the cruelties inflicted by German upon German . . . all that is primarily a matter for Germany herself . . . In all of this there is nothing yet to indicate that the new Chancellor intends to be immoderate in his foreign policy.'[17] Hitler in fact intended to be more immoderate in his foreign policy than any other European of the twentieth century, though he no longer referred publicly to the huge ambitions for 'living space' in Eastern Europe he had set out in *Mein Kampf*. In March 1933, however, the Security Service was no more alarmed than *The Times*. Its main immediate response to Hitler's rise to power was to accept, with no visible soul-searching, an invitation from Berlin to discuss the haul of material on Comintern operations captured during the raid on KPD headquarters.[18] On 22 March the SS opened its first, infamous concentration camp at a disused powder-mill in a suburb of Dachau, about 12 miles from Munich. A week later Guy Liddell, a fluent German-speaker, arrived in Berlin 'to establish contact with the German Political Police' and seek access to the Comintern documents. SIS volunteered to pay half the expenses of Liddell's visit as well as providing assistance from the head of its Berlin station, Frank Foley.[19]

Liddell's host, during his ten days in Berlin, was Hitler's Harvard-educated foreign-press liaison officer, Ernst 'Putzi' Hanfstaengel, whom Liddell found 'on the whole an extremely likeable person' but 'quite unbalanced' about both Jews and Communists: 'He is under the erroneous impression that Communism is a movement controlled by the Jews.' Liddell was deeply sceptical about Nazi claims that, thanks to tough action by the new regime, 'a serious Communist outbreak had just been averted':

In fact all our evidence goes to show that, although the German Communist Party may have contemplated a peaceful street demonstration which might have provoked violent counter-demonstrations by the Nazis, Moscow had issued definite instructions that no overt act was to be committed which could in any way lead to the wholesale repression of the Party.

Liddell was equally unconvinced by 'a map which purported to show that International Jewry was being controlled from London', and took an instant dislike to the thirty-three-year-old head of the political police (soon to become the Gestapo), Rudolf Diels:[20]

His face is scarred from the sword duels of his student days. His jet black hair, slit eyes and sallow complexion give him a rather Chinese appearance. Although he had an unpleasant personality he was extremely polite and later when he came round on a tour of inspection gave orders to all present that I was to be given every possible facility.

The few documents from KPD headquarters seen by Liddell, however, were deeply disappointing: 'Most of the raids were carried out by the Sturm Abteilung [SA], who just threw the documents into lorries and then dumped them in disorder in some large rooms.' Ironically therefore Liddell concentrated instead on records of a Soviet front organization, the League Against Imperialism (LAI), which had been captured during a police raid over a year before Hitler came to power and, unlike those seized from KPD headquarters, had been carefully filed away. Liddell found further evidence in these files both of Soviet funding for the LAI and of Comintern instructions to Indian Communists.[21]

Liddell left Berlin with no illusions about the brutality of the Nazi regime. 'A number of Jews, Communists and even Social Democrats', he reported, 'have undoubtedly been submitted to every kind of outrage and this was still going on at the time of my departure.' But Liddell wrongly believed that the current brutality was likely to prove a passing phase, and that the Comintern remained a more serious problem than the Nazi regime:

In their present mood, the German police are extremely ready to help us in any way they can. It is, however, essential, that constant personal contact should be maintained ... so that when the present rather hysterical atmosphere of sentiment and brutality dies down, the personal relations established will outweigh any forms of bureaucracy which would normally place restrictions on a free interchange of information.

The most disturbing part of Liddell's report on his visit to Berlin is a prejudiced appendix on 'The Anti-Jewish Movement' which, while dismissing Nazi anti-Semitic conspiracy theories, claimed that there was a serious basis for claims that official corruption during the Weimar Republic was due chiefly to the Jews:

There have undoubtedly been some very serious cases of corruption in Government institutions where the Jews had a firm foothold. For the last ten years it has been extremely noticeable that access to the chief of any department was only possible through the intermediary of a Jew. It was the Jew who did most of the talking and in whose hands the working out of any scheme was ultimately left.[22]

Liddell's denunciation of German-Jewish corruption did not derive from a more general anti-Semitism. It was at his proposal that Victor Rothschild was later invited to join the wartime Security Service.[23] His memorandum was none the less the lowest point in a distinguished career.

The first Security Service officer to grasp the seriousness of the Nazi threat was John 'Jack' Curry, who joined B Branch in 1934 after a quarter of a century in the Indian police.[24] Curry was also the first B Branch officer to pay serious attention to the British Union of Fascists (BUF), founded in 1932 by the political maverick, fencing champion and former Labour minister Sir Oswald Mosley, who modelled the BUF black-shirt uniform on his fencing tunic. Curry joined Mosley's January Club, led by two former Indian army officers, which organized dinner parties for those thought likely to be receptive to Fascist ideas and was believed to be targeting other retired officers from the armed services. After a series of tedious dinners, Curry concluded that the Club had little appeal to former servicemen and was not worth further investigation.[25]

The Security Service's main source of intelligence on the BUF came from Maxwell Knight's contacts and agents inside the movement, some of whom dated back to his earlier membership of the British Fascisti.[26] His early reports, however, were somewhat distorted by his belief in the BUF's genuine, if wrong-headed, patriotism. Until the spring of 1934 he refused to believe reports from Rome that the BUF was receiving secret subsidies from Mussolini.[27] On 13 April Knight admitted his mistake. He reported that before Mosley's visit to Italy in March the BUF had been in dire financial straits with talk of Mosley having to sell his late wife's jewels. Since his return from Italy, however, BUF finances had suddenly returned to health. Knight's sources within the BUF reported that it had an active membership of 35,000 to 40,000.[28] A majority, however, probably did no more than pay subscriptions and purchase *Blackshirt* and other BUF publications. The Security Service later estimated the BUF's *active* membership, at its peak in 1934, at only about 10,000.[29]

The evidence of foreign funding for the BUF, combined with street fighting between black-shirted Fascists and Communists, chiefly in the East End of London, prompted Kell to prepare his first full-scale report for the Home Office and other government departments on 'The Fascist Movement in the United Kingdom'. Early in May 1934 he wrote to chief constables in England, Scotland and Wales asking them to supply details at regular intervals of BUF membership, together with 'their opinion as to the importance to be attached to this movement in their areas'. From their replies he concluded that 'the Fascists have been more active and successful in the industrial areas and that their achievements in the majority of the Counties may be regarded as negligible'. He reported to the Home Office that the prospect of a Fascist coup was still far away, but detected 'various tendencies' which were 'bringing Sir Oswald Mosley and his followers more to the front of the stage'. Their propaganda was 'extremely clever'.[30] The Fascist threat, such as it was, appeared to reach its peak at the Olympia rally in June 1934, extravagantly proclaimed beforehand by the BUF as 'a landmark, not only in the history of fascism, but also in the history of Britain'. Most of the choreography for the rally was borrowed from Hitler and Mussolini. Mosley marched to the platform lit by a spotlight through a forest of Union Jacks and BUF banners while uniformed Blackshirts gave the Fascist salute and chanted 'Hail Mosley!' Fights between hecklers and Fascist stewards started almost as soon as Mosley began to speak, and continued intermittently for the next two hours. 'The Blackshirt spirit', declared Mosley afterwards, 'triumphed at Olympia. It smashed the biggest organised attempt ever made in this country to wreck a meeting by Red violence.' The Communist *Daily Worker* also claimed victory: 'The great Olympia counter-demonstration of the workers against Blackshirts stands out as an important landmark in the struggle against Fascism in this country.'[31] Though virtuously disclaiming all responsibility for the violence, both the BUF and the CPGB, in MI5's view, used 'illegal and violent methods': 'In fact, both . . . were delighted with the results of Olympia.'[32]

Despite the evidence of foreign Fascist funding for the BUF, the Home Secretary, Sir John Gilmour, refused a Security Service application for an HOW on Mosley,[33] apparently in the belief that he remained a staunch patriot who posed no threat to national security. His successor, Sir John Simon, continued to refuse an HOW even when, two years later, Mosley married his second wife, the former Diana Mitford, in a private ceremony attended by Hitler in Goebbels's drawing room. Hitler gave Diana a signed photograph in an eagle-topped silver frame which she kept in the marital bedroom.[34] MI5 later concluded that 'Before the outbreak of war Lady Mosley was the principal channel of communication with Hitler. Mosley himself has admitted she had frequent interviews with the Fuhrer.'[35] But until their internment in 1940 both, remarkably, were not subject to HOWs, though copies of letters to and from them turned up in the correspondence of other, less well-connected Fascists on whom MI5 did obtain HOWs.

After the Olympia rally of June 1934 the cabinet briefly turned its attention to ways of preventing further rallies in which Fascists paraded in political uniforms. But the problems of framing new legislation to prevent such rallies were complicated by the difficulty of defining what 'political uniforms' were. Possibly reassured by Security Service reports, the cabinet gradually lost its sense of urgency. Kell reported to the Home Office in October 1934:

It is becoming increasingly clear that at Olympia Mosley suffered a check which is likely to prove decisive. He suffered it, not at the hands of the Communists who staged the provocations and now claim the victory, but at the hands of Conservative MPs, the Conservative Press and all those organs of public opinion which made him abandon the policy of using his 'Defence Force' to overwhelm interrupters.

The BUF had been publicly disowned a month after Olympia by the press baron Lord Rothermere, previously its most prominent Conservative supporter. Mosley himself was said by MI5 to be in a state of 'acute depression' and the deputy leader of the BUF, Dr Robert Forgan, who later left the movement, was reported 'to have doubts as to his leader's sanity'.[36] MI5 reported in March 1935 that, according to a trustworthy source, Fascist 'cells' had been formed in 'various branches of the Civil Service'. But the general tenor of Kell's intelligence continued to be reassuring. Reports to MI5 from chief constables showed that, in all major cities except Manchester, BUF membership had declined, branches had closed, sales of the *Blackshirt* had dropped and enthusiasm had cooled.[37] Aware of the BUF's lack of electoral appeal (though unwilling to accept that violence at its rallies had damaged its reputation), Mosley fielded no candidates at the November 1935 general election. The landslide victory of the National Government underlined the BUF's increasing irrelevance in British politics.

Mussolini's subsidies did little or nothing to arrest the steady decline of the BUF during the two years after the Olympia rally. A Nazi ideologue of Scottish extraction, Colin Ross, visited England in April 1936 to report on the state of the British Fascists. According to the Special Branch, which kept him under close surveillance, Ross concluded that the BUF had 'a fine policy and a splendid leader, but absolutely no organisation'. There were signs, none the less, of growing German influence among the Blackshirts. In July, despite Hitler's unwillingness to provide secret funding, the BUF changed its full title to the British Union of Fascists and National Socialists. 'Mosley', MI5 noted, 'has also shown a closer approach to the German spirit in his more pronounced attacks on the Jews during recent months'.[38] Kell reported to the Home Office in July 1936 that the monthly Italian subsidies had been cut from £3,000 to £1,000, and that the BUF was in 'general decline':

It is true that in the East End Fascist speakers have had a better welcome than elsewhere, but there is a good deal of anti-semitic feeling there and anti-semitic speeches are therefore welcome. There does not seem to be any reason for believing that public opinion in the East End is becoming seriously pro-Fascist.[39]

The Security Service emphasized the growing influence within the BUF of the pro-Nazi William Joyce who, it reported, had greater influence on militant Blackshirts than Mosley himself. It continued for several years to rely on a rather optimistic appreciation of Joyce by Knight (identified in reports to the Home Office only as 'someone who knows him well'), written in September 1934, which claimed that, though Joyce was 'a rabid anti-Catholic' and 'a fanatical anti-Semite' with 'a mental balance . . . not equal to his intellectual capacity', it was unlikely that anything 'could occur to shake his basic patriotism'.[40] In fact Joyce was dismissed from the BUF in 1937, formed the stridently pro-Nazi (but small) British National Socialist League, took German citizenship in 1940 and became infamous as 'Lord Haw-Haw', broadcasting Nazi propaganda to wartime Britain.

On 4 October 1936 the attempt by four columns of Blackshirts to march to meetings in Shoreditch, Stepney, Bethnal Green and Limehouse led to the 'battle of Cable Street' when anti-Fascists threw up a barricade in the Blackshirts' path, fought with police and forced Mosley to divert his march along the Embankment. The day produced, according to the Special Branch, 'undoubtedly the largest anti-Fascist demonstration yet seen in London'. It also led the government to recover the sense of urgency it had lost after the Olympia rally two years before. Though still unwilling to authorize an HOW on Mosley, Sir John Simon told the cabinet: 'There cannot be the slightest doubt that the Fascist campaign . . . is stimulating the Communist movement so that the danger of a serious clash is growing.' A Public Order Bill prohibiting political uniforms and empowering the police to forbid political processions was rushed through parliament and came into effect on 1 January 1937.[41]

The battle of Cable Street, condemned by the BUF as 'the first occasion on which the British Government has surrendered to Red Terror', gave Mosley just the publicity he was looking for. The Security Service reported that at meetings organized by Mosley in the East End immediately afterwards 'the display of pro-Fascist sentiments on the streets surprised a number of experienced observers.' But the BUF resurgence was short lived. At the end of November 1936 MI5 put BUF membership at 'a maximum of 6,500 active and 9,000 non-active members'; the Special Branch put it rather higher, and probably less accurately, at a total of nearly 20,000.[42] With the banning of the Blackshirts the BUF dwindled into peacetime insignificance.[43] The Security Service, however, regarded it as a potential wartime threat. Holt-Wilson drafted an amendment to the Government War Book (a classified compendium of legislation, regulations and other measures to be introduced in wartime) which was intended to ensure that British citizens should not, as in the First World War, be exempt from internment. In July 1937 the Committee of Imperial Defence approved the terms of a draft Bill providing for 'the detention of persons whose detention appears to the Secretary of State to be expedient in the interests of the public safety or the defence of the Realm', so laying the groundwork for the internment of Mosley and many of his followers three years later.[44]

By the time the British Blackshirts lost their shirts, Germany had, for the first time since the First World War, replaced Soviet Russia as the main target of British foreign intelligence. The Soviet menace slipped into fourth place in the SIS 'Order of Priorities' behind the more important threats to British interests from Germany, Italy and Japan.[45] German rearmament also produced a modest revival of British government interest in its intelligence services. On 16 March 1935, in defiance of the Versailles Treaty, Hitler announced the introduction of conscription. On the 25th he made the exaggerated boast that the Luftwaffe had already 'reached parity' with the RAF. An investigation by the Ministerial Committee on Defence Policy and Requirements discovered a serious shortage of intelligence on the Luftwaffe and 'brought out very clearly the need for increased financial provision for Secret Service funds'. Without debate in parliament the Secret Vote was raised from £180,000 in 1935 to £250,000 (with a supplementary vote of £100,000) in 1936, to £350,000 in 1937, to £450,000 in 1938 and to £500,000 in 1939.[46]

The most committed Whitehall supporter of both MI5 and SIS was Sir Robert Vansittart, permanent under secretary at the Foreign Office from 1930 to early 1938. 'Van' was much more interested in intelligence than his political masters were. Unlike Simon and Sir Nevile Henderson, the British ambassador in Berlin, he 'felt that we indulged in it all too little',[47] dined regularly with Quex Sinclair,[48] was also in (less frequent) touch with Kell,[49] and built up what became known as his own 'private detective agency' collecting German intelligence.[50] More than any other Whitehall mandarin, Van stood for rearmament and opposition to appeasement. His suspicions of Germany were of long standing. As a student in Germany, he had been challenged to, but succeeded in declining, a duel. A generation later he was among the first in Whitehall to forecast, in May 1933, that 'The present regime in Germany will, on past and present form, loose off another European war just so soon as it feels strong enough ... We are considering very crude people, who have few ideas in their noddles but brute force and militarism.'[51] Van later described his German sources as 'a few brave men' who 'knew that I realised a war to be nearing': 'They thought that, if they fed me with sufficient evidence, I might have influence enough to arouse our Government and so stop it. Of course they were wrong, but we tried.'[52]

With Vansittart's encouragement, the Security Service began for the first time to develop sources within the German embassy.[53] By far the most important was the aristocratic diplomat Wolfgang zu Putlitz, proud of the fact that his family had owned the castle at Putlitz in Brandenburg since the twelfth century. Putlitz's first experience of Britain, on arriving to learn English in 1924 to prepare for a diplomatic career, was mixed. Though he had a letter of introduction to Lady Redesdale (mother of the Mitford sisters), when he went to call on her the door was shut in his face.[54] Putlitz did, however, become close friends with a German journalist in London, Jona Ustinov, who was recruited as an MI5 agent (codenamed U35) early in 1935,[55] six months after Putlitz (then aged thirty-five) was posted to the German embassy in London. Both men were committed anti-Nazis, though Putlitz later had to join the Party in order to keep his job. Putlitz (code-named PADGHAM by the Security Service) later recalled that he met Ustinov every fortnight:

I would unburden myself of all the dirty schemes and secrets which I encountered as part of my daily routine at the Embassy. By this means I was able to lighten my conscience by the feeling that I was really helping to damage the Nazi cause for I knew [Ustinov] was in touch with Vansittart, who could use these facts to influence British policy.[56]

Vansittart put Kell in touch with Ustinov, doubtless intending the Security Service to use him as its point of contact with Putlitz.[57] Ironically, in view of the fact that Van listed homosexuality (along with Communism and 'Deutschism') as one of his three pet hates,[58] Putlitz was gay; his partner, Willy Schneider, also acted as his valet.[59]

Jona Ustinov strongly disliked his given name and, rather oddly, much preferred the unappealing nickname 'Klop' (Russian for 'bedbug'). In his twenties his build was so slight that his Russian-born wife, the artist and designer Nadia Benois, called him by the diminutive 'Klopic' ('little bed bug'); as he became more portly in appearance, she reverted to 'Klop'.[60] Ustinov's first case officer, Jack Curry, had his portrait painted by Nadia.[61] Dick White, who later succeeded Curry as case officer, called Klop Ustinov the 'best and most ingenious operator I had the honour to work with'.[62] While running Ustinov, Curry rarely saw Vansittart but had frequent contact with two high-flying young diplomats, William Strang and Gladwyn Jebb, who briefed him on foreign policy. As a result, Curry became the first Security Service officer to have regular access to British diplomatic documents – in particular despatches from the ambassadors in Berlin and Rome: 'This gave me an inside view of the situation created in Europe by Hitler and the Nazi leaders, and it enabled me to indicate to [Klop] questions on which it was desirable for Putlitz to develop sources of information.' For several years, Curry sent regular reports to Vansittart on the information supplied by Putlitz and other sources in the German embassy.[63]

As well as providing important intelligence on German foreign policy, Putlitz, and other Security Service sources in the German embassy, supplied information on the British section of the Auslands Organisation, the association of Nazi Party members living abroad. An application by the Security Service for an HOW on the London office of the Auslands Organisation had been turned down in January 1934. The permanent under secretary at the Home Office, Sir Russell Scott, told Kell that 'unless we [MI5] discovered in the ordinary course of our work any case of subversive propaganda or other inimical steps against the interests of this country we were to leave them alone.'[64] Kell himself was initially reluctant to become involved in the investigation of the Auslands Organisation. 'Perhaps', thought Curry, 'he felt that in these matters he was getting into deeper waters than those which surrounded the simpler issue of dealing with espionage by a foreign power and its agents.' The Director was finally persuaded by Vansittart and B Branch.[65] By 1935 the Security Service had identified 288 Nazi Party members resident in Britain, as well as 870 Italian Fascists (members of the Fasci all'Estero).[66] In May 1936 MI5 called a meeting attended by representatives from the Home Office, Foreign Office, Colonial Office, SIS and several other government departments, at which it laid out its concerns about the Auslands Organisation:

Since the Nazi machine has unprecedented power over the individual it can direct the energies of every member of the Party in any desired direction. If, as at present, the Führer desires friendship [with Britain] every man is adjured to act and speak with that in view. We cannot lose sight of the fact that in certain eventualities the whole energy of the machine could be directed in the reverse direction. It is, for instance, a ready-made instrument for intelligence, espionage, and ultimately for sabotage.[67]

Though Security Service concerns about the Auslands Organisation were shared by Winston Churchill, who called it the 'Nazitern', they made little impact on Whitehall.[68] MI5's repeated calls for it to be banned were rejected.[69] Curry, however, was instructed to prepare detailed plans for the arrest of all important members of the organization 'if and when the Home Secretary decided that this should be done'. Copies of the Security Service card index of Auslands Organisation members were supplied to police forces, with instructions to arrest them on receipt of telegrams containing the codeword ANSABONA (constructed by Curry from the phrase 'Anti Sabotage Nazis'). The telegrams were not sent until the organization was officially banned on the outbreak of war.[70]

Among the Auslands Organisation reports to Berlin supplied by Putlitz which had the greatest impact on Curry was one correctly predicting that when Hitler ordered German troops into the Rhineland in March 1936, in contravention of Versailles (as well as of the Locarno Treaty signed by Weimar Germany), Britain would take no military action. The German ambassador in London, Leopold von Hoesch, made the opposite prediction and was condemned for his timidity by Hitler, who praised the more clear-sighted vision of London Nazis. In the aftermath of the remilitarization of the Rhineland, greeted by cheering German crowds and the pealing of church bells, Curry – strongly influenced by warnings from Putlitz trans-mitted by Klop – 'began to feel that there was danger of another great war'.[71] In June 1936, Kell submitted to the Committee of Imperial Defence a 'Memorandum on the possibilities of sabotage by the organisations set up in British countries by the totalitarian governments of Germany and Italy', drafted by Curry, which may well have been the first document circulated in Whitehall to warn that negotiations with Hitler were likely to achieve nothing and that the vast territorial ambitions set out in *Mein Kampf*, even if at variance with his current rhetoric, must be taken seriously as a guide to his future conduct:

No reliance can be placed on any treaty which has been signed, or may be signed, by Germany or Italy; any obligation which they have undertaken is liable to be repudiated without warning if it stands in the way of what their dictators consider at any moment to be the vital interests of their nations . . . If Hitler is the lord of Germany with a power for which history offers few examples, the question of the exact significance to be attributed to his book *Mein Kampf* has some bearing on his attitude to the supreme direction of foreign-policy-cum-military-strategy or Wehrpolitik . . . It is emphatically not a case of irresponsible utterances which have been discarded by a statesman on obtaining power.[72]

Putlitz insisted, and B Branch believed, that the only way to deal with Hitler was to stand firm. Appeasement would not work.[73]

By the time Hoesch died suddenly in April 1936, Hitler had probably already decided to replace him as German ambassador with the former wine and spirits trader Joachim von Ribbentrop, who arrived in London in August. Ribbentrop (the 'von' was fraudulent) compensated for his crude grasp of international relations by skilful sycophancy in telling Hitler what he wanted to hear. He became better known in London for a series of social gaffes which led *Punch* magazine to refer to him as 'Von Bricken-drop'. Putlitz, however, reported that Hitler continued to call him 'a foreign policy genius' (*ein aussenpolitisches Genie*).[74] By a curious coincidence, Klop Ustinov's son, Peter, spent the school year 1936–7 in the same class at Westminster School as the son of Ribbentrop, sitting at the next desk.

Peter Ustinov's first success as a budding journalist was to earn seven shillings and sixpence from the *Evening Standard* for his lurid account of an artwork by the young Ribbentrop devoted to an enthusiastic depiction of warfare, murder and mayhem.[75]

Putlitz reported that Ribbentrop's arrival transformed the previously staid atmosphere of the London embassy into 'a complete madhouse'. Staff discovered that their desks were being regularly searched at night by SS men whom the new ambassador had brought to London. After an early meeting with the Prime Minister, Stanley Baldwin, Ribbentrop announced contemptuously that 'the old fool does not know what he is talking about.' In September 1936 Putlitz reported that Ribbentrop and his staff regarded a German war with Russia as being 'as certain as the Amen in church', and were confident that Britain would not lift a finger when Hitler began his invasion. Ribbentrop placed high hopes in King Edward VIII, who had come to the throne at the beginning of the year. Because of his ignorance of the British political system, he greatly exaggerated the King's ability to influence relations with Germany. As the abdication crisis loomed, Putlitz reported that Ribbentrop was trying to send the King a message via the pro-German Lord Clive that the 'German people stood behind him in his struggle.' 'King Edward must fight,' Ribbentrop told his staff, 'and you will see, Gentlemen, that he is going to win the battle against the plotters!' After the abdication in December 1936, Ribbentrop blamed 'the machinations of dark Bolshevist powers against the Führer-will of the young King', and informed his staff: 'I shall report all further details orally to my Führer.' Exasperated at the ambassador's obsession with applying conspiracy theories to British politics, Putlitz told Ustinov: 'We are absolutely power-less in the face of this nonsense!'[76]

In May 1937, when Neville Chamberlain succeeded Baldwin as prime minister, Ribbentrop was once again briefly optimistic. According to Putlitz: 'He regarded Mr Chamberlain as pro-German and said he would be his own Foreign Minister. While he would not dismiss [the Foreign Secretary] Mr Eden he would deprive him of his influence at the Foreign Office. Mr Eden was regarded as an enemy of Germany.' Chamberlain did indeed dominate the making of British foreign policy. Eden eventually resigned in February 1938, exasperated by the Prime Minister's interference in diplomatic business, and was succeeded as foreign secretary by Lord Halifax. Chamberlain, however, initially proved less accommodating towards Germany than Ribbentrop had forecast. During the later months of 1937 Ribbentrop struck Putlitz as increasingly anti-British and anxious to leave London. Early in 1938 Putlitz reported that Hitler, probably prompted by Ribbentrop, had lifted an earlier moratorium on German espionage in Britain. (The moratorium had in fact been lifted in the previous year.)[77] The only way to deal with the English, Ribbentrop maintained, was to give them 'a kick in the behind' (*ein Tritt in den Hintern*).[78]

In February 1938 Hitler made Ribbentrop his foreign minister, a post he retained for the remainder of the Third Reich. Ustinov summed up Putlitz's assessment as follows:

The Army will in future be the obedient instrument of Nazi foreign policy. Under Ribbentrop this foreign policy will be an aggressive, forward policy. Its first aim – Austria – has been partly achieved . . . Austria falls to [Hitler] like a ripe fruit. After consolidating the position in Austria the next step will be against Czechoslovakia.

Putlitz's constant refrain during 1938 was that '. . . Britain was letting the trump cards fall out of her hands. If she had adopted, or even now adopted, a firm attitude and threatened war, Hitler would not succeed in this kind of bluff. The German army was not yet ready for a major war.'[79] When the Wehrmacht crossed into Austria on 12 March, it left in its wake a trail of broken-down vehicles ill prepared even for an unopposed invasion. The probability is that it would also have proved ill prepared for a war over Czechoslovakia in the following autumn.

In May 1938 Putlitz left London and was posted to the German embassy in The Hague. Since the Security Service had no authority to run agents abroad, he was transferred by mutual agreement to SIS. SIS agreed, however, that Putlitz had built up such a close relationship with Klop Ustinov that 'there could be no question of substituting any other intermediary.' During a visit to London by the SIS head of station in The Hague, Major Richard Stevens, Curry was instructed to introduce him to Ustinov. Curry thought it likely that Stevens had been identified as an SIS officer by the German embassy in The Hague and that he might therefore be shadowed by SS security officers based in the London embassy. While going by taxi with Stevens to meet Ustinov at his London flat, Curry looked out of the rear window:

As we drove off a man jumped into a taxi on the rank immediately behind us and followed us closely as far as the rear of St George's Hospital. Here I instructed our driver to make two or three quick turns into side streets and was relieved to see that the taxi following us became entangled in the traffic at one of these corners. Although he appeared to make special efforts to disentangle himself he failed to do so.

After a long detour, making further checks for surveillance en route, Curry and Stevens eventually reached Ustinov's flat. Though Curry had no proof that their would-be pursuer was from the German embassy,[80] his suspicions that the Germans had identified Stevens as the head of the SIS station at The Hague were well founded. It was later discovered that they had also identified both of Stevens's two predecessors, Major H. E. Dalton and Major 'Monty' Chidson.[81] SIS in The Hague had a troubled history. Dalton had committed suicide in 1936 after embezzling official funds.[82] Abwehr penetration of the SIS station was to bring Putlitz's career as a British informant to an abrupt end soon after the outbreak of war.[83] Until then he continued to provide Klop Ustinov with important intelligence on German policy. Ustinov passed on Putlitz's intelligence to MI5 as well as SIS.

To maintain regular contact with Putlitz, Ustinov found a job as the European correspondent of an Indian newspaper with an office in The Hague. During the summer of 1938 Whitehall received a series of intelligence reports, some of them from Putlitz, warning that Hitler had decided to seize the German-speaking Czech Sudetenland by force.[84] There were contradictory reports, however, on when Hitler planned to attack.[85] Putlitz apart, Ustinov's most important source from mid-August onwards was 'Herr von S'.[86] One evening, while he was studying at drama school, Peter Ustinov arrived home to find Klop in 'an unusual state of agitation', with an open cigar-box on the table and a bottle of champagne on ice. Peter was sent off to spend the evening in the cinema, passing on his way out a mysterious group of visitors who were still in the flat wreathed in cigar smoke when he returned. Years later, Klop revealed to Peter that the leader of the mysterious visitors had been the former German military attaché in London, General Baron Geyr von Schweppenburg ('Herr von S'), who had told him: 'We simply must convince the British to stand firm ... If they give in to Hitler now, there will be no holding him.'[87] Among the material handed over to Ustinov by Schweppenburg which the Security Service forwarded to the Foreign Office was a memorandum by Ribbentrop of 3 August, reporting that a decision to settle the Czechoslovak question *in unserem Sinne* ('in accordance with our wishes') would be taken before the autumn, and expressing confidence that Britain and France would not intervene. Even if war followed, Germany would be victorious.[88]

At the beginning of September Sir Alexander Cadogan, who had succeeded Vansittart as PUS in January, arrived back in the Foreign Office after a disturbed French holiday to find 'enough in the Secret Reports to make one's hair stand on end'. 'It's obviously touch and go,' he believed, 'but not gone yet.' On 6 September Whitehall received the most direct warning so far. The German chargé d'affaires, Theodor Kordt, previously one of Van's 'private detectives' and, in Cadogan's view, a brave man who 'put conscience before loyalty', paid a secret visit to 10 Downing Street, where he was admitted through the garden gate, and warned Chamberlain's close adviser, Sir Horace Wilson, that Hitler had decided to invade Czechoslovakia. Next day he returned to Number 10 and repeated the same message to Lord Halifax. Kordt called for a firm statement to be 'broadcast to the German nation' that Britain would help the Czechs resist a German attack.[89] He failed to convince his listeners. On 8 September Chamberlain announced to an inner circle of advisers – Halifax, Horace Wilson, Simon and Cadogan – a secret 'Plan Z' for him to visit Hitler in person to try to settle the crisis without war. To Vansittart, brought into the meeting at Halifax's request after Plan Z had been announced, 'it was Henry IV going to Canossa again.' But Van had become a voice crying in the Whitehall wilderness. 'We argued with him', Cadogan smugly told his diary, 'and I think demolished him.'[90]

On 15 September the Prime Minister made a dramatic flight to Munich to parley with the Führer in his grandiose mountain retreat at Berchtesgaden. *Le Matin* caught the mood of both the French and British press when it applauded the courage of 'a man of sixty-nine making his first aeroplane journey . . . to see if he can banish the frightful nightmare which hangs over us and save humanity'. Within Van's entourage, Chamberlain's attempts at appeasement by shuttle-diplomacy gave rise instead to the cynical ditty:

> If at first you can't concede
> Fly, fly, fly again.

On the day of Chamberlain's first flight to Munich, Schweppenburg contacted Ustinov with an updated account of Hitler's war plan, which the Security Service forwarded to the Foreign Office:

It is Hitler's intention to bring about the dissolution of the Czechoslovak state by all or any means . . . Secret mobilisation will have been developed by Sunday, 25th September, to a stage at which it is only necessary for Hitler to press the button to set the whole military machine in motion with a view to destroying the Czechoslovak state by force.

It is part of Hitler's plan that up to and until the 25th September every possible means should be adopted to put pressure on Czechoslovakia and the other powers . . . and if by that date he has not gained his object he intends to order the attack on Czechoslovakia on or at any time after that date.

But Hitler did not need to 'press the button', although he seems to have been disappointed not to. After Chamberlain had made three round-trips by air and attended a disorganized four-power conference at Munich, the Prime Minister returned to a hero's welcome in London on 30 September, brandishing an agreement which surrendered the Czech Sudetenland to Germany and meant, he claimed, not only 'peace with honour' but 'peace for our time'. Jack Curry later recalled the 'growing sense of dismay' in the Security Service as the negotiations with Hitler continued: 'When Chamberlain returned from Munich waving his piece of paper we all had an acute sense of shame.'[91]

SIS saw things differently. Before and during the Munich Crisis, Quex Sinclair – probably to a greater degree than ever before – set out to influence government policy. SIS's own policy was set out in a memorandum of 18 September entitled 'What Should We Do?', drafted by the SIS head of political intelligence Malcolm Woollcombe and personally approved by Sinclair. SIS argued strongly that the Czechs should be pressed to accept 'the inevitable' and surrender the Sudetenland. They should 'realise unequivocally that they stand alone if they refuse such a solution'. Britain, for its part, should continue with a policy of calculated appeasement. It should not wait until German grievances boiled over and threatened the peace of Europe. Instead the international community should take the initiative and decide 'what *really legitimate* grievances Germany has and what surgical operations are necessary to rectify them'. Some of Germany's colonies, confiscated after the last war, should be restored. If genuine cases for self-determination by German minorities remained in Europe they should be remedied:

It may be argued that this would be giving in to Germany, strengthening Hitler's position and encouraging him to go to extremes. Better, however, that realities be faced and that wrongs, if they do exist, be righted, than leave it to Hitler to do the righting in his own way and time – particularly if, concurrently, we and the French unremittingly build up our strength and lessen Germany's potentialities for making trouble.

Britain should try to ensure '*that Germany's "style is cramped", but with the minimum of provocation*'. Sir Warren Fisher, head of the civil service and chairman of the currently inactive Secret Service Committee, told Sinclair that 'What Should We Do?' was 'a most excellent document'.[92]

MI5 disagreed. B Branch followed the Munich Crisis by preparing a very different report on the intelligence from Putlitz and other German sources (none of them identified by name) which it had forwarded to the Foreign Office over the previous few years.[93] On 7 November the note was handed to Kell, who personally delivered it to Vansittart. Van, who earlier in the year had been kicked upstairs to the post of (not very influential) chief diplomatic adviser to the Chamberlain government, forwarded the note to Cadogan, who made a few comments on it, then passed it to Lord Halifax, the Foreign Secretary.[94] This unprecedented report represented probably the first (albeit implicit) indictment of government foreign policy by a British intelligence agency. Page 1 of the MI5 report included the provocative statement that, in view of the intelligence the Service had provided from 'reliable sources' over the past few years:

There is nothing surprising and nothing which could not have been foreseen in the events of this summer in connection with Czechoslovakia. These events are a logical consequence of Hitler's Nazi Weltanschauung and of his foreign policy and his views in regard to racial questions and the position of Germany in Europe.

The report went on, with unusual frankness, to record the frustration of Putlitz ('Herr Q') at the failure of the British government to stand up to Hitler:

Our intermediary [Klop Ustinov] has frequently found that, on occasions when the attitude or actions of the British Government have seemed to indicate their failure to see the real nature of what he describes as the Machiavellian plans of Hitler, [Putlitz] has given expression to the greatest exasperation and even to feelings of dismay. There have been times when he has said that the English are hopeless and it is no use trying to help them to withstand the Nazi methods which they so obviously fail to understand, but after reflection he has always returned to the attempt.

. . . It is important to emphasise that the information which we have received from him has always proved to be scrupulously accurate and entirely free from any bias in the presentment of facts.

Apart from Putlitz, the MI5 report placed most emphasis on the intelligence received from 'Herr von S', who had also called for a 'stiff attitude on the part of Great Britain' to resist Hitler's demands:

It need hardly be emphasised that in giving us . . . information Herr von S. has been risking his life. On the 28th September so strong was his desire to do everything possible to bring about the defeat of the Nazi regime in the event of war – that he was attempting, in spite of the immense difficulties in the way of rapid and safe communication, to send through information which he hoped would have given the British Air Force a few hours more warning than they would otherwise have received.

Schweppenburg reported that, in the event of war, the German General Staff intended to launch 'immediate aerial attacks' against France and Britain. This information was confirmed to MI5 by 'a [Nazi] Party source' in London.[95] Curry later recalled that, though feeling 'an acute sense of shame' at the Munich agreement, 'we felt too some relief that we were not to be subjected to an immediate aerial bombardment.'[96] On this point Schweppenburg's information, which perhaps derived from boasting by Göring, was wrong. The Luftwaffe was in no position to launch a serious air attack on Britain until it gained forward bases after the conquest of France and the Low Countries in 1940. The illusion persisted, however, until the outbreak of war in September 1939, reinforced by a series of subsequent intelligence reports from various sources, that the Luftwaffe would attempt an immediate 'knock-out blow' against London as soon as hostilities began.[97]

British policy during the Munich Crisis, MI5 reported, had convinced Hitler of 'the weakness of England': 'There now seems to be no doubt he is convinced that Great Britain is "decadent" and lacks the will and power to defend the British Empire.' The aim of the report was to stiffen Chamberlain's resolve by demonstrating that appeasement had encouraged rather than removed Hitler's aggressive designs:

Hitler . . . remarked in a circle of his friends and ministers: 'If I were Chamberlain I would not delay for a minute to prepare my country in the most drastic way for a "total" war, and I would thoroughly reorganise it. If the English have not got universal conscription by the spring of 1939 they may consider their World Empire as lost. It is astounding how easy the democracies make it for us to reach our goal.'[98]

Hitler, the Security Service correctly concluded, was only in the early stages of a massive programme of territorial expansion:

It is apparent that Hitler's policy is essentially a dynamic one, and the question is – What direction will it take next? If the information in the [report], which has proved generally reliable and accurate in the past, is to be believed, Germany is at the beginning of a 'Napoleonic era' and her rulers contemplate a great extension of German power.[99]

In order to try to ensure that the MI5 report attracted Chamberlain's attention, it was decided, at Curry's suggestion, to include samples of Hitler's insulting references to him.[100] Halifax underlined three times in red pencil Hitler's reported description of Chamberlain as an 'arsehole' (*arschloch*)[101] and was reported to have shown it to the Prime Minister.[102] According to Curry, the insult made, as he had intended, 'a considerable impression on the Prime Minister',[103] who was known to be infuriated by mockery and disrespect.[104] Hitler was also reported to have mocked Chamberlain's trademark umbrella as a symbol of his feebleness and to be 'very fond of making jokes about the "umbrella-pacifism" of the once so imposing British world empire'.[105]

The impact of the MI5 report was heightened by evidence from one of its informants that George Steward, Number Ten press spokesman, had secretly hinted to Fritz Hesse, the press attaché at the German embassy, that Britain would 'give Germany everything she asks for the next year'. On 28 November 1938 Kell called personally at the Foreign Office to show Cadogan the secret evidence. Cadogan could scarcely bring himself to repeat Kell's message to Halifax, who, he believed, was 'getting rather fed up' and contemplating resignation, but decided he had to do so. 'We must stop this sort of thing,' he told his diary. When Halifax tackled the Prime Minister next day, Chamberlain appeared 'aghast'. Cadogan suspected Sir Horace Wilson of complicity in the contact with Hesse, but he agreed with Kell that Steward should be 'spoken to' by Wilson. 'This', he believed, 'will put a brake on them all.'[106]

At Liddell's request, Curry also prepared a brief, updated digest of Putlitz's intelligence to present to the Home Secretary, Sir Samuel Hoare, who was part of Chamberlain's inner circle of foreign policy advisers. Hoare was the first former MI5 (and SIS) officer to become a cabinet minister,[107] but had little sympathy with the current views of the Security Service on the perils of appeasement. Curry accompanied Kell on a visit to the Home Secretary – partly to support the Director, partly because, when Secretary of State for India in the early 1930s, Hoare had praised a book by Curry on the Indian police. They received a frosty welcome from the Home Secretary. When Kell reminded Hoare of his previous acquaintance with Curry, there was no flicker of recognition. The Director then handed over the digest of Putlitz's intelligence. According to Curry's later recollection: 'As Hoare read it, the colour faded from his cheeks. He made a few brief comments, showed no desire to have the matter discussed or elaborated, and dismissed us.' Curry believed that Hoare had been shocked by Putlitz's insistence that 'if we had stood firm at Munich, Hitler might have lost the initiative.'[108] In reality, the Home Secretary was not so much shocked as in denial. Even in early March 1939 he was still looking forward to a new European 'golden age'.[109]

Klop Ustinov reported that Putlitz was 'extremely disconcerted' by the Munich agreement, complaining that, in passing on, at great personal risk, intelligence about Hitler's plans and intentions, he was 'sacrificing himself to no purpose'.[110] In January 1939, Curry and Ustinov arranged a secret meeting for Putlitz with Vansittart in the hope of reassuring him. According to Putlitz's account of the meeting, Van told him:

Well, Putlitz, I understand you are not too pleased with us. I know Munich was a disgraceful business, but I can assure you that this sort of thing is over and done with. Even our English forbearance has its limits. Next time it will be impossible for Chamberlain to allow himself to be bamboozled by a scrap of paper on which Hitler has scribbled a few words expressing his ardent desire for peace.

Vansittart promised Putlitz asylum if he ever decided to defect.[111]

Curry was told, probably by Vansittart, that MI5's intelligence from Putlitz and other German sources 'contributed materially – if only as a minor factor – towards Mr Chamberlain's reformulation of policy', including his decision in April 1939 to introduce conscription.[112] Curry was well aware, however, that, in general, MI5 intelligence had only a limited impact on Number Ten:

I do not wish to attach too great importance to our reports. The Prime Minister and the Foreign Secretary had available to them a mass of information obtained from foreign statesmen and experienced and well informed officials in our Embassies and Consulates abroad. These no doubt furnished a fuller and better-informed assessment of the whole situation than Putlitz could offer from his somewhat restricted point of view . . .

None the less Putlitz's intelligence was 'so far as we knew unique in that it gave us inside information based on German official documents and the remarks of Hitler and some of his principal followers'.[113] Putlitz was certainly far better informed than the British ambassador in Berlin, Sir Nevile Henderson, who was, Cadogan believed, 'completely bewitched by his German friends', and reported myopically that the German compass was 'pointing towards peace'.[114]

The Prime Minister was equally misinformed. 'All the information I get', wrote Chamberlain cheerfully on 19 February, 'seems to point in the direction of peace.' Vansittart pointed emphatically in the opposite direction.[115] Next day he sent Halifax a report, probably based chiefly on intelligence from Putlitz,[116] that Hitler had decided to liquidate Czechoslovakia. By early March Van was predicting a German coup in Prague during the week of the 12th to the 19th.[117] Kell called at the Foreign Office on 11 March 'to raise [Cadogan's] hair with tales of Germany going into Czechoslovakia in [the] next 48 hours'. That evening Cadogan's private secretary, Gladwyn Jebb, rang up with further 'hair-raising' reports from SIS of a German invasion planned for the 14th. On 13 March SIS reported that the Germans were about 'to walk in'. Neither Chamberlain nor his Foreign Secretary, Lord Halifax, was yet convinced by the intelligence warnings. Halifax could still see no evidence that the Germans were 'planning mischief in any particular quarter'. But he added as an afterthought: 'I hope they may not be taking, even as I write, an unhealthy interest in the Slovak situation!' The German interest by now was very unhealthy indeed. On 15 March Hitler's troops occupied Prague and announced the annexation of the Czech provinces of Bohemia and Moravia. Slovakia became a vassal state. Van was bitter about the rejection of his warnings. 'Nothing seems any good,' he wrote morosely when he heard the news from Prague, 'it seems as if nobody will listen to or believe me.' Cadogan admitted to his diary that he had been wrong and Vansittart right: 'I must say it is turning out – at present – as Van predicted and as I never believed it would.'[118] On 18 March Chamberlain finally acknowledged to the cabinet that 'No reliance could be placed on any of the assurances given by the Nazi leaders'[119] – a conclusion which the Security Service had put formally to the cabinet secretary almost three years earlier.[120]

The Security Service's intelligence, however, still carried little weight in the Foreign Office. In early April, Dick White, now Klop Ustinov's case officer,[121] visited the Foreign Office to deliver a warning from Putlitz that Italy was preparing to invade Albania. He was given a sceptical reception.[122] At a cabinet meeting on 5 April Halifax discounted reports of an impending Italian invasion. Two days later, on Good Friday, Italy occupied Albania. After attending a three-hour Good Friday service Halifax met Cadogan and 'decided we can't *do* anything to stop it'.[123] Chamberlain took the invasion as a personal affront. 'It cannot be denied', he wrote rather pathetically to his sister, 'that Mussolini has behaved to me like a sneak and a cad.'[124]

The limited impact of the Security Service's intelligence on German policy reflected the broader confusion of British intelligence assessment. The Joint Intelligence Committee, set up in 1936 on the initiative of the Chiefs of Staff, had yet to establish itself, lacked an intelligence staff and was still largely ignored by the Foreign Office. The confusion of Easter 1939 when the Admiralty took seriously wholly unfounded intelligence reports of Luftwaffe plans to attack the Home Fleet in harbour, while the Foreign Office dismissed accurate warnings of the invasion of Albania, brought matters to a head. The Chiefs of Staff now demanded that, as a minimum response to current intelligence problems, all intelligence – both political and military – which required quick decisions should be collated and assessed by a central body on which the Foreign Office would be represented.[125] Cadogan acknowledged that he was 'daily inundated by all sorts of reports' and found it virtually impossible to sort the wheat from the chaff. Even when he correctly identified accurate intelligence reports, 'It just happened that these were correct; we had no means of evaluating their reliability at the time of their receipt.' After the traumatic Easter weekend the Foreign Office gave way to service pressure for a Situation Report Centre (SRC) under a Foreign Office chairman which would assess intelligence and issue daily reports 'in order that any emergency measures which may have to be taken should be based only on the most reliable and carefully coordinated information'.[126] Two months later, the SRC proposed its own amalgamation with the JIC. In July the Foreign Office, hitherto only an irregular attender at the JIC, agreed to provide the chairman.[127] There were, however, no overnight miracles. Serious improvement in intelligence assessment had to await the Second World War.

There were also significant pre-war weaknesses in counter-espionage. The official history of British security and counter-intelligence in the Second World War by Sir Harry Hinsley and the former Deputy Director General of MI5, Anthony Simkins, published in 1990, makes the remarkable claim, since widely repeated, that before the war neither the Security Service nor SIS even knew the name of the main German espionage organization, the Abwehr, or of its head Admiral Wilhelm Canaris.[128] In reality there are pre-war references to both the Abwehr and Canaris in MI5 records. The Service also referred to the Abwehr in liaison reports to the United States.[129] Judging from pre-war MI5 and SIS records, however, in the mid-1930s both Services still regarded the Abwehr as first and foremost a *counter-espionage* service.[130] So far as Britain was concerned, this belief was broadly true. The Abwehr did not begin its transformation into a fully fledged foreign intelligence service until after the Nazi conquest of power,[131] and, following the signature of the Anglo-German naval agreement in 1935, Hitler temporarily forbade the Abwehr to conduct espionage against Britain in order not to risk prejudicing further improvements in Anglo-German relations.[132]

Though reduced in scale until reauthorized by Hitler in 1937, some German espionage in Britain continued.[133] Among the Abwehr's British agents was Major Christopher Draper, a First World War fighter ace who had won both the Distinguished Service Cross and the French Croix de Guerre, had had a brief post-war career in the RAF (which still used military ranks) and subsequently became a stunt pilot and film actor. Draper's penchant for flying under bridges (including Tower Bridge) earned him the nickname the 'Mad Major', which he later used as the title of his autobiography. In 1933, a year after meeting Hitler at a Munich air show, he was asked by the London correspondent of the Nazi newspaper

Völkischer Beobachter to provide intelligence on the RAF. Draper reported the approach to the Security Service and agreed to become a double agent – the first to operate against Germany since the First World War. In June 1933, with MI5's approval, he travelled to Hamburg to meet his Abwehr case officer. For the next three years he sent disinformation prepared by MI5, disguised (as instructed by the Abwehr) as correspondence on stamp-collecting, to a cover address (Box 629) in Hamburg. Lacking the interdepartmental system for assembling disinformation developed for the Double-Cross System in the Second World War, however, MI5 began to run out of plausible falsehoods of interest to the Germans. By 1937 the Abwehr was expressing 'grave dissatisfaction' with the quality of Draper's information. In the course of the year it broke contact with him.[134]

By maintaining an HOW on letters to the Hamburg box number used by Draper to correspond with his case officer, the Security Service discovered that a Scottish hairdresser, Mrs Jessie Jordan, was being used by the Abwehr to forward correspondence to some of its foreign agents. In January 1938 an HOW on Jordan's address led to the discovery of a letter from an Abwehr agent in the United States, codenamed CROWN, which contained details of a bizarre plot to chloroform and kidnap an American army colonel who had in his possession classified documents on US coastal defences. CROWN was identified as Guenther Rumrich, a twenty-seven-year-old US army deserter, who was convicted with several of his accomplices in an Abwehr spy-ring at a highly publicized trial.[135] As a result of US inter-agency confusion, others who had been indicted succeeded in escaping. J. Edgar Hoover, the FBI Director, and the prosecuting attorney blamed each other. The judge, to Hoover's fury, blamed the FBI. Leon G. Turrou, the FBI special agent in charge of Rumrich's interrogation, was so poorly briefed that he confused the Abwehr with the Gestapo.[136]

Though the Security Service was far better informed than the FBI, there were large gaps in its understanding of the organization of pre-war German intelligence.[137] Possibly the largest was its lack of awareness of the Etappe Dienst naval network, eventually discovered as a result of German records captured in 1945. Post-war analysis revealed that, though the pre-war Security Service had been unaware of the network to which they belonged, it had successfully identified a number of Etappe Dienst agents. Among them was Otto Kurt Dehn, who arrived in Britain in 1936 as managing director of a newly founded cinematographic film company, Emelco, despite – as B Branch noted when applying successfully for an HOW on him – having no previous experience in cinematography, film or advertising.[138] When the Etappe Dienst was taken over by the Abwehr in 1939, it had a total of thirty-one agents operating against British targets.[139] But most of these must have been visiting rather than resident agents, since, after a small number of arrests on the outbreak of war, it now appears that German intelligence had no significant agents operating in Britain, except for a British-controlled double agent and his three sub-agents.[140] Some of the pre-war attempts by the Abwehr to obtain intelligence on RAF installations which were known to the Security Service probably provided information of value to the Luftwaffe. However, most of the German espionage detected by MI5 during the 1930s was, Curry later concluded, 'run on a very crude basis'. Many of the agents provided 'information of no importance in order to extract the maximum of reward for the minimum of effort'.[141]

The Security Service remained understandably worried that 'a cloud of agents of low quality served to hide a few good ones' which it had failed to detect.[142] One of the pre-war networks which most impressed MI5 when it was revealed by post-war interrogations was the Abwehr naval intelligence station in Bremen, which seems to have modelled its operations, at least in part, on those of the Etappe Dienst, using members of German steamship companies and other businessmen travelling from Bremen to the UK. Its head, Captain Erich Pfeiffer, was proud of what it achieved after its expansion in 1937. He claimed that there was much excitement in the Kriegsmarine when his agents discovered that the King George V class of battleships were to be fitted with quadruple gun turrets. Pfeiffer further claimed that intelligence from his agents had influenced the design of the anti-aircraft defences on the pocket battleships *Gneisenau* and *Scharn-horst*.[143] Such claims are difficult to corroborate. The general impression created by the evidence currently available is that Pfeiffer ran a well-organized Abwehr network, more remarkable for the quantity than for the quality of the intelligence it gathered. The file of one of Pfeiffer's agents, Fritz Block, an engineer working for the Hamburg/Bremen Africa Line, contains 117 intelligence reports, with photographs, on British seaports, airports, industry, shipbuilding, warships, radio stations and troop movements, for which he was paid large amounts of money.[144] It is highly unlikely, however, that any of Pfeiffer's agents were actually in Britain when war began.

By the outbreak of war, the Security Service had begun to operate a double agent against Nazi Germany who was to prove far more successful than Major Draper. The man whom MI5 considered the 'fons et origo' of what became known as the Double-Cross System was a Welsh-born electrical engineer codenamed SNOW who had emigrated to Canada as a child and returned to live in London. Early in 1936 he had begun to work part-time for SIS, reporting on his business visits to German shipyards. Later in the year, however, MI5 discovered a letter from SNOW during a routine check of correspondence addressed to Box 629, Hamburg, the Abwehr cover address previously used by Draper. When challenged, SNOW confessed that he had joined the Abwehr but claimed unconvincingly that he had done so only to penetrate it in the interests of SIS. His English interrogators condescendingly described him as 'a typical Welsh "underfed" type, very short, bony face, ill-shaped ears, disproportionately small for size of man, shifty look'. Though SNOW continued to supply SIS and MI5 with details of some of his dealings with the Abwehr, his 'shifty look' continued to inspire suspicion. T. A. 'Tar' Robertson, SNOW's MI5 case officer, decided to leave him on a loose rein in the knowledge that, if war came, he could be arrested under emergency regulations. However much SNOW concealed from MI5, it is clear that he also defrauded the Abwehr, claiming to have at least a dozen sub-agents in England who, MI5 concluded, probably all 'existed only in SNOW's imagination'.[145]

In August 1939 SNOW left for Hamburg in the company of his lover (an Englishwoman of German extraction) and a man whom MI5 believed he intended to recruit for the Abwehr. On 4 September, soon after his return to England, he arranged a meeting with a Special Branch inspector at Waterloo Station. To his surprise, he was served with a detention order and taken to Wandsworth Prison. Once in jail, SNOW quickly revealed that his radio transmitter was in the Victoria Station left-luggage office and offered to use it to communicate with the Abwehr under MI5 control. Robertson agreed. SNOW's transmitter was installed in his cell and, after some difficulty, he succeeded in sending what proved to be a momentous message to his Abwehr controller, Major Nikolaus Ritter: 'Must meet you in Holland at once. Bring weather code. Radio town and hotel Wales ready.' The 'weather code', SNOW explained, was for transmitting the daily weather reports he was expected to send. The reference to Wales related to an assignment given him by Ritter to recruit a Welsh nationalist to organize sabotage in South Wales. Ritter quickly agreed to a meeting.[146] Though of only minor importance at the time, the deception of the Abwehr begun in SNOW's Wandsworth prison cell was eventually to grow into the Double-Cross System, which played a crucial role in the D-Day landings in Normandy in 1944.

Unknown to the Security Service, however, just as its deception of the Abwehr was beginning, the penetration of the SIS station in The Hague by German intelligence had begun to put at risk MI5's most important source, Wolfgang zu Putlitz. In October 1938, a twenty-six-year-old Dutchman, Folkert van Koutrik, who was working as the trusted assistant of SIS's head agent in the Netherlands, was turned by the Abwehr and worked thereafter as a double agent, submitting weekly reports which included details of British agents in the Netherlands and what the SIS station knew about German agents.[147] Soon after the outbreak of war, Putlitz realized that the station had been penetrated and that he must accept Vansittart's offer of asylum.[148]

On the eve of war, however, Putlitz, still with no inkling that he was in danger, was in unusually confident mood, buoyed up by the belief that Britain was at last resolved to stand up to Hitler. Guy Liddell noted in his diary on 30 August:

Klop has sent in a report which indicates that the Germans have got the jitters. It is rather a case of order, counter-order, disorder. There have been recriminations between Nazi Party and non-Party men. Non-Party men are saying: 'We always told you that you get us into this mess, and you will be the first people to suffer for it.' P[utlitz] has the impression that Hitler is on the run and that nothing should be done to provide him with a golden bridge to make his getaway.[149]

Putlitz's was one of a number of over-optimistic intelligence reports from various sources which reached Whitehall during the final days of peace, prompted by a delay in the planned German attack on Poland, which suggested that Hitler or his high command were having last-minute doubts about going to war. 'I can't help thinking', Cadogan told his diary on 30 August, '[that the] Germans are in an awful fix. In fact it's obvious even if one discounts rumours of disturbances.' 'It *does* seem to me', he wrote at about midnight on 31 August, '[that] Hitler is hesitant and trying all sorts of dodges, including last-minute bluff.'[150] A few hours later, at dawn on 1 September, German troops crossed the border into Poland and the last hopes of peace were dashed. Two days later Britain was at war.

Section C
The Second World War

Introduction

The Security Service and its Wartime Staff:
'From Prison to Palace'

During the first year of the Second World War the Security Service made what one of its staff called a transition 'from prison to palace'.[1] The prison was Wormwood Scrubs, the Service's first wartime headquarters. Blenheim Palace, to which most staff transferred in October 1940, was the birthplace of Winston Churchill, who had become prime minister five months earlier. MI5's arrival at the Scrubs on 27 August 1939, made necessary by the need for more wartime office space than was then available in Thames House, was so sudden that some staff found unemptied chamberpots in the cells which became their offices.[2] Prisoners remained in several of the cell blocks and were sometimes seen exercising in the yard. 'Don't go near them,' one of the warders warned female staff. 'Some of them ain't seen no women for years.'[3] Other prisoners, however, had. The ex-public-school 'Mayfair Playboys', who had been imprisoned earlier in the year for robbing high-class jewellers, had danced with some Registry staff at debutantes' balls during the London season.[4] The Playboys' leader, the twenty-two-year-old Old Etonian Victor Hervey, the future sixth Marquess of Bristol, was later said to have provided some of the inspiration for the 'Pink Panther'.[5]

The prison buildings, complained Milicent Bagot, 'appeared never to have been ventilated since their erection and their smell was appalling.'[6] The cell doors had no handles or locks on the inside. So, as one Wormwood Scrubs veteran recalls, staff 'stood a good chance of being locked in by unwary visitors turning the outside door handle on leaving. At first there were no telephones in the cells, and with the rooms themselves sound-proofed, it was possible for you to be shut in for hours before anyone noticed that you were not around.'[7] The dreariness of the prison sur-roundings was reinforced by the strict secretarial economy measures ordered by Kell, in line with those implemented in the War Office: 'Single spacing must be used, wide margins avoided, and both sides of the paper used whenever practicable. Quarto size paper must be used in the place of foolscap whenever this will effect economy.'[8] A Branch sent further instructions on the conservation of used blotting paper, which, for security reasons, had hitherto been destroyed at the end of every working day. Henceforth it was to be placed in a locked cupboard overnight and reused for as long as possible.[9] In an attempt to maintain morale amid these straitened working conditions, Kell's secretary arranged for a ladies' hairdresser to visit the prison.[10] Miss Dicker, the Lady Superintendent, also relaxed the previously inflexible female dress code. Because of the open prison staircases, visible from below, women were for the first time allowed to wear trousers.[11] For the only time in MI5 history, the working day ended with the blowing of a bugle to remind staff to draw the curtains before the beginning of the night-time black-out.[12]

Wartime restrictions were briefly suspended at Christmas. Constance Kell, who helped run the canteen, later recalled:

We managed to have a Christmas dinner at the office canteen and another branch of our large community gave a Christmas party and presents were handed out . . . it was a real break in our busy days to have this gay afternoon – there was a splendid spirit everywhere, a spirit of camaraderie, which drew together the whole people . . . There was something about Kell himself that inspired that will to do and to help in every way possible.[13]

Despite the personal affection he inspired in most staff and his wife's rose-tinted recollections of Christmas in the Scrubs, Kell, though less than a year older than Churchill, was well past his best. By the outbreak of war he had been director for thirty years, longer than the head of any other British government department or agency in the twentieth century. Thirty-six years old when he founded the Service in 1909, he was nearly sixty-six when the Second World War began. In December 1938, having reached what he called 'the respectable age of 65' in the previous month, he wrote to Sir Alexander Cadogan, PUS at the Foreign Office and *ex officio* member of the (then inactive) Secret Service Committee, to ask, 'in the interests of the Security Service, that something definite should be ordained with regard to my future': '. . . I would suggest, if my work has been approved of, that my services should be retained on a yearly basis, provided I am compos mentis and do not feel the burden too heavy.'[14]

The response to Kell's letter suggests that no serious thought had been given in Whitehall to the future management of the Security Service. Cadogan passed the letter on to Sir Warren Fisher, head of the civil service and chairman of the Security Service Committee, with the comment that Kell seemed 'active enough to carry on his present work efficiently, though one cannot of course tell how long that will continue to be the case. I should be quite content to see him continue for as long as he can . . .'[15] Fisher saw Kell in January 1939 and agreed that he should stay on, apparently on the yearly contract he had proposed.[16] A year later, however, Kell was in declining health and finding it difficult to cope with the huge increase in wartime work.[17]

Among the clearest evidence of Kell's shortcomings was his failure to learn from his own past experience. He made no serious preparation for the rapid recruitment which the experience of the First World War should have taught him would follow the outbreak of the Second. According to a later report by his main wartime successor, Sir David Petrie:

When the war broke out, each officer 'tore around' to rope in likely people; when they knew of none themselves, they asked their acquaintances. Occasionally recruits who were brought in knew of other 'possibles'. Various Ministries also contributed surplus staff. In much the same way, retired officers came to notice, and new people continued to be got by the same processes . . . If I am correctly informed, there have been cases in which recruits have been taken on by divisions (or sections) without so much as informing Administration.[18]

Though somewhat chaotic, 'tearing around' by MI5 officers succeeded in bringing into the Service a remarkable array of academic, legal and other talent. Dick White recruited his former history tutor at Christ Church, (Sir) J. C. Masterman, later vice chancellor of Oxford University.[19] Guy Liddell's recruits included the brilliant young zoologist Victor (third Baron) Rothschild, heir to a banking dynasty, an accomplished jazz pianist and one of Britain's most gifted polymaths, who was assembling the finest collection of eighteenth-century English books and manuscripts in private hands. Rothschild founded MI5's first counter-sabotage department (B1c) in a cell in Wormwood Scrubs, as well as maintaining a laboratory at his own expense. He in turn talent-spotted a friend he had first met at Trinity College, Cambridge: the leading (though traitorous) art historian Anthony Blunt. Rothschild's first wife asked early in their marriage whether it was really necessary to invite Blunt so frequently to dinner. 'Darling,' replied Rothschild, 'you are talking of a saint.'[20] MI5's wartime recruits from the law included six future judges – Patrick Barry, Edward Cussen, Helenus 'Buster' Milmo, Henry 'Toby' Pilcher, Edward Blanchard Stamp and John Stephenson – as well as a series of other able barristers and solicitors. Among the solicitors was Martin Furnival Jones, who went on to become director general of MI5 from 1965 to 1972.[21] One of the barristers, Sir Ashton Roskill QC, later commented that the overall calibre of the wartime recruits was 'too high'.[22] In retrospect Dick White agreed. 'In the national interest', he told Masterman, 'I think that we appropriated too much talent. The demand for men of ability in other departments was enormous and perhaps we were a bit greedy.'[23]

The number of officers in the Security Service grew from thirty-six in July 1939 to 102 in January 1940 (not including Security Control personnel in ports), 230 in January 1941, 307 in January 1942 and a wartime peak of 332 in January 1943. Secretarial and Registry staff increased from 133 in July 1939 to 334 in January 1940 (not including Security Control personnel in ports), 617 in January 1941, 934 in January 1942 and a wartime peak of 939 in January 1943.[24] Security Control officers at ports grew steadily throughout the war from twenty-nine in September 1939 to 117 in May 1943 and 206 in April 1945.[25] There was also a significant expansion in MI5's imperial presence. At the outbreak of war it had six defence security officers (DSOs) permanently stationed abroad, in Cairo, Gibraltar, Malta, Aden, Singapore and Hong Kong. By the end of hostilities in 1945 the total number of Security Service officers in the Empire and Commonwealth had risen to twenty-seven, supported by twenty-one secretaries despatched from London.[26]

There was no wartime expansion, however, in the number of female MI5 officers. At the outbreak of war, the Security Service had only one such officer: Jane Archer (née Sissmore), its main Soviet expert, who married the Service's RAF liaison officer, Wing Commander John 'Joe' Archer, during the lunch-hour on the day before war was declared.[27] Her interrogation of the Russian defector Walter Krivitsky, early in 1940, was a model of its kind – the first really professional debriefing of a Soviet intelligence officer on either side of the Atlantic.[28] In November 1940, however, she was sacked after denouncing the incompetence of Kell's successor as director, Jasper Harker.[29] Though Guy Liddell believed that Archer 'had unfortunately gone too far', he had no doubt that Harker was mainly to blame: 'but for his incompetence, the situation would never have arisen, and he had, moreover, over a period of many years, encouraged frank criticism from Jane Archer.'[30] Harker was himself replaced a few months later. Archer moved on to SIS.[31] No other woman was given officer rank for the remainder of the war, even if a substantial number performed officers' jobs. Though the surviving evidence is fragmentary, new regulations introduced in 1941 (for which the then Director General, Sir David Petrie, bore ultimate responsibility) seem to have made it impossible for women to be promoted to officer rank.[32]

Women continued to be actively employed as agents. The Security Service's leading pre-war penetration agent in the CPGB had been Olga

Gray, run by Maxwell Knight.[33] Early in the Second World War, Knight succeeded in placing three female agents (among them his secretary, Joan Miller, who lived with him for several years)[34] in the pro-Nazi Right Club, some of whose members identified themselves by the initials 'P.J.' ('Perish Judah').[35] Knight's section also ran a number of women, employed by London embassies and diplomats suspected of assisting the Nazi cause. Among them was an agent described as an 'exceptionally capable, reliable and discreet woman', who between 1941 and 1945 worked for, and reported on, employers of six different nationalities.[36] Knight appears to have been the first MI5 officer to put on paper his views 'On the subject of Sex, in connection with using women as agents'. Female agents, he argued, should 'not be markedly oversexed or undersexed':

It is difficult to imagine anything more terrifying than for an officer to become landed with a woman agent who suffers from an overdose of Sex.

What is required is a clever woman who can use her personal attractions wisely. Nothing is easier than for a woman to gain a man's confidence by the showing and expression of a little sympathy. This cannot be done by an undersexed woman. However, it is important to stress that I am no believer in what may be described as Mata-Hari methods. I am convinced that more information has been obtained by women agents by keeping out of the arms of the man, than was ever obtained by sinking too willingly into them.

. . . It is frequently alleged that women are less discreet than men: that they are ruled by their emotions, and not by their brains: that they rely on intuition rather than on reason; and that Sex will play an unsettling and dangerous role in their work. My own experience has been very much to the contrary. During the present war, M.S. [Knight's department] has investigated probably hundreds of cases of 'loose-talk': in by far the greater proportion of these cases the offenders were men. In my submission this is due to one principal factor: it is that indiscretions are committed from conceit. Taking him generally, Man is a conceited creature, while Woman is a vain creature: conceit and vanity are not the same. A man's conceit will often lead him to indiscretion, in an endeavour to build himself up among his fellow men, or even to impress a woman: women, being vain rather than conceited, find their outlet for this form of self-expression in their personal experience, dress etc.[37]

Wrongly believing at the outbreak of war that it faced a far more dangerous challenge from German intelligence than in the First World War, the Security Service was deeply frustrated at having to spend most of its time dealing with enemy aliens in Britain rather than with counter-espionage. Government policy for most of the First World War, though not always enforced, had been to intern all enemy aliens unless they could prove that they presented no threat.[38] The Service favoured the same policy at the beginning of the Second World War, largely because it saw no practicable alternative.[39] With a mere thirty-six officers in July 1939, rising to only 102 by January 1940, it lacked the resources required to distinguish rapidly those enemy aliens who posed a potential threat to national security from those who did not. Two days before the declaration of war, however, the PUS at the Home Office, Sir Alexander Maxwell, informed the Service that, instead of mass internment, tribunals would be set up to review individually the cases of all male enemy aliens over the age of sixteen.[40] Four hundred and fifteen enemy aliens were arrested immediately under the Emergency Powers (Defence) Act of September 1939, and all others were required to report to the police. By the end of the year 120 tribunals had divided resident German and Austrian nationals into three categories. The 569 placed in Category A were interned; the 6,800 in Category B were made subject to restrictions such as curfews and limitations on their movements; those in Category C (64,000) were subject to no restriction.[41] The Service, wrote Jack Curry, was given 'the impossible task of obtaining concrete evidence against individual enemy aliens, and this process contributed to overwhelm it in a mass of detailed enquiries.'[42] Liddell complained that much of the evidence it did collect was ignored:

The proceedings were laughable ... Our records were not consulted, except to a small extent in the metropolitan area; the Chairmen had no standards and no knowledge of the political background of those who came before them; no record[s] of the proceedings were kept.[43]

In December 1939, by Liddell's jaundiced calculations, four-fifths of MI5's time was spent dealing with the alien population, leaving it with inadequate resources to investigate the potentially serious threat from German espionage.[44] The refusal of successive home secretaries to authorize HOWs on British Fascists, and the consequent lack of Security Service eavesdropping on them, had left the Service, as Curry later acknowledged, with 'no definite knowledge whether there was any organized connection between the German Secret Service and Nazi sympathisers in this country, whether British or alien nationality'.[45]

By the time Hitler invaded France and the Low Countries on 10 May 1940, the dramatic growth in the demands placed on the Security Service had brought its administration close to collapse. Kell had failed to heed the warning contained in an MI5 report at the end of the First World War that in the next war it would be deluged with 'a flood of paper'. Even had Kell been more far-sighted, however, his pre-war budget was too small to have funded adequate preparations for wartime conditions. During the second quarter of 1940 MI5 received, on average, 8,200 requests a week from newly security-conscious government departments for the vetting of individuals and the issue of exit permits. Curry later described some of the demands made on the Service as 'almost Gilbertian' in their bureaucratic absurdity – such as the attempt to insist that it vet individually all enemy aliens (even in Category C) who were permitted to post parcels abroad.[46]

Government policy on internment changed dramatically as a result of Germany's six-week conquest of France and the Low Countries. The extra-ordinary rapidity of the German victory was mistakenly ascribed, in part, to large 'fifth columns' supposedly working behind the lines. Sir Nevile Bland, the British minister in the Netherlands, cited a report, reminiscent of the spy scares of the First World War, that a German maid had led paratroopers to one of their targets. Bland warned that Britain faced the same danger from the 'enemy in our midst': 'Every German or Austrian servant, however superficially charming and devoted, is a real and grave menace . . .' There was, he claimed, a fifth column of enemy aliens in Britain who, when the signal was given, would 'at once embark on wide-spread sabotage and attacks on the civilians and the military indiscriminately'. Bland's warning was taken seriously. When his report was presented to the War Cabinet by the Foreign Secretary, Lord Halifax, on 15 May, Churchill, now Prime Minister, declared that 'urgent action' was required.[47] A Home Intelligence report to the Ministry of Information concluded on 5 June: 'Fifth Column hysteria is reaching dangerous proportions.'[48] The Security Service was overwhelmed by a torrent of deluded reports from the public. Marks on telegraph poles were frequently interpreted as codes designed to guide a German invasion; investigation revealed that some were the work of Boy Scouts and Girl Guides who 'readily agreed to refrain from the practice'.[49] Pigeons were widely suspected of secret intercourse with the enemy; counter-measures included the use of British birds of prey to intercept suspicious pigeons in mid-air.[50] One new recruit spent his first day in the Security Service in June 1940 dealing with a series of time-wasting reports which began with 'a letter from lady pointing to the danger of sentries being poisoned by ice-creams sold by aliens'.[51] The Security Service's lack of preparedness to deal with public paranoia about German-inspired subversion reflected a failure, once again, to remember the lessons of the First World War. In the autumn of 1914, wrote Sir Basil Thomson, then head of the Special Branch, spy mania had 'assumed a virulent epidemic form accompanied by delusions which defied treatment'.[52] As in 1914, spy mania in 1940 afflicted some in high places and government departments as well as the general public. Shortly before being replaced as C in C Home Forces in July, Field Marshal Sir Edmund (later Baron) Ironside, warned that there were 'people quite definitely preparing aerodromes in this country' for use by the Luftwaffe.[53] One of the lessons drawn by Sir David Petrie, who became director general in 1941, was:

the need to have people ready to deal with alarmist rumours about wireless, lights, pigeons and so on; in fact all the scare stories that are bound to descend like a flood. Such material must be kept away from and not allowed to clog the wheels of the real counter-intelligence machinery.[54]

None of the reports sent to MI5 led to the discovery of any real fifth column or the detection of a single enemy agent. Fear of fifth columnists, however, produced insistent demands for mass internment from the military authorities. On 19 June the Chiefs of Staff called for all enemy aliens to be interned 'immediately'.[55] Their most influential supporter was Churchill. Guy Liddell noted on 25 May: 'It seems that the Prime Minister takes a strong view about the internment of all Fifth Columnists at this moment and that he has left the Home Secretary in no doubt about his views. What seems to have moved him more than anything else was the Tyler Kent case.'[56] Tyler Kent was a cipher clerk in the US embassy in London who had previously been stationed in Moscow and struck the British writer and wartime SIS officer Malcolm Muggeridge as 'one of those intensely gentlemanly Americans who wear well-cut tailor-made suits, with waistcoat and watch-chain, drink wine instead of high-balls, and easily become furiously indignant'.[57] Kent directed much of his fury against President Franklin D. Roosevelt who, he believed, was in danger of compromising American neutrality, of which he was a strong supporter. With the aim of discrediting Roosevelt's foreign policy, he amassed a private collection of about 1,500 US diplomatic documents, including cables exchanged between Churchill, while first lord of the Admiralty, and FDR. Publishing these documents, he believed, would expose a plot hatched by Roosevelt and Churchill to bring the United States into the war.[58]

Maxwell Knight had discovered Kent's activities as a result of his penetration of the pro-German, anti-Semitic Right Club, of which Anna Wolkoff, a British associate of Kent, was a leading light. One of Knight's three agents (all female) in the Right Club, codenamed M/Y, was so successful in posing as a pro-Nazi that Wolkoff called her 'the little Storm Trooper' and fantasized about 'a triumphal procession' in which she would ride in the same car as the SS chief, Heinrich Himmler.[59] Wolkoff introduced Kent to the head of the Right Club, Captain Archibald Ramsay, a maverick Tory MP who had been seduced by the anti-Semitic conspiracy theories of *The Protocols of the Elders of Zion* and was obsessed by his self-imposed mission 'to clear the Conservative Party of Jewish influence'.[60] On 23 April 1940 M/Y reported that Kent was passing Wolkoff classified information. Wolkoff told M/Y that she had seen 'the signature of one Liddell of the Military Intelligence to a letter concerning American radio detectors and Hoovers [*sic*]'. What she had actually seen was correspondence between Guy Liddell, then deputy head of B Branch, and J. Edgar Hoover, Director of the FBI, on the purchase of US radio direction-finding equipment.[61] Wolkoff was also in contact with the ardently pro-Nazi William Joyce, who had fled to Germany on the eve of war. Knight concluded that, in view of her correspondence with Joyce, 'there was . . . abundant evidence that Anna Wolkoff was indeed to be classed as an enemy agent.'[62] On 2 May M/Y reported to Knight: 'There is no doubt that Tyler Kent is a definite Fifth Column member.'[63] Kent had developed such close links with the Right Club that it was later discovered he had been entrusted with a locked red-leather-bound book containing the names of its 235 members. At the time neither MI5 nor Churchill had any means of knowing that the Kent–Wolkoff case was not the tip of a much larger, as yet undiscovered fifth-column iceberg.

Anna Wolkoff was not content simply to be passed US diplomatic documents by Kent. On 11 May, the day after Churchill became prime minister, she boasted to M/Y that she had secretly purloined and copied some of his private hoard of documents.[64] The documents copied by Wolkoff were messages exchanged between Churchill (then first lord of the Admiralty) and Roosevelt, some of them dealing with secret Anglo-American co-operation,[65] which she planned to pass to Nazi Germany and Fascist Italy. Since Italy remained officially neutral until June, she gave them in the first instance to the Italian embassy in London which was, she believed, 'charmed to receive the copies of the letters'.[66] Italian diplomatic telegrams decrypted by British codebreakers revealed that Rome was passing to Berlin 'practically everything from Ambassador Kennedy's despatches to President Roosevelt, including reports of his interviews with British statesmen and officials'.[67] Churchill must have been seriously alarmed. Had his secret dealings with Roosevelt been publicly exposed, they would, at the very least, as Kent intended, have strengthened the hand of American isolationists whose influence Churchill was struggling to diminish.

On 18 May 1940, Knight called on Herschel Johnson at the US embassy to explain the case against Kent. Johnson, Knight reported, was 'profoundly shocked' and 'promised the fullest co-operation'. An application for Wolkoff's detention under Regulation 18B of the Emergency Powers (Defence) Act was approved the following day by the Home Secretary. On 20 May 1940 the State Department dismissed Tyler Kent from government service and waived his diplomatic immunity. The same day, Knight, accompanied by a US embassy official and three officers from Scotland Yard, surprised Kent at his flat and found 'an amazing collection' of US diplomatic documents. Knight reported, possibly with some exaggeration: 'It is quite clear that some of the information relating to the military position of the Allies was so vital that in the event of its being passed on to Germany, the most disastrous consequences would ensue.' Other documents found included correspondence in which Kent requested a transfer to the Berlin embassy, as well as the secret Right Club membership list.[68] Kent was arrested after being interrogated by Knight at the US embassy in the presence of Ambassador Kennedy.[69] 'Nothing like this has ever happened in American history,' wrote the shocked US Assistant Secretary of State, Breckinridge Long. 'It means not only that our codes are cracked . . . but that our every diplomatic manoeuvre was exposed to Germany and Russia . . . It is a terrible blow – almost a major catastrophe.'[70] Kennedy, however, informed the State Department that, in order to avoid embarrassing Roosevelt, Kent would be kept incommunicado during the forthcoming US presidential election campaign.[71]

On 21 May Maxwell Knight and Guy Liddell visited the Home Office to brief Sir John Anderson, the Home Secretary, and other senior Whitehall figures on the Kent–Wolkoff case as well as the 'underground activities of the BUF' and the Right Club discovered by Knight's agents. In Liddell's view, 'Max was extremely good and made all his points very quietly and forcibly':

Anderson agreed that the case against Ramsay was rather serious but he did not seem to think that it involved the BUF. Max explained to him that Ramsay and Mosley were in constant touch with one another and that many members of the Right Club were also members of the BUF.

By the end of the meeting, according to Liddell, the Home Secretary was 'considerably shaken'.[72] Next day, 22 May, Anderson reported to the War Cabinet that, though the Security Service had no concrete evidence, it believed that 25 to 30 per cent of the BUF would be 'willing if ordered to go to any lengths' on behalf of Germany. The War Cabinet agreed to amend Defence Regulation 18B to allow the internment of those showing sympathy to enemy powers.[73] Later the same day orders were signed for the detention of Mosley and thirty-two other leading members of the

BUF.[74] An opinion survey by Mass Observation reported overwhelming public support: 'Indeed, very seldom have observers found such a high degree of approval for anything.'[75] Though extremely few in number, would-be German agents did exist in Whitehall. In 1940–41 two Nazi sympathizers in the Ministry of Supply, Molly Hiscox and Norah Briscoe, attempted to pass on classified information to the Germans but supplied it instead to an agent of Maxwell Knight posing as a German agent. Both received five-year jail sentences.[76]

To iron out what he called the 'overlaps and underlaps' in the various agencies dealing with counter-espionage and counter-subversion, Churchill founded the Home Defence (Security) Executive, better known as the Security Executive, which was formally constituted by the War Cabinet on 28 May. Its first head was the Conservative politician Lord Swinton, a former minister of air, whom Churchill instructed to 'find out whether there is a fifth column in this country and if so to eliminate it'.[77] At the time Swinton had no doubt that there was and that large-scale internment was required to deal with it. By July the internment of BUF members had reached a peak of 753. Mass internment of enemy aliens was on a much greater scale. Between May and July 1940 about 22,000 Germans and Austrians and about 4,000 Italians were interned.[78] Some Security Service officers knew personally of cases of anti-Nazi Germans and anti-Fascist Italians being interned with supporters of Hitler and Mussolini. The future judge (Sir) John Stephenson later recalled how 'Heddy, my mother's Austrian Jewish cook, was carried screaming off to internment'.[79]

Jack Curry later acknowledged in an in-house history, 'By the time of the fall of France the organisation of the Security Service as a whole was in a state which can only be described as chaotic.'[80] The main blame fell on Kell. On 10 June Sir Horace Wilson, who had succeeded Fisher as head of the civil service, summoned Kell to his office in the Treasury and told him that 'it had been decided to make certain changes in the controlling staff of the Security Service'.[81] Kell wrote in his diary, 'I get the sack from Horace Wilson,' added his dates of service, '1909–1940', and drew a line beneath them. Then he vented his feelings on the Italians: 'Italy comes into the war against us. Dirty Dogs.'[82] It had already been decided that Kell's deputy, Sir Eric Holt-Wilson, who was only two years younger and had served under him since 1912, was too old to succeed him.[83] Though Holt-Wilson was due to retire in only a fortnight's time, he decided to resign immediately so that he and Kell would 'both go together'. Lady Holt-Wilson, over thirty years younger than her husband, saw his resignation as a sacking:

... I cried to think of the hurt to you. You who have worked so wonderfully, who have been so repeatedly told that nobody else has your knowledge in your special line, who spared nothing to give your best – to be given 48 hours notice – why not even a Kitchen Maid gets thrown out like that![84]

Before the war Kell had 'very strongly' recommended Jasper Harker, the head of B Branch, as his eventual successor.[85] Probably because of B Branch's successes during the 1930s in penetrating the German embassy, the CPGB and the BUF, the Secret Service Committee had agreed.[86] On the evening of 10 June Harker was summoned by Churchill and told that he was to succeed Kell[87] – a clear indication of the priority which the Prime Minister attached to uncovering and uprooting the (non-existent) fifth column. Harker was also informed that he would be 'responsible' – in other words subordinate – to Swinton, the head of the Security Executive.[88]

Holt-Wilson, though scarcely an impartial judge, wrote on hearing that Harker was to take over: 'God help the Service as he hasn't a real friend here and knows *nothing* about the machinery ...'[89] Harker proved to have little idea about how to restore order and improve morale amid the confusion which he inherited at Wormwood Scrubs. A nineteen-year-old MI5 typist was overheard complaining to a friend in a restaurant that:

A new Director – a new broom – had arrived and the place had been plastered with pamphlets [entitled] 'GO TO IT'. These had proved very irritating to the female staff who were putting in a lot of overtime and on finishing work feeling very tired came across this 'GO TO IT'. Some had been removed, others torn and scribbled on, and when action was threatened some 20 girls tendered their resignations.[90]

One of MI5's wartime recruits, Ashton Roskill, compared Harker to 'a sort of highly polished barrel which, if tapped, would sound hollow (because it was). Swinton saw through him in a flash.'[91]

In July, apparently on Churchill's personal instructions, Swinton was formally given 'executive control' of MI5, with responsibility for helping Harker reorganize the Service.[92] Swinton's most important contribution was to recruit a business-efficiency expert, Reginald Horrocks, formerly London manager and European director of Burroughs Adding Machines Ltd (later part of Unisys) as deputy director (organization). Horrocks's main task was to modernize MI5's antiquated filing system, introduce a Hollerith punch-card system, and assimilate a large number of untrained recruits into the Registry. In Curry's view, he 'brought about a great improvement in the mechanics of the Office and gradually introduced order where there had been disorder and confusion'.[93] Though more efficient, however, the new Registry was also more impersonal. A member of staff who had joined the Registry in 1937, complained: 'Horrocks told me it was to be something like Ford's factory where each worker had only one job to do, and this reminded me of Charlie Chaplin in *Modern Times* when he used a spanner to screw a nut and bolt as the machine belt brought the pieces of machinery around.'[94] A review by the future director general Sir David Petrie concluded early in 1941:

It is interesting to note that some of the Registry staff who are dissatisfied with their conditions of employment admit, even while voicing a complaint, that the new system has enormously improved speed and efficiency ... The old Registry was small, it was then what has been called the 'family party' period and the system probably answered its purpose well. But a system that may be satisfactory for the running of a private house may not be adequate for a large hotel.[95]

But if Swinton understood the need to reform the Registry, he had little grasp of the problems facing B Division, which complained that he seemed to think of MI5 as 'a large detective agency carrying out frequent raids in fast cars'. At a stormy meeting in early August he declared B Division's investigative capacity to be quite inadequate and insisted on appointing as joint head of the Division, alongside Guy Liddell, a London solicitor, William Crocker, who had no previous intelligence experience.[96] The appointment, according to Curry, 'helped to reduce B Branch to a state of chaos and ... seriously damaged the morale of its officers'. In September Crocker resigned after a row with Swinton, leaving Liddell in sole charge of the Division.[97] Liddell went on to win a reputation as one of the war's outstanding intelligence officers. Hugh Trevor-Roper (later Lord Dacre), a wartime recruit to SIS, who got to know Liddell well and was usually a hard judge, found him 'a remarkable and very charming man who gave the B Division its special character: open, genial, informal, but highly professional'.[98]

Initially, Swinton's Security Executive did more to exacerbate than to resolve intelligence confusion over the supposed threat from the (non-existent) fifth column which preoccupied Churchill at the beginning of his premiership. Liddell complained on 3 July that the Executive was 'really pandering to the Fifth Column neurosis, which is one of the greatest dangers with which we have to contend at the moment'.[99] By the end of July, however, fifth-column 'neurosis' had passed its peak. Mass internment reassured most of both Whitehall and the public that the fifth column had been neutralized, and MI5 noted a welcome decline in alarmist reports with which it was expected to deal. The establishment in late June, at the suggestion of Liddell and B Branch, of twelve regional security liaison officers (RSLOs) also enabled such reports to be filtered locally, with the result that only a minority reached MI5 headquarters in Wormwood Scrubs.[100]

Reports by Swinton and the Security Executive on 'the danger of retaining alien internees in this country', where they might help a German invasion, led some to be deported to Canada. Deportations ceased after a former luxury liner, *Arandora Star*, carrying 1,200 German and Italian internees across the Atlantic, was torpedoed on 2 July by a German submarine and sank with heavy loss of life.[101] On 24 July further mass internment was suspended due to lack of accommodation, and was never resumed. Early in August a government spokesman admitted that, due to official blunders, many innocent people had been interned.[102] Later in the month, Churchill told the Commons, with what one historian has called 'an impressive display of amnesia', that he had always thought the fifth-column danger exaggerated.[103] By late October just over 20 per cent of the aliens interned had been released.[104]

The Security Service, like the military authorities, was unhappy with the extent of the releases. Its main concern was the potential support of those released for a German invasion. British intelligence did not know that German invasion plans (codenamed Operation SEALION) had been indefinitely postponed on 17 September and cancelled on 12 October. Military intelligence declared on 29 September that 'the time will never come when it will be safe to say that there will be no invasion.' On 10 October, though reporting that the threat of invasion had declined, the JIC concluded that it would persist as long as the Luftwaffe remained larger than the RAF.[105] Harker, as the Service director, did not put the case for maintaining mass internment well. When the Security Executive discussed a recommendation by the Advisory Committee on Internment on 24 October that interned domestic servants of established repute should be released, Harker declared that 'experience had shown that German and Austrian domestic servants were not always as harmless as they appeared.'[106] Apart from unsubstantiated claims after the conquest of France and the Low Countries that German maids had led paratroopers to their targets,[107] it is difficult to guess what 'experience' Harker had in mind.

Influenced by the treachery exposed by the Kent–Wolkoff case (which at the time the Security Service could not know was as untypical as it now appears), the Service exaggerated the potential threat to national security posed by the phasing out of mass internment. But it is still impossible to be certain how loyal enemy aliens and British Fascists would have been if

Operation SEALION had gone ahead. 'It must never be forgotten', wrote Sir David Petrie later, that many of those British Fascists who had protested their patriotism 'might have behaved very differently if ever a German invasion had become a reality'.[108] A (probably small) minority of enemy aliens and British Fascists, consisting mainly of those who remained interned throughout the war, might well have supported it. At the Peveril internment camp in the Isle of Man on Hitler's birthday in April 1943 'there was community singing of the Horst Wessel Lied in the Camp canteen.'[109]

In the midst of the controversy over ending mass internment, the Security Service was forced to move its headquarters. As soon as the London Blitz began in September 1940, it became clear that Wormwood Scrubs was insecure. During air-raids three-quarters or more of the staff on upper floors were ordered to leave their rooms; only the ground floor was regarded as being reasonably safe.[110] The Registry index and files were particularly vulnerable, following the unwise decision to house them in a glass-roofed workshop which had formerly been the prison laundry. One member of staff recalls arriving at the Scrubs on 29 September:

to find firemen and hosepipes everywhere. An incendiary bomb had dropped on the Registry and apparently the night duty officer could not find the keys quickly enough so the hosepipes had to be worked through the barred windows and doors and the mess was simply awful. The half-burnt files were soaking wet and there was a disgusting smell of burnt wetness.[111]

The whole central card index and about 800 files were badly damaged. Though the index had been microfilmed at the suggestion of Victor Rothschild, the quality of the film was so poor that registry clerks could work on it for only a few hours at a time and the index took nine months to reconstruct.[112]

In October 1940 the greater part of the Security Service moved to the safer and far more scenic surroundings of Blenheim Palace at Woodstock, near Oxford, which had just been vacated by the boys of Marlborough College. The Director, some other senior officers and the counter-espionage operations officers stayed in London at a building in St James's Street whose role was camouflaged by a large 'To Let' sign outside. St James's Street was known as the 'town office' and Blenheim Palace as the 'country office'.[113] After the miseries of Wormwood Scrubs and the London Blitz, one member of staff found arriving at the Palace during 'wonderful autumn weather' a 'blissful' experience:

At Blenheim the trees were gold with autumn and the sky was blue, the palace pale yellow, really lovely. Our desks were set up under the tapestries which were still on the walls. The Duke had his own wing and we had the run of the grounds in the lunch hour ... I swam in the lake occasionally and, when it snowed, a lot of the staff tobogganed using the intrays, or skated on the frozen lake to the confusion of the sentries stationed at the edge to repel intruders.[114]

The Registry occupied most of the ground floor, including the Great Hall, the Long Library and some of the state rooms. Anthony Blunt, who was based in St James's Street, came from time to time to lecture on the architecture of Blenheim Palace.[115] Not all staff, however, worked in the Palace itself. John Stephenson's office was a hut in the courtyard, 'inadequately warmed by paraffin and imperfectly ventilated. Though draughts of cold air came in, fumes of paraffin and tobacco were unable to get out.'[116]

Initially, 250 female staff[117] (later considerably more) were lodged in rooms at Keble College, Oxford, usually two to one undergraduate set. Since there were no telephones in the rooms, messages had to be left with the college porters, who would stand in the quad and bellow the names of the recipients. Coal for the coal fires in rooms was rationed; cold and condensation were constant problems in the winter months. After a usually Spartan breakfast in the College Hall, served by the scouts (male servants), buses were waiting in a side road to take staff to Blenheim Palace.[118] In May 1941 Keble's Bursar complained that Service staff were responsible for considerably more breakages than undergraduates. M. B. Heywood replied on behalf of the Service:

It is difficult to envisage that, among other things, our staff have broken 28 large coffee pots, 740 plates of [all] sorts and 104 dishes of [all] sorts in the dining room, unless there has been a free fight.

I feel that the bulk of the breakages must occur between the kitchen and the dining room and be attributable to the College staff.[119]

A minority of female staff, as Milicent Bagot later recalled, lived in greater comfort in nearby country houses:

One of our hostesses startled her billetees on their arrival, wearied by many sleepless nights in London, by enquiring whether any of them fished, shot or hunted. She herself went off regularly once a week for hunting. Her domestic staff included a butler, personal maid, cook and housemaid, as well as a girl especially detailed to look after the billetees. It was a strange world for most of us![120]

Telephone No.:
OXFORD 48411-6.

Telegraphic Address:
SNUFFBOX, OXFORD.

BOX No. 500,

G.P.O.,

OXFORD.

5th May, 1941.

Dear Colonel Milman,

    Thank you for your letter of May 3rd. Before I discuss the question of china damages with my chief, perhaps you could clarify the following points.

    In comparing our staff with undergraduates, has a true comparison been taken? Our staff have been in continuous residence for six months, whereas undergraduates are only in residence for a period of eight weeks at a time.

    It is difficult to envisage that, among other things, our staff have broken 28 large coffee pots, 740 plates of sorts and 104 dishes of sorts in the dining room, unless there has been a free fight.

    I feel that the bulk of the breakages must occur between the kitchen and the dining room and be attributable to the College staff. I am painfully aware, as no doubt you are, what wholesale breakages can occur in washing up, dropping trays, etc, even in one's own home.

    I have made enquiries regarding breakages in the rooms, and am assured that they were all paid for at the time.

    As far as normal breakages are concerned, I was under the impression that the 28/- per week covered wear and tear to College property.

        Yours sincerely,

Colonel Milman,
   Keble College,
      Oxford.

MI5 defends itself against complaints that its female staff occupying rooms at Keble College, Oxford, destroy more crockery than the students.

Though the staff worked long hours, the office circulars at Blenheim provide evidence of a working environment unimaginable at the Scrubs. For example: 'The practice of leaving bunches of flowers in the fire buckets militates against the efficiency of our fire fighting arrangements, and causes much extra work for the fire fighting staff. Will all members of the staff therefore please refrain from placing their flowers in the fire bucket.'[121] Staff also had to be reminded about the rules of the road in the Palace grounds:

A great deal of horn-blowing, mud-splashing and general confusion would be avoided if both pedestrians and car-drivers would conform to the normal rule of the road, viz where no footpath is provided, pedestrians should walk on the RIGHT hand side of the road, so as to face oncoming traffic, while car-drivers should proceed on the LEFT hand side of the road. Car owners are also reminded that in order to avoid excess damage to the drive and unnecessary splashing of pedestrians, a speed limit of 10 MPH is in force in the Palace Grounds.[122]

In addition to swimming, tennis and cricket in summer, as one member of staff recalled:

There was plenty of entertainment in the evenings for those who wanted it . . . There were lists that you could sign should you wish to be what was called a 'hostess' at parties given by the RAF and the American [Army] Air Force stationed at the many airfields near by; we were usually picked up, and of course returned, in a five (or was it a ten) ton lorry. We were herded like cattle on benches at the back all in our finery for an evening out. As the lorries were far from clean, we feared that our own dresses, skirts etc would be ruined and stained before we even got to the party. On arrival, there was certainly no shortage of drink, the one idea was to get us, shall we say, more than merry.[123]

At Blenheim Palace, the Security Service had its first royal visitor, Queen Mary (widow of George V), who was shown round by the Duke of Marl-borough, but disconcerted staff by 'looking through' them.[124] Other visitors included Winston Churchill, who was an occasional weekend guest of his cousin the Duke.[125] As one member of staff wrote:

Churchill was born in the downstairs room where Constant and Mounsey had their office. These two ladies (no one would call them girls) gave us our monthly salary in pound notes in envelopes ('no lady talks about her pay' we were told). New faces appeared on the staff. Strange Mr Croft-Murray with the booming voice started up a little orchestra which gave lunchtime concerts. He was once seen playing the violin in an open car as it sped along near Marlow . . . The first time I saw Lord Rothschild (Sabotage section) must have been a Sunday morning. He was wearing an open neck shirt and carrying a leather holdall. I thought he was a plumber until he asked the way in beautiful educated English.[126]

Despite the dramatic improvement in working conditions at Blenheim, during the early months administration remained confused, further complicated by the need to ferry files to and fro between the Palace and the St James's Street headquarters. Confidence in Jasper Harker's leadership continued to decline. The controversy over the release of a majority of the internees also continued. The leadership of the Security Service knew that despatch of a new wave of Abwehr agents to Britain which began in September had been intended as part of the preparations for a German invasion,[127] and feared that freed internees might assist the invading forces. The Service objected to 111 of the 199 cases in which the Advisory Committee on Internment recommended the release of British Fascists interned under Defence Regulation 18B. At a meeting of the Security Executive on 6 November, however, it was forced to back down and, faced with opposition from both Swinton and the Home Secretary, dropped its objections to all but fifteen cases.[128] By the end of 1940 almost a third of enemy alien internees had been released.[129]

Churchill complained to the Foreign and Home Secretaries on 25 January 1941 that 'the witch-finding activities of MI5 are becoming an actual impediment to the more important work of the department.'[130] This harsh criticism was coloured by the Prime Minister's more general unease at the state of the Security Service. In late November he had received a cryptic handwritten letter from an old political ally, Baron Croft of Bournemouth, Parliamentary Under Secretary for War in the House of Lords, reporting that all was not well 'in certain quarters' and urging him to send for Major Gilbert Lennox, MI5's liaison officer with military intelligence, and ask him to speak freely. 'Do not consult *anyone*,' he added.[131] After retiring from the Indian army in 1932 at the age of forty-four, Lennox had begun a successful new career as a playwright. His pre-war play *Close Quarters*, about a left-wing couple who commit suicide after being wrongly accused of the assassination of a Fascist dictator, had been a hit in the West End and also played more briefly on Broadway. Lennox joined the Service at the outbreak of war on the recommendation of Jane Archer and Dick White. In Archer's view, as well as being 'a playwright of some standing', Lennox was 'an extremely "hearty soul" . . . a man of the world, shrewd and of sound judgement with a taking manner'.[132] Harker's decision to sack Archer in November 1940 probably brought to a head Lennox's dissatisfaction with the management of the

Security Service.[133] Lennox was taken aback, however, to be summoned to see Churchill on 26 November.[134]

When shown into the Prime Minister's study, Lennox explained his views about MI5 and the Security Executive. He was then further taken aback to be asked by Churchill why he had come, and replied, 'Because you sent for me.' Churchill said that he left such matters to his intelligence adviser, Major Desmond Morton, and sent Lennox to see Morton in his room in Number Ten.[135] Lennox told Morton that the Service was suffering from inadequate leadership and internal jealousies. On Churchill's instructions, Morton then consulted the directors of intelligence in the three armed services. He reported to the Prime Minister on 3 December that the directors believed the Security Service was close to collapse, that Harker was not up to the job, and that Swinton's 'executive control' of the Service was unsatisfactory. In their view, MI5 required a strong civilian, non-political head who would report to a minister, not to Swinton. By this time the former Home Secretary Sir John Anderson, then Lord President, had taken the initiative in commissioning an inquiry into the Security Service from the former head of the Delhi Intelligence Bureau and chairman of the Indian Public Service Commission, Sir David Petrie, a sixty-year-old Scot.[136] Petrie was also asked if he would be willing to take over from Harker. But, he wrote later, 'I refused outright to take charge until I had examined things for myself.'[137] Once he had completed his review, Petrie agreed to take charge.

Petrie's report, completed on 13 February 1941, concluded, unsurprisingly, that the rapid and poorly planned wartime expansion of the Security Service had led to organizational breakdown and confusion, best exemplified in B Division, which currently had 133 officers distributed among twenty-nine sections, which were themselves divided into approximately seventy to eighty sub-sections. Crocker's appointment as joint head of the Division had only increased the confusion. Petrie strongly supported proposals (implemented after he took over) to lighten B Division's load by moving 'alien control' (including internment issues) and counter-subversion to, respectively, a new E Division and a new F Division (both based at Blenheim). His report also implied that giving Swinton 'executive control' of MI5 had been 'an unfortunate mistake'. Outside interference had lowered MI5 morale.[138] Before becoming director general in April 1941, wrote Petrie later, 'I got the principle of the D.G. being master in his own house recognised and endorsed.'[139] Kell and Harker had had the title of director; Petrie was the Service's first director general.[140] Harker, who stayed on as Petrie's deputy, became deputy director general (DDG). Charles Butler, head of A Division (administration and Registry),[141] Guy

Liddell, head of B Division (counter-espionage), and H. I. 'Harry' Allen, head of C Division (mainly vetting) and D Division (protective security and travel control), were given the title of director. Theodore 'Ted' Turner, head of the new E Division, and Jack Curry, head of the new F Division, were made deputy directors.[142]

Dick White, Assistant Director of B Division when Petrie took over, later described the new Director General as 'one of the best man managers I ever met'.[143] Ashton Roskill agreed: 'Solid in appearance and in mind, [Petrie] made it his business to know the essentials of his job, but did not hesitate to delegate. I doubt if he had more than a B+ mind but he used it, made few – if any – mistakes, and combined courtesy with firmness.'[144] Norman Himsworth, an officer in Maxwell Knight's section, remembered him as 'A real gentleman. He would speak broad Scots when he was annoyed but perfect English when he was not.'[145] Catherine Weldsmith (née Morgan-Smith), later the last lady superintendent, who was deputed to show Petrie around Blenheim, found him 'very easy and nice about it – he was rather a shy man.'[146] The DG was acutely security-conscious. One of the secretaries at St James's Street recalls that 'He always burned his own Top Secret stuff in a fire bucket.'[147] Almost all accounts of Petrie's appointment as DG agree with Curry that he 'restored confidence – almost immediately internally and more gradually among the officers and Departments with whom [MI5] was in external relation . . .'[148]

By the autumn of 1941 the Security Service had completed an internal transformation as striking as the move of its main premises 'from prison to palace'. Its resources on the eve of war – with only thirty-six officers and 133 secretarial and Registry staff – were below the level that would nowadays be considered necessary for a security service with such wide responsibilities and the reasonable expectation of a major enemy intelligence offensive to function at all. The Secret Service Committee had given no serious thought to its future leadership, allowing Kell to continue on a yearly basis as long as, in his own words, he remained 'compos mentis' in order to avoid having to take a longer-term decision. Its choice of Harker to succeed him in June 1940 appears to have been taken without any attempt to seek the views even of senior staff who would very probably have expressed some of the reservations which surfaced soon after he became director. During the first year of the war, even with effective leadership, the Service would have been unable to cope with the unreasonable demands made of it. What remains surprising is less that, by the time of Kell's dismissal, as Curry acknowledged, MI5 had been reduced to 'a state which can only be described as chaotic' than that, over the next year, it achieved a total dominance over German intelligence which it retained for the rest of the war.[149]

The transformation of the Security Service was made possible, in part, by new leadership in the person of Sir David Petrie. At least equally important was the ability of a group of able pre-war officers – Guy Liddell, Dick White and Tar Robertson chief among them – to win the respect and harness the often remarkable talents of the wartime recruits. One of the keys to the Service's wartime success from 1941 onwards was its *esprit de corps*. It was, recalled the Oxford historian Sir John Masterman a genera-tion later, 'a team of congenial people who worked together harmoniously and unselfishly, and among whom rank counted for little and character for much'.[150] Though not all were as enthusiastic as Masterman,[151] many were.[152] An opinion survey by outside consultants in 2000 reported that 98 per cent of staff believed in the importance of their work and 87 per cent expressed pride in working for the Service – among the highest ratings the consultants had recorded inside or outside the public service.[153] A similar survey in 1945 might well have produced a similar result. Even for Victor Rothschild, who had no shortage of glittering careers ahead of him, leaving the Service after the Second World War was a deeply emotional moment. He wrote to Petrie's successor as DG, Sir Percy Sillitoe, who was appointed from outside:

I have been in the Security Service now for six years, and the idea of officially resigning from it is painful and distressing in a way which perhaps you, who have not seen much of us, may find difficult to understand. Most of the people who have been as intimately associated with it as I have been, have developed an affection for the Office as a whole and the staff in particular which I am certain is most unusual in a large Government Department.[154]

Few of the Security Service's wartime successes were known to other government departments. The reasons for the Service policy of hiding its light under a bushel went some way beyond the demands of operational security. Petrie preferred to keep his contacts with Whitehall to a minimum. Two years after becoming director general, he admitted to Duff Cooper (Swinton's successor as head of the Security Executive) that he was a bad 'publicity merchant' for the Service:

I have lived so long abroad that I had comparatively few contacts in London, and I never cared to extend them beyond what was necessary for business purposes. So it is a fact that many people, even some who ought to know better, have only the vaguest idea of M.I.5 and what it does. This certainly does not hurt our work –

quite the contrary – but it bears rather hardly on the department and the many able officers it comprises.[155]

Unlike Stewart Menzies, the Chief of SIS, Petrie made no attempt to forge a personal relationship with Churchill, though there was much about the Security Service's wartime work which would have fascinated (and eventually did fascinate) the Prime Minister. Had Petrie briefed Churchill, he would have been able to counter dismissive comments by Desmond Morton, as late as 1943, that 'MI5 tends to see dangerous men too freely and to lack that knowledge of the world and sense of perspective which the Home Secretary rightly considers essential.'[156] At the very moment when Morton made this claim, MI5's double agents were achieving unprecedented success in deceiving the enemy. It did not occur to Petrie to send Churchill a monthly report until Duff Cooper suggested it in March 1943.[157]

One of the few parts of Security Service work to come to Churchill's attention from other sources was the extraordinary bravery of Victor Rothschild as head of its counter-sabotage department in defusing German bombs, meticulously recording his every move by field telephone in case he was killed in the attempt. (Rothschild owed much of his success to the expertise in micro-manipulation which he had acquired as a young zoologist at Cambridge University dissecting frogs' eggs and sea-urchins.) But, when Churchill asked Petrie in February 1944 about Rothschild's success in defusing a German bomb hidden in a crate of Spanish onions which was timed to explode in a British port, the DG's response was so off-hand that it amounted to a brush-off – or, as Rothschild described it, 'a raspberry'.[158] The head of Churchill's Defence Office, General Sir Hastings 'Pug' Ismay, replied that the Prime Minister would not be content with the information supplied and asked for more.[159] When it was provided, Churchill took the personal decision to award Rothschild the George Medal.[160]

Petrie's relations with Churchill were less successful than Kell's had been thirty years before. Churchill's willingness as home secretary in 1910–11 to make a major extension to the HOW system and his encouragement to chief constables to collaborate with Kell were crucial to the successes of MI5 counter-espionage before the First World War.[161] Since Petrie regarded the early history of the Security Service as an irrelevance,[162] he may well have been ignorant of Churchill's important role in it. His reluctance to take the Prime Minister fully into his confidence during the Second World War, however, had some justification. Petrie probably believed that, if Churchill knew more about Service operations, he might jump to hasty conclusions and interfere, as he did in the North African campaigns in 1941–2 when German decrypts convinced him that Rommel was much weaker than he was.[163] Though Churchill's enthusiasm for intelligence far exceeded that of any previous British prime minister, Petrie was right to be nervous about where that enthusiasm might lead him.[164]

I

Deception

The Second World War, like most of its predecessors, found Britain at best half ready. The War Office knew so little about Germany's immediate plan of campaign that, misled by mistaken intelligence reports over the past year,[1] it feared the Luftwaffe would attempt an immediate 'knock-out blow' against London. At 11.27 on the morning of Sunday 3 September, barely a quarter of an hour after the Prime Minister, Neville Chamberlain, had broadcast the news that the nation was at war, air-raid sirens wailed over the capital. War Office staff in Whitehall from top brass to junior clerks filed down to the air-raid shelter in the basement. There they listened apprehensively to a series of muffled explosions above them which a former military attaché with first-hand experience of air-raids during the Spanish Civil War identified as a mixture of anti-aircraft fire and bombs dropping. When the all-clear sounded, the War Office staff emerged from the basement and discovered to their surprise that there had been no air-raid, and that the 'explosions' had been caused by the noise of slamming office doors echoing down the lift shafts.[2] In reality, the Luftwaffe was not yet capable of launching a 'knock-out blow'. It was unable to begin the London Blitz until after the conquest of France and the Low Countries in the following year. The intervening eight months in the west were a period of 'Phoney War', sometimes almost as surreal as the first hours of the war in the War Office basement. On 5 September the Secretary of State for Air insisted that 'there was no question of our bombing even the munitions factories at Essen, which were private property.' Leaflets were dropped instead. Until Churchill succeeded Chamberlain as prime minister in May 1940 no British bombs were dropped on German territory.[3]

The intelligence war, however, began immediately, and for some months Germany seemed to have the upper hand. In less than a fortnight, the Security Service lost its most important German source. The diplomat Wolfgang zu Putlitz, who for the past sixteen months had been stationed at the German legation in The Hague,[4] realized that the security of the local SIS station must have been breached when the German ambassador showed him a list of German agents in the Netherlands identical to one he had given SIS.[5] Putlitz concluded that it 'could only be a matter of time before he was discovered and dealt with', and sought refuge in Britain with his partner and valet, Willy Schneider. On 15 September they arrived in London and were welcomed by Dick White, who found them temporary accommodation in his brother's flat. Though Putlitz's belief that the SIS station in The Hague must be penetrated was later shown to be correct, at the time it was not taken very seriously. 'The general impression', noted Guy Liddell, 'is that the whole situation had rather got on his nerves and that he felt he could not go on.'[6]

For the Security Service the only compensation for the loss of Putlitz was that another of its agents, a German-born British subject, Mrs 'Susan Barton' (the name by which she was usually known within the Service), seemed on the point of penetrating the German legation in The Hague. 'Barton' had been working as a 'casual agent' for several years, providing information on the German colony in Britain before moving to the Netherlands in 1939.[7] Once in The Hague 'Barton' renewed contact with Lili, an old friend from Germany who was working as the secretary of the German naval attaché, Captain Besthorn. Besthorn took a liking to the attractive Mrs 'Barton', who encouraged his interest in her. Lili wrote to her on one occasion, 'The Captain wants to be remembered [to you], he was very pleased about your letter written specially for him! Oh these men . . .' When Ustinov returned to Britain after Putlitz's defection, 'Barton' moved in with Lili and reported on 25 October that Besthorn was seeking authorization from Berlin to offer her a job. Lili, however, seemed jealous since 'she believes herself to be in love' with Besthorn.[8]

For several months SIS in The Hague mistakenly believed that it was on the verge of a spectacular success which would more than compensate for the loss of Putlitz. Soon after the outbreak of war Major Richard Stevens, the SIS head of station, and his colleague Captain Sigismund Payne Best were contacted by Germans claiming to be senior army officers engaged in a plot to remove Hitler from power. The plotters were in reality officers of the Sicherheitsdienst (SD, the SS security service) who successfully deceived Whitehall as well as SIS. Sir Nevile Bland, the British minister in the Netherlands, wrote to congratulate the Chief of SIS, Admiral Quex Sinclair, on the choice of Stevens to conduct the negotiations with the plotters: 'Stevens is being quite admirable: you couldn't have done better when you chose him.'[9] Lord Hankey, Minister without Portfolio but with special responsibility for the intelligence services in Chamberlain's

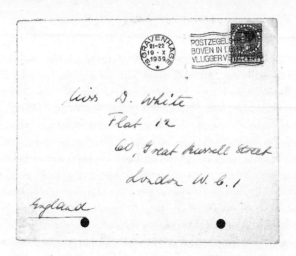

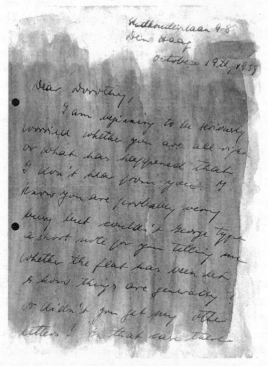

Extract of letter (tested for invisible ink) from the German-born British subject and MI5 agent 'Susan Barton' in the Netherlands to her case officer in London, 'Dorothy White' (the pseudonym by which she addressed Dick White). 'Barton' seemed on the point of obtaining a job with the German naval attaché in The Hague but was recalled for fear that she had been compromised, following the capture of two SIS officers.

War Cabinet (and previously a long-serving cabinet secretary), was equally enthusiastic, describing a secret report by Sinclair on Stevens's and Best's negotiations with the bogus German conspirators as 'one of the most cheering documents I have read'.[10] Chamberlain too was in optimistic mood, apparently interpreting the German overtures as evidence of growing awareness by the enemy that 'they *can't* win.' 'I have a "hunch"', he wrote on 5 November, 'that the war will be over by the spring.' Four days later, at a meeting with the supposed German dissidents at Venlo on the Dutch–German border, Stevens and Best were kidnapped by the SD and taken to Germany where they were later given starring roles by the Gestapo in a publicity stunt involving an alleged attempt on Hitler's life.[11]

The first that John Curry (probably like other Security Service officers) knew of what had happened was when he read a report in *The Times* that two British officers had been captured at Venlo. Curry immediately rang up SIS to ask if Stevens and Best were the officers concerned.[12] The main immediate anxiety of the Security Service leadership in the wake of the Venlo kidnap was for its agent 'Susan Barton',[13] whose identity was known to Stevens. Liddell noted on 12 November: 'The danger is that Stevens generally carried a list of agents in his vestpocket. Nobody knows at the moment what he had on him.' For her own safety Dick White recalled 'Barton' to England, thus ending her hope of penetrating the German embassy.[14] Despite the kidnap of Stevens and Best, SIS and the Foreign Office still failed to realize they had been taken in. Radio messages from the bogus conspirators, making no mention of Venlo, continued to reach SIS. Finally, on 22 November the SD tired of continuing the charade and sent a mocking radio message to tell SIS it had been duped. 'So that's over,' Cadogan noted in his diary, though he still thought the original approach from anti-Hitler plotters might have been genuine but subsequently 'taken over' by the Gestapo.[15] The SD's tactical triumph, however, was a strategic mistake. Instead of kidnapping Best and Stevens, German intelligence could have maintained the illusion of SIS and Whitehall that they were in contact with influential opponents of Adolf Hitler and used that illusion as the basis of a long-term deception.

Even after the Venlo débâcle, there seems to have been no serious attempt by either SIS or MI5 (both at the time heavily overstretched) to examine the evidence for Putlitz's conviction that the SIS station in The Hague was either penetrated or, at the very least, leaking highly classified intelligence.[16] In particular, no suspicion fell on the assistant to the SIS head agent, Folkert van Koutrik, who had been recruited by the Abwehr as a double agent (codenamed WALBACH) in October 1938.[17] Van Koutrik had betrayed both Putlitz and SIS's longest-serving German agent, Dr Otto Krüger, a retired naval officer who was run by the SIS station in The Hague. Krüger committed suicide in prison shortly after confessing that he had worked for SIS for twenty-one years.[18]

After the German invasion of the Low Countries in May 1940, van Koutrik and his wife fled to Britain, probably at the instigation of the Abwehr, which doubtless hoped to continue using him as a double agent.[19] Van Koutrik, who still aroused no suspicion in SIS or MI5, gave a heroic (though fraudulent) account of his selfless devotion to duty while working as an SIS agent in the Netherlands before his flight:

Certainly within the last two years I worked in constant danger, as the Nazi-power grew bigger and bigger, but I stayed on the job and did my utmost.

When we had to leave Holland which was a matter of hours, together with my wife, (who expected a baby) I destroyed all reports, lists and valuable documents, which took us all the availalble [sic] time. . . . I drove my wife and children as well as the family [of the SIS head agent Adrianus] V[rinten] t[h]rough the town, whilst bombing and machinegunning was going on, safe aboard of the ship which brought us over to England.

I am proud to say that, for my part, not a piece of paper, which could lead to the arrest by Germans of our agents, was left in my house. My wife and I, we did not think of ourselves but of the people we left behind. We left the house only with a small case with some children-cloth[e]s.[20]

Once in England, van Koutrik was quickly taken on by the Security Service to work for E1c, making 'special enquiries' about the flood of foreign refugees.[21] To protect himself against any possible suggestion of responsibility for leaking intelligence from the SIS station, van Koutrik pointed a finger of suspicion at Vrinten, who, he claimed, had destroyed only 'a small part' of his files, seeming more interested in packing 'six or eight big cases' of his possessions to take with him to England.[22] While working for the Security Service, van Koutrik sought to strengthen his claim that Vrinten, currently employed by the security service of the Dutch government in exile, was unreliable; he reported on a number of occasions that Vrinten was asking him 'indiscreet questions'.[23]

For the first time in its history, MI5 was thus penetrated in May 1940 by a German agent – a month before it recruited the Soviet agent Anthony Blunt, of whose past record it was also unaware.[24] While van Koutrik was not in the Blunt class, his previous record as the Abwehr's most successful agent operating against British targets, combined with his continuing ability to avoid attracting suspicion, demonstrate that he posed a serious potential security risk to the Security Service. Though very few details survive of his work for MI5, a note of December 1940 records E1c's total confidence in his commitment to the Allied cause: 'Since his employment by this Office his duties have been varied, though his greatest success has been as an Agent. In that capacity he has always been very resourceful and I should say that he has always displayed a perfectly genuine faithfulness.' What caused concern in E1c was not van Koutrik's loyalty but his abrasive personality: 'He has frequently antagonised and offended Officials who might otherwise have been extremely helpful.'[25] In August 1941 van Koutrik was sacked from the Security Service with one month's salary on the pretext that there was no longer work for him to do. 'Is this the way the Government shows her appreciation?' he wrote sarcastically. 'Very generous indeed.'[26] For several months in 1942 Koutrik went on to work for SIS, also interrogating refugees.[27]

Scarcely had van Koutrik been dismissed than the pre-war German agent William John 'Jack' Hooper, a British-Dutch dual national who had also worked for the SIS station in The Hague, was taken on by the Security Service. Hooper had been dismissed by SIS in September 1936 – he claimed unfairly – after the scandal caused by the suicide of the head of station, Major H. E. Dalton, and the discovery that Dalton had embezzled SIS funds.[28] After his dismissal Hooper volunteered his services to Soviet intelligence, which employed him as an agent during 1937 before breaking contact with him – probably as the result of the defection of a GRU officer who knew of his recruitment. While working for Soviet intelligence, Hooper had also made contact with the Germans and worked as an Abwehr agent in 1938–9. A post-war investigation, largely based on the interrogation of German intelligence officers, revealed that Hooper had disclosed to the Abwehr both that Dr Otto Krüger was an SIS agent (probably shortly after van Koutrik had already done so), and that Soviet intelligence had penetrated the Foreign Office Communications Department (a fact he had learned while working for the NKVD). While working for the Abwehr, Hooper simultaneously tried to mend his fences with SIS by revealing to them also the existence of a Soviet spy in the Communications Department. Initially his intelligence was not taken seriously. When it was shown to be correct, SIS revised its view of Hooper and re-engaged him as an agent in October 1939. After the German conquest of the Netherlands, Hooper, like van Koutrik, moved to Britain. In 1941 he was taken on by the Security Service as an agent-recruiter based (after a trial period in London) in Glasgow.[29]

Though the Security Service had, unwittingly, taken grave risks in employing van Koutrik and Hooper, it seems to have suffered little, if any, damage from either case. During post-war interrogations senior Abwehr officers were frank about van Koutrik's work for them up to his departure for England in May 1940 but gave no indication that it continued afterwards. It would have been difficult as well as very risky for van Koutrik to have renewed contact with the Abwehr from Britain, and he may well have been unwilling to take the risk. A post-war inquiry by SIS concluded, however, that, while working for the Dutch security service, he had been 'disloyal to the Dutch Government in exile', though it gave no details:

He was released after a period of detention by the Dutch authorities after returning to Holland after its liberation merely because the Dutch found it impossible on the existing evidence to bring him to court.

. . .

The man has blood on his hands.[30]

As in the case of van Koutrik, Hooper's previous career as a German agent was eventually discovered by the Security Service as a result of post-war interrogations of Abwehr officers.[31] Again like van Koutrik, it seemed highly improbable that Hooper had tried to renew contact with the Germans after his move to Britain. In August 1945, a month before Hooper was confronted with the evidence against him and sacked, Petrie reported to 'C':

With the exception of one incident involving rather serious indiscretions with a woman [Hooper's mistress] and a general tendency to high expense claims, I have had no trouble with Hooper and have no reason to suspect that he has been acting other than in the interests of this country. His work, which has been carefully supervised, has in fact been extremely good.[32]

The success of both van Koutrik and Hooper in penetrating the Security Service, following the earlier humiliation of SIS at Venlo, demonstrates the opportunities available to German intelligence during the first year of the war to mount its own Double-Cross System.[33] It would not have been difficult for the Abwehr to make arrangements for van Koutrik to communicate with it after he moved to England, for example by writing under a pseudonym to a cover address in a neutral country. The threat to reveal to the British that he had betrayed both Krüger and Putlitz would have been likely to ensure van Koutrik's continued collaboration. But the opportunity was missed. Nor is there any evidence of a sustained attempt to retain Hooper as an Abwehr agent after the outbreak of war.[34]

During the first year of the war there was an extraordinary transformation in the balance of intelligence power between Germany and Britain, marked most dramatically by the fact that ULTRA, the SIGINT obtained from decrypting the variants of the German 'Enigma' and other high-grade enemy ciphers, began to come on stream in May 1940, the month when Churchill became prime minister. While Germany threw away at Venlo the opportunity for a major, long-term penetration of British intelligence, the Security Service was in the early stages of establishing the spectacularly successful British Double-Cross System.[35] The Double-Cross began a few weeks after the outbreak of war when the double agent SNOW met his Abwehr case officer, Major Nikolaus Ritter, in Rotterdam and arranged a further meeting in October to which he promised to bring a Welsh saboteur.[36] MI5 sent to the second meeting a retired Swansea police inspector, codenamed GW,[37] who successfully posed as a Welsh nationalist explosives expert anxious to sabotage English targets. SNOW and GW returned to England with money, an Abwehr code and microphotographed instructions which included leads to what turned out to be the only two remaining German agents still resident in Britain.[38] MI5 identified both. The first, Mathilde Krafft, a German-born British national who was used by the Abwehr to forward money, was put under surveillance but not arrested immediately for fear of compromising SNOW and in the hope that she might produce leads to other agents; she was later interned in Holloway Prison.[39] The second, codenamed CHARLIE, was a British businessman who had been pressured into working for the Abwehr by threats to a German relative and was easily turned into a double agent by MI5.[40] The code supplied to SNOW and GW later helped GC&CS to discover the basic construction of Abwehr hand ciphers, which were later regularly broken and assisted the capture of other German agents. The first Abwehr decrypt was circulated by GC&CS (which had relocated to Bletchley Park at the outbreak of war) on 14 April 1940. To produce the decrypts, which continued for the rest of the war, a new section was set up at Bletchley, headed by the veteran codebreaker Oliver Strachey. The decrypts became known as ISOS ('Intelligence Service Oliver Strachey'), informally referred to by some of those with access to it as 'ice'; its initiates were said to be 'iced'.[41]

In May 1940 SNOW's eight-month-old career as a double agent came close to disaster. His German case officer, Major Ritter, asked SNOW to meet him on a trawler in the North Sea and to bring along another potential Abwehr recruit who was then to proceed to Germany to be trained in sabotage and espionage. The bogus recruit chosen by B1a, the double-agent section of B Division, was a reformed petty criminal (codenamed BISCUIT) who had previously been used as an MI5 informant.[42] SNOW and BISCUIT proved a nearly disastrous combination. Even before their trawler left Grimsby, BISCUIT told his B1a case officer that SNOW had admitted 'double-crossing us'.[43] Once at sea, the two men had a violent quarrel. SNOW – at BISCUIT's insistence – was placed under guard in the cabin, and the trawler returned to Grimsby.[44] On MI5 instructions SNOW sent a radio message to Ritter claiming that the trawler had turned up at the rendezvous but had become lost in North Sea fog. BISCUIT travelled to Lisbon, posing as a dealer in Portuguese wine, to meet Ritter and repeated the same excuse. Ritter seemed satisfied with the explanation, but confided in BISCUIT that, though SNOW's past performance had been excellent, he was now past his best.[45] Running the SNOW case taught the Security Service vastly more than it had previously known about Abwehr operations. According to Dick White, it 'saved us from absolute darkness on the subject of German espionage'.[46]

B1a was run by Thomas Argyll 'Tar' Robertson, one of the Security Service's ablest agent-runners. Born in Sumatra in 1909 but brought up in Tonbridge and educated at Charterhouse and Sandhurst, Robertson had begun his career in the Seaforth Highlanders before working in the City in the early 1930s and joining the Security Service in 1933.[47] Among his first assignments was mingling with sailors in pubs in the Cromarty Firth in order to assess their mood in the aftermath of the Invergordon Mutiny.[48] In MI5 headquarters Robertson continued to wear his tartan Seaforth trews, thus earning the nickname 'Passion Pants'.[49] Tar's natural air of authority did not suffer from the nickname. Sir Michael Howard describes him as 'a perfect officer type, who could have been played by Ronald Colman'.[50] He had a remarkable gift for selecting case officers (all previously inexperienced wartime recruits) who were capable of entering into the personalities of their double agents. Tar later recalled that 'one golden rule in running an agent was that his personality should be stamped on every message he transmitted' to the Abwehr.[51] B1a staff were devoted to him and remained so for the rest of their lives. Reminiscing half a century later, one of them, Christopher Harmer, wrote to his former B1a colleague Hugh Astor: 'Thank God for TAR I say. He gave us all our heads and encouraged us . . .'[52] Robertson's judgement, though usually very good, was not, of course, infallible. At his first meeting in October 1941 with Jack Hooper, later discovered to be a former agent of both Soviet and German intelligence, Tar 'formed a favourable opinion of him' and recommended that he be taken on trial.[53]

B1a's successes owed much to the leads provided by the 'Beavers' in B1b, who analysed ISOS decrypts, Abwehr communications with the double agents and other intelligence relevant to the Double-Cross System.[54]

Headed initially by the future judge Helenus 'Buster' Milmo, B1b contained some of the Security Service's most formidable intellects: among them Herbert Hart, later professor of jurisprudence at Oxford and principal of Brasenose College, and his fellow Oxford philosopher Patrick Day of New College. In August 1940 ISOS decrypts enabled the Beavers to give B1a advance warning of the imminent despatch of a new wave of Abwehr agents. The attempted expansion of the German agent network in Britain was part of the preparations for Operation *SEELÖWE* ('SEALION'), the planned but never implemented German invasion of Britain. During the three months from September to November twenty-five agents landed by parachute or small boat, most of them inadequately trained and poorly equipped. The Security Service found them 'an easy prey',[55] all the easier to detect since some of their forged identity documents were based on misleading information supplied by MI5. In August SNOW provided the Abwehr, at its request, with names and numbers for a dozen forged identity cards; two months later he was asked for more.[56]

B1a rapidly turned four of the twenty-five German agents into double agents. Central to the turning process was the Security Service's wartime interrogation centre, Camp 020 (known within the Service as B1e), based in Latchmere House near Ham Common in west London and run by Captain (later Colonel) Robin 'Tin-eye' Stephens. Tin-eye owed his nickname (never used to his face) to the monocle which seemed permanently glued to his right eye – he was rumoured to sleep in it. Born in 1900, he had spent fourteen years in the Indian army and political service, latterly working in the Judge Advocate's department. After returning to England in 1932, he went to Lincoln's Inn; though (for unknown reasons) not qualifying as a lawyer, he co-authored law books as well as working as a journalist. Like many other MI5 officers, Stephens was a keen sportsman, working from 1937 to 1939 for the National Fitness Council. He was also a good linguist, fluent in French, German and Italian, with an interpreter's qualification in Urdu and what he described as a 'poor' knowledge of Somali and Amharic.[57] He took a dim view of most Europeans. Italians were 'undersized, posturing folk', Belgians overweight, 'weeping and romantic', the French corrupt, Polish Jews 'shifty' and Icelanders 'unintelligent'. Stephens had a particular dislike of Germans. But, for all his ethnic prejudices, he proved a remarkable judge of individual character. 'National Characteristics in spies', he acknowledged, 'are inconclusive ... The interrogator must treat each spy as a very individual case ... a very personal enemy.'[58]

In January 1941, the London Reception Centre (LRC) was established at the Royal Victoria Patriotic School in Wandsworth to act as a screening centre for aliens arriving from enemy territory. In the course of the war, approximately 33,000 refugees passed through the LRC (known in the Security Service as B1d), where they were questioned about their methods of escape, the routes they had followed, safe houses, couriers, helpers and documentation. Their statements were meticulously indexed and cross-checked against those of their companions and earlier arrivals. Intelligence was extracted and circulated to Whitehall departments. Any inconsistencies in their stories were rigorously followed up. Though SIS and SOE officers were also present at the LRC, MI5 reserved the right to carry out the first interview. As Dick White put it, the function of the LRC was to separate the 'sheep from the goats'.[59] The goats – those suspected of being Axis agents – were transferred to Camp 020.

Camp 020's first major contribution to the construction of the Double-Cross System was to turn, in the space of only a few days, two of the first wave of Abwehr agents, codenamed SUMMER and TATE (both Scandinavians), who landed in England in September 1940. SUMMER was caught soon after landing by parachute in the Northamptonshire countryside in the early hours of 6 September by a farmhand who found him asleep in a ditch, together with his parachute, radio transmitter, £200 in banknotes, a false identity card and a loaded pistol. During interrogation at Camp 020, Stephens assessed him as 'a fanatical Nazi'. Within two days, however, SUMMER had agreed to work as a double agent in return for a promise that the life of his friend TATE would be spared. This was the only time in the history of Camp 020 that such a promise was made to a prisoner. It proved to be the key to the recruitment of TATE, who was dropped by parachute in the Cambridgeshire fens in the early hours of 20 September. As SUMMER had done, he landed heavily, spraining an ankle, and quickly aroused suspicion when he hobbled into the village of Willingham, wearing a smart blue suit. When arrested, TATE was found in possession of both a genuine Danish passport in his own name and a forged British identity card in the name of 'Williams'. The interrogation of TATE at Camp 020 followed a quite different pattern from that of SUMMER. He claimed to have landed by boat from Denmark three weeks earlier, fleeing persecution by the Germans – in the process infuriating a military intelligence officer from MI9, Colonel Alexander Scotland, who was present at the interrogation.[60] The sequel is described in Guy Liddell's diary for 22 September:

I have just been told that the officer from MI9 who was present at the interrogation of TATE yesterday took it upon himself to manhandle the prisoner without saying anything to Colonel Stephens, Dick White or Malcolm Frost [all of MI5]. The interrogation broke off at lunchtime, when Colonel Alexander Scotland left the room. Frost, wondering where he was, followed him and eventually found him in the prisoner's cell. He was hitting TATE in the jaw and I think got one back for himself. Frost stopped this without making a scene, and later told me what had happened. It was quite clear to me that we cannot have this sort of thing going on in our establishment. Apart from the moral aspect of the whole thing, I am quite convinced that these Gestapo methods do not work in the long run. We are taking the matter up with DMI [Director of Military Intelligence] and propose to say that we do not intend to have that particular military intelligence officer on the premises any more.[61]

Henceforth all interrogations, save on some matters of technical detail, were conducted exclusively by Camp 020 officers.[62] Stephens remained completely opposed to physical violence during interrogation (a principle later restated by the post-war Security Service). Guy Liddell noted an example of his punctiliousness. One of the officers at 020 was a qualified dentist, who carried out any dental work required at the camp, which occasionally included extracting a secret ink capsule hidden in a hollow tooth. Before doing so, the dentist would first obtain the prisoner's written consent.[63]

Stephens was, however, a firm believer in the use of psychological pressure to isolate the prisoner, intimidate him and demonstrate his powerlessness.[64] Potential double agents were told they could either work for the British or be sent for trial and hanged. Of the 440 people despatched to Camp 020, only fourteen were executed; Stephens was disappointed there were not more.[65] He was also a strong advocate of deception as a tool of the interrogator. The information given by SUMMER to gain a guarantee that TATE's life would be spared, including details of the arrangements for them to meet at the Black Boy Inn at Nottingham, was used to persuade TATE that his friend had betrayed him. TATE, wrote Stephens, 'lost all his previous composure, cursed "the swine [SUMMER]" and blurted out that he would tell the whole truth. He held back little.'[66] After only two days' interrogation,[67] TATE began a career as the longest-serving of all B1a's double agents, exchanging wireless messages with the Abwehr in Hamburg continuously from October 1940 until May 1945. His German controllers described him as a 'pearl' among agents, sent him large sums of money and had him awarded the Iron Cross, both First and Second Class.[68]

In the course of the Second World War, B1a, which usually had five case officers, ran a total of nearly 120 double agents. On average, five of its officers were running twenty-five agents at any one time.[69] Only six double agents were German nationals. The Abwehr deployed against Britain agents of thirty-four different nationalities. Though only eleven of the double agents were turned by Camp 020, they included some of the most successful: among them (in addition to TATE and SUMMER) the Briton Eddie Chapman (ZIGZAG) and the Norwegian Helge John Niel Moe (MUTT).[70]

Though the Security Service retained the lead role in the Double-Cross System, its successful expansion depended on an unprecedented degree of collaboration within the British intelligence community, on a scale and with a sophistication not matched by any other wartime power. ISOS decrypts from GC&CS led directly to the capture of five of the twenty-three German agents despatched to the UK during 1941, identified two more and provided valuable guidance in devising the disinformation with which the double agents deceived the Abwehr.[71] In December 1941 the veteran codebreaker 'Dilly' Knox, though terminally ill with cancer, succeeded in breaking the Abwehr variant of the Enigma cipher. The decrypts were given the codename ISK (Intelligence Service Knox) to distinguish them from the ISOS decrypts of Abwehr hand cipher messages, which had been circulated for the past twenty months. Most recipients, however, did not understand the distinction and referred to all Abwehr decrypts as ISOS. By the spring of 1942, Tar Robertson was able to state categorically, on the basis of the intelligence derived from the decrypts, that the Security Service controlled all German agents operating in Britain.[72] ULTRA provided crucial evidence that the Germans were successfully deceived by much of the disinformation fed to them by their turned agents.

The Double-Cross System also involved SIS, which both recruited and assisted double agents in neutral capitals. Its first major recruit was Dušan 'Duško' Popov, a young Yugoslav working for the Abwehr who contacted the SIS station at Belgrade. In December 1940 Popov travelled to London via Lisbon, telling the Abwehr that he was going to collect intelligence from a friend in the Yugoslav legation but with the real intention of making contact with MI5. Codenamed TRICYCLE because of his fondness for three-in-a-bed sex, Popov became the centre of a considerable network of agents, some imaginary (invented by B1a). After the war he was given British citizenship and presented with the OBE by Robertson at an informal ceremony in the bar of the Ritz.[73]

Like TRICYCLE, the Catalan businessman Juan Pujol Garcia (GARBO), the most successful of all the double agents run by B1a, began as an SIS recruit. Pujol, whose experience of the Spanish Civil War had left him with a loathing of both Fascism and Communism, first offered his services to the British in Madrid in January 1941 but was turned down. He then approached the Abwehr, told them he was travelling to England, and was eventually taken on as Agent ARABEL. Pujol got no further than Lisbon, from where, claiming to be in England, he despatched to the Abwehr plentiful disinformation on non-existent British troop and naval movements, spiced with details of 'drunken orgies and slack morals at amusement centres' in Liverpool and the surprising revelation that Glasgow dock-workers would 'do anything for a litre of wine'. By February 1942 Section V (counter-intelligence) of SIS had identified Pujol as the author of these colourful reports, which were decrypted by Bletchley Park. A month later SIS recruited him as a double agent.[74]

By cutting across the demarcation line which confined MI5 to British soil and SIS to foreign territory, the double agents necessitated closer operational co-operation between the two Services than ever before. Unsurprisingly, the collaboration did not always run smoothly. In March 1942 Felix Cowgill, the head of SIS Section V, told Liddell that he wished to bring GARBO to London to be debriefed in SIS headquarters but wanted a guarantee that the Security Service would then allow GARBO to return to Lisbon to be run by SIS. Liddell was outraged:

[Cowgill] did not wish to give [GARBO] up or to allow us to have access to him even though in all our interests it might be better that he should remain here. Fundamentally, his attitude is 'I do not see why I should get agents and then have them pinched by you.' The whole thing is so narrow and petty that it really makes me furious.[75]

Liddell won the interdepartmental battle which followed. Since Pujol's reports to the Abwehr claimed that he and his partially mythical agent network were based in Britain, it made better sense for him to be run by the Security Service in London than by SIS in Lisbon. On 24 April GARBO arrived in London and was transferred to the control of B1a.[76]

Relations with Cowgill remained tense. B Division, which had hitherto believed it was receiving all ISOS and ISK Abwehr decrypts, discovered in April 1942 that Cowgill had been withholding all those which mentioned SIS agents – in all over a hundred decrypts, including some reports from Pujol. Though the Security Service had got on well with the previous head of Section V, Valentine Vivian, it found Cowgill difficult to deal with. So did some other sections of the intelligence community. Commander Ewen Montagu, the naval intelligence representative on the newly established Twenty Committee, complained to Tar Robertson that Cowgill was possessed of a 'pathological inability to inform anyone of anything that he can possibly avoid'.[77] Kim Philby told Herbert Hart of B1b 'how he had argued with Major Cowgill that the secret abstraction of these messages from the circulation of ISOS and ISK was quite wrong, since it mutilated the total series, and in any case some of the considerable amount of information in these messages might reasonably be held to concern us'.[78] Cowgill was eventually overridden by 'C', Stewart Menzies, who assured Masterman on 11 June that all decrypts relevant to double agents would henceforth be passed to the Twenty Committee.[79]

In order to run double agents successfully, B1a needed to have available a mixture of information and disinformation with which they could both impress and deceive German case officers. In January 1941 the Wireless Board (also known as the W Board) was set up to decide what to tell the Abwehr. On it sat Guy Liddell (who had succeeded Harker as head of B Division), Stewart Menzies and the three service directors of intelligence. This elevated committee, while considering broad policy issues, inevitably lacked the time to provide the detailed, sometimes daily, operational guidance which became necessary following the expansion of the Double-Cross System in the autumn and winter of 1940.[80] The Wireless Board therefore quickly delegated day-to-day selection of information and disinformation to the Twenty Committee, so called because the roman numeral for twenty (XX) is a double cross. The Committee, which had representatives from the Security Service, SIS, the War Office, the three service intelligence departments, GHQ Home Forces and, when necessary, other interested departments, began meeting in January 1941 and thereafter met weekly for the remainder of the war.[81]

The MI5 chairman of the Twenty Committee, the Oxford history don J. C. Masterman (later knighted), was, like the two other key figures in the Double-Cross System, Robertson and Stephens, an inspired choice. Born in 1891, Masterman was considerably older than most other B1a officers, and owed his recruitment in November 1940 to Dick White, who had been his pupil at Christ Church. While a young fellow of Christ Church, Masterman was studying in Germany in August 1914, and was interned for the remainder of the war.[82] He first came to the Security Service's attention as the result of an officious postal censor who in August 1918 reported to the Chief Constable of Hampshire that Masterman's mother had been ordering 'suspicious books' from a Dutch bookshop to be sent to her son during his internment. Kell was subsequently informed that the books, mainly poetry and on the origins of the war, had been ordered by Masterman himself with a request for the bill to be sent to his mother. No further investigation followed.[83]

As well as being an academic, Masterman was probably the best all-round games player ever to join the Security Service. As an undergraduate he had won an athletics Blue. Between the wars he played hockey and tennis for England and at the age of forty-six was still a good enough cricketer to tour Canada with the MCC.[84] In his reports on the Double-Cross System, Masterman sometimes used cricketing analogies. 'Running a team of double agents', he believed, 'is very like running a club cricket side. Older players lose their form and are gradually replaced by new-comers.' He compared the leading double agents to well-known cricketers: 'If in the double-cross world SNOW was the W. G. Grace of the early period, then GARBO was certainly the Bradman of the later years.'[85]

Though there were some tensions when Masterman rejected risky pro-posals from the young case officers of B1a, he won the respect of all and, at least in retrospect, they conceded that his caution was necessary.[86] Guy Liddell noted at the end of the war: 'Apart from his ability he is an extremely delightful personality and has been liked by us all.'[87] Masterman was also an excellent chairman. He preceded the first meeting of the Twenty Committee with what he later called 'a small but important decision, to wit that tea and a bun should always be provided for members':

In days of acute shortage and of rationing the provision of buns was no easy task, yet by hook or crook (and mostly by crook) we never failed to provide them throughout the war years. Was this simple expedient one of the reasons why attend-ance at the Committee was nearly always a hundred per cent?

Despite some early tension between MI5 and SIS and the difficulties of reconciling the sometimes conflicting interests of deception, security and intelligence-gathering, the Twenty Committee worked remarkably smoothly. Masterman had a gift for creating consensus. At only one of its 226 meetings was a disagreement pressed to a vote.[88] From its very first meeting it began to suspect the astonishing truth that, in Masterman's words, 'we actively ran and controlled the German espionage system in this country'. The Abwehr's instructions to SUMMER and TATE in the autumn of 1940 suggested, even if they did not prove, that the only German agents then operating in Britain had already been turned by the Security Service. The B1a-controlled SNOW network was asked to act as SUM-MER's paymaster, and TATE was given contact details of the double agent RAINBOW.[89] Though the Twenty Committee and B1a remained alert to the possibility that there were German agents at large outside its control, it did not occur to either that the Security Service itself had been penetrated by two of the Abwehr's previously most successful agents.[90]

Though Folkert van Koutrik and Jack Hooper chose to remain inactive, both were a serious potential threat to the Double-Cross System.

Despite their ignorance of van Koutrik and Hooper, however, the Twenty Committee and B1a were acutely aware of how easily the System could go wrong. In January 1941, SUMMER, who was living under guard in a house near Cambridge, attempted to escape. He attacked the only guard on duty, telling him unhelpfully, 'It hurts me more than it hurts you,' tied him up and tried to make his getaway on a motorbike belonging to another guard. Strapped to the motorbike was a canoe in which SUM-MER planned, optimistically, to cross to the continent. 'Fortunately', wrote Masterman, 'the motorbike, being government property, was not very efficiently maintained,' and broke down.[91] The MI5 Regional Security Liaison Officer (RSLO) in Cambridge reported to Dick White that the pursuit of SUMMER was quickly over:

At the first cross roads we came to we met some roadmen who stated that they had seen a man on a motorcycle carrying a canoe turn left down the Newmarket Road. We proceeded until we got to Pampisford Station, where we met Mr F. Brown, a roadman of Pampisford, who said that he had seen the man on the motorcycle with the canoe – in fact he had seen a lot of him because the man on the motorcycle had fallen off just by him and he had helped the man to throw the canoe over a hedge.[92]

SUMMER was caught soon afterwards and his career as a double agent brought to an abrupt conclusion. Comic-opera though his escape attempt was, it emphasized the danger that a successful escape could undermine the whole Double-Cross System.

B1a strongly suspected that SUMMER was not the only double agent who, if the opportunity presented itself, might well return to the German side. Elaborate plans were therefore made to remove most to secret locations in North Wales in the event of a German invasion, which early in 1941 was still regarded as a real possibility. The operation was initially codenamed 'Mr Mills' Circus' in honour of the B1a officer originally put in charge, the Old Harrovian and Cambridge engineering graduate Cyril Mills, son of Britain's leading circus-owner, Bertram Mills. The officer responsible for the North Wales end of the operation, Captain P. E. S. Finney, sometimes used circus metaphors in his correspondence with Head Office, writing from Colwyn Bay in April 1941: 'I have now completed arrangements for the accommodation of the animals, the young and their keepers, together with accommodation for Mr Mills himself.' All were to be housed in hotels at Betws-y-Coed, Llanrwst and Llandudno, whose owners had been vetted.[93]

The top priority of 'Mr Mills' Circus' was SUMMER's friend TATE, who, it was believed, 'would probably attempt to escape in case of an invasion'.[94] Next came SNOW who, in Masterman's cricketing metaphor, had hitherto 'always batted at number one' but slipped down the batting order in January 1941 after a visit to Lisbon to meet his German case officer, Major Nikolaus Ritter (alias 'Dr Rantzau'). The main purpose of SNOW's meeting with Ritter was to introduce him to CELERY, an MI5 agent posing as a new recruit to the Abwehr's agent network. On his return from Lisbon, however, SNOW claimed that he had been accused by Ritter of double-crossing him and had admitted doing so. But there were many contradictions in SNOW's account, which did not square with CELERY's version of the trip. In the end, B1a concluded that the most likely explanation was 'that SNOW had not in fact been "rumbled" at all, but had invented this part of the story because the complications of his position were getting too much for him'.[95] SNOW, it was believed, was so confused about his loyalties that it was difficult to determine whether he was '(a) genuinely friendly to this country, or (b) really pro-German, or (c) anxious to work with both sides and come out on the right side in the end'. A German invasion, however, would almost certainly resolve SNOW's mental confusion: 'As he is a great believer in German efficiency, it is highly probable that he would attempt to join the Germans immediately if invasion occurred. He should therefore be arrested on the first news of invasion and transferred to a safer part of the country . . .'[96] SNOW's case officers also found him personally tiresome, with disagreeably plebeian habits which included 'only wearing his false teeth when eating'.[97]

Some of the double agents, notably GW, were trusted to make their own way to North Wales in the event of a German invasion and given car passes, petrol coupons and money for their journeys.[98] Those who were not trusted, TATE and SNOW chief among them, were to be handcuffed and taken by car under armed escort to their chosen hotel. The handcuffs (later returned) were loaned by Scotland Yard.[99] Tar Robertson informed Tin-eye Stephens: 'If there is any danger of the more dangerous cases falling into enemy hands they will be liquidated forcibly' – in other words, shot. If any one of them was able to contact the enemy, it 'could blow our whole show'.[100] The DG, Sir David Petrie, personally instructed TATE's escort: 'As it is of vital importance that TATE should not fall into the hands of the enemy, you must be prepared to take any step necessary to prevent this from occurring.'[101] This and similar instructions to the escorts of other double agents are the only known occasions on which a DG has authorized executions (though in the event none was carried out). The legal justification was presumably that any double agent attempting to assist an invading army would have been regarded as, in effect, an enemy combatant.[102] As fear of a German invasion receded, 'Mr Mills' Circus' gradually wound down. Even TATE, though still not fully trusted, was regarded as unlikely to change sides once there was no longer any serious prospect of a German invasion. The untrustworthy SNOW, however, was imprisoned in Dartmoor and stayed there for the rest of the war.

The success of the Double-Cross System depended not merely on capturing all, and turning some, of the Abwehr agents landed in Britain, but also on preventing the emergence of an alternative base for German espionage. The best potential base was the London embassy of Fascist Spain, where a number of pro-Nazi diplomats protected by diplomatic immunity were willing to spy for Germany in association with other Spaniards in London. Had the embassy become a successful base for German espionage, the intelligence collected would at some point have contradicted, and therefore risked compromising, the disinformation supplied by the double agents. The fact that Spanish espionage in the German interest achieved little of significance was due in large part to the Security Service's successful penetration of the embassy. The Service discovered that it was up against mostly low-grade, somewhat eccentric opposition, and that embassy security was gratifyingly weak.

The first breakthrough into what MI5 believed was 'the heart of the Spanish espionage network' came as the result of an SIS lead in the autumn of 1940. On 27 September Miguel Piernavieja del Pozo arrived in London on an espionage mission, posing as a journalist and observer for the Spanish Instituto de Estudios Políticos; he achieved instant notoriety by publicly forecasting a German victory. Shortly afterwards, following an SIS report that del Pozo was a German agent, the Security Service obtained an HOW on him. His intercepted phone calls and correspondence, combined with B6 surveillance, led MI5 to categorize him as 'a dissolute and irresponsible young man, aged 26, of the playboy type', who had little or no knowledge of journalism, of the Instituto de Estudios Políticos, or – it soon transpired – of espionage. Del Pozo greatly simplified MI5 surveillance by writing to GW, the double agent whom the Abwehr believed was a fanatical Welsh nationalist recruited for them by SNOW. With the agreement of the Security Service, GW met del Pozo on 10 October at his flat in Athenaeum Court, Piccadilly. To his surprise, del Pozo handed him a talcum-powder tin containing £3,500 in large-denomination banknotes, over £100,000 at current values and probably the largest sum yet handed to a twentieth-century British agent (other than funds intended for the Communist Party and other organizations). Part of this large sum, GW was told, was for his own personal use; part was to be held in safe-keeping for del Pozo and returned to him as and when required. GW was instructed to send weekly reports on the activities of the Welsh Nationalist Party and on arms and aircraft production to the hall-porter at the Spanish embassy, who would forward them to del Pozo.[103]

Del Pozo revealed to GW at one of their regular meetings that he took his orders from a more senior Abwehr agent, Angel Alcázar de Velasco (a close friend of Franco's pro-Nazi Foreign Minister, Ramón Serrano Suñer), who, despite knowing no English, was posted to the London embassy as press attaché in January 1941. According to a Security Service assessment:

Alcázar is a most remarkable character. He is of gipsy extraction and, as a boy, worked as a bootblack in Madrid. He was extremely ambitious and in order to earn money to educate himself he became a bullfighter. He joined the [Fascist] Falange at its inception and claims that his first real step-up in politics was his assassination of [a] Republican police officer . . .

By sheer force of personality, this self-educated ex-bullfighter immediately dominated and terrorised the Spanish colony [in London] and Embassy personnel – with the single exception of the Duke of Alba [the ambassador]. He behaved in a manner which, had he been a less formidable figure, would have made him ridiculous. He went to an interview at the Foreign Office wearing Falange uniform; he accepted hospitality at smart London clubs and insisted on paying for the drinks; he ate fish with his fingers at the Savoy; he gave a demonstration of bull fighting technique at the Turkish baths. The acutely embarrassed Spanish diplomats adapted themselves as best they might to the role of yes men, fearing Alcázar's power in Madrid. In addition he made no attempt to conceal his strong pro-German feelings and his desire for an Axis victory.

By the time Alcázar arrived in London, del Pozo, according to Security Service surveillance, 'was devoting his time almost exclusively to the girls at the Café de Paris and acquired such a reputation as a drunkard, waster and buffoon' that in February he was recalled to Spain. Alcázar returned temporarily to Madrid in the same month. Though the Security Service asked for him to be declared *persona non grata*, the Foreign Office was reluctant to do so for fear of retaliation against British embassy staff in Madrid. It did, however, adopt delaying tactics which prevented Alcázar's return to London until July 1941.[104]

In May 1941, in an attempt to discover the extent of Spanish espionage in Britain in the Nazi interest, MI5 instructed GW to renew contact with the embassy porter to whom he had previously sent reports destined for del Pozo. In Alcázar's absence the porter put GW in touch with Luis Calvo, a leading Spanish journalist. At his first meeting with GW, Calvo revealed that he was using journalism as a cover for espionage. 'You and I', he told GW, 'are going to work very well together,' and boasted that on a recent trip to North Wales he had obtained 'very useful information' on aircraft factories and aerodromes. B1g, which was responsible for countering Spanish espionage, believed that, but for GW, 'it is at least doubtful whether we should have got on to Calvo at all, and certain that we should not have learned about him so soon.' Other counter-espionage successes followed. B1g commented: 'It is a remarkable fact that in the few months between September 1941 and the middle of February 1942, we . . . gained not only a general outline but a fairly precise picture of the [Spanish] Espionage network in this country . . .'[105]

The B Division officer most actively concerned with the penetration of neutral embassies, particularly those most likely to assist the enemy, was Anthony Blunt. As Blunt informed Soviet intelligence, MI5 port security officers 'were able to get hold of many [diplomatic] bags which were being carried out by couriers':

In some cases . . . it was possible to persuade the courier – extraordinary though it may seem – to put his bag in the care of the security officer at the port rather than leave it in the hotel overnight. This method works particularly well with the Spaniards and the Portuguese who go out from Poole or Bristol to Lisbon.[106]

Within neutral embassies, Blunt informed Moscow, MI5's best agent was an employee in the Spanish embassy who 'gets us cipher tape, clear versions of cipher telegrams, drafts of the ambassador's reports, private letters, notes on dinner parties and visitors, and general gossip about members of the embassy'.[107] In December 1941 the employee was recruited as Agent DUCK. A post-war B1g report described DUCK as 'of inestimable value' with wide-ranging access to diplomatic documents, thanks to the fact that, 'Most fortunately for us, the security arrangements in the Embassy were nil.'[108] In January 1942[109] and on at least two subsequent occasions,[110] DUCK was able to walk out of the embassy with the current Spanish diplomatic cipher tape in a bag to hand over to an MI5 car waiting around the corner. Each cipher tape remained in use for some months, thus enabling GC&CS to decrypt communications between the embassy and Madrid. Another agent inside the embassy, run by Maxwell Knight's section, sometimes let in Security Service staff through a window on nights when acting as firewatcher for 'a little discreet burglary'.[111]

As with counter-espionage operations against Germany and the running of the Double-Cross System, SIGINT was also crucial in revealing the activities of Spain's London embassy. In January 1942 decrypted telegrams from the Japanese ambassador in Madrid to Tokyo revealed that Alcázar claimed to be running a twenty-one-man agent network in Britain. Reports from some of the agents were cited in ISOS decrypts of reports to Berlin from the Abwehr station in Madrid. Only two of the agents were Spanish: Luis Calvo and an unnamed individual whom the Service believed must be the Spanish embassy porter contacted by GW. Calvo, who, unlike Alcázar, had no diplomatic immunity, was arrested on 12 February and quickly admitted his dealings with GW.[112] He was able to throw little light on most other members of Alcázar's spy-ring, some of whom were identified by B1a as fictitious sub-agents of GW which it had invented to deceive the Abwehr. The Service gradually realized that Alcázar's other agents were his own fraudulent inventions. He later admitted to SIS that for two years he earned about £4,000 a month by selling bogus intelligence to the Japanese as well as the Germans, some of it from another non-existent spy-ring in the United States At one point, on Alcázar's instructions, his secretary even succeeded in selling some of his fabricated intelligence reports to the SIS Madrid station.[113] The Spanish embassy in London, however, no longer represented any potential threat to the Double-Cross System.

1. The earliest surviving photograph of Vernon Kell as first head of MI5. He became the longest-serving head of any twentieth-century UK government agency or department.

2. Major (later Brigadier General Sir) James Edmonds, who assembled the evidence of German espionage which led to the creation in 1909 of the Secret Service Bureau, forerunner of both MI5 and SIS.

3. William Le Queux (standing), the Walter Mitty of pre-war counter-espionage, pictured here with his publisher, who paid him the same rate per thousand words as Thomas Hardy. His best-selling books persuaded many readers that Britain was being overrun by 'spies of the Kaiser'.

4. Kell's 'Chief Detective', William Melville, on a surveillance mission on board a cross-Channel ferry (probably to keep track of Gustav Steinhauer's pre-war British agent, George Parrott).

5. The 'Kaiser's Spy', Gustav Steinhauer, head of the British section of the German Admiralty's foreign intelligence service, posing in one of the disguises he used on operations in Britain.

6. (*above*) Winston Churchill (seen here centre-left in top hat at the 'Siege of Sidney Street' in 1911) was Kell's leading supporter in government during the early years of MI5. As home secretary in 1910–11 Churchill introduced the Home Office Warrants which still play a key role in MI5 investigations.

7. (*left*) William Hinchley Cooke in German military uniform. Son of a British father and German mother, he was one of Kell's first wartime recruits and masqueraded as a German officer to obtain intelligence from German POWs.

8. MI9 staff testing suspicious correspondence for secret ink (commonly used by German agents) during the First World War.

9. Carl Lody, the first German spy to be caught during the First World War (following the interception of his letters), also became the first man for one and a half centuries to be executed at the Tower of London. Kell regarded him as a 'really fine man' and 'felt it deeply that so brave a man should have to pay the death penalty'.

10. Karl Müller, though less admired by Kell, also showed great bravery; he is reported to have shaken hands with the firing squad before his execution at the Tower in June 1916. Without realizing it, Müller became the precursor of the Second World War Double-Cross System. MI5 earned enough money from sending bogus reports in his name to German intelligence to buy a car which it called the 'Müller'.

11. MI5's first graduate recruit, Lieutenant Colonel Maldwyn Haldane (*front row, right*), head of Registry and Administration, with senior Registry staff on the roof of MI5 HQ, Waterloo House, in 1918.

12. Kell and MI5 heads of Branches in 1918. Front row (*left to right*): Lieutenant Colonel Eric Holt-Wilson (Kell's deputy); Kell; Haldane. Back row (*left to right*): Major Sidney Chaytor Welchman (F: preventive intelligence); Major James Sealy Clarke (G: investigations); Major Francis Hall (D: imperial and overseas intelligence); Major Herbert Eames Spencer (E: port and frontier control).

WATERLOO HOUSE.
16. CHARLES STREET.
HAYMARKET.
LONDON. S.W.1.

11TH NOVEMBER, 1918.

ARMISTICE DAY.

ON this historic occasion, when we have at last reached the goal set before us during the last four years, I desire to express to all in this office, ladies, officers, and staff, my heartfelt thanks for the splendid efforts which have been made by one and all.

Your loyalty and devotion to duty have been the outstanding features of your work and your cheerfulness during the dark days a very real help.

It has been my good fortune to have had the pleasure of working together with such a staff, and during the period of demobilisation, as and when you leave this office, I trust you will take away with you the pleasantest reminiscences of M.I.5.

V.G.W.Kell

General Staff.

(*above*) 13. Armistice Day 1918 on the roof of Waterloo House. The Stars and Stripes is amongst the Allied flags on display.

(*left*) 14. Kell's Armistice Day letter of thanks to 'ladies, officers, and staff' of MI5.

15. Maxwell Knight, MI5's leading agent-runner from 1931 to the early 1950s, with one of his household pets. Visitors to his home might, as one recalled, 'find him nursing a bush-baby, feeding a giant toad, raising young cuckoos or engaging in masculine repartee with a vastly experienced grey parrot'. Some of his intelligence tradecraft derived from the study of animal behaviour. Knight later became a popular BBC naturalist.

16. Jane Archer (née Sissmore), MI5's first female officer. Recruited as a wartime 'temporary clerk', she qualified as a barrister (pictured here in 1924) in her spare time and became MI5's chief Soviet expert. In 1940 she took the lead role in interrogating Walter Krivitsky, the first major Soviet defector.

17. The Communist Party official Percy Glading, photographed while serving a prison sentence for running a Soviet spy-ring in Woolwich Arsenal. Glading's diary, examined by MI5 after his arrest in 1938, contained a reference to Melita Sirnis (later Norwood) which was not followed up. Nor was a lead from the agent M2, who reported that Norwood was an active Communist engaged in 'especially important' secret work and provided a drawing of her.

18. Sketch of Melita Norwood by agent M2 in 1938. She went on to become Soviet intelligence's longest-serving British agent.

19. Norwood, after she was publicly exposed by the KGB defector Vasili Mitrokhin in 1999.

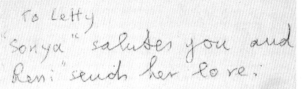

20. Her wartime Soviet controller, 'Sonya' (Ursula Beurton, née Kuczynski), then living in retirement in eastern Germany, sent Norwood a message of support after her exposure (extract).

2

Soviet Penetration and the
Communist Party

On 4 September 1939, the day after Britain declared war on Germany, deeply depressing intelligence on Soviet agent penetration arrived at the Foreign Office. The PUS, Sir Alexander Cadogan, received what he described as a 'very unpleasant' telegram from the British chargé d'affaires in Washington, Victor Mallet, which gave 'a line on the "leaks" of the last few years'.[1] The telegram contained allegations of Soviet penetration made to Mallet by the American journalist Isaac Don Levine, who had collaborated with the Soviet intelligence officer Walter Krivitsky, who had defected to the United States, in a series of sensational magazine articles. Krivitsky, Levine revealed, knew of two major Soviet agents operating in London: 'One is King in the Foreign Office Communications Department, the other is in cypher department of Cabinet Offices but name unknown.' According to Krivitsky, King was 'selling everything to Moscow'. The other agent had bought forty or fifty planes for the Republican side in the Spanish Civil War. Mallet reported:

Krivitsky knows his name, I understand, but likes him and so far won't tell it, because the man was not acting for mercenary motives but through idealism and sympathy for the 'loyalists' [Republicans] and may now be on our side owing to Stalin's treachery. This man is a Scotsman of very good family, a well-known painter and perhaps a sculptor. He was sent on a trip ostensibly to Holland with his wife and mother-in-law whom he left there and then went on to Yugoslavia where he bought the planes and arranged for their transfer to Spain.[2]

Though Krivitsky's description of the second agent, as reported by Levine, turned out to be confused and misleading, the agent in the Foreign Office Communications Department was quickly identified as the cipher clerk Captain John King. Cadogan asked Jasper Harker and Colonel Valentine Vivian, head of Section V (counter-espionage) in SIS, to conduct a joint investigation and was shocked by the 'awful revelations of leakage' which they uncovered.[3] Initially, however, it seemed unlikely that there would be enough admissible evidence for a prosecution.[4] On 25 September Harker and Vivian subjected King to 'a "Third Degree" examination' (psychological pressure rather than physical brutality).[5] Cadogan wrote in his diary next day: 'I have no doubt he is guilty – curse him – but there is no absolute proof.' Unaware of the legal limitations of the evidence against him, King cracked under further interrogation. At a trial in camera at the Old Bailey in October, kept secret for the next twenty years, King was sentenced to ten years' imprisonment. Harker and Vivian suspected others in the Communications Department, but failed to find enough evidence for prosecution. Two officials, however, were dismissed for 'irregularities'. Cadogan agonized for the remainder of the year about how to remedy the appalling breaches of security uncovered by Harker and Vivian. 'I *shall* be glad when it's over!' he wrote despondently on 30 November. The Foreign Secretary, Lord Halifax, decided that he had no option but to move all the existing members of the Communications Department to other jobs and bring in fresh staff. Halifax broke this 'most painful' news to the Department on 1 December and, in Cadogan's view, 'he did it very well.'[6]

Despite the accuracy of Krivitsky's intelligence on Captain King, Harker correctly concluded after investigation that, at least as reported by Levine, Krivitsky's information on the second Soviet agent was seriously garbled. He told the Foreign Office on 8 November: 'We know the identity of the man who bought the aeroplanes for Spain, whom we believe not to be identical with the Scottish artist and idealist, who is a totally different person.'[7] On 10 November Jane Archer (née Sissmore),[8] the Security Service's main Soviet expert, wrote to Vivian, 'Personally, I am convinced from [Krivitsky's] articles, and the scraps of information that Levine has obtained from Krivitsky and given to our Ambassador in Washington, that if we wish to get to the bottom of Soviet military espionage activities in this country, we must contact Krivitsky.'[9] Harker agreed. He told the Foreign Office on 20 November, 'It is imperative that Krivitsky should be seen as early as possible.'[10] Next month Krivitsky accepted an invitation to visit Britain.

By the time Krivitsky landed at Southampton in January 1940 under the alias 'Mr Thomas', he had begun to suspect that he was walking into a trap. He was welcomed by a Russian-speaking Security Service officer, Major Stephen Alley, who invited him to tea. Because of wartime shortages, there was no sugar and Alley offered him a saccharine tablet. As Guy Liddell noted afterwards, Krivitsky 'sheered right off this, obviously thinking it was dope or poison'.[11] To try to put him at his ease, Harker, Archer and Vivian began the questioning on 19 January 1940 not in a Whitehall office but in the relative comfort of his room at the Langham Hotel in Portland Place. The debriefing, however, began badly: 'He obviously feared lest any admission from him of participation in Soviet espionage activities against the United Kingdom would lead to a "full examination" as understood by citizens of the U.S.S.R.'[12] Krivitsky eventually admitted that he was aware of a Soviet intelligence network operating in Britain, but 'was very anxious to point out that he himself was not responsible for the direction of activities against the U.K.', and wanted 'to know what action we would take on his information, as he was convinced that anything we did in the way of arrests, etc., would at once be attributed by the Soviet Government to his activities'. Harker and Vivian assured Krivitsky that he would not have to give evidence in court and that whatever he told them 'would be treated as regards its source with absolute confidence'.[13]

Thus reassured, Krivitsky began to talk about the first agent in the Foreign Office. It had already been decided that, as one of the tactics to try to persuade him to open up, an attempt would be made to impress him with how much his questioners already knew. He was told that British intelligence were 'perfectly aware' of the agent, that his name was King, and that he had already begun a ten-year prison sentence. As Harker observed, 'This rather took the wind out of [Krivitsky's] sails.'[14] Thereafter, with Jane Archer taking the lead role in the questioning, Krivitsky began to open up. Liddell noted on 2 February: 'Krivitsky is coming out of his shell and has told us quite a lot. He has as far as possible given us a detailed picture of the 4th Department [Soviet military intelligence] and the OGPU [NKVD].'[15]

As a post-war report acknowledged, Krivitsky provided the Security Service 'for the first time with an insight into the organisation, methods and influence of the Russian Intelligence Service'.[16] Though Krivitsky was a military intelligence officer, from 1935 to 1937 he had been involved in NKVD as well as Fourth Department operations in Western Europe. During his four weeks' debriefing, he identified over seventy Soviet intelligence personnel and agents operating abroad, most of them previously unknown to MI5.[17] There were, however, limitations to his knowledge. Since all NKVD legal and illegal officers serving in Britain before Krivitsky's defection in 1937 had been withdrawn, he was unable to provide any information on the current London residency. His information on illegals operating in Britain during the mid-1930s – among them the two main controllers of the Cambridge Five, Deutsch and Maly – was of mainly retrospective interest. The only British agent on whom he was precisely informed was Captain King. Though Krivitsky did not speak English and had never been stationed in Britain, he had, curiously, been chosen to run

King in 1935 (in the event he did not do so) and briefed on the case before it was reassigned.[18] He was unaware, however, that in 1937, during the paranoia of the Great Terror, the Centre had absurdly concluded that King had been betrayed to British intelligence by (the wholly innocent) Teodor Maly, and the NKVD had since made no contact with him.[19]

With the exception of the King case, Krivitsky's information on Soviet agents still operating in Britain was too muddled to make identification possible. Claims that the Security Service should have been able to identify Maclean and/or Philby after the debriefing are ill founded.[20] Krivitsky was confused about both the background and the role of the second spy in the Foreign Office. Harker noted on 23 January that, according to Krivitsky, 'there had been for some time a leakage of valuable information which emanated from what he described as the *Council of State* – but which *we* think must be the C.I.D. [Committee of Imperial Defence] Offices.'[21] On 3 February, however:

. . . Thomas [Krivitsky] suddenly said 'Ah, I now remember this man must be in the Foreign Office'. He then told me a story . . . of how a third man was approached by a Dutchman from Holland, and offered to supply material from the Foreign Office. He says he now remembers that he refused to allow this man to be taken on because they already had *two* good sources in the Foreign Office and he thought to take on a doubtful third would imperil those two. The two agents in the Foreign Office were King and the Imperial Conference man, of that he seems now quite certain.[22]

Krivitsky's information about the second agent in the Foreign Office was inconsistent, not least in his confused references to the 'Council of State' and 'Imperial Conference'. He no longer described the agent (correctly) as a Scotsman or (incorrectly) as 'a well-known painter and perhaps a sculptor' who had purchased planes for the Spanish Republicans. According to the final version of his shifting recollections:

He is certain that the source was a young man, probably under thirty, an agent of Theodore Mally [*sic*], that he was recruited as a Soviet agent purely on ideological grounds, and that he took no money for [his] information . . . He was almost certainly educated at Eton and Oxford. Krivitsky cannot get it out of his head that the source is a 'young aristocrat',[23] but agrees that he may have arrived at this conclusion because he thought it was only young men of the nobility who were educated at Eton. He believes the source to have been the secretary or son of one of the chiefs of the Foreign Office.[24]

With the gift of hindsight, this now seems to have been a garbled description of Maclean, who had been educated at public school and Oxbridge (though at Gresham's and Cambridge rather than Eton and Oxford), and was the son of a knight (though not an aristocrat) who had also been a cabinet minister (though not 'one of the chiefs of the Foreign Office'). At the time, however, Krivitsky's information could not have enabled the Security Service to identify Maclean. There were other young British diplomats who were a closer fit than Maclean – who really had been to Eton and Oxford, who did come from aristocratic families, and whose fathers were, or had been, senior Foreign Office officials.

At one point, while talking about the Foreign Office agent, Krivitsky began to 'harp on the suggestion that [the agent's] name began with P'. It is possible that Krivitsky was confusing Maclean with Kim Philby. At another point in the debriefing, a clue provided by Krivitsky can be seen, again with the gift of hindsight, to refer to Philby. He recalled that the Foreign Office agent was 'amongst the friends' of another 'English aristocrat who was to go to Spain to murder Franco'.[25] By 'aristocrat', Krivitsky, who lacked a sophisticated understanding of the British class system, meant no more than of 'good family'. He subsequently recalled that Franco's intended assassin was also a journalist. According to the final report on Krivitsky's debriefing:

Early in 1937 the OGPU received orders from Stalin to arrange the assassination of General Franco. Hardt [Maly] was instructed by the OGPU chief, Yezhov, to recruit an Englishman for the purpose. He did in fact contact and sent to Spain a young Englishman, a journalist of good family, an idealist and a fanatical anti-Nazi. Before the plan matured, Mally himself was recalled to Moscow and disappeared.[26]

When Philby later saw this report, he recognized himself.[27] In 1937, he had been entrusted by Maly with a mission to assassinate Franco (later abandoned) and had operated under journalistic cover. Even if the Security Service had had the resources in 1940 to follow up this and the many other imprecise leads provided by Krivitsky, however, it is unlikely that Philby would have been unmasked. Since the NKVD had at its disposal the trained assassins of Serebryansky's Administration for Special Tasks, the Security Service would have found it difficult to credit that the inexperienced Philby could have been selected for the highest-profile foreign assassination it had yet attempted. Maly himself made clear to the Centre that he did not believe Philby was capable of carrying out the mission entrusted to him.[28]

One name mentioned by Krivitsky proved too sensitive to include in the report on his debriefing. Jane Archer, who drew up the report, assured Valentine Vivian that she had left out all references to a current SIS agent,

Jack Hooper. Krivitsky had claimed that, while working for SIS in the Netherlands, Hooper had shown Christiaan Pieck, a Dutch agent-runner working for Soviet intelligence, 'a document purporting to incriminate him. Pieck was frightened of him from that time.' According to Krivitsky, Hooper had subsequently asked Pieck to find him work with Soviet intelligence.[29] Both Vivian and his successor as head of SIS Section V, Felix Cowgill, believed Hooper to be innocent and were thus anxious that he should not be incriminated in Archer's report. Hooper had admitted to pre-war contact with both Soviet and German intelligence but had what Vivian and Cowgill regarded as a satisfactory explanation.[30] After his admitted contact with Pieck, Hooper had provided intelligence which, as MI5 later acknowledged, 'should have enabled us to identify J. H. King', the Soviet agent run by Pieck in the Foreign Office Communications Department, well before the outbreak of war.[31] When Hooper was recruited as an MI5 agent in 1941, Cowgill 'said that, above everything, he is certain that he is absolutely loyal'.[32] Hooper, it was later discovered, was in reality the only MI5 employee who had previously worked for both Soviet and German intelligence (as well as SIS).[33]

Despite Krivitsky's inability to provide clear leads during his debriefing to any current Soviet agents or intelligence personnel in Britain, he none the less transformed the Security Service's understanding of the nature and extent of Soviet intelligence operations.[34] As recently as January 1939 Kell had confidently declared that '[Soviet] activity in England is non-existent, in terms of both intelligence and political subversion.'[35] Once its eyes were opened by Krivitsky a year later, the Security Service was handicapped in investigating Soviet espionage by lack of resources. B Division (counter-espionage) was wholly occupied with enemy (chiefly German) spies. War-time Soviet counter-espionage, which was considered a much lower priority, was initially relegated to a single officer (F2c) in F Division (counter-subversion).[36] The Service's main handicap in countering Soviet penetration, however, was that, with the recruitment of Anthony Blunt in June 1940, it was itself penetrated.

Blunt had been the only one of the Cambridge Five to attract the pre-war attention of the Security Service. After he joined what his brother Wilfrid called 'left-wing pilgrims' on a visit to the Soviet Union in 1935,[37] Blunt's name was discovered on the passenger list of the Russian M/V *Sibier*, which left London Bridge for Leningrad on 10 August, and was recorded again when he returned from Russia just over a month later. Though Blunt himself was not put under any form of surveillance, the HOW on Marx House in London revealed that on 15 March 1936 he volunteered to give a lecture to the Marx Memorial Library.[38] After his recruitment by Arnold Deutsch early in 1937,[39] he was more cautious, 'trying to create the impression that I didn't share left-wing views' while simultaneously talent-spotting left-wing students for the NKVD. His most successful recruit was a Communist student at Trinity College, Leo Long, who later became a wartime military intelligence officer and was run by Blunt as a sub-agent.[40]

On the eve of war, after taking advice from the NKVD resident in London, Anatoli Gorsky, Blunt applied to join the Intelligence Corps.[41] His first attempt was unsuccessful. Following a Security Service report on 29 August 1939 that it would be 'inadvisable to employ him on Intelligence duties' he was expelled from a training course at Minley Manor, near Aldershot.[42] Blunt told Gorsky that there were two possible reasons for his expulsion: his past Communist activities or his homosexuality.[43] A fellow of Trinity College later told the Security Service that 'it was basically on the score of homosexuality that the College Council had turned down the suggestion that Blunt should be elected to a permanent Fellowship of the College.'[44] Blunt's expulsion from the Intelligence Corps training course, however, was due not to his indiscreet gay love life but to the MI5 record of his Communist associations before he left Trinity in 1937 to work as an art historian at the Warburg Institute. He told Gorsky that, with the help of a friend in Whitehall, he had talked his way back on to the training course by claiming that he was interested only in 'the applications of Marxism to art history' and did not hold Marxist 'political views'.[45] In June 1940 Blunt succeeded in moving from the Intelligence Corps to the Security Service. Though the contemporary record of Blunt's recruitment does not survive, a later account concludes: 'The exact circumstances in which he joined M.I.5 are obscure, but do not appear to be unusual or sinister.'[46] Blunt's Cambridge friend and contemporary Victor Rothschild, the Security Service counter-sabotage expert, introduced him to the head of B Division, Guy Liddell, who took to him and offered him a job in the St James's Street office.[47] Liddell seems to have been convinced by Blunt's claim that his interest in Marxist theory did not extend to politics. Just over a decade later when Blunt first began to come under suspicion, Liddell still believed that, though 'he had associated with a number of Communists [at Cambridge] and believed in the Marxist interpretation of history and art, ... he had no sympathy with Marxist theories as applied by the Russians'. He was convinced that 'Blunt had never been a Communist in the full political sense, even during his days at Cambridge.'[48]

From the moment that he arrived in the Security Service, Blunt embarked on a remarkably successful charm offensive. Dick White later recalled:

He made a general assault on key people to see that they liked him. I was interested in art and he always used to sit down next to me in the canteen and chat. And he betrayed us all. He was a very nice and civilised man and I enjoyed talking to him. You cannot imagine how it feels to be betrayed by someone you have worked side by side with unless you have been through it yourself.[49]

The secretary of Courtenay Young, who shared a room with Anthony Blunt and was 'in and out of their room all the time', later recalled:

My God, he was a charmer! Poor Anthony! We were all a bit in love with Anthony, you know . . . He used to wander around with his cod-liver oil and malt, saying 'That's what Tiggers like for breakfast.' He knew *Winnie the Pooh* very well. He had a Leslie Howard face – a matinée idol – a rather thin and drawn looking face but it was the face of Leslie Howard. Everyone was in love with Leslie Howard at that time.

When she heard a quarter of a century later that Blunt had confessed to being a Soviet agent: 'It was exactly like being in an earthquake – or on a quicksand, I couldn't believe it. I really, truly, couldn't believe it . . . Really, I mean the whole world shook. It really shook for me. You started thinking, "Who else? What about me? Was I one too?"'[50] Another secretary in St James's Street remembers being equally charmed by Blunt and equally shocked when she later discovered his career as a Soviet agent: 'Very tall, very good-looking, *extremely* charming always. You couldn't fault him in any way. And I was absolutely astounded when [news of his treachery] broke. Incredible!'[51]

A few months after Blunt joined the Security Service, he moved into a flat off Oxford Street belonging to Victor Rothschild, which he later shared with his close friend and fellow Soviet agent Guy Burgess.[52] Late in 1940 Blunt recruited Burgess, who had just been dismissed by SIS and was working as a BBC radio producer, as a Security Service agent with the codename VAUXHALL. Though the BBC had previously agreed that Burgess should be called up for military service,[53] Blunt successfully argued in 1941 for the call-up to be cancelled: 'Burgess has been working for us for some time and has done extremely valuable work – principally the running of two very important agents whom he discovered and took on. It would, therefore, be a great pity from our point of view if he was called up . . .'[54] Blunt seems to have persuaded Guy Liddell that, following Burgess's success as an agent, he should be recruited as a Service officer. Liddell told Curry, then head of F Division, that, though Burgess had 'completely abandoned' his former support for Communism, he retained

OFFICIAL SECRETS ACTS, 1911 and 1920.

2. " (1) If any person having in his possession or control any secret official code word, or pass word, or any sketch, plan, model, article, note, document, or information which relates to or is used in a prohibited place or anything in such a place, or which has been made or obtained in contravention of this Act, or which has been entrusted in confidence to him by any person holding office under His Majesty or which he has obtained or to which he has had access owing to his position as a person who holds or has held office under His Majesty or has held a contract made on behalf of His Majesty or as a person who is or has been employed under a person who holds or has held such an office or contract,—

(a) communicates the code word, pass word, sketch, plan, model, article, note, document, or information to any person, other than a person to whom he is authorised to communicate it, or a person to whom it is in the interest of the State his duty to communicate it, or

(aa) uses the information in his possession for the benefit of any foreign power or in any other manner prejudicial to the safety or interests of the State, or

(b) retains the sketch, plan, model, article, note, or document in his possession or control when he has no right to retain it or when it is contrary to his duty to retain it, or fails to comply with all directions issued by lawful authority with regard to the return or disposal thereof, or

(c) fails to take reasonable care of, or so conducts himself as to endanger the safety of the sketch, plan, model, article, note, document, secret official code, or pass word or information ;

that person shall be guilty of a misdemeanour.

(1a) If any person having in his possession or control any sketch, plan, model, article, note, document, or information which relates to munitions of war, communicates it directly or indirectly to any foreign power, or in any other manner prejudicial to the safety or interests of the State, that person shall be guilty of a misdemeanour.

(2) If any person receives any secret official code word, or pass word, or sketch, plan, model, article, note, document, or information, knowing, or having reasonable grounds to believe, at the time when he receives it, that the code word, pass word, sketch, plan, model, article, note, document, or information is communicated to him in contravention of this Act, he shall be guilty of a misdemeanour, unless he proves that the communication to him of the code word, pass word, sketch, plan, model, article, note, document, or information was contrary to his desire.

8 (2). Any person who is guilty of a misdemeanour under the Official Secrets Act 1911 and 1920 shall be liable on conviction or indictment to imprisonment, with or without hard labour, for a term not exceeding two years, or, on conviction under the Summary Jurisdiction Acts, to imprisonment, with or without hard labour, for a term not exceeding three months or to a fine not exceeding fifty pounds or both such imprisonment and fine."

I understand that the above clauses of the Official Secrets Act 1911 and 1920, cover also articles published in the press and in book form, and I undertake not to divulge any official information gained by me as a result of my employment, either in the press or in book form.

Signature ....

Guy Burgess signs the Official Secrets Act while working as a Soviet agent.

'an extraordinary knowledge' of it as well as of 'the work of the Communist Party' which could make him 'very useful'. After investigation, Curry decided not to recruit Burgess – partly because of his promiscuous homosexuality, partly because he was 'not satisfied that his claim to have abandoned Communism could be accepted at its face value'. Liddell told Curry he thought he was mistaken, but did not press the point. Curry later recalled that this was their only disagreement during his twelve years in the Service. After Burgess had defected to Moscow with Donald Maclean in 1951, Liddell congratulated Curry on the judgement he had shown a decade earlier. The recruitment of Burgess, he acknowledged, 'might have been a catastrophe'.[55]

During Blunt's first six months in the Security Service, he received no guidance from the NKVD. Because of a recurrence in the Centre of paranoid suspicions that the London residency was being fed 'disinformation' by its agents, it was closed in February 1940 and the resident, Anatoli Gorsky, recalled to Moscow. In December 1940 the residency reopened, and Gorsky returned to London. On 28 December Blunt met him and made 'a good impression'. Among the first MI5 documents which Blunt handed over to Gorsky in January 1941 was the final report on the debriefing of Krivitsky.[56] Boris Kreshin, who took over from Gorsky as the case officer for Blunt (then codenamed TONY) and the rest of the Five in 1942, reported to the Centre: 'TONY is a thorough, conscientious and efficient agent. He tries to fulfil all our tasks in time and as conscientiously as possible.' Blunt met Kreshin about once a week in various parts of London, usually between nine and ten o'clock in the evening. The head of the British department at the Centre, Elena Modrzhinskaya, complained that Blunt was taking 'incomprehensible' risks by bringing many original MI5 documents as well as copies on film to the meetings with his case officer. According to KGB files, from 1941 to 1945 he provided a total of 1,771 documents.[57]

The prodigious amount of intelligence supplied by Blunt and the rest of the Five aroused suspicion among the Centre's conspiracy theorists, who included Modrzhinskaya. By November 1942, she suspected that the Double-Cross System which she knew, chiefly from Blunt, was being successfully used against Germany was also being targeted against the Soviet Union, using the Five as double agents. There was also what she believed was 'suspicious understatement' in the Five's reports on British intelligence operations against Soviet targets: 'Not a single valuable British agent in the USSR or in the Soviet embassy in Britain has been exposed with the help of this group, in spite of the fact that if they had been sincere in their cooperation they could easily have done [so].'[58] It did not occur to Modrzhinskaya or other representatives of the Centre's paranoid tendencies that no such agents had been reported for the simple reason that none existed. The lack of British agents working against Soviet targets, though due largely to the overwhelming priority of operations against Nazi Germany, was due partly to restrictions on covert activities imposed by the Foreign Office after Hitler's surprise attack on Russia in the summer of 1941 turned Britain and the Soviet Union into allies.

Despite its failure to penetrate Soviet intelligence, however, the Security Service had considerable success throughout the war in penetrating the Communist Party (CPGB). It had a ring-side seat as the Party leadership coped with the shock of the Nazi–Soviet Non-Aggression Pact signed in Moscow on 25 August 1939. Stalin, previously lauded by the CPGB as the world's most dependable opponent of Fascism in all its forms, told Hitler's Foreign Minister, Joachim von Ribbentrop: 'I can guarantee, on my word of honour, that the Soviet Union will not betray its partner.' Though the CPGB initially announced qualified support for the war against Hitler, a week later it turned the Stalinist somersault required by Comintern and adopted a policy of 'revolutionary defeatism'. The Central Committee minutes recording its ideological contortions were seized during a police raid on its King Street headquarters in June 1940. The Security Service later urged unsuccessfully that they be published to provide proof of the Party's subservience to Moscow.[59]

Among those who penetrated the CPGB early in the Second World War was Norman Himsworth, a journalist recruited to the Security Service by Maxwell Knight. Himsworth had great admiration for Knight, later recalling affectionately how he and others had sat on the bank of a pond listening to Knight explaining tradecraft while he was fishing. Among Himsworth's early targets was the Workers' Music Association, a cultural society founded by the CPGB primarily as a cover organization in case the Party's 'revolutionary defeatism' led to its being banned.[60] Within the Association Himsworth passed himself off as a civil servant in War Office public relations: 'Gradually I got to know them, and I was gradually accepted as part of them.' The Association's Communist president, Alan Bush, then invited Himsworth to become its secretary and told him all office-holders were expected to be Party members. Himsworth agreed on the spot. Knight, he later recalled, 'gave us a free hand; he had great faith in his staff.' Bush gave Himsworth the cover name 'Ian Mackay', and urged him to keep his Party membership secret.[61] Himsworth discovered that the Musical Association had set up a secret interview room in central London to collect classified information about weapons and military operations from Communists and sympathizers in the armed forces.[62]

On 15 July 1942 Himsworth was unexpectedly summoned to King Street by the head of the Control Commission, Robert 'Robby' Robson, whose responsibilities included Party security.[63] F2a, which was responsible for monitoring the CPGB, regarded Robson as a 'particularly wily' character, 'in charge of the Party's undercover work', and had discovered he was receiving classified documents from an unidentified civil servant. As well as being subject to an HOW, he was under surveillance by B6, which tried unsuccessfully to find a vacant apartment in his block of flats at Parliament Hill from which to keep him under observation.[64] After putting a few innocent questions to Himsworth about his background and how he came to join the Musical Association, Robson suddenly asked him: 'How many reports have you sent in for MI5?' He then quoted from a report which Himsworth had submitted to MI5 on 23 March 1941, unwisely writing it in the first person – thus making it easier to identify him as the author. According to a Security Service report on the meeting, Himsworth 'gave as good as he got', adopted an attitude of outraged innocence and tried to deflect suspicion on to the president of the Association. At one point Robson, 'a violent man' according to Himsworth, pushed him against a wall and was about to hit him. Himsworth believed that only the arrival of another member of the Control Commission, Jimmy Shields, prevented a fight breaking out. The meeting ended with Himsworth still protesting his innocence. He continued to do so during three further meetings.

The last meeting was requested by Himsworth himself in the hope that, if he succeeded in making Robson angry, he might reveal clues about the source of the leak in MI5. Robson was unaware that, thanks to eavesdropping devices recently installed by the Security Service at King Street, his conversation with Himsworth was being recorded. Contrary to usual regulations, the head of the transcription section, Mrs Evelyn Grist, listened in live to Himsworth's last meetings with Robson, apparently because of fears for his personal safety. By prearranged signal, while at King Street, Himsworth hummed the tune to 'Non piu andrai . . .' from the finale to Act One of Mozart's *Marriage of Figaro* in order to reassure her that all was well.[65]

The best clue to the source of the leak within MI5, however, came not from Himsworth's final showdown with Robson but from an earlier transcription of Robson talking to his assistants at King Street:

Yes, they're MI5 we've got inside the Party – very clearly . . . And this is one of them and the system we've got is just beginning to operate. [Identifying] Mackay

[Himsworth] is the first fruits ... Unfortunately the person that was able to do it got the bloody sack after getting this Mackay. And I had to send an urgent message that she was to get the job back at any bloody cost.

Robson described the female MI5 employee who had got the sack as 'one of these something or other liberals who have conscientious scruples and begin to come over a bit and start telling us things'. A hunt (codenamed the VIPER investigation) began for a secretary who had 'got the bloody sack' and found one possible suspect whose flat was searched without revealing incriminating evidence.[66] It later turned out that the clue which led to the search was misleading. The secretary who had leaked classified information had not been sacked but had resigned.

On 23 December 1942 further eavesdropping at King Street produced what MI5's Legal Adviser, Edward Cussen, called 'a Christmas gift'. The transcript revealed not merely that a female Party agent was still operating in MI5 but that Robson had asked her to look up his own file. Robson's file was then used as bait in the Security Service Registry and a twenty-three-year-old secretary in C3 (the vetting section) was observed looking through it 'but not in the way of someone looking for a trace'. Subsequent surveillance of the secretary left 'no doubt' that she was a Communist.[67] Blunt reported to his Soviet case officer that colleagues involved in the investigation had heard references to 'our girl' through the eavesdropping devices installed at King Street and were 'absolutely sure that the Communist Party still has an agent inside MI5'. With his own security in mind, Blunt added: 'It is good that it is a girl they speak about.'[68]

On 19 January 1943 the secretary was questioned by Cussen, Reginald Horrocks, the Director of Establishments and Administration, and William Skardon, a detective seconded from the Met, and she eventually made a partial confession. Three days later, the hidden microphones at King Street picked up the following conversation between Robson and one of Wheeler's Communist contacts, Philip McLeod:

McLEOD: I wouldn't do this unless it was very important. The girl came home last night and she's been grilled

ROBSON: She's been what?

McLEOD: Grilled

ROBSON: Which is the person you're talking about?

McLEOD: Oh, she's been with Norman [a Communist contact], you see

ROBSON: Oh that person we're getting the stuff from?

McLEOD: Yes

ROBSON: O-o-o-oh!

McLeod said the girl had had to make a written statement but thought she had succeeded in concealing 'some matters of importance'. Her statement, however, had raised suspicions about another secretary who had resigned from the Security Service early in July 1942, at precisely the point when Robson had been overheard saying that his MI5 informant had got the sack. Henceforth, wrote Cussen, 'We assumed that [this other secretary] was the Party's original agent within the Service and that it was upon her departure that the C3 secretary had been recruited . . . as a replacement.'[69]

Investigation of this other secretary revealed that, while in the Security Service, she had been closely involved with a group of four Communist militants: two officers in the RAF medical branch, Wing Commander Robert Fisher and Squadron Leader John Norman Macdonald, Mary Peppin (who was married to Fisher) and her sister Geraldine. An HOW on the secretary also revealed that she had just had an illegal abortion and had been called to give evidence at the trial of the abortionist. Since she was no longer able to pass material from MI5 to the CPGB, it was decided not to interview her until after the trial. In the meantime the DG, Sir David Petrie, decided that prosecution of the C3 secretary, who had been dismissed on 24 January, would be 'inexpedient', probably because of the nature of the evidence needed to secure a conviction.

When Cussen and Skardon on 15 July interviewed the other secretary, after the trial of her abortionist, they found her 'in that untidy state which', they condescendingly observed, 'was usual for her when no special occasion was involved'. Cussen began by telling her they knew about her involvement with the abortionist as well as the fact that she had concealed it from her family. She must, said Cussen, have been through hell. But 'When you were working in our office you betrayed us. You used to visit Fisher and Macdonald and the Peppins and you used to tell them things which were in our files. I know exactly what you told them and I will tell you about it in a minute.' He implied that, if she co-operated, there would be no prosecution. She begged Cussen and Skardon 'never to say a word about the abortion matter', then 'broke down completely and cried, and we spent a good deal of time in restoring her'. When she recovered, she made a statement admitting passing information to the CPGB. Her interrogators were impressed by her ability to recall much of the contents of the MI5 document with which Robson had confronted Himsworth. Cussen wrote later:

Having regard to her character and 'make-up' we both thought the account which she gave of being unable to resist the temptation of mentioning its contents to Fisher in the presence of Mary Peppin was true. She is a mixture of an intelligent and a naive person. It is quite possible that Fisher got further information out of her, but I am inclined to think that the C3 secretary proved a much better agent when circumstances brought about the replacement of this girl.[70]

Though the Security Service did not uncover any wartime Soviet spy as important as Blunt or the other members of the Five, it successfully resolved a number of other espionage cases. The first began with the chance discovery by the Special Branch of photographs of classified War Office documents while searching the London home of a Communist named Oliver Green, who was arrested in May 1942 on a charge of forging petrol coupons and later sentenced to fifteen months' imprisonment. When questioned in prison in August by Hugh Shillito of F2c, Green admitted that he had been recruited as a Soviet agent while fighting for the International Brigade in the Spanish Civil War.[71] Green had first been identified as a CPGB member in 1935,[72] but told Shillito that, after his recruitment, he had (like the Five) 'cut right away from the Party and has had nothing to do with it from that day'.[73] Though he refused to identify any of his sub-agents by name, he said that they included an informant in the army, a merchant seaman, a fitter in an aircraft factory, an official in a government department, a member of the RAF and a man who supplied figures on aircraft construction. Green claimed that he had forged petrol coupons only because he needed his car to maintain contact with his agent network. 'Ideologically', noted Guy Liddell, 'he is a curious character, and not altogether unlikeable.'[74]

Potentially the most worrying information provided by Green was his claim that 'Russian Intelligence had an agent in the Security Service.' He had been assured that, 'if British Intelligence had any suspicion about them as Soviet agents, the Centre would come to know very quickly.'[75] Since it is inconceivable that any of Green's case officers would have compromised Blunt's role in MI5 by making any reference to him, it is far more likely that they were referring to the fact (already known to Shillito and Liddell) that the CPGB had informants within the Security Service. On Green's release from prison, he went to report to Robby Robson, the head of the Party Control Commission, at King Street. Unaware that everything he said was being picked up by MI5 microphones, Green revealed the names of his sub-agents.[76] Though all were made subject to HOWs and physical surveillance, the evidence obtained against them was inadequate for a prosecution, perhaps because they had become more cautious after Green's imprisonment.[77]

The most important Soviet espionage case solved by the wartime Security Service was that of a spy-ring headed by the CPGB's national organizer, Douglas Springhall, who was sentenced to seven years' imprisonment in July 1943 for offences under the Official Secrets Act. Though the Service believed that Soviet agents normally 'cut themselves off from the Party', Springhall took the 'unusual step of using the Party apparatus for espionage'.[78] Like Green, Springhall was discovered as the result of a lead which came from outside MI5. John Curry later concluded, 'There was reason to think that he had been active for some years and had excellently placed informants, and might have escaped detection but for a piece of negligence on his part.'[79] Among Springhall's sources was a secretary in the Air Ministry, Olive Sheehan, who passed him details of a new anti-radar device, codenamed WINDOW. Sheehan's flatmate, Norah Bond, heard her discussing classified information with Springhall, saw her handing him material and succeeded in obtaining an envelope which Sheehan planned to pass to Springhall. Bond gave the envelope to an RAF officer who steamed it open, discovered that it contained information on WINDOW and informed the Air Ministry, which told MI5.[80]

Security Service examination of Springhall's diary led to the discovery of two further members of his spy-ring: Ormond Uren, a staff officer in the Special Operations Executive (SOE), and Ray Milne, a secretary in SIS. In November 1943 Uren, who was found to have revealed the entire 'organisational lay-out of SOE' to Springhall, was sentenced, like Springhall, to seven years' imprisonment.[81] Guy Liddell noted that, as a secretary in Section V of SIS, Ray Milne was 'right in the middle of ISOS [Abwehr decrypts] and everything else'.[82] During interrogation by Roger Hollis and the head of Section V, Felix Cowgill, Milne confessed to very little but claimed, like Springhall and Uren, that passing intelligence to Moscow was merely sharing information with an ally.[83] She was dismissed but never prosecuted.[84]

The CPGB leadership reacted with shocked surprise to Springhall's conviction, expelling him from the Party and publicly distancing itself from any involvement in espionage. David Clarke (F2a) reported that both Pollitt and Willie Gallacher, the Party's only MP, were 'clearly anxious to clean the Party of such activities'. In order to emphasize its British identity, at the Sixteenth Party Congress in July 1943 the Party decided to call itself the 'British Communist Party'. Clarke, however, saw the Party's attempts to distance itself from Soviet espionage as primarily cosmetic: 'The Soviet authorities have from time to time obtained information from most of the leading members of the Communist Party who have shown various degrees of willingness to do this work.'[85] The Home Secretary told the War Cabinet in August that the Springhall case emphasized the 'great risk of the Party trading on the current sympathy for Russia to induce people . . . to betray [secrets]', and raised once more the question of barring Communists from access to classified information.[86] Whitehall, however, still had a rather casual attitude to protective security. In February 1940 the Foreign Office had taken the long-overdue step of appointing a retired diplomat, William Codrington, as chief security officer. But Codrington was given neither a salary nor, until 1942, any assistant. Not until after the war did the Foreign Office at last establish a Security Department.[87]

After 'lengthy and intricate investigations', David Clarke reported in October 1943 that fifty-seven Communist Party members working in government departments, the armed forces and scientific research had 'access to secret information and in some cases to information of the highest secrecy'. Three Communists were employed on the TUBE ALLOYS project, Britain's top-secret atomic research programme. Clarke urged that all should be moved to non-classified work:

The whole experience of the Security Service shows that members of the Communist Party place their loyalty to the Party above their loyalty to their Service and that their signature of the Official Secrets Act always carries a mental reservation in favour of the Party. The fact that the Communist Party is at present supporting the war would not prevent them from using any secret information in their possession irresponsibly and without regard to the true interests of the country.[88]

Most of the fifty-seven Communists identified by Clarke had gained access to classified information because the departments concerned had no coherent vetting procedures for Party members and had failed to follow Security Service guidelines.[89] The Home Secretary proposed that all Communists identified by the Security Service should be moved from secret work. Churchill was initially inclined to agree. He seems to have been persuaded otherwise by his intelligence adviser, Desmond Morton, a former SIS officer who had become hostile to the Security Service. A secret Whitehall panel which contained no Security Service representative was given responsibility for examining all cases of Communists in government departments submitted to it by the Service. The Security Service believed, probably correctly, that the panel was not up to its job. Before the panel was wound up in July 1945, it referred only one case to it.[90]

As well as being seriously dissatisfied with Whitehall's approach to protective security, the leadership of the Security Service was also well aware that it was failing to keep track of Soviet espionage. With at least partial justice, it blamed its failure on the severe restrictions placed by the Foreign Office on investigation of the Soviet embassy and Trade Delegation, and therefore of the intelligence residencies for which they provided cover. In March 1943 Liddell noted in his diary:

I had a talk this morning with Hollis about Soviet espionage. There is no doubt to my mind that it is going on and sooner or later we shall be expected to know all about it. On the other hand if we take action and get found out there will be an appalling stink.[91]

MI5 decided not to risk 'an appalling stink'. Blunt reported to his case officer that the Security Service had no agents inside the Soviet embassy and that even surveillance of callers at the embassy had been suspended. Only telephone calls were monitored. MI5 energies were overwhelmingly directed against Nazi Germany. Instead of welcoming this news, the Centre was incredulous. Convinced that intelligence operations against Soviet targets must be as high a priority for British intelligence as operations in Britain were for the Centre, it concluded that Blunt (like others of the Five) must be deceiving them. 'Our task', the Centre instructed its London resident, Anatoli Gorsky, 'is to understand what disinformation our rivals are planting on us.' Modrzhinskaya concluded in October 1943 that 'all the data' indicated the Cambridge Five were part of an organized deception mounted by British intelligence. In reality, much of the data indicated the opposite. Before the great victory of the Red Army at Kursk in June 1943, the GRU had reported that ULTRA intelligence on German operations forwarded by Blunt from Leo Long, his sub-agent in military intelligence, was 'very valuable'. Most of it was later 'confirmed by other sources'. Further ULTRA intelligence from Long, the GRU concluded, was 'highly desirable'.[92] The Centre's conclusion that the Five were trying to deceive it derived not from a rational assessment of the intelligence they supplied but from its own paranoid tendencies.

To try to discover the exact nature of the British deception, the Centre sent an eight-man surveillance team to London to trail the Five and other supposedly bogus Soviet agents in a vain attempt to discover their contacts with their non-existent British controllers. The team, all conspicuously dressed in Russian clothes and unable to speak English, were inevitably and hilariously unsuccessful.[93] The Centre's suspicions of the Five did not disappear until Operation OVERLORD, the D-Day landings of 6 June 1944.[94] On 26 May that year Blunt passed on a complete copy of the entire deception plan devised as part of OVERLORD. On 7 July he provided a comprehensive account of B Division's role in the deception and, in particular, its use of double agents.[95] The stress of his own double life took a greater toll on Blunt than on the rest of the Five. He was under such visible strain that the Centre did not object to his decision at the end of the war to return to his career as an art historian and accept appointment as Surveyor of the King's Pictures.[96]

F Division was acutely aware that both its successful wartime prosecutions of Soviet spies – the Green and Springhall cases – were the result of outside leads, and that there must be a series of others it had failed to detect. It was worried also by the commitment shown by both men and by their sub-agents. The head of the Security Executive, now Duff Cooper, wrote to Churchill in October 1943, reflecting the MI5 view: 'These agents differ fundamentally from the very poor type employed by the Germans who belong to the dregs of civilisation. Communist agents are intelligent and are inspired by altruistic, idealistic motives. Their first duty is to the Soviet Union.'[97] The senior MI5 officer most alert to the continued threat from Soviet espionage was Roger Hollis, who as F2 was responsible for monitoring Communism and other left-wing subversion. Hollis had regarded the main SIS Communist expert, Valentine Vivian, head of Section V until January 1941, 'with the veneration of a pupil for a master',[98] but disliked his successor, Felix Cowgill. Philby, who worked under Cowgill, told the Centre that he was shy but combative, had 'few social graces' and was unable to delegate. In one respect, however, Philby likened Cowgill to Karl Marx: both smoked pipe tobacco 'in prodigious quantities' (an irreverent comparison which cannot have amused the NKVD).[99] In April 1942 the Security Service, which had hitherto believed it received all ISOS material, discovered that Cowgill had been withholding Abwehr decrypts containing references to SIS agents, thus depriving the Service of a large amount of relevant intelligence. Philby ingratiated himself with MI5 by attacking Cowgill's failure to share all Abwehr decrypts with it.[100] Hollis told Petrie in April 1942 that he probably saw more of the product of Section V than Vivian (then Deputy Chief of SIS). But 'To be honest even I do not see much.' Hollis was highly critical of what he did see:

I can think of no document produced by SIS which makes it appear that international communism had been seriously studied by them since the outbreak of war. We, on the other hand, have started, rather belatedly, to follow the activities of the Comintern wherever it appears, and it was we who drew the attention of SIS to the growth of a settlement of refugee Comintern leaders in Mexico, and not SIS who told us . . .

It may be said that our job is internal security, and that we are going outside our charter. To that I should misquote Litvinoff and say 'Communism is indivisible.'

You cannot study the CPGB and the refugee communists in this country without knowing what the Comintern is doing.[101]

After the signing of the 1942 British–Soviet Treaty, which bound both powers not to make a separate peace with Germany, Petrie circulated a memorandum by Hollis warning that the Soviet Union and international Communism had not changed their spots: 'Once Russia is safe and out of the battle, our Communists will seize every chance to make trouble, as they did in the past.'[102]

Within the Security Service the main pressure for keeping record cards on all Communist Party members came from Hollis, who argued that Soviet intelligence often selected rank-and-file Party members with 'clear records' for espionage.[103] The more than threefold wartime expansion of the Party from the 15,000 members at the end of the era of 'revolutionary defeatism' in June 1941, however, made it impossible for the Registry to cope, and Hollis had to settle for selective registration.[104] In the final stages of the war Petrie had a series of meetings with Hollis to discuss the post-war threat from Soviet espionage. On the morning of 5 September 1945, they discussed, at length, the 'leakage of information through members of the Communist Party'.[105] Their meeting turned out to be remarkably well timed. Later the same day a GRU cipher clerk in Ottawa, Igor Gouzenko, defected with dramatic evidence of the 'leakage of information'.[106]

Hollis's most remarkable insight into Soviet intelligence penetration was that, probably alone within the Security Service, he became suspicious of Blunt. Philby later recalled that 'Hollis was always vaguely unhappy about him.'[107] After Blunt eventually confessed to working as a Soviet agent, he told his interrogators, Peter Wright and Arthur Martin, 'I believe [Hollis] disliked me – I believe he slightly suspected me.' Blunt recalled one particularly dramatic example of Hollis's suspicions. After Gouzenko had revealed the existence of an unidentified Soviet agent codenamed ELLI, Hollis turned to Blunt and said, 'Isn't that so, ELLI?'[108] It was sadly ironic that Wright and Martin, the most damaging conspiracy theorists in the history of the Security Service, should later persuade themselves that the unidentified Soviet agent was Hollis himself.[109]

3
Victory

In the middle of the Second World War, the Double-Cross System, like the British war effort as a whole, moved up a gear. Masterman later listed seven main aims which the double agents were intended to serve:

(1) To control the enemy [espionage] system, or as much of it as we could get our hands on
(2) To catch fresh spies when they appeared
(3) To gain knowledge of personalities and methods of the German Secret Service
(4) To obtain information about the code and cypher work of the German Service
(5) To get evidence of enemy plans and intentions from the questions asked by them
(6) To influence enemy plans by the answers sent to the enemy [by the double agents]
(7) To deceive the enemy about our plans and intentions.[1]

It was not until the summer of 1942 that the Twenty Committee began to make its priority strategic deception (the deception of the enemy high command, not merely of its forces in the field). Tar Robertson informed the W Board on 15 July:

It is reasonably certain that the only network of agents possessed by the Germans in this country is that which is now under the control of the Security Service ... The combined General Staff in this country have, in MI5 double agents, a powerful means of exercising influence over the OKW German High Command.[2]

Strategic deception began not in the European theatre but in the Middle East, where early in the war the British Commander in Chief, General Sir Archibald Wavell, appointed an intelligence officer, Lieutenant Colonel Dudley Clarke, to devise deception plans.[3] Clarke's 'A Force' set the tone for deception campaigns throughout the Middle East, and ultimately for all other theatres during the war. The official historian of British wartime deception, Sir Michael Howard, concludes:

A small acorn planted by Dudley Clarke in December 1940 in the shape of a few bogus units in the Western Desert was to grow into a massive oak tree whose branches included the non-existent British Twelfth Army in Egypt (and the barely existent Ninth and Tenth Armies in Syria and Iraq) and the First United States Army Group (FUSAG) in the United Kingdom.[4]

Dudley Clarke's capacity for deception extended even to his still mysterious private life. In November 1941 Kim Philby, who enjoyed retailing personal scandals to Soviet intelligence, reported that Clarke had been arrested in Madrid, dressed in women's clothing.[5] Philby occasionally perplexed Moscow, probably after heavy drinking sessions, by sending, along with high-grade intelligence, bizarrely improbable scandal such as a report that Germany was infiltrating cocaine and other hard drugs, probably by parachute, into the Irish Republic, whence they were smuggled into Britain by Welsh fishermen in motor launches and supplied to London clubs where RAF officers 'under the influence of drugs, alcohol, sexual orgies or Black Mass are induced to part with information'.[6] By contrast, Philby's report of Clarke's transvestite tendencies, which led to his temporary imprisonment in Spain, was quite correct.[7] Despite his personal eccentricities, Clarke's deception operations in the Middle East inspired the creation of the London Controlling Section (LCS), headed from May 1942 by Lieutenant Colonel J. H. Bevan, in order to 'prepare deception plans on a worldwide basis with the object of causing the enemy to waste his military resources'. Though given the grand title of 'Controlling Officer', Bevan lacked executive authority; his role was to plan, co-ordinate and supervise.[8]

Strategic deception co-ordinated by the LCS was central to the first major Allied offensive of the war: Operation TORCH, the invasion of French North Africa, for which planning began in July 1942. The two main deception plans devised by Bevan, OVERTHROW and SOLO 1, successfully persuaded the Germans that Allied preparations for landings in, respectively, northern France and Norway were at an advanced stage.[9] Throughout the deceptions, the LCS maintained close contact with the Twenty Committee and B1a. Eight double agents were used to pass disinformation to the enemy.[10] The most inventive disinformation came from the Spanish double agent GARBO and his full-time case officer, Tomás 'Tommy' Harris,[11] the bilingual son of an English father and Spanish mother, who formed one of the most creative and successful agent–case-officer partnerships in MI5 history.[12] Harris had established himself before the war as a wealthy London art dealer, artist and socialite, and had been recommended to MI5 early in 1941 by Anthony Blunt, with whom he shared artistic interests.[13] Throughout the war Harris and his wife kept open house at their Mayfair home, with generous supplies (despite wartime rationing) of champagne and canapés for friends in the intelligence and art worlds: among them Blunt, Guy Burgess, Kim Philby, Guy Liddell, Dick White, Victor Rothschild, Bond Street art dealers and Sotheby's auctioneers. Harris's friendship with three leading Soviet agents did not impair, though it adds piquancy to, his operational effectiveness in MI5.[14]

Before Operation TORCH, GARBO sent the Abwehr numerous reports from fictional sub-agents invented by Harris and himself. Sub-agents in Scotland reported on mountain warfare training for Canadian, Scottish and Norwegian troops which pointed to preparations for an invasion of Norway. GARBO's contacts in the Ministry of Information were said to have revealed that officially inspired rumours of an expedition to Dakar were intended to distract attention from an attack elsewhere, possibly Norway or France. On 29 October GARBO reported, correctly, that a convoy had just set sail from the Clyde. Three days later, on 1 November, he informed the Abwehr, also correctly, that intelligence from the Ministry of Information pointed to an Allied invasion of French North Africa. B1a, however, arranged for the letters containing these reports to be delayed in the post. They did not reach GARBO's case officer until 7 November, a few hours before the Allied landings and after the invasion force had already been spotted by the Germans. It did not occur to the Abwehr to blame GARBO for the delay or to suspect the involvement of British intelligence. 'Your last reports are all magnificent,' they told him, 'but we are very sorry they arrived late.'[15] General Alfred Jodl, Chief of the Operations Staff of the German High Command (OKW) and Hitler's closest military adviser, told Allied interrogators after the war that the landings in North Africa had come as 'a complete surprise'.[16]

No agency in British history, probably none in the history of intelligence, had ever devised such a wide range of ingenious deceptions with such a high success rate as B1a during the Second World War. Most new recruits to the section were so enthused by the ethos created by Tar Robertson that they learned the art of deception with unusual speed. Among them was the twenty-five-year-old Oxford-educated Flight Lieutenant Charles Cholmondeley, who joined MI5 from the Intelligence Directorate at the Air Ministry in 1940[17] and was later described by Tar as 'a most extraordinary and delightful man who worked in my section largely as an ideas man'.[18] Robertson's less enthusiastic deputy, John Marriott, found him 'an incurable romantic of the old cloak and dagger school'.[19] The most ingenious cloak-and-dagger deception devised by Cholmondeley, soon after the beginning of TORCH, was a scheme to plant bogus documents on the enemy designed to mislead them about the target of a forthcoming Allied operation in the Mediterranean:

A body is obtained from one of the London hospitals (normal peacetime price £10). It is then dressed in uniform of suitable rank. The lungs are filled with water and the documents disposed of in an inside pocket. The body is then dropped by a Coastal Command aircraft at a suitable position where the set of the currents will probably carry the body ashore in enemy territory . . . Information in the form of the documents can be of a far more secret nature than it would be possible to introduce through any other normal B1a channel.[20]

Cholmondeley quickly won the support of Lieutenant Commander Ewen Montagu, the naval representative on the Twenty Committee (whose pro-Russian brother Ivor was later identified as a Soviet agent). On 4 February they informed the Committee that a suitable corpse had been found (that of Glyndwr Michael, a homeless Welshman who had died by ingesting rat poison), and won approval for what became known as Operation MINCEMEAT. Michael was given the fictitious identity of Major William 'Bill' Martin of the Royal Marines, an officer on the staff of the Chief of Combined Operations, Vice Admiral Lord Louis Mountbatten.[21]

Some modifications were made to Cholmondeley's original plan. In order to ensure that the bogus official documents on the body were not overlooked, they were placed in a briefcase attached to the belt of 'Martin's' trenchcoat rather than in his pockets, which contained personal items and letters from his fiancée. It was also decided that, instead of being dropped into the sea from an aircraft, the corpse should be taken by submarine to a point near Huelva on the Spanish coast where the local currents could be relied on to wash it ashore.[22] As controlling officer of the LCS, Colonel Bevan called on Churchill at 10 a.m. on 15 April to gain his consent to MINCEMEAT. He found the Prime Minister sitting up in bed, smoking a cigar, 'surrounded by papers and black and red Cabinet boxes'. Churchill quickly gave his enthusiastic support for the deception (subject to the agreement of General Dwight D. Eisenhower, Allied commander in the Mediterranean theatre, which was also obtained). If the operation did not succeed at the first attempt, he said, not entirely seriously, 'we shall have to get the body back and give it another swim.'[23]

Though the implementation of Operation MINCEMEAT was not MI5's responsibility, it provided considerable assistance. Montagu invited secretaries in B Division to submit photographs from which he chose a suitable candidate to become 'Major Martin's' fiancée, 'Pam'. His choice fell on a B1b secretary. An attractive photograph of her in a swimsuit was placed in 'Martin's' wallet.[24] Other secretaries helped draft love letters from 'Pam' to place in 'Martin's' pocket.[25] The photograph in 'Martin's' identity card was of a B1a officer, Ronnie Reed, who bore some resemblance to the unfortunate Glyndwr Michael.[26] 'Martin's' pockets also contained stubs of London theatre tickets dated 22 April, as evidence that he had left England after that date.[27] In reality, the corpse had been loaded several days earlier on to the submarine, HMS *Seraph*, which took it to the Spanish coast. On 22 April Montagu and Cholmondeley presented the secretaries mainly responsible for the love letters and the swimsuit photograph with the theatre tickets whose stubs had been planted on the corpse, and the four of them celebrated 'Bill Martin's farewell' with a show and dinner.[28]

Just over a week later, on 30 April, the corpse was picked up offshore near Huelva by a local sardine fisherman. Though the body was handed over to the British for burial, pro-German Spanish officials, as expected, allowed the Abwehr to photograph the documents in the briefcase. Among them were letters by Mountbatten and the Vice Chief of the Imperial General Staff, Lieutenant General Sir Archibald Nye, as well as proofs of a manual on Combined Operations to which Eisenhower had, supposedly, been asked to write a foreword. The letters falsely indicated that the Allies were planning a landing in Greece, codenamed Operation HUSKY. Soon afterwards ULTRA decrypts revealed that the Germans had been comprehensively deceived. A message sent to Churchill during a visit to Washington said simply: 'MINCEMEAT swallowed rod, line and sinker.' Even when the Allied attack came in Sicily rather than Greece, the Germans did not doubt the authenticity of the MINCEMEAT documents but concluded that Allied plans had changed.[29]

The preparations for Operation MINCEMEAT persuaded the head of the Security Executive, Duff Cooper, that the time had come to brief Churchill on some of the other deceptions devised by B1a and the double agents which it ran.[30] As late as March 1943, Guy Liddell noted in his diary that the Prime Minister, despite his regular meetings with 'C' and close interest in the work of Bletchley Park and SOE, still knew nothing about Security Service operations.[31] The double-agent case chosen by Duff Cooper as most likely to enthuse the Prime Minister during his first briefing on the work of B1a was that of Eddie Chapman.[32] Before the war Chapman had been a flamboyant London career criminal, who drove a Bentley and dressed in Savile Row suits. While on the run from the Met in 1939, he fled to Jersey where he was jailed for house-breaking and larceny. His fortunes were changed by the German occupation of the Channel Islands. Chapman's offer to spy for Germany after his release from prison was eventually accepted by the Abwehr. In the early hours of 16 December 1942 he was dropped by parachute over the Cambridgeshire countryside, equipped with false identity cards, £990 in used notes, a wallet taken from a dead British soldier, a radio set and a suicide pill. By morning he had contacted the local police and told them he wished to tell his story to the 'British Intelligence Service'. Chapman was taken to Camp 020, where it took the commandant, Tin-eye Stephens, only a few days to turn him into a double agent, codenamed ZIGZAG. Though no detailed account survives of Churchill's briefing on ZIGZAG, the Prime Minister was almost certainly told that early in 1943 he had carried out a sabotage operation against the de Havilland aircraft factory at Hatfield which built the Mosquito bombers then pounding German cities. Dramatic photographs were taken of wrecked factory buildings covered in tarpaulins with debris strewn around. ZIGZAG's exultant German case officer, Stephan von Gröning, comfortably ensconced in a large mansion at the French port of Nantes, celebrated by ordering 'champagne all round'. At a secret ceremony in Oslo later in 1943 ZIGZAG became the first British subject to be awarded the Iron Cross in recognition of his 'outstanding zeal and success'. The 'sabotage' of the de Havilland factory, however, was a hoax, orchestrated by B1a.[33]

The second case on which Churchill was briefed by Duff Cooper in March 1943 was that of a senior Abwehr officer, codenamed HARLEQUIN, who had been captured in North Africa in November 1942 and brought to Britain as a POW. Though it was not possible to run him as a double agent, since the Germans knew he had been taken prisoner:

he was turned round to a point where, convinced of the inevitability of a German defeat, he placed in our hands a written offer of his services, subject only to the reservation that he should not be compelled to take up arms against the German Forces. He has supplied a wealth of intelligence, much of which is subject to check [that is, can be corroborated], though this fact is unknown to him. He has also been used in a consultative capacity and has contributed helpful and informative comments on cases submitted to him.[34]

The Security Service believed that HARLEQUIN had 'a none too rigid conscience' and had agreed to co-operate partly because he lacked the 'moral courage' to face up to life as a POW and wanted the war over as quickly as possible. But Petrie reported in April: 'So far he has played well by us and it is anticipated that provided we hold to our side of the bargain he will continue to do so.'[35]

Struck by Churchill's evident fascination with ZIGZAG, HARLE-

QUIN and other colourful MI5 operations, Duff Cooper proposed that the Security Service send the Prime Minister a monthly report of two or three pages.[36] Like Petrie, Liddell was anxious that Churchill might be carried away by what he read: 'There are obvious advantages in selling ourselves to the PM who at the moment knows nothing about our department. On the other hand, he may, on seeing some particular item, go off the deep end and want to take action, which will be disastrous to the work in hand.'[37] On balance, largely in the interests of Security Service staff, Petrie decided in favour of a monthly report to Churchill:

It is a disadvantage of Security work, by and large, that the results are apt to be mainly negative, that is to say the better it is done, the less there is to show for it. Also from its very nature, its secrets can be confided only to the few. It is only fair, therefore, that the good work of the Service, to which I would like to pay my own tribute, should be brought to the notice of the Prime Minister and certain other high quarters.[38]

The Service leadership was particularly concerned by the likely reaction of the Labour Home Secretary in Churchill's coalition government, Herbert Morrison. A meeting of Liddell, Dick White, Tar Robertson and Roger Hollis agreed not to include counter-subversion in the monthly reports, on the grounds that 'The PM might speak to the Home Secretary about it and if the latter was not also informed we should find ourselves in trouble.'[39] Their reluctance to send reports on subversion to Morrison was heavily influenced by the Zec case in the previous year. In March 1942 the Home Secretary had been enraged by a cartoon by Philip Zec in the *Daily Mirror*, showing a torpedoed sailor, his face smeared with oil, lying on a raft in the Atlantic. Morrison interpreted the cartoon, probably wrongly, as implying that the sailor's life had been sacrificed to increase oil companies' profits. Though no evidence survives in Security Service files, it seems likely that Morrison asked the Service to investigate.[40]

Probably fearful of provoking more demands for more investigations of alleged subversives, the Service leadership decided that the monthly reports to Churchill should be confined, almost exclusively, to its role in the war against the Axis powers. For the first monthly report, the various sections of the Service (excluding Hollis's) produced drafts totalling about sixteen single-spaced typed pages. Anthony Blunt prepared a précis, and the final draft of about two and a half pages was produced in collaboration between him and Dick White.[41] Since Blunt continued to draft the monthly reports to Churchill for the remainder of the war,[42] it is highly probable they went to Soviet intelligence as well – and quite possibly to Stalin personally.[43] Indeed,

A. Spies arrested since September 1939

It is believed that while the many Germans who returned to their country on the outbreak of war took back with them a most exact knowledge of the state of our re-armament and of the potential output of our factories, they left no live spy organisation behind them. Being without up-to-date information, after their defeat in the Battle of Britain, the Germans again resorted to their former system of individual spying. Since September, 1940, attempts at penetration have been persistent. In all 126 spies have fallen into our hands. Of these eighteen gave themselves up voluntarily; twenty-four have been found amenable and are now being used as double-cross agents. Twenty-eight have been detained at overseas stations, and eight were arrested on the high seas. In addition twelve real, and seven imaginary persons have been foisted upon the enemy as double-cross spies. Thirteen spies have been executed, and a fourteenth is under trial.

B. New Arrests.

(1) MENEZES

This spy was a clerk in the Portuguese Embassy, London. He was working for the German and Italian Secret Services, to whom he sent reports written in secret ink in private letters sent through the Portuguese diplomatic bag. For a period during which we were able to assure ourselves that the reports which he was sending were harmless, we watched his operations and finally on an occasion when he had obtained an interesting item of news which duly showed up in a letter, his career as a spy had to be ended. Through the wholehearted collaboration of the Portuguese Ambassador MENEZES was arrested and made a full confession. The Portuguese Government having waived his diplomatic privilege, he has now been committed for trial.

(2) DE GRAAF

This Canadian traitor, of Dutch parentage, was detected by our interrogation staff on entering this country. He confessed to having worked for the German Secret Service for more than two years, during which he had insinuated himself into an Allied escape organisation for our prisoners of war which he is believed to have betrayed to the enemy. He was in addition a well trained saboteur.

(3) BATICON, LASKI, PACHECO Y CUESTA

The existence of these three spies on ships bound for South America was revealed by material supplied from special sources. They were successfully identified at our Trinidad control, and are being sent to this country for interrogation.

C. Agents Expected

Similar material reveals German plans for despatching two new spies to this country and two saboteurs to be landed by submarine on the coast of Palestine. Suitable arrangements have been made for their reception.

D. Controlled German Spies ("Double-Cross Spies")

(1) Through a double-cross spy in this country a deal was concluded with the German Secret Service in Madrid, by which £2,500 were paid to the spy here and 250,000 pesetas were put at our disposal in Madrid. This deal was arranged through the unconscious help of the Spanish Assistant Military Attaché in London, who took with him in the diplomatic bag a letter of introduction to the principals in Madrid, on the back of which was a message to the German Secret Service in secret ink.

(2) "ZIGZAG", an Englishman was dropped as a spy by parachute in December 1942 near Thetford. Extensive information was already in our

/possession

Extract from first monthly 'Report on Activities of Security Service', dealing mainly with counter-espionage and double agents, submitted to the Prime Minister in the spring of 1943. Churchill was much impressed and annotated 'deeply interesting. WSC' at the end. Since the draft reports were prepared by Anthony Blunt, copies may well have gone to Stalin also.

possession before his arrival, so that his confession on giving himself up could be immediately checked. It was found possible to collaborate with this spy in deceiving his former masters, who were persuaded to believe that he did in fact perform the mission for which he was sent here, namely to sabotage the de Havilland Mosquito factory at Hatfield. The agent has now been sent back to the Germans via Lisbon, and it is expected that he will be given another similar mission in British or Allied territory.

(3) On the night of 20.2.43. a wireless set of new design, £200 in notes, and sabotage equipment were dropped by parachute in Aberdeenshire for MUTT and JEFF, who are double-cross spies of Norwegian nationality. The German aircraft flew low over the exact spot indicated by us to the German Secret Service.

(4) On 10.3.43. one of our agents who has been recruited by the German Sabotage Service in Spain had a faked explosion arranged for him in Gibraltar. The German Sabotage Service gave him some S.O.E. equipment with which to carry out this act of sabotage. As in a previous case where an act of sabotage was staged for another of our Gibraltar agents, this apparently successful enterprise has caused extreme satisfaction in German and Italian circles.

F. German Spies ready to collaborate with Britain

Important new information about the organisation and methods of the German Secret Service has been obtained from two of its former members. Both these individuals have been induced to collaborate, and as one of them, an officer of the German General Staff, had been chief of an enemy Secret Service base, his revelations were particularly sensational. As a "book of reference", it is believed his services will continue to prove of great value.

G. General Security measures

(1) The Security Service has prepared a memorandum, running to sixty-eight printed pages, including diagrams, on the technical counter-measures to be taken against possible enemy sabotage. This memorandum has been circulated to our Defence Security Officers in the most important posts in the Empire. A special section dealing with the defence of shipping against sabotage has been further circulated to all ports in which we have representatives, both in England and overseas.

(2) On the strength of information about "Torch" supplied by the Security Service, the Director of Military Intelligence has issued a strong warning against careless talk about future operations. This warning was based on Security Service investigations which showed that a disturbing amount of loose talk had taken place before the invasion of North Africa.

(3) On the return of a special adviser who had been sent to the Middle East to survey the security position there, the Security Service are implementing his recommendations by sending three officers to the area, two of whom will plan and direct the examination of aliens, who arrive in that area from occupied Europe at the rate of about 900 a month, and the collection of intelligence from them. The third officer will supervise the investigation of Axis espionage. The existing organisation in Middle East requires strengthening on both these sides of the work.

(4) By arrangement with the Director of Military Intelligence the Security Service is supplying certain of its officers who have recently been put through special training courses in preparation for their future work, which will be to act as advisers on general security measures and on the technical aspect of counter-espionage and counter-sabotage work, both to the G.H.Q. Ib staff of future expeditionary forces and to the staff of the Chief Civil Affairs Officer in the area behind the lines. The Director General considers that, with diminishing risks at home, these officers should be released for the purposes stated.

Moscow may well also have received the longer version before it was condensed by Blunt and thus have seen more detailed reports than Churchill.

The first monthly 'Report on Activities of Security Service', submitted on 26 March 1943,[44] was an instant success with the Prime Minister.[45] Churchill wrote on it in red ink: 'deeply interesting'.[46] Henceforth, Petrie wrote later, Churchill 'took a sustained personal interest in our work'.[47] The first report began with a summary of counter-espionage successes since the outbreak of war:

In all 126 spies have fallen into our hands. Of these eighteen gave themselves up voluntarily; twenty-four have been found amenable and are now being used as double-cross agents. Twenty-eight have been detained at overseas stations, and eight were arrested on the high seas. In addition twelve real, and seven imaginary persons have been foisted upon the enemy as double-cross spies. Thirteen spies have been executed, and a fourteenth is under trial.

As examples of how comprehensively the Germans were being deceived by the 'double-cross spies', the Report revealed that GARBO (like other agents, not identified by name) had been sent £2,500, as well as having a further 250,000 pesetas put at his disposal in Madrid by the Abwehr, and that a radio set of new design, sabotage equipment and £200 in banknotes had been dropped by parachute in Aberdeenshire for MUTT and JEFF.[48]

The case which Churchill seems to have found of greatest interest in the first monthly report was that of HARLEQUIN, and he asked for more information from MI5 on the intelligence HARLEQUIN had provided.[49] On the additional report submitted to him, Churchill marked the following passage in red: 'HARLEQUIN states that when the German [1942] summer offensive failed to bring about the annihilation of the Russian armies, every single officer of the Abwehr was convinced, as was HARLEQUIN, that Germany had lost the war.' The Abwehr believed that the growing superiority of arms production by the Grand Alliance (the United States, Great Britain and the Soviet Union) made its victory inevitable.[50] Two months later, however, the Security Service reported to Churchill that, though HARLEQUIN had provided 'invaluable' intelligence, he had ceased to co-operate, had put on his German military uniform and had been sent to a POW camp:

He asked to be released from his bargain because it had become evident to him that the Allies were determined to impose crushing terms on a defeated Germany and he did not want to feel that he had played any part in bringing about the oppression of the German people.[51]

The written reports to Churchill did not, however, mention that after his capture HARLEQUIN had been assured by military intelligence that, in return for his co-operation, he would be allowed to travel to a neutral country to meet the head of the Abwehr, Admiral Wilhelm Canaris, whom he saw as 'the centre of a future anti-Nazi organisation' which would succeed the Hitler regime. After reading British press reports in April that Canaris had been dismissed, HARLEQUIN abandoned his plan and lost interest in co-operation with the Security Service. The press reports, however, had been planted by the Political Warfare Executive. Though Canaris's influence was being rapidly supplanted by that of Himmler, he was not dismissed as head of the Abwehr for another year. The Service regarded HARLEQUIN's decision to cease co-operation as 'singularly fortuitous', since it had no interest in his scheme to meet Canaris and believed it had already obtained 'all but an infinitesimal part' of the intelligence he was able to provide.[52]

The second MI5 monthly report, submitted to Churchill on 1 May, contained further exciting news of ZIGZAG. After arriving in Lisbon to begin a lengthy period abroad working for the Abwehr, he had been given an explosive device camouflaged as a large lump of coal with instructions to place it in the bunkers of a British ship.[53] Instead ZIGZAG handed it to the captain and MI5 later staged an incident designed to demonstrate that ZIGZAG had carried out his sabotage mission.[54] Duff Cooper sent for a full copy of ZIGZAG's MI5 file which he discussed 'at some length with the Prime Minister, who', he told Dick White, 'is showing considerable interest in the case'.[55] Some of Churchill's 'considerable interest' was probably aroused by ZIGZAG's plan to assassinate Hitler when he visited Berlin while working for the Abwehr. Improbable though his plan appeared, ZIGZAG's case officer, Ronnie Reed, did not dismiss the possibility that he might succeed. ZIGZAG claimed that, having convinced his Abwehr case officer that he was an enthusiastic pro-Nazi, he had been promised a seat near the podium at a rally addressed by Hitler. According to Reed, ZIGZAG knew that the assassination attempt would cost him his life but liked the idea of going out in a blaze of glory: 'He can think of no better way of leaving this life than to have his name prominently featured throughout the world's press, and to be immortalised in history books for all time – this would crown his final gesture.' There is no evidence that B1a encouraged or even welcomed ZIGZAG's plan. Tar Robertson told him: '. . . I am most anxious for you not to undertake any wild sabotage enterprises.'[56] But he probably suspected that, if the opportunity arose, ZIGZAG might go ahead with the assassination plan. The only surviving report to Churchill on ZIGZAG's plan, submitted to him over a year later, describes it as 'his own proposal' and, rather obscurely, as 'a parergon' – in other words, as subsidiary to his main aim of operating as a B1a double agent within the Abwehr.[57]

Following HARLEQUIN's decision to cease co-operation with MI5 and the beginning of a lengthy period during which ZIGZAG was out of contact, the Security Service judged – no doubt correctly – that the double agent most likely to capture Churchill's imagination was GARBO.[58] Service reports to the Prime Minister emphasized the extraordinary creativity and productivity of GARBO, his case officer Tomás Harris and their MI5 support team, who were able to convince the Abwehr that GARBO had a network of highly productive sub-agents, eventually numbering twenty-eight, mostly in the UK but some as far afield as North America and Ceylon:[59]

Apart from the work of those of our officers who forge the letters of the sub-agents and from the work of the case officer, who spends his entire time in controlling, organising and developing the case, living GARBO's life and thinking GARBO's thoughts, GARBO himself works on average from six to eight hours a day – drafting secret letters, enciphering, composing cover texts, writing them and planning for the future. Fortunately he has a facile and lurid style, great ingenuity and a passionate and quixotic zeal for his task. This last quality has indeed caused an outburst of jealousy on the part of his wife, who, considering herself neglected, was with difficulty persuaded not to ruin the whole undertaking by a public disclosure.[60]

As well as feeling neglected, Mrs Pujol (known to B1a as Mrs GARBO or Mrs G) was also extremely homesick. 'Her one desire', noted Liddell, 'is to go back to her home country,' where she was thought likely to reveal all and thus sabotage the entire Double-Cross System:

We have ... thought of warning the Spanish embassy here anonymously that a woman of Mrs G's description is anxious to assassinate the ambassador. This would, we hope, ensure her being flung out if she attempted to go to the Embassy. It would however result in the police being called in, which would be a bore.

That scheme, however, was abandoned in favour of a cruel charade devised by GARBO himself. A senior Scotland Yard officer called on Mrs G on 22 June to say that her husband had been arrested after deciding to end his career as a double agent because of his wife's objections and threatening to 'give the whole show away'. Later that day GARBO's radio operator, Charles Haines, found Mrs G in a room full of coal gas. Though Haines suspected that this was 'a bit of play-acting', Tommy Harris's wife spent

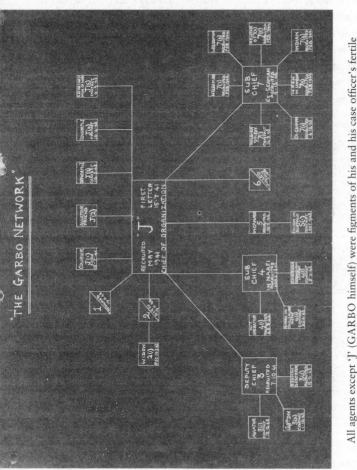

"THE GARBO NETWORK"

All agents except 'J' (GARBO himself) were figments of his and his case officer's fertile imaginations. The principal sub-agents, 3 (a Venezuelan 'of independent means' normally resident in Glasgow but currently in London), 4 (a Gibraltarian working for the NAAFI in Chislehurst), 5 (the brother of 3, currently in Canada) and 7 (a retired Welsh seaman), ran fictitious sub-networks, all of whom deceived the Abwehr.

the night trying to 'calm her down'. Next day, 23 June, after a tearful interview with Tar Robertson, she signed a statement 'saying that the whole of the incident was due to her fault and that on no account would she behave badly in future', and was then taken to see her husband who was masquerading as a prisoner in a cell in Camp 020. On the 24th the Security Service's Legal Adviser, Edward Cussen, explained to Mrs G in what Liddell considered 'masterly style' that she had escaped arrest only by 'a hair's breadth', and that, if there were any repetition, she and her husband would be interned for the remainder of the war. GARBO returned home, somewhat shaken by the deception practised on his wife, but resumed his career as a double agent with undiminished enthusiasm.[61]

What Churchill learned about GARBO and the double agents during 1943 left him with the conviction that, 'In wartime, truth is so precious that she should always be attended by a bodyguard of lies.' No military operation in British history has ever been so successfully protected by deception as OVERLORD, the Allied invasion of occupied northern France in 1944. Late in 1943 conferences of the British and American Combined Chiefs of Staff in Cairo and Tehran took the decision to launch the invasion in May 1944 (a date later deferred until the D-Day landings on 6 June). Colonel Bevan of the LCS was instructed to prepare the deception plans for OVERLORD. The key aims of the deception were:

a. To induce the German Command to believe that the main assault and follow up will be in or east of the Pas de Calais area, thereby encouraging the enemy to maintain or increase the strength of his air and ground forces and his fortifications there at the expense of other areas, particularly of the Caen area [in Normandy].
b. To keep the enemy in doubt as to the date and time of the actual assault.
c. During and after the main assault, to contain the largest possible German land and air forces in or east of the Pas de Calais for at least fourteen days.[62]

All three aims were achieved.

The two main deception plans which became an integral part of OVERLORD were FORTITUDE SOUTH and FORTITUDE NORTH. FORTITUDE SOUTH was intended to reinforce the belief of most German commanders that the Calais region was the logical place for the Allied attack. As well as requiring the shortest sea crossing, the Pas de Calais was also the best landing point from which to advance on the German industrial heartland in the Ruhr. FORTITUDE NORTH was designed to play on Hitler's obsession with Norway as his 'Zone of Destiny' and persuade him and his high command that the Allies were planning a major diversionary attack on Norway that would require them to keep large forces there which might otherwise be redeployed to meet the Allied attack on northern France. Many elements went into the deception plans: among them bogus radio messages from non-existent army units which the Germans were intended to intercept, disinformation abroad spread by British diplomats and agents, and dummy military installations. Shepperton Studios built a huge fake oil-storage complex near Dover, designed by Basil Spence (later one of Britain's leading architects), which received official visits from King George VI, General Eisenhower, supreme commander of the Allied Expeditionary Forces for OVERLORD, and Montgomery, commander of land forces.[63] The role of B1a's double agents was crucial.

The double agent who contributed most to the success of the FORTI-TUDE deceptions was, once again, GARBO. During the first six months of 1944, working with Tomás Harris, he sent more than 500 messages to the Abwehr station in Madrid, which, as German intercepts revealed, passed them to Berlin, many marked 'Urgent'. Right up to D-Day, however, B1a was acutely aware that the Germans might discover that they were being deceived. The greatest threat of discovery appeared to come from Johann Jebsen, the Abwehr case officer of the double agent TRICYCLE. After seeing his case officer in Lisbon in the autumn of 1943, TRICYCLE was 'absolutely sure' that Jebsen knew he was working for the British. However, he also reported that Jebsen had anti-Nazi sympathies and had discussed with him the possibility of taking refuge in Britain. Late in September, Jebsen was recruited as a double agent and given the codename ARTIST. In January 1944 ARTIST confronted B1a and the Twenty Committee with a difficult dilemma when he revealed the names of some of the agents being run against Britain by the Abwehr's Lisbon station. At the top of his list was GARBO (known to the Abwehr as ARABEL). If the British authorities took no action against GARBO, ARTIST might well realize that he was a double agent. And even if ARTIST did not tell his Abwehr colleagues about GARBO, what would happen if he was interrogated by the Gestapo, which was known to be suspicious of him? Tomás Harris was so concerned at the risk posed by ARTIST to the whole Double-Cross System that at the end of February he recommended that GARBO should no longer be used for deception operations.[64] The Twenty Committee even considered, but rejected, the possibility of asking SIS to arrange ARTIST's assassination.[65] A Security Service report to Churchill on 7 March 1944 concluded, however, that the problem could probably be managed:

[ARTIST's] zeal and ability . . . has verged upon the embarrassing. He has begun to provide us with information about the networks maintained by the Germans in this country. Of these it appears that the principal one is the GARBO organisation of which it is clearly undesirable that he should make us too fully aware. We are engaged at the moment in the delicate operation of diverting this valuable agent's attention elsewhere. There is good promise of success.[66]

The attempt to divert ARTIST's attention failed. By mid-April he was in no doubt that GARBO was a double agent working for the British.[67] GARBO and his fictitious agent network were so highly rated by both B1a and the Twenty Committee, however, that, despite the risk that ARTIST would expose them, they were allowed to retain their key role in the FORTITUDE deceptions.

The next most important double agent in the FORTITUDE deceptions was the former Polish fighter-pilot Roman Garby-Czerniawski (codenamed BRUTUS), who had been captured by the Germans while running an agent network, the Réseau Interallié, in occupied France in 1941. The head of Abwehr counter-intelligence in Paris, Colonel Oscar Reile, recruited Garby-Czerniawski as a German agent (or so he believed) by playing on his hostility to Communism and the Soviet Union, and by promising that, if he worked as an Abwehr agent in Britain, no members of his network would be harmed.[68] Soon after he arrived in England in October 1942, he turned himself in and asked to work as a double agent for the British. Though his MI5 interrogators found Garby-Czerniawski 'intensely dramatic and egotistical', they eventually recommended he be taken on. Masterman, however, argued that the risks were too great. BRUTUS's primary loyalty was to Poland; the Germans might well suspect that he had decided to work for the British rather than the Abwehr; and the Russians were intensely suspicious of the British use of Polish agents.[69] BRUTUS was the cause of probably the biggest dispute between Masterman and B1a case officers in the history of the Double-Cross System. Whereas Masterman was initially preoccupied by the risks, the young Turks of B1a were determined not to waste the deception opportunities which BRUTUS offered. BRUTUS's first case officer, Christopher Harmer, claimed later that 'old JC' (Masterman) was 'hell bent on chopping him and intrigued behind my back'. On 5 March 1943, the day before his wedding Harmer found time to send Masterman 'one of the rudest letters I have ever written . . . it took some time to heal the breach.' The breach was healed because Masterman knew B1a had to be adventurous and B1a realized Masterman had to be cautious. 'I loved the old boy,'

Harmer wrote later, 'and I suppose he was only doing his job – of exercising a wise and mature restraint on the irresponsibilities of the hot-headed youngsters of those days.'[70]

The memoirs of Oscar Reile, BRUTUS's Abwehr recruiter, strongly suggest that Masterman's fears of the risks involved in running him as a double agent were fully justified. Reile claims to have realized that it was a 'probability bordering on certainty' that BRUTUS (codenamed ARMAND by the Abwehr) was under British control: 'Not the least of my reasons for arriving at this conclusion was that none of the radio messages which came from England contained any enquiry about the 66 members of the Réseau Interallié who were still in the hands of the Germans.'[71] BRUTUS also became involved in a dispute in London with the head of the Polish air force which led to his court martial in the summer of 1943.[72] As Reile complained, however, German military operations officers had no doubt that BRUTUS's reports contained important intelligence and dismissed his own suspicions of a British deception. BRUTUS's service background made it possible for B1a to include in his messages more military detail than would have been credible in GARBO's reports. Hugh Astor, who succeeded Harmer as his case officer in December 1943, wrote later:

Undoubtedly GARBO sent a far greater volume of traffic but the traffic sent by BRUTUS was much more professional in style and it was obvious from ULTRA that the Germans attached importance to his messages. Certainly I was under the impression that their projection of our order of battle was chiefly derived from BRUTUS.[73]

After reporting on (non-existent) preparations in Scotland for an attack on Norway, BRUTUS radioed the good news to the Abwehr on 26 May that he had been posted as a member of an Allied mission to the HQ of the (equally non-existent) First United States Army Group (FUSAG) at Wentworth, near Ascot, and had obtained its complete order of battle. TATE complemented and corroborated BRUTUS's battle-order intelligence by providing a schedule of FUSAG troop movements which he claimed to have acquired from a railway clerk in Ashford, Kent.[74] The size of the non-existent FUSAG, whose reality was never doubted by the German high command, was greater than that of all the US forces which actually took part in the Normandy landings.[75]

The most recently recruited double agent to play an important part in the FORTITUDE deceptions was Nathalie 'Lily' Sergueiev, a French Abwehr agent of White Russian origins who changed sides after being sent on a mission to England in November 1943.[76] Masterman wrote later that Sergueiev was 'intelligent but temperamental' and eventually 'proved exceptionally troublesome'.[77] B1a's choice of TREASURE as her code-name seems to have been deliberately satirical. As well as being one of the few female double agents of the war, TREASURE was the only one with a female case officer, Mary Sherer, who was not, however, allowed officer rank.[78] Though the two women sometimes operated as an effective professional partnership, they never bonded. TREASURE later complained that her determination to undermine the Nazi war effort had been weakened by the unfeeling attitude of the British authorities to her and her dog Babs.[79] From the moment she arrived in London, she was preoccupied with the treatment of Babs, whom she had left in Gibraltar in order to avoid having to subject her to six months in English quarantine kennels. TREASURE believed she had been given a promise that a way would be found, despite quarantine regulations, to bring Babs, to whom she was devoted, to join her in London. In December 1943 she refused to send more letters to the Abwehr until her dog arrived. Sherer, who does not seem to have been particularly sympathetic, reported that TREASURE was being 'very unreasonable'.[80] It is difficult to believe that the whole affair could not have been better handled.

TREASURE eventually suspended what Sherer called her 'strike' after falling ill at the end of the year and spending a week in hospital. In March 1944 she flew to Lisbon to meet her Abwehr case officer and collect a radio transmitter[81] – a fact of sufficient importance to be reported to Churchill.[82] While in Lisbon she was also given money and codes for her mission in England, presented with souvenir photographs of herself and her case officer, and rewarded with a diamond bracelet.[83] After returning to London TREASURE reported to the Abwehr by radio that, during regular week-end visits to Bristol, she had seen very few troop movements in south-west England,[84] thus reinforcing the German belief that the main Allied troop concentrations were in the south-east, preparing for an invasion of the Pas de Calais. (In reality, in preparation for D-Day, most Allied forces were in the south-west.) The Abwehr attached great importance to TREASURE's reports. Bletchley Park reported in May that 'The messages of TREASURE and BRUTUS are being so consistently relayed verbatim on the German Intelligence W/T [wireless telegraphy] network that, with the assistance of this "crib", there has been a very considerable saving of time and man-power in deciphering Most Secret [SIGINT] Sources.' This, the Security Service told Churchill, was proof that the double agents 'have, at a critical period, acquired a value which it is scarcely possible to overestimate'.[85]

TREASURE

Description of Code

The code is based on a French book "Montmartre" by Pierre Frondaie, published by "Baudiniere, 27 bis, rue du Moulin-Vert, Paris."

For the purpose of this description we will assume that message number 1 is to be sent on the 12th of November, 1943. The message is:-

"Arrived safely Bristol 6th November. Authorities satisfied. Address Cambridge."

The messages should always be sent in French, so it is preceded by the number of the message and becomes:-

"Un. Bien arrivee Bristol six un un. Autorites satisfaites. Adresse Cambridge."

A special key for the Day is then prepared from the book.

On odd months from pages 100 to 130.
" even " " " 210 " 240.

November being an odd month, pages 100 to 130 are used, and as it is the 12th day we take page 112. The last line on the page having not less than 20 letters is then taken and the first 10 letters are written down:-

CONNUDAUTR

These are numbered according to their position in the alphabet, and underneath the numbers an ordinary alphabet is written commencing from left to right and continuing underneath from right to left on the next line. The remainder of the alphabet being grouped on the next line from left to right under the numbers from 1 to 6.

```
        C O N N U D A U T R    (10 = 0)
        2 6 4 5 9 3 1 0 8 7
        A B C D E F G H I J
        T S R Q P O N M L K
        U   V W   X Y Z
```

A page and line from the book is then selected for the construction of a coding square. The length and breadth of the square is decided according to the length of the message to be coded. In the given example a square with a length of side of 11 spaces will be sufficient.

Assume that page 90 line No. 8 is taken with a square of 11 per side. These numbers are then written down to provide a key for decoding, e.g.

Page	Line	Square
90	8	11 = 90811.

This key is then enciphered twice with the prepared key for the day by taking any two letters of the key under its appropriate number, e.g. number 9 would be letter E and P, and number 0 would be H and Z, so that the complete group is:

```
9 0 8 1 1
Z R G N
F Z N G
```

The letters in the square are then split up into five letter groups commencing by reading downwards under column headed 1 and following with column 2, column 3, etc.   First group is PBVSY, second SUGNT, etc. The two key groups previously obtained are written in the space reserved for the 3rd and 9th groups as November is an old month.

The number of letters in the final message plus the key groups precede the telegram with the morse sign KA going in front.

KA 115

PBVSY   SUGNT   EHLGN   TIRIU

SRBCR   TF·IUS   EXGST   IRYII

FZING   MDSNN   YLFLC   GAOAB

RRIMY   BIATE   WSVWO   MEUEE

OODWN   SKAET   BTNUY   SWABA

RYAEU   RIIDE   SRAIE

When transmitting the message KA is sent twice, and so are the number of letters in the message.

The Call Signs.

The agent's call sign is made up of the first three consonants of the left hand side of the first line of the page taken for the key for the day reading from left to right, i.e. page 112, call is C.M.P.

The call sign for the control station is also taken from the first line, but reading from right to left and is D.S.R.

If a change of frequency is made the call sign is taken from the next line, both for the agent and the control station, i.e. they call L.S.G. agent calls P.L.M.   If a change of frequency is requested by the agent three letters are sent.

    1st letter is taken from the key for the day indicating a number.
    2nd   "   is any dummy letter.
    3rd   "   is C.

e.g. If the agent requires the control station to change to frequency number 2, a letter corresponding to 2 under the key for the day is taken, i.e. letter T, a dummy letter is say K.

Then the sign TKC is sent, which means: "Please change to frequency number 2 (QSU2)."

If the agent wishes to indicate that a change is to be made on the transmitter this end, then the same procedure is followed except that the last letter is D, i.e. TGD means: "I am going to change to frequency number 2".

In selecting the lines for the key for the day, the key for the square and the call sign, indented lines and those starting with words in italics are omitted.

Two five letter groups are thus obtained EHIGN and PZING. These are subsequently inserted in the final coded groups in the following position:-

On even months in the 4th and 10th group.
" odd " " " 3rd " 9th "

The Key Square.

The first 11 letters of the 8th line are written two lines above the top of the key square. These are numbered underneath according to their position in the alphabet. On the 1st line of the square a mark is made directly after the square beneath the figure 1. On the second line a mark is made after the square beneath the figure 2. On the third line a mark is made after the square beneath the figure 3, etc. These lines are then joined up dividing the square into two parts. Blank positions are then marked in the square based on the two highest numbers taken from the key for the day. In this case 9 and 8 - starting with the left hand side of the divided square and blanking out square number 9, and then number 8 and continuing into the right hand section. Any dummy letters are then placed in the squares immediately following the blank squares. If the blanked square is the last on the line before the dividing position, or is at the end of the line, the dummy letter is placed on the next line (c.f. line number 8. The dummy letter is placed in the first square on line number 9).

Any three letters are then written in the first three spaces of the left hand crossword, followed by the message. A full stop is represented by the letter W, and a comma by the letter Y.

Proper names and important numbers are always repeated and quoted by placing the letter Y before and after them.

If the message does not fill up the square a line is drawn to terminate the message and the rest of the spaces are blanked out.

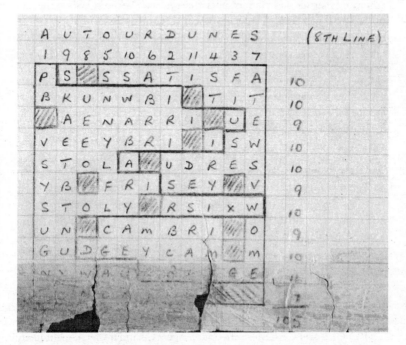

Coded radio message from TREASURE to her Abwehr case officer falsely reporting her arrival in Bristol in November 1943.

Churchill was also given evidence of how much German intelligence valued the disinformation sent them by TRICYCLE and TATE. Pride of place in the double-agents section of MI5's April monthly report to the Prime Minister went to TRICYCLE, just returned from visiting 'his German masters' in Lisbon: 'He has once more succeeded in convincing them of his complete reliability and has extracted from them a large sum in dollars as an advance against his future services.'[86] Churchill was told that, when TATE transmitted his thousandth radio message to the Abwehr on 24 May:

He took the opportunity of referring to this fact and expressing his loyal devotion to the Führer. A cordial reply has been received, and it is hoped that this will be followed up by the further advancement of TATE in the Order of the Iron Cross, of which he already holds the First and Second Class.[87]

During the month before D-Day, however, the Double-Cross System suffered two near-disasters. The first derived from the death in Portugal of TREASURE's much loved dog Babs, for which she blamed the uncaring British. On 17 May TREASURE startled her case officer, Mary Sherer, by admitting that she had planned a terrible revenge. While in Lisbon she had obtained from her Abwehr case officer a 'control signal' to add to her transmissions; if she omitted it, that would be a sign that the British had taken over her transmitter:

She had meant, on her return, to get the W/T working well and then blow the case by omitting the signal. She confessed that her motive was revenge for the death of her dog for which she considered we were responsible. On return from Lisbon she had changed her mind about blowing the case. She refused to divulge what the signal was.[88]

Tar Robertson was thus faced, less than three weeks before D-Day, with an appalling dilemma: either to arouse German suspicions by abruptly ending TREASURE's transmissions or to allow her to continue in the hope, but without the certainty, that she really had 'changed her mind about blowing the case'. Probably after consultation with Masterman, Robertson chose the second option.[89]

An even greater threat to the Double-Cross System arose from the arrest by the Gestapo in early May of TRICYCLE's Abwehr case officer in Lisbon, ARTIST, who had himself become a double agent.[90] Before his arrest ARTIST had made clear to his British case officer that he knew TRICYCLE and GARBO were double agents,[91] and it was thought likely that he suspected other German agents in Britain had also been turned.

Only three days before D-Day Churchill was warned by the Security Service that 'the TRICYCLE case is passing through a most critical phase and must be handled with the greatest care in view of Overlord'.[92] ARTIST was believed to have been arrested for embezzlement rather than because the Gestapo suspected him of being a British agent. But, as Masterman wrote later:

That belief was small consolation. Under interrogation it was to be presumed that much, if not all, of the history of [ARTIST's] activities would come to light, and in that case many of our best cases were doomed.

. . . We were saved by time and fortune. D Day arrived before the Germans had succeeded in unravelling all the tangled skein of the ARTIST case, and presumably there was little opportunity after D Day for patient research into such matters in German offices.[93]

On 1 June Bletchley Park produced reassuring evidence that, despite the potential threats posed by ARTIST and TREASURE, the key elements of the strategic deception on which the D-Day landings depended were still intact. A Japanese decrypt revealed that Hitler had told the Japanese ambassador, Baron Hiroshi Oshima, that eighty enemy divisions had been assembled in Britain for the invasion. In reality there were only forty-seven, but the Führer, like his high command, had been deceived into believing in the non-existent FUSAG as well as misled about where the main Allied attack would come. Hitler told Oshima that after 'diversionary attacks . . . in a number of places', the Allies would then use their main forces for 'an all-out second front across the Straits of Dover'.[94]

The final act in the pre-D-Day deception was entrusted, appropriately, to its greatest practitioners, GARBO and Tomás Harris. After several weeks of pressure, Harris finally gained permission for GARBO to be allowed to radio a warning that Allied forces were heading towards the Normandy beaches just too late for the Germans to benefit from it. Though the Abwehr radio station in Madrid normally shut down from 11.30 p.m. to 7.30 a.m., GARBO warned it to be ready to receive a message at 3 a.m. on 6 June (D-Day).[95] But, for unknown reasons, Madrid did not go on air until after 6 a.m., and received the warning several hours later than intended.[96]

At noon on 6 June, Churchill, watched by his wife and eldest daughter from the Speaker's Gallery, announced to a packed and expectant House of Commons: 'During the night and early hours of the morning, the first of the series of landings in force upon the European continent has taken place.' The Prime Minister must have thought his reference to other

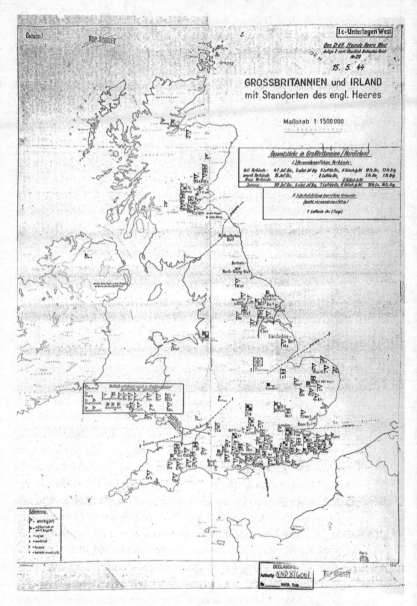

The Security Service's August 1944 report informed Churchill that a German map (*above*), captured in Italy, showing the location of Allied forces in the UK, accorded 'precisely' with the disinformation fed to the enemy by the double agents and wireless deception pointing to an attack in the Calais region. The map opposite shows the real deployment of Allied forces preparing for the Normandy landings.

OVERLORD

DISPOSITION OF MAJOR US GROUND UNITS
AND CERTAIN BRITISH/CANADIAN FORCES

15 MAY 1944

35 ADV DET ONLY

7 ADV DET ONLY

SCALE

1000 FOOT CONTOUR
CONIC PROJECTION

WEST LONGITUDE   0   EAST LONGITUDE

GOODE'S SERIES OF BASE MAPS
HENRY M. LEPPARD, EDITOR

Prepared by Henry M. Leppard
Published by the University of Chicago Press, Chicago, Illinois
Copyright 1944 by the University of Chicago

landings which were to follow D-Day would help to reinforce the German belief that an even bigger Allied assault was being planned in the Calais region. Tar Robertson and others in B1a, however, were shocked by Churchill's statement, which – though he did not realize it – contradicted an earlier message sent by GARBO to the Abwehr reporting a bogus Political Warfare Executive (PWE) directive on the need to avoid any public reference to 'further attacks and diversions'.[97] The Prime Minister's faux pas seemed to justify Petrie's and Liddell's earlier fear that, if Churchill was informed of a deception operation (as he was in this case), he might take some rash initiative of his own.[98] At 8 p.m. on D-Day GARBO radioed Madrid, saying that he had spoken to the PWE Director, who was dismayed that Churchill had ignored his directive. The Prime Minister, claimed GARBO rather lamely (without, however, arousing the suspicions of the Abwehr), had felt obliged not to distort the facts when announcing the invasion to the Commons and to the country.[99] GARBO rounded off his radio message with a withering denunciation of the failure of Madrid to come on air at 3 a.m. that day to receive vital intelligence on the imminent Allied landings on the Normandy beaches: 'This makes me question your seriousness and sense of responsibility. I therefore demand a clarification immediately as to what has occurred.' By the following morning, after a supposedly sleepless night, GARBO radioed a further message of recrimination, this time combined with self-pity:

I am very disgusted as in this struggle for life and death I cannot accept excuses or negligence ... Were it not for my ideals and faith I would abandon this work as having proved myself a failure. I write these messages to send this very night though my tiredness and exhaustion due to the excessive work I have had has completely broken me.

The errant Abwehr case officer in Madrid, who had failed to ensure that the radio station came on air at 3 a.m., replied apologetically with a fulsome tribute to the quality of GARBO's intelligence: 'I wish to stress in the clearest terms that your work over the last few weeks has made it possible for our command to be completely forewarned and prepared.'[100] That tribute, which probably caused GARBO and Harris to laugh out loud, was quoted in the Security Service's June report to the Prime Minister.[101]

Before D-Day it had been expected that the fiction of a planned attack on the Pas de Calais could not be maintained for more than ten days after the Normandy landings. ULTRA, however, revealed that the deception remained firmly embedded for far longer in the minds of both Hitler and his high command.[102] For the rest of June GARBO and BRUTUS continued to send alarming intelligence reports on the waves of fresh American forces supposedly flooding into Britain and the growing troop concentrations in the south-east of England, apparently poised for an assault on the Pas de Calais. Four weeks after D-Day the German high command still had twenty-two divisions waiting to repel an attack by the non-existent FUSAG.[103] The Security Service's monthly report for June, despatched to Churchill on 3 July, concluded:

It is known for a fact that the Germans intended at one time to move certain Divisions from the Pas de Calais area to Normandy but, in view of the possibility of a threat to the Pas de Calais area, these troops were either stopped on their way to Normandy and recalled or it was decided that they should not be moved at all.

Churchill was also informed that Berlin had awarded GARBO the Iron Cross (Second Class); the following German radio message was cited as an example of the praise lavished on him and his imaginary sub-agents: '. . . I reiterate to you, as responsible chief of the service, and to all your collaborators, our total recognition of your perfect and cherished work and I beg of you to continue with us in the supreme and decisive hours of the struggle for the future of Europe. Saludos.' The Security Service's June report to the Prime Minister also cited 'an effusive message of encouragement' to TATE from his German case officer: 'Your messages about concentrations and movements (more especially signs of troops preparing for action) can be not only fabulously important, but can even decide the outcome of the war.'[104] A month after D-Day Eisenhower declared: 'I cannot overemphasize the importance of maintaining as long as humanly possible the Allied threat to the Pas-de-Calais area, which has already paid enormous dividends and, with care, will continue to do so.'[105] Not till the last week of July did the HQ of Field Marshal Gerd von Rundstedt, Commander in Chief West, conclude that 'The more ground Montgomery gains southward from the [Normandy] bridgehead, and the quicker he does this, the less probable it will be that the forces still in England will carry out a seaborne landing at a new point.'[106]

Since February 1944 copies of the Security Service's reports to the Prime Minister had also gone to the Foreign Secretary, Anthony Eden,[107] to whom in December 1943 Churchill had given ministerial responsibility for MI5.[108] On 26 June 1944 Petrie wrote to Eden that since becoming director general in 1941 he had 'perhaps said more hard things of the Service than almost anyone else', but now wanted to pay tribute to it:

The role of the Security Service has been particularly important and particularly difficult ... Before and even after D-Day in the recent operations, the German Abwehr has continued to show unbounded and almost pathetic confidence in reports of agents, which have been described as vitally affecting 'the whole course of the war' and in similar terms.

Eden replied on 7 July that MI5 'could take legitimate pride in what has been achieved'.[109] For the Security Service the aftermath of the FORTI-TUDE deceptions brought a stream of congratulations and gratitude not often seen in the organization's history and far removed from the open criticism of the early war years. On 21 August, Colonel Bevan wrote, as controlling officer of the LCS: 'I honestly believe that whatever success may have been achieved in our line of business is due in very large measure to the support given by B1A.'[110]

The Security Service's August report informed Churchill that a German map, captured in Italy, showing the location of British ground forces in the UK, accorded 'precisely' with the disinformation fed to the enemy by the double agents and wireless deception.[111] It added, with an understand-able air of triumph: 'Conversations between Hitler and his generals . . . show that the threat to the Pas-de-Calais caused Rommel to delay committing the full weight of his armour until the bridgehead had become sufficiently established to enable us to repel his attack.' Churchill minuted 'Let me see' against this passage, and wrote 'Good' on the report as a whole.[112]

Later in the year, having already been promised the Iron Cross by his German case officer, GARBO became the first British agent (as opposed to intelligence officer) to be awarded the MBE. Since it was thought inappropriate for a double agent to meet the King, the presentation was made instead by the DG, Sir David Petrie, in a private ceremony attended by Tomás Harris and senior members of B1a. Petrie, noted Liddell, 'made a nice little speech': 'Later we lunched at the Savoy when GARBO responded to the toast in halting but not too bad English. I think he was extremely pleased.'[113]

B1a continued to use double agents for deception purposes until the last week of the war. The most serious German threat to which the Security Service had to respond in the aftermath of the Normandy landings was the V-weapons (*Vergeltungswaffen*) which were mainly targeted on London. The first V-1 flying bombs (small pilotless planes) hit London on 13 June, only a week after D-Day. GARBO complained that, despite being a London resident, he had not been given advance warning of the attack (for which the Abwehr apologized), but applauded 'this fantastic reprisal weapon, the creation of German genius'. On Sunday 18 June a V-1 landed on the Guards Chapel at Wellington Barracks in the middle of morning service, killing 121 of the worshippers. The explosion was heard in MI5's St James's Street offices. Since the attack was publicly announced, GARBO duly reported it but added the improbable claim that the initial public alarm generated by fear of flying bombs had none the less 'disappeared'.[114] Though a majority of the V-1s crashed or were shot down before they reached the target area, 2,419 hit London, about thirty Southampton and Portsmouth, and one Manchester, killing 6,184 people and injuring 17,981.[115]

GARBO reported that 17 per cent of the V-1s to reach England during June had hit the Greater London area; in fact the figure was over 27 per cent. Though it was believed that the V-1s were aimed at central London, probably Charing Cross, the Ministry of Home Security located their 'mean point of impact' (MPI) as around North Dulwich Station, where large expanses of open ground reduced the level of casualties. Since only a slight correction would bring the MPI into central London, both the Air Ministry and Home Defence Executive attempted to devise ways not merely to discourage the Germans from correcting their aim but also to persuade them to worsen it by using the double agents to send reports that they were overshooting their targets in the hope that they would then conclude that they needed to shorten their aim, with the result that fewer of the V-1s would reach central London. Meeting on 29 June, the Twenty Committee welcomed this deception, which fitted in well with reports already sent by GARBO to his case officer that the flying bombs were falling mainly in an arc to the north and west of London.[116]

It was decided, however, that continuing to use GARBO to send disinformation on the flying bombs carried too great a potential risk to the credibility of B1a's star double agent. A pretext had therefore to be found for him to cease reporting on the V-1s. On 5 July a radio transmission to the Abwehr from GARBO's (non-existent) second in command reported him missing, followed by an even more alarming report two days later that he had been arrested. Decrypted Abwehr traffic made clear its consternation and its qualified relief on 10 July when GARBO's deputy reported his release. On the 14th GARBO sent details of his arrest by courier to the Abwehr office in Madrid. While investigating flying-bomb damage in Bethnal Green, he had been stopped by police and taken into custody after being caught attempting to dispose of his notes. Happily he had been released after a protest by his supposed employers in the Ministry of Information (MoI); GARBO enclosed both the warrant for his arrest and a letter from the Home Office to the MoI apologizing for the officiousness of the police. Joy was unconfined in the Madrid Abwehr, which, as expected, insisted that GARBO take no more risks reporting on the V-1s: 'Cease all investigations of the new weapon.' He was told there must be 'a period of complete inactivity' during which he suspended contact with his extensive network of (non-existent) sub-agents. The apparent near-disaster to the GARBO network led the Abwehr to send similar instructions to BRUTUS, whom it considered its second most valuable agent, for fear that he too might put himself at risk. To reassure GARBO of the high regard in which he was held in Berlin, his case officer informed him on 29 July 'with great happiness and satisfaction' that the Führer had decided to award him the Iron Cross for his 'extraordinary merits'. It is easy to imagine the secret hilarity with which, assisted by Harris, GARBO composed his reply: 'I cannot at this moment, when emotion overwhelms me, express my gratitude in words.'[117]

In the absence of GARBO and BRUTUS, the main double agents left to report on the impact of the V-weapons were TREASURE, TATE and ZIGZAG. TREASURE, however, was no longer trusted by B1a to transmit even under supervision.[118] While TREASURE's career as a double agent was being abruptly ended,[119] the Abwehr was completing final preparations forZIGZAG's return to Britain, one of his assignments being to report where V-1s were landing and the damage they caused.[120] The Security Service informed Churchill that the 'outstanding event' of the last week of June was the triumphant homecoming of ZIGZAG, who had landed by parachute in Cambridgeshire from a Junkers 88 after fifteen months of extraordinary adventures with the Abwehr:

For his sabotage of the Hatfield works (organised by us)[121] and other services, he appears to have received rather more than 100,000 marks as a bonus from the Germans. Since that date he has been given an extended holiday in Norway, where he has indulged in yachting and other recreations and has successfully withstood various psychological and other tests, all of which have served to fortify German belief in him.

ZIGZAG described Berlin as a 'complete shambles resembling the ruins of Pompeii', and German morale as visibly low. But during none of his three visits to the capital had there been an opportunity to carry out his plan to kill the increasingly reclusive Führer.[122] During ZIGZAG's first month back in Britain, most of his radio messages to the Abwehr, apart from complaining about transmission problems, consisted of reports on the times and places of impact of flying bombs.[123] B1a judged him 'indis-

pensable to the bomb damage deception scheme'.[124] The deception, however, had to be suspended on 25 July after London evening papers published
maps showing where V-1s had actually fallen.[125] To provide a pretext for
failing to provide further reports on the flying bombs, ZIGZAG told the
Abwehr that he was concentrating on trying to acquire a sample of secret
equipment it had tasked him to obtain.[126]

For two months after the beginning of the flying-bomb offensive, the
cabinet balked at a full-scale deception which would lead the Germans to
believe they were overshooting and unintentionally target the south of
Greater London. Though total casualties and disruption would be reduced
(a claim contested by some), the deception would be directly responsible
for the deaths of Londoners who would otherwise have survived. The main
aim was therefore initially to prevent the Germans from improving their
aim rather than to persuade them to redirect the V-1s to south London. In
mid-August, however, the cabinet finally approved a deception designed
to persuade the enemy to shift his aim 'to a slight extent . . . towards the
south-east'.[127] By then, however, the main V-1 offensive had only a fortnight to go. On 18 August the Germans began closing down the V-1 launch
sites in northern France before they were overrun by the Allied advance.
The last flying bombs in the initial offensive were fired on the night of
30/31 August, nine of them hitting central London.[128]

The threat from the V-2 rocket missile offensive, of which intelligence
had provided advance warning, was much more serious than that from the
flying bombs. Unlike the V-1s, they could not be shot down before they
reached their targets and worst-case forecasts of casualties by the Ministry
of Home Security reached 100,000 fatalities a month (vastly more than
actually occurred); in August there were mass evacuations from London.[129]
Guy Liddell took the threat from the V-2s so seriously that he favoured
using the threat of atomic retaliation to deter Hitler from continuing with
it. He noted on 25 August 1944:

I saw 'C' [Menzies] today about the uranium [atomic] bomb and put to him the
suggestion that it should be used as a threat of retaliation to the Germans if they
used V.2. 'C' said that he had no reason to think V.2 was imminent although it was
possible to think that it might start in the near future. He felt however that there
was nothing to be lost and that he would put this suggestion to the P.M.[130]

What Churchill said in reply is not recorded. V-2 attacks were more
imminent than Menzies realized. The first to reach England crashed on
Chiswick only a fortnight later, on 8 September. To Liddell in MI5's
St James's Street headquarters, it sounded much nearer than it was and

was followed by an echo: 'It is said that the [V-2] fragments found at Chiswick were in part so hot you couldn't touch them and in part coated with ice. The rocket is supposed to have gone 38 miles high.'[131] Liddell noted a week later: 'V2 continues at the rate of two or three per twenty-four hours. The remarkable thing is that the explosions are heard quite definitely even when the rocket falls at a distance of up to twenty miles away.'[132]

Though implemented by B1a and the double agents, the deception plan designed to convince the Germans that the V-2s had overshot their targets (a more complex deception than for the V-1s, involving precise calculation of bogus timings for the hits they achieved), was devised by the Security Executive.[133] After GARBO's reported arrest during his investigations of the V-1 attacks, the Abwehr decided not to take the risk of asking him to report on the V-2s. For 'data about place and time of the explosions', it initially relied mainly on ZIGZAG[134] and TATE.[135] ZIGZAG's inquiries were cut short by the abrupt end of his career as a double agent. Tin-eye Stephens had great respect for ZIGZAG's bravery and nerve but regarded him as a 'vain crook' and moral degenerate: 'He did not blush when he related how, having infected a girl of eighteen with VD, he blackmailed her by threatening to tell her parents that she had given it to him!'[136] As ZIGZAG renewed old acquaintances in the criminal underworld after his return to London, he was discovered to have bragged about the secrets of his double life to a convicted safe-breaker (as well as earlier to a girlfriend while in Norway).[137] Probably the final straw came at the end of October, when he was found discussing the publication of a book of his experiences with a convicted pre-war Soviet agent, Wilfred Macartney.[138] Only four months earlier the Security Service had described ZIGZAG to Churchill as one of its finest double agents. Early in November he was abruptly dismissed.[139] Eddie Chapman (no longer double agent ZIGZAG) and Macartney were later fined £50 each plus expenses at a trial in camera for the breaches of the Official Secrets Act involved in the writing of Chapman's memoirs which, MI5 acknowledged in a report to Number Ten, were 'very readable and very accurate'.[140]

With ZIGZAG's demise, the main role in the V-2 deception passed to TATE. The chief supporting role was taken by a new recruit to the double-agent stable: ROVER, a Polish naval officer who had joined the Abwehr in order to find an opportunity to escape to Allied territory. ROVER was probably the last Abwehr agent to arrive in England during 1944.[141] Masterman wrote later: 'What made him attractive to us was the fact that he had had a year's training in morse, the construction of wireless sets, and secret writing; we could not believe that the Germans would lavish so much care on someone in whom they did not believe.' To the surprise and disappointment of B1a, however, the Abwehr initially failed to reply to ROVER's early transmissions. In September B1a decided to abandon the case and send ROVER to rejoin the Polish navy. 'We were no doubt too impatient', wrote Masterman, 'for hardly had this been done when the Germans started to call ROVER.' Further disruption followed. Though communication between ROVER and his German case officer began in October 1944, it had to be suspended in November when his B1a radio operator went into hospital and later died. Via a second radio operator early in January, ROVER explained that he had been knocked over by a lorry and spent some time in hospital, suffering from broken ribs, a dislocated collarbone and internal injuries. It was hoped that, if the Abwehr noticed the changed rhythm of his transmissions (frequently detectable when a radio operator was replaced), they would put it down to his damaged shoulder. In the event the new radio operator seems to have aroused no suspicion.[142]

The Security Service reported to Churchill that during January 1945:

TATE and ROVER have been successfully supplying misleading information about the fall of V.1. and V.2., and there is some reason to believe that their messages are having an effect on the places where these missiles are falling. TATE has also been used at the Admiralty for Naval deception with great success.[143]

Masterman wrote later:

Over a period of some months we contrived to encourage the enemy steadily to diminish his range; thus in the four weeks from 20 January to 17 February 1945 the real M.P.I. moved eastward about two miles a week and ended well outside the boundary of London region.

. . . A captured German map shows a schedule of results for a fortnight based on agents' reports and gives the M.P.I. in the Charing Cross area. This is, of course, exactly what we wished the enemy to believe.[144]

The monthly report to Churchill for February 1945 concluded:

TATE and ROVER have continued to supply misleading information about the fall of V.2 and it is now possible to conclude with some certainty that the shift to the north-east of London of the mean point of impact of V.2 is due to reports from Special Agents. The renewed use of V.1 was foreshadowed by a message sent to TATE a week before the event.[145]

By the time the last V-2 was launched on 27 March 1945, a total of 1,054 of the rockets had hit English targets, about half of them in Greater London.

Over 2,700 Londoners were killed.[146] Later analysis for the Ministry of
Home Security concluded that, if the MPI of the V-2s had not altered
when it did, about 1,300 more people would have been killed and 10,000
more injured – in addition to the disruption which would have been caused
to government and the economy by many more V-2s landing in the area
between Westminster and the docks.[147]

While sending misleading reports on the V-weapons, TATE simultaneously took the lead role in the most important naval deception of the
war. During 1944 German U-boats were fitted with the Schnorchel ('nose')
device, a combined air-intake and diesel gas-outlet which enabled them to
remain submerged indefinitely and be virtually undetectable by radar.[148]
They were thus able to lie in wait for convoys in mine-free channels. In
November 1944 TATE reported to his Abwehr case officer that he had
learned from a Royal Navy mine-laying specialist, who sometimes spent
the night at his flat, that mines of a new design were being laid near the
sea bottom at depths which allowed convoys to pass over them unscathed
but would trap submarines diving to avoid surface attack. The deception
gained added credibility when TATE sent accurate reports of U-boat
sinkings in areas where the non-existent mines had supposedly been laid.[149]
The Security Service informed Churchill on 19 February 1945 that TATE's
deception was having 'great success'.[150] Early in March, off Fastnet, a
U-boat hit a real mine which was mistaken by the Germans for one of the
imaginary deep-water mines reported by TATE. As a result, U-boats were
instructed to avoid an area of 3,600 square miles south-east of Fastnet.[151]
Masterman later concluded: 'On a modest estimate TATE must have
ensured the safety of many of our vessels which would otherwise have run
considerable risks in that area, and it is not impossible that his misinfor-
mation moved U-boats from areas where they were safe to areas where
they emphatically were not.'[152] TATE's German controllers were so pleased
with the reports which deceived them that they described him as a 'pearl'
among agents. A few hours before Hamburg fell to the Allies on 2 May
1945, his case officer appealed to him by radio to keep in touch.[153]

For some in the St James's Street offices of the Security Service, the final
weeks of the war, when they were no longer faced with any serious threat
to national security, were an anti-climax. Hugh Astor, formerly the highly
motivated case officer of BRUTUS and other double agents who had
played a key role, found himself becoming bored as his case-work ran
down.[154] So did Guy Liddell, who wrote in his diary on 4 May: 'The end
of the war is falling rather flat, and VE Day is undoubtedly going to be a
colossal bore, with no food and no transport. The only thing to do is to

tie a Union Jack to the bedpost and go to bed.'[155] The mood in Blenheim
Palace, where most members of the Service were based, was different. On
the last Sunday of the war, 6 May, the church bells, which earlier in the
war were to have been the warning signal of a German invasion, rang out
to celebrate victory. The double doors in the Duke's dining room were
thrown open and staff allowed on to the palace terrace to listen to the
bells. One member of Registry, who had 'sweated through four years of
war', recalls that for her and her colleagues it was 'a very tremendous
occasion . . . a real thanksgiving.'[156]

Contrary to Liddell's pessimistic expectations, 'Victory in Europe' (VE)
Day on 8 May was one of the most extraordinary national celebrations in
British, especially London, history. Churchill spent the morning in bed at
Number Ten preparing his great Victory broadcast, having been assured
by Scotland Yard and the Ministry of Food that there was no shortage of
beer in the capital – though 'individual public houses here and there may
run dry'. At 3 p.m. the Prime Minister began his broadcast, announcing
the unconditional surrender of all German forces. Some from MI5's
London offices were in the crowd in Parliament Square listening to the
speech being relayed through loudspeakers. When Churchill spoke of 'the
evil-doers, who are now prostrate before us', there was an audible gasp
from the crowd. As he began his peroration, his voice broke as he declared,
'Advance Britannia!' But it was firm and confident once more as he ended
with the words: 'Long live the cause of freedom! God save the King!'
Churchill made his final speech that day from the balcony of the Ministry
of Health to the vast crowds thronging Whitehall, some members of MI5
again among them. 'This is your victory,' he told them. 'No – it is yours!'
they shouted back. Churchill continued: 'It is the victory of the cause of
freedom in every land. In all our long history we have never seen a greater
day than this!'[157]

VE Day was the greatest day too in the history of the Security Service.
Its members did not rank their own contribution to victory as high as those
of the armed services and their allies who had risked, or lost, their lives in
battle. But they were right to believe that, by their comprehensive victory
over German intelligence, they had saved many lives. Few, if any, of those
who knew the secret of the Double-Cross System believed that it would
ever be revealed. When Sir John Masterman (knighted in 1959) published
his now celebrated history of it in the United States a quarter of a century
later, many past and present members of the Service were deeply shocked.
The Director General, Sir Martin Furnival Jones, who had joined the
Service a few months after Masterman, wrote to him: 'I consider your

action disgraceful and have no doubt that my opinion would have been shared by many of those with whom you worked during the war.'[158] Though Tar Robertson was dead, his former deputy John Marriott refused to speak to Masterman again.[159]

The wartime success of the Double-Cross System initially raised exaggerated expectations about the potential use of deception in the Cold War against Britain's former wartime ally, the Soviet Union. As early as February 1944, the LCS argued that 'organised deception should henceforth form an essential part of any modern war machine';[160] its Controlling Officer, Colonel Bevan, argued in some detail in a post-war report that strategic deception 'may almost be classed as a new weapon'.[161] The LCS was directed in 1949 to 'lay the necessary foundations to ensure the immediate use of deception from the start of any future war'.[162] Post-war service chiefs showed great interest in the use of double agents. Guy Liddell warned in April 1951: 'Our main difficulty may not be so much to persuade senior officers to allow us to run double-agents, but to prevent them from making us run everything in sight as a double-agent.' There was, however, never any prospect that a Double-Cross System directed against the Russians could achieve anything approaching the level of success achieved against the Germans. 'It would', wrote Liddell, 'be extremely difficult to "do it again" on the Russians.'[163] When his friend, the former MI5 agent Guy Burgess, and the diplomat Donald Maclean defected to Moscow the following month,[164] Liddell must have realized that a Cold War Double-Cross System would be even more difficult than he had supposed.

Section D
The Early Cold War

Introduction
The Security Service and its Staff in the Early Cold War

For the small circle of those indoctrinated into the Double-Cross System, the Security Service emerged from the Second World War trailing clouds of glory from the most successful deception in the history of warfare. But for many of the Labour MPs elected in the landslide victory of 1945, who knew nothing of MI5's contribution to victory, its reputation was clouded with suspicions dating back to the Zinoviev letter of 1924, which they blamed for the fall of Ramsay MacDonald's first Labour government.[1] When Petrie retired as DG in the spring of 1946, the internal candidates to succeed him were passed over in favour of the Chief Constable of Kent, Sir Percy Sillitoe, whom the new Prime Minister, Clement Attlee, trusted to keep the Security Service, so far as possible, on the straight and narrow path of political impartiality. Sillitoe was a large man with a powerful physical presence and a reputation as a crime-buster.[2] Attlee was far from his only supporter in Whitehall. At interview in November 1945 Sillitoe outperformed the rest of a strong shortlist which included General Sir Hastings 'Pug' Ismay, who had been Churchill's Chief of Staff, General Kenneth Strong, Eisenhower's British intelligence chief (to whom Ike was devoted), and William Penney, Mountbatten's intelligence chief (also highly regarded). The PUS at the Foreign Office, Sir Alexander Cadogan, noted in his diary that the Whitehall interviewing committee 'were unanimous in choosing Sillitoe . . . I certainly thought he was very good.'[3]

Few senior officers in the Security Service agreed with the Whitehall committee. Apart from being disappointed not to become DG, Guy Liddell, head of B Division (intelligence),* believed:

---

* Within MI5 'branch' and 'division' had often been used interchangeably. In internal administrative documents 'division' predominated from 1943 to 1950. From 1953 onwards the accepted term was 'branch'. On changes in division/branch nomenclature and responsibilities, see Appendix 3, p. 000.

(1) It is a mistake to appoint a policeman since the work of this office is entirely different from police work.

(2) It puts the stamp of the Gestapo on the office.[4]

(3) It creates a false impression in the minds of police forces generally and of the Services that MI5 is a kind of police dept.

(4) It generally down-grades the office.

Liddell did not think Sillitoe had sufficient stature for his influence in Whitehall to compensate for his lack of intelligence experience. And it was 'extremely discouraging for the younger members of the office and for others coming in, to feel that the head of the office is likely to be appointed from outside'.[5]

Sillitoe made no secret of his distrust of 'Oxbridge types' and 'long-haired intellectuals'. Since the two senior MI5 officers who were to succeed him as DG – Dick White and Roger Hollis – were both 'Oxbridge types' (though not long-haired), the omens were bad. Sillitoe's son later recalled an occasion when, convinced that his directors were trying to humiliate him by quoting Latin epigrams he could not understand, the DG stormed out of the Security Service headquarters, white-faced with rage: 'When we got into the car I asked, "What was that all about?" He said, "One word – bastards!" He would return home to the flat in Putney night after night and tell my mother, "Dolly, I can't get to grips with a brick wall!" '[6] Even Bill Magan (later one of the Service's leading directors), who got on well with Sillitoe personally, recalls that the DG 'never understood MI5 and was surrounded by men more intelligent and better educated than himself'.[7] According to Norman Himsworth, Sillitoe did not help himself by swearing 'like a fishmonger's wife'.[8]

The powers which Sillitoe acquired on his appointment as DG were constitutionally remarkable by present-day standards with no basis in statute. A report by Sir Findlater Stewart, chairman of the Security Executive, had concluded on 27 November 1945: 'The purpose of the Security Service is the Defence of the Realm and nothing else ... There is no alternative to giving [the DG] the widest discretion in the means he uses and the direction in which he applies them – always provided he does not step outside the law.'[9] Since the Security Service's powers were not defined by statute, however, it was unclear what their legal limits were. Though it was supposed that the authority for the interception of mail and telephone calls through Home Office Warrants (HOWs) ultimately derived from royal prerogative, the precise origin of the power to conduct telephone intercepts was 'a little hazy'.[10] A Committee of Privy Counsellors twelve years later could find no basis for the power to intercept communications other than 'long usage', but recommended that the practice continue subject to HOWs. 'This means', Sir David G. T. Williams QC later concluded, 'that the Security Service, itself a body unrecognised by law, continues to rely upon a practice which is also not recognised by law.'[11]

Sir Findlater Stewart's November 1945 report also called for the reform of the confused chain of ministerial responsibility for the Service established during the war:

It was controlled by the Home Secretary so far as it used the special postal powers, and the Treasury was responsible for providing it with funds. But the responsibility for its direction *as a Service* was a more difficult matter. From the summer of 1940 it rested with Lord Swinton, as Chairman of the Security Executive (he was, of course, not a Minister), then with Mr Duff Cooper, while he was Chancellor of the Duchy [of Lancaster]. It then went to Mr Eden, but only in his personal capacity and *not* as Foreign Secretary.

... I feel strongly that the time has come to regularise the position ... The Minister responsible for it *as a Service* (though not for action taken by other Ministers on its advice) should be the Minister of Defence, or, if there is no Minister of Defence, the Prime Minister as Chairman of the Committee of Imperial Defence.[12]

Probably because of his initial suspicions of the Security Service, Attlee wished to keep personal control of the Service rather than delegate to the Minister of Defence. Sillitoe was instructed before taking office on 1 May 1946: 'You will be responsible to the Prime Minister to whom you will have the right of direct access. It will be your responsibility to keep the Prime Minister constantly informed of subversive activities likely to endanger the security of the State.'[13]

Soon after his appointment as DG, Sillitoe told Liddell that 'He would be seeing the PM at least once a fortnight on the latter's special instructions.'[14] Though they do not seem to have met quite so often, Sillitoe saw the Prime Minister far more frequently than any subsequent DG for the remainder of the twentieth century. Sillitoe's right of direct access to Attlee was a considerable asset for the Security Service which, as Dick White later acknowledged, he and other senior officers with a low opinion of the DG failed to exploit adequately.[15] Sillitoe was a rare (perhaps unique) example of a DG who inspired greater confidence in Number Ten than in his own staff. After succeeding Harker as DDG in October 1946, Liddell sometimes stood in for Sillitoe (notably during the DG's lengthy visits to the Empire and Commonwealth) at meetings with the Prime Minister. He too won Attlee's confidence but, like other visitors to Number Ten, sometimes found the Prime Minister's taciturn manner disconcerting: 'You say your piece and when you come to the end there is a long pause – you then begin the next item on the agenda. I think it is to some extent due to a curious shyness, which he radiates, and indeed imparts to his visitors. He does not often look you in the face.'[16]

The traditional culture of the Security Service, however, was to keep ministers at arm's length. Guy Liddell wrote dismissively in 1950:

Intelligence matters were usually of such complexity that the less Ministers had to do with them the better. It was far better to get things settled, if possible, on a lower level; Ministers had not really got the time to go into all the details. If therefore they were required to make a decision, it is as likely as not that it would be the wrong one![17]

The head of the civil service, the cabinet secretary and the Home Office PUS were each far better informed about the Security Service than most of the cabinet. During the Attlee government and most of the three following Conservative administrations, the Service benefited from the confidence of the immensely influential Sir Norman Brook, assistant cabinet secretary from 1945 and cabinet secretary from 1947 to 1963. In 1950 Brook was asked by Attlee to carry out an inquiry into the Service. He told Liddell afterwards that 'there was really practically nothing that he could criticise.' Brook had initially been 'inclined to think that the manpower and efforts devoted to the work of B1 [counter-subversion] were perhaps out of proportion with those of B2 [counter-espionage] but in arguing his case with the officers concerned he had been entirely persuaded that this was not so.'[18] Brook went on to become one of the closest confidants and advisers to both Winston Churchill and Harold Macmillan.[19]

Soon after Sillitoe's appointment as DG, he was instructed to inform the Prime Minister and him alone about any MP of whatever party who 'is a proven member of a subversive organisation'.[20] Attlee also expected to be kept informed about signs of subversion among ministers' families. When, under Churchill's peacetime government in 1952, the DG was made directly responsible to the Home Secretary (then Sir David Maxwell Fyfe) rather than the Prime Minister, Sillitoe told him that he had been 'accustomed to confide in the Prime Minister certain delicate matters which came to the notice of the Security Service from time to time and which concerned the personal affairs of Ministers', such as the case of 'a Minister's son who had become involved with certain people under investigation by the Security Service and who had given information to these people in return for some kind of reward'.[21]

The 1952 Maxwell Fyfe Directive (kept secret until it was published in the wake of the Profumo scandal a decade later), which the Security Service regarded as its charter, reaffirmed 'the well-established convention whereby ministers do not concern themselves with the detailed information which may be obtained by the Security Service in particular cases, but are furnished with such information only as may be necessary for the determination of any issue on which guidance is sought'. The Service's role was defined as follows:

The Security Service is part of the Defence Forces of the country. Its task is the Defence of the Realm as a whole, from external and internal dangers arising from attempts of espionage and sabotage, or from actions of persons and organizations whether directed from within or without the country, which may be judged to be subversive of the state.

Though instructed to avoid any political or sectional bias, the DG was left free to judge what was 'subversive of the state'. Unlike SIS and GCHQ (the successor to GC&CS), the Security Service was thus essentially self-tasking.[22]

When Guy Liddell retired from the Service in 1952 at the age of sixty to become head of security at the Atomic Energy Authority, Dick White succeeded him as DDG. Relations between White and Sillitoe did not improve. White later recalled, 'I found Sillitoe vapid and shallow and frequently wrong. I was close to leaving to try my hand at something else.'[23] Before retiring as DG on 31 August 1953, Sillitoe cut his ties to the Security Service in dramatic and unprecedented fashion by ordering the destruction of his record of service.[24] Maxwell Fyfe delegated the shortlisting and interviewing of candidates for the succession to Sillitoe to a high-powered committee of Whitehall mandarins, chaired by the head of the civil service and former cabinet secretary Sir Edward Bridges.[25] The Committee acknowledged that Guy Liddell had 'unrivalled experience of the type of intelligence dealt with in MI5, knowledge of contemporary Communist mentality and tactics and an intuitive capacity to handle the difficult problems involved'. But 'It has been said that he is not a good organiser and lacks forcefulness. And doubts have been expressed as to whether he would be successful in dealing with Ministers, with heads of department and with delegates of other countries.'[26] The Committee concluded that the two strongest candidates were Dick White and General Sir Kenneth Strong (who had been shortlisted in 1945). Following interviews with both, Maxwell Fyfe told Churchill that he agreed with a majority on the Committee in recommending White:

Particularly since the last two appointments were made from outside the Service, there would be substantial advantage, from the point of view of the internal morale of MI5, in making an appointment from within if there is a suitable candidate there. I have seen a good deal of the work of MI5 since I have been Home Secretary and I have formed the highest opinion of Mr White's capabilities.[27]

White's appointment as DG at the age of forty-six was welcomed with relief as well as pleasure within the Security Service. The future DDG, Anthony Simkins, probably spoke for many of his colleagues when he said, 'We've got a professional and not a policeman in charge!'[28] Among the fairest judges of White's character was the Oxford historian and wartime intelligence officer Hugh Trevor-Roper, who had an unblemished reputation for never conferring unmerited praise. Trevor-Roper singled out White's 'liveliness, the genial equanimity, the sense of humour – and of the absurd – which carried him through every crisis'. It was precisely these characteristics which underpinned White's popularity within the Service. Of his intellect, Trevor-Roper wrote, probably also fairly: 'His mind was not original but it was always open. He enjoyed discussing ideas, literature and the arts.'[29]

Sillitoe had been a semi-public figure, whose photograph occasionally appeared in the press and who sometimes seemed to court publicity. As the features editor of the *Sunday Express*, J. L. Garbutt, told Maxwell Fyfe, Sillitoe's ineffectual attempts to disguise his appearance by, for example, wearing dark glasses at football matches or walking backwards out of aeroplanes merely increased media interest in him: 'The way he went about the job simply cried out for publicity. It was Sillitoe's unwisdom that was responsible for it all. I know this myself. He would even seek out the editors.' Garbutt advised the Home Secretary: 'Just let the Chief of M.I.5 fade into obscurity. It has been done. It can be done again. It all depends on the man.'[30] White was of the same mind. Though a naturally clubbable man, he was determined that both he and the Security Service should return to the shadows as soon as possible after Sillitoe's departure. While Sillitoe's appointment had been publicly announced, White's was not. Admiral George P. Thomson, the head of the D-Notice Committee (which advised on the publication of matters affecting national security), asked newspaper editors, 'in the national interest', not to publish his name.[31]

Though the media also made no reference to the Service's shabby Mayfair headquarters at Leconfield House,[32] to which it moved late in 1948, bus conductors and taxi drivers were less inhibited. A member of Registry recalls:

When you got off the bus in Park Lane the conductor would shout down the bus 'Curzon Street and MI5' and all the girls would troop off looking somewhat embarrassed! We also had to contend with some of the 'ladies of the night' in Curzon Street as Shepherds Market was a very red light district in the 60's and I think they might have thought they had some competition.[33]

Post-war cutbacks reduced the total size of the Service from 897 in July 1945 (down from a wartime peak of 1,271 early in 1943)[34] to 570 in 1947.[35] MI5 remained heavily male-dominated. In May 1945, though there were no female officers, fifty-nine women were doing officers' jobs.[36] As in the rest of British society, progress to equal opportunity was slow. In March 1952 fifty-four officers and twenty-four 'other' staff in B Division (intelligence) were male; three officers and 172 'others' were female.[37] As staff numbers increased with the worsening of the Cold War, the Service had to seek additional accommodation at a number of other central London sites.

Dick White began his term as DG with what became known as the 'October Revolution': a major reorganization in which the three existing Divisions – Establishments and Administration (A); Intelligence (B); Protective Security (C), supplemented in 1950 by an Overseas Division (OS) – were replaced by six Branches. Surveillance staff, formerly part of the Intelligence Division, became part of a new A Branch charged with technical support. B Branch became Personnel and Establishments; C Branch was Protective Security; D Branch took over Counter-Espionage; E Branch was responsible for Counter-Subversion in the Empire and Commonwealth; F Branch was charged with Counter-Subversion at home.[38]

As DDG White chose Roger Hollis,[39] a much more reserved personality than himself. High among his reasons for doing so was the fact that, during the Second World War, Hollis had been foremost in the Security Service in foreseeing the post-war threat from Soviet espionage and Communist subversion, the Service's two main targets at the time when White took over.[40] Despite his reserve, Hollis had also won the confidence of Britain's two most important Commonwealth intelligence allies. Both the Australian secretary of the Department of Defence, Sir Frederick Shedden and the Canadian under-secretary for External Affairs, Norman Robertson, became personal friends and – White believed – 'greatly respect his ability and judgement'.[41]

Since Hollis was a year older than White, his prospects of becoming DG appeared remote. But for Sir Anthony Eden's dissatisfaction with the leadership of SIS when he succeeded Churchill as prime minister in 1955, White would probably have remained DG until his retirement in 1968. Eden's desire to move White to SIS is usually explained by his annoyance at the embarrassment caused by the death of an out-of-condition SIS diver, 'Buster' Crabb, while secretly inspecting the hull of a Soviet warship in Portsmouth Harbour during the state visit of the Soviet leaders, Nikita Khrushchev and Nikolai Bulganin, in April 1955. In reality, Eden had already made up his mind in December 1954 to move White on the retirement of the current 'C', Sir John 'Sinbad' Sinclair, in June 1956. On being told the news by Eden,[42] the Home Secretary Gwilym Lloyd George described it as 'a great blow to me':

Sir Dick White has grown up in MI5 and I do not think it is an irresponsible statement to say that he is, in the opinion of the Home Office, far and away the best that that Department has ever had. He made the most excellent impression when he appeared recently before the Conference of Privy Counsellors on Security.[43]

White himself was reluctant to leave the Security Service, telling Sir Frank Newsam (PUS at the Home Office) that he was happy for 'as strong a counterargument as possible' to be put to the Prime Minister:

Basically, I really do believe that ... Security and Counter-Espionage are more important than Espionage in the present world context. The latter is faced by the totalitarian security measures of the Soviet bloc countries and I imagine is becoming progressively less feasible. On the other hand the Russians and their Satellites are increasing their efforts to obtain our secrets and this puts the emphasis on defence.[44]

Both White and the Home Office, however, gave way to the Prime Minister's insistence that he succeed Sinclair as chief of SIS.[45]

Gwilym Lloyd George told Eden that, as the next DG, 'I can only think of one man in MI5 who would be in the running, viz Mr R. H. Hollis, who is Sir Dick White's deputy.'[46] At the time White gave Hollis his enthusiastic support.[47] He later changed his mind, writing in a sympathetic obituary that, though respected within the Service during his nine years as DG, Hollis 'did not enjoy easy personal relations with its ordinary members who tended to find him reserved and aloof'.[48] Some, probably many, did not meet him at all. One staff member who encountered Hollis in the lift and failed to recognize him, said: 'Oh, we haven't met. What section are you?' 'I am the DG,' replied Hollis.[49]

Perhaps the ultimate example of Hollis's remote management style came during the thirteen days of the Cuban Missile Crisis in October 1962, the most dangerous moment in British history. Though the crisis was caused by the American discovery of Soviet nuclear missile bases under construction in Cuba, the threat to Britain, the United States' chief ally, was even greater than to America itself. There must have seemed to many Service staff, as to much of the British population, a real danger that the crisis would end in thermonuclear warfare and the obliteration of the United Kingdom. Most staff knew no more about the crisis than they read in the press and saw on television news. Once the BBC (slightly ahead of US television channels) broadcast photographs of the Soviet missile sites under construction on Cuba taken by American U-2 spy planes,[50] staff knew that intelligence was likely to play a crucial role in the resolution of the crisis. But, as they worried about the fate of themselves and their families, they heard nothing from the DG or senior management.[51] The DG had decided six years earlier, without informing most staff, that in a nuclear war 'it was no good envisaging an organised Head Office existing anywhere; indeed there would be nothing to do.' Any surviving senior officers were expected to go to help the wartime regional commissioners to preserve what survived of local administration. No plans were made for the rest of staff.[52]

Had war seemed likely in 1962, Hollis would have had to select two or three representatives of the Service (of whom he might have been one) to join the Prime Minister, the War Cabinet and senior defence and intelligence staff in a large underground bunker, codenamed TURNSTILE, near Corsham in the Cotswolds.[53] Before the Missile Crisis, Harold Macmillan, who had succeeded Eden as prime minister in 1957, directed that TURN-STILE was to 'act as the seat of government' in what he optimistically described as 'the period of survival and reconstruction' following a nuclear attack. More realistically, in a Third World War the bunker would probably have provided no more than a short-lived underground refuge for the remnants of British government while Britain was obliterated above them. Such thoughts must surely have been in the Prime Minister's and DG's minds at the height of the Missile Crisis. Macmillan planned an exceptional Sunday cabinet meeting on 28 October at which he probably intended to authorize the move to a 'Precautionary Stage' in the countdown to war. Shortly before the cabinet was due to meet, however, the Soviet leader Nikita Khrushchev brought the crisis to a dramatic end by giving in to US demands to dismantle the Cuban missile bases.[54] Security Service staff were not briefed about the Missile Crisis even when it was over. By contrast, their former DG, Sir Dick White, now 'C', was believed to have congratulated SIS staff on the role they had played.[55]

At a personal level, Hollis's final years in office and much of his comparatively brief retirement were among the most difficult experienced by any DG. In 1963 he authorized the surveillance and secret investigation of Graham Mitchell, whom he had made DDG in 1956, on what turned out to be the unfounded suspicion of being a Soviet agent. By 1964 Hollis had fallen under suspicion himself from a small but determined minority of Service conspiracy theorists.[56] The tiny but influential circle of Whitehall mandarins privy to these extraordinary suspicions might perhaps have been expected to favour an outside appointment to succeed Hollis as DG on his retirement in December 1965. That an insider was preferred was due partly to the fact that Hollis, at least in operational matters, retained the confidence of the Home Office and, in particular, its powerful PUS, Sir Charles Cunningham. Equally influential was the unhappy precedent set by the appointment of Sir Percy Sillitoe – 'a clear illustration', in Cunningham's view, of the dangers of appointing an outsider: 'I am satisfied that an outside appointment would be wrong so long as there is a suitably qualified successor to Sir Roger Hollis in the Security Service itself – and fortunately there is.' The successor Cunningham had in mind was Martin Furnival Jones (FJ), both the first Cambridge graduate and the first man with a law degree to become DG, widely regarded as the cleverest man in the Security Service.[57] FJ had succeeded Mitchell as DDG in 1963 and was strongly backed by Hollis.[58]

In 1965, as a result of continued staff expansion, the Service leased a new headquarters from Great Universal Stores at 15/17 Great Marlborough Street near Oxford Circus, to which the new DG, his secretariat and A, B and D Branches moved.[59] Furnival Jones was a shy man with much the same reserved manner as Hollis. One female member of staff recalls that when he came to office bridge evenings, 'You would be his partner and he would not even talk to you.'[60] FJ's main visible enthusiasms were bird-watching and *The Times* crossword.[61] The aloof management style of Hollis and FJ did little to diminish the sociable work culture of the rest of the Service, many of whose members never met the DG. One new recruit was told in 1953 by Bill Foulkes, a personnel officer in the newly founded B Branch, 'One of the best things about working here is that the percentage of bastards is extremely low.'[62] Extensive interviews with retirees and staff opinion surveys since the end of the Cold War[63] strongly suggest that this has remained ever since the view of a considerable majority of the Service.

The earliest known post-war attempt to sum up the qualities expected of a Security Service officer is a note prepared in the mid-1950s by Antony Simkins, then B1 (personnel), for German liaison. Though an intellectual himself, with a first-class honours degree in history from Oxford University, Simkins began by emphasizing that, while 'a good standard of ability is required', 'intellectual arrogance is a grave fault since matters of opinion bulk large in the work of the Security Service':

While integrity is no doubt the first qualification, it is closely followed by stability, sense of responsibility and purpose, stamina, humour, tolerance and generosity which go to make a good colleague. A Security Service officer must work as a team. To be humourless, opinionated or personally over ambitious is a serious defect. Maturity is essential and a man will rarely be suitable before he reaches the middle twenties at the earliest ... The hall mark of a good security officer is judgement, which is generally the product of a trained mind and well rounded personality.[64]

A sense of humour was regarded, as it had been since the earliest days of the Service,[65] as indispensable both for preserving a sense of proportion when dealing with fraught issues of national security and for maintaining team spirit. A secretary who worked at Leconfield House from 1949 to 1958 still had vivid memories half a century later of 'a lot of humour' in the Service.[66] A member of the Registry in the 1950s remembers 'endless laughter, particularly working with Dolly Craven, oh my goodness!'[67] Many other female staff recall beginning the working day by listening to the extrovert Ms Craven, who was in charge of outgoing mail, frankly recounting to gales of laughter the latest episodes in her adventurous private life.[68] A secretary who worked at Leconfield House from 1959 to 1965 remembers Service culture as a mixture of humour and hard work: 'Life was fun for young secretaries, even on £9 a week.'[69] After making due allowance for the fact that fond memories tend to become fonder still as the years go by, it is impossible to mistake the affection with which the Security Service is still regarded by so many of its surviving post-war veterans. Even the disaffected memoirs of Peter Wright, though permeated by personal grievances and conspiracy theories, record that 'in the main, the 1950s were years of fun, and A Branch [of which he was an officer] a place of infectious laughter.'[70]

Post-war Service recruitment remained largely by personal recommendation. Following earlier informal contacts with the careers services (then called Appointments Boards) at Oxford and Cambridge Universities, formal contact was established in 1949. Ironically, in view of what later became known about the KGB's recruitment of Cambridge graduates in particular, the DDG, Guy Liddell, was not in favour of going further afield for university recruits with the possible exception of Edinburgh: 'London is something of a breeding ground for Left Wingers and Manchester and Birmingham, as far as I know, produce specialists such as chemists, engineers, etc.' The Service preferred its officer recruits, however well educated, to have experience of the outside world and to be in at least their mid-twenties. It thus took relatively few direct from university. The

Oxbridge Appointments Boards were cultivated partly because their advice continued to be sought by some graduates when changing jobs in the course of their careers. A circular to Service officers in 1953 concluded that 'a personal introduction ... still remains the most satisfactory form of introduction'. Recruitment procedures were somewhat perfunctory. A preliminary interview with the Director of Establishments and Adminis-tration, if it was recorded at all, usually amounted to only a few lines, sometimes with dismissive comments such as 'a small man of a retiring disposition'.[71]

Of the 164 officers in the Service in 1955, thirty had joined after demobil-ization from the wartime armed forces, twenty-three had come from the police, twenty-two from the professions, twenty-one from the regular armed forces, twenty from business, seventeen from the colonial and home civil services, nine from other parts of the intelligence community and one from the BBC. Eleven were listed in the statistics as 'direct entry' (probably from university). By 1955 there were ten women officers (listed as a separ-ate category), all of whom had achieved their rank as a result of internal promotion within the Service.[72] The most influential of them was Milicent Bagot, the Service's first female Oxford graduate, who had joined the Service from the Special Branch during the 1931 reorganization.[73] In 1949 she was promoted from administrative assistant to the rank of officer,[74] in recognition of her extraordinary memory for facts and files on international Communism which passed into Service folklore.[75] Bagot was a stickler for meticulously correct office procedure, terrifying some young officers to whom she pointed out their shortcomings.[76] Though a powerful personality within the office, she was a quite different person at home. A male col-league, who for a time lodged at Bagot's house, later recalled:

Milicent had the most extraordinary domestic arrangements because she shared a house in Putney with her Nanny, and Nanny was boss ... She looked after Milicent and was not afraid to correct or criticise her ... Milicent, I think, adored her ... Milicent in fact on her own could hardly boil a kettle of water.[77]

Officers who joined the Service early in the Cold War could expect to spend a quarter to a third of their careers on overseas postings in the Empire and Commonwealth.[78] This, for many recruits, was one of the attractions of a Service career in an era before the invention of the package holiday had brought foreign travel within the reach of most of the British population. An officer who joined in 1949 remembers overseas postings as 'definitely the cream on the pudding'.[79] Most secretaries were equally enthusiastic. One of them recalls that, when offered a two-year posting in

Colombo soon after joining, 'I could hardly believe my luck.' The cautionary advice given to women posted abroad by the last of the lady superintendents, Catherine Weldsmith,[80] has passed into Service folklore. The
warning most frequently attributed to her was 'Beware of men in hot
climates!' She also advised wearing a girdle at all times 'just in case', though
its precise function as a defence against hot-blooded males was never
spelled out.[81] At various times during the thirty years after the Second
World War, the Service had forty-two outposts abroad, the great majority
in the Empire and Commonwealth.[82]

By 1965, some 65 per cent of officers recruited during the previous ten
years had come from the administrative services of newly independent
colonies.[83] The Indian civil service and police had long provided recruits
to MI5, chief among them the wartime DG Sir David Petrie. In the spring
of 1947, shortly before Indian independence, Liddell, then DDG, visited
India[84] and recruited eight policemen, three of whom later reached
high rank in the Service.[85] From the mid-1950s contact with the head of
the Re-employment Bureau of the Sudan Political Service led to a stream
of recruits nicknamed the 'Sudanese souls'.[86] In 1955 Director B, J. H.
Marriott, wrote to the head of the Cambridge University Appointments
Board:

What we want in fact is the sort of combination of brains and character that was
looked for in the I[ndian] C[ivil] S[ervice] or the Colonial Service in its palmy days.
Our chaps frequently find themselves in a position where, since they have no
authority, their ability to put across the point of view of the Service depends almost
entirely upon themselves.[87]

At the beginning of 1957 the DDG, Graham Mitchell, and B1 visited
Malaya to make job offers to officers of the Malayan civil service, who
were known after their arrival in MI5 as the 'Malayan mafia'. Stella
Rimington, the first female DG, later complained that, though some of the
colonial recruits rose to senior positions, a minority, with the security of a
pension and a lump sum to buy a house, 'seemed to do very little at all,
and there was a lot of heavy drinking.'[88] Others claim that that heavy
drinking was limited to a few notorious cases – chief among them a director
whose alcoholism led to his early retirement.[89]

By the time Furnival Jones became DG in 1965 there was growing
dissatisfaction among Security Service officers with their confused salary
and career structure. Though many had pensions from previous employment in addition to their Service salaries, most were in their forties or fifties
with poor promotion prospects. Some had remained at the top of their pay

scale for ten years or more. After an internal inquiry, FJ approved a new career structure in which officers in charge of sections were renamed assistant directors, and a new rank of senior officer was created as an intermediate grade. For the first time directors, hitherto paid at different rates, were to receive the same salary, and the DG's salary scale was raised to that of a deputy secretary in the civil service. Unusually, Treasury officials agreed to the proposals without a quibble. In fact they were so taken aback by the Service's confused salary scales that one official asked Director B, John Marriott, 'Why haven't you had a mutiny?' Already privately distressed by the investigation of his predecessors as both DDG and DG on suspicion of working for the KGB, FJ seems to have been shocked to discover how far behind the times the Service had fallen in providing a coherent career structure for its staff. At a meeting of about twenty officers selected for promotion to the new-style senior-officer grade, Furnival Jones burst into tears in the middle of his announcement. Few members of the Service had previously realized the strong emotions concealed by FJ's stiff upper lip and shy exterior.[90]

During the early Cold War, the Security Service's training policy, like its management style, was old-fashioned. Ironically, when Training Section was set up in 1955, its job was to train not Service staff but police and administrative personnel in colonies on the verge of independence and other parts of the Commonwealth.[91] Though new entrants were given two or three days' practical training on administration and the running of the office, there was no attempt to address broader issues.[92] It was only during this brief initial training that some staff discovered the identity of the organization they had joined. An officer recruit relates how he had been in the office several days before he was told by Director B, John Marriott, 'I suppose someone told you this is MI5?' In fact, no one had.[93] One new entrant to the Registry recalls that she had been in the Service for several weeks before she was told. The training recollections of those officers who joined during the early Cold War are mostly very similar: 'In all my career in the Service I had very little training – what I knew I picked up';[94] 'Training was something you didn't have or you did it on the job';[95] 'Training when I joined was sitting with Aunt Nellie . . . It was briefing not training.'[96]

By the mid-1950s most new entrants to the Security Service started in what was called the 'Study Group', successively designated F1A, F2C and F1C. This section, also known as the 'nursery', was responsible for identifying members of the Communist Party of Great Britain (CPGB), using both intelligence and open sources,[97] and was thus seen as an ideal training ground for learning the basic investigative work of the Service, file-making, indexing, source evaluation, and liaison with local police forces. Newcomers lived in dread of the Registry Examiners who sent back files with green slips pointing out their errors. As Stella Rimington later recalled, 'The arrival of files one thought one had got rid of, covered in green notes, was a sort of ritual humiliation that one was required to suffer as an embryo desk officer.'[98]

During the early Cold War the 'watchers' of A4 (as they became in the White reorganization of 1953)[99] came from working- or lower-middle-class backgrounds very different from those of most of the officers. Their social separation was emphasized by the fact that they were housed separately from most of the Service. By the time he retired in 1947, Harry Hunter, who had joined MI5 in 1917 and headed the surveillance department since 1937, was the longest-serving male member of the Service. In Hunter's view:

From experience it has been found that the ideal watcher should be 5' 7" or 8" in height, looking as unlike a policeman as possible. It is likewise a mistake to use men who are too short as they are just as conspicuous as tall men. We favour shadowers of a nondescript type; good eyesight is essential, also hearing, as it is often vitally important to overhear a suspect's conversation; active and alert, as it frequently happens that a suspect hastily boards or alights from a fast moving vehicle; hardy enough to withstand cold, heat and wet during the long hours of immobility in the street, and, more important, to escape being spotted by the suspect himself.[100]

Hunter's successor, David Storrier, was a former policeman. A4's total size in December 1946 was only fifteen (including a male secretary); by 1956 it had increased to fifty. Instead of dressing casually, the watchers were expected to wear suits, trilby hats and raincoats. In winter they were sometimes forced to stuff newspapers under their shirts in an attempt to stay warm. Brown envelopes containing their weekly wages were frequently delivered to A4 staff in the street by bicycle from Head Office. They worked a five-and-a-half-day week with no Sunday working until 1956 when mobile watchers were required to work one weekend in four (from 1963 two weekends in five).[101]

The main surveillance target was the Soviet embassy and intelligence residencies in Kensington Palace Gardens (KPG). Soviet personnel initially travelled mostly on foot, or by bus and taxi. So did A4 surveillance personnel, communicating with each other by hand signals. Immediately after the war, A4 had no car, though it sometimes pressed into service the DG's Wolseley. By the end of the 1940s it had acquired three or four Hillmans.[102]

When the Russians started to use embassy cars, a watcher (usually one who could not drive) would alert A4 surveillance cars to their movements by radio-controlled buzzers. Equipment allowing speech communication was not installed until 1951.[103] The head of A4 from 1953 until his retirement in 1961 was William (known as Jim) Skardon, a former detective inspector in the Met whose record of service notes that, since joining the counter-espionage division of the Service in 1947, he had shown himself 'perhaps the most foremost exponent in the country' of the interrogation of suspects.[104] But for his ability to extract confessions, the atom spy Klaus Fuchs could not have been successfully prosecuted.[105] It was an indication of the continued lowly status of A4 that, despite Skardon's achievements as interrogator and the crucial role of surveillance in Service investigations, he was never given promotion to senior officer.[106]

Since the Second World War the Service had had an outstation, in a Post Office building in St Martin's Le Grand near St Paul's, headed in the 1950s by Major Albert Denman (remembered by Peter Wright as 'an old-fashioned military buffer with a fine sense of humour'), which was responsible for postal interception and the installation of telephone taps under Home Office Warrants. Technicians, wearing rubber gloves to avoid leaving fingerprints, sat at long trestle tables, equipped with powerful lamps and large kettles, steaming open mail and producing photostats of their contents with pedal-operated cameras. During the early 1960s the outstation moved across the road to Union House, another Post Office building, and replaced the photostat machines with less cumbersome 35mm film and Kodak cameras. The number of postal items opened in London and at other units around the country increased from 135,000 in 1961 to 221,000 in 1969. In 1966 a letter to the Ministry of Public Building and Works condemned the working conditions in Union House as 'so far below the Shops and Railway Premises Act that it is little short of disgraceful'; after heavy rain the sinks were said to overflow and the parquet flooring began to lift. There was no major improvement until 1969, when the unit joined a refurbished laboratory in Union House.[107]

The recording and transcription of telephone calls intercepted under HOWs and the product of eavesdropping devices was carried out on the sixth floor of Leconfield House in A2A, a section closed to most members of the Service. In the 1950s Dictaphone cylinders were used to record telephone intercepts and acetate gramophone disks for microphone circuits.[108] The work of the mainly female transcribers in A2A was supervised during this period by a redoubtable assistant officer, Mrs Evelyn Grist, noted for her powerful personality and fondness for hats, necklaces and shawls.[109] A2A was known in her honour as 'The Gristery'.[110] There was some alarm in 1950, before the introduction of shredders, when fragments of secret waste from the Gristery which had been placed in a malfunctioning incinerator blew up the chimney and scattered in the street outside.[111] After Mrs Grist's retirement, A2A was put under the control of an officer. By 1964 it had ninety-four members: fifty-three English-language transcribers, thirty linguists, eleven managerial and office staff. With the intensification of operations against Soviet Bloc targets and counter-subversion in the mid-1960s, its total staff jumped by half in only two years to reach 140 in 1966.[112] The Russian transcribers came mainly from White Russian émigré families. To Peter Wright they seemed to have turned their sixth-floor hideaway into 'a tiny piece of Tsarist Russia . . . Some even installed icons in their rooms.'[113] Until 1970 the threat from Arab terrorism seemed so remote that A2A contained only one Arabic linguist.[114]

A Branch's lack of funds and state-of-the-art technology for its early Cold War operations was partly compensated for by the technical virtuosity of some of its members. A1 acquired a 'burglar' of genius, a former sergeant major, who set up a locksmith's workshop in the 'Dungeons' (basement) at Leconfield House with neatly arranged rows of numbered keys acquired or duplicated in the course of operations against offices, hotels and private homes.[115] He was passionate about his work, spending many evenings and nights of unpaid overtime on operations. Christopher Herbert (A1) wrote of him in 1968:

One is asked to avoid superlatives. I find it difficult to do so in writing about the work of this officer. For over a year he has been engaged in a series of difficult operations involving a high degree of engineering skills, apart altogether from running his workshop and participating in what one might call more routine operations. I can only pay tribute to his determination, professional ability and qualities of leadership. He refuses to be beaten by technical difficulties and has inspired his subordinates to work as they have never worked before. He is one of the greatest operational assets possessed by the Service.[116]

His admirers included Peter Wright who, after some years' part-time work, was recruited in 1955 as the Service's first scientist to advise A Branch on the operational use of electronic and other scientific equipment. Wright appears to have had considerable success in improving the performance and deployment of eavesdropping technology. Cleve Cram, who as deputy head of the US Central Intelligence Agency (CIA) station in London had regular contact with Wright, subsequently said that he would give him a mark of 8½ out of 10 for his work in A2 – despite his distaste for

Wright's later conspiracy theories of Soviet penetration.[117] Shorn of self-dramatization, Wright's celebrated claim in his disaffected memoirs to have 'bugged and burgled our way across London at the state's behest' is broadly true.[118] There was no HOW system for the installation of eavesdropping devices, which usually required burglary (though the Service did not use the word), mostly against Communist and Soviet Bloc targets. Approval was given instead by the Home Office PUS.[119] The belief at the time that 'bugging and burgling' in defence of the realm was covered by the royal prerogative was probably mistaken. Following publication of Peter Wright's memoirs in New York in 1987, according to Stella Rimington, the DG, Sir Antony Duff, argued – in the end successfully – that new legislation was needed to give the Security Service authority for operations which required 'entry on or interference with property'.[120]

During the early Cold War the integration of science and technology into Security Service culture and operations proceeded slowly. In 1962, after a series of discussions with SIS, a former senior government scientist was appointed joint director of science for the two Services.[121] Wright quickly fell out with him, claiming that he 'wanted to integrate scientific intelligence into the Ministry of Defence. He wanted the Directorate to be a passive organization, a branch of the vast inert defence-contracting industry, producing resources for its end users on request.'[122] In 1963 Wright and two SIS scientists formed a joint scientific directorate which in the following year was based in the new SIS headquarters at Century House in Lambeth. In 1966 the joint directorate broke up and the Service established a new scientific R&D section as A5.[123] In 1970 A5 had only six members, one of them a non-scientist, but its services were rapidly in heavy demand. Director A reported in August of that year that A5 officers were 'run off their feet'.[124]

The largest section of the Security Service, the Registry, was an exclusively female preserve. The first men did not join until 1976. In the immediate post-war years the daughters of former officers and debutantes were a major source of recruits. The Director of Establishments claimed in 1948 that 'the general atmosphere . . . is that in which ex-officers would like to find their daughters working.' According to Service folklore, 'a job in the Registry was as much a step in a debutante's progress as Queen Charlotte's Ball.' Though the folklore exaggerates the proportion of debs, there was no shortage of individuals who fitted the stereotype. One young woman in the Registry in the 1950s lived in the Curzon House Club (which then had no casino but was widely used by ladies from county families on shopping trips to Harrods), conveniently situated for the Service's then HQ at Leconfield House. Another Registry deb is said to have arrived each morning accompanied by her boyfriend in the Household Cavalry, with whom she had just been riding in the Park. Partly because of what were then termed the 'hazards of marriage' (normally followed by resignation) among its young and eligible female employees, turnover was always heavier in the Registry than anywhere else in the Service.[125] In 1960 the DG, Sir Roger Hollis, was asked informally by Burke Trend of the Treasury (later cabinet secretary) if he would consider the possibility of a building south of the river in the Elephant and Castle area. He replied that it was a rather 'slummy' district. Hollis wrote subsequently that 'since most of our girls come from the Kensington and Bayswater area', a move to the Elephant and Castle would have an adverse effect on recruiting.[126] Some of the working- and middle-class girls in Registry were initially rather intimidated by the novel experience of working with debs.[127]

By the later 1960s the younger generation of women graduates and professionals felt less content with life in the Service than most previous female recruits. Their discontents were increased by John Marriott's successor as Director B, who told at least one group of new entrants at the end of the 1960s: 'Women are happier in subordinate positions.'[128] Women were not included in the agent-running sections of the Service for another decade. When Stella Rimington became junior assistant officer in 1969:

The nearest women got to the sharp end of things in those days was as support officers to the men who were running the agents. They would be asked to go and service the safe-house where the agent was met – making sure there was milk and coffee there and the place was clean and tidy, and very occasionally they might be allowed to go with their officer to meet a very reliable, long-standing agent on his birthday or on some other special occasion.[129]

The first area where women played operational roles was in surveillance. By 1955 there were three female members of A4. At first none was allowed to drive. Their role was essentially to act as camouflage, accompanying male officers when it was necessary to strengthen their cover.[130] Until 1975, when sex discrimination legislation made the restriction unlawful, no woman was allowed to remain in A4 for more than five years because, as Director B wrote in 1967, 'Once we allow a woman to stay for over five years we should find it very difficult in practice to get rid of her at all.'[131] One of the victims of the five-year rule later recalled:

. . . I was dreadfully upset when my time came to leave. Looking back I remember all the good times – riding my motor-bike, map reading from helicopters, exhausting

days and very amusing evenings. Of course there were boring times but they soon
passed . . .[132]

Male and female surveillance staff in the early Cold War tended to come
from different class backgrounds, with the A4 women coming from much
higher up the social scale. Veterans believe that the class difference (a far
bigger social barrier half a century ago than it has since become) was 'a
deliberate ploy' devised by the management so that, despite being cooped
up in cars together for hours on end, the single women would not break
up the marriages of their male colleagues. One female member of A4 recalls
that collecting the surveillance cars from Clapham (where they were parked
overnight in the basement of Arding and Hobbs department store) took
for ever 'because we lived in Kensington, you know . . . We were always
meeting our friends if you were rushing through Harrods.'[133]

Throughout the early Cold War the Security Service continued to see
itself as standing apart from Whitehall and needing to keep its distance to
avoid unwelcome interference. The contrasting managerial mindsets of
Whitehall and the Service were epitomized by their very different responses
to the 1968 Fulton Report on the Civil Service.[134] There was much in the
report which was relevant to the Security Service as well as to Whitehall:
the need for more skilled and professional managers, career planning,
training and accountability. Whitehall responded by setting up a new Civil
Service Department, founding the Civil Service College and increasing
management training by 80 per cent in a year. The Security Service simply
filed the Report away.[135] When Sir Burke Trend suggested in 1966 that the
Civil Service Commission might be able to help the Service fill staff shortages in ancillary grades, FJ's frosty reply was one that Kell might well have
given a generation earlier – 'that we were not Civil Servants and that
technically speaking, the staff were in his personal employment'.[136] New
recruits were told they were Crown servants – not civil servants. Though
operationally effective with mostly good morale, the Service had a management which, largely because of its isolation from Whitehall, was behind
the times.

I

Counter-Espionage and Soviet Penetration: Igor Gouzenko and Kim Philby

The transition from war to Cold War brought with it a transition from intelligence feast to intelligence famine. During the Second World War, British intelligence had discovered more about its enemies than any state had ever known before about a wartime opponent. The Soviet Union, though less successful at penetrating the secrets of its enemies, discovered more of its wartime allies' secrets than any power had done before. When the war ended, four of what were later called the 'Magnificent Five' – the most successful group of foreign agents in Soviet history – were still in place in Britain. Kim Philby in SIS, some believed, had the potential to become a future 'C'. Donald Maclean and Guy Burgess were both supplying large quantities of classified Foreign Office documents. John Cairncross, though the peak of his career as a Soviet agent was past, was well positioned in the Treasury to provide intelligence on British defence expenditure. Anthony Blunt left the Security Service and returned to academic life as director of the Courtauld Institute, but continued to carry out occasional part-time missions for Soviet intelligence.[1]

On the eve of the Cold War, by contrast, the Security Service and SIS had not a single Soviet agent worth the name, were woefully ignorant about the extent of Soviet wartime intelligence penetration, and lacked even much basic information about Soviet intelligence agencies. SIGINT, for several years, provided little assistance and never came close to replicating against the Soviet Union the spectacular wartime successes against Nazi Germany.[2] The Security Service's first major post-war insight into Soviet intelligence operations in the West was the result of a defection in Canada.

On the evening of 5 September 1945 Igor Gouzenko, a twenty-six-year-old cipher clerk working for the GRU (Soviet military intelligence) at the Soviet embassy in Ottawa, secretly stuffed more than a hundred classified documents under his shirt and attempted to defect. He tried hard to hold in his stomach as he walked out of the embassy. 'Otherwise', his wife said later, 'he would have looked pregnant.' Defection turned out to be more difficult than Gouzenko had imagined. When he sought help at the offices of the Ministry of Justice and the *Ottawa Journal*, he was told to come back next day. But on 6 September both the Ministry of Justice and the *Ottawa Journal*, which failed to grasp it was being offered the spy exclusive of the decade, showed no more interest than on the previous evening. By the night of the 6th, the Soviet embassy realized that both Gouzenko and classified documents had gone missing. While Gouzenko hid with his wife and child in a neighbour's flat, Soviet security men broke down his door and searched his apartment. It was almost midnight before the local police came to his rescue and the Gouzenko family at last found sanctuary.[3] Though Gouzenko later persuaded Guy Liddell that he was an ideological defector,[4] at the time his decision to defect was thought to derive chiefly from fears for his own fate if he returned to the Soviet Union. He had breached GRU security regulations by failing to lock up classified material in the Ottawa residency and had been summoned back to Moscow.[5]

Ignorance about the extent of Soviet intelligence penetration of its Western allies contributed to the shock produced by Gouzenko's revelations in both London and Ottawa. Among those most shocked was the Canadian Prime Minister, William Mackenzie King, who naively told his diary:

As I dictate this note I think of the Russian embassy being only a few doors away and of them being a centre of intrigue. During the period of war, while Canada has been helping Russia and doing all we can to foment Canadian–Russian friendship, there has been one branch of the Russian service that has been spying on [us] . . . The amazing thing is how many contacts have been successfully made with people in key positions in government and industrial circles.[6]

As well as providing some further evidence of Soviet espionage in the United States, Gouzenko revealed the existence of a major GRU Canadian spy-ring which had penetrated parliament, External Affairs, air force intelligence, the Department of Munitions and Supply, and scientific research.[7] Gouzenko's most shocking revelation, only a month after Hiroshima, was that Soviet intelligence had obtained 'documentary materials of the atomic bomb: the technological process, drawings, calculations'.[8] The documents he provided included GRU telegrams on an agent codenamed ALEK, soon identified as the British atomic scientist Alan Nunn May. A secret Communist and contemporary of Donald Maclean at Trinity Hall, Cambridge, May was the first of the 'atom spies' to be unmasked.[9] In January 1943 he had joined an Anglo-Canadian nuclear research laboratory at Montreal. Despite the fact that he had made contact with the GRU in

Britain during the previous year, it took the local GRU some time to grasp his importance. Not till late in 1944 was Pavel Angelov of the Ottawa GRU residency selected as his case officer. At some point during the first half of 1945, Angelov asked May to obtain samples of the uranium used in the construction of atomic weapons – an assignment which a Canadian agent of the GRU, Israel Halperin, had described as 'absolutely impossible'. May, however, succeeded. On 9 August 1945, three days after Hiroshima, he gave Angelov a report on atomic research, details of the bomb dropped on Hiroshima and two samples of uranium: an enriched specimen of U-235 in a glass tube and a thin deposit of U-233 on a strip of platinum foil. The GRU resident in Ottawa, Nikolai Zabotin, sent his deputy to take them immediately to Moscow. Soon afterwards Zabotin was awarded both the Order of the Red Banner and the Order of the Red Star. Angelov gave May about 200 Canadian dollars in a whisky bottle.[10]

The intelligence officer best equipped to interrogate Gouzenko after his defection was Jane Archer, née Sissmore. But for her move from MI5 to SIS in 1940,[11] she would probably have done so. In 1944 Archer was posted to the newly established SIS Section IX, which was responsible for Soviet and Communist counter-intelligence. Unluckily for British intelligence, but luckily for Soviet espionage, the head of Section IX was none other than Kim Philby. As one of Philby's SIS colleagues, Robert Cecil, later acknowledged, his remarkable success in becoming head of Section IX 'ensured that the whole post-war effort to counter Communist espionage would become known in the Kremlin. The history of espionage records few, if any, comparable masterstrokes.'[12] One of Philby's first priorities was to neutralize the potential threat from Jane Archer, for whom he had a healthy respect: 'After Guy Liddell, Jane was perhaps the ablest professional intelligence officer ever employed by MI5. She had spent a big chunk of a shrewd lifetime studying Communist activity in all its aspects.' Archer's interrogation of the Soviet defector Walter Krivitsky in 1940 had produced 'a tantalizing scrap of information about a young English journalist whom Soviet intelligence had sent to Spain during the Civil War', which Philby, but no one else, had immediately recognized as a reference to himself. 'Jane', he realized, 'would have made a very bad enemy.' Philby therefore diverted her formidable energies to analysing the large amount of intercepted radio traffic on Communist activities in Eastern Europe,[13] thus ensuring that she had no involvement in either the Gouzenko or (almost immediately afterwards) the Volkov defection cases, where her exceptional skills would have been far more productively used.

The lead roles in the British response to the Gouzenko case were thus taken within SIS not by Archer but by Philby, as head of Section IX, and within the Security Service by the head of F Division (counter-subversion), Roger Hollis (later Director General from 1956 to 1965). Philby's first response on hearing the news from Ottawa was one of personal alarm that Gouzenko might have evidence which could lead to his own exposure. His Soviet controller, Boris Krötenschield, reported to the Centre:

STANLEY [Philby] was a bit agitated . . . I tried to calm him down. STANLEY said that in connection with this he may have information of extreme urgency to pass on to us. Therefore STANLEY asks for another meeting in a few days. I refused a meeting but I did allow him to pass on urgent and important information through HICKS [Burgess].[14]

Philby was even more alarmed by news from Istanbul on 19 September about the attempted defection of an NKGB officer stationed in Turkey, Konstantin Dmitrievich Volkov. In late August 1945, a matter of days before Gouzenko defected in Ottawa, Volkov had written to the British vice consul in Istanbul requesting an urgent appointment. Receiving no reply, Volkov had turned up in person on 4 September – the day before Gouzenko first attempted to defect – and in return for political asylum for himself and his wife and £50,000 (about a million pounds at today's value) he offered important files and information which he had obtained while working on the British desk in the Centre. As an indication of the importance of the intelligence he had on offer, Volkov revealed that among the most highly rated British Soviet agents were two in the Foreign Office (no doubt Burgess and Maclean) and seven 'inside the British intelligence system', including one 'fulfilling the function of head of a section of British counter-espionage in London', which was almost certainly a reference to Philby himself.[15] Philby quickly warned Krötenschield of Volkov's threatened defection.[16]

In response to Philby's warning, the Centre took predictably drastic action. On 21 September the Turkish consulate in Moscow issued visas for two Soviet diplomatic couriers (in reality hitmen from the Centre) to travel to Istanbul. The British investigation into the Volkov case would normally have been handled by the head of Security Intelligence Middle East (SIME), whose head, Sir Douglas Roberts, then happened to be in London. Luckily for Philby, Roberts hated flying. Using this as a pretext for involving himself in the case, Philby succeeded in gaining authorization from 'C', Sir Stewart Menzies, to fly to Turkey and deal personally with Volkov. Due to travel delays, Philby did not arrive in Istanbul until 26 September.[17] By then it was too late. Volkov had asked the British vice consul to contact him by phone at the Soviet consulate. But, as Guy Liddell noted in his diary:

The telephone was answered by the Russian Consul General on the first occasion and on the second by a man speaking English claiming to be Wolkoff but [who] clearly was not. Finally contact was made with the Russian telephone operator who said that Wolkoff had left for Moscow.[18]

By then, the Soviet hitmen had done their job. Volkov and his wife, both on stretchers and heavily sedated, had been carried on board a Soviet aircraft bound for Moscow.[19] Under brutal interrogation in Moscow before his execution, Volkov admitted that he had asked the British for political asylum and £50,000, and confessed that he had planned to reveal the names of no fewer than 314 Soviet agents, probably including Philby.[20] As Philby later admitted, the Volkov case had 'proved to be a very narrow squeak indeed'.[21] With slightly less luck in Ottawa earlier in September, Gouzenko would not have been able to defect. With slightly more luck in Istanbul, Volkov would have succeeded in unmasking Philby and disrupting Soviet intelligence operations on a much larger scale than Gouzenko was able to do.

Reassured by Volkov's forcible removal to Moscow that he himself was not in danger, Philby was able to concentrate on limiting the damage to Soviet intelligence caused by Gouzenko's revelations. His first priority was to try to prevent a successful prosecution of his Cambridge contemporary Alan Nunn May, who was unaware that he had been identified by Gouzenko. Philby reported to Moscow that Gouzenko's evidence against May was unlikely to be adequate to secure a conviction. He sent a warning, however, that Gouzenko had revealed that, after returning to Britain, May had a series of meetings scheduled with his Soviet controller in London, beginning on 8 October outside the British Museum, where he was to identify himself by carrying a copy of *The Times* under his left arm.[22] Sir David Petrie took the personal decision that May was to be caught in the act.[23] Though MI5 and the Special Branch kept the meeting point outside the British Museum revealed by Gouzenko under surveillance, neither May nor his new Soviet case officer appeared. Philby reported, doubtless with relief, to his controller on 18 November:

According to MI5, May has not put a foot wrong from the time he arrived in England. He did not establish any suspicious contacts. He does not show any signs of being afraid or worried and continues to work quite normally on his academic research. Bearing this in mind, MI5 came to the conclusion that May is a tough

customer who will not break down under questioning until he is confronted with
fresh and convincing evidence.[24]

But no 'fresh and convincing evidence' turned up. MI5's Legal Adviser,
Colonel Cussen, later acknowledged that, as Philby had indicated to
Moscow:

it was not likely that any evidence against Primrose [May] obtained in Canada
would be admissible without the calling of a Russian official, since it was contained
in telegrams exchanged between Ottawa and Moscow ... If Corby [Gouzenko]
were called at Bow Street [magistrates' court] himself, he would not be able to
identify Primrose whom he had never seen.[25]

Not until the defection of Burgess and Maclean in 1951, which cast suspicion on Philby for the first time, did MI5 begin to suspect that May's
failure to meet his controller after his return to London was due to the fact
that Philby had warned the Centre. Philby probably also warned the Centre
about other Soviet agents identified by Gouzenko who were under British
and American surveillance. Within SIS, Philby was responsible for co-
ordinating intelligence on the case emanating from the FBI and other US
sources, with the assistance of the SIS representative in Washington. On
at least one occasion, an agent identified by Gouzenko was able to escape
from America, probably to the Soviet Union, despite being under active
surveillance by the FBI.[26] A warning to the Centre from Philby may well
have prompted the escape.

For a year and a half before Gouzenko's defection, Philby's aim had
been to establish himself as the leading Soviet counter-espionage expert
within the British intelligence community. As head of Section IX, Philby
had met regularly with Roger Hollis, to discuss Soviet and Communist
affairs. Philby wrote patronizingly in his memoirs: '[Hollis] was a likeable
fellow of cautious bent ... Although he lacked the strain of irresponsibility
which I think is essential (in moderation) to the rounded human being,
we got on well together, and were soon exchanging information without
reserve on either side.'[27] Philby passed on to Moscow the information
which Hollis supplied 'without reserve'. Within a few days of Gouzenko's
defection, Hollis had flown to Ottawa to liaise with the Royal Canadian
Mounted Police (RCMP) and was treated 'as one of their own investigating
team'.[28] The fact that Gouzenko had defected in a Commonwealth capital,
rather than on foreign territory, meant that the Security Service, rather
than SIS, had the lead role in responding to it. Although Hollis's presence
in Canada was unpublicized, he was present during the questioning of

witnesses by the Canadian Royal Commission on the Gouzenko case, and was allowed to examine all the documents and other evidence gathered by the RCMP.[29] When Mackenzie King arrived in Southampton on 7 October 1945 on board the *Queen Mary*, at the beginning of a four-week stay in Britain, Hollis came on board and showed him a telegram from the British ambassador in Washington, Lord Halifax, reporting President Truman's wish that May, who, Gouzenko had revealed, was due to meet his Russian contact next day outside the British Museum, should not be arrested 'unless it was obviously necessary for security reasons and then only if he were discovered to be communicating some document of a Top Secret nature to the man he was to meet':

The President felt very strongly that there should be an agreement on the matter . . . Every effort should be made to secure further information in the US and also Britain before action was precipitated. [It was] also most important to have complete understanding between the countries immediately concerned first.[30]

Mackenzie King told Hollis that he agreed with Truman. In the event, of course, neither May nor his Soviet controller turned up for the meeting outside the British Museum. Unaware of Philby's treachery, MI5 was left agonizing over the reasons why the prearranged rendezvous did not take place.

During Mackenzie King's stay in London, the Canadian permanent secretary for external affairs, Norman Robertson, agreed at a meeting with the DG, Sir David Petrie, that no action should be taken on Gouzenko's revelations until after Attlee and Mackenzie King had conferred with Truman in Washington.[31] Meanwhile, the role of the Security Service in the Gouzenko case, as in most other cases, remained entirely secret. When the case was publicly discussed again five years later after the conviction of the atom spy Klaus Fuchs, the Commonwealth Secretary, Patrick Gordon Walker, still believed it 'particularly important to avoid saying that we have or did have security officers in Canada'.[32]

May was first questioned at Harwell, Britain's first atomic energy research centre, by Commander Leonard Burt of Scotland Yard on 15 February 1946, the day after the Gouzenko case became public knowledge. Burt informed Guy Liddell that, when told by the Harwell security officer that someone wanted to see him, May 'turned as white as a sheet, and was very near collapse'. During questioning by Burt:

He failed to answer any questions except in a plain negative. He made one rather curious remark when asked whether he would be prepared to assist the authorities:

'Not if it's counter-espionage.' Asked what he meant he was unable to explain. His usual answer was 'The answer is no,' after several minutes of silence.

Liddell noted, 'There is no doubt from his demeanour that he is guilty.'[33] On 20 February skilful interrogation by Burt convinced May that the case against him was very much stronger than it actually was. Liddell observed in his diary: 'The point I think that shook May more than anything was Burt's reference to the proposed meeting [with a GRU officer] in London.' May signed a statement admitting he had been approached by a 'Soviet agent', whom he refused to identify, and had given him a report on atomic research together with two samples of uranium:

He had done this because he thought it was in the general interest that the Russians should be kept in the picture, and should share in the experimental work. He knew about the appointment in London but had not kept it as he felt that since so much information had been public on atomic research there was no need to communicate any more.[34]

May's explanation for missing the rendezvous with his London controller was a lie. Over half a century later, shortly before his death, he finally admitted that he had received a warning from Soviet intelligence (no doubt prompted by Philby's warning to Moscow) 'and so did not turn up to this meeting'.[35]

Mackenzie King was surprised as well as delighted by May's confession on 20 February 1946. It was, he wrote, 'the best piece of news we have had yet'. It would demonstrate that there were British as well as Canadian lapses of security and enable a trial which, the Canadian Prime Minister was confident, would lead to similar trials in the United States. May pleaded guilty at the Central Criminal Court on 1 May to charges of breaking the Official Secrets Act by handing to a person unknown 'information which was calculated to be or might be useful to an enemy'. After a trial lasting only a day, he was sentenced to ten years' penal servitude. When news reached Los Alamos of May's arrest, the wife of one of the British scientists commented, 'I knew him fairly well. But I don't know how you would describe him. He was like – why he was rather like Klaus [Fuchs] here.' Fuchs, who was later revealed as the most important of the British atom spies, is said to have smiled politely and commented that he did not think May could have told the Russians anything of real importance.[36] Though Fuchs did not say so, he probably concluded correctly that Gouzenko had no intelligence which incriminated him. When the net began to close around Fuchs in 1949, Philby was able once again to warn the Centre.[37]

Philby's repeated attempts to dominate the British handling of the Gouzenko case eventually led to complaints from the Security Service. On 19 February 1946, Philby prepared a draft memorandum on Gouzenko's defection which he claimed that Sir Stewart Menzies, 'C', wished to circulate to the directors of intelligence in the armed services.[38] Hollis was quick to protest:

I feel that the question of circulating this document from your office to the Directors of Intelligence is a matter of some embarrassment. The case took place in Canada and has ramifications in this country and in both Canada and here the security responsibility rests on our office and not on yours. The close cooperation which we have had over this case has, of course, given you just as much information as we have about it and as you know, we have welcomed this. But when it comes to putting out such a paper to the Directors of Intelligence, it may, I am afraid, give the impression that the responsible department is yours and not M.I.5.

Hollis suggested sending a covering letter to the service directors making it clear that MI5, not SIS, was 'the department responsible for dealing with counter-espionage in the Empire' and had approved the circular. He also noted a number of misleading statements in Philby's draft which he politely termed 'small inaccuracies'. Philby had failed to give the service directors a clear indication of the kind of intelligence which the GRU was collecting in Canada. Hollis generously, but mistakenly, assumed that Philby had been motivated by a desire to protect the security of the Gouzenko case. 'Perhaps you hedged on this', he told Philby, 'so as to avoid giving the Directors of Intelligence too much detailed information.' Other inaccuracies in Philby's draft included his failure to mention that the Canadian Communist Party had acted as talent spotters for Soviet intelligence – a revelation which might have caused the service directors to investigate the wartime role of British Communists in the armed forces.[39] Philby's reputation in the Security Service, none the less, remained high. Liddell was 'profoundly sorry' to be told in September 1946 that Philby was leaving to become head of station in Istanbul and doubtful whether his successor would be nearly as good.[40]

Liddell also had great respect for Gouzenko, whom he found 'extremely alert and intelligent' during a visit to Canada in March 1946:

I asked him how it was that Russia had been going on in its present state for 28 years and how it was that the Russian people fought so well. He said that if I had been brought up on Marxian dialectics from the age of 6, if I had heard nothing but Soviet press and radio telling me that conditions abroad were far worse than any conditions in Russia, in fact that the rest of the world was living in squalor and revolution, if I had known what it was to walk down a street with my best friend and feel I could not talk freely, and if I had had no opportunity of comparing my standards with those of anybody else, I should have been thinking as he did before he came to Canada. The impact of Canadian conditions was so ter[r]ific that he had been completely converted and had realised that from his youth up he had been deceived. He said that although he was under guard day and night by 3 officers of the RCMP he had never felt freer.

Gouzenko added that Liddell could have no idea what it meant to him just to be able to go out and buy a bag of oranges and a pound of hamburger. Liddell noted in his diary that, with rationing in force in Britain, it actually meant 'quite a lot' to him too.[41]

Gouzenko's evidence contained one puzzle which continued to confuse, and at times torment, MI5 for over thirty years. He revealed that there had been two Soviet agents codenamed ELLI. One was quickly identified as Kay Willsher, deputy registrar in the British high commission in Ottawa, who was sentenced to three years' imprisonment in March 1946 for breaches of the Official Secrets Act. The identity of the second and more important ELLI remained a mystery until the 1980s.[42] A series of conspiracy theorists, chief among them the maverick MI5 officer Peter Wright, succeeded in convincing themselves and many of their readers that ELLI was none other than Roger Hollis, who had been working as a Soviet agent throughout the Gouzenko investigation.[43] In reality, probably no other senior MI5 officer during the Second World War had placed more emphasis on the continuing threat from Soviet espionage and the need to maintain comprehensive surveillance of the British Communist Party. The KGB found the Hollis conspiracy theory so bizarre that some of its foreign intelligence officers suspected that it derived from 'some mysterious, internal British intrigue'.[44]

The second ELLI was finally uncovered only after the high-flying SIS penetration agent Oleg Gordievsky was posted to the KGB London residency in 1982. Gordievsky identified ELLI as Leo Long, whom Anthony Blunt had run as a sub-agent in military intelligence during the war. Long, like Blunt, had been an NKGB (later KGB) agent – thus accounting for the fact that Gouzenko (who had worked for the GRU, not the NKGB) could provide only fragmentary information about him. Long had probably come briefly to Gouzenko's attention because the GRU had made an approach to him in 1943, only to be warned off by the NKGB from making further contact with its agent.[45] It is now clear that an important clue which could have identified Long much earlier was overlooked by

British intelligence for almost forty years. A substantial minority of Second World War KGB codenames contained important clues to the identities of the agents. The first codename of the Fifth Man in the Cambridge Magnificent Five, John Cairncross, MOLIÈRE, was derived from the subject of his academic research, on which he published two books. Anthony Blunt's remarkably unimaginative first codename was TONY. The youngest major KGB agent of the Second World War, Ted Hall, one of the leading atom spies, was codenamed MLAD, 'Youngster'. The Hollywood producer Boris Morros was codenamed FROST – the English translation of the Russian word *moroz*. The codename ELLI can be translated from Russian as 'Ls', the plural of the roman letter 'L'. LL were the initials of Leo Long. Had this clue been spotted during the original investigation, Peter Wright's conspiracy theories might well have grown to less preposterous proportions.

In addition to leaving behind one major puzzle which took British intelligence nearly forty years to solve, the Gouzenko case also helped to generate one serious misunderstanding. An early report on the case, circulated by Philby, considerably exaggerated the quality of Soviet intelligence which it appeared to reveal: 'The general impression of the GRU obtained from Corby [Gouzenko] is that it is an extremely efficient intelligence system, demanding the highest standards of work and security, and suffering partly from over-centralisation.'[46] Throughout the Cold War, as in the aftermath of the Gouzenko case, the British and American intelligence communities regularly failed to grasp the huge gulf which separated Soviet intelligence collection, which enjoyed some remarkable successes, from Soviet intelligence assessment, which (save in the sphere of scientific and technological intelligence) was frequently dismal. As in all one-party states, Soviet political intelligence assessment was constrained by the need to tell the political leadership what it wanted to hear. 'Telling truth to power' was not a serious option.

As well as uncovering a major Soviet espionage network in Canada with British connections, the Gouzenko case made the more far-sighted in the Security Service realize how much they still did not know about Soviet intelligence operations. In October 1946 John Curry sent a forceful memorandum to the DDG, Guy Liddell, arguing that the Service must make a strong and convincing case for extra counter-espionage resources: 'We are now in a position vis-à-vis Russia similar to that we had vis-à-vis Germany in 1939/1940 in the sense that we have little positive knowledge of the basic structure of the organisation which we have to counter.'[47] Not until SIGINT began providing important clues in 1948 did the Service's hunt for Soviet agents start to make real progress.[48]

2

Zionist Extremists and Counter-Terrorism

The Security Service's main concern at the beginning of Sir Percy Sillitoe's term as director general was not, as is usually supposed, the looming Cold War with the Soviet Union but the threat from Middle Eastern terrorism during the final years of the Palestine mandate (given to Britain by the League of Nations in 1922). The terrorists came not, as later in the twentieth century, from Palestinian or Islamist groups but from the Zionist extremists of the Irgun Zvai Leumi and the Stern Gang (also known as Lehi after its Hebrew acronym), who believed that the creation of an independent Jewish state required and legitimated the use of terror against the British administration. Both, the Security Service believed, were increasing in size. The Stern Gang was thought to have an active membership of about 500, the Irgun several times as many.[1] The Stern Gang was among the last groups in the world to describe itself publicly as a 'terrorist' organization.[2] Both it and the Irgun, the Service believed, were planning to extend their operations to Britain. For the only time before the closing years of the Cold War, counter-terrorism thus became a higher Service priority than counter-espionage.

The Security Service had no specialist counter-terrorist department. B3a in the Intelligence Division[3] at Leconfield House was mainly responsible for dealing with Zionist terrorism and other Middle Eastern matters. In the Middle East the responsibility fell to the interdepartmental SIME (Security Intelligence Middle East) in Cairo, which controlled a network of defence security officers (DSOs), later renamed security liaison officers (SLOs), and liaised with B3a. Though SIME had been primarily a military organization during the war, in December 1946 it was transferred to the control of the Security Service with the flamboyant Alex Kellar as its head.[4] Kellar is thought to have been the inspiration for the 'man in cream cuffs' in John le Carré's *Call for the Dead*, played in the film by Max Adrian wearing a dragon-patterned silk dressing gown with a purple handkerchief and a rose in his buttonhole.[5] In the summer of 1947 he suffered a breakdown after being diagnosed with suspected amoebic dysentery and returned to London. Kellar's far more robust successor, Bill Magan, who had begun his career in an Indian cavalry regiment, was admiringly described to his wife Maxine before their wedding in New Delhi in 1940 as 'a Cavalry officer who actually reads a book'. Though suffering on the day of the wedding from a relapse of malaria with a temperature of 103°, Magan characteristically declined to postpone the ceremony.[6] He was well aware that his views did not commend themselves to the Jewish Agency, which was preparing for the foundation of the State of Israel: 'I said, "You may pack a couple of million Jews into your little Jewish state, but you will be for ever more surrounded by two hundred million Muslims who will never leave you alone."' Magan also knew that he was high on the Zionist terrorist target list.[7]

In March 1946, B3a received information from a 'reliable' source in Palestine, in 'direct contact' with the Stern Gang, that 'terrorists are now training their members for the purpose of proceeding to England to assassinate members of His Majesty's Government'.[8] The wartime track record of Zionist terrorists ensured that such reports were taken seriously. In November 1944 the Stern Gang had assassinated the British Minister of State in the Middle East, Lord Moyne, and Zionist extremists had made several attempts to murder the British high commissioner for Palestine, Sir Ronald MacMichael. Shortly before Sir David Petrie was succeeded as DG by Sillitoe, he concluded in a minute on the Zionist threat that 'the red light is definitely showing.'[9] In July 1946 Irgun, headed by the future Israeli prime minister Menachem Begin, blew up the British Palestine HQ in the King David Hotel in Jerusalem with 500 pounds of explosives packed into milk-churns.[10] Ninety-one lives were lost,[11] five of them staff engaged locally by the Security Service. All staff from Head Office survived. One eyewitness later recalled three of the 'London ladies' staggering from the ruins of the hotel with ceiling plaster in their hair and 'looking like the wrath of God'. They showed 'no hysteria – they were marvellous'.[12]

Both Irgun and the Stern Gang were also believed to be plotting the assassination of the British Foreign Secretary, Ernest Bevin, who became a figure of hate for many Zionists during the first year of the Attlee government. On his arrival at the Foreign Office in July 1945, proud of his pre-war record as Britain's most successful trade union negotiator, Bevin had rashly boasted that he would stake his 'political future' on securing a settlement between Jews and Arabs in Palestine. He also had a reputation as a committed supporter of the establishment of a Jewish state. Within days of becoming foreign secretary, however, he had changed his mind.

'Clem,' he told the Prime Minister, 'about Palestine. According to my lads in the Office, we've got it wrong. We've got to think again.' Though President Truman urged Attlee to admit 100,000 Jewish refugees to Palestine immediately, the Labour government imposed a limit of 1,500 immigrants a month (a limit Labour leaders had previously opposed). With remarkable insensitivity, Bevin joked to the Labour Party conference in June 1946, little more than a year after the liberation of the last Nazi concentration and death camps, that the United States supported mass Jewish immigration into Palestine 'because they did not want too many of them in New York'.[13]

According to an intelligence report from Palestine on 23 August 1946, a month after the bombing of the King David Hotel: '. . . Irgun and Stern have decided to send 5 cells to London to operate in a manner similar to I.R.A. To use their own words "beat the dog in his own kennel".'[14] Sillitoe included this warning written in red ink as a stop-press addition to a note entitled 'Threatened Jewish Activity in the United Kingdom, Palestine and Elsewhere', which he handed to Attlee shortly afterwards. He added that Bevin was believed to have been marked out for assassination.[15] The Security Service reported in September 1946 that most Stern Gang recruits were 'desperate men and women who count their own lives cheap':

In recent months it has been reported that they have been training selected members for the purpose of proceeding overseas and assassinating a prominent British personality – special reference having been made several times to Mr Bevin in this connection.[16]

The apparent threat to Bevin was given added emphasis by reports in the autumn of 1946 that the leader of the Irgun, Menachem Begin, had disappeared from the Middle East; MI5 and SIS sources believed that he was in Paris and intending to travel secretly to Britain. (In reality Begin remained in Palestine until late in 1948.) An SIS source reported that Begin had undergone plastic surgery to alter his appearance – though, SIS noted, 'We have no description of the new face.'[17] Though Begin had not in fact undergone plastic surgery, there was considerable confusion about his appearance. Jerusalem CID had obtained two photographs of him. One, in Begin's view, was a fairly good likeness; the other, which the CID believed to be Begin's military identity card, 'bore only a slight resemblance' to him but had a somewhat villainous appearance. Largely for that reason, Begin believed, the CID relied on the latter photograph when hunting for him. Begin confused them further by growing a beard and drastically limiting the circle of those able to identify his bearded self. When he agreed to give a secret interview to the writer Arthur Koestler, his security guards insisted that they meet in a darkened room. Koestler chain-smoked throughout the interview, drawing heavily on his cigarettes in the vain hope of generating enough glow to enable him to catch a glimpse of Begin. According to Begin, the myth of his plastic surgery was confirmed in the minds of British intelligence when a leading Irgun activist, imprisoned in Cairo, was asked about the surgery during interrogation and replied in apparent alarm (but with the real intention of adding to British confusion): 'How did you know that? No, no, it's not true!'[18]

Irgun dramatically demonstrated its ability to carry out attacks in Europe in October 1946 by blowing up most of the British embassy in Rome – a clear indication, the Security Service believed, of what Irgun was planning in the UK. MI5 reasonably assumed that if Irgun and the Stern Gang set up terrorist cells in Britain, they would be assisted by British Zionist extremists.[19] In addition to intelligence from SIME and agent reports in Britain, B3a depended on intercepted communications and 'technical coverage' of some British Zionists which led to the identification and surveillance of a number of individuals involved with Irgun and the Stern Gang. SIGINT had been a major part of British intelligence-gathering in the Middle East ever since the establishment of an intercept station at Sarafand in Palestine in 1923. Alastair Denniston, the interwar head of the Government Code and Cypher School (GC&CS), the predecessor of GCHQ, paid tribute in 1944 to the 'close liaison between GC&CS and Sarafand' over the previous twenty years.[20] MI5's Middle Eastern section found the wartime SIGINT derived from intercepted Zionist communications of 'considerable assistance'.[21] It continued to do so after the war.

In Palestine, Begin wrote later, 'There is no disputing that . . . the names of many hundreds of officers and men of the Irgun Zvai Leumi were given to the British police by official Jewish institutions and their liaison officers.'[22] Among those who provided names was Teddy Kollek, later famous as a long-serving mayor of Jerusalem, who in 1942 had become the Jewish Agency's deputy head of intelligence. From January 1945 to May 1946 Kollek was the Agency's chief external liaison officer in Jerusalem, in regular touch with both the main MI5 representative, DSO Palestine, and SIME, to whom he gave intelligence on 'intended terrorist activities'.[23] In November 1946 the DDG, Guy Liddell, briefed Attlee on the Service's relations with Kollek and other Jewish Agency representatives in Palestine and Cairo:

I told him that the measure of this co-operation was limited; it had never led to the actual pin-pointing of terrorists – it had generally taken the form of notifying us that something was likely to happen somewhere within the next 24 or 48 hours, or that the terrorist was believed to be in Jerusalem. In fact, the Agency told the authorities just as much as they thought was good for them and had always endeavoured to keep the strings in their own hands and to imply that they were the people who were governing Palestine and not the British Government. The P.M. remarked that they were singularly tortuous people to deal with.[24]

In fact the intelligence supplied by the Jewish Agency had sometimes been more specific than Liddell suggested. On 10 August 1945, for example, Kollek revealed the location of a secret Irgun training camp near Binyamina and told an MI5 officer it would be 'a great idea to raid the place'. The raid led to the arrest of twenty-seven Irgun members.[25]

The Security Service also had contacts in London with the Jewish Agency and official British Zionist organizations whose leaders were anxious that terrorism in Palestine should not spread to Britain and were willing to provide intelligence on Irgun and the Stern Gang.[26] Service co-operation with mainstream British Zionism, however, was combined with close surveillance. MI5 successfully applied for Home Office Warrants (HOWs) to enable it to intercept the correspondence and tap the telephones of all the important Zionist organizations in Britain: both the mainstream Jewish Agency and Jewish Legion and the smaller, extremist United Zionist Revisionists (UZR) and United Zionist Youth Organization (better known by its Hebrew acronym, Betar).[27] The Security Service became particularly concerned about Betar, of which Begin had been a teenage militant in interwar Poland, and which trained its post-war members to 'go into Palestine in order to build, defend and fight for the Jewish state'. According to reports reaching MI5, the Betar organization in Palestine had close links to the Irgun. The Service feared that the British Betar would establish similar links.[28] The HOW on its London HQ identified a number of visitors who had connections with the Stern Gang and Irgun, and were involved in the illegal purchase of arms.[29] By September 1946 the Security Service was receiving detailed reports on support for terrorism by British Zionist extremists from two agents, one in the UZR and the other in Betar, both run by Captain F. C. Derbyshire.[30] More reassuringly, Security Service investigations concluded that the Jewish Agency and other mainstream official bodies had distanced themselves from the extremist UZR and Betar.[31]

In November 1946 an Irgun defector, who claimed to have been 'shocked by the King David Hotel operation', provided important intelligence on other planned attacks, as well as revealing the location of the Irgun's

Jerusalem headquarters (which contained only files when it was raided) and a large arms cache.[32] The defector knew far less about planned attacks in Britain. After being brought to London for questioning by the Security Service and the Metropolitan Police Special Branch (MPSB), he claimed that 'Attempts to carry out acts of sabotage in U.K. will definitely be attempted.' When asked for details by his interrogators, he replied, not very helpfully, 'All I can say is that if they attempt anything they will try to sabotage buildings.'[33] The warning, while vague, turned out to be well founded – though the main threat came from the Stern Gang rather than Irgun.[34]

On 15 April 1947 the Stern Gang almost succeeded in blowing up the Colonial Office in Whitehall. A bomb containing twenty-four sticks of explosive failed to detonate only because the timer failed. Commander Leonard Burt, head of the Special Branch, believed that if the bomb had gone off, the damage might have been as bad as that inflicted on the King David Hotel in Jerusalem nine months earlier.[35] In June 1947, following earlier death threats, the Stern Gang posted twenty-one letter bombs from Italy to Bevin, Attlee, Churchill, Anthony Eden and other British notables.[36] Several reached their destination but failed to explode; the GPO was then warned and the others were intercepted before they could be delivered.[37] Explosives experts at the Home Office reported that all were potentially lethal.[38] On 2 June, shortly before the letter bombs reached England, two Stern Gang terrorists, Betty Knouth (also known as Gilberte or Elizabeth Lazarus) and Jacob Elias, were arrested at the Belgian frontier as they were about to cross into France. Envelopes addressed to British officials, together with detonators, batteries and a time fuse, were discovered in the false bottom of Knouth's suitcase.[39] Knouth was sentenced to a year's imprisonment and Elias to eight months for carrying concealed explosives. At a Stern Gang press conference in Tel Aviv after her release, the twenty-two-year-old Knouth said in reply to questions: 'Did I post letter bombs? Unfortunately, the Belgian police got me before I could do so. They are a Stern Gang patent, you know . . . Belgian experts said they were deadly. I'm sorry none of them was delivered.' Among the intended recipients of the letter bombs was the former Chief Secretary of the Palestine administration, Sir John Shaw, later head of the Security Service Overseas Division.[40]

'Elias' had a much longer track record as a terrorist than Knouth. When his fingerprints were sent to London, his real identity was discovered to be Yaacov Levstein,[41] who had been a Stern Gang terrorist in Palestine throughout the war and was believed to be responsible for the deaths of a number of police officers as well as an attempt on the life of the high

STERN GANG GIVE BOMB GIRL A PARTY

From ERIC GREY

TEL AVIV, Tuesday.—The Stern Gang threw a café party today for a 22-year-old girl from Paris.

Mlle. Betty Knouth was sentenced to a year in a Belgian prison, as Elizabeth Lazarus, for smuggling gelignite to be used in terrorist letter-bombs.

She served eight months, returned to Paris, and is now in Palestine as a reporter for a Paris newspaper. The Stern Gang's party was to let her meet the Press.

She fought with the French Maquis when she was 15. After the war, she says, " I was asked to join Haganah, Irgun and Stern "—three Jewish armed organisations. " I chose the Stern group—it seemed the best of the three.

" Did I post letter bombs ? Unfortunately, the Belgian police got me before I could do so.

I'M SORRY

" They are a Stern Gang patent, you know. One was addressed to Sir Alan Cunningham, another to Sir John Shaw [former Chief Secretary of the Palestine Government and now Governor of Trinidad]. I forget to whom the others were addressed.

" Belgian experts said they were deadly. I'm sorry none of them was delivered."

I asked her if she had anything to do with the bomb in the Colonial Office last March.

" Scotland Yard could give you very precise details about that," she replied, " but I don't consider this the right time to talk about it. We are still at war with Britain. But my terrorist days are over and done with now. I'm just a reporter. I hope to settle down in Israel one day."

BETTY KNOUTH
' Bombs were deadly '

Daily Express, 25 August 1948.

commissioner. He had been sentenced to life imprisonment (subsequently commuted to ten years) in 1942, but had escaped from jail after eight months.[42] Levstein's fingerprints were discovered on the timing device of the bomb which failed to explode at the Colonial Office on 15 April. The Security Service believed, however, that the bomb had been planted by Betty Knouth. She fitted the description of an attractive young woman who had been seen at the Colonial Office, carrying a distinctive blue-leather mitre-shaped handbag, which was still in her possession when she was arrested. Knouth admitted arriving in London on 11 April and leaving on the 15th.[43] When asked at the Stern Gang press conference after her release from prison whether she 'had anything to do with the bomb in the Colonial Office', Knouth replied: 'Scotland Yard could give you very precise details about that, but I don't consider this the right time to talk about it. We are still at war with Britain. But my terrorist days are over and done with now.'[44]

While investigations were continuing on the continent, the Security Service simultaneously discovered within Britain a group of Zionist 'conspirators' led by two north London Jews, Leo Bella and Harry Isaac Presman, whose aim, it reported, 'was undoubtedly to organise acts of terrorism in this country'. Bella was a stateless company director of Russian origin; Presman was a British subject also of Russian origin, and the director of a firm of chemical manufacturers.[45] 'Bella and his associates' were believed to be involved in the April 1947 letter-bomb campaign.[46] Telephone tapping (telechecks) of Bella and Presman revealed that, though both usually spoke in guarded terms, they were obtaining explosives which, it was believed, were intended for terrorist attacks in Britain.[47] The summary of a telecheck on 15 July records: 'Pressman [sic] says that he has got that Barium nitrate potassium chloride. Bella asks if it is possible to get a pound or two. Presman thinks so – he will post them to Bella, unless somebody is going that way in which case he will send them by hand.'[48]

Covert surveillance of Presman's attempts to stockpile weapons and explosives were interrupted by the unexpected discovery on 19 July by Presman's chauffeur, Charles Whiting (who was unaware of his employer's terrorist connections), of twenty-four hand grenades and twenty-four detonators in a lock-up garage recently vacated by Presman. What followed provides a striking and somewhat comic illustration of post-war London's unpreparedness for terrorist attacks. Since this was an era when 'bobbies on the beat' were a much more visible part of life in the capital than they have since become, Whiting went out into the street to look for one and saw Pc 560N passing on horseback. After inspecting the grenades and detonators, Pc 560N told Whiting to take them to Stoke Newington police station in Presman's Rover, which he duly did.[49] When questioned by the police, however, Presman denied all knowledge of the weapons in the garage:

. . . Presman now declares that he is not responsible because he recently sub-let the garage No. 2 to an unknown man. He cannot now produce the man concerned and we cannot accept his story. He appears to have made some moves to support his alibi in the event of disclosure . . .[50]

Improbable though Presman's explanation was, there was insufficient evidence for a prosecution – particularly after Whiting made a further statement on 22 July in support of his employer's alibi. Presman, he declared, had 'refreshed my memory [about] certain incidents and I feel sure this is the true story . . .'[51] Probably as a result of the discovery of the weapons in the garage and questioning by the Special Branch on his 'possession of extremist Jewish literature',[52] Presman seems to have decided to lie low. No further evidence came to light of his links to terrorist groups.[53] Unlike Presman, Bella appears to have been unaware that he was under suspicion. The Security Service continued to regard him as 'the chief organiser in the UK of a Revisionist movement reported to be in contact with the HQ of a terrorist organisation in Paris, consisting of members of the Irgun Zvai Leumi and Stern Gang'.[54]

By the beginning of 1947 Bevin's rash initial optimism that he could engineer a negotiated settlement of the Palestinian problem had evaporated. 'I am', he confessed, 'at the end of my tether.'[55] In February, unable to devise a settlement acceptable to both Jews and Arabs, Britain handed over the Palestine problem to the United Nations, which voted nine months later for partition. British attempts to stop 'illegal' Jewish immigration which exceeded the 1,500 monthly quota, however, continued to exacerbate the mutual antagonism between Zionists and the British authorities. David Ben-Gurion, later Israel's first prime minister, declared that Britain had 'proclaimed war against Zionism'.[56] The earlier flow of intelligence from the Jewish Agency in Palestine seems to have dried up. In June Guy Liddell inveighed in his diary against what he believed was the 'duplicity' of the Agency, which regarded as equally duplicitous British restrictions on Jewish immigration. The British administration in Palestine, Liddell believed, lacked the intelligence necessary to wage a successful counter-terrorist campaign:

What was really lacking was positive information on what the Irgun were going to do next Friday. Only with information of this kind was it possible to suppress terrorism. It was difficult, or almost impossible, to obtain owing to the hostile or terrorised attitude of the population. The Police clearly [had] been let down over a long period both in strength and efficiency, and it was difficult to build them up in the present circumstances.[57]

In July 1947, a month after Liddell's diary entry, the Irgun captured two British sergeants from British military intelligence in Natanya and used them as hostages to try to secure the release of three of their members awaiting execution after being convicted of terrorist attacks.[58] When the Irgun members were executed, the bodies of the two British sergeants were found hanging in an orange grove. Their corpses had been booby-trapped and a British officer was seriously injured when he attempted to cut them down.[59]

Intelligence had greater success in restricting what Britain declared was illegal Jewish immigration. The Security Service believed that, as a result of its penetration of the Jewish organizations in London and other intelligence sources, 'only one out of some thirty ships carrying illegal immigrants reached their destination.'[60] The most controversial case was that of the *Exodus*, intercepted off Palestine in July 1947 with 4,500 Jewish 'illegal immigrants' on board, whom Bevin ordered to be forcibly returned to refugee camps in Germany. As the captain of the *Exodus* later recalled, Zionist intelligence officers 'gave us orders that this ship was to be used as a big demonstration with banners to show how poor and weak and helpless we were, and how cruel the British were'. Newspaper photographs around the world showed apparently brutish British soldiers manhandling defenceless Jews.[61]

Though attacks on British forces and officials in Palestine continued right up to the end of the mandate in 1948, both Irgun and the Stern Gang failed to mount a major attack within the United Kingdom. By the end of 1947, with the approach of Israeli independence and a looming Arab–Jewish conflict in Palestine, the Security Service believed that the threat of Zionist terrorist attacks in the UK had passed the acute phase. In order to 'lighten the load' on the transcribers, the labour-intensive telephone check on the UZR head office had been suspended, along with checks on three leading Revisionist militants. Of the four militants on whom telephone checks remained in place, only two, Samuel Landman and Leo Bella, still gave rise to serious concern – neither, however, in connection with an imminent terrorist threat to Britain:

We are at present investigating what appears to be an attempt to set up an international service designed to collect funds and intelligence on behalf of the Irgun Zvai Leumi. The [telephone] check on Landman, who appears to be taking the lead in organising the projected service, keeps us informed of his numerous contacts, of the nature of the business he is discussing with them, and, at the moment, of what appears to be a leakage at Cabinet level.

Although Landman figures as the chief conspirator in this scheme, Bella remains the chief suspect by reason of his past association with the terrorist organisation in Paris and the liaison which he is believed to maintain with the Irgun Zvai Leumi, through the medium of his brother in Paris.[62]

That the Security Service was right to take the continued threat of extremist Zionist terrorism seriously was shown by the assassination in Palestine in the summer of 1948 of the president of the Swedish Red Cross, Count Bernadotte, for allegedly siding with the British in his recommendations to the UN for the future partition of the country.[63] The failure of Irgun and the Stern Gang to achieve their ambition of killing Bevin or another senior figure in London reflected both the lack of serious support for terrorism among British Zionists and the stronger protective security in Britain compared with Palestine.

The intelligence obtained from an HOW on Samuel Landman initially suggested that one of his contacts was passing him information from a Jewish member of the Attlee government, Emmanuel 'Manny' Shinwell, in 1947 successively Minister of Fuel and Power and Secretary of State for War. B3a reported in November 1947:

There have been various indications that Landman has contacts with, and is getting information from, official Government circles, through a friend of his named 'Stanley' ... not definitely identified ... The first mention of these contacts is on 31st October, when Landman mentions that 'he' (probably Stanley) is going to the House of Commons to see Shinwell and has also had a telephone conversation with Bevin's secretary.

On the next day Stanley gives Landman an account of his meeting with 'Mannie' (probably Emmanuel Shinwell) who has promised to do everything in his power during the moving [of a parliamentary Bill] for which he will have entire responsibility.[64]

... Stanley says he has an appointment to see the Prime Minister on Tuesday afternoon (4th November) if the latter is back from Holland. If he is not back by then Stanley will see 'Ernie' [Bevin] instead. Landman will give Stanley all the necessary material for presentation to the Prime Minister or to Stanley's friend (presumably Shinwell) who, according to Stanley, has been given full power by Attlee (?) to deal with the whole problem.[65]

Further investigation revealed that Landman's claims of influence via Stanley on Shinwell and the Attlee government were based on a mixture of invention and exaggeration. The Service regarded Landman as deeply untrustworthy. As a solicitor in 1938 he had been suspended for three years by the Disciplinary Committee of the Law Society for misappropriation of clients' funds.[66] During the Second World War Landman was regarded by both the Service and Scotland Yard as 'a rogue who has been preying upon ignorant clients and upon anyone else who offers a chance of making easy money'.[67]

Landman's friend 'Stanley' was discovered to be the confidence trickster and undischarged bankrupt Sidney Stanley, a Polish Jew who was probably the most flamboyant fraudster to prey on post-war British public life. His claims of influence with the Attlee government were characteristically overblown. He had indeed made the acquaintance of Manny Shinwell, then Secretary of State for War, who had sought his services as a fixer to find his son Ernie a job.[68] Stanley acquired confidential information on the disbandment of the Transjordan Frontier Force,[69] for which the War Office may (or may not) have been the source.[70] Stanley also met Ernie Bevin at a dinner party which he had organized and paid for, while arranging for the invitations to go out in the name of a prominent Labour Party member.[71] On the strength of their conversation, he later tried unsuccessfully to arrange a private meeting with Bevin through his private secretary.[72] Stanley's claim to Landman that he had an appointment with Attlee and would see Bevin instead if the Prime Minister failed to return in time from abroad was pure invention – as was Stanley's alleged ability to sway votes 'in an area where the Government need support'.[73]

Late in 1948 Sidney Stanley was the star witness at a tribunal set up to investigate allegations of corruption among members of the government and Whitehall officials. Presided over by Mr Justice Lynskey, the Tribunal heard sixty witnesses and a million words of evidence in an oak-panelled hall at Church House, Westminster. The sometimes exotic revelations of high-living and subterranean intrigue in an era of post-war austerity so captured the imagination of newspaper readers that they were dubbed 'the great breakfast serial'. John Belcher, Parliamentary Secretary at the Board of Trade, who had received lavish hospitality and presents from Stanley, as well as seeing him or speaking to him on the phone at least once a day,[74] announced his resignation even before the Tribunal concluded, on the grounds, said his Counsel, 'that although he did not receive these bribes corruptly, nor did he allow them to influence him in any way in any decision he had to make, they are incompatible with his position as a Minister of the Crown'.[75] Belcher acknowledged that he had 'found Mr Stanley to be interesting, amusing, generous in his nature and in general a good companion'. Stanley's geniality and flamboyance during the Tribunal were almost as striking as the unreliability of his evidence. Under questioning by the Attorney General, Sir Hartley Shawcross, he replied at one point, 'Do not try to trap me with the truth.' After Shawcross's final address to the Tribunal, Stanley told him, 'That was a fine speech. Thank you, Sir Hartley. I have been a fool, I admit it.' 'If you say so, Mr Stanley,' replied the Attorney General, 'I am sure it must be true.' Stanley was equally gracious to the Scotland Yard superintendent who had been in charge of investigating his affairs. 'Thank you very much,' Stanley told him. 'You have played the game.'[76]

Stanley's cheerfulness at the end of a tribunal which had exposed him as a fraud probably reflected his relief that he had not also been exposed as a member of the Irgun intelligence network in Britain. During the Tribunal hearings, the Chief of SIS, Sir Stewart Menzies, personally informed Sillitoe that he had 'learned from a reliable informant' that Stanley was 'part of a group of extreme Zionists intent on running arms to Palestine'.[77] In the Commons debate on the findings of the Lynskey Tribunal on 3 February 1949, Attlee announced that the government had decided that it would be 'conducive to the public good' for Stanley to be deported. What he did not reveal to the House was that the main threat which Stanley posed was far less the much reduced risk that he would corrupt people in public life than that he would assist Irgun.[78]

Kim Philby, like his masters in Soviet intelligence, secretly welcomed the terrorist campaign against the British mandate in Palestine as a blow to British imperialism in the Middle East inflicted by 'progressive' Jews of Russian and Polish origin. According to a B3a report, the newly appointed secretary general of the United Zionist Revisionists, C. Ben Aron, told the UZR North-West London Area Council on 19 May 1947:

There is every hope that the Russians will succeed in helping the Jews against the British, by demanding the withdrawal of British troops from Palestine. The tasks of the Revisionists at present [are] to foster unrest and difficulties in Palestine, and to thus force Britain to give up the mandate.[79]

The arms supplied to the Zionists from Czechoslovakia with Moscow's blessing during the first Arab–Israeli War in 1948 (known to Israelis as the War of Independence and to Arabs as al-Nakbah, 'the Disaster'), as well as Soviet diplomatic support, were of crucial importance to the birth of Israel. That same year the Soviet Union was the first to recognize the new state. Stalin, however, had miscalculated. The State of Israel rapidly built up a special relationship not with the Soviet Union but with the United States. Stalin spent the final years of his life consumed by anti-Semitic conspiracy theories.

Security Service concern at the threat of Zionist terrorism in Britain did not entirely disappear with the establishment of the State of Israel. Sillitoe informed SIME that during a discussion of terrorism in November 1949:

The [Service] Directors agreed that, on the basis of information at present available, there was still a need to study it. They decided that the focal point for such a study was to be this office. There is not much that we can do, but we are going to attempt to stimulate SIS to make enquiries in foreign countries, and we shall also have to look to you for any information which may come your way in the Middle East. Our main task will be to pass on to the Police any information we get about organisations or individuals who may make trouble in the UK.[80]

The loathing which Menachem Begin inspired within the Security Service was rekindled by the publication of an English translation of his memoirs in 1952. The outraged Director of the Overseas Division, Sir John Shaw, former Chief Secretary in Jerusalem, gave his verdict on the memoirs in a minute on Begin's file:

It is a revolting document which glories in the flogging of British officers, the hanging of British sergeants, &c. by Jewish terrorists during the latter days of the Mandate. I took legal opinion as to whether I should take proceedings for libel in connection with [Begin]'s account of the King David Hotel episode in 1946, but I was advised not to do so for technical reasons. The book had no sale or circulation in this country and it is not worth the notice of this Office now.[81]

No other officer of the Security Service is known to have contemplated a libel action against a Service target.

The one inexcusable aspect of the Security Service's post-war attitudes towards Zionism was its policy on the recruitment of Jews. During the war a small number of Jews had served with distinction in the Security Service – chief among them Victor Rothschild. Though MI5's own investigations had shown that mainstream British Jewish associations were wholly opposed to terrorism, the post-war Service refused to recruit Jews on the grounds that their dual loyalty to both Britain and Israel might create an unacceptable conflict of interest. In 1955 John Marriott, Director B (personnel), stated that 'our policy is to avoid recruiting Jews if possible unless they have very strong qualifications which are necessary for our work.'[82] He went on to tell a staff board that 'as a matter of general policy Jews were not now recruited to the Service.'[83] In 1956 a potential female recruit was rejected on the grounds that she was a practising Jew,[84] but in 1960 a Jew who was a member of the Church of England was appointed as a transcriber.[85] As late as 1974, when it was agreed that there was 'no general bar on the recruitment of Jews of British nationality', there was still prejudice against particularly observant Jews and those of distinctively Jewish 'physical appearance and demeanour'.[86]

The discrimination practised by the Security Service against potential Jewish recruits has, at least in the early Cold War, to be seen within the context of the low-level anti-Semitic prejudice which, even after Auschwitz, was still common in British public life. Attlee commented during a discussion on new ministerial appointments in 1951, 'There were two who were always being recommended as knowing about industry – [Ian] Mikardo and [Austen] Albu – but they both belonged to the Chosen People, and he didn't think he wanted any more of *them*.'[87] Neither, alas, did the Security Service.[88]

3

VENONA and the Special Relationships with the United States and Australia

The most important counter-espionage breakthrough of the early Cold War came from SIGINT. Whereas wartime ULTRA had been a primarily British success shared with the Americans, the first major SIGINT break-through of the Cold War was an American success shared with the British. The assistance which MI5 counter-espionage received from SIGINT thus derived from the peacetime continuation of the Special Relationship with the United States which had shortened the Second World War. As Roose-velt's vice president, Harry Truman had been kept in ignorance of the ULTRA secret. After succeeding Roosevelt in April 1945, however, he was so impressed by the insight which ULTRA gave him into the closing weeks of the war with Germany and the final months of the war against Japan that in September 1945 he secretly authorized the continuation of the SIGINT alliance with Britain. The details of peacetime SIGINT collabor-ation between the United States and the British Commonwealth were settled by a top-secret agreement concluded in London in March 1946 (later updated on a number of occasions).[1]

One of Petrie's few blind spots as DG was his failure, unlike Guy Liddell, to foresee the post-war importance of the Special Relationship, which Liddell was anxious to reinforce by personal contact. When Liddell sought the DG's approval for a liaison visit to America in February 1946, Petrie 'was not supportive, thought others could do it . . . In the end he said that if I would pay half my passage he thought I could go.' Though Liddell decided to go on these humiliating terms, he told his diary:

I feel somewhat insulted by the whole incident. It just goes to show how much value is attached by the DG to one's efforts to try and build up a liaison with the Americans. I feel rather like a schoolboy who has been accused of wangling a day's holiday on the excuse that he is going to his aunt's funeral.[2]

Even Liddell can have had little idea how important intelligence from the United States was to be to British counter-espionage for the rest of his term as DDG. The most important source was VENONA, the most closely guarded intelligence secret on both sides of the Atlantic during the early Cold War.

VENONA was the final codename[3] given to almost 3,000 intercepted Soviet intelligence and other classified telegrams sent during the period 1940 to 1948, which used the same (theoretically unbreakable) one-time pads more than once and thus became vulnerable to cryptanalytic attack.[4] Most were decrypted in the late 1940s and early 1950s, usually in part only, by a team led by a cryptanalyst of genius, Meredith Gardner, at the Army Security Agency (ASA) at Arlington Hall, Virginia, assisted from 1948 by GCHQ.[5] The first approach to GCHQ from ASA came as the result of Gardner's discovery in 1947 that some of the telegrams between the Centre (Soviet intelligence headquarters) and its Canberra residency were still reusing one-time pads.[6] Though GCHQ was not yet informed about the decrypted traffic between the Centre and its US residencies (probably because of its acute political sensitivities), in May 1947 it was invited to send a liaison officer to Washington to collaborate in the ASA attack on the Canberra traffic.[7] As a later CIA study noted, 'It speaks volumes about inter-allied signals co-operation that Arlington Hall's British liaison officers learned of the breakthrough even before the FBI were notified.'[8] On 25 November Liddell was informed that the decrypt of a Soviet telegram 'dated about 1945' had revealed a serious leak of British classified information, probably from the Australian Department of External Affairs.[9] Even more remarkable was the fact that the CIA was not informed of the Soviet decrypts until five years later.[10]

Though the decrypts provided important information on Soviet espionage in regions of the world as far apart as Scandinavia and Australia, the most numerous and most important concerned intelligence operations in the United States. VENONA revealed that over 200 Americans were working as Soviet agents during and sometimes after the Second World War, and that the leadership of the American Communist Party was hand-in-glove with the KGB. The decrypts showed that every section of the wartime administration of Franklin D. Roosevelt had been penetrated by Soviet intelligence. The US Office of Strategic Services (OSS, forerunner of the CIA) was the most penetrated intelligence agency in American history. Thanks to Soviet agents in the top-secret laboratory at Los Alamos near Santa Fe, which designed and built the world's first atomic bomb, the first Soviet atomic bomb, successfully tested in 1949, was a copy of the American original tested at the Alamogordo test site more than four years earlier.[11]

VENONA was an even more closely guarded secret than ULTRA.

There had never been any question of withholding ULTRA from President Roosevelt. By contrast, for at least three years President Truman was not briefed on VENONA.[12] Attlee, however, was. Late in 1947 he was personally informed by Sillitoe that VENONA decrypts revealed that Soviet intelligence had obtained top-secret British documents on post-war strategic planning from 'friends' in the Australian Department of External Affairs. Attlee authorized the DG to visit Australia, accompanied by Roger Hollis (then B1), in order to brief the Australian Labor Prime Minister, J. B. 'Ben' Chifley, and some of his senior officials about the leakage of classified information in Canberra (though not about the Soviet decrypts which had revealed it), and to discuss ways to improve Australian security.[13] On 21 January 1948 Attlee wrote to Chifley: 'Sir Percy Sillitoe, who has my complete confidence, will explain orally a most serious matter which I should like you to consider personally.'[14] Chifley did not take to Sillitoe. He rang up Sir Frederick Shedden, the secretary of the Department of Defence, and told him: 'There is a fellow here with a bloody silly name – Sillitoe. As far as I can make out he is the chief bloody spy – you had better have a look at him and find out what he wants.'[15] In order to conceal the SIGINT source from Australian ministers and officials, Sillitoe and Hollis used a somewhat feeble cover story, claiming that the evidence of high-level penetration of Australia had been provided orally by a Soviet defector. At a meeting with Chifley, Dr H. V. 'Bert' Evatt, Minister of External Affairs, John Dedman, Minister of Defence, and Shedden, the cover story quickly began to fall apart as it was skilfully probed by the abrasive Evatt. As Hollis ruefully acknowledged:

The point made by Dr Evatt was in fact unanswerable on the basis of the cover story. He suggested that it would be a reasonable Russian cover to attribute a leakage to Australia if the Russians had in fact a well-placed agent in some other part of the Empire, and that if the defector had accepted in good faith the attribution of the leak to Australia, no amount of examination by the U.K. authorities could go further than establish that the defector genuinely believed what he had been told . . . There was a very considerable risk that Dr Evatt and his colleagues would regard us either as fools for failing to see his point, or as knaves for knowing a great deal more than we were prepared to tell them, and it is by no means certain that they do not have suspicions in regard to the latter alternative.[16]

Since the cover story had failed to convince Chifley and his ministers, the only solution appeared to be to reveal the true source. On Attlee's instructions Sillitoe visited Washington to seek American consent to do so. With the support of the Secretary of State, George Marshall, he eventually gained US agreement to telling Chifley, Evatt and Dedman, in the strictest confidence, of the SIGINT evidence.[17]

By the time this permission was obtained, however, United States alarm at the state of Australian security had led it to place an embargo on the transfer to Australia of all classified information – a decision communicated to the Australian ambassador in Washington 'suddenly and without any reason given'.[18] When Hollis paid a further visit to Australia in August and September 1948, accompanied by Robert Hemblys-Scales of B2, he found the Defence Ministry and service chiefs deeply concerned by the embargo and anxious to reform Australian security – a 'most refreshing change' from what Hollis regarded as the 'lethargy' of most of the Canberra government, Evatt and Chifley in particular. The source of much of the 'lethargy', he believed, was Longfield Lloyd, head of the Commonwealth Investigation Service (CIS), Australia's post-war security service:

He . . . claims already to know and understand the workings of the M.G.B. [fore-runner of the KGB] and Russian espionage methods generally and to be able to cope with them adequately. In fact he demonstrably knows nothing of these matters and has almost no resources to cope with them . . . I think we must assume that the ostrich-like attitude towards security of Evatt and the P.M. probably comes in part from such assurances from Lloyd. I am quite convinced that the C.I.S. with its existing staff and Lloyd at its head has no possibility of ever becoming an effective counter-espionage service.[19]

Once briefed on the existence of the Canberra decrypts, Chifley and Dedman, who between them determined Australian security policy, dropped their earlier objections to the reform of the CIS and set out to mend their fences with Britain and the United States. The impact of the Soviet decrypts was, almost certainly, greater on Dedman than on Chifley. The Defence Department had suspected since late 1944 that there had been leakages of classified information from External Affairs to the Soviet Union. The post-war Australian SIGINT agency, the Defence Signals Bureau, headed by a British GCHQ officer, came under the authority of the Defence Department, whose powerful secretary, Sir Frederick Shedden, jealously protected its control of SIGINT. The able but morbidly distrustful Evatt was a controversial figure even in External Affairs and was loathed by Shedden.[20] Though Hollis had been authorized to reveal VENONA to Evatt as well as Chifley and Dedman, the External Affairs Minister was away during his visit and there is no evidence in Security Service files that he was ever briefed.[21]

On 17 September, shortly before Hollis returned to London, the Australian Defence Committee formally acknowledged that the CIS did not have the required 'counter-espionage capacity' and recommended the establishment of a new security organization. Three days later, Chifley approved the founding of an agency 'similar to MI5' and said he would write to Attlee asking him to station a Security Service officer in Australia to 'provide advice' to it. When Hollis left Australia, Hemblys-Scales remained to give advice on both the new organization and the Australian spy-hunt. Though lacking physical presence and described by an Australian colleague as 'skinnyish' with a 'pimply, pasty face', Hemblys-Scales played a major role in the reform of Australian security.[22] So strong was Security Service influence on the setting up of the Australian Security Intelligence Organization (ASIO) that Shedden referred to it in a secret memorandum of December 1948 as a 'proposed MI5 section'.[23]

Hollis's reason for returning to London in September 1948 was to take part in a secret Commonwealth Security Conference, largely prompted by what he called 'the dangers to which bad security can expose us', as demonstrated by the Australian experience.[24] Hollis reported afterwards to Sillitoe that the dominions* had little grasp of counter-espionage and 'look to the Security Service for guidance and leadership':

In our discussions on counter-espionage at the Conference, we put forward the proposal that it would be redundant for each constituent member of the Commonwealth security services to undertake the basic study of the Russian Intelligence Service which is now carried on in B2b, and that on this matter B2b should act as a coordinating point. Canada was unable to agree that B2b in London should have a formal directing function in Canadian counter-espionage work, though the other dominions raised no objection to this direction. In order to meet the Canadians, the final recommendation was drafted to read as follows:-

There should be the fullest exchange among these security services of information on counter-espionage and upon the organisation, personnel, methods and targets of all hostile intelligence services.

There was general agreement that London would be in possession of very much more information than the other parts of the Commonwealth and that the information which we put out would in fact fulfil a directing function.

. . . The security services of the Dominions do not have access to much of the material which is available to us, nor are most of them in close enough contact with

* The dominions in 1948 were Australia, Canada, Ceylon/Sri Lanka, India, New Zealand, Pakistan, South Africa. Though technically a dominion until 1949, Ireland had long ceased to be an active member of the Commonwealth.

the United States services to share the product of their work. It is therefore only through London that the whole available supply of intelligence information on the Russian Intelligence Service can be made available to the Dominions.[25]

Early in 1949 Hollis returned to Australia to give detailed advice on the charter, organization and senior personnel of ASIO, which was formally established on 16 March by a directive from Chifley to its first head, Mr Justice Reed. Hollis was accompanied by Courtenay Young, who was to replace Hemblys-Scales as the MI5 representative and to become the first security liaison officer (SLO) with ASIO. For its first fifteen months almost all ASIO's energies were devoted to following up leads from VENONA provided by the Security Service. Young kept the decrypts themselves in a huge Chubb safe to which no one in ASIO had access.[26] When passing on information to ASIO, he guaranteed its authenticity but concealed the SIGINT source. In consultation with Courtenay Young and with the approval of the Prime Minister (initially Chifley; from December 1949, Sir Robert Menzies), ASIO instituted telechecks on the main suspects identified by VENONA.[27] Director B (Dick White) noted with evident satisfaction after a visit to Australia in November 1949: 'ASIO never embark upon a new line of enquiry without first consulting the SLO. On his side Mr Courtenay Young has displayed great patience and ability and I feel sure that he is personally liked and respected by all members of the ASIO.'[28] On becoming the second head of ASIO in 1950, Charles Spry, previously Director of Military Intelligence, was indoctrinated into VENONA (of which he had previously been unaware) by Courtenay Young.[29] Derek Hamblen, Young's successor as SLO in 1951, had a major row during his first week in Australia as a result of Spry's insecure handling of a decrypt. They subsequently became firm friends and Hamblen was given an office next to Spry's in ASIO's Melbourne headquarters, where they spent many hours discussing the VENONA leads.[30]

Though there was no Australian system of Home Office Warrants, approval for telechecks on suspects named by the SLO was 'sought and granted orally'. One of the first telephones to be tapped was that of Fyodor Andreyevich Nosov, a TASS journalist and Soviet intelligence co-optee, who under the codename TEKHNIK was identified by the VENONA decrypts as the main point of contact with the Australian spy-ring. Though ASIO also obtained authority to bug Nosov's flat, it lacked MI5's experience in planting microphones. The team which bored a hole in Nosov's ceiling from the flat above to insert a microphone were horrified to discover not merely that the microphone was easily visible in the ceiling but that plaster disturbed by the drilling had fallen on the floor. Having persuaded the caretaker of the apartment block to let them into Nosov's flat, they removed the microphone and cleared up the mess, but had no doubt that Nosov would realize that an attempt had been made to bug his flat.[31]

Apart from Nosov, the main initial targets of the MI5–ASIO investigation were two Australian diplomats identified by VENONA decrypts as ideological Soviet agents: Ian Milner (codenamed BUR), who had joined the Communist Party while a Rhodes Scholar at Oxford in 1934 and had been seconded to the UN secretariat in New York in December 1946; and Jim Hill (TOURIST), brother of a leading Communist lawyer, who was posted as first secretary to the Australian high commission in London early in 1950 so that he could be kept under surveillance by the Security Service.[32] In May 1950 Hill was visited in his Aldwych office by MI5's leading interrogator, Jim Skardon, who a few months earlier had coaxed a confession out of the atom spy Klaus Fuchs. Though plainly shocked, Hill protested his innocence. Guy Liddell noted in his diary: 'There is no doubt in our minds that Hill is a guilty party. He telephoned to his wife from a callbox immediately after the first interview, but said no more than that something extremely serious had happened in regard to something that he had done.'[33] Having heard that Hill had been questioned, Ian Milner fled to Prague, where he spent the rest of his career teaching English literature at Charles University. Though never prosecuted, Hill returned to Australia and left External Affairs early in 1951.[34]

VENONA revealed that, in one important respect, Soviet intelligence operations in Australia differed from those in most Western countries. Virtually all Soviet espionage was organized by a leading Australian Communist Party official, Wally Clayton (codenamed KLOD), described by one member of his spy-ring in External Affairs as 'a shadowy figure' who 'wouldn't look at me when I was reporting'. A fellow Communist who lent Clayton his flat for meetings with his agents said later that 'the mysterious quality in his work . . . was mirrored in his face, which nearly always wore a furtive expression, although Clayton was not unlikeable.' Clayton ceased being a Party functionary in 1951, probably as the result of the compromise of his spy-ring.[35] Though he refused to confess to espionage and there was no evidence capable of convicting him (since SIGINT was regarded as too secret to use), the KGB was believed to be 'disturbed that so important and (to them) potentially dangerous a witness should remain at large'. Plans appear to have been made later for him to defect to Moscow, but Clayton's passport was revoked before he could leave the country.[36] Thereafter ASIO showed only intermittent interest in him.

In the autumn of 1948 Arthur Martin (B2b), a former wartime army signals officer, and others in the small circle of Security Service officers indoctrinated into the VENONA decrypts had begun to realize that the American ASA must be decrypting Soviet wartime intelligence traffic with residencies in the United States as well as in Australia.[37] ASA remained unwilling to discuss American VENONA with GCHQ until early in 1949, when decrypted telegrams exchanged between the Centre and its residencies in Washington and New York during the final year of the war revealed that there had been a Soviet spy within the British embassy who could not be identified without British assistance. Once informed of the existence of the decrypts early in 1949, Liddell sought the help of Sir Edward Travis, the Director of GCHQ, in persuading the United States Communications Intelligence Board (USCIB), which was responsible for co-ordinating the US SIGINT effort (a mission in which it had limited success), to disclose how many more telegrams dealing with Soviet intelligence operations in the United States had been decrypted and to make them available in London. In addition, he asked Travis to arrange with USCIB for the SLO in Washington, Dick Thistlethwaite, to be given access to all available decrypts and authorized to discuss what action was to be taken on them with 'appropriate' American colleagues.[38]

Travis, however, discovered to his surprise that even USCIB had not been informed of the American VENONA.[39] He then approached General Carter W. Clarke, the head of ASA, with whom he had worked closely on ULTRA during the war. Clarke appeared surprised that the GCHQ representative in Washington was not already seeing all available VENONA decrypts and gave instructions that he was to have full access. It was also agreed that the FBI should give Thistlethwaite and the SIS liaison officer in Washington all the intelligence derived from VENONA on Soviet espionage in the United States.[40] The case officer with whom they dealt was Robert Lamphere, the FBI's chief liaison with ASA (and its successor AFSA) on VENONA investigations. Thistlethwaite found him 'exceptionally friendly and able'.[41] He and his SIS colleague did, however, agree that they should not receive 'details of purely United States domestic' interest.[42] Geoffrey Patterson, who succeeded Thistlethwaite as SLO in June, later reported to Sillitoe: 'The raw [VENONA] material, when processed, is liable to produce most startling information about American domestic affairs, and I cannot see the authorities here allowing it to reach the hands of another country, however friendly that country may be.'[43]

Despite this restriction, it was an extraordinary comment on the close-ness of the transatlantic Special Relationship that ASA, the FBI and the

Armed Forces Security Agency (AFSA), which took over responsibility for VENONA production on its foundation in July 1949, should have been prepared to share with all three British intelligence agencies intelligence affecting US interests which they were not prepared to communicate to the CIA and most of the American intelligence community. After his meeting with Clarke, Travis telegraphed to Sillitoe and Menzies:

Only very few of American Military Intelligence [of which ASA was a part], A.S.A. and F.B.I. are in [the VENONA] picture, and nobody in any other Department. Imperative, therefore, no mention this line of information be made to any American even though he be indoctrinated, e.g., United States personnel at G.C.H.Q., members C.I.A., F.B.I. representative in U.K. etc.[44]

Thistlethwaite telegraphed a further warning that even Rear Admiral Inglis, head of USCIB and Director of US Naval Intelligence, then visiting Britain and the continent, knew nothing of the American VENONA decrypts: 'We are therefore not at liberty to discuss it with him. Grateful if you would ensure "C" also appreciates this.'[45]

On becoming first head of AFSA in July 1949, Rear Admiral Earl F. Stone, also a member of USCIB, appears to have been seriously put out to discover that he had previously been kept in ignorance of VENONA. He was also – to quote a doubtless euphemistic FBI memorandum – 'very much disturbed' to discover that, though ASA had called in the Bureau in an attempt to identify the codenames of the Soviet agents mentioned in the VENONA decrypts, it had failed to inform either the President or the Director of Central Intelligence (DCI). Stone insisted that ASA do so promptly. Carter Clarke 'vehemently disagreed'. After what was probably a blazing row, Stone and Clarke took their dispute to the Chairman of the Joint Chiefs of Staff, General Omar Nelson Bradley.[46]

Truman was a strong supporter of Bradley, and had enthusiastically supported his appointment as army chief of staff in succession to Eisenhower a year earlier.[47] In 1949, however, Bradley was guilty of an extraordinary act of insubordination to the Commander in Chief, siding with Clarke in his dispute with Stone over whether to reveal VENONA to Truman and the CIA. Bradley announced that if, in his opinion, the contents of the decrypts ever warranted it he 'would personally assume the responsibility of advising the President or anyone else in authority'.[48] Clarke assured Patterson that, even if Bradley did decide to pass on VENONA material to Truman or the National Security Council, he would do so in a 'suitably dressed up form' which would conceal its SIGINT origin.[49] Bradley was even more anxious to keep the VENONA secret from the CIA – and in particular

from its head, Rear Admiral Roscoe H. Hillenkoetter, DCI from 1947 to
1950. Clarke doubtless reflected Bradley's views as well as his own when
he told Patterson that he had 'very good reason for suspecting that it is not
safe to pass such secret material to C.I.A.'. That 'very good reason' was,
almost certainly, the evidence contained in the decrypts that OSS had
been heavily penetrated during the war and the understandable (though
mistaken) fear that its peacetime successor, the CIA, was also penetrated.[50]
The Director of the FBI, J. Edgar Hoover, was equally suspicious of CIA
security and viewed the Agency as an upstart rival.[51] Hillenkoetter was
frequently Truman's first caller of the day, bringing with him the intelligence briefing which later became known as the President's Daily Brief. If
Truman were informed of VENONA, he would be likely to raise the subject
with his DCI. Only by keeping the secret from the President, therefore, could
Bradley and Hoover be sure that it was kept from the DCI.[52]

VENONA revealed much less about NKVD/NKGB intelligence operations in the United Kingdom than in the United States, chiefly because far
fewer wartime messages were intercepted between Moscow and London
than between Moscow and the US. Even before the Soviet entry into the
war, the Foreign Office had agreed that the Soviet embassy in London
could communicate with Moscow by radio on set frequencies. These radio
messages were initially intercepted and recorded in the hope that they
could eventually be decrypted, but interception (save for that of GRU traffic,
which continued until April 1942) ceased in August 1941[53] because of the
need to concentrate resources on the production of ULTRA intelligence
based on the decryption of Enigma and other high-grade enemy ciphers.
Interception of Soviet traffic did not resume until June 1945. In the United
States, by contrast, there was no agreement allowing the Soviet embassy and
consulates to communicate with Moscow by radio. Instead, Soviet messages
were written out for transmission by cable companies, which, in accordance
with wartime censorship laws, supplied copies to the US authorities.[54]

The most important British VENONA breakthrough was the decryption
in whole or in part of all but one of the radio messages sent by the Centre
to London from 15 to 21 September 1945.[55] The intercepts revealed the
existence of an inner ring of British agents referred to by the Centre as 'the
valuable agent network', which had access to British intelligence. Some
years later, following lengthy analysis of collateral evidence, the codenames
for three members of the network were identified as those of Philby, Burgess
and Blunt. At the time, however, clues to the identities of the agents were
sparse. By the mid-1950s Burgess was the only one of the three whose
codename had been correctly identified in the decrypts.[56] Even in the

mid-1970s, twelve of the twenty-four codenames in the September 1945 decrypts had still not been identified.[57] The unidentified included JACK and ROSA, an apparently important agent couple of whom no significant identifying details were given but who were, at various times, wrongly suspected of being Herbert and Jenifer Hart or Victor and Tessa Rothschild; and a high-level atom spy, KVANT ('QUANTUM'), who it was later thought might be Bruno Pontecorvo, who defected to Russia in 1950.[58] The importance of the intercepts during this single week in September 1945 provided graphic evidence of the serious intelligence loss sustained as a result of the non-interception of Soviet traffic for most of the previous four years. With the exception of that week, only five other telegrams exchanged between the Centre and the London residency were (partially) decrypted. The lack of British VENONA covering the most successful period of Soviet intelligence collection in Britain in the history of the Soviet Union was to prove an enormous handicap to post-war British counter-espionage. Had British VENONA been on the scale of its US counterpart, a number of the Security Service's most important counter-espionage investigations – chief among them the Cambridge Five – would undoubtedly have been both more successful and more rapidly concluded. The first two important British Soviet agents discovered as a result of VENONA, Klaus Fuchs and Donald Maclean, were both identified not from messages intercepted in Britain but from decrypts of traffic between the Centre and its residencies in Washington and New York relating to their time in the United States.

Access to VENONA was tightly restricted. A list dated 2 October 1952, five years after the Security Service's first involvement in it, records that only nine officers had unrestricted access to the decrypts; another nineteen had restricted access or were aware of their existence.[59] Secretaries were not allowed to open envelopes containing VENONA material.[60] As a result of Soviet penetrations of both AFSA and SIS, however, these security precautions were fatally undermined. In 1950 AFSA was shocked to discover that one of its employees, William Weisband, had been a Soviet agent ever since he joined the wartime army SIGINT agency in 1942.[61] The son of Russian immigrants to the United States, Weisband was employed as a Russian linguist and roamed around first ASA, then AFSA, on the pretext of looking for projects where his linguistic skills could be of assistance. Cecil Phillips, one of the cryptanalysts who worked on VENONA, remembers Weisband as 'very gregarious and very nosy':

He would come around and ask questions about what you were doing . . . He was never aggressive. If you said, as I often did, 'Nothing important,' or 'I'm doing something as dull as hell,' he would wander off . . . I never heard him offer a political thought. He was around everywhere all the time. He cultivated the senior officers.

Meredith Gardner recalls Weisband looking over his shoulder at a critical moment in the project late in 1946, just as he was producing one of the first important decrypts – a telegram from the New York residency to Moscow of December 1944 listing some of the scientists who were developing the atomic bomb.[62] It seems to have been over a year, however, before Weisband was able to pass on this dramatic news to Moscow. After the defection of the American KGB courier Elizabeth Bentley in 1945, the Centre ordered contact with Weisband to be broken as a security measure. Contact was not resumed until 1947.[63] It was probably as a result of Weisband's warning that the Soviet reuse of one-time pads ceased in 1948.[64]

By the time Weisband was arrested in 1950, the Centre had an even better-informed source on the progress being made by Meredith and his colleagues. In September 1949, a month before he arrived in Washington as the SIS liaison officer, Kim Philby was indoctrinated into VENONA.[65] Soon afterwards he reported to Moscow that the atom spy successively codenamed REST and CHARLES, referred to in a number of the decrypts, had been identified as Klaus Fuchs – thus enabling Moscow to warn those of its American agents who had dealt with Fuchs that they might have to flee through Mexico. Among those who made their escape were Morris and Lona Cohen, who later reappeared in Britain using the aliases Peter and Helen Kroger and were convicted of espionage in 1961.[66] After his death in 1995, Morris Cohen was posthumously declared a Hero of the Russian Federation by President Boris Yeltsin.

Soon after his arrival in Washington, Philby was taken to AFSA by the departing SIS liaison officer, Peter Dwyer, and introduced to Gardner. On this, as on a number of previous visits, Dwyer provided information which helped Gardner fill in gaps in one of the decrypts. Almost half a century later, Gardner still vividly recalled the meeting:

. . . I was very much pleased [with progress on the decrypts] and so was Dwyer, of course. Philby was looking on with no doubt rapt attention but he never said a word, never a word. And that was the last I saw of him. Philby was supposed to continue these visits, but helping me was the last thing he wanted to do.[67]

Despite discontinuing meetings with Gardner, however, Philby contrived to increase his access to VENONA decrypts. His anxiety to do so grew in June 1950 after the first partial decryption of telegrams to the London residency from Moscow in September 1945 referred to the existence of a 'valuable' British agent network, of which, as he was well aware, he had been a prominent member.[68] The Security Service SLO, Geoffrey Patterson, wrote to the DG on 18 July 1950:

Philby has signalled 'C' to suggest that an extra copy of any material which G.C.H.Q. send to [their Washington liaison] should be enclosed for Philby and myself. At the moment [their liaison] receives only one copy which he, of course, shows to us, but he has no time in which to sit down and copy it for us. If Philby and I can have our own copy it will give us more time for studying it before we approach the F.B.I. on the subject.[69]

Armed with his own copies of VENONA decrypts, Philby was able to pass them on to Moscow.[70] At the time he was the only person in either London or Washington able to identify a particularly important Soviet spy in Britain, codenamed STANLEY in the September 1945 telegrams from Moscow to London,[71] as himself.

Thanks to Weisband and Philby, the VENONA secret was communicated to Moscow well before it reached either the President of the United States or the CIA. From 1950 onwards, following Weisband's arrest,[72] Clarke, Bradley and Hoover must have been aware that the secret they had kept from Truman and the Agency was known to Stalin and the Centre. Though American and British security procedures both failed miserably to prevent Moscow learning of the VENONA decrypts, however, they were remarkably successful in keeping the secret within the United States and Britain.

Despite the fact that VENONA probably identified more Soviet agents than any other Western intelligence operation of the Cold War, it was too secret to be mentioned in American or British courts, even in camera, and therefore led to very few convictions. It was possible to mount successful prosecutions against Soviet agents identified in the decrypts only if they could be persuaded to confess or if alternative evidence could be discovered from non-SIGINT sources. Among the few who admitted their guilt when confronted by the evidence against them (which they had no idea was based on SIGINT) were two of the atom spies at Los Alamos: the German-born British physicist Klaus Fuchs and the American Technical Sergeant David Greenglass. Greenglass also implicated his wife's brother-in-law, Julius Rosenberg, whom VENONA had identified as the organizer – with some assistance from his wife Ethel – of a highly successful Soviet spy-ring in New York producing a wide range of scientific and technological intelligence. When the Rosenbergs' trial opened in 1951, Greenglass was the chief witness for the prosecution. Unlike Fuchs, who was sentenced to fourteen years' imprisonment in 1950, the Rosenbergs were sentenced to death, though the execution was not carried out until 1953.[73] They were the only Soviet spies executed during the Cold War.

When the flow of VENONA decrypts reduced to a trickle during the early 1950s, however, the Security Service senior management largely ceased to pay detailed attention to them. In October 1955 an important clue to Philby in a newly decrypted message from Moscow to the London residency of September 1945 was missed.[74] The value of VENONA as a counter-espionage tool was diminished, sometimes seriously, by the extreme secrecy with which it was handled. As Peter de Wesselow, who had the main day-to-day responsibility in MI5 for handling VENONA, later recalled, it 'was considered as of exceptional delicacy' and the decrypted messages from Moscow to London were 'ten times more delicate than the rest'.[75] The Director of GCHQ, Group Captain E. M. Jones, made life more difficult for his cryptanalysts by denying them the real names and biographical details of the British citizens whom de Wesselow and others in MI5 suspected of being referred to by codenames in the VENONA traffic.[76] In April 1956 both the DG, Sir Dick White, and the future DDG Graham Mitchell, then Director D (counter-espionage), unaware of the important clue to Philby which had been overlooked only six months earlier, mistakenly concluded that VENONA was no longer 'worth the effort'. Though GCHQ continued to work on VENONA, the Security Service 'virtually abandoned it' for the next five years.[77]

Service interest in VENONA revived in the early 1960s as the result of the acquisition of new intelligence from the KGB defector Anatoli Golitsyn and from Swedish intelligence. Though Golitsyn had little precise intelligence on the so-called 'Ring of Five', he identified it as the 'valuable agent network' mentioned in decrypts of September 1945.[78] Following requests during 1960, the Swedes supplied copies of wartime GRU telegrams exchanged between Moscow and the Stockholm residency, some of which were discovered to have employed the same one-time pads used in hitherto unbroken GRU traffic with London.[79] One hundred and seventy-eight GRU messages from the period March 1940 to April 1942 were successfully decrypted in whole or part. After a gap of almost three and a half years, another 110 decrypts were produced for the period from September 1945 to March 1947.[80] The main discovery from this new VENONA source was the existence of a wartime GRU agent network in Britain codenamed the 'X Group', which was active by, if not before, 1940. The identity of the leader of the Group, or at least its chief contact with the GRU London residency, codenamed INTELLIGENTSIA, was revealed in a decrypted telegram to Moscow on 25 July 1940 from his case officer as one of the CPGB's wealthiest and most aristocratic members, educated at Westminster School and King's College, Cambridge:

[The Honourable] Ivor Montagu, brother of Lord [Ewen] Montagu, the well known local communist, journalist and lecturer. He has [*several words not decrypted*] contacts through his influential relations. He reported that he had been detailed to organise work with me, but he had not yet obtained a single contact.

All that Ewen Montagu reported at this meeting was general political gossip. His GRU controller made clear his dissatisfaction in a telegram to Moscow on 16 August:

INTELLIGENTSIA has not yet found the people in the Military Finance Department. He has been given the address of one officer but has not found him yet . . . I have taken the liberty of pointing out to the X Group that we need a man of different calibre and one who is bolder than INTELLIGENTSIA.

Montagu did, however, provide classified reports from his friend, the scientist J. B. S. Haldane, educated at Eton and New College, Oxford, and, like Montagu, a Communist with aristocratic connections, whose war service for the Admiralty included work at the Royal Navy's secret underwater research establishment near Gosport.[81] Most other members of the X Group proved harder to identify. BARON, who was a prolific source of intelligence on German forces and troop movements in Czechoslovakia, was thought likely to be a member of the intelligence service of the Czechoslovak government in exile in London.[82] There was speculation that BOB, another member of the X Group, was the future trade union leader Jack Jones, though a report of 1969 concluded that there were 'few pointers to the identity of "BOB" and the most that can be said is that Jones cannot be eliminated as a candidate.'[83] A decade after work on the GRU decrypts began, the Security Service's VENONA experts were still uncertain what the X Group's precise function had been:

We have not established what the X Group represents. It is not the Communist Party as such, but it is probably some fraction or undercover group of the C.P. Moscow obviously visualised it as a source of military intelligence but it is difficult to trace the connection between Ivor Montagu (whose interests were largely in Film Production, Jewish affairs, International Table Tennis etc.), a Colonel in the R[oyal] A[rtillery], a girl in a Government Department and NOBILITY, a journalist.[84]

The Service devoted no significant further resources to unravelling either the connection between Montagu and the rest of the X Group or the identity of NOBILITY, which remains unknown.[85]

4

Vetting, Atom Spies and Protective Security

The most unwelcome increase in the Security Service's responsibilities during the early Cold War was in vetting. Even at the end of the Second World War there was little sign of what was to come. The future DG, Roger Hollis, noted in February 1945, 'The Civil Service has in the past shown an extreme and understandable reluctance to have its intake vetted by us.'[1] Though most government departments consulted the Service about the employment of temporary personnel on secret work, they rarely did so about established staff. In at least one case, a Whitehall failure to consult Service records led to the appointment of a Communist as private secretary to a cabinet minister.[2] Even when a Communist was discovered in a sensitive post, there were no grounds for dismissal. 'All that a Department could do was to transfer him to non-secret or less secret work, if it could do this without rousing the man's suspicions.'[3]

The Attlee government was initially reluctant to grapple with the problem of keeping Communists away from classified information for fear of being accused of witch-hunts by the Labour left. It was gradually spurred into action by the sensational revelations of Soviet espionage which began with the arrest of Alan Nunn May in March 1946, followed a few months later by the report of the Canadian Royal Commission on Igor Gouzenko's disclosures of Soviet spy-rings in Canada.[4] In May 1947 the newly founded Cabinet Committee on Subversive Activities (GEN 183) concluded that 'what was done in Canada might be attempted with comparable if not equal success in any other democratic country, including our own', and that the May case showed 'the existence of a Soviet espionage machine in this country':

The ideology of the Communist involves, at the least, a divided loyalty, which might in certain contingencies become active disloyalty; the Canadian case has amply demonstrated the reality of this danger. This is not to say that all Communists would be prepared, even after long exposure to Communist indoctrination, to betray their country by consenting to work for Russian espionage agents; but there is no way of separating the sheep from the goats, at least until the damage has been done or suspicion is aroused . . . We are, therefore, forced to the conclusion that the only safe course is to decide that a member of the Communist Party is not to be employed on work where he may have access to secret information.[5]

Attlee brooded for some months before deciding to grasp the nettle. He minuted in December 1947: 'We cannot afford to take risks here, and the general public will support us. Fellow travellers may protest, but we should face up to this. Action should be taken in regard to Fascists as well as Communists although the former are feeble.'[6] Feeble though the tattered remnants of British Fascism were, they proved of some use for public relations purposes in enabling the government to claim that it was protecting the state against extremists of both left and right. In March 1948, following cabinet discussion, the Prime Minister announced in the House of Commons the introduction of what became known as the 'Purge Procedure' excluding both Communists and Fascists from work 'vital to the Security of the State'. The Communist MP Willie Gallacher interjected defiantly, 'So raise the scarlet banner high!'

The Security Service was unenthusiastic. It would have preferred a more systematic use of the existing informal vetting system which, it believed, could 'produce as good security' as the Purge Procedure. The Service was predictably anxious that a more public vetting system might prejudice the secrecy of its sources, especially in the Communist Party.[7] But there was also a deep sense of grievance at the way in which Labour ministers, embarrassed by the unpopularity among many of their own supporters of the extension of the vetting system, seemed reluctant to take full political responsibility, preferring to let the opprobrium fall as far as possible on MI5. On 25 March 1948 Herbert Morrison, the Lord President, told Guy Liddell, the DDG, 'I hope you chaps will be very careful in [vetting] all these Civil Servant cases.' Though Morrison's tone seems to have been light-hearted, Liddell gave an indignant reply:

I said that I should like him to know that all these cases are handled with scrupulous care and impartiality, and that so far from being a set of irresponsible autocrats in these matters, it was our Department which was exercising a restraining hand not only on the Working Party set up by the Cabinet, but also on all Government Departments. It seemed to me that in the Press, Parliament and in the public mind generally a totally false impression was being allowed to grow up about the work of our Department. This could not be otherwise than extremely damaging to our work in the future, particularly to the cooperation we get from the Police,

Government Departments and various administrations overseas. It seemed to me that there was a serious risk of our being used as a whipping boy . . .[8]

A few weeks later, Liddell put the same point to the Prime Minister but found Attlee unsympathetic: 'I pointed out to him that in the minds of the Press and the public we appeared as a bunch of irresponsible autocrats who, without authority, were empowered to victimise unfortunate Civil Servants. He said he was afraid that this was to some extent un-avoidable . . .'[9] A still indignant Liddell wrote to the Treasury, 'There is a strong belief that MI5, staffed by black reactionaries, is in a position to influence Government departments against their better judgement.'[10]

The Security Service therefore welcomed the appointment in April 1948 of a three-man Advisory Tribunal, chaired by Sir Thomas Gardiner, former Director General of the Post Office, which took some of the responsibility for purge decisions from its shoulders. The other two original members of the Tribunal were both retired civil servants, though one was soon replaced by a former trade union official. While the final decisions on dismissals remained with ministers, the Tribunal was given the task of reviewing the evidence on which decisions were based. The Service immediately agreed to reveal to the Tribunal full details of its intelligence on those purged and the sources on which it was based.[11] A new sub-division, B1E, was set up to investigate Communism in the civil service and the professions, with responsibility for preparing purge cases. Its head, Graham Mitchell (soon to take over all B1), usually appeared before the Tribunal and quickly reached an understanding with Gardiner, who remained chairman until 1958. In the Service's view, Gardiner 'was impartial but showed a ready understanding of Security Service problems and the protection of sensitive sources'. Sitting alone with the three Advisers and their secretary (usually a Treasury official), Mitchell showed them raw intelligence of a kind still never shown to ministers or government departments, such as transcripts of intercepted telephone calls and bugged conversations, agent reports (with comments on the agent's reliability and access) and photographs of Communist Party registration cards. Gardiner voluntarily proposed that the Service should have the opportunity of checking in draft the Tribunal's reports to ministers to ensure that they did not unwittingly compromise an intelligence source. The three Advisers on the Tribunal also took care to protect the source when asking questions. It quickly became Service practice never to recommend a purge case which it was thought the Tri-bunal might reject. On one occasion Gardiner told Mitchell he was worried that the fact that the Tribunal usually found in favour of the cases put to it by the Security Service might undermine public confidence in its impartiality. Mitchell, however, did not respond to Gardiner's suggestion that the Service put forward weaker 'Aunt Sally' purge cases which the Tribunal could use to reassure public opinion by rejecting.[12]

The Purge Procedure initially involved only what later became known as 'negative vetting': the checking of those engaged in 'secret work' against Security Service records, especially its increasingly complete files on Communist Party membership.[13] The Service, however, was alarmed by the increase in its workload. In June 1948 Hollis complained that the Purge Procedure was placing an 'intolerable burden upon the Security Service'.[14] The burden increased further as the procedure was extended to List X firms (those working on classified government contracts). Hitherto the only course of action open to the Security Service when it discovered those it regarded as security risks employed on secret work outside the public service was to try to persuade the contractors concerned to move them discreetly into other jobs. Since this was not always possible, in 1949 the cabinet agreed that in the last resort a minister (in practice usually the Minister of Supply) should have the right to instruct a firm to remove a suspect from work on a secret contract. Unlike the Purge Procedure in the government service, what became known in Whitehall as the 'Industrial Purge' was never publicly announced.[15]

In January 1949 Attlee announced that, under the Purge Procedure, eleven government officials had been removed from sensitive work. Though ten had Communist connections, the eleventh – no doubt to the Prime Minister's relief – was found to be a Fascist, thus reinforcing official claims that the procedure was even-handed.[16] By September the Purge Procedure had acquired still greater importance. 'The event of the year', Liddell wrote later, was the first Soviet atomic test,[17] about two years earlier than had been expected in Washington and London, which ended the US nuclear monopoly and began a new and much more dangerous phase in the Cold War. On 3 September a US weather-reconnaissance aircraft detected abnormally high levels of radiation over the North Atlantic. Over the next week the US Air Force and Royal Air Force together tracked the radioactivity as it was blown at high altitude across North America and the Atlantic towards the United Kingdom.[18] The discovery was announced to the JIC by its Foreign Office chairman, William Hayter, under what Liddell described as 'a melodramatic bond of secrecy':

Hayter cleared the room of secretaries and then said if there was anyone present who could not keep what was going to be said to himself, would he kindly leave the room ... It was then announced by [Sir Michael] Perrin of atomic energy that the explosion of an atomic bomb had occurred in Russia, it is believed somewhere in the vicinity of Lake Baikal.[19]

Though Liddell, like the rest of the JIC and the Prime Minister, wanted to keep the news secret,[20] Truman announced publicly on 23 September that 'We have evidence that within recent weeks an atomic explosion occurred in the USSR.' The shock caused by the Soviet Union's sudden emergence as a nuclear superpower was heightened by the triumph of Communism in the most populous state on earth. On 21 September Mao Zedong announced the establishment of the People's Republic of China.

For the small group of those on either side of the Atlantic with access to VENONA the news of these two Communist triumphs coincided with the discovery from newly decrypted Soviet telegrams that plans of the first US atomic bomb had been betrayed to Soviet intelligence late in the Second World War by a British scientist, codenamed successively REST and CHARLES. The FBI quickly concluded that the scientist was the German-born Klaus Fuchs, who, unlike Alan Nunn May, had been at the heart of the MANHATTAN atomic project at the Los Alamos laboratories in the New Mexico desert and was currently working at Harwell.[21] Though the Security Service also considered the possibility that the Soviet agent might have been Fuchs's Harwell colleague Rudolf Peierls, who had a Russian wife, Liddell noted on 20 September that the odds were 'heavily on Fuchs'.[22] The case was particularly embarrassing for the Security Service since Fuchs had previously been vetted by the Service on three separate occasions: before joining the British TUBE ALLOYS atomic project in 1941, the MANHATTAN project in the United States in 1943 and Britain's post-war atomic project in Harwell in 1947. On the last occasion there was a division of opinion within the Service. C Division, which was responsible for vetting, concluded that Fuchs was a serious potential security risk who should be immediately removed from atomic research. Some of the leading officers in B Division (counter-espionage) – among them Dick White, Roger Hollis and Graham Mitchell – argued that, on the contrary, the evidence against Fuchs was purely circumstantial and was outweighed by outstanding references from two of Britain's leading physicists, Professor (Sir) Neville Mott, a future Nobel Laureate, and Professor Max Born. The case was passed up to the DDG, Guy Liddell, who ordered a further investigation and obtained HOWs on both Fuchs and Peierls. When no further evidence against either emerged from the 1947 investigation, Liddell had concluded that 'we have no case on which to make any adverse recommendation.'[23] As was not uncommon with academic references, however, Mott had been economical with the truth. He later recalled how, while he had supervised Fuchs's research at Bristol University in the mid-1930s, Fuchs had enjoyed playing the part of the chief prosecutor, Andrei Vyshinsky, in dramatized readings of the Stalinist show trials, 'accusing the defendants with a cold venom that I would never have suspected from so quiet and retiring a young man'.[24]

The receipt of the VENONA evidence of Soviet atomic espionage at Los Alamos by the Security Service on 12 September 1949[25] prompted renewed and more intensive surveillance of Fuchs. His telephones were tapped and his correspondence intercepted at both his Harwell home and office, and many letters tested for secret ink. Concealed microphones were installed in Fuchs's home in Harwell, and three B Division officers relayed daily surveillance reports by scrambler telephone from a Newbury hotel to Head Office.[26] Fuchs was tailed by B4 surveillance teams, who reported that he was a 'bad driver' and difficult to follow.[27] Though much was discovered about Fuchs's private life, including his affair with the wife of his line manager,[28] the investigation failed to produce any evidence of espionage. Fuchs had, however, told the Harwell security officer, Henry Arnold, that his father had been offered an academic post in Communist East Germany (which he accepted soon afterwards). Liddell therefore thought that the most practicable solution would be to tell Fuchs 'with the deepest regrets that it would be embarrassing both for us and for him if he remained any longer in atomic energy, but that we would do our utmost to find him other suitable employment'. Sillitoe, by contrast, remained anxious to secure a conviction.[29]

The only hope of a successful prosecution depended on using the information about Fuchs's espionage contained in the VENONA decrypts to persuade him to confess.[30] When Skardon began his interrogation on 21 December, Fuchs flatly denied that he had given the Russians any information.[31] Skardon's persistence, however, eventually made a successful prosecution possible. Instead of following normal procedure and attempting to achieve a speedy breakthrough, he correctly judged that Fuchs was more likely to confess once his confidence had been won. Had the strategy failed, Skardon might well have been severely criticized for his dilatory approach. At the beginning of his fourth meeting with Fuchs on 24 January 1950, this time at Fuchs's Harwell home, Skardon himself must have wondered whether he had made the right decision. Fuchs began the meeting by saying, 'I will never be persuaded by you to talk.' After lunch, however, he abruptly changed his mind, told Skardon that 'he had decided it would be to his best interests to answer my questions'[32] and admitted giving the Russians 'all the information in his possession about British and American research in connection with the atomic bomb'.[33] In the hope that Fuchs would provide leads to other spies, Skardon decided not to arrange with Special Branch for his immediate arrest. Fuchs was so reassured by Skardon's manner that he mistakenly believed that he would be allowed to remain at Harwell 'or, as a possible second best, obtain . . . a senior university post'.[34] Instead, on 1 March, Fuchs was sentenced to fourteen years' imprisonment. According to Chapman Pincher's sensational account of the trial, 'In 90 minutes at the Old Bailey yesterday, a riddle was solved: How did Russia make the atomic bomb so quickly? Dr Klaus Emil Julius Fuchs . . . gave them the know-how.' What Fuchs had failed to realize was that, but for his confession, there would have been no case against him. Skardon's knowledge of his espionage, which had so impressed him, derived from SIGINT unusable in court.

Fuchs's conviction alarmed the leadership of the British Communist Party (CPGB), which feared damaging publicity about his links with other British Communists and was immensely relieved when the press failed to pick up the story. Security Service eavesdropping devices in the Party headquarters overheard the following conversation between the Party's industrial organizer, Peter Kerrigan, and Reuben Falber, later CPGB assistant general secretary:

PETER KERRIGAN (reading, apparently from press report): 'He [Fuchs] seemed to have taken no active interest in politics in this country, nor is [he] known at any time to have associated with British members of the Communist Party in this country.' That's a bloody let-off!
REUBEN FALBER: Phew![35]

The Fuchs case led to a crisis in the Special Relationship. Already critical of British security, J. Edgar Hoover took it as a personal affront that, for legal reasons, Fuchs's statements, which were formal evidence for the prosecution, could not be made available to the FBI until his trial was over. He was further enraged by the Home Office's refusal to allow a Bureau representative to visit Fuchs after his conviction, largely for fear that he might disturb the close relationship between Fuchs and Skardon. Hoover informed London that he was 'outraged at the lack of cooperation by the British Government and MI5 on the Fuchs case'. A bitter controversy followed. The SLO in Washington, Geoffrey Patterson, reported that he had had 'some interesting interviews' with Hoover: 'At times I feel like a sandwich – a very small bit of chewed meat between two crusts.' Lish

Whitson, the unfortunate FBI officer who had been despatched to London in an unsuccessful attempt to interview Fuchs, was summoned back in disgrace. On his return he discovered that his name-plate had been removed from his office door and that he had been posted out of Washington.[36]

During a visit to London on 27 March 1950, the SIS representative in Washington, Kim Philby, told Liddell (and, doubtless, the KGB) that Hoover remained adamant the FBI must interview Fuchs: 'He was afraid that if it could not be agreed, Hoover was quite capable of reducing our liaison to a pure formality, regardless of the loss that it might be to his own organisation.'[37] After Patterson sent a similar warning from Washington, Sillitoe called on Attlee to emphasize the importance of resolving the dispute, which might put the prospects for renewed atomic co-operation as well as intelligence liaison at risk, by allowing the Bureau access to Fuchs.[38] The Home Office gave way, and two FBI officers, Hugh Clegg and Robert Lamphere, arrived to interview Fuchs on 19 May. Sillitoe, however, then revived the dispute by complaining to the FBI officers about the behaviour of the Bureau and delivering what Clegg claimed was a 'dressing down'. A further furious correspondence with Hoover followed, and Patterson reported that he was being 'officially boycotted'. The dispute calmed down in the autumn of 1950 after a ceremony at the Washington embassy in which Hoover was invested with an honorary KBE.[39] The success of the FBI interview with Fuchs also helped to improve relations with the Security Service. Information from Fuchs made it possible to identify his most important Soviet intelligence contact in the United States as the industrial chemist Harry Gold, who provided further evidence on the Rosenberg spy-ring and other Soviet agents in America.[40]

As well as adding to the tensions of the early nuclear age, the Fuchs case produced pressure for active investigation – 'positive vetting' – of those with access to important classified information, in addition to the usual checks based on Security Service files. After a discussion at the Cabinet Committee on Subversive Activities (GEN 183), chaired by the Prime Minister, on 5 April 1950, Attlee appointed a Committee on Positive Vetting under the senior Treasury official John Winnifrith, 'to consider the possibility of listing a limited number of posts in regard to which positive vetting could be undertaken and to assess the risks and advantages of embarking upon any such system of positive enquiry'.[41] The Security Service found itself in a dilemma. On the one hand it believed in the need 'to make more searching enquiries' about those engaged in important secret work. On the other hand it continued to fear being overwhelmed by an expansion of the vetting system. Sillitoe told GEN 183 that if MI5 'were asked to undertake, either direct or through the police, positive enquiries about the persons referred to them [by service departments], then even the numbers coming from the headquarters staffs would be far more than they could cope with'.[42]

Soviet atomic weapons, noted Liddell on New Year's Day 1950, had 'thrown everyone's calculations out of date', and 'would necessitate the revision of all former JIC assessments'. Within seven years, he forecast, 'the Russians should have sufficient atomic bombs to blot this country out entirely.'[43] The JIC feared that the Soviet Union might attempt a surprise nuclear attack much earlier. On 12 June 1950 it considered the nightmare scenario of a Soviet atomic weapon being smuggled into Britain and detonated in a densely populated area. The JIC believed that it would be comparatively easy for a Soviet atomic weapon to be broken down into its component parts, smuggled undetected into Britain on board a merchant ship, reassembled in as little as twenty-four hours, and detonated by remote control or time delay.[44]

Such fears were heightened by the unexpected outbreak of the Korean War less than a fortnight later. Communist North Korea's invasion of the South in the early hours of 25 June was as big an intelligence surprise as Pearl Harbor.[45] In its early stages there seemed a real prospect that it might herald a Third World War. A secret committee in the Ministry of Defence (MoD) with the misleadingly innocuous title of the Imports Research Committee, examined the possibility of a Soviet atomic bomb being detonated 'in a "suicide" aircraft flying low over a key point', such as London. Though less likely than a bomb arriving by ship:

nevertheless it is possible and there does not seem to be any answer to it. The crew of the aircraft in order to detonate the bomb at the right time would have to know what their cargo was and would therefore be a 'suicide' squad. Short of firing on every strange civil aircraft that appears over our shores we know of no way of preventing an aircraft that set out on such a mission from succeeding.[46]

The Korean War also increased demands on the vetting system. An internal review of B Division in July concluded that 'The constantly increasing mass of business to transact here has led to a crisis in management and a crisis in manpower.' The Fuchs case had shown that, when investigating Soviet espionage, old Communist affiliations had to be taken into account as well as current Party membership, and this became the responsibility of B1E.[47] Sillitoe was informed on 1 August that:

a number of our industrial contacts were showing a very welcome keenness in getting rid of their Communist employees, and are now taking the initiative in dealing with them rather more quickly than in the past. They have, in fact, already dealt with a case which it was proposed to submit for the industrial purge ... Non-Communist employees at de Havillands, Stag Lane, had threatened to strike if the Communist employees were not sacked![48]

In late September 1950, Henry Arnold, Harwell's security officer, informed the Security Service that one of Fuchs's former colleagues at Harwell, the Italian-born atomic physicist Bruno Pontecorvo, had failed to return to the UK after a family holiday abroad. It was later discovered that he and his family had flown to Finland and from there had defected to the USSR. The Pontecorvo case dramatically illustrated once again the limitations of negative vetting. Until a few months earlier, he had been 'No Trace' in MI5 files.[49] Positive vetting, however, would have revealed that some of his Italian family were well-known Communists.[50] Pontecorvo had first become a cause for concern to the Security Service on 2 March when it received intelligence from Sweden reporting that both he and his wife were Communists. When questioned by Arnold, Pontecorvo denied the report but admitted that some of his relatives were Communist sympathizers. He acknowledged, however, that he might be seen as a bad security risk and said that he would prefer to leave Harwell for a university post. By the time he defected, a post had been found for him at Liverpool University.[51]

Pontecorvo's defection led to another fierce exchange of correspondence between MI5 and the FBI. Shortly before Pontecorvo began work for the wartime Anglo-Canadian atomic research team in Montreal in 1943, the FBI had reported to British Security Co-ordination (BSC) in New York, whose responsibilities included intelligence liaison with the United States, that it had found Communist literature in his home in the United States. 'Nobody knows what happened to these reports,' wrote Liddell in October 1950, 'since the records of B.S.C. have been destroyed.'[52] Because Pontecorvo had never lived in Britain, BSC had not referred his case to MI5. An investigation led by Hollis after Pontecorvo's defection concluded that, because of bureaucratic mismanagement at BSC, the FBI report must have been misplaced.[53] Hollis's investigation also revealed that in February 1950 Sir John Cockcroft, the head of Harwell, had been informed by a US official that the Italian-born nuclear physicist Emilio Segrè had reported that 'several members of Pontecorvo's family in Italy were Communists, some quite prominent, who "had influence on him".' Segrè also claimed that Pontecorvo's decision to remain in atomic research could have been 'for the wrong purposes'. Incredibly, before Pontecorvo's defection, neither Cockcroft nor Arnold had passed on this report to the Security Service, which did not reveal their lapse to the FBI for fear of strengthening its suspicions about British nuclear security.[54]

Just as the new dispute arose with the FBI over Pontecorvo's defection, Sillitoe was in Washington, attempting to resolve the earlier problems created by the Fuchs case. Geoffrey Patterson gloomily reported to London that the goodwill created by awarding Hoover an honorary KBE was in danger of being dissipated: 'Now we are faced with another case which can, to put it bluntly, upset the apple-cart.'[55] While in Washington, Sillitoe was briefed on SIS reports of Pontecorvo's defection by the SIS representative, Kim Philby. As Calder Walton has noted, the DG was thus, unwittingly, in the extraordinary position of being briefed on the movements of one Soviet agent by another Soviet agent.[56] Philby doubtless sent a full report to Moscow. Though Attlee had been sympathetic during the Fuchs case, he was exasperated by MI5's failure to prevent another atomic security scandal so soon afterwards. At a meeting with the Prime Minister, Sillitoe made the unlikely claim that it was 'quite probable that Pontecorvo had no intention of decamping to Russia' when he went on holiday.[57] The later defector Oleg Gordievsky, who knew KGB officers acquainted with the case, later revealed that Pontecorvo had first volunteered his services to Soviet intelligence soon after he arrived in Montreal during the war and was highly rated by his case officers.[58]

In the aftermath of Fuchs's conviction and Pontecorvo's defection, Attlee was anxious not to be taken by surprise again, and asked to be personally informed of any further 'cases of persons holding positions of great importance about whom there were unusual security doubts'. His attention was drawn to the case of Boris Davison,[59] a scientist who had been employed at Harwell after negative vetting had revealed no evidence against him in Security Service files. Davison's personnel file at Harwell, however, disclosed that, though his parents were British by birth, he himself had been born and brought up in Russia. Further investigation by MI5 then revealed that Davison's father currently lived in Moscow, that Davison himself had had 'Communist associations' at university (unsurprisingly, since the university was Leningrad), and that he had come under pre-war pressure to become a Soviet agent. In 1938, because he had refused to give up his British passport, his Soviet passport had not been renewed and he had moved to Britain. The Security Service concluded that 'Because he had undoubtedly had a complete conversion and was almost certainly completely trustworthy, no real risk had been run on this occasion; but . . . we ought to have got evidence of his conversion before deciding to accept him as a good risk.'[60] Given the Service's view that Davison was currently 'a good risk' and the difficulty of finding a replacement for him, Attlee agreed in January 1951 that he could remain at Harwell and 'personally accepted responsibility for any political consequences'.[61]

Both the Pontecorvo and Davison investigations strengthened the case for positive vetting, which was accepted by the Cabinet Committee on Subversive Activities, chaired by Attlee, on 13 November 1950. An attempt was made, however, to limit the demands on Security Service resources:

If Departments found themselves unable, from their own resources and from routine enquiry of the Security Service, to reach a certain conclusion, they should ask the Security Service to have specific enquiries made through the local police: such enquiries ought, however, to be exceptional and only taken in the last resort.[62]

With its parliamentary majority reduced to single figures after the February 1950 elections, the Attlee government dared not risk backbench claims that it was conducting a witch-hunt in the civil service. The Cabinet Committee on Subversive Activities therefore decided that the introduction of positive vetting (PV) would not be publicly announced, nor would individuals subject to it be informed that inquiries were being made about them.[63] The secrecy of the PV system inevitably limited its effectiveness. As Winnifrith later acknowledged, vetting inquiries could be directed only to 'third parties who were unlikely to blow the gaff'. Initially, it was expected that only 1,000 government posts would be subject to positive vetting, all of them ones in which 'the holder [was] privy to the whole of a vital secret of crucial value to an enemy'.[64]

The main pressure for extending positive vetting and making it publicly known came from the United States, whose concerns about weaknesses in British security were strengthened by the defection of Burgess and Maclean in April 1951.[65] In July 1951 the Americans called a Tripartite Conference on Atomic Energy with the British and Canadians in London. The Conference recommended that 'in future no one should be given access to classified atomic energy information unless he passed an open enquiry into his loyalty, character and background'[66] – thus extending the numbers subject to positive vetting in Britain from 1,000 to 11,000.[67] According to Winnifrith, the British delegation backed these proposals 'in the hope that they would lessen American doubts about the efficacy of our security arrangements and remove obstacles to greater co-operation in atomic energy matters'.[68] During its final months in power before losing the October 1951 election, the Labour government was reluctant to implement most of the proposals of the Tripartite Conference. It was left to Churchill's

Conservative administration to announce publicly in January 1952 a much expanded positive-vetting programme.[69]

Under the Churchill government the question arose for the first time of whether ministers with access to atomic secrets should be positively vetted. In retirement Attlee admitted that he had thought some of his cabinet 'were not fit to be trusted with secrets of this kind'.[70] As a result the momentous decision on 8 January 1947 to build the British atomic bomb was taken not by the full cabinet but by a specially convened Atomic Energy Cabinet Committee (GEN 163) consisting only of Attlee and five trusted ministers.[71] News of the decision was not made public until an answer by the Minister of Defence, A. V. Alexander, to a parliamentary question in May 1948. Alexander, however, was economical with the truth. Even Churchill was amazed after the 1951 Conservative election victory to discover that Attlee had concealed from the Commons the £100 million cost of the atomic bomb programme. Breaking with the precedent set by his predecessor, Churchill submitted the decision on whether to build a hydrogen bomb to the full cabinet, which approved it on 26 July 1954. His friend and adviser on nuclear policy, Lord Cherwell, then suggested that ministers, like everyone with access to 'the most vital atomic energy secrets', should be positively vetted. While Conservative ministers, he believed, were 'perfectly secure', a Labour prime minister, 'whose colleagues might not always be quite so exceptional', might well be grateful for the requirement that they undergo the PV process. The United States, Cherwell reported, did not wish to share atomic secrets with socialists. That, Churchill replied, was a problem not for him but for the Labour leadership: 'The Socialists must win the Americans' confidence like anyone else.' The best solution was for the British electorate 'not to elect them'. Churchill rejected the proposal to vet ministers.[72] It became the practice, however, immediately after every election for the DG to provide the PUS at the Home Office (later the Prime Minister) with a dossier on prospective cabinet ministers about whom MI5 had security concerns.[73]

American pressure was partially responsible for strengthening protective security as well as for the introduction of positive vetting. At tripartite discussions on security with the United States and France in 1953, the US delegates criticized the lack of any central UK authority responsible for setting and enforcing standards of protective security. In discussions with the cabinet secretary, Sir Norman Brook, the DDG Roger Hollis acknowledged that there was some force to the American criticism. Though the Security Service had produced a booklet of guidance on protective security, there was no mechanism to ensure that Whitehall departments acted on it. On Brook's proposal an official committee was established under his chairmanship with a membership consisting of the DG and department heads most concerned with protective security.[74] Thereafter much of Whitehall asked the Security Service to inspect security arrangements and recommend improvements. The main thrust of the Service's advice was that 'full-time security officers with authority to follow up security instructions are a necessity in any Government Department which has a substantial amount of classified material to protect.'[75] The part of government least interested in Security Service advice was the Houses of Parliament, whose security remained woeful until the beginning of the twenty-first century.[76]

In November 1954 the Security Service informed the Whitehall Personnel Security Committee that they had 'moved somewhat from their original position' on positive vetting and 'now appreciated more fully the advantage to be derived' from it.[77] 'At the risk of being smug,' wrote Sir John Winnifrith in a memorandum on vetting to the Security Conference of Privy Counsellors in 1955, 'I would like to say in the first place that, particularly given the speed with which it has been evolved, the present system is a pretty good one.'[78] Eleven thousand working in the atomic field had so far been positively vetted, with 3,000 PVs still to be completed. In other sensitive posts, 7,000 had been PV'd, with another 6,000 to follow.[79] There was no anti-Communist witch-hunt in Britain comparable to that led by Senator Joseph McCarthy in the United States. Two years after his election defeat, Attlee gave a withering response in an American journal to McCarthy's criticism of the Purge Procedure he had introduced: 'The Labour Party has had nearly 40 years of fighting Communism in Britain, and despite war and economic depression, the Communists have utterly failed. We are pardonably annoyed at being instructed by a beginner like Senator McCarthy.'[80] Between 1947 and 1956, US purges led to the sacking of 2,700 federal employees and the resignation of another 12,000.[81] By American standards, the numbers purged in Britain were small. The declared number of dismissals in the civil service (which probably included resignations and reassignment to non-sensitive work) during the period from 1948 to 1954 was 124. The main impact of vetting, however, was at the point of entry. Almost certainly more were refused entry, or were deterred from applying, than were dismissed.[82] The psychological impact was also considerable. Positive vetting was alien to the work culture of Whitehall. When Arthur de la Mare became head of the Foreign Office Security Department in 1955, it was still widely considered to be 'unBritish' and regarded by many diplomats with 'contempt and derision'. He complained that many of the referees nominated by members of the Diplomatic

Service who were being vetted 'protested to us and their MPs at being interrogated by "snarks" on the background and integrity of their friends'.[83]

Far more remarkable than the distaste felt by the Diplomatic Service was the opposition within the Security Service to applying positive vetting to itself. Among the leading opponents was Roger Hollis, who minuted as DDG in 1954 his opposition even to seeking referees for Service staff:

The secrecy of one's employment influences one's private life, and I doubt if any of us who have spent a number of years in the Security Service could produce referees whose testimonial would be really valuable. I am sure I could not and I should not like to ask my friends to act as referees in a matter of this importance because I do not think it would be fair to them . . .[84]

At a subsequent Directors' Meeting Hollis was overruled and staff were required to provide the names of two referees.[85] The requirement that all Security Service staff undergo positive vetting seems to have followed an embarrassing incident in its relations with the Atomic Weapons Research Establishment at Aldermaston, probably in 1957. Shortly before four of its officers were about to inspect security at Aldermaston, the Service was asked if all had been PV'd. They had not and rapid vetting had to be arranged. One of the four, who came from the north-east of England and had joined the Service two years earlier, recalls the irritation of Director B (personnel and organization), John Marriott, at his inability to provide London referees and the need to carry out hasty PV interviews in New-castle.[86] Even after the Aldermaston embarrassment, however, positive vetting of existing Security Service staff proceeded painfully slowly – so slowly that Hollis decreed as DG in 1957 that it was unnecessary to investigate staff who had joined before the introduction of PV, 'if there is evidence that references were taken up'.[87] Remarkably, Hollis also ruled that A4 (formerly B4) surveillance personnel and other staff members who did not have access to files need not be subject to the PV process.[88]

Positive vetting was not fully implemented within the Service until the early 1960s. Following spy scandals at the beginning of the decade,[89] an inquiry headed by Lord Radcliffe 'to review procedures and practices currently followed in the public service', which reported in 1962, led to an extension of vetting within the civil service. Hollis gave the cabinet secretary an undertaking that the whole Service would be PV'd. The Service officer who was asked to devise a PV system later recalled that John Marriott wanted nothing to do with it, and in any case 'hated' Hollis. Marriott was overridden. The officer who devised the system recruited a team of interviewing officers, mainly retired senior officers from the armed services, and interviewed the officer grades himself.[90]

The Radcliffe inquiry was deeply impressed by a Security Service briefing paper which reported that in the major civil service unions one-third of the permanent and one-quarter of the elected officials were Communists or sympathizers.[91] It concluded that Communist penetration of these unions was 'most dangerous to security' and recommended that:

Departments should have the right in respect of establishments or staff employed on secret work to deny access to or refuse to negotiate with trade union officials whom they had reason to believe were communists. This would require a formal challenge, in each case, with a right of appeal to the Three Advisers [on the vetting Tribunal].

Nine trade union officials were identified by the Security Service under the Purge Procedure as Communists who should be excluded from civil service negotiations, though two names were withdrawn before they had been formally submitted to ministers. The three-man Advisory Tribunal, under a new head, Sir Henry Hancock, former chairman of the Board of Inland Revenue, and with a changed membership, no longer had the harmonious working relationship with the Security Service of a decade earlier. The union officials who were purged had no official access to secrets, were not government servants and their livelihood was at risk. The Advisers, perhaps understandably, seemed to find their task distasteful. Challenging some of the Security Service evidence, one Adviser claimed that he had experience of 'distortion by security people'. At one of the hearings, when a photograph was produced as evidence of a union official's attendance at a Communist meeting, the Tribunal insisted on the appearance of a member of A4 who would be prepared to swear to the date on which the photograph was taken. It also became clear that the Advisers sometimes had their Security Service briefs before them when interviewing suspects, and put intelligence sources at risk by referring to surveillance photographs or to Communist Party registration cards. The Service none the less regarded the outcome of the Tribunal hearings as a success. Five of the union officials identified as Communists resigned their posts; two others were moved to jobs which involved no contact with sensitive departments.[92]

In the wake of the Radcliffe Report, the Security Service was anxious to limit the drain on its resources caused by increase in vetting. In October 1962 the DG, Sir Roger Hollis, attended a long meeting with the Chiefs of Staff to repel proposals that the Service should take over responsibility for vetting throughout Whitehall. In theory, each government department was responsible for organizing most of its vetting requirements in-house. In practice much vetting within Whitehall was done by the Ministry of Supply, which had accumulated relevant experience as a result of its involvement in the nuclear field. Hollis spoke for the Service as a whole when he told the Chiefs of Staff that vetting was a thankless task which was likely to become steadily more onerous.[93]

The Security Service also had to resist pressure for increased vetting from the British Broadcasting Corporation.[94] The main initiative for the introduction of vetting in the 1930s had come from the BBC's first director general, Sir John (later Lord) Reith, an authoritarian Calvinist, 6 feet 7 inches tall (aptly described by Churchill as 'the wuthering height'), whose interpretation of the requirements of public service broadcasting led him to seek MI5 assistance in excluding Communists and Fascists from the Corporation.[95] Kell agreed that 'general vetting' was required. Initially informal, negative vetting was formalized in 1937[96] and changed little over the next two decades. MI5 reported to the cabinet secretary, Sir Norman Brook, in 1952 that it was responsible for vetting about 5,000 of the BBC's 12,000 staff: all those who received monthly salaries, all non-British employees and about half the engineering staff.[97] The Security Service was then sending the BBC 'adverse reports' on about 10 per cent of its applicants.[98] Though it was up to the BBC whether to act on these reports,[99] during the early Cold War it seems to have done so. The Home Office forwarded to the Prime Minister, Winston Churchill, a 1952 MI5 report which concluded: 'Our considered opinion is that communist influence in the BBC is very slight and does not constitute a serious security danger.' The Security Service calculated that less than 1.5 per cent of BBC staff were known or suspected Communist Party members or sympathisers.[100]

The appointment of Sir Hugh Greene as BBC director general in 1960 was followed by a 'long dispute' with MI5. Despite his success in giving the Corporation a less stuffy image and his support for satirical programmes mocking establishment values such as That Was The Week That Was, Greene, according to a Security Service minute, 'wanted us to vet far more widely than we were prepared to do because they did not wish to employ anyone who might damage their reputation for impartiality'.[101] Hollis noted after a meeting with Greene that there was 'an irreconcilable difference' between them over the purpose of vetting: 'We were concerned with defence interests but they were really concerned with the avoidance of embarrassment.' The Home Office sided with MI5 and supported Hollis's refusal to extend vetting in the BBC.[102] The fact that vetting occurred at all remained a closely guarded secret. Both Greene and his head of administration, John Arkell, steadfastly refused to admit its existence. Arkell told a senior colleague in 1968 that he 'might like to gain a bit of credit for the BBC next time you talk to MI5' by telling them that, despite 'pointed and penetrating questions' in a recent press interview, 'I still denied that we had any vetting procedures.'[103] Though Sir Charles Curran, who became DG in 1969, lacked Greene's liberal reputation, he attached less importance to vetting. For the first few years of the Curran era, C3 complained that the BBC frequently ignored vetting advice: 'it was their deliberate policy to offer jobs to some people with ultra left records whom they considered to be imaginatively creative and desirable.'[104] The mood changed after Sir Michael Swann, former principal and vice chancellor of Edinburgh University, became BBC chairman in 1973. Swann told the Prime Minister, Harold Wilson, in 1975 that, though the situation in the Corporation 'was a picnic compared with Edinburgh University', he was concerned 'about "hippie" influences in the BBC':

. . . He thought that too many young producers approached every programme they did from the starting point of an attitude about the subject which could be summed up as: 'You are a shit.' It was an attitude which he and others in the management of the BBC deplored, and they would be using their influence as opportunity offered to try to counter it.[105]

C3 noted that the BBC now, once again, usually took its vetting advice.[106]

There was a case for some degree of vetting in the Corporation. It is scarcely imaginable, for example, that loyal adherents of the CPGB pro-Moscow line should have been employed in news rooms during the Korean War and the Hungarian Uprising. But the scale of the mass vetting of BBC staff (drastically cut back after it gave rise to public controversy in the mid-1980s)[107] now seems seriously disproportionate – though at the time it was accepted by successive governments. The fact that, in contrast to the Whitehall Purge Procedure, BBC management refused even to admit that it practised vetting added to the sense of injustice felt by those who believed, sometimes with good reason, that their careers had been damaged by it.[108]

Probably the most pointless vetting for which the Security Service was responsible was of homosexuals in the public service. The initial criteria for positive vetting had identified homosexuals as inherently untrustworthy.[109] In 1951, Graham Mitchell, then in charge of the Service' departmental security section, had produced the first detailed case for the vetting of gays. Though acknowledging that 'all lay generalisations are or should be suspect', Mitchell proposed as less suspect than other generalizations the claims that homosexuals were:

(a) maladjusted to the social environment and may therefore be of an unstable character;

(b) they stick together and are backward in giving information even though it is their duty to do so; and

(c) in so far as their activities are felonious they are at least in theory open to blackmail by a hostile intelligence agency.[110]

As the 1957 report of the Wolfenden Committee on Homosexual Offences and Prostitution made clear, at least the first two claims were ill founded.

Controversy over the alleged security risks posed by gays was revived by the case of John Vassall, who confessed in 1962 that, while working as a clerk in the office of the British naval attaché in Moscow, he had been blackmailed by the KGB and recruited as a Soviet agent after being secretly photographed (in his words) 'having oral, anal or a complicated series of sexual activities with a number of different men'.[111] In the aftermath of the Vassall affair, Director C (Bill Magan) was impressed by an alarmist report to the May 1963 Commonwealth Security Conference by Mr Kelly of the RCMP:

Kelly said that the Canadian Government has an absolute rule against the employment of homosexuals on sensitive work ... A purge has been going on on an extensive scale. It has not led to embarrassment or administrative difficulty. Investigations point to some 10% of Government servants being homosexuals. The practice is not concentrated in any identifiable types of people; it is spread pretty evenly involving the highest and the lowest, administrative, executive, clerical staffs, service officers, other ranks and so on. A considerable number of high officials and armed forces officers have been purged. (One very senior Foreign Affairs official was thought to have had homosexual associations with one of HMG's ambassadors.) In Kelly's own words, 'Shoals of people have been brought back from behind the Iron Curtain.'[112]

To assess the problem in Britain, HOWs were obtained for telephone checks in 1964–5 on four suspected homosexuals in the public service. Three were discovered to be relatively discreet in their relationships. The telecheck on the fourth, however, generated an 'immense amount of material' involving over 250 men engaged in 'long telephone conversations which were often of a revolting nature'. The transcribers found the whole exercise a stressful experience: 'The regular members of [his] circle were much given to referring to each other by girls' names (Maud, Kitty, Alice and so on). This transposing of the sexes, and the use of other homosexual slang, at times made for difficulties of interpretation.'[113] The Security

Service, however, saw no reason to follow the Canadian example: 'It was concluded that the present criterion was right, i.e. that homosexuality raises a presumption of unfitness to hold a P.V. post but the presumption can be disregarded by the Head of the Department if he is satisfied in all the circumstances that this can be done without prejudice to national security.' In 1965 the Security Service successfully resisted the Treasury view that it might be necessary to treat homosexuality as an absolute bar against holding any post which required positive vetting.[114]

Though its criteria were never fully spelt out, the Service seems to have been relatively unconcerned during positive vetting by the presence of gays in the government service, provided that they did not actually identify themselves as homosexual and remained discreet about their sexual liaisons (which, until 1967, remained illegal). After the passage in 1967 of the Sexual Offences Act, which embodied the ten-year-old Wolfenden recommendation to legalize gay sex between consenting adults, C Branch recommended to Whitehall's Personnel Security Committee (PSC) that the issue of homosexuality should continue to be considered during the PV process because the risk of blackmail remained. The PSC agreed. In guidance to government departments, however, it was suggested that, since lawbreaking was no longer involved, they might now be able to decide in favour of individuals who would previously have failed positive vetting. Much of Whitehall none the less remained anxious. The Service continued to receive numerous requests from government departments for advice on whether individual homosexuals were security risks. As late as 1969 almost 50 per cent of the 'character defect' cases passed to the Service concerned homosexuality.[115]

5

The Communist Party of Great Britain, the Trade Unions and the Labour Party

Pressure of work had forced the wartime Security Service to give up the attempt to keep a comprehensive database of all CPGB members. The Service told chief constables in 1942 that henceforth it would concentrate on maintaining records on Party officials and keeping track of Communist activity in the armed forces and other sensitive areas. That policy, reaffirmed in another circular to chief constables in December 1945, changed three years later with the onset of the Cold War. Attlee's announcement to the Commons in March 1948 of the Purge Procedure, designed to exclude Communists and Fascists from work 'vital to the Security of the State', made it necessary to identify all Communists as well as the few remaining Fascists. The Service concluded in October 1948, 'Our ultimate aim must be the keeping of accurate records of all members of the [CPGB].'[1] In most respects the CPGB was 'a political party like other political parties', with officials who spent most of their time on humdrum administration. But, because of its loyalty to Moscow, there was a danger that, in wartime, it would 'prove a formidable fifth column'.[2]

The Service had extraordinary success in gaining access to Party membership records through both agents and a series of operations collectively codenamed STILL LIFE which gained covert entry into all British and Northern Irish local Party offices. The first major operation, RED KNIGHT in 1949, succeeded in copying Party registration forms for the London district.[3] An even more successful operation, PARTY PIECE, followed the discovery that a large collection of Party records were stored in the house of the Communist Berger family[4] at 5 Grove Terrace, Highgate Road, in north-west London.[5] Roland Berger had first been identified as an undercover Communist and member of a Communist cell in the civil service during the Second World War.[6] After working for the United Nations from 1947 to 1952, he established the British Council for the Promotion of International Trade, which at one point was believed to be a conduit for Soviet funding of the CPGB.[7] An MI5 officer, who became tenant of a flat in the Berger household, organized the first phase of Operation PARTY PIECE in June 1955, during which about 6,000 documents were copied inside the house. Three months later, 48,000 documents were secretly removed at night in suitcases to be photographed at Leconfield House and returned before their absence was noticed. Security Service files were regularly updated by further covert entries into local Party offices, at first every three years, later at five-year intervals.[8] Such was the expertise of the STILL LIFE operations that they passed virtually undetected.

Sillitoe told Attlee in May 1949 that 'we now had quite a number of agents in the Communist Party who were well-placed and gave us good coverage.' 'The P.M.', noted Liddell, 'seemed particularly pleased about this.'[9] Like Olga Gray in the 1930s,[10] the most successful penetration agent in the early Cold War was probably one of Maxwell Knight's women agents.[11] She applied to join MI5 after the war but said she could not make ends meet on the salary she was offered and accepted a better-paid post elsewhere. Norman Himsworth, an officer in Knight's section who had himself successfully penetrated the Party early in the war, then recommended her recruitment as an agent.[12] Knight invited her to lunch at Canuto's and told Dick White afterwards, 'I feel very strongly she is the sort of agent for whom we have been looking for so long.'[13] Himsworth, who became her case officer, called her his 'Number 1' agent.[14]

Within a year of joining the Party, the agent had been asked to work for it and, like Olga Gray, 'was treated as part of the furniture, which is what she wanted'.[15] For a decade she provided regular reports (eventually filling thirty-two volumes) as well as, intermittently, Party records. Though highly motivated, she eventually became depressed by the atmosphere within the CPGB: 'When she saw it at close quarters she saw the deceit, ruthlessness and double standards of CPGB officials. She admitted that by working for "the elite" of the CPGB she might see these aspects more clearly than a rank and file member.'[16] To maintain her cover, she lived in what she found depressing working-class accommodation, rarely went on holiday, lacked opportunities to make new friends, and had to fend off sexual harassment by a Communist colleague.[17] Once it was clear that she had become burned out, it was mutually agreed that she should cease work as an agent.[18] Probably with Kipling's Kim in mind, she wrote to the DG, 'It has always been a deep satisfaction to me to be able to play a small part in the game.'[19]

As late as the summer of 1950, the CPGB leadership gave no sign of realizing either the level of Security Service penetration or that the Service had gained extensive access to its membership records. The Party's industrial organizer, George Allison, told a closed (but bugged) meeting of Communist trade union officials that he believed:

MI5 coverage of the Party was extremely haphazard so far as the purge was concerned, and that they relied upon liaison with the heads of firms, etc, for their information [about Party membership], which, he thought, was obtained through suggestion boxes, i.e. in some factories and firms fellow workers put notes in these boxes, probably with malicious intent, saying that so-and-so is a Communist, etc.

Allison's misconceptions were greeted with delight by the Service leadership.[20] At the end of 1950, however, the detailed knowledge of Party members displayed during the Purge Procedure at last led the CPGB leadership to conclude that the Service must have gained access to some of its membership records. Alerted to this discovery by agents and technical intelligence, the Service requested that the Purge Procedure be pursued less energetically. Attlee agreed to instruct permanent under secretaries to try for the time being to avoid purging Communists in some districts and merely move them to less sensitive posts.[21]

In 1952 the Security Service reported that a comparison of its existing files on the CPGB with the latest sample of current Party membership records it had purloined indicated that it had identified approximately 90 per cent of the 35,000 CPGB members. The missing 10 per cent were thought to be mostly young or new members 'who have not yet come to notice and who are so far of minor security significance'.[22] The Service's main difficulty was in coping with the sheer volume of CPGB records it obtained. F4 reported in 1970 that over the past year it had 'handled approximately 20,000 items of Still Life. Often Still Life from several districts may arrive together with a result that a backlog of valuable security information builds up in F4.'[23]

The Service's most reliable way of keeping track of the Party leadership was through hidden microphones and tapping telephones at the CPGB's London headquarters in King Street, Covent Garden. In 1943 Blunt revealed to his Soviet controller that a microphone had been placed in King Street. Soviet intelligence passed this report to the CPGB, which searched its premises but failed to find any eavesdropping equipment.[24] After the war, eavesdropping detected 'periodic scares about the presence of microphones'. On one occasion all the floorboards were taken up in an attempt to find them – but to no avail.[25] From time to time eavesdropping in King Street revealed an awareness that the telephones were tapped. On 22 January 1948, for example, the future general secretary John Gollan was heard complaining to an unidentified Party member: 'That bloody phone there – the fact that you phoned me, they know. What I said to you, they know. They open our letters. They go to our meetings. We are spending more on the bloody Secret Service now than we ever spent in the years of British history. The spies are everywhere!' Gollan added that none of this would become public knowledge 'until we've cracked the [intelligence] archives one day. Then you'll know what was going on!'[26] 'In practice,' the Security Service noted in 1968, 'the Party has never taken any prolonged counter-measures other than the development [in 1965] of Room 10 as a safe room.' The Party was unaware that Room 10 was also bugged, though sound quality from the hidden microphone was poor.[27]

The Security Service had 'good coverage' of the secret Soviet funding of the CPGB, monitoring by surveillance and telecheck the regular collection of Moscow's cash subsidies by two members of the Party's International Department, Eileen Palmer and Bob Stewart, from the north London address of two ex-trainees of the Moscow Radio School.[28] The Service was also well informed about the Party leadership's attempts to deal with ideological dissidence among its members. One of its best sources, apart from its coverage of King Street, was an HOW on the formidable Betty Reid, who from 1946 was in charge of 'membership' issues – a euphemism for checking members' loyalty and identifying those who failed to follow the Party line. Even a sympathetic history of the CPGB describes her as 'the party's witchfinder general'. In public Reid was uncompromising on the need to confront heresy: 'Political differences, if they are not challenged and thrashed out, can over a period become so deep that in the end disciplinary action is the only solution.'[29] Security Service surveillance revealed a more human side to Ms Reid. According to an assessment forwarded to the Home Office by the DG:

In spite of her bulk and apparent lack of beauty she is a feminine personality . . . [who] tends to have a disarming effect on comrades who have been summoned to see her, and have mounted the stairs to the Org[anisation] Dept. prepared for severity. As far as I know, she has been entirely responsible for the elaborate machinery for the vetting of party comrades . . . Her patience and robust sense of humour are more than a match for the leg-pulling to which she is constantly subjected, and her great weakness is a profound liking for cheese cake![30]

Reid also had a weakness for cream cakes, which was regularly indulged by her contact at the Soviet embassy, Nikolai Timofeyev, whom she called her 'cream cake pal'. Though playing a key role in Party security, Reid became convinced that her own security had been compromised, believing that the home help she employed from 1950 onwards was a Security Service agent.[31]

It did not require secret intelligence to detect the CPGB's subservience to Soviet dogma. The Party continued to perform almost instantaneous ideological somersaults at a word of command from Moscow. When the Yugoslav Communist leader, Josip Tito, was officially unmasked as a heretic, James Klugmann, his long-time friend and admirer, denounced him in a rapidly composed polemic entitled *From Trotsky to Tito*. The price of the Party's servility to Soviet interests at the beginning of the Cold War was electoral disaster. At the 1950 general election both the Communist MPs elected in 1945, Willie Gallacher and Phil Piratin, lost their seats. The Party's general secretary, Harry Pollitt, went immediately to Moscow to seek advice from Stalin, whom he regarded as a friend, as well as from Soviet Communist Party apparatchiks. After a second trip to Moscow he returned with a document which formed the basis of a new Party manifesto, *The British Road to Socialism*, published in February 1951 and pledging it to a parliamentary route to power.[32] At the general election eight months later, standing on this manifesto, all ten CPGB candidates lost their deposits.

Telechecks, eavesdropping and agent penetration gave the Security Service a secret ringside seat at the disputes within the CPGB provoked by Khrushchev's admission of some of the horrors of the Stalin era during his 'Secret Speech' to the 1956 Soviet Party Congress, which was published in the West (though not in the Soviet Union). During a bugged conversation at the home of the Communist Berger family in Highgate, Nan Berger (Roland Berger's wife, née Whittaker) was heard to tell a Polish visitor that 'A great many people had been completely knocked out by it [the Secret Speech] and just could not believe it. Another very large group were now saying "Well, really we've known this all the time. This is what the capitalist press have been saying, and we've been pretending it hasn't been so." '[33] The crushing of the Hungarian Uprising by Soviet tanks in the autumn of 1956 provoked an even greater crisis of confidence among Party members than the Secret Speech. In the course of the year, 7,000 people – over a quarter of the membership – left the Party.[34] John Gollan, who succeeded Pollitt as general secretary, and the rest of the Party leadership, however, remained unswervingly loyal to the Soviet Union. Gollan 'used to say in difficult moments that he could have done with a direct telephone line to Moscow'.[35]

Late in 1947 the cabinet secretary, Sir Norman Brook, had initiated a review of the 1939 Government War Book, which included preparations for internment.[36] In the early Cold War the Security Service used its extensive records on the CPGB to identify the Moscow loyalists most likely to support the Soviet Bloc in a conflict with the West. Some, undoubtedly, would have done so. The editor of the *Daily Worker*, William Rust, declared at the beginning of 1948, 'There are now two camps in the world: the imperialist camp and the democratic camp.'[37] His loyalties and those of his comrades, he declared, belonged to the 'democratic camp', led by the Soviet Union. By August 1950 the Security Service had identified about 980 British men and 100 women (one-third of them in London), 150 Soviet citizens and 'at least' 1,500 male and 1,300 female other 'enemy aliens' for internment 'when the flag falls'.[38] As in the Second World War, the main internment centre during war with the Soviet Bloc was to be the Isle of Man, where two holiday camps 'could be made available at 48 hours notice by arrangement with the owners'. The core of the Service's list of British detainees was its Category A list of Communists, defined as:

All full-time employees of the Communist Party, the Young Communist League and the Daily Worker (editorial and reporter staff only); all members of the Executive Committee of the Communist Party; all members of the National Committee of the Young Communist League; and all members of the District Committees of the Communist Party. [39]

The JIC, as well as the Security Service, was confident that internment would prevent the emergence of a significant British Communist fifth column supporting the Soviet war effort.

Organised sabotage before the war is most unlikely because the Soviet leaders will be unwilling to give away their plans to Communists in the United Kingdom. No organised sabotage will take place after the outbreak of war because, as at present planned, the whole known organisation of the British Communist Party will have been smashed [by internment].[40]

The elaborate preparations during the 1950s for wartime internment looked back to the experience of the Second World War rather than forward to the unprecedented horrors of thermonuclear warfare. The JIC calculated in 1955 that the Soviet Union would not use H-bombs against Britain until it could launch a devastating nuclear attack against the United States, which, it estimated, was unlikely before 1960.[41] Defence reviews in the later 1950s produced a fundamental change in internment policy. The Service's Legal Adviser noted after a meeting at the Home Office in March 1959:

We were now to plan for a war of very short duration and complete devastation, and we were not to plan for any long-term war. In the circumstances it seemed to the Home Office that it was quite impracticable to carry out any detention and internment policy involving the present number of persons . . .

Plans for internment camps were abandoned because of the impossibility of installing their inmates before the bombs started falling.[42] Detention was to take place in prison instead. As in the preparation of previous internment plans, the cabinet played no part. Sir Charles Cunningham, PUS at the Home Office, wrote to Hollis: 'The present arrangements do not seem to have been approved by any Official or Ministerial Committee. You may agree, therefore, that arrangements for implementing any revised plans can similarly be made without submission for any formal approval.'[43] Hollis approved, indeed doubtless welcomed, the continued lack of ministerial interference.[44] By May Day 1959, the Security Service had reduced its list of wartime internees to 110 British subjects (mostly Communists) and eleven aliens. The total included ten women.[45] The drastic scaling down of plans for internment meant that, for the first time, the Security Service had no major role in the preparations for war set out in the current War Book.[46]

By the 1950s the Service no longer saw the CPGB as a major subversive political threat. Norman Himsworth wrote dismissively in January 1951:

The British Communist Party at the moment is led by a group of old men unable, or unwilling, to pass on the responsibilities of office to younger and more energetic comrades. Never before, perhaps, in the history of the Party has the leadership been so poor, so incapable of carrying the masses with it, as it is today.[47]

The Service regarded the main subversive threat from the CPGB as industrial rather than political. Attlee too was deeply concerned about Communist influence in the trade unions. By 1947 the government had a tendency to identify all industrial stoppages with Communist subversion.[48] At the height of post-war shortages and rationing in November 1947, Attlee was counting on popular enthusiasm for the wedding in Westminster Abbey between the heir to the throne, Princess Elizabeth, and Lieutenant Philip Mountbatten to help lift the spirits of the country, and he feared the CPGB was planning to depress them. The Prime Minister 'expressed great anxiety' to Sillitoe 'about the Communists; he thought they were promoting strikes to threaten the Royal Wedding.'[49] In May 1948 the Security Service warned the cabinet that the CPGB aim was 'to secure control of each individual union and, through the union, of the General Council and the Annual Assembly of the Trades Union Congress, potent forces in political life'. In view of the fact that only 30,000 of the 8.7 million union members were

21. The First World War fighter ace Christopher Draper (*left*), meeting Adolf Hitler at a Munich air display in 1932. Between them are two German pilots. After Hitler came to power in 1933, Draper was asked to supply intelligence on the RAF to the Abwehr He informed MI5 and began work as its first double agent to operate against Germany since the First World War.

22. Draper was known as the 'Mad Major' because of his penchant for flying under bridges. He is shown here approaching Westminster Bridge.

23. (*above left*) Wolfgang zu Putlitz, MI5's most important source in the pre-war German embassy in London. He communicated with MI5 via his friend Jona 'Klop' Ustinov (24. *above right*), a German journalist in London who became an MI5 agent (codenamed U35) in 1935. (The illustration shows Ustinov's Alien's Registration Card issued by the London City Police in 1920.) MI5's leadership was strongly influenced by Putlitz's insistence that the only way to deal with Hitler was to stand firm; appeasement would not work.

25. Dick White (a future head of both MI5 and SIS), who became Ustinov's case officer in 1939, called him the 'best and most ingenious operator I had the honour to work with'. White did not take easily to wearing uniform in wartime. An MI5 colleague once found him with 'his Sam Browne the wrong way round; the front was at the back and it was filthy'.

26. (*above*) The calm before the bombs. Staff relaxing at Wormwood Scrubs in the summer of 1940 before the London Blitz forced MI5 to leave.

27. (*left*) Wormwood Scrubs, 1939. A Civilian officer at work in one of the cells at Wormwood Scrubs. Cell doors had no handles or locks on the inside, so, as one MI5 veteran recalls, staff 'stood a good chance of being locked in by unwary visitors'.

28. An isolated Vernon Kell at Wormwood Scrubs at about the time he was sacked in June 1940, after thirty-one years as head of MI5.

29. Folkert van Koutrik was recruited by the Abwehr as a double agent in 1938 while working for the SIS head-agent in The Hague. After the German invasion of the Low Countries in May 1940, van Koutrik fled to Britain and was taken on by MI5 to make 'special enquiries' about foreign refugees. For the first time in its history, MI5 was thus penetrated by a German agent, though in the event van Koutrik did not take the risk of renewing contact with the Abwehr after moving to Britain.

30. In June 1940 MI5 recruited the Soviet agent Anthony Blunt, shown here in the uniform of the Intelligence Corps at about the time he joined the Security Service.

31. Surveillance photo of John Gollan (centre, later CPGB general secretary), leaving a meeting of the CPGB Central Committee, 30 January 1942. Blunt was able to warn his Soviet case officer of surveillance of the CPGB leadership, including the bugging of its King Street headquarters.

32. (*above*) MI5's wartime interrogation centre, Camp 020, based in Latchmere House near Ham Common in west London. Some of the most successful double agents were 'turned' during interrogation here.

33. (*left*) Robin 'Tin-eye' Stephens, Commandant of Camp 020, wearing the monocle that gave him his nickname.

34. Thomas Argyll 'Tar' Robertson, head of MI5's double-agent section, B1a. A former Seaforth Highlander, Tar continued to wear his tartan Seaforth trews in MI5, thus earning the nickname 'Passion Pants'.

35. The Oxford historian J. C. Masterman, recruited to MI5 by his former pupil Dick White. Masterman chaired the Twenty Committee, which was at the heart of the Double-Cross System, feeding disinformation to the enemy.

36. Juan Pujol (GARBO), probably the most successful of the wartime double agents, outside Buckingham Palace on the fortieth anniversary of D-Day in June 1984, after being congratulated by the Duke of Edinburgh. Pujol is wearing the MBE awarded to him forty years earlier.

37. GARBO's wartime case officer, Tomás 'Tommy' Harris, the bilingual son of an English father and Spanish mother. The two men formed one of the most creative agent/case officer partnerships in MI5 history.

38. MI5's first female agent-runner, Mary Sherer was allowed to run only a small number of female agents: chief among them the able but temperamental double agent Nathalie 'Lily' Sergueiev (TREASURE).

39. Nathalie 'Lily' Sergueiev (TREASURE), shown here with her Abwehr case officer, Major Kleimann, blamed the British for the death of her dog Babs (40. *above right*), which she had been forced to leave in Portugal because of British quarantine regulations. She admitted to Sherer that, in revenge, she had planned to blow the double-agent operation to the Germans – though she finally decided not to do so.

42. Victor, third Baron Rothschild, heir to a banking dynasty and one of Britain's most gifted polymaths, founded MI5's first counter-sabotage department in a cell in Wormwood Scrubs. Rothschild owed much of his success in defusing German bombs to the expertise in dissection he had learned as a zoologist at Cambridge University.

41. Guy Liddell (pictured here with his brother David, also an MI5 officer) was Director of B Division (counter-espionage) from 1940 to 1946 and DDG from 1946 to 1952. Even Kim Philby remembered him as 'an ideal senior officer for a young man to learn from'.

43. In February 1944, Rothschild defused a bomb concealed in this crate of onions imported from Spain, reporting by field telephone that he had found a 'characteristic block of German TNT' (arrowed). Churchill took the personal decision to award him the George Medal for bravery.

Communist, the Service believed that the CPGB had acquired astonishing influence in the labour movement, thanks, in part, to the 'apathy' of most non-Communist trade unionists. It had adopted an insidious strategy of entryism into the trade union movement, sometimes flagrantly falsifying ballot papers. The Service claimed to have abundant evidence of electoral malpractice. It gave the example of a recent ballot of the Boilermakers Society when only 4,000 of the 80,000 members cast their vote and many blank ballot forms were 'filled in at Party headquarters'.[50]

Attlee was alarmed by such reports and turned for assistance to the Foreign Office Information Research Department (IRD), founded in January 1948 to expose the aims of Soviet Communism and its Western disciples. In June 1948 the Minister of Labour, George Isaacs, told a cabinet committee that one of 'the most urgent tasks was to organise effective opposition to the election of Communists to key positions in the Executives of the Unions'.[51] The International Department of the Labour Party, then headed by the former Communist and future deputy Labour leader Denis Healey, proved adept at passing on anonymous IRD briefing materials to trade unions and other sections of the labour movement.[52]

In October 1948 the TUC General Council accused the CPGB of pursuing a strategy of industrial disruption on orders from Moscow.[53] Vic Feather, assistant secretary (later general secretary) of the TUC, gave a well-received address to a joint MI5–SIS Russian Studies Weekend at Worcester College, Oxford, in September 1951 on 'Communism in the Trade Unions':

Mr Feather said that the TUC 'had tabs' on all those known to it as Communists ... Though Mr Feather said nothing that was new from our point of view, he reflected the feeling of confidence of the TUC in its powers to handle the situation and shewed that it is very much alive to what is going on. He obviously did not disclose all that he knew and it seems that the TUC have good sources of information, at least on the more purely industrial side of Communism. Probably it runs a few agents.

Feather believed that, in the midst of the Korean War, the CPGB was out to disrupt British rearmament by making its priority targets for strike action:

(1) Engineering (the hub of the rearmament programme)
(2) Docks (the focal point of rearmament transport, since railways are not concentrated and can be operated by troops, or replaced by road transport)[54]

The Security Service agreed. Following Churchill's return to power after the Conservative election victory in October 1951, the Service reported that the CPGB was trying to promote a new strike wave. In July 1952, Sillitoe told the Home Secretary, David Maxwell Fyfe:

Since the end of 1951 the Communist Party has been following a militant policy in industry. The Party instructions to its followers in British industry are that strike action must be achieved where possible.

A disturbing feature of Communist Party tactics in industry is their apparent concentration on engineering firms engaged on work affecting the rearmament programme.[55]

The Industrial Desk of F1 supplied the Ministry of Labour and its successor, the Department of Employment and Productivity (DEP), with intelligence on Communist and Trotskyist penetration of the executive committees and full-time official positions of major unions and involvement in industrial disputes – mostly derived from a mixture of eavesdropping at CPGB HQ, telephone checks and F4 agent reports.[56] In May 1953 the Confederation of Shipbuilding and Engineering Unions demanded a 15 per cent wage increase. Sillitoe informed Maxwell Fyfe at his room in the Commons: 'Communist inspiration for and interest in the demand is clear; and, though we do not know the full story, it is difficult to escape the conclusion that, but for the Party's efforts, the present demand might never have been formulated.'[57]

In the spring of 1956 the Security Service circulated to the Official Committee on Communism (Home) a memorandum on 'Communism and the Trade Unions' which set out what became a recurrent theme in its reporting on the subject: that CPGB strategy was to use industrial unrest as a means of capturing and consolidating positions of power and influence in the trade union movement. Partly as a result of this strategy, one in eight union officials and members of executive committees were either Party members or Communist sympathizers. The Minister of Labour discussed this report with three leading anti-Communist trade unionists, who argued that the most effective means of countering Communist influence in the union movement would be to publicize evidence of Communist ballot-rigging. A working group with representatives of the Security Service was established under the aegis of the Official Committee on Communism (Home) with the aim of publicizing such abuses and halting the run of Communist successes in union elections.[58]

During his brief and ill-fated term as prime minister in succession to Churchill, Sir Anthony Eden took a close interest in the Service's work on counter-subversion.[59] In June 1956 he formally commended the Service memorandum on 'Communism and the Trade Unions'. The Home Secretary told the DG, Sir Roger Hollis, that 'M.I.5's reputation stood very high, and that in discussion with the Prime Minister about the frogman case [the bungled SIS attempt to use 'Buster' Crabb to inspect the hull of the Soviet cruiser *Ordzhonikidze* during its goodwill visit to Portsmouth in April], the Prime Minister had told the Home Secretary he was sure M.I.5 was much more disciplined than M.I.6 and that we would be unlikely to take any risky action without Ministerial authority'.[60] One 'unfortunate' risk was, however, taken in 1957. Intelligence on a leading Communist rail-wayman, obtained in anticipation of a Home Office Warrant which the Home Secretary was expected to sign, was given to the chairman of the British Transport Authority, who used it to help settle a dispute. The Home Secretary, however, then declined to sign the warrant. Such incidents were very rare. According to a memorandum of 1970, there had also been no subsequent example of industrial intelligence being passed directly to an employer.[61]

From 1957 onwards, the Service provided much of the material which was covertly used by Whitehall to orchestrate publicity campaigns against Communist influence in the union movement. By far the most successful of these campaigns was against Communist ballot-rigging in the Electrical Trades Union (ETU),[62] which was exposed by two ETU officials, Les Cannon and Frank Chapple, who left the CPGB in protest against the Soviet suppression of the 1956 Hungarian Uprising. Though ousted from his job as the ETU education officer, in 1957 Cannon beat a Communist candidate, John Frazer, for a place on the ETU executive. The election results, however, were falsified and Frazer declared the winner.[63] Cannon was barred for five years from holding union office, but began a long, exhausting and eventually victorious battle against ETU ballot-rigging. Two BBC *Panorama* programmes presented by the Labour MP Woodrow Wyatt made the ballot-rigging scandal front-page news.[64] Cannon's main ally within the ETU was Frank Chapple, who succeeded in gaining a place on the executive in 1958 and survived a campaign of intimidation to force him out.[65]

The ETU scandal reached its peak when the Communist general secretary, Frank Haxell, was declared to have been re-elected in 1959. Eaves-dropping at King Street revealed that, in reality, his anti-Communist opponent Jock Byrne had won the election. Haxell was heard reassuring Party comrades that he would fix the result.[66] The Security Service was able to listen in on a series of meetings between the Communist members of the ETU executive and Party leaders. Hollis informed the Home Office early in 1960:

We know from our coverage of Party Headquarters and of two or three of the private meeting places chosen by it that twelve meetings were held during 1959 of the Party's Advisory Committee for the E.T.U. This committee consists of 9 communist members of the Union including the President, General Secretary and Assistant General Secretary, and is chaired by [Peter] Kerrigan, the Party's National Industrial Organiser. On one or two recent occasions [John] Gollan himself has attended. This information has been made available to the Ministry of Labour.[67]

The Service's access to the inner workings of both King Street and the ETU goes far to explain why Hollis felt able to assure the Home Secretary: 'On the subversive side I thought we had the British Communist party pretty well buttoned up.'[68]

The climax of the media outcry which followed Haxell's re-election as general secretary was a television interview by the former Labour junior minister John Freeman (later ambassador in Washington) with the ETU president, Frank Foulkes, on BBC's *Face to Face*. The good offices of the Labour MP and television presenter Christopher Mayhew, who as a junior minister had helped to found the IRD, were used to arrange the interview. The Security Service was kept informed.[69] Freeman challenged the evasive Foulkes to sue him and the BBC if the charges of election-rigging which he made against the ETU leadership were untrue. The TUC General Council also called on the union to take legal action to defend the good name of the labour movement. According to Chapple, the atmosphere on the ETU executive, of which he was still a member, 'dripped with venom'.[70]

Victory in the campaign against Communist ballot-rigging came with the civil case brought in 1961 by Cannon and Chapple against Foulkes and others in the ETU leadership. Appearing for the plaintiffs, Gerald Gardiner QC (later a Labour lord chancellor), claimed that the defendants were guilty of 'the biggest fraud in the history of trade unionism'. A Service officer spent what he later described as 'a very enjoyable fortnight' attending the trial,[71] during which the ten defendants who appeared in the witness box were discredited one by one. The judge, Mr Justice Winn, dismissed the evidence of Haxell and Frazer as 'puerile mendacities', and condemned the other eight for their lack of truthfulness. He ruled that Haxell and his colleagues had rigged the ballot, and declared Byrne the winner of the election for general secretary. The CPGB was also implicated. Mr Justice Winn found that 'not only was the ETU managed and controlled by Communists and pliant sympathisers, but it was so managed in the service of the Communist Party and the ideas of the Party.'[72] Subsequent claims by sympathetic historians that there was in fact no 'evidence implicating King Street in the affair'[73] are contradicted by the evidence of Security Service files. King Street, however, sought to distance itself from the ballot-rigging by holding an inquiry. Haxell, probably under CPGB pressure, resigned his Party membership. The TUC followed the court case by demanding that Foulkes, who had been named as party to the fraud by the court, submit himself to re-election for the post of ETU president. When Foulkes refused, the ETU was expelled from membership of the TUC.[74] In fresh elections to the executive every Communist candidate was defeated.

By the beginning of the 1960s the leadership of the Labour opposition was probably more concerned about Communist subversion than the Conservative government. Ever since its landslide election victory in 1945, Labour leaders had been worried by the presence of what they believed were 'crypto-Communists' on their backbenches. The *Daily Worker* news editor, Douglas Hyde, later recalled answering the phone on the morning after the election:

The man at the other end announced himself as the new Labour member for his constituency. He followed it with a loud guffaw and rang off. I had known him as a Communist Party man for years ... By the time the list [of Labour MPs] was complete, we knew that we had at least eight or nine 'cryptos' in the House of Commons in addition to our two publicly acknowledged M.P.s.[75]

Francis Beckett's history of the Communist Party concludes that, after the 1945 election, 'About a dozen of the 393 Labour MPs were either secret CP members or were close to the CP, sharing its beliefs and enjoying the company of its leaders.'[76] In November 1946, Attlee instructed the DDG, Guy Liddell, to inform him whenever 'we had positive information that a Member of Parliament was a member of a subversive organisation'. Liddell believed that Attlee felt 'he had a responsibility to the House and country to see that such members did not get into positions where they might constitute a danger to the state.'[77] Morgan Phillips, general secretary of the Labour Party, kept a 'Lost Sheep' file on pro-Soviet MPs who 'used their positions and their prestige, as members of the British House of Commons, in a manner inimical to the work of the party and in support of policies which, time and again, had been rejected by the Annual Party Congress'. Information on the misbehaviour of the Lost Sheep came from a great variety of open sources: among them other MPs, Party members and the press.[78] It also drew on material supplied by the intelligence communities on both sides of the Atlantic.[79] In 1948–9 four of the Lost Sheep – John Platts-Mills, Konni Zilliacus, Hugh Lester Hutchinson and Leslie Solley –

were expelled from the Party by the Labour National Executive Committee.[80] Platts-Mills, the first to be expelled, later acknowledged in his unpublished autobiography that he had 'hurled himself at Ernie Bevin like a clenched fist whenever he appeared ... to be acting ... more abjectly servile than usual to United States foreign policy. This was only about once a day.'[81] Morgan Phillips had another fifteen MPs[82] on his Lost Sheep list marked down for possible expulsion, though none was in the end expelled.

Among the evidence in the Service's possession which suggests that Zilliacus may have been a secret member of the Communist Party in the immediate aftermath of the Second World War was a notebook belonging to Mrs Margaret Thornhill, who was suspected of involvement with 'an undercover department of the C.P. run by [D. N.] Pritt and [Jack] Gaster'. Thornhill had written 'Dues' on the cover of the notebook in which she recorded monthly payments from a list of individuals headed by Zilliacus. The next two names on the list appeared to be those of the pro-Soviet Labour MPs Stephen Swingler and William Warbey (though only their surnames were listed).[83] Both were on Morgan Phillips's list of Lost Sheep. Attlee told Sillitoe in 1947 that he was 'certain that Swingler was a C.P. member'.[84] Zilliacus ceased to be a Lost Sheep after he sided with Tito against Stalin and was denounced as a Fascist by the Soviet press; he was readmitted to the Labour Party in 1952.[85] The other three Lost Sheep expelled in 1948–9 were defeated in the 1950 election and did not return to the Commons.

The concern of the Labour leadership with the Lost Sheep on its backbenches declined somewhat after the Party's 1951 election defeat but revived in the early 1960s as it scented the prospect of a return to power after more than a decade in opposition. In August 1961 Hugh Gaitskell, the Party leader, agreed with George Brown, the deputy leader, and Patrick Gordon Walker, his closest associates within the shadow cabinet, that Gordon Walker should approach the Security Service to seek help in identifying secret Communists within the Parliamentary Labour Party (PLP). No other member of the shadow cabinet, including Gaitskell's eventual successor, Harold Wilson, was informed of their intention.[86] Gaitskell and his colleagues knew so little about the intelligence community, however, that they had little idea how to approach MI5. Since they were unwilling to ask the Conservative government for fear of alerting it to their plans for a purge of crypto-Communists, it was decided that George Brown should approach the journalist Chapman Pincher, who supplied him with contact details for both Sir Roger Hollis and the Chief of SIS Sir Dick White.[87] Following a letter to Hollis from Gordon Walker, Graham Mitchell, the

DDG, saw him on 5 September. Gordon Walker brought with him a handwritten list on House of Commons notepaper of sixteen Labour MPs who, he believed, 'were in effect members of the CPGB pretending to be Labour members or men under Communist Party direction' and nine 'possible' crypto-Communists.[88]

The name at the top of the list was that of Will Owen, who nine years later was put on trial for spying for the Czechoslovak security and intelligence service, the StB. Though Owen was acquitted, he was, almost certainly, guilty as charged.[89] Ironically, in 1961 Owen aroused less suspicion in the Security Service than in the Labour leadership. According to a Service assessment, he was 'not known to be CP but CP officials say he has no hesitation about being in touch with CP.' Owen was not one of the ten MPs whom the Service regarded as 'of most significance' on Gordon Walker's list.[90]

According to Mitchell's note of their meeting on 5 September, Gordon Walker told him:

The Labour leaders were aware that there were quite a lot of Communists within their ranks in the House but they had in mind to expel only about 6 or 8. When it came to taking this action they would take it openly, expelling the Members as being Communists. They hoped that if they made these examples 'the others would be very careful' . . .

Before he had got as far as this, Gordon Walker may have gathered from my expression that his project was not meeting with much enthusiasm. He said that the Labour leaders were very ready for us to say 'no' and indeed half expected it. They would fully understand if the D.G. found that he could not comply with their request [for information on Communist penetration of the PLP]. In that event Gordon Walker would volunteer a one-way traffic, through safe channels, from him in person to any member of the Security Service whom we cared to nominate and whose identity he need not know, indicating without expectation of information in return Labour Party members whom the Party had reason to suspect of Communist sympathies.

Mitchell did not respond to Gordon Walker's offer but said that 'it was incumbent on the Security Service to be very careful to do nothing which could be represented as partaking of a party political nature.' Its records 'could be used only in the interests of the security of the realm as a whole' – and therefore, by implication, not to help the Labour Party conduct a purge. Though he did not mention it to Gordon Walker, Mitchell was also afraid that any secret project known to George Brown 'might not stay secret for long'.[91] Mitchell no doubt had in mind Brown's notorious indiscretions

Sir Roger Hollis

CP:-   W. Owen ✓   Possible   Zilliacus ✓
       Warbey ✓   V. Yates ✓
       Leo Abse ✓   A. Lewis ✓
       R. Allaun ✓   S.O. Davies. ✓
       J. Silverman ✓   B. Stross ✓
       J. Baird *Bridge MP.*   Emrys Hughes ✓
       J. Mendelson ✓   W. Griffiths ✓
       T. Driberg *No.*   S. Silverman ✓
       D. Ross   E. Fernyhough ✓
       R. Parkin ✓   9
       S. Swingler - ✓
       J. Rankin ✓
       H. Davies - *Not on W.D. list* ✓
       L. Plummer *Bridge MP*
       R. Kelly ✓
       T. Swain. ✓
18.   J. Hart ✓

Handwritten list on House of Commons notepaper given to MI5 by the Labour Party
leadership in 1961 of sixteen (not eighteen as indicated bottom left) MPs who, it believed,
were secret Communists and nine further 'possibles'. The names of individuals to whom the
list was sent have been redacted.

when 'tired and emotional' (a euphemism for heavy drinking later invented for his benefit by *Private Eye*). It was later discovered that, having been denied Security Service assistance in tracking down crypto-Communists, George Brown had turned instead to Chapman Pincher.[92]

Pincher later alleged that, after being warned by the Labour leadership of the crypto-Communists on its backbenches, the Security Service began an investigation which lasted 'many months' and involved 'surveillance, the tapping of phones and the opening of mail'.[93] Walter Terry also claimed in the *Daily Mail* that '15 Labour MPs were shadowed by security men and had their phones tapped.'[94] In reality the Security Service made no investigations of any of the MPs on Gordon Walker's list and sought not a single HOW.[95]

Soon after Gordon Walker's approach to Mitchell, however, the Security Service discovered that Arthur Bax, chief press officer at Transport House, Labour Party headquarters, was working for several Soviet Bloc intelligence services. The discovery was the result of information from one of Bax's controllers, the Czechoslovak journalist Antonin Buzek (codenamed BROADSHEET), who worked for the StB as a co-optee.* Over the previous few years, while working in London, Buzek had been variously described in Security Service reports as a 'communist devoted to his cups', having 'national deviationist [Slovak] views' and being extremely fond of England. After unsuccessful attempts to use an elderly Czech émigré to contact him, Buzek was approached by an officer from D4 (which was responsible for counter-espionage agent-running), who offered to arrange for him to remain in England. Though Buzek did not accept the offer, he showed no hostility to the approach. In August 1961 an A4 officer personally delivered a letter inviting him to a rendezvous at a public house in Surrey and giving a phone number to confirm the meeting. A few days later Buzek met a D4 officer at the Jolly Farmer near Reigate. Following further meetings over the next few weeks, Buzek finally agreed to defect with his family in September. His most important counter-espionage lead was to Arthur Bax who, when questioned by the Security Service, confessed to working for the Russians, Romanians and Bulgarians as well as for the Czechoslovaks.[96] In November 1961 Hollis had a series of meetings with George Brown at which he revealed details of Bax's espionage[97] – some of which were subsequently passed on by Brown to Chapman Pincher.[98]

The most senior Labour politician on whom the Security Service held a

---

* Most co-optees were Soviet Bloc officials who agreed to combine work on behalf of their intelligence service with their declared jobs. Officials rarely became agents.

file was Harold Wilson who, at the time of Gordon Walker's approach to the Security Service, was shadow chancellor and chairman of the Labour Party National Executive Committee. In 1961 he had stood unsuccessfully against Hugh Gaitskell for the Labour leadership. The file had been opened soon after his election as MP in 1945 and appointment as parliamentary secretary at the Ministry of Works. In 1947, at the age of only thirty-one, Wilson became president of the Board of Trade and the youngest member of the Attlee cabinet. Because of its unusual sensitivity, his file was kept under the pseudonym 'Norman John Worthington'.[99] Graham Mitchell, then B1a (responsible for studying Communism in the UK), noted when Wilson became a cabinet minister: 'The security interest attaching to Wilson and justifying the opening a P[ermanent] F[ile] for him derives from comments made about him by certain Communist members of the Civil Service which suggested an identity or similarity of political outlook.'[100] A telecheck on a Communist civil servant at the Ministry of Works recorded him bemoaning Wilson's move to the Board of Trade in 1947: 'He and I were getting you know – quite a plot, but it has all gone west now.'[101] Such evidence, Mitchell minuted, did not establish that Wilson himself had Communist sympathies and he noted an attack on him in the *Daily Worker* for having 'inexcusably failed to conclude a trading agreement with the Soviet Union'.[102] In April 1951 Wilson followed Aneurin 'Nye' Bevan out of the Attlee cabinet in a bitter dispute over health service charges and defence expenditure which threatened to split the Party. In October 1954, a year before Attlee retired as Labour leader, a bugged discussion at King Street revealed that opinion at the CPGB headquarters favoured Wilson rather than Bevan as Attlee's successor.[103] (In the event, Attlee was succeeded in 1955 by Hugh Gaitskell, whose wife Dora had once amused King George VI by claiming that her husband was 'rather right-wing'.)[104]

King Street's misplaced hopes in Harold Wilson doubtless owed much to his unusually frequent contacts with the Soviet Union.[105] While at the Board of Trade, Wilson had paid three official visits to Moscow for trade negotiations, claiming after a game of cricket near the River Moskva 'to be the only batsman ever to have been dropped at square leg by a member of the NKVD [KGB]'.[106] His Russian contacts increased during his years in opposition after the Conservative election victory in October 1951. From 1952 to 1959 he worked as economic consultant for Montague L. Meyer Ltd, timber importers from the Soviet Union, paying a series of visits to Moscow, partly on Meyer business but increasingly with the main aim of meeting Soviet leaders and establishing himself as Labour's main

Soviet expert. In May 1953 the *Daily Worker* reported that he had had 'Warm and Friendly Talks' with Vyacheslav Molotov, the Soviet Foreign Minister.[107]

Though the Security Service never suspected Wilson of being a secret crypto-Communist or fellow-traveller, it looked askance at some of the Communist connections he developed in the course of his Russian travels and work for Montague L. Meyer. Among Wilson's contacts was the veteran undeclared Communist Roland Berger, who figured prominently on MI5's list of those selected for internment in the event of war with the Soviet Bloc. In 1954 Wilson suggested to Berger the names of businessmen who might join his British Council for the Promotion of International Trade (BCPIT), which, on Security Service advice, was later officially identified as 'Communist controlled'.[108] Surveillance as well as other sources revealed that Wilson was also in friendly contact during the 1950s with a KGB officer operating under diplomatic cover at the London residency, Ivan Federovich Skripov,[109] and another Soviet diplomat later suspected of KGB affiliation, Nikolai Dmitrievich Belokhvostikov.[110] Though Wilson did not know that either was a KGB officer, he must surely have suspected it. He later claimed that he had operated under the assumption that any Soviet diplomat with whom he had dealings might be working for the KGB.[111] According to Wilson's KGB file, his gossip on British politics, though it doubtless did not include classified information, was so highly valued by the KGB that reports on it were passed to the Politburo.[112]

In January 1956, just back from his sixth visit to Moscow, Wilson told Skripov he was sure he would like an article he had written for the *Liverpool Daily Post* on his meeting with the Soviet First Deputy Prime Minister, Mikoyan.[113] Skripov was probably even more impressed by two articles by Wilson in the *Daily Mirror* on his meeting in Moscow with the Soviet leader, Nikita Khrushchev. After denouncing those Western diplomats and journalists who wrote off Khrushchev as 'garrulous, boorish, given to wild statements and even to clowning', Wilson declared: 'THEY ARE WRONG. THE WEST MUST NOT UNDERRATE THIS MAN. In a team of strong, able men, Khrushchev stands out as the undoubted chief.' Wilson eulogized the extraordinary Soviet achievement in rapidly modernizing a previously backward economy which was now moving to 'mechanisation, electrification and automation': 'Let no one think that we can halt this industrial revolution inside Russia by our footling restrictions on exports from the Western world ... In the next generation Russia's industrial challenge may well dominate the world economic scene.'[114]

In June 1956 Wilson was back in Moscow and had further meetings with senior Soviet figures. The *Sunday Dispatch* reported, probably accurately, that though his visit to Russia was ostensibly on Montague Meyer business, he was believed to be establishing his claims to become foreign secretary in the next Labour government by building up contacts with Soviet leaders.[115] In order not to prejudice those contacts, Wilson rather cravenly refused to sign a letter by other left-wing Labour MPs condemning the Soviet invasion of Hungary in October.[116] He appears to have gone even further in his campaign to establish himself as the British politician best qualified to conduct a dialogue in Moscow. According to his KGB file, one of the firms with which he was involved breached the Western CoCom embargo on 'strategic' exports to Soviet Bloc countries.[117] Wilson's official biographer, Philip Ziegler, accepts that this was probably the case: 'The export of many items was forbidden; inevitably a grey area grew up in which trading might or might not be illegal. Some of Wilson's associates strayed into that area or even beyond it.'[118]

The high value placed in Moscow on Wilson's political gossip, the dubious nature of some of his business contacts, his probable involvement in the breach of the CoCom embargo and his public praise for Soviet achievements probably explain the KGB's decision in 1956 to give him the codename OLDING and open an 'agent development file' in the hope of recruiting him. The OLDING file records, however, that 'The development did not come to fruition.'[119] Though the CPGB leadership's unfounded optimism earlier in the 1950s in its ability to influence Wilson had markedly declined by the end of the decade, traces of it still recurred in Security Service transcripts of discussions at the Party's King Street headquarters. In October 1959:

Reuben [Falber] . . . remarked that he wished he knew where Wilson stood as he had been very quiet, and he rather felt himself that if there were a genuine possibility of the sort of more Trade Union and working class elements in the Parliamentary Labour Party 'getting any place', then Wilson would be the leader of it. Wilson was a very, very clever manoeuvrer.

Betty Reid, more bizarrely, now believed that Wilson was a Trotskyist.[120]

After losing a leadership election to Gaitskell in October 1961, Wilson sought to position himself in the middle ground between the Gaitskellites and the left-wing Tribune Group led by Michael Foot. On becoming shadow foreign secretary in January 1962 he was much more guarded in his comments about the Soviet Union than during his visits to Moscow in the 1950s. When Wilson was elected Party leader after Gaitskell's sudden death in January 1963, the *Daily Worker* was distinctly unenthusiastic. Since becoming shadow foreign secretary, it complained, 'Mr Harold Wilson has moved steadily to the right.' It was particularly outraged by the fact that he had visited West Berlin and, standing at the Berlin Wall, had denounced the (East) German Democratic Republic.[121] The KGB was equally outraged. So far from regarding Wilson as a potential recruit, as it had done in 1956, and probably for several years afterwards, once Wilson became prime minister in 1964 it inspired a number of press articles attacking his policies.[122]

6

The Hunt for the 'Magnificent Five'

Kim Philby, Guy Burgess, Donald Maclean, Anthony Blunt and John Cairncross – all recruited at, or soon after leaving, Cambridge University in the mid-1930s – were the ablest group of British agents ever recruited by a foreign power. It was not until the spring of 1951 that the partial VENONA decrypt of a seven-year-old NKGB telegram from the Washington residency to Moscow at last identified one of the Five.[1] That discovery, which took the Security Service completely by surprise, began the most complex and longest-drawn-out investigation in its history, taking over thirty years to complete.

Aware since the unmasking of the atom spies of the extraordinary quality of some of the ideological agents working for Moscow, the Security Service formed a greatly exaggerated view of the sophistication of late-Stalinist foreign intelligence operations. In reality, Soviet agent-running in the West during the 1940s and early 1950s, though able to draw on an impressive pool of highly motivated Western recruits, was frequently of poor quality. After the recall to Moscow of their inspirational early case officers (Arnold Deutsch and Teodor Maly in particular),[2] many of the remarkable successes of the Cambridge Five were achieved in spite, rather than because, of their controllers. For almost two years in the middle of the Second World War, the Centre, amazingly, believed that the Five were an elaborate anti-Soviet deception operation by British intelligence. Though that became a minority view in the Centre after the war, there were still senior Soviet intelligence officers who argued that the Five were part of a 'fiendishly clever' British plot.[3] In the early Cold War both Maclean and Philby were badly let down by their controllers at crucial moments. It is inconceivable that either the Security Service or SIS would have shown a similar level of incompetence in the running of such important agents.

After Maclean's posting to Cairo in October 1948 as counsellor and head of Chancery at the age of only thirty-five, apparently on a path which might take him to the top of the diplomatic service but with his double life placing him under increasing strain, he became deeply depressed by the local Soviet residency's insensitive handling of him. In December 1949 he attached to his latest bundle of classified documents a note asking to be allowed to give up work for Soviet intelligence. The Cairo residency gave so little thought to running Maclean that it forwarded his note unread to Moscow. Incredibly, the Centre also ignored it. Not till Maclean sent another appeal in April 1950, asking to be released from the intolerable strain of his double life, did he at last succeed in attracting the Centre's attention. While the Centre was still deliberating on its response, Maclean went berserk. One evening in May, in a drunken rage, he and his drinking companion, Philip Toynbee, vandalized the flat of two female members of the US embassy, ripped up their underwear, then moved on to destroy the bathroom. There, Toynbee later recalled, 'Donald raises a large mirror above his head and crashes it into the bath, when to my amazement and delight, alas, the bath breaks in two while the mirror remains intact.' A few days later Maclean was sent back to London where the Foreign Office gave him the rest of the spring and the summer off, and sent him to see a Harley Street psychiatrist.[4]

Atrocious though the Soviet handling of Maclean had been, it had helped to reduce him to such a desperate mental state that the last thing which either the Foreign Office or the Harley Street psychiatrist were likely to suspect was his involvement in espionage. The psychiatrist reported to the FO that Maclean's psychological problems were so serious that he thought they might have a physical origin which should be investigated at the Maudsley Hospital:

... I found it very difficult to believe the man I saw on Saturday morning has got on as well as he has in the Foreign Office. I thought for a man in his position he was somewhat slow and retarded, and, of course, I had no account either from his wife or from the other people in Cairo as to how bad he was.[5]

The Treasury's medical adviser told the Foreign Office Personnel Department, after examining Maclean: 'Personally I think a solution is going to be difficult to find as the whole family ... are definitely unbalanced & there is a marked alcoholic tendency which is surprising with such a family background.' Matters were made worse by Maclean's insistence on being treated by a psychoanalyst of his own choice, Dr Erna Rosenbaum, rather than by the Foreign Office psychiatrist, possibly because he feared he might give something away in meetings with a psychiatrist chosen by the Foreign Office.[6] The choice of Dr Rosenbaum did not please the Treasury medical adviser; she was 'not qualified in England and he therefore feared she might be a quack.'[7] Treatment by her, however, seems to have partly stabilized Maclean's condition. Remarkably, he was considered sufficiently recovered by the autumn of 1950 to be appointed head of the FO American desk. There, despite alcoholic evenings in the Gargoyle Club and a drunken description of himself as 'the English Hiss' (a former Soviet spy in the State Department), Maclean's work in office hours, as his deputy later recalled, was meticulously efficient.[8]

  Philby's handling by the Centre during his two years as SIS liaison in Washington from 1949 to 1951 was as bad as that of Maclean. The chaotic post-war state of the Soviet residency in Washington, which led to the recall of two successive residents in 1948–9, made Philby refuse any contact with legal Soviet intelligence officers in the United States. For almost a year his sole contact with the Centre was via messages sent to Burgess in London. In the summer of 1950 he received an unexpected letter from Burgess. 'I have a shock for you,' Burgess began. 'I have just been posted to Washington.'[9] Burgess, like Maclean, was showing the strain of his double life. His behaviour had become so outrageous that he had come close to dismissal from the diplomatic service. A trip to Gibraltar and Tangier in the autumn of 1949 had turned into what his friend Goronwy Rees called a 'wild odyssey of indiscretions': among them failing to pay his bills, publicly identifying MI5 and SIS officers and drunkenly singing in local bars, 'Little boys are cheap today, cheaper than yesterday.'[10] The Security Service representative in Gibraltar wrote to the DG to complain about Burgess's 'extremely indiscreet' behaviour: 'Burgess appears to be a complete alcoholic and I do not think that even in Gibraltar have I ever seen anyone put away so much hard liquor in so short a time as he did.'[11] On his return Burgess was summoned for interview by the FO Personnel Department, denied that he had behaved indiscreetly and blamed his troubles on the fact that he was 'on bad terms' with 'the Security authorities' (presumably the Security Service).[12] The Security Service's Legal Adviser, Bernard Hill,[13] told the FO that Burgess could be prosecuted under the Official Secrets Act but that 'it would be undesirable to proceed,' chiefly 'to avoid further publicity about SIS's affairs'. Burgess also sought the help of Guy Liddell, who believed all that was required was 'a severe reprimand from somebody [Burgess] respected': 'I did not think he often got wholly out of control, but there was no doubt that drink loosened his tongue.' Burgess, he mistakenly believed, was 'not the sort of person who would deliberately pass confidential information to unauthorised parties'.[14]

  Philby later claimed in his memoirs that he agreed to have Burgess as a lodger at his large neo-classical house on Nebraska Avenue during his tour of duty at the Washington embassy in order to try to keep him out of the spectacular alcoholic and other 'scrapes' for which he was increasingly notorious. There was, however, a more important reason which Philby did not mention. Though the 'scrapes' continued, Burgess fulfilled an important role as courier between Philby and his newly appointed case officer, Valeri Makayev, a Soviet illegal codenamed HARRY, in New York.[15] The establishment of an apparently secure line of communication to Moscow via Burgess and Makayev encouraged Philby to try to extend still further his already remarkable access to British and US intelligence. During a visit to London in September 1950 he had a long talk with Guy Liddell, whom he tried to convince that his job in Washington did not really give him 'enough scope' (despite the fact that he was working for both SIS and Soviet intelligence). Liddell noted in his diary: 'I thought I discerned a fly thrown over me in the form of a suggestion that it was really unnecessary for us to have a Washington representative, and that he could carry the whole business, but I may have been wrong.' In fact Liddell was very probably right. Ever since the Second World War, Philby had obtained Security Service intelligence on a series of counter-espionage cases on the grounds that it was necessary for him to ensure effective collaboration between the Service and SIS.[16] For him to become Security Service as well as SIS liaison officer in Washington would have marked a triumphant conclusion to this strategy. Though it did not occur to Liddell to suspect Philby's motives, he did not rise to the bait: '. . . I told him that whatever the flow of information, I was quite convinced that we ought to have a man in the Western hemisphere.'[17]

Some of the most important intelligence which Philby supplied to HARRY, his Soviet case officer, concerned Donald Maclean. The VENONA decrypts to which he had access contained references to an agent codenamed HOMER operating in Washington at the end of the war, but initially gave only vague clues to his identity. Philby quickly realized that HOMER was Maclean, but was informed by the Centre that 'Maclean should stay in his post as long as possible' and that plans would be made to rescue him 'before the net closed in'. In April 1951 a telegram decrypted by Meredith Gardner finally identified HOMER as Maclean. It revealed that in June 1944 HOMER's wife was expecting a baby and living with her mother in New York – information which fitted Maclean's wife Melinda, but not the wife of any other suspect.[18] There still remained a breathing space of at least a few weeks in which to arrange Maclean's escape. The search for the evidence necessary to convict him of espionage, complicated by the decision not to use VENONA in any prosecution, made necessary a period of surveillance by the Security Service in the hope of discovering him in contact with a Soviet case officer. A plan to warn Maclean that he had been identified as a Soviet agent was worked out not by the Centre but by Philby and Burgess.[19] In April 1951 Burgess was ordered home from Washington in disgrace after a further series of escapades had aroused the collective wrath of the Virginia State Police, the State Department and the British ambassador. On the eve of Burgess's departure from New York aboard the *Queen Mary*, he and Philby dined together in a Chinese restaurant where the piped music inhibited eavesdropping and agreed that Burgess would convey a warning to both Maclean and the London residency as soon as he reached Britain.[20]

Philby was even more concerned by the possibility of his own detection than by the fate of Maclean. If Maclean cracked under interrogation, as seemed possible in view of his overwrought condition, Philby and the rest of the Five would also be at risk. Philby sent a message to the Centre demanding Maclean's immediate exfiltration to the Soviet Union, so that he himself would not be compromised.[21] He also extracted an assurance from Burgess that he would not accompany Maclean to Moscow, for that too would compromise himself. Immediately after his return to England on 7 May, Burgess called on Blunt and used him to deliver a message to the current controller of the Five at the London residency, Yuri Modin, whom Blunt knew as 'Peter'. According to Modin, Blunt's anxious appearance, even before he spoke, indicated that something was desperately wrong. 'Peter,' he said, 'there's serious trouble. Guy Burgess has just arrived back in London. HOMER's about to be arrested ... Donald's now in such a state that I'm convinced he'll break down the moment they question him.' Two days later the Centre agreed to Maclean's exfiltration. Since it seemed clear that Maclean would need an escort, the Centre insisted that Burgess accompany him to Moscow. Burgess initially refused to go, recalled his promise to Philby not to defect and seemed to Modin 'close to hysteria'. The London resident, Nikolai Borisovich Rodin, seems to have persuaded Burgess to go by giving the impression that he would not need to accompany Maclean all the way, and would in any case be free to return to London. In reality, the Centre believed that Burgess had become a liability and was determined to get him to Moscow – by deception if necessary – and keep him there. 'As long as he agreed to go with Maclean,' wrote Modin later, 'the rest mattered precious little. Cynically enough, the Centre had ... concluded that we had not one but two burnt-out agents on our hands.'[22]

On 17 April Herbert Morrison, who had succeeded Bevin as foreign secretary in March, agreed to Maclean being placed under Security Service surveillance.[23] Not long after Burgess's return to London an A4 surveillance team observed him meeting Maclean. Since Maclean was head of the American desk and Burgess had just returned from the Washington embassy facing the prospect of dismissal, their meeting was not in itself suspicious. Though Burgess was obviously worried, it was reasonable to suppose that the cause of his worries was the fact that he was facing the sack and the end of his Foreign Office career. The very outrageousness of his behaviour protected him against suspicion that he, like Maclean, was a Soviet agent. According to an A4 surveillance report:

... Guy Burgess appears to have something on his mind and is, in fact, obviously deeply worried. He will order a large gin (his favourite tipple) and will then pace the bar for a few seconds, pour the neat spirit down his throat and walk out, or order another and repeat the performance.

In the open he frequently shows indecision with, apparently, his mind in turmoil.

With CURZON [Maclean] there is an air almost of conspiracy between the two. It is quite impossible even in a bar to hear a word of what they are saying. It would seem likely that Burgess has unburdened himself to CURZON as the latter does not display any normal emotion when they are together.[24]

Maclean was observed leaving the Foreign Office after work on Friday 25 May, carrying a large cardboard box, and tracked to Victoria Station, where 'After a drink he boarded the 6.10 p.m. train.'[25] That was to be the last A4 saw of him. Security Service surveillance of Maclean was fatally flawed as a result of its lack of resources. The London residency knew from studying the watchers' working pattern that they clocked off each evening and stopped work for the weekend at Saturday lunchtime with no Sunday working.[26]

Unknown to Maclean, in the course of that day, Friday 25 May, the Foreign Office proposed he should be interrogated by the Security Service on some date between 18 and 25 June.[27] The London residency, however, mistakenly believed that Maclean was to be arrested on Monday 28 May, and made plans for his exfiltration with Burgess during the previous weekend, in the correct belief that A4 would not attempt to resume surveillance until Monday morning.[28] (It may or may not have realized that there was no surveillance at all of Maclean at his home at Tatsfield on the Kent–Surrey border, for fear that its isolated location might lead to the detection of the watchers.)[29] The residency also discovered that the pleasure-boat *Falaise* made round-trip weekend cruises from Southampton to French ports, which did not require passports. Burgess was instructed to buy tickets for himself and Maclean under assumed names for the cruise leaving at midnight on Friday 25 May. Next morning they left the boat at Saint-Malo, made their way to Rennes and caught the train to Paris. From Paris they took another train to Switzerland, where they were issued with false passports by the Soviet embassy in Berne. In Zurich they bought air tickets to Stockholm via Prague, but left the plane at Prague where they were met by Soviet intelligence officers. By the time that Melinda Maclean reported that her husband had not returned home after the weekend, Burgess and Maclean were behind the Iron Curtain.[30]

The Centre congratulated itself that the successful exfiltration of Burgess and Maclean had 'raised the authority of the Soviet Intelligence Service in the eyes of Soviet agents'. That, however, was not Philby's view. At a meeting on 24 May, Makayev (HARRY) had found him 'alarmed and concerned for his own security', and insistent that he would be put 'in jeopardy' if Burgess, his friend and former lodger at his Washington home, fled with Maclean to Moscow. The first that Philby learned of Burgess's defection with Maclean was during a briefing about five days later by the Security Service SLO, Geoffrey Patterson, in Washington. 'My conster-nation [at the news]', wrote Philby later, 'was no pretence.' Later that day he drove into the Virginia countryside and buried in a wood the photographic equipment with which he had copied documents for Soviet intelligence – an action he had mentally rehearsed many times since arriving in Washington two years earlier. Just when Philby most needed his con-troller's assistance, however, Makayev let him down. The New York resi-dency left a message and $2,000 in a dead letter-box for HARRY to deliver to Philby. Makayev failed to find them, and Philby never received them. An inquiry by the Centre into Makayev's conduct in New York, prompted by his failure to help Philby, concluded that he was guilty of 'lack of discipline', 'violations of the Centre's orders' and 'crude manners'.[31]

The Centre calculated that, since their recruitment in 1934–5, Philby, Burgess and Maclean had supplied more than 20,000 pages of 'valuable' classified documents and agent reports.[32] As Philby had feared, however, the defection of Burgess and Maclean did severe, though not quite terminal, damage to the careers in Soviet intelligence of the other three members of the Magnificent Five. At the insistence of General Walter Bedell Smith, the Director of Central Intelligence (DCI, head of the CIA), Philby was recalled from Washington.[33] On his return to London, he was officially retired from SIS with a golden handshake, though a majority of his colleagues continued to believe in his innocence. Dick White as Director B (counter-espionage) asked Philby to come to Leconfield House to help in the investigation of 'this horrible business with Burgess and Maclean'.[34] White's friendly manner left Philby off his guard when summoned to a further meeting at the Security Service. This time the interrogator was H. J. P. 'Buster' Milmo KC, later a High Court judge, a wartime member of the Service with a confrontational style, who warned Philby that this was a 'judicial enquiry' and instructed him not to smoke.[35] Milmo concluded after a four-hour interrogation: 'I find myself unable to avoid the conclusion that Philby is and has been for many years a Soviet agent.'[36]

Philby's sense that he had been worsted by Milmo, despite the lack of the evidence against him required for a successful prosecution, doubtless accounts for the fury he expressed afterwards to his friends in SIS. B4 (M. E. D. Cumming) noted on 14 January 1952:

Nicholas Elliott [of SIS] again referred to PEACH [Philby]'s intense anger with M.I.5 over the Milmo interrogation. He said that PEACH did not in any way object to such an independent interrogation being carried out but he did resent the fact that after his friendly conversations with Dick White, he should be virtually enticed to London under false pretences and then thrown straight into what proved to be a formal enquiry at which even his request to smoke was refused.[37]

In the hope of extracting a confession or usable evidence against him, the Service sent its leading interrogator, Jim Skardon, to call on Philby at home. Philby found Skardon 'scrupulously courteous, his manner verging on the exquisite; nothing could have been more flattering than the cosy warmth of his interest in my views and actions.' In the previous year, however, Philby had followed with great attention the way that 'Skardon wormed his way into Fuchs's confidence' in meetings at his home and was thus forewarned about his subtle interrogation methods: 'During our first long conversation, I detected and evaded two little traps which he laid for me with deftness and precision. But I had scarcely begun congratulating myself when the thought struck me that he may have laid others which I had not detected.'[38] Skardon, however, was at least partly taken in. Philby, he reported, 'created a much more favourable impression than I would have expected'. He concluded that the case against Philby was unproven.[39]

The flight of Burgess and Maclean in May 1951 and the recall of Philby from Washington, like the Fuchs case a year before, produced another crisis in the Special Relationship. Sillitoe flew to Washington to brief, and attempt to mollify, the irascible J. Edgar Hoover in person. As well as undertaking the difficult task of trying to reassure a sceptical Hoover about the current state of British security, he quickly found himself caught in cross-fire between the Bureau and the CIA. Hoover was affronted that the

DCI, General Bedell Smith, had learned from British liaison of the existence of the VENONA decrypts which identified Maclean as Agent HOMER.[40] Though Hoover had been content for MI5 to have access to VENONA, he was determined that the supposedly insecure CIA should not.[41]

For the small circle of those indoctrinated into the VENONA secret, the consequences of Philby's presumed treachery were particularly devastating. If Philby was indeed a Soviet agent, then the actual text of some of the VENONA decrypts must have been passed on to Moscow. In January 1952 Arthur Martin (B2b) had the unenviable task of going to GCHQ (then at Eastcote in the London suburbs) to tell the Director, Group Captain Jones, that 'it should be assumed that Philby was a spy throughout his service with SIS': 'It was quite clear that this came as a considerable shock to Jones. Whatever he had been told by "C" he had certainly not realised that our conclusions were as definite as this, nor had he been told that the Americans were being kept informed.'[42]

As well as ending Philby's career as an SIS officer (though not his contacts with his former Service), the defection of Burgess and Maclean also cast suspicion on John Cairncross and Anthony Blunt. Immediately after the defection, Blunt went through Burgess's flat, searching for and destroying incriminating documents. He failed, however, to notice a series of unsigned notes describing confidential discussions in Whitehall in 1939. In 1952, in the course of a lengthy Security Service investigation, Sir John Colville, one of those mentioned in the notes, was able to identify the author as Cairncross.[43] During questioning by Jim Skardon, Cairncross acknowledged that he had written the notes (he could scarcely do otherwise) but denied that he knew Burgess was a Soviet agent. An SIS officer, who had himself been a Communist at Cambridge, however, identified Cairncross as a Party member while at Trinity College. Cairncross was suspended from the Treasury and soon afterwards forced to resign.[44]

A4 began surveillance of Cairncross and followed him to the location of a hurriedly arranged meeting with his controller, Yuri Modin, on 7 April 1952.[45] Just in time, Modin noticed the surveillance and turned back. Cairncross, however, proceeded to Gunnersbury Park (presumably the rendezvous agreed with Modin) where, though a non-smoker, he was observed for some time chain-smoking. When later questioned by Skardon about this incident, Cairncross initially produced no coherent explanation. Next day he claimed that he had been on his way to a secret assignation with a married French woman, who had failed to turn up. Owing to what he claimed were his lover's strict security precautions during their affair, he did not even know where she lived. Skardon, remarkably, was taken in by this improbable tale and reported: 'I think he has told me the truth.' His great strength as an interrogator – his ability, as in the case of Fuchs, to gain the confidence of some of those he questioned – was also his weakness.[46]

Immediately after the defection of Burgess and Maclean, the Centre instructed Modin to press Blunt, whom it knew to be under suspicion as Burgess's friend and former flatmate, to follow them to Moscow. Unwilling to exchange the congenial, prestigious surroundings of the Courtauld Institute for the bleak socialist realism of Stalin's Russia, Blunt refused. 'I know perfectly well how your people live,' Blunt told his controller, 'and I can assure you it would be very hard, almost unbearable, for me to do likewise.' Modin, by his own account, was left speechless. Blunt was rightly confident that MI5 had no hard evidence against him.[47] Like Cairncross, Blunt successfully deceived Skardon, though for different reasons. In Blunt's case, Skardon believed that his concealment of much of what he knew about Burgess was to be explained by gay culture rather than by recruitment as a Soviet agent. He reported on 21 April 1952:

As the result of my discussions with Blunt, I left with the strong impression that the overwhelming loyalty of one homosexual for another will be a bar to a successful examination of this man until these inhibitions are broken down and the obsessions removed from his mind. Whether I am the best person to conduct this psychoanalytic exercise time alone will show.[48]

Three weeks later, Skardon had given up hope of learning more from Blunt: 'I am left with the strong impression that whatever Blunt knows he has passed on to the authorities. There may be incidents of tremendous significance yet to be unearthed but they will probably only be developed in the course of time as the result of further information coming our way.'[49]

The search for further evidence against both Philby and Blunt was complicated by misinterpretation of fragmentary clues in the VENONA decrypts. It was a number of years before the Security Service realized that Philby was the agent STANLEY, who – as one of the September 1945 decrypts implied – was the most important of the 'valuable' British agent network. For several years those indoctrinated into VENONA misidentified Philby as the agent codenamed JOHNSON (who was in reality Anthony Blunt), though HICKS was correctly identified as Burgess. J. C. Robertson (D1, in charge of investigating Soviet espionage) minuted to Hollis, the DDG, in May 1954, 'We have for some time thought that "HICKS" might be Burgess and "JOHNSON" Philby. I now definitely favour this theory.'[50]

For three years after Philby's recall from Washington, his controller in London, Yuri Modin, considered it too dangerous to resume direct contact with him because of Security Service surveillance. In 1954 Modin made contact through what Philby called 'the most ingenious of routes'. The route was Anthony Blunt. One evening after a talk by Blunt at the Courtauld Institute, Modin approached him, probably for the first time since 1951, handed him a postcard reproduction of a painting and asked for his opinion of it. On the reverse was a message in Burgess's distinctive handwriting giving a rendezvous for the following evening at the Angel public house on the Caledonian Road. At the Angel, Modin asked Blunt to set up a meeting for him with Philby. The main message which Modin passed to Philby at their meeting, the first for several years, was one of reassurance which, so Philby later claimed, left him 'with refreshed spirit'.[51]

Philby's immediate need for spiritual refreshment sprang from the well-publicized defection of the KGB resident in Australia, Vladimir Petrov, and his wife Evdokia (then being extensively debriefed by a Security Service officer),[52] who provided intelligence on Burgess and Maclean, including the first hard (as opposed to circumstantial) evidence that both were in Moscow. Modin was able to reassure Philby that Petrov knew nothing about his career as a Soviet agent.[53] Philby was further reassured by support from former colleagues in SIS. Ronnie Reed, who worked on the VENONA material in D Branch, later recalled 'the intense disagreement between our two services on Philby':

... MI6 felt strongly that we had as good a candidate for the leakages from British Intelligence in the person of Guy Liddell. He said that MI6 were at pains to point out that Liddell had parted from his wife, had a faintly homosexual air about him and, during the war, had been a close friend of Burgess, Philby and Blunt.[54]

On 20 July 1955 'C', Major General Sir John 'Sinbad' Sinclair, wrote to the DG, Sir Dick White, arguing that there was mounting evidence that, as a result of Milmo's supposedly biased interrogation, Philby had been the victim of a miscarriage of justice.[55] Two days later, White agreed to a joint MI5–SIS re-examination of the Philby case. Philby said that he welcomed the chance to clear his name. On 7, 10 and 11 October two SIS officers questioned Philby at length. The Security Service officer and transcribers present were deeply dissatisfied with the proceedings, putting on file their belief that one of the questioners was prejudiced in Philby's favour, repeatedly helping him find answers to awkward questions and never pressing questions which he failed to answer.[56]

By the time the questioning took place, both MI5 and SIS were aware that claims that Philby was the 'Third Man' who had tipped off Burgess and Maclean before their flight to Moscow were about to become public. J. Edgar Hoover had been outraged at the failure of a White Paper on the defection of Burgess and Maclean, published on 23 September, to make any reference to the suspicions surrounding Philby, and set out to force a full-scale British official investigation by leaking the story to the press. On 23 October, the New York *Sunday News* named Philby as the Third Man. Though Philby's house was quickly surrounded by the press, forcing him to take refuge in his mother's flat where he buried the telephone under a pile of cushions, British newspapers were deterred from identifying him by fears of being sued for libel. Two days later the Labour MP Marcus Lipton asked at Prime Minister's Question Time in the Commons:

Has the Prime Minister made up his mind to cover up at all costs the dubious third man activities of Mr Harold Philby who was First Secretary at the Washington embassy a little time ago, and is he determined to stifle all discussion on the very great matters which were evaded in the wretched White Paper, which is an insult to the intelligence of the country?

Philby first realized that he had been named in the Commons while travelling on the London tube and seeing the story on the front page of a neighbour's *Evening Standard*.[57] Lipton's question played into Philby's hands. Harold Macmillan, Foreign Secretary in the Eden government, who was forced to comment on the allegation during the debate on the White Paper on 7 November, had no realistic option but to clear him of the charges against him.[58] Next day Philby gave a triumphant press conference in his mother's living room, shamelessly telling the assembled journalists: 'The last time I spoke to a Communist, knowing he was one, was in 1934.'[59]

Macmillan was unaware that, almost a month before, new evidence had emerged which strengthened the case against Philby. While working at GCHQ as liaison officer for NSA, the US SIGINT agency founded in 1952, Meredith Gardner produced, for the first time for several years, an important VENONA decrypt of a message from the Centre to the London residency. The decrypt, dated 17 September 1945, was first shown to D1A (C. P. C. de Wesselow), one of the small circle of VENONA initiates in the Security Service, at GCHQ on 10 October 1955. It read as follows: '[Eight groups unrecovered] STANLEY about the events in Canada in the line of the Neighbours' work. [B% Report] STANLEY's information.' Given the date and the reference to the 'Neighbours' (GRU), the 'events in Canada' were plainly the Gouzenko case, with which Philby was closely involved. De Wesselow argued that, taking into account another reference to STANLEY in a decrypt of the following day, 18 September 1945, he was 'clearly a long established Soviet agent':[60] 'There is no record in our files that any officer in S.I.S. was aware of the [Gouzenko] case, other than "C" himself and Mr Philby'.[61]

A re-examination of the case by Director D (A. M. MacDonald) a decade later concluded:

What does appear strange is the fact that although Philby's case was very much under review in September 1955 when the first [version of the] decrypt was available, no one in the Security Service or MI6 directly related STANLEY to Philby. There were admittedly other candidates but I should have thought that in the light of our knowledge of the Philby case at the end of 1955 he would have been regarded as a strong candidate for STANLEY.[62]

The DDG, Anthony Simkins, also found 'this apparent boob' surprising. The DG, Furnival Jones, noted: 'I agree.'[63] Like MacDonald, they seemed unaware that, so far from 'no one in the Security Service' realizing that Philby was 'a strong candidate for STANLEY', de Wesselow had written a paper saying precisely that. De Wesselow could not later recall to whom he had showed his paper, but 'thought it inconceivable that he would not have discussed this with D1 [J. C. Robertson] who would have instructed him to make the researches on which his note was based'. Neither Robertson nor any other Service officer, however, could remember having seen the paper.[64] The confusion over this important episode reflects a broader failure in the Service's management of the VENONA project, as well as the extreme secrecy with which it was handled.[65] The failure to identify STANLEY as Philby was so remarkable that Peter Wright and others later claimed that the identification must have been deliberately suppressed and therefore pointed to possible Soviet penetration of the Service. An investigation in 1967 by D1/Inv reached the more sensible conclusion 'that there could have been explanations other than a sinister one but whatever they were did indicate a lack of professionalism on the part of those who were aware of the message'. De Wesselow lived almost in a world of his own within the Service, working on material too secret to mention to most of his colleagues.[66]

Given Philby's knowledge of Security Service procedures, he can have been in no doubt since Milmo's interrogation that the Service would have obtained Home Office Warrants for letter and telephone checks against him. For that reason both checks yielded slim intelligence pickings – though his lack of contact with the KGB until his undetected meeting with Modin in 1954 meant in any case that there was little of importance about his current activities to discover. An analysis of thirty-three volumes of checks for the five years from 1951 to 1956 concluded that 'The only intelligence dividend . . . is the extent to which PEACH [Philby] is still in touch with, and subsidised by, M.I.6.'[67] The checks did, however, also reveal much about Philby's sometimes squalid private life which has escaped the attention of his biographers, 'show[ing] that PEACH is apt to get blind drunk and behave abominably to his best friends'.[68] Philby's most abominable behaviour was towards his mentally fragile second wife, Aileen, by whom he had five children. Aileen Philby's psychiatrist told the Service that among her problems was her belief in her husband's guilt – which was at least partly responsible for Philby's attempts to 'smash Aileen up': 'He is convinced that she possesses important security information about her husband and her own Communist past . . . In [Aileen's] opinion and that of her psychiatrist, Philby had by a kind of mental cruelty to her "done his best to make her commit suicide".'[69]

In the absence of useful intelligence, however, cruelty to Aileen Philby did not constitute an adequate case for continuing the HOWs, which were suspended in 1956.[70] There is other evidence that Aileen had finally realized her husband's treachery and had thus become a potential threat to him. One of her friends later claimed that she had heard her blurt out one evening to Kim, 'I know you're the Third Man!' That realization, combined with Kim's mental cruelty, accelerated her decline into alcoholism and despair. She died on 12 December 1957 from congestive heart failure, myocardial degeneration, a respiratory infection and pulmonary tuberculosis.[71] After her death, her psychiatrist said 'that he suspected that Aileen might have been murdered' by Philby.[72] That is highly unlikely – not least because by then Philby had moved to Beirut to work as a journalist. But Kim's callous treatment of Aileen, which probably hastened her end, was symptomatic of the cold brutality with which he treated those who threatened his security. He never forgave Burgess for having accompanied Maclean to Moscow and so cast suspicion on him. Philby refused to see him even on his deathbed.[73]

By the mid-1950s, those in the Security Service working on the Philby, Blunt and Cairncross cases seem to have been losing heart. The Service leadership saw little point in further work on the British VENONA material. Director D (Graham Mitchell) wrote to Sir Dick White in April 1956:

I am beginning to come regretfully to the conclusion that it is not worth the effort. All the messages on which progress has been made since Gardner came here and, I understand, on which there is hope of further progress are in the direction Moscow–London. Even if there were substantial further recoveries [decryption] on these, the odds are that the practical value to us would not be great. What we need, and can hardly hope to get, is recovery of the London-to-Moscow traffic.

White replied that he was inclined to agree.[74] Though GCHQ continued to work on VENONA, the Service 'virtually abandoned it until 1961'.[75] Given Gardner's success in October 1955 in decrypting a message from Moscow to the London residency which pointed to the strong likelihood that, at the time of Gouzenko's defection, Philby was Agent STANLEY, the Service's loss of interest in VENONA only six months later now appears inexplicable. The probability must be that both White and Mitchell had ceased to pay close attention to the VENONA project. When, some years later, GCHQ was asked to work further on the partially decrypted message from the Centre to the London residency of 17 September 1945, it produced a fuller version which revealed that STANLEY had been able to provide information on the Gouzenko affair and thus identified him even more clearly as Philby: '[c% Consent] [one group unrecovered] was given to verify the accuracy of your telegram containing STANLEY's data about the events in the Neighbours' sphere of activity [Gouzenko affair]. STANLEY's information corresponds to the facts.'[76]

By the beginning of the 1960s the Security Service had still discovered very little about how any of the Magnificent Five had been recruited or controlled as Soviet agents. Its ignorance led it to exaggerate, sometimes very greatly, the quality of Soviet intelligence in the Stalin era. Unaware of the bungling by the Centre and some of its residencies in handling the Cambridge spies, the Service wrongly assumed that the successes of the Five reflected careful planning and exemplary tradecraft by the KGB. (Not until 1992, for example, did it discover from the material smuggled out of KGB archives by Vasili Mitrokhin both the Centre's lamentable failure to respond to Maclean's pleas for help from Cairo and the incompetence of the Soviet illegal HARRY as Philby's controller during his Washington posting.)[77] The gaps in the Service's knowledge of the Five and their handlers provided increasing opportunities for its small but disruptive group of conspiracy theorists. It was possible to argue, for example, that the tip-off to Maclean, instead of coming from Philby via Burgess, had been given instead by an undiscovered Soviet agent inside the Security Service. In the imagination of Peter Wright the KGB became transformed into an agency of extraordinary operational subtlety and sophistication. As Wright began to descend into his conspiratorial wilderness of mirrors, Hollis warned him, 'They're not ten foot tall, you know, Peter!'[78] That warning, however, merely strengthened Wright's suspicions of Hollis himself.

The defection of a KGB major, Anatoli Golitsyn, to the CIA in December 1961 both provided significant new intelligence on the Five and sent the Service investigation as a whole seriously off course. According to a note prepared, somewhat reluctantly,[79] by the Service for the Home Secretary in 1966:

In 1962 a defector [Golitsyn] from the R[ussian] I[ntelligence] S[ervice] stated that in the 1930s there was a very important spy network in the United Kingdom called the Ring of Five because it originally had five members all of whom knew each other and had been at the university together. He knew that Burgess and Maclean were members of the ring. He thought that the network had expanded beyond the original five.

Remarkably, the DG, Furnival Jones, told the PUS at the Home Office, Sir Charles Cunningham, that he 'very much hoped that the Home Secretary would not feel he had to inform the Prime Minister'.[80]

By 1964 the Service had obtained confessions of varying frankness from Philby, Blunt and Cairncross. The breakthrough in the prolonged and generally dispiriting Security Service investigation of the Philby case came as a result of a chance meeting at the Weizmann Institute in Israel in 1962 between the former MI5 officer Victor Rothschild and Flora Solomon, a Marks and Spencer executive and former lover of Alexander Kerensky, head of the Russian Provisional Government overthrown by the Bolshevik Revolution. Solomon was outraged by Philby's anti-Israeli and pro-Arab newspaper articles, and revealed that Philby had tried to recruit her as a Soviet agent before the war.[81] Armed with Solomon's information, Philby's friend and former SIS colleague Nicholas Elliott flew out from London at the beginning of 1963 to confront him in Beirut, where he was working as a journalist. According to Philby's later version of events given to the KGB after he escaped to Moscow, Elliott told him:

You stopped working for them [the Russians] in 1949, I'm absolutely certain of that . . . I can understand people who worked for the Soviet Union, say before or during the war. But by 1949 a man of your intellect and your spirit had to see that all the rumours about Stalin's monstrous behaviour were not rumours, they were the truth . . . You decided to break with the USSR . . . Therefore I can give you my word and that of Dick White that you will get full immunity, you will be pardoned, but only if you tell it yourself. We need your collaboration, your help.

Philby assured the KGB that he had steadfastly resisted all attempts to persuade him to admit that he had ever been a Soviet agent.[82]

The truth was quite different. Philby's version of events after he reached Moscow was a fabrication designed to avoid discrediting himself in the eyes of the KGB by admitting that, when offered immunity from prosecution by Elliott in return for a confession, Philby (probably tempted by the offer) had admitted working as a Soviet agent from 1936 to 1946. In 1946, he told Elliott, he had seen the error of his ways and broken off contact with Soviet intelligence, though he had sent a warning to Maclean in 1951 for reasons of personal friendship. Philby, one of the twentieth century's most accomplished liars, made his bogus confession (part of it recorded by Elliott) so persuasively that, in addition to Elliott, the heads of both MI5 and SIS, Sir Roger Hollis and Sir Dick White, were deceived by it. Hollis wrote reassuringly to J. Edgar Hoover on 18 January 1963:

In our judgment [Philby's] statement of the association with the R.I.S. is substantially true. It accords with all the available evidence in our possession and we have no evidence pointing to a continuation of his activities on behalf of the R.I.S. after 1946, save in the isolated instance of Maclean. If this is so, it follows that damage to United States interests will have been confined to the period of the Second World War.[83]

The fact that less than a week later Philby secretly fled to Russia aboard the Soviet freighter *Dolmatova* made Hollis's and White's subsequent relations with the US intelligence community all the more embarrassing.

Philby's defection probably helped to increase the psychological pressure on both Cairncross and Blunt to confess secretly to the Security Service, since neither was willing to take refuge in Moscow. Early in 1964 Cairncross accepted a teaching post at Western Reserve University in Cleveland, Ohio. At a meeting in Cleveland, Arthur Martin (D1) persuaded Cairncross to confess that he had spied for the Russians until 1951. Unsurprisingly, Cairncross declined a request to return to Britain and be interviewed under caution. Later in 1964 he took up a job in Rome with the UN Food and Agriculture Organization. For some years Cairncross was given to understand that he returned to the UK at his peril; not until 1970 did the DPP authorize the Service to give him some assurance of immunity from prosecution. In the meantime, 'Although the information he provided seemed sometimes vague, confusing and contradictory, he appeared to co-operate honestly during the numerous interviews which followed his initial admission.'[84]

The decisive breakthrough in the Service's investigation of Anthony Blunt came when the American Michael Straight admitted that Blunt had

PHILBY IN RUSSIA?

"We'll soon have enough there to start a cricket team"

Daily Mail, 2 July 1963.

recruited him while he was an undergraduate at Trinity College, Cambridge. Arthur Martin called on Blunt at the Courtauld Institute on the evening of 23 April 1964 and asked him to recall all he knew about Michael Straight. Martin 'noticed that by this time Blunt's right cheek was twitching a good deal' and 'allowed a long pause before saying that Michael Straight's account was rather different from his'. He then offered Blunt 'an absolute assurance that no action would be taken against him if he now told me the truth':

He sat and looked at me for fully a minute without speaking. I said that his silence had already told me what I wanted to know. Would he now get the whole thing off his chest? I added that only a week or two ago I had been through a similar scene with John Cairncross who had finally confessed and afterwards thanked me for making him do so. Blunt's answer was: 'give me five minutes while I wrestle with my conscience.' He went out of the room, got himself a drink, came back and stood at the tall window looking out on Portman Square. I gave him several minutes of silence and then appealed to him to get it off his chest. He came back to his chair and [confessed].[85]

Once Philby had fled to Moscow and Cairncross and Blunt had confessed to working as Soviet agents, the Security Service had, without realizing it, identified all of the Ring of Five. The tragedy was that the Service failed to grasp that it had actually solved the case – chiefly because those involved in the investigation took literally Golitsyn's statement that all five had been at university together. Blunt had not been recruited until after Philby had ceased talent-spotting at Cambridge. That and the fact that Blunt had been allowed by Moscow to leave MI5 after the war was thought to indicate that he did not qualify as the 'Fourth Man'. The fact that Cairncross had not arrived at Cambridge until after Philby and Maclean had left was similarly regarded as ruling him out of contention as a candidate for the 'Fifth Man'. Until 1974 James Klugmann, Maclean's contemporary at both Gresham's School and Cambridge as well as (at the time) one of Britain's most active young Communists, was regarded as the most likely Fourth Man.[86]

For some years after 1964 the Service seemed to move further away from, rather than closer to, an identification of the two missing members of the Ring of Five and an understanding of the circumstances of Burgess's and Maclean's defection. Though the pool of able ideological Soviet recruits began to dry up during the early Cold War, KGB tradecraft and professionalism improved considerably. Some of the Security Service officers involved in the investigation of the Five and the cases of other suspected agents recruited during the 1930s and 1940s made the mistake of supposing that Soviet intelligence had operated then with the same level of sophistication as it did by the 1960s. The relatively simple fact that Burgess's main objective on his return to London in May 1951 had been to warn Maclean was thus erroneously reinterpreted as an elaborate Soviet deception. K7, one of the Service's experts on Soviet penetration, wrote in 1972: 'That Burgess was sent back to London in May 1951 to warn Maclean as the R.I.S. would have us believe, is nonsense. We are justified in assuming the R.I.S. had other means to care for Maclean.' Had K7 been aware of the gross mishandling of Maclean by Soviet intelligence in 1949–50 and of its numerous other limitations at that period, she would have realized that her 'justified' assumption was in fact unjustified. On the basis of that unjustified assumption, however, she and others constructed an elaborate conspiracy theory according to which Burgess's defection, so far from being motivated by the Centre's desire to ensure both that Maclean got to Moscow and that Burgess did not have the opportunity to get into more trouble in London, was actually motivated by a desire to increase Blunt's opportunities to monitor MI5's investigations of the Ring of Five:

By disappearing with Maclean, [Burgess] threw suspicion on Blunt. Blunt's obvious course of action was to be seen to cooperate with the Security Service. In this way he was able to maintain his bona fides as a loyal citizen in the eyes of the Security Service. The contact had the additional advantage of permitting him to monitor Security Service action to some extent, and giving him access to safeguard R.I.S. interests if he could do so without endangering his own position . . .[87]

Peter Wright's attempts to get Blunt to admit to this and other things he had not done increasingly disrupted serious investigation of his actual career as a Soviet agent. It was tragic that the lead role in interviewing Blunt was taken over by Wright, whose conspiracy theories arguably did as much damage to the Service as Blunt's treachery.

Though Blunt had a considerable liking for gin and tonic before he had to deal with Wright, pressure to provide non-existent evidence to validate Wright's misconceived conspiracy theories helped to turn him into an alcoholic. The more Wright questioned him, the more Blunt drank. The telecheck on Blunt's flat in the Courtauld Institute recorded his partner, John Gaskin, saying in December 1965: 'His drinking problem has been growing and growing . . . beyond all reasonable proportions. [Anthony has an] enormous drink bill – over £100 a month.'[88] £100 a month in 1965 was more than the salary of a young academic. In January 1966 Blunt was heard telling a friend that he was 'not feeling very well and [got] through yesterday solely on gin'.[89] Within a few years Blunt's drinking was making further questioning increasingly difficult. Wright noted in June 1970: 'He is obviously drinking like a fish and consumed an incredible amount of gin during the lunch hour that I spent with him.'[90] Four months later Wright reported that, after further heavy gin consumption at the beginning of another bout of questioning, 'Blunt was in such a state that it was not worthwhile pursuing [further questions].'[91]

The fact that Golitsyn's definition of the Ring of Five was taken so literally not merely by Wright and the small band of conspiracy theorists but by other Service investigators seems in retrospect remarkable, given both Golitsyn's known tendency to exaggerate and his admission that he had not seen the files of any of the Five. In reality, the KGB's habit of referring to them collectively with expressions such as 'the Five', 'Ring of Five' and 'Magnificent Five' did not mean, as Golitsyn claimed, that all had been at Cambridge at the same time. The Five were so called simply because they had established themselves as the five star performers among a larger group of Cambridge recruits. Had the Security Service adopted this common-sense definition and concentrated simply on identifying the most successful of the Cambridge recruits, it would have identified Blunt and Cairncross as the Fourth and Fifth Men far more rapidly than it did.

The failure to complete the identification of the Five increased fears that there were other undetected Soviet moles in high places who, like the Five, had been recruited at, or soon after leaving, university. In 1967 the Service's newly founded University Research Group (URG) was given the mammoth task of tracking down all students at British universities who had been Communists or Communist sympathizers during the quarter-century from 1929 to 1954 and identifying their current employment. Hitherto the systematic study of Communists in British universities had been largely confined to Oxbridge. Had it been less sensitively carried out, the URG's work might well have appeared as a McCarthyite witch-hunt of dedicated civil servants who were being persecuted simply because of their left-wing sympathies as university students. Remarkably, the URG attracted virtually no complaints or publicity. Most of those who were approached co-operated with the inquiry. Though the inquiry was well conducted, however, it achieved little of importance apart from adding to the Service's contextual knowledge of past Communist and Comintern activities in British universities. Five years of investigations identified not a single additional Soviet spy.[92]

Not until 1974 was Blunt at last identified, initially tentatively, as the Fourth Man.[93] Even then, however, the hunt for the Fifth Man still did not appear in sight of success. One of the few, rather slim, remaining hopes after the Service recovered its interest in VENONA during the 1960s[94] was that a new Soviet decrypt might provide the solution. On 22 June 1977 the DG, Sir Michael Hanley, was asked by the Prime Minister, James Callaghan, if he knew the identity of the Fifth Man. Hanley's response was somewhat defeatist:

I replied that I did not, though there were many theories. The only independent source on which I could rely was VENONA. There was still a chance that we should get enough VENONA messages from the London [residency] of the KGB in 1945 to enable us to discover more about the Ring of Five. NSA were doing a great deal of work on this and I had already emphasised to our American friends the importance, at least from our point of view, of bringing this to a successful conclusion.[95]

The identity of the Fifth Man was eventually to be established, not through a belated VENONA breakthrough, but as a result of intelligence from Oleg Gordievsky, an SIS agent in the KGB recruited late in 1974. From September 1975 SIS passed all intelligence received from Gordievsky to K Branch (counter-espionage), where, in the Service's view, K6 made 'a fundamental contribution to the collation and assessment' of his information.[96] It was not, however, until after Gordievsky returned to Moscow at the end of the 1970s to work at the Centre that he discovered the identity of the Fifth Man.[97] After his posting to the London residency in 1982, he revealed that the Fifth Man was John Cairncross, who had confessed his role as a Soviet agent to the Security Service eighteen years earlier. The Service then discovered that a major counter-espionage problem which had continued to preoccupy it for over twenty years had been resolved in 1964.

7

The End of Empire: Part 1

The post-war retreat from the greatest empire in world history without a single military defeat sets the British experience apart from the humiliations suffered by other European imperial powers. Britain's decolonization, unlike that of its main imperial rival, France, began before it was too late for an orderly withdrawal. The transfer of power in India and Pakistan in 1947, despite the horrendous inter-communal carnage which accompanied it, happened in time to preserve a degree of official goodwill for post-imperial Britain. The last Viceroy, Lord Mountbatten, was asked to stay on as governor general and the framework of the civil service of the British Raj was largely preserved in independent India. What was not made public, however, was that, during a visit to India in March 1947, the DDG, Guy Liddell, obtained the agreement of the government of Jawaharlal Nehru for an MI5 security liaison officer (SLO) to be stationed in New Delhi after the end of British rule.[1] Though the first SLO, Lieutenant Colonel Kenneth Bourne, who had served in India with the Intelligence Corps during the war,[2] stayed for only six months, he set an important precedent for the subsequent history of British decolonization. In all other newly independent Commonwealth countries, as in India, the continued presence of an SLO became a significant, though usually undisclosed, part of the transfer of power. For almost a quarter of a century, relations between the Security Service and its Indian counterpart, the Delhi Intelligence Branch (DIB or IB), were closer and more confident than those between any other departments of the British and Indian governments.

In 1948, shortly after Bourne had been succeeded as SLO by Bill U'ren, an old India hand with twenty-two years' service in the Indian police,[3] a dispute between the British high commissioner in India, General Sir Archibald Nye, and SIS led to the reaffirmation of the principle that the Empire and Commonwealth were the exclusive preserve of the Security Service. After Nye had complained in the autumn of 1948 that SIS activities in India risked prejudicing 'delicate negotiations' he was conducting in New

Delhi, the Prime Minister issued what became known as the 'Attlee Directive' (an oral instruction which was never put in writing) formally precluding SIS from conducting clandestine operations in Commonwealth countries.[4] An annexe to the 1952 Maxwell Fyfe Directive to the DG (this time in writing) allowed for a more flexible interpretation of the Attlee Directive:

Broadly speaking, the activities of the Security Service relate to British, Colonial and Commonwealth territory, and those of SIS to foreign territory but it is recognised that in certain circumstances it is expedient that each conducts operations on the other's territory, on the understanding that both parties are kept informed.[5]

Not till the late 1960s, with decolonization almost complete, did the Security Service surrender the lead intelligence role in India and most of the Commonwealth to SIS.[6]

In June 1950 U'ren's successor as SLO, Eric Kitchin, another old India hand, reported that the first head of the independent DIB, T. G. Sanjevi, lost 'no opportunity of stressing the value which he places on maintaining our relationship on a professional and personal basis'.[7] Liddell and Sanjevi were united in their deep distrust of the first Indian high commissioner in London, V. K. Krishna Menon, the Congress Party's leading left-wing firebrand who had spent most of his previous political career in Britain, founding the India League in 1932 to campaign for Indian independence and serving as a Labour councillor in London.[8] In 1933 the Security Service had obtained an HOW on Menon on the grounds that he was an 'important worker in the Indian Revolutionary Movement' with links to the CPGB.[9] To outward appearance, Menon seemed an Anglicized figure. The only language he spoke by the time he became high commissioner in 1947 was English, he disliked curry and much preferred a tweed jacket and flannel trousers to Indian dress. But Menon also had a passionate loathing for the British Raj which independence did little to abate.

Though the JIC discussed the question of Communist influence at the Indian high commission, the discussion was considered so sensitive that no record was made of it. Liddell, however, noted in his diary that he told the JIC, 'We were doing what we could to get rid of Krishna Menon.'[10] The attempt failed. Though Menon was reported to be threatening to resign after press attacks in India, he was able to count on Nehru's support and did not do so.[11] Fears of Menon's pro-Soviet sympathies were well founded. On at least one occasion during his later political career in India, the KGB paid his election expenses.[12]

Sanjevi's successor as head of the DIB, B. N. Mullik, was also an enthusiastic supporter of close liaison with the Security Service.[13] In 1951, despite South African opposition, India (represented by Mullik), Pakistan and Ceylon (Sri Lanka) were invited to the Second Commonwealth Security Conference in London along with the white dominions.[14] Since the election victory in 1948 of Dr Daniel Malan's white-supremacist Nationalist Party it had proved more difficult to maintain intelligence liaison with South Africa than with India. The Security Service had no SLO in Pretoria. Sir Percy Sillitoe, who had spent his early career in the British South African and Northern Rhodesian police forces, visited South Africa in 1949 and told Attlee afterwards that he was strongly opposed to the creation of a local security service:

The improper uses to which a Security Service might be put by the Nationalists might well include its employment against the Parliamentary Opposition and against those members of the British community out of sympathy with the Nationalist political programme. It would certainly be used to keep down the black races.[15]

Though in favour of intelligence co-operation with South Africa against Communism, the Security Service remained intermittently nervous about the political uses to which the Pretoria government might put its intelligence. The case of the campaigning anti-racist cleric the Reverend Michael Scott, who had contacts in the CPGB but was not at all the Communist stooge imagined by Pretoria, gave rise to particular anxiety. In December 1951 Sillitoe sent an unusually direct rebuke to the SLO in Salisbury (later Harare), B. M. 'Bob' de Quehen, for providing information on Scott to the South African authorities:

The Commonwealth Relations Office, the Foreign Office and our own High Commissioner at Pretoria have already said that they are opposed to allowing the South African Government the use of information about Scott received from British sources, because of political objections.

Would you please therefore refrain from giving further information about Scott to the South African High Commissioner without first referring to us. Scott's case is one of exceptional political delicacy, which is a source of embarrassment to us no less than to the South Africans, and it is essential that our Service should not allow itself to become involved in its political aspects.[16]

Stung by the criticism, de Quehen replied plaintively to the DG: 'Could not your letter have been expressed a little more graciously?'[17]

There were no such sensitivities in sharing Security Service intelligence on Communist 'subversion' with Mullik and the DIB. When Walter Bell became SLO in New Delhi in 1952, he was encouraged by Mullik to visit DIB outstations as well as its headquarters.[18] Bell found Mullik 'such an exceptional man, both personally and in the position which he held, that he was the fount of all knowledge that I wanted'.[19] When Mullik visited London for the Third Commonwealth Security Conference in 1953, he told Hollis (then DDG) 'that he thought the Intelligence Bureau was reasonably well informed about subversive activities within India, but he was not so well satisfied about his position on the counter-espionage side'. Mullik asked for an experienced counter-espionage officer to visit DIB headquarters and for help in training transcribers.[20] During 1955, probably to Mullik's dismay, an exchange of state visits by Nehru and Nikita Khrushchev opened a new era in Indo-Soviet relations. American reliance on Pakistan as a strategic counterweight to Soviet influence in Asia encouraged India to turn to the USSR. The newly appointed SLO, John Allen, was understandably concerned about the possible impact on his relations with the DIB. He reported to Hollis in December:

As you know, Mullik has always been anxious not to draw the attention of the Ministry of External Affairs (excluding [N. R.] Pillai, the Secretary-General, who, I suppose, is more in our confidence than any other Indian civil servant) to the existence of an SLO here. Mullik's opinion is that there are too many people in this Department who would be happy to break up the liaison. The fact that neither Mullik nor Pillai have sufficient confidence in the Prime Minister's continuing approval of the liaison willingly to draw his attention to it is a fair indication of the delicate path we tread.[21]

In 1956 Nehru declared that he had never encountered a 'grosser case of naked aggression' than the Anglo-French invasion of Suez, but failed to condemn the brutal Soviet suppression of the Hungarian Uprising in the same year. The chill in Indo-British diplomatic relations, however, had little impact on collaboration between the DIB and MI5. A steady stream of DIB officers attended Security Service training courses in London.[22] At Mullik's request, a D Branch officer was sent to India in 1957 to undertake a detailed review of the DIB's counter-espionage operations against the Soviet Union and propose improvements.[23] Arrangements were also made for a Service expert on the CPGB to visit New Delhi to study DIB records on the finances of the Communist Party of India (CPI),[24] which received regular secret subsidies from Moscow.[25] After returning to London for the 1957 Commonwealth Security Conference, Mullik wrote to Hollis, who had succeeded White as DG: 'In my talks and discussions, I never felt that I was dealing with any organisation which was not my own. Besides this, the hospitality and kindness which all of you showed me was also quite overwhelming.'[26] Hollis visited the DIB in May 1958 and noted afterwards that Mullik's views on Communist penetration were closer to his own than to those of the Indian government.[27] But the SLO, John Allen, feared that, with 'so many unfavourable political winds blowing' between India and Britain, if Nehru realized how close collaboration between the DIB and MI5 was, he would probably forbid much of it.[28] Nehru, however, either never discovered how close the relationship was or – less probably – did discover and took no action.

In the view of the Security Service, the DIB was increasingly unequal to coping with the growing Soviet intelligence presence in India, greater than in any other country in the developing world. In February 1964, three months before Nehru's death, Director E (then responsible for overseas counter-subversion, intelligence organization and liaison), a veteran of the Indian police under the British Raj, visited New Delhi to discuss training and counter-espionage with the DIB:

Despite minor successes, the overall impression of the Bureau's work against the huge Soviet Embassy staff is depressing indeed. Politicians and many officials do not even recognise that there is any threat, and there is no attempt to limit the movements of Russians. In effect they are having an almost free run for their money both in the espionage and subversive fields.[29]

KGB records reveal that his assessment was well founded. Its residency in New Delhi was rewarded for its operational successes by being upgraded to the status of 'main residency'. Oleg Kalugin, who became head of counter-intelligence in KGB foreign intelligence (and its youngest general) in 1973, remembers India as 'a model of KGB infiltration of a Third World government'. India under Nehru's daughter and successor, Indira Gandhi, was probably also the arena for more KGB 'active measures' than anywhere else in the world.[30] Successive SLOs' close relations with the DIB made their inside information on Indian politics and government policy of increasing value to the British high commission at a time when the Soviet Union, through KGB as well as overt channels, was attempting to establish a special relationship with India. In 1965, a year after Nehru's death, the high commissioner, John Freeman, wrote to Hollis to say how much he valued the SLO's information: 'his liaison is one which continues unaffected by changes in Indo-British relations.'[31] Most of the SLOs appointed to New Delhi were gregarious people, fond of India and good at getting on with both the DIB and their high commission colleagues. In 1967 the SLO recruited as his clerical assistant the future DG, Stella Rimington, whose husband was a first secretary at the high commission. The SLO lived in some style. 'He was', Rimington recalls, 'best known for his excellent

Sunday curry lunches, which usually went on well into the evening, and for driving round Delhi in a snazzy old Jaguar.'[32]

By trying to maintain close links with the governments of its former empire, Britain sought (unsuccessfully in the case of India) to prevent them gravitating into the Cold War orbit of the Soviet Union.[33] Though rarely mentioned in public, one of the most important of those links was in security and intelligence. During the early Cold War the wartime defence security officers (DSOs) were succeeded by a network of MI5 SLOs operating under civilian rather than military cover, who reported to the local colonial administration (usually the governor) and sometimes the British military commanders, as well as passing intelligence to and from London.[34] After independence, as in India, they became part of the British high commission. Sillitoe frequently felt more at home in the Empire and Commonwealth, where he made a number of lengthy tours as DG, than he did in his office at Leconfield House.[35] In January 1950, both to improve the co-ordination of the imperial security network and to bolster his own authority over it,[36] Sillitoe brought in a leading colonial administrator, Sir John Shaw, to head a new division, the Overseas Service (OS). Over the next two years, Shaw went on lengthy tours of inspection of the Middle East, Far East, the Indian sub-continent and Anglophone Africa.[37] Within the Security Service his beanpole appearance and time spent in the air earned him the nickname the 'Flying Pencil'.[38] Most of Sillitoe's directors, however, resented the way that Shaw and OS interfered with direct communication between the SLOs and the intelligence departments. When Dick White succeeded Sillitoe as DG in August 1953, he lost no time in disbanding the Overseas Service.[39]

The imperial historian John Darwin rightly emphasizes 'the wide variation in British attitudes and policy between one region and another, and the very different kinds of accommodation which they reached, or sought, with different nationalist movements'.[40] The Security Service played a part in many of the 'accommodations'. The first great challenge to an orderly post-war retreat from Empire was the guerrilla war begun by the Malayan Communist Party, composed mostly of ethnic Chinese, in 1948. The colonial administration was ill equipped to deal with it. One of the greatest successes of pre-war imperial intelligence had been the recruitment of the Vietnamese Communist Lai Teck, who became secretary general of the Malayan Communist Party in 1939. Chin Peng, who uncovered his treachery in March 1947 and succeeded him as secretary general, later described Lai Teck's agent career as 'surely one of Britain's greatest spying triumphs'. Lai Teck was assassinated shortly after he was unmasked.[41] The problems of Malayan intelligence were exacerbated by a power struggle between the interdepartmental Security Intelligence Far East (SIFE),[42] based in Singapore, and the ambitious Colonel John Dalley, head of the Malayan Security Service (MSS) founded in 1946. In the view of the Security Service:

... Dalley was an empire builder, could not delegate responsibility and was convinced that he was the sole expert on intelligence in the Far East ... The shortcomings of MSS seriously hampered the work of SIFE and the personality of Dalley thwarted any attempt to remedy the situation.

Following complaints by Sillitoe to the Colonial Office in 1947, high-level negotiations ensued in both London and the Far East but failed to find a solution.[43] Liddell's distrust of Dalley was so acute that he believed there was a 'strong indication that if, as we intend to do, we put in an informant [in the Malayan Communist Party], Dalley will sabotage him'.[44]

On 14 June 1948 Dalley reported, 'At the time of writing there is no immediate threat to internal security in Malaya although the position is constantly changing and is potentially dangerous.' Two days later Communist guerrillas killed two British managers and an assistant at two rubber plantations. At one of the plantations the guerrillas signalled their intentions by shouting to the Malay labourers who witnessed the killings, 'We will shoot all Europeans!' The Governor, Sir Edward Gent (soon to be replaced), responded by declaring a State of Emergency, and blamed a Communist 'organised campaign of murder'.[45] Intended as a purely temporary measure, the Emergency was to last twelve years. What was not known at the time was that, though the Communist leadership had issued a rather imprecise programme for guerrilla war, the killings on 14 June were the result of a decision by local Communists not authorized by the Party leadership.[46]

At the beginning of the Emergency, Sillitoe sent the flamboyant Alex Kellar[47] to Malaya to advise on changes to the intelligence structure and spend almost a year as head of SIFE. Soon after his arrival he claimed from Head Office the cost of assembling a tropical kit which included 'two Palm Beach and one Saigon linen suitings, white shirts, drill, sharkskin dinner jackets'.[48] Kellar's rather camp manner grated with some of the military. Sillitoe himself received an unusually frosty welcome during a visit to Malaya early in the Emergency. When he heard that Dalley had described him as a Glasgow street-corner boy (a slighting reference to Sillitoe's gangbusting days as chief constable of Glasgow in the 1930s), he demanded and obtained an apology. The Governor's secretary reported that he had 'seldom witnessed so tense a scene'.[49] As Sillitoe and Kellar had recommended, however, the Malayan Security Service was replaced by a new Special Branch within the Malayan Criminal Investigation Department, which liaised with SLOs in Kuala Lumpur and the neighbouring British colony of Singapore.[50]

The creation of the Special Branch proved insufficient to solve the problem of intelligence during the Emergency. Lieutenant General Sir Harold Briggs, who became director of operations in Malaya in 1950, complained: 'Unfortunately our Intelligence organisation is our "Achilles heel" . . . when it should be our first line of attack. We have not got an organisation capable of sifting and distributing important information quickly.'[51] At the heart of the problem was poor civil–military co-ordination; the Chief of Police and the Director of Military Intelligence were not on speaking terms. Faced with a flurry of attacks by Communist guerrillas and declining morale among the European population in 1950 and 1951, there were moments when the British feared they might be losing the war. In October 1951 the high commissioner, Sir Henry Gurney, was killed by guerrillas while being driven in his Rolls-Royce.[52] Oliver Lyttelton, who had just become colonial secretary in Churchill's government, had no doubt that Malaya was his most pressing problem: 'It was evident that we were well on the way to losing control of the country, and soon.'[53] Lyttelton, however, was too pessimistic. During the latter part of 1950, Briggs had begun establishing throughout the squatter areas of Malaya fortified 'new villages', floodlit at night and constantly monitored during the day to prevent guerrilla penetration. As Chin Peng, the guerrilla leader as well as secretary general of the Communist Party of Malaya, later acknowledged, during the first half of 1951 the 'Briggs Plan' 'began directly affecting our food supplies' and eventually severed the supply lines.[54]

The problems of civil–military co-ordination in Malaya were largely solved by the appointment in February 1952 of General (later Field Marshal) Sir Gerald Templer, a former director of military intelligence in London, to the combined post of high commissioner and director of operations, which gave him greater power than any British general since Oliver Cromwell three centuries before.[55] 'The Emergency', he declared, 'will be won by our intelligence system – our Special Branch.'[56] The Special Branch, however, required urgent reform and he turned for assistance to the Security Service. 'Special Branch people here are tricky,' Templer wrote to Sillitoe. '. . . They pout like a lot of petulant children and cannot bear criticism.'[57] Templer asked Dick White, who, like Sillitoe, had made a personal tour of inspection in Malaya, to become his director of intelligence. Doubtless with one eye on the succession to Sillitoe, White refused.[58]

Templer then chose another senior MI5 officer, Jack Morton, previously head of SIFE in succession to Kellar, to become director of intelligence with responsibility for intelligence co-ordination and advising him on the reorganization of the Special Branch.[59] The two men worked remarkably closely together.[60] Templer accepted Morton's recommendation to split the Special Branch from the CID to allow it to concentrate wholly on counter-insurgency.[61]

The Communist guerrillas became steadily less effective as Templer's counter-insurgency campaigns and disruption of their supply lines forced them to withdraw deeper and deeper into the jungle. Agent penetration of the guerrillas by the reformed Special Branch achieved some striking successes. In the summer of 1953, after two months of 'slogging through the world's thickest jungles', Chin Peng set up a new headquarters at Grik in Northern Malaya, not far from the Thai border, only to be told by the local guerrillas that, though he had yet to be identified, there must be a traitor in their midst. For the past year: 'Intended guerrilla operations had been thwarted by the British before they could be launched. Weapons, ammunition and food supplies had been revealed to the enemy and seized. Key Party officials had been betrayed and arrested.' Soon after Chin Peng's arrival in Grik, the traitor was identified when a government cheque for $50,000 was found in the shirt pocket of a local Party secretary. Late in 1953 Chin Peng was forced to move his headquarters into deep jungle across the Thai border.[62] In February 1954 Morton reported to Templer, 'There has been a very real all-round progress in the development of the intelligence machine in the last two years.'[63] Templer agreed. Morton, he wrote later, 'has done an absolutely first-class job of work and I have a very high opinion of him indeed.'[64]

Templer's leadership and the close co-ordination of the Special Branch with the security forces turned the Malayan campaign into probably the most successful counter-insurgency campaign of modern times. 'Winning hearts and minds', though the phrase was not invented until after the campaign, was an essential part of Templer's strategy. A major programme of road and electricity-grid construction 'resulted in an infrastructure that few countries in Asia could match'. There was also, as a senior police officer acknowledged in 1954, 'less beating up' of suspects.[65] The Security Service accepted that 'an Interrogation Centre cannot be run as a welfare institution. It is a place where firm discipline needs to be maintained.' During decolonization, as in the wartime Camp 020,[66] however, the Service was firmly opposed to physical violence during interrogation: 'Moral consideration alone should suffice to prohibit it. Further, it is the purpose of interrogation to elicit valid intelligence, whereas extorted confessions are likely to be unreliable.' 'Less beating up' thus produced, in the Service's view, better intelligence.[67] Particular care was needed when interrogating women. The SLO in Malaya commended guidelines drawn up in 1957 by the Malayan Special Branch: 'In order to command respect from the prisoners, the interrogator must exercise self-respect and avoid foul language. It is completely erroneous for the interrogator to threaten the removal of a female prisoner's clothing and to threaten to expose the prisoner in the nude.'[68]

By the time Chin Peng emerged from the jungle in 1955 in a vain attempt to seek an amnesty from the Malayan government, it was clear that he had lost the war.[69] In the run-up to the independence of the Malayan Federation in 1957, the SLO developed such a close relationship with the future leader of the Federation, Tunku Abdul Rahman, that he was entrusted with the numbers of the combination locks to the Tunku's security safes. Two Security Service officers were seconded to Special Branch in 1958 to help train a new generation of Malay officers.[70] When the Emergency was formally ended in 1960, three years after independence, a despondent Chin Peng abandoned his base in the border region and retreated to Beijing.[71]

While the Malayan Emergency was continuing, Security Service intelligence was also influencing British policy on decolonization in West and East Africa. Soon after the riots in Accra of February 1948 which marked the active beginning of the struggle for independence in the Gold Coast (the future Ghana), Robin 'Tin-eye' Stephens was appointed SLO with direct access to the Governor, Sir Charles Arden-Clarke.[72] Stephens's influence in Accra owed much both to his own powerful personality (previously demonstrated as head of MI5's wartime interrogation centre, Camp 020) and to the fact that for the previous two years the Security Service had been supplying the Colonial Office with reports on the activities of the West African National Secretariat (WANS), founded in London late in 1945 to campaign for independence.[73] The politically astute WANS secretary general (and future first Ghanaian prime minister), Kwame Nkrumah, later described the WANS office as the London 'rendezvous of all African and West Indian students and their friends. It was there that we used to assemble to discuss our plans, to voice our opinions and air our grievances.'[74] Thanks to an HOW,[75] many of these plans, opinions and grievances were overheard by the Security Service. The grounds for obtaining the HOW on WANS had been its contacts with the British Communist Party. Telechecks on the CPGB and eavesdropping on its King Street HQ provided further evidence of these links. A note on Nkrumah's file records that, when he called King Street, he spoke with a 'foreign sounding accent' (presumably to disguise his identity), making it difficult for MI5's transcribers to understand him.[76] In November 1947, an intercepted telephone conversation between Nkrumah and King Street revealed that he was planning to leave Britain for the Gold Coast.[77]

When riots broke out in the Gold Coast in February 1948, Nkrumah was arrested and imprisoned by the colonial authorities. After his arrest, he was found to be carrying an unsigned CPGB membership card, together with notes on an organization called the 'Circle', led by Nkrumah, whose aim was to establish in West Africa a Union of African Socialist Republics.[78] Plans for the Union reflected Nkrumah's own grandiose but unrealistic vision of a united post-imperial Africa, which he claimed implausibly was 'probably better equipped for industrialization than almost any other region in the world' and would develop its own distinctive brand of socialism.[79] Hampered by the almost complete lack of reliable intelligence from Moscow during the early years of the Cold War, however, MI5 desk officers admitted to Accra that, though they had never previously heard of the Circle, they thought it possible that Nkrumah's plans might have derived from 'outside' (Soviet) guidance.[80] In reality, the KGB – unlike the British Communist Party – still took so little interest in sub-Saharan Africa that it was not until 1960 that its foreign intelligence arm established a department to specialize in that region.[81]

The Security Service view of Nkrumah and of African nationalism in general, however, was far from alarmist. The DDG, Guy Liddell, told the JIC in December 1949:

in so far as West and East Africa were concerned, there was no evidence of Communism as it was understood in Europe, there was no local Communist Party. There was, however, a lot of nationalism, which received considerable encouragement from all sorts of people who went out to preach British democracy. It was true that niggers coming here often went to the C.P. This did not mean that they were Communists or that they understood anything about Karl Marx or dialectical materialism: it merely meant that they found the Communists sympathetic because they had no racial discrimination and were all in favour of the niggers running their own show.[82]

Though 'nigger' was less outrageously insulting in 1949 than it later became, it was clearly derogatory. Liddell would have been highly unlikely to use it in a formal report to the JIC.

The Security Service concluded in June 1948 that Nkrumah's main motivations were African nationalism and personal ambition: 'His interest in Communism may well be prompted only by his desire to enlist aid in the furtherance of his own aims in West Africa ... Although an undoubted nationalist, N'krumah's aims are probably tainted by his wishes for his own personal advancement.'[83] Nkrumah's periods in jail after his return to Accra for leading strikes and demonstrations against the colonial administration merely added to his popularity as the Gold Coast's leading nationalist politician. In June 1949 Stephens forecast accurately that, when a general election was held, Nkrumah's newly established Convention People's Party (CPP) was likely to win.[84] Over the next year he reported growing popular support for Nkrumah's demands for 'Self Government Now'.[85] Like Whitehall and the colonial administration, however, the Security Service failed to foresee the pace of change in both the Gold Coast and the rest of the African empire. Liddell wrote dismissively in his diary after a visit to West Africa in December 1950:

There is no doubt in my mind that the West African natives are wholly unfitted for self-rule ... You need only to try to buy a set of stamps for 1/- at the Accra Post Office on a hot afternoon; the place is a seething mass of blacks milling round the counter. After a long delay a black clerk will endeavour to add up the sum; it will come out wrong, but it is better not to argue as the delay and frustration would only be greater![86]

The head of the Security Service Overseas Service, Sir John Shaw, as well as the SLO, remained in close personal touch with the colonial administration in Accra. On New Year's Eve 1951, Shaw stayed up until 2 a.m. talking on the telephone with the Governor, Sir Charles Arden-Clarke, about the political situation. The future of the Gold Coast, he noted on New Year's Day, depended on Arden-Clarke's ability to get on with Nkrumah. The Governor doubtless welcomed the evidence provided by MI5 from the bugging of the CPGB HQ that Nkrumah had fallen out of favour with the Party. In October 1950, the *Daily Telegraph* ran a story entitled 'Red Shadow over the Gold Coast', which claimed that the CPP was orchestrated from Moscow, 'using Ju Ju of darkest Africa'. Nkrumah's intercepted correspondence in both Britain and the Gold Coast told a quite different and far more reassuring story, showing his intention, when he became prime minister in March 1952, to follow the constitutional path to independence. In Shaw's view, intelligence provided grounds for 'quiet optimism'.[87] As Shaw had forecast, Arden-Clarke's ability to build a successful relationship with Nkrumah was crucial to the smooth transfer of power which led to Ghana becoming the first of Britain's African colonies to achieve independence in 1957.[88]

The main issue for the Security Service in the months leading up to independence was whether Nkrumah would set an example to other future leaders of Anglophone Black Africa by keeping on the current SLO, R. J. S. (John) Thomson. In September 1956 Thomson identified himself to Nkrumah as a Security Service officer and quickly persuaded him of the advantages of maintaining a link with the Service to keep him informed of subversion sponsored by Colonel Nasser's regime in Egypt (of which Nkrumah was then increasingly suspicious) and by the Soviet Bloc countries, which were Nasser's main foreign backers. Referring to Egypt and its Soviet backers (though not by name), Nkrumah declared: 'Colonialism and imperialism may come to us yet in a different guise.'[89] When Thomson's tour of duty came to an end in November 1959, it was extended until June 1960 at the request of Nkrumah, who sent a personal letter of thanks to the DG. Nkrumah's Interior Minister, Asford Emmanuel Inksumah, said that, ideally, they would have liked Thomson to stay 'for ever'.[90] Thomson shared the optimism of a senior Colonial Office official who said proudly of Nkrumah, 'We have turned an LSE Communist into a progressive Socialist.'[91] The remainder of Britain's former African colonies followed Ghana's example after independence in keeping a Security Service SLO, usually until the late 1960s.

The Kenyan leader, Jomo Kenyatta, aroused greater fears among the colonial administration than Nkrumah. Like its counterpart in Malaya at the beginning of the Emergency, the Special Branch in Kenya was unprepared for the outbreak in 1952 of the Mau Mau rebellion, which its head described as a 'most dangerous subversive organisation'.[92] As Oliver Lyttelton, the Colonial Secretary, read reports from Kenya of 'bestial, filthy' Mau Mau atrocities, he felt that he saw 'the horned shadow of the Devil himself'.[93] Some officials in Nairobi, the Colonial Office and other parts of Whitehall believed from the outset that the Mau Mau rebellion was a Communist plot. Kenyatta, whom they wrongly regarded as 'leader' of Mau Mau, was, they had no doubt, a 'Communist'.[94] The Governor, Sir Evelyn Baring, was convinced that, 'With his Communist and anthropological training, *[Kenyatta] knew his people* and was directly responsible [for Mau Mau]. Here was the African leader to darkness and death.'[95] The Security Service strongly disagreed. Sillitoe wrote in January 1953: 'Our sources have produced nothing to indicate that Kenyatta, or his associates in the UK, are directly implicated in Mau Mau activities, or that Kenyatta is essential to Mau Mau as a leader, or that he is in a position to direct its activities.'[96] Some Colonial Office officials as well as Baring were unconvinced.[97]

Suspicions of Kenyatta's Communist connections went back to the moment when he first arrived in Britain to study at the London School of Economics in 1929 as the leader of the Kikuyu Central Association. His activities had been monitored by the Special Branch, which compiled a 'large file' on him.[98] In April 1930 it reported that he was believed to have joined the CPGB and that a leading British Communist, Robin Page Arnot, had called him 'the future revolutionary leader of Kenya'.[99] The Security Service opened its own file on Kenyatta three months later after receiving a report from SIS that he was off to Hamburg to attend a 'negro conference'.[100] Unknown to British intelligence, he went on from Germany to Moscow to study at the secret Comintern-run Lenin School and Communist University of the Toilers of the East under the alias 'James Joken'.[101] MI5 first learned of Kenyatta's time in Moscow soon after his return to Britain late in 1933 from a Special Branch informer, who reported that, while studying at the Lenin School, he had received 'instructions' to become a Comintern agent.[102] (Training in underground work, espionage and guerrilla warfare were indeed on the secret Lenin School curriculum.)[103] Sir Vernon Kell personally informed both the Colonial Office and the Commissioner of Police in Nairobi.[104] MI5 simultaneously obtained an HOW on Kenyatta, who was then living in London. So prompt was postal delivery in pre-war London that, on two occasions over the next few months, Kenyatta complained to the Post Office that he believed his mail was being opened because of the delay in receiving it. To calm his suspicions, the HOW was suspended in July 1934.[105]

MI5 did not discover for almost twenty years that Kenyatta had been disillusioned by his period in Moscow. While at the University of the Toilers of the East he had joined in a written protest at the 'derogatory portrayal of Negroes in the cultural institutions of the Soviet Union' as 'real monkeys', and had complained to his lecturers that 'in all respects' their teaching was inferior to that in 'bourgeois schools', which encouraged pupils to think for themselves. When an earnest South African Communist in Moscow accused him of being a 'petty-bourgeois', Kenyatta was said to have replied: 'I don't like this "petty" thing. Why don't you say I'm a big bourgeois?'[106] In the course of the Second World War, the monitoring of CPGB headquarters and intermittent surveillance of Kenyatta, who in 1940 moved to West Sussex, gave the Security Service other evidence of his declining links with Communist politics. O. J. Mason, soon to become the first SLO in East Africa, reported to the Colonial Office after Kenyatta spoke at the Pan-African Congress in Manchester in 1945: 'During the last few years, Kenyatta appears to have led a fairly quiet and non-political life, but previously he had been known as something of an anti-British agitator. It is believed that he was at one time a Communist, but is thought to have quarrelled with that Party . . .'[107]

After Kenyatta's return to Kenya in 1946, the intelligence available to the Security Service, much of it from intercepted communications passing between Britain and Kenya, continued to be reassuring. In July 1951 a report from the SLO in Salisbury, Bob de Quehen, belatedly disclosed the disillusion experienced by Kenyatta during his period in Moscow almost twenty years earlier. Kenyatta had revealed to a South African police source how he had witnessed the first black secretary general of the Communist Party of South Africa, Albert Nzula, being dragged out of a meeting in Moscow by two OGPU officers. He was never seen alive again.[108] Kenyatta must have reflected that he had been fortunate to leave Moscow in 1933. Had he still been there a few years later during the Great Terror, his political incorrectness and unconcealed preference for 'bourgeois' education would probably have led him to share the fate of Nzula. Sillitoe, however, believed that ill-informed accounts of Kenyatta's period at the Lenin School in Moscow twenty years before continued to be mainly responsible for claims in Nairobi and Whitehall of 'Communist influence behind Mau Mau'.[109]

Shortly after the declaration of a State of Emergency in Kenya by the Governor, Sir Evelyn Baring, on 20 October 1952, Sillitoe wrote to the Colonial Office to offer the Service's assistance. The PUS, Sir Thomas Lloyd, declined the offer, saying that what was needed instead was 'a good man from some Special Branch'. The head of OS, Sir John Shaw, had no doubt that Lloyd's proposal would prove 'futile': 'Sooner or later, too late, we shall be asked for help.' The request for help came earlier than Shaw expected. On 20 November, at the request of the Governor, Sillitoe and A. M. MacDonald flew to Nairobi, where they were joined by Alex Kellar, who arrived from the Middle East. 'So', remarked Shaw to Lloyd, 'the first XI of MI5 is to play the Mau Mau.' The Service delegation arrived on a Friday, their recommendations were drafted by the following Tuesday and accepted by Baring the same morning. MacDonald stayed on as security adviser 'to concert all measures to secure the intelligence Government requires' and to 'co-ordinate the activities of all intelligence agencies operating in the Colony and to promote collaboration with Special Branches in adjacent territories'. His first task was to reorganize the Special Branch, which he found 'grossly overworked, bogged down in paper, housed in offices which were alike impossible from the standpoint of security or normal working conditions. The officers were largely untrained, equipment was lacking and intelligence funds were meagre.' Reform proceeded so rapidly that in August 1953 MacDonald recommended that his post as security adviser be abolished. He wrote to Head Office in October, 'Special Branch goes from strength to strength and we now have some excellent sources operating. I have no qualms at leaving this lusty infant to look after itself.'[110]

Like Whitehall and the colonial administration, however, the Security Service did not grasp the complexities of the rebellion. Mau Mau grew out of internal factionalism and dissent among the Kikuyu people as well as opposition to British rule. What the British called Mau Mau was not a single movement born of primeval savagery (an image created by the obscene oath-taking ceremonies for new recruits and a series of horrific murders) but a diverse and fragmented collection of individuals, organizations and ideas.[111] Given the Security Service's slender East African resources, it is unreasonable to expect it to have understood Kenyan complexities which eluded the experienced and far more numerous colonial administration. But, unlike Government House in Nairobi, MI5 did not make the mistake of lumping together all those campaigning for independence. Kenyatta told a mass meeting of the Kenya African Union (KAU) in July 1952: 'KAU is not a fighting union that uses fists and weapons. If any of you here think that force is good, I do not agree with you . . . I pray to you that we join hands for freedom and freedom means abolishing criminality . . .' The prevailing opinion in Government House, however, was that Kenyatta and all senior figures in the KAU must somehow be responsible for Mau Mau.[112] The SLO in East Africa, C. R. Major, wrongly believed that Kenyatta had indeed helped to organize some Mau Mau incidents before October 1952, but that thereafter 'they had a snowball effect' which Kenyatta was powerless to prevent.[113] He opposed the decision by Government House to put Kenyatta on trial, which, he reported, was motivated by political expediency and the need to find a culprit to placate the settlers.[114] As Major had feared, Kenyatta was given what amounted to a show trial. Crown witnesses, it was later claimed, were carefully coached before giving evidence and effectively bribed with substantial 'rewards'. Kenyatta was sentenced to seven years' imprisonment.[115]

During the Emergency all Security Service staff in Kenya, female secretaries included, were issued with hand-guns and given target practice. The secretaries were also warned to be careful whom they slept with. As SLO in Nairobi, Robert Broadbent slept with a revolver under his pillow,[116] unaware, however, that a Mau Mau arms dump was hidden in his kitchen. The dump was discovered during a reception at Broadbent's house after a waiter dropped a tray of drinks and, in the ensuing commotion, Mau Mau guerrillas who had come to retrieve some of their arms were discovered in the kitchen threatening staff.[117] Despite the fact that the British media gave most publicity to Mau Mau atrocities against Europeans, only thirty-two white settlers were killed during the Emergency – fewer than died in traffic accidents in Nairobi during the same period. Over 90 per cent of those killed were Kikuyu, in what turned into a civil war between the loyalist Kikuyu Guard and Mau Mau guerrillas. Though the Emergency lasted until 1959, Mau Mau was effectively defeated by the end of 1956. In the view of a number of Service officers, a key step in its defeat was the appointment as director of security and intelligence from 1955 to 1958 of John Prendergast (later knighted), a Kenya police officer who had previously served in Palestine, the Gold Coast and the Canal Zone.[118] Black Kenyans, however, paid a terrible price for both the rebellion and the brutality with which it was crushed. During the Emergency Kenya became a police state which imprisoned a higher proportion of its population than any other colony in the history of the British Empire. On a conservative estimate, one in four adult Kikuyu males were held in often brutal camps and prisons at some point during the Emergency.[119]

During the mid-1950s, in the wake of the Security Service's role in the Malayan and Kenyan emergencies, Eric Holt-Wilson's pre-war vision of a great imperial security network dominated by the Service began to become a reality. Other African colonies facing nationalist unrest became used to seeking the Security Service's usually reassuring advice. In September 1953, for example, Sir Geoffrey Colby, Governor of Nyasaland (the future Malawi), became concerned that local political agitators 'might be merely the tool of some dangerous anti-British organisation inspired from outside Africa':

After most careful thought I feel sure it is imperative that all available material should be examined by a high level expert from M.I.5 as soon as possible ... The Special Branch have no knowledge of this situation. They have neither the capacity nor the time to investigate it properly. They are flat out in coping with day-to-day security intelligence.[120]

Sir John Shaw reassured the Colonial Office of the improbability of a 'dangerous anti-British organisation' inspiring unrest from abroad and recommended that Bob de Quehen, the SLO for Central Africa, be called in from Salisbury to advise the Nyasaland administration.[121] While serving in Kenya in 1953, A. M. MacDonald too was asked for advice by neighbouring colonies. That experience prompted him to write a paper on the imperial role of the Service which concluded, 'The Security Service, with the full support of the Colonial Office, must now undertake the task of surveying the entire field of intelligence organisation.'[122] In June 1954 MacDonald was seconded to the Colonial Office to serve as full-time security intelligence adviser to the Secretary of State with the additional task of setting up or reorganizing Special Branches in every colony which would prevent further imperial intelligence surprises such as that in Malaya in 1948 and provide advance warning of any threatened insurgencies.[123] On his return from Malaya in 1954, Templer was instructed to investigate the state of colonial security around the globe. By April 1955, in consultation with the Security Service, he had completed a mammoth investigation for the cabinet, visiting potential trouble spots from Cyprus to Uganda. His lengthy report placed heavy emphasis on the importance of improving imperial intelligence:

It is possible that, had our intelligence system been better, we might have been spared the emergency in Kenya, and perhaps that in Malaya. It must be our objective so to improve the present system that we are, so far as is humanly possible, insured against similar catastrophes in future.[124]

Templer insisted that in the Empire as a whole Communism was not the principal problem:

Our enemy in the cold war is of course Communism. But in the Colonies this threat is for the most part indirect and intangible; it operates, if at all, through the medium of other anti-British manifestations which would be present even if the Communist Party had never been invented. Such manifestations are created by a wide variety of irritants, of which some of the most obvious are nationalism, racialism, religion, frustration, corruption and poverty. In Malaya, it is true, the fight is to keep a frontier against Communism. But in the other colonies its immediate impact is small or non-existent.[125]

The one colony in which Whitehall saw a serious prospect of a Communist takeover was British Guiana, where, Templer reported, 'The root of the problem, and consequently the way to deal with it, is a political matter outside my competence.'[126] In April 1953, following the victory at the first elections held under universal suffrage of the People's Progressive Party (PPP), led by Cheddi Jagan, an American-educated dentist descended from ethnic Indian sugar-plantation workers, British Guiana had become the first British colony with a Marxist prime minister. Jagan and his wife, Janet (née Rosenberg), a Chicago Marxist, had first attracted the attention of the Security Service in 1947 when he made contact with the Soviets in

Washington. From 1948 onwards he was in touch with British Communist Party headquarters.[127] In 1950 the SLO in Trinidad, whose responsibilities also included British Guiana, described Jagan as an 'astute politician', who 'wields great influence over a large number of people who have never been, and in all probability never will be, communists or have the slightest sympathy with communist aims and ideals'. Jagan's support was based on popular opposition to the 'selfish and high-handed' sugar-plantation owners (most of them British agribusinesses) and other big employers.[128] There was, the Security Service reported in 1951, 'no evidence that the PPP is controlled or directed by any Communist organisation outside the Colony'.[129] The Jagans, however, remained in touch with CPGB head-quarters, which Janet Jagan visited soon after the 1953 PPP election victory.[130]

Immediately following the formation of the PPP government, Winston Churchill began to consider seeking US assistance in ousting Jagan from power. He wrote to Lyttelton, the Colonial Secretary, on 2 May: 'We ought surely to get American support in doing all that we can to break the Communist teeth in British Guiana.' He added satirically, 'Perhaps they would even send Senator McCarthy down there.'[131] At the same time Churchill was enthusiastically supporting preparations for British–American covert action ('Special Political Action' in British parlance) to overthrow the supposedly pro-Communist Iranian Prime Minister, Muhammad Mussadeq.[132] Though Mussadeq was duly overthrown, Chur-chill decided it would not, after all, be necessary to seek CIA assistance in British Guiana (CIA involvement was, however, later approved by the Macmillan government).[133] In late September 1953 Lyttelton informed the cabinet that Jagan's government 'have no intention of working the present constitution in a democratic manner nor have any real interest in the good of the people of British Guiana. They have taken every opportunity to undermine the constitution and to further the communist cause.'[134] On 27 September Churchill approved Operation WINDSOR: the unheralded landing of British troops in British Guiana on 9 October, accompanied by the dismissal of the Jagan government and the suspension of the consti-tution. (The SLO in Trinidad later paid tribute to his wife and the wife of the Commissioner of Police in Trinidad for preparing 600 sandwiches for the troops embarking on a British warship en route to Georgetown.)[135] News of Operation WINDSOR, however, leaked out ahead of time and on 7 October, before the British Governor in Georgetown had been informed, *The Times* carried the dramatic headline: 'Danger of Communist Coup in British Guiana: Troops Sent to Avert Risk of Bloodshed'.[136]

After only 133 days as chief minister, Cheddi Jagan was ousted from office and the Governor given emergency powers which continued for the next three years. Churchill's government justified Jagan's overthrow by claiming that 'the intrigues of Communists and their associates' in the PPP government had threatened to turn British Guiana into 'a Communist-dominated state'. Despite some support for Jagan on the Labour back-benches, the Leader of the Opposition, Clement Attlee, also dismissed Jagan and his PPP colleagues as 'either Communists or Communist stooges'.[137] In 1955 Jagan's former ally, the black lawyer Forbes Burnham, split the PPP into two factions and two years later formed the People's National Congress. Thereafter British Guianan politics increasingly divided along ethnic lines with the PPP deriving most of its support from ethnic Indians and the PNC from urban blacks.[138] Though the Security Service had told the Colonial Office some years earlier that Burnham was not of the same calibre as Cheddi and Janet Jagan,[139] both the colonial adminis-tration and the CIA increasingly saw support for Burnham as one of the keys to defeating the Jagans.[140] In most of the Empire, the Security Service contributed to a relatively smooth transfer of power. British Guiana, how-ever, was to be a notable exception. The dominant intelligence agency there in the fraught years leading up to independence in 1966 was to be not the Service but the CIA.[141]

8

The End of Empire: Part 2

As DG in the later 1950s, Roger Hollis found security in colonies and British-administered territories overseas of greater concern than security in Britain itself. On the eve of one of his many imperial tours in May 1958, he told the Home Secretary, R. A. 'Rab' Butler, that colonial 'Special Branches undoubtedly needed all the help they could have, and we were getting a number of requests for assistance.' Rab agreed that, as colonies approached independence, 'it was right to devote considerable time to this aspect of our work.'[1] The total number of colonial and Commonwealth police and administrative officers trained in Britain by the Security Service jumped from an average of 250 a year in the period from 1954 to 1958 to 367 in 1959.[2] The Service felt it necessary to remind the JIC in 1960 that:

The task of the Security Service at home differs markedly from its role overseas. In this country it is both producer of intelligence and consumer of its own product; overseas its representatives are not primarily intelligence producers. They are trainers and advisers of those who are purveyors of intelligence to them . . .[3]

The most serious imperial intelligence challenge after the Malayan Emergency came in Cyprus. As in Malaya in 1948, there had been little advance warning before open warfare erupted in April 1955 between the EOKA guerrillas led by Colonel George Grivas, fighting for union with Greece, and British forces. The lack of intelligence available to the British authorities was due chiefly to the disorganization of the under-resourced Cyprus Special Branch, which had earlier been described by a head of Security Intelligence Middle East (SIME) as a 'right royal muddle'.[4] The EOKA 'Death to Traitors' campaign targeted the Special Branch and CID, as well as their agents and informers, in an attempt to break their morale.[5] In May 1955 Donald Stephens of the Security Service was seconded to the Cyprus government to take up the new post of director of intelligence. The appointment in September as governor and commander in chief of Cyprus of Field

Marshal Sir John Harding, a Malayan veteran who – like Templer – bridged the political–military divide, greatly strengthened Stephens's authority. Philip Kirby Greene, who had become head of SIME earlier in the year, reported that Stephens was at the 'very centre' of the struggle against EOKA 'and enjoying every minute of it'.[6] Masked informers, unflatteringly known as 'hooded toads', were used to identify EOKA guerrillas when suspects were rounded up.

In December 1955 Operation FOXHUNTER uncovered a cache of EOKA documents including part of Grivas's remarkably verbose diaries and almost succeeded in capturing Grivas himself, who at one point was hiding behind a tree within arm's length of a British soldier. Operation LUCKY ALPHONSE in June 1956 captured seven members of Grivas's entourage, his favourite Sam Browne belt and a further 250,000 words (two-thirds as long as this book) of his diaries. Once again Grivas had the closest of shaves, escaping just in time after being alerted to the arrival of British forces by a barking patrol dog. Sections of the diaries, which were read out at a London press conference and then published, provided damning evidence of the links between Archbishop Makarios III, the leader of the Greek Orthodox Church in Cyprus, and EOKA (though Grivas personally distrusted him), and helped to justify the decision taken in March to deport the Archbishop to Mahe, the most remote island in the Seychelles.[7]

In November 1956 Harding declared for the first time a formal State of Emergency, and began a new intelligence-led offensive against EOKA which achieved a series of successes. Among the tactics employed were 'Q patrols' (so named after the disguised British armed merchant ships which had lured some German U-boats to their destruction during the First World War) composed of turned EOKA guerrillas and anti-EOKA Greek Cypriots who arrived in villages pretending to be guerrillas fleeing from British forces and asked to be put in touch with those who could shelter them.[8] In his role as security intelligence adviser, A. M. MacDonald wrote to the Security Service after an operation which had, he believed, ended in 'the complete destruction of the terrorist organisation in Nicosia and the disruption of the [EOKA] Central Courier System' to say that both Stephens and the head of the Special Branch, W. D. 'Bill' Robinson, 'both deserve the highest praise'.[9] In March 1957 alone thirty EOKA bases were uncovered and twenty-two senior guerrillas killed or captured – among them Grivas's second in command, Gregory Afxentiou, who was killed after an eight-hour firefight. Grivas agreed to a ceasefire in return for the release of Makarios, who was flown back from the Seychelles to begin tortuous negotiations for a political settlement.[10] Stephens returned to

London in July 1957 and was succeeded as director of intelligence by Bill Robinson, who, in the Service view, proved unequal to his job, particularly in coping with the emergence of a terrorist organization in the minority Turkish community and the growth of intercommunal violence.[11]

Because of the need to reconcile the conflicting interests of Greek and Turkish Cypriots, the search for a political solution proved much more complex than in Malaya. Macmillan later called the 'Cyprus Tangle' 'one of the most baffling problems I can ever remember'.[12] Though the ceasefire lasted until October 1957, the first attempts to negotiate with Grivas and Makarios ran into the ground. The new governor appointed in December, Sir Hugh Foot, brother of the left-wing Labour MP Michael Foot and reputedly a left-winger himself, seemed better fitted than his predecessor to seek a political solution. He also sought to reform the intelligence system, which the former head of SIME, Philip Kirby Greene, who became SLO in Cyprus when SIME was wound up in 1958, told him in July was in 'an appalling state of affairs'. In October Foot sent a personal request to the DG for a 'high grade research officer' to collate and assess all available intelligence with the aim of capturing Grivas and the entire EOKA leadership. To the delight of Foot and the Colonial Office, Hollis approved the appointment of Director E, Brigadier Bill Magan, for a six-month secondment. As soon as Magan arrived in Cyprus, Foot asked him to take over 'the full intelligence task', including heading the Special Branch; Magan declined but agreed to act as temporary special adviser to the Branch.[13]

Hollis wrote to Magan shortly after his arrival, 'If we could seize Grivas this would surely knock the stuffing out of Eoka.'[14] Magan set up a re-search team to go through the large accumulation of reports and captured documents on Grivas. Kirby Greene reported to the DG on 25 November: 'Already he has found a considerable amount of intelligence, some of it of importance, which, it seems, passed unnoticed and certainly was not prop-erly recorded or filed and to all intents and purposes was lost.'[15] Magan acknowledged Grivas's 'exceptional singlemindedness' and the way in which he had imposed his own austere lifestyle and passion for order on the EOKA guerrillas, but believed that he had serious limitations as a commander. As a result, his guerrillas had killed surprisingly few British soldiers:

Had the spirit of EOKA been more offensive, had there been more courage in their hearts, they could, shielded as they were by nearly the whole Greek Cypriot population, have on any day of the week carried out as many murders as they did in a month, and forced the British, as was the case a decade ago in Palestine, into a life of barbed wire cages, enormously increasing the static guarding commitment of the army.

Magan produced a lengthy personality profile of Grivas which, he acknowledged, might 'in parts be thought a trifle colourful for an official paper. But I am writing about a man – an unusual man, and not, shall we say, about a gasworks.'[16]

In February 1959 tense and difficult negotiations on the future constitution of an independent Cyprus opened in the ornate setting of Lancaster House, London, whose 'dignity and splendour' were thought to exert 'a potent and helpful influence' on colonial delegations.[17] While talks were proceeding at Lancaster House, Operation SUNSHINE in Cyprus succeeded in tracking down Grivas to an area in Nicosia where the security forces believed that he could be seized by a snatch squad. Had Grivas been caught, however, he would probably – like his second in command two years earlier – have died in a gun battle with the security forces. Over dinner during the Lancaster House conference, Macmillan inquired of the Greek Foreign Minister, Angelos Averoff, what the consequences would be if Grivas was captured. Averoff replied that the negotiations would collapse and a bloodbath would follow. Later the same evening, Macmillan gave instructions that Grivas was to be left undisturbed in his Nicosia hiding place.[18] Magan, whose insight into Grivas's mind and operations had made a major contribution to his discovery, was thus robbed of the prey he had hunted since his arrival in Cyprus. Sir Hugh Foot, who was one of Magan's greatest admirers, wrote afterwards:

Just when [Magan] was establishing his mastery of the subject and moving into the stage of positive action, the powers that be were inconsiderate enough to settle the whole thing. I never see him without a feeling of guilt that I had some hand in this! But though his opponent was saved by the bell he is the first to recognise that what has happened has been very much for the best.[19]

The Lancaster House conference eventually agreed on the establishment of an independent Cyprus republic with a Greek president, a Turkish vice president and a House of Representatives with 70 per cent Greek and 30 per cent Turkish membership, the proportions reflecting the relative size of the two communities in the Cypriot population. Even at the eleventh hour Macmillan feared that Archbishop Makarios, later the first president of Cyprus, was about to torpedo the negotiations. The final difficulties, however, were resolved early on 19 February 1959. Macmillan noted in his diary, 'An extraordinary day. Colonial Secretary rang at 9 a.m. (followed quickly by Foreign Secretary). The answer is "Yes". The Cyprus agreement is therefore made.'[20]

The Security Service intelligence most appreciated by Whitehall during the series of negotiations in London during the late 1950s and early 1960s came from the surveillance of the colonial delegations. The Foreign and Colonial Secretaries both sent personal thanks to the Service via the Home Secretary, Rab Butler, for the intelligence obtained during the conferences which negotiated the independence of Cyprus and, a year later, began three years of intermittent negotiations over Kenyan independence. Hollis confessed to Butler that the surveillance of visiting delegations meant 'we were moving a little outside the strict terms of my Directive.' Butler immediately condoned this enlargement of Security Service operations on the grounds that 'obviously the product was of great importance and of great value to the government negotiators.'[21]

In 1960, with Jomo Kenyatta still in jail, black and settler delegations from Kenya were invited to another conference at Lancaster House during which the Macmillan government committed itself to African majority rule.[22] The Kenyan delegate of most interest to the Security Service during the negotiations was the firebrand future Deputy President of independent Kenya, Oginga Odinga. A bugged conversation at the CPGB's King Street HQ on 19 February 1960 revealed that Odinga had asked Idris Cox of the Party's International Department and one of his colleagues to draft a constitution for a new Kenyan political party of which he intended to be the leading figure.[23] There was much in the uncompromising programme of Odinga's Kenya African National Union (KANU), founded after the Lancaster House conference, of which his CPGB advisers undoubtedly approved. Unlike the more moderate Kenya African Democratic Union (KADU), KANU demanded confiscation of all settler estates and property, the ending of foreign investment and nationalization of industry. How far the KANU programme was actually influenced by the CPGB, however, is uncertain. A Kenya Special Branch 'research paper', forwarded to London by the SLO in Nairobi in September 1960, did not take Odinga's Communism very seriously:

Throughout it has been manifest that Odinga is not an ideological convert to Communism, but has regarded the Eastern Bloc as a new and untapped source of financial aid with which to bolster his political prestige in Kenya ... Odinga by himself is not of sufficiently high calibre to subvert African nationalism in Kenya to Communism, although an attempt might be made to groom him for that role.[24]

Odinga's fundraising success in the Soviet Bloc and China soon led him to be taken more seriously. According to an intelligence report forwarded to London by the SLO in November:

The assistance he has already obtained, although substantially less than he alleges has been promised him, is enough to ensure that his influence in the next few months will be very disruptive. In the longer term he could become a vehicle for external subversion on a familiar pattern, and as a means for the ultimate return to Kenya of a cadre of trained Communist agents.[25]

At the 1961 general election, KANU won a sweeping victory but refused to form a government until Kenyatta was freed. Kenyatta was finally released in August 1961 and entered the legislature after a by-election as president of KANU. Odinga had probably expected him to emerge from prison as a shadow of his former self – about seventy years old (no one knew his exact age), physically feeble, alcoholic, out of touch and a figurehead whom Odinga could dominate. Instead Odinga quickly found himself outmanoeuvred by Kenyatta, who distanced himself from KANU's election programme, reassuring white settlers that they would be welcome to stay in an independent Kenya and that their property would not be confiscated. 'Many of you', he told them, 'are as Kenyan as myself.' 'The mastermind of Mau Mau', as Baring had mistakenly called him, proved instead to be a master of magnanimity.[26] In June 1963, six months before independence, Kenyatta was sworn in as Kenya's first prime minister. Two months later he made a celebrated appeal to white settlers to 'forgive and forget' and stay on in an independent Kenya – as most of them did.

In October 1963 Kenyatta led a KANU delegation to London to complete independence negotiations at Lancaster House. The Security Service was informed by a Colonial Office official that Duncan Sandys, Secretary of State for Commonwealth Relations from July 1960 to October 1964 (as well as Colonial Secretary from July 1962), 'attached great importance to the service of intelligence we were giving him about the activities and views of the delegates to the Kenya conference'.[27] Hollis complained that Sandys had risked compromising the intelligence by referring to some of what it revealed during the negotiations. According to a Colonial Office official, the Kenyan delegation 'looked a little stunned' after one of Sandys's indiscretions. The PUS at the Colonial Office, Sir Hilton Poynton, agreed that Hollis's complaint about Sandys's misuse of intelligence was well founded. Sooner than 'attempt to rebuke my Secretary of State', he told Hollis that he was trying to ensure that Sandys did not make the same mistake again.[28]

Though Kenyatta was thought to suspect that his delegation was under surveillance, these suspicions, remarkably, did not affect his relations with the Security Service. While in London, he and his attorney general, Charles Njonjo, called on Hollis in Leconfield House, apparently at their own request. Hollis began by saying he was pleased that Kenyatta had got to know the SLO in Nairobi, Walter Bell.[29] Kenyatta replied that 'he had had interesting talks with Mr Bell,' who lived next door to his daughter. He had been pleased to learn that two Kenyan policemen were currently on MI5 training courses and said he would like to send more. He asked whether the Security Service might also send officers to conduct less advanced training courses in Kenya. Though Kenya already had its own police training college, 'he thought it very useful to have trainers from outside. They carried greater authority and might have fresh ideas.' 'It was', Hollis informed the Colonial Office, 'a friendly meeting.'[30] Kenyatta had clearly signalled his desire for continuing liaison with, and advice from, the Security Service after independence. In December 1963 he became the first prime minister of independent Kenya with Odinga as his deputy. A year later, Kenya became a republic with Kenyatta as president.

Intelligence obtained from the surveillance of colonial delegations was also highly valued by British negotiators during the protracted and fraught negotiations which eventually led to the winding up in 1963 of the Central African Federation, whose ill-considered creation in 1951 had lumped together Nyasaland and Northern Rhodesia, both overwhelmingly black, with the white supremacist regime in Southern Rhodesia. Macmillan developed a personal dislike for the volatile and pugnacious white Prime Minister of Southern Rhodesia, Sir Roy Welensky (a former prize fighter), and seems to have taken a particular interest in the transcripts of his private conversations. He later recalled an occasion during negotiations in March 1961 when Welensky's room at the Savoy Hotel was bugged: '. . . Welensky always thought he was very clever . . . [He] would say to his entourage, "We pulled a fast one on the British Government." But this was immediately relayed to me . . . so he was not so clever as he thought . . .'[31] The Security Service officer responsible for providing intelligence to ministers on the Southern Rhodesian delegation recalls that Duncan Sandys reacted in such an 'impetuous' manner that he decided to ration what the Secretary of State was told.[32]

The Security Service relationship with Kenya and most other newly independent African colonies in the early 1960s followed the pattern established in Ghana in 1956 when the SLO, John Thomson, had introduced himself to Kwame Nkrumah.[33] Alex Kellar noted in 1962: 'It is our custom to declare the role of the Security Service, and in particular of its S.L.O.s, when the office of Chief Minister is first held by an indigenous politician. It is our normal practice to do this at the same time as indigenous ministers are officially informed of the Special Branch and the local intelligence community as a whole.' Before the independence of Tanganyika in 1961 and Uganda in 1962, Kellar personally assisted the local Governors in briefing their leaders, Julius Nyerere and Milton Obote.[34] Following the acrimonious winding up of the Central African Federation, however, Hastings Banda, the leader of independent Malawi (formerly Nyasaland), declined to continue the existing arrangement under which a Central African SLO based in Salisbury also had responsibility for the other two states in the former Federation. After discussions between Banda and the DDG, Furnival Jones, early in 1964, it was agreed to station a new SLO in Zambia (formerly Northern Rhodesia) who would also be accredited to Malawi.[35] In Asia, as well as in Africa, some of the SLOs won high praise from their newly independent hosts. In 1962, for example, Hollis showed the Home Secretary a letter from Lee Kuan Yew in Singapore 'thanking us for [SLO] Christopher Herbert's work'.[36]

For Kellar, as Director E from 1958 to 1962, the success of SLOs in winning the confidence of newly independent governments, 'so strikingly recognised at each Commonwealth Security Conference', was a matter of enormous pride:

In the case of the African Commonwealth countries, I have felt – profoundly so – that the contributions that we as a Security Service have been making to their own security by our training facilities, by our service of information, and by the close links which we are building up in running joint agent operations, together constitute a record of which we can be legitimately proud ... we have built up in these new emergent territories cadres of indigenous officials who admire, respect and trust us and who can do much to influence their political masters in the right direction.

... We shall never be able to make any African country pro-West but, by this kind of support, we can at least assist them to sit on the fence and not to fall over on the wrong side.[37]

The close relations between SLOs and a number of independent governments and their security departments increased their value to British high commissions, which no longer had the direct access to all branches of the local administration that they had enjoyed during the colonial era.[38] SLOs were thus formally given the additional responsibility in 1962 of providing political intelligence (not, however, involving the use of agents) to high commissions – as had happened informally in New Delhi and some other Commonwealth capitals for some years.[39] The increased Soviet presence in newly independent Commonwealth countries also strengthened the importance of SLOs' liaison with their special branches and security services:

Newly independent countries invariably loom large in the Cold War; they are targets of a political and economic offensive by the Communist Bloc and they often welcome embassies, delegations and advisers from these countries. This creates a demand for intelligence about the Communist Bloc from the newly independent Commonwealth countries.[40]

Some security liaisons with former colonies, however, proved short lived. The SLO in Uganda reported in 1962 that ministers were 'unwilling or unready to absorb our advice'.[41] The SLO in Tanganyika, who also failed to establish a productive relationship with the post-independence government, was withdrawn in 1964.[42] The SLO in Zambia in 1965–7 found himself frozen out when an African head of Special Branch took over from a British expatriate. The posts in both Uganda and Zambia were closed in 1967.[43]

The relationship between the SLO in Accra and the Nkrumah regime was also under threat. When the first SLO in independent Ghana, John Thomson, had left Accra in June 1960, he had regarded Nkrumah as 'a bastion against communism'. On his return for a second posting in June 1962, he discovered what the British high commissioner dramatically called 'a lurch to the left'.[44] Nkrumah was deceived by forged KGB documents which purported to reveal that the CIA had assassinated the Prime Minister of Burundi and attempted a coup in Tanganyika. After an assassination attempt against him in 1962 Nkrumah became obsessed by the belief that the Agency was plotting his overthrow, gave visitors copies of a book denouncing CIA conspiracies,[45] and accepted a Soviet offer to send a KGB officer to give advice on his personal security.[46] Other officers from the KGB and the East German Stasi followed to train a new National Security Service which ran a large network of informers (a particular speciality of the Stasi).[47]

In November 1963 Thomson reported that the head of the Special Branch, J. W. K. Harlley, and his deputy, A. K. Deku, had told him they were convinced that Nkrumah was turning Ghana into a Soviet satellite. In January 1964 a Ghanaian policeman fired at Nkrumah, causing him only minor injury but killing a security guard. A bogus letter from a supposedly disillusioned US military intelligence officer, rapidly fabricated by the KGB, persuaded Nkrumah that the CIA was, once again, plotting his overthrow. He wrote an angry personal letter of protest to President Lyndon Johnson, accusing the CIA of devoting all its energies to 'clandestine and subversive activities among our people'.[48] The high commissioner in Accra, Hugh Smedley, tried unsuccessfully to persuade Hollis to extend Thomson's tour of duty beyond the planned departure date of May 1964. The Commonwealth Relations Office wrote to Hollis:

Our High Commission in Accra view Thomson's departure with some dismay because they regard him as a key man in the Mission, with excellent knowledge and judgment of Ghanaian affairs and having contacts, especially with Special Branch, which are of crucial importance ... It looks as if we may be entering one of those phases in our relations with Ghana when Thomson's advice would be particularly helpful.[49]

In 1965, a year after Thomson's departure, the post of SLO in Accra was abolished on the grounds that, because of the worsening of relations with the Nkrumah regime, it no longer served any significant purpose.[50] Over farewell drinks in the house of a Ghanaian general, Harlley invited Thomson's successor as SLO to ask London to send him telephone interception and eavesdropping equipment. London did not respond.[51]

On 24 February 1966 Harlley succeeded in organizing a combined military and police coup which overthrew the Nkrumah regime. Next day Sir Arthur Snelling of the Commonwealth Relations Office rang the DG, Furnival Jones, to ask him to despatch Thomson urgently to Ghana. Snelling believed that 'through his knowledge of personalities in Ghana [Thomson] would be able to find out what was going on and in particular what the prospects were for a resumption of diplomatic relations'.[52] Arriving in Accra on the 28th, Thomson was welcomed with open arms by Harlley, who was now deputy chairman of the National Liberation Council (NLC). After a brief tirade from Harlley upbraiding Her Majesty's Government for having abandoned him in 1963 and put his life in danger, as well as failing to supply the equipment he had asked for in 1965, the two men settled their differences and renewed their friendship over a bottle of brandy. Thomson went on to be welcomed by, and deliver unofficial congratulations to, the NLC chairman, General Ankrah, and the other NLC members. On 2 March, following a favourable report from Thomson, Britain formally recognized the new Ghanaian regime, establishing full diplomatic relations three days later. This was the only occasion on which a Security Service officer was charged by HMG with making the first contact with a new government which had seized power in a *coup d'état*.[53]

In some other African Commonwealth countries, the SLO remained an influential figure throughout the 1960s. By 1966 the SLO in Lagos had been given one of the twenty secret government telephones allocated to senior Nigerian figures. After the coup which brought General Gowon to power in July 1966, he was asked, with the approval of the new regime, to arrange the escape of the number two in the previous government, which he successfully effected during 'an amusing few hours reminiscent of wartime . . . with launch trips after dark and ladders over the seaward side of the mailboat'.[54] The SLO also reported that his small office, 'through our liaison contacts, were virtually the only source of real intelligence throughout the coup and that [the] huge official edifice, with its forty-four British diplomats and over one hundred non-diplomats, relied on us for almost all of their factual information'.[55] The high commissioner, Sir Francis Cumming-Bruce, told the DG in November that the SLO was 'the High Commission's lifeline for information on day-to-day developments in the internal security situation, through his contacts with the Nigerian police'.[56] A new SLO, who was appointed in 1967 at the beginning of the Nigerian Civil War which followed the attempted secession of Biafra, was taken aback by the amount of inside information on the Gowon regime which he acquired from his contacts in the Nigerian Special Branch,[57] including its head whom he had first met on a colonial administrator's course in Oxford in the 1950s. When he accompanied the high commissioner to see the President, General Gowon made a point of asking the SLO to stay behind so that he could thank him for his help.[58]

The former African colony in which the Security Service's role remained of greatest significance was Kenya. The intelligence in which Kenyatta took most interest concerned the activities of the pro-Communist deputy president of his ruling KANU party, Oginga Odinga. With assistance from former senior members of the colonial Special Branch, whom Kenyatta had asked to stay on after the end of British rule, at least one of Odinga's houses was bugged.[59] On the first anniversary of Kenyan independence in 1964, Kenyatta asked the former Commonwealth Secretary, Duncan Sandys, 'if we, the British, could produce any documentary proof of Odinga receiving money from the Chinese. Kenyatta said that he was perfectly well aware of these subventions but he could not effectively deal with Odinga unless he could confront him with specific evidence.'[60] Though no usable evidence seems to have been forthcoming, the Special Branch successfully identified the main conduit by which Odinga received funds from China.[61] In April 1965 the Kenyan Attorney General, Charles Njonjo, informed the British high commissioner, Malcolm MacDonald, of reports that Odinga and his associates were planning a coup, and requested the intervention, if necessary, of British troops. The coup, however, never materialized. Odinga's offices were searched, and several crates of machine guns, grenades and other arms were seized. Soon afterwards Kenyatta gave the Soviet ambassador a furious dressing down after the arrival of a Soviet arms shipment apparently arranged by Odinga. The arms were sent back to Russia. Odinga was replaced as deputy president in 1966 and lost a trial of strength with Kenyatta over the following year.[62]

Soon after Odinga's sacking, the Head of Training in the Security Service[63] was asked to carry out a review of Kenyan intelligence. He recommended the secondment of a British intelligence officer to head a 'research' desk which would co-ordinate intelligence assessment and produce reports for Kenyatta and other members of his administration, and the creation of a National Security Executive to oversee the intelligence community. His report was accepted in its entirety and an MI5 officer was appointed in January 1967 as both head of the research desk and secretary of the new National Security Executive. The Ministry of Overseas Development paid the officer's salary on the possibly dubious grounds that he was providing 'technical assistance'.[64] He later recalled that Kenyatta had asked him 'to keep an eye on Oginga Odinga'.[65] The Nairobi SLO reported in July 1968 that the MI5 officer had acquired an access to the Kenyan Special Branch and its files 'which is almost unique in Africa in this day and age'.[66]

The two most fraught transfers of British imperial power in the 1960s were in Aden and British Guiana. In both areas the Security Service had only a limited influence. The aim of the Macmillan government in the late 1950s and early 1960s was to consolidate British influence in the Arab world by maintaining the British base in its Aden colony and setting up a federation of British protectorates in South Arabia ruled by traditional tribal chiefs. Though Macmillan sensed what he called 'the wind of change' leading Africa to independence, he greatly underestimated the force of Arab nationalism in the Middle East, inspired by the charismatic Egyptian leader Gamal Abdel Nasser, who was widely believed to have humiliated both British and French imperialists during the Suez crisis of 1956. So far as South Arabia was concerned, Macmillan believed: 'We must get rid of this horrible word "independence". What we want is a word like "home rule". The thing to do is to think of the Arabic for "home rule" and then work backwards from it.'[67]

In 1959 six states in the Western Arab Protectorate were persuaded to form a Federation of Arab Emirates of the South and sign a treaty of friendship and mutual co-operation with Britain accepting the continuation of the British military base in Aden. By the end of 1962 the total number of states in the Federation had grown to eleven. Aden Colony joined as the State of Aden in January 1963 and the Federation was renamed Federation of South Arabia.[68] There was never any realistic chance, however, of stemming the rising tide of Arab nationalism. In June 1962 Nasser sponsored the foundation in Aden of the People's Socialist Party (PSP), an offshoot of the Aden Trade Unions Congress, led by Abdullah al-Asnag, whose aim was to cause labour unrest, provoke a government crackdown and radicalize Adeni opinion. A year later Nasser provided support for the newly founded and more radical National Liberation Front (NLF), which from its base in Yemen began to plan a nationalist rebellion in Aden through a network of secret operational cells. By late 1963 Nasser was beginning to tire of al-Asnag and the PSP, whom he condemned as 'too moderate', and to place greater confidence in the NLF. On 10 December, however, al-Asnag sought to demonstrate his revolutionary credentials by leading an assassination attempt at Aden Airport against Sir Kennedy Trevaskis, the high commissioner. Trevaskis survived but his aide, George Henderson, was killed, attempting to shield him from the attack.[69]

As the PSP and NLF had doubtless hoped, the Federation Government declared a State of Emergency and arrested over fifty PSP members, prompting protests at the United Nations, from the Soviet Bloc and from a wide range of anti-imperialist groups. During a visit to neighbouring Yemen in April 1964, Nasser declared: 'We swear by Allah to expel the British from all parts of the Arabian Peninsula.'[70] The British authorities in Aden failed to learn the lessons of the Malayan insurgency more than a decade earlier. Intelligence organization was confused and no overall director of intelligence was appointed until 1965. The Security Service was not asked to play a role which approached the significance of its participation in previous counter-insurgencies in Malaya, Kenya and Cyprus. Trevaskis favoured extensive use of Special Political Action (SPA) against Arab nationalists. The Aden high commission, he claimed, 'would be able to bring about a clash between the PSP and SAL [the rival South Arabian League] which will encourage them to slit each other's throats'. Trevaskis was authorized by the Secretary of State, Duncan Sandys, to spend £15,000 'penetrating their organizations, suborning their key figures, stimulating rivalries and jealousies between them, encouraging dissension and the emergence of splinter groups and harassing them generally, for example by breaking up public meetings'.[71]

In July 1965 the high commission reported to the Colonial Office that 'the casually aimed grenade and the incompetently assembled explosive device are giving place to planned and selective assassination. Presumption is that new cadre of skilled and carefully trained operatives are now on the job.'[72] Trevaskis was thought to be in favour of retaliating against the NLF murder campaign by a covert assassination campaign against known terrorists. At a meeting at the Colonial Office, Director E, Bill Magan, argued that, as 'in the Malayan jungle' and against 'Mau Mau in the Kenyan forests', the correct strategy in Aden was not to kill terrorists but to capture and interrogate them.[73] When asked by the Colonial Office to clarify his proposals for targeting terrorists, Trevaskis dropped the subject. Magan believed that the original proposal had come from the armed services and MoD, which had pressed it on the high commission.[74] The SLO in Aden reported that he too was inclined to favour the selective targeting of known terrorists.[75] Magan did not. 'For myself,' he replied, 'I think that experience shows that to counter terrorism with terrorism is for the authority administering the law a two-edged and dangerous weapon, and the temptation to use it is best avoided.'[76] The SLO continued to argue his case: 'I am not advising anything drastic: all I would suggest at present is that [Trevaskis] be advised to inform Head of Special Branch that if a very few NLF suspects were shot whilst resisting arrest there would be nothing more than a formal inquest.' Magan noted his (probably exasperated) dissent on the SLO's letter.[77]

A JIC Working Party on Intelligence Organization in Aden concluded that, despite some improvements, the intelligence organization 'still does not work smoothly'.[78] Among the reports which led it to this conclusion was one from the Political Adviser Middle East Command in December 1965:

There is no Intelligence Service, properly speaking, covering and targeting the Protectorate. The nearest thing to an Intelligence Service is the Special Branch, which is confined to Aden State, which has been gravely weakened by assassinations and which, because of these assassinations and through intimidation of the population, is receiving far less than the normal flow of information.

. . . Security Service material is available as necessary, but Security Service coverage outside Aden is very small indeed. The Security Service does not of course run its own intelligence network.[79]

In February 1966 Harold Wilson's Labour government announced that South Arabia was to be fully independent by 1968 at the latest, that Britain would withdraw from its Aden military base and end its defence commitment to the Federation. Sandy Stuart, who had become SLO four months earlier, wrote to Head Office: 'The political side is thoroughly confused both locally and amongst the exiles abroad; and the decisions concerning the base here and the absence of a defence treaty after independence have added to the confusion. My impression is that everyone is at present rather rudderless . . .'[80] Stuart was also concerned by the brutality of some of the interrogations conducted by the Federal Ministry of Internal Security, and believed it necessary to:

emphasise that it is both morally wrong as well as being unproductive to torture or subject to third degree treatment the subjects of interrogation but, in so doing, also seek to have it clearly understood by the Federal Government that such procedures are not practised by ourselves in the Aden Interrogation Centre at Fort Morbut.[81]

The announcement of British withdrawal from South Arabia, which the Labour government had expected to diminish the insurgency, served only to intensify it. NLF spokesmen declared, 'Some may ask, "Why fight for independence when the British will grant it freely?" Comrades, true independence is not given away, but taken.'[82] On 28 February 1967 the Security Service suffered the only fatality of a member of staff or of staff family in the entire retreat from Empire (though some locally engaged staff had been killed in Palestine) during an Aden drinks party in the fourth-floor apartment of a British diplomatic couple. Sandy Stuart had reassured his wife Judi that the apartment was too high up for gun or grenade attacks. A Czech-manufactured anti-personnel mine, however, had been concealed in a bookcase and exploded during the party. Two of the guests, one of them Judi Stuart, were fatally wounded. As Sandy Stuart waited at the hospital, where his wife died on the operating table, John Prendergast, the Director of Intelligence, brought him a change of clothing ('a Christian act', Stuart said later, because his own clothes were saturated with his wife's blood).[83] 'Swallowing all emotion', he bravely sent back to Head Office the forensic report on Judi's death. Stuart accompanied his wife's body back to the UK for the funeral but then insisted on returning to his post. An investigation concluded that the bomb had been planted by a servant with 'a grudge against the British', probably related to his treatment by a previous employer. A diagram of what was believed to be the electric circuit used for the bomb detonator was found in an exercise book in his room.[84]

Judi Stuart's death was part of an escalating pattern of violence during the final year of British rule. By September 1967 the Foreign Secretary, George Brown, had washed his hands of South Arabia. 'It can't be helped,' he said privately. 'Anyway, we want to be out of the whole of the Middle East as far and as fast as we possibly can.' Richard Crossman, Leader of the House of Commons, noted cynically in his diary that the fact that 'the regime . . . should have been overthrown by terrorists and has forced our speedy withdrawal, is nothing but good fortune'.[85] On 30 November South Arabia became independent as the People's Republic of South Yemen.

In British Guiana, unlike South Arabia, Special Political Action had a major influence on the transition to independence in 1966. But for SPA, the first prime minister of independent British Guiana would almost certainly have been Cheddi Jagan, the Marxist leader of the People's Progressive Party (PPP), rather than the supposedly moderate, pro-Western Forbes Burnham. After being dismissed as chief minister a few months after the 1953 PPP election victory,[86] Jagan returned to office when the PPP won the 1957 elections under a new colonial constitution. As elsewhere in the Empire and Commonwealth, the Security Service's role in SPA in British Guiana was peripheral. Unlike most other imperial troublespots, British Guiana lacked a resident SLO. The SLO in Trinidad from 1960 to 1963 visited British Guiana about once a month but regarded it as 'the bane of my life – a ghastly place'.[87] He reported in February 1961 that Jagan and his wife Janet were in effective control of the PPP. While some PPP office-holders had been committed members of the CPGB during their time in Britain, there was no evidence that the Jagans themselves, though undoubtedly Marxists, were members of any Communist organization. After independence, however, they could be expected to seek close relations with Castro's Cuba, to whom Cheddi Jagan paid an official visit in 1960, as well as with the Soviet Union and China. The SLO believed the PPP were likely to win the October 1961 elections, though by too small a majority to form a stable government. He was strongly opposed to the use of SPA to try to ensure Jagan's defeat; it would be unlikely, he warned in April, to influence the outcome of the elections and 'the results of failure would probably be disastrous.'[88]

Contrary to the SLO's expectation, the PPP won a clear majority in the elections and Jagan became prime minister. Eavesdropping at the CPGB's London headquarters revealed that Jagan had approached it for help in recruiting financial, taxation and social security staff to work in British Guiana.[89] Soon after his election victory, he went to visit President John F. Kennedy in the Oval Office to seek US support for British Guianan independence. Cheddi Jagan might be a Marxist, Kennedy said afterwards, 'but the United States doesn't object, because that choice was made by an honest election, which he won.' In private, JFK said the opposite. Following the humiliating failure to overthrow Fidel Castro by the CIA-backed landing of an anti-Castro brigade at the Bay of Pigs six months earlier, the President was determined not to allow the emergence of another potential Castro in the Caribbean.[90] The US Secretary of State, Dean Rusk, wrote to Lord Home, the British Foreign Secretary, on 19 February 1962, 'I must tell you now that I have reached the conclusion that it is not possible for us to put up with an independent British Guiana under Jagan.'[91] Macmillan told Home that Rusk's letter was 'pure Machiavellianism', exposing a 'degree of cynicism' which he found surprising in view of the fact the Secretary of State was 'not an Irishman, nor a politician, nor a millionaire'. Home replied sharply to Rusk:

You say that it is not possible for you 'to put up with an independent British Guiana under Jagan' and that 'Jagan should not be allowed to accede to power again.' How would you suggest that this can be done in a democracy? And even if a device could be found, it would almost certainly be transparent . . .[92]

Macmillan and Home, however, gave way to American pressure. In no other British colony was the United States allowed to take the lead in covert action (the US term for SPA).[93] On 15 August 1962 President Kennedy authorized a covert $2 million CIA operation to drive Jagan from power before British Guiana became independent.[94] On 15 October, the Colonial Secretary, Duncan Sandys, agreed that the CIA should approach Jagan's two main political opponents, Forbes Burnham, leader of the People's National Congress (PNC), and Peter D'Aguiar, leader of the pro-business United Force (UF), which campaigned for 'people's enterprise capitalism'.[95]

At a meeting with the Governor of British Guiana, Sir Ralph Grey, on 7 November, Hollis reaffirmed traditional Security Service policy on SPA: 'that [head] office and the SLO should keep out of any direct association with the implementation of the plans, but that we were doing what we could at some remove from the actual site to see that the facts on which plans were based were accurate'.[96] Director E, Alex Kellar, however, was passionately opposed to the use of Special Political Action against any colonial or Commonwealth government:

Despite the political stresses and strains that occur between the countries of the Commonwealth, there are factors that continue to bind the individual members together to make the Commonwealth still a powerful force with which to be reckoned in world affairs. Among these factors, none is more important than the Commonwealth security complex in which the Security Service and its SLO play so dominant and influential a role. Our SLOs, in particular, have taken a leading part because, whatever the personal contributions they have made in the field as individuals, all have conducted themselves with a complete honesty of purpose and, by so doing, have gained and retained the trust, confidence and respect of the indigenous officials, administrative as well as police, that matter so much; and no more so than in the case of those new Commonwealth countries who, sensitive about their newly acquired independence, can so easily go sour on us should they identify us in, or even suspect us of, activity behind their backs.

This danger becomes more and more real as pressures . . . for clandestine action within these emergent territories gain momentum with the inevitable, as it now seems, involvement of the SLO and consequent corruption of his position.

. . . I accept that there are recalcitrant members of our Commonwealth and that they try our patience to the full but the UK, with its greater maturity, political experience and pivotal position, has a special responsibility for exercising patience.[97]

SPA in British Guiana during 1963 went some way to justifying Kellar's fears about the 'corruption' of the SLO's role. In January 1963 the White House was reported to be 'well satisfied with the development of covert operations' in British Guiana.[98] On 10 April the British Guiana TUC began a crippling general strike which was to last ten weeks – longer than any general strike anywhere in the world had ever lasted before.[99] On 8 May Jagan confronted the Governor with the dramatic claim that 'US Intelligence agents with large sums of money' were trying to use the strike to bring down his government.[100] Unknown to Jagan, after his 1961 election victory the head of the TUC, Richard Ishmael, had secretly lobbied Dean Rusk for support for future strike action against the 'Jaganite Communist threat'.[101] In response to Ishmael's request, US financial support for the TUC was channelled through American trade unions during the general strike. But the TUC leadership was told that the support would 'cease the minute strike becomes political'.[102] US covert action aimed, with British consent, at securing Jagan's electoral defeat – not at using a general strike to overthrow him.

In August 1963, a month after the end of the strike, the SLO called on Janet Jagan, Minister of Home Affairs in her husband's government, and told her he was 'available to advise on security matters', in particular 'protective security and the organisation of security intelligence'. He predictably failed to mention, however, that the main security threat to the Jagan government was CIA covert action designed to ensure that it was out of office by the time British Guiana became independent. At this and subsequent meetings with the SLO, Mrs Jagan 'listened politely' and was 'very friendly'. She said, however, that she had been 'struck by the paucity of information she was receiving from Special Branch'. The SLO forbore to mention that the Special Branch had penetrated the PPP, though its head privately complained that it was currently 'short of well placed agents'. After his August meeting with Mrs Jagan, the SLO reported to Head Office:

From my point of view, the meeting went off well. I believe that I was able to give a fairly plausible account of the SLO's functions (within the limits agreed with the Governor) without giving rise to embarrassing questions from the Minister. I have no doubt that she surmised there was more to it than I had outlined but I have no reason to suppose that her position will prevent me from doing a worthwhile job in British Guiana.[103]

SPA in British Guiana achieved its main objective of removing Jagan from power without the direct involvement of the SLO. The electoral system was changed to a system of proportional representation which favoured Burnham's PNC and D'Aguiar's UF,[104] both of which received advice and funding from the CIA. After the Labour victory in the October 1964 British elections, Harold Wilson and an inner group of his ministers (including the Foreign Secretary, Patrick Gordon Walker, and the Colonial Secretary, Anthony Greenwood) approved the continuation of SPA in British Guiana.[105] The PPP lost the December 1964 election, and Jagan's government was succeeded by a coalition of the PNC and UF, headed by Forbes Burnham, which led Guyana (as British Guiana was renamed) to independence in 1966.

Among at least some Security Service officers, the experience of observing SPA in British Guiana from the sidelines left a bitter taste. E5 minuted on the eve of independence that the Service was not being kept fully informed.[106] Burnham's corrupt and incompetent rule was to wreck the Guyanese economy as well as to reinforce enmity between the Afro-Caribbean and Indian communities. Ironically by the 1970s he was to announce that Guyana was 'on the road to socialism', nationalize the sugar plantations and form friendly ties with the Soviet Bloc.[107] How far Cheddi Jagan would have aligned himself with the Soviet Union had he, rather than Burnham, led Guyana to independence is a matter of conjecture. It is significant, however, that after the suppression of 'Socialism with a human face' in Czechoslovakia by the tanks of the Warsaw Pact in August 1968, he, like Fidel Castro, aligned himself with the destroyers of the Prague Spring. Jagan declared in Moscow in 1969, 'Not only theory, but practice also, has taught us that this is where we belong.'[108]

With a few notable exceptions such as Aden and British Guiana, a majority of SLOs later looked back with nostalgia on their experience of the end of Empire and the friendships they had made with local security personnel. Service in the Empire and Commonwealth was part of the experience of most of the post-war generation of Security Service officers. At the end of the 1960s, however, most of the Service's post-imperial role came to an unexpectedly abrupt conclusion. In 1968 a newly appointed Committee on Overseas Representation began looking for economies. As part of its inquiries, the distinguished retired diplomat Sir Frank Roberts prepared a top-secret report on British intelligence stations abroad. In the ten countries which had both MI5 and SIS representation, Roberts proposed a single combined station headed by an officer of the Service with the main interest in the country concerned. Furnival Jones resisted the Roberts Report, arguing that, because of the different priorities of MI5 and SIS, combined stations would not necessarily produce real economies. Save for India, where the SLO post was already scheduled for closure, all the high commissioners in the countries covered by the Roberts Report recommended the maintenance of SLOs. The FCO reported to the Security Service that its geographical departments had 'confirmed the striking vote of confidence which you have received from the High Commissioners'. The Service, however, was less good than SIS at arguing its case in Whitehall. In most countries where it had been represented, SLOs were phased out in favour of sole representation by SIS.[109]

The recall of the SLOs was greeted with dismay by many, perhaps most, of the Commonwealth security services to which they were accredited. The Delhi Intelligence Bureau, then headed by S. P. Varma, was warned personally by the DG, Furnival Jones, that the current SLO would not be replaced at the end of his tour of duty. Varma's reaction was 'immediate and strong'. He would regard it as a disaster if the post closed and he 'did not know how they would manage without it'.[110] The DIB subsequently wrote in a formal letter to FJ: 'Since its establishment, we have had nearly 20 years of uninterrupted liaison with your organisation through the Resident SLO in New Delhi. The withdrawal of this officer now would break the longstanding contact at a personal level which has proved invaluable to us.'[111]

The Service's Overseas (E) Branch was wound up in 1971 and its remaining responsibilities divided between the Secretariat and the intelligence branches.[112] In the long run, since SIS was Britain's foreign intelligence service, there was a good case for transferring to it most of the Security Service's responsibilities in former colonies. It increasingly made little sense, for example, for MI5 to have the dominant role in an African country which belonged to the Commonwealth and for SIS to take the lead in its non-Commonwealth neighbours. The abrupt disappearance of the SLOs, however, left too little time for an orderly transfer of responsibilities, and led in some countries to a gap in intelligence collaboration which was not immediately filled by SIS. In May 1969, the Kenyan Director of

Intelligence, James Kanyotu, was reported to be 'very resentful' of the way in which the changes were made.[113] So were some members of the Security Service.

9

The Macmillan Government: Spy Scandals and the Profumo Affair

Relations between Harold Macmillan and the Security Service never recovered from Sir Dick White's move to SIS in 1956 and his replacement by Sir Roger Hollis, who remained DG throughout Macmillan's seven years as prime minister (1957–63). White found Macmillan 'marvellous to deal with'. Macmillan in turn liked and respected White. But Macmillan took a dislike to the far less clubbable Hollis, later claiming that he had found him 'insignificant' and inept.[1] Had White remained DG, the Service's relations with Macmillan would doubtless have run more smoothly. Rab Butler, Macmillan's first Home Secretary, had much greater sympathy for Hollis and MI5 but took office with little grasp of their work. Most ministers who dealt with the Security Service during at least the first half of the Cold War were poorly informed, if not actually misinformed, about its operations. Rab was no exception. He told Hollis at their first meeting in January 1957, that 'he knew already that the Security Service was doing a very good job, and promised us all the support he could give us.' It turned out, however, that Butler did not even know where the Service was based. When told that its headquarters was in Leconfield House, he expressed surprise 'as he imagined we operated under cover' – presumably supposing that MI5 had a series of safe houses hidden around London rather than a conventional office building. He accepted Hollis's invitation to see the premises for himself.[2]

The basis of counter-espionage against KGB and GRU operations in London was the wearisome surveillance by various means of the Soviet embassy and Trade Delegation, which provided cover for intelligence officers. Though few significant leads emerged from this activity in the later 1950s, it provided interesting insights into the lifestyle of Soviet officials – sometimes including comments on their favourite London restaurants. On one such occasion Provotoroff, an official at the Trade Delegation, was heard discussing with Kaplin, the visiting chairman of the Soviet fur-trading association, Soyuzpushnina, where he would like to have dinner. 'Provotoroff suggests the Savoy Grill. Kaplin thinks it would be too crowded. Provotoroff suggests the Mirabelle. Kaplin says it was the first one he ever visited . . . Provotoroff sings praises of the Mirabelle – it is downstairs, wealthy, fresh, has a fountain, [and is] comfortable.' These comments aroused the interest of a Security Service staff member with a particular interest in fashionable London restaurants. When Kaplin was heard saying a few days later that the Caprice Restaurant was 'evidently run by the Ritz', the staff member commented: 'This is not accurate. Mario, previously head waiter of the Ivy, runs it and it is backed by Robert Morley and others.'[3]

Macmillan hated spy scandals and, partly for that reason, disliked direct contact with the Security Service on counter-espionage matters. As foreign secretary in 1955, he had been forced, reluctantly, to clear Philby in the Commons of charges that he was a Soviet spy, because of lack of proof of his guilt. He had loathed and despised the media 'hue and cry' which followed. It was, he believed, 'dangerous and bad for our general national interest'[4] – as well as embarrassing for the government – for such matters to be discussed in public. To his relief, no spy scandals disturbed the first three halcyon years of his premiership from which he emerged with a reputation as 'Supermac' and a convincing electoral victory in 1959.

The Security Service had little success during the later 1950s against the Soviet target. Its investigation of the case of the Magnificent Five was making slow progress.[5] The KGB residency, by contrast, was running a major penetration agent in SIS.[6] The Service's main counter-espionage successes during the later 1950s were achieved not against the KGB but against the Polish UB intelligence station in London. No doubt to Macmillan's relief, they attracted no publicity. By 1958 thirty-one UB agents had been identified and a number turned into double agents. As a result of the achievements of the double agents and the intelligence obtained from several Polish defectors, the DDG, Graham Mitchell, proudly declared that D2's operations against the UB were 'of a quality which no security organisation could hope to better'.[7] The leads which led to the resolution of the two main Soviet counter-espionage cases of the early 1960s also came from a Polish intelligence officer, Michal Goleniewski, who was recruited not by the Security Service but by the CIA with the codename SNIPER, and who later defected to the United States.

In April 1960 Goleniewski reported that an agent recruited by Polish intelligence in the British naval attaché's office in Warsaw in about 1951 had been handed over to the KGB when he returned to Britain. The prime suspect was quickly identified as Harry Houghton, a clerical officer at the

Underwater Detection Establishment (UDE) at Portland, who had served as clerk to the naval attaché in Warsaw in 1951–2 and had been sent home for alcohol abuse. In 1956 the Admiralty had reported to the Security Service claims by Houghton's wife that he was revealing classified information, but raised the possibility that her allegations were made because their marriage was breaking up. The Security Service vetting section concluded without serious investigation that the claims were prompted by spite and left it to the Admiralty to pursue them. After Houghton's conviction in March 1961, Director D, Martin Furnival Jones, concluded that if his wife's allegations had been properly followed up by the Service in 1956, there was 'a fair chance that Houghton would have been revealed as a Russian spy at that time'. When Mrs Houghton, who had since remarried, was questioned for the first time after Goleniewski's lead was passed from the CIA to the Security Service in 1960, she provided convincing evidence that her former husband had been engaged in espionage. He had brought classified papers home with him from work at the UDE, and made regular weekend trips to London, returning with bundles of pound notes. Mrs Houghton had been afraid to go to the police for fear of being attacked by her violent husband. Though Houghton had little direct access to classified information, he was discovered to be having an affair with a record-keeper at the UDE, Ethel 'Bunty' Gee, who regularly handled top-secret documents. In July 1960 an A4 surveillance team followed Houghton and Gee on a weekend trip to London and observed them meeting a man, at first wrongly identified as a Polish intelligence officer, on a park bench near Waterloo Station. The man drove off after the meeting in a car which was found to be registered in the name of Gordon Lonsdale. A4 kept Houghton and Lonsdale under surveillance at their next meeting in a café near Waterloo Station, saw Houghton surreptitiously hand over an envelope concealed inside a newspaper, and overheard snatches of conversation between the two men on arrangements for their next meeting.[8]

All previous post-war Soviet espionage cases in Britain investigated by the Security Service had involved intelligence officers based at the KGB and GRU London residencies. Investigation of Lonsdale revealed, however, that he was a deep-cover Soviet illegal using a bogus nationality and identity, though his real name – Konon Trofimovich Molody – was not discovered until after he had been convicted of espionage. The son of two Soviet scientists, Molody seems to have been selected in childhood as a potential foreign intelligence officer. In 1932, at only ten years of age, he was sent with official approval to live with an aunt in California and attend secondary school in San Francisco, where he became bilingual in English before returning to Moscow in 1938. During the Great Patriotic War he joined the NKVD and, to quote the stilted language of his official hagiography, 'brilliantly displayed such qualities as boldness and valour'. After the war Molody graduated in Chinese and worked as a Chinese-language instructor before beginning training as an illegal in 1951.[9] Three years later he was sent to establish a fictitious identity in Canada, where he obtained a passport in the name of a 'dead double', Gordon Arnold Lonsdale, who had been born in Ontario in 1924, emigrated as a child to the Soviet Union with his Finnish mother, and died in 1943. In March 1955, Molody travelled to London under his new identity as 'Gordon Lonsdale' and enrolled as a student on a Chinese course at the School of Oriental and African Studies (SOAS). As a qualified lecturer in Chinese, Lonsdale had no difficulty in coping with the course requirements and was able to spend most of his time developing his cover and establishing the KGB's first post-war illegal residency in Britain. Using KGB funds, he set himself up as the director of several companies operating juke boxes, vending machines and one-arm bandits. An electronic locking device produced by one of the firms in which he was a partner won a gold medal at the 1960 International Inventors Exhibition in Brussels. In retirement, Molody later made the wildly exaggerated claim that his business ventures had been so successful that he had become the KGB's first multi-millionaire illegal resident.[10]

On 26 August 1960 Lonsdale was seen by A4 taking packages to a safety deposit box at a bank, then observed soon afterwards leaving the country, probably en route for Russia and a rare visit to his family. While Lonsdale was abroad, the DDG, Graham Mitchell, gained permission to open his safety deposit box. Charles Elwell, the Security Service case officer, was present as the contents of the box were investigated by Peter Wright and Hugh Winterborn. Among them was a briefcase containing a Ronson table-lighter, in which X-ray examination revealed a secret compartment with one-time cipher pads, a list of London locations and map references.[11] Also in the briefcase, to Elwell's surprise, was a photograph of him talking to a 'rather pretty girl', which he reported to Furnival Jones, then Director D. When Elwell arrived at the office next day, he was told to report immediately to FJ, who demanded, 'How do you account for the fact that there is a photograph of you in Lonsdale's briefcase?' His wife was collected from home by office car and interviewed separately. There was a curious but innocent explanation for the photograph. The Elwells had let their flat to a Canadian diplomat studying at SOAS who had invited them to a party with some of his lecturers and fellow students. One of the students was Lonsdale, who went round taking photos of the other guests. It was,

Elwell believed, 'unique in the annals of counter-espionage' that an intelligence officer investigating an illegal should unwittingly have been photographed by his target.[12]

By the time Lonsdale returned to London from Russia in October 1960, A Branch had installed listening devices in his flat in Albany Street. A search of the flat revealed that some of the one-time pads in the Ronson table-lighter had been used, showing that he had been in contact with Moscow.[13] After a meeting with Houghton in November, Lonsdale was tailed by A4 and seen entering a bungalow in Cranley Drive, Ruislip, belonging to an antiquarian bookseller and his wife, Peter and Helen Kroger. An observation post (OP) was set up in a house opposite. Not until the Krogers' fingerprints were taken after their arrest two months later was it discovered that they were in reality the veteran American KGB illegal agents Morris and Lona Cohen, who had been acting as Lonsdale's radio operators and technical support team.[14] Like Lonsdale, the 'Krogers' were extroverts with an active social life which strengthened their cover. One of their friends in the London book trade later recalled many convivial evenings and 'the most wonderful hospitality' at their house in Ruislip.[15]

On 4 January 1961 Goleniewski defected to the CIA in Berlin. The Security Service feared that, if the Russians realized that he had known about Houghton's espionage, they would withdraw Lonsdale and the Krogers, and decided to wind up the case quickly. On 7 January Houghton, Gee and Lonsdale were arrested by the Special Branch in Waterloo Road shortly after Gee had handed over classified documents. The Krogers were arrested in their Ruislip home. In their possession was a cigarette lighter with a secret compartment similar to Lonsdale's, containing one-time pads. When Mrs Kroger asked to stoke the boiler, a vigilant female police officer searched her handbag and found incriminating evidence of espionage – letters from Lonsdale. Five days after the Krogers' arrest, their radio transmitter was discovered in a cavity under their floor.[16] During a six-day trial at the Old Bailey in March 1961, an unprecedented number of Security Service officers, both A4 surveillance and technical experts, none of them publicly identified, gave evidence in court. All five of the 'Portland spies' were convicted. The Lord Chief Justice, Lord Parker, sentenced Lonsdale to twenty-five years' imprisonment, the Krogers to twenty years each, Houghton and Gee to fifteen. The Attorney General, Sir Reginald Manningham-Buller (father of a future DG), who had led the prosecution, sent congratulations to the Service's Legal Adviser, Bernard Hill, on 'the wonderful work done by the Security Service'.[17] The intelligence from Portland passed by Lonsdale to Moscow was believed by the Admiralty to have helped in the manufacture of a new and more silent generation of Soviet submarines.[18]

Once in jail, Lonsdale agreed to be interviewed by Elwell, who began by producing the photograph taken of them at the party in his rented flat. Instead of revealing that the photo was the result of an extraordinary coincidence, Elwell used it to give Lonsdale the impression that the Security Service had long been on his trail.[19] Lonsdale jumped to the conclusion that Houghton must have been a Security Service agent whom the Service had ended by double-crossing. Elwell did not disabuse him.[20] Remembering his own wartime imprisonment as a POW in Colditz, Elwell was deeply affected by the length of Lonsdale's sentence. He believed that he could have 'turned' Lonsdale but for 'the hopelessness of the Home Office', who made 'no effort whatever to collaborate with us'. Elwell's hopes were finally dashed when Lonsdale was freed in a spy exchange in 1964.[21] By contrast, Elwell never had any hope of turning the Krogers. He later remembered Kroger as a 'horrid man' and his wife as 'even more horrid'.[22]

Just as the trial of the Portland spy-ring was reaching its conclusion in March 1961, the Security Service received news of an even more serious Soviet penetration. In November 1959 Goleniewski had told his CIA case officer that the KGB had an agent in SIS, but there were doubts about the reliability of his intelligence until his lead to Houghton was confirmed in the summer of 1960.[23] The investigation of his warning of a penetration of SIS, though henceforth taken seriously, initially led to misplaced suspicions that the agent was in the SIS Brussels station.[24] Following Goleniewski's defection early in 1961, however, he provided further leads which pointed to the thirty-nine-year-old SIS officer George Blake. Né Behar, Blake had been born in Rotterdam of a naturalized British father (by origin a Sephardic Jew from Istanbul) and a Dutch mother who called their son George in honour of King George V. During the Second World War, Blake served successively in the Dutch Resistance and in the Royal Navy, before joining SIS in 1944. There was much that SIS had failed to discover about its new recruit, notably the influence on him of his older cousin Henri Curiel, co-founder of the Egyptian Communist Party. In 1948 Blake was posted by SIS to South Korea, working under diplomatic cover as vice consul in Seoul. A year later, shortly after the outbreak of the Korean War, he was interned by the invading North Koreans.[25]

In the autumn of 1951 Blake handed his captors a note written in Russian and addressed to the Soviet embassy, saying that he had important information to communicate. At a meeting with Vasili Alekseyevich Dozhdalev of the KGB, he identified himself as an SIS officer and volunteered to work as a Soviet agent, codenamed DIOMID. According to Sergei Aleksandrovich Kondrashev, who became Blake's controller in Britain after the end of the Korean War in 1953, the Centre considered him so important that no other member of the London residency was permitted to know either DIOMID's identity or the fact that he was an SIS officer.[26] How Blake had been recruited by the KGB was still unknown to SIS investigators when they came to seek the advice of Director D (Furnival Jones) on 20 March 1961. FJ noted afterwards:

In order to resolve their suspicions they intended to bring Blake back [from a language course in Lebanon] to the UK on an administrative pretext at the end of the Easter weekend, when they would subject him to interrogation. Their first question was whether it would be in order for them at an appropriate stage in the interrogation to tell Blake, as an inducement, that he would not be prosecuted if he confessed. I gave them advice on the handling of the interrogation and said that no doubt the DG [Sir Roger Hollis] would wish to discuss the matter with 'C' [Sir Dick White].[27]

To the combined relief of both SIS and MI5, late on the afternoon of 5 April Blake confessed to his SIS interrogators without being offered immunity from prosecution. He admitted that he had offered his services to the KGB while interned in North Korea in October 1951 and had spied 'for purely ideological motives, although he was on many occasions offered large sums of money'.[28] Once he resumed his career with SIS in April 1953, he used a Minox camera to take about 200 exposures a month of classified documents which he passed on to his controller. In order not to arouse suspicion, he was careful to limit himself to documents to which he would be expected to have access.[29]

Both White and Hollis must have groaned inwardly at the thought of having to tell their American allies that for the previous ten years an SIS officer had been working as a KGB agent. Hollis agreed that the SLO in Washington would personally deliver a letter from White on the STAR-FISH (Blake) case to J. Edgar Hoover.[30] The fact that the Security Service had just achieved a major success in uncovering the Portland spy-ring and securing the evidence to convict three KGB illegals (two of them Americans) may have made Hoover's response to the news of Soviet penetration less irascible than usual. The SLO was surprised to find the FBI director in a 'genuinely sympathetic and understanding' mood. The Blake case, Hoover told him, was 'a further illustration of how constantly alert we had to be to the dangers which beset us. After all, he said, Christ Himself found a traitor in His small team of twelve . . .'[31]

Harold Macmillan's usual irritation as prime minister at having to deal with spy scandals was compounded by the need in the Blake case to inform personally the new President of the United States, John F. Kennedy, with whom he was attempting to establish a personal Special Relationship.[32] Whatever critical views the President may have formed about the Blake case, however, were swiftly submerged by the farcical failure of the CIA-backed landing of the anti-Castro 'Cuban Brigade' at the Bay of Pigs on 17 April. There followed what Kennedy called 'two full days of hell . . .' the most excruciating period of my life'. He despairingly asked his special counsel, Theodore Sorensen, 'How could I have been so stupid, to let them go ahead?'[33]

KGB files give Blake the credit for two major successes as a Soviet agent. First, his intelligence, together with that supplied by Heinz Felfe, a KGB agent in the West German intelligence service BND, and previous information from Philby, is said to have made possible the 'elimination of the adversary's agent network in the G[erman] D[emocratic] R[epublic] in 1953–55'.[34] SIS calculated that at least forty agents identified by Blake were executed.[35] Blake's second major achievement as a Soviet agent was to alert the Centre to one of the most remarkable Western intelligence operations of the Cold War – the secret construction of a 500-metre underground tunnel from West to East Berlin to intercept landlines running from the Soviet military and intelligence headquarters at Karlshorst in the East Berlin suburbs. At a meeting with his controller on the top of a London double-decker bus in January 1954, Blake handed over the minutes of a conference on the tunnel project, codenamed Operation GOLD.[36] Blake was posted to Berlin station on 14 April 1955,[37] one month before the tunnel became operational. The Centre, however, dared not interfere either with the tunnel's construction or with its early operations for fear of compromising Blake, who had established himself as by far its most important British agent. By the time the KGB staged an 'accidental' discovery of the tunnel in April 1956, Operation GOLD had yielded over 50,000 reels of magnetic tape recording intercepted Soviet and East German communications. The intelligence yield was so considerable that it took more than two years after the end of the operation to process all the intercepts. Though the KGB was able to protect the security of its own communications, it was curiously indifferent to the interception of those of the rival GRU and of Soviet forces.[38]

The Security Service Legal Adviser, Bernard Hill, represented SIS as well as the Service at meetings with the Director of Public Prosecutions and the law officers of the Crown before Blake was put on trial at the Old Bailey on 3 May 1961.[39] To general astonishment, the Lord Chief Justice, Lord Parker, sentenced Blake to forty-two years' imprisonment, the longest sentence ever imposed by a British court. Blake appeared stunned. Sir Dick White later said that he too had been shocked by the severity of the sentence.[40] J. Edgar Hoover, by contrast, was delighted, telling the Washington SLO approvingly: 'Anyway, the British have guts!'[41] Macmillan, however, found the spy scandals of the early 1960s even more distasteful than the furore which had surrounded his clearing of Philby in 1955. Instead of congratulating MI5 for its part in tracking down a series of Soviet spies, he blamed the Service for causing him public embarrassment. The Prime Minister complained in his diary after Blake's conviction that the public, already shocked by media reports, 'do not know and cannot be told that he belonged to MI6, an organisation which does not theoretically exist. So I had a rather rough passage in the House of Commons . . .'[42] Though the British press did not reveal that Blake was an SIS officer when reporting the verdict, the foreign press had no such inhibitions and the secret soon leaked out. The Security Service got little more credit from the British media than from the Prime Minister. The *Washington Post* reported from London:

The outfit which is likely to catch it in the neck as a result of this and other recent cases is MI5, the counter-intelligence organization charged with tracking down enemy agents in this country. They already are under fire following the discovery that a group of agents, including two Admiralty employees, had been busy peddling British naval secrets to the Russians for an extended period.[43]

The steady growth in the size of the KGB and GRU London residencies during the 1960s[44] made counter-espionage progressively more difficult. The Security Service was handicapped not merely by its own overstretched resources but also by the difficulty (which it was, understandably, not anxious to advertise) of bringing successful prosecutions. Unless it could obtain confessions or catch agents in the act of handing over material, it was usually impossible to secure convictions. Its difficulties were exemplified by the trial in 1963 of Dr Giuseppe Martelli, a thirty-nine-year-old Italian physicist employed for the previous year at the Culham Laboratories of the Atomic Energy Authority. Arrested as a result of a lead from a KGB defector, Martelli was found in possession of a record of meetings with Nikolai Karpekov and other KGB officers, a set of partly used one-time pads for cipher communications hidden inside an ingeniously constructed cigarette case, and instructions for photographing documents. But possession of espionage paraphernalia (unlike housebreaking equipment) is not in itself a crime, and Martelli had no official access to classified information, though he was in contact with people who had. Martelli admitted meeting Karpekov, but claimed he was engaged in an ingenious scheme to turn the tables on a blackmail attempt by the KGB. He was acquitted.[45]

Just as the discovery of the atom spies had prompted the early Cold War transformation of protective security, so the spy cases of the early 1960s led to its further development. The conviction of George Blake and the Portland spy-ring in 1961 prompted the appointment of the Radcliffe Committee, which carried out a comprehensive review of the protective-security system. The Security Service was to be responsible for advice on security training and technical education in the public service and step up security education in industry. C Branch's lead role in protective security thus received official recognition.

In the 'Night of the Long Knives', Macmillan's major cabinet reshuffle of July 1962, Rab Butler was promoted to the post of deputy prime minister and first secretary of state, and was succeeded as home secretary by the accident-prone Henry Brooke. Though more supportive of the Service than Macmillan, Brooke caused some anxiety by requesting a list of the names and addresses of those individuals and organizations in his Hampstead constituency which had HOWs authorizing the monitoring of their post and telephones. The Security Service reluctantly provided the details but remonstrated with Brooke's PUS, Sir Philip Allen, over the Home Secretary's request. According to a note by the DDG, Graham Mitchell: 'Allen said that the Home Secretary felt that he needed it because he meets a lot of people in his constituency and would be fortified in knowing if he had any one of them on check. I said I thought this was a rotten reason.'[46]

The arrest of another Soviet spy, John Vassall, an Admiralty clerk,[47] only a few months after the convictions of the Portland spy-ring and George Blake, was greeted with further irritation by Macmillan. The initial lead in the investigation was one of the few provided by the troublesome KGB defector Anatoli Golitsyn, later supplemented by further intelligence from another Soviet intelligence source. The case officer, as in the Portland spy case, was initially Charles Elwell. An eavesdropping operation against Vassall's Dolphin Square flat, A4 surveillance of his journeys to and from work on the Number 24 bus and searches of his desk at the Admiralty uncovered no evidence of espionage. However, a search of his flat in September 1962 revealed two cameras and exposed film concealed in a hidden compartment. Vassall was arrested later the same day. An A4 veteran, who accompanied the Special Branch officer making the arrest, recalls during the car journey to Scotland Yard that Vassall was 'panting with fear' and confessed his guilt. Since his recruitment in Moscow in 1955, he had operated continuously as a Soviet agent, save in the aftermath of the Portland case, when he had been told to lie low. He was later sentenced to eighteen years' imprisonment.[48]

Macmillan later claimed that, after Vassall's arrest, Hollis had called on him to announce, 'I've got this fellow [Vassall], I've got him!' When Macmillan failed to show any enthusiasm for this MI5 success, Hollis allegedly remarked, 'You don't seem very pleased, Prime Minister.' Macmillan, by his own account, replied:

No, I'm not at all pleased. When my gamekeeper shoots a fox, he doesn't go and hang it up outside the Master of Foxhounds' drawing room; he buries it out of sight. But you just can't shoot a spy as you did in the war. You have to try him . . . better to discover him, and then control him, but never catch him . . . There will be a terrible row in the press, there will be a debate in the House of Commons and the government will probably fall. Why the devil did you 'catch' him?[49]

In fact, Macmillan's memory played him false. The news of Vassall's detection had been conveyed to him not at a personal meeting with Hollis but by a written report channelled through the cabinet secretary, Sir Norman Brook.[50] Following Vassall's conviction in 1963, the Radcliffe tribunal made further protective-security recommendations about the staffing of missions behind the Iron Curtain as well as about the PV process.

Macmillan's annoyance at the embarrassment caused by MI5 spycatching seems to have been in striking contrast to his appreciation of SIS's success in recruiting and running jointly with the CIA perhaps the most important Western agent of the Cold War, Colonel Oleg Penkovsky, deputy head of the foreign section of the GRU. During a visit to Britain as head of a Soviet delegation in April 1961, Penkovsky was secretly debriefed at Mount Royal Hotel near Marble Arch by a team of SIS and CIA officers, whom he astonished by declaring, 'The great desire which I have carried in my soul . . . is to swear my fealty to my Queen, Elizabeth II, and to the President of the United States, Mr Kennedy, whom I am serving as their soldier.' In Moscow, London and Paris, Penkovsky provided large quantities of highly classified documents (many photographed with a Minox camera) as well as important insights into Soviet policy and the Soviet armed forces. In April 1961 and again during a further visit to London in July, he had personal meetings with Sir Dick White. President Kennedy was informed of Penkovsky's role (though not of his name) by the Director of Central Intelligence in July.[51] Macmillan was probably briefed personally by White, with whom he had a warm personal relationship. Though Hollis and six other members of the Security Service were fully indoctrinated into the Penkovsky case, the Service remained on the sidelines and had no direct contact with the colonel.[52] Despite Penkovsky's arrest by the KGB in September, his intelligence continued to be of the first importance during the thirteen days of the October Missile Crisis. All the top-secret 'Evaluations of the Soviet Missile Threat in Cuba' supplied at least daily to President Kennedy and his advisers carried the codeword IRONBARK, indicating that they made use of Penkovsky's documents. The Penkovsky case was an extraordinary example of the Cold War Special Relationship, to which Macmillan was deeply committed.[53]

The last straw, as far as Macmillan's relations with Hollis were concerned, was the DG's warning in the spring of 1963 that his own deputy, Graham Mitchell, was suspected of being a Soviet penetration agent. According to Macmillan's later, confused recollection of his briefing on the evidence against Mitchell: 'He'd been spotted wandering round the loos in the park . . . passing things, probably it was opium or something, he seemed to be somewhat unhinged, probably not working for the Communists. Fortunately he retired before we could do anything about it, but it was all a great worry . . .'[54] Macmillan's suspicions about Mitchell's behaviour were without foundation, but bear witness to his resentment of the scandals in which the Security Service seemed to be involving him. He must have been further annoyed by the humiliation of having to report the investigation of Mitchell to President Kennedy, because of the possibility that the DDG had betrayed American as well as British secrets.[55]

The Profumo affair, however, was a far greater worry. Its combination of sexual and spy scandal made this the most difficult episode of Macmillan's premiership. The element of sexual scandal, despite the enormous media coverage of it, was in reality very small. Though the Secretary of State for War, John Profumo, had an affair with a prostitute, Christine Keeler, the affair was quickly over. Had he not lied to the Commons by denying the affair and instead simply refused to comment on his private life, many in the Chamber might have hesitated to throw the first stone. The brief affair with Christine Keeler by a GRU officer in London, Evgeni 'Eugene' Ivanov, operating under cover as assistant Soviet naval attaché, also never came close to threatening national security. Keeler was never in any position to obtain state secrets from Profumo and pass them on to Ivanov. A later Security Service investigation plausibly concluded that it must have been obvious to Ivanov from the outset that Keeler had no information of significant value to him: 'Although undoubtedly attractive, Keeler was vacuous and untruthful. Ivanov had no need to sleep with her to discover that.'[56] The Service was aware that Ivanov had been arrested for drunkenness during a previous posting in Norway and it seemed likely by early 1961 that the Admiralty would be asking the FO to make a strong protest to the Soviet embassy about his behaviour in London.[57] The Director of Naval Intelligence reported to the Security Service on 18 January that Ivanov's 'Character weaknesses are apparent when under the influence of alcohol, notably his lack of discretion and loss of personal control, his thirst for women and his tactless bluster.'[58]

The history of the Profumo affair has been distorted by claims that Stephen Ward, a sexually eccentric society osteopath and portrait painter who introduced Profumo to the nineteen-year-old Keeler at a party around the swimming pool on the Cliveden estate of Lord ('Bill') Astor on 8 July, was later 'framed' by the police and driven to suicide, and that the Service used Keeler as a 'honey-trap' to try to lure Ivanov into defection. In reality, Ward was of interest to the Service only because of his involvement with Ivanov. He first came to the attention of MI5 early in 1961 when intelligence disclosed that a man called Ward was trying to strengthen his acquaintance with Ivanov by boasting of his society connections.[59] Ward later claimed that he had introduced Ivanov to the highest in the land and that they became 'close friends': 'Eugene [Ivanov] also met Jack Profumo with me socially and on another occasion he met Princess Margaret. He admired her lovely hair and she was furious when he pretended he did not think it was her real colouring.'[60] It took several months for MI5 to track down the right Stephen Ward. The Special Branch initially directed the Service to another Stephen Ward, who, on being summoned to a meeting with a D1 operations officer who used the alias 'Keith Wood' on 29 May, said 'that there must have been some mistake since he had never met a Russian in his life . . . He was at present engaged in writing a history of the Durham Light Infantry. He was not, and never had been, an osteopath.' 'Wood' apologized and offered him a cup of coffee.[61]

A member of the Service was able to provide 'Wood' with information about the right Stephen Ward obtained through an acquaintance:

the information was that Ward was a difficult sort of person, inclined to be against the government. This attitude stemmed from the war years, when the Army refused to recognise his American medical degree. At some time or other Ward had been declared a bankrupt and he is also believed to have been involved in a call-girl racket.[62]

'Wood' met Ward on 8 June, noting afterwards: 'Ward, who has an attractive personality and who talks well, was completely open about his association with Ivanov. Despite the fact that some of his political ideas are certainly peculiar and are exploitable by the Russians, I do not think that he is of security interest . . .' 'Wood' also reported that Ward had introduced him to a girl who 'was obviously sharing the house with him. She was heavily painted and considerably overdressed and I wondered . . . whether this is corroborating evidence of the allegation . . . that he has been involved in the call-girl racket.'[63] Since Ward's alleged involvement with prostitutes appeared to have no relevance to national security, however, the Service made no attempt to investigate it.

On 12 July Ward invited 'Wood' to lunch in order to expound his views about Soviet policy (to which he, but not the Security Service, attached great importance). 'Wood' was more interested in Ward's description of Ivanov's drunken behaviour at the now celebrated Cliveden weekend a few days earlier when, Ward claimed, Ivanov and Christine Keeler had drunk two bottles of whisky between them. 'Wood' noted afterwards: 'My opinion of [Ward] has not changed. I do not think he is a security risk in the sense that he would be intentionally disloyal, but his peculiar political beliefs combined with his obvious admiration of Ivanov might lead him to be indiscreet unintentionally.'[64] The fact that Profumo had also been at the Cliveden party with Ward, Keeler and Ivanov caused some anxiety in Leconfield House. At Hollis's suggestion, the cabinet secretary, Sir Norman Brook, saw Profumo on 9 August 1961 to warn him that Ward might be trying to pick up information from him to pass on to Ivanov. Profumo wrongly jumped to the conclusion that the Security Service knew of his affair with Keeler. Doubtless as a result of the cabinet secretary's warning, he broke off contact with Ward.[65]

Remarkably, the Foreign Office continued to see Ward, because of his friendship with Ivanov, as a useful intermediary with the Soviet embassy. At a meeting with Ward on 28 May 1962, 'Wood' discovered that 'Without our knowledge Ward was used by the Foreign Office . . . to pass off-the-record information to the Russian embassy.'[66] A fortnight later D1, Arthur Martin, wrote to Philip Adams of the Foreign Office Security Department to check the truth of Ward's claim that he and Sir Godfrey Nicholson MP (a distant relative) had 'assisted the Foreign Office by passing official reports to Ivanov'.[67] Adams confirmed that suitably tailored FO material had been channelled to Ivanov via Ward.[68] Ward had been used as an intermediary with the Soviet embassy with the personal approval of both the Foreign Secretary, Lord Home, and the PUS, Sir Harold Caccia. The Security Service warned the Foreign Office that Ward was 'both naive and indiscreet',[69] thus implying that the FO had also been naive to use him. The Foreign Office paid little, if any, attention to the warning.

During the Cuban Missile Crisis in October 1962, Ward was used once again, this time on the initiative of the Russians, as a confidential channel for communications between Moscow and London. MI5 'again drew the attention of the Foreign Office to the dangers of using Ward for such purposes'.[70] Already fond of boasting about his close contacts with the highest in the land, Ward interpreted his use as a back-channel between Moscow and London at the most dangerous moment of the Cold War as proof that Whitehall had assigned him a major role as an intermediary between East and West. MI5 was informed by a source whom it believed to be reliable:

Ward says that at the height of the Cuban missile crisis . . . Ivanov brought another Russian official, (Vitalij) Loginov [chargé d'affaires] to see Ward: 'We had practically a Cabinet meeting one night. That was the night when Kennedy made his famous speech on the radio [revealing the existence of the Cuban missile bases].' Ward tried to give Source the impression that whatever had been discussed at his flat with the Russians had been passed on to the Prime Minister and the Foreign Secretary, Lord Home.

Ivanov, he said, had come to him because he knew that Ward would be able to put information through to the Prime Minister: 'You should have seen what happened. Eugene rang me up in a very worried state and later brought round this man Loginov. Certain messages they gave me they wanted to go to the Foreign Office. The Prime Minister was informed. It had quite a bearing on what transpired later.'[71]

Though Ward's boasts were characteristically exaggerated, there was a core of truth to them. On 24 October, at one of the tensest moments of the Missile Crisis, Ward passed a message from Ivanov to Caccia at the Foreign Office 'that the Soviet Government looked to the United Kingdom as their one hope of conciliation'. Caccia forwarded it to the British ambassador in Moscow, who was 'sceptical about both the information and the initiative'. On the 27th, Ward accompanied Ivanov to the home of a Foreign Office official, the Earl of Arran, in order 'to get a message to the British government by indirect means asking them to call a Summit conference in London forthwith'. Lord Arran passed on the message to Number Ten as well as to the Foreign Office.[72] Next day, however, Khrushchev agreed to remove the missile bases from Cuba and the crisis was resolved.

The Security Service was less well informed about Profumo than it was about Ward and Ivanov. It did not discover that Profumo had had a liaison with Keeler until 28 January 1963, almost eighteen months after their first meeting round the Cliveden swimming pool. At that point, though rumours were circulating round Fleet Street and Westminster, there was still some reason to believe that Keeler would not publicize the affair. On 6 February F4 (counter-subversion agent-running) informed the DG that 'our news-paper source' had reported that 'The courtesan, Christine Keeler, has told source that she has no intention of putting her name to anything that would embarrass Mr Profumo.'[73] It was not long before she changed her mind.

By the end of March the Home Secretary, Henry Brooke, was so alarmed by the wild rumours flying round Westminster that he summoned Hollis to ask him what MI5 was up to:

He said that . . . the latest story to reach him was that, in 1961, MI5 had been so worried that both Profumo and Ivanov were sleeping with Christine Keeler that they had sent anonymous letters to Valerie Hobson [Profumo's wife] with the hope of breaking up Profumo's liaison. The Home Secretary said he felt he ought to know the facts.

Hollis forbore to ask Brooke how he could possibly have supposed there might be any truth to the preposterous rumour that the Service had been sending anonymous letters to a cabinet minister's wife. Instead, he replied that MI5's sole concern had been to ensure that Profumo should be warned that Ivanov was a Soviet intelligence officer out to steal British defence secrets. Hollis handled a very difficult case and an excitable Home Secretary well. The Service stuck to its remit of not investigating political or sexual scandal unless it threatened national security. Despite sometimes hysterical media claims that the Profumo affair posed such a threat, it never did. As Hollis told Henry Brooke on 28 March 1963: 'Security Service interest in the whole case was limited to Ivanov and his contacts, and it was no part of our business to concern ourselves with what Ward was up to in connec-tion with the girls with which he was associated.' Brooke agreed.[74]

When Profumo admitted lying to the Commons about his relations with Keeler and announced his resignation from the government on 5 June, the combination of sexual scandal in high places (real and imagined) and wide-ranging conspiracy theory produced an extraordinary media feeding frenzy, which in retrospect seems further evidence for Macaulay's dictum, 'We know of no spectacle so ridiculous as the British public in one of its periodical fits of morality.' The evidence in support of Macaulay's dictum was not diminished by a *Times* leader, personally written by the editor Sir William Haley, pompously pronouncing: 'It *is* a moral issue.'

On 3 July 1963 Ward was committed for trial on a charge of living off the earnings from prostitution of Christine Keeler and Mandy Rice-Davies in 1961–2. Convinced that only nine months before he had played a crucial role in the Cuban Missile Crisis, he now claimed that he was being framed by an Establishment plot. Though the claim has been regularly repeated since, it is not supported by any evidence in MI5 files. On 31 July he was found unconscious after taking an overdose. Though Ward was found guilty in his absence, he died before sentence could be passed.

A distressed Macmillan told his diary after Profumo's resignation, 'I do not remember ever having been under such a sense of personal strain. Even Suez was "clean" – about war and politics. This was all "dirt" . . .' Lord Hailsham, Leader of the House of Lords, told the Young Conservatives in a reference to some of the assorted sexual scandals which the media associated with the affair: 'I am not the man without a head, the man in the iron mask, the man who goes about clad only in a Masonic apron, or a visitor to unnamed orgies.'[75] Lord Denning, Master of the Rolls, who conducted an inquiry into the Profumo affair, which became an instant best-seller on its publication in September, later recalled:

I saw Ministers of the Crown, the Security Service, rumour-mongers and prostitutes. They all came in by back doors and along corridors secretly so that the newspapers should not spot them. Some of the evidence I heard [while preparing the Denning Report] was so disgusting – even to my sophisticated mind – that I sent the lady shorthand writers out, and no note of it was taken.[76]

Denning's Report vindicated the role of the Security Service. His judgment, though challenged by numerous conspiracy theorists, has stood the test of time: 'This was an unprecedented situation for which the machinery of government did not cater. It was, in the view of the Security Service, not a case of a security risk, but of moral misbehaviour by a Minister. And we have no machinery to deal with it.'

But there was one important and potentially highly controversial intelligence lead on the Profumo case from a Western double agent in Soviet intelligence (whose name remains classified) of which neither Denning nor the Security Service was aware. On 14 June 1963, nine days after Profumo's resignation, the agent reported overhearing a Soviet intelligence officer say that 'the Russians had in fact received a lot of useful information from Profumo from Christine Keeler, with whom Ivanov had established contact, and in whose apartment Ivanov had even been able to lay on eavesdropping operations at the appropriate times.' Though the double agent did not realize it, the Soviet intelligence officer's boast was based on deeply improbable speculation rather than reliable intelligence. Ivanov was a GRU officer and it is highly unlikely that detailed reports on his operations would have been sent to the KGB residency where the double agent was stationed. At the time, however, the boast was taken seriously and the agent's report forwarded to the US Attorney General, Robert Kennedy, to pass on to his brother, the President, who was due to meet Macmillan in July.[77]

The probability is, however, that Robert Kennedy, who sometimes disregarded Hoover's advice, did not tell the President and that therefore Macmillan did not learn of the double agent's claim. Hoover himself did not inform the Security Service for several years, probably because of his belief in 1963, in the wake of the series of spy scandals over the past year, that 'the British leak like a sieve.' The SLO in Washington, who was told of the double agent's report in 1966, was rightly relieved that it had not been available in London when Denning was conducting his inquiry:

I imagine that if it had reached us [in 1963], it would have been difficult to do other than to accept that it had emanated from a genuine source who had proved reliable in the past, even though our own material gave us no reason to believe that there had been security breaches as a result of Profumo's infatuation with Keeler, and the latter's involvement with Ivanov in 1962.[78]

If the contents of the double agent's report had been mentioned by Denning in 1963, the conspiracy theorists would have had a field day.

After the sensational spy cases of the early 1960s, culminating in (for Macmillan) the almost unbearable embarrassment of Profumo, the usually well-balanced Prime Minister began to succumb to conspiracy theory. He summoned Dick White, in whom he continued to place far more confidence than he did in Hollis, and asked him if he was being set up by Soviet intelligence.[79] White did not believe so, but to set the Prime Minister's mind at rest, on 17 June a joint MI5–SIS working party was instructed 'to look into the possibility that the Russian Intelligence Service had a hand in staging the Profumo affair in order to discredit Her Majesty's government'. By the time that it reported in the negative, ill health had forced Macmillan to resign.[80]

As a result of the spy scandals and the Profumo affair, protective security became a convenient political stick with which the Opposition could beat the government. The establishment of the standing Security Commission in January 1964, initially chaired by Mr (later Lord) Justice Winn, with a remit 'to advise whether any change in security arrangements is desirable', was intended to remove protective security from the arena of party politics. The disadvantage for C Branch was that it sometimes found its own lead role in protective security challenged by what it tended to regard as the well-intentioned, enthusiastic amateurs on the Security Commission.[81]

A year after the Profumo affair, the Conservative government headed by Macmillan's successor, Sir Alec Douglas-Home (who had given up his peerage), was threatened by the prospect of another sexual scandal – this time involving the promiscuously bisexual senior Conservative politician Lord Boothby, who had been MP for East Aberdeenshire for over thirty years before being given a life peerage in 1958. On 19 July 1964 the lead story in the *Sunday Mirror*, published under the banner headline 'THE PICTURE WE DARE NOT PRINT', referred to an incriminating photograph of a prominent politician in the Lords in the company of the leader of London's biggest protection racket, and claimed that Scotland Yard was investigating a homosexual relationship between the two. Three days later, uninhibited by British libel laws, the German magazine *Stern* identified the two men concerned as Lord Boothby and the gay psychopath Ronnie Kray, who, together with his twin brother Reggie, ran north London's leading criminal gang as well as moving in showbusiness and celebrity circles. Even before *Stern* named Boothby and Ronnie Kray, D4 noted that an 'unpaid source of ours who is a semi-reformed homosexual' had reported stories going round Fleet Street linking Boothby, the gay Labour MP Tom Driberg and the Kray twins. Director D minuted that 'the content of the report appears to be of no security interest as Lord Boothby and Mr Driberg do not have access to classified information.' A D Branch Fleet Street source, however, reported that the links between Boothby and the Krays 'might blow up into another minor Profumo affair'.[82] That was also the fear of some members of the Douglas-Home government, though – with an election less than three months away – they feared that the scandal might prove more than minor. On 22 July, the day *Stern* named Boothby and Ronnie Kray, the DG was summoned to see the Home Secretary, Henry Brooke, who told him that he and some of his colleagues felt that the scandal might develop along the lines of the Profumo affair. Hollis acknowledged that the Security Service had heard numerous rumours, some of them about Boothby's homosexuality, but added that, since he had no access to official secrets, his private life was no concern of the Service.[83]

Boothby publicly denied that he had any close or homosexual relations with Ronnie Kray and issued a writ for libel against the *Mirror*. On 7 August the *Mirror* made a public apology and paid £40,000 damages as well as Boothby's costs. Thereafter the media were scared off pursuing the story. In reality, Boothby's relations with the Krays, who five years later were sentenced to life imprisonment for murder (with minimum terms of thirty years), were much closer than he admitted.[84] Had those relations been made public at the time, the resulting scandal would have been even more deeply embarrassing for Harold Macmillan than the Profumo affair. What Hollis and Brooke almost certainly knew but did not mention, when they met on 22 July, was that the bisexual Boothby was the long-term lover of Lady Dorothy Macmillan.

FLUENCY: Paranoid Tendencies

The most traumatic episodes in the Cold War history of the Security Service – the prolonged investigations as suspected Russian agents first of a DDG, Graham Mitchell, then of a DG, Sir Roger Hollis – had their improbable immediate origins in Kim Philby's heavy drinking. After Philby's interrogation, partial confession and defection in January 1963, his third wife Eleanor revealed that he had become very nervous during the previous summer and had begun drinking even more heavily than usual. The obvious explanation for his anxiety was an entirely rational fear that the recent KGB defector to the CIA, Anatoli Golitsyn (codenamed KAGO), might be able to identify him as a Soviet agent.[1] Conspiracy theory, however, triumphed over common sense in explaining Philby's anxiety. It was perversely claimed that he must have been warned by someone in the Security Service that he was once again under suspicion and likely to be questioned. Plans for Philby's interrogation were known to five members of the Service, of whom only Hollis and Mitchell had long enough service and good enough access to classified information to fit the profile of a long-term penetration agent.[2] The Service's fear of penetration was strengthened by the continuing failure to resolve the case of the Magnificent Five and to identify ELLI, as well as by the discovery in 1961 that the SIS officer George Blake was a Soviet spy.[3]

Security Service conspiracy theorists were further encouraged by Golitsyn, whose passionately paranoid tendencies made him an increasing liability to the US and British intelligence communities, which had originally welcomed him with open arms. The Service's leading conspiracy theorist at the time of his defection, Arthur Martin (D1), head since January 1960 of the Soviet counter-espionage section, later acknowledged that it was Golitsyn who had 'crystallised' his long-standing suspicion that there was a major Soviet mole within the Service. Yet, as Martin also acknowledged, Golitsyn could offer only 'circumstantial evidence' with 'no precise information' to back up his theories.[4] Ironically, Martin's own career offered tempting material for the conspiracy theorist. He had originally been recommended to the Security Service in 1946 by Kim Philby, who had met him when he was working for the wartime Radio Security Service.[5] Whatever Philby's motives, they cannot have been to advance MI5's interests. Martin was a skilful and persistent counter-espionage investigator who was awarded the CBE in 1963, but he lacked the capacity for balanced judgement and a grasp of the broader context. Director B, John Marriott, had written of him in 1955: 'In spite of his undeniable critical and analytical gifts and powers of lucid expression on paper, I must confess that I am not convinced that he is not a rather small minded man, and I doubt he will much increase in stature as he grows older.'[6]

A shrewder judge than Martin noted after questioning Golitsyn in April 1962, four months after his defection to the CIA, that his 'knowledge ranges over a wide field but nowhere has it any great depth'.[7] Even Peter Wright, who transferred to D3 in 1964 and was to succeed Martin as the Service's leading conspiracy theorist, later acknowledged that 'the vast majority of Golitsyn's material was tantalisingly imprecise. It often appeared true as far as it went, but then faded into ambiguity . . .'[8] Golitsyn, however, sought with messianic zeal to try to persuade both the American and British intelligence communities that they were falling victim to a vast KGB deception from which only he could save them. His malign influence on MI5 was increased by his decision in December 1962, after one of his periodic disputes with the CIA, to move to Britain. On the recommendation of Graham Mitchell and a senior SIS officer, Golitsyn and his family were accepted for resettlement and arrangements made to obtain a licence for his revolver and organize quarantine for his Alsatian dog. SLO Washington was one of a number of Service officers who thought Golitsyn overrated, dismissing him as a 'psychopath believing he is a gift from heaven to the Western World'. Following a leak in Washington and press publicity about his presence in Britain, Golitsyn decided in July 1963 to return to the United States. His months in Britain, however, coincided with Martin's successful pressure for the investigation and surveillance of Mitchell and the beginning of his active collaboration with Peter Wright. Golitsyn remained in contact with Martin and other Security Service officers following his return to the United States, writing to Martin with characteristic immodesty after Kennedy's assassination in November, 'Both CIA and FBI are doomed without my help.'[9]

Martin unreasonably regarded Hollis's lack of sympathy for his conspiracy theories of Soviet penetration not merely as 'complacency towards the threat of Russian espionage' but as further grounds for suspecting him

"Everything's all right, Prime Minister—this chap's very kindly brought our secrets back!"

The presence in Britain of the KGB defector to the CIA Anatoli Golitsyn attracts unwelcome media attention (cartoon by John Jensen in the *Sunday Telegraph*, 14 July 1963). Shortly afterwards, Golitsyn decided to return to the United States.

of involvement in it. His other chief suspect, Mitchell, Martin claimed, 'had had the reputation of being a Marxist during the war' – an assertion which, he later acknowledged, rested only on (inaccurate) hearsay evidence. Because of his suspicions about both the DG and DDG, Martin – by his own admission – 'deliberately ignored the proper channels' and took his conspiracy theories to the former DG, Sir Dick White, then Chief of SIS. If Martin's account is to be believed, White's response marks one of the lowest points in his long and distinguished intelligence career. According to Martin, White pronounced as plausible his baseless belief that the KGB had been tipped off about Philby's impending interrogation by a senior source in MI5, and said he would like to reflect on how to proceed. Next day he rang Martin to say he should report his suspicions about Mitchell (though not about Hollis) directly to Hollis.[10]

At 6 p.m. on 7 March 1963 Martin called on Hollis by appointment in his office at Leconfield House. The DG sent his secretary home and spent the next half-hour listening as Martin outlined his conspiracy theories about Soviet penetration of the Service and Mitchell's possible treachery, but failed to mention his suspicions about Hollis himself. According to Martin:

Throughout the telling the D.G. interrupted hardly at all. He sat hunched up at his desk, his face drained of colour and with a strange half-smile playing on his lips. I had framed my explanation so that it led to the conclusion that Graham Mitchell was, in my mind, the most likely suspect. I had ended by saying that while the suspicion remained unresolved I did not see how I could take responsibility for KAGO's [Golitsyn's] safety in the U.K.

I had expected that my theory would at least be challenged but it received no comment other than that I had been right to voice it and that he would think it over. With that he invited me to have dinner at his club [the Travellers] . . . As we settled down into [his] car I said something like: 'I must say I admire your phlegm, sir!' This seemed to galvanise him and his response has remained one of my most vivid memories of that evening. It was as though this somewhat lame conversational gambit had caught him out. Metaphorically he squared his shoulders, his withdrawn, pensive expression changed to one of challenge and he said: 'You must not think I do not take your theory seriously; I take it very seriously indeed.'

It seems much more likely that, since the allegation had been made by the head of the Security Service's Soviet counter-espionage section, Hollis concluded that it would have to be properly investigated but groaned inwardly at the thought of pursuing such an implausible and potentially embarrassing line of inquiry. To Martin's annoyance, Hollis kept well away from the subject during their dinner conversation at the Travellers Club. Though Martin was 'itching to debate', they were reduced to 'painful small-talk'.

He clearly wanted to get rid of me as quickly as possible and, for my part, I had no wish to prolong the embarrassment. We agreed that neither of us wanted coffee.

Only after we had left the club and were standing in Pall Mall did he mention again the subject of our interview. He said that he would get in touch with me again about the middle of the following week and that, in the meantime, I was to tell no one of our conversation. He got into his car and drove away.[11]

Five days later Martin was summoned to a meeting at Hollis's home, also attended by Director D, Martin Furnival Jones (FJ). Martin was authorized to begin 'discreet enquiries' into Mitchell's background, which he was to report only to FJ. At the beginning of May, having obtained evidence of what he claimed was 'suspicious behaviour' by Mitchell, Martin was given a case officer to work under him.[12] FJ was initially persuaded by Martin's evidence. A D Branch officer recalls that he and several colleagues were told by FJ in the summer of 1963 that Mitchell had been a Soviet agent. When pressed, FJ declined to give details. His authority lent credence to a statement which, the officer recalls, they would not have believed if it had come from anybody else.[13]

In mid-May 1963 Arthur Martin compared notes for the first time with Peter Wright, then in the Science Directorate, who had wrongly deduced from apparent oddities in a number of counter-espionage cases that there must be a high-level penetration of the Service and that Mitchell was the most likely culprit.[14] Coached by Golitsyn, Peter Wright rapidly emerged as the Service's witchfinder general, becoming as great a liability as Golitsyn and an even greater menace than Martin. In his memoirs, *Spycatcher*, Wright, while not abandoning his conspiracy theories, later came close to admitting that he and Golitsyn had been consumed by *folie à deux*: 'In the tense and almost hysterical months of 1963, as the scent of treachery lingered in every corridor, it is easy to see how our fears fed on his theories.'[15]

From 10 May until 14 June that year a number of searches were made of Mitchell's office and a specially recruited surveillance team[16] kept him under observation for part of his journey home each evening.[17] Though initially unwilling to seek an HOW on the DDG,[18] Hollis changed his mind. After meeting the Home Office PUS, Sir Charles Cunningham, at Cunningham's flat on 5 June, he appears to have obtained an HOW for telechecks on both Mitchell's home and office. Hollis and the Home Secretary, Henry Brooke (who was briefed on 24 June),[19] had three meetings with the Prime Minister, Harold Macmillan – on 28 June and 19 and 27 July – to discuss the unprecedented investigation of the DDG.[20] Macmillan, who already had a low opinion of Hollis, seems understandably to have been appalled.[21] The only other minister briefed on the investigation was the Foreign Secretary, Lord Home, on 1 July.[22]

Until his retirement on 6 September 1963, Mitchell (codenamed PETERS at the suggestion of Golitsyn, whose own codename it had once been)[23] was kept under both visual and audio surveillance in his office. A small hole was bored through his office wall to enable him to be continuously observed while at his desk by CCTV.[24] Hollis also approved 'barium meal' operations against him, during which bogus intelligence was fed to him which, had he been a Soviet spy, he might have been expected to pass on to Moscow.[25] Mitchell's habit of muttering to himself when he was alone in his office added to the suspicions of Martin and Wright – though his mutterings proved difficult for the transcribers to decipher. On 30 August, for example, when he was fed a 'barium meal' story of a projected operation against two GRU officers, the transcriber produced two alternative versions of Mitchell's muttered response:

(i) Well I must tell ?Yu-Yuri that they are. I am sure – (slight laugh) – he'll laugh if the Russians (??have booked).

(ii) Well I am most terribly curious if they are. I am sure – (slight laugh) – he'll laugh if the Russians (??have booked).

The transcriber felt unable to guarantee the accuracy of either version, but preferred the first. Some of the case against Mitchell was constructed of even feebler material. For example:

It was noticed that the bottom left-hand drawer of his desk had recently been unlocked. On examination this drawer, like all the others, contained a thick layer of dust, but this one also contained marks as if a small object on legs had been placed in the drawer and subsequently removed. No satisfactory evidence has yet been advanced to explain these marks.[26]

Peter Wright, inevitably, saw a sinister significance in the marks in the dust. They had, he suspected, been made by a KGB camera given to Mitchell to photograph Security Service documents.[27]

When the new Director of D Branch, Malcolm Cumming (who had talent-spotted Dick White almost thirty years before), was indoctrinated into the PETERS case on succeeding FJ in June 1963,[28] he discovered that Martin had fed him some of the bogus 'barium meal' intelligence, which he had passed on to Mitchell believing it to be genuine. Martin saw Director D's irritation at this discovery as evidence of a character defect – 'a bitter pill for a vain man to swallow'. The new Director D's lack of enthusiasm for the Mitchell investigation, though in retrospect a sign of balanced judgement, was proof in Martin's less balanced view that he was simply not up to the job of directing counter-espionage.[29] By August, a fourth Security Service officer, Hugh Winterborn (A2), had joined the PETERS investigation. All, according to Martin, had no 'serious doubts about Mitchell's guilt', but feared that 'we would not be able to produce evidence sufficient for a prosecution except by successful interrogation.'[30] Martin insisted that the interrogation take place before Mitchell's retirement and that both the 'CIA and FBI should be told at once so that in the weeks of climax we could make our moves in concert with them.' Hollis, however, was 'not yet convinced either that the case was strong enough to justify interrogation or that it was necessary to inform the Americans at all'. Martin, Wright, Winterborn and a colleague then decided between themselves to force Hollis's hand. At a Saturday-morning meeting at Hollis's house, each in turn made a personal statement saying that he would resign from the Service unless the Americans were told. Hollis gave no immediate reply, but seems to have decided over the next few days that he had little option but to give in to their demand. At the beginning of the year, less than a week before Philby's defection, he had assured Hoover that there was no evidence Philby had worked as a post-war Soviet agent. Having so recently and so seriously misinformed Britain's main intelligence ally, Hollis probably decided that he could not take the risk of concealing the investigation of Mitchell. After consulting White, he went to see Macmillan who agreed that he should brief the Americans soon after Mitchell's retirement.[31]

In late September, Hollis flew to Washington and was faced with the unprecedented embarrassment of informing both the CIA and FBI of the investigation of his own deputy. Martin followed a day later to explain the 'implications for certain American intelligence sources who, if Mitchell was a spy, must be considered either compromised or provocateurs'.[32] Both the CIA and FBI were deeply sceptical about the case against Mitchell – largely because the many current US or joint UK–US operations of which he was aware showed no sign of being compromised.[33] Their scepticism was shared by the RCMP.[34] It was a remarkable sign of the closeness of the transatlantic intelligence alliance that President Kennedy and his brother Robert, the US Attorney General, were also briefed on an investigation known to only three British ministers and to no member of Her Majesty's Opposition.[35] Their reaction is not recorded.

By the time Martin flew to Washington, the direction of the PETERS case had been taken out of his hands. The investigative part of his section, D1, was split off as D1/Inv,[36] whose head became increasingly doubtful about the case against Mitchell, partly as a result of the scepticism of the CIA and FBI. Michael Straight's revelation of his pre-war recruitment by Anthony Blunt, followed by Blunt's confession to Martin in April 1964,[37] also provided an explanation for much of the hitherto mysterious evidence of wartime penetration. The discovery of Blake's treachery similarly accounted for much post-war evidence.[38] A D1/Inv report in March 1964 concluded that 'on present evidence PETERS is more likely to be innocent than guilty. I think that, while continuing the PETERS investigation, we should make a determined effort to look for other candidates.'[39]

In the course of 1964, Martin's relations with his colleagues became increasingly fraught. As even Wright later acknowledged, Martin was both temperamental and obsessive, and 'never understood the extent to which he had made enemies over the years'.[40] On the Tuesday after Whitsun he was summoned to the DG's office, where he found Hollis 'choking with anger', though, in Martin's view, 'it seemed an artificial, rehearsed anger for it was not reflected in his eyes.' Hollis told Martin that he was 'a focal point for dissension in the Service, and in D Branch in particular, and that he could not tolerate this any longer'. Martin was suspended for two weeks.[41] After further disagreements over the next few months, including a complaint by D1/Inv that Martin was undermining his authority, in November he was once again summoned by the DG. Hollis told Martin he had made D1/Inv's life 'a misery' and was 'at the centre of all the unrest in the office'. The directors had originally intended to dismiss him but had decided instead to second him to another section of the intelligence community for a period of two years.[42]

With Martin's transfer, Peter Wright emerged as the Security Service's leading conspiracy theorist. His investigations, however, uncovered nothing against Mitchell save for personal eccentricities which provided no evidence of treachery.[43] A later investigation by the former cabinet secretary Lord Trend concluded: '. . . Mitchell's curious behaviour is reasonably explicable on the assumption that it represented the natural reaction of a highly strung and rather "odd" individual to the strain of working for a DG with whom he was increasingly out of sympathy.'[44]

After leaving the Security Service, Martin continued to co-operate with Wright in their pursuit of imaginary traitors within the intelligence community. By the beginning of 1964 both were convinced that Hollis, not Mitchell, was the most likely suspect. Martin persuaded himself that Hollis had engineered the investigation of Mitchell in order to throw them off the scent and 'protect himself'.[45] During the early stages of their investigation of Hollis, Wright narrowly avoided dismissal from the Service. Before Hollis's retirement in 1965 he asked an A1 operations officer to stay behind one evening, then told him, 'There's a drawer in the DG's office I want to look into.' 'But I can't do that,' the officer replied. 'Oh yes, it's all above board,' Wright improbably assured him. The officer later recalled that he agreed to open the drawer, only to discover that it was empty: 'I thought, "What the devil is he on about?" '[46] Had Wright's break-in been discovered, he might well have been sacked and the Service would have been rid of its most troublesome and conspiratorially minded member. Hollis's empty drawer remains as a striking visual symbol of the baselessness of the allegations against him.

In November 1964 a joint Security Service–SIS working party code-named FLUENCY, chaired by Peter Wright (but excluding Martin), was directed to examine all available evidence of penetration of both Services.[47]

The report of the FLUENCY Working Party to Hollis and White on 28 May 1965 concluded not merely that both Services had been penetrated by Soviet intelligence but that the penetration continued.[48] D3 (responsible for counter-intelligence research and collation) simultaneously sent a note to Hollis indicating that the DG himself was under suspicion.[49] There followed a meeting between Hollis and Wright on about 11 June which was unprecedented in Security Service history. According to a later note on file by Peter Wright, Hollis asked him, 'Why do you think I am a spy?' They went on to discuss two of the leads which Wright believed made the DG a suspect.[50] On 5 July 1965 Hollis and Sir Dick White agreed that the Working Party had 'established a *prima facie* case for penetration of British Intelligence which requires further investigation', and formally instructed the FLUENCY Working Party to continue an inquiry which the DG knew was bound to make him the first British intelligence chief in modern times to be investigated on suspicion of treason. Golitsyn remained a malign influence on the inquiry. Though admitting that 'details of penetration of [British] intelligence were particularly tightly held in the KGB' and therefore mostly unavailable to him, 'as a result of his intensive reading of KGB files over a period of sixteen years he was certain that British Intelligence on both sides [MI5 and SIS] had been continuously and widely penetrated by the KGB.'[51] Wright's faith in Golitsyn was unaffected by such inconsistencies in his behaviour as the fact (reported by SLO Washington) that, despite claiming to fear assassination by the KGB, he dined in New York restaurants frequented by Soviet officials.[52] The root cause of the conspiracy theories which did such damage to the Security Service, apart from the unbalanced judgement of a minority of its officers, was the lack of good defector intelligence on Soviet penetration of the quality later provided by Oleg Gordievsky, which would have demolished the case against Hollis and Mitchell. Tragically, the most important KGB defector apparently able to provide leads on Soviet penetration, Anatoli Golitsyn, so far from dispelling the myths which obsessed Wright and the head of the CIA's Counter-Intelligence Staff, Jim Angleton, encouraged their conspiracy theories.

In January 1966, a month after Hollis's retirement, a FLUENCY report concluded that the most likely penetration agent in the Security Service was either Hollis himself or a 'middle grade spy', to whom a lead had been given by the Polish defector Goleniewski.[53] According to Peter Wright, the new DG, Furnival Jones, dismissed the suspicions against Hollis as 'grotesque', and instructed that the allegations about a 'middle grade spy' be investigated. The Director of C Branch (protective security), Michael

Hanley, a future DG, seemed a possible fit. FJ questioned Hanley himself and quickly declared him innocent. Wright agreed.[54] The next candidate for the 'middle grade spy', 'Gregory Stevens' (as Wright later referred to him), was less fortunate. As during his investigation of Hollis,[55] and probably other cases, Wright instructed an A1 operations officer to break into the suspect's desk, in this case to read 'Stevens's' personal diaries. The interrogation was conducted by Wright and John Day. In addition to Wright's published account in Spycatcher (which misidentifies Day),[56] later unpublished recollections survive by both Day[57] and 'Stevens'.[58] Despite some discrepancies on other points, all accounts agree that, under great strain after several days' interrogation, 'Stevens', for reasons he could never later fully explain, made, then retracted, a bogus confession. He also accused his interrogators of being worse than the KGB. Soon afterwards, 'Stevens' left the Service. Though subsequently reinstated, he never fully recovered from the trauma of having his unblemished loyalty to the Security Service called into question. His position became even more invidious when news leaked out to his colleagues that he had been grilled by Wright, and he took early retirement.[59] Wright's own reputation within the Service never recovered. As he later acknowledged in Spycatcher: 'There was talk of the Gestapo. Younger officers began to avoid me in the canteen. Casual conversation with many of my colleagues became a rarity.'[60]

After the fiasco of the hunt for the 'middle grade spy', the FLUENCY Working Party once again focused its attention on Hollis. As well as recommending a full-scale investigation of Hollis (who in September 1967 was assigned the codename DRAT), the Working Party also decided to make a final attempt to resolve the case against Mitchell.[61] By this time US intelligence, chiefly in the person of Jim Angleton, was also involved in the investigation. The point at which Angleton finally became lost in a conspiratorial wilderness of mirrors from which he was never to escape came in 1965 when Golitsyn persuaded him of the absurd proposition that the Sino-Soviet split, one of the turning points of the Cold War, was a mere charade designed to deceive the West. For Angleton to have believed that both the Soviet Union and the People's Republic of China could have convincingly maintained over a series of years the pretence of a bitter quarrel between them to deceive the West is proof that his obsession with Soviet penetration and disinformation had led him to lose all sense of proportion. Golitsyn, however, dismissed all agents, defectors and other Soviet sources who disputed his deception theories as part of the KGB deception – and Angleton believed him. At the time of his defection Golitsyn had not claimed that the Sino-Soviet split was a fraud. During a visit to Washington late in 1965, Peter Wright 'asked Angleton why he thought KAGO [Golitsyn] had held back so long, if he really thought all this when he came out. [Angleton] said that KAGO was afraid of being laughed at (as indeed he was).'[62]

The extraordinary scale of the Soviet deception which Angleton believed had taken hold in the West was, in his view, proof that Western intelligence had been penetrated. He was anxious to be involved in the investigation of that penetration on both sides of the Atlantic.[63] On the morning of 14 March 1966 A. M. MacDonald, who had succeeded Cumming as Director D, was rung up by Maurice Oldfield of SIS (of which he later became chief) with the 'somewhat unexpected news that Jim [Angleton] and Anatol [Golitsyn] had turned up unheralded in London' and were leaving next day. Their visit was so secret that Angleton insisted that even the CIA London station must not be informed of their presence. He asked for an urgent meeting with Sir Dick White, Furnival Jones and some of their senior officers, and said that he brought with him a:

brief from [the DCI Richard] Helms to discuss with certain Liaison Services the problems of disinformation and penetration and to explore whether arrangements could be made both to step up investigations in the countries which they were visiting and to make arrangements for pooling, transmitting and distributing the results.

The DG cancelled an appointment with the PUS at the Home Office, and went with MacDonald and Wright for a meeting with Angleton and Golitsyn at White's flat. FJ and MacDonald agreed later that 'the whole performance was somewhat extraordinary, but then Jim and Anatoly are quite extraordinary chaps.' MacDonald noted afterwards:

The D.G. and 'C' indicated very tactfully that while they accepted the facts of penetration and disinformation, they did not consider that it was therefore necessary to subscribe to the Sino-Soviet deception theory. I said that even if we agreed to differ on the Sino-Soviet split, this would not really invalidate the remainder of Jim's proposals.

After the meeting ended at 6.30 p.m., MacDonald and Wright accompanied Angleton and Golitsyn to Maurice Oldfield's Marsham Street flat, where discussions continued until the early hours with a break for dinner. According to MacDonald, 'Nothing very new emerged during these talks but Jim emphasised that he was convinced there was penetration of his own organisation . . .'[64]

The willingness of non-conspiracy theorists in the Security Service such as MacDonald to collaborate with Angleton, despite rejecting his insistence that the Sino-Soviet split was a Soviet deception, reflected both their sense of the importance of the intelligence 'Special Relationship' and a personal regard for Angleton himself. Golitsyn too could be good company when he chose. MacDonald wrote after their visit: 'I liked Jim and I was, of course, pleased to see Anatol again. He gave me a very warm welcome and I presented him with a book on wine, a subject in which I know he is interested, as a memento of the many good meals we had together in the past.'[65] Even after Angleton entered the wilderness of mirrors, he remained personally popular with his British colleagues. As Peter Wright later recalled, 'He drank us all under the table and played sharper poker and still sat up and argued politics hours after younger men had lost control and fallen asleep.' He also had a well-deserved reputation as an orchid breeder.[66] Angleton was a highly cultured man with an impressive range of literary interests. A BBC producer with a first-class honours degree in English literature who tried to arrange an interview with Angleton for a radio documentary in 1980 found himself being questioned in detail about twentieth-century English poetry for over half an hour on the telephone. 'My God!' the producer said afterwards. 'That was a better viva than I ever had at Oxford!'[67]

During the year following the surprise visit to London by Angleton and Golitsyn, talks in Washington between representatives of MI5, SIS, CIA and FBI, some attended by FJ, agreed on British–American collaboration in an investigation of Soviet disinformation and penetration by a small group of intelligence officers who exchanged highly classified information. Though J. Edgar Hoover rejected formal FBI membership of the group, the head of the Bureau's Communist desk, Bill Sullivan, collaborated with it and attended its first conference in Washington in June 1967. A Security Service review two years later concluded that the collaboration had been kept so secret that the other intelligence allies – ASIO, RCMP and the New Zealand Security Service (NZSS) – were not, 'as far as is known', aware of its existence. All were, however, involved with the CIA, MI5 and SIS in a larger secret association with a similar agenda, codenamed CAZAB, which held its first meeting in Melbourne in November 1967.[68] The meeting agreed to set up a joint counter-intelligence group (in association with the FBI) to seek to identify high-level Soviet penetration in the West, especially of intelligence agencies, and to uncover Soviet disinformation campaigns.[69]

Angleton brought Golitsyn with him to Melbourne, where, according to Peter Wright, Golitsyn 'laid special emphasis on Britain, and the many penetrations which, he claimed, were as yet undiscovered, and which only he could locate. FJ was smiling the smile he reserved for particularly tiresome people.'[70] Security Service officers continued to consult Angleton personally about the search for traitors in MI5's own ranks. In February 1968, D1/Inv wrote to the SLO in Washington, updating him on the Mitchell investigation and adding:

I think it would be well worth discussing all this with Jim. This would, first, demonstrate that we are trying to get to grips with the case and bring it to a conclusion. Secondly it would enable you to ask for any help CIA can possibly give us in filling in the strange gap [in Mitchell's career] between 1936 and 1938.[71]

In September 1968 the second CAZAB meeting, this time in Washington, reviewed general progress in the search for high-level penetration of Western intelligence.[72] In the case of the Security Service, since there was in reality no high-level Soviet penetration left to uncover, there was inevitably no significant progress to report. For the conspiracy theorists, however, the difficulty in finding proof of penetration was evidence of how successful it had been.

The witch-hunt within the Security Service, though the details were known to few, made Peter Wright increasingly unpopular. At a conference of senior Security Service officers in 1969 at the Sunningdale Civil Service College, Wright was taken aback by the 'bitter attacks' on him and some of his colleagues in D1/Inv. 'How do I go into the office', he asked FJ, 'facing this level of hostility?' 'That is a price you have to pay for sitting in judgment on people,' FJ replied.[73] The FLUENCY Working Party continued, however, to press the DG to authorize the investigation of Hollis. Though deeply sceptical of the case against his predecessor, FJ finally agreed in the summer of 1969. As the DRAT and PETERS cases proceeded,[74] Angleton's advice continued to be sought on both.[75]

Stella Rimington later concluded that Wright and Angleton 'fuelled each other's paranoia'.[76] Angleton, however, provided very little hard information for the FLUENCY investigations. A Security Service review of CAZAB concluded in 1969: 'We have not received any intelligence which seems to match the bait produced by Angleton in earlier discussions, when he said that C.I.A. had information relevant to United Kingdom interests which they were unable to pass, in the absence of an indoctrination forum.' The Service considered, however, that there had been a general gain in the closeness of liaison on counter-intelligence among the five intelligence allies:

The ... CAZAB networks, although having something of a precedent in the VENONA exchanges ... are probably unique in conception, at least in peacetime.

There is acceptance by the participating organisations of the threat from penetration and from disinformation and the professions of complete frankness appear to be reflected in the actual exchanges of intelligence.

. . . The frank discussions on the threat, the exchanges of ideas on the methods to combat the threat have so far been valuable. Now that the proceedings of the Commonwealth Security Conference tend to be inhibited by the large number of delegates in attendance, it has been useful to include Australia, Canada and New Zealand in this intimate circle. It has resulted in them devoting more resources to work on disinformation and penetration.[77]

In May 1970 FJ agreed to invite Golitsyn to Britain and give him access to material from Security Service files in order to identify the penetrations which he claimed to be able to uncover.[78] The operation was run by an MI5 officer who had met Golitsyn while SLO in Washington. Helped by an assistant, the officer transported documents from Leconfield House for inspection by Golitsyn at a safe house on the south coast. Golitsyn was first booked into a hotel in Bournemouth but walked out, convinced he was being spied on by building workers. He was then put into a rented house near Christchurch where he was looked after by an A4 officer and his wife. His paranoid tendencies made him a nightmare to handle; he insisted on drinking only Perrier water for fear of being poisoned, and would go out only at night. After a while he asked to move into the family home of the former Washington SLO, where his behaviour alarmed both the MI5 officer's daughter and one of their neighbours. The officer found the whole time-consuming operation a complete waste of time.[79]

From the summer of 1969 to the summer of 1970 the Security Service DRAT and PETERS investigations proceeded in tandem.[80] The Mitchell case was finally closed after he was questioned in FJ's office in August 1970.[81] No evidence of guilt emerged and the DG told Mitchell he had been cleared.[82] John Day (K7), who took part in the questioning, later recalled that afterwards, presumably in a half-hearted attempt to make amends, the DG took Mitchell to lunch at his club. Day, who was also present, remembered the meal as, unsurprisingly, 'rather a strain'.[83] The investigation of Hollis, which eventually involved more than fifty interviews (including two with Hollis himself), also turned up no credible evidence since there was none to find.[84] FJ's personal embarrassment over this miserable episode was reflected in his failure to inform either the Home Secretary or the Prime Minister that Hollis was under investigation. By contrast, three ministers had been told about the investigation of Mitchell while it was still in its early stages.[85]

'The Case against DRAT' submitted on 18 June 1970, drafted by John Day, who was to lead the interrogation of Hollis early in the following year, unintentionally exposes how threadbare the evidence against Hollis was. It remains a shocking document – a classic example of a paper written to support a conclusion already arrived at which excludes important evidence to the contrary and turns on its head evidence which does not fit the preconceived conclusion. There was no mention of the fact that during the Second World War Hollis had been one of the members of the Service most alert to the threat of Soviet penetration of Whitehall and the armed services, even criticizing the DG, Sir David Petrie, for his lack of attention to the dangers which this posed. Hollis had also been almost the only – perhaps the only – wartime member of the Service suspicious about Blunt. Day, however, turned this evidence on its head as pointing to a KGB plot to divert suspicion from Hollis.[86] Nor could the conspiracy theorists credibly explain how a series of highly successful operations against the KGB of which Hollis had knowledge – among them the defection of the Petrovs in 1954 – could have been possible if Hollis had been a Soviet spy.

All three of the supposed leads pointing to Hollis's guilt cited in the 'Case against DRAT' were later shown, as could reasonably have been inferred at the time, to refer to others. Hollis was alleged to be the most likely candidate for the 'acting head of a department of British Counter-Espionage (or Counter-Intelligence) Directorate' mentioned by Volkov in September 1945 before his failed attempt to defect. It should have been clear well before 1970 that by far the most likely candidate was Philby, who at the time had recently been acting head of SIS Section V (counter-intelligence), whereas Hollis had been the substantive (not acting) head of F Division (counter-subversion) in MI5 for five years. (In addition Philby was known to have been responsible for ensuring the failure of Volkov's attempt to defect.) Hollis was also identified as the most likely candidate for a 'cadre worker' (serving officer) in MI5 able to bring out files on Russians at will who was mentioned by the Soviet resident in Stockholm to the future defector Petrov in early 1954. It should have been obvious that the prime candidate was not Hollis but Blunt, who had confessed in 1965 that during the war he had taken MI5 files out of headquarters in a suitcase. Hollis was also alleged to be the agent codenamed JOHNSON mentioned in London VENONA decrypts of September 1945. As even Wright later acknowledged, this also was Blunt.[87]

Despite his own scepticism about the 'Case against DRAT',[88] FJ at last informed Sir Philip Allen, PUS Home Office, and Sir Burke Trend, the cabinet secretary, of the investigation of Hollis. Though pressed by Allen, the DG remarkably refused to tell either the Home Secretary, Reggie Maudling, or the Prime Minister, Edward Heath. Since Hollis had had three meetings with the last Conservative Prime Minister, Harold Macmillan, to discuss the investigation of Mitchell, it is difficult to see the justification for FJ's refusal to inform Heath. No minister was informed of the investigation of Hollis until Harold Wilson was told in August 1975; he too had not been informed of the suspicions against Hollis during his first administration.[89] In keeping with the terms of the CAZAB counter-intelligence collaboration, FJ did, however, inform his US allies. During a visit to the DCI, Richard Helms, at CIA headquarters in November 1970:

He said that he did not suspect DRAT of having been a spy. He added, however, that others in the Service did not share his view and that in the near future DRAT would be interviewed. Because he might be thought to be prejudiced, to which he admitted, he did not intend to conduct the interview personally.[90]

In 1970 the FLUENCY codeword was changed.[91] (The new codename remains classified.) FJ finally authorized the interrogation of Hollis by Day and a colleague in K7 in February 1971, but gave Hollis advance notice and refused to seek HOWs for letter and telephone checks.[92] As even Wright acknowledged, the interrogation of Hollis effectively brought the case to an end: 'We knew we had not brought the case home.' At the end of the interrogation, Hollis 'said goodbye, and meant it. He travelled back to Somerset, back to his golf, and his cottage.' FJ declared that the case was closed and that it was time to move on. Very few within the Service apart from Peter Wright disagreed. Wright, however, had lost most of his influence. He later wrote in his memoirs that, though he did not formally retire until 1976, his retirement really began on the day that Hollis's interrogation ended: 'What came after was mostly going through the motions.'[93] Hollis died in 1973.

While 'going through the motions', Wright's conspiracy theories continued to grow. He convinced himself 'that the Ring of Five stood at the centre of a series of other concentric rings, each pledged to silence, each anxious to protect its secrets from outsiders'.[94] Stella Rimington and some of her friends in the Security Service called Wright 'the "KGB illegal", because, with his appearance and his lisp we could imagine that he was really a KGB officer himself, living under a false identity . . .'.[95] After the investigation of Hollis and Mitchell was concluded, about one hundred leads pointing to possible other penetrations – half of them provided by Golitsyn – remained. By 1973 it was generally recognized within D Branch that only five of these leads merited investigation; only one was still thought worth pursuing three years later. Between 1973 and 1978, however, the leading SIS conspiracy theorist repeatedly complained that the investigations into Soviet penetration had been improperly conducted, on one occasion appealing directly to the Prime Minister, Harold Wilson. Though he did not succeed in seeing Wilson, he put his case to the cabinet secretary, Sir John Hunt. Partly in response to the SIS officer's complaints, the previous cabinet secretary, Lord Trend, was asked to review the investigation, and reported in May 1975 that there was no evidence to show that either Hollis or Mitchell had ever been a Soviet agent.[96] Wright, Martin and the SIS officer were unconvinced. Conspiracy theory of the kind contracted by all three is an incurable condition. What J. A. Allen (Director KX) wrote of the SIS officer was equally true of Wright and Martin: 'Involvement in counter-espionage cases induces in some a form of paranoia which causes them to find only pusillanimity, or worse, in others who see through different eyes.'[97] The damage done to the reputation of the Service in the eyes of the four Prime Ministers privy to the charges against Hollis or Mitchell or both – Macmillan, Wilson, Heath and Callaghan – was inevitably substantial. The charges against Hollis in particular became the main theme of Wright's best-selling intelligence memoirs, which succeeded in spreading the author's conspiracy theories around the world.

After the publication during the 1980s of books by several authors, in particular Peter Wright's *Spycatcher* (which appeared in 1987), which publicized the charges against Hollis and Mitchell, a number of Service reports reviewed the earlier investigations. Those reports represent probably the most damaging indictment ever produced within the Service of any of its investigations. An officer in K10R/1, which was responsible for research into old espionage cases, concluded in June 1988: 'In our estimation the case originally against Hollis which culminated in two interviews with him was so insubstantial that it should not have been pursued.'

It may well be asked why belief in high-level penetration continued so long in the UK, directed first at Mitchell . . . and later at Hollis. The reasons are complex:

(a) a lack of intellectual rigour in some of the leading investigators . . .

(b) dishonesty on the part of Wright, who did not scruple to invent evidence where none existed . . .

(c) the baleful influence of Golitsyn who realised in 1963 that he had told all he knew and set about developing his theory of massive and co-ordinated Soviet deception ('disinformation') supported by high-level penetration of all western intelligence and security services[98]

Among the instances of Wright's dishonesty in fabricating or distorting evidence to fit his conspiracy theories which came to light after his retirement in 1976 were the following:

  (i) Wright has quoted an incident in 1961 when the KGB Resident Korovin was said to have been watching television [news] on the evening of the day when Lonsdale and the Krogers etc were arrested – and showed no emotion [the implication being that he had been forewarned]. This is quite untrue. Korovin was having a party with his two deputies and they were not watching television or listening to the radio.

 (ii) Wright 'led' his witnesses most unscrupulously in, for example, his interviews of the Petrovs, Elsa Bernaut[99] and Blunt (in one interview he suggested to Blunt that Hollis was a spy, causing Blunt considerable anxiety for his own safety).

(iii) His tendency to select a solution, then tailor the evidence to fit it (as in his 1965 investigation of the fire at the Moscow Embassy in 1964).

(iv) His standard manoeuvre when worsted in argument of taking refuge in mystery ('If you knew what I know'). This was a characteristic shared by Angleton in CIA. In both cases this was later shown to be a dishonest charade.[100]

Though all these points were well taken, the 1988 and other investigations did not address the underlying strategic failures which gave such free rein to the witch-hunts against Hollis and Mitchell. Overawed by the discovery of the atom spies, the Cambridge spies and (to those with access to VENONA) the Soviet wartime penetration of OSS and much of the Roosevelt administration, the Service formed a greatly exaggerated view of the efficiency of the Stalinist intelligence system and paid far too little attention to defector evidence (from, for example, the Petrovs) on its numerous inefficiencies, thus making itself susceptible to conspiracy theories which took no account of the frequency of Soviet cock-ups. Secondly, the Service had no mechanism for challenging the passionately held but intellectually threadbare conspiracy theories of a disruptive minority – particularly one which was so willing to fall back on claims of superior information ('If you knew what I know') which it refused to expose to critical examination. Thirdly, the lack of such a mechanism was ultimately the result of a managerial failure – particularly by FJ, who, despite his deep scepticism about the DRAT investigation, failed to appoint a Team B from within the Service to review the deeply flawed evidence on which it was based. Fourthly, the introverted work culture of the Service made it deeply reluctant to call in an experienced, senior figure from Whitehall to provide a second opinion. But that, in the end, a decade too late, is what it was forced to do.

There was thus one long-term gain from the decade of otherwise futile and disruptive FLUENCY investigations. In 1975, at the suggestion of the cabinet secretary, an independent 'assessor' was appointed to oversee all current and future investigations of alleged penetration of the Security Service or SIS. Having completed his inquiry into the Hollis and Mitchell cases, the first incumbent continued as assessor until his death in 1987. Successive incumbents have been appointed by the home secretary, with the agreement of the prime minister and the foreign secretary.[101] Had such a system been in place at the beginning of the 1960s, it would doubtless have brought to an early conclusion the witch-hunts of the Service's conspiracy theorists.

The Wilson Government 1964–1970: Security, Subversion and 'Wiggery-Pokery'

Labour returned to power in 1964 with many of the suspicions about the Security Service which had troubled it in 1945. Even among the Service's supporters in the government there was a widespread delusion that their correspondence and telephone calls were intercepted. Tony Benn, whom Wilson made postmaster general, noted in his diary after a discussion with his future cabinet colleague Dick Crossman fifteen months before Labour's election victory:

Dick, who worked for Intelligence during the war, is a fierce security man and said that, as a Minister, he would think it right that his phones should be tapped and all his letters opened. This is quite mad. I am terrified that George Wigg may be made Minister for Security and given power over all our lives.[1]

Wigg, a former colonel in the Education Corps, told journalists in 1963 that he was out to 'get Profumo' (in his view a bad secretary of state for war as well as a security risk), and gave himself much of the credit for forcing Profumo out of office.[2] Benn had good reason to be alarmed about Wigg's future role in a Wilson government. As Wilson's official biographer observes: '[Wigg's] passion was secrets, the more malodorous the better. He was at his happiest in the twilight world of spies, counter-spies and Chapman Pincher, and viewed his fellow MPs with the same ferocious suspicion as he would have lavished on an accredited agent of the KGB.'[3] What Wilson did not know was that, as well as claiming (with little justification) to be an expert in security matters, Wigg combined prurience about the sex lives of others with the use of prostitutes.[4] Ironically, during the Attlee government Wigg had been on the list of 'Lost Sheep' pro-Soviet Labour MPs marked down for possible expulsion from the Party by its general secretary, Morgan Phillips.[5] By 1964, at least as regards the Soviet Union, Wigg's 'Lost Sheep' days were far behind him.

On Saturday 19 October 1964, the day after Harold Wilson was sworn in as prime minister, the PUS at the Home Office, Sir Charles Cunningham, phoned the DG, Sir Roger Hollis, to tell him that the new Home Secretary would be Sir Frank Soskice but that Wilson proposed to transfer responsibility for security to George Wigg as paymaster general (in effect minister without portfolio). Hollis and Cunningham both saw 'substantial objections' to (in other words, were appalled by) Wilson's plan, which would have thrown the whole Home Office Warrant system, on which the Security Service depended, into disarray: 'It would be impossible for Colonel Wigg, who would not be a Secretary of State, to sign warrants.'[6] In the course of the weekend, however, Wilson was persuaded to reconsider Wigg's role – probably by the cabinet secretary, Sir Burke Trend, for whom he had enormous respect.[7] On the morning of Monday 21 October, Trend summoned Hollis and Sir Dick White to his room in the Cabinet Office to inform them:

that it had been agreed that the Home Secretary would continue to be the Minister responsible for the Security Service and that [its] charter would be re-affirmed. Nevertheless the Prime Minister did intend to give Wigg a charge to assist him from time to time on questions of security. Apparently what he had in mind was that Wigg should safeguard the Prime Minister against scandals taking him unaware and he did not want to be caught in the position of Macmillan at the time of the Profumo case.[8]

Wilson sought to justify Wigg's role to the probably sceptical head of the civil service, Sir Laurence Helsby, by claiming that he was to have an important role in strengthening protective security.[9] The Security Service file on liaison with the Paymaster General is, however, very thin and contains little of substance – doubtless because, in reality, Wigg made no significant contribution to protective security.[10] Roy Jenkins, who was to succeed Soskice as home secretary, later recalled Wigg's role with derision.

[Wilson] employed the half-comic, half-sinister George Wigg nominally as Paymaster-General, but in fact as a licensed rifler in Whitehall dustbins and interferer in security matters. Wigg as an unofficial emissary of the Prime Minister used to pay me occasional Home Office visits during which he delivered cryptic messages. As they increasingly came to refer back to previous ones which had passed over my head the crypticism became compounded. Out of a rash mixture of boredom and supineness (for I did not wish to embroil with Wilson over him) I decided to roll with his punch, particularly as nothing ever seemed to follow from what he said. 'You know that matter I talked to you about last time,' a typical conversation would begin. 'It hasn't moved much, but I'll keep watching it.' If one nodded sagely he went off quickly away, apparently satisfied, and no harm (or good either) ever seemed to result. But his activities hardly conduced to a coherent control of security policy.[11]

Despite Wigg's insignificant contribution to national security, for some time he saw Wilson more often than any other minister – more frequently even than the Chief Whip.[12] The frequency of their meetings was due chiefly to what Barbara Castle, who held a series of portfolios in the Wilson cabinet, called Wilson's 'obsession with "plots" against him'.[13] Wigg kept the Prime Minister up to date with plotting within, and sometimes outside, the Labour Party, as well as with sexual and other irregularities on Labour benches which might erupt into public scandals.[14]

Some of the material which Wigg supplied to the Prime Minister was bizarre. Early in Wilson's first administration, Wigg sent him a large envelope marked 'Not to be opened by female staff'. Understandably disregarding this curious instruction, the duty clerk, Anne Kiggell, now an Anglican priest, recalls opening the bottom of the envelope and re-moving from it the photograph of a public figure, whom she was able to identify, in the act of removing the corset of a female companion. She then replaced the photograph in the envelope, resealed it and sent it on to the Prime Minister.[15] The purpose of the photograph was presumably to alert Wilson to the possibility of a public scandal involving the man who appeared in it. It is difficult to imagine a more bizarre relationship between a prime minister and his security adviser than that between Wilson and Wigg. A decade later Wilson was to go to the extraordinary lengths of personally hiring private detectives to follow Wigg to the home of his (Wigg's) mistress and illegitimate child.[16] Soon afterwards Wigg was stopped a number of times for kerb-crawling, on one occasion – according to police evidence – accosting six women in the Park Lane area of London in the space of only twenty minutes.[17]

Despite Wigg's unpopularity on Labour benches in the Commons, he caused few problems to the Security Service. At his first meeting with Hollis in October 1964, Sir Frank Soskice assured the DG that he 'did not propose ever to ask to see Security Service files or their contents, nor to ask for the source of our information'. Wigg gave the same assurance, though adding the self-important claim that he 'did get a good deal of information about security' from his own sources. 'All he intended to do with it', however, 'was to hand it to [Hollis] and he would not expect to be told what action was to be taken on it.'[18] At the end of his three years as paymaster general, Wigg wrote to thank the DG (by then Furnival Jones) for the 'wonderful support' he had received from the Service: 'You have enlisted me as a supporter and whenever the wellbeing of the Security Service is an issue I shall be on your side.'[19]

Wigg's confidence in the Security Service merely served to strengthen the suspicions of some of his fellow ministers. Even the law officers of the Wilson government believed that the Security Service kept files on them as a matter of routine. Lord Gardiner, the Lord Chancellor, had been told by an unidentified and misinformed informant some years earlier that, on joining the cabinet, ministers were allowed to see their own files. On taking office, he therefore asked for his Security Service file, 'thinking that this would give me a good opportunity to judge the efficacy of MI5. After all, I would be able to judge what they said about me in comparison with what I knew about myself.' When his department failed to obtain the non-existent file, Gardiner went to see the Home Secretary.[20] Despite his legal expertise and personal charm, Soskice was, in the view of his successor Roy Jenkins, 'a remarkably bad Home Secretary' – 'extremely indecisive' with 'practically no political sense'.[21] Both these failings were in evidence when the Lord Chancellor asked to see his file. Soskice wrongly assumed that such a file existed but was unwilling to reveal to Gardiner that he had given Hollis an assurance that he would never ask to see the contents of *any* Security Service file. Soskice's response to the Lord Chancellor's request was thus confused. According to Gardiner: 'Frank Soskice was embarrassed and said that he couldn't agree and that he wasn't allowed to see the files either. When they wanted to show him anything, they photographed a page and gave it to him but he never saw the complete file. He was so upset about it that I just let it drop.'[22]

Soskice's embarrassment reinforced the Lord Chancellor's suspicions about the Security Service. Gardiner later revealed that he 'thought it more likely than not that MI5 was bugging the telephones in my office'. When he had really confidential business to discuss with the Attorney General, Sir Elwyn Jones, he would ask his chauffeur to drive them around during their discussion, confident that 'she would never have allowed the car to be bugged without my knowledge.'[23] The law officers' naivety was as breathtaking as their ignorance. Had the Security Service really decided to break the law and bug the Lord Chancellor's car, it is scarcely likely that the chauffeur would have seen them do it. Most extraordinary of all is the fact that, though the law officers thought it 'more likely than not' that the Security Service was acting illegally in breach of its charter, they believed themselves powerless to prevent the Service breaking the law. From such bizarre delusions by Labour ministers, Tony Benn drew the alarming conclusion 'that there is no political control whatsoever over the security services. They regard a Minister – even the Home Secretary – as a transitory person, and they would feel under no obligation to reveal information to him.'[24]

The most senior minister on whom the Security Service did have a file (though not one based on active investigation) was the Prime Minister himself.[25] Hollis must have been relieved when, at their first meeting on 9 November, Wilson failed to follow the Lord Chancellor's example and inquire about his file. The DG tried to allay Wilson's suspicions by insisting that the Service strictly observed the restrictions of its directive and avoided 'Party political matters'.[26] Wilson is unlikely to have been entirely convinced. Though he probably did not know the full story, he may well have discovered from Wigg that in August 1961 the then Labour leader, Hugh Gaitskell, and his closest associates had sought Security Service assistance in tracking down 'crypto-Communists' on Labour benches.[27] Wilson questioned Hollis about 'an official at Labour Party Headquarters who claimed to be in contact with the Security Service and to be compiling a black list. Did I know anything about this? I said I did not and that I would be very surprised if it were true.'[28] The official whom Wilson had in mind was probably John Franklin Clarke, administrative officer at Labour HQ in Transport House, whom – doubtless with Gaitskell's approval – Gordon Walker had suggested in 1961 as a reliable working-level contact for the Security Service. The Service, however, did not take up the suggestion.[29]

Soon after Wilson took office, Sir Burke Trend 'told him in general terms about the use of microphones and similar techniques to obtain intelligence in the U.K.'.[30] Wilson was 'anxious that Ministers should not be told about the techniques although some, including the Home Secretary, the Foreign Secretary and the Commonwealth Secretary, should occasionally see the product'.[31] Wilson's developing fascination with bugging, which a decade later was to become an obsession,[32] was reflected in his belief that, when he was on holiday in the Isles of Scilly, a Russian SIGINT-gathering trawler was monitoring his phone calls – as indeed may have happened. Wilson amused himself by devising cryptic messages, such as 'The fox has a black cloak,' designed to confuse Soviet intelligence. When the zip on his shorts jammed after swimming, he declared for the benefit of any KGB eavesdropper: 'You can tell the Russians there are no flies on the British Prime Minister.'[33]

Early in 1965 Wilson raised the question of telephone checks on MPs. On 3 March Hollis told Soskice that 'during the last few years 4 M.Ps had been on check, 3 from the Labour Party and 1 Conservative.'

We then proceeded to No. 10 and saw the Prime Minister, who said he was very strongly opposed to tapping the telephones of M.Ps. The Home Secretary said that he was satisfied that the Security Service had asked for such facilities in the case of M.Ps only in the most exceptional circumstances and that, in each case, the Home Secretary had been consulted and had authorised interception for a strictly limited period only. He mentioned the fact that 4 M.Ps had been on check and the proportion as between the political parties, and the Prime Minister accepted his advice that it would be wrong to ask for names ... In reply to a direct question [from the Prime Minister], I gave him an assurance that telephones to the Houses of Parliament were never tapped.[34]

Soskice had just signed an HOW on the left-wing Labour MP Bob Edwards, who was later revealed by Oleg Gordievsky to be a long-term KGB agent. Wilson, however, countermanded the warrant, thus probably delaying Edwards's discovery by over a decade. Late in 1965 Edwards became chairman of the Defence, Foreign and Commonwealth Affairs Sub-Committee of the Parliamentary Estimates Committee and in 1966 vice chairman of the Western European Union (WEU) Defence Committee. The Security Service later concluded that 'Both would have been of interest to the KGB and there is no doubt Edwards would have passed on all he could get hold of. We know Edwards' motivation was ideological, though he occasionally accepted money ...'[35]

Despite his reluctance to allow the investigation of MPs and trade unionists suspected of links with the KGB and his slighting references to what he called MI5's 'gentlemen in raincoats and black boots', Wilson came to depend on Security Service intelligence on industrial subversion. In May 1966, two months after an election victory had raised its majority in the Commons from three to ninety-seven, the Labour government was 'blown off course' by a strike called by the National Union of Seamen (NUS) which threatened to cripple overseas trade and wreck the government's prices and incomes policy. Wilson's last-minute attempt to avert the strike by summoning the seamen's leaders to Number Ten on 13 May ended with acrimonious accusations that he was supporting capitalist shipowners against the workers.[36]

F1A (counter-subversion) later recalled that the Security Service initially regarded the seamen's strike as 'a straightforward industrial dispute – nothing to do with us'. Then two NUS militants were overheard by A2A transcribers visiting the CPGB's King Street headquarters to ask the Party's chief industrial organizer, Bert Ramelson, for advice on how to run the strike: 'From the day-to-day coverage of King Street it was clear they were

getting quite a lot of advice.'[37] The advice they were given was decided by
Ramelson in consultation with the Party leader, Johnny Gollan, and the
Political Committee.[38] A4 began surveillance of several NUS leaders to
obtain evidence of their contacts with Communist 'trouble makers'.[39] Following two reports by F1A to the Cabinet Office on CPGB involvement
in the seamen's strike, he and the DG, Furnival Jones, were summoned to
see Sir Burke Trend, who then decided to inform the Prime Minister of the
intelligence the Service was obtaining. F1A, Furnival Jones and Director F
briefed Wilson and Wigg in the Cabinet Room.[40]

From 24 May onwards, the Security Service provided both the Prime
Minister and the Home Secretary with regular reports on the seamen's
strike,[41] which convinced Wilson that the NUS was controlled by an inner
core of Communist militants who were manipulating the strike for their
own subversive purposes. No previous Prime Minister had shown such
enthusiasm for regular up-to-the-minute Service reports during an industrial dispute. He was sometimes briefed daily, or even twice daily, by
varying combinations of Furnival Jones, Director F and F1A.[42] The
briefings were conducted in the greatest secrecy with the door between
Wilson's office and that of his political secretary, Marcia Williams, kept
locked.[43] Director F already had a reputation as a popular briefer with a
more extrovert manner when dealing with Whitehall audiences than most
of his Service colleagues; Wilson's private secretary Michael Halls, who
had heard him speak on previous occasions, called him 'Comic Cuts'.[44]
Director F was worried by the 'danger that the Government would look at
these problems through Communist eyes as we were forced to do' and take
too little account of the non-Communist influences on the strike which
MI5's charter did not allow it to cover.[45]

On 26 May, following Wilson's decision to declare a state of emergency,
eavesdropping in King Street revealed that the CPGB Political Committee
had set up a secret committee, headed by Ramelson, to co-ordinate Party
activities in support of the strike.[46] The first meeting of this committee
monitored by the Service decided to campaign for the recall of the NUS
Executive Council with the aim of persuading it to transfer control of the
strike, so far as movements of ships within port were concerned, from the
National Disputes Committee, on which the Party was not represented, to
the strike committee which had Communist members. It was announced a
few days later that the Executive was to be recalled.[47] On 3 June the bugging
of King Street revealed the decision of the CPGB Political Committee
that, for the strike to succeed, it had to be expanded. Ramelson was also
overheard reporting that he was to meet the Communist chairman of the

NUS Negotiation Committee, Gordon Norris, at 4.30 p.m. that day, and would press on him the need for the militants on the NUS Executive Council, whatever the outcome of a court of inquiry into the strike, to oppose any return to work without 'a satisfactory agreement' – one, in other words, which defied the government's prices and incomes policy. Norris was also to be told that the Executive Council must be persuaded as a matter of urgency to 'black' all oil tankers arriving in the UK and ask the International Transport Workers Federation (ITF) to black all British ships arriving in foreign ports. Whether or not as a result of Norris's persuasion, the Executive Council did indeed declare the court of inquiry's proposals insufficient to justify a return to work, and agreed to black the use of foreign oil tankers to replace strike-bound British tankers, as well as to appeal to the ITF to black all British ships in foreign ports.[48]

On 10 June, at a meeting attended by Wigg, Trend, the DG and F1A (but not by Roy Jenkins, the Home Secretary), 'The Prime Minister opened the discussion by expressing his satisfaction with the series of intelligence reports submitted . . .'[49] When passing on Wilson's warm thanks to the Service, FJ singled out for praise the secretaries, transcribers and officers of A Branch: 'I know that many have worked early and late during the past three weeks.'[50] By 10 June eavesdropping revealed that King Street realized that its efforts to extend the strike on behalf of the NUS through the other unions, notably the Transport and General Workers Union (TGWU), had failed, and that it must concentrate its efforts on bringing about a stoppage in all British docks with or without official union support.[51]

Despite the fact that the Security Service played a more active part in briefing the government than during any previous industrial dispute, Roy Jenkins as home secretary was scarcely involved.[52] George Wigg played a much more active role. When Director F took the latest situation report to Sir Burke Trend in the Cabinet Office on the morning of Saturday 11 June, the day of the Queen's Birthday Parade, Trend asked him to wait until after the parade (of which he had an excellent view) to speak to the Prime Minister and Paymaster General. Wigg was the first to arrive and briefed Director F on his use of the media in an attempt to discredit the strike. Impressed by John Freeman's celebrated television interview with the ETU president Frank Foulkes during the ballot-rigging scandal six years earlier,[53] Wigg reported that, as well as arranging for ITV coverage of a strike meeting in the docks that morning, he had made 'tentative' arrangements for Gordon Norris, and possibly Ramelson as well, to be interviewed on television that evening. Wigg had ensured that he would supply all the questions for the interview. Director F was appalled:

I said I thought this was not a very happy project and compared it with the ETU case. There were two main difficulties. In the ETU case they had a first-rate interviewer in the form of John Freeman and although Foulkes had, in fact, stood up well in the beginning he finally cracked because he was trying to hide corruption in his union. In the present case, Norris and, for that matter, [the dockers' leader, Jack] Dash, who are quite open Communists, had nothing to hide because they behaved with reasonable correctitude throughout the strike. Norris, moreover, was something of a personality and, if he was put on TV, the result might be in his favour instead of the other way round.

The probably crestfallen Wigg accepted Director F's arguments but said that he had 'already made certain overtures to the Press, which he could not withdraw'. When Wilson arrived after a party which followed the Birthday Parade, he agreed with Director F and ordered that no further action be taken until after the weekend. In Director F's view, however, Wigg's influence on coverage of the strike in the following day's *Sunday Times* was 'obvious'.[54]

On 20 June, after the strike had dragged on for six weeks without an end in sight, Wilson denounced the seamen's leaders in the Commons as a 'tightly knit group of politically motivated men' – a phrase, like other parts of his speech, coined by the Security Service.[55] F1A, the chief drafter, was present in the Chamber, occupying one of the three seats below the Speaker's chair reserved for civil servants who may be needed to brief ministers. He remembers it as 'one of the most fascinating days of my life'.[56] The Communists, Wilson declared, had at their disposal 'an efficient and disciplined industrial apparatus controlled by headquarters':

No major strike occurs anywhere in this country in any sector of industry in which the apparatus does not concern itself . . . For some years the Communist Party have had as one of their objectives the building up of a position of strength, not only in the seamen's unions, but in others concerned with docks and transport.

The central figure, Wilson declared, following his Security Service brief, was the CPGB's industrial organizer, Bert Ramelson. He gave details of Ramelson's staff, his contacts in the NUS and the address where he met them.[57] 'I couldn't find anyone in the Cabinet who thought it very clever,' a sceptical Barbara Castle told her diary. 'Elwyn [Jones, the Attorney General] and Roy Jenkins [the Home Secretary] both assured me they had not been consulted.' Next day Wilson informed the cabinet that he and Ray Gunter, the Minister of Labour, believed that, but for 'outside pressures', many members of the NUS Executive would have supported a return to work. When Mrs Castle asked 'if we could be given more details of the conspiracy', Wilson replied that 'there were some things that were better not revealed even to the Cabinet.'[58] Crossman, like Castle, suspected 'Wiggery-pokery'.[59] Wilson's speech was better received outside Westminster. It either coincided with or helped to prompt a change of mood in the NUS. The moderates in the leadership voted down the 'extremists' and the strike was called off at the end of June.[60]

Labour suspicions of the Security Service were revived by the sensational, though garbled, revelation on 15 February 1967 of the attempt in 1961 by the then Labour leadership to seek the Service's assistance in tracking down crypto-Communists among Labour MPs. Chapman Pincher wrongly claimed in the *Daily Express* that the approach by the Party leadership had prompted a major Security Service investigation: 'The enquiry lasted many months. The standard methods employed in such enquiries involve surveillance, the tapping of phones and the opening of mail.'[61] In reality none of these methods had been used against a single Labour MP on the 1961 leadership list of 'crypto-Communists'. Wilson had already been enraged by Pincher's campaign against Labour defence cuts which, as Pincher later acknowledged, used 'as many embarrassing leaks from angry service chiefs as possible',[62] and suspected that the latest story might be the result of a plot between Pincher and the Secretary of the D-Notice Committee, Colonel L. G. 'Sammy' Lohan. The Home Office PUS Sir Philip Allen did not take Wilson's conspiracy theory seriously, telling the DG 'it was difficult to see how [Lohan] could possibly have come into the picture.'[63]

When Pincher published another front-page attack on the Labour government in the *Daily Express* on 21 February, Wilson came close to losing self-control. The article accused him of using 'Big Brother methods' and moving towards 1984-style surveillance by demanding copies of all cables and overseas telegrams for inspection by the security authorities. Wilson was convinced that the publication of this story should have been prevented by a D-Notice and was convinced there had been collusion between Pincher and Lohan. Marcia Williams wrote later: 'Now began the time when Number Ten was dominated by the D-notice affair . . . We all became obsessed with the matter. The whole lamentable affair . . . hung like a heavy cloud over us for many months. It . . . sapped the energy of the Prime Minister and his morale.'[64] Wilson's conspiracy theory, as on other occasions, turned out to have little foundation. Lohan, instead of colluding with Pincher, had tried to dissuade him from publishing the article, though admitting that it did not breach any D-Notice.[65] Under

Opposition pressure, Wilson agreed to hand the matter over to a committee of Privy Counsellors chaired by Lord Radcliffe. But when the committee found in favour of Pincher, the Prime Minister refused to accept its findings. Wilson accused Lohan of 'overclose association with journalists and especially with Mr Chapman Pincher', then fired him.[66] After lengthy research into this bizarre episode, the official historian of the D-Notice Committee later concluded: 'One is left with a strong image of a Prime Minister at bay, alone in his study except for his faithful bloodhound George Wigg occasionally licking his writing hand.'[67]

Chapman Pincher's source for his story about the search for crypto-Communists on Labour benches had been George Brown, and his informant about cable interception a disaffected former employee of two cable companies.[68] Wilson, however, appears to have harboured suspicions that the Security Service was somehow involved. Even the Home Secretary, Roy Jenkins, who did not share Wilson's conspiratorial mindset, seems to have suspected on this occasion that the Service had been up to no good. On 24 February the DDG, Anthony Simkins, was summoned to see Jenkins and his PUS. The Home Secretary asked for, and received, an assurance that two recent applications for HOWs did not have a 'political inspiration' intended to damage the Prime Minister. Jenkins also said that Jackie Kennedy's sister, Princess Lee Radziwill, 'was positive that their telephone was tapped when President and Mrs Kennedy stayed with them in 1961' during their visit to Britain. Simkins assured the Home Secretary, without perhaps entirely convincing him, that the Radziwills' phone had never been tapped. Jenkins said that he was anxious to reduce the number of HOWs in operation.[69] Obituaries after Jenkins's death plausibly reported that his numerous love affairs had included one with Lee Radziwill.[70]

As well as causing severe damage, never wholly repaired, to Wilson's once excellent relations with the media, the D-Notice affair also helped to terminate Wigg's career as Wilson's security adviser. Probably like a majority of the cabinet, Castle and Crossman concluded that 'The evil genius had once again been George Wigg – "Harold's Rasputin".'[71] It seems likely that Wilson too put some of the blame on Wigg for what he realized in retrospect had been a major error of judgement. In November 1967 Wigg was appointed chairman of the Horserace Betting Levy Board, resigned as both paymaster general and MP and was made a life peer. With Wigg's departure, Wilson lost his main early-warning system of potential scandals on Labour benches, in particular within the cabinet. The head of the civil service, Sir Laurence Helsby, informed the DG that Wilson wanted to know: 'How would chit-chat about the activities of Ministers now reach the Prime Minister?' Furnival Jones, predictably, declined to help, telling Helsby: 'I hoped that I would not be instructed to seek out or report on information on the morals of Ministers unless there were some security aspect to them.'[72] Wilson's interest in 'chit-chat' extended to the staff at Number Ten. In July 1968 the Prime Minister informed FJ via the newly appointed head of the home civil service, Sir William Armstrong, that his private and political secretary, Marcia Williams (later Lady Falkender), was expecting a child by the political correspondent of the *Daily Mail*, Walter Terry. The DG was asked to make inquiries about Terry and replied that nothing to his detriment was known. Armstrong and FJ then jointly agreed that the Prime Minister should be advised not to keep Mrs Williams as his secretary because of 'the obvious risk that sensitive information would leak from No. 10 to the Daily Mail. Even if Mrs Williams were the soul of discretion, the general public, if this became a scandal, would certainly think a risk existed.' Wilson rejected the advice.[73]

To his later regret, Wilson also rejected security advice about Jeremy Thorpe, who in 1967 became leader of the Liberal Party. Thorpe was aware from his early days in the Commons (if not before) that his career might be ended by sexual scandal. He wrote in 1961 to a gay lover he had met in San Francisco: 'How I adored S[an] F[rancisco]. SF has everything, & certainly is about the one city where a gay person can let down his defences and feel free and unhunted. If I'm ever driven out of public life in Britain for a gay scandal then I shall settle in SF!'[74] The risk of 'gay scandal' at a time when gay sex, even between consenting adults, was still illegal laid Thorpe open to the risk of blackmail, and it was this threat which led the Security Service to issue a warning to the Foreign Office early in Wilson's first administration when it was suggested that Thorpe join a group of experts with access to secret material who would advise the Foreign Secretary on policy to the United Nations.[75] In April 1965 Thorpe's friend and fellow Liberal MP Peter Bessell warned the Home Secretary, Sir Frank Soskice, 'that Thorpe's mother had received a letter from a young man [presumably claiming to be a gay lover] asking for £30 and making statements about his relations with Jeremy Thorpe'. Soskice informed the DG 'that this confirmed him in his belief that Thorpe should not be given any position which would give him access to Government secrets, and that we should report to the Home Secretary if it came to our notice that there was any intention to put him in any such position'.[76]

Following Thorpe's election as Liberal leader in January 1967, Furnival Jones informed Soskice's successor as home secretary, Roy Jenkins, of earlier complaints of 'buggery' made against Thorpe to the police by

Norman Scott (then known as Norman Josiffe), a sometime male model, while working as a horse trainer. Though Scott was regarded as unstable and likely to make an unreliable witness, the police attached 'some credence' to his allegations.[77] FJ told the Home Secretary: 'We had never investigated Thorpe and would not at all welcome a request to do so now.' Jenkins replied that 'Thorpe's homosexuality was common knowledge in the House.'[78]

Thorpe's predecessor as Liberal leader, Jo Grimond, had had to wait five years before being made a privy counsellor, with access under certain circumstances to classified information on national security. Despite the warnings from the Security Service, Wilson made Thorpe a privy counsellor only two months after he became Party leader. He did so partly because he enjoyed Thorpe's company. Marcia Williams later recalled that 'Harold and I used to giggle at his impersonations. He was a colourful addition to any dinner party.'[79]

After Wigg's departure from Number Ten, Wilson made clear his anxiety that there should be no interruption in the flow of intelligence on 'Communist activities in the industrial field', of which Wigg had previously been the most frequent conduit. The Prime Minister remained deeply interested in intelligence on industrial subversion. So did James Callaghan, who succeeded Jenkins at the Home Office in November 1967. In retirement Callaghan later sought to distance himself from the surveillance he had authorized as home secretary. According to his distinguished official biographer, Kenneth O. Morgan: 'No one ever needed to bug him. He also did what he could to prevent the bugging of others. Thus as Home Secretary he forbade MI5 from engaging in the surveillance of certain prominent trade union leaders and dismissed the idea that they were in any way security risks.'[80] This claim does not square with the evidence of Service files.

Speaking to Furnival Jones unofficially ('as a private citizen') on 7 March 1969, Callaghan said that he had 'two ploys in mind' to diminish Communist influence in the unions:

(a) To unseat [Hugh] Scanlon [the hard-left leader of the Amalgamated Engineering Union] and replace him by [John] Boyd at the next elections due in Spring 1970. He wanted to have a broadsheet printed and distributed unattributably. This involved getting damaging material together and arranging for its printing and distribution. Could the Security Service help?

(b) The governing body of the London Cooperative Society was now wholly Communist and some members suspected that [a leading official] was misappropriating some of the £80,000 p.a. that the Society was supposed to provide the Labour Party with for political purposes, either into his own pocket or the Morning Star [the Communist newspaper]. A body of members . . . was manoeuvring to unseat the present governing body and take over control. Could the Security Service help with information about this?

Somewhat taken aback, FJ replied that he would see 'whether we had any dirt on Scanlon' but 'thought the second question was getting perilously near the field of party politics', with which the Security Service had a duty not to become involved. Allen, the Home Office PUS, agreed with the DG that Callaghan's proposed 'ploy' to unseat Scanlon was 'rather alarming'. It was decided that FJ 'would assemble such intelligence as we had' which would assist the two 'ploys', but would take no further action until he heard from Allen.[81]

Both Wilson and Callaghan showed much the same ambivalence towards industrial intelligence, being keenly interested in obtaining 'damaging material' from eavesdropping operations on pro-Communist union leaders but at the same time reluctant to take the political risks of signing HOWs. On 19 November 1969 Furnival Jones discussed with Callaghan proposals for telephone checks on a number of trade unionists, chief among them Jack Jones of the TGWU and Ernie Roberts of the AEU.[82] Jones had been an open CPGB member from 1932 to 1941 and, the Service believed, did not leave the party until 1949. FJ reported (chiefly on the basis of eavesdropping at King Street) that there was 'no doubt that Jones, after fifteen years' disassociation from the Party, has resumed active and regular contact with it':

Ramelson, the Party's chief industrial organiser, claimed in August 1969 that Jones had said that although there would be tactical differences between himself and the Party, they were going in the same direction and wanted the same things . . . It has become clear that [Jones] is prepared to pass to the Party Government and other information which has been passed to him confidentially in his trade union capacity.[83]

FJ told Callaghan that the Czech StB defector to the United States, Josef Frolik, who had served in London in 1964-6, had revealed that he had been told to abandon his plan to cultivate Ernie Roberts on the grounds that he was already 'in touch with friends' (the KGB). Roberts had subsequently apologized to Frolik for causing him trouble: 'If Frolik did not form a mistaken impression this information would indicate that Roberts was a recruited agent by that time.'[84]

Callaghan did not challenge, or even query, the Service's assessment of

Jones and Roberts but was worried by the potential political fall-out of investigating either.[85] On 28 November FJ was informed by Sir Philip Allen that, after long discussion, Wilson and Callaghan had decided not after all to authorize a telecheck on Jack Jones: 'They felt that the case just fell short of what was required to justify such a delicate operation.'[86] Had the case involved a civil servant rather than a trade union leader, it is unlikely that they would have hesitated. Oleg Gordievsky later reported that Jones had been regarded by the KGB as an agent from 1964 to 1968, providing confidential Labour Party documents which he obtained as a member of the NEC and the Party's international committee as well as information on his colleagues and contacts. Though the KGB believed that Jones's motives were ideological, his case officer noted that he accepted, without visible enthusiasm, modest contributions towards holiday expenses. Jones broke contact with the KGB after the crushing of the Prague Spring by Soviet tanks in August 1968.[87]

Despite Labour's criticisms while in opposition of the laxity of Conservative policy on protective security, Wilson's government showed no great enthusiasm for it after its 1964 election victory. Wigg's intended role as a protective-security supremo who would ensure that 'security procedures were efficient and were kept up to date' came to nothing. The main initiative emerged instead from the Security Commission, which had been set up in the wake of the Profumo affair.[88] The Commission's first report[89] followed the conviction in 1965 of two heavily indebted mercenary spies, Frank Bossard, a project officer in the Guided Weapons (Research and Development) Division of the Ministry of Aviation recruited by the GRU,[90] and Peter Allen, a chief clerk at the MoD, who had contacted the United Arab Republic and Iraqi military attachés in London offering to supply top-secret documents for money.[91] Though C Branch, then headed by the future DG Michael Hanley, approved of most of the Security Commission's proposals, it argued strongly against a few recommendations which 'might be superficially attractive to the layman in that they might hamper or deter a spy, but which in practice the Public Service would find intolerable'. Chief among them was a proposal for periodic searches of civil servants. In January 1966 Harold Wilson announced that it had been decided not to pursue the Security Commission's proposal.[92]

The Commission returned to the charge in 1967 after the conviction of Helen Keenan, a secretary in the Cabinet Office, on charges of passing classified material to an agent of South African intelligence.[93] As well as reviving the proposal for periodic searches of staff, the Commission proposed that, in order to prevent the unauthorized removal of documents, officials should not be allowed to carry the keys to their own briefcases when they went to meetings in other government offices. Instead, designated officials in every government department would unlock briefcases at the beginning of every meeting and lock them at the end. C Branch believed that, as well as being remarkably cumbersome, these procedures also carried security risks. 'God help us', minuted Furnival Jones, 'if the Government accepts these proposals.' The government, however, required little persuasion from C Branch before turning the proposals down.[94]

The Security Commission was in action again after Douglas Britten, an RAF chief technician, was sentenced in 1968 to twenty-one years in jail for giving the KGB highly classified information from RAF signals units in Cyprus and Lincolnshire. Partly because Britten pleaded guilty, his case attracted only minimal publicity. A Security Commission inquiry after Britten's conviction, however, discovered a series of vetting failures. Twenty years earlier he had served six months' hard labour for fraud; since leaving prison he had had a history of financial problems and a record as an 'accomplished liar'.[95] By the time of the Commission's report, however, Whitehall had become seriously concerned by the cost of increasing protective security and was disinclined to fund further improvements. In 1968 a costing exercise, initiated by the head of the home civil service, Sir William Armstrong, estimated that the total cost might be £40 to £50 million a year, and that it was at present impossible to judge its cost effectiveness. At FJ's suggestion, a committee chaired by Armstrong's predecessor, Lord Helsby, was appointed in 1969 'to review the scope of protective security and review what changes if any are desirable'. The head of C4 (then physical and document security) was made secretary of the Committee – but to little effect. Though the Helsby Committee produced some radical proposals, few were implemented.[96]

Doubtless to Wilson's relief there were no spy cases during his first two administrations which came close to emulating the sensational publicity which had surrounded the trials of the Portland spy-ring and George Blake during the Macmillan government. The greatest espionage-related embarrassment of this period was Blake's escape from Wormwood Scrubs after serving only five years of his forty-two-year sentence. The escape, it was later discovered, had been made possible by three former prisoners who had befriended him in jail: the Irish Republican Sean Bourke and the peace protesters Michael Randle and Pat Pottle. On 22 October 1966 Blake knocked a loosened iron bar out of his cell window, slid down the roof outside and dropped to the ground, then climbed over the outer wall with a nylon rope-ladder thrown to him by Bourke. Blake was later driven, hidden in the Randle family Dormobile, to East Berlin, where he was joined by Bourke before continuing to Moscow.[97] Highly critical though press coverage of the jail-break was, Wilson was not greatly dismayed by it since the minister who attracted most press criticism was Roy Jenkins, whom he had identified as a potential rival. 'That', the Prime Minister told Dick Crossman, 'will do our Home Secretary a great deal of good. He is getting complacent and he needs taking down a peg.'[98] Jenkins later tried to put some of the blame on the Security Service: 'We thought Blake had probably been taken out through London Airport on the run, but in fact he went to ground in Paddington for several weeks. I consider that MI5 and the Special Branch contributed little skill to the attempt to find him.'[99] Security Service records tell a somewhat different story. FJ rang Jenkins's private secretary on 28 October to say that it was believed 'Blake had been in London at the beginning of the week' (not that he had made for Heathrow), and that information received by the Service had been passed to Scotland Yard.

Though spy scandals caused Wilson, unlike Macmillan, no significant political embarrassment, there were three cases involving Labour MPs (in addition to that of the as yet unidentified long-term KGB agent Bob Edwards) which would have caused a sensation if the media had discovered the Security Service investigation of them. The first was that of Bernard Floud, who had been elected MP for Acton in 1964. His case was part of a larger investigation into the possibility that before the Second World War Soviet intelligence had recruited a major spy-ring in Oxford as well as in Cambridge. One of the chief Oxford suspects was Floud, who had been an undergraduate at Wadham College from 1934 to 1937 and, though not formally a Party member, had been heavily involved in Communist campaigns. One of his Communist Oxford contemporaries, Jenifer Fischer Williams, revealed to the Security Service that Floud had advised her to join a civil service department from which she could secretly pass on valuable information to the CPGB, and had put her in touch with a Central European later identified as Arnold Deutsch, the recruiter and first controller of the Cambridge Five. (Ms Fischer Williams, who subsequently married Herbert Hart, wartime member of the Security Service and later professor of jurisprudence at Oxford University, also said that after a few clandestine meetings she had broken off contact with Deutsch.) The fact that in 1938 Floud had gone on a three-month visit to China with the leading Cambridge Communist James Klugmann strengthened D Branch's suspicions of him. D3 wrote in March 1966:

The case for suspecting that Floud may have worked for the Russians as a talent spotter when an undergraduate rests on his early association with James Klugmann – who is known to have so acted – and certain analogies between the two men's pre-war careers. It seems highly possible that what Klugmann was doing at Cambridge was echoed by Floud at Oxford. Floud's direction of Jenifer Fischer Williams . . . lends credence to this hypothesis.[100]

Further investigations concluded that, while Floud worked in the Ministry of Information from 1942 to 1945, the CPGB 'regarded him as an intelligent and amenable source of information'. At the post-war Board of Trade, where he rose to become assistant secretary, Floud was 'reported to have organised and taken part in secret meetings of Communist civil servants until some time in 1948', though there was no evidence of Communist involvement after 1952, by which time he had left the civil service.[101] In May 1966 the DG, Furnival Jones, reported to the PUS at the Home Office, Sir Charles Cunningham, 'On the face of it Mr Floud's record is disturbing and he may well be extremely sensitive about it.'[102]

In July 1966 Jenkins and Wilson authorized the Security Service to question Floud.[103] An ingenious variant of the soft man/hard man technique was devised for the start of the questioning on 4 August in a Service flat in South Audley Street. In Operation ROAST POTATO, A1 concealed a microphone in the flat which enabled the interview to be both recorded and monitored in real time at Leconfield House. The interview was to be begun by F4 (who used the name 'Derek Hammond') and listened to in Leconfield House by D3 (Peter Wright), who would turn up in the Service flat if he judged that a point had been reached at which Floud might be persuaded to confess by tougher questioning.[104] In the event, no such point was reached and Wright did not put in an appearance.[105] Floud began by asking if the interview was being taped. 'Hammond' replied untruthfully, as he felt bound to do, that he was 'not conscious of this'. Floud, who was apparently being considered for appointment as junior minister, was understandably anxious that the interview might prejudice his career prospects. He told 'Hammond' that he hoped the Prime Minister would not be informed that he was being investigated. 'After all,' he added, 'one is not wholly without ambition.' 'Hammond' found Floud 'uneasy, evasive and less than frank' about his Communist activities at Oxford and in the civil service:

The explanation of his drift away from Communism has a ring of truth about it – unless it is a subtle cover story – and could be genuine. If this is so, his wish not to tell us the whole truth about his Communist past and about any work he may have done for the R[ussian] I[ntelligence] S[ervice] could spring from a natural desire not to prejudice his new career as a politician.[106]

After two further interviews with Floud by 'Hammond' and Wright, questioning was suspended in January 1967 after the death of Floud's wife, a former student Communist whom he had met at Oxford.[107] Two final interviews took place in March. On the 17th Wright confronted Floud with Fischer Williams's account of his contacts with her at Oxford (largely confirmed by their Oxford contemporary Phoebe Pool, who had since become a colleague of Blunt at the Courtauld Institute).[108] According to Wright, Floud immediately became 'very agitated' and took some time to recover his composure, but did not 'break'.[109] At an interview three days later Floud was told that, because of lack of frankness about his past Communist associations, he was regarded as a 'full security risk' and could not therefore be given security clearance.[110] Floud can have been in little doubt that his prospects of a ministerial career had gone. Six months later he killed himself.[111] Press reports made no mention of his questioning by MI5, and his family were convinced, probably correctly, that his suicide was the result of long-term depressive illness (of which the Security Service seems to have been unaware), exacerbated by his wife's death.[112] The collapse of his ministerial ambitions, following his failure to gain security clearance, however, probably added to his despair.

Save for the personal tragedy with which it was associated, the investigation of Floud was of less importance than it seemed to the Security Service at the time. There was – and is – no evidence that he had any Communist contacts after 1952. His pre-war contacts with Soviet intelligence are also unlikely to have been of great significance, though it would have been very different if, after he had put Jenifer Fischer Williams in touch with Arnold Deutsch, she had decided to become a long-term penetration agent in the Home Office. She had been placed third out of 493 applicants in the 1936 civil service entrance examinations (the highest ranking so far obtained by a female candidate), quickly established herself as a high-flier, and in 1939 was appointed private secretary to the PUS at the Home Office, Sir Alexander Maxwell. In 1940 she was asked by the Director, Jasper Harker, who was unaware of her Communist background, to recommend the names of suitable recruits to the Security Service.[113] Had Fischer Williams become an NKVD agent, Harker's request would have represented an extraordinary recruitment opportunity for Soviet intelligence. It had been reasonable to speculate, when the Security Service investigation of Floud began, that he might have been a member of a major

Oxford spy-ring recruited before the Second World War on the Cambridge model. The investigation, however, uncovered no evidence of an Oxford recruitment remotely comparable in importance to the Cambridge Five.[114]

The Security Service was unaware, at the time when Floud committed suicide, that two other Labour MPs, one of them a minister, were agents of the Czech StB. As the Centre seems to have recognized, until the suppression of the Prague Spring by the tanks of the Warsaw Pact in August 1968 the StB residency in London was often more successful than the KGB in approaching British politicians and trade unionists, who tended to be both less suspicious of Czechoslovaks than of Russians and sympathetic to a people betrayed by the West at Munich in 1938.[115] The most worrying intelligence of StB penetration of parliament concerned the case of John Stonehouse, successively Parliamentary Secretary at the Ministry of Aviation, Parliamentary Under Secretary of State for the Colonies, Minister of Aviation, Minister of State for Technology, Postmaster General and Minister of Posts and Telecommunications in the Wilson government. In July 1969 US liaison reported that Josef Frolik had said during debriefing that, though he had never seen any StB report on Stonehouse, he was '90 per cent sure' that he was a Czech agent. When questioned by the Security Service in the United States on 1 August, Frolik no longer seemed '90 per cent sure'. He told his debriefers he was 'not sure that Stonehouse *is* an agent' – only that one of his StB colleagues had been ordered to make an approach to him. When Security Service investigators interviewed Stonehouse on 4 August, they found him 'as calm and assured as anyone in his position could be expected to be in the circumstances'. He dismissed any suggestion that he had ever assisted Czech intelligence in any way. The Service reported to the Prime Minister that 'There is no evidence that Mr Stonehouse gave the Czechs any information he should not have given them, much less that he consciously acted as an agent for the [StB].'[116] On the evidence available in 1969, that was a reasonable conclusion. It was, however, incorrect. A decade later another StB defector provided convincing evidence that Stonehouse had indeed been a Czech agent.[117] Had that information been available in 1969, Wilson would have been faced with an intelligence scandal worse than the Profumo affair.

Frolik's evidence in 1969 against another Labour politician, Will Owen, MP for Morpeth, was much more convincing. Though Owen's official StB codename was LEE, he was also known by its London residency as 'Greedy Bastard'. Frolik had seen some of Owen's product while stationed in London in the mid-1960s:

'Lee' was interested solely in the five hundred pounds a month retainer which we gave him . . . In spite of the obvious danger, he was always demanding free holidays in Czechoslovakia so that he might save the expense of having to pay for the vacation himself. He even went as far as pocketing as many cigars as possible whenever he came to the Embassy for a party.[118]

It may well have been Owen's close relations with the Czechoslovak embassy which had led the previous Labour leadership to place him at the top of its list of suspected crypto-Communists in 1961.[119] What neither the Labour leadership nor the Security Service had realized before Frolik's revelations, however, was that Owen was a long-serving Czechoslovak agent, recruited soon after his election in 1954 to the Commons by an StB officer working under diplomatic cover. Since then Owen had had regular meetings with successive case officers while taking his dog for an early-morning walk in London parks. Though only a backbencher, Owen became a member of the Commons Estimates Committee and provided what Frolik described as 'top-secret material of the highest value' on the British Army of the Rhine and the British contribution to NATO.[120]

When FJ informed the Prime Minister on 29 July 1969 of Frolik's evidence that Owen was an StB agent: '[Wilson] described Owen as "a drip" . . . saying that he was an ineffective member of the House, moderately intelligent but very naive. It would not in the least surprise him to learn that Owen would pass on to anyone any information that came his way.'[121] Telephone and letter checks combined with surveillance would have increased, probably greatly, the prospect of a successful prosecution – particularly in view of Owen's regular early-morning meetings with an StB officer in a London park. Over the next few months, however, 'The Prime Minister was emphatic that he would not authorise a telephone check at this stage.' Though Wilson conceded that he might authorize one after Owen had been questioned,[122] a telecheck then would inevitably have been less productive because Owen would have realized he was under suspicion. Wilson's motives for thus diminishing the chances of a successful prosecution were probably twofold. First, as in the case of union leaders, he feared the potential for political embarrassment in what was expected to be an election year. Secondly, he had given an assurance to the Commons that 'there was to be no tapping of the telephones of Members of Parliament' and that, if developments required a change in this policy, he would make a statement to the House when the security of the country permitted. Wilson therefore feared that he would have to tell the House, possibly before the election, that he had authorized the tapping of an MP's phone.[123]

The Legal Adviser, Bernard Sheldon, however, obtained the consent of the Attorney General, Sir Elwyn Jones, to a search warrant and police interrogation of Owen. When Owen was questioned in January 1970, he made a partial admission – acknowledging that he had been paid by Czech officials for information he had provided over a period of years, but claiming that he had only done so under pressure and denying that he had ever handed over classified information. When examination of his bank account revealed large sums on which he had never paid tax, he decided not to fight the next election and resigned his seat in April – thus greatly diminishing the political embarrassment to the Labour Party. Frolik was flown over from the United States with a CIA escort to give evidence at Owen's trial on official secrets charges in May under the pseudonym 'Mr A'. Though Frolik feared he might be poisoned while in London by his former StB or KGB colleagues, the Service considered that he performed well in the witness box. Since, however, he had seen none of the classified documents allegedly handed over by Owen, the judge dismissed this crucial part of his evidence as hearsay and therefore inadmissible. The defence successfully maintained that Owen was a foolish old man who, under pressure, had given information to the Czechs but had never betrayed classified information. Though Owen was acquitted, he emerged discredited from a case which both judge and defence counsel said had been properly brought.[124]

Section E
The Later Cold War

Introduction

The Security Service and its Staff in the Later Cold War

The aloof management style of two successive DGs, Sir Martin Furnival Jones, and his predecessor, Sir Roger Hollis, combined with the unprecedented investigations of Hollis and Mitchell on suspicion of being Soviet agents, built up strong support within the Home Office in favour of an outside appointment following FJ's retirement in 1972. The PUS, Sir Philip Allen, told the Home Secretary, Reggie Maudling, in January 1972, 'My own view is that the Service would benefit from a breath of fresh air, and that it would particularly benefit from someone who had some political nous.'[1] The case for a DG with 'political nous' was reinforced by the fact that the Prime Minister, Edward Heath, had taken a personal dislike to FJ at their first meeting after his election victory in June 1970.[2] Allen's candidate for the succession was a senior Home Office official, J. H. Waddell, who was considered unlucky not to have become a PUS.[3] The main argument against an outsider, as Allen acknowledged, was the malign precedent set a quarter of a century earlier by Sir Percy Sillitoe, who 'had a distinguished record as a Chief Constable, but was pretty disastrous as Director General of the Security Service'.[4]

At a meeting with Maudling on 5 January 1972 FJ argued against an outside appointment with some passion and 'at very considerable length'. 'Members of the Service', he insisted, 'were not civil servants . . . They were a professional body who ought to be professionally led – just like the Army or the Police.' In addition to the effect on Service morale:

To appoint an amateur at this stage would have a bad effect on our allies . . . At the moment, MI5 was regarded in the USA, Western Europe and the old British Commonwealth as being the best Security Service in the Free World, and arguably better than the KGB. This was because it was professionally staffed and had been professionally led for the last 18 years. It was the Service which was the most favoured by the CIA (the Israeli secret service being next). All this would be badly affected if an appointment were now made from outside, and the head of CIA would regard such an appointment as showing that the powers that be in this country thought there was something wrong with MI5.

FJ countered Home Office claims that the Service 'would benefit from a breath of fresh air' by linking them to similar statements by the discredited Sillitoe:

Sir Percy Sillitoe had said in his memoirs that the Security Service were 'a bunch of introverts', and other people had said that they would benefit from a breath of fresh air. Furnival Jones refuted both statements which he thought were nonsense. Their recruits tended to be fairly mature, with experience of the outside world; a good many of them were extroverts.[5]

The DG's arguments failed to make any impression on the Home Secretary, who wrote to the Prime Minister recommending the Home Office candidate as the next DG. Heath, however, after speaking to FJ, 'saw some force in the argument that the Service be professionally led'.[6] At interview, Heath found Waddell 'if anything too balanced and careful' to make a good DG and preferred the internal candidate, Michael Hanley, currently DDG: 'It had been suggested that he might be a little heavy-footed; but I must say that was not the judgement I formed in our admittedly short talk.'[7] Hanley was a large, powerfully built man who had acquired the nickname 'Jumbo' early in his career, and was 'amazed' to discover how small Heath was: 'He sized me up. Asked me a few personal questions. I hit it off with him, always did.'[8] On discovering that he had been overruled by the Prime Minister and that Hanley was to be the next DG, Maudling simply 'shrugged his shoulders'.[9]

Hanley was a less remote DG than his two immediate predecessors (or his two immediate successors). When Stella Rimington returned to work in 1971 from maternity leave, she 'was surprised to be called into [Hanley's] office to be welcomed back to work and to the counter-espionage branch. His kindly interest was unusual in those days when personal contact between directors and junior staff was rare.'[10] As DG, Hanley said later, 'I made a point of circulating but I did not do enough.'[11] Director B had noted in 1971: 'We are committed to a significant expansion in the size of the Service, primarily in K Branch and our operational resources.' Because of numerous retirements of wartime and post-war recruits and the drying up of some traditional sources of staff, particularly from the colonial administration of the now nearly defunct British Empire, Director B argued that the Service 'could be required to make a major change in recruitment by seeking officer candidates among graduates leaving university'.[12] Some continued to oppose direct entry from university, among them B2, who argued that 'Officers require qualities of maturity, common sense and knowledge of the world, which are rarely to be found in young men.'[13] From 1975 to 1979, however, an average of fifteen staff officers a year were recruited direct from university.[14]

In 1976 testing was introduced to assess applicants' potential. The tests were a curious mixture of current business practice and occasional throwbacks to a bygone era. Candidates were subjected to the American 'Wonderlic' test: fifty questions to be answered in only twelve minutes, which purported to measure verbal ability, numeracy and analytical skill. Though Kell would probably have been appalled by Wonderlic, he would have had more sympathy with a drafting exercise in which candidates were asked to imagine that they were the personal assistant to a wealthy landowner and had been instructed to write a letter designed to return to his possession 'a beautifully inlaid desk which had been given to one of his ancestors by George IV'.[15] After preliminary sifting and testing, officer selection was by interview and final selection board.[16]

Training section moved from B Branch to the newly formed S Branch in 1976. The first step towards structured training was taken with the introduction of a four-week induction course under the direction until 1980 of an extrovert K Branch investigator, who was seldom without a black cigarette holder which she used for dramatic gestures as well as for smoking brown More cigarettes. 'Her performance in training section', it was noted, 'won huge praise from the start.'[17] One of her former pupils describes the use of the word 'performance' as unusually apt.[18] Those taking her course arrived at Grosvenor Street, next door to the Estée Lauder salon, where they were given lectures on the 'Threat of Espionage' and 'Counter-Espionage', illustrated with slides of Philby, Burgess and Maclean, and were shown a film entitled *Sweetie Pie*, depicting a lonely secretary being cultivated by a scheming Soviet agent. They also went on a surveillance exercise, and were introduced to letter checks by being taken to see the Post Office Investigation Department steaming open envelopes with giant kettles. Agent-running courses for new entrants started in 1975 and rudimentary management training began in 1977.[19]

Those members of the Security Service who were least happy with its management, recruitment and training at the start of the Hanley era were the female graduates, who felt – one of them recalls – that they were expected 'to develop into good NCOs' rather than senior managers.[20] Their views were shared by many professional women throughout British society, who complained of the 'glass ceiling' which kept them out of top jobs and the 'golden pathway' to promotion signposted by and for men. Expectations in Whitehall were raised by the introduction in January 1971 of a new civil service training grade for both male and female honours graduates direct from university.[21] The Service failed to follow suit. Growing resentment among its female graduates led to a meeting in November 1972 to discuss a petition (known to some as the 'Women's Charter') complaining against the career discrimination to which they were subject.[22] One of the women present believes the meeting was bugged and is convinced she heard the 'blow back' from the microphone.[23] Some signed the petition; others recorded their general agreement with its contents.[24] One of the signatories later acknowledged: 'Our meeting caused some justified ill-feeling amongst the non-graduate women; they should have been included, as the lack of career prospects affected them as much as us. However, we, being young and thoughtless, had not considered this.'[25]

One of the women not invited was widely reported to have said of the rebellious graduates, 'My dear, they're ten a penny! If they don't like it, they can leave.'[26] The petition became known to male management as 'The Women's Revolt'. Some male responses to the 'Revolt' were sympathetic; others recalled by one of the signatories included the following: 'Are you *preaching* about your *rights*?'; 'You're just like my daughters, always saying: "It's not fair!" Life isn't fair and you've just got to accept it'; 'You mustn't, ah, lose your sense of humour about this . . .'; and 'Think of Milicent Bagot!' The implication of the last remark was 'that at the merest whiff of power, all women would undergo a Hydran transformation into Milicent Bagot clones, which would then terrorise the Office'.[27]

The biggest obstacle to female promotion was the general conviction throughout the British intelligence community that women were unsuitable for agent-running (despite the fact that the leading atom spy Klaus Fuchs, before leaving Britain for Los Alamos, had been successfully run by a female GRU controller). The minutes of a meeting in February 1973, attended by the DG, DDG and senior staff (all male), to discuss the qualities required of agent-runners record: 'It was the unanimous view of the meeting (supported by MI6 experience) that agent-running was predominantly a male preserve,' though the married male agent-runner ('ideally not a teetotaller') would be helped by having 'a "conscious" and understanding wife'.[28] The only woman selected for the first agent-running training course in 1973 was Stella Rimington, later the first female DG.[29] Rimington believed that, in the aftermath of 'The Women's Revolt', senior management 'were genuinely surprised at the strength of feeling and sufficiently concerned that so many of their good female staff, essential to the running of the Service, appeared to be disgruntled, that the policy was changed'. A number of female assistant officers, Rimington among them, were promoted to full officer rank and women began, like men, to be recruited at officer level,[30] a policy change accelerated by the 1975 Sex Discrimination Act. In 1978 women were allowed to become agent-runners. Rimington was one of the first. Her first agent, however, was a Soviet Bloc seaman who initially refused to see a female case officer. Just when Rimington was beginning to imagine a return to a desk-bound existence, he changed his mind.[31]

Even for most female graduates, office life in the 1970s did not revolve around gender warfare. One of the prime movers of the 'Women's Charter', despite her justified grievances about promotion prospects, found the Security Service, 'principally because of the people, a good place to work, and I got on well with c.99% of those with whom I dealt'.[32] A sense of humour remained a valued characteristic of Service work culture.[33] In the corridors of power, however, the image of the Service was quite different. In their limited contacts with the rest of Whitehall, desk officers usually had to deal with unwelcome matters involving security risks and security lapses. They thus tended to impress some of their official contacts, such as the diplomat George Walden, not as a Service which prized its sense of humour but as 'a rather repressed group of people, suffering from low morale on account of how nobody understood them, still less the trouble they'd seen'.[34]

In the mid-1970s the Service, already dispersed in a number of buildings around central London, suddenly found itself with an accommodation crisis. In 1974 Great Universal Stores, landlords of 15/17 Great Marlborough Street, unexpectedly gave notice that the Service's lease, due to expire in 1977, would not be renewed. Late in 1975 the Service began moving into drab new headquarters at Babcock House at the northern end of Gower Street. Simultaneously, it began planning a large new computer installation at Curzon Street House, a bunker-like building at the opposite end of the street from Leconfield House, formerly occupied by the Department of Education and Science, to which the Registry and A and F Branches, together with the vetting section of C Branch, moved in March 1977.[35] In addition to the installation of a new main-frame computer, the paper-filing system, which had changed little since the war, was updated by the introduction of an ingenious miniature single-track railway used for moving files around the building.[36] Unable to find a headquarters large enough to house all its staff, by the mid-1980s the Service occupied nine separate buildings scattered around central London. A fleet of vans was required to run a continuous shuttle service ferrying often highly classified files from building to building, sometimes resulting in urgently needed papers being stuck in Mayfair traffic jams.[37]

When Hanley was asked after his retirement what he thought he had achieved during his six years as DG, he replied: 'I was on the Whitehall map – certainly a change!' His easiest Whitehall relationships were with successive Home Secretaries, which he called 'my bread and butter'. During the Heath government he began the practice of seeing the Home Secretary monthly. Though the regular monthly meetings lapsed when Labour returned to power in 1974, Hanley and the new Home Secretary, Roy Jenkins, got on well,[38] and Jenkins sometimes invited him to lunch at his London club, Brooks's.[39] When Jenkins was succeeded by Merlyn Rees in 1976, he told Hanley in a handwritten letter: 'I enjoyed working with you.'[40] Rees resumed the practice of monthly meetings with the DG.[41]

Hanley made much less effort to cultivate the rest of Whitehall. As deputy head of the Permanent Under Secretary's Department at the FCO (the Foreign Office had merged with the Commonwealth Office in 1968) and responsible for liaison with the Security Service, David Goodall found the DG 'a bit of a bruiser'.[42] Though he always attended Joint Intelligence Committee meetings, Hanley later admitted that they 'bored me stiff'.[43] It is likely that he communicated his boredom to colleagues on the JIC. 'He was', recalled one of his directors, a 'good bull in a china shop sort of fellow and he did not mince his words.'[44] While Hanley 'hit it off' with Heath, by his own admission he did not hit it off with the Wilson and Callaghan governments: 'I didn't think much of them, not that I'm anti-Labour – on the contrary – but I thought they were just amateurish.' Though Hanley later admitted that he made too little effort to establish good relations with Number Ten, winning over Harold Wilson was probably beyond his power. During Wilson's second term from 1974 to 1976, he became preoccupied with what the cabinet secretary, Sir John Hunt, called 'paranoiac suspicions' of a Security Service plot against him.[45] Hanley had what he acknowledged was 'a terrible row' with Wilson. James Callaghan (whom Hanley privately described as a 'bull frog') and the DG also disliked each other.[46]

'I was quite unhappy', Callaghan said later, 'with the way in which [Hanley] was conducting [MI5's] affairs and when he was due to retire I determined to bring someone into the office from a different culture.' Instead of promoting the DDG, John Jones, he decided that the next DG should be the ambassador in Moscow, Sir Howard Smith,[47] who was intended to bring into the Security Service the 'breath of fresh air' for which Waddell's Whitehall backers had hoped in 1972. Senior officials in the Home Office, Cabinet Office and FCO collaborated in an unprecedented secret operation, codenamed LORELEI, to ensure that the Security Service had no inkling of Smith's impending appointment until it was a fait accompli. Smith informed the Soviet Foreign Minister, Andrei Gromyko, in Moscow on the morning of 19 December 1977 that he was to become DG of the Security Service just as the news was being broken to Hanley in London. Though the Service's main target was Soviet intelligence, Gromyko took the news more calmly than Hanley, giving Smith his good wishes.[48] Meanwhile in London Sir Robert Armstrong (now PUS at the Home Office) reported to the cabinet secretary, Sir John Hunt: 'The decision obviously came upon Hanley as a thunderstroke – which speaks well for our security precautions – and was received with a very bad grace.'[49] Probably no DG has ever been so furious at a meeting with the Home Secretary. An eyewitness in Merlyn Rees's outer office remembers Hanley bursting into the Home Secretary's room declaring, 'It's a fucking disgrace!'[50] The DG insisted that his appointed successor was not merely unpopular in the Security Service but 'had an abominable reputation':

Sir Howard Smith was by reputation a weak man, an appeaser. When he had been head of the former Northern Department in the FCO, he had done nothing to respond to the Service's warnings about the expansion of Soviet and satellite espionage. Similarly, during his time in Northern Ireland, Sir Howard Smith had been too ingratiating towards the minority community and acquired a reputation for spending more time with the Cardinal than with anyone else.[51]

In an obvious snub to his successor, Hanley appointed several new directors before his departure. Armstrong tried to persuade him simply to recommend the appointments to Smith and leave the new DG to make the final decision. Hanley refused and went ahead with the installation of the new directors.[52] He also took the unprecedented step of asking to see the Leader of the Opposition, Margaret Thatcher: 'I met Maggie and poured out my woes. I think she took note of one or two things. I was just about to retire so I was very frank.'[53]

Among the areas where Whitehall was most convinced that the Service would benefit from a 'breath of fresh air' was in its recruitment procedures. The Service had traditionally resisted proposals that it take part in the Civil Service Selection Board (CSSB) because, as B1/0 put it in 1978, 'We are looking for candidates with qualities different in some respects to those of a Civil Servant . . .'[54] The Service preferred, as it had always done, to rely as far as possible on personal recommendation. That same year 30 per cent of officer candidates interviewed had been recommended by members of staff[55] (down from 36 per cent in 1970).[56] On Sir Howard Smith's appointment as DG in 1978, Callaghan made clear that he expected him to 'institute closer control, better management and more acceptable and accountable methods of recruitment'.[57] The blueprint for change was provided in the summer of 1978 by a report by Lord Croham, who had been asked to lead an inquiry into Service management and recruitment, to which, unprecedentedly, both the Prime Minister and Home Secretary gave evidence. Croham's report seems to have been more favourable than Callaghan had expected; his criticisms were confined to the tendency for Security Service recruits 'to be drawn from a somewhat narrow group'.[58] Though Smith believed that Croham had failed to appreciate 'how wide a range of recruiting contacts the Security Service has nowadays in universities and polytechnics', he agreed in September 1978 to make CSSB 'a central feature of the recruitment procedure' for officers. The Croham reforms introduced a four-stage selection system: paper sift of applications; formal board chaired by a former director; CSSB with a Security Service observer; and final selection board chaired by the DG.[59]

Though CSSB provided external, independent assessment of applicants, its Director, Clarence Tuck, acknowledged that 'The staff of the Security Service are not Civil Servants and ultimately responsibility for selection and appointment remains with the Security Service.'[60] Croham accepted that, in addition to new graduates, 'the Service needed recruits who had seen something of life – the mature man.' Among the most mature entrants was a former colonial Special Branch officer, long acquainted with MI5 and SIS, who joined at the age of fifty in 1981:

I was somewhat taken aback at my Final Selection Board to be asked, 'Have you any objection to reading other people's mail?' What did the Board think I had been doing for the past 20 odd years! Anyway, my reply was that, unlike the American President who said that 'Gentlemen do not read other Gentlemen's mail,'[61] I had no objection to reading 'other Gentlemen's mail', if it was in accordance with the law. A member of the board responded, 'I assume this applies to Ladies as well.' (It was Eliza [Manningham-Buller] – yes her!)[62]

In the recruitment of female officers the Service moved ahead of much of Whitehall and most employers in the private sector. By the early 1990s some 40 per cent of its officers were women.[63]

Smith's term as DG saw an extensive revision of the training programme for 'General Duties and Staff Officers', which for the first time included residential courses. The reforms of the Smith era owed little, if anything, to the DG himself, who did not prove to be the great reformer for which his Whitehall backers had hoped in 1978. As one of his directors recalls: 'He did not immerse himself in the business as he would have had to have done to make a great reform.'[64] Though less disastrous than Hanley had predicted, Smith was none the less unsuited for the role of DG, more aloof and less at ease with staff than Hanley had been. He began badly at his first meeting with directors and senior staff on 7 April 1978. One of his successors, Sir Patrick Walker, later recalled, 'It was awful. He stood on the stage while we sat in rows. No message came across. He was ill at ease and stilted.'[65] Smith's declining influence in Whitehall was shown in 1980 by the collapse of plans for the first ever visit by the Queen to Security Service headquarters, which was expected to boost staff morale. The visit, which initially aroused no opposition within Whitehall, was agreed with Buckingham Palace but then cancelled on the insistence of the FCO which declared that, since it was inappropriate for the Queen to pay even a secret visit to SIS (for fear of compromising its unavowable status), it would be unfair to SIS for her to visit the Security Service.[66] Smith seems to have accepted this snub to the Service from the FCO, of which he was a distinguished former member, without making a serious attempt to fight its corner. A senior diplomat who had had high expectations of Smith believes that his lack of impact as DG was due partly to the fact that he was constantly preoccupied by the long-drawn-out terminal illness of his wife, to whom he was devoted.[67]

Smith gave a widespread impression within the Service of distaste for some of the operations for which he was responsible as DG. One of his senior officers recalls resenting the way in which 'he kept far away from A Branch and left it all to John Jones [a former Director A], regarding it as dirty work.'[68] Smith's lacklustre performance raised the reputation of Jones, the unsuccessful internal candidate to succeed Hanley, who had remained DDG and had a closer involvement in the running of the Service than the DG. One of the directors remembers Jones's period as DDG under Smith as 'his finest hour . . . John Jones kept the whole thing afloat.'[69] In November 1980, Willie Whitelaw, who had become home secretary after the 1979 Conservative election victory, told Mrs Thatcher that he was strongly in favour of Jones becoming DG after Smith's retirement in March 1981: 'I have given a lot of thought to this appointment and have made a point of observing Mr Jones at close quarters over the last eighteen months. I am satisfied that he is the right man for the job . . . Another outside appointment would upset the Security Service and damage their morale.'[70]

Mrs Thatcher accepted the case for an internal candidate but was unenthusiastic about Jones. After a visit to the Service's Gower Street headquarters in December 1980, partly intended to give her an opportunity to
assess internal candidates for the succession to Smith, she 'thought [Jones]
lacked the dynamism and imagination which one would expect in the man
who was going to run the Security Service'.[71] The Prime Minister found it
hard to believe that there was not an abler younger candidate for DG.[72] It
emerged, however, after inquiry by the Home Office, that under Smith
(and probably Hanley too) 'virtually no career planning had been done;
the younger able Assistant Directors were not being brought on in time.'
Though criticizing the lack of forward planning,[73] the Prime Minister seems
to have accepted that there was no realistic alternative candidate to Jones.

In addition to his record in keeping 'the whole thing afloat' under Smith,
Jones seemed to have much to recommend him. He was a rare example of
a miner's son who had won a place at Cambridge on the eve of the Second
World War. After an undergraduate career at Christ's College interrupted
by war service, he had graduated with first-class honours in history, and
won another first class when qualifying as a teacher with a Cambridge
Postgraduate Certificate in Education. He then spent eight years in the
Sudan Government Service, rising to become senior inspector in the Ministry of Education, where, according to a confidential report, he 'proved
quite outstandingly successful'. After joining the Security Service in 1955,
he continued to receive glowing reports.[74] Despite his considerable talents,
however, Jones was far less successful as DG than as DDG. As one of his
obituaries later acknowledged, 'Jones was by inclination as well as by
professional training a deeply private man.'[75] 'I had a lot of time for John
Jones,' recalls his first DDG. 'Only trouble was he was a terribly shy man.
I could not get him to get out and talk, especially to rank and file. It was
beyond him.'[76] As DG, he was invisible to many members of the Service.
One graduate who joined in 1983 recalls that she did not even know his
name.[77] 'Even when John Jones came to see what we were doing,' recalls
a long-serving member of the Registry, 'we didn't feel he was really interested in us. He seemed to be doing it simply because he felt he ought to.'[78]
Cecil Shipp, who became DDG in 1982, failed to compensate for the DG's
aloofness. He combined, the same member of Registry recalls, 'a very
distant manner with an air of superiority'.[79] He was given the unaffection-
ate nickname 'Lettuce' (derived from his initials 'COS', also used as an
alternative nickname).[80] To many of the staff – even at middle-management
level – senior management seemed remote and out of touch.

MI5's uncommunicative management proved incapable of responding adequately to the damage to morale caused by the arrest in September 1983 and conviction in April 1984 of a disaffected Security Service officer, Michael Bettaney, who had unsuccessfully offered his services to the KGB.[81] It was clear from an early stage of the inquiry into the Bettaney case by the Security Commission that there would be criticisms of Service management style. Director C recalls attending a session of the Security Commission at which the DG was questioned about management training in the Service. He believes that Jones 'torpedoed himself' by replying airily that such training did, of course, take place – though, in Director C's view, 'this was not true in any meaningful sense . . . The mood of the Commission changed from one of sympathy to one of criticism.'[82]

Leon Brittan, who succeeded Whitelaw as home secretary in June 1983, spent some time getting to know the Service. Though admiring its operational effectiveness, he found its management style backward. He was confirmed in both views by the Bettaney case, writing to Mrs Thatcher in December 1984:

The management style of the Service needs to become more communicative, and with a more corporate approach. Relations with the other intelligence agencies and with Whitehall could with advantage be more forthcoming . . . At the same time we need to sustain the present high level of operational efficiency in the Security Service, on which so much depends. The professionalism and dedication of the staff are first class.[83]

The, at first sight improbable, agent of reform was Jones's successor as DG in 1985, Sir Antony 'Tony' Duff: war hero, ex-ambassador, former chairman of the JIC and Intelligence Co-ordinator in the Cabinet Office, and, at sixty-five, over the Service retirement age. Duff was widely believed within the Service to be Thatcher's choice,[84] but this was not the case. Though an admirer of Duff, she thought him too old for the job and favoured an internal candidate.[85] So, initially, did Leon Brittan, his PUS Sir Brian Cubbon, and the cabinet secretary Sir Robert Armstrong. All three initially preferred Director K, John Deverell,[86] but eventually concluded that none of the internal candidates was suitable. At a meeting on 23 January 1985:

the Prime Minister said that she was now persuaded that the best course was to offer the post to Sir Antony Duff for 2–2½ years: the precise term could be left open within this range. It should be made clear to him that one of his most important roles would be to bring on and establish his successor from the candidates within the Service.[87]

Despite the managerial problems which led to Duff's appointment, not all was doom and gloom in the Security Service. A rare public glimpse of the Service in one of its leisure moments appeared in a *Guardian* account of a performance of Dvořák's Mass in D in St John's Wood Church on 28 June 1984 by the Service choral society, conducted by Director F.[88] At the suggestion of Sir Robert Armstrong the society had taken the name 'The Oberon Singers' – an allusion to Oberon's words in *Midsummer Night's Dream*, 'We are invisible, we will o'er hear their conference.'[89] Ian Black told *Guardian* readers in an article entitled 'The spy catchers strike a new note':

More than 100 spy-catching singers and musicians worked their way through a varied programme. The conductor, who could easily pass for a gung-ho school housemaster, lived up to his reputation for amusing eccentricity. 'I must tell you', he announced as an expectant hush fell over the elegant London church where the performance took place, 'that we are waiting for a horn.'

... Mindful of the Official Secrets Act, the Guardian feels unable to reveal the work name of the choir or the venue of its performances. But the concert was most enjoyable, and, as it was not paid for out of the Secret Vote, we made a modest contribution to help to defray expenses.

The *Guardian*, however, did not gain entry after the performance to the Oberon Singers' drinks and buffet dinner in a nearby church hall.[90]

Despite such moments of conviviality, morale within the Service during the final year of Jones's term as DG was lower than it has ever been since. Following Bettaney's conviction in April 1984, he issued a statement claiming that the Security Service 'cynically manipulates the definition of subversion and thus abuses the provision of its charter so as to investigate and interfere in the activities of legitimate political parties, the Trade Union Movement and other progressive organizations'. Though Bettaney's denunciation was widely discounted as an attempt to justify his treachery, the subsequent comments by two young members of the Service who had resigned from it had much greater impact both on the media and on Service morale. Miranda Ingram, a former colleague of Bettaney in K Branch, declared that, though counter-espionage was 'the acceptable face of MI5', working in F Branch meant 'monitoring one's fellow citizens' and engaging in activities of dubious legality. But, 'in the prevailing right-wing atmosphere, an officer who dissents from the official line does not feel encouraged to voice his concerns. He feels that it will be futile or detrimental to his career.' The second former MI5 officer to go public, Cathy Massiter, had worked in F Branch and made much the same points as Ingram in greater detail and with greater force on television as well as in print, claiming that the Service had been 'violating' the rules against political bias in operations against the Campaign for Nuclear Disarmament (CND), had launched investigations in all major industrial disputes and had put under surveillance two prominent members of the National Council for Civil Liberties, Harriet Harman and Patricia Hewitt, both later leading Labour politicians.[91]

The Massiter case, recalls Stella Rimington:

came as a massive shock to everyone in MI5, so unused were we in those days to any form of public exposure or to any member of the Service breaking cover . . . And here was this erstwhile colleague, someone we all knew well, talking about her work on nationwide TV and what's more giving an interpretation of it which to us seemed distorted and unrecognisable. It was breathtaking.[92]

The Prime Minister was personally 'very concerned' by Massiter's appearance on television and asked Sir John Jones for 'an absolute assurance that there had been no unauthorised interception of subversives'. The DG replied that there had been 'none since 1972 when it was within his knowledge'. On 4 March 1985, in her last meeting with Jones before his retirement as DG, Mrs Thatcher asked him if he thought there were 'any more Massiters' in the Service: 'She said she was very concerned about *the morale of the Security and Intelligence Services* and offered more money or any other help that was needed.'[93]

Sir Tony Duff's arrival as DG a few weeks later brought about an almost instantaneous improvement in Service morale. Duff was a man of great personal charm (even if he annoyed Stella Rimington and possibly other female staff by calling them 'Dear') and became the first DG to go round all sections of the Service, asking staff at all levels what they thought needed changing and what their ideas were for reform.[94] He also had the great advantage of being the first DG since Sir Dick White thirty years earlier (save, briefly, for Hanley in the last two years of the Heath government) to establish a rapport with the Prime Minister. In the nearly unanimous view of those past and present members of the Service who recall the Duff era, it marked a turning point in Service history. Like Sir David Petrie, another outsider and the most successful of his predecessors, Duff became DG at an awkward moment. He was quick to see the parallel between the main problems facing him and those confronting Petrie in 1941: the Service's difficulty in responding to all the demands made on it, poor morale and lack of leadership. 'I think we have an easier task than [Petrie] had,' he minuted in September 1985, 'but the nub of the problem is very much the same.'[95]

On 2 May 1985 Duff created a new P (for 'policy') Branch 'to make recommendations to me on changes in the Service's management, personnel and security policies and procedures'.[96] At a meeting for staff and spouses three years later, Director P was able to report that, though reform was still continuing, 'we can look with some satisfaction to the new personnel arrangements that have been devised,' among them:

– a permanent 10% 'edge' over Civil Service pay [which subsequently proved to be temporary]. This was a significant achievement at a time when the Government was looking for ways of reducing expenditure; and it points to the value the Government attaches to the Service.
– clearer and more rational career structures
– more training of all kinds
– improved welfare arrangements, ranging from health checks to better staff restaurants
– more open staff reporting systems, indeed more openness generally.[97]

Following the reforms of the Duff era, length of service also had much less influence than previously on promotion.[98]

There were also significant shifts in Service priorities. Though counter-espionage remained its most important activity, counter-subversion declined rapidly and counter-terrorism became more important than ever before. The officer appointed by Duff as Director F, who had never previously worked in the Branch, had no doubt that his remit was 'to run the Branch down': 'I read a lot of the papers when I got there. It seemed to me we had always overstated the threat since Communists at no stage would have filled a Football Stadium.'[99] Whitehall's growing recognition of the threat from international terrorism in the mid-1980s produced a major change in Security Service culture as well as a shift of Service resources.[100] Patrick Walker, an Oxford graduate who had joined MI5 from the colonial service in 1963 and became Director FX (counter-terrorism) in 1984, was struck by the way during the decade the Service 'moved from being an introvert organisation with few Officers (and certainly not the more junior) in touch with Whitehall Departments to a Service at ease in Whitehall and confident in its expertise'. With the appointment, on Walker's initiative, of an out-of-hours duty officer from his branch to deal with terrorist incidents (in addition to the regular Service night duty officer), the Security Service completed its transformation into an operational service capable of operating around the clock.[101] Stella Rimington, who became Director FX in 1988, was similarly impressed by the emergence of a new generation of officers 'quite different from those who had been around when I first entered the Service':

The new breed of MI5 officer was comfortable in Whitehall, sitting on committees and discussing issues with ministers and their advisers. As more and more counter-terrorist operations were successful and ended with the arrest and trial of the suspects, giving evidence in court became much more common. Those who were able to meet these new requirements thrived and advanced, those who couldn't either left or became back room players.[102]

Whereas changes under Smith had been introduced from on high, the changes of the Duff era were introduced after wide consultation within the Service. In the autumn of 1985 Stephen Lander, then deputy head of B2 (personnel), reported a widespread belief among new entrants that the traditional practice of placing them in F2 to learn to identify members of the CPGB was outmoded and boring. He proposed recasting the General Intelligence Duties (GID) training package, arguing that, with the contraction of F Branch, GID staff would in future 'spend less of their careers on counter-subversion work'.[103] Director F, perhaps voicing a generational divide within the Service, strongly disagreed:

Basic to all intelligence work is the investigation of individual suspects and basic to that work are what some lightly dismiss as the routine work of identification and the type of studies which F2C engage in. It is as fundamental in my view as learning to shoot for a potential infantry officer.[104]

On the initiative of P Branch, mentoring was introduced in 1986 (initially on a trial basis) to provide training on the job, but with the proviso that 'Mentoring is learning from experience; it is not a replacement for conventional training but an additional training tool.'[105]

Well before Duff retired on 6 January 1988, all the internal candidates for the succession at the time of his appointment had ceased to be in contention. Duff's choice as DDG (Organization) was Patrick Walker. Though Walker had not been in the running to succeed Sir John Jones, he had impressed Duff by his success as Director FX and by his insistence on the need for the Service to have a round-the-clock operational capability. By May 1987 Duff had concluded that he was 'the only real contender' to become the next DG.[106] Walker's nomination was accepted by the Home Office and Number Ten. He was the last DG with a colonial background. Among his recreations was cricket; playing for the MI5 team, he and Stephen Lander opened the batting together.

On 7 January 1988, the day after his retirement, Duff drew up 'a sort of valedictory' on his period as DG, which he sent to the PUS at the Home Office, Sir Brian Cubbon, who forwarded it with his personal commendation

Making the right career choice can be difficult, even for Graduates

If there's one thing all graduates should do before choosing a career, it is to look very carefully before they leap.

Because what might seem like the ideal opportunity from the outside can prove to be very different once you are in. Too many graduates find that their skills are not fully used. Their potential is unexploited. And they end up frustrated and bored, looking for a way out.

If this sounds like you, or if you would like to avoid the pitfalls first time around, our client may be able to help you.

They have plenty of opportunities for those aged 21-26 with good honours degrees in any discipline; opportunities that offer a London-based career in a congenial environment, job security, good prospects and occasional travel.

Initially working as part of a team, you will need to demonstrate sound analytical powers and well-developed interpersonal and communications skills. And if you show determination, sound judgement, enthusiasm and a practical but imaginative approach to problem-solving you can look forward to a rewarding career.

Salaries start in the range of £11,000-£15,000 dependent on your age and previous experience, so even if you haven't graduated yet, we would like to hear from you. Find out more by contacting Bob Gunning at Austin Knight Selection on 01-588 6452 or write to him at 17 St. Helen's Place EC3A 6AS (or 01-256 6925 evenings and weekends). Quoting reference JRG/173/88.

Austin Knight Selection

An eye-catching job advertisement in the *Guardian* in 1988. *Guardian* readers were unaware that the jobs were in MI5, which did not identify itself by name in such advertisements for another nine years.

to the Home Secretary.[107] Some of it, Duff believed, was 'not suitable for Security Service eyes' – though he later slightly relented and sent a copy to Patrick Walker for his personal information only. The core of what Duff considered unsuitable for Security Service eyes concerned its relations with government. Despite the emergence of a new generation of officers more at ease in Whitehall, Duff still saw a danger that the Service might return to old ways:

It seems to me that in the past there has been a tendency within the Service to regard itself as being a thing apart, an entity that should exist in its own right and that should perform its given functions regardless of the views, activities, and indeed requirements of the government. In terms of maintaining a proper political neutrality, and of not being diverted from a proper concentration on the requirements of national security, it is right that the Service should maintain a certain detachment. But this must not be exaggerated. If the Service is to perform effectively and usefully, it must understand the politics and needs of the government of the day, and consider its own work in that context, and if it is to be able to make an appropriate contribution to the counsels of government, and to have its views listened to with attention, it must take pains to obtain and retain the esteem of ministers, officials, the military and the police.

This is possibly the most difficult lesson for members of the Security Service to learn. They are learning it – but unless they are encouraged from within and without the Service to join willingly and actively with other departments and agencies in the consideration and discussion of matters on which they have a contribution to make, or from which they can gain experience or advantage, they will slip back.[108]

Cubbon agreed, telling the Home Secretary, 'The Security Service will slip back into its shell unless Whitehall itself is organised to encourage it in the opposite direction.'[109]

Duff was also concerned about the Service's public image. That image had been severely damaged by the public relations fiasco of the unsuccessful attempt to prevent the publication of Peter Wright's memoirs, which reached a humiliating climax in Australia late in 1986. The well-publicized proceedings in the New South Wales Supreme Court, some of which combined the entertainment value of *Yes Minister* and *Fawlty Towers*, ended in victory for Wright and exposed the Service to public ridicule.[110] Duff saw no easy way to restore MI5's reputation:

In the face of the sustained criticism and vilification of the last year or two, arising chiefly from the ramifications of the Peter Wright case, the Service has kept up its spirits pretty well. But these unremitting attacks do have their effect and my fear is that in the longer term the Service will be damaged in a number of ways.[111]

"YOU'RE A DECEITFUL, CUNNING POOFTER, SMITHERS—EVER THOUGHT OF JOINING MI5?"

An example of the sometimes dismissive tabloid image of MI5 in the wake of the unmasking of Anthony Blunt, the treachery of Michael Bettaney, the *Spycatcher* affair and other damaging publicity (Bernard Cookson, *Sun*, 29 April 1987).

To provide a secure outlet for future complaints by discontented intelligence officers, Mrs Thatcher announced in November 1987 the appointment of an 'ombudsman' or 'staff counsellor' for the intelligence services to whom any of its members could take 'anxieties relating to the work of his or her service'.[112] For the Security Service to win public confidence it also required a statutory basis. Duff argued, as he had done since his early days as DG: 'A good Security Service Act is now essential.'[113] Before he became DG the main impetus for reform of Security Service management had come from Whitehall, sometimes encountering opposition from the Service. After 1985, however, pressure for putting the Security Service on a legal footing came from the Service itself and was initially resisted by Whitehall. Nothing better epitomized the transformation of the Service during the 1980s than its ultimately successful campaign for the passage of the Security Service Act of 1989.[114]

1

Operation FOOT and Counter-Espionage in the 1970s

Operation FOOT, the mass expulsion of Soviet intelligence officers from London in September 1971, marked the major turning point in Security Service counter-espionage operations during the Cold War. As a retrospective Service report on FOOT recalls: 'The steady and alarming increase in Soviet official representation in the UK during the 1950s (from 138 in 1950 to 249 in 1960), accompanied as it was by a proportional increase in the number of Russian intelligence officers (IOs) threatened to swamp our then meagre resources.'[1] To expand its counter-espionage capability, the Service was authorized in 1962 to recruit an additional fifty officers, 150 'other ranks' and a hundred in secretarial and clerical grades.[2]

However Soviet representation continued to grow and it soon became clear that the only effective way of containing the R[ussian] I[ntelligence] S[ervice] threat lay in a limitation of the number of Russian officials. We therefore set about a long and painstaking process of educating the Foreign and Commonwealth Office and other departments at all levels about the reality of the threat and the need to impose a ceiling on the numbers of Russians. An important feature of this programme of education was the consistent and well-documented presentation of recommendations for the expulsion of individual Russians and for the refusal of visas to others. Not all our recommendations were accepted but between 1960 and 1970 we secured the expulsion of 25 Russians for engaging in inadmissible activities and the refusal of about 40 visas.[3]

Some senior FCO officials, however, persuaded themselves during the later 1960s that the threat from the KGB was declining rather than rising. In May 1967 the future PUS, Sir Denis Greenhill, told a Service symposium that, in the less tense climate of East–West relations which had followed the Missile Crisis, he expected the Golden Age of the KGB to draw to a close and its influence to diminish.[4] His timing could scarcely have been worse. The newly appointed KGB Chairman, Yuri Andropov (later the only intelligence chief to become Soviet leader), was one of the leading advocates within the Politburo of the Soviet invasion of Czechoslovakia in the following year.[5]

The first major success of the Security Service campaign to 'educate' Whitehall on the threat of Soviet espionage was the decision by the Wilson government in November 1968, three months after the crushing of the Prague Spring by the forces of the Warsaw Pact, to allow no further increase in the size of the Soviet embassy. The KGB and GRU, however, managed to circumvent this ceiling by sending more 'working wives' to the embassy and stationing more intelligence officers in other Soviet offices in London, in particular the Trade Delegation. Service attempts to limit the growth of the Trade Delegation ran into 'considerable opposition' from both the Department of Trade and Industry and the British embassy in Moscow.[6] The Conservative victory at the June 1970 general election greatly assisted the Security Service campaign. The incoming Prime Minister, Edward Heath, and his Foreign Secretary, Sir Alec Douglas-Home, were convinced that the size of the Soviet intelligence presence in London had become 'a real threat to our national security'. For some months Douglas-Home hoped to resolve the problem by private negotiation. But when he raised the issue with his Soviet opposite number, Andrei Gromyko, in the autumn, Gromyko gave the absurd reply: 'These figures you give cannot be true because the Soviet Union has no spies.' In December Douglas-Home wrote to Gromyko formally requesting a curb in 'the scale and nature of the intelligence activities conducted by Soviet officials in this country'. He received no response.[7]

Within the Foreign Office, the strongest support for the mass expulsion of Soviet intelligence officers came from George Walden, who became Soviet desk officer shortly after the election. Walden was convinced that Moscow would not take British diplomacy seriously until the British government summoned up the nerve to deal with its bloated espionage network in London:

The Russians knew that we were swamped with spies and that we didn't dare to do anything about it. The will to resist their pressures in the field of espionage was rightly seen by the Russians as a gauge of the country's resolution overall, and by 1970 the KGB regarded the British as broken-backed.[8]

By the spring of 1971, most if not all FCO under secretaries and heads of department had been won over to the Security Service proposal for a mass expulsion of Soviet intelligence officers if, as seemed increasingly likely, private persuasion failed.

The KGB attempted to discredit one of the few public figures to campaign publicly for a reduction in the Soviet intelligence establishment in London, the former Tory MP Commander Anthony Courtney, by circulating photographs of his seduction by an Intourist guide in a Moscow hotel room fitted with a concealed KGB camera. The operation, codenamed PROBA,[9] merely increased support for Courtney's campaign among Conservative backbenchers. The minister in Edward Heath's government whom the Service found hardest to win over was the Home Secretary, Reggie Maudling, to whom it reported. Like the previous Wilson government, Maudling initially took the view that a public protest over Soviet espionage would simply prejudice more important issues in East–West relations: 'After a mass expulsion the government would be the laughing stock of the British public and we should all look very foolish.'[10] The Home Secretary, however, was eventually convinced by the Security Service case. FJ noted, after meeting him on 24 May 1971, that Maudling 'was surprised that we were able to identify so many Russian IOs so positively' and 'much struck by the size of the effort needed to follow an IO'.[11] In a joint memo to the Prime Minister on 30 July, Maudling and Home argued that the numbers of KGB and GRU officers were 'more than the Security Service can be expected to contain'.[12] Based on the Service's estimate of 130 Soviet intelligence officers in London, the FCO agreed on a target of a hundred expulsions.[13] On 4 August Douglas-Home sent Gromyko what amounted to a final warning that the 'inadmissible Soviet activities' in Britain which had continued unabated since his previous letter to him eight months earlier must cease. Once again, Gromyko did not reply.[14]

The defection of Oleg Lyalin from the KGB London residency on 3 September provided what the Service regarded as 'a convenient additional justification' for the mass expulsion of Soviet intelligence officers.[15] On 21 April 1971 Lyalin had walked into Hampstead police station, claiming to be a member of the Russian Trade Delegation. He asked to see Special Branch officers, identified himself to them as a Soviet intelligence officer and said he had important information to reveal. He was subsequently debriefed in a safe flat by Security Service officers during the first of many meetings which continued until his defection.[16] Lyalin disclosed that he was the senior representative in the London residency of Department V, the section of KGB foreign intelligence specializing in sabotage and covert attack 'in periods of crisis or war':[17]

It was his task to select and report on sites to be used for the infiltration by air and sea of Soviet sabotage groups and to build up a locally recruited support organisation. In 1971 he completed a comprehensive plan for the seaborne landing of a sabotage

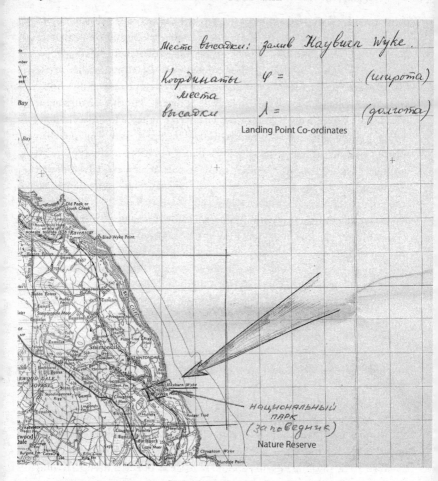

Место высадки: залив Наувил Wyke.

Координаты места φ =   (широта)
высадки   λ =   (долгота)

Landing Point Co-ordinates

НАЦИОНАЛЬНЫЙ ПАРК
(заповедник)

Nature Reserve

Map provided by Oleg Lyalin after his defection, showing plans for the
seaborne landing of a sabotage group (or groups) at Hayburn Wyke on
the north Yorkshire coast.

group (or groups) at Hayburn Wyke on the north Yorkshire coast. At the same time
he was giving consideration to the selection of a dropping zone for an airborne
landing north of the Caledonian Canal. Using locally domiciled agents recommended
by his Department V predecessors, Aleksandr Savin and Vladislav Savin, he built
up a network (including a Moscow trained radio agent) to support the arrival and
operations of the sabotage groups to be infiltrated through Hayburn Wyke. He had
the formation of a second support network in mind.[18]

Lyalin revealed that the primary purpose of the planned sabotage operations was to demoralize and terrorize the civilian population. By sabotaging railways, for example, Department V believed it could 'make people too afraid to travel on them, thereby paralysing the economic life of the community'.[19]

Lyalin told his Security Service debriefers that by the time he arrived in London he was already disillusioned with Department V and despised his fellow Line F officers (as the Department's officers were known when stationed in residencies) for their fraudulent expense claims. He also wrongly believed that his cover had been blown when on arrival in London as, ostensibly, a knitwear representative in the Soviet Trade Delegation, he was met by his Line F colleague Vladislav Savin, whom he assumed had been identified by the British authorities. He told his debriefers that thereafter he fully expected to be contacted by the Security Service. In September 1970 Kentish Town police station attempted to contact Lyalin at the Trade Delegation, but only to verify his address in connection with a minor incident which had occurred some weeks earlier. Lyalin was out but called at the police station to confirm his address. He later rang 999 from a telephone booth in Highgate and, with the intention of offering information, said he wanted to get in touch with anyone who knew anything about the Soviet Union. The operator misunderstood the purpose of the request and offered to give him the number of the Soviet embassy. Lyalin rang off.[20]

During meetings in a Security Service safe flat which began on 21 April 1971 and continued for over four months, Lyalin's attitude was assessed as 'always friendly but never relaxed', frank and responsive to all the questions put to him with no intelligence topic off limits. He usually drank beer at a 'steady rate' during the meetings but did not become visibly drunk (as he regularly did after his defection). The debriefing sessions were recorded with a tape recorder which Lyalin saw being switched on and off. What he did not realize, however, was that a second, hidden tape recorder kept recording even when the other was switched off. Lyalin's debriefers initially found it difficult to understand his motives. Though he accepted £10 or £15 at each meeting, he showed no interest in larger sums, and took considerable personal risks to stay in contact with his debriefers. Lyalin's complicated private life added to the problems of dealing with him. He revealed in his first debriefing that he planned to leave his wife and marry his Russian lover. In May, after a heated argument, his wife was observed by A4 standing in front of Lyalin's car to try to stop him driving away. Lyalin was summoned by the head of security in the London residency to discuss this episode and the scandal likely to result from his divorce. Lyalin appealed to the Security Service to arrange for his expulsion from Britain so that he could return to Moscow and try to ensure that divorce did not damage his career. He refused to defect to Britain but declared himself anxious to work in Russia as a British agent inside the KGB.[21] The Service, however, believed Lyalin to be too unpredictable to be run for long in Moscow.[22] To revive his flagging career as a KGB officer, the Service devised a scheme for him to recruit a bogus agent in the MoD, codenamed AFT, with access to classified information.[23]

The complications in Lyalin's private life continued to increase, as he conducted a simultaneous affair with a married English woman, as well as with his Russian lover. On 27 August he had a 'particularly frank session' with his case officers about the three women in his life, revealing that his Russian lover had hinted she was willing to live with him in Britain. Lyalin, however, said he was still determined to return to the Soviet Union. A few days later he changed his mind. In the early hours of 30 August, Lyalin was arrested for drunken driving in Tottenham Court Road, spent the night in a police cell after refusing to give a blood or urine sample, and was remanded on bail next morning at Marlborough Street Magistrates' Court. At a meeting with his handlers in the safe flat on 1 September, Lyalin seemed unconcerned about his arrest, which the residency had reported to the Centre as a provocation stage-managed by the British authorities. But he was worried by a letter from a KGB colleague in Moscow saying that his estranged wife was claiming that Lyalin was disaffected with the KGB and that he would be in serious trouble if she told the authorities. Unhappily for Lyalin, the letter had been delivered in error to a colleague in the London residency who had passed it to the security officer. Two days later, having been ordered back to Moscow, Lyalin decided to defect. At 9.50 a.m. on 3 September Lyalin rang his English lover but failed to persuade her to leave her husband and move in with him. He then phoned his Russian lover, who agreed. At 2.15 p.m. Lyalin contacted the Security Service, saying that he wished to defect, together with a friend. After removing classified documents from a KGB safe in the residency, he and his Russian lover arrived at the safe flat and signed applications for political asylum.[24]

As well as revealing details of Department V's sabotage plans in Britain, Lyalin provided a powerful insight into the success of the KGB London residency in detecting A4 mobile surveillance. In 1967 Lyalin's predecessor, Aleksandr Savin, had recruited as an agent a disaffected clerk in the Greater London Council (GLC) motor licensing department, Siroj

Hussein Hassanally Abdoolcader. Born into a well-to-do Malaysian family, Abdoolcader had arrived in London ten years earlier to study at Lincoln's Inn. As a result of his repeated failure to pass his law exams and dissatisfaction with his social life, he became – according to a later Service assessment – steadily 'more bitter and resentful'. In 1967 Savin struck up an apparently chance conversation with Abdoolcader in a pub, introducing himself as a Pole named 'Vlad' who had lived in England for many years. After further convivial pub evenings, with 'Vlad' buying most of the drinks, he revealed himself as a Russian and persuaded Abdoolcader to look up for him in GLC records the owners of a series of cars whose registration numbers he supplied. Among them were a number which belonged to A4 and the MPSB, which KGB officers were henceforth able to identify. When Savin was recalled to Moscow in July 1969, he handed Abdoolcader over to Lyalin, whom he introduced as 'Alex'. Lyalin began to use Abdoolcader as a talent spotter, trained him in the use of dead letter-boxes and gave him presents and regular payments (mostly small, though one was £100). A fortnight after Lyalin's defection, Abdoolcader was arrested with, in his possession, a postcard addressed to Lyalin and further details of A4 surveillance vehicles. He was later sentenced to three years' imprisonment.[25]

Despite the London residency's success in identifying A4 mobile surveillance, however, Lyalin had apparently reassuring news about its lack of success in penetrating the Security Service. Discussions with the KGB resident, Yuri Nikolayevich Voronin, and other residency officers convinced him that there had been no Soviet penetration of the British intelligence community since the Douglas Britten case in 1968.[26] K7, which was responsible for investigating Soviet penetration, urged caution. It noted that Lyalin knew little about either past penetrations or the structure of the British intelligence community. If there were a current penetration, he 'would hardly be on the indoctrination list'. It was none the less ironic that, at a time when Peter Wright and other conspiracy theorists were pursuing their hunt for imaginary KGB moles within the Security Service, Lyalin should be insisting that penetration of the Service was regarded by the Centre as 'virtually impossible'.[27]

Operation FOOT had been planned for October 1971 but was brought forward by a few weeks following Lyalin's defection on 3 September. The Centre was caught completely off-guard both by the defection and by the implementation of Operation FOOT. On 24 September 1971 the PUS at the FCO, Sir Denis Greenhill, who a few years earlier had told the Service he expected the KGB's influence to go into steady decline, summoned the Soviet chargé d'affaires, Ivan Ivanovich Ippolitov (a KGB co-optee), and

"In the old days it used to be just cigarette packets and bus tickets. Now ninety per cent. of this rubbish is flamin' micro film!"

A satirical comment by Bernard Cookson on the espionage debris supposedly left in London parks after the mass expulsion of Soviet intelligence officers (*Evening News*, 1 October 1971)

informed him that ninety KGB and GRU officers stationed in Britain under official cover were to be expelled. Another fifteen then on leave in the Soviet Union would not be allowed to return, making a grand total of 105 expulsions.[28] That evening there was a celebration party at Security Service headquarters. Among the guests was the head of the FCO Russian desk, George Walden, whose previous dealings with MI5 officers had given him the impression of a rather depressed group of introverts. This time, however, he found them in high spirits. Initially he was concerned by the lack of drink at the party. 'Then one of them opened a vast imposing safe. It was chock-a-bloc with bottles.'[29]

Almost immediately after Ippolitov's return from his meeting with Greenhill at the FCO on 24 September, A4 reported that a Soviet intelligence officer had been seen in Kensington Palace Gardens sprinting across the road to the embassy from the GRU residency opposite, no doubt

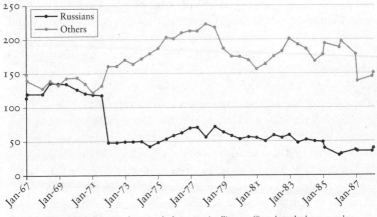

Identified hostile intelligence personnel in London, 1967–1988

NOTE: Figures include co-opted personnel who are not intelligence officers but who have agreed to co-operate with an intelligence service.

The increase in non-Soviet intelligence personnel after the 1971 expulsions was due largely to appeals by the KGB for assistance by its Soviet Bloc allies.

summoned by telephone for an urgent briefing on the mass expulsion.[30] On the day after the expulsions, Sir Alec Douglas-Home flew to New York for a meeting at the United Nations where he was confronted by an angry Gromyko, who warned him that it was very dangerous for Britain to threaten the Soviet Union. According to a diplomat who witnessed the encounter, the Foreign Secretary burst out laughing. 'Do you really think', he asked, 'that Britain can "threaten" your country? I am flattered to think that this is the case.' Douglas-Home added that the KGB had plainly not told Gromyko what it was up to and hoped it had been helpful for him to be informed how many Soviet officials in Britain were actually intelligence officers. Gromyko appeared deflated by the put-down.[31]

In the short term Lyalin's defection probably caused the KGB even greater concern than Operation FOOT. The Centre informed the Soviet leadership that Lyalin was likely to compromise Department V operations in other countries as well as Britain. Though the British government released few details about Lyalin after his defection, the Attorney General told the Commons that he was responsible for 'the organisation of sabotage within the United Kingdom' and 'the elimination of individuals judged to be enemies of the USSR'. According to a later KGB defector, Vladimir Kuzich-kin, on 27 September the Soviet leader, Leonid Brezhnev, cut short a tour of

Eastern Europe for an emergency meeting of the Politburo in the VIP lounge at Moscow airport. Shortly afterwards most Line F officers were recalled from Western capitals, leaving Department V effectively crippled and unable to fulfil its task of co-ordinating sabotage operations abroad in time of crisis.[32] Department V found itself in limbo pending a reorganization which took three and a half years to complete. The files on operations in Britain seen by the KGB archivist (and later defector) Vasili Mitrokhin record no new sabotage plans during the few years after Lyalin's 'treachery'.[33]

Following traditional KGB practice, the Centre's investigation into the London débâcle denounced Lyalin, like previous defectors, as depraved, claiming that he had seduced the wives of a number of his Soviet colleagues in London. The Centre chose as chief scapegoat Voronin, the former London resident in London, who was accused of having covered up Lyalin's misdeeds in order to avoid a scandal in the residency.[34] Despite the fact that only a few months earlier Voronin had been promoted to head the Third Department of the First Chief Directorate (foreign intelligence), he was dismissed from the KGB – a certain indication of its fury at the damage done by Lyalin's defection.[35] 'In all,' as one well-informed commentator later observed, 'Lyalin's revelations caused quite the most satisfactory panic that had occurred in KGB/GRU ranks for years.'[36]

Operation FOOT had an extraordinary international impact on Western as well as Soviet Bloc intelligence services, enhancing the Service's prestige with its foreign friends and allies. On 5 October 1971 FJ reported to Sir Philip Allen, PUS at the Home Office, that reactions from Commonwealth and foreign liaison services had been enthusiastic. At the FBI the autocratic seventy-six-year-old J. Edgar Hoover had 'received the news with delight' and intended to propose to President Nixon that he take similar action.[37] The SLO in Washington, Cecil Shipp, who was due to return to London in October, had his last meeting with Hoover in the wake of the expulsions and was rewarded with a two-hour audience. Even more remarkably, he reported that – unlike previous occasions – this meeting 'was not a monologue'.[38] The DCI, Richard Helms, sent 'hearty congratulations': 'It is not often we receive such good news!' Helms, however, failed to persuade the State Department to follow the British example. The Canadian liaison in London said that the information he had received on FOOT 'would, he hoped, lead to those Ministers (not Trudeau [the Prime Minister, possibly considered a hopeless case]) who were still starry-eyed about the Russians being finally disillusioned'. The Belgian liaison officer sent 'very warm and heartfelt congratulations' and hoped that his own government would be stimulated to take similar action. The French DST (security service) expressed its own delight and forwarded the personal congratulations of the Interior Minister; a 'delighted' SDECE (French foreign intelligence) intended to propose a similar expulsion to President Pompidou. The German BfV (security service) was reported to be 'electrified' as well as delighted but pessimistic that the Willy Brandt government would follow suit; the BND (German foreign intelligence), whose first reaction was one of astonishment, described FOOT as both 'courageous and revolutionary'. The Dutch also intended to use FOOT to press their government to take a tougher line against Soviet intelligence and declared themselves 'thunderstruck at the toughness and courage of H.M.G.': 'This was a real and damaging blow at the structure of the K.G.B. in the West.'[39]

After Operation FOOT, the security case which most concerned the Heath government during the remainder of its period in office was the threat of a new Profumo affair. On 29 April 1973 the *News of the World* reported that (unnamed) peers were involved with prostitutes and drugs. The Met informed the Security Service that they were investigating claims by a prostitute, Norma Levy, and her husband Colin that the Parliamentary Under Secretary for the RAF, Lord Lambton, had been using drugs 'and had needle marks on his arms'.[40] Colin Levy alerted the *News of the World*, which concealed a microphone in a teddy bear on Norma Levy's bed and placed a cameraman in her bedroom cupboard. The photographs and recording, which in the end the *News of the World* decided not to use, ended up in the hands of the police.[41] The DG, Sir Michael Hanley, saw the risk of a major security scandal.[42] Colin Levy also made allegations against Lord Jellicoe, Lord Privy Seal and Leader of the House of Lords, and another Conservative minister (later judged to be innocent). On 2 May the DDG was summoned to the Home Office and told that the Prime Minister wished to know if the Security Service had 'any security doubts about the three Ministers'.[43] Next day the Legal Adviser, Bernard Sheldon, informed the Home Office that there was 'no adverse information' in Service records against any of the three but, unusually for an MI5 officer, expressed concern about the likely political embarrassment for the Prime Minister.[44]

On 7 May, at the direction of the Home Office (and, no doubt, with the approval of Heath), Sheldon was provided by the police with a longer list of public figures named by Colin Levy. Once again, 'no adverse information' against any of them on security grounds was discovered in Service records. The fear of another Profumo affair, however, remained. On 14 May the government Chief Whip, Francis Pym, received an alarmist report from an assistant whip that Rupert Murdoch, owner of Britain's best-selling tabloids, the *Sun* and the *News of the World*, 'has a "Profumo" type story on the stocks *with photographs* about a junior minister who is involved in sexual orgies with back benchers. The official car is involved. The story is about to break.'[45]

A meeting of senior ministers and officials chaired by the Prime Minister on 18 May was informed that the police intended to interview Lambton on the 21st, and agreed that 'a decision on further action by the Security Service' should wait until after the interview.[46] After being questioned by the police, Lambton told the Chief Whip that 'He had agreed that a photograph showing a man on a bed with two women was of him and that the cigarette which he was smoking in the photograph was of cannabis.' Since the 'small amount of cannabis' in his possession might lead to criminal charges, Lambton announced his immediate resignation from the government.[47] K2 (Charles Elwell) noted after interviewing him on 13 June:

Lambton immediately assured me that absolutely nothing of security significance had taken place during the course of his association with tarts, that [there was] no attempt to blackmail him and that he had never discussed his work with any of the tarts ... Asked about the official briefcase he said he had never taken any of his papers out of the office. Indeed he had no need to since he had so little work to do. He rather implied that the futility of the job was one of the reasons that he had got up to mischief ('idle hands' etc).[48]

Lambton was possibly more frank about the 'mischief' during a television interview. When asked by the well-known television presenter Robin Day why he had 'to go to whores for sex', Lambton replied, 'I think that people sometimes like variety. Don't you?'[49]

Anxious not to allow the sex-in-high-places scandals to develop into another Profumo affair, Heath also took a tough line with Lord Jellicoe, who admitted paying for prostitutes from the Mayfair Escort Agency. Though a report to the Prime Minister concluded that 'There is nothing in his conduct to suggest that the risk of indiscretions on these occasions was other than negligible,' Jellicoe resigned from the government on 24 May.[50] The DDG emphasized at a meeting with Heath that, as he was no doubt well aware, because of the risk of blackmail, ministers' involvement with prostitutes always involved a potential security threat.[51]

For several years after Operation FOOT the mass expulsions threw Soviet intelligence operations in Britain into disarray. Most Soviet agents were put on ice.[52] The Centre asked Soviet Bloc and Cuban intelligence services to help plug the intelligence gap in London. The KGB also sought to strengthen the residency by co-opting diplomats and staff of the London embassy. By 1973 nineteen members of the embassy were listed in Centre files as KGB agents and co-optees, among them the ambassador's deputy, Ivan Ippolitov.[53] Security Service eavesdropping at the CPGB's King Street headquarters revealed that the KGB was also using senior Party officials, in particular the industrial organizer Bert Ramelson, to obtain confidential TUC documents. During a month's all-expenses-paid holiday in the Soviet Union in July 1973, Ramelson was approached by Igor Klimov, one of the KGB officers expelled during FOOT, and agreed to supply him with copies of the minutes of the TUC General Council's International Committee (to which Ramelson had gained unauthorized access) via Valeri Rogov, the London correspondent of the Soviet trade union paper *Trud*. On 6 August, soon after his return to London, Ramelson met Rogov and handed over several previous sets of minutes. Thereafter they met regularly for the same purpose. As with previous cases of leaked TUC documents, the Department of Employment, when informed by the Security Service, took 'a relaxed view of this since they have long recognised that any information given to the TUC is likely to leak – one has only to consider the composition of the General Council.'[54]

Since Ramelson was willing to pass TUC documents to the KGB, it seems likely (though proof is lacking) that he also provided confidential information from the Labour Party National Executive Committee (NEC). In the autumn of 1971 he began receiving reports of the proceedings soon after every NEC meeting from one of its trade union members, Alexander Kitson, executive officer of the Transport and General Workers' Union and Treasurer of the Scottish TUC. The DG informed the Home Office that Kitson had collaborated closely on industrial matters with the CPGB since about 1960: 'His political aims and views appear to be substantially in line with those of the Communist Party though he has never formally joined it. He has also for many years enjoyed close friendships with officials of Communist embassies in London.' One of Kitson's closest contacts was Igor Klimov of the KGB. After Klimov's expulsion, he intervened unsuccessfully with the Foreign Office in an attempt to have the ban overturned. Klimov's other regular contacts in the Labour Party had included Joan Maynard MP,[55] nicknamed 'Stalin's Granny' for what one Labour historian calls 'her devotion to the Soviet cause'.[56] When Maynard was elected to the NEC in 1972, she too began supplying Ramelson with regular accounts of its meetings.[57]

The DG told the Home Office:

Ramelson's activities in obtaining for the CPGB documentary and other information, presumably confidential to the TUC and Labour Party, and his readiness to
pass at least some of this information to the Russians and other Communist Parties,
are not illegal in that Government secrets are not at risk. Nevertheless, the fact that
Russian intelligence officers are involved with Ramelson, and with members of trade
unions and of the Labour Party, in obtaining information about the TUC (and
probably about Labour Party policies) carries with it some danger for the future
and, in particular, if and when a Labour Administration is returned to power.[58]

In March 1974, a month after Labour's election victory, Hanley found Roy
Jenkins, then beginning his second term as home secretary, 'exceedingly
interested' in intelligence on Communist attempts to penetrate the NEC
and TUC. When Hanley revealed that Ramelson had the minutes of a
meeting between the new Employment Secretary, Michael Foot, and the
TUC, Jenkins announced that he intended to inform the Prime Minister.[59]
Wilson's reaction is not recorded.

Probably the KGB's most important British agent for much of the 1970s,
Geoffrey Prime, was run exclusively outside the UK and was therefore
unaffected by the expulsions of Operation FOOT. Prime was a sexual and
social misfit who blamed many of his personal problems on the capitalist
system and, as he later acknowledged, had 'a misplaced idealistic view of
Russian Communism'. In 1968, while an RAF corporal at the Gatow
SIGINT station in West Berlin, he left a message at a Soviet checkpoint
asking Soviet intelligence to make contact with him. Prime's note was
passed not to the KGB First Chief [foreign intelligence] Directorate (FCD)
but, though he did not realize it, to the Third Directorate, which was
responsible for the surveillance and security of Soviet armed forces and
sometimes succeeded in recruiting (usually low-level) agents among
Western troops stationed in Germany. Anxious to steal a march over the
more prestigious FCD, the Third Directorate recruited Prime as one of its
own agents. In agreement with his case officers, he successfully applied for
a job at GCHQ after leaving the RAF and was trained at the KGB
compound at Karlshorst in the East Berlin suburbs in radio transmission,
cipher communications, microdots, photography with a Minox camera
and the use of dead letter-boxes. He served for almost nine years as a
Soviet agent at GCHQ in Cheltenham and elsewhere, spending much of
that period transcribing and translating intercepts. A later Security Service
assessment summed up the Third Directorate's handling of the case as
'incompetent and inept; had it been run more effectively the damage done
by Prime (which was anyway very considerable) would have been even

worse.' Since he was given no tasking by his case officers, who showed little understanding of GCHQ, he simply set out to pass on 'all information that seemed to him significant'. By 1975 Prime had access to what was officially described as 'intelligence from a very sensitive source',[60] which included details of British successes and failures in decrypting Soviet traffic.[61] His KGB case officers, however, failed to pay attention to the stress on Prime caused by his double life and remarriage. In the summer of 1977, having come close to breaking point, he made plans to defect and bought an air ticket to Helsinki but turned back on his way to the airport.[62] Though GCHQ colleagues were struck by his morose appearance, they put it down to his problems at home and career frustrations. In September 1977 Prime resigned from GCHQ, broke contact with the KGB and began work as a Cheltenham taxi driver. The London residency seems to have been unaware of his existence – as was the Security Service until his arrest for sexually abusing small girls in 1982.[63]

The first section of the KGB London residency to resume something like normal operations after the expulsions, albeit slowly and on a reduced scale, was Line X (scientific and technological intelligence, or S&T). During 1972 plans were made to renew contact with six of its most highly rated agents: the veteran HOLA (Melita Norwood), a secretary in the British Non-Ferrous Metals Research Association (BNFMRA) recruited in 1937;[64] HUNT, a civil servant recruited by Norwood in 1967; ACE, an aeronautical engineer; NAGIN, a chemical engineer; STEP, a laboratory assistant; and YUNG, an aeronautics and computer engineer. Evidence from KGB files later provided by the defector Vasili Mitrokhin suggests that the reactivation of the six agents was a lengthy business, probably preceded by prolonged investigation to ensure that none was under Security Service surveillance. By 1974 Line X at the London residency had nine operations officers, seven fewer than before Operation FOOT.[65]

The peak of Mrs Melita 'Letty' Norwood's career as a Soviet agent was long past. In March 1945, when the BNFMRA won a contract on the TUBE ALLOYS (atomic bomb) project, Norwood was working as personal assistant to its director and gained vetting clearance.[66] Though the Security Service had received earlier, unconfirmed reports that she had been a pre-war Communist, her 1945 vetting 'interview did not substantiate those concerns and raised the possibility that some of the information held by the Service about Melita might have referred to her sister Gertrude',[67] who had joined the CPGB in 1931 and been an active student Communist at the London School of Economics at a time when Melita was a member of the Independent Labour Party.[68] After Norwood was publicly exposed as a former Soviet agent in 1999, a Security Service assessment of the intelligence she had provided on TUBE ALLOYS concluded that 'its significance to the Soviet atomic bomb programme would have been marginal'.[69] Though that was a reasonable interpretation of the evidence in Service files, BNFMRA records at the National Archives and other British sources, the Centre had arrived at a different conclusion in 1945. Norwood's atomic intelligence, it told the London residency, was 'of great interest and a valuable contribution to the development of work in this field'.[70]

A review of Norwood's case in 1951, which re-examined pre-war reports that she was an active Communist engaged in 'especially important' secret work led Director B (John Marriott) to conclude 'that the [1945] vetting of this lady was unsatisfactory'.[71] Her security clearance was revoked, though her access to atomic intelligence had been effectively terminated in 1949 when BNFMRA's classified contract came to an end.[72] Letty Norwood, however, remained an active Soviet agent, even though her access was reduced to commercially sensitive but unclassified information. According to Vasili Mitrokhin's notes on her KGB file, some of the S&T which she supplied 'found practical application in Soviet industry'. (His notes give no further details.) In 1958 Norwood was awarded the Order of the Red Banner by the KGB. Two years later she was rewarded with a life pension of £20 a month, payable with immediate effect. HOLA, however, was an ideological agent who did not work for money.[73]

By 1965 the Security Service had strong grounds for suspecting her past involvement in espionage. It was now known that there had been a wartime Soviet spy in the BNFMRA and it had also been discovered that Mrs Norwood was related to a BNFMRA metallurgist connected to the atom spy Klaus Fuchs. (Not until Mitrokhin's defection, however, did the Security Service discover that in the middle of the Second World War Norwood and Fuchs had the same female Soviet case officer, Ursula Beurton, née Kuczinski.)[74] In 1965 letter and telephone checks on Norwood authorized by an HOW revealed no evidence of espionage and were discontinued after a year. D1/Inv noted in April 1966: 'The investigation has proved unrewarding. Such information as we have gleaned seems to suggest that Norwood is a harmless and somewhat uninteresting character.'[75] A4 surveillance revealed that she left home at 8.30 every morning to catch the train to the BNFMRA HQ in Euston Street and spent the whole day in the office (including the lunch break) except for about ten minutes' hurried shopping before returning home to Bexleyheath between 6.30 and 7 p.m.[76] Letty Norwood seemed to have few friends. By contrast, her husband

Hilary, a science master at Bexley Grammar School, had many friends (most of them Communist) and, unlike Letty, was an active Party member. Mrs Norwood's only identified Communist contact, apart from her immediate family, was an elderly doctor whom she had known since both were members of the pre-war Independent Labour Party: 'Her contact with him seems to be only out of kindness of her heart for old times' sake.'[77]

Unaware that Mrs Norwood remained a disciplined and dedicated Soviet agent, active Security Service investigation of her ceased in April 1966,[78] a year before she recruited HUNT to the KGB. In order to detect her contacts with the KGB it would have required intensive long-term physical surveillance on a scale which would have scarcely been practicable in the pre-FOOT era when A4 resources were seriously overstretched. For security reasons, Norwood tended to meet her Soviet controller only four or five times a year, usually in the south-east London suburbs, to hand over Minox photographs of BNFMRA documents.[79] The Service had no proof of her career as a KGB agent until the defection of Vasili Mitrokhin in 1992.[80] Even then, since Mitrokhin's notes from KGB files included no original documents, the evidence would have been insufficient for a successful prosecution.

When the London residency renewed contact with Letty Norwood in 1974, her case officer discovered that she had retired from the BNFMRA two years earlier. Since she no longer had access to S&T material, contact was discontinued. Norwood, however, retained a high reputation in the Centre as probably its longest-serving British agent with a very productive record which had included intelligence on the British nuclear programme. According to a report which reached the Security Service a quarter of a century later, HOLA's file had been used in the FCD as a 'study/training aid to show how a productive case could be developed from inauspicious beginnings'.[81] Letty Norwood remained throughout her career a dedicated Communist and true believer in the Soviet Union. After ceasing to be an active agent, no longer needing to conceal her political beliefs, she became an open Communist and joined the Party. A number of reports of her CPGB activities were entered on her Security Service file.[82] During her first visit to Moscow with her husband in 1979, forty-two years after her recruitment as a Soviet agent, Mrs Norwood was formally presented with the Order of the Red Banner awarded to her over twenty years earlier.[83] She was also offered but refused a further financial reward, saying she had all she needed to live on.[84] Even when publicly exposed as a KGB agent in 1999, she told an interviewer that she had no regrets: 'I would do everything again.'[85]

The intelligence supplied by HUNT, whom Norwood had recruited as an agent while he was working for the Department of Trade and Industry in 1967, which was most highly rated by the KGB, seems to have been on British arms sales (though Mitrokhin's brief notes on his FCD file give no details). After he was put on ice following Operation FOOT, KGB contact with him was not re-established until 1975, and even then it thought it safer to do so via a French agent, MAIRE, rather than an operations officer from the London residency. In the late 1970s the London residency gave him £9,900 to found a small business, probably in the hope that he could use it to supply embargoed technology. By 1981, however, the Centre was dissatisfied with the quality of HUNT's intelligence and apparently fearful (wrongly) that he was under Security Service surveillance.[86] He died soon afterwards from a heart attack. The Service did not discover HUNT's existence until Mitrokhin's defection eleven years later. Another source in the 1990s claimed that, at one stage in his career, HUNT had produced 'very valuable copies of departmental classified telegrams'. A Security Service investigation concluded, however, that 'It is unlikely that [HUNT]'s activities caused any significant damage to the UK.'[87] Nor, in the Service's view, did STEP,[88] NAGIN[89] and YUNG.[90]

By far the most productive of the Line X agents reactivated after FOOT was the aeronautical engineer, codenamed ACE, who had first come to the Security Service's attention in October 1964 as a result of his contacts with a Soviet delegation visiting Farnborough Air Show. Various other contacts between ACE and Soviet officials (not an uncommon occurrence in the aircraft and airline businesses) were recorded over the next four years, but no evidence emerged that he was a Soviet agent and Service interest in him lapsed in 1968.[91] Late in 1981 a French agent in the KGB codenamed FAREWELL revealed that the London residency was running a Line X agent, codenamed ACE, whose work was highly praised in Moscow, especially by the Soviet Aviation Ministry.[92] But no connection was made with ACE, and FAREWELL's information was too general to provide a significant intelligence lead. ACE's career as a KGB agent came to an end with his death in 1982. ACE's identity was not discovered until after Mitrokhin's defection a decade later. According to Mitrokhin's notes on his multi-volume KGB file, ACE was Ivor Gregory, a senior aircraft engineer who had been recruited for money by Line X of the London residency in 1967.[93] His 'product file' alone consisted of about 300 volumes, each of about 300 pages. Most of these 90,000 pages comprised technical documentation on new aircraft (among them Concorde, the Super VC-10 and Lockheed L-1011), aero-engines (including Rolls-Royce,

Olympus-593, RB-211 and SPEY-505) and flight simulators. ACE's material on the flight simulators for the Lockheed L-1011 and Boeing 747 was believed to be the basis for a new generation of Soviet equivalents. ACE also recruited under false flag (probably that of a rival company) an aero-engines specialist codenamed SWEDE.[94] The Security Service investigation of Gregory was hampered by the fact that he had been dead for ten years by the time it received Mitrokhin's notes on his KGB file. An initial assessment in 1992 concluded: 'He must have saved the Soviets millions of roubles in research and development, not least in the field of flight simulators. His motivation it seems was financial.'[95] There is no evidence in the files, however, that the Service attempted to identify and talk to ACE's former employers to establish exactly what he did have access to – probably because the case was an old one and the Service had many more pressing current priorities. Unsurprisingly, therefore, subsequent assessments of ACE's significance fluctuated. A 1996 assessment suggested that Gregory had passed information on commercial aviation only to Russians with whom he had 'legitimate dealings' and was not involved in espionage. The most recent assessment in 2003 concluded, on the contrary, that the suggestion that Gregory 'was an unwitting tool of the Russians is completely unjustified ... He was quite clearly aware of what he was doing and was guilty of knowingly working for a foreign power.' There is no evidence that Gregory had access to classified information. But, as the 2003 assessment concluded, 'this need not have prevented him causing significant economic damage.'[96]

The intelligence from KGB files provided by Vasili Mitrokhin in 1992 suggests that there were fewer new British Line X recruits during the 1970s than in the decade before Operation FOOT. The most important new recruit was, almost certainly, Michael John Smith (codenamed BORG), a Communist electronics engineer. The secretary of the Surrey Communist Party in the early 1970s, Richard Geldart, later described Smith as an 'out-and-out Tankie' – a hardline supporter of the crushing of the Prague Spring by Soviet tanks in 1968: 'Not to put too fine a point on it, he was the total nerd. There was socialising going on, but he was not part of it.'[97] A Line X officer at the London residency, Viktor Alekseyevich Oshchenko, made initial contact with Smith in a pub near Smith's flat at Kingston-on-Thames in May 1975. On instructions from Oshchenko, Smith left the Communist Party, ceased trade union activity, became a regular reader of the *Daily Telegraph*, joined a local tennis club and – as his KGB file quaintly puts it – 'endeavoured to display his loyalty to the authorities'.[98]

Michael John Smith first came to the attention of the Security Service in

November 1971 at the age of twenty-three, when surveillance of the CPGB revealed a membership application from a 'Michael Smith' in Birmingham. Both the Service and the local police, however, failed to identify him. In January 1973 the Service received a report that an engineer called Michael John Smith with an address in Chessington had attended a district congress of the CPGB in Surrey. Because the surname was so common and the address was different, no connection was made with the Birmingham Smith. By a remarkable coincidence, the Surrey Communist Party contained another Michael John Smith and the 1973 report, like some subsequent reports, was wrongly placed on his file. In July 1976 the Michael John Smith recruited by Oshchenko began work as a test engineer in the Quality Assurance department of EMI Defence Electronics, a job which required a normal vetting (NV) security clearance giving him access to material classified up to secret. Since C Branch, because of the filing error, had no knowledge of Smith's Communist background, he was given the clearance. In the spring of 1977 the Service's earlier filing error was corrected when it was discovered that the Smith working for EMI had been active in the Surrey District Communist Party from 1973 to 1976. The C2 adviser to EMI, a List X firm (that is, working on classified government contracts), did not, however, raise the case with them until February 1978 – a delay understandably criticized in a later Security Commission report. After a series of discussions between the Service, EMI and MoD, Smith's security clearance was revoked and he was moved to unclassified work.[99]

One reason for C2's lack of urgency was almost certainly, as a later Director K acknowledged, 'the perception in K Branch that by the 1970s the KGB did not recruit members of the CPGB as agents . . . I remember absorbing it myself in my early years in the Branch.'[100] Earlier in the Cold War, following well-publicized cases on both sides of the Atlantic in which Communists had either conducted or assisted Soviet espionage, the Centre had become much more wary about recruiting Party members. Lyalin had reported to the Security Service after his defection: 'The KGB are not supposed to cultivate or recruit known Communists. If after recruiting an agent they discovered that he was a Communist, they would try to modify his behaviour as far as the outside world was concerned and renounce his Communist views.'[101] But though Directorate K did not realize it for over a decade, Lyalin had been far too categorical. As in the case of Smith, the Centre was quite capable of making exceptions.[102]

For a year before Smith lost his security clearance in 1978, he had been working on the top-secret Project XN-715, developing and testing radar fuses for Britain's free-fall nuclear bomb.[103] The KGB passed the documents on Project XN-715 provided by Smith to N. V. Serebrov and other nuclear weapons specialists at a secret Soviet military research institute codenamed Enterprise G-4598, who succeeded in building a replica of the British radar fuse. Smith's intelligence, however, seemed too good to be true. Serebrov and his colleagues were puzzled as to how Smith had been able to obtain the radio frequency on which the detonator was to operate. This information, they believed, was so sensitive that it should not have appeared even in the top-secret documents on the design and operation of the detonator to which Smith had access. Armed with a knowledge of the radio frequency, Soviet forces would be able to create radio interference which would prevent the detonator from operating. The Centre, like the Soviet nuclear weapons specialists, also seems to have been suspicious of the ease and speed with which an engineer with a previous reputation as a staunchly pro-Soviet Communist had been able to gain access to one of Britain's most highly classified nuclear secrets so soon after going through the motions of leaving the Party and switching from the *Morning Star* to the *Daily Telegraph*. Its suspicions that Smith's intelligence on the radar fuse might have been a sophisticated deception seem to have strengthened when he told his controller in 1978 that he had lost his security clearance and, for the time being, could no longer provide classified information.[104]

To try to resolve its doubts the Centre devised a series of tests to check Smith's reliability. The most detailed, personally approved by the KGB Chairman, Yuri Andropov, and termed in KGB jargon 'a psycho-physiological test using a non-contact polygraph', was conducted by KGB officers in Vienna in August 1979. Smith was asked more than 120 questions (all 'yes' or 'no') and his replies secretly recorded. Subsequent analysis of the recording reassured the Centre that he was not, as it had thought possible, engaged in a grand deception orchestrated by British intelligence. Though Smith had been led to suppose that the 'psycho-physiological test' was a routine formality, it had never before been used by the KGB outside the Soviet Union. The Centre was so pleased with its success that it decided to use the same method to check some other agents.[105] The excitement of working for the KGB seems to have appealed to Smith. A hint of the exotic began to enliven a hitherto drab lifestyle. In 1979 he got married, took up flamenco dancing, began cooking Spanish and Mexican cuisine, and gave dinner parties at which he served his own home-made wine.[106] Smith also began a campaign to recover his security clearance at EMI, even drafting a personal appeal to Mrs Thatcher, to whom he complained, 'There is a cloud over me which I cannot dispel.' He had made little progress in dispelling the cloud by the time he was made redundant in

1985. No doubt because of his lack of access to classified material, the KGB had broken contact with him at least a year previously, though it was later to recontact him.[107] In November 1993 Smith was sentenced to twenty-five years' imprisonment (reduced to twenty on appeal) for collecting and communicating material in the period 1990–92 while working for GEC 'for a purpose prejudicial to the safety or interests of the state'.[108]

Despite Line X success in running Michael John Smith and ACE, Operation FOOT had turned the United Kingdom into a hard target for Soviet intelligence. It remained so for the rest of the Cold War. Material smuggled out of KGB archives by Vasili Mitrokhin later revealed that, because of the difficult operating conditions in London, at least six (probably more) British Line X agents either met their case officers outside the UK or were controlled by residencies elsewhere in Europe.[109] Operating conditions were also made more difficult by the C Branch advisers to List X firms. The uncharacteristic error made in the Michael Smith case was an exception which proved the rule – evidence of how important protective security was as a defence against Soviet S&T operations. There was a striking contrast with the United States, where failure to limit the size of KGB and GRU residencies combined with widespread weaknesses in US defence contractors' protective security to produce a haemorrhage of S&T to the Soviet Union. By 1975 FCD Directorate T had seventy-seven agents and forty-two confidential contacts working against American S&T targets both at home and abroad, some of them inside leading defence contractors such as IBM, McDonnell Douglas and TRW. Christopher Boyce, a TRW employee who passed the operating manual of the latest Rhyolite spy satellite to the KGB via his drug-addict friend Andrew Daulton Lee, later testified to a Senate committee that security was so lax in TRW that he and his colleagues 'regularly partied and boozed it up during working hours within the "black vault"' housing the Rhyolite project. Bacardi, he reported, was kept behind the cipher machine and a cipher-destruction device used as a blender to mix banana daiquiris and Mai Tais.[110] Boyce also claimed that one employee successfully gained entrance to top-secret TRW offices with a security pass containing the photograph of a monkey superimposed on his own.[111] Though such extreme lapses in protective security are unlikely to have been common, Soviet intelligence collected more S&T from the United States than from the rest of the world put together. The Pentagon estimated in the early 1980s that probably 70 per cent of all current Warsaw Pact weapons systems were based in varying degrees on Western – mostly US – technology. *Both* sides in the Cold War – the Warsaw Pact as well as NATO – depended on American know-how.[112]

2

The Heath Government and Subversion

Edward Heath did not take to Sir Martin Furnival Jones, who continued as director general during his first two years as prime minister. Like Macmillan during the Hollis era, Heath compared the DG unfavourably with the far more clubbable Sir Dick White, whom he had first met while lord privy seal at the Foreign Office during the Blake case in 1961:

Almost a decade later, I was again much impressed by [White, then Intelligence Co-ordinator]. The head of MI5 was not so convincing. Having described his work, he told me that he had a particular point to make. His people had heard that a church organist was being sent from Poland to London to give a recital, to which I would be invited, in the hope that he could have an interview in order to obtain the latest political information from me. As I had never heard of the organist, nobody else was able to identify him and there was no evidence whatsoever of any such organ recital in London, this kind of nonsense hardly seemed to represent a fruitful way of occupying either my time or that of MI5.[1]

Heath's recollection may well have been garbled. There appears to be no record in Security Service files of any warning to the Prime Minister about a Polish organist's visit to London.

Despite his personal dislike for FJ, however, Heath paid close attention to Security Service reports on industrial subversion and proved anxious for more. The first major industrial dispute with which the Heath government had to deal, less than a month after the Conservative election victory, was a dock strike which the TGWU, led by Jack Jones, declared official on 15 July. Next day, because of disruption to food supplies, the government declared a state of emergency. On 17 July Lord Justice Pearson was appointed to head an inquiry which, less than a fortnight later, recommended a 7 per cent pay rise for the dockers. 'It was', Heath wrote later, 'far from an ideal settlement, but we had yet to publish our proposed union legislation and this was not the time or the issue for a bruising struggle . . .'[2]

Heath was determined not to be taken by surprise by other industrial disputes. The cabinet secretary, Sir Burke Trend, noted with some concern the new Prime Minister's 'propensity to want action and to supply it himself if it was not forthcoming from his Ministers'. After reading a Security Service report entitled 'Prospects for Industrial Unrest',[3] Heath called for new machinery to provide advance warning of industrial unrest and plan the government response to it. The Whitehall response was unenthusiastic. Sir Philip Allen, PUS at the Home Office, commented that it was not possible to foresee disruption with sufficient precision to make meaningful plans to deal with it: 'Life was not like that.' Heath also appeared determined to deal with the 'evil men' who, he believed, were out to cause industrial disruption. Trend tried to persuade him that this too was impracticable. He cited what he believed was the cautionary example of Harold Wilson's public denunciation of seamen's leaders in 1966 as a 'tightly knit group of politically motivated men', only to discover that this was almost the only one of his predecessor's actions of which Heath wholeheartedly approved. Director F shared Trend's scepticism about the Prime Minister's proposals. In present circumstances, he believed, publicly exposing the Communist connections of leading trade unionists might actually be counter-productive.[4] Whitehall responded to the Prime Minister's 'propensity to want action' against industrial disruption by the time-honoured device of setting up two new committees – one composed of ministers, the other of senior officials – to consider government strategy to deal with current and pending wage claims and associated industrial disruption. The Official Committee on Subversion at Home, founded in 1969, was to consider the longer-term threats posed by 'communist and other subversive activities in the United Kingdom'.[5]

At a meeting with the Home Secretary, Reginald Maudling, on 26 October 1970 FJ renewed the application for an HOW on the general secretary of the TGWU, Jack Jones, which had been turned down by Wilson a year earlier. FJ noted afterwards:

I said that I did not think it at all likely that an investigation of Jones would result in his being charged with espionage under the O[fficial] S[ecrets] A[ct] and this was not the purpose of the proposed exercise. We did, however, think it possible that he was being manipulated by the Russians or was at least under their strong influence . . . At the very least an operation against Jones and his wife would produce intelligence which could be of great value in particular to the Department of Employment and to the Government generally in the field of industrial disputes.

Maudling was hesitant about agreeing to an HOW, chiefly because of the risks involved: 'If the operation went astray it would create an intolerable situation between the Government and the Trade Unions.' However, he agreed to consult Heath,[6] who approved the application.[7]

Though Jones was not, in fact, 'being manipulated by the Russians', the Security Service was right to consider the possibility that he was. Intelligence six years later from the most important British agent of the later Cold War, Oleg Gordievsky, revealed that from 1964 to 1968 the Centre had regarded Jones as an agent.[8] The product of the HOW on Jones, discontinued after just over a year, proved to be reassuring, revealing not merely no sign of a continuing Soviet connection but also positive evidence of growing distance between him and the CPGB. The Security Service came to the conclusion that, 'In present circumstances the realities of Jones' position as General Secretary of the largest trade union in the country press more heavily on him than any influences the CPGB could bring to bear upon him.'[9]

The centrepiece of Heath's policy on the trade unions was the much heralded Industrial Relations Bill, published on 3 December. The Bill provided for the establishment of an Industrial Relations Court with wide-ranging powers to enforce ballots and cooling-off periods on registered unions, and, as Heath acknowledged, provoked 'fractious exchanges between government and unions for the rest of the parliament'. Even when the Bill became law, unions were able to remain outside the reach of the new court by refusing to register under it.[10] The second great industrial crisis of the Heath government began only four days after the publication of the Bill, when power-station workers began a work-to-rule which threatened to disrupt electricity supplies. At midday on 12 December the DDG, Anthony Simkins, was informed by the Service's duty officer that Maudling had sent a message out of a cabinet meeting to say that he would like to see the DG as soon as the meeting was over:

As the DG could not be reached, I drove up to London and saw the Home Secretary in his flat at Admiralty House. He told me that the Cabinet had decided to declare a State of Emergency and went on to say that a very important meeting of the four Unions involved in the power go-slow was to be held at the Electricity Council offices on the morning of December 13th ... The Home Secretary said it was of the highest importance to get intelligence as early as possible about what went on at the meeting.

... The Home Secretary then said that the Prime Minister had enquired about the possibility of getting a device into the room [at the Electricity Council]. I replied that an eavesdropping attack against this target would take us right outside the field in which the Security Service had operated throughout my twenty-five years with it.

It would be a departure of great significance to seek intelligence from a target which could not properly be regarded as subversive. The Home Secretary wondered whether our view of what was subversive needed bringing up to date: the Unions were seeking to blackmail H.M.G. and in so doing were threatening the security of the State. This was a point which might be considered at greater leisure.

Sir Burke Trend asked to see Simkins after his meeting with Maudling and told him that Sir Philip Allen was 'very uneasy' about the suggestion of bugging the meeting at the Electricity Council. Simkins noted afterwards: 'In my presence [Trend] telephoned Allen to let him know that the Prime Minister's proposal was not being pursued. I emphasized that it was both outside the Charter and could also run very great risks of discovery.' Though Trend appeared to agree,[11] the Home Secretary did not. Three days later Allen reported that Maudling wanted 'an examination undertaken of the role of the Security Service in relation to industrial action which brought pressure on the government'.[12]

On 27 January 1971 FJ sent Maudling, via Allen, a memo entitled 'Industrial Action: The Role of the Security Service' which firmly restated the traditional limits to the Service's involvement in industrial intelligence collection:

The tendency over the sixty years of the Security Service's existence has been to keep the Service within narrow limits and at once to insulate it from involvement in politics while bringing it increasingly under formal controls. Both tendencies have been healthy. Because the work of the Security Service has to remain secret, there is a special obligation to see that it is kept within strict limits erring, if at all, on the side of caution.

... What are the motives of the leaders of Unions, e.g. in the Electrical Power industry, in seeking to obtain what many regard as excessively large wage increases? Their principal motive is the perfectly proper one of ensuring that their members do not lose ground in the inflationary race. The fact that by adopting this course they increase the pace of inflation, does not impugn their motives ... They are performing the task for which they were elected and, though they may be damaging the State, they cannot properly be described as subversive.

Nevertheless, the recent tendency towards the use or threat of industrial action as a political weapon introduces a different factor. This has so far been advocated and encouraged by subversive organizations and by individuals on the extreme left ... It is possible that in an endeavour to outflank the militants, the T.U.C. and Trade Union leaders would give tacit or even open encouragement to such industrial action.

Would such action with such an objective properly be regarded as subversive and therefore within the sights of the Security Service?[13]

That final question seems never to have been answered because the issue did not arise. The dialogue between government and Security Service was confused by some ambiguity over what subversion meant. On 1 February 1971 FJ admitted to Maudling that 'he had always refrained from trying to define subversion.'[14] Subversion was eventually defined in 1972 by Director F (John Jones) as 'activities threatening the safety or well-being of the State and intended to undermine or overthrow Parliamentary democracy by political, industrial or violent means': a definition incorporated in an F Branch instruction in January 1973 and quoted in the Lords by a government minister two years later.[15]

During Simkins's farewell call as DDG on the Home Secretary on 28 June 1971, Maudling 'remarked that he was grateful for the discussions with us about the investigation of subversion in industry. He and the Prime Minister had been a little brash in their approach, but he thought we had kept things on the right lines.'[16] The deputy head of Registry minuted to FJ: 'Further to the earlier request of Mr Maudling for improper investigation you will wish to note that ... he, & the P.M., recanted!'[17] The leadership of the Security Service remained anxious to avoid what it saw as ill-judged Whitehall attempts to change its counter-subversion responsibilities. F1/0 (the Assistant Director in charge of monitoring the CPGB and other subversive organizations) noted the 'almost complete absence' in the Annual Review of Intelligence for 1972 by the Intelligence Co-ordinator of any reference to the Service's counter-subversion role.[18] FJ responded: 'We deliberately omit a great deal that the Security Service does from the annual review on the ground that we do not want the J.I.C. or the Intelligence Co-ordinator to concern themselves with it.'[19]

Despite the Heath government's anxieties about industrial subversion, at the beginning of 1972 Whitehall gravely underrated the threat from the National Union of Miners (NUM). The miners were the last union from which the government had expected a serious challenge to its pay guidelines. 'What we did not anticipate', Heath later admitted, 'was the spasm of militancy from a union which had been relatively quiet for so long.'[20] Over the previous decade the NUM had tamely acquiesced in the closure of over 400 pits and the reduction of the labour force from 700,000 to less than 300,000. Militancy in the coalfields seemed a thing of the past. While strikes in the dockyards and on the railways had become a regular feature of the industrial landscape, there had been no miners' strike since 1926. From their traditional place at the top of the earnings league, the miners had slipped steadily down the table. Neither the government nor most of the media initially took the miners' challenge seriously. Bernard Levin in

The Times insisted that the miners could not defy the inexorable decline of their industry: 'The doomed miners' strike has started exactly one year to the day after the no less doomed post-workers' strike.'[21]

Despite extensive experience of mediating industrial disputes since 1945, the Department of Employment had never handled a miners' strike. As the Secretary of State for Employment, Robert Carr, later acknowledged, 'There was no doubt about it, our intelligence about the strength of opinion within the miners' union generally was not as good as it should have been . . .'[22] But it was not the role of the Security Service to provide much of the intelligence which the government wanted. MI5's responsibilities were limited to the role of the Communists, Trotskyists and fellow-travellers, and it resisted suggestions that it go beyond the limitations imposed by its directive. The government was thus better informed about the role of the extremists and their sometimes secret discussions than it was about the mood of the NUM rank and file. The telecheck on the Communist leader of the Scottish miners, Mick McGahey, revealed that he spoke freely, if not always comprehensibly, over the phone about the strike plans and tactics of the Scottish Area NUM. The English transcribers' difficulty in understanding McGahey's thick Scottish accent was compounded by his heavy drinking; they noted his habit, when drunk, of going to sleep it off in the Ladies' Rest Room at NUM headquarters.[23] Eavesdropping at King Street revealed that the Party leadership was concerned about how he paid for his binge-drinking. Gollan, the Party leader, was heard to say that 'McGahey must do a lot of his drinking at the expense of the union.'[24]

The bugging of the CPGB's King Street headquarters revealed that McGahey was in close touch with the Party's industrial organizer Bert Ramelson. As well as having a first-class degree in law, the Ukrainian-born and Canadian-educated Ramelson had an engaging manner. Even the *Sunday Times* called him 'a charming and erudite man with a keen sense of humanity'. The sympathetic history of the CPGB by Francis Beckett, published in 1995, concludes, like Service reports in the 1970s, that Ramelson, rather than any of the Party's general secretaries, was its most influential post-war member, becoming 'the face of British Communism in the only place after 1956 where it really mattered, the trade unions'. Pre-war Communists had tried to appeal to the union rank and file over the heads of union leaders. Ramelson pursued the opposite strategy, writing in 1967 that it was 'tremendously important' for the Party to realize 'that it's no good having militants at the bottom and not at the top. For the first time in history there is now a very important minority of left-wingers at the

TUC.'[25] Apart from McGahey, Ramelson's other contacts in the NUM included its general secretary, Lawrence Daly, a Scottish former Communist. According to a Security Service assessment of Daly:

He by no means slavishly follows Ramelson's advice, but is prepared, when it suits him, to work closely with the Party . . . Daly can perhaps best be described as an aggressive extreme left wing militant of no fixed ideological abode, articulate and shrewd, but not an intellectual. He is a very heavy drinker but appears able to remain sober when he is involved in critical negotiations.[26]

Ramelson believed that, unlike McGahey, Daly did not finance his heavy drinking from NUM funds: 'When Daly bought him a drink, it had been out of his own pocket.'[27] Following Daly's election to the TUC General Council in September 1971, he regularly supplied Ramelson with copies of its minutes.[28]

Though anxious to avoid strike action, the NUM president, Joe Gormley, was outvoted by his own executive.[29] The Security Service noted that Ramelson was 'particularly secretive' about his meetings with Daly and other NUM contacts, and 'rarely committed anything to paper'.[30] At the beginning of the miners' strike in January 1972, the NUM was much better prepared than the Heath government. The devastating use of a novel industrial weapon, the 'flying pickets', marauding from Yorkshire under the flamboyant leadership of the thirty-four-year-old Arthur Scargill, the youngest member of the NUM executive committee, succeeded in closing a major supply depot as far away as Saltley in the West Midlands.[31] As Scargill later admitted: 'We took the view that we were in a class war. We were not playing cricket on the village green like they did in '26. We were out to defeat Heath and Heath's policies . . . We wished to paralyse the nation's economy.'

With coke unable to reach the power stations, it looked as if the flying pickets might succeed.[32] The Heath government declared a State of Emergency and took powers to put industry on a three-day week to conserve energy.[33] Brendan Sewill, special adviser to the Chancellor of the Exchequer, Anthony Barber, later recalled:

At this time, many of those in positions of influence looked into the abyss and saw only a few days away the possibility of the country being plunged into a state of chaos not so very far removed from that which might prevail after a minor nuclear attack. If that sounds melodramatic I need only say that – with the prospect of the breakdown of power supplies, food supplies, sewage, communications, effective government and law and order – it was the analogy that was being used at the time.

This is the power that exists to hold the country to ransom: it was fear of that abyss which had an important effect on subsequent policy.[34]

The government capitulated to the miners' demands, conceding the large pay rises rapidly recommended by a committee of inquiry. During 1972 miners' earnings increased by up to 16 per cent, double the rate of inflation. More working days were lost in strikes during 1972 than during any year since 1919 – another year when the government had been preoccupied by the apparent menace of subversion.[35]

Heath strongly suspected that there was some undiscovered subversive masterplan behind the industrial unrest. His principal private secretary, Robert Armstrong, wrote to Trend on 21 February 1972:

The Prime Minister finds it hard to believe that the way in which the miners' dispute developed was unplanned, and has asked for the preparation of an analysis to show who was responsible for the organization of this episode. Such an analysis would ideally show how the decisions were taken that the NUM should not give strike pay, who was responsible for the decision to try to bring power supplies to a standstill, and who planned and organized the programme of picketing.

The Security Service was asked to prepare an answer to the Prime Minister's questions and agree it with the Department of Employment.[36] On 16 March FJ sent Trend, 'as a basis for a discussion between the Prime Minister and some of his colleagues, a memorandum describing the present state of subversive activity in this country to cover industry, education, communications and so forth'. The tone of the memorandum, entitled 'Subversion in the U.K. – 1972', was resolutely unalarmist:

The number of people who may be described as committed supporters of the various subversive organizations or who are violently inclined Anarchists, is little more than 40,000 or well below 0.1% of the population. This figure bears little relationship to the temporary, wider support which subversive organizations sometimes obtain when they adopt causes of the day which enjoy a broad appeal.

By far the largest subversive organization remained the CPGB with 29,000 members:

Having consistently failed to attract the electorate, it is pursuing political power through infiltrating the trade unions. Using union representation, the Communists hope to influence Labour Party policy to the point where an alliance, which they would try to dominate, became possible . . . Although, through its industrial influence, its size and its relatively strong organization, the C.P.G.B. remains the major long term subversive threat in this country, it is weakened by internal dissension.

Trotskyist groups currently had only about 4,000 members but their numbers were increasing. Maoists and anarchists together totalled about 4,500. Fascist groups represented 'only an occasional problem for law and order rather than a threat to national security'.

The main subversive threat was in industry:

For complex reasons an atmosphere prevails in industry in which militancy and disruptive activities flourish, particularly at shop floor level. This provides continuing opportunities for exploitation by the different subversive groups, though there is no significant collaboration between them in this field; on the contrary they regard themselves as rivals for the allegiance of left-wing workers . . . Despite extensive penetration of the largest trade unions the Communist Party does not yet control any union or exercise a decisive influence on the T.U.C. Its attitude to industrial disputes is tactical and it exploits rather than creates them, preferring to work through union leadership where it has a vested interest, than through the shop floor level. It sees an opportunity in current disputes for forcing a General Election, its principal aim since June 1970. The Party's secret caucuses within the major unions and in some industries provide effective electoral machinery for Communist supported candidates for union office and thus bring influence to bear on union policies. The present Industrial Organiser of the C.P.G.B. [Bert Ramelson] is a competent, natural militant with wide contacts at the top levels of unions.

The Service view was that there was no novel dramatic solution to the menace of subversion but that good intelligence was of central importance:

There is no panacea for subversive activities. Government is limited in what it can do . . . It has sometimes been expedient to encourage the Press to expose subversive activities but this and other forms of action which draw attention to subversive organizations risk playing into enemy hands, as publicity is often what those concerned in subversive activities are looking for. Suitable openings for exposure tend to be rare.[37]

Heath criticized the Security Service memorandum on subversion for taking 'too relaxed a view'. Burke Trend told the DG that '[Heath] and some of his ministerial colleagues were worried by the growing lack of respect for authority and were convinced that there was a number of evil minded men particularly in the unions. Some of them must, the Prime Minister said, be "done".' According to Trend, Maudling supported the less alarmist Security Service view 'but he was almost the only member of the Cabinet to take a relaxed attitude.'[38] Maudling told FJ on 13 June: 'He disagreed with most of his colleagues who thought that industrial disputes could be blamed on a subversive conspiracy. He read our Subinds [reports on subversion in industry] with much interest and thought that they, and notably those dealing with the railways dispute, supported his point of view.'[39] On 18 July 1972 Maudling was succeeded at the Home Office by Robert Carr. The senior management of the Security Service was doubtless relieved to hear from Allen, the Home Office PUS, that the new Home Secretary 'is not given to gossiping'.[40]

Soon after Carr became home secretary, the new DG, Michael Hanley, who inspired far greater confidence in Heath than FJ had done,[41] proposed to Allen the establishment of a new committee under Home Office chairmanship which would be responsible for assessing the internal security situation in the UK:

With the growth of violence and with increasing industrial relations trouble, the Security Service was in a very exposed position. Traditionally we had provided assessments but under the present conditions it seemed possible that something more authoritative was required which could not be so easily rejected by Ministers who might have other views.[42]

The purpose of the new committee, in Hanley's view, was to keep subversion and 'increasing industrial relations trouble' away from the Joint Intelligence Committee. Despite the fact that the JIC's terms of reference included a duty 'to keep under review threats to security at home and overseas and to deal with such security problems as may be referred to it', Hanley thought it had 'bugger all to offer except on Ireland'. Its Assessments Staff was 'packed by the FCO, where the JIC chairman was an FCO official and so was the Intelligence Coordinator', who since 1969 had been responsible for producing an annual review on the 'state of intelligence' and the intelligence community.[43] Hanley agreed that a suitable chairman for the new committee would be the unsuccessful Home Office candidate for the succession to FJ.[44] The Service would supply the committee staff and continue to co-ordinate information from the police. On 31 July 1972 Trend informed a meeting attended by the DDG that Heath wanted more to be done to expose the hidden hand of the Communists in industrial subversion and for the Security Service to extend its investigations into industrial unrest. Trend asked whether, for example, the Service could tap the phones of key individuals involved in the current dock dispute. The DDG insisted that the Service stick to its charter and investigate only those with 'subversive affiliations': mainly defined as Communists, Trotskyists and sympathizers. There was, however, already an HOW on one of the dockers mentioned by Trend who came into the 'subversive' category.[45]

In September 1972 the new interdepartmental committee proposed by Hanley to study Subversion in Public Life (SPL) came into being 'to supervise and direct the collection of intelligence about threats to the internal security of Great Britain arising from subversive activities, particularly in industry and to make regular reports to the Ministers concerned'. Draft reports were initially jointly prepared by an official of the Department of Employment and a Security Service officer. Trend told the Committee that 'The Prime Minister attaches particular importance to Ministers receiving comprehensive reviews of the position at regular intervals and not merely when some critical situation has already developed.'[46] For the remainder of the Heath government, at approximately two-monthly intervals, SPL issued a series of major studies of industrial subversion, concentrating on those unions or industries thought most likely to become involved in disputes,[47] with titles including 'Impact of Subversive Groups on Trade Union Activity', 'Potential Disputes in the Public Sector – October 1972', 'Claimants and Unemployed Workers Union', 'National Union of Mineworkers', 'Labour Relations at Ford Motors', 'Industrial Relations in British Rail', 'The Security Significance of the Ultra Left in the UK in 1973', 'The Amalgamated Union of Engineering Workers', 'The Construction Industry' and 'The Transport and General Workers Union',[48] The papers included considerable background information on unions and industry from the Department of Employment, and some from the FCO's Information Research Department. However, the SPL paper on 'The Communist Party of Great Britain in 1973'[49] was a purely Security Service production. Circulation of these reports was initially restricted, on Heath's instructions, to only eight ministers (Prime Minister, Foreign Secretary, Chancellor of the Exchequer, Home Secretary, Secretaries of State for Defence, Scotland, Trade and Industry, and Employment) and their senior officials.[50] The Lord President of the Council was later added to the circulation list.[51]

At the end of 1972 there was further ministerial pressure on the Service (though not from Carr, the Home Secretary) to go beyond its charter in the investigation of subversion and industrial unrest. In December 1972 Allen told Hanley that he and other officials were resisting pressure from ministers to change the Service's terms of reference in order to allow it to collect more industrial intelligence. Provided the DG was 'able to take not too narrow a view of our Charter', he thought they would be able to persuade ministers to accept the position as it stood. Hanley replied that he stuck to the charter but did not interpret it 'legalistically'. He was prepared to 'stretch the Charter as far as it would go', but could not, for example, put an application for an HOW on someone against whom there was no adverse security information.[52] Trend also reported to Hanley that

Heath had said that the Security Service charter 'ought to be enlarged', but that he had dissuaded him.[53]

In the summer of 1973 another confrontation with the miners began to loom over NUM opposition to the latest phase of the government's statutory incomes policy. Heath became suspicious that the moderates on the union's executive were being manipulated for political ends by the hard left and in particular the Scottish Communist Mick McGahey. At the NUM conference in July 1973, McGahey called for 'agitation in the streets' to defeat the Heath government. He made an even more dramatic impression at a private meeting at Number Ten of some senior ministers and officials with the entire NUM executive, nearly thirty strong, on 28 November. Though McGahey claimed his words had been distorted, according to Heath:

> When I asked him what he really wanted, he proclaimed that he wanted to bring down the government. During the election campaign, even the Labour Party had to disown McGahey when he demanded that any troops which might be called out to deal with a national emergency should support the miners.[54]

On 14 November the Service obtained an HOW on Arthur Scargill, whom it regarded as a Communist sympathizer, 'to help establish the extent of communist influence on present negotiations in the mining industry'.[55]

This time the government was well prepared – or thought it was – for another miners' strike. In December 1973 it pre-emptively declared a three-day working week, instead of delaying as in 1972. On 12 December the Secretary of State for Employment, Willie Whitelaw, summoned a group of senior Security Service officers to his office and told them that intelligence was 'one of the keys of success in handling the present situation'.[56] The Service view of the origins of the latest conflict with the NUM, summarized in a note of 8 January 1974, was very similar to its analysis of the seamen's strike almost eight years earlier and was once again drafted with a possible Commons statement in mind. Its author had had the lead role in drafting Harold Wilson's celebrated Commons denunciation of the seamen's leaders in 1966 as a 'tightly knit group of politically motivated men':[57]

> Communists in the [NUM] were largely responsible for framing the pay claim which is the subject of the present dispute. This originated from the Communist-controlled Scottish Area and was subsequently endorsed by the NUM's National Conference in July 1973. The Party's aim was to try to ensure that this claim would ultimately result in a strike ... Throughout the whole of this period leading Communist

members of the Executive have kept closely in touch with the Party's National Industrial Organiser, Ramelson, and continue to discuss their tactics with him. Before meetings of the NUM National Executive Committee, McGahey, the Vice-President of the NUM, usually consults privately with Ramelson and agrees with him the policy which the Communist Party would wish to see pursued by the Executive as a whole.[58]

The transcribers within the CPGB transcribing room, who provided much of the highly sensitive raw intelligence on which this assessment was based, worked inside a glass partition which separated them from the other transcribers. The young English graduate who transcribed Mick McGahey's phone calls during the three-day week had the same difficulty as her predecessors with his sometimes impenetrable Scottish accent. Though already aware of his alcoholic tendencies, she had the impression that at the height of the crisis he 'more or less reinvented heavy drinking'.[59]

With a miners' strike due to begin on 9 February, Heath called an election to be held on the 28th. Unlike Wilson, Heath decided not to use Security Service intelligence to launch a public attack on 'a tightly knit group of politically motivated men'. Instead he chose to fight the election on the larger constitutional issue of 'Who Governs Britain?' After an indifferent campaign Heath lost the election and Labour emerged with five more seats than the Conservatives. 'The miners yet again appeared triumphant, indeed in the euphoric view of young left-wingers like Arthur Scargill virtually invincible.'[60]

Counter-Terrorism and Protective Security in the Early 1970s

The main shift in Security Service priorities during the last two decades of the Cold War was from counter-espionage (CE) and counter-subversion (CS) to counter-terrorism (CT). The transition, however, was very gradual. The Service had no sense during the 1970s, or even for much of the 1980s, that CT was destined to become its main priority. Counter-terrorism was initially regarded as 'the violent side of subversion'[1] and was included in the responsibilities of the counter-subversion F Branch. The first step towards the creation of an independent CT Branch did not begin until 1976 and was not fully implemented until 1984. Protective security against terrorist as well as other threats remained throughout the responsibility of C Branch.[2]

After long periods of quiescence, Middle Eastern terrorism and the IRA (the two main targets of the Service's CT operations in the later Cold War) both re-emerged as threats almost simultaneously at the end of the 1960s. For historical reasons, the counter-terrorist responsibilities of the Security Service against the IRA were quite different from those against Middle Eastern terrorism. Ever since the foundation of the Metropolitan Police Special Branch (originally Special Irish Branch) in 1883 during the Fenian 'Dynamite Wars' in London, it had held the lead intelligence role against Irish Republican terrorism on the British mainland. The lead role in Northern Ireland belonged to the Special Branch of the Royal Ulster Constabulary (RUC). Within the United Kingdom the Security Service thus had only a supporting role against the IRA. Against all other terrorist threats to mainland Britain (even including those from Northern Ireland *Loyalist* paramilitaries) the Service had the lead intelligence role, though that role was not formally acknowledged until 1972.[3]

For twenty years after the disappearance of the post-war threat to London from Zionist extremists,[4] Middle Eastern terrorism ceased to be a significant Security Service concern. In 1968, however, it suddenly became front-page news. This time the threat came from Arab rather than Zionist terrorists. The leading terrorist strategist was Dr Wadi Haddad, deputy leader and head of foreign operations in the Marxist-Leninist Popular Front for the Liberation of Palestine (PFLP), headed by Dr George Habash. From the day Israeli forces had destroyed his family home in Galilee, Haddad had sworn that the rest of his life would be devoted to liberating Palestine from Zionist occupation. Convinced of the futility of attacking military targets in Israel after the humiliating Arab defeat in the 1967 Six-Day War, Haddad devised a new strategy of aircraft hijacking and terrorist attacks on Jewish and Zionist targets in Europe which attracted worldwide publicity. The first hijack, in July 1968, took place on board an El Al Boeing 707 bound for Tel Aviv which two PFLP guerrillas forced to land in Algiers and renamed (with no acknowledgement to James Bond) 'Palestinian Liberation 007'. After more than a month's negotiations, the Israeli passengers on board were exchanged for sixteen Palestinians in Israeli jails.[5] Because there was as yet no evidence that British airlines were at risk from the PFLP, Whitehall showed little urgency in responding to the hijacking menace. Following a second PFLP hijack in September, however, this time of a TWA Boeing 747 also en route to Tel Aviv, the cabinet secretary, Sir Burke Trend, set up a working party to study hijacking and other attacks on civil aircraft. Progress was slow. C Branch issued threat assessments to El Al and Jordanian Airlines, which were thought to be most at risk from the PFLP, but did not yet think it necessary to contact British airlines.[6]

The first PFLP attacks on Jewish targets in London were so amateurish that they failed to give a greater sense of urgency to British counter-terrorism. Incendiary devices planted in Oxford Street at Selfridge's and Marks and Spencer on 18 July 1969 caused minimal damage. A third PFLP bomb attack, not far away at the Israeli Zim Shipping Office in Regent Street, was slightly more successful, breaking several windows and causing minor injuries to a member of staff. None of these incidents was thought serious enough to merit investigation by the Security Service, which left inquiries to the MPSB.[7] The Service, however, expected further, more dangerous 'Arab Terrorist Attacks'. The DG, Sir Martin Furnival Jones, was pessimistic about the prospects for preventing them:

It is not difficult for terrorists previously unidentified as such (as they usually are) to gain entry to Britain for short periods, possibly carrying explosives with them. There are a large number of pro-Arab supporters of different nationalities in Britain, including many Arab students, who would be prepared, or could be induced, to give help in minor ways or provide cover, even though they themselves condemn the use of violence as bad publicity for the cause. In our view, attempts to perpetrate terrorist attacks, not excluding assassination, are likely to continue and not to diminish.[8]

The Security Service was even more pessimistic about the prospects for ending the violence of the 'Troubles' in Northern Ireland, which began at almost the same time as the terrorism of the PFLP.

The last IRA bombing campaign in mainland Britain dated back to 1938–9. The most recent campaign in Northern Ireland, which began along the border with the Republic in 1958, had little impact and passed almost unnoticed in London. Although the Security Service, at the request of the Unionist government at Stormont Castle, sent a liaison officer to Belfast,[9] the RUC were able to cope with the threat from the IRA with only limited assistance from the British army. The IRA blamed public indifference as one of the reasons for ending its campaign in 1962.[10] The Stormont government remained cocooned within the complacency generated by almost half a century of one-party Unionist rule in Northern Ireland committed to maintaining the union with Great Britain, and by the Unionist sense of superiority over the supposedly backward Republic in the south, some of whose citizens continued to emigrate in search of a better life overseas. Westminster mostly looked the other way, doing its best not to become involved in Northern Ireland. Long-established convention forbade the tabling of questions by MPs concerning any issue within the direct responsibility of a Stormont minister. Until the late 1960s, despite the presence of Northern Ireland MPs at Westminster, the Commons usually devoted less than two hours a year to discussing the Province.[11]

Until violence began in the summer of 1968, provoked by some of the supporters and opponents of civil rights campaigns against discrimination affecting Ulster's Catholic minority, there seemed little in Northern Ireland to concern the Security Service. On 6 November the Home Secretary, James Callaghan, asked Furnival Jones for 'an up-to-date appreciation of the prospect of violence in Northern Ireland from the IRA'.[12] FJ seems to have been somewhat taken aback by the request. The DDG, Anthony Simkins, told the PUS at the Home Office, Sir Philip Allen, that Callaghan's request placed the Service in 'a rather Gilbertian situation as we derived our information from the [RUC] and had no independent coverage'. MI5's own inquiries would therefore require 'discreet handling'.[13] The Service appreciation, entitled 'The Threat of Violence in Northern Ireland', completed in December, implied that the Home Secretary had too narrow a perspective. Though Callaghan had asked only for an assessment of the threat from the IRA, Furnival Jones insisted that 'The threat from the IRA cannot be viewed in isolation from the other factors making for violence in Northern Ireland.' The Service concluded that 'The IRA may well see in the Civil Rights Movement the broader base necessary for the achievement of its political aims,' thus provoking a violent backlash from Loyalist extremists. The tone of the appreciation was gloomy and implied that little could be done to resolve the root causes of the violence:

In basic terms the security problem in Northern Ireland is simple. It springs from the antagonism of two Communities with long memories and relatively short tempers. Their differences, originally religious and cultural, largely coincide with political divisions and, with the passage of time since the formal constitution of the Northern Ireland state, have been aggravated by social and economic grievances. Thus, the Roman Catholic and Nationalist minority almost instinctively attributes its problems to what it believes to be the inherent and deliberate bad faith of the Protestant and Unionist majority, while the latter, conscious of the minority's Southern orientation, with almost equal instinct believes that the demand for the remedying of grievances is a preliminary to the dissolution of the State itself. In this atmosphere attempts to improve relations, however genuine and well founded, only too often are greeted with suspicion by both groups.[14]

Following the worsening of the Troubles in the spring of 1969, a Head Office Newsletter told staff:

Until very recently the interest of this Service in the security situation in Northern Ireland has been both limited and indirect. In practice we have been almost wholly dependent for information on the Royal Ulster Constabulary who, for good reason, have always regarded the Irish Republican Army as their primary security target. The fact that responsibility for the investigation of I.R.A. activity in Great Britain rests upon the Metropolitan Special Branch has tended to reduce our interest yet further. The total effort deployed by F. Branch in matters Irish was until recently confined to one part-time desk officer in F.1.C.[15]

Whitehall responded to the beginning of the Troubles with a predictable flurry of committee meetings: among them the newly founded Official Committee on Northern Ireland, chaired by Allen, the Home Office PUS, on which the DDG, Anthony Simkins, represented the Service. In addition, at the prompting of the cabinet secretary, Sir Burke Trend, the JIC set up a Current Intelligence Group on Northern Ireland, which as the JIC (A) Ulster Working Group held its first meeting on 30 April 1969. On 25 April 1969 Simkins told a meeting of Allen's committee, which acted as the main Whitehall channel for advice to ministers:

The [RUC] Inspector General had told [the Service] a few days ago that [RUC] Special Branch was overwhelmed and that he wished we could help them by posting an officer as we had done in a previous emergency. If we took up this suggestion we should probably get a very good idea of the reliability of the RUC's intelligence about the IRA. Allen said the Home Secretary approved of our doing so, and the meeting warmly endorsed the idea.[16]

Four days later a Security Service officer arrived in Northern Ireland as security liaison officer (SLO) and was given an office in RUC headquarters at Knock near Belfast.

At about the same time as this posting, a full-time desk to cover all Irish security intelligence, with particular emphasis on the North, was set up in F1B at Leconfield House.[17] By the autumn, F1B consisted of one female assistant officer (then the highest rank usually open to female staff) and the young Stella Rimington, who – after part-time work for the Service in India – had begun full-time work at Head Office only a few months earlier. Rimington recalls in her memoirs:

My boss and I very rapidly became almost submerged, trying to make sense of the information that began to come in . . . I began to have to stay late into the evenings just to keep up with the flow of paper. My colleague had a habit of talking out loud all the time, telling herself what to do next and, as the days wore on and the pressure mounted, her instructions to herself became more and more manic. Anyone coming into the room was faced with two dishevelled-looking women, one chattering like a parrot and the other peering squirrel-like from behind a tottering pile of paper.[18]

Northern Ireland, previously rarely discussed by the JIC,[19] became a regular item on its agenda. In June 1969 it concluded, like Furnival Jones's report to Callaghan six months earlier, that 'the potential disorder in Northern Ireland comes from the interaction of three distinct groups': the IRA, the civil rights movement and the 'ultra Protestant' supporters of the Reverend Ian Paisley. It also noted increasing Communist influence in the IRA and Trotskyist infiltration of the civil rights movement.[20]

On 14 August 1969 the Wilson government took the fateful decision to send British troops to keep the peace in Ulster, thus beginning what almost no one foresaw would become the longest-lasting military operation in British history. Despite the army's early welcome from Catholics in Belfast and elsewhere, it inevitably came to be seen by nationalist supporters of Irish unity as the defender of the Unionist one-party state. Callaghan realized as much when he gloomily told his cabinet colleague Dick Crossman on 11 September that 'There was no prospect of a solution. He had anticipated the honeymoon wouldn't last very long and it hadn't. The British troops were tired and were no longer popular, and the terrible thing was that the only solutions would take ten years, if they would ever work at all.'[21]

Despite the fact that the constitution of the Irish Republic claimed sovereignty over the North as well as the South, Dublin was even less prepared than London for the beginning of the Troubles. 'Northern Ireland in 1969', writes Eunan O'Halpin, the leading historian of Irish security, 'might as well have been North Korea, so sparse was the reliable information available.' Irish military intelligence did not even possess an organization chart of the RUC and made strenuous efforts to assemble one based chiefly on gossip of varying reliability – only to discover that the information it required was freely available in Northern Ireland official publications which were on sale in Dublin.[22]

Counter-terrorism would have been a higher priority for the Security Service had it known that both the PFLP and the IRA were seeking arms from its main counter-espionage target, the KGB. The first contacts between Wadi Haddad and the KGB took place in 1968 – probably in the aftermath of the first PFLP hijacking. By the spring of 1970 Haddad had been recruited as Agent NATSIONALIST. The KGB Chairman Yuri Andropov proudly reported to the Soviet leader Leonid Brezhnev (whom he was to succeed twelve years later): 'The nature of our relations with W. Haddad enables us to control the external operations of the PFLP to a certain degree, to exert influence in a manner favourable to the Soviet Union . . .' With Brezhnev's approval, an initial delivery to Haddad of five RPG-7 hand-held anti-tank grenade launchers in July 1970 was followed by the elaborately planned Operation VOSTOK ('East'), during which a large consignment of arms and ammunition was handed over to the PFLP at sea near Aden under cover of darkness. Thanks to Haddad, the KGB almost certainly had advance notice of all the main PFLP terrorist attacks for which he was responsible.[23] News of his recruitment was very tightly held within the Centre. Though Oleg Lyalin began supplying the Security Service in April 1970 with intelligence on the activities of the First Chief Directorate Department V, which was responsible for 'special operations' of the kind discussed with Haddad, he appears to have been unaware of the KGB's links with the PFLP when he defected in September.[24]

Lyalin was, however, aware that Seamus Costello, a Marxist member of the IRA Army Council, had submitted a request for arms to the Soviet embassy in London but had been rebuffed.[25] The Security Service does not seem to have discovered until much later that, following the rebuff, another appeal for arms from Costello and Cathal Goulding, the IRA chief of staff, was forwarded to the KGB by the general secretary of the Irish Communist Party, Michael O'Riordan, confirming earlier Service reports on links between the IRA and Irish Communists. O'Riordan claimed that there was now a serious possibility of civil war between the two communities in Northern Ireland and of serious clashes between British troops and the Catholics. Yuri Andropov, however, was doubtful of O'Riordan's and the IRA's ability to keep secret the supply of Soviet arms. It was two and a half years before he was sufficiently reassured to go ahead with the shipment requested by Goulding and Costello. Several consignments of weapons and munitions in waterproof wrapping were submerged by a Soviet intelligence-gathering vessel, disguised as a trawler, on a sandbank 55 miles from the coast of Northern Ireland and attached to a marker buoy of the kind used to indicate the presence of fishing nets below the surface. The consignments, picked up by a fishing vessel manned by what the KGB called 'Irish friends' (Communists) who were unaware of their contents, went undetected by the British intelligence community.[26]

Shortly after O'Riordan delivered the request for Soviet arms, the IRA – as the RUC and Security Service had anticipated several years earlier – split into Marxist and nationalist wings: the Officials under Goulding and the Provisionals led by Seán Mac Stíofáin. The sympathies of the KGB were with the Marxist Officials rather than the nationalist Provisionals. But it was the Provisionals, not the Officials, who were to establish them-selves as the major protagonists in the Troubles. By the time Soviet arms arrived, the Officials had given up the 'armed struggle'. The probability is that the weapons smuggled into Ireland by the KGB were used not against the British but in internecine warfare between Republican paramilitaries.[27]

A mid-air explosion which destroyed a Swiss airliner bound from Zurich for Tel Aviv on 21 February 1970 with the loss of forty-seven lives gave modest impetus to the development of a Security Service anti-hijack strat-egy. Though responsibility for the attack was never claimed, it was believed to be the work of a breakaway group within the PFLP. The destruction of the airliner at last prompted C Branch to set up a liaison system to enable urgent threat assessments to be passed to British airlines. By later standards, however, these arrangements were primitive. Implementation of protective-security recommendations was left solely in the hands of the airlines, with no supervision or co-ordination by either the Security Service or the Department of Trade and Industry (DTI). A proposal for a director of security who would oversee arrangements at airports came to nothing.[28]

C Branch (protective security) still had an ambivalent status within the

Security Service. Though few high-fliers had been attracted to MI5 by the prospect of a career in protective security, new entrants were told that if 'one wanted to get on in the Service one had to do a stint in C Branch', which then had the closest contacts with government departments, especially the Cabinet Office. When the future DDG Julian Faux was posted to C Branch in 1971, Personnel 'went to great lengths to tell me how lucky I was'. The post did indeed provide Faux with far more frequent opportunities for contact with Whitehall than most of his contemporaries enjoyed. Though all government departments were issued with copies of the Service bible, 'Security in Government Departments', they frequently required assistance on how to interpret particular cases. 'I really did not enjoy this esoteric and arcane work,' Faux later recalled. 'It all seemed like splitting hairs to me.'[29] Whitehall still thought of the Security Service's role in protective security primarily in terms of vetting and safeguarding classified information rather than protection against terrorist attack. During the 1970s, C Branch dealt with an average of about 300,000 vetting inquiries a year.[30]

During the last thirty years of the twentieth century, protective security became a steadily more important part of the Security Service's counter-terrorist strategy. But the change occurred gradually and it began slowly. At Furnival Jones's first meeting with Edward Heath in July 1970, he raised the subject of protective security exclusively in the context of counter-espionage. During a wide-ranging survey of Service priorities, the DG mentioned terrorism only briefly, and solely in the context of Northern Ireland. Whitehall, for its part, was unenthusiastic about a major extension of protective security in any context. When FJ stressed its role as a 'security weapon against espionage', Burke Trend intervened to say that this was a 'vexed question' in the civil service. FJ believed, no doubt correctly, that what really concerned Whitehall was the fact that 'the complexity and cost of protective security were both very large.'[31]

PFLP terrorism, however, made clear the need for greatly improved aircraft security. On 6 September 1970 the PFLP hijacked four airliners bound for New York (a feat unequalled by any other terrorist organization until the Al Qaida hijacks on 11 September 2001) and took them to a remote former RAF airbase in Jordan known as Dawson's Field. Wadi Haddad gave the most difficult assignment on the day of the hijacks to the world's best-known female terrorist, Leila Khaled, still photogenic despite plastic surgery to change her appearance after her first hijack a year earlier, and the Nicaraguan-American Patrick Arguello, who together posed as a newly married couple. Their aircraft, an El Al Boeing 707 departing from Tel Aviv, was the only one of the four which carried an air marshal.

Though they succeeded in smuggling aboard both handguns and grenades, the hijack failed. Arguello was shot dead by the air marshal and Khaled, who was prevented by other passengers from removing grenades hidden in her bra, was arrested when the plane made an emergency landing at Heathrow. The hijackers aboard a TWA Boeing 707 and a Swissair DC-8, however, successfully diverted their aircraft to Dawson's Field, which they promptly renamed 'Revolution Airstrip'. A hijacked Pan Am Boeing 747, which was discovered to be too large to land at the Airstrip, was forced to land instead at Cairo where passengers and crew were evacuated and the aircraft blown up. A fifth plane, a BOAC VC-10, was hijacked three days later and flown to the Airstrip to provide the PFLP with British hostages. As the PFLP had planned, the hostages were eventually exchanged for Khaled and six Palestinian terrorists imprisoned in West Germany and Switzerland.[32] The aircraft were destroyed by the hijackers. Discussions within Whitehall about how to deal with future hijacks were confused and sometimes bizarre. The future cabinet secretary Richard Wilson, then working in the Private Office of the Minister for Civil Aviation, recalls 'surreal discussions' which included the use of blow-darts to overpower hijackers.[33]

The September hijackings swiftly led to further mayhem in the Middle East. King Hussein of Jordan, infuriated by the hijacking of aircraft to a Jordanian airfield and by the emergence of the Palestine Liberation Organization (PLO), led by Yasir Arafat, as a virtually independent state within his kingdom, used the Jordanian army to drive it out. Thousands of Palestinians were killed during what became known as Black September. A shadowy terrorist organization of that name was set up within Arafat's Fatah movement at the heart of the PLO when it regrouped in Lebanon. Following the hijacks, the JIC concluded that the danger to UK interests from Arab terrorism had 'significantly increased'. A series of JIC and MI5 assessments over the next month envisaged the possibility of further hijackings, kidnappings, sabotage of aircraft, ships and oil terminals in the Persian Gulf, and armed attacks on tankers in the Gulf and Eastern Mediterranean. The Home Secretary was informed that, as 'the responsible authority for advice on counter sabotage', the Security Service, sometimes acting in conjunction with the MPSB, the DTI and the armed services, had provided protective-security advice at oil installations in the Gulf as well as in the United Kingdom.[34]

For almost two years, however, aircraft and airports seemed the only British interests at serious risk from Arab terrorists. The C Branch Assistant Director responsible for counter-sabotage, Cecil Shipp (a future DDG), took the initiative in the creation of the National Aviation Security Committee, whose first meeting took place in May 1971 with representatives of the police, the British Airports Authority (BAA), the principal airlines and trade unions. C4 officers provided a comprehensive threat assessment and took the lead in discussions on counter-measures. Agreement was reached with BAA that security surveys should be carried out by C4, beginning at Heathrow, and that the implementation of protective security required effective supervision.[35]

On 14 December 1971 MPSB reported information that a group of PFLP terrorists had arrived in London with plans 'either to hijack a plane or to assassinate members of the Jordanian Royal Family'.[36] The target, however, turned out to be the Jordanian ambassador. Next day, as the ambassador's car was passing down Holland Street, Kensington, a bystander saw 'a young man pull a Sten gun from under his coat': 'I couldn't believe my eyes. He levelled it at hip level and pulled the trigger and fired about 40 rounds . . . It was like a scene out of a Chicago film.'[37] The ambassador, remarkably, escaped with an injury to one hand.[38] Like earlier PFLP attacks in London, the attempted assassination was not planned as a direct attack on British interests. Changes in the Whitehall machinery for dealing with intelligence on terrorism owed far more to the resumption during 1972 of PFLP attacks on aircraft and airports than to the attempt on the life of the ambassador.

On 8 May four PFLP hijackers diverted a Belgian Sabena aircraft to Tel Aviv's Lod Airport, where they demanded the release of 317 jailed Palestinians. In the first ever assault on a hijacked plane, Israeli special forces disguised as airport workers freed the passengers and killed or captured the hijackers. The successful counter-terrorist operation at Lod provided evidence of contingency planning in Israel of a kind which did not yet exist in Britain. Haddad, however, took a terrible revenge. On 31 May three members of the Japanese Red Army Faction working for the PFLP walked into the baggage-reclaim area at Lod Airport, removed two suitcases from the conveyor belt, took from them grenades and machine guns, killed twenty-six passengers, most of them Puerto Rican Catholic pilgrims, and wounded seventy-six others. The Lod massacre shocked the Security Service into undertaking a major reappraisal of aviation security, which had hitherto concentrated on preventing hijacks rather than protecting airports. By the end of the year C4 had completed a survey of security at thirteen British airports.[39]

Counter-terrorism, however, was not as yet a major priority either of the Heath government or of the Security Service. As the Special Air Service

(SAS) officer Peter de la Billière (later Director SAS) noted, the government was more concerned about industrial unrest than about the terrorist threat. After the Lod massacre de la Billière ordered the preparation of a paper on the use of the SAS for counter-terrorist operations. Once forwarded to the MoD, however, the paper was quietly shelved.[40]

For a brief period in the early 1970s the Security Service feared that Britain, like some continental countries, was developing its own home-grown international terrorist group. On 12 January 1971 two bombs exploded at the Hertfordshire home of the Secretary of State for Employment, Robert Carr. Responsibility for the attack was claimed by a group calling itself the Angry Brigade which declared in a communiqué: 'Robert Carr got it tonight. We're getting closer.' 'Before Carr's house was bombed,' wrote Britain's best-known anarchist, Stuart Christie, 'nobody had heard of the Angry Brigade. Now, overnight, it had become headline news and every pundit had his own explanation of its origin.'[41] Security Service files, however, contained no likely leads.[42] Over the next six months there were further Angry Brigade bomb attacks, on the London offices of the Ford Motor Company, the Biba dress boutique, the Metropolitan Police computer unit, the home of Ford's managing director, an electricity sub-station near Ford's Dagenham factory, and the home of the Secretary of State for Trade and Industry. Forensic evidence collected by the Met pointed to links with the Spanish First of May Group and other continental anarchists involved in terrorist attacks. The explosive used in most Angry Brigade bombings, as in some First of May attacks, was nitramite, a French-manufactured explosive unavailable in the UK.[43]

The first major breakthrough in the police investigation was a lead from a prisoner on remand in Brixton Prison who claimed that a fellow remand prisoner, Jack Prescott, had admitted involvement with the Angry Brigade.[44] On his release from Brixton, Prescott went to a commune in Islington, which was raided by the police, who, according to Prescott's friend Stuart Christie, discovered diaries and address books which 'provided material for many a happy "fishing trip" for the police in months to come'.[45] The description of the commune in Security Service files was unusually censorious:

The inhabitants were found to consist of revolutionaries who had dropped out of conventional society. They were living promiscuously, the only acknowledged relationship being that of 'brothers and sisters'. A child in the commune was claimed to be the child of all the women in the house. Addiction to hashish and L.S.D. is part of the way of life . . .

The material found during the police raid, combined with subsequent observation of the commune, eventually led the police to a flat in Stoke Newington which documents, weapons and sticks of nitramite identified as the base of the Angry Brigade. Among the weapons was a Beretta machine carbine which forensic examination showed to have been used in an attack on the US embassy in Grosvenor Square in 1967 for which the First of May Group had claimed responsibility.[46] As F1 later acknowledged, 'We ought to have been quicker in connecting the Angry Brigade with the First of May Group.'[47] The documents found in the Stoke Newington flat disclosed 'a great deal of research into future targets': among them cabinet ministers, judges, civil servants, police and prison officers, property companies, computer services and private security agencies.[48]

Eight inhabitants of, or visitors to, the Stoke Newington flat were charged with conspiring to cause explosions. Four were later sentenced to ten years' imprisonment, the remainder found not guilty. With the trial, Angry Brigade attacks and communiqués came to an abrupt end. As Stuart Christie acknowledged, the Brigade had won few friends even among those in favour of revolutionary violence abroad: 'A lot of the political left began to turn against the Angry Brigade. Power might grow out of the barrel of a gun in Vietnam and Bolivia but not in Barnet. What was hailed as an urban guerrilla action in Peru was fascist propaganda in Poplar.'[49] At the CPGB's 'bugged' King Street HQ, Bert Ramelson was overheard denouncing the Angry Brigade as 'nutcases'.[50]

The Security Service accepted that it had taken too long to track down the Angry Brigade. When Robert Carr's house was bombed in January 1971, E1 (later F3), which was responsible for investigating the international dimensions of subversion, was still located outside Leconfield House and in irregular contact with F1 inside Leconfield House, which dealt with domestic subversion. 'This', a post-mortem acknowledged, 'was an immense handicap, slightly reduced but not altogether overcome when F3 joined F1 in Leconfield House.' Had F1 and F3 been in closer contact, F Branch might well have been quicker to see the links between the British Angry Brigade and the Spanish First of May Group.[51] F Branch's main expertise, however, lay in counter-subversion rather than in counter-terrorism. Once Carr's house was bombed, the lead role in investigating anarchism passed to the Special Branch.[52] Since a crime had been committed, however, the MPSB investigation of the Angry Brigade was directed by the CID. The Security Service had files on three of the 'Stoke Newington Eight',[53] and provided some information which assisted the police. But, as F1B acknowledged, the Security Service and Special Branch were to some extent 'duplicating each other's work'.[54] The Angry Brigade bombings provided further evidence of the hesitancy with which the Security Service in the early 1970s was adjusting to a counter-terrorist role. Though the Brigade has since become a mere footnote in British history, there was no means of knowing in 1971 whether or not the bombings presaged something as serious as the terrorist campaign waged in West Germany during the 1970s by the Baader–Meinhof gang and its pretentiously named successor, the Red Army Faction, against leading representatives of 'the imperialist feudal system', such as those on the Angry Brigade target list.

In 1972 Sandy Stuart, one of the few Security Service officers to have been the target of a terrorist attack, was drafted in to C Branch to carry out a review of counter-terrorist protective security.[55] As SLO in Aden in 1967 he had survived a bomb attack in which his wife Judi had been killed.[56] Stuart found that little had changed since the counter-sabotage measures devised during the Second World War.[57] While he was in the middle of his review, an attack by Black September on Israeli athletes competing at the 1972 Munich Olympic Games dramatically heightened the priority given by the Heath government to counter-terrorism. On 5 September seven Arab terrorists (three of whom, thanks to poor security at the Games, had obtained jobs in the Olympic village) burst into the athletes' dormitory, killing two and taking nine hostage. Though the Israeli government refused to negotiate with the terrorists, the West German authorities agreed to give them safe passage to fly to Egypt with their hostages. At the airport, however, German sharpshooters began a firefight which ended in the deaths of five of the terrorists, a policeman and all of the hostages.[58] As a Palestinian refugee told a British reporter, 'From Munich onwards nobody could ignore the Palestinians or their cause.' Palestinian terrorists inspired other frustrated ethnic and nationalist groups to follow their example. Though the international terrorist groups which multiplied during the 1970s varied greatly, all had in common 'a burning sense of injustice and dispossession alongside a belief that through *international* terrorism they too could finally attract worldwide attention to themselves and their causes'.[59]

As well as demonstrating the unpreparedness and confusion of the German government when faced with a major terrorist attack, the Munich massacre also highlighted the need for further contingency planning and counter-terrorist precautions in the UK. On 8 September, the Director of Military Operations, Major General Bill Scotter, rang de la Billière to tell him that the Prime Minister wanted to know what the army could contribute to counter-terrorism. The earlier paper commissioned by de la Billière after the Lod Airport massacre on the use of the SAS for counter-terrorist operations was promptly rescued from an MoD filing cabinet; he was authorized to create an SAS counter-terrorist unit and told that money was no object.[60] The deputy head of a C Branch section, David Sutherland, took an active part in the creation of the unit.[61] Julian Faux, who had been bored by his post in another part of the Branch, was delighted to be transferred to Sutherland's section in 1972 and was much impressed by Sutherland.

Maudling's successor as home secretary, Robert Carr, asked the Security Service for an assessment 'of the likelihood of a Munich-type terrorist operation happening in this country'. Carr can scarcely have been reassured by the pessimistic estimate of the Security's capacity to provide advance warning of terrorist attacks sent to him by Director F, John Jones (later DG), on 8 September:

We have no current intelligence to indicate that any Arab terrorist group is currently planning an operation in the U.K. of the kind recently carried out by the Black September group of Al Fatah in Munich. There is, however, some recent intelligence of preliminary planning by the PFLP of sabotage operations directed against El Al aircraft at a number of places including London Airport . . . It is difficult to predict the likelihood of terrorist operations in the U.K. We do not control directly the amount or quality of intelligence we receive about Arab terrorist plans and intentions. The planning of such operations is undertaken in highly secure conditions in the Middle East. Because of this tight security the intelligence we receive from friends and liaison services (including the Jordanians and the Israelis and West European security services) is usually imprecise as regards targets, timing and the identities of those involved. It is in any case the practice of terrorists to travel on false passports . . .[62]

How difficult it remained 'to predict the likelihood of terrorist operations in the U.K.' was demonstrated only eleven days later when the agricultural counsellor at the Israeli embassy in London, Dr Ami Shachori, was killed by a Black September letter bomb. Seven other letter bombs sent to British addresses were successfully intercepted before they reached their targets.[63] On looking through Security Service files, Sandy Stuart found a paper written some years previously by Anthony Simkins saying that giving advice on countering letter bombs was not a Service responsibility. Stuart thought that was 'crap' and obtained permission from Simkins, then DDG, to rewrite the paper. He successfully argued that advising on letter bombs was part of the Service's protective-security responsibilities. Stuart believed that his paper on 'Postal bombs and measures for identifying them' had the widest circulation of any document yet produced by MI5; its recipients included all British embassies abroad and numerous security liaisons. He was flattered to find himself referred to as 'Mr Counter-Terrorism UK'.[64] 'Terrorist activity', wrote Stuart, 'looks to be here to stay for some time.'[65]

The development of British protective security during 1972, however, was more influenced by the massacres at Lod Airport and Munich than by letter bombs in Britain (the only form of international terrorist attack against targets in the UK in the course of the year). In the aftermath of the Munich massacre, Edward Heath called for an immediate and comprehensive report on the current state of counter-terrorism ranging from military and police contingency plans to the use of advanced equipment and devices. The Cabinet Office working group originally set up in 1969 was reconstituted with broad terms of reference as GEN 129, later to become the Official Committee on Terrorism, under the chairmanship of the PUS at the Home Office. For some time the DG, Michael Hanley, attended its meetings. The first meeting on 2 October 1972 agreed on the pressing need for contingency planning and an immediate study of anti-terrorist techniques.[66]

A report by GEN 129 on 20 October 1972 broke new ground by recommending that existing contingency plans for Heathrow and other airports should be extended to cover all attacks on aircraft in British airspace, and that officials be authorized to call in the military; the decision to commit the military to action, however, would be reserved to ministers. These new proposals would require joint training exercises involving police forces throughout the country, the military and the Security Service.[67] Following ministerial approval of the recommendations, study groups were set up to prepare contingency plans for action on the ground in the case of a terrorist incident, operational control and communications (based in a windowless Cabinet Office briefing room, henceforth known by the acronym COBR), and the use of state-of-the-art technology.[68] The Security Service was represented on all three study groups and its key position was emphasized by its chairmanship of a further group formed to consider what guidance on handling terrorist incidents could be derived from past experience. Under new alert arrangements COBR was to be manned by officials at one hour's notice. Director C and C Branch officers were thus for the first time placed on call outside office hours; in 1974 the Post Office provided them with 'bleepers' similar to those supplied to hospital doctors.[69]

On 13 November 1972 the Joint Intelligence Committee issued a notice which for the first time formally established the Service's lead intelligence role in counter-terrorism:

44. The German-born British physicist Klaus Fuchs, who, while working at Los Alamos in 1945, gave Soviet intelligence the plans of the first atomic bomb – the most important secret ever betrayed by a British citizen. While Fuchs was working at Harwell four years later, decrypted Soviet telegrams provided evidence of his treachery.

45. MI5's chief interrogator, William 'Jim' Skardon (*left*), with the Harwell security officer, Henry Arnold. Though there was no usable evidence capable of convicting Fuchs, Skardon's sympathetic questioning eventually coaxed a confession from him.

46. Sir John Shaw (*centre*), Director of Overseas Division (1950–53), with President Harry S. Truman in the United States. Shaw was known in MI5 as the 'Flying Pencil' because of his tall, lean physique and the amount of time he spent in the air In the early Cold War MI5 officers could expect to spend a quarter to a third of their careers on imperial and Commonwealth postings.

47. SLO staff in Aden survey the bleak landscape of the Thirra pass in 1963. On the eve of Aden's independence in 1967 the wife of the SLO became the only member of MI5 or of staff family to be killed in a terrorist attack during the retreat from empire.

48. (*left*) Roger Hollis (DG 1956–65), photographed at his desk in Leconfield House, acknowledged in 1960 that MI5's surveillance of colonial delegations during independence negotiations went 'a little' beyond its Charter. Because of the importance of the intelligence gained, MI5's action was approved by the Home Secretary.

49. (*below*) Jomo Kenyatta (*centre*) at Lancaster House during the Kenya Independence Conference in October 1963. During the Conference Kenyatta asked Roger Hollis to keep the MI5 SLO in Kenya after independence.

50. Konon Molody, a deep-cover KGB illegal who while in London took the identity of a Canadian 'dead double', Gordon Lonsdale.

51. Surveillance photograph of Lonsdale's most important British agents, Harry Houghton and Ethel Gee, who were seen by A4 handing him highly classified documents from the Underwater Detection Establishment (UDE) at Portland.

52. Lonsdale's case officer, Charles Elwell, was amazed to discover in Lonsdale's briefcase a photo of himself. He later discovered that he had been at a party at which Lonsdale took photos of the guests. After Lonsdale had been convicted and imprisoned, Elwell used the photo to give him the misleading impression that the Security Service had long been on his trail.

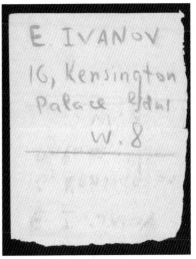

53. Evgeni Ivanov, a GRU officer in London operating under cover as Soviet assistant naval attaché.

54. Ivanov's address at the Soviet service attachés' office (which housed the GRU residency) written by him in pink lipstick characteristically borrowed from a woman at a party whom he wanted to contact him.

55. Portrait of Ivanov by the society osteopath and portrait painter Stephen Ward, who introduced him to Christine Keeler, with whom both Ivanov and the Secretary of State for War, John Profumo, had brief affairs. MI5 concluded that, contrary to claims made during the 'Profumo affair', Keeler was never in any position to obtain state secrets from Profumo and pass them on to Ivanov.

56. Milicent Bagot (*right*) at Buckingham Palace in 1967 after receiving the CBE. An Oxford classics graduate, she became MI5's chief expert on international Communism. With Bagot is her former nanny, who lived with her in Putney. Though Bagot was a powerful personality within MI5, at home 'Nanny was boss.'

57. An A4 surveillance photograph of Bert Ramelson (*right*), the influential CPGB industrial organizer, with Lawrence Daly, the NUM general secretary, in the Prince of Wales pub, Warren Street, London, in 1969. MI5 believed that Daly, a former Communist, 'by no means slavishly follows Ramelson's advice, but is prepared, when it suits him, to work closely with the Party'.

58. A 1972 surveillance photograph of Betty Reid en route to a meeting with a Soviet Bloc official. Since 1946 she had been responsible for identifying CPGB members who failed to follow the Party line.

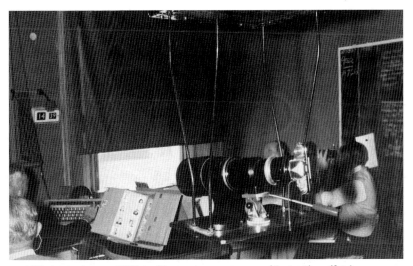

59. MI5 observation post (OP) tracking movements *c.* 1970 of Soviet Bloc officials, intelligence officers and suspected agents. To the right of the camera is a blackboard with target list; to the left photos to aid identification.

60. Oleg Lyalin before his defection in 1971. Lyalin was the senior representative in the KGB London residency of Department V, which specialized in sabotage and the covert use of violence.

61. Some of the record number of Soviet intelligence officers expelled from Britain in Operation FOOT, leaving for Moscow with their families in September 1971. The expulsions marked a turning point. Henceforth, for the first time, Britain became a hard target for the KGB and GRU.

62. Registry staff carrying out 'look-ups' in the card index in the 1970s.

63. (*left*) Two future DGs, Patrick Walker (*foreground*) and Stephen Lander, prepare to open the batting for the MI5 cricket team in 1984 and go on to score a century partnership (64. *below*). 'Running a team of double agents,' the wartime chairman of the Twenty Committee, J. C. Masterman, believed, 'is very like running a club cricket side.'

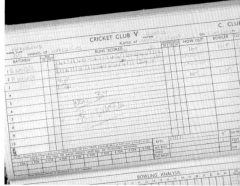

The Security Service is the focal point for the receipt, assessment and distribution of intelligence on terrorist activities affecting British security and for the provision of advice to the appropriate authorities on precautions and counter-measures against the threat.

The role of the [JIC] Current Intelligence Groups is confined to the field of assessment. In that field they are not concerned with the assessment of intelligence of an operational nature relating to specific threats to British security. Assessment of such material is . . . the responsibility of the Security Service.[70]

This clear and unambiguous definition of the Service's central part in the study of terrorism in effect brought up to date the 1952 Maxwell Fyfe Directive and allowed the Service formally to add counter-terrorism to its existing responsibilities for counter-espionage and counter-subversion. A month later the JIC's Notice was amended to make clear the Service's international responsibility as 'the focal point for the receipt and recording of all information on terrorist activities in other countries'.[71] So confused, however, was Whitehall about the divided responsibilities for dealing with Irish terrorism that it was another two years before anyone noticed that the JIC Notice failed to take account of the MPSB's lead role in dealing with Republican terrorism on (but not beyond) the British mainland. The Notice was duly amended.[72]

A report on the handling of terrorist incidents was approved by GEN 129 on 23 February 1973.[73] The first full-scale exercise to test the new procedures, codenamed ICON, devised and controlled by C Branch, took place on 10 April 1973, and was based on a simulated terrorist hijack of an aircraft to Stansted Airport with demands by the hijackers for the release of prisoners held both in the UK and overseas. Though the exercise involved the police, armed services, ministers and officials, F3, despite having responsibility for intelligence on Arab and Middle Eastern terrorists in the UK, surprisingly declared itself too busy to take part. The postmortem on the exercise unsurprisingly emphasized the need for intelligence involvement in dealing with future hijacks and exercises, recommending the inclusion of 'an intelligence officer and an electronics expert from the Security Service' in the teams assembled to deal with hijackers. A Branch responded to the call for an electronics expert by setting up a technical surveillance team, equipped with cameras, CCTV, radio-microphones and other advanced technology. The team, which at full strength numbered fifteen men and three vehicles, took part in all subsequent exercises. Though the Home Office Police Department took over the co-ordination of CT exercises, C Branch continued to play a central role.[74]

The first opportunity after ICON to test the new procedures during a real terrorist incident did not arise for some time. On 5 March 1974 a BOAC VC-10 from Bombay to London was hijacked over Greece.[75] Two Arab men brandishing pistols burst into the cockpit and forced the pilot to land at Amsterdam. The hijackers then released the passengers, set fire to the aircraft and surrendered to the Dutch police. A Dutch court later jailed them for five years.[76] The incident was over so quickly that there was no opportunity for British involvement on the ground. On 21 November 1974, another BOAC VC-10 was hijacked, and forced to land at Tunis. This time the incident lasted for several days and the Service sent an officer from F Branch, who assisted in interviewing hostages as they were gradually released, in order to obtain intelligence about conditions on board the aircraft. The main lesson learned was the need to try to prevent the release of information by the media which might prove helpful to hijackers. At Tunis the hijackers heard a report on the cockpit radio that the Dutch Prime Minister would be willing to release the two hijackers arrested at Amsterdam in March.[77]

Despite the emergence during the early 1970s of international terrorism as a significant feature of international relations for the first time since the beginning of the Cold War and the official recognition of the Security Service's lead intelligence role in countering it, the proportion of Service resources devoted to counter-terrorism remained surprisingly small. Indeed, it was embarrassed to reveal to Whitehall just how small the proportion was. Director S noted early in 1974 when preparing material for the Intelligence Co-ordinator's Annual Review:

The proportion of total Service effort devoted directly to the investigation of terrorist organisations is approximately 3% while another 4½% is directly concerned with Northern Ireland.

... DDG agreed that to use these figures in the Intelligence Co-ordinator's Review ... could not pass without startled comment from the Chiefs of Staff and their advisers. Even if we were to use figures reflecting the effort in the field of counter subversion (without giving any figure for that) we should still only be talking about something under 10% on counter terrorism and approximately 15% on Northern Ireland, figures which again DDG considered were subject to a similar objection.[78]

By contrast, 52 per cent of the Service's resources went on counter-espionage and 28 per cent on counter-subversion. As Director F from 1972 to 1974 John Jones had responsibility for both counter-subversion and counter-terrorism, but was far more interested in the former. The officer who established the counter-terrorist section in F Branch found Jones 'not really interested in terrorism as a subject ... Skulduggery in counter-terrorism was not really his scene.'[79]

The terrorist debut in Britain in 1973 of the man who became the best-known terrorist working for the PFLP, Ilich Ramírez Sánchez, alias 'Carlos the Jackal', was memorable mainly for its incompetence. 'Carlos' had first arrived in Britain in 1966, accompanied by his wealthy Venezuelan mother and two brothers, as a sixteen-year-old student of the English language. The immigration officer who interviewed them at Heathrow noted that they were 'a well-dressed family' but correctly deduced that the 'unusual forenames of the children' – Vladimir, Ilich and Lenin – 'might have some bearing on the political colour of the family ...'.[80] 'Carlos' subsequently studied at Moscow University but told the MPSB that he had been expelled in 1970 for 'anti-Soviet sentiments'.[81] Following intelligence on his involvement with the PFLP, in December 1971 he was made subject by HOW to letter- and telechecks. F Branch later reported:

Neither check ... has produced significant information to connect Ramírez Sánchez with Arab terrorist activity and it is probable that once he became aware that the authorities were interested in him (his home had been searched in December 1971 and he was aware of A4 surveillance) whatever plans had been made for him by the PFLP were abandoned.

A4 reported that he appeared 'very edgy' during visits to the ophthalmic department of St George's (then at Hyde Park Corner) and later to an optician, from which he emerged wearing dark glasses.[82]

Though the Special Branch and Security Service lost track of 'Carlos' during 1972, it was later discovered that he spent the next few years travelling, often on forged passports, in Europe, the Middle East and Latin America, on operations for the PFLP and paying several visits to Britain.[83] On 30 December 1973, during one of these visits, 'Carlos' knocked on the door of the surprisingly unprotected St John's Wood home of Joseph Edward 'Teddy' Sieff, an ardent Zionist and chairman of Marks and Spencer. The door was opened by the butler, whom 'Carlos' ordered to take him to his victim. 'Carlos' fired a single shot which was deflected by Sieff's front teeth and failed to kill him. The gun then jammed and 'Carlos' ran away. A month later 'Carlos' tried to throw a bomb packed in a shoe box over the front counter of the Israeli Hapoalim Bank in the City of London but his aim was poor; the box bounced off the door, missed the counter and made a small crater in the floor, causing minor injuries to a nineteen-year-old secretary. 'Carlos' ran off once again.[84] Though the PFLP claimed responsibility for both attacks, it was only in the summer of 1975 that the Security Service discovered that the terrorist involved had been 'Carlos'.[85] By that time he had emerged as a far more formidable terrorist elsewhere than he had proved to be in London.

Though what Walter Laqueur later called the 'Age of Terrorism' had begun, Middle Eastern terrorists still made far more impression on the media than on most Western governments. 'Future historians', wrote Laqueur, 'will be intrigued and puzzled by the staggering disproportion between the enormous amount of talk about terrorism and the tiny effort made to combat it and the minute sums of money allocated for this purpose.'[86]

Those who do not remember past mistakes, it has been said, are doomed to repeat them. Historical ignorance goes far to explain British policy and intelligence failures in Northern Ireland in the 1970s. If Whitehall or the various components of the security forces had been aware of the serious damage done to British operations against Sinn Fein and the IRA in the years between the Easter Rising of 1916 and the founding of the Free State in 1922 by the lack of co-ordination between the military, the police and the metropolitan intelligence agencies,[87] similar kinds of confusion would have been less likely to recur half a century later. The Security Service officer appointed as SLO in Belfast in July 1970 later recalled that when he arrived 'the scene was chaotic. With mutual distrust between the police and the army, the Home Office was responsible but not in effective political control.'[88] The Provisional IRA (PIRA), on its foundation in 1970, suffered from the opposite defect, paying too much – rather than too little – attention to historical memory (and myth), recreating the outmoded and clumsy structure of the IRA of the 1920s. Its pseudo-military terminology of 'battalions' and 'brigades', ill applied to units a fraction of the size of their military equivalents, was intended to persuade the nationalist community of its legitimacy as an army of liberation.[89]

Furnival Jones was pessimistic about what intelligence could achieve in Northern Ireland. He told Heath at their first meeting in July 1970 that 'no amount of intelligence could cure Northern Ireland's ills. The most intelligence could do was to define the problem and help the security forces to confine the troubles.'[90] With the escalation of violence in 1970–71, both the army and the RUC began to suffer heavy losses. For the army to mount effective counter-terrorist operations, it required intelligence which the under-resourced RUC Special Branch was unable to provide.[91] Before the Troubles began, the IRA had been small in size and drawn from Republican families well known to the Special Branch. Between the arrival of the first British troops on the streets of Belfast in August 1969 and the end of 1971, according to credible Republican estimates, IRA 'Volunteers' in the city grew from about fifty to around 1,200. Though ridiculed for their failure to act as the 'armed defender' of the nationalist community during the violent sectarian summer of 1969, in September 1971 they were able to launch 200 bomb attacks.[92] The sudden introduction of internment without trial by the Stormont government on 9 August 1971 exposed the confused state of intelligence in Northern Ireland. In a series of dawn swoops, the army arrested 342 Republican suspects, many from the Official IRA, but 105 were released within two days. Heath complained that the intelligence supplied by the RUC Special Branch before internment proved to be 'hopelessly out of date'.[93] The limited security benefits of internment were far outweighed by the upsurge of sectarian violence which in three days caused twenty-two deaths and left up to 7,000 people (a majority of them Catholic) homeless as their houses were burned to the ground. For the Provisionals in particular internment produced an upsurge in recruitment.[94]

The division of Irish responsibilities between the MPSB and Security Service was all the more bizarre in view of the fact that the Service had the lead intelligence role on the British mainland for intelligence operations against Irish Loyalist paramilitaries, whose largest pockets of support were in Strathclyde and Merseyside. In the early 1970s F5, whose responsibilities included 'subversive activities' by 'extreme Protestant groups', as well as IRA arms smuggling, had some major intelligence successes which led to convictions for smuggling arms and explosives to Loyalist paramilitaries in Ulster from mainland Britain.[95] Julian Faux, who was involved in these operations, believed that their success was due largely to close co-operation with local Special Branches (SBs), authorized by successive home secretaries. 'There was a real sense', he wrote later, 'in which the SBs were the field agents of the Service.'[96] In order not to infringe MPSB's prerogatives, there were as yet no comparable A4 operations against the more serious threat posed by Irish Republican supporters in mainland Britain.

One further element of confusion in the organization of British counter-terrorism was the fact that, though the Security Service did not have the lead role in countering PIRA mainland attacks, it had the main responsibility for devising protective-security measures against them.[97] The counter-sabotage section of the Service had long had a remit to advise on the protection of military 'key points' in the UK in time of international tension and war.[98] Fear that the IRA might extend its bombing campaign to mainland Britain prompted the C Branch counter-sabotage section on 30 March 1971 to propose to MPSB that the list of 'key points' be extended to include potential non-military terrorist targets which were of 'vital importance to the economy'. When MPSB showed no interest in the idea, the section took it up with the chairman of the Key Points Sub-Committee of the Official Committee on Terrorism, who was equally unresponsive.[99] The DG then raised the issue with the PUS at the Home Office, Sir Philip Allen. In 1972 the Home Office agreed to support the compilation of a list of what later became known as 'Economic Key Points' (EKPs) which required special protection.[100] Due to what the Security Service considered Home Office procrastination, no action to begin assembling the list was taken for several years.[101]

At the beginning of 1972, despite continuing confusion in the organization of intelligence in Northern Ireland, both the RUC and the army were still optimistic that Republican terrorism in all its manifestations could be defeated.[102] Most of that optimism evaporated during a Derry civil rights rally on what became known as 'Bloody Sunday', 30 January. The rally led to riots in which part of the crowd tried to climb over a street barrier and were forced back by rubber bullets and water cannon. More than a hundred youths engaged in a running battle, hurling stones and iron bars at soldiers of the Parachute Regiment. Then the shooting began. Major General Robert Ford, Commander of Land Forces, insisted that 'There is absolutely no doubt that the Parachute Battalion opened up only after they were fired on.' Nationalists were convinced that, on the contrary, the British soldiers were guilty of premeditated murder. Thirteen men (all apparently unarmed) were shot dead by the Parachute Regiment; eighteen more were wounded, one of whom died later. According to the *Irish Press* on 31 January 1972, 'If there was an able-bodied man with Republican sympathies within the Derry area who was not in the IRA before yesterday's butchery there will be none tonight.'[103] On 2 February, after a series of anti-British demonstrations in Dublin, the British embassy was burned down.

On 22 February 1972 Republican terrorism spread to the British mainland for the first time since the IRA attacks of 1938–9. A bomb planted by the Official IRA in the HQ of the Parachute Regiment at Aldershot, in revenge for Bloody Sunday, missed its target and, instead of blowing up paras, killed five cleaners, an army chaplain and a gardener. The Aldershot killings marked the beginning of a Republican bombing campaign on the mainland which was to continue intermittently for the next quarter-century. On 24 March, following two serious terrorist attacks in Belfast, Heath announced the suspension of the Stormont government when it refused to surrender voluntarily control of law and order to London. In its place a secretary of state for Northern Ireland (SOSNI), initially Willie Whitelaw, assisted by junior ministers, took over the functions of the Unionist government which had ruled at Stormont for the past half-century.

In response to the urgent request of the PUS in the newly established Northern Ireland Office (NIO), Sir William Neild, for more intelligence from the Province,[104] an Irish Joint Section (IJS) was established by MI5 and SIS with jointly staffed offices in Belfast and London.[105]

The fact that SIS had a larger role than the Security Service in running the IJS during the early years of direct rule from London reflected not an ambition to encroach on MI5 responsibilities within the UK but the Security Service's own lack of readiness for a major role in Northern Ireland. One of the Service officers posted to Northern Ireland in the mid-1970s contrasted his own Service, which as yet lacked experience of conducting operations in hostile territory, unfavourably with SIS.[106] Though many MI5 staff had experience of working in Africa, Asia and/or the West Indies, Ulster still seemed more alien territory than outposts of Empire thousands of miles away. The story was told of an air stewardess who, before landing at Belfast's Aldergrove Airport, advised passengers to put their watches back 300 years. The unreadiness of the Security Service for Northern Irish responsibilities at the beginning of direct rule was graphically demonstrated when Whitelaw established the post of director and co-ordinator of intelligence (DCI) in Belfast to act as both his personal security adviser and his main link with the senior army general and the RUC Chief Constable. Though the post was offered to the Security Service, no one of sufficient seniority was willing to fill it. The first DCI, appointed on 31 October, thus came from outside MI5. His Security Service successor remembers him as 'the right man really to establish the post': 'He was there for a year and he did it in tremendous style ... He lived like a king, he entertained like a king, he used to drink with Willie [Whitelaw] all night.'[107]

As Director F from 1972 to 1974, with responsibility for counter-terrorism as well as counter-subversion, John Jones showed no desire to expand the Service's role in Northern Ireland. While on the Irish desk, a former Security Service officer recalls that he 'never had one conversation with Jones about Ireland in my whole time'.[108] The title 'Director and Co-ordinator of Intelligence', held by Security Service officers from 1973, was a partial misnomer. DCIs never directed intelligence operations in Northern Ireland. Their main function was intelligence liaison and co-ordination,[109] which in the early 1970s were difficult and sometimes thankless tasks. At the end of 1973, after two years' work on the Irish desk and the Irish Current Intelligence Group on the JIC, an F5 officer gave 'a somewhat sanguine forecast that it is possible that in due course the Provisionals, already badly mauled, will cease-fire, that the Army will be partly withdrawn from Northern Ireland and will diminish its intelligence effort':

We, and indeed the southern Irish also, regard [the Official IRA] as a greater long-term threat to UK and the Republic than the Provisionals, chiefly because of its greater political sophistication, its Marxist orientation, and its links abroad.[110]

In fact the Official IRA, which in May 1972 had declared what became a permanent ceasefire, rapidly lost influence to PIRA.

Despite its secondary role in countering Republican attacks in Britain, the Security Service had the lead intelligence role in monitoring Republican activities outside the UK, in particular the crucial issue of arms procurement. Unlike the Official IRA, which in 1972 received undetected arms shipments from the KGB, the Provisionals failed in a series of attempts in 1972–3 to smuggle arms from Europe.[111] PIRA's most willing potential supplier was Colonel Qaddafi of Libya, whom the veteran Republican and PIRA chief of staff Joe Cahill found possessed of 'an awful hatred of England': '[He] said he did not understand why we did not speak in Irish, and why did we speak in English, the language of our enemies?'[112] In August 1972 MPSB discovered that the freighter *Elbstrand*, soon to be renamed the *Claudia*, was involved in smuggling weapons to Ireland. For the next seven months the vessel was kept under intelligence surveillance. Cahill himself took part in chartering the *Claudia* for a first arms shipment from Libya in March 1973. F5 later 'speculated', almost certainly correctly, that Cahill and Dáithí Ó Conaill 'personally supervised the negotiations [with Qaddafi] and the shipment itself to ensure that it did not go wrong'. Colonel Qaddafi was believed to have offered PIRA as many arms as it could carry away.[113]

The Security Service was not informed of the surveillance of the *Claudia* until 26 March when F Branch received a hand-delivered copy from the FCO of an urgent telegram sent three days earlier by the Foreign Secretary, Sir Alec Douglas-Home, to the British ambassador in Dublin, informing him that intelligence reports over the past twenty-four hours indicated:

that the Claudia left North Africa a few days ago carrying up to 100 tons of small arms and explosives reported to have been provided free by the Libyans for delivery to the IRA in the Republic. At least one senior member of the IRA is believed to be on board. The ship is due to rendezvous with two Irish fishing trawlers off the coast between Dungarvan and Waterford . . .

Claudia is to be located and kept under discreet surveillance by British maritime forces. The latter will not repeat not attempt to intercept or board on the high seas, nor take any action in the final stages which would infringe Irish sovereignty. The primary purpose of the surveillance operation is to establish beyond all reasonable doubt that Claudia is proceeding to the rendezvous. We consider that interception of this arms shipment should be a matter for the Irish government . . .

You should take urgent steps to inform [the Taoiseach, the Irish Prime Minister] Mr Cosgrave of the above . . .[114]

Since the Security Service was responsible for collating intelligence on Republicans' foreign arms procurement, F Branch reacted with understandable indignation to the discovery that it had previously been kept in the dark over surveillance of the *Claudia*. 'This mistake', minuted a probably furious head of section, 'must not be made again.'[115] His point appears to have been taken.

During the voyage from Tripoli neither Joe Cahill nor the other PIRA members on board the *Claudia* suspected that they were being tracked by a British surveillance operation.[116] When they were intercepted by the Irish navy off the coast of County Waterford on 28 March, there was, according to a report from the British embassy in Dublin, 'apparently complete surprise and consternation amongst those on *Claudia* when the boarding party came alongside'.[117] Cahill, who was in the ship's galley, later recalled being unaware even that the *Claudia* had been boarded until he felt a gun muzzle pressed against his temple and heard a young Irish navy officer say, 'Don't move.' Five tons of arms, ammunition and explosives were discovered in the hold – far less than had been expected. Intelligence reports that the Libyans had originally intended to supply much more were, however, correct. Qaddafi had been deterred by poor PIRA security and had scaled down the shipment.[118] If the 5 tons had got through safely, they would no doubt have been quickly followed by more and larger consignments. The capture of the *Claudia* was thus of major significance in limiting PIRA's ability to expand its operations.[119] When large-scale arms smuggling from Libya began in 1985, it was to transform the Provisionals' operational capability.[120]

During 1973 PIRA seemed to be losing ground in Northern Ireland. Despite angry protests by the Provisionals and Sinn Fein, Willie Whitelaw succeeded in drawing the nationalist Social Democratic and Labour Party (SDLP) into power-sharing negotiations. In November 1973 the Official Unionist Party, the SDLP and the small Alliance Party agreed on setting up a power-sharing executive to restore power at Stormont and end direct rule from London. The framework of the new Executive was set out a month later in the Sunningdale agreement between the three parties and the British and Irish governments. Many Unionists, however, were almost as suspicious of Sunningdale as the Provisionals were. The new Executive lacked popular support from the moment it took office on New Year's Day 1974. In the general election to the Westminster parliament at the end of February the pro-Sunningdale Unionists were routed by the hardliners. What finally brought the Executive down was the Ulster Workers Council (UWC), founded by Unionist trade unionists who controlled most of the key services in Northern Ireland, with the backing of the Loyalist paramilitaries. A combination of telechecks and local Special Branch reports on the paramilitaries' Merseyside supporters, from whom the UWC attempted to drum up support, provided advance warning of UWC plans before it called a general strike on 14 May.[121] A State of Emergency was declared on the 19th. Good intelligence made little difference to the outcome. Though 2,000 British troops were flown in to help run the power stations and deal with the Emergency, it was clear that power had passed from the Executive to the UWC. 'This', concluded Merlyn Rees, SOSNI in the final Wilson government, 'was the Protestant people of Northern Ireland rising up against Sunningdale.' On 28 May the power-sharing Executive resigned and Northern Ireland returned to direct rule from London.[122]

Though PIRA's violence continued to be concentrated in Northern Ireland, in February 1974 it made its first lethal attack on a British mainland target, planting a 50-pound bomb on a coach carrying soldiers to Catterick Military Camp, which exploded on the M62 killing nine soldiers, one civilian and two children. The lack of intelligence on PIRA operational planning made the Irish Joint Section pessimistic about the prospects for countering the mainland bombing campaign.[123] The 1974 campaign cost more lives in Britain than any other in the history of the Troubles. The forty-four deaths (twenty-nine civilians, fourteen members of the security forces and one PIRA bomber blown up by his own bomb) accounted for 38 per cent of those killed in England during the entire period from 1973 to 1997. A majority of the civilian deaths took place on a single day, 21 November 1974, when PIRA bombs in two Birmingham pubs killed nineteen people and wounded 182 (two of whom died later from their injuries). The Security Service's credibility with the RUC was enhanced by a PIRA bomb attack on the home of the Service representative at RUC headquarters. After a farewell dinner at his home on 5 January 1975 for a departing colleague, attended by army and police officers, a brigadier pointed to a plastic bag outside the house and, with a feeble attempt at humour, called to his host: 'I see someone has left you a bomb!' The officer thought it more likely that the bag contained his wife's shopping or a salmon from a friend. On closer inspection, he discovered that the contents consisted of five sticks of gelignite and a timer which had run its course but failed to detonate the explosive. Thereafter he had the impression that the RUC considered him 'one of us'.[124]

Despite the bombing campaigns in Britain and Northern Ireland, a secret back-channel had been established to the Provisional leadership which was to play a major role in later ceasefire and peace talks involving the Security Service as well as SIS. The main intermediary (the 'Contact') through whom clandestine talks with the Provisionals were intermittently conducted was a Derry businessman, Brendan Duddy, who knew Ruairí Ó Brádaigh, the president of Sinn Fein.[125] Duddy said later that his 'mission' of 'replacing violence with dialogue' was driven by his 'Christian faith': 'I was completely opposed to the bombs, the blood and the bullets on all sides.'[126] Contacts with the Provisionals were among Whitehall's most tightly held secrets. When Harold Wilson returned to power in March 1974, he instructed that only he and the Secretary of State for Northern Ireland, Merlyn Rees, should be kept informed of them.[127] In January 1975 Duddy helped to arrange direct talks between NIO officials and PIRA representatives. Intelligence briefings by the DCI and others to Rees identified two other initiatives which helped to make the talks possible:

First, as a direct result of a meeting at Feakle in the Republic with some Northern Protestant clergymen, the Provisionals declared a temporary ceasefire over Christmas 1974. They indicated to the clergymen that this was to give us a chance to open negotiations for an indefinite 'truce'. Secondly, David O'Connell [Dáithi Ó Conaill], then the Provisional IRA Chief of Staff, made a similar proposal in a letter to the Prime Minister delivered through the intermediary of Dr John O'Connell, a Labour Deputy in the Dail.[128]

On 9 February the Provisionals announced an indefinite ceasefire. Rees concluded, chiefly on the basis of his intelligence briefings, that PIRA's motives, though not known with certainty, were probably, in declining order of importance:

a) A belief that the British Government and people were so fed up with Ireland that all they were looking for was an honourable way out;

b) An awareness that a number of incidents, notably the Birmingham bombs, had eroded some support from the Provisionals in the South. This meant there was a need to take stock and show a responsible face to the Catholic community;

c) An element of war weariness;

d) A desire to re-group and re-equip.[129]

Even if, as proved to be the case, the ceasefire did not prove to be indefinite, in addition to saving lives it served, in Rees's view, 'two vital short-term objectives'. First, it provided a period of peace in which elections could be held on 1 May 1975 for a Constitutional Convention at which it was hoped that all parties, including those linked to paramilitaries, would debate the future of Northern Ireland. Though Sinn Fein boycotted the elections and the Convention achieved little, it was able to meet during a period of comparative peace. Rees's second objective during the truce, also successfully accomplished, was to end internment without trial in Northern Ireland – which would probably have been politically impossible in the middle of a major PIRA bombing campaign.[130]

By the time the PIRA truce began, the early confusion over the role of the Director and Co-ordinator of Intelligence had been largely resolved. Though the DCI never directed intelligence in Northern Ireland, his liaison and advisory functions made him nonetheless an influential figure. He became SOSNI's chief intelligence adviser with regular access to him, ran an office which produced daily intelligence summaries, and acted as the channel for passing intelligence on Northern Ireland to the JIC, travelling every fortnight to London to brief the Assessment Staff. The DG, Sir Michael Hanley, also showed increased interest in intelligence on PIRA. The desk officer responsible for monitoring the threat of renewed Republican terrorism during the 1975 ceasefire saw Hanley at 9 a.m. every Thursday – partly to ensure that the DG was fully briefed in case he was summoned to the Home Office or, occasionally, to Number Ten before the weekly Thursday cabinet meetings.[131] On instructions from the Prime Minister, however, the DG did not brief the Home Secretary, Roy Jenkins, on the talks with the Provisionals which continued during the truce. Harold Wilson insisted, as before, ignoring the 1952 Maxwell Fyfe Directive (which made MI5 directly responsible to the Home Secretary), that only he and the Secretary of State for Northern Ireland should be briefed on them.[132] On occasion the Prime Minister took a personal, somewhat conspiratorial interest in intelligence on PIRA. When the DCI reported that, unusually, he had obtained a copy of an important PIRA document, he found himself summoned, not to Number Ten (which Wilson had mistakenly come to believe was bugged),[133] but to Chequers where, to his surprise, the door was opened by the Prime Minister himself. Wilson asked him if he thought the document was genuine. The DCI said it was. Later in Whitehall he found himself criticized for having bypassed the JIC to deal directly with the Prime Minister.[134]

4

The 'Wilson Plot'

Harold Wilson returned to power in February 1974 after a narrow election victory which left Labour only four seats ahead of the Conservatives, with no overall majority. During his preceding four years in opposition, some of the business friends Wilson had made while involved in East–West trade during the 1950s attracted the unfavourable attention of the Security Service. The friend who gave the Service most cause for concern was the Lithuanian-born Joseph (later Lord) Kagan, whose company Kagan Textiles made the Gannex macs which became one of Wilson's trademarks. While chancellor of the exchequer in the later 1960s, Roy Jenkins had once been 'practically run over' by a sports car as he was walking along Downing Street to his official residence at Number Eleven. A stocky figure emerged from the car and hurried to the door of Number Ten which was promptly opened for him. Finding the figure faintly familiar but unable to identify him, Jenkins asked the policeman outside Number Ten 'Who was that?' 'Oh, don't you know, sir?' was the reply. 'That's Mr Kagan. He's *very* well known here.'[1]

In August 1970 a Lithuanian officer in the KGB residency, Richardas Vaygauskas, was reported to have congratulated Kagan on his knighthood (awarded on Wilson's recommendation), claiming to be 'so proud' that Britain had at last a Lithuanian knight.[2] Kagan returned the compliment by inviting Vaygauskas to his investiture at Buckingham Palace, possibly the first ever attended by a KGB officer.[3] The KGB defector Oleg Lyalin[4] confirmed that Kagan was being actively cultivated by Vaygauskas, who in September 1971 was among the Soviet intelligence officers expelled from Britain in Operation FOOT. When interviewed by a K5 (counter-espionage operations) officer two months later, Kagan said that Vaygauskas had visited his flat almost every week since being posted to London in 1964, and that he had introduced Vaygauskas to all his friends (including a number of MPs), not realizing that he was a KGB officer.[5] At a subsequent meeting with Tony Brooks (K5B/1), Kagan admitted that Vaygauskas had asked him to use his influence with leaders of the Jewish community in Britain to call off demonstrations and the media campaign against trials of Russian Jews in Leningrad. Kagan had agreed to do so, having been convinced by Vaygauskas that 'If the outcry in the Western world were stopped the sentences would be light and further action against Jews would probably be stopped.' Brooks noted after the meeting:

I thanked Kagan for telling me this as it was a first class example of the KGB exploiting him as an agent of influence, because surely he was not so naive as to believe that calling off the legitimate protest in the West would have any effect on the fate of Jews in the USSR . . . Kagan was by now subdued and very worried and he quietly asked me whether what he had done was indictable. I said not in this country . . .[6]

Kagan also admitted that, if Vaygauskas had been collecting 'dirt' on people in public life, he would have provided him with a great deal: 'You know what it is in our sort of world, we gossip a lot and tend to make and destroy people's reputations.' Among the gossip was Harold Wilson's alleged affair with a female member of staff (whom he did not name). Vaygauskas would sometimes interrupt his evening chats with Kagan in order to go and see his 'ambassador' (in reality, almost certainly the KGB resident) before returning with 'a shopping list of questions'.[7]

In October 1972, Wilson himself requested a meeting with the Service to discuss information given him by Kagan. He was visited in his Commons office not by the DG or DDG (as he would have been had he still been prime minister), but by K5. Though Kagan's information was of little significance, K5 used the meeting to brief Wilson on Kagan's contacts with Vaygauskas:

It seemed clear to us that Kagan was being used unconsciously by Vaygauskas to supply items of news or scandal and as a medium for obtaining access to the famous. Kagan now accepts this.

Here Wilson interrupted to say that Kagan has two main faults – he cannot stop gossiping or chasing women . . . Wilson said that Kagan was a very sharp Jewish businessman and that he wished that he would stick to business.

. . . Wilson asked if it would help us in any way if he was to have a word with Kagan and warn him about talking to the Russians. I said that I thought it might be a good thing to do because nobody's secrets were safe when they were in the hands of a man as garrulous as Kagan.[8]

One of K5's main impressions from the meeting was 'Wilson's high regard for this Service which he has mentioned on a number of occasions'. This impression, however, may have been somewhat misleading. Presumably disconcerted by the discovery that a friend who had been one of the most regular visitors to Number Ten throughout his previous six years as prime minister had been passing on gossip about the Labour government to the KGB, Wilson was anxious to show that he himself had a proper regard for national security. He told K5 that, while at Number Ten, he had asked Security Service technicians to investigate the television set because of his concern that it could be used for 'technical attack' by a hostile intelligence service. 'This', noted K5, 'enabled me to mention the case of . . . a Lithuanian employed in the Electrical Dept. in the House of Commons who had been introduced to Vaygauskas by Kagan. Wilson seemed startled by this information but I assured him that it was under investigation.' Wilson, K5 concluded, 'is obviously under no illusions about Kagan's business honesty'.[9]

Immediately after K5's meeting with Wilson, Hanley discussed the Kagan case with the PUS at the Home Office, Sir Philip Allen. Both were baffled as to why, despite being well aware of Kagan's dishonesty and indiscretion, Wilson continued to see him regularly.[10] Director KX (John Allen) concluded that Kagan was: 'clearly a target of the highest importance for the K.G.B. because of his close association with Mr Wilson and other Labour Party leaders. I do not believe Kagan has been, or is now likely to become, a conscious Soviet agent but I am sure he has been a valuable source of intelligence.'[11]

Why Wilson was attracted to such dubious characters still remains something of a mystery. His official biographer, Philip Ziegler, concludes that 'He enjoyed the company of flamboyant self-made men; and where he would have been ill at ease in the company of a traditional backwoods Tory peer, a swashbuckling adventurer, especially if Jewish, appealed to him.'[12] Wilson continued to enjoy their company even when, as with Kagan, he was 'under no illusions about [their] business honesty'. When Wilson's press officer, Joe Haines, surveyed the Prime Minister's personal guests at the Guildhall ceremony on 12 December 1975 to confer on him the Freedom of the City of London, he 'looked around to see if Inspector Knacker of the Yard was keeping the ceremony under observation'.[13] Even after Kagan was sentenced to ten months in jail for fraud in 1980, Wilson's friendship with him continued. On at least one occasion after Kagan emerged from jail, the two men jointly entertained a member of the Soviet Trade Delegation at the House of Lords.[14] As late as 1986 two major British embassies complained to the FCO Security Department of Wilson's personal involvement with another company which had 'a dodgy reputation', was notorious for 'sharp practice' and had a chairman whose 'disgraceful' behaviour had caused diplomatic problems.[15]

Apart from Kagan, the business friend of Wilson of most concern to the Security Service during his final term as prime minister was Rudy Sternberg who, like Kagan, had made a fortune out of trade with the Soviet Bloc and had received a knighthood in 1970 on Wilson's recommendation. In the Service's view, Sternberg had made his money 'by methods which seem frequently to have been on the fringe of respectability'.[16] In 1961, he led a committee otherwise composed of MPs and peers to the Leipzig Trade Fair, to the great satisfaction of the East German Communist regime, which was not recognized in the West. As Sternberg's entry in the *Dictionary of National Biography* records: 'It was a role he clearly relished and he drove around Leipzig in a Rolls-Royce flying the Union Jack. Whether or not he intended it, the delegation's presence provided a valuable propaganda coup for a regime craving international recognition and acutely embarrassed the British government.'[17]

In May 1974 Robert Armstrong, then Wilson's principal private secretary, asked the DG, Sir Michael Hanley, whether there was 'anything we ought to know' about Sternberg, who was currently 'seeking to bend the Prime Minister's ear' – apparently 'to seek accreditation as an unpaid, unofficial, confidential and irregular liaison between the Prime Minister and the top leadership of the Soviet Government/Communist Party and other Eastern European Governments/Parties'.[18] Hanley replied that, though there was no evidence that Sternberg had been recruited as an agent:

It is a measure of the interest taken in him by the Soviet bloc intelligence services that of the many Soviet bloc officials with whom he had been in contact over the years, at least thirty-two are intelligence officers or suspected intelligence officers. With some of these he has been on first name terms and remained in touch after they have left the UK.[19]

The Security Service strongly advised that Sternberg should not be given access to any information classified 'Confidential' or above.[20] 'Sternberg's ambitions', it believed, 'render him vulnerable to Soviet bloc pressure.'[21]

Despite opposition from Robert Armstrong,[22] Sternberg received the peerage he appeared to crave in the 1975 New Year Honours List. As Philip Ziegler observes, his elevation as Lord Plurenden 'caused particular offence, since it was well known that Sternberg had contributed generously to Wilson's office expenses during the period in opposition'.[23] Strange and sinister rumours about Sternberg circulated around Whitehall. Bernard Donoughue, Wilson's senior policy adviser, noted in his diary that Sternberg was 'reported by the Downing St private office as being a Soviet spy', and on another occasion that 'The Foreign Office have told me privately that he is a double agent.'[24] Joe Haines also recalls that, when Wilson announced his intention to make Sternberg a peer, 'a shocked Foreign Office official protested to me, knowing I would tackle Wilson about it, that Sternberg was a Soviet spy. When I raised it with Wilson, he said cheerfully that he had always thought so too, but that when he checked with the security services he had been told Sternberg was a double agent.'[25] There is no evidence that the Security Service ever suggested to the Prime Minister that Sternberg was a double agent. Wilson's tendency to conspiracy theory may have led him to reach that conclusion for himself.

Among Wilson's other disreputable business friends who had made their fortunes from East–West trade was Harry Kissin, who, like Kagan and Sternberg, had helped to finance his private office.[26] Kissin was one of Wilson's confidants during his final term.[27] Soon after Wilson returned to Number Ten, the cabinet secretary, Sir John Hunt, asked Hanley for a report on Kissin. Hanley replied that, though, unlike Kagan, Kissin's security record 'hardly amounts to an adverse one', he was 'obviously not a man to be trusted with confidences' – in other words, entirely unsuited for a role as Prime Minister's confidant.[28] The DG doubtless had in mind Kissin's indiscretions to, and corrupt use of, prostitutes. According to an agent whom the Service considered reliable, 'When Kissin comes to [a brothel] on pleasure bent – always two girls at a time – he invariably uses the telephone in his Rolls Royce . . . to establish that the talent at his disposal has already arrived.'[29] Kissin also employed prostitutes to entertain foreign business contacts. In August 1968, according to an agent report, he asked 'a fashionable tart' to 'be nice' to one of his business friends. She was reported to have been 'nice to him shortly afterwards'.[30] Kissin also hired call-girls to entertain Asian contacts as well as a senior diplomat of an Asian country where he had business interests.[31] He appears to have passed on confidential information acquired during his conversations with Wilson to at least one call-girl agency. He was reported to have boasted (accurately or inaccurately) to one prostitute in September 1973 'that he is contributing money in support of Wilson's mounting campaign to boost the Liberal Party and so alienate wavering Tories [from voting Conservative] before the next election. At the same time, Kissin said that "Wilson is not the man he was. He is ill."'[32]

After Wilson's return to Number Ten in February 1974, Kissin was confident of a peerage in the Birthday Honours List. Unsurprisingly, however, his nomination ran into opposition – probably (as in the case of Sternberg) from Robert Armstrong or Sir John Hunt, or both.[33] The peerage, however, duly arrived – doubtless at Wilson's insistence. On receiving congratulations from one of the brothels he frequented,[34] the newly ennobled Lord Kissin of Camden promised to call round for a champagne celebration.[35] Kissin continued both to use call-girls to entertain his foreign contacts (as well as himself)[36] and to talk indiscreetly to them about his confidential conversations with the Prime Minister. In January 1975, for example, he was reported to have revealed 'a lot' about the John Stonehouse case, though claiming that he was now 'fed up with Harold Wilson'.[37] Wilson, however, was not fed up with Kissin and continued to meet him regularly.[38]

Sitting in his study at Number Ten on his first day back in office, Wilson told Kissin: 'There are only three people listening – you, me and MI5.'[39] Though MI5 was not, of course, listening in to the Prime Minister and had never actively investigated him, it still had a file on him which recorded, *inter alia*, his past contacts with Communists, KGB officers and other Russians. Hanley went to even greater lengths than Hollis or FJ to conceal its existence within the Security Service. In March 1974 the DG instructed that the card referring to the file should be removed from the Registry Central Index, with the result that: '*A look-up on Harold Wilson would therefore be No Trace.*' Outside the DG's private office and – probably – the Board of Directors, the existence of the file was known only to F2, K10 and the Legal Adviser, Bernard Sheldon.[40] Access to it required the personal permission of the DG. Though the file was never used to undermine Harold Wilson, Hanley's decision to preserve it, approved by Sheldon, would doubtless not have been approved by either the Home Secretary or the Prime Minister.

Wilson's main suspicions on returning to power, however, were directed far less at the Security Service than at the CIA and the South African intelligence service, BOSS, both of which, he believed, were up to no good in London. The CIA, he wrongly suspected, partly as a result of misleading press reports, was seeking to penetrate British trade unions.[41] Hanley responded to the Prime Minister's suspicions by submitting two reports. The first concluded that 'The reports of alleged CIA activities in trade unions are unsubstantiated. The head of the London CIA station has specifically denied them, and we have no reason to disbelieve him.' The second report stated that the Security Service had no liaison with South African intelligence but kept a close watch on its activities in Britain, 'mainly, but not entirely, for the purpose of keeping Ministers informed about South African activities which could cause political embarrassment'.[42] Wilson was unconvinced.

Wilson and Marcia Williams (ennobled in 1974 as Lady Falkender) were also preoccupied by the belief that the Prime Minister's former security adviser George Wigg was behind press attacks on her. Without informing the Security Service, Wilson went to the extraordinary lengths of hiring private detectives to put Wigg under surveillance. Wilson's press officer, Joe Haines, recalls that:

One evening in the middle of the [May 1974] Ulster crisis, Wilson went off to have a private dinner with George Wigg, leaving behind in Number 10 a gathering of ministers and top military brass who were discussing the total collapse of civil order and authority in Northern Ireland . . . Wilson took with him information on Wigg's mistress and second family, collected by private detectives. He threatened to expose Wigg if he did not lay off Marcia. The visit was a curious priority for a Prime Minister in the middle of an Ulster crisis.[43]

Among other scandals which Wilson contemplated publicizing through planted parliamentary questions in order to distract the media from what he saw as its persecution of Marcia Williams were allegations that the Liberal leader, Jeremy Thorpe, had been threatened with blackmail as a result of his homosexuality. Donoughue told him 'he should forget this muckraking and not stoop to the gutter levels of the press.'[44]

Despite Wilson's conspiracy theories about intelligence, the Security Service regarded its relationship with him as 'perfectly friendly' until soon after the election of October 1974 (the second of the year), which gave Labour, previously without an overall majority, a majority of three (less precarious than it seemed because of the apparent improbability of all the minority parties in the Commons combining with the Conservatives to oppose the government). Over the past few months the Prime Minister had been brooding over an article by Chapman Pincher entitled 'Ministers in Security Risk Shock', published on 21 May, claiming that security doubts about some junior ministers had led to restrictions on their access to classified material. During his first period in office, Wilson had become enraged and obsessed by leaks to Pincher, wrongly suspecting that the source was the Security Service.[45] He made the same mistake during his final term. On this occasion, the probable source for Chapman Pincher's story was the maverick, extreme right-wing, retired Deputy Chief of SIS, George Young, who had become an embarrassment to his former Service and had lunch with Pincher on the day before the article appeared. Wilson, however, told the cabinet secretary, Sir John Hunt, on 17 October that he knew the story had been leaked to Pincher by the Security Service. Hunt replied that the Service was unlikely even to know what restrictions had been imposed,[46] but warned Hanley that he doubted whether he could shake the Prime Minister's conviction that the Service was to blame.[47] Wilson continued, however, to seek information from the Security Service about some of his own colleagues. In November 1974 he made inquiries about Defence Secretary Roy Mason's mistress.[48] In February 1975 he asked that the Labour MP Eric Heffer 'be warned off having contacts with the Communist Party', of which he had once been a member, but did not wish to issue the warning himself. Hunt and Hanley agreed that, on the contrary, any warning should come from the Prime Minister.[49] Wilson was also anxious that Ron Hayward, general secretary of the Labour Party, whom he privately regarded as 'one of the vainest and silliest men' he knew,[50] should be warned about his contacts with the CPGB.[51]

Wilson's suspicions about the Security Service were inevitably strengthened by his briefings on the sensational FLUENCY investigations into Hollis and Mitchell. The impact on Wilson was all the greater because during his first term as prime minister he had not been told about the investigation of Hollis – despite the fact that Hollis had been DG for his first year at Number Ten.[52] Wilson was entitled to feel that he should have been informed of the suspicions that Hollis had been a Soviet agent. In early August 1975 Wilson wrote on Sir Burke Trend's review of the Hollis and Mitchell cases, 'This is very disturbing stuff, even if concluding in "not proven" verdicts.'[53]

The discovery that important secrets had been kept from him by Hanley's predecessor and the inevitable suspicion that there might have been more that he was still not being told encouraged Wilson's belief that the Security Service was concealing from him its habit of leaking discreditable information about his government to Chapman Pincher. Soon after reading Trend's report, the Prime Minister complained to Hanley 'about the sort of things which Chapman Pincher seemed to know about'. These included alleged security concerns about the Minister for Overseas Development, Judith Hart, and – in Hanley's words – 'something, I could not make out what, about Lady Falkender'.[54] Joe Haines was told by Robert Armstrong that 'the security services still had not completed Marcia's positive vetting and that the PM was intervening to try to stop it. Robert is not certain that she would pass and is very jumpy about what to do.'[55] Though Hanley assured Wilson that no member of the Security Service was authorized to have any dealings with Chapman Pincher, Wilson's suspicions deepened and darkened. Sir John Hunt was so concerned by Wilson's continuing 'paranoiac suspicions' of the Security Service that he arranged a meeting between Wilson and Hanley in the summer of 1975 in an attempt to clear the air – but to no effect.[56] As Hanley later recalled, they had 'a terrible row': 'I could not get off the hook. He got the idea I was his worst enemy. I did not know what to do.' For a time the DG contemplated, but in the end rejected, the idea of resignation.[57]

Wilson's undisguised loathing of Hanley was, in many ways, out of character. Donoughue wrote of the Prime Minister: 'He could be accessible, warm, kind and humorous, which drew the affection and loyalty of those who worked for him. He had absolutely no side or any of the pretensions or assumptions of grandeur that sometimes accompany high office.' But, Donoughue noted, Wilson was also a conspiracy theorist who suffered from 'near paranoia about plots by various imaginary and genuine enemies'.[58] Conspiracy theorists are inherently unfitted for the ultimate responsibility which fell to Wilson as prime minister for the management of the British intelligence community.

By December 1975, a crisis-ridden month which he later described as 'the most hectic and harrowing' of his time as prime minister, Wilson was convinced that there was a plot to discredit and destroy him and his government, probably involving more than one intelligence service. Wilson's official biographer describes him as 'reasonably certain that elements of MI5 were doing the donkey work, though at what level he did not know'. He suspected that BOSS and a dirty-tricks department in the CIA were also involved.[59] In the United States 1975 became known as the 'Year of Intelligence', during which, according to the Director of Central Intelligence (head of the CIA), William Colby, 'The CIA came under the closest and harshest public scrutiny that any such service has ever experienced . . . anywhere in the world.' Revelations of a series of sensational CIA dirty tricks made front-page news around the world – among them assassination plots against Fidel Castro and several other foreign leaders. Senator Frank Church, chairman of a Senate committee of investigation, compared the CIA to 'a rogue elephant on the rampage' – conveniently overlooking that most of the rampage, assassination plots included, had been authorized if not instigated by the White House.[60] Though there was no authenticated evidence of dirty tricks targeted against Britain, Wilson believed that he was a victim of them. When Senator Church visited London, Wilson made a series of 'wild insinuations' about CIA operations.[61]

The paranoid strain in Wilson's view of intelligence was further strengthened by the attempted assassination of Jeremy Thorpe's former lover, the male model Norman Scott.[62] The inexperienced would-be assassin, Andrew Newton, a former airline pilot, succeeded only in killing Scott's Great Dane. Early in 1976, a hysterical Scott, who was being prosecuted for benefit fraud, claimed in open court that he was 'being hounded all the time by people just because of my sexual relationship with Jeremy Thorpe'.[63] Thorpe succeeded in persuading Harold Wilson that he was being framed by an elaborate plot orchestrated by the South African intelligence service, BOSS – a deception for which Marcia Williams later said she 'could not forgive him'.[64] Wilson required little persuasion by Thorpe – despite the fact that two years earlier he had contemplated publicizing stories about Thorpe's homosexuality and vulnerability to blackmail.[65] In Donoughue's view, the Prime Minister had become obsessed by the belief 'that the South African espionage system – BOSS – is doing dirty tricks'.[66]

Such evidence as there was for the claim that Thorpe was the victim of BOSS dirty tricks derived from the activities of an ex-Yorkshire burglar, South African freelance journalist and BOSS agent Gordon Winter, who had slept with Norman Scott and learned of his affair with Thorpe.[67] Wilson believed that Winter's attempts to publicize Scott's story were part of an elaborate plot by BOSS. The Security Service concluded that, on the contrary, they were a private initiative by Winter.[68] The Prime Minister was convinced that he understood BOSS better than the Security Service. The Intelligence Co-ordinator, Sir Leonard 'Joe' Hooper (formerly director of GCHQ), noted after being summoned to a meeting with Wilson on 23 February: 'PM suspects authors [of an MI5 report] do not know much about the subject and fears that friendly relations with S[outh] A[frican] diplomatic and intelligence people in London preclude their being watched properly.'[69]

Like some of the media, which bizarrely regarded BOSS as 'arguably the most efficient intelligence service in the world',[70] Wilson had a greatly inflated view of the sophistication of its foreign operations. Its use of the mendacious and unreliable Winter tends to support the contrary view of the Security Service that these operations were, in reality, 'comparatively crude and unsophisticated'. Wilson may also have been misled by Rhodesian threats to blackmail an 'immoral' Labour MP into believing that BOSS operated in a similar way. In an attempt to uncover the (non-existent) evidence for South African involvement in fabricating a gay scandal involving Thorpe, Wilson once again approached Sir Leonard Hooper,[71] without – apparently – gaining any support for his conspiracy theories.

The supposed South African connection in the Thorpe case was one of Wilson's chief preoccupations during his final two months in power. Donoughue noted: 'The PM is loving it all, since it appeals to his obsessions with plots, spies, conspiracies, etc.' One of Wilson's late-night meetings with Thorpe lasted three hours, from 10.30 p.m. to 1.30 a.m.[72] On 9 March, one week before he announced his resignation, Wilson declared, in reply to a parliamentary question he had planted himself: 'I have no doubt that there is a strong South African participation in recent activities relating to the leader of the Liberal Party.' Though Wilson avoided accusing the South African government directly, he claimed that 'massive resources of business money and private agents of various kinds and various qualities' had been involved in the campaign against Thorpe. Donoughue stated in his diary: 'Nobody knows if he has any evidence, and he did not consult anyone before planting a question with Jim Wellbeloved.'[73] The unknown source of some, perhaps much, of Wilson's information on the supposed South African conspiracy was his private and political secretary Lady Falkender. At a lunch only days before his resignation, he declared that he had proof that South African money had been involved in the plot to discredit Thorpe: 'It's been a great detective exercise, I can tell you. Detective Inspector Falkender has been up to her eyes in it.'[74]

Wilson's mental decline during the year before his resignation in April 1976 was obvious to all around him. Once impressively quick on his feet, he now found it difficult even to improvise a short constituency speech. 'For someone who had prided himself on his quickness of mind, his legendary memory,' writes Philip Ziegler, 'to slow up, to be at a loss for words or to grope for a statistic was not merely galling but a blow to his confidence.' Physically too, he became increasingly run down, consulting his doctors far more frequently than before, and suffering increasingly from psychosomatic stomach pains before difficult meetings (of which there were many).[75] Wilson's mental and physical decline was accompanied by, and may partly explain, his increasing tendency (long present in more muted form) to conspiracy theory. One of his colleagues recalls standing next to him in the lavatory at Number Ten, and watching in some astonishment as the Prime Minister pointed to the electric light fitting and gestured to indicate that, because it might well be bugged, it was unsafe to mention anything confidential. During his last few months in office, Wilson appears rarely to have said anything in the lavatory without first turning on all the taps and gesturing at imaginary bugs in the ceiling.[76] The Prime Minister also suspected that a hole in the wall of the Cabinet Room behind a portrait of Mr Gladstone contained a listening device. Apparently not trusting either the Security Service or any other government agency to examine it, he called in a firm called Argon Ltd. The hole turned out to be have been caused by nothing more sinister than the removal of an earlier picture light.[77] Wilson was also convinced that his study was bugged and on

16 February 1976, only a month before his resignation, arranged for a private security expert to search the room.[78] Wilson's obsession with bugging by now infected much of Number Ten. Bernard Donoughue, who distanced himself from many of Wilson's conspiracy theories, wrote in his diary, 'I believe that my room is bugged. Certainly my phone is tapped.'[79] He was wrong on both counts.

Though the various searches in 10 Downing Street predictably discovered no bugs, the Prime Minister's suspicions remained. In February 1976 he sent his publisher, George Weidenfeld, on a mission to the former US Vice President Hubert Humphrey, to ask him to try to discover whether the CIA had been involved in a smear campaign against him.[80] George Bush the elder, then Director of Central Intelligence, flew to London to reassure the Prime Minister in person, but emerged from a meeting at Number Ten asking, 'Is that man mad? He did nothing but complain about being spied on!'[81] Wilson's conspiracy theories about the involvement of the British intelligence services in plots against him were powerfully reinforced on 9 March when the maverick former Deputy Chief of SIS, George Young, gave a speech alleging that three of Wilson's ministers were crypto-Communists and that a prominent Conservative had been run by a KGB officer in London during the Heath government. On the 15th, the day before he announced his resignation, Wilson was briefed about Young's extreme right-wing activities and his connections with Chapman Pincher. A later Security Service inquiry concluded that a confused recollection of this briefing might have been responsible for Wilson's subsequent denunciation of a plot to discredit him by 'a very small MI5 mafia who had been out of the Service for some time who still continue the vendetta for no doubt very right wing purposes of their own'.[82] There was, in reality, no plot by any Service officer, serving or retired, to conspire with George Young against Wilson. Indeed, F Branch were becoming increasingly worried about Young's clandestine organization of the extreme right-wing group UNISON (not to be confused with the later trade union of the same name).[83]

Ironically, Wilson's resignation on 16 March 1976 gave rise to ill-informed speculation among some of his colleagues that the knowledge that the Security Service had obtained discreditable material on him had forced him to step down. At a dinner given by Michael Foot there was talk of 'very strong rumours' to this effect. 'Some funny things have evidently been happening,' believed Tony Benn. He himself suspected dirty dealing by South African intelligence.[84] Wilson's controversial Resignation Honours List, drafted on lavender (some say lilac or pink) notepaper by

Lady Falkender, added to the conspiracy theories. Along with the usual quota of the great and good were some inappropriate names and a few subsequently exposed as criminals: among them Sir Joseph Kagan (given a peerage) who was imprisoned for fraud in 1980, and Eric Miller (knighted) who committed suicide in 1977 while under official investigation for financial irregularities.[85]

Shortly after his resignation Wilson invited two young BBC journalists, Barrie Penrose and Roger Courtiour, whom he had never previously met but knew to be searching for evidence of South African interference in British politics, to investigate the 'grave danger' to British democracy from 'anti-democratic agencies in South Africa and elsewhere'. Thorpe's accuser, Norman Scott, was, he told them, a South African agent, like others in the international conspiracy to discredit the Liberal leader. He also claimed to have discovered in 1975 that MI5 had been trying to discredit both him and Lady Falkender in the belief that both were Communists. Wilson offered to help Penrose and Courtiour ('Pencourt' as they became collectively known) discreetly with their inquiries:

I see myself as a big fat spider in the corner of the room. Sometimes I speak when I'm asleep. You should both listen. Occasionally when we meet I might tell you to go to the Charing Cross Road and kick a blind man standing on the corner. That blind man may tell you something, lead you somewhere.[86]

In the three centuries since Sir Robert Walpole became Britain's first prime minister, no holder of that office has given a stranger interview.

After an exhausting year pursuing Wilson's and other conspiracy theories that the case against Thorpe had been fabricated by BOSS and its agents, Pencourt concluded that there was no substance to them. Unwilling to reveal these conclusions to Wilson for fear that he might break off contact with them, they approached Lady Falkender instead. 'Harold', she told them, 'certainly won't be happy to hear that.'[87] Pencourt, however, continued to believe Wilson's story, supported by Falkender, that the Security Service had plotted against him. That story was the most sensational item in their book, *The Pencourt File*, whose serialization rights were bought by the *Observer*. On Sunday 17 July 1977 the *Observer* led with a front-page story headed 'World Exclusive': 'Wilson: "Why I Lost My Faith in MI5"'.[88]

For the Security Service, Wilson's most damaging claim to Penrose and Courtiour, reported by the *Observer*, was Hanley's alleged admission to Wilson in 1975 that MI5 did indeed contain 'a disaffected faction with extreme right-wing views' capable of plotting against him. The Home

Secretary, Merlyn Rees, informed Wilson's successor, Jim Callaghan, that, on the contrary:

I am assured by Sir Michael Hanley that, at his meeting with Sir Harold Wilson* in the summer of 1975, he did not confirm 'the existence within his Service of a disaffected faction with extreme right-wing views'. Sir Harold Wilson apparently suggested to him that, because there were a number of former army officers in the Service, there was likely to be some sort of bias against Labour Ministers; Sir Michael Hanley acknowledged that there were a number of retired [army] officers in the Security Service, but did not accept that that meant that their loyalty and integrity as public servants was in question.

Nor was there any evidence that, as Wilson claimed, the Service had ever confused Will Owen (who had been lucky to be acquitted of espionage for the Czechoslovak StB) with his fellow MP David Owen or the Soviet spy Edith Tudor-Hart with the Labour minister Judith Hart. But because some of the other information passed by Wilson to Penrose and Courtiour was correct – including the highly embarrassing revelation that Wilson had sought the help of the head of the CIA in investigating the supposed plot against him – Rees believed 'it would not be possible to deny the whole of the article.' He suggested simply a general statement reaffirming 'confidence in the competence and integrity of the Security Service'.[89]

The DDG, John Jones, noted on 27 July 1977:

Since no one has yet fathomed Harold Wilson's devious purpose in making allegations against the Security Service, the Prime Minister [Callaghan] thought it highly desirable for the record to have a talk with the DG for the specific and formal purpose of going over all the allegations in The Observer articles.[90]

Hanley briefed Merlyn Rees on 3 August, then had an unusually long meeting with Callaghan, lasting one and a half hours. Both struck the DG as 'friendly and relaxed, and very supportive of the Security Service', but – especially in Callaghan's case – deeply suspicious of Wilson. Callaghan thought Wilson perfectly capable of causing horrendous embarrassment by publicly revealing the lengthy investigations of Hollis and Mitchell based on suspicions that they were Soviet agents. If Wilson did decide to publicize this story, Callaghan feared that he 'would do so to the hilt'.[91]

On 23 August a press statement from 10 Downing Street announced:

The Prime Minister has conducted detailed inquiries into the recent allegations about the Security Service and is satisfied that they do not constitute grounds for

---

* Wilson was made a Knight of the Garter on resigning as prime minister in 1976.

lack of confidence in the competence and impartiality of the Security Service or for instituting a special inquiry. In particular, the Prime Minister is satisfied that at no time has the Security Service or any other British intelligence or security agency, either of its own accord or at someone else's request, undertaken electronic surveillance in No 10 Downing Street or in the Prime Minister's room in the House of Commons.

Callaghan repeated the same statement to the Commons, adding that there were no grounds for doubting Wilson's loyalty and that he was also 'quite satisfied ... with what is going on in the security services'. Callaghan's official biographer, Kenneth Morgan, comments: 'On the face of it, the affair implied a rebuke of his predecessor by the Prime Minister. One of his main concerns, however, was to protect Wilson who was already showing signs of the illness that was to dog his later years.'[92]

After the front-page story in the *Observer* in July 1977, Wilson seems to have lost the desire to publicize his claims of a Security Service plot against him. Part of the explanation probably lies in his growing, though reluctant, awareness of the declining credibility of his claims that the allegations against Jeremy Thorpe were part of a great conspiracy by BOSS to undermine British democracy. On 19 and 20 October the *Evening News* led with confessions by Andrew Newton and Peter Bissell, headlined respectively: 'I was hired to kill Scott. Exclusive: Gunman tells of incredible plot – a murder contract for £5,000' and 'Former MP reveals murder plot. Exclusive: He [Scott] must be bumped off.' The *Observer* followed on 23 October with more in the same vein from Penrose and Courtiour. Next day the Home Secretary asked Hanley if the Security Service had 'any hard security information against Jeremy Thorpe other than allegations of homosexuality'. The DG 'said there was none. We had known about these allegations for some time but Thorpe was not otherwise a security case.'[93]

The 'Wilson plot' conspiracy theory was given continuing currency by allegations of dirty tricks by the Security Service and other sections of the intelligence community made by a number of others including Colin Wallace, an MoD information officer in Northern Ireland from 1968 to 1975, and Captain Fred Holroyd, who had served for a year as military intelligence officer in the Province in 1974–5.[94] The DG, Sir Antony Duff, assured staff in 1987 that Wallace's and Holroyd's allegations of dirty tricks were 'equally baseless'.[95] Duff also declared that claims that the Security Service had tried to encourage the Ulster Workers strike were 'completely untrue', and that the allegation by the future Labour minister

Peter Hain that his arrest on an unfounded charge of robbery in October 1975 might have had assistance from an element in the Service was 'rubbish'.[96]

The longevity of belief in the Wilson plot owes as much to Peter Wright as to Harold Wilson. A decade after Callaghan's public statement that he was 'quite satisfied' with the role of the Security Service, Wright claimed in Spycatcher that thirty MI5 officers 'had given their approval to a plot'. During a television interview Wright admitted that this figure was exaggerated: 'The maximum number was eight or nine. Very often it was only three.' When pressed further and asked, 'How many people, when all the talking died down, were still serious in joining you in trying to get rid of Wilson?', Wright replied, 'One, I should say.' In reality, instead of orchestrating a plot, he spent his final years in MI5 before retiring in January 1976 'mostly going through the motions'.[97] Though Wright had effectively discredited his own evidence, Spycatcher persuaded many who had dismissed Wilson's conspiracy theories a decade earlier that there must have been something to them after all. The former Home Secretary Roy Jenkins noted that 'the publication of Peter Wright's tawdry book ... nonetheless chimed in with a chorus of other allegations.'[98] Callaghan reached a similar conclusion. So did the official biographers of both Wilson and Callaghan. The DG, Sir Antony Duff, recorded after a meeting on 31 March 1987 with Callaghan and the then leader of the Labour Party, Neil Kinnock: 'Callaghan fixed me with a fairly penetrating, not to say hostile glance, and said that even if only a tenth of what Wright had said about destabilising the Wilson government was true, it was still a "bloody disgrace" that it had happened. I said that it was all in any case untrue.' Though not all Callaghan's suspicions seem to have been laid to rest, he acknowledged 'Wilson's "paranoia" and said that Marcia and others had been responsible for a lot of it'.[99]

The stringent internal inquiry ordered by Duff, which examined all relevant files and interviewed all relevant Security Service officers, both serving and retired, concluded unequivocally that no member of the Service had been involved in the surveillance of Wilson, still less in any attempt to destabilize his government. When Stella Rimington became director general, she tried 'once and for all to knock on the head the Wilson plot allegation' by inviting former Labour home secretaries and other senior Party figures to her office. The attempt failed. 'Though I did my best to convince them that they were wrong,' she recalls, 'I knew that further efforts would be fruitless.'[100] A decade later she also failed to convince the Guardian, which accompanied the serialization of her memoirs in 2001 with an article claiming that, while there might have been fewer than the thirty plotters claimed by Peter Wright, 'there is no doubt that some MI5 officers were out to destabilise Labour ministers.' Old conspiracy theories never die. This one has not even begun to fade away.

5

Counter-Terrorism and Protective Security in the Later 1970s

By late 1975 the secret talks with the Provisionals, in the view of the British negotiators, had become 'largely meaningless':

Our interlocutors were unable or unwilling to control their followers and there was nothing we could plausibly say to them which would materially affect events – except in so far as their continuing contacts with us gave them a certain status within the Provisional movement which itself enabled them to exercise a limited restraining influence.[1]

Though PIRA did not formally end the ceasefire until early in 1976, during the final months of 1975 it embarked on a bombing campaign against restaurants and hotels in the West End of London. A detective in the Met's Anti-Terrorist Squad identified a distinctive pattern in the PIRA attacks. Most occurred between 6.30 and 9.30 p.m. on weekdays, none took place at weekends, and the bombers sometimes attacked the same target more than once. The Security Service played little part in defeating the London bombing campaign. The campaign was successfully brought to an end by the Metropolitan Police's Operation COMBO, which for an eight-day period early in December saturated the West End with patrols. When PIRA bombers launched a second attack on Scott's Restaurant in Mayfair on 7 December, they were spotted by a police unit and pursued to a flat in Balcombe Street where they held the occupants hostage during a six-day siege before surrendering to the Met. The Balcombe Street siege proved to be a turning point in PIRA operations in Britain. Though sporadic attacks by the Provisionals on mainland targets continued, there was no further sustained mainland bombing campaign until 1989.[2]

On Harold Wilson's instructions, James Callaghan, like all other cabinet ministers except for Rees, had been kept in ignorance of the negotiations with the Provisionals during the previous government. His first briefing on the now moribund negotiations did not take place until shortly after he became prime minister in April 1976.[3] At the same time Merlyn Rees

(SOSNI) sent Callaghan a confident account of the functioning of the intelligence system:

The first point I should like to make is that we now have a well-established, single machine for processing intelligence and covert work in Northern Ireland. The overall responsibility for the coordination of intelligence operations is exercised by the Director and Coordinator of Intelligence (DCI) . . . [in] the Northern Ireland Office in Belfast. He is responsible to me through the Permanent Under Secretary.[4]

Rees had announced to the Commons in March 1976 that henceforth the RUC was to have 'primacy' in counter-terrorist operations in Northern Ireland,[5] and he told Callaghan that its intelligence collaboration with the army was working well.[6] He also praised the 'breadth of view and . . . knowledge of social and political background' shown by the DCI and Security Service officers in the Irish Joint Section (IJS).[7]

In May 1976 the DG, Sir Michael Hanley, made a three-day tour of the Province – his first extended visit for eighteen months – and was impressed both by the improved performance of the RUC Special Branch (of which he had earlier been critical) and by the new Chief Constable, (Sir) Kenneth Newman, formerly of the Met. Hanley wrote on his return:

The main emphasis of our support must now be switched to the RUC. Since the NIO was formed in 1972 I have followed a policy of helping the Army first. Of course we must still help the Army, but henceforth our first priority must be the RUC, and we ought to pursue an active and positive policy towards them and be on the alert for any ways in which we can be of assistance.[8]

PIRA, Hanley concluded, was losing the 'armed struggle':

The bombing and shooting had not diminished and the PIRA continued to possess a considerable capacity for violence, but their sterile tactics were taking them relentlessly along the road to isolation. It would take time to complete the process, but that must be the aim. The PIRA/PSF [Provisional Sinn Fein] should be hit hard and their claims to 'respectability' should be utterly destroyed. It was encouraging that it was now considered practicable to press ahead with the concept of the primacy of the Police, the intention being gradually to return the Province to a system of normal policing with crimes being investigated and criminals brought to court . . . The process would inevitably be a gradual one, but at least it held out the prospect of success in the long term, lowering the security temperature as it progressed. The joker in the pack was the politician.[9]

Hanley probably had in mind politicians at Westminster as well as in the Province. James Callaghan, burdened with unhappy memories of his experience of Northern Ireland in the previous Wilson government,[10] did not share the cautious optimism of Rees and Hanley that PIRA was losing the 'armed struggle'. The newly appointed DCI reported after briefing the Prime Minister during his visit to Belfast in July 1976:

I had the impression that he found the problem of Northern Ireland dispiriting and frustrating and that it was not one that was likely to engage a great deal of his personal attention. In the middle of the talk we were silenced by the noise of the G[eneral] O[fficer] C[ommanding]'s helicopter taking off from the lawn outside the S[ecretary] of S[tate]'s office and the PM somewhat wearily remarked that it reminded him of 'last days in Vietnam' [the removal by helicopter of the last occupants of the US embassy in Saigon as the city fell to the Vietcong].[11]

Like the DCI, Callaghan saw little point in maintaining the secret back-channel to the Provisionals. On 3 August he approved the DCI's proposal 'to distance ourselves' from further dealings with Brendan Duddy, the 'Contact' who had been the main conduit to the PIRA leadership (and over a decade later was to play a significant part in the peace process).[12] The IJS concluded at the end of the year: 'It seems certain that the leadership today is less sophisticated and more hard line than it was when the talks were progressing.'[13]

The DCI, probably like many other British intelligence officers, believed that the underlying political problem was the lack of a coherent long-term strategy by the Westminster government: 'HMG has no clear cut or agreed long term policy for dealing with Northern Ireland and the Irish problem. Its short to medium term policies are based on the fact that Northern Ireland is part of the UK and the assumption that it is likely to remain so for some time.'[14] Callaghan's senior policy adviser, Bernard Donoughue, was equally critical of the government's lack of a long-term policy.[15] The problems posed by PIRA and the Troubles are scarcely mentioned in Security Service records of Callaghan's occasional meetings with the DG after the summer of 1976.

Despite the improved co-ordination of intelligence in Belfast by the DCI, Northern Ireland remained an unpopular posting for many in the Security Service. Because of the shortage of volunteers, the letter of appointment issued to new officer recruits in the mid-1970s formally obliged them, for the first time, to serve anywhere 'including Northern Ireland'.[16] Few current staff who had, sometimes reluctantly, accepted postings in Belfast had any previous experience of Ireland, North or South. In the mid-1970s, at a time of horrendous sectarian killings, most probably sympathized with the Service's assessment at the beginning of the Troubles that the root of the security problem, which the security forces could not solve, was 'the antagonism of two Communities with long memories and relatively short tempers'.[17]

In February 1976, Hanley announced in the DG's Newsletter that he intended to establish in the summer a new FX Branch to handle all the aspects of Irish counter-terrorism for which the Security Service was responsible: a decision prompted not by any dramatic event but by a gradual increase in F Branch business during the early 1970s. Though F Branch was to retain responsibility for 'alien' (international) counter-terrorism, FX was to run agents against both Irish and international terrorists as well as against domestic subversives. Director FX was to act as the deputy of Director F, who would continue to have overall control of the work of both Branches.[18] This clumsy reorganization left a blurred division of responsibility which was not satisfactorily resolved until FX became a fully counter-terrorist Branch eight years later. Confusingly, FX sections kept the prefix 'F'.[19] The Registry sometimes found it difficult to know whether to route incoming correspondence to F Branch or FX.[20]

By the time FX Branch began work, 'the height of the Arab terrorist threat' in Britain, retrospectively dated as from 1971 to 1974, was believed to have passed.[21] FX agent penetrations of terrorist groups in the later 1970s revealed no plans for direct attacks on British interests.[22] Protective security against international (as opposed to PIRA) terrorism thus declined in priority. Given both the decline in the threat and the ease with which Palestinians could use false names or travel on passports issued by other Arab states, it was decided, with some exceptions, that 'general vetting by the Security Service of Arab visa applications be discontinued'.[23]

Counter-terrorism ranked low among Callaghan's priorities as prime minister. Probably his only CT initiative followed the hijacking in October 1977 of a Lufthansa Boeing 737 by four Arab terrorists. Callaghan personally authorized a secret meeting at 10 Downing Street between the commander of a German commando unit and SAS officers to discuss co-operation in ending the hijack. Soon afterwards two members of SAS took part in storming the hijacked plane at Mogadishu airport. Crucial to the success of the operation was the use of stun grenades which temporarily blinded and deafened those on board the aircraft as it was being stormed. All the passengers were rescued (though the pilot had been shot earlier by the hijackers), three of the terrorists were killed and the fourth captured.[24] Callaghan's decision to publicize British involvement at Mogadishu was questioned by both Hanley and Merlyn Rees, who had left the NIO to become home secretary in September 1976. Rees asked the DG whether he thought the publicity had increased the risk of terrorist attack in Britain. Hanley noted afterwards: 'I said I thought it was right to suppose that the threat to Britain and British interests had been greatly increased. I had no intelligence to this effect, but it was a reasonable supposition.'[25] In fact the Mogadishu operation, following the spectacular success of the Israelis in rescuing hijacked hostages at Entebbe in the previous year, seems to have acted as a deterrent. There were no further terrorist hijacks for the remainder of the decade.

During Merlyn Rees's period as home secretary from September 1976 to May 1979, counter-terrorism does not appear to have been discussed at any length during his meetings (usually monthly) with the DG. Those attacks by international terrorist groups which took place in Britain – usually in London – were mostly a spill-over from conflicts in the Middle East rather than being targeted specifically against British interests. Among the most operationally effective groups were tight-knit Armenian terrorist cells whose ultimate aim was to establish an independent Armenia. Their first attack in the UK was the bombing of a Turkish bank in north London on 10 February 1978. The F3 desk officer noted 'the ruthless efficiency and determination of Armenian terrorists in striking against Turkish diplomatic personnel and premises' in a number of countries.[26] All but one of the terrorist killings in London during the later 1970s were related to rivalries in the Middle East. In 1977 a PFLP assassin killed a former Yemeni prime minister, Abdullah al-Hejiri, his wife and the minister at the Yemeni embassy, and two Syrian intelligence officers planning an attack on an Egyptian office in London were killed when their bomb exploded prematurely. In 1978 the moderate PLO representative in London, Said Hammami, who was being used by Yasir Arafat to sound out Israeli liberals, was assassinated by the Abu Nidal Organization; General al-Naif, a former Iraqi prime minister, was killed by Saddam Hussein's secret service; and the Bulgarian dissident Georgi Markov was murdered by Bulgarian intelligence, assisted by its Soviet allies. Despite the fact that the KGB had felt bound to assist its Bulgarian ally in assassinating Markov, it was less directly involved with Middle Eastern terrorism than it had been at the start of the decade. After the death of the two main Soviet agents within the PFLP in 1978, the KGB's direct connection with it appears to have died away.[27]

The main lesson learned by the Security Service from the international terrorist attacks in London was the importance of foreign liaison. In F Branch's view:

International terrorist activity is not just a series of incidents scattered through various countries taking place on various dates but it is a constant and ongoing affair involving a high degree of mobility on the part of those involved, who, together with their support workers and contacts, are invariably difficult to locate and identify. Therefore when a Western service apparently scores a hit ... it is important that the service concerned should:–

i. not repeat not think solely in domestic terms since it may be that other friendly services have unattributable collateral available and/or comments of assistance in assessing the significance of the hit.

ii. should interpret the need to know criteria as liberally as possible particularly where there is a likelihood that possible targets ... may transit the country of a friendly service.[28]

Unlike international terrorist groups, PIRA was not responsible for a single death in mainland Britain during the later 1970s.[29] Though sectarian and terrorist violence continued in Northern Ireland, deaths attributable to the Troubles declined from an average of 264 a year in 1974–6 to 102 a year in 1977–9.[30] The Provisionals emerged from the ceasefire of 1975 apparently weaker than before. The IRA veteran and former PIRA chief of staff Joe Cahill later acknowledged: 'The second half of the 1970s were not good years for republicans. The armed struggle was continuing alright, but there were many volunteers being killed and lifted [captured]. In many ways, the Brits' strategy was working and the movement had been caught flatfooted.'[31] IJS intelligence revealed that the Provisionals were also going through a financial crisis, due to a quarrel with Colonel Qaddafi, probably their main source of funds over the previous five years. In keeping with the eccentric division of responsibilities for dealing with Irish Republican terrorism, since the Qaddafi funds came from outside the UK the Security Service had the main responsibility for monitoring them. According to an IJS report: 'Libyan–PIRA cooperation had initially gone smoothly, but PIRA [broke] off the contact in 1978 when it became clear that the Libyans were trying to lay down what policy PIRA should follow. The particular Libyan interest had been to promote a bombing campaign in England.'[32] Roy Mason, who had succeeded Merlyn Rees as secretary of state for Northern Ireland in September 1976, publicly announced at the end of 1977 that 'the tide has turned against the terrorists and the message for 1978 is one of real hope.'[33] The total of eighty-one deaths in Northern Ireland in 1978 was to be the lowest since 1970.

In the summer of 1978, however, PIRA succeeded in extending its operations to the continent, where the Security Service, not the MPSB, had

the lead intelligence role. Its continental campaign began in earnest on the
night of 18–19 August with bomb attacks on eight British army barracks
in north-west Germany. No lives were lost. On 24 August two further
explosive devices were discovered in a car in a NAAFI car park at Rhein-
dalen. Two days later a bag containing PIRA bomb-making equipment
was found on the banks of the Rhine at Düsseldorf. Though not surprised
that the British Army on the Rhine (BAOR) was being targeted, neither
the Security Service nor the rest of the British intelligence community
gained any advance warning of the beginning of the bombing campaign.[34]
The Service's liaison arrangements on the continent against Irish Republican terrorism, a major element in its later strategy, were less developed
than those against international terrorism. A decade later, it had still not
'conclusively' identified the 1978 bombers.[35] PIRA, however, lacked the
capacity for a sustained continental campaign. There were no further
attacks on the continent for the remainder of 1978. It was not until
December that PIRA claimed responsibility for the August bombings in
Germany, grandly declaring that it had 'established [its] ability to strike at
British Imperialism anywhere at any time'.[36]

Roy Mason's confidence that the war against PIRA was being won was
undimmed by its relatively unsuccessful bombing campaign in Germany.
He wrote optimistically on 23 November:

There should be no relaxation of the security profile in present circumstances, but
we should recognise that PIRA are also being undermined by general Government
policy and Government measures outside the immediate ambit of the Security Forces.
Purely security objectives should not be regarded as paramount: it is important to
pursue the general Government policy of encouraging progress towards normality.
Improvements in the economic situation in the Province help to reduce any remaining
authority enjoyed by PIRA in the minority community.[37]

Only a week later, however, PIRA stepped up its bombing campaign in
Northern Ireland. On the night of 30 November to 1 December sixteen
towns were bombed in a nine-hour period. Simultaneously the Provisional
Army Council ordered a pre-Christmas bombing campaign in mainland
Britain. On 17–18 December 1978 a total of thirteen bombs exploded or
were defused in English cities. Seven people were injured in Bristol, two in
London and two in Liverpool. There were no fatalities. Despite the fact
that the MPSB retained the lead role, the Security Service was for the first
time able to make a significant contribution to intelligence on a mainland
bombing campaign as a result of the Irish Joint Section's success in penetrating PIRA. In the early twenty-first century, the issue of penetration became

a major theme in the Republican historiography of the Troubles, with informers – both real and imagined – being blamed for a variety of PIRA failures. Because of the guarantee given to Security Service and SIS agents that their identities will be kept secret indefinitely, all information about them remains classified.

The pre-Christmas bomb attacks on English cities were intended to be the prelude to a sustained New Year bombing campaign. On 17 January 1979 a bomb blew a hole in a tank containing aviation fuel at a Texaco oil terminal on Canvey Island, though the fuel failed to ignite as PIRA had intended. In the early hours of the 18th a bomb attack at a gas-holder near the south entrance of the Blackwall Tunnel ignited the escaping gas and caused a major explosion.[38] A third bomb, discovered on the verge of the M6 in Leicestershire, was made safe by army bomb-disposal experts.[39] Then the bombing campaign ground to an abrupt halt. According to IJS intelligence, the PIRA active service unit (ASU) responsible for the bomb attacks claimed that none of the promised preparations had been made for their arrival in England, thus limiting their capacity to mount operations. Because they were not provided with bogus identity documents, in order to hire a car the ASU had purchased a false driving licence which turned out to have been used before and began a trail which enabled the police to track down the flat they were using. The ASU had devised, but failed to implement, plans for bomb attacks on both Roy Mason and Margaret Thatcher (the latter, ominously, at a Conservative Party conference).[40] The relative lack of impact of PIRA mainland operations was emphasized by a spectacular terrorist success by the much smaller Irish National Liberation Army (INLA) at the Houses of Parliament. Barely a fortnight after becoming prime minister in May 1979, Thatcher delivered the memorial address for her friend Airey Neave, whom she had intended to make her Northern Ireland secretary. Neave had been killed by an INLA bomb with a mercury tilt-switch attached to his car as he drove out of the Commons car park on the eve of the Conservatives' victorious election campaign.

Though the Provisionals' planned 1979 bombing campaign had been disrupted in Britain, it continued on the continent. On the morning of 22 March, the British ambassador in The Hague, Sir Richard Sykes, and his valet, Karel Straub, were shot dead. The same afternoon a Belgian banker, André Michaux, who had been mistaken for the British minister to NATO, was killed in Brussels. PIRA refused to acknowledge its responsibility for the bungled operation.[41] Its only continental attacks in the remainder of the year were the bombing of a BAOR base in Dortmund on 10 July, which caused superficial damage, and an explosion beneath a

Brussels bandstand where a British military band was due to play, which injured eighteen people.[42] Unsurprisingly, the PIRA leadership was reported to be seriously dissatisfied with the progress of its continental campaign.[43]

There seemed good reason to fear, however, that PIRA would be more effective in the 1980s than in the 1970s. A British army assessment of 'Future Terrorist Trends' by Brigadier (later General Sir) James Glover of the military intelligence staff, which fell into the hands of the Provisionals and was published in the Republican newspaper *An Phoblacht* on 10 May 1979, concluded that PIRA was becoming an increasingly dangerous opponent: 'The mature terrorists, including, for instance, the leading bomb makers, are sufficiently cunning to avoid arrest. They are continually learning from mistakes and developing their expertise.' The Provisionals were acquiring weapons at a faster rate than the army could recover them. Glover predicted that PIRA might also succeed in acquiring sophisticated Soviet SA-7 anti-aircraft missiles, similar to those used by Joshua Nkomo's guerrillas in 1978 to shoot down two Rhodesian Viscounts.[44] IJS sources reported that Glover's assessment was in most respects 'remarkably accurate' and that 'its flattering picture of PIRA effectiveness had had a strong effect on morale throughout the movement'. The IJS believed, however, that there was no foreseeable prospect of PIRA obtaining Soviet SA-7s.[45]

In the summer of 1979 PIRA's Irish operations achieved their most spectacular successes so far. The Provisionals had identified the Queen's cousin, Earl Mountbatten, who had a holiday home in Sligo with no resident bodyguard, as the softest of prestige targets and killed him (as well as his fourteen-year-old grandson and two others) on 27 August by detonating by remote control a 50-pound bomb placed beneath the floorboards of his boat, *Shadow V*, as it sailed in Sligo Bay.[46] An attack a few hours later on British troops near Warrenpoint in County Down underlined Brigadier Glover's warning of increasing PIRA technical expertise. A first explosion, triggered by remote control from across the border of the Irish Republic, blew up a British army vehicle. PIRA correctly calculated that the troops who came to the scene of the explosion would take cover in an old gatehouse near by, where a second bomb was also detonated by remote control from the Republic. A total of eighteen soldiers were killed – more than in any other PIRA operation in the history of the Troubles.[47] IJS intelligence indicated that the Mountbatten killing as well as Warrenpoint had been carefully considered and approved by the Provisional leadership.[48]

Though the management of the Security Service reasonably regarded it as illogical that the only aspect of counter-terrorist intelligence in mainland Britain in which it did not possess the lead role was against PIRA and other Republican groups, it was not ready to campaign within Whitehall for the transfer of that lead role from the MPSB. The Service's main counter-terrorist successes in the later 1970s were in operations against Loyalist paramilitaries on the mainland, for which it had the main intelligence responsibility. An intelligence briefing prepared for Callaghan soon after he became prime minister reported:

There are numerous Loyalist paramilitary organisations varying in size and nastiness. Their objectives are very simple. First to ensure that the Protestant majority in Northern Ireland does not become the Protestant minority in Ireland. Secondly, within the boundaries of Northern Ireland, to try to cow the Catholics.[49]

Some of the Loyalist paramilitaries were responsible for what the DCI called 'particularly vicious murders'. Eleven of the sadistic 'Shankhill butchers', who tortured and killed their Catholic victims with surgically sharp knives and axes, later received a total of forty-two life sentences for crimes which included nineteen murders. The paramilitaries had, however, one major weakness, noted by the DCI: 'Fortunately they are ill armed by the standards of the IRA (though they have a worrying capacity for manufacturing machine guns) and have difficulty in getting hold of either weapons or explosives.'[50]

Combined operations by the police and the Service during 1977 had considerable success in preventing arms supplies from the British mainland reaching the paramilitary Ulster Defence Association (UDA) and Ulster Volunteer Force (UVF) in Northern Ireland. According to a later A4 report on operations in Scotland:

The [Loyalist] targets habitually drank at run-down inner-city bars, where the clientele generally had criminal tendencies, were unemployed, were heavy drinkers and could spot a policeman immediately. A4 officers did not generally have the same build and demeanour as police officers. They also spoke with an English accent and were generally considered non-threatening.[51]

In June 1978 the UDA commander in Scotland, Roddy MacDonald, a former soldier, was sentenced to eight years' imprisonment for his part in the robbery of an Edinburgh gunshop.[52] In June 1979, at two separate trials in Glasgow, twelve members of the UDA received long prison sentences after being convicted on firearms and conspiracy charges. Though the involvement of the Security Service was not mentioned during the trials,[53] an undercover police officer described in court how he had penetrated the Paisley UDA and witnessed punishment beatings administered with a red, white and blue pickaxe handle inscribed 'Snoopy'.[54] MacDonald's successor as Scottish UDA commander, James Hamilton, was sentenced to sixteen years' imprisonment. The Security Service reported to its Whitehall contacts that the length of the sentences had shocked both the UDA's Belfast headquarters and its Scottish supporters: 'The removal of the Scottish leadership will incapacitate the organisation for some time. The deterrent effect of the sentences is likely to be considerable.'[55] In February 1979 Scottish UVF members bombed two pubs in Glasgow frequented by Catholics. Ten were later given long prison sentences. In June the local UVF leader, William Campbell, was sentenced, like Hamilton of the UDA, to sixteen years. In the Security Service view, 'The main UVF structure in Scotland has been almost totally destroyed during the last 6 months.' The Service expected it to be rebuilt.[56]

The main contribution made by the Security Service to countering PIRA mainland operations in the later 1970s was in the field of protective security. Though memories of the IRA's last bombing campaign in England in 1938-9 had faded, it had then targeted both factories and the electricity-supply system. One attack early in 1939 had cut off electricity supplies to 25,000 people in north London.[57] From 1972 onwards C Branch argued that PIRA or other terrorist groups might well, once again, attack economic targets. Whitehall's response to its protective-security proposals was unenthusiastic. The chairman of the Key Points Sub-Committee of Whitehall's Official Committee on Terrorism, which oversaw preparations for the protection of vital installations during war or periods of severe international tension, was reluctant to add protection against peacetime terrorist attack to his already large responsibilities.[58] In 1972 an attempt by the Service to persuade the Home Secretary, Reggie Maudling, of the need for better protection of what later became known as Critical National Infrastructure (CNI) produced only what it considered 'a lethargic response'. However, the discovery in 1975 in London and Liverpool of PIRA target lists which included public utilities changed Whitehall attitudes and marked a turning point in the history of British protective security. Harold Wilson was sufficiently concerned to ask the Official Committee on Terrorism to review the terrorist (in particular PIRA) threat to North Sea oil and gas supplies.[59] By October 1976 a list of Economic Key Points (EKPs) which required protection against peacetime terrorist attack had been completed and added to the responsibilities of the Official Committee on Terrorism. The Committee approved a C Branch proposal for the establishment of a working group to supervise a phased programme of work for the protection of these installations. In 1977 a C Branch section assumed responsibility for the first time for assessing the sabotage capabilities of PIRA, as well as Welsh and Scottish extremists. Papers on this subject were passed to the working group planning the protection of EKPs.[60]

This section was staffed mainly by outside experts, mostly with a military background, who joined it in the early 1970s. Lieutenant Colonel David Sutherland, who was appointed head of the section in 1970, had won the Military Cross for his exploits in wartime operations. Its first explosives expert, recruited from the MoD in 1973, assembled forensic evidence which helped to convict some of the perpetrators of PIRA's mainland bombing campaign in that year. The Service officer who chaired the inter-departmental Forcible Attack Working Group (FAWG), founded on C Branch's initiative, had had an adventurous career in SOE during the Second World War, which included travelling through Crete dressed as a shepherd with explosives hidden in animal dung. FAWG specialized in devising and testing perimeter fencing and intruder-detection systems.

Its expertise found a growing market during the 1970s, some of it in Northern Ireland. By 1978 it had provided protective-security training for every member of the RUC Security Section.[61] The DG reported to the Home Secretary in the same year that C Branch was also providing advice to the Saudis on 'the protection of their Economic Key Points'.[62] Improvements to protective security at British EKPs, however, proceeded slowly, largely because of the expense involved. The budget crises of the Callaghan years and the cuts in government spending necessary to secure an IMF loan made it difficult to argue for extra funds in a field which aroused so little enthusiasm in Whitehall. The fact that not a single EKP was successfully attacked probably owed less to improved protective security than to PIRA's failure to identify their continued vulnerability.

6

The Callaghan Government and Subversion

Though the Callaghan government ended in, and is nowadays chiefly remembered for, the strikes of its final 'Winter of Discontent', it began with a period of unprecedented industrial peace. Its first year saw the lowest number of industrial disputes so far recorded in the twentieth century. Callaghan was (and still remains) the only trade union official to become post-war Labour leader. As prime minister, 'He was no intellectual, he appeared avuncular to the point of maddening complacency, and behind the scenes he was a fixer and a bit of a bully; to the average trade union official he was almost as good as one of their own.'[1] In the summer of 1976 the TUC was persuaded – reluctantly – to extend what had been a virtual wage-freeze policy by agreeing to a limit of 5 per cent for wage increases over the next twelve months.

Despite the apparent industrial calm of the early Callaghan government, however, there was a renewed emphasis within Whitehall on the need for more active counter-subversion, prompted in large part by an F2 threat assessment of April 1976 which identified the CPGB, despite its lack of success as a political party, as a major subversive threat within the trade union movement out to disrupt the economic policy of the elected government. Approximately one in five of the leading full-time officials and executive committee members in thirty-four major trade unions was a Communist or Communist sympathizer (as compared with only one in 500 of the rank and file). F2 argued that even this statistic underestimated the extent of Communist influence. A small, disciplined Communist group, backed by the CPGB's industrial apparatus, was capable of exerting disproportionate influence on any union executive whose other members did not act in concert. Communist penetration of the union movement had also increased the Party's political influence on the Labour left. Over the past decade, the threat assessment argued, the CPGB had shown an increasing ability to exploit traditional trade union opposition to interference in free collective bargaining and government attempts to reform industrial relations. The Security Service believed there was a strong Communist influence in the NUM and AUEW (the Amalgamated Union of Engineering Workers, formerly the AEU), both of which had been in the forefront of opposition to wage restraint and industrial-relations legislation. Since Labour's return to power in 1974, TUC participation in the government's counter-inflation policy had given the CPGB the opportunity to attempt to drive a wedge between the government and the left wing of the labour movement with the aim of forcing the TUC into opposition to any form of wage restraint.[2] The key figure in CPGB industrial strategy remained its industrial organizer Bert Ramelson, who succeeded in assembling a powerful left-wing caucus within the TUC.[3] Ramelson was to achieve his greatest influence during the years of the Callaghan government.

Economic crisis acted as the catalyst to industrial disruption. Economic growth from 1974 to 1979 averaged only 1.4 per cent a year, less than half the rate of the previous decade. Annual inflation in 1976 reached 16 per cent with a record budget deficit and government spending apparently out of control. Despite public spending cuts in April 1976, a sterling crisis in September forced the Callaghan government to seek a loan from the IMF, which demanded further cuts. Henceforth the life of the government was dominated by the linked problems of inflation and union challenges to its economic policy.[4]

In December 1976 new intelligence arrived on links between the KGB and Britain's best-known trade unionist, Jack Jones, general secretary of the TGWU from 1969 to 1978. Oleg Gordievsky reported that after being targeted for recruitment by the London residency, Jones had been regarded by the KGB as an agent for a number of years in the 'latter half of the '60s'. All contact with him had been dormant for some time.[5] It was not, however, until Gordievsky was stationed in London in 1982 after several years working on the British desk in the Centre that he was able to provide more detail on Jones's contacts with the KGB.[6] This intelligence on Jones was very tightly held, known only to a very small number of officers in K Branch and to none in F Branch.[7] Eavesdropping at King Street no longer provided evidence of significant contact between Jones and the CPGB. In 1969 Ramelson had been overheard praising Jones as 'sound politically', with 'courage and guts'.[8] 'The only dishonest thing about Jack', said Ramelson, 'was that he gave the impression that he was never in the [Communist] Party.'[9] By 1976 Ramelson had changed his mind. Far from being a member of the left-wing caucus in the TUC, Jones was now regarded by the Callaghan government as, on balance, a force for moderation.[10]

In June 1976 a meeting convened in the Home Office to consider the Security Service's latest threat assessment of subversion decided to reactivate the interdepartmental group to study subversion in public life (SPL). Founded by the Heath government, it had been virtually moribund since Labour returned to power in 1974.[11] Chaired by Robert Armstrong (then deputy secretary at the Home Office) with members from the FCO, Department of Energy, Scottish Office, Security Service, Scotland Yard and the Cabinet Office, the revived SPL was provided with an MI5 assessments officer to prepare reports.[12] Its new terms of reference were 'to give guidance on the collection and to co-ordinate the assessment of intelligence about threats to the internal security of Great Britain arising from subversive activities, and to make periodic reports to the officials concerned'.[13] The existence of the group was to be kept secret and its reports so closely held that they were not to be placed on normal departmental files. To advise on counter-subversion policy, the Subversion at Home Committee (SH) of permanent secretaries, which had also become moribund, was revived under the chairmanship of the cabinet secretary, Sir John Hunt, with the permanent secretaries of the Home Office, FCO and Department of Energy, the DG of the Security Service and the chairman of SPL as regular members, with other PUS being invited as necessary.[14]

In December 1976 SPL recommended a more positive and systematic approach to devising counter-subversion initiatives, probably with the covert release of damaging information on subversives to the media chiefly in mind. The DDG, John Jones, was extremely wary, arguing from the experience of the Heath administration that such initiatives were 'in the main ineffective':

The whole concept of trying to manage counter subversion in the media [is] of very doubtful value. It is natural for Ministers and senior officials to attempt to manipulate the news and the media. This is part of the stuff of politics. The results of such attempts have almost invariably been unforeseen and I think it unrewarding that officials should attempt to plan and launch in the media campaigns to counter subversion.

. . . In the field of counter subversion generally I see the Security Service as the provider of objective and factual information and comment to official departments and agencies about the security status of individuals and groups . . . We should be very chary of becoming involved in schemes to use our information publicly or through non official bodies. If we are consulted about such proposals our first concern must be to protect our sources and to preserve our non-partisan status in political matters.[15]

Fearing that the definition of subversion was in danger of being confused with opposition to the policies of the Callaghan government, Jones
warned the DG, Sir Michael Hanley, before his first attendance at the SH
in February 1977:

There is a natural tendency for senior officials (and in this they reflect the views of
the Ministers they serve) to equate subversion with activity which threatens a
Government's policies or may threaten its very existence . . . In the heat of the day
the objective impartiality in these matters which we must observe tends to become
blurred, certainly in the minds of politicians and sometimes in those of their officials.
It is in the long term interests of the Security Service that we adhere firmly to
the objective non-partisan approach of our Charter and the current definition of
subversion assists in this.[16]

The Communist-influenced left-wing minority on the TUC General
Council had its greatest impact during the final two years of the Callaghan
government. The Alternative Economic Policy adopted by the TUC in
1977 began as a Communist initiative, proposed by Ken Gill, the Communist leader of the draughtsmen's union, TASS. At its annual conference in
September, the TUC voted for a return to 'unfettered collective bargaining'.
Gill recalls an occasion when he was part of a TUC delegation to 10
Downing Street and had to ring his office during a break in the meeting.
He felt a tap on his shoulder, turned round and saw the grinning face of
the Chancellor of the Exchequer, Denis Healey, who had presumably been
reading MI5's Box 500 reports (so called after the Service's SW1 Post
Office box). 'Reporting back to King Street, Ken?' Healey asked him. In
addition to the Communists Ken Gill and, briefly, Mick McGahey on the
TUC General Council, there was a core of non-Communist union leaders
with a high regard for Ramelson, who listened to his policy advice and
took part in the left-wing caucus which he organized: among them the
public employees' leader Rodney Bickerstaffe, the seamen's Jim Slater,
print union leader Bill Keys, Alan Sapper of the television technicians, Ken
Cameron of the Fire Brigades Union and the tobacco workers' Doug
Grieve.[17]

Initially, however, some members of the Callaghan government were
more concerned by political than industrial subversion. At his first meeting
with Hanley on 11 November 1976, the new Home Secretary, Merlyn
Rees, raised the issue of Trotskyist penetration of the Labour Party.[18] In
1971 the 'total hard membership' of Trotskyist and other 'Far Left' groups
had been estimated as 'probably no greater than one-sixth that of the
CPGB'.[19] Though Trotskyists increased in number during the remainder

of the decade, they showed their usual capacity for internecine ideological warfare. The Security Service monitored three main overt Trotskyist groups – the Workers Revolutionary Party (which stole a march over its rivals by purchasing Trotsky's death-mask), the International Socialists (from 1977 the Socialist Workers Party) and the International Marxist Group – and the more clandestine Militant Tendency, the name usually given in public to the Revolutionary Socialist League, which sought to infiltrate the Labour Party. In 1975 Director F had tasked F1A with a wide-ranging investigation of the extent of subversive infiltration and influence in the Labour Party. F1A/1 noted that previous work in this field had been 'primarily concerned with the Communist threat. Now, however, it is to comprise intrusions by the Ultra Left.'[20] In 1961 the Labour leadership had sought the help of the Security Service to identify 'crypto-Communists' within the parliamentary party.[21] By 1976, however, its main concern was attempted 'entryism' by the Militant Tendency (MT), under the autocratic leadership of Ted Grant. According to his one-time Trotskyist comrade Roger Protz, 'Grant looked like a tramp, always wore a dirty raincoat from which old copies of the *FT* bulged, and looked as though he slept under a hedge.'[22] Cocooned in his self-declared ideological infallibility, however, Grant was one of the most single-minded fanatics in British politics, absurdly telling Tony Benn in 1973 that, himself apart, 'there is no one else in the world who follows Trotsky correctly'.[23] The basis of Grant's political strategy was the secrecy of his organization. The Revolutionary Socialist League, unlike its Trot-skyist rivals, which Grant despised, denied that it existed. Militant Tend-ency kept up the public pretence that it was not an organization at all but simply an informal group concerned with the production and sale of the weekly newspaper *Militant*. In private, however, MT members were instructed to join their local Constituency Labour Parties (CLPs) and try to take them over.[24] Militant was thus unquestionably subversive: a secret organization with a covert strategy designed to undermine the future of Labour as a democratic political party and turn it against the 'parliamen-tary road to socialism'. Though smaller than the Workers Revolutionary Party and the International Socialists during the 1970s, MT was far more influential, able to exploit both the moribund state of many CLPs and the reluctance of Labour's left-dominated National Executive Committee (NEC) to embark on the round of proscriptions and expulsions necessary to remove Militant 'entryists' from Party membership.

At his meeting with Merlyn Rees on 11 November 1976, Hanley found the new Home Secretary, unlike the NEC, 'fully seized of the importance of subversive penetration of the Labour Party'.[25] Rees told the DG that

'He had spent his life in the Labour Party but unfortunately the Party was no longer what it had been.' Rees's most immediate concern was Trotskyist penetration of the CLP in his own constituency, Leeds South. A Security Service note on 'Subversive Influences in the Labour Party in Leeds', forwarded to him on 22 November, reported that the CLP chairman in Leeds South-East was an MT member and that the CLP secretary was believed to be a leading member of the Trotskyist Socialist Charter Movement (SCM). In Leeds North-East the CLP chairman was said to work closely with Militant. In Leeds South, the chairman of the Young Socialists was 'in touch' with Militant, and the CLP delegate to the 1975 Party conference (who had since moved to Leeds South-East) was an SCM member.[26] Further details of leading Militant Tendency activists in Leeds were sent to Rees on 17 December.[27] Callaghan also had to deal with vociferous, though less influential, MT critics in his Cardiff constituency.[28] The Security Service provided the Home Secretary, at his request, with a list of the forty-three constituencies in which Trotskyist groups were most active,[29] as well as details of nine constituencies in which Trotskyist influence was considered sufficiently strong to pose a threat to a sitting Labour MP.[30]

Thanks to letter and telephone checks, eavesdropping on the MT annual conferences and agent penetration, the Service believed it had identified about 75 per cent of the Militant membership.[31] The Militant Tendency, it discovered, was secretly run by a thirty-strong Central Committee, elected at its annual conference, which met every two to three months and was mainly composed of full-time MT workers. Although, for security reasons, the MT did not give formal titles to the officials it claimed it did not possess, Ted Grant remained its acknowledged leader with Peter Taaffe, the editor of *Militant*, as his deputy (and later rival).[32] In 1976 MT secretly claimed to have increased membership from 765 the previous year to 1,030, organized in eighty branches under a system of district and regional committees. MT employed thirty-seven full-time workers but considered it needed six more.[33] In May 1976 it held its first ever National Council (NC) meeting in conditions of great secrecy, taking elaborate security precautions to ensure its venue was not disclosed to outsiders and appointing stewards to verify the credentials of all who attended. The precautions, however, failed to prevent Security Service technical and agent penetration, which revealed that the NC agreed an optimistic target figure of 2,000 members by the end of 1976 and decided that all members should attend MT training courses.[34]

The first major success of Militant entryism was in the Labour Party Young Socialists (LPYS), where it had won control by 1970.[35] From 1972 the LPYS annual conference was able to elect a representative to the NEC, thus giving Militant in effect a reserved seat on it for the remainder of the 1970s and most of the 1980s.[36] The Young Socialists also became a springboard for Militant penetration of local Labour Parties. The secret annual MT policy statement of 1974 declared:

We must dig roots in the wards and the Y[oung] S[ocialists]. Many are still shells dominated by politically dead old men and women. They are now ossified little cliques. They will begin to change with an influx of new members. The YS branches where we have support are already a springboard for work in the wards and G[eneral] M[anagement] C[ommittee]s.

The 1975 policy statement instructed: 'We must consciously aim to penetrate every constituency party in the country.'[37] In 1976 Militant's youth organizer, Andy Bevan, was appointed Labour Party national youth officer, a position he retained for the next twelve years. On Bevan's first day at Transport House he had to walk past a demonstration by his new colleagues, protesting against his appointment. The colleagues, however, were protesting not against his Trotskyism but against what they claimed was a breach of closed-shop agreements. Within a few years he had made himself sufficiently popular among the same colleagues to be elected chief shop steward.[38] The Security Service reported in 1976 that, encouraged by its success in the LPYS, Militant had appointed a full-time organizer to co-ordinate penetration of CLPs and urge its members to influence the choice of resolutions and delegates to Labour Party regional and annual conferences and to gain seats on their General Management Committees. In 1976 members of the MT Central Committee were selected as prospective Labour Party candidates in Liverpool Crosby and Edinburgh North, and MT sympathizers were selected in Croydon Central and the Isle of Wight.[39]

The Security Service took a more relaxed view of CPGB and Trotskyist penetration of universities and the media: 'When Communists and Trotskyists do become involved in disturbances directed at the university authorities, their activities are rarely co-ordinated by party headquarters.' The Service calculated that the proportion of students with 'subversive affiliations' remained constant throughout the 1970s at about 0.6 per cent. Though the executive and officials of the National Union of Students included 'a considerable number of subversive individuals', 'In practice, subversive elements in the NUS leadership have never been able to turn the union into an effective instrument for mobilising mass militant activity by students.' Within the media, the Security Service believed that 'a Trotskyist element' in Granada Television was responsible for a small number of 'distorted' *World in Action* current affairs programmes in the mid-1970s – but that 'this element subsequently dispersed.' In 1976–7 it reported that 'Ultra Left' production staff were responsible for three or four 'similarly distorted programmes' on Thames Television's *This Week*. But:

There have been virtually no instances of subversive bias in the presentation of news bulletins by the BBC or the I[ndependent] B[roadcasting] A[uthority] companies. The reason no doubt lies in the careful selection of key personnel by management, their careful monitoring of the product in the interests of objectivity, and, not least, the competition that has grown up between the BBC and the independent companies in the presentation of news.[40]

Successive governments of both political complexions did not always succeed in taking such a balanced view.

In August 1977 Merlyn Rees visited the Security Service, together with his PUS, Robert Armstrong, for extensive briefing by the DG, DDG, Director F and two senior F Branch officers on Communist and Trotskyist subversion within the Labour Party, industry and the unions. Rees revealed that he favoured a scheme to redraw constituency boundaries in order to get rid of the city-centre constituencies which, he believed, were those most easily exploited by subversives.[41] By 1977 Militant Tendency was believed to have gained a foothold in some eighty-eight CLPs and to pose a threat to twelve sitting MPs.[42] Secretly recorded by the Security Service, Peter Taaffe told the annual conference that Militant cadres, despite disappointing recruitment figures, were the 'spinal column of the future mass revolutionary organisation', which would be 'an indispensable weapon of the Revolution in Britain'.[43] Militant members of CLP delegations to the annual Labour Party conference increased from thirty-five in 1976 to fifty-five in 1978.[44] Though MT membership was still below 1,500 in 1978,[45] Taaffe made the wildly exaggerated claim that year that MT played a decisive influence in 100 CLPs and a significant role in 225.[46]

Despite the concern felt by Rees and Callaghan about Militant entryism, there were powerful voices on the NEC opposed to any serious action to prevent it, among them those of Callaghan's two immediate successors as Labour leader, Michael Foot and Neil Kinnock. In November 1975 the Labour Party national agent, Reg Underhill, presented a report to the NEC on extreme left-wing infiltration of the Labour Party which concluded that Militant was an independent political organization and therefore clearly contravened the prohibition in Labour's constitution on Party members joining organizations with their 'own programmes, principles, and policy for distinctive and separate propaganda'.[47] The MT leadership gave much of the credit for sidelining the Underhill report to one of its members, Nick Bradley, the LPYS representative on the NEC, who, it believed, succeeded in persuading the Organization sub-committee that the report should 'lie on the table'.[48] When the report eventually reached the NEC, the Committee voted by sixteen to twelve to take no action.[49] As late as 1981 Neil Kinnock believed that, within the Labour Party organization, 'there was neither the will nor, more important, the organisational capacity to undertake a systematic attack on Militant.'[50] The divided views within the Labour leadership about the threat of Militant entryism produced frustration among the F Branch officers concerned with the investigation of subversion in the Labour Party. It was unclear to the Security Service how much of the Callaghan government shared Rees's close interest in MT. F1A/1 commented in January 1978 that F1A/9 had written nine papers over the past two years, often without knowing for whom they were intended and based on the 'haziest of requirements'. Without feedback from Whitehall, F1 was unable to judge whether its work was of value to government.[51]

The Security Service had far less doubt about government interest in its intelligence on industrial subversion. During the summer of 1977, with the industrial harmony of the early Callaghan government at an end, television news was dominated by daily confrontations between mass pickets and police outside the Grunwick photo-processing plant in north London, where a hundred mostly Asian female workers had been sacked for joining a union. Despite the fact that several ministers had appeared on the picket line, Callaghan told a meeting at Chequers on 26 June: 'If things continue on the present basis there could well be fatalities and in circumstances which might be in danger of bringing the Government down ... The government was not dealing with respectable unionism but rent a mob.'[52] Callaghan was particularly worried by the use of mass flying pickets by Arthur Scargill, the Yorkshire miners' leader, who had been arrested on the picket line, and he asked the cabinet secretary for a note on Scargill's first use of them during the 1972 miners' strike. On 5 July he issued a handwritten note asking: 'Was Scargill at Grunwick today ...[?] Keep me informed about Scargill's movements. He may have to be warned off.'[53] Callaghan was reported to be showing a personal interest in intelligence on 'future action on mass pickets at Grunwick'.[54] Eavesdropping and telechecks at King Street showed that Ramelson saw Scargill's flying pickets of Yorkshire miners as a key element in winning the strike.[55] A 'Day of Action', involving the Yorkshire miners, planned for 8 August, however, was called off by the Grunwick strike committee in response to an appeal for calm by Lord Scarman, who had been appointed to head an inquiry.[56]

When told the news, Ramelson was heard to 'mutter a curse'. 'Once the level of activity was reduced in any campaign,' he believed, 'it was difficult to restore it.'[57] The Scarman Report's recommendation to reinstate or recompense the strikers was turned down by the Grunwick plant owner.[58] When the strike committee asked Scargill at short notice to bring the miners to a mass picket on 7 November 1977, he was reported to have replied that there was not time to make the necessary arrangements.[59] A furious Ramelson was heard complaining about Scargill's absence: 'If the fucking miners had been there they [the picket] would have topped 10,000.'[60] The strike was eventually called off in the following year.

By the autumn of 1977 Callaghan's main concern was the threat of a police strike. The Police Federation had demanded a massive pay rise of between 78 and 104 per cent.[61] The Home Secretary, Merlyn Rees, warned that a 10 per cent offer would lead to an immediate showdown. In some areas, notably Merseyside, there was likely to be an all-out strike. In London police withdrawal from traffic duties risked causing chaos. The overall impact could be as devastating as the miners' strike which had brought down the Heath government. Rees was in favour of a 15 per cent pay offer. Callaghan refused, telling Rees that 'people would laugh at such a breach in government pay policy.' He was 'prepared to resign rather than . . . give in to the threat of a strike'.[62] The Prime Minister heavily censored a draft speech which Rees intended to give to the Police Federation. In the margins of a proposed reference to the police as a 'special case', the Prime Minister scrawled an emphatic 'NO. So is beating inflation. Don't use this terminology.'[63] On Callaghan's insistence, the Police Federation were offered, and finally accepted, a 10 per cent pay rise with the promise of a committee of inquiry to look at longer-term pay settlements.[64] The threat of a police strike vividly illustrates the limits of the Security Service's investigation of labour disputes. Despite the fact that Callaghan feared it might force his resignation, the Service provided no significant intelligence because it did not regard either the Police Federation or its leaders as subversive.

In the 1977–8 pay round settlements averaged over 15 per cent. When Callaghan tried to impose a 5 per cent pay-rise ceiling in July 1978, the relationship between Labour and the unions suffered a spectacular breakdown, despite the attempts of the TUC general secretary, Len Murray, to win support for government policy. There seemed no cure for the 'British disease' of repeated strike action and chaotic industrial relations.

Early in 1978, Ramelson was succeeded as CPGB industrial organizer by his deputy, Mick Costello, a hardline Communist whose New Zealand father Desmond ('Paddy'), a former diplomat turned professor of Russian at Manchester University, was assessed by the Security Service as a KGB agent.[65] Security Service Box 500 reports to Whitehall and Special Branches concluded that 'The Party leadership has had some misgivings about [Mick] Costello's rather brash manner and an habitual unwillingness to admit to error. Ramelson himself has frequently expressed doubts about his political judgement.'[66] The CPGB leadership was reported to be worried that the 'wages struggle' against the 5 per cent ceiling on pay rises was insufficiently political (in other words, not adequately focused on attacking the Callaghan government) and that, while the Party maintained 'continued strength of influence at senior levels among trade union officials', it was losing ground to the Trotskyists on the shop floor.[67] It was also dismayed at the end of 1978 by the extent of Trotskyist influence on the national executive committee of the Civil and Public Service Association (CPSA).[68] As the industrial disruption of the Winter of Discontent proceeded, the CPGB mood brightened. A Box 500 report on 29 January described the Party as 'increasingly enthusiastic about the effects of the public services dispute which it believes could be a significant factor in bringing about opportunities for its political advance'.[69]

Box 500 reports made clear, however, that the Winter of Discontent was not the result of either a Communist or a Trotskyist masterplan:

Trotskyist groups are finding difficulty in keeping pace with events and in some places are being told by Party officials to concentrate their attention entirely on selling their newspapers. Deason, the industrial organiser of the Socialist Workers Party (SWP), believes that many of their members are daunted by the scale of the action and are not clear how to take advantage of it.

In the four unions at the centre of the Winter of Discontent, the Service reported 'relatively little subversive influence at national level'. 'Subversive influence' was strongest in the thirty-nine-member general executive council of the Transport and General Workers Union (TGWU), which contained nine Communists, two Communist sympathizers and two Trotskyist sympathizers. By contrast, the only 'subversive' among the thirty members of the executive council of the General and Municipal Workers Union (GMWU) was a single Trotskyist. Though the National Union of Public Employees (NUPE) had 'in recent years become notably militant', its executive council of twenty-six contained only one Communist sympathizer. The Confederation of Health Service Employees (COHSE) had 'no subversives at executive or full time national official level'.[70] The Winter of

Discontent was followed by a private 'acknowledgement by the Communist Party that it has in recent years lost much of its industrial influence at the shop-floor level and that it needs to revitalise its organisation of workplace branches'.

The leading casualty of the Winter of Discontent was James Callaghan. 'The belief that he enjoyed a unique relationship with the unions, and was a supremely effective agent of industrial partnership, collapsed.'[71] Because the Security Service collected intelligence only on the comparatively minor 'subversive' influences, its reports did not cover most of the industrial disruption which led Labour to defeat at the polls and were of only secondary importance to the ministers responsible for dealing with the Winter of Discontent.

The Security Service's 1972 definition of subversive activities as 'those which threaten the safety or well being of the State and are intended to undermine or overthrow Parliamentary democracy by political, industrial or violent means' had been accepted both by the Heath government and by its Labour successors during the 1970s. It was quoted in parliament in 1975 and defended by the Home Secretary in 1978.[72] In some respects the Service, so far from exaggerating the threat of subversion, had a more realistic view of it than ministers and was less likely than successive governments to see subversion as a key element in industrial disruption. The Service was justified in the mid-1970s in identifying Militant entryism as a subversive threat to Labour Party democracy. Neil Kinnock's ferocious attack as Labour leader on Militant in the mid-1980s[73] strongly suggests that Service assessments during the Callaghan government, at a time when Kinnock had taken a much more relaxed view of the entryist problem, showed prescience rather than alarmism.

The Security Service did, however, devote too much of its resources during the 1970s to monitoring often insignificant political activities of the CPGB and its sympathizers. Part of the explanation was that keeping as full a record as possible of CPGB membership had become one of the Service's best-established routines and was needed for the vetting process approved by successive governments. In a small but significant minority of cases, Party membership did pose security risks.[74] Many of the young desk officers who spent part of their early careers in the Service studying the membership and activities of CPGB branches felt, however, that the detailed attention lavished on them was out of all proportion to their actual importance. As a trainee desk officer in 1969, Stella Rimington was set to study the CPGB in Sussex where she discovered, despite the cornucopia of radical and 'revolutionary' movements at Sussex University, that there were few Communist Party members and a high proportion were elderly: 'As far as I could see not much of interest was happening so, after I had found out what I was supposed to be doing, I whiled away the time reading Dornford Yates novels under the desk.'[75] Six years later, little had changed, as one recruit recalls:

As a newly recruited desk officer in September 1975, I spent only 6 weeks in F1C before being fortunate enough to obtain an early release from the sentence of relentless tedium of paper procedures in the section . . . I found it hard to understand why we were spending as much time as we did investigating the activities of Communist districts/branches in, for example Surrey, Sussex or Hampshire, let alone worrying about attempting to identify someone who was presumed to have sympathies with Communism, perhaps by writing for a leaflet, but of insufficient strength to join the organisation itself . . . My contemporaries were of a similar opinion . . . However, what is surprising is that we did not seriously challenge the assumptions of the [Communist] threat. We merely concentrated on escaping as soon as possible to more interesting/challenging desks. We had no doubt that the Trotskyists were a far more interesting target.[76]

The strongest supporter within the Security Service of detailed monitoring of the CPGB and its fellow-travellers during the Callaghan era was Charles Elwell, F1/0 from April 1974 until his retirement in May 1979. Elwell believed that 'many' Communists and their sympathizers were 'able to exert influence in, for example, education, local government, religious organisations, political parties, local pressure groups etc'. He therefore called for even greater resources to be used to investigate them than they were already receiving.[77] Shortly before Elwell retired, he 'abandoned bureaucratic niceties' and fired off a minute to the DG and DDG complaining that the Service was not paying enough attention to the threat of subversion:

The Communist threat has become more insidious because of the 'blurring of the edges between Communism and democratic socialism'. It is therefore more difficult to recognise and to counter. The job of identifying Communists outside the Party – generally known as 'sympathisers' – has become more important. It requires in those responsible for it discrimination, judgement, investigating ability, a knowledge of Marxism and the ability to recognise the significance of an indication, which may often be fleeting, of Communist sympathy.[78]

Elwell's views, however, were those of a small and dwindling minority within the Service. They were opposed even by Elwell's deputy from 1976 to 1979, who believed that the ample flow of intelligence from technical and agent penetration of the CPGB clearly demonstrated its declining political influence and that 'the subversive threat as a whole was greatly over-hyped, particularly by Charles Elwell.' When he told Elwell, whom he liked personally, that he did not consider the Communists a serious subversive threat to the Labour Party, Elwell 'hit the roof'.[79]

After the May 1979 election, the main pressure for more energetic counter-subversion came not from within the Service but from the new Conservative Prime Minister.[80]

7

The Thatcher Government and Subversion

Margaret Thatcher took greater interest in the intelligence community than any prime minister since Winston Churchill. But, as her Home Secretary, Willie Whitelaw, told the DG, Sir Howard Smith, at their first meeting after the Conservative election victory, much of Mrs Thatcher's information about the Security Service's counter-subversion role during her years as Leader of the Opposition had come from 'people who knew little or nothing about our work'. Whitelaw told Smith that he wished to be sufficiently well briefed to be able to counter 'some of the rather extreme advice' Mrs Thatcher had received.[1]

The Service's briefing was relatively reassuring. The rise in Trotskyism during the 1970s, it reported, was more than counterbalanced by the decline in Communist Party membership: 'Taking the position as a whole, though the threat from subversion is serious and in some ways more evident, it is not greater than 10 years ago.'[2] Mrs Thatcher was not convinced. Smith at his first meeting with the Prime Minister found, as he expected, 'that Mrs Thatcher assumes a greater role and influence on the part of the Communist Party and Trotskyists in the trade union and industrial field than they did in fact enjoy'.[3] The Winter of Discontent had strengthened the Prime Minister's belief in the importance of counter-subversion in dealing with industrial disruption. Whitelaw, though more sympathetic to the Security Service view, also believed that secondary picketing and other militant activism during the strike wave 'showed marks of skilled and highly-coordinated direction'.[4]

Mrs Thatcher demanded prompt action to deal with the 'wreckers' in British industry, and summoned a meeting of the DG, 'C' (Sir Arthur 'Dickie' Franks) and Lord Rothschild (with whom she had discussed the problem),[5] chaired by the cabinet secretary, Sir John Hunt, to come up with 'solutions'. The Prime Minister, Hunt told the meeting, wanted all the 'wreckers' to be identified – which would breach the Security Service charter (the Maxwell Fyfe Directive) of 1952, limiting its role to 'the

Defence of the Realm as a whole, from external and internal dangers arising from attempts of espionage and sabotage, or from actions of persons and organizations whether directed from within or without the country, which may be judged to be subversive of the State'. Non-subversive industrial 'wreckers' were not covered. Hunt suggested that the twenty-seven-year-old directive, written at a time when subversion 'loomed less large in the country's problems', might now benefit from revision. Smith's arguments in favour of the existing definition of subversion and against attempting to extend it to include all industrial disruption, however, carried the day. The meeting also failed to come up with the straightforward solutions for dealing with the 'wreckers' which Mrs Thatcher wanted. The DG argued that ending industrial strife was far more an issue for government policy than for action by the Security Service.

Early in October 1979 Smith learned that Mrs Thatcher had summoned a meeting at Chequers later in the month with Whitelaw, the Foreign Secretary Lord Carrington, the Secretary of State for Trade and Industry Sir Keith Joseph, Sir John Hunt and his successor as cabinet secretary, Sir Robert Armstrong, to 'consider action to counter hostile forces working for industrial unrest'. The DG was not invited. The meeting was so secret that all three ministers were forbidden to show the Prime Minister's summons to anyone except their permanent under secretaries.

The Chequers meeting on 21 October decided to set up a small unit in the Cabinet Office to use information from both open and secret sources to try to forestall industrial disruption. The new unit was to report to the cabinet secretary and be subject to the authority of the Home Secretary (with recourse, when necessary, to the Prime Minister). Whitelaw expressed his willingness to increase the number of HOWs to provide intelligence for the unit. In addition to the ministers present at the Chequers meeting, only the Secretary of State for Employment, Jim Prior, was to be informed of its existence. When it was necessary to give other ministers information from the unit, the source would be concealed. F2, John Deverell, then considered one of the Service's younger high-fliers, was seconded to run the unit, which Service records suggest became a one-man band.[6] Sir Robert Armstrong agreed with Deverell that they would 'firmly eschew any thoughts of black propaganda' as the risks would far outweigh the likely gains.[7] Deverell was tasked instead with submitting proposals for countering specific cases of industrial subversion for approval by the Home Secretary and, if appropriate, the Prime Minister. Whitelaw was enthusiastic, telling Deverell to come and see him whenever he considered there were 'political angles to be explored'. Mrs Thatcher too made clear her personal interest in the new unit.[8] Deverell devised the unit's first successful 'ploy' in response to a strike-call by the Amalgamated Union of Engineering Workers (AUEW) at the government-owned British Leyland (BL) Long-bridge plant, following the dismissal on 19 November of the convenor of the shop stewards, Derek 'Red Robbo' Robinson, regarded by Thatcher as 'a notorious agitator'. The strike, she believed, 'threatened the very survival of BL'.[9]

Red Robbo, who regarded his nickname as a 'badge of honour', had become synonymous with the repeated strikes and disputes which crippled much of Longbridge's increasingly uncompetitive car production.[10] On 21 November 1979 Deverell devised a plan to publicize the record of a September meeting of the CPGB Midland District Committee, attended by Robinson and the Party's industrial organizer Mick Costello, held to discuss opposition to the BL recovery plan. Costello was horrified to discover that detailed minutes had been taken, believed they would do serious damage to the CPGB if they became public and ordered all copies to be recovered and destroyed. The Security Service, however, had obtained a copy, and, at a meeting with Thatcher and Whitelaw, Deverell gained their approval for it to be passed to the BL chairman, Sir Michael Edwardes. To disguise the source of the minutes, they were placed inside a brown envelope with a Birmingham postmark. Edwardes showed them to the president of the AUEW, Terry Duffy, who was sufficiently impressed to postpone strike action. Edwardes also contacted the *Sunday Times*, whose journalists tracked down some of those mentioned in the minutes. Eaves-dropping and telephone-tapping in King Street provided ample evidence of the dismay of the CPGB leadership.[11]

Probably inspired by the success of the 'ploy' against Red Robbo, Sir Keith Joseph returned to the idea that the Security Service, at least in the public sector, might warn employers when subversives applied for jobs with them. When Deverell ruled this out, Joseph suggested channelling warnings to employers through the Economic League, using the 'dirty brown envelope technique we had used with Edwardes'.[12] Deverell found fewer opportunities for 'ploys' than Thatcher and Whitelaw had hoped. Sir Robert Armstrong, however, reported to the Prime Minister in May 1980 that, although comparatively few counter-subversion operations had been mounted, Deverell's work had had a 'significant and beneficial effect on the course of events'. Since Deverell was not fully occupied in the Cabinet Office, he was allowed to return to the Security Service, on the understanding that his first priority, when opportunities arose, would remain counter-subversion operations.[13] In July 1981, when Deverell was posted out of F Branch, responsibility for these operations was taken on by David Ranson, who had been appointed Director F.[14]

Besides industrial disruption, the area where the Thatcher government – the Prime Minister and the MoD in particular – most feared the hidden hand of subversion during the early 1980s was in the peace movement, which organized mass protests over the deployment of US cruise missiles on British soil as a dangerous escalation of the nuclear arms race. Though Mrs Thatcher believed that support for CND had passed its peak in 1981, it remained, in her view, 'dangerously strong'.[15] Of especial concern was the possibility of KGB and Communist subversion within the peace movement. Though rarely alarmist in its assessments, the Security Service had taken the view that 'as CND grew more influential, the potential for subversives to threaten national security through it also increased'. By the mid-1970s CPGB members occupied eight of the fifteen seats on the CND national executive.[16] While monitoring Communist influence in CND was clearly within the Service's remit, the case for opening a temporary file on Monsignor Bruce Kent as a 'possible Anarchist' when he became CND chairman in 1977 and for converting this into a permanent file on his election as CND secretary general from 1979 now appears distinctly dubious.[17] In April 1982 F1A reported that CND was expanding at such a rate that Kent no longer knew precisely how large its membership was – possibly 30,000 in the national organization and as many as 250,000 in independent local groups. CND would remain a target for Communist and Trotskyist groups because it offered 'not only access to a broad-based popular movement with growing influence in political fields, but also an opportunity to challenge Government policies in key areas'.[18]

The section of the peace movement which attracted the greatest international media attention was the Greenham Common Women's Peace Camp set up in September 1981 outside the airbase near Newbury in Berkshire which had been selected as a site for cruise missiles. For the next two years, the women protesters attempted – in the end unsuccessfully – to disrupt the construction of the missile site by blockading the base and cutting down parts of the perimeter fence. In May 1983 a temporary file on the Camp was converted into a permanent file on the grounds that it was 'subject to penetration by subversive groups'.[19] No significant subversive penetration, however, came to light.[20] The dominant element in the Peace Camp was believed to be militant feminists who saw nuclear arms as a problem created by a male-dominated world order. Though Communists, Trotskyists and their sympathizers (all members of male-dominated organizations) had an important role in organizing mass demonstrations in support of the protest, they were reported to disapprove of the Camp's exclusion of men. F2R/1 (whose responsibilities involved investigating possible subversion in the peace movement) minuted in March 1984, four months after the first cruise missiles were deployed at the airbase, that 'we are now able to state with some authority, that the subversive influence on the founding and continuing life of the camp has been slight'.[21]

KGB directives passed by Oleg Gordievsky to SIS after he arrived at the London residency in the summer of 1982[22] demonstrated that Moscow regarded the anti-nuclear movement in Britain (as in the rest of the West) as 'our natural allies' and believed it could exercise considerable influence over it.[23] When 'C' gave Mrs Thatcher her first briefing on Gordievsky on 23 December, at Security Service request he made no mention of his reporting on the peace movement – presumably because of fears that the Prime Minister would take too literally exaggerated KGB claims of its ability to influence the movement. After the briefing, however, 'C' reported to Smith's successor as DG, John Jones, that the Prime Minister had herself in passing raised the issue of KGB involvement with the CND and the peace movement. In these circumstances he had asked SIS to discuss with Director K whether any of Gordievsky's reports needed to be rewritten and whether substantive desk comments should be added before they were presented to the PM. In the meantime Gordievsky would be asked to clarify and update his information on KGB attempts to manipulate the peace movement.[24]

On 25 February 1983 the DDG, Cecil Shipp, and the Deputy Chief of SIS presented to Sir Robert Armstrong, the cabinet secretary, a résumé of Gordievsky's intelligence on the Soviet Union and the British peace movement which they had jointly prepared for Mrs Thatcher.[25] The Security Service added a commentary designed to emphasize the contrast between some KGB claims for its ability to influence the peace movement and what it had actually achieved. Gordievsky's intelligence on the paucity of effective KGB contacts in the movement, as well as the limited influence of the Soviet embassy, was, it reported, both reassuring and in line with previous Service assessments. When the London residency was urged by the Centre in the autumn of 1982 to increase its efforts, the only 'confidential contact' it was able to cite with substantial influence on the peace movement was the ninety-four-year-old left-wing Labour politician Lord Brockway, co-founder three years earlier of the World Disarmament Campaign, whose efforts to persuade local authorities to declare themselves 'nuclear-free zones' were applauded by the Centre. Brockway was estimated to agree with 70 to 80 per cent of Soviet policy decisions. He had monthly meetings with Mikhail Bogdanov, a Line PR (political intelligence) officer operating under journalistic cover, and accepted presents from him – though it was thought that Brockway probably did not realize he worked for the KGB.[26] Bogdanov, then in his early thirties and the son of a Leningrad musician, was rated by Gordievsky as 'the most polished and sophisticated member' of the London residency.[27]

The joint SIS–Security Service brief for the Prime Minister also emphasized some of the failures of KGB and other Soviet attempts to influence the peace movement. The KGB was so suspicious of the willingness of the European Nuclear Disarmament Movement (END), founded by Professor E. P. Thompson, to criticize Soviet as well as Western policy that it concluded perversely that END was inspired by Western intelligence. In January 1983 the chairman of the Soviet Peace Committee sent a letter to CND accusing it and other British groups of dividing the world peace movement and playing into the hands of the Americans. Gordievsky reported that Bruce Kent visited the Soviet embassy to register his disagreement.[28] Service investigation of attempted Soviet penetration of the peace movement eventually reached the reassuring conclusion that efforts by KGB officers and other Soviet officials to enter into a dialogue with its leading figures achieved little, since most – like Joan Ruddock and Bruce Kent – were fiercely independent and critical of some aspects of Soviet policy.[29]

In 1982, however, Ruddock, then CND chairman, had a temporary file opened on her by Cathy Massiter, which was converted into a PF (personal file) in 1983 because of her meetings with Mikhail Bogdanov, whom Ruddock was doubtless unaware was a KGB officer.[30] After reviewing several years later the claims made by Massiter of excessive surveillance of the peace movement, a senior MI5 officer (a future DDG) concluded that there was some force to her argument that the case for beginning a telephone check in 1983 on John Cox, a member of the CPGB National Executive Committee and one of the CND vice chairmen, was inadequate: 'I am not sure what I think. There were certainly solid and respectable reasons at the time for proceeding as we did but I feel in retrospect that Massiter may be right in questioning whether the warrant was strictly justified.'[31] At the time, however, the telephone check on Cox was viewed as the Service's 'most important source on Communist involvement in the peace movement and a useful source of intelligence on Trotskyist activities within CND and on Soviet attitudes towards CND':

It enabled us to conclude, among other things, that members of the CPGB were not manipulating CND or exercising decisive influence within it. The warrant was cancelled in 1985 when we were in a position to make a full assessment of the level of subversive influence in CND and, in that light, reduce our coverage.[32]

The Security Service reported that, because of the KGB's failure to influence the leading figures within CND, its London residency tended to rely instead on less influential contacts more receptive to the Soviet viewpoint. None, apart from Fenner Brockway, had a significant influence on CND or public opinion. The Service found no evidence that KGB funding to the British peace movement went beyond occasional payment of fares and expenses to individuals.[33]

As with industrial disruption, there was some ministerial pressure on the Security Service to go beyond the terms of its charter in investigating the peace movement. According to a later internal investigation, prompted by Cathy Massiter's allegations: 'It was plain to the Service in 1983 that MoD was anxious to obtain ammunition against CND and would have liked us to assist actively. But our response was very cautious ... If there was political pressure on us to do more than was justified, we appear to have resisted it.'[34] At the time, however, some members of the Service believed that the resistance was inadequate. Director FX later claimed that the DG, John Jones, gave into MoD pressure to provide unclassified 'dirt' on CND.[35] In March 1983 the Service provided the MoD with open-source material on the political affiliation of seven leading members of CND.[36] One of the desk officers at the time recalls her and some of her colleagues' 'discontent' at the decision to do so.[37]

Like its Labour predecessor, the Thatcher government's main fears about subversion centred on industrial disruption. Its fears reached a climax during the year-long miners' strike of 1984–5, the longest in British history. The Service was less alarmed than the Prime Minister. Director F told the Directors' Meeting on 13 March 1984 that 'so far there did not appear to be significant subversive involvement in the current miners' strike.'[38] He reported on 4 April that 'subversive organisations were not making a significant impact on events.'[39] Mrs Thatcher and some of her ministers seem to have been unpersuaded. Though the Service continued to monitor contacts between the CPGB and the miners' leader, Arthur Scargill, Director F believed that the Party was seeking – unsuccessfully – to exert 'a moderating influence' on him, rather than to inflame the dispute further. 'In general,' he told his fellow directors on 4 June, 'the prospect of a settlement of the strike appeared to be remote.'[40] Scargill had been the subject of an HOW, continued by successive home secretaries since November 1973, on the grounds of his contacts with the CPGB.[41] The former

MI5 officer Cathy Massiter later recalled that Scargill 'would occasionally shout abuse into the phone at the people who were tapping him'. The NUM's Communist vice president Mick McGahey had been subject to an HOW for most of the period since 1970.[42] According to Massiter:

The tapping of his home telephone . . . gave rise to an office joke about the girls who had to listen to Mrs McGahey's interminable telephone conversations with friends and relatives. But we were able to get information from her chatting about his movements, which he himself was careful to conceal.[43]

It has been claimed that during the miners' strike 'Every single NUM branch and lodge secretary had his phone monitored. So did the entire national and area union leaderships, as well as sympathetic trade unionists and support-group activists all over the country.'[44] These claims are fanciful. Most phone tapping, authorized in every case by HOWs, was limited to leading Communist and Trotskyist militants and those judged to have close links with them. Stella Rimington, then F2, later recalled 'agonising' over the justification for continuing the HOW on Scargill, before categorizing him as 'an unaffiliated subversive' on the grounds that, after calling a strike without a ballot, his declared aim was to overthrow the democratically elected Thatcher government.[45]

The Service's regular (often daily) Box 500 situation reports on the miners' strike were originally sent only to senior Whitehall officials. In late June 1984, however, Mrs Thatcher discovered their existence and it was agreed that henceforth copies of all the reports should be sent to her through the cabinet secretary.[46] She seems to have read them attentively, complaining on one occasion that a Box 500 report of 4 September that Scargill was planning a statement blaming the National Coal Board (NCB) for withdrawing from proposed talks had arrived too late for the government to be able to counter it immediately. The government, said the Cabinet Office, 'were anxious not to lose propaganda points' during a strike which was unusual in 'being to a large extent conducted through the media'.[47] Rimington recalls a visit to the Gower Street headquarters by Leon Brittan, after he succeeded Whitelaw as home secretary in June: 'I remember telling him, "We will accumulate information and, in so far as it is our responsibility, pass [it] to Whitehall but then it is up to you and you must decide how you are going to deal with it."'[48]

A best-selling history of the miners' strike later claimed that Rimington was heavily involved in orchestrating dirty tricks against the NUM. According to a Commons motion by a group of Labour MPs, Roger Windsor, the NUM chief executive officer during the strike, was 'an agent of MI5 under Mrs Rimington, sent into the NUM to destabilize and sabotage the union at its most critical juncture'. After the allegation had been denied by both Rimington and the Prime Minister, John Major, Windsor won substantial damages from the *Sunday Express* for repeating the claim that he had been an MI5 'mole' during the miners' strike.[49] As during many previous industrial disputes, though the government was anxious for a wide range of intelligence, the Security Service refused to violate its charter by targeting union leaders and activists who were not Communists, Trotskyists or assessed by the Service as sympathizers. It was also unwilling to monitor picket lines or the miners' wives' association.[50]

Rimington noted in September that, according to Peter Gregson, deputy secretary at the Cabinet Office responsible for 'civil contingencies', Service reports, though not 'of vital significance to HMG', 'were of value as background information and some were of particular interest':

The Government regarded it as a dispute that they must win. If the Nottinghamshire coalfield continued to work and the power stations continued to receive fuel, the Government felt confident that coal stocks would last through the winter. In March [1985] new nuclear and oil burning power stations came on stream and coal supplies would become of decreasing significance. It followed that the intelligence of greatest interest to the Government would be on the following subjects:–

a. Indications of the strike spreading to Nottinghamshire

b. Information about the return to work movement

c. Indications of action likely to prevent the movement of coal into the power stations

d. Any advance information that Scargill was planning a propaganda coup of any kind which might have the effect of causing an all out strike.[51]

From the viewpoint of the Thatcher government, the most critical moment of the miners' strike came in the autumn of 1984 with the threat of a strike by the National Association of Colliery Overmen, Deputies and Shotfirers (NACODS), who bore the main responsibility for mine safety.[52] Since the law required that coal could be mined only in the presence of trained safety personnel, a NACODS strike threatened to bring the whole coal industry to a halt. Because there were no Communists or Trotskyists at the top of NACODS, however, the Security Service had no HOWs on its leaders and could provide little useful intelligence on their intentions. The government thus had to rely largely on the rather ill-informed assessments of the NCB, which was initially far too optimistic about the likely outcome of a strike ballot in late September. Contrary to NCB predictions the ballot produced a pro-strike majority of 82.5 per cent. After negotiations with the NCB, however, the NACODS executive called off the strike before it was due to begin on 24 October. The absence of Box 500 reports on NACODS left Mrs Thatcher 'unclear' about what had caused the change of heart.[53]

Until (and, in lesser degree, even after) NACODS called off its strike, Arthur Scargill seemed in confident mood. *The Economist* believed he had some reason to be so, declaring on 6 October, 'Mrs Thatcher is not now going to win the miners' strike outright.' One of the recurrent themes in Box 500 reports was Scargill's intransigence. The situation report for 24 October 1984 concluded: 'He remains determined not to concede any points to the National Coal Board (NCB) and expects the strike to continue until the NCB meets all the NUM's demands.'[54] Box 500 reports also kept the government informed about Scargill's successful attempts to obtain funds for the NUM from Colonel Qaddafi. After reports of his Libyan connections appeared in the *Sunday Times* on 28 October, Scargill, even 'in private . . . appeared unconcerned and highly amused by the publicity, claiming not to understand what the fuss was about'.[55] 'Leading Communists and Communist sympathisers within the NUM' were, however, reported to be 'privately critical of the union contacts with the Libyans'. Though the NUM's Communist vice president Mick McGahey supported Scargill in public, in private he was 'extremely angry and embarrassed' about the contact with Libya.[56] By contrast, McGahey was happy to take part, with Scargill and other NUM leaders, in contacts with Soviet representatives. 'It seems likely', the Service reported on 1 November, 'that the Soviet Union may also provide funds for the NUM.'[57] As during previous industrial disputes, transcribing McGahey's telephone and other conversations was complicated by the effect of his phenomenal drinking on what seemed to English ears his already difficult Scottish accent.[58] On 5 November the Service reported that McGahey was 'ill in bed from alcohol poisoning'.[59]

The main intelligence source on these contacts was almost certainly Oleg Gordievsky, by then head of political intelligence (Line PR) in the KGB London residency. 'I see the Russian connection has now come out [in the press],' McGahey told a Scottish miners' rally. 'In case you don't know, I'm the guy. I had discussions with Soviet comrades. I will tell you the figure – it's $1,138,000. It's coming from Soviet trade unionists.'[60] Gordievsky revealed, however, that the decision to give the money to the NUM – against the advice of the KGB – had in reality been made by the Central Committee of the Soviet Communist Party.[61]

After the resolution of the NACODS crisis, the Security Service reported increasing pessimism among both Communists and Trotskyists at the likely outcome of the strike. A Communist on the NUM South Wales executive committee was reported to believe that 'the loyalty of striking miners in South Wales is . . . being seriously undermined by the intransigence of the national leadership.'[62] A Box 500 situation report on 29 November declared: 'Although they are still encouraging their full-time workers to continue their efforts to support the NUM, some leading [Militant Tendency] figures, including Peter Taaffe, editor of "Militant", are beginning to admit privately that the strike may be a lost cause.'[63] Service reports in the closing weeks of 1984 emphasized the CPGB's increasing pessimism about the prospects for the strike and the growing rift between Scargill and the Party leadership. Scargill privately complained of CPGB attacks on him. Bert Ramelson, the Party's former industrial organizer to whom Scargill had once been close, was asked by the Party leadership to meet him 'to try to persuade him of the importance, for public relations, of his being seen to be flexible and reasonable'. Ramelson produced a paper outlining a basis for resumption of talks between the NUM and NCB which he claimed was welcomed by McGahey. Scargill's reaction to the paper, when Ramelson met him on 12 December, was hostile: 'Ramelson found Scargill tired and strained. He recognises that Scargill is unable to admit when his strategy is wrong but hopes that he will read the document seriously. He hopes to meet Scargill again to continue to try to exert influence on him.'[64]

On 10 December the Security Service received intelligence that in early November the Soviet Foreign Trade Bank had attempted to transfer the equivalent of almost US$1.2 million to the NUM via banks in Switzerland and London, but had abandoned the attempt after the Swiss bank began to suspect a Soviet money-laundering operation. The report gave Mrs Thatcher the opportunity a week later to raise the question of Soviet financial support to the NUM, without compromising Oleg Gordievsky, during her talks in London with Mikhail Gorbachev, the Soviet heir apparent.[65] Gorbachev 'claimed to be unaware' that financial support was being given. Subsequent intelligence reports to the Prime Minister indicated that, on the contrary, Gorbachev 'was among those who authorised payment'.[66]

By early January 71,000 of the 187,000 miners were back at work. Though Scargill refused to accept defeat and sought further funds from Libya, the end of the strike was now only a matter of time. The miners' return to work in April 1985 was a defining moment in the history of both the Thatcher government and the union movement. It also marked the beginning of the end of counter-subversion as one of the Service's main priorities. The shift in priorities was hastened by the appointment of Sir

Antony Duff as DG just as the strike was ending. At a meeting with Brittan's successor as home secretary, Douglas Hurd, in October 1985 Duff discussed how far counter-subversion could be cut back.[67] The main obstacle which Duff had identified to reducing the resources required for counter-subversion was the Security Service's responsibility for vetting, which made it necessary to have comprehensive lists of members of, and people known to be sympathetic to, subversive organizations. F Branch received some 3,000 negative vetting inquiries a day.[68]

In May 1987 Duff reported to the Home Secretary that, almost certainly for the first time in the Cold War, the threat from subversive groups was assessed as 'low'. There had, however, been some shift in F Branch work from the declining Communist Party to growing Trotskyite groups, especially the largest of them, Militant Tendency.[69] In the short term Militant's growth appeared little affected either by the scathing denunciation of it by the Labour leader, Neil Kinnock, at the 1985 party conference, or by its expulsion from the Party before the June 1987 general election. After a recruitment campaign in the spring of 1986, Militant membership reached about 7,800 (roughly 2,000 more than in 1984).[70] At a national conference held on Merseyside, one of its regional strongholds, Militant claimed to have passed the 8,000 mark and to employ 267 full-time workers (as compared with Labour's 180).[71] Overtaken by revolutionary enthusiasm, the executive committee convinced itself that Militant Tendency was now poised to 'prepare ourselves for the future role of leadership of the British revolution and the conquering of power at the earliest opportunity, both nationally and internationally'.[72] Despite Militant's expulsion from the Labour Party, three of its members – Dave Nellist, Terry Fields and Pat Wall – were returned as Labour MPs in the June elections, one more than in 1983. All were given a rapturous reception at Militant HQ, which also congratulated itself on the election of a Militant sympathizer, Ronnie Campbell, at Blyth.[73]

Militant was also confident of its growing ability to penetrate the union movement. In July 1986 a Militant sympathizer, John Macreadie, had been elected general secretary of one of the main civil service unions, the CPSA, with a seat on the TUC General Council (a triumph somewhat marred by allegations of ballot rigging).[74] For the past decade, the civil and public service had been assessed as particularly vulnerable to subversive activity. At the end of 1984 approximately 1,800 civil servants and employees of public corporations were identified by the Security Service as having subversive records. The effect of vetting had been to concentrate those judged to be subversives in departments such as the Department of Health and Social Security, where they had little access to classified information but significant opportunities to cause disruption.[75] Duff's report to the Home Secretary in May 1987 on the prospects for subversion, however, was resolutely unalarmist. The threat from Militant and other subversive organizations, as well as from subversive individuals in sensitive areas of public life, was likely to remain low. The DG did, however, forecast that the Trotskyist groups would continue to grow and remain very active.[76]

Duff's forecast proved too pessimistic. Nineteen-eighty-seven was to be Militant's high water mark. Over the next few years, increasingly impaled on its own ridiculous rhetoric and preposterous policies, the very epitome of the 'Loony Left' which many mainstream Labour supporters blamed for playing into the hands of the Tories and keeping their own party out of power, Militant saw its appeal and influence dwindle steadily. According to Security Service reports, Ted Grant, the founder of Militant Tendency, came to be derided even within Militant ranks as a 'Worzel Gummidge' who had 'lost his marbles'.[77]

Margaret Thatcher's appetite for intelligence actually increased during her eleven years in office. At a meeting with the new DG, Patrick Walker, in January 1988 she mentioned with approval 'but some irritation' the President's Daily Brief which Ronald Reagan received from the CIA each day before breakfast. The Prime Minister also seemed annoyed by the fact that, at meetings with Jacques Chirac, the French Prime Minister (later President), 'Chirac always seems able to come out with some piece of intelligence which she has not received.' Henceforth, it was agreed that the DG should see the Prime Minister every four months.[78] What had previously been *ad hoc* and occasional visits by the DG to Number Ten became routine for the first time since the era of Sir Percy Sillitoe. Little of Mrs Thatcher's briefings, however, any longer had to do with subversion, which had been her main intelligence preoccupation when she took office. Walker emphasized to her in January 1988 'the low level of the current threat assessment' of subversion. The Prime Minister does not seem to have challenged that assessment.[79]

8

Counter-Terrorism and Protective Security in the Early 1980s

The Security Service's counter-terrorist responsibilities were sufficiently confusing for Director F to think it necessary in January 1980 to remind the DG, Sir Howard Smith, what they consisted of:

You have responsibilities for the collection of intelligence:

(a) on International Terrorism, its impact on the UK and her interests

(b) in relation to Irish Republican Terrorism:

    (i) because the DCI is a Security Service officer;

    (ii) because of our responsibilities for covering the overseas links and source of supply of Irish terrorists;

    (iii) through our joint effort with SIS in the IJS to collect intelligence particularly in support of the effort to suppress Republican Terrorism in Northern Ireland

(c) on Northern Ireland Protestant extremist and terrorist activities in Great Britain[1]

Dealing with these diverse responsibilities was made more difficult by the confused division of counter-terrorist responsibilities between F and FX Branches.[2] In 1980 Smith reversed the previous priorities of the two branches by making FX the main counter-subversion branch and handing over responsibility for Irish as well as international terrorism to F.[3] Illogically, however, Smith decreed that FX remain responsible for all counter-terrorist agent-running. Director FX from 1981 to 1984 later acknowledged that, until a further reorganization in 1984 made the Branch's responsibilities solely counter-terrorist, it lacked internal coherence.[4]

The most straightforward of the Security Service's CT responsibilities was surveillance through a variety of means, in association with local Special Branches, of members and supporters in mainland Britain of Ulster's Loyalist Protestant paramilitaries, most of whom were concentrated in Strathclyde and Merseyside. Neither the UDA nor the UVF had recovered from the long prison sentences passed on some of their leading

British members in 1978–9.[5] The Service assessed their general level of activity in the early 1980s as low. It reported to ministers in 1983 that UDA and UVF activities consisted 'mainly of attempts, frequently unsuccessful, to smuggle arms and explosives to Northern Ireland'.[6]

PIRA was a much more dangerous opponent outside Northern Ireland than the Loyalist paramilitaries. The Security Service continued to feel hampered in its response to them by the fact that, illogically in its view, the MPSB possessed the lead intelligence role on the British mainland.[7] The Service also believed that the Special Branch paid too little attention to long-term investigation. Director FX complained in 1980: 'Until MPSB's modus operandi changed i.e. until they organised themselves on what we would call a Desk Officer system – involving continuous intelligence study – they would never be able fully to carry out their intelligence, as opposed to police, functions.'[8]

The Security Service none the less had a larger role to play against PIRA in the 1980s than in the 1970s, partly because of PIRA operations on the continent and arms procurement from abroad – both areas in which the Service had the lead intelligence role. Though the lead intelligence role in Northern Ireland remained with the RUC Special Branch, the position of the DCI as SOSNI's chief intelligence adviser also enhanced the role of the Service. The Irish Joint Section (IJS) Belfast station possessed a combination of human and technical sources (both still classified) which sometimes provided important insights into PIRA policy and operations. Director F, a former DCI, reported to the DG in November 1980:

[IJS] officers are already more directly involved with RUC S[pecial] B[ranch] in producing operational intelligence on all aspects of the security scene in Northern Ireland; and that involvement extends to dealings with SB officers both at RUC HQ and elsewhere in the Province . . . In short [the IJS] is increasingly seen by both Army and the RUC as a significant part of the intelligence gathering organisation in the Province.

. . . The RUC suspicion of the Security Service operations in Northern Ireland apparent some years ago has now gone and the Security Service maintains close contacts with the RUC through two sections, F5 (principally) and F3, which already have an acknowledged responsibility for parts of Irish Republican and Protestant extremism . . .[9]

The IJS Belfast station was by now wholly funded and mainly staffed by the Security Service.[10] There had been a remarkable transformation in the Security Service's view of its role in Northern Ireland since the founding of the IJS eight years earlier. In 1972 the Service had not even been able to find a credible candidate for the post of DCI, and SIS had taken the lead role in the IJS.[11] By 1980, Director F believed that the IJS had outlived its usefulness.[12] Though it was not to be wound up for another four years, the Security Service was ready to take sole control of the operations in Northern Ireland which for the past eight years it had shared with SIS.

During the early 1980s 'international' terrorists, against whom the Security Service retained the lead intelligence role, mounted considerably more attacks in mainland Britain than the Provisionals. Unlike PIRA operations, however, their operations were usually spill-overs from conflicts in other parts of the world, mainly the Middle East, and rarely targeted British interests directly. One of the main problems faced by the Service in confronting international terrorism during the 1980s was the diffuse and often unpredictable nature of the threat. The first major terrorist incident of the decade – an attack on a London embassy – took the Service by surprise. Because of the contingency planning of the 1970s, however, it was far better handled than it would have been less than a decade earlier.

On 30 April 1980 six armed terrorists burst into the Iranian embassy at Prince's Gate in Knightsbridge and seized twenty-six hostages, one of whom was a member of the Metropolitan Police's Diplomatic Protection Group.[13] The terrorists, who called themselves the 'Group of the Martyr' and supported the movement for autonomy in Iranian 'Arabistan', demanded that ninety-one members of the movement imprisoned by the Khomeini regime (which had taken power in Iran after the fall of the Shah) should be released, that the regime should recognize the 'legitimate rights of the Iranian peoples', and that a special plane should be provided to carry the terrorists and their hostages to an unspecified Middle East country. If their demands were rejected, they threatened to destroy the Iranian embassy and kill the hostages. According to Margaret Thatcher's memoirs, she and the Home Secretary, Willie Whitelaw, were agreed from the outset on their counter-terrorist strategy: 'We would try patient negotiation; but if any hostages were wounded we would consider an attack on the embassy; and if a hostage were killed we would definitely send in the Special Air Service (SAS).'[14] During the eighteen months before the hostage crisis there had been increasing contact between the Security Service and SAS, due in part to the personal friendship between David Sutherland, head of a C Branch section, and Brigadier (later General Sir) Peter de la Billière, the SAS director.[15]

After the terrorist attack on the Iranian embassy, Security Service officers took part, as usual, in the COBR crisis-management group in the Cabinet Office, chaired by the Home Secretary, which was manned around the clock throughout the hostage crisis.[16] COBR was told there was reliable intelligence that the terrorists had been recruited and trained by the Saddam Hussein regime in Iraq, then at war with Iran.[17] Though the regime, unsurprisingly, did not admit responsibility for the operation, the terrorists' demands were publicly supported by the government-controlled Iraqi press.[18]

Following the Service's well-rehearsed procedures for dealing with terrorist hostage-taking, an intelligence team together with a large A Branch technical support group was quickly deployed to the scene of the embassy siege to support the Metropolitan Police and to obtain intelligence to help plan an assault on the Iranian embassy.[19] A variety of ingenious eavesdropping devices were used to gather intelligence on the state of mind of the terrorists and their captives, as well as to identify their precise locations in a six-floor embassy with over fifty rooms.[20] The Arabic- and Farsi-speaking transcribers who listened in to the conversations inside the embassy were asked to work long and exhausting shifts in the belief that 'it was preferable for a small number of linguists to build up a detailed mental picture of the gunmen and their hostages, their attitudes and actions, rather than a larger number of linguists being deployed with a resulting loss of continuity'.[21] A Branch deployed a total of thirty-five staff in its technical support team, supplemented by sixteen staff seconded from other parts of the intelligence community.[22]

Thanks to astute negotiation by the police, assisted by intelligence from the Security Service, a series of deadlines set by the terrorists came and went without incident. Once it became clear to the terrorists, however, that their demands were not going to be met, eavesdropping revealed the growth of acute tensions between them. On 5 May they announced that two hostages would be shot, and others killed at regular intervals unless their demands were met. Shots were heard from within the embassy later the same day but negotiations continued because it could not initially be established whether anyone had been killed. However, when the body of a hostage was pushed through the front door, Whitelaw rang the Prime Minister, then on her way back to Downing Street from Chequers, to seek her authority to send in the SAS. Given the sophistication of the eavesdropping operations in Prince's Gate, it was ironic that, because of poor reception on Mrs Thatcher's car-phone, she was unable to hear what the Home Secretary said. Once she had told her driver to pull into a lay-by, however, she was brought up to date with the critical situation in the Iranian embassy and replied with characteristic decisiveness, 'Yes, go in'[23] – thus authorizing the first ever use of the SAS in Britain to resolve a crisis by the use of force.

The Security Service post-action assessment concludes that its intelligence from within the Iranian embassy 'played a vital part'.[24] As de la Billière later recalled:

The aim was to attack every floor of the building simultaneously, and to break in so fast on all levels that the gunmen would not have time to execute anyone. Success depended on every SAS man knowing his task precisely: the soldiers had to be able to pick out the terrorists, recognise every hostage (from memorizing photographs), and keep within pre-set boundaries so that there was no risk of shooting each other.[25]

When the assault began, de la Billière was the only person in COBR to be in touch, via headphones, with Prince's Gate, and kept up a running commentary: 'They're on the roof ... They're laying out the ropes ... They've got the charges down the light-well ... They're ready.' Next came the codeword 'Hyde Park', telling the abseilers on the roof to hitch themselves to their ropes, ready for the signal 'London Bridge', instructing them to drop down from the roof and break in through the windows on every floor. Unlike much of the nation which was glued to live coverage of the break-in on television, no one in COBR saw the storming of the embassy. It did not occur to any of those present that, if they had switched on one of the row of television sets fixed to the wall above head-height, they would have been able to see the assault team in action. De la Billière was soon able to report to COBR that, after a brief struggle, five of the terrorists had been killed and the sixth captured alive. Of the twenty-six hostages, five had been released during the siege, one had been killed by the terrorists before the attack and a second after it began; the other nineteen were freed by the SAS. As de la Billière gave the news, everyone in COBR leaped to their feet, papers flew in the air and bottles of whisky appeared from a cupboard.[26] The successful ending of the siege and the enormous publicity given to it, shown on television around the world, may well have deterred other terrorist attacks in London.[27]

Willie Whitelaw sought to reinforce the deterrent effect of the assault by telling the Commons: 'The way in which this incident was conducted and resolved demonstrates conclusively the determination of the British Government and people not to allow terrorist blackmail to succeed.'[28] Twenty years later (or less) the Home Secretary would have paid public tribute to the role of the Security Service in bringing the siege to an end. But in 1980 public mention of its role was still taboo. Whitelaw, however, wrote privately to the DG to express 'deep appreciation' of the part played by the Service and 'the enormous value of the intelligence which was being produced'.[29] The DG and his senior management, however, were criticized within the Service for their failure either to appear on the ground during the siege to provide moral support for hard-pressed staff or to express adequate thanks for their work after the siege was over.[30] The Iranian embassy siege provided further evidence of the remote management style of Sir Howard Smith and his DDG, John Jones.[31]

Aircraft hijacks were as difficult to predict as the attack on the Iranian embassy, but proved less of a problem in the early 1980s than a decade earlier. The contingency planning developed during the 1970s[32] was first put to the test on British soil in 1982. On 26 February an Air Tanzania Boeing 737 on an internal flight was hijacked by a group claiming to be representatives of the previously unknown Tanzanian Youth Democratic Movement. The aircraft with about eighty passengers was diverted to Nairobi, where inconclusive negotiations took place, then to Jeddah for refuelling, then to Athens, and finally to Stansted, where the plane landed on 27 February.[33] COBR convened, initially chaired by the Prime Minister for the only time during her years in office,[34] and the other elements of the contingency plan were put into action, including the assistance of an A Branch technical support group and Security Service intelligence analysis. Though the motives of the hijackers appeared confused, their principal demands were for the resignation of President Nyerere of Tanzania and for a meeting with Oscar Kambona, a former Tanzanian foreign minister living in exile in London. Eavesdropping on the hijackers suggested that there was a good prospect of a peaceful settlement. After patient negotiations, the passengers were released in groups and the hijackers surrendered. There was no damage to the aircraft and the only injury was to the co-pilot, who was accidentally shot in the back by one of the hijackers. Five hijackers were tried, convicted and sentenced to prison terms of between three and eight years. Among the Security Service team at Stansted was a former member of the Colonial Service who was one of the few people in England able to understand the local Tanzanian dialect used by some of the hijackers in their overheard conversations.[35]

Also difficult to predict was the extent to which foreign authoritarian regimes would use state-sponsored terrorism to silence dissidents who had fled abroad. The most persistent, though not quite continuous, state-sponsored terrorist threat in Britain during the 1980s came from Colonel Qaddafi's Libya.[36] Qaddafi's vanity was exemplified by a flamboyant wardrobe which enabled him, for example, to change in the same day from naval uniform adorned with gold braid and medals to Arab dress with exotic Bedouin headgear to a gold cape over a red silk shirt. Its more vicious side was shown by a determination to hunt down critics of his personal dictatorship (misleadingly entitled the 'Socialist People's Libyan Arab Jamahiriya') who had taken refuge abroad. Qaddafi was responsible for a series of attacks on Libyan émigrés in Britain, which included three killings at the beginning of the decade. By the spring of 1980 F Branch possessed 'conclusive evidence' that the Libyan embassy in London (renamed the 'Libyan People's Bureau') was 'directing operational and intelligence gathering activities against Libyan dissidents'.[37] The first dissident to be killed was Muhammad Ramadan, who was shot dead outside the Regent's Park Mosque in April 1980. The gunman, Ben Hassan Muhammad El Masri,[38] and his accomplice, Nagib Mufta Gasmi,[39] were arrested near the scene of the killing by two passing police officers and later sentenced to life imprisonment. A fortnight later another of Qaddafi's assassins, Mabrook Ali Mohammed Al Gidal, murdered the dissident Libyan lawyer Mahmoud Abbu Nafa in his Kensington office. Al Gidal had formerly shared a flat with El Masri and Gasmi; like them he was caught and sentenced to life imprisonment.[40]

The assassinations were intended as a warning to other Libyan dissidents to obey Qaddafi's demand for them to cease their opposition and return to Libya. The deadline for their return on 11 June was marked by a dissident demonstration outside the London People's Bureau which caused predictable outrage in Tripoli. Reliable intelligence revealed that the Libyan Foreign Liaison Bureau (Foreign Ministry) reprimanded Musa Kusa, the effective head of the London People's Bureau, for failing to use force to disrupt the demonstration. He was told that, in order to demonstrate that all opposition would be mercilessly crushed, at least one of the demonstrators should have been killed. Probably in response to this reprimand, Kusa gave an interview to *The Times* declaring that Libya was prepared to support the IRA and approving a decision by the Libyan 'Revolutionary Committee' in the UK to sentence two dissidents to death. Following the publication of Kusa's interview on 13 June, he was given forty-eight hours to leave the country. That night there was a petrol-bomb attack on the British embassy in Tripoli. No one was hurt and the Libyan authorities absurdly blamed the damage on an electrical fault.[41] After Kusa's expulsion, reliable intelligence continued to suggest that the People's Bureau was engaged in the surveillance of dissidents in the UK and planning assassinations. Potential targets were warned by the police, and the Service passed intelligence on likely Libyan assassins to the MPSB.[42] The fact that no leading dissident was killed or wounded by the People's Bureau hitmen in the remainder of the year strongly suggests that this was a case in which intelligence saved lives.

Late in October F Branch received further reliable intelligence that the People's Bureau had poison in powder form with which to assassinate dissidents.[43] The first Libyan hitman to attempt to use the poison appears to have been Hosni Sed Farhat, who was reported to be targeting dissidents in the Portsmouth area.[44] Though F Branch was aware of Farhat's activities, it had no means of predicting that his first target would be Farj Shaban Ghesouda and his British wife Heather Clare, who were not members of any dissident group and appeared to be low in the rank order of Qaddafi's émigré opponents. Farhat probably selected the Ghesoudas partly because the precautions taken by leading dissidents had made them hard targets, partly because his previous acquaintance with the Ghesoudas gave him a pretext for a social call. During Farhat's visit on 7 November he quickly aroused suspicion by offering to go into the kitchen and prepare coffee. Fearing a poisoning attempt, the Ghesoudas declined his offer but did not suspect that a packet of peanuts which he brought as a present might have been tampered with.[45] As Mrs Ghesouda said later, 'Arab visitors usually bring nuts or sweets with them.' The peanuts, however, were laced with thallium. After the Ghesoudas' children ate them, their central nervous systems were affected, their hair fell out, and only prompt diagnosis and treatment saved their lives. The family's pet Pekinese, which picked up some of the peanuts from the floor, died. Farhat was arrested four days after his visit to the Ghesoudas and, like the assassins of Ramadan and Abbu Nafa, sentenced to life imprisonment for attempted murder.[46]

The final victim of Qaddafi's hitmen in Britain during 1980 was Ahmed Mustafa, a Libyan student at Manchester University, who was found murdered on 29 November. According to the police, there were elements of ritual killing in the murder.[47] The assassins were believed to be Libyan language students who returned to Tripoli immediately after the killing. This time the People's Bureau was not thought to be involved. 'Our intelligence', the future DG, Patrick Walker (then F3), told the police, 'suggested that the attack on Mustafa was initiated from Libya.'[48] An FCO assessment concluded that Mustafa's assassins might have chosen the wrong target.[49] After the killing there was an unexpected lull in Qaddafi's assassination campaign in Britain, perhaps reflecting irritation that his hitmen during 1980 had either been caught or had killed the wrong man.

Among the known terrorist targets in London were several ambassadors, the Israeli and the Turkish chief among them. On 3 June 1982 the Israeli ambassador, Shlomo Argov, was shot in the head by a gunman as he was leaving a diplomatic reception at the Dorchester Hotel. The gunman was then himself shot and wounded by the ambassador's police protection officer.[50] Two other men left the scene rapidly by car but were later arrested. All three were convicted of attempted murder, and sentenced to prison terms of at least thirty years. The ambassador survived, though with terrible injuries. The Service quickly identified as the group responsible for the attack the Abu Nidal Organization (ANO), then sponsored by Iraq, later by Libya,[51] which subsequently admitted responsibility.[52]

Born into a wealthy Palestinian family in Jaffa which was forced to flee its home during the Arab–Israeli War of 1948, Abu Nidal (born Sabri al-Banna) split from the Palestine Liberation Organization (PLO) in the early 1970s on the grounds that it was too moderate. After assassinating several of its leading representatives, he was sentenced to death by the PLO in 1974. By the time Abu Nidal ordered the killing of Shlomo Argov in June 1982, he was the most feared terrorist in the Middle East. Two months later an ANO group machine-gunned a kosher restaurant in Paris, killing six people and wounding thirty.[53] The way that Abu Nidal had selected the three intended assassins of Argov (one Iraqi and two West Bank Palestinians) made the Service pessimistic about the prospects of detecting future ANO terrorists in Britain. All were students at a London language school with valid passports and visas issued by British embassies in the Middle East. None was known to the Security Service or had any contact with groups the Service was investigating: 'It is unlikely', F3/6 concluded afterwards, 'that they would have come to our notice in the ordinary course of events . . .' The quartermaster of the Argov assassination team lived inconspicuously in a YMCA hostel, where he stored his weapons: 'The fact is nothing short of a blanket refusal to admit Arab students can prevent an assassination team in that guise entering the UK.'[54]

As a result of Security Service success in identifying and investigating several members in London of the Marxist-Leninist Armenian Secret Army for the Liberation of Armenia (ASALA), it was able to forestall an assassination attempt on the Turkish ambassador three months after the shooting of Argov. Between 1975 and 1985 more than forty Turkish diplomats and members of their families worldwide were killed by Armenian terrorists.[55] On 4 September 1982 a telephone intercept revealed that an unidentified Armenian gunman had travelled to London to carry out a terrorist attack.[56] The intercept also revealed that the gunman was staying at the Lancashire Hotel, Norfolk Square, where a police search of the register identified him as a Syrian national, Zaven Bedros.[57] A white plastic bag found in his hotel room contained a machine pistol, a Russian-made hand grenade, detonators and ammunition.[58] Bedros was later sentenced to eight years' imprisonment for firearms possession.[59] Although the Security Service role in the intelligence case was not relevant to the criminal proceedings a police source revealed the Service's involvement. *The Times* commented:

Only a brilliant undercover operation started by MI5, continued by the Special Branch, and completed by Scotland Yard's anti-terrorist squad (C13) prevented Zaven Bedros from [carrying out] a terrorist attack in London . . . it was a brilliant piece of work. It is often said what a lot of duffers the Security Service people are, but this is a classic case of how effective they have been.[60]

Technical and A4 surveillance of ASALA almost certainly prevented a serious terrorist attack in London similar to those which took place in France and Turkey. In July 1983, while Bedros was on trial, an ASALA bomb attack at Paris's Orly Airport killed seven people and wounded fifty-six at the Turkish Airline check-in desk. In August ASALA killed eleven and injured over a hundred in separate attacks on Ankara's Esenboğa Airport and the Grand Bazaar in Istanbul.[61] The rapid and unexpected decline in Armenian terrorism thereafter, due to a series of arrests, the revulsion of much of the Armenian diaspora at the loss of life, and faction-fighting among the terrorist groups, illustrates the difficulty faced by MI5 and all other security services and police forces in foreseeing the rise and fall of terrorist groups.

Despite the great variety of international terrorist groups operating in Britain at various times in the early 1980s, PIRA continued to pose the greatest direct threat to UK security. On 10 October 1980 Republican prisoners in Long Kesh Prison near Belfast, many of whom were already refusing to wear prison uniform and were engaged in a 'dirty protest', wearing only blankets and smearing excrement on the walls of their cells, issued a statement which inaugurated what has been rightly called 'one of the most dramatic and terrible episodes in Irish history':

We, the republican prisoners of war in H-Blocks, Long Kesh, demand as of right political recognition and that we be accorded the status of political prisoners.

. . . We wish to make it clear that every channel [of negotiation] has now been exhausted and, not wishing to break faith with those from whom we have inherited our principles, we now commit ourselves to a hunger strike.[62]

At the time it was widely believed in both London and Belfast that the initiative for the hunger strike, which began on 27 October, had come from the Provisional and Sinn Fein leadership. The IJS Belfast station, however, had reliable intelligence that the hand of a reluctant Republican leadership had been forced by the prisoners in Long Kesh.[63] On 18 December, with one of the H-Block hunger strikers, Sean McKenna, close to death, the strike was called off. The official explanation given by

Belfast Sinn Fein leaders was that a note from the British (whose contents were in reality vague and ambiguous) had met the strikers' demands.[64] The PIRA prisoners' disillusionment with the terms of the British note, which failed to resolve their demands for 'political' status, led to a new and more determined hunger strike, begun on 1 March 1981 by the twenty-seven-year-old Provisional officer commanding (OC) in Long Kesh, Bobby Sands. This time the hunger strike was staggered, with other prisoners joining in, usually in groups of two, every two or three weeks. The strike won world-wide publicity with the handsome, long-haired Sands achieving cult status as a revolutionary icon – especially after he was elected Westminster MP for Fermanagh-South Tyrone in a by-election on 7 April. Streets were named after him in cities as far apart as New York and Tehran. IJS sources reported that, shortly after Sands's election, in order not to distract attention from the hunger strike, the PIRA leadership had given instructions to suspend attacks on off-duty members of the security forces and commercial targets in Northern Ireland.[65]

On 5 May, with rosary beads sent by the papal envoy around his neck, Bobby Sands died what Republicans and his many foreign supporters believed was a martyr's death. By 7 July five more hunger strikers had died. The IJS Belfast station reported to London that PIRA had decided to end its earlier ban on attacking off-duty members of the security forces and business premises:

The reason for this about-face was the pressure from rank-and-file members of the IRA in the North. They had reported to their commanders that they were being jeered at in the streets for their inaction ... They were also burning to retaliate for the deaths of the ten republican prisoners.[66]

Despite reliable intelligence reports that the initiative for the hunger strike had come from the strikers themselves, Mrs Thatcher was sceptical. Even when told in July 1981 by the Catholic Primate of Ireland, Cardinal Tomás Ó Fiaich, that he believed 'the hunger strikers were not acting under IRA orders', she was 'not convinced'.[67] Recent historians of the Provisionals, however, corroborate the intelligence provided at the time by the IJS. Most of the PIRA leadership feared that the hunger strike might prove an unwinnable battle, play into the hands of the British government and do severe damage to Republican morale.[68] They proved wrong on all counts. Though the hunger strike ended on 3 October after a total of ten deaths without winning major concessions from the British, the IJS reported that PIRA believed the hunger strike 'was the greatest unifying force the Republican movement had had for decades'.[69] The death of Bobby Sands turned Margaret Thatcher, though she did not realize it at the time, into PIRA's main target.[70] It took over three years, however, for PIRA to put itself in a position to make a serious assassination attempt during a Conservative Party conference – a strategy first devised, according to IJS intelligence, even before Mrs Thatcher came to power.[71]

Four days after the death of Bobby Sands, due to a lapse in protective security by British Petroleum (BP), PIRA came close to achieving one of its most spectacular coups. On 9 May 1981, the Queen on the Royal Yacht *Britannia* and the King of Norway on board the *Norge* arrived at Sullom Voe in Shetland for the official inauguration of the BP oil terminal, the largest in Europe. Other top brass were conveyed on a P&O ship chartered by BP. Because of several days of dense fog, however, most of a large police contingent from the Scottish mainland was unable to arrive in time to complete more than brief physical security checks before the opening.[72] Just as the Queen appeared there was a small explosion at the power station some 500 yards away from the oil terminal, which was believed at first to be an electrical fault and passed unnoticed during the ceremony. The explosion, however, turned out to have been caused by a bomb, though this was not made public at the time. There was very little structural damage and no casualties.[73] The Queen was characteristically unruffled. The PIRA Overseas Department was deeply disappointed not to hear news that the inauguration ceremony had been disrupted. Several news agencies received phone calls from people speaking with an Irish accent, asking if they had been sent reports of an incident at Sullum Voe.[74] PIRA claimed afterwards to 'have breached the English Queen's security'.

It was later discovered that the large construction team at Sullum Voe, many of them Irish, had included a number of known or suspected Republicans. After forensic examination of more than sixty dustbin loads of debris, the bomb detonator was identified as coming from the Irish Republic. Subsequent police inquiries established that two parcels, each containing a bomb, had been posted to a Republican militant working on the construction of the terminal. When the second parcel was delayed in the post, he appears to have panicked, believing that it had been intercepted en route, and fled without collecting either his cards or his bonus pay for two years' service at the construction site. The Republican militant stayed only long enough to plant the first bomb (or possibly give it to an accomplice). The second parcel, containing a 6-pound bomb and a twelve-day timing device, arrived after his departure and remained uncollected in the construction village post office until, absurdly, it was forwarded to (but failed to reach) his address in Northern Ireland.[75]

A C Branch officer, who was present at the opening ceremony, had previously paid several visits to Sullum Voe, producing a report on protective security which had been agreed by both BP and Whitehall's Official Committee on Terrorism. It included a specific recommendation for the security of the power station. BP, however, balked at the cost of implementing all the recommendations, which ran into seven figures, and detailed discussions were still continuing at the time of the attack.[76] Cost remained, as it had been for the past decade, the main obstacle to implementing the Security Service's protective-security recommendations in the private sector. Throughout the 1980s the Security Service believed that, of the hundreds of Economic Key Points (EKPs), 'only a small number were even reasonably protected.'[77] C Branch went by helicopter to inspect most North Sea oil platforms and organized a series of exercises with the Royal Marines to practise recapturing a platform in case one was ever taken over by a terrorist group.[78] Whitehall showed little interest. C Branch complained that Whitehall found counter-terrorist protective security boring as well as expensive:

Security organisations in departments are not staffed by high fliers. The Departments of Transport and Energy seem to find particular difficulty in making decisions quickly on the protection of EKPs. This is frustrating not only for C Branch but also for the industries and organisations concerned. On a number of occasions recently, after lengthy and frustrating delays, both departments have eventually taken the action recommended by C Branch.[79]

Security Service staff found arguing the case for improved protective security to unresponsive Whitehall committees a wearisome business.[80] The Provisionals, however, failed to grasp how vulnerable many EKPs remained. The Cabinet Office concluded in 1982 that PIRA had no coherent strategy (such as it developed in the 1990s) for causing serious damage to the economy and national infrastructure:

There has been no attempt to study supply systems, such as electricity or telecommunications. PIRA is therefore unlikely to be able to identify and simultaneously destroy mutually dependent targets in supply systems in Great Britain, although it might be able to do so in Northern Ireland.[81]

Even the attack on Sullum Voe seems to have been designed as a spectacular demonstration of PIRA's ability to penetrate royal security rather than as an operation to do serious damage to the North Sea oil industry. PIRA's 'armed struggle' did not yet aim at undermining the British economy.

As with the attempted bombing of Sullum Voe, the Security Service had no advance intelligence on the targets of PIRA's continental campaign, which resumed on 16 February 1980 when Colonel Mark Coe was shot dead at Bielefeld. On 1 March a Royal Military Police patrol in Münster was fired at while approaching traffic lights and the driver wounded. Nine days later a corporal in the BAOR was shot, but not seriously wounded, at Osnabrück. No further attack took place until 3 December when two shots from a slow-moving car were fired at Christopher Tugendhat, a British EEC commissioner in Brussels. It was another month before PIRA admitted responsibility. The Service concluded that there had been a major reappraisal of PIRA strategy, stemming from the fear that further operations might compromise the propaganda success on the continent of Sinn Fein's campaign to exploit sympathy for the hunger strikers.[82] There were no further PIRA attacks on British targets on the continent until 1987.

PIRA had no such inhibitions about its operations in Britain. In the final months of 1981 there was a series of bomb attacks in London.[83] In December the Chief Constable of the RUC, Sir Jack Hermon (who had succeeded Newman in January 1980), proposed that 'the Security Service should assume responsibility for the investigation of Republican terrorism in Great Britain just as they had responsibility for co-ordinating its investigation outside the UK.'[84] The IJS Belfast station supported the proposal. Despite its private criticisms of the MPSB, however, the Security Service leadership was still unwilling to provoke a conflict with the Met by claiming the lead intelligence role against Republican terrorism on the mainland. The DG, John Jones (who had succeeded Smith earlier in the year), was 'most anxious' that Hermon's views 'should not get back to the Metropolitan Police, who might well suspect us of propagating them'.[85] Stephen Lander, then in F5, was struck by what he saw as the generational divide between the cautious Jones and his DDG in London on the one hand and the able, ambitious, proactive young Security Service officers of the Belfast station.[86]

For three years after the end of the bombing campaign in London during the final months of 1981, the PIRA threat to the mainland appeared to decline. In 1982 the weekly Directors' Meetings spent more time discussing the terrorist threat in Britain from Welsh extremists (for which it had the lead role)[87] than that from PIRA (for which it did not). After a visit to Ulster in January, the DDG told the directors that 'On the security side everyone had been relaxed, taking the view that by and large the level of violence had, at least for the present, been reduced to what was about the practicable minimum.'[88] Thereafter the Directors' Meeting did not discuss PIRA operations on mainland Britain for over six months.

After failing to launch any mainland operation during the first half of 1982, an active service unit (ASU) despatched by the England Department succeeded on 20 July in planting both a car bomb near Hyde Park Corner, which killed four members of the Household Cavalry, and a bomb beneath a bandstand in Regent's Park, which killed seven bandsmen of the Royal Green Jackets.[89] Director F told a Directors' Meeting held on the day of the Knightsbridge–Hyde Park and Regent's Park bombs that 'It had been expected for some time that PIRA would launch a new bombing campaign in London.'[90] The IJS later reported that the ASU responsible for the London bombings had returned by fishing boat to the Irish Republic on 30 July, and that its leader was planning further mainland attacks to coincide with the Conservative Party conference in October and the parade celebrating victory in the Falklands War a few days later. Both operations, the IJS believed, were vetoed by the PIRA leadership, which had noted the widespread revulsion both in Ireland and around the world at the graphic media photographs of the carnage on 20 July and wished to avoid damaging Sinn Fein's prospects during the October elections to the Northern Irish Assembly by further bombing.[91]

The main focus of Security Service operations against the Provisionals during 1982 was less the immediate threat of mainland bombing (which remained the primary responsibility of MPSB) than arms procurement in the United States and PIRA operations on the continent (which the Service had the lead role in monitoring). The hunger strikes and the death of Bobby Sands produced a wave of anti-British feeling among the Irish diaspora, especially in the United States, where there were demonstrations in many American cities. In New York a picket mounted by supporters of the Irish Northern Aid Committee (NORAID) outside the British consulate on Third Avenue continued for some years.[92] In September 1982, SLO Washington reported to the DG: 'The FBI investigative effort against the Irish target in New York over the last eighteen months has been most heartening and rewarding and fully vindicates the cajoling and pressure we have placed upon them to pursue this target.'[93] The problem remained, however, to persuade New York juries to convict, as the *Guardian* reported on 6 November:

Five Irish Americans including the 80-year-old president of the Irish Northern Aid Committee (NORAID), Mr Michael Flannery, were found not guilty here yesterday of conspiring to supply guns to the IRA.

There were cheers from over 100 spectators in the New York Eastern District Court in Brooklyn when the verdicts were announced. The jury had deliberated for nearly three days.

The defendants freely admitted that over the past twenty years they had smuggled more than 1 million dollars worth of guns and ammunition. But they claimed in their defence that their main arms supplier was a CIA agent, and that the operation therefore had US Government approval.

The CIA and the federal prosecutor denied that the US intelligence community was in any way involved either with the defendants or with the arms smuggling, nor was any evidence produced to show that it was. The jury, however, appeared to accept the argument of Flannery's attorney that 'It is up to the government to prove the CIA was not involved with the defendants, not our burden to prove it was.'[94]

By April 1983, SLO was less pessimistic about the prospects for prosecuting PIRA gun-runners: 'It is clear that the US attorneys are learning by their mistakes . . .'[95] Soon afterwards he reported 'convictions against PIRA and INLA arms procurers in three separate trials in New York'. Director F asked SLO to forward to the FBI an 'expression of our appreciation'.[96] There was continuing disappointment, however, at the Bureau's limitations in investigating Irish Republicans. Patrick Walker's successor as F5 wrote in 1984:

Our exchange of intelligence with the FBI on Irish matters is surprisingly one-way given that the concentration of support for Irish republicanism is greater in the USA than anywhere else in the world outside Ireland. While we supply a great deal of information to assist them we get relatively little back. This is partly because the FBI are legally constrained from passing information about US citizens to us and partly because they suffer from considerable investigational difficulties (eg even doing a reverse telephone enquiry [identifying a subscriber from the number] is a laborious process). However they also seem not to appreciate the value of more open exchanges, and it has to be said that some of their officers are very much 'Police oriented' and take exception to our 'intelligence' approach to investigations.[97]

There was, however, one major limitation in the Security Service's own understanding of PIRA's support base in the United States. The widespread publicity given to NORAID misled the Service into believing that it was the main North American Irish Republican fundraiser. Not until the beginning of the 1990s did it discover that NORAID was of less significance than Clan na Gael, a secret Republican society which successfully avoided publicity. Whereas most NORAID supporters were Irish-Americans born in the United States, Clan na Gael's members were Republican Irish immigrants. According to a Security Service report in 1990: 'Clan na Gael finds it relatively easy to raise funds for the IRA as many of older generation Irishmen would rather support the military than the political wing.'[98]

During the 1980s, Security Service collaboration with some continental services in counter-PIRA operations became closer than that with the FBI and an increasingly important component of its CT strategy. Though the Provisional Army Council suspended attacks on British targets on the continent early in 1982, it decided to set up bases in France and Belgium, using local sympathizers as well as PIRA members, to support bomb attacks in mainland Britain, to conduct arms-procurement operations in France and Belgium, and to assist in the transfer to Ireland of weapons and equipment obtained in the United States.[99] The Security Service's foreign liaisons were crucial to its continental counter-terrorist operations. In June 1982, after an operation involving close collaboration with the Belgians and French a large consignment of arms was discovered near Nantes in a Toyota camper van apparently abandoned by the driver after he detected surveillance.[100] Another PIRA arms-procurement operation culminated in the arrest of the Provisional Patrick McVeigh, who was caught red-handed in Limerick by the Garda unloading a container of arms which had been shipped from New York to Dublin via Rotterdam.[101]

Intelligence was also accumulating on the renewal of PIRA arms procurement from Libya, which was thought to have virtually ceased in 1978.[102] Colonel Qaddafi appears to have been so impressed by the H-Block hunger strikers that he agreed to resume the supply of money and arms. Forensic examination after the Knightsbridge–Hyde Park bombing in July 1982 identified a British-made electronic switch used in the bomb which had been bought by an engineer in Hemel Hempstead who, police inquiries revealed, had purchased a number of the switches at the request of a PIRA volunteer.[103] Patrick Walker, then F5, noted in April 1983: 'Reports are accumulating that Libya is providing money and/or weapons to PIRA. Weapons and grenades of Soviet and East European origin have been appearing in Northern Ireland and in the recent . . . weapons consignment recovered on the Continent.'[104]

According to intelligence reports, PIRA's England Department had to abort a series of planned attacks during 1983, partly as a result of disruption caused by two major arms finds. The mainland bombing campaign eventually resumed in December after a gap of almost eighteen months. There was no advance intelligence on the intended targets. Of the three bombs planted by an ASU, by far the most damaging was a car bomb outside Harrods which killed six people and injured many Christmas shoppers. International public revulsion at the carnage of the innocent was so great that, according to intelligence reports, there was even talk within the PIRA leadership of suspending all mainland operations.[105] F5 concluded that the head of the PIRA Overseas Department had personally given the go-ahead for the Harrods bombing, despite the fact that it had not been approved by the Provisional Army Council.[106]

In April 1984 the Irish Joint Section was wound up. By agreement with SIS, the Security Service, which had become the dominant partner in the IJS, gained sole control of its Belfast station and set up a new section, F8, at its London headquarters to take over responsibility for the day-to-day management of Northern Irish operations.[107] Simultaneously FX Branch was reorganized under a new director, Patrick Walker, as a fully independent branch no longer subordinate to F, with, for the first time, undivided responsibility for counter-terrorism.[108] The Northern Ireland Office wrote to Walker soon afterwards:

Statistics show the considerable decrease in violence in the Province over the last 10 years. For example, nearly 500 people were killed in 1972 in over 10,000 incidents; whereas last year fewer than 80 people were killed in a few hundred incidents. The latter figure of casualties represents less than half the number of people killed on the roads of Northern Ireland each year. Therefore, unacceptable though the present situation is, it is not as bad as some of the media or the terrorists themselves would have the world believe.[109]

For the first nine months of 1984, the PIRA threat to mainland Britain occupied the weekly Directors' Meetings far less than Libyan terrorism.

Early in 1984 Qaddafi ordered a new campaign against dissident émigrés – or, as he preferred to call them, 'stray dogs'.[110] Over the next few months intelligence reports of Libyan plans for a new wave of attacks on dissidents in Britain led to a series of operations by the Security Service and the Met to thwart the planned attacks. On 9 March the Service informed MPSB by telex of a reliable intelligence report on a meeting in the People's Bureau in London to discuss further 'revolutionary' action against opponents of the Qaddafi regime. But there was no clear indication as yet that the Bureau itself might open fire on demonstrators gathered outside in St James's Square, London.[111] Instead, from 10 to 12 March there was a series of bomb attacks against Libyan dissidents in London and Manchester. The People's Bureau, F3 noted, 'has strenuously denied complicity. It is quite clear, however, that they both directed and planned the bombing campaign.'[112] A Security Service telex to MPSB on 13 March reported reliable intelligence that the Bureau was in high spirits and prepared to step up its campaign against dissidents, though it appeared to be running short of bomb-making equipment.[113]

On 16 April MPSB discovered that an anti-Qaddafi group had planned a demonstration outside the People's Bureau on the following day. A request from the Bureau to the Met for detailed information about the planned demonstration was refused.[114] It was not until after the demonstration on the 17th that the Service learned that on the evening of the 16th the People's Bureau had proposed three options to Tripoli for dealing with the demonstrators:

(i) To clash directly with the demonstrators from outside the Bureau
(ii) To fire on them from inside the Bureau
(iii) To prevent the demonstration by diplomatic pressure[115]

The People's Bureau began by pursuing the third option. At 1.15 a.m. on 17 April a delegation from the Bureau visited the FCO and asked for action to stop the demonstration. The delegation declared that neither they nor their government could be held responsible for the consequences if the demonstration went ahead. Tripoli that night authorized the Bureau's second option – firing on the demonstrators.[116] That is what happened on 17 April. What began as a peaceful demonstration ended in tragedy. While policing the demonstration WPC Yvonne Fletcher was killed by machine-gun fire from a first-floor window of the People's Bureau. Her killer was no doubt influenced by the knowledge that the Bureau had been heavily criticized by Tripoli for not firing on a similar demonstration four years earlier.[117]

Next day, 18 April, the KGB residency in London was informed by telegram from the Centre that it had reliable information that the shooting had been personally ordered by Qaddafi. The residency's head of political intelligence, Oleg Gordievsky, a long-serving British agent, passed on the information to his case officer.[118] The Thatcher government broke off diplomatic relations with Libya and, after a siege of the People's Bureau, expelled more than sixty of Qaddafi's officials and supporters. The expulsions effectively brought to an end the Libyan terrorist campaign in mainland Britain. On 14 May the Home Secretary, Leon Brittan, formally expressed to the DG, Sir John Jones:

his personal appreciation not only of the extremely valuable professional contribution which the Service had made throughout the operation involving the Libyan People's Bureau, but the quality of the advice on the handling of the situation as a whole offered by the Security Service representatives at the meetings which he had chaired in COBR.[119]

Whitehall's anxiety about the increased threat from international terrorism in the mid-1980s produced a major change in Security Service culture. Patrick Walker recalls that, during his years as Director FX from 1984 to 1986, the Service:

> moved from being an introvert organisation with few Officers (and certainly not the more junior) in touch with Whitehall Departments to a Service at ease in Whitehall and confident in its expertise. The interdepartmental arrangements following the Libyan People's Bureau siege helped to bring us closer to other departments.[120]

In the aftermath of the killing of WPC Fletcher and the siege of the People's Bureau, the Prime Minister was chiefly concerned not with PIRA but with the increasing threat from non-Irish terrorism. At a meeting with the DG on 18 May, Mrs Thatcher inquired about the Service's need for increased surveillance resources to assist in combating terrorism. In response, the Service requested four more staff in the international terrorism section of FX Branch; eight additional linguist/transcriber posts to 'enable us to operate effectively in any of the likely languages on a 24 hour basis and at the same time to improve our normal coverage of terrorist or potential terrorist targets; and an increase of twelve in the mobile surveillance teams'. The DDG, Cecil Shipp, informed the cabinet secretary that 'Our use of mobile surveillance against terrorist targets has more than doubled proportionally over the last few years.'[121] A review by the Intelligence Co-ordinator, Sir Tony Duff (soon to succeed Jones as DG), approved the proposed increase in staff. The Security Service became at last an operational service capable of operating around the clock.[122]

For Qaddafi the assassination campaign against 'stray dogs' in Britain had a humiliating sequel. Ali Al Jahour, a corrupt Libyan businessman who had been involved in organizing the London bombing campaign and was arrested shortly afterwards, broke down in court when initially denied bail and burst into tears.[123] The fact that he was later allowed bail seems to have aroused suspicions in the Qaddafi regime that he was co-operating with the British authorities. On 20 August he was found dead in a flat which he had rented. Forensic evidence showed that he had been forced to his knees and shot at close range in the back of the head.[124] A note in Arabic left by his body declared: 'This is the punishment for the one who is employed to do a job and does not succeed in doing it.' It was signed 'Al Fatih Forever and the Committees Everywhere'. Al Fatih ('The Conqueror') was a title sometimes used to flatter Qaddafi; the People's Committees were the democratic figleaf used by Qaddafi to conceal his dictatorship.[125] 'We and the Police know a great deal about Jahour,' wrote F3/4. 'He appears to have tried unsuccessfully to keep in touch with both the pro and anti [Q]addafi factions.'[126] Further Special Branch inquiries revealed that Jahour was also 'well known at the Hilton Hotel as a resident with a penchant for drinking sessions and entertaining prostitutes'.[127] In October another Libyan bomber, Salhen Ramdan Salem El Tarhuni, was arrested and charged with causing explosions in London in March. Though El Tarhuni denied having been in London at the time of the bombing, he had left his fingerprints on bomb-parts and batteries. He was later sentenced to fifteen years' imprisonment.[128]

In November 1984 Tripoli Radio announced a major success in the campaign to liquidate émigré dissidents which Qaddafi probably felt outweighed the setbacks in London. It reported that the former Libyan Prime Minister Abdul-Hamid Bakoush, leader of the anti-Qaddafi Libyan Liberation Organization, had been 'executed' in Egypt for 'selling his conscience to the enemies of the Arab nation'. Dramatic pictures were sent to Libya of what appeared to be Bakoush's blood-stained corpse. Qaddafi, however, was the victim of a particularly humiliating sting. No sooner had Tripoli celebrated the assassination of Bakoush than he appeared alive and well on Egyptian television to reveal that the team sent to assassinate him by Qaddafi had been caught and had made a full confession.[129]

Qaddafi took his revenge for the humiliations of 1984 by publicly announcing, and dramatically increasing, his support for PIRA: 'We do not consider the IRA a terrorist army; they have a just cause, the independence of their country ... We are not ashamed of supporting it with all the means we have.'[130] Qaddafi's emergence in the mid-1980s as the main arms supplier to PIRA posed a far greater threat to national security than his homicidal campaign against Libyan dissidents in Britain. The weapons and explosives which he secretly supplied to the Provisionals over the next three years greatly enhanced their capacity to continue the 'armed struggle'. Failure to detect and prevent these arms shipments until 1987 was a major weakness in British counter-terrorist strategy.[131]

Arms supplies from Libya were all the more important to the Provisionals as a result of disruption in the arms flow from the United States, due in large part to intelligence co-operation. On 29 September 1984 a major PIRA arms shipment was seized by the Irish navy off the coast of County Kerry on board the Irish trawler *Marita Ann*. The *Marita Ann* operation, originally codenamed CARDOON, had begun in the early summer when the Garda learned that Martin Ferris, then OC Kerry PIRA (promoted shortly afterwards to OC Southern Command), was planning to use the trawler to bring arms from the United States. In the early hours of 28 September, however, an RAF Nimrod observed arms being transferred to the *Marita Ann* from an American trawler which had crossed the Atlantic with its port of registration painted out. The Nimrod also detected some signs of panic as the two trawlers attempted to keep their distance in heavy seas by facing into the wind with a hawser between them. The whole operation was followed in real time by senior FX officers both at the RAF Northwood Command Centre and in Curzon Street, who informed the Garda that the *Marita Ann* had been seized even before the news was received from the Irish navy.[132] When the *Marita Ann* was intercepted by the Irish naval vessel *Emer*, its crew initially believed they had been boarded by a fisheries protection vessel and shouted, 'We have no salmon on board!' The hold was found to be packed with weapons and ammunition. Martin Ferris, John Crawley, a former US marine and PIRA member who had arranged the arms deal, and Michael Browne, the trawler skipper, were later each sentenced to ten years' imprisonment at the Special Criminal Court in Dublin, sitting without a jury.[133]

Less than three weeks after the capture of the *Marita Ann*, PIRA's England Department, after several ineffective years, achieved its most spectacular success so far. The Northern Ireland Office had correctly identified a trend for PIRA attacks in Britain, following a series of setbacks, to 'become less frequent but more sophisticated'.[134] For several years, the Security Service had been reporting intelligence that PIRA intended to bomb one of the annual Tory conferences – though the fact that no attempt was made until 1984 may have damaged the credibility of these warnings.[135] In the early hours of 16 October a 20-pound bomb with a long-delay timer (the first to be used on the mainland) exploded at the Grand Hotel at Brighton, where Mrs Thatcher and most of her cabinet were staying during the Conservative Party conference.[136] The 'Brighton bomber', Patrick Magee, had been wanted for the past five years for his part in the bombings in the London area in the winter of 1978–9. In September 1980 he had been arrested in the Netherlands but in January 1981 a Dutch court rejected an application for his extradition to stand trial in England.[137] Two years later he had another narrow escape. In April 1983 he was discovered at an address in Lancashire and secretly photographed in the company of a suspected PIRA associate. While driving towards Preston on the motorway at over 90 mph, however, the two men realized they were being tailed, abandoned their car at Preston railway station with the key still in the ignition, and disappeared.[138] The bomb planted by Magee in the Grand Hotel in 1984 killed five Conservative Party members and injured more than thirty, some seriously. Though Thatcher survived unscathed, PIRA issued a statement afterwards, directed chiefly at the Prime Minister: 'Today we were unlucky, but remember we only have to be lucky once. You will have to be lucky always.'

9

Counter-Espionage in the Last Decade of the Cold War

During Mrs Thatcher's first term as prime minister, the longest-drawn-out investigation in Security Service history – the hunt for the Ring of Five – was finally laid to rest. In November 1979, fifteen years after Blunt's secret confession and the promise of immunity from prosecution, he was exposed as the Fourth Man in a Commons statement by Mrs Thatcher issued after strong hints to his identity had appeared in the press. Blunt was almost everything the media then hoped for in a Soviet mole: a traitor from a good public school and Trinity College, Cambridge, with a record of sexual deviance (by the standards of the times) and connections with the Royal Family as Surveyor of the Queen's Pictures. 'TRAITOR AT THE QUEEN'S RIGHT HAND', thundered the headline in the *Daily Mail*. 'Treacherous Communist poof', declared John Junor in the *Daily Express*.[1]

The public exposure of Blunt occurred some years later than either the Security Service or Number Ten had expected. Under the Heath government, when he had been seriously ill with cancer and thought unlikely to survive, preparations had been made to deal with the media furore which was expected to follow the revelation after his death of his role as a Soviet agent. In March 1973 Heath had asked for the Queen to be given a detailed report, only to discover that Her Majesty had been informed of Blunt's treachery in more general terms about a decade earlier.[2] At a press conference after his 1979 exposure, Blunt's penitence was qualified. Though accepting that he had been 'totally wrong', he several times insisted that he had 'acted according to my conscience'. Over the next few years some of the enormity of his betrayal gradually sank in. Blunt told a confidant before his death in 1983, 'I made a terrible intellectual mistake, and should have been shot for what I did.'[3]

In the wake of Blunt's sensational unmasking in 1979 there was a world-wide media demand for more British traitors. Imaginary moles, identified as the result of mistaken leads, began to multiply rapidly in print: among them Donald Beves,[4] Frank Birch, Andrew Gow, Sir Roger Hollis, Guy Liddell, Graham Mitchell and Arthur Pigou (all dead), Sir Rudolf Peierls (who denied claims that he too was dead and sued successfully for libel), Lord Rothschild (the victim during his lifetime of innuendo rather than open allegation in case he also sued) and Wilfred Mann (who did not sue but wrote a book to prove his innocence). Though the Service knew that all were innocent, it was not until August 1982 that, thanks to intelligence from Oleg Gordievsky, it finally identified John Cairncross as the Fifth Man in the Ring of Five.[5] Though Cairncross had secretly confessed to espionage in 1964, the Service had failed to realize just how highly the KGB rated him. Gordievsky's public identification of Cairncross as the Fifth Man during the closing months of the Thatcher government in 1990 (later confirmed by extracts from his KGB file released by the SVR, the post-Soviet Russian foreign intelligence service), while attracting substantial media attention, also caused some disappointment. Cairncross was a Trinity graduate who had published a scholarly study of polygamy, but his background as the son of a Scottish shopkeeper was disappointingly modest and contained no connection with the Royal Family. Though he was an even more important spy than Blunt, his media profile has consequently remained much lower.[6]

In 1980 evidence from a Czech StB defector identified the only British politician (so far as is known) to have acted as a foreign agent while holding ministerial office: John Stonehouse, who had served in the Wilson governments of 1964–70 (without cabinet rank). Though an earlier StB defector, Josef Frolik, had reported his suspicions about Stonehouse in 1969, the Security Service had informed Wilson after interviewing both Frolik and Stonehouse that there was 'no evidence that Mr Stonehouse gave the Czechs any information he should not have given them, much less that he consciously acted as an agent'.[7] The Service repeated that conclusion to Edward Heath.[8] Stonehouse's subsequent behaviour, however, under-mined the credibility of his previously persuasive protestations of inno-cence. In 1974, faced with serious business problems, he abandoned his wife, faked his own suicide, adopted a new identity and disappeared with his mistress to Australia. Having been successfully tracked down and brought back to England, he was sentenced in 1976 to seven years' impris-onment on eighteen charges of theft and fraud. Once out of jail he published a somewhat absurd spy novel, *Ralph*, which, if it is at all autobiographical, tends to support the claims in Frolik's memoirs that Stonehouse had been recruited by the StB after falling victim to a honey trap during a visit to Czechoslovakia in the late 1950s. The novel (which would later have been a strong contender for the *Literary Review*'s Bad Sex Award) describes the entrapment of a senior British civil servant in the European Commission, Ralph Edmonds, by the seductive Lotte of East German intelligence. ('One of our best operators,' Ralph's controller later tells him. 'What she did was strictly in the line of duty.') Ralph spends an enjoyable evening with Lotte, who (strictly in the line of duty) 'sent sensations of joy to every crevice of his brain'. After one last 'magnificent thrust', 'Ralph noticed their reflections in a huge, oval ceiling mirror.' He is later handed souvenir photographs of the evening taken through the one-way mirror in the ceiling, and agrees to co-operate. Inept though Stonehouse's storytelling was, the account of Ralph's entrapment may have drawn on his own experience at the hands of the StB.[9]

In 1980 evidence from an StB defector codenamed AFFIRM persuaded both the Security Service and the Thatcher government that Stonehouse had been a Czech agent. Since, however, it was decided that the defector's evidence could not be used in court, Mrs Thatcher agreed that Stonehouse should not be prosecuted.[10] AFFIRM's evidence was largely corroborated a quarter of a century later when some of the contents of Stonehouse's lengthy StB file were revealed in the Czech Republic. As AFFIRM had claimed,[11] his original codename had been KOLON ('Colonist', a reference to two years he had spent in Uganda). Stonehouse had been recruited while an Opposition backbencher to provide 'information from Parliament and Parliamentary committees', using the money he received to fund his social life. The StB, however, were disappointed by the amount of intelligence Stonehouse provided once he became a minister.[12]

Counter-espionage in the Thatcher era was distinguished by closer collaboration with SIS than ever before. K3, the section which recruited and ran Soviet agents, was staffed by both male and female agent-runners from both Services. The KGB London residency had no experience of being targeted by front-line female intelligence officers and seems to have taken several years to realize this was happening. K3 operations enabled both Services to learn from and about each other. According to Stella Rimington: 'We learned from MI6 the skills of agent-running and agent recruitment, in which they then had more experience than we did. They learned from us how to behave when they were up against a sophisticated security service – of great value when working undercover in a foreign posting.'[13] A case which strikingly exemplified MI5–SIS collaboration was that of the most important British agent of the later Cold War, Oleg Gordievsky, a KGB officer recruited by SIS in 1974. To the delight of the minority of indoctrinated members in K Branch as well as SIS, in January 1982 the FCO received a visa application from the Soviet embassy on behalf of Gordievsky following his appointment as counsellor (in reality as a senior KGB political intelligence officer) in London.[14] Soon after his arrival in London on 28 June 1982, Oleg Gordievsky renewed contact with SIS.

The KGB documents which he smuggled out of the residency to meetings with his case officer stunned the small circle of intelligence officers who had access to them. They revealed that for the past year, jointly with the GRU, the KGB had been engaged in the largest peacetime operation in its history. In a secret speech to a major KGB conference in May 1981, the visibly ailing Soviet leader Leonid Brezhnev denounced the policies of the US President Ronald Reagan, who had taken office at the beginning of the year, as a serious threat to world peace. He was followed by the long-serving Chairman of the KGB, Yuri Andropov, who was to succeed him as Soviet leader eighteen months later. To the astonishment of most of the audience, Andropov announced that, by decision of the Politburo, for the first time in their history the KGB and GRU were to collaborate in a global operation codenamed RYAN (a newly devised acronym for *Raketno-Yadernoye Napadenie*, 'Nuclear Missile Attack'). Its purpose was to collect intelligence on the plans by the United States and NATO for a surprise nuclear first strike against the Soviet Union. In reality, no such plans existed. RYAN derived from the paranoid tendencies of the Soviet and KGB leadership at a tense period in the Cold War, fuelled by the anti-Soviet rhetoric of President Ronald Reagan, who had denounced the Soviet Union as an 'evil empire'. Gordievsky reported that his colleagues in the Line PR (political intelligence) in London were considerably less alarmist than the Centre about the threat of nuclear war and viewed Operation RYAN with some scepticism. None, however, was willing to put his career at risk by challenging the Centre's assessment of the aggressive designs of the Reagan administration and its NATO allies. RYAN thus created a vicious circle of intelligence collection and assessment. Residencies felt, in effect, obliged to report alarming information even if they themselves were sceptical of it. The Centre was duly alarmed by what they reported and demanded more.[15] Gordievsky's intelligence had a considerable impact on Margaret Thatcher, who was indoctrinated into the Gordievsky case on 23 December 1982.[16] Sir Geoffrey Howe, who was also informed about the case on becoming foreign secretary six months later, recalls:

One powerful impression quite quickly built up in my mind: the Soviet leadership really did believe the bulk of their own propaganda. They did have a genuine fear that 'the West' was plotting their overthrow – and might, just might, go to any lengths to achieve it. This near obsession, it became clear, was fuelled by the rhetoric (and sometimes more than rhetoric) which accompanied ... the more or less simultaneous arrival in power of Margaret Thatcher and Ronald Reagan.[17]

The only other cabinet minister indoctrinated into the Gordievsky case (on

24 January 1983) was the Home Secretary.[18] With one extraordinary exception which comes close to second sight, there is no known case of a Security Service officer not indoctrinated into the case who suspected that Oleg Gordievsky was a British agent. The exception was an officer involved in identifying Soviet intelligence officers operating under diplomatic cover, who was indoctrinated on 15 March 1983 to help monitor Gordievsky's security and provide other forms of support. She explained to the colleague who had indoctrinated her that a few nights earlier she had dreamed that she was walking along a corridor in the Service's Gower Street headquarters and went into a small office directly ahead of her. 'There, sitting at the desk, was Gordievsky.'[19]

Though Gordievsky was run by SIS rather than by the K3 joint section, his case was very much a combined operation with the Security Service providing various forms of support. In collaboration with SIS, the small group in the Security Service who were indoctrinated into the case set out to strengthen Gordievsky's position within the London residency in two ways. The first was by giving him apparently impressive (though unclassified) information designed to enhance his reputation within the KGB as a political intelligence officer – work for which his role as a British agent left him too little time. K6 sometimes lacked the resources to give all the assistance requested. This caused almost the only friction between the two Services in the history of the Gordievsky case.

The second way in which the Security Service sought to advance Gordievsky's career was by finding reasons to justify the expulsion of more senior officers in the London residency in the hope that he would be able to take their place. The two KGB officers it was most anxious to expel were the head of Line PR, Igor Titov, and the resident, Arkadi Guk. In March 1983, after discussion with Gordievsky, Titov was declared *persona non grata*. To avoid arousing any suspicion of the real motive for the decision, the case against Titov was submitted to the FCO at the same time as that against two GRU officers who had already been earmarked for expulsion and were also PNG'd.[20] As had been hoped, Gordievsky succeeded Titov as head of Line PR.

Gordievsky reported to his SIS case officer that Line PR at the London residency was running half a dozen agents and more than a dozen confidential contacts, with only modest success. (At this stage he had only limited knowledge of operations by other Lines.)* Neither of the London resi-

---

* The main Lines (departments) in KGB residencies during the later Cold War were: KR (counter-intelligence and security), N (illegals support), PR (political intelligence), SK (Soviet colony) and X (S&T). Line F ('special actions') had been wound up in its existing form following the scandal which resulted from Lyalin's defection. For further details, see Andrew and Mitrokhin, *Mitrokhin Archive*, appendix E.

dency's two most prominent Line PR agents, Jack Jones and Bob Edwards MP, was any longer of much significance.[21] Gordievsky reported that Jones had been regarded by the KGB as an agent only from 1964 to 1968. Though contact was later re-established, Jones no longer held clandestine meetings with his case officer or passed on confidential material.[22] He ceased to be general secretary of the TGWU in 1978 and left the TUC General Council in the same year. As his case officer five years later, Gordievsky found that, unsurprisingly, Jones no longer had access to inside information of much significance. On one occasion, however, Gordievsky's report on a meeting with Jones made a considerable impression in the Centre:

One day I took with me a brochure from the Trades Union Congress which gave a long list of union leaders, and asked [Jones] to comment on them. This he did to such effect that I was later able to write a three-page summary, which I added to my report of our meeting. 'Our agent's information on trade union personalities was so extensive', I wrote, 'that I am attaching it as an appendix.' The combined document made it appear that he had been outstandingly helpful and volunteered many facts of the greatest value. You can see from this what the facts really were and how, by careful reporting, success can be created out of very little.[23]

Though the KGB was believed to have assessed Jones's motives as ideological during the period when it regarded him as an agent, Gordievsky found him willing to accept gifts, some of them in cash.[24] The DG, Sir Tony Duff, reported to the cabinet secretary in October 1985 that Jones 'last received money (£250) from his case officer [Gordievsky] on the instructions of the KGB Centre in May 1984'. Thereafter the Centre issued instructions that, given Jones's lack of access to confidential information, he was to be contacted only at six-monthly intervals.[25]

Unlike Jack Jones, the veteran KGB agent Bob Edwards MP was almost unknown outside Westminster and the ranks of the hard left. He remained, however, an enthusiastic participant in Soviet 'active measures' (influence operations). Though there is no evidence that these had any significant impact, the KGB rated him highly and awarded him the Order of the People's Friendship, the third-highest Soviet decoration, in 1980.[26] The medal remained in his file at the Centre but on one occasion was taken by his case officer, Leonid Zaitsev, to show him at a meeting in Brussels. Zaitsev, who had run Edwards while he was stationed at the London residency in the 1960s, was by then head of FCD Directorate T (science and technology) but continued as his controller – partly, Gordievsky believed, because he regarded Edwards as an old friend, partly because he liked trips to the West as an operations officer.[27] Remarkably, the KGB made arrangements to stay in contact with Edwards by radio and dead letter-box (DLB) in the event of war.[28] Gordievsky reported that most of Line PR's political reporting from London to the Centre was based not on secret sources but on the press and conversations with journalists and politicians – though some contacts received substantial payments.[29]

Though the arrival of Gordievsky at the London residency in 1982 and the remarkable quality of the intelligence he supplied marked one of the high points of British intelligence during the Cold War, the public image was one of Soviet rather than British intelligence successes. In 1981 Chapman Pincher, with the secret assistance of the disaffected former Security Service officer Peter Wright, revealed publicly for the first time that Sir Roger Hollis had been investigated on charges of being a Soviet agent, and claimed that the charges were accurate.[30] Gordievsky was able to confirm what earlier Security Service investigation had already shown[31] – that the charges were nonsense. The Centre was deeply puzzled as to why Hollis had ever been investigated and why the charges against him, which it knew to be false, had aroused a media storm in Britain. Igor Titov told Gordievsky after he had been PNG'd from London, 'The story is ridiculous. There's some mysterious, internal British intrigue at the bottom of all this!'[32] Though ridiculous, the Hollis story was front-page news in Britain and widely believed.

A Security Service brief to Mrs Thatcher dubbed 1982 'the year of the security scandal'.[33] The most damaging security scandal was that of Geoffrey Prime, formerly of GCHQ, whose career as a Soviet agent came to light only after he was arrested in the summer of 1982 for sexually abusing under-age girls. He handed over to the police a 2,000-card index of girls whose telephone numbers or photographs he had obtained from local papers. His wife told the police that he had also been engaged in espionage and handed to them two plastic sachets containing one-time pads, typed instructions for reading microdots, and twenty-six envelopes containing letters addressed to East Berlin. A search of the house uncovered further espionage paraphernalia. Prime eventually admitted that after leaving GCHQ and breaking contact with the KGB in September 1977 he had been recontacted by telephone in April 1980. Regretting that he had earlier 'let the Russians down', he flew to a meeting with a new case officer in Vienna, taking with him a series of Minox films and handwritten notes he had made during his last sixteen months at GCHQ. A Security Service assessment later concluded that, 'Though espionage did not give him a sense of purpose, it provided a feeling of importance.' Prime spent several days being debriefed in Vienna, mostly on board a Russian cruise ship, where he was kept apart from other passengers until the final evening when he dined on the captain's table and was introduced as a British businessman. He was questioned about, but not criticized for, his resignation from GCHQ and asked if it would be possible to rejoin. Prime said he did not wish to do so. Though told that most of the films he had brought with him had not come out, he was given £600 before returning to England. After one further meeting with a case officer in West Berlin in October 1981, the KGB ended contact with him.[34]

In November 1982 Prime was sentenced to thirty-eight years' imprisonment. Over the next five months he was interviewed in Long Lartin Prison by K Branch officers on thirteen occasions. His interrogators were puzzled by some of what he told them, in particular by the off-hand manner and lack of understanding shown by his Soviet case officers by contrast with the much greater professionalism shown by the KGB in running most other British agents investigated by the Security Service. Prime described, for example, how during a meeting in the Turkenschanze Park in Vienna in September 1975 the more senior of his KGB case officers, 'Mike A', became visibly bored with the highly classified intelligence he was providing. While the more junior 'Anatoli' carried on talking to Prime, 'Mike A' walked away and began a game of chess with a total stranger.[35] Such episodes seemed so contrary to KGB practice that the K Branch interrogators began to doubt Prime's version of events. Their doubts dissolved when it was realized that Prime had been run not by case officers of the First Chief Directorate, which was responsible for most espionage operations, but by the Third Directorate, which was out of its depth with an agent of Prime's importance.[36]

In the wake of Prime's arrest, a Security Service brief for the Security Commission, which was also passed on to the Prime Minister, reviewed the forty-three cases since 1952 of British Soviet Bloc agents who had been convicted, had confessed or had defected. The brief concluded that sixteen had primarily mercenary motives, fourteen (including Prime)[37] were ideological and ten had been recruited through 'emotional blackmail'. Three Soviet agents (who, interestingly, included George Blake) were regarded as having 'other' motives. A majority of the most important cases, however, were ideological.[38] The Service's categorization of motives was arguably less satisfactory than the FBI MICE acronym (money, ideology, compromise, ego); ego, omitted in the Security Service analysis, has frequently been an important subsidiary motive in cases ranging from the Cambridge Five to the Americans Aldrich Ames and Robert Hanssen. In sixteen of the forty-three cases the main initial lead to detection had come from Service sources, eleven from defectors, eight from liaison and eight from other sources.[39]

By far the most serious counter-espionage case for the Security Service in the final decade of the Cold War began on Easter Sunday 1983 when Michael Bettaney, a heavy-drinking, disaffected officer in K4 (the department responsible for the investigation and analysis of Soviet London residencies), pushed through the letter-box in Holland Park of Arkadi Guk, the KGB resident, an envelope containing the case put by the Security Service for expelling three Soviet intelligence officers in the previous month, together with details of how all three had been detected. The envelope also contained the offer of further secrets as well as instructions on how to contact him. Bettaney did not reveal his identity but signed himself 'Koba', a name once used by Joseph Stalin.[40] Fortunately for the Security Service, Arkadi Guk had a penchant for conspiracy theories about its operations: among them his claim that many advertising hoardings on the London Underground concealed secret observation posts from which MI5 monitored the movements of KGB officers and other suspicious travellers. Presented by Bettaney with the KGB's first opportunity for a quarter of a century to recruit an MI5 or SIS officer, Guk demonstrated an ability of heroic proportions to look a gift horse in the mouth. With a greatly exaggerated belief in the extent of Security Service surveillance, he must have found it difficult to believe that an MI5 officer could put a packet through his letter-box without being observed. Guk therefore concluded that Bettaney's offer must be a provocation designed to trap him and did not respond to it.[41]

On 11 April the small circle of Security Service officers with access to Gordievsky's intelligence learned that Guk was aware of the Service case for the expulsion of the three Soviet intelligence officers in March – though he had not told Gordievsky how the information had reached him.[42] It was not immediately clear that the leak had come from within the Service since the case for the expulsion had been passed on to both the Foreign Office and the Home Office as well as (probably) to Number Ten. The first person to fall (wrongly) under suspicion was a Foreign Office official whose contacts with a Line KR (counter-intelligence and security) officer operating under diplomatic cover in the London residency had already caused some security concern.[43]

The course of the investigation changed dramatically after a report from Gordievsky on 17 June revealed that the KGB residency had received a document listing KGB and GRU staff in London.[44] Gordievsky had been shown the document by the residency reports officer, Slava Mishustin, who sought his help in translating it and commented that KGB officers at the Centre were never given 'such precise information' about the personnel of Western intelligence stations in Moscow: 'This shows how much better they work than we do.'[45] Gordievsky was able to describe the document he had seen in enough detail for it to be identified as one of about fifty copies of a recent chart of the KGB London residency produced by K4. The hunt (codenamed ELMEN) for the source of the top-secret information reaching the residency henceforth concentrated on the Security Service.[46] Important additional information from Gordievsky arrived on 21 June in a report entitled 'An official from British Counter-Intelligence offers his services to the KGB (Early April–mid June 1983)'. Gordievsky had been told by Guk and the head of the Line KR, Leonid Nikitenko, that the original information on the expulsions of Soviet intelligence officers had arrived in an envelope pushed through Guk's letter-box in April which contained an offer of further classified material and suggested a signalling system and DLB for maintaining contact. Both Guk and Nikitenko believed the approach was a carefully planned British provocation and had decided (with the Centre's approval) not to respond to it. Between 10 and 14 June a further packet had been pushed through Guk's letter-box containing the document listing the personnel of the KGB and GRU residencies, as well as renewing the offer of more top-secret material and making detailed proposals for establishing contact. Guk remained convinced that the whole affair was a devious Security Service plot.

On 24 June, in agreement with the DDG (Cecil Shipp), Director K (John Deverell) decided to concentrate the search for the traitor in K Branch.[47] The ELMEN investigators (later known to each other as the 'Nadgers')[48] were chosen from the ranks of those indoctrinated into the Gordievsky case on the grounds that, since he had not been betrayed, the culprit could not be one of them. The investigation was led personally by John Deverell, and meetings of the Nadgers took place in his rooms in order not to attract attention in the rest of the Branch.

K's suite, with office conference room, secretary's room and three doors to the corridor, proved to be a suitable, indeed the only suitable, place where full discussions could regularly take place, and although towards the end of the investigation doors were opening and shutting furtively as in a French bedroom farce . . . nobody outside the team noticed anything out of the ordinary.[49]

On 27 June the ELMEN investigators received a further important lead from Gordievsky. He had learned that the second letter pushed through

Guk's letter-box about a fortnight earlier asked the residency to give a series of signals on 4 (or possibly 6) July to indicate that it was now willing to make contact – among them parking Guk's car in a London square not far from the Soviet embassy.[50] Deverell and the Nadgers unanimously agreed that the officers who had been identified as the most likely suspects (one of them Bettaney) should be put under surveillance on their way to work on 4 July to see if any of them checked whether the KGB residency was displaying any of the signals requested in the second letter to Guk. The surveillance was expected to be difficult since Bettaney in particular was known to be very surveillance conscious. Because A4, still in ignorance of the case, could not be used, the Nadgers proposed to conduct the surveillance themselves with the assistance of ELMEN indoctrinees in SIS. Assistance by SIS, however, was vetoed by the DDG. Remarkably, and with the full support of the Nadgers, Deverell deliberately ignored Shipp's ruling (an act of disobedience for which there are few parallels in Security Service history).[51] One member of the Nadger surveillance team recalls, 'I was five months pregnant at the time and had a very hard time keeping up.' Her baby, who took part in the surveillance while still in the womb, was christened 'Little Nadger' by her colleagues.

In the event none of the suspects deviated from their normal routes to work on 4 July. Bettaney, however, took a two-hour lunch break during which it was thought he might have gone to check whether the KGB residency was displaying the signals which indicated its willingness to make contact.[52] By this time Gordievsky was on leave in Moscow and unable to provide any further leads until after his return on 10 August.[53] From 4 July onwards, however, Bettaney's bizarre behaviour combined with his pursuit of files of particular interest to the KGB increasingly persuaded the Nadgers of his guilt. K6/7 noted on 7 July that he was showing an obsessional interest in Guk, joking that the Service really needed to recruit him.[54] Next day Bettaney told K4C/1 that, even if the KGB were offered a 'golden apple' or 'peach' of a source inside British intelligence, they would reject it.[55] Director K noted on the same day that, as well as asking odd questions about individual Soviet intelligence officers, Bettaney had begun to talk at length about what had led Philby, Blake and Prime to work for the KGB.[56]

Henceforth, the Nadgers referred to Bettaney by the unofficial and pejorative codename TRAFFIC after the tiresome traffic noise which disturbed their non-air-conditioned Gower Street offices when they were forced to open the windows during the long, hot summer of 1983. He was later assigned the official codename PUCK, but, as one of the Nadgers recalls, 'The Shakespearean connection was deemed highly inappropriate by all members of the team and the word itself was too close to a well-known Anglo-Saxon expletive for comfort.'[57] On 14 July Bettaney provided clinching evidence of his guilt when he asked K4C/1 how he thought Guk would respond if a British intelligence officer put a letter through the door of his house.[58] But, like the other circumstantial evidence so far gathered, it did not begin to provide the basis for a successful prosecution.[59] Neither an HOW 'to monitor Bettaney's movements'[60] nor a secret search of his house uncovered any significant evidence against him.[61] The Nadgers hoped that he would make a further attempt to contact the London residency and be caught in the act.[62] Bettaney, however, had finally despaired of Guk.[63] Evidence began to accumulate that he was planning an approach to the KGB residency in Vienna instead. In late July he mentioned to K4/0 that he was considering taking a holiday in Austria and discussed with her the effectiveness of Austrian security. The DG ruled that under no account must Bettaney be allowed to go abroad.[64] There was worrying evidence that Bettaney continued to make plans to do so. A search of his cupboard in K4 revealed that he had prepared a study of KGB agent-running abroad, including one case (in which Bettaney had shown particular interest) involving a KGB officer expelled from London during Operation FOOT who was currently stationed in Vienna.[65]

Without adequate evidence for a prosecution, it was therefore decided to gamble on a confrontation with Bettaney designed to extract a confession from him. Planning for the confrontation in the DG's conference room, codenamed Operation COE, began early in August.[66] It was clear from the outset that COE was a high-risk strategy. The Service Legal Adviser Bernard Sheldon warned that Bettaney could not be forced to answer any questions. So long as Bettaney remained a member of the Service, he could be ordered not to leave the country. But, if he resigned during the questioning, nothing could be done to prevent him leaving the building.[67] The DDG warned SIS that 'We could not guarantee success; it was possible that TRAFFIC may walk away at the end of the day free to do what he wants – even to defect. We cannot in the last resort be sure that we can prevent this.'[68]

Throughout the preparations for the confrontation, it remained a major priority to avoid any suspicion among non-Nadgers within the Service that the lead which led to Bettaney's discovery had come from an agent in the London residency. In order to conceal Gordievsky's role, Director K and SIS agreed in early August to invent a fictitious reason for the hunt for the traitor in K Branch by concocting a K6 source report of 28 June from 'a very delicate and reliable liaison source', which stated that 'In early 1983 the KGB received an offer of service from a person purporting to be an official in the Russian Department of British Counter-intelligence. It is not known whether the offer was taken up.'[69] Protecting Gordievsky was regarded as so important that, when the Security Commission later investigated the Bettaney case, it too was informed that the original lead was 'a report from a liaison service' (though it is possible that the chairman of the Commission may have been better informed). Even Bernard Sheldon was not briefed on the Gordievsky case until two months after the agent's defection in July 1985.[70]

The operational plan for Bettaney's interrogation was intended to take him by surprise. At the time he was on a course run by SIS, and was summoned to Gower Street in order to discuss an urgent (but fictitious) K3 case which had just arisen.[71] Bettaney was completely deceived. Even after the interrogation began he was not sure whether it had all been a ploy or whether the operational emergency was genuine. Though visibly surprised when ushered into the DG's conference room on 15 September Bettaney initially remained calm as Director K set out the case against him, using a series of visual aids which were intended to shock him into confessing. As Deverell referred to 'an offer which was made to the RIS in the Spring of this year', he showed a photo of Guk's front door taken from an observation post, which was doubtless intended to give Bettaney the false impression that he had been observed pushing packets through the letter-box.

After about three-quarters of an hour, as the apparent weight of evidence against him began to sink in, Bettaney became for the first time visibly nervous. The turning point in the interrogation came when he could offer no explanation for a page torn from his office diary on which he had written coded telephone numbers for two KGB officers. Five minutes later Bettaney started referring to a hypothetical spy who might have done what Director K was saying he had done and would, he thought, have had ideological motivation. In responding to further questions from both Director K and the DDG, he sometimes slipped into the use of the first person singular when referring to the hypothetical spy. By saying that he did not think it was in his interest to confess, Bettaney implicitly admitted his own guilt. After a lunch-break during which he refused the offer of food, he admitted sympathizing with Philby and Blake, referring to them familiarly as Kim and George. He also commented that he assumed there could be no question of an offer of immunity from prosecution as in the case of Blunt – a further implicit admission of guilt.[72] An implicit admission, however, was not enough. Since all the evidence against him was circumstantial, only an actual confession, made or repeated to the police, would make a prosecution possible. K6/7, who was listening to the interrogation in the monitoring room, later recalled:

We had a very real fear that Bettaney would succeed in bluffing it out. When he started to talk 'hypothetically' about what the guilty person might or might not have done, those of us in the monitoring room were at the edge of our seats, urging him to go further. Listening to his attempts to avoid admitting anything, but indulging in musings about motivation and actions which tied in with what we knew but couldn't use as evidence, was an excruciating experience.[73]

At the end of the first day's questioning, Bettaney agreed to spend the night in a Service flat at the top of its Gower Street headquarters and resume on the following day. On entering the flat, his first action was to check the windows. All had been secured to guard against the possibility that he might commit suicide by jumping into Gower Street. Bettaney was already on friendly terms with two of his three overnight minders, and developed a particularly close rapport with K4A/1, who listened sympathetically to what he said, occasionally asking disingenuous questions designed to elicit further admissions. Having already refused lunch, Bettaney also turned down the offer of supper and non-alcoholic drinks. Instead, he demanded a bottle of whisky, drank most of it by 3 a.m., and rejected the advice of his minders to try to get some sleep.[74]

As Bettaney reflected aloud in the course of the night on the past day's questioning, it became clear to his minders that he had been greatly impressed by what he called the 'battery of evidence' deployed against him.[75] He failed entirely to realize that, unless he confessed, the evidence was quite inadequate to secure a conviction. In the course of the night, though making no formal confession and showing no contrition, he abandoned all pretence of innocence, telling his minders that his aim had been to warn Soviet intelligence which of its officers were at risk. He began referring to the British as 'you' and the Russians as 'us'. Bettaney admitted informally to K4A/1 that he had approached Guk but had received no response.[76]

Bettaney refused any breakfast before the interrogation resumed in the DG's conference room on the morning of 16 September. After a sleepless night, a bottle of whisky and no food for the past twenty-four hours, he was, unsurprisingly, in a bad temper, telling K4A/1 he had no intention of making a confession. When K4A/1 replied that this was not the impression he had given overnight, Bettaney became agitated and asked if he could tell him something off the record. Director K intervened to say nothing

was off the record. Eventually, probably through exhaustion, Bettaney said
he wanted to get the whole business over quickly. While Director K was
out of the room contacting the MPSB, Bettaney told the sympathetic K4A/1
he was past caring about the admissions he was making and identified the
places in his home where he had hidden incriminating material later used
in evidence at his trial. At 11.42 a.m. he announced, 'I think I ought to
make a clean breast of it. Tell Director K I wish to make a confession.'
Detective Superintendent Westcott of the Special Branch subsequently took
Bettaney to Rochester Row police station, where he recorded his confession
and he was charged under the Official Secrets Act.[77]

What remained most obscure both to the Nadgers and to his other
colleagues when they were informed of his arrest was Bettaney's motivation. His favourable references to 'Kim' and 'George' during interrogation
showed the extent to which he identified with Philby and Blake and their
work for the KGB. But he was not, like them, a committed pro-Soviet
Communist. 'There was no simple motive,' he told his interrogators, 'it
was a cumulative process.' He did not even appear particularly hostile to
the Security Service, saying at one point: 'I have put the Service in a bloody
position – but it wasn't my intention.'[78] Even during the tense night between
the first and second days of his interrogation, he seemed genuinely to enjoy
the company of colleagues, despite the fact that he had spent the last few
months attempting to undermine Service operations against the KGB.

The ELMEN investigation, though conducted under very difficult conditions, was remarkably successful. Bettaney made a confession, despite
the lack of the evidence against him required to mount a successful prosecution.[79] Neither he nor any other non-indoctrinated member of the
Service had the slightest suspicion that the investigation was taking place.
The surprise when Bettaney's arrest was announced by a DG's circular on
16 September was total.[80] Nor was there any suspicion that his detection
was the result of leads from an agent inside the London residency.

Sir Robert Armstrong, the cabinet secretary, rang the DG, Sir John Jones,
on 16 September 1983 to convey the Prime Minister's congratulations on
'how well the case had been handled. She was very pleased that Bettaney
had been detected and that he had been stopped.'[81] Alone in the cabinet
save for the Foreign and Home Secretaries, Mrs Thatcher knew that
Bettaney had been detected thanks to intelligence supplied by Oleg Gordievsky. The DG sent Gordievsky a formal letter of thanks which was shown
to him by his SIS case officer. The Nadgers also sent a personal message of
gratitude, telling Gordievsky 'how warmly we feel about him'. Gordievsky
replied with equally warm congratulations on the success of the Bettaney

investigation, saying that he dreamed of the day when he would be able to meet and talk to the officers of the Security Service:

I don't know whether such a day will come or not – maybe not. Nevertheless, I would like this idea to be recorded somewhere: that I have underlined my belief that they are the real defenders of democracy in the most direct sense of the word. Therefore it is natural for me to give them whatever help and support I can.[82]

The contrast between Gordievsky's spontaneous warmth and the DG's stiffness struck all the Nadgers. As one of them later recalled: 'John Jones, not the chummiest of DGs, called the team in for a drink on conclusion of the case. Given how closely the team had worked below DG and DDG level, it was a curiously stiff, sad, anticlimactic moment for us all. It all seemed very hollow.'[83]

Bettaney's arrest occurred just as the Cold War was approaching its most dangerous moment since the Cuban Missile Crisis of 1962. With Operation RYAN at its peak, Gordievsky provided extraordinary intelligence on the state of near-paranoia which prevailed in the Centre. The silver lining, so

The scathing press comment in the Bettaney affair contrasted with Mrs Thatcher's congratulations on how well the investigation had been handled
(*Daily Mail*, 23 April 1984).

far as the Security Service was concerned, was the evidence of the extent to which the London residency was being distracted from more productive espionage by the time-consuming and sometimes bizarre requirements placed on it to find non-existent evidence of US and NATO preparations for a nuclear first strike. Among twenty 'tasks' imposed on the residency on 17 February 1983 in order to monitor supposed British preparations for a thermonuclear Armageddon were regular checks on the number of lights on at night and the cars parked at official buildings, the identification of possible evacuation routes for government officials and checks on the state of readiness of bomb shelters. The Centre's requirements were informed by ignorance as well as paranoia. 'Immediate task' number three instructed the residency:

One important sign that preparations are beginning for RYAN could be increased purchases of blood from donors and the prices paid for it ... In this context, discover the location of the several thousand blood-donor reception centres and the price of blood donated, and record any changes. Time limit: 2nd quarter [by 30 June 1983]. If there is an unexpectedly sharp increase in the number of stationary and mobile blood donor centres and in the prices paid, report at once to the Centre.

It had not occurred to the Centre that British blood donors are unpaid, and the residency was reluctant to cause embarrassment by drawing attention to its ignorance. Almost as bizarre was the Centre's suggestion that leading clerics and international bankers might be given advance warning of the NATO nuclear first strike.[84]

On 28 September the terminally ill Soviet leader, Yuri Andropov, issued from his sickbed a denunciation of US and NATO policy couched in apocalyptic language unprecedented since the depths of the Cold War: 'The Reagan administration, in its imperial ambitions, goes so far that one even begins to doubt whether Washington has any brakes at all preventing it from crossing the point at which any sober-minded person must stop.' The KGB took its cue from Andropov. The Centre's alarmism reached its peak during the NATO command-post exercise ABLE ARCHER 83, held from 2 to 11 November to practise nuclear-release procedures, which it feared might be used as cover for beginning the countdown to an actual first strike. Gordievsky passed to his SIS case officer, who informed MI5, a telegram from the Centre to the London residency on 5 November warning that, once the preliminary decision was taken to go ahead with a first strike, nuclear missiles were likely to be launched within a week to ten days. During this period that secret decision was bound to 'be reflected in the pattern of work in [British] state institutions which are involved in safeguarding the defence capability and security'. Guk was therefore instructed to pay particular attention to 'unusual activity at the Prime Minister's residence at 10 Downing Street, where there will be energetic consultations without informing the press'.[85] Gordievsky, wrote Sir Geoffrey Howe later, 'left us in no doubt of the extraordinary but genuine Russian fear of real-life nuclear strike'.[86]

Gordievsky reported that in the annual review of the work of the London residency at the end of 1983, Guk felt forced to admit 'shortcomings' in failing to obtain the (non-existent) intelligence demanded by the Centre on 'specific American and NATO plans for the preparation of surprise nuclear missile attack against the USSR'. During the early months of 1984, however, helped by the death of Andropov on 9 February and reassuring signals from London and Washington (prompted, particularly in the British case, by knowledge of the fears generated by ABLE ARCHER 83), the mood in Moscow gradually lightened. Andropov's successor and former rival, Konstantin Chernenko, was already in failing health and had only a year to live, but he was less morbidly suspicious of Western surprise attack than Andropov had become at the end of his life. A marginal lessening of East–West tension was evident even at Andropov's funeral, attended by Mrs Thatcher and other Western dignitaries. The Soviet ambassador in London, Viktor Popov, told a meeting of embassy and residency staff that Mrs Thatcher had gone out of her way to charm her hosts. In March Nikolai Vladimirovich Shishlin, a senior foreign affairs specialist in the Central Committee (and later an adviser to Mikhail Gorbachev), addressed the staff of the London embassy and KGB residency on current international problems. Gordievsky reported to his case officer that Shishlin made no mention of the supposed threat of surprise nuclear attack which had been the residency's chief preoccupation for the past three years. The bureaucratic momentum of Operation RYAN, however, took some time to wind down. When, in the early summer of 1984, the London residency grew lax about sending its pointless fortnightly RYAN reports, it received a reprimand from the Centre (passed on by Gordievsky to his SIS case officer) telling it to adhere 'strictly' to the original RYAN directive.[87]

Bettaney's conviction and sentencing to twenty-three years' imprisonment in April 1984, later followed by a report of the Security Commission, provided public embarrassment for both the Security Service and the KGB. The revelation that the Service had harboured a traitor in its midst and tolerated his binge drinking exposed it to media ridicule. Arkadi Guk received at least equally unwelcome publicity as a bungling KGB resident. The Attorney General, Sir Michael Havers, told the jury that Bettaney had written to inform Guk that, if his offer to work for the KGB were accepted, 'he would find in the first-floor gents lavatory at the Academy One Cinema in Oxford Street, taped under the lid of the cistern, a canister containing exposed film of classified information'.[88] Guk was publicly revealed to have turned down the KGB's first opportunity since the Second World War to recruit a penetration agent inside the Security Service.

Despite the fact that Bettaney's offer had been ignored, both the Security Service and SIS argued strongly that the publicity given to Guk's role as KGB resident should be used as justification for declaring him *persona non grata* with the secret aim of furthering Gordievsky's career. With Service backing, 'C' (Sir Christopher Curwen) sought Sir Robert Armstrong's assistance in gaining the support of Mrs Thatcher for what he said was a unique opportunity to get rid of the resident 'since Guk has always been most careful not to become directly involved in KGB agent running operations and is likely to be even more careful in the future' – thus making it difficult to prove his active involvement in espionage.[89] Gordievsky believed that after Guk's expulsion, his deputy, Leonid Nikitenko, head of Line KR, who was likely to become acting resident, might well confide in him more – and that his own chances of becoming resident would be improved.[90] Unlike some FCO officials, Sir Julian Bullard, deputy PUS and political director, was enthusiastically in favour of seizing the opportunity: 'The stakes are very high; nothing less than the chance of access to all, or practically all, the KGB operations against this country. For such a prize it is, in my opinion, worth paying the price of sacrificing our own PSO [post security officer] in Moscow . . .'[91] Sir Robert Armstrong informed the PUS at the FCO, Sir Antony Acland, that the Prime Minister 'would be grateful if the Foreign and Commonwealth Office, in consultation with the Security Service, would as a matter of urgency consider the expulsion of Mr Guk without delay'.[92] The Soviet embassy was informed of Guk's expulsion on 14 May. As Bullard had anticipated, Moscow retaliated by expelling the British PSO.[93] At Guk's farewell party before returning to Moscow, Gordievsky was asked to deliver a tribute to him. 'I must', he recalls, 'have sounded just a touch too smooth, and very slightly insincere, because all Guk said, immediately, was "You've learnt a lot from the Ambassador." In the art of making insincere speeches, Popov was undisputed champion.'[94] As Gordievsky had expected, Nikitenko as acting resident almost immediately gave him increased access to residency files and regularly sought his advice. During Nikitenko's absences from London, Gordievsky stood in as acting resident.[95]

Probably no British prime minister has ever followed the case of a

British agent with as much personal attention as Mrs Thatcher devoted to Gordievsky. In October 1984 she expressed concern at the strain he must be under after ten years as a British agent, supposing that he might 'jump at any time', and sought assurances that he and his family would be well looked after when he decided to defect. The Prime Minister emphasized her concern for Gordievsky as an individual – not just as an 'intelligence egg layer'.[96] Gordievsky expressed his warm appreciation when the Prime Minister's concern was reported to him by his case officer.[97] The insights into Soviet policy provided by Gordievsky's intelligence were of particular importance to Mrs Thatcher in December 1984 during the visit to Britain of Mikhail Gorbachev, heir apparent to the ailing Konstantin Chernenko, at the head of a delegation from the Supreme Soviet – a visit which proved to be a turning point in Soviet–British relations. To assist Gordievsky in writing briefs during the visit which would impress both Gorbachev and the Centre, his case officer showed him the brief prepared by the FCO for Sir Geoffrey Howe. Gordievsky later recalled:

We knew that Gorbachev was reading what we wrote with close attention, because one morning, after we had included a flattering paragraph about his wife, Raisa, which recorded how [British] people had admired her, he made his first and only correction, crossing out five lines, to leave only two lines of modest, matter-of-fact tribute, and adding a note: 'It is very dangerous to make other members' wives jealous.'[98]

Gorbachev's visit began a slow thaw in the glacial Soviet–British relations of the early Thatcher era. 'His personality', Margaret Thatcher later recalled, 'could not have been more different from the wooden ventrilo-quism of the average Soviet *apparatchik*.'[99] 'I like Mr Gorbachev,' she told the press. 'I think we can do business together!' The Prime Minister must also have been reassured by the knowledge that the best-informed political briefing provided to Gorbachev during his visit came from a dedicated, long-serving British agent in the KGB.

Gordievsky's briefs doubtless impressed the Centre as well as Gorbachev, almost certainly influencing the decision of the FCD Third Department in January 1985 to recommend his appointment as London resident in succession to Guk.[100] Plans considered by Director K to declare Nikitenko, the acting resident, *persona non grata* in order to clear the way for Gordievsky's promotion were abandoned as unnecessary and possibly counter-productive.[101] On 28 April, despite unsuccessful lobbying by Nikit-enko to press his own claims to succeed Guk, Gordievsky formally became resident-designate.[102] The reasons for the Centre's almost simultaneous realization that Gordievsky was a British agent still remain obscure. Though Aldrich Ames, a Soviet agent in the CIA, betrayed Gordievsky to his controller in Washington, Gordievsky believes that the original KGB lead may have come from another, as yet unidentified, source outside the British intelligence community. On 16 May 1985 he was called back to Moscow, ostensibly for high-level briefings and formal confirmation as resident but in reality for an interrogation intended to secure a confession that he was a long-serving British agent. His last KGB operation on 18 May, the eve of his departure from London, was to leave £8,000 for an illegal codenamed DARIO hidden in a large brick which he deposited on a grassy verge near Coram's Fields children's playground in Bloomsbury.[103] DARIO was photographed picking up the brick by a female K Branch officer using a camera concealed in a baby's pram. A week later, immediately after Gordievsky's interrogation in Moscow, the Centre – for the first time in KGB history – recalled all its (apparently underperforming) illegals from Britain, realizing that they had been compromised.[104]

Despite being drugged by KGB interrogators after his return to Moscow to weaken his defences, Gordievsky did not confess and was allowed to go on leave, doubtless in the hope that he would be caught red-handed contacting British intelligence. Remarkably, Gordievsky succeeded in evading KGB surveillance and, with SIS assistance, escaped across the Finnish frontier.[105] On 22 July Gordievsky arrived at Heathrow to be greeted with champagne by a reception committee which included John Deverell, whom he remembers as 'a man of exceptional intelligence and charm, who became a staunch friend and ally'.[106] He spent the next five days at a Security Service safe house in the Midlands where he was visited by 'C' and questioned about his two months in Russia by Deverell and his SIS case officer. On 27 July Gordievsky moved to an intelligence training centre, where he began a marathon two-month debriefing session. A later Security Service assessment concluded: '[Gordievsky]'s commitment to his work with SIS and the Security Service never wavered. He was patient and thorough in dealing with detailed questions at a time of extraordinary tension and anxiety. His judgement and analysis seemed unaffected.'[107] Gordievsky's escape, probably the most remarkable of the Cold War, was so extraordinary that the DG, Sir Tony Duff, felt it prudent to send the cabinet secretary, Sir Robert Armstrong, a memorandum to counter suggestions from a small number of Whitehall sceptics that Gordievsky might have been turned into a double agent during his time in Moscow, then deliberately sent back to Britain.[108]

It was later discovered that for several weeks after Gordievsky's escape the KGB had no idea what had happened to him and thought he might have committed suicide. Moscow was officially informed of Gordievsky's defection on 15 August without any public announcement in the hope that negotiations could begin to enable his wife and two small daughters to join him in Britain. Following its usual practice with defectors, however, the KGB was determined not to allow Gordievsky's family to leave Russia.[109] Preparations thus began for Operation EMBASE, the public announcement of the defection and the expulsion of KGB and GRU officers in London identified by Gordievsky.[110] Margaret Thatcher did not want the press statement to 'mince words'.[111] On 12 September, the day the news of Gordievsky's defection (though not as yet of his escape from Russia) was made public, twenty-five Soviet intelligence officers were expelled.[112] When the Russians retaliated with twenty-five British expulsions (not all intelligence personnel) from Moscow, Sir Robert Armstrong proposed four further expulsions from London. Mrs Thatcher did not consider this 'an adequate response' and raised the number to six, once again matched by Moscow.[113]

The first apparent sighting of a Soviet illegal in Britain after the recall of KGB illegals to Moscow in May 1985 came on 19 April 1986 when a member of the Soviet Trade Delegation suspected (probably wrongly, it was later concluded) of being a GRU officer was followed to Hampstead Heath and seen to behave 'in a generally furtive manner' before entering the Old Bull and Bush public house. Half an hour later another man appeared and searched an area of ground before he too went into the Old Bull and Bush. The second man was followed to his home address in Friern Barnet, north London, and identified as a forty-year-old Dutch citizen named Erwin Van Haarlem. Initially, Van Haarlem was suspected of being an agent of the GRU 'legal' residency. As investigations continued, however, it was concluded that he was an unidentified illegal who had taken the identity of the real Erwin Van Haarlem, the illegitimate wartime son of a Dutch mother and a German soldier who had been killed fighting in France. In October 1985, after ten years working for the Hilton hotel group, he had become a self-employed art dealer. This, however, was simply a cover profession which generated very little income; Van Haarlem paid tax on sales he had not made simply to keep up his cover.[114]

Van Haarlem's main intelligence work as an illegal was to penetrate British supporters of the Jewish 'refuseniks' in the Soviet Union who were prevented from emigrating to Israel. During a visit to Russia with a refusenik-support group, he impressed his colleagues by the bravado with which he denounced the KGB and the iniquities of the Soviet system. The KGB's known obsession with monitoring Western support for Jewish dissidents in the Soviet Union strengthened the belief that he was an illegal agent (probably Czech rather than Dutch) working for the Russians.[115] K Branch later concluded, however, that, though the StB passed all Van Haarlem's intelligence reports to the Soviet 'friends', he himself had 'no direct contact with the KGB'.[116] A Special Branch raid on Van Haarlem's flat on the morning of Saturday 2 April 1988 caught him, still in his pyjamas, sitting on a stool in the kitchen in the act of taking down a coded message from Prague through an earphone. As the police entered, he leaped to his feet in surprise, knocking over the stool and dropping the earphone, from which the morse transmission from Prague was clearly audible to the officers in the room. Clearly in a state of shock, Van Haarlem made no attempt to keep up the pretence of Dutch nationality, admitted he was Czech, asked for the Czechoslovak embassy to be informed, and produced a bar of soap from a bedroom drawer containing one-time pads for his cipher communications.[117]

The Van Haarlem case led to the last major espionage trial of the Thatcher era and the first of an illegal since Gordon Lonsdale in 1961. At his trial in February and March 1989, the main Security Service witness was 'Miss J' (Stella Rimington), described by the judge as 'a very senior and experienced person involved in intelligence', who explained the role of illegals.[118] Court appearances were still very rare for Security Service officers and Rimington found it a disorienting experience. To protect her identity she was permitted what was termed a 'light disguise' – a curly-haired wig, make-up which aged her by about ten years, and clothes unlike any in her wardrobe. (When, a few months later, she met the trial judge at a dinner party, he failed to recognize her without the disguise.)[119] Rimington told the jury it was unlikely that Van Haarlem had been posted to London simply to report on refusenik-support groups. He was a 'sleeper' intended for a front-line intelligence role in time of war or East–West crisis when the legal residencies could no longer operate normally. The jury took only three-quarters of an hour to find Van Haarlem guilty of committing an act preparatory to espionage. He was sentenced to ten years' imprisonment.[120] Van Haarlem had little idea how he had been tracked down. A Service officer who questioned him in prison reported that he 'showed great ignorance about Security Service practice and displayed signs of paranoia'. Van Haarlem claimed to be well aware that his television had been 'fiddled' with, that he had been frequently followed by a silver Mercedes, and that Service personnel 'were in and out of his flat quite often'.

534

92263 36198 94101 60612 13119
·33959 62102 93816 15931 15003
18117 27611 77908 21086 94901
91990 89816 01161 13373 06068
63362 80903 67102 90067 90079
25925 72503 82562 11930 975621
68811 16270 29912 02028 27992
79225 18977 18691 71198 03930
92963 60090 62909 60257 57192
32293 55818 29596 60309 71893
26385 17911 92987 11163 79219
72532 81269 90916 93255 60699
51088 69692 25138 38636 82315
73112 90795 06911 64295 17015
29871 87297 50067 71922 90260
62728 36968 11012 23960 72968
30067 80611 39021 26398 09295
57908 82959 98299 77870 37123
68109 86611 76362 33912 01659
89310 07880 05097 78761 71791
91999 61283 57631 5095 48869
07931 91067 00057 90857 26256
77225 97023 03287 02857 78222
03906 61967 16711 79556 60991
11592 61591 33198 93022 05356
06189 39286 66211 66756 71181
09801 671

"WE (ALREADY) KNOW THE ORGANISATION OF CZECH EMIGRATION ABROAD. Z4. ON THAT SUBJECT, SEND ONLY INFORMATION ABOUT PREPARED OPERATIONS (or CHANNELS) TO CZECHOSLOVAKIA, THEIR ?DEFRAYMENT FOR SPECIAL SERVICES AND THE SOURCES OF FINANCE FOR THEIR ACTIVITIES. QSL 50 to 53 (ie we have received your 50-53). WE ARE INTERESTED IN THE "IOC". PREPARE A REPORT FOR DELIVERY (OR TRANSMISSION) TO VIENNA, LET ME KNOW BY WHAT MEANS YOU CAN OBTAIN THE IOC MICROFICHES, THEN WE SHALL DECIDE WHAT TO DO NEXT. DO NOT DEVELOP A MORE PROMINENT INITIATIVE TOWARDS CZECH EMIGRATION WITHOUT OUR PRIOR AGREEMENT. FIRST LET ME KNOW THE NEXT POSSIBILITY FOR A MEETING".

The coded radio message being received by Van Haarlem from the Czech StB as police entered his flat on 2 April 1988.

He was wrong on all counts.[121] Van Haarlem's real name, the Service discovered, was Václav Jelínek.[122]

On 17 May 1988, almost three years after Gordievsky's exfiltration, Director K reported to the Management Board that the Security Service debrief of Gordievsky had finally been completed: 'It had been the longest and most comprehensive debrief ever undertaken by the Service; over 1300 specific briefs from sections had been answered and 2500 reports issued within the Service.'[123] Mrs Thatcher continued to attach great importance to Gordievsky's assessments of Soviet policy. Sir Geoffrey Howe later called him 'a secret weapon in our drive for better East–West relations': 'His invaluable (not least because it was so regular) commentary on thinking in the Kremlin ... played an important part in shaping our own strategy.'[124]

In the short term the expulsion of thirty-one Soviet intelligence officers in September 1985, following Gordievsky's escape, though less dramatic than Operation FOOT fourteen years earlier, was thought to have temporarily 'paralysed' the KGB residency in particular and caused the other Soviet Bloc residencies in London 'to lie low for a while'.[125] K Branch realized, however, that, even with Gordievsky's 'invaluable help' in identifying intelligence personnel, it would only be a matter of time before the KGB and GRU residencies resumed something approaching the level of activity before the expulsions. It reported in June 1988: 'The KGB has now clawed back to half its pre-expulsion strength. Both residencies are now once again viable intelligence-gathering units and growing more active. While continuing to contain them as far as possible we must also now move to operations to disrupt them.'

During the 1980s Line X (scientific and technological intelligence) in the KGB London residency had greater success than Line PR.[126] The last major success of the residency in the Thatcher era, in the autumn of 1990, was to resume running the electronics engineer Michael John Smith, who had so far escaped detection by the Security Service.[127] S&T was also a field in which the intelligence services of the Soviet Bloc were of particular importance to the Centre.[128] In 1980, possibly an exceptional year, just over half the S&T obtained by the KGB came from the intelligence services of the Soviet Bloc, the East Germans and the Czechoslovaks chief among them.[129] Only a decade later, however, with the collapse of the Soviet Bloc, the KGB lost all its main European intelligence allies. By 1990 some of the Soviet Union's closest Cold War intelligence allies had begun to co-operate with Western agencies. The illegal Václav Jelínek, alias 'Erwin Van Haarlem', who had previously refused to talk to the Security Service, was instructed to do so by the post-Communist Czech intelligence service.[130]

During the final years of the Cold War, Chinese espionage in Britain was probably more difficult to monitor than KGB operations. The Service reported in 1988:

At around 500 [the Chinese] are the largest official community in London. There are over 2,000 students at some 300 establishments and colleges; and delegations visiting the UK run into thousands. Both the Chinese Intelligence Services have substantial resources and both are represented here with their officers and co-optees working within the diplomatic community and outside it. We cannot therefore pretend to anything like satisfactory coverage.[131]

According to Chinese defectors, there was a dramatic increase in Beijing's scientific and technological intelligence-gathering in the later 1980s. In 1986 Beijing rated Britain as the fourth most important source of S&T. By 1988, the S&T unit at its London embassy was rated the 'most productive in terms of reporting' anywhere in the world.[132] An Interdepartmental Working Group convened by the Cabinet Office in 1987 concluded, after considering detailed evidence from K6 and K8, that List X firms showed insufficient awareness of 'the weight and intensity of the Chinese Intelligence effort in the United Kingdom'. One cautionary example used by C Branch in 1988 concerned a leading hi-tech company with classified defence contracts which, to strengthen its commercial links with China, gave a 'scholarship' to enable a young Chinese weapons engineer, whose father had an important job in Beijing, to train with it. A C Branch security adviser agreed with the List X company's security controller a training programme which would keep 'Mr Zhang' (not his real name) away from sensitive areas. When the adviser visited the company in April 1988, however, he found that for the past four months 'Mr Zhang' had been working in a secure area with engineers who were in the habit of discussing classified projects and in the vicinity of filing cabinets containing documents marked SECRET. 'The assumption has to be made', the C Branch adviser concluded, 'that [Zhang] will have been working to a detailed intelligence brief.'[133]

Chinese espionage never came close, however, to equalling the threat from Soviet Bloc espionage during the Cold War. A Cabinet Office assessment concluded in 1988:

The Chinese Government is not hostile to the British Government or NATO in the way the Soviet Government and the Warsaw Pact are. We should recognise the distinction between [Soviet] spying with the hostile intent of gaining an advantage over an enemy, and [Chinese] spying with the purely selfish intent of gaining a national advantage.[134]

The Chinese military threat to British interests was rated so low that, as K8 (whose responsibilities included monitoring Chinese intelligence operations) reported to the DG: 'The Chinese enjoy an access to the MoD and Armed Forces that is not afforded to any other Communist country. For example, the Chinese are now authorised to receive Confidential information from MoD. Also Chinese students are increasingly attending [military] courses in the UK . . .'[135]

At the end of the Cold War, the overall threat to national security from foreign espionage appeared to be low. Since Operation FOOT in 1971, the United Kingdom had been a hard target for the intelligence services of the Soviet Bloc. One of the most effective weapons in MI5's armoury had proved to be the policy of refusing a visa to any known hostile intelligence officer applying to work in or visit the UK. A counter-espionage officer, who became Director K in 1992, recalls:

Over the years this policy kept hundreds of experienced I[ntelligence] O[fficer]s from entering the country . . . The result of this policy was that the opposition was increasingly forced to post inexperienced intelligence officers to the UK – officers who had never served in the West before, or who had never drawn attention to themselves through operational activity, the espionage equivalent of 'clean skins' – who were more likely to make mistakes or who would be reluctant to risk being caught and expelled ignominiously.[136]

The KGB's difficulty in appointing competent, experienced residents in London probably explains its choice of the inadequate Arkadi Guk in 1980. A more competent resident might well have accepted Bettaney's offer to work as a Soviet agent and have succeeded in bringing about the only major Cold War penetration of the Security Service. There were of course some able KGB officers who succeeded in slipping through the net. Possibly the ablest was Viktor Oshchenko of Line X, who was responsible for the recruitment of Michael John Smith, probably the most important espionage case in Britain still unresolved at the end of the Cold War.[137] There were fewer restrictions on the GRU. In order to facilitate the posting of British military attachés in Moscow, there was a policy of giving visas to Soviet military attachés posted to London – all of them GRU officers – provided that they had not previously been identified acting operationally (including, but not limited to, running agents) against the UK or a close ally.

In tandem with the visa-refusal policy, the ceiling on the numbers of Soviet officials allowed in the UK prevented the unchecked expansion of the London residencies, forcing the KGB and the GRU to compete with other departments for slots in the embassy, Soviet Trade Delegation and other Soviet offices. A retrospective analysis of Service counter-espionage in the later Cold War concluded:

When a hostile IO arrived in this country, he faced an intimidating array of counter-measures, ranging from a sophisticated protective security programme to intensive surveillance and double-agent operations or 'stings'. We watched, analysed, made deductions, followed up every lead, interviewed their contacts, even put officers alongside them under cover. This was the bread and butter of our work against the so-called 'legal' Residencies – those IOs who operated under diplomatic or trade cover in the embassies, trade delegations, international organisations etc. At the outset, of course, we did not know whether a particular individual was an IO or not, so the first priority was to confirm his status. Once identified as an IO, he would become the focus of more intensive study to determine the nature of his duties and contacts. Finally we would decide whether and how to disrupt his espionage activity. The defensive system that we developed over the years put enormous pressure on hostile IOs, most of whom felt apprehensive and intimidated even before they arrived here, such was our reputation.

Perhaps the clearest evidence that the KGB found it hard to operate in Britain was the fact that in the latter years of the Cold War, it diverted a significant amount of its operations against UK targets to third countries, where British personnel were more exposed and vulnerable and where the local security service might not be as effective. The Security Service sought to counter this by briefing likely targets. Soviet Bloc intelligence agencies also moved many meetings with British agents to other countries, which made them more difficult to detect. To some extent, one Director K believes, 'the Service may thus over time have become the victim of its own success.'[138]

Counter-Terrorism and Protective Security in the Later 1980s

Stella Rimington later argued that the aftermath of the Brighton bombing would have been the moment for the Security Service to claim from the MPSB the lead intelligence role in combating Irish Republican terrorism in Britain. The opportunity, if it existed, was missed. Rimington blamed senior management, who, she claimed, 'had not wanted to take on the responsibility, because they were afraid of criticism if they failed'.[1] Though the claim that Sir John Jones and the Service leadership did not possess the courage to make the change may be unjust, they lacked the confidence to argue their case within Whitehall in a way which would have given it any real prospect of success. The ineffectiveness of PIRA mainland operations after the Brighton bombing also lessened what pressure there was for a radical reorganization of counter-terrorism. Neither the Security Service nor the MPSB could have foreseen that the attack on the Grand Hotel was to be the last major success by a mainland ASU for the next four years.

From the mid-1980s onwards, the decline in the Cold War and in the perceived threat from domestic subversion was matched by increasing awareness of the terrorist menace. FX Branch's work was evenly divided between Irish and international terrorism. Director FX, Patrick Walker, told the Home Secretary and his PUS in July 1985: 'The threat posed by international terrorism was less intense and sustained, but it was, on the other hand, more diffuse and, in intelligence terms, tougher to crack. The threat posed by Irish terrorism was more sustained, but in this area the Security Service shared responsibility with MPSB . . .'[2] The Service found it particularly difficult to assess the threat from the most active and brutal international terrorist group of the time, the Abu Nidal Organization (ANO), then based in Libya,[3] which was committed to the destruction of the State of Israel and to an international Arab revolution. In an unsuccessful attempt to secure the release of the jailed hitmen responsible for the attempted assassination in 1982 of the Israeli ambassador in London, Shlomo Argov, the ANO threatened a series of attacks on British interests.[4]

The Service, however, had no means of knowing whether the increasingly mentally unstable and unpredictable Abu Nidal was planning operations in Britain as horrendous as his murderous attacks in the mid-1980s on Rome and Vienna airports, and on Istanbul's largest synagogue. F3/8 told an intelligence conference in September 1984:

It has always been extremely difficult to achieve a sound estimate of the size of AN[O] either as a whole or in a particular country such as the UK. The group has been very effective in securing the anonymity of its members in European countries and it has been exceptionally difficult to penetrate. Although we are constantly in receipt of lists which purport to name Abu Nidhalists, they are usually worthless. We have received over twelve such lists in 1984 alone, some of them being repeated from one security service to another, the names being increasingly garbled in transmission. Few of the names ever prove to be of men who can be positively identified.[5]

'I am the evil spirit of the secret services,' boasted Abu Nidal in an interview with *Der Spiegel* in 1985. 'I am the evil spirit which moves at night causing nightmares.' The greatest nightmare for the Security Service was his threat to the Prime Minister: 'We are working with all our forces against Thatcher, for example with the IRA. She escaped with her life from the last assassination attempt in Brighton, but I can assure you that she will not be able to avoid the next attacks.'[6] Improbable though the threat to Mrs Thatcher might appear, Abu Nidal's terrorist track-record was such that it could not be ignored. In the event, instead of mounting further attacks in Britain, he chose softer British targets abroad. In 1984 ANO assassins killed Kenneth Whitty, the British cultural attaché in Athens, and Percy Norris, the British deputy high commissioner to India in Bombay. Abu Nidal's most ambitious operation against a British target, probably prompted by his Libyan hosts, seems to have been the attack on Sunday 3 August 1986 by three small groups identified by the Security Service as ANO terrorists on the living quarters and recreational area of RAF Akrotiri in the British Sovereign Base Area of Cyprus. The attackers claimed to be retaliating against the US air-raid on Libya a few months earlier, which Qaddafi wrongly believed had been launched from Akrotiri. Though the terrorists used a rocket launcher and mortars, damage to the RAF base was slight. The only injuries were minor shrapnel wounds suffered by two wives of service personnel.[7] The Security Service continued to investigate the possibility that ANO had established a network in Britain capable of mounting a major terrorist attack.[8] Though the Service found no evidence of any, it could not be certain that – as now seems highly probable – none existed. During the later 1980s, Abu Nidal increasingly dissipated his homicidal energies in a feud with the leader of the PLO, Yasir Arafat, whom he bizarrely called 'the Jewess's son', and in a paranoid hunt for mostly imaginary Arab traitors. He subjected his mostly innocent victims to sadistic torture and execution.[9]

The newly introduced Security Service Annual Report to the Home Secretary for 1985–6 noted that counter-terrorist staff were 'under great pressure' and 'fully extended':

The main thing to be said about our work in the counter-terrorist field is that it increases monthly ... One welcome result of the diminution of activity by the Russians since [the] September [1985 expulsions of KGB and GRU personnel][10] has been the greater availability of the [A4] mobile surveillance teams for action against terrorist targets. [Director FX, Patrick Walker, wrote on his copy of the report: 'But still not enough'][11]

The main features of the year have been –

i. the increase in violent attacks against Western targets, both in the Middle East and Europe;

ii. the increasing danger of Sikh (and other sub-continental) terrorism in the UK;

iii. the intense political pressure, mainly from the US, for more active retaliation against terrorist groups and governments sponsoring terrorism;

iv. the continuing and increasing need to take part in inter-departmental [counter-terrorist] work in Whitehall and in a variety of international meetings;

v. a further increase in the quality of our links with liaison services, especially on the European continent. These embrace not only the exchange and assessment of intelligence but a number of cases of fruitful, though sometimes unsuccessful, operational cooperation.[12]

Sikh extremism, which the DG, Sir Tony Duff, put at the top of the list of current terrorist threats in mainland Britain in the 1985–6 Annual Report, illustrated once again the often unpredictable rise and fall of the threat from international terrorist groups. In the early 1980s terrorism by Armenian extremists, who attempted to assassinate the Turkish ambassador in 1982, had been a serious problem. Within a few years, however, the problem had virtually disappeared.[13] By contrast, terrorism by Sikh extremists in the UK, which scarcely existed at the beginning of the decade, suddenly emerged as a major threat during the summer and autumn of 1984. In early June the Indian Prime Minister, Indira Gandhi, sent troops into the Punjab where they stormed the Sikh holy of holies, the Golden Temple of Amritsar. On 31 October two of her Sikh guards took their revenge by shooting her dead in the garden of her house. While Mrs Gandhi's body lay in state, with Indian television cameras broadcasting live pictures of her decomposing remains, Hindu mobs looted and torched Sikh neighbourhoods and businesses, hacking or burning to death Sikh men in front of their wives and children. The Indian police, save for a minority who joined in the massacre, were nowhere to be seen.[14] In Britain the invasion of the Golden Temple and the massacres produced an upsurge of support within the Sikh community for the creation of an independent Sikh state of Khalistan on the Indian sub-continent. The Service reported 'a wave of support among Sikhs in UK for the Khalistan National Organisation', led by Dr Jagjit Singh Chauhan, who formed the Khalistan 'Government in Exile'.

Before the state visit to Britain in October 1985 of Indira Gandhi's son and successor as prime minister, Rajiv Gandhi, a year later, the Service reported to the Home Office: 'Since June 1984 there have been a number of relatively minor attacks in the UK by Sikh extremists against Indian official targets and moderate Sikhs. The level of support for the extremists has diminished considerably but this is making the hard core increasingly frustrated and could lead to further violence.'[15] Good intelligence, combined with the arrests of Sikh and Kashmiri extremists, was believed to have frustrated plots to attack Rajiv Gandhi during his state visit.[16] In April 1986 the DG, Sir Tony Duff, warned the Home Office that the minority of 'violence-prone extremists' within the Indian Sikh Youth Federation and the fundamentalist Dam Dami Taksal 'form a small intensely security-conscious group who, because of the nature of the Sikh community, are a difficult target':

We cannot at present increase our technical coverage ... because we do not have enough transcribers. This is chiefly a question of finding suitably qualified linguists. I would also like to see our agent running effort improved but again it takes time to find the right staff for the difficult task of recruiting and running this kind of agent.[17]

By 1987, despite its lack of success on the British mainland since 1984, PIRA was far better armed than it had been at the time of the Brighton bombing. Between August 1985 and October 1986, four large arms and explosives shipments from Libya were secretly landed on the coast of County Wicklow, south of Dublin.[18] However, a fifth and even larger shipment (including SAM-7 missiles capable of downing British army helicopters), loaded on board the rickety fifty-year-old Panamanian-registered *Eksund* at Tripoli on 13 and 14 October 1987, was successfully intercepted off Ushant. On 27 October the *Eksund*'s steering failed and it began drifting closer and closer to the French coast. Next day, after attempts to repair the steering had failed, the senior Provisional on board,

Gabriel Cleary, took the decision to sink the ship and its cargo before it ran aground, go ashore with the crew on an inflatable dinghy and catch a ferry back to Ireland. Shortly after leaving Tripoli, Cleary had fitted a timing power unit (TPU) to twelve explosive charges below the *Eksund*'s waterline to enable him to scuttle the ship if it was intercepted before it reached its destination. When Cleary was unable to activate the TPU, he concluded that it had been sabotaged and that there must be a traitor on board. At various stages during the voyage he had noticed what seemed to be spotter aircraft. At Gibraltar one had swooped so low that he been able to see the pilot. As the *Eksund* ran into difficulties off Ushant, another spotter plane monitored its movements. The ship was surrounded by motor launches and boarded by armed French customs officials, who arrested the crew.[19] During questioning, the crew revealed that over the previous two years they had brought 120 tons of arms from Libya to the Irish Republic – including many tons of Semtex, about twenty SAM-7s and other sophisticated weaponry.[20] Despite the loss of the *Eksund* arms shipment, PIRA already had a total arsenal of about 150 tons of weaponry – enough, it believed, 'to prosecute its "Long War" almost indefinitely'.[21] A gloomy Security Service assessment concluded that 'PIRA has acquired from Libya more weapons etc than it can use.'[22] Only one of the SAMs, however, was ever fired. It missed.[23]

The Security Service retained the lead intelligence role in monitoring the mainland activities of Loyalist paramilitaries as well as PIRA overseas operations and funding. UDA members in Britain increased from about 200 to 800 from 1985 to 1988 and those of the UVF from 70 to 200 during the same period. The Service reported that in London the UDA had 'attracted members of the skinhead movement of the extreme right'. But it believed the UDA had no formal links with right-wing extremists of either the National Front or the British National Party: 'Indeed, at leadership level, there is mutual suspicion.' The Service reported to the Prime Minister in 1988: 'A hard core of activists within the UDA and UVF will continue to attempt to obtain arms and explosives for shipment to Northern Ireland.' As in the past, the Service remained cautiously optimistic about its ability, in co-operation with local police forces, to disrupt the shipments. Arms seizures in 1987 led to the conviction and imprisonment of a number of UDA and UVF activists on firearms charges.[24]

Within Northern Ireland the Security Service was usually successful in keeping a low profile for its operations, which included increasing (and still classified) technical assistance by A1 to the RUC. One instance of this assistance, whose details cannot be revealed, led to considerable soul-searching and a fraught internal inquiry which found that several Service officers had been at fault. It is reasonable to conclude with the gift of hindsight, though the inquiry did not reach that conclusion at the time, that the errors of individuals reflected a larger management failure. Sir Patrick Walker remembers the whole affair as 'a gruesome business' which kept him awake at nights.[25] The most controversial aspect of Northern Irish counter-terrorist operations in the 1980s concerned the RUC's alleged preference for shooting, rather than arresting, suspected Republican terrorists. In May 1984 John Stalker, Deputy Chief Constable of Greater Manchester, was appointed to investigate three specific allegations that the RUC was conducting a shoot-to-kill policy. In June 1986 Stalker was replaced as head of the inquiry by the Chief Constable of West Yorkshire, Colin Sampson. Though the official explanation for Stalker's replacement were charges (later dismissed) that he had associated with 'known criminals', it was widely alleged that the real reason for his dismissal was that he was close to discovering illegal acts which the authorities wished to conceal. The fact that Stalker had already concluded that the RUC had no shoot-to-kill policy was generally lost sight of amid a spate of ill-founded conspiracy theories.[26]

There is no evidence in Security Service files that it countenanced or assisted a shoot-to-kill policy in Northern Ireland. In 1988, however, it became embroiled in the shoot-to-kill controversy as a result of Operation FLAVIUS, which successfully prevented a PIRA attack on the Gibraltar garrison. In Gibraltar, as on the rest of the continent, the Service had the lead counter-PIRA intelligence role which it did not yet possess in the United Kingdom. On 6 March 1988 the three members of a PIRA active service unit, Seán Savage, Danny McCann and Mairéad Farrell, who were preparing an attack, were shot dead in Gibraltar by military personnel in civilian clothes who said they believed that the ASU was about to detonate a car bomb by remote control and/or to draw their weapons. The confusion which followed encouraged claims that the military believed no such thing but were following a deliberate shoot-to-kill policy, in league with the Security Service and the Thatcher government. BBC Radio 4 News reported at 7 a.m. next day: 'It's now known that the three people shot and killed by Security Forces in Gibraltar yesterday were members of the Provisional IRA. It's thought they were challenged while trying to leave Gibraltar after planting a huge car bomb in the centre of the colony.' After the news, the Armed Forces Minister, Ian Stewart, interviewed on the Radio 4 *Today* programme, congratulated the Gibraltar government and added: 'There was a car bomb found which has been defused.' All the morning newspapers also reported that a bomb had been found and that the terrorists had been armed. Some claimed that there had been a shoot-out. Later that day, however, the Foreign Secretary, Sir Geoffrey Howe, gave a different account of the deaths of Savage, McCann and Farrell:

On their way to the [Spanish] Border, they were challenged by the Security Forces. When challenged, they made movements which led the military personnel, operating in support of the Gibraltar police, to conclude that their own lives and the lives of others were under threat. In the light of this response, they were shot. Those killed were subsequently found not to have been carrying arms.

Howe added that no car bomb had been discovered on the Rock.[27]

Savage and McCann had been under surveillance for some time since intelligence had revealed that they were preparing for a continental oper-ation. The Security Service considered the introverted Savage 'probably PIRA's most effective and experienced bomb-maker'.[28] A later Republican obituary described him as 'a quiet and single-minded individual who neither drank nor smoked and rarely socialised', but attended Mass regu-larly and helped his parents care for his Down syndrome brother.[29] The much more extrovert McCann was later remembered by friends as a good family man and devout Catholic who 'liked nothing better than a bit of *craic* at the local pub'.[30] The RUC and Security Service saw a different side of McCann. Though aged only twenty-nine, he was regarded as one of the Provisionals' most experienced and ruthless hitmen, and was thought to be responsible for as many as twenty-six killings. A stamp in his passport which revealed that in mid-November 1987 he had been at the La Línea border crossing between Spain and Gibraltar was one of a number of pieces of intelligence which pointed to preparations for an attack on the Rock. By this time the Security Service had discovered that the ASU had gained a third member: Siobhan O'Hanlon, an explosives expert, devout Catholic and committed feminist who would always insist on doing her share of the digging when constructing weapons hides. On 25 November F5 warned the Gibraltar authorities by telex of the danger of a PIRA attack. At a meet-ing with the Governor soon afterwards, it was concluded (correctly) that the ASU probably intended to bomb the ceremonial changing of the guard, involving up to fifty soldiers and bandsmen. PIRA preparations for the bombing, however, were delayed for several months by cancellations of the changing of the guard due to renovation of the Guard Room and roadworks along the route of the procession.[31] In mid-December F5/0 and A4/0 visited Gibraltar to discuss A4's role when the ASU returned – which it now seemed clear would not be until the changing of the guard resumed in the New Year.

A4's surveillance team sent to the Rock during Operation FLAVIUS was to be its biggest deployment so far, either at home or abroad.[32]

It was believed that, if the members of the ASU were arrested in Spain before they were ready to go ahead with an attack on the Gibraltar garrison, they would face only minor charges. All were regarded by the Security Service as ruthless terrorists who remained at liberty in the UK only because of the lack of usable evidence against them and would kill again unless brought to justice on this occasion. At a meeting in Gibraltar on 15 February, the Governor, Director FX, F5/0 and a JIC representative therefore agreed that the ASU should be allowed to travel to Gibraltar with their explosives, so that they could be caught red-handed. This strategy, however, would require the assistance of the military: 'The Gibraltar police had never fired a shot in anger and simply did not have the manpower. It was common sense to deploy the most professional body against such hardened terrorists.' On 18 February, after Mrs Thatcher had approved a secret military deployment on the Rock (whose details remain officially classified), F5/0 and the army commander flew to Gibraltar to brief the Governor and the Police Commissioner. The military team arrived from Britain a few hours later and began joint exercises with the A4 surveillance team next day.

On 20 February Siobhan O'Hanlon was spotted at the La Línea border crossing. She was kept under surveillance as she walked into Gibraltar, studied a poster announcing the resumption of the changing of the guard, then – confident in the justice of her homicidal cause – entered the cathedral to pray and light a candle. Next day she phoned McCann to say she had very good news and would be staying until 23 February (the date when the changing of the guard resumed). The Governor and Mrs Thatcher agreed that the ceremony could go ahead since McCann would not arrive in Gibraltar in time for an attack to be mounted on the 23rd. The A4 surveillance team reported that, when O'Hanlon turned up for the changing of the guard on that day, she remained expressionless throughout the ceremony. Her mood became more animated when she left the Rock and phoned McCann, telling him excitedly, 'Everything went great today!' On 24 February, however, she noticed Spanish surveillance, returned to Northern Ireland and dropped out of the ASU. O'Hanlon was replaced as the third member of the ASU by Mairéad Farrell, later remembered by a journalist who knew her as 'small, determined, angry, ready to sacrifice her life and anyone else's to her cause, ready for whatever comes her way'. During the 'dirty protest' Farrell had been officer commanding thirty PIRA women prisoners.[33]

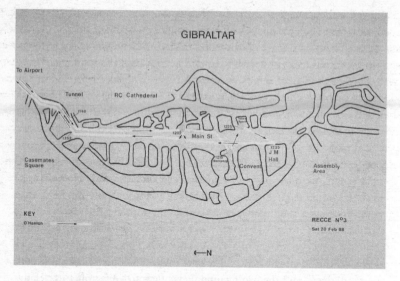

A4 surveillance map of the route taken by Siobhan O'Hanlon in Gibraltar on 20 February 1988 while making preparations for a PIRA attack on the British garrison.

On 4 March McCann, Savage and Farrell were seen meeting at Málaga airport. Within hours a Command Group, chaired by the Gibraltar Commissioner of Police and including representatives of the various security forces involved in Operation FLAVIUS, was operational in The Convent, the Office of the Governor General, in constant radio communication with a seventy-strong response team on the ground. The role of the Security Service throughout FLAVIUS was to co-ordinate intelligence collection, circulate intelligence assessments, plan the response to the ASU, and 'guide and advise the [Police] Commissioner as the operation unfolded'. The Spanish security service, the DSE, was asked not to follow McCann, Savage and Farrell after their meeting at Málaga on 4 March, for fear that, like O'Hanlon eight days earlier, they would spot the surveillance. As a result, contact with them was lost until they arrived on the Rock on Sunday 6 March.

A4 set up an observation post (OP) overlooking the Spanish border in the hope of detecting the arrival of the ASU. They had a difficult task. On Sundays more than 25,000 people crossed into Gibraltar, and the OP had only five to ten seconds to observe each car. As a result it failed to spot Savage crossing the border in a rented Renault 5 on the morning of 6 March. At 12.50 p.m. Savage parked the Renault near the assembly point for the changing of the guard ceremony due to take place on the morning of Tuesday the 8th. It was another two and a quarter hours, however, before he was clearly identified. McCann and Farrell crossed the border on foot and were observed entering Gibraltar at 2.25 p.m. At 3.10 McCann, Farrell and Savage were seen sitting on a park bench looking intently at the Renault parked by Savage. When they began heading back towards the Spanish border, the Commissioner signed a warrant instructing the military to arrest all three. Meanwhile the EOD (explosive ordnance disposal) commander mistakenly reported, after a hurried inspection of the Renault, that it appeared to contain a bomb and that an old aerial on the car might be part of a radio-controlled detonation system. As Savage, McCann and Farrell approached the outskirts of Gibraltar, they suddenly spotted the military team keeping them under surveillance. The sequence of events which followed quickly became, and still remains, highly controversial.

Republicans claimed that the three were gunned down in cold blood, victims of the Thatcher government's alleged shoot-to-kill policy in Ireland. A much publicized Thames Television documentary, 'Death on the Rock', produced eyewitnesses who claimed that the Provisionals had been shot while trying to surrender. The soldiers' version of events, given later at an inquest, was quite different. The movements of Savage, McCann and Farrell had convinced the military team that they were either about to detonate a car bomb or about to produce weapons, and the team took the split-second decision to shoot to kill. There is no persuasive evidence that the decision was premeditated. F5/o later recalled: 'News of the shooting was greeted with a stunned silence in the [FLAVIUS] Ops room. Then bedlam broke out as the police had to arrange the evacuation of the area of the [supposed] car bomb and A4 arranged to pack up. At 1606 hours control was passed back to the police.' Press lines had been prepared to announce the arrest of the ASU. Had there been a premeditated shoot-to-kill policy, press lines would have been ready to cover the shootings. But there were none. Hence the confusion which followed the 'stunned silence' in the Gibraltar Operations Room when news of the shootings was received. The muddled sequence of news stories which preceded the Foreign Secretary's statement on the following day was evidence of official cock-up rather than, as some alleged, conspiracy.

The fact that McCann, Farrell and Savage were shot rather than arrested derived from the incompleteness of the intelligence available at the time (a common characteristic of even the best intelligence). There was very good intelligence on the identity of the ASU members, their previous movements and their target. The fact that they were unarmed, however, was not discovered until after they had been shot. McCann's past record as a ruthless gunman, probably responsible for twenty-six deaths, made it reasonable to believe that he and his colleagues would be carrying guns. There was good reason also to believe that the ASU was planning 'a button not a clock job' – a bomb detonated by remote control rather than by timer. It now seems probable that this had been the original intention of the Gibraltar operation and that the decision to use a timing device came as the result of a PIRA change of plan of which the Security Service was unaware. It was not until after the shootings that a Ford Fiesta rented by the ASU was discovered in an underground Marbella car park containing a partly constructed car bomb with 64 kilos of explosive, 200 rounds of Kalashnikov ammunition and a timing mechanism. Only then was it realized that Savage's Renault 5 had, in all probability, been used simply to reserve a parking space in Gibraltar for the Fiesta which was to be driven on to the Rock during the morning rush hour on 8 March before the changing of the guard. Had the bomb in the Fiesta exploded during the ceremony, there would have been civilian as well as military deaths. Operation FLAVIUS undoubtedly saved many lives.

Though the attempted bombing of the Gibraltar garrison had ended in operational disaster for the Provisionals, they probably had the better of the prolonged media controversy which followed. While acknowledging that Farrell, McCann and Savage were PIRA 'volunteers', Republican spokesmen also claimed that they were victims of a British shoot-to-kill policy, similar to that which was alleged to operate in Northern Ireland. The Thames Television *World in Action* documentary 'Death on the Rock', broadcast on 28 April, reached no definite conclusion but, lacking full information, lent some support to that claim. The presenter announced: 'We have interviewed four key witnesses to the shootings. Their accounts raise serious questions about what really happened that afternoon; for they say that the British soldiers opened fire without warning, and none of them saw the IRA bombers make any threatening movements.' A later independent inquiry commissioned by Thames Television found that the claim that 'none of them saw the IRA bombers make any threatening movements' was 'not a fair reflection' of the statements made by two of them.[34] 'Death on the Rock' also ignored the possibility that there might have been good reason for the security authorities to fear that Savage's car contained a remote-controlled bomb. Unaware that the Spanish DSE had been asked not to follow the members of the ASU after their rendezvous at Málaga airport on 4 March for fear that they would detect surveillance,[35] the programme included a dramatic but inaccurate reconstruction of how both Savage's Renault 5 and a red Fiesta hired by McCann and Farrell were 'expertly tailed' by 'plain-clothes officers of Spain's elite anti-terrorist squad' to the Gibraltar border on 6 March while 'a police helicopter made sure that the watchers [in the cars] made no mistake', keeping the British constantly informed of the cars' progress.[36] Another inaccuracy in 'Death on the Rock' was its assertion that 'British security officials' identified Savage from the moment that his car entered Gibraltar and allowed him 'to drive through unhindered'. The presenter told viewers: 'Just why the British security men did not stop a car that only two hours later came under suspicion as a dangerous car bomb is one of the key questions . . .'[37] Though founded on a basic misunderstanding about the sequence of events, that question has since been frequently repeated in studies of the Gibraltar shootings by writers unaware that Savage was not identified until more than two hours after he had parked the Renault 5.[38]

On 30 September the jury at a Gibraltar inquest ruled by nine to two that the three members of the ASU had been 'lawfully killed'. Mrs Thatcher wrote formally to the DG asking him to pass on her 'warm appreciation' to the members of the Service who had given evidence in the Gibraltar inquest and 'to the Service as a whole for its part in thwarting an action which would have caused untold loss of life'.[39] The DG replied that in recent months the Service had 'received much ill-founded public criticism', and that the Prime Minister's letter was therefore 'particularly valued'.[40] 'Death on the Rock', however, had a greater public impact than the Gibraltar inquest, winning 'best documentary' awards from both the Broadcasting Press Guild and the British Academy of Film and Television Arts (BAFTA).[41]

Operation FLAVIUS provided dramatic, if somewhat inaccurate, public evidence of the Security Service's growing counter-terrorist role. A brief prepared for Patrick Walker's first meeting as DG with Margaret Thatcher in January 1988 concluded: 'The most significant recent development has been the marked growth in the number of staff employed in FX Branch (Counter-Terrorism) in the last two years. This growth has been achieved partly at the expense of K Branch (Counter-Espionage) and F Branch (Counter-Subversion).'[42] The DG's 1986–7 Annual Report to the Home Secretary showed that FX Branch now had 171 staff as compared with 192 in K and 110 in F Branch.[43] The priority of counter-terrorism continued to rise. During 1987–8 the Security Service produced 1,100 terrorist threat assessments as compared with 750 in the previous year, but believed that, because of lack of resources, this still fell short 'of what we would wish by way of background research'. In 1988 FX was renamed G Branch, a minor administrative change which, however, emphasized the increased status of counter-terrorism within the Security Service and removed the confusion caused by the fact that both F and FX Branches previously had F sections.[44] The first Director G, Stella Rimington, was also the first woman to become a Security Service director.[45] G Branch won some support within senior management for its belief that it needed more resources to deal with the growing terrorist threat. Director P noted in September 1988: 'If we are not to seriously reduce the effort of our management reforms, the increase in terrorism means we must *EITHER* increase our resources *OR* cut back on non-terrorist intelligence activity.'[46]

Three months later came the most homicidal terrorist attack ever to take place in Britain. On the evening of 21 December 1988 a PanAm Boeing 747, flight PA 103 en route to New York, crashed on the Scottish town of Lockerbie, killing all 259 passengers and crew as well as eleven people on the ground. Though most of the passengers had boarded at Heathrow, over thirty had started their journey in Frankfurt on a Boeing 727 which connected with the 747 and bore the same flight number; other passengers transferred from other flights and joined PA 103 at either Frankfurt or Heathrow.[47] Surveys of the wreckage and analysis of information from the air-traffic control radar recordings and the aircraft's flight recorders showed that PA 103 suffered catastrophic damage while cruising at 31,000 feet, breaking up as it fell to the ground.[48] A bomb attack was immediately suspected. After a hunt for debris over an area of some 800 square miles stretching to the east coast of Scotland, detailed forensic examination found traces of explosive in a metal luggage container. Further painstaking forensic and intelligence investigation eventually identified the suitcase which had contained the bomb. The bodies and body parts strewn for many miles around Lockerbie had also to be identified, then linked to particular items of baggage. The Service sent several officers to join the intelligence cell at Lockerbie run by the Strathclyde police. With support from Service headquarters, they acted as the link between the front-line investigators on the scene and the foreign security and intelligence agencies whose assistance proved of crucial importance in pinning down responsibility for the attack. Most of the immensely difficult and harrowing investigation into the disaster would have proved impossible had the explosion occurred over the Atlantic. The fact that PA 103 was brought down over land was an accidental by-product of the weather conditions. The flight to New York from Heathrow frequently took other routes which would have left the aircraft wreckage on the seabed at a depth which would probably have made recovery of the flight recorder and forensic examination impossible. Chance as well as good intelligence thus played a crucial part in the resolution of the case.

Numerous time-consuming (and frequently time-wasting) lines of inquiry had to be followed up, many of them involving individual passengers who were either on the plane or had left it at London. One of a series of misleading leads which received extensive publicity was a telephone call to the US embassy in Helsinki two weeks before the crash, threatening an attack on an unspecified PanAm flight. Though some media reports seized on this as an important clue, it was in reality only one of a series of similar calls which had been fully investigated by the Finnish authorities, who correctly concluded that the calls were the result of a personal vendetta and had nothing to do with the attack on PA 103. Later reinvestigation confirmed this assessment.[49]

Though claims of responsibility for the attack were quickly made by a series of terrorist organizations and denials issued by others, initial suspicions focused on a breakaway group from the Popular Front for the Liberation of Palestine, the PFLP–GC based in Syria, a number of whose members had been arrested in Germany in late October 1988 with an explosive device including a barometric detonator. Although the possibility of Libyan (or Iranian) involvement was considered,[50] it was not at first thought very likely. No significant hard evidence pointed towards Libya until some fragments of clothing classed as 'category one blast-damaged', and therefore from inside the case containing the bomb, were eventually traced to an outlet in Malta, where the shopkeeper recalled selling the clothing to a man resembling a suspected Libyan intelligence officer, Abdelbaset Ali Mohmed Al Megrahi.[51] Subsequent analysis of airport baggage-handling showed that the case containing the bomb was not first loaded at Heathrow but had joined PA 103 from the connecting flight from Frankfurt, where records suggested that in all probability one item of luggage had been loaded on to the aircraft from a flight out of Malta. Some months later a tiny fragment of electronic printed circuit board found by a forensic scientist in one of the charred pieces of clothing – the neckband of a shirt – was identified by the Service's main explosives and weapons expert as coming from a long-delay Swiss-manufactured timing mechanism. Other evidence implicated Libyan intelligence and a Libyan Airlines representative in the operation to put the suitcase containing the bomb on the flight from Malta.[52]

Though no one could have predicted it at the time, the Lockerbie tragedy marked the climax of Libyan terrorism against Western targets rather than the first stage in a new and particularly lethal campaign. Tired of his status as an international pariah, Qaddafi began to show signs of a desire to distance himself from his terrorist past.[53] After lengthy and wearisome negotiations between Britain and Libya, Al Megrahi and another alleged Libyan intelligence officer, Lamen Khalifa Fhimah, were tried by a Scottish court sitting in the Netherlands for their part in the Lockerbie disaster. In January 2001 Al Megrahi was convicted and sentenced to life imprisonment. Fhimah was acquitted. Without the Security Service's analysis of intelligence leads and use of its international liaison contacts, there would have been insufficient evidence to convict Al Megrahi.[54]

International liaison was also crucial to the Security Service's counter-PIRA operations. In 1988 G5 officers made more than fifty liaison visits lasting a total of 250 days, to nine different European security and intelligence services; G5 reported at the end of the year: 'Most if not all of these liaisons have stated that they look to the Security Service to take a lead on Irish terrorist matters and to play a co-ordinating role in determining the response to specific threats.'[55]

Following the failure of their Gibraltar operation, the Provisionals sought to demonstrate their continued ability to strike at British targets on the continent. ASUs living under cover in holiday cottages set out to reconnoitre and attack British bases and military personnel in the Netherlands, Germany and Belgium. In a two-and-a-half-year continental campaign beginning in May 1988 PIRA killed eight British servicemen and members of service families, but in the same campaign fifteen ASU members were arrested or shot dead.[56] 'In the end', Director G (Stella Rimington) wrote later, 'the Provisional IRA decided that the losses they were sustaining made their European operations not worth the cost . . .'[57] The Provisionals also suffered the humiliation of having to issue public apologies for several bungled attacks, among them the killing in May 1990 in the Dutch town of Roermond of two Australian tourists.[58] For the Security Service, PIRA's largely unsuccessful continental campaign had the great advantage of strengthening its collaboration with other European security and intelligence services. Stephen Lander, then G5, wrote in 1990:

Since 1988, PIRA has come to dominate the exchanges of terrorist intelligence between the security intelligence services in the centre of Western Europe. Both French services, the Belgians, the Dutch, the Danes and the Germans now all have staff working full time on PIRA, while on the periphery, the Portuguese, Spanish, Italians, Austrians, Swedes and Norwegians devote resources to PIRA work when approached for help . . . In all this work, European services work closely with the Security Service.[59]

Improved collaboration between the Security Service and the FBI[60] led to a major success at the end of the decade against PIRA high-tech arms procurement in the United States. In 1989 the FBI arrested Richard Clark Johnson, an expert in electronic counter-measures with top-secret clearance, employed by a major US defence contractor; Martin Peter Quigley, an Irish electronics expert employed by a computer software company in Philadelphia; Christina Leigh Reid, a computer technician from California; and Gerald Hoy, a computer science lecturer in Philadelphia.[61] They were later sentenced to prison terms of, respectively, ten years, eight years, forty-one months and two years for conspiracy to violate federal arms export controls. Johnson, the first to be investigated, was believed by the Security Service to have been involved with PIRA since 1978. The first breakthrough in the long investigation which culminated in the convictions came as a result of the efforts orchestrated by the Security Service's main arms expert to track PIRA weapons components back to source. In 1984 the FX401 tone frequency switch used by the PIRA Engineering Department to protect its radio-controlled bombs from counter-measures by the security forces was traced back to an English manufacturer. An investigation by MPSB at the request of the Security Service revealed that one order of fifty switches had been sent, via the manufacturer's US subsidiary, to Richard Clark Johnson in California.[62] That the investigation continued for the next five years, despite numerous difficulties in obtaining the evidence necessary for a successful prosecution, was due largely to the persistence of the Service's main arms expert.[63]

Johnson was arrested in the car park of his current employer, Mitre Corporation. On the morning of 12 July 1989 he looked out of his office window, saw two men tampering with his car and rushed downstairs to confront them. The men turned out to be FBI agents examining the car.[64] A possibly over-dramatized account of what happened next was relayed to Head Office by SLO Washington. The FBI officer supervising the agents was reported to have been told by his field office: 'Either you arrest the two FBI agents interfering with the car or you arrest Johnson.' Having decided, without much difficulty, on the second option, the FBI officer was said to have informed Johnson, 'Only in America do you interrupt two men breaking into your car and find that you are the one who is arrested!'[65] Following the conviction of Johnson, Quigley, Reid and Hoy a year later, the FBI thanked the Service for its assistance in a prolonged investigation whose 'successful prosecution in the US was dependent on an outstanding international cooperative effort'.[66] 'This success', it believed, 'has significantly damaged PIRA's capability to produce new types of remote controlled bombs, and has completely disrupted a programme to develop anti-aircraft rockets.'[67]

The series of operational successes achieved by MI5 and the security forces against PIRA in the late 1980s did not, however, bring them within sight of victory. As the Security Service's Legal Adviser reluctantly acknowledged, the Provisionals' leadership was effectively beyond reach of the law because of the near-impossibility of obtaining enough usable evidence for a successful prosecution:

The sum of the intelligence gathered about Irish terrorism has identified all the leaders, the majority of the activists and details of many of their operations. If this intelligence were converted into evidence it should act as an effective deterrent by enabling many successful prosecutions. Yet in twenty years of terrorism, the upper terrorist echelons have become a bedrock, the stability of which nurtures the ranks, draws recruits and attracts steady financing.[68]

At the end of the Thatcher era there was clear evidence that the Provisionals were embarking on a new mainland campaign. During the spring and summer of 1990 PIRA was responsible for fifteen (mostly small-scale) mainland bomb attacks and shootings.[69] The best-known fatality was Ian Gow, Conservative MP for Eastbourne, who was killed on 30 July by a bomb as he started his car in the driveway of his house. Gow was probably chosen as a target because he was both a vociferous, long-standing critic of PIRA and a friend of Margaret Thatcher. The Prime Minister felt 'deep personal grief' at his death: 'I could not help thinking . . . that my daughter Carol had travelled with Ian in his car the previous weekend to take the Gows' dog out for a walk: it might have been her too.'[70] On 18 September Air Chief Marshal Sir Peter Terry, who had been governor of Gibraltar during Operation FLAVIUS, was shot and wounded at his home in Staffordshire. Next day Mrs Thatcher's private secretary, Charles Powell, wrote to the Home Office:

The Prime Minister is most exercised about the recent increases in PIRA attacks or attempted attacks on the mainland, which seem to indicate both a stepping up of their campaign and a change in tactics with greater emphasis on the use of firearms. She thinks that Ministers need to examine urgently whether existing measures, both to protect those who are vulnerable, to apprehend those responsible and to deter further attacks, are adequate.[71]

Mrs Thatcher dismissed the Home Office response[72] as 'wet' and complacent.[73] At a meeting with ministers, the DG and the Commissioner of the Met on 25 October, a month before her resignation, a clearly dissatisfied Prime Minister 'said that the steps which had been taken to investigate and counter PIRA activities in mainland Britain had not been sufficient'.[74]

The future DG Stephen Lander had argued for some time that, in dealing with the threat from PIRA, the MPSB were hampered by their 'natural wish to pursue criminals rather than to obtain information': 'The police should leave us to do the intelligence work while they, in the form of SO13 [Anti-Terrorism Branch], should do what they are internationally respected for, the after-crime investigations.'[75] The Service leadership sympathized with Lander's argument but could not bring itself to try to wrest the lead intelligence role on the mainland from the MPSB. The DDG (Operations), Julian Faux, minuted to the DG, Sir Patrick Walker, in January 1990:

We have consistently over the last 18 months or so told the Home Office about our unease concerning the ability of MPSB to effectively investigate the PIRA threat on the mainland, and to analyse the intelligence of that threat. At the same time we have made it clear that we did not wish to unnecessarily disturb our improving relations with MPSB on the Irish question.[76]

For the Service to take over the lead role was 'perhaps the ideal solution but totally impractical at the present time because we do not have the resources'.[77] Walker agreed, telling the cabinet secretary, Sir Robin Butler, that 'The Service accepted that the MPSB were in the lead and should remain in the lead on the mainland.'[78]

Given the decline of the Cold War, the decreasing significance of subversion and the growing threat of terrorism, Sir Tony Duff came to the conclusion while DG that both the Security Service and Whitehall needed to reassess the priorities of its work in protective security. In December 1986 Duff set out the case for a root-and-branch review of vetting in a letter to the cabinet secretary, Sir Robert Armstrong. He reported that in 1985 the Service had handled over 327,000 vetting inquiries, making about 700,000 individual checks in its records. The total number of man-hours devoted to the process came to sixty-four years. Only in 913 cases (0.28 per cent of those submitted to it) had the Service found security concerns.[79] A Cabinet Office review, completed in November 1988, though more restricted than Duff had hoped, accepted the need, 'in the light of the diminishing threat from subversion and the increasing threat from terrorism', to 'ensure that the effort devoted to security vetting is commensurate with the threat'. Vetting, previously covert, was to be replaced by an overt two-tier system: a reliability check for access to confidential material and positive vetting for access to secret information. A new vetting category, counter-terrorist checking (CTC), was introduced for individuals not cleared for classified material who had access to unclassified targeting or other information of interest to terrorists, or who made regular, unescorted visits to the MoD and other likely terrorist targets. The fact that, under the new clearance system, finally approved in 1990, the Security Service was not involved in reliability checks dramatically decreased its workload: from 360,000 vetting inquiries in 1990 to about 250,000 in 1991. A Home Office memorandum noted, almost nostalgically, in 1990:

The most striking change is that almost 100 bodies which fell within the old criteria for checking against Security Service records now fall outside the criteria ... Old friends who thus appear no more include the National Bus Company, the Rural Development Commission, the Sports Council and the Agricultural and Food Research Council.[80]

11

The Origins of the Security Service Act

Intelligence was the last taboo of British politics. For the Security Service's first seventy years it was protected from public gaze and parliamentary scrutiny by a bipartisan consensus built around two dubious constitutional principles. The first was that intelligence was wholly undiscussable in public – even in parliament. As the Foreign Secretary, Sir Austen Chamberlain, told the Commons in 1924: 'It is of the essence of a Secret Service that it must be secret, and if you once begin disclosure it is perfectly obvious to me as to hon. members opposite that there is no longer any Secret Service and that you must do without it.'[1] The inflation of the common-sense doctrine that all intelligence operations require secrecy into the bizarre requirement that intelligence must never be mentioned at all originated not as carefully considered policy but as an inherited taboo, akin to the Victorian belief that civilized life might crumble if sex were mentioned in public. In 1985 Sir Michael Howard, one of the official historians of wartime intelligence, explained the traditional British view of intelligence thus:

In Britain the activities of the intelligence and security services have always been regarded in much the same light as intra-marital sex. Everyone knows that it goes on and is quite content that it should, but to speak, write or ask questions about it is regarded as extremely bad form. So far as official government policy is concerned, the British security and intelligence services do not exist. Enemy agents are found under gooseberry bushes and intelligence is brought by the storks.[2]

It followed from the storks-and-gooseberry-bush tradition that the mysteries of intelligence must be left entirely to the grown-ups (the agencies and the government) and that the children (parliament and the public) must not meddle in them. The second constitutional doctrine which underpinned the traditional British view of intelligence was thus that parliament must entirely abdicate its powers in this field to the executive.

The most astonishing thing about these two dubious doctrines is that there was no serious challenge to them until the 1980s. They were defended after his retirement even by Harold Wilson, despite his fears of a Security Service plot against him.[3] In 1977, as these fears were reaching their peak, he published his distillation of the constitutional wisdom of the ages in a volume grandly entitled *The Governance of Britain*. The chapter on 'The Prime Minister and National Security' may be the shortest ever written by a British politician. It is barely a page long and begins by quoting approvingly Macmillan's warning to the Commons after Philby's defection in 1963: 'It is dangerous and bad for our general national interest to discuss these matters.' Wilson concluded his mini-chapter thus:

The prime minister is occasionally questioned on [security] matters arising out of his responsibility. His answers may be regarded as uniformly uninformative.

There is no further information that can usefully or properly be added before bringing this Chapter to an end.[4]

The Callaghan government, despite the Prime Minister's private dissatisfaction with the management of the Security Service,[5] was an equally stout defender of intelligence storks and gooseberry bushes. 'Parliament', it declared, 'accepts that accountability must be to Ministers and trusts Ministers to discharge that responsibility faithfully.'[6]

During the Thatcher decade, a series of public controversies involving the intelligence services gradually eroded the all-party storks-and-gooseberry-bush consensus, which was still intact when the Conservatives returned to power in 1979. The unmasking of Sir Anthony Blunt as the Fourth Man by Mrs Thatcher in the Commons shortly afterwards forced the government to concede for the first time a parliamentary debate on security of the kind previously denounced by Macmillan and Wilson as 'dangerous and bad for our general national interest'. After the first publication of the sensational claim that Sir Roger Hollis had been a Soviet mole in Chapman Pincher's *Their Trade is Treachery* in 1981, Mrs Thatcher, to her visible dismay, was forced to breach the traditional taboo once again and make another statement to the Commons, this time to declare Hollis innocent. Further government statements followed the conviction of Geoffrey Prime, formerly of GCHQ, in 1982 and of Michael Bettaney of the Security Service in 1984. While periodically disregarding Harold Wilson's dictum that the Prime Minister's remarks to parliament on security and intelligence should be as rare as possible and 'uniformly uninformative', Mrs Thatcher none the less insisted that the principle remained intact. She told the Commons in November 1986: 'I repeat: the practice and the custom of all prime ministers of all parties is to adhere to the normal rule of not commenting on security matters.'

The Falklands conflict in 1982 led to a further breach of the old intelligence taboos. Faced with Opposition charges that the government had ignored intelligence warnings of an Argentinian invasion, the government appointed a commission of six Privy Counsellors (two of them Labour politicians), headed by Lord Franks, to carry out the 'Falkland Islands Review'. The Prime Minister did not do so willingly. According to David Owen, 'It was like dragging teeth out of her to agree to the Franks enquiry.' Mrs Thatcher's reluctance was understandable. For by establishing the Franks Committee she virtually conceded in practice the principle of an oversight committee for the intelligence community which she continued to resist. The Committee was given unrestricted access to relevant intelligence files and personnel. Having accepted the Franks Committee's findings on the Falklands conflict and its recommendations on the joint intelligence system in 1983, the Thatcher government could scarcely argue credibly that a standing committee of similar structure (such as the Intelligence and Security Committee set up a decade later) would be unworkable. It did, however, argue precisely that.[7] On intelligence accountability, as on statements to parliament, Whitehall sought to preserve a status quo which had already been breached. At a meeting on 23 February 1983, chaired by the Intelligence Co-ordinator (and future DG), Sir Antony Duff, to discuss the case for and against changing the current system of oversight and accountability:

Sir Antony Acland [PUS at the FCO] began by saying that his own view and that of the Foreign and Commonwealth Secretary was that there was no need to change the present policy on accountability and oversight unless there was very strong Parliamentary pressure to do so and that it was desirable to resist the attempt by various Select Committees to encroach in this area. This was a matter of political judgment but both the Foreign and Commonwealth Secretary and the Chief Whip considered that the present position could be maintained.[8]

The case for a body on the lines of the future Intelligence and Security Committee was thus on the political agenda for the first time (though the model then most frequently suggested was a parliamentary select committee). When Christopher Andrew had suggested the idea in 1977, it had been received in Whitehall, according to Peter Hennessy in The Times, with all the enthusiasm normally reserved for insulting references to the Royal Family. By 1983, however, it was Party policy for both Labour and the Liberal–SDP Alliance.

A third area in which the intelligence taboos suffered significant erosion during the first two Thatcher governments concerned their use of the

Security Commission. Previous administrations had used it only to report on security breaches within Whitehall and the armed services, including those associated with sexual irregularities by ministers. Between 1982 and 1985, however, the Commission produced, at government request, four major reports on the intelligence community reviewing security procedures both in the community as a whole and individually in GCHQ, the Defence Intelligence Staff and the Security Service after the convictions of, respectively, Geoffrey Prime, Philip Aldridge and Michael Bettaney. A summary of the first report's recommendations and the bulk of the other three reports were published. They pulled few punches. Though reassuring as regards operational effectiveness, the 1985 report on the Security Service called for 'a thorough-going re-examination of the personnel management services' – an unprecedented official public criticism of the running of the Service.[9]

The most influential attack on the traditional taboos came, however, from the courts. By the mid-1980s British juries were reluctant to convict under the old discredited Official Secrets legislation. The government also came under pressure from the European Court of Human Rights. In 1984 the Court upheld a complaint about the tapping of his phone by a British businessman, James Malone, who had been acquitted on a charge of receiving stolen goods. Article 8 of the Human Rights Convention requires respect for the privacy of citizens' private and family lives, homes and correspondence, but recognizes the right of public authorities, 'in accordance with the law', to infringe these rights on specified grounds which include 'the interests of national security' and 'the prevention of disorder or crime'. Since, however, telephone tapping in Britain was not 'prescribed by law', the Court found that Article 8 had been contravened. That judgment led directly to the 1985 Interception of Communications Act, which provided for a commissioner to monitor warrants for telephone tapping and a tribunal to investigate complaints.[10]

During the passage of the Act government spokesmen claimed that it reflected the cabinet's desire for openness and accountability in the use of the HOWs. The shadow Home Secretary, Gerald Kaufman, attacked these claims as 'effrontery':

The Government . . . have been dragged kicking and screaming all the way. They would have continued to resist if it had not been for the Malone case. It was Mr. James Malone who, when tried for dishonestly handling stolen goods, discovered that his telephone had been tapped by the police. It was he who brought a High Court action against the Metropolitan police. It was he who, even though he lost the case, heard the judge, Sir Robert Megarry, state in court that telephone tapping is a subject that cries out for legislation, who took his case to the European court and who then, almost a year ago, saw the House of Lords pass, against the Government's wishes, a Labour amendment to the Telecommunications Bill placing controls on interception. That is why the Government is legislating. It is not because they want to; it is because they have to.[11]

There was a certain amount of 'effrontery' on Opposition benches too from former Labour ministers who protested against the breadth of the powers for the interception of communications contained in the Act. The Home Secretary, Leon Brittan, reminded them that HOWs under Labour governments had operated under 'precisely the same criteria'. The Act did not confer 'any additional powers whatsoever', but simply provided, 'for the first time, a clear and comprehensive statutory framework for the interception of communications'.[12]

Media attacks on telephone tapping by the Security Service continued. In the 20/20 Vision television documentary 'MI5's Official Secrets', broadcast on Channel 4 just prior to the Commons debate on the Interception of Communications Bill, the former Security Service officer Cathy Massiter claimed that some prominent members of the peace movement and trade unions were under MI5 surveillance. Massiter, whose claims were supplemented by those of an anonymous, retired Service secretary, was clearly in breach of Section 2 of the Official Secrets Act. Both Massiter and the secretary were prohibited by the terms of their employment and declarations they had signed on their retirement from disclosing any information they had acquired while working for the Service. After an advance viewing on 20 February 1985, the Independent Broadcasting Authority decided, on the advice of its lawyers, to stop the programme being transmitted until it became clear whether or not the government intended to prosecute Massiter or the producers. In the event, the Attorney General, Sir Michael Havers, decided there was to be no prosecution, almost certainly chiefly because of the belief after the trial earlier in February of the MoD official Clive Ponting that, however clear the law, a jury would not convict. So discredited had Section 2 of the Official Secrets Act become that, despite the fact that Ponting admitted leaking confidential documents on the Falklands conflict to Tam Dalyell MP and a near instruction from the judge to convict, the jury returned a verdict of not guilty.[13]

The delay in broadcasting 'MI5's Official Secrets' merely generated further publicity for it. Within hours of the IBA's decision to stop transmission on 20 February, videos of the programme were being shown to journalists at a London hotel and to MPs at the House of Commons.

Copies of the video were marketed by Richard Branson under the Virgin label with the title *MI5's Official Secrets – The Programme That Couldn't Be Shown*, and a lengthy extract from the script was published in the *Guardian*. On 6 March, the day after the announcement that there was to be no prosecution, the IBA lifted the ban on the programme, which was transmitted on the 8th. The government response to Cathy Massiter's televised charges against the Security Service was to ask the chairman of the Security Commission, Lord Bridge of Harwich, to investigate whether the Service had obtained the necessary warrants for telechecks and whether the criteria for phone tapping were being complied with. The investigation, like the rest of the Massiter affair, was a public relations disaster. Lord Bridge began his inquiry on 28 February and, despite sitting as a judge in the House of Lords for two days during the inquiry, reported on 6 March that all was well and that there had been no wrongdoing by either government or Security Service. In view of the fact that 6,129 HOWs had been issued over the previous fifteen years, the speed of his conclusion that the regulations were being fully observed inspired widespread scepticism. The *Daily Telegraph* described Lord Bridge's report as 'hasty and bland', 'the Bench's answer to fast food, a juridical Big Mac'. The former Home Secretary Roy Jenkins said that Lord Bridge had been made to appear a 'poodle of the executive'.[14]

Many Opposition MPs believed that the Security Service had become a political tool of the right. Gerald Kaufman charged in the Commons on 12 March that MI5 had 'deliberately and wrongfully classified Joan Ruddock, the chairman of CND, as a subversive so that they could open a file on her' – the first time a shadow Home Secretary had ever made so serious a public charge against the Security Service. The charge, to which the government made no substantive response, was mistaken. What concerned the Service was not an erroneous belief that Ruddock was subversive but her meetings with a Soviet journalist who, though she did not know it, was a KGB officer.[15] Some Labour backbenchers made even fiercer criticisms than Kaufman. David Winnick thought it 'quite likely that MI5 is out of control', while Ian Mikardo claimed that Britain was 'catching up fast' with the Soviet Union in its use of state repression.[16] Mikardo's charges of Soviet-style repression were particularly ironic in view of intelligence from Gordievsky that prior to 1967 he had been a Soviet agent.[17]

Sir Antony Duff, who became DG soon after the passage of the Interception of Communications Act, became convinced that further legislation was needed. Though telephone and postal interception were legislated for under the Act, other eavesdropping had been omitted because any mention

65. An A4 surveillance photograph of the KGB officer Oleg Gordievsky taken on 4 November 1982, while he was stationed at the London residency; like most of MI5, the photographer was unaware that Gordievsky was a British agent.

66. In 1983 Gordievsky revealed that a Security Service officer, later discovered to be Michael Bettaney, had pushed top-secret material through the letter-box of the KGB resident Arkadi Guk (shown here with his wife), who mistakenly believed MI5 was trying to trap him and did not reply to Bettaney's offer of more intelligence.

67. Surveillance photograph of the last Soviet Bloc illegal discovered in Britain during the Cold War: Václav Jelínek of the Czech StB, who had taken the identity of a Dutch citizen, Erwin Van Haarlem.

68. A Special Branch raid on Jelínek's flat on 2 April 1988 caught him sitting on a stool in the kitchen, taking down a coded message from Prague through an earphone attached to his radio. He leapt to his feet, knocking over the stool and dropping the earphone, from which the StB transmission was clearly audible.

69. On 7 February 1991 a mortar, fired from a white Ford Transit van parked by a PIRA active service unit in Horse Guards Avenue at the junction with Whitehall, exploded on the Downing Street lawn in the middle of a cabinet meeting. The Prime Minister, John Major, was told that, if the mortar had landed 10 feet closer to the Cabinet Room, 'half the Cabinet could have been killed'.

70. Surveillance of Operation AIRLINES in July 1996: Donal Gannon (PARADISE NEWS, *left*) and Gerard Hanratty (TULIP STEM) preparing for a foiled PIRA attack on the electricity supply of Greater London.

71. An A4 surveillance photograph of Siobhan O'Hanlon, an IRA explosives expert, devout Catholic and committed feminist, reconnoitring Gibraltar in February 1988 in preparation for a bomb attack on the British garrison during the changing of the guard ceremony (72.*below*). While in Spain on 24 February O'Hanlon noticed local surveillance, returned to Northern Ireland and took no further part in the operation. The three members of the IRA active service unit who continued with the operation were shot dead in Gibraltar on 6 March.

73. (*left*) In July 2000 Operation LARGE uncovered the first Islamist bomb factory to be detected in Britain. Moinul Abedin, codenamed PIVOTING DANCER (shown here in an A4 surveillance photo), was later sentenced to twenty years' imprisonment.

74. (*below*) In 2003–4 Operation CREVICE uncovered the first bomb plot by British Islamists against British targets since 9/11. This A4 surveillance photo, taken at Heathrow on 20 February 2004, shows the leading British plotter, Omar Khyam (*right*), meeting the Canadian Islamist extremist Mohammed Momin Khawaja, from whom he hoped to obtain electronic bomb-triggers.

75. (*left*) Surveillance photo of Dhiren Barot, the chief plotter in Operation RHYME in 2004, later sentenced to a minimum life sentence of thirty years in prison. Believed to have been handpicked by Khalid Sheikh Mohammed, the chief Al Qaida planner behind 9/11, Barot's ultimate aim was to explode a radioactive dirty bomb, but he admitted that for the moment he lacked the contacts necessary to construct one.

76. (*right*) As on 7/7, MI5 had no advance warning of the failed London suicide bomb attacks on 21 July 2005. Its intelligence, however, contributed to the arrests of the four would-be suicide bombers. Muktah Said Ibrahim (*left*) and Ramzi Mohammed were seen live on television emerging in their underpants from Mohammed's London flat.

77. (*right*) Yassin Hassan Omar was arrested in Birmingham, dressed in a burka. Hussein Osman was later tracked down in Rome.

78. (*below*) A photograph used in evidence at their trial showing Ramzi Mohammed (*left*) and Yassin Omar (*hooded, right*) at a military-style training camp in Cumbria, 2004.

79. (*left*) Surveillance photograph of Dr Bilal Abdulla, a twenty-six-year-old doctor at the Royal Alexandra Hospital, Paisley, shopping for a gas canister to use in bomb attacks in 2007.

80. (*below*) Gas canister with detonator and nails (to increase injuries) left in a car by Abdulla and his associate, Kafeel Ahmed, in preparation for attacks on a London nightclub and other targets. Abdulla was arrested after an unsuccessful attack on Glasgow airport and sentenced in December 2008 to life imprisonment with a minimum of thirty-two years.

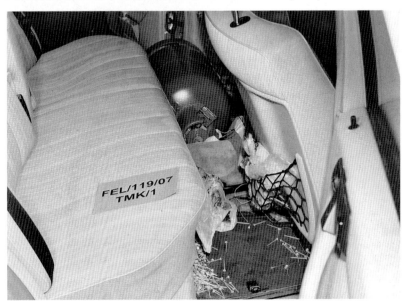

81. A night-time training exercise for covert entry into a target building.

82. The Director General, Jonathan Evans, in the Intelligence Operations Centre at Security Service headquarters in May 2009.

of it was thought too politically sensitive by the government. Mrs Thatcher and some of her ministers initially 'took the view, not altogether surprisingly, that setting out to legislate to allow the secret state to break into people's property for the purpose of planting microphones to overhear their conversations would cause a terrible furore and do the government no good at all'. Following the extensive publicity given to Peter Wright's boast in *Spycatcher* that 'we bugged and burgled our way across London at the state's bequest, while pompous, bowler-hatted civil servants looked the other way', Stella Rimington recalls that Duff suspended operations which required 'intrusion on property': 'The result was a sudden loss of intelligence, just at a time when terrorist and other hostile activity was at its peak.'[18] In fact, existing eavesdropping operations continued but it became more difficult, and often required several months, to obtain Home Office approval for further operations. Duff used the legal uncertainties over eavesdropping to press the case for a Security Service Act to provide a statutory basis for the Service itself as well as for its intrusions on property.[19]

The case for a Security Service Act was further strengthened by the judgment of the European Court of Human Rights in the case brought by Torsten Leander, a Swedish Marxist who had been sacked from the Karlskrona Naval Museum in 1979. Because the Museum was next to a large naval base, the Swedish security police, the Säpo, concluded that Leander was a security risk and informed his employer. The Säpo was cleared of any wrongdoing under Articles 8 (respect of privacy) and 10 (freedom of conscience) of the Human Rights Convention. The Court found greater difficulty in deciding whether there had been a breach of Leander's rights under Article 13 (denial of an effective remedy), since he had no means of redress under Swedish law. In March 1987, it decided by seven votes to five that there had been no transgression. The Court, however, concluded in its summing up:

The expression 'in accordance with the law' in paragraph 2 of Article 8 requires, to begin with, that the interference [with human rights] must have some basis in domestic law. Compliance with domestic law, however, does not suffice: the law in question must be accessible to the individual concerned and its consequences for him must also be foreseeable (see, *mutatis mutandis*, the Malone judgment of 2 August 1984 . . .).[20]

All security services were thus held to require a statutory basis, failing which the Court would not recognize the state's power to violate citizens' personal privacy in the interests of national security. The law regulating the work of security services had to be 'sufficiently clear in its terms to give an adequate indication as to the circumstances in which and the conditions on which the public authorities are empowered to resort to this kind of secret and potentially dangerous interference with private life'. Citizens must also have 'adequate protection against arbitrary interference':[21] 'In view of the risk that a system of secret surveillance for the protection of national security poses of undermining or even destroying democracy on the ground of defending it, the Court must be satisfied that there exist adequate and effective guarantees against abuse.'[22]

Though the Leander case made a deep impression on the Security Service's Legal Adviser Bernard Sheldon and his team, it was little noticed by the media and most politicians. By contrast, the prolonged litigation deriving from the government's misjudged attempts to prevent the publication of Peter Wright's memoirs made front-page news. Wright had retired in 1976 embittered both by resentment over the fact that his pension took no account of his fifteen years' employment by the Admiralty before joining the Security Service and by the fact that his conspiracy theories of Soviet penetration were no longer treated seriously. Short of working capital for the stud farm in Tasmania to which he had retired, Wright wrote to his friend, the wartime MI5 officer Lord (Victor) Rothschild, who warned the DG that Wright was thinking of writing his memoirs. He wrote again to Rothschild in 1980, telling him that he had thought of a way of publishing and avoiding prosecution:

It is not the Official Secrets Act that concerns me. With all the books written it would be very difficult to make it stick. But I was made to sign a document when I retired, never to disclose anything I knew as a result of my employment, whether classified or not. I can avoid action against me by staying in Australia and never returning to my beloved England.

Instead of dissuading Wright, Rothschild encouraged him. Though his motives remain difficult to fathom, they included a desire for a written statement by Wright exonerating him and his wife from whispered rumours that they had been Soviet spies. He may also have concluded that public revelation of the sensational charges against Sir Roger Hollis, of whose innocence he had no doubt, would distract attention from the innuendoes accusing him of involvement with the KGB, with which he had become obsessed. In August 1980, without telling the Security Service, Rothschild sent Wright a return air ticket from Tasmania to London. He arrived bearing a three-page testimonial and a ten-chapter typescript on Soviet penetration dramatically entitled 'The Cancer in our Midst'. Having devised a plan for a more readable version of the book to be produced by an author who would make no mention of Wright but share the proceeds with him, Rothschild introduced him to Britain's best-known spy-writer, Chapman Pincher, who was amazed by Wright's 'willingness to tell me secrets for publication on a scale which I knew to be unprecedented in the entire history of the secret services'. The result, in March 1981, was Pincher's rapidly written book, *Their Trade is Treachery*, devoted chiefly to the case against Hollis. As Rothschild's biographer observes, 'So little guilt did Victor feel in procuring that colossal breach of security that he continued to address letters to *The Times* deploring the steady leak of classified documents to the press.'[23]

Wright first informed the Security Service that he was writing a memoir in June 1981 when he reported an approach by a British writer seeking information on Hollis and Blunt. He said that he had told the writer that 'for my own satisfaction and for the record, I am writing an accurate history of what happened but that it would not be published in my life-time'.[24] Wright failed to mention, however, that he had already secretly collaborated with Pincher on *Their Trade is Treachery*. Director B (John Allen) replied with what was intended as an 'unambiguous letter of warning': 'To avoid any uncertainty, I must tell you that your obligation not to make such a record, whether for publication or not, remains unchanged. I have little doubt that the authorities here would respond to a breach of your obligation by invoking any available remedy, under civil as well as criminal law.'[25]

On 16 July 1984 Wright appeared in a Granada *World in Action* tele-vision documentary on MI5 and for the first time made public his allega-tions that Hollis was a Soviet spy. Press reports revealed that he was writing a book, eventually entitled *Spycatcher*; his ghost-writer was to be the *World in Action* producer Paul Greengrass. Sir Robert Armstrong sent an outraged letter to the DG, Sir John Jones, written in his usual elegant hand:

I hope you are reviewing the possibility of discontinuing the payment of Peter Wright's pension. His contribution to the World in Action programme on 16 July was self-evidently in flagrant breach of his obligations under the Official Secrets Act ... He is, moreover, in open and defiant breach of trust on which your service depends: we have surely to consider the effect on others if he escapes scot free.[26]

The DG replied, after taking legal advice, that he did not believe Wright's pension could be withheld but wondered, following the precedent set by stripping Blunt of his knighthood, 'if there is any way in which HMG's displeasure might be shown by depriving [Wright] of the CBE which he was awarded in the 1972 New Year Honours'.[27] Armstrong told Mrs Thatcher that, regrettably, no such action was possible: 'Mr Wright would present himself as a[n] aged patriot striving to do his duty and protect his country, and victimised for his pains.'[28] The correspondence between Armstrong and Jones vividly reflects both fury at Wright's betrayal and frustration at their inability to take action against him.

The press reported on 2 August 1984 that the Attorney General, in consultation with the Director of Public Prosecutions, had decided to prosecute Wright for unauthorized disclosure if (which was doubtless considered unlikely) he returned to the UK.[29] Bernard Sheldon initially hoped to prevent publication by warning off potential publishers. Wright's literary agent, Anthony Sheil, was successfully identified,[30] and two publishers lost interest in Wright's memoirs after being warned off. On succeeding Jones as DG in the spring of 1985, Sir Antony Duff approved a similar attempt to warn off Heinemann, the third publisher to enter the *Spycatcher* arena.[31] Heinemann, however, sought to avoid an injunction preventing publication by transferring the book to their Australian subsidiary. On 17 June 1985 Sir Robert Armstrong chaired a meeting attended by, among others, 'C' (Sir Colin Figures), the DDG (Cecil Shipp) and Sheldon to consider how to proceed. The Treasury Solicitor, John Bailey, said there was 'some reason to hope that an action in Australia might be successful':

He cited the judgment in the Fairfax case where the court had said it would be prepared to grant an injunction if it could be proved that disclosure would be inimical to the public interest . . . Summing up, Sir Robert Armstrong said that there was general agreement that legal action should be taken, both in Australia and the United Kingdom, if there was a reasonable chance that it would be successful, both to prevent the damage that would be caused by this particular book and to deter others.[32]

As the action to prevent publication proceeded, however, Armstrong's condition that there must be 'a reasonable chance that it would be successful' tended to be lost sight of in Whitehall. In Stella Rimington's view, 'It was decided to pursue the book through every possible legal channel, whether there was any hope of success or not.'[33]

In September 1985, the Attorney General, Sir Michael Havers, acting in the name of the British government, began proceedings in Australia against Wright and Heinemann Australia, seeking an injunction to prevent publication on the grounds that Wright was in breach of his duty of confidentiality to the Crown. In order to avoid having either to confirm or to deny the accuracy of any of Wright's allegations, the Attorney General decided to admit – for the purpose of these proceedings only – that all the allegations in *Spycatcher* were correct. Though this was intended only as a legal tactic, the Australian judge, Mr Justice Powell, pronounced the admission 'quite dramatic'. The effect was to make it much more difficult for the British government to argue that publication was contrary to the Australian public interest – as it had to do if it was to win its case. The tactical acceptance of Wright's most sensational allegation – that Sir Roger Hollis had been a Soviet spy – was of considerable public interest in Australia since Hollis had had a major role in the foundation of ASIO, the Australian security service.[34]

The *Spycatcher* trial, which was to last five weeks, opened in Sydney in November 1986 and attracted a level of global publicity unequalled by any other book since the British government's equally ill-fated attempt to ban the publication of *Lady Chatterley's Lover* on the grounds of obscenity a quarter of a century earlier. Heinemann's British solicitor, David Hooper, 'could not avoid gaining the impression that the British government over-estimated the deference that they thought would be accorded to them by the Australian courts and government'.[35] 'It was an enormous lark', re-called Wright's counsel, the able, aggressive thirty-two-year-old Malcolm Turnbull, 'and I enjoyed every minute of it.'[36] The part of the 'lark' he enjoyed most was probably questioning Sir Robert Armstrong, who had been selected, rather than a senior Security Service officer, as the principal witness in support of the government case.[37] Though Armstrong was the accounting officer for the funds received by the Service under the Secret Vote, he had no first-hand information about any of the operations described by Wright and, even with the voluminous briefing material pro-vided for him, he was placed, as Stella Rimington, then Director K, later acknowledged, 'in a very difficult if not impossible position'.[38] The urbane, patrician Armstrong made an irresistible target for much of the Australian media. Turnbull positioned his lectern so that, when answering his ques-tions, Armstrong was facing a press gallery who, wrote Turnbull, 'were laughing at him and some were sneering too'.[39]

The exaggerated levels of British official secrecy made it easy for Turnbull to ridicule the government case. Though the existence of ASIS, the Austra-lian foreign intelligence service, was officially admitted, like most other intelligence services around the world, the Thatcher government, like its predecessors, refused to acknowledge the existence of SIS. Armstrong was therefore bound to stick to that position. When reminded by Turnbull that he had admitted that Sir Dick White had been Chief of SIS, he was forced

A cartoon by Nicholas Garland shows the *Spycatcher* affair leading to shipwreck
for the Thatcher government. The cabinet secretary, Sir Robert Armstrong, who
had been sent to Australia to give evidence in the *Spycatcher* trial, is already
overboard (*Independent*, 26 November 1986).

to give the surreal reply that, while acknowledging the existence of SIS
when White was at the head of it, he could not admit that it had any prior
or subsequent existence. Though Armstrong handled most of his impossible
brief skilfully, he was caught out in one minor evasion which was seized
on by the media as well as Turnbull. Armstrong acknowledged that, when
writing to the publisher of *Their Trade is Treachery* in March 1981 asking
for a pre-publication copy, he had failed to mention that he already had a
copy from a confidential source. Since he had felt bound to protect his
source, he could scarcely have done otherwise. In reply to a question
from Turnbull, Armstrong denied that he had lied in his letter to the
publisher, but acknowledged (quoting Edmund Burke) that he had been
'economical with the truth' – a memorable phrase which the media made
instantly infamous as evidence of deception at the heart of Whitehall. The
Australian cabinet secretary, Michael Codd, in evidence at the trial, offered
support for the British case by testifying that, if *Spycatcher* were to be
published in Australia, the intelligence agencies of Britain and other friendly
countries would be unwilling to exchange secret intelligence with Australia.
Codd's evident unfamiliarity with the details of the Wright case, however,
made his support somewhat counter-productive. True to form, Turnbull

dismissed Codd's evidence as 'codswallop'. Mr Justice Powell avoided puns but was equally unflattering, describing parts of the cabinet secretary's testimony as 'complete and utter moonshine', 'ridiculous' and 'totally without foundation'.[40]

The government, unsurprisingly, lost its case in the New South Wales Supreme Court. It continued, however, for well over a year to try to maintain and enforce injunctions forbidding publication of extracts from *Spycatcher* by the British media – even at a time when the book was top of the best-seller list in the United States. The Labour MP David Winnick asked the Attorney General whether Wright had yet 'expressed his gratitude to the British government for helping to boost the sales and publicity of his book'.[41] The government case for a permanent injunction was successively rejected in the High Court, then by a majority in the Court of Appeal, and finally, in the summer of 1988, by a majority in the House of Lords. The Law Lords accepted the government argument that the book constituted a serious breach of confidentiality but concluded that, since it had already been published abroad, publication in Britain would cause no further damage to national security. The European Court of Human Rights later found that continuing the injunction against publication in Britain even after *Spycatcher* had been published in the United States contravened Article 10 of the Human Rights Convention.[42]

The argument that Wright had compromised national security by breaking his undertaking 'never to disclose anything I knew as a result of my employment' was well founded. The government's decision 'to pursue the book through every possible legal channel, whether there was any hope of success or not'[43] was not. The affair did lasting damage to the Service's reputation, chiefly perhaps in reviving the conspiracy theory of the Wilson plot.[44] Mr Justice Powell appeared to take Wright's unreliable evidence at face value, declaring in his summing up: 'Mr Wright went to see Sir Michael Hanley and told him [about the plot], and there was some dressed up little enquiry that got nowhere. Michael Hanley took a degree of delight in its getting nowhere.'[45] Never before or since has the Security Service suffered the level of public ridicule provoked by the long-drawn-out *Spycatcher* saga. Some of the ridicule came from unexpected quarters. Possibly the most surprising was Edward Heath, who told the Commons that there were officers in MI5 'whose whole philosophy was ridiculous nonsense. If some of them were on the tube and saw someone reading the *Daily Mirror*, they would say, "Get after him, that is dangerous. We must find out where he bought it."'[46] Few if any MPs were aware that during Heath's term as prime minister the main pressure for increased surveillance of trade union militants had come not from the Security Service but from his government.[47]

The public embarrassments of the Peter Wright affair left most members of the Security Service with the conviction that things could not go on as before. The Master of the Rolls, Sir John Donaldson, said, when giving judgment in an action against newspapers which had published *Spycatcher* extracts, 'It may be that the time has come when Parliament should regularise the position of the Security Service.' The Service agreed. Its Annual Report for 1987–8 concluded that 'There is complete acceptance among staff of the desirability of legislation for the Security Service.'[48] Ministers took longer to convince. The main credit for convincing the government and senior civil servants of the need for the Security Service Act belongs to Sir Tony Duff. As the Home Secretary, Douglas Hurd, hitherto opposed to legislation, later acknowledged, Duff persuaded him over lunch on 8 January 1987 that 'the time had passed when the Security Service could successfully operate on the basis that it did not exist. The pretence had worn threadbare, making it increasingly difficult to recruit and train men and women of quality for the Service.'

Duff then thought it would take another two years to win over the Prime Minister and the cabinet secretary. In fact, Sir Robert Armstrong was on side by April, probably as a result of the Leander case as well as his own experience in the New South Wales Supreme Court, but both he and the Foreign Secretary, Sir Geoffrey Howe, believed another year would be required to persuade Mrs Thatcher. In July, however, she agreed to the drafting of a Security Service Bill, though without any commitment that she would accept it. In April 1988 she finally agreed to the draft Bill. Hurd was convinced that Duff's advocacy was crucial: 'He was one of those good-looking, grand-mannered officials who could exercise great influence over her once they had gained her trust . . .'[49]

Also influential in changing the government's mind was the case pending before the European Court of Human Rights brought by two former officers of the National Council for Civil Liberties, Harriet Harman and Patricia Hewitt. In support of their case Cathy Massiter swore an affidavit that the Security Service held files containing personal details on both which, they claimed, infringed their human rights. The case was especially sensitive because Harman and Hewitt were rising Labour politicians.[50] Harman was elected as Labour MP for Peckham in 1982; Hewitt joined the staff of the Leader of the Opposition, Neil Kinnock, in 1983. Both later became cabinet ministers under Tony Blair. The Security Service realized that, because of the lack of the statutory basis for its actions which the European Court in the Leander case had held to be essential, Harman and Hewitt were likely to win their case (as they eventually did).[51]

The Queen's Speech of 22 November 1988 announced that 'A Bill will be introduced to put the Security Service on a statutory basis under the Secretary of State.'[52] The Security Service Act of 1989 at last placed MI5 on a statutory footing, elegantly sidestepping the contentious issue of the previous legal basis for the Service's operations by the use of the brilliantly equivocal formula 'There shall continue to be a Security Service.' The Service remained under the authority of the Home Secretary. Its tasking also remained quite different to that of SIS and GCHQ. A 1993 briefing for the Queen informed Her Majesty: 'Unlike the intelligence collection agencies (SIS and GCHQ) which respond solely to outside tasking, the Security Service is required under the Act to assess threats to national security and to deploy its resources accordingly.'[53] The definition of the role of the Service, unlike the 1952 Maxwell Fyfe Directive, referred specifically to the threat from terrorism and the need to safeguard Britain's economic well-being:

The function of the Service shall be the protection of national security and, in particular, its protection against threats from espionage, terrorism and sabotage, from the activities of agents of foreign powers and from actions intended to overthrow or undermine parliamentary democracy by political, industrial or violent means.

It shall also be the function of the Service to safeguard the economic well-being of the United Kingdom against threats posed by the actions or intentions of persons outside the British Islands [the UK, Channel Islands and Isle of Man].

To the statutory authority under HOWs for letter-opening and telephone-tapping established by the 1985 Interception of Communications Act, the Security Service Act added the authority, also under HOWs, for 'entry on or interference with property'. The Director General had a duty 'to ensure that no information is obtained or disclosed by the Service, except in so far as is necessary for the proper discharge of its functions'. The Act established a tribunal of experienced lawyers to deal with most complaints against the Service save those concerning 'interference with property', which were referred to the Security Service Commissioner. Over the next few years none of the complaints to the Tribunal and the Commissioner was upheld.[54]

With the sensational publicity provoked by the *Spycatcher* affair now largely abated, the Security Service Act attracted less public interest and parliamentary attention than the government had anticipated. During the passage of the Act there were never more than forty-two MPs in the Chamber. Passions in the poorly attended debates ran less strongly than during the passage of the Interception of Communications Bill four years earlier. Even the authorization for 'entry on or interference with property', which had been thought too contentious to include in the 1985 Act, failed to generate major controversy.[55] Within Whitehall, however, the Act was recognized as a turning point in the history of the British intelligence community and was celebrated by a party at Gower Street attended by both Margaret Thatcher and the Lord Chancellor, Lord Mackay. The Prime Minister spent much of her time at the party denouncing media sensationalism over the previous few years.[56]

The Act left behind unfinished business. All Britain's main intelligence allies now had oversight committees in or associated with their parliaments. In Australia the Director General of ASIO, Alan Wrigley, welcomed the foundation of the Joint Parliamentary ASIO Committee and the office of inspector general of intelligence and security in 1987 as a means of restoring public confidence in ASIO. The lack of public confidence in the Thatcher government's response to the Cathy Massiter and Peter Wright revelations had shown a similar need for an all-party oversight committee in Britain. In 1988 a private conference at Ditchley Park attended by senior politicians from the three major parties and retired Whitehall mandarins (serving mandarins were forbidden to attend) agreed on the desirability of a British oversight committee. The Thatcher government, however, was not yet ready to follow the example of its intelligence allies.[57]

Section F
After the Cold War

I

The Transformation of the Security Service

What made the greatest impression on many, perhaps most, MI5 staff in the final months of 1989 was not the secret intelligence to which they had access but the images on television news of the fall of the Berlin Wall and the rapid, unexpectedly peaceful collapse of the Communist one-party regimes of Eastern and Central Europe. The Security Service, like all Western governments and intelligence agencies, was caught off guard. The end of the Cold War, the collapse of the Soviet Bloc and the disintegration of the Soviet Union transformed the priorities of the Security Service. It reported to the Home Secretary that 'between 1989 and 1991, the already declining subversive threat reached a new low and the espionage threat from some countries (with the notable exception of Russia) all but disappeared.'[1] In the early 1990s the Service became for the first time in its history primarily a counter-terrorist rather than a counter-espionage agency. It could not complete the transition, however, until it gained the lead intelligence role against the main current terrorist threat, PIRA's mainland campaign.

On 7 February 1991 a mortar, fired from a white Ford Transit van parked by a PIRA ASU in Horseguards Avenue at the junction with Whitehall, exploded on the Downing Street lawn in the middle of a cabinet meeting. The Prime Minister, John Major, was told that, if the mortar had landed 10 feet closer to the Cabinet Room, 'half the Cabinet could have been killed.'[2] Immediately after the explosion, recalled the cabinet secretary, Sir Robin Butler, 'We didn't even know it was a mortar. The French windows at the end of the room were burst open by the blast. My first impression was that men were going to dash in with masks on and submachine guns.'[3] Though two other mortars were off-target, one of the most worrying features of the PIRA attack was its technical sophistication, grudgingly acknowledged in a later report by the Service's main weapons expert:

The positioning of the [mortar] baseplate at the firing point was done with remarkable precision and the range calculations had clearly been carried out with extreme
care. It was no mean feat to place round one on target, which argues for the presence
of a highly experienced and capable operator.[4]

The fact that none of the cabinet was killed or injured was due largely
to the protective-security expertise of C Branch, which kept up to date
with PIRA's weaponry and bomb technology. During a routine visit to
Number Ten in 1990, Director C had mentioned that PIRA had begun to
use mortars. C Branch, which was called in to advise, recommended that
the windows be fitted with reinforced laminated glass. The fitting (save for
the top floor, where work had not yet begun) had only just been completed
when the PIRA attack took place. Several members of C Branch heard the
crump of the mortars landing while at a meeting in their Assistant Director's office. One of those present recalls a colleague saying, 'That sounds
like mortars. I hope my glazing has stood up!' It had. Another C Branch
veteran believes that 'Had it not been for the windows, the place would
have been shredded.' At the very least, some ministers would have been
badly injured by flying glass. After the mortar attack, C Branch became
heavily involved in advising on the measures needed to protect Number
Ten and the surrounding area against further attack.[5]

Following the Brighton bombing seven years earlier, PIRA had now
come close to killing two British Prime Ministers. The near success of the
mortar attack strengthened the case for Service primacy over MPSB in
mainland operations against Irish Republicans.[6] That case was powerfully
reinforced by the Security Service's successes against PIRA on the continent, where it already had the lead intelligence role. Less than a week after
the mortar attack on Downing Street, the DG, Sir Patrick Walker, was
able to report to the Prime Minister the arrest of a three-man ASU in
Brussels after a combined operation with the Belgian Sûreté:[7] 'Lives were
probably saved. The operation demonstrated the close cooperation which
exists among European security authorities in countering Irish terrorism.'[8]
The Service presented the Belgian Sûreté with a case of whisky.[9] Combined
operations by the Security Service and the French DST also led to the
discovery of PIRA arms caches hidden in the French countryside and the
disruption of further Provisional operations.[10]

As Director G from 1988 to 1990, Stella Rimington was the last head
of counter-terrorism to be responsible for dealing with the threats from
both PIRA and international terrorism. In 1990 the Service's Irish CT
responsibilities were hived off to a new T Branch.[11] A ministerial meeting

on 11 April 1991 approved a Service request for increased counter-terrorist resources and considered a range of possible threats from PIRA. Interestingly, in view of the Islamist terrorist threat a decade later, the worst-case scenario envisaged by the meeting was of Provisional suicide bombers.[12] By June T1 had begun preparing a detailed case for the transfer of the lead intelligence role against Republican terrorism from the MPSB. The most influential Whitehall supporter of the Service case was Sir Gerry Warner, who became intelligence co-ordinator in July 1991. Warner persuaded the chairman of the JIC, Sir Percy Cradock, to visit the Service for briefing by Stephen Lander (then T5/0) and Director A. The DG was subsequently invited to a meeting with Cradock and the cabinet secretary, Sir Robin Butler, to discuss how the Service would handle the lead role if it was offered it.[13] On 14 October, after consulting Butler, Warner asked the DG to provide a written statement of Service plans for taking over the lead role from MPSB.[14] From this point on, recalls Lander, who prepared a draft response two days later,[15] he and his colleagues were confident that the decision would go in favour of the Service.[16]

A policy file to plan the transfer of intelligence primacy in counter-PIRA operations on the British mainland, codenamed ASCRIBE, was opened on 16 October. Next day the Service despatched a written case for the transfer to Sir Robin Butler, stressing the experience it had gained in the lead intelligence role on the mainland against international terrorist groups for the past two decades.[17] Butler told a meeting on 21 October, attended by the DG, Cradock, Warner and Sir Clive Whitmore (PUS at the Home Office):

Both Ministers and officials had previously taken the view that the responsibility for pre-emptive intelligence to counter Republican terrorism on the mainland would more logically rest with the Security Service than the Metropolitan Police. However, they had on previous occasions concluded that the disruption involved in a transfer of responsibility outweighed the benefits of the change. That might no longer be the case.[18]

Butler's minute for the Prime Minister was franker. He acknowledged the strengths of the Met in operational policing and post-incident investigations, but concluded that they could not match the intelligence skills and experience of the Security Service.[19] On 21 November Major decided there was an 'a priori case for the Security Service to take over intelligence operations against Republican targets on the mainland', but, in view of the complexities of the changeover, asked for a detailed report.[20] It was to be another six months before a formal decision was taken.

At almost the same moment that Major decided in principle on the transfer of the lead role against PIRA, Sir Patrick Walker told the DDG for Administration (DDG(A)),[21] Stella Rimington, who had joined the Service as clerical assistant to the SLO in New Delhi nearly a quarter of a century earlier, that she was to succeed him as DG on his retirement in February 1992. By later (and some previous) standards, the selection process was remarkably casual. No applications were invited, there was no selection panel and no interviews. Rimington was not even asked whether she wanted the job.[22] The Home Secretary, Kenneth Baker, consulted Walker (as well as, doubtless, his PUS and the cabinet secretary), then wrote to the Prime Minister on 12 November, recommending Rimington's appointment. Major agreed next day.[23] Rimington first heard the news soon afterwards from a senior New Zealand intelligence officer visiting London who had been informed under liaison arrangements.[24]

Though Rimington was the first female head of any of the world's leading intelligence or security agencies, there is no convincing evidence that her gender had a significant influence on her appointment. For some years the Security Service had been recruiting probably a higher proportion of women at officer/executive level than any other branch of British government.[25] Rimington believes that by the time she became DDG(A), 'The fact that I was female had almost ceased to be relevant to the progress of my career . . . As far as colleagues in the Service or in Whitehall went, I did not think it was an issue.'[26] She was chosen as DG because there was good reason to believe she was the best candidate. Stephen Lander, who served under Rimington in the mid-1980s, remembers her as 'far and away' the best assistant director he ever had, 'decisive, easy, confident, assertive, supportive'.[27]

Walker surprised Rimington by saying that she was to be the first British intelligence chief whose appointment was publicly announced. When Rimington raised objections, the DG replied that the decision in favour of publicity had already been approved by the Prime Minister. She then rang up Sir Clive Whitmore, who she recalls exclaiming, 'My God, have you only just found out? We thought you had known for ages.' Told that if she wanted to challenge the decision, she must speak to Sir Robin Butler, she decided to accept publicity as a fait accompli.[28] Among those taken aback by the public announcement of her appointment was Rimington's elder daughter, then a university student. 'I thought you must have done something wrong', she told her mother, 'because I knew you were not supposed to talk about your work.'[29] But, though Rimington's name was published, no photograph was released – despite the fact that the New Statesman already had a blurred picture of her. The DG's protective-security advisers insisted that to publish a clearer photograph would increase the risk from PIRA. 'That', Rimington later realized, 'was amazingly naive because it was inevitable that the press would get a photograph. In the end it was me personally who thought, "Stuff it, I'm going to stand there and let them take a picture because I'm fed up with all this."' The day after she allowed a picture to be taken, the *Evening Standard* published it with a black band superimposed across her face to conceal her identity.[30]

Thereafter, Rimington recalls, her pursuit by paparazzi 'became ludicrous'. For a few days she moved to a hotel with her younger daughter in the vain hope that the reporters and photographers camped outside her Islington house would lose interest while she was gone. But they were still there when she returned home, and she was forced to move to secure accommodation. Every detail of her unremarkable private life became a news story from shopping at Marks and Spencer to her bank account (into which a private investigator made a deposit in the name of a KGB chief).[31] An unflattering photograph of Rimington shopping in old clothes, this time without her face concealed, was used to illustrate an article in the *Evening Standard* entitled 'Success and the Dowdy Englishwoman'. Rimington was advised to visit 'a decent hairdresser on a regular basis' and use 'some subtle make-up'.[32] The *Sun* broke the news that she was separated from her husband in a front-page story under the sensational banner headline 'MI5 WIFE IN SECRET LOVE SPLIT'. Other newspaper headlines included 'HOUSEWIFE SUPERSPY' and 'MOTHER OF TWO GETS TOUGH WITH TERRORISTS'.[33] Thanks to this mostly unwelcome publicity, Rimington was the first intelligence chief in modern British history to become something approaching a household name. The *Sun* invited readers to become 'Sun secret agents': 'Did you go to school with her or have you met her since? Phone the special Sun spy hot-line . . . Don't worry about the cost. We'll ring you straight back.'[34]

The most important change in the Security Service's role during Rimington's term as DG was the implementation of ASCRIBE. Like John Major, Ken Clarke, who became home secretary after the Conservative election victory in April 1992, was convinced that 'only a transfer of the lead responsibility would allow the Security Service to make their maximum contribution in this crucial area.'[35] The decision to give the Security Service the lead role against PIRA, taken on 30 April,[36] was announced by Clarke to the Commons on 8 May. Fraught negotiations followed before the official handover from the MPSB to the Security Service on 1 October. Stephen Lander, who had become Director T in February and, as one of his fellow directors recalls, was 'not known for being a shrinking violet', recalls the negotiations as 'just awful, awful, awful . . .'.[37] He urged staff to be conciliatory and understanding in their dealings with MPSB: 'The ASCRIBE review has been a wounding experience for some B [Special Branch Irish] Squad staff and they are naturally disappointed at the outcome.' The Met's local knowledge and expertise in law enforcement would continue to be irreplaceable in operations against PIRA[38] – as was recognized by the Home Secretary's instructions for the Service's intelligence on mainland Republican terrorism to be shared with MPSB. Eliza Manningham-Buller, who was appointed first head of the newly founded T2 to take responsibility for mainland Republican terrorism, wisely brought in a number of Met officers on secondment.[39] Her success in T2 helped to mark her out as a possible future DG. A Home Office official wrote soon after the formal handover of the lead role from Special Branch to the Security Service: 'I have heard it said that senior police officers regard her appointment as "inspired".'[40]

Rimington wrote in July 1992, four months after becoming director general:

The Service itself has changed out of all recognition since the late 1960s and 70s. In those days the intelligence cadre was almost entirely male, with many ex-military or Colonial Service officers in their middle years. Now we are a younger Service – the average age of our intelligence officers is 36 – drawn from varied backgrounds. Half of the Directors are under 50 and over 40% of the intelligence officers are women (the figure for the whole Service is 55%). Our detractors who accuse us of being conservative, old fashioned, Cold War warriors are a very long way from the truth. We would like to see such myths blown away.[41]

Once Rimington had got over the shock of her early encounter with the paparazzi, she began to see her unprecedented public visibility as DG and the media interest in her as a possible advantage to be exploited – a means of helping to 'blow away' myths about the Service. Without seeking any advice from PR consultants, she and her advisers set out to develop an openness programme. The first step in what she called 'the Service's debut before the wider public' was the publication of the first ever official booklet on its work with the first official photograph of the DG, which showed a smartly dressed, well-groomed woman who bore no resemblance to the 'dowdy Englishwoman' previously mocked by the *Evening Standard*.[42] Unremarkable though the booklet now appears, its secret gestation caused angst in Whitehall, where every word of the draft text was minutely scrutinized. 'The process of getting the first edition off the stocks', Rimington recalls, 'would have made a good episode of *Yes Minister*.' In July

1993, the media were summoned without explanation to the Home Office, where, to their surprise, they were handed copies of the Security Service booklet and briefed by the DG, who also answered questions. Though Rimington took a photocall after the briefing with the Home Secretary and was filmed working at a desk, she was not allowed to speak on camera and the media were forbidden to mention that she had conducted the briefing. These farcical requirements, she believed, derived from 'the nightmare in Whitehall at the time that if they did not keep a very close rein on me, I would end up answering questions about security policy and usurping the Home Secretary's role'.[43]

The impact of the Service booklet and Rimington's briefing was heightened by the almost simultaneous arrest in a London street, following Security Service and MPSB surveillance, of a leading Provisional, Robert 'Rab' Fryers, who was about to begin a major bombing campaign in the City of London and provincial cities.[44] Thereafter Rimington started to accept invitations to lunch with the media and to give off-the-record briefings. Jon Snow of *Channel 4 News* expressed surprise that she was not more like Rosa Klebb, the fearsome female KGB officer in the James Bond film *From Russia with Love*.[45] The DG reported after a year of such briefings: 'Silly press speculation can never be removed entirely, but the Service's continuing, controlled contact with senior editors and others is helping to shape a better informed and more considered attitude to the Service in the more responsible quarters of the media.'[46]

As well as developing contacts with the media, Rimington became the first DG to take part in the weekly Wednesday-morning meetings of permanent under secretaries. In June 1994, with Whitehall apparently no longer fearful that Rimington might upstage the Home Secretary, she was allowed to talk in public for the first time and deliver the annual televised BBC Dimbleby Lecture on 'Security and Democracy: Is There a Conflict?' As the DG appeared before a hand-picked audience of 340 at Whitehall's Banqueting House, she was probably helped by her long experience of amateur dramatics. (Her memoirs include photographs of her playing Marcelle in *Hotel Paradiso* in 1968 and celebrating her sixty-fourth birthday in 1999 by appearing in Tom Stoppard's *The Fifteen-Minute Hamlet* at a barge theatre in Copenhagen.)[47] Though Rimington was, by her own admission, 'extremely nervous' before giving the Dimbleby Lecture, even the *Guardian*, one of the Security Service's most frequent critics, reported that 'The first, superficial, impression was of a brilliantly accomplished performance, almost a culture shock.' As usual, Rimington's wardrobe aroused intense media interest:

Commentators, including fashion editors, have dwelt at length on her power-dressing – her rather severe primrose yellow jacket – offset by her body language with the use of large, unblinking, eyes reminiscent of Princess Diana as she paused to drive a point home, or completed a well-rehearsed delivery of a light-hearted anecdote.[48]

Thereafter, there was a perception in Whitehall that 'Stella enjoyed being in the limelight' – though she disapproved of all other members of the Service, past or present, making public appearances and vetoed a BBC invitation to her predecessor, Sir Patrick Walker, to appear on *Desert Island Discs*. Late in 1994, Rimington appeared for the first time before the newly established oversight committee of parliamentarians, the Intelligence and Security Committee (ISC), for whose creation support had been growing since the final years of the Thatcher government. Michael Howard, who had become home secretary earlier in the year, was initially anxious that the Security Service might prove politically inept in its dealings with the ISC, and asked his PUS, Sir Richard Wilson, to spend some time with the DG explaining what the Committee would expect from her. Rimington, however, proved a confident and assured performer.[49] At least one of the MPs on the ISC initially believed that the Service was 'inbred and not open to outside influences'. He and the rest of the Committee seemed reassured by meeting members of staff. 'You are obviously sane and ordinary people' was one comment, apparently intended as a compliment.[50]

Rimington believed that one of the major achievements of her term as DG was 'the demystification of the Service and the creation of a more informed public and media perception'.[51] Eliza Manningham-Buller, the next female officer to become DG, was struck by Rimington's concern for what she called the Service's 'shop window'.[52] The Service's new image was epitomized by its move, publicly announced, to a new, light and airy headquarters at Thames House on Millbank where two buildings had been fused into one and skilfully modernized behind the interwar façade. Staff, who had previously been dispersed between Gower Street, Curzon Street and seven other central London offices, linked by a continuous shuttle service ferrying classified files and documents back and forth, were at last able to work together in the same building. Atriums with glass roofs at both ends of the building allowed even those rooms which had no outside window to have a view of the sky. An automated miniature monorail (an improved version of the one used at Curzon Street two decades earlier) brought files up from the basement. The official opening of the Thames House headquarters by the Prime Minister, John Major, on 30 November 1994 provided a further photo-opportunity. Less than forty years earlier

Rab Butler, on becoming home secretary, had had no idea where MI5 headquarters were.[53]

The new public profile of the Security Service was part of a more general transformation. The Service changed more during the 1990s than in any previous decade since the Second World War. Change, however, was an uncomfortable process. The end of the Cold War, which had been MI5's chief preoccupation for much of the previous half-century, left an initial sense of disorientation which complicated H Branch's attempt to plan the Service's new role.* H1/0, who was asked in February 1990 by Sir Patrick Walker to prepare a strategic review of the Service's future, noted that when he began his review 'there was reason to fear that world events might run away from us and that the Service would be left with its role and objectives inadequately defined in radically new international circumstances.'[54] H1/0's review, which took almost a year to complete, was, he reported, 'without precedent in our Service':

Of course, major reorganisation of the Service took place in 1941 following Sir David Petrie's report; and in 1953, following Sir Dick White's appointment as Director General. Very great improvements in management style and policy were introduced by Sir Antony Duff. But, as far as I know, this is the first occasion on which, addressing radical changes in the world, the top management of the Service has sought to formulate a coherent strategy.[55]

The Service, however, was still unused to strategic thinking. Though H1/0's strategic review drew heavily on discussions with a small circle of fellow enthusiasts, in general he found little enthusiasm within the Service for 'addressing radical changes', and was disappointed by the lack of imagination shown by many of his colleagues when he discussed the future with them:

We must recognise the fact, unfortunate though it is, that the need for us to respond to the new situation by devising an articulate and coherent strategy is appreciated by few colleagues in the Service . . . For the Service as an institution, a lack of interest in, or a hostility to, demanding strategic thinking will not do. How to overcome these incapacities is a serious question for us.[56]

The future DG Jonathan Evans, then H1B/1, recalls the initial discussion of H1/0's strategic review by the Management Board as '*stormy!*' He and

* When P Branch, founded by Duff in 1987 to review internal organization and procedures, was wound up in 1990, its policy and planning function was transferred to H Branch. See Appendix 3, p. 000.

H1/0 wondered whether the Legal Adviser, David Bickford, who had clashed with Walker at the meeting, might resign (though, in the event, he did not do so).[57] The controversies aroused by the review helped to produce an important cultural shift. By 1992 it was accepted that:

Strategic planning is the principal role of the Management Board, supported by H1. Board members have corporate, non-partisan responsibilities in this regard in addition to their individual command roles.

. . .

Strategic planning [is] now part of annual resources management cycle of objective setting, planning and performance review. A review of strategy each summer begins the cycle.[58]

(Along with the Service's increased capacity for strategic thinking went a growing acceptance of jargon – even a belief among some staff that it was expected of them.) Debate on how far the Service should move into new areas of work – countering the proliferation of weapons of mass destruction, supporting the police against organized crime, defending the UK's 'economic well-being', investigating animal-rights extremists – continued into the mid-1990s.

In March 1992, the Security Service proposed to the Interdepartmental Working Group on Subversion in Public Life (SPL) that it cease keeping a record of 'rank-and-file members of subversive organisations', once the first assignment of most new graduate entrants. The SPL agreed that 'this change will not involve any increased risk to national security.' The proportion of subversives detected by the Security Service during vetting had declined from 2.7 per cent of all applicants in 1971 to 0.06 per cent in 1990. 'This decline', it reported, 'parallels the national decline in subversive organisations.' Since the 1970s the number of organizations identified as subversive had fallen from over seventy to around forty-five, and their total membership from 55,000 to around 14,000. Only six of the organizations had more than 400 members. None represented any significant threat to national security. The Service had found no evidence in recent years that any subversive group had deliberately set out to obtain classified information.[59]

The illusion within Whitehall that the 'peace dividend' produced by the end of the Cold War should extend to the intelligence community as well as to the armed services led to budget cuts for the Security Service (as for SIS and GCHQ) which made necessary the first compulsory redundancies since the Second World War.[60] Like Washington and the government machines of other allies, Whitehall failed to grasp that, even though the threat of thermonuclear war was far lower than it had been for forty years, the increased diversity of potential threats to national security, especially from terrorism, pointed to a need for more, rather than less, intelligence. The culmination of the intelligence budget negotiation was a 'Star Chamber' in which ministers whose departments were the main intelligence consumers put to the heads of the agencies, as it seemed to Rimington, the most awkward questions their officials could devise:

You knew that whatever you were proposing, you would be given less, and drawing attention to the comparative cost to the country of a successful IRA bomb in the City of London and a few more thousands of pounds spent on counter-terrorism never seemed to work. I came away wondering ruefully why I had put so much effort into stopping them all getting blown up.[61]

In November 1993 the DG announced to staff the depressing news that the Major government had decided, on the recommendation of the PUS Committee, 'that over the next three financial years we must find the funding for additional work necessary against PIRA from within our own resources, as well as producing some further savings on top of those already presented in our [financial] Plan, as a contribution towards reducing Government expenditure'. In the view of Stephen Lander, who became Director H in 1994,[62] Rimington's negotiating skills within Whitehall helped to 'fight off the worst cuts'.[63] Over the next two years, however, almost 300 staff were retired early. In all, the Service lost over 400 jobs, nearly 20 per cent of its total strength. As Lander later acknowledged, 'Our success at handling this painful episode was mixed.'[64] Despite Rimington's skill in dealing with Whitehall, she seemed a somewhat remote figure to those in Thames House worried about their jobs. In Manningham-Buller's view, she was 'better externally than internally as DG, not always comfortable with staff'.[65] The painful problems of redundancy were compounded by the travails of moving towards a record-keeping system increasingly based on computerization rather than paper files. When Lander became Director H, the Service used a Unix word-processing system called GIFTED CHILD, which malfunctioned so frequently that it was nicknamed SPOILED BRAT. Lander took the risky but ultimately successful decision to buy Linkworks, which, as well as working with Unix, enabled the Service to switch to PCs and use Microsoft software.[66]

The dramatic post-Cold War shift in the Service's operational priorities and public profile, combined with painful staff and budget cutbacks, prompted the unprecedented decision by the Board in April 1993 to put staff morale on its agenda every six months.[67] Concern for morale also led three months later to the first Staff Attitude Survey.[68] Seventy per cent of respondents found the Service's work 'a source of satisfaction'; 79 per cent described relationships with colleagues in similar terms. The staff management section found 'the overall feedback from the survey positive and encouraging', but must have been disconcerted to discover that only a bare majority of line managers (52 per cent) rated the support it provided to them as 'good' or 'very good'.[69]

In the aftermath of ASCRIBE, PIRA posed a greater mainland threat than ever before. A Cabinet Office review of the 'United Kingdom Response to Irish Republican Terrorism' by Joe Pilling (later PUS in the Northern Ireland Office), completed in February 1993, was the most wide-ranging since the start of the Troubles. Pilling concluded that: 'The cost of Northern Ireland is high. But although it continues to go up it is of broadly the same order as we have been used to for many years.' The frequency – though not the lethality – of PIRA mainland attacks, however, was steadily increasing. Between 1977 and 1989 there was no year during which there were more than four days on which 'Irish Republican terrorist acts took place in Great Britain'. In 1990, however, there were nineteen days – more than during the whole of the 1980s. The total rose to a record forty-seven days in 1992. The outlook appeared bleak – not least because PIRA had begun a bombing campaign against the City of London. A Whitehall report commented:

1992 saw the introduction to Great Britain of devices consisting of a large quantity of HME [home-made explosive]. One [at the Baltic Exchange] in the City of London led to insurance claims of around £800m. Only a combination of good intelligence, good policing and good luck prevented several more incidents on a similar scale. The cost of four or five similar explosions such as they intended last summer would have been equivalent to the contingency reserve for a financial year. There is every reason to think that PIRA see the pressure that this places on HMG . . .[70]

The Service's role in preventing a series of City bombings on the scale of that at the Baltic Exchange made an important and perhaps crucial difference to the struggle against PIRA.

On 22 February 1993, John Major received, via the intelligence link used for secret communications between Whitehall and PIRA, a message which marked the beginning of the long and tortuous path leading eventually to the Good Friday Agreement of 1998. The remarkable fact that, only two years after coming within 10 feet of killing perhaps half the cabinet, the Provisionals (though they later disputed the wording of the message quoted by Major in his memoirs) were seeking an end to the 'armed conflict' reflects, in part, the role of intelligence in limiting the success of their operations. It also reflected the success of Operation CHIFFON, whose aim was 'to achieve a ceasefire and talks' with PIRA. The principal channel through which CHIFFON operated was Brendan Duddy, the Derry businessman who had provided a back-channel to the Provisionals in the 1970s and had direct access to a senior figure in the PIRA leadership.[71]

Since 1981 there had been little contact with Duddy. Early in 1991, however, he had renewed contact to say that Republican leaders were interested in peace talks.[72] Thereafter the case was taken over by T Branch, which began regular meetings with Duddy, usually at fortnightly intervals.[73] Martin McGuinness later acknowledged, 'I was given the responsibility of building a bridge to the British government, building contacts, which I worked away at from the late 1980s . . .'[74] On 20 February 1993 McGuinness declared publicly that the British government privately believed in the need for 'inclusive dialogue'. He added that Republicans, for their part, would have to apply 'new and radical thinking' to their understanding of the Unionists. Compromise was in the air.[75] Duddy's Security Service contact wrote in a briefing for the Prime Minister in March: 'I think it is most unlikely that we would have been able to launch CHIFFON had it not been for [Duddy] . . . He is a remarkable man who is devoted to achieving peace in Northern Ireland despite the high risk to himself . . .'[76] The back-channel process, however, encouraged ambiguity. As Duddy's first British intelligence contact had acknowledged almost twenty years earlier, 'ambiguous phrases' were 'very much the currency we were involved in'.[77] After the *Observer* revealed in November 1993 that the British government had a secret back-channel to the Provisionals, the contacts between them collapsed in acrimony with each side publishing different accounts of what had been said. John Major wrote later: 'I regretted the loss of the back channel. It gave us some difficult moments, but it played its part. Making peace is a tricky business.'[78] In Lander's view, without the back-channel 'there would have been no peace process.'

While the secret contacts were still continuing, PIRA had begun a major new offensive against the City of London. On 24 April 1993 a bomb containing over a ton of HME exploded at the NatWest Tower in Bishopsgate London, killing one person, injuring more than thirty and causing damage estimated at £350 million. Stephen Lander, then Director T, remembers it as one of the low points in his career. However, Major, to whom he sent a detailed report, was sympathetic.[79] In July the Provisionals made public their strategy to frighten foreign financial institutions from maintaining offices in the City of London. PIRA letters to foreign-owned City institutions warned them that the newly established security zone around the City would be powerless to prevent more attacks as devastating as those against the Baltic Exchange and the NatWest Tower. The Security Service reported: 'The sending of these letters was not only a propaganda exercise by PIRA, but also a continuation of its campaign to damage the British economy. PIRA hopes that foreign companies will either move away from London, or be discouraged from making further investments there.'[80]

Had the bombing campaign in the City continued, PIRA might well have succeeded in its aim. Scarcely had the PIRA letters been posted, however, than surveillance of one of the leading figures in the mainland bombing campaign, Robert 'Rab' Fryers, a senior Belfast Provisional, led to a major breakthrough. Fryers was tracked down in Scotland staying at a flat occupied by Hugh Jack, a Scot with no known PIRA links who had been chosen as his support worker.[81] Surveillance revealed that, as well as preparing an attack on the City, Fryers was planning a prolonged bombing campaign in Birmingham and Manchester. Fryers was overheard telling Jack that he was going to plant a bomb within the 'ring of steel' which had been erected to protect the City of London from further PIRA attacks. He planned to drive south to Neasden, park his car near the Ox and Gate public house, then travel into the City with the bomb by bus, convinced that the police were stopping and searching only private vehicles.[82]

After telling Hugh Jack that he had put a 'couple of bits and pieces' in a 'wee bag',[83] Fryers left Jack's flat early on the evening of 13 July, carrying a box which he appeared to be trying to conceal under his coat, and was heard telling Jack that he was driving south to the Scratchwood Service Area on the M1, where, after sleeping in his car, he would head for Neasden and catch a bus for the City. A4 followed Fryers to the Service Area, then handed over surveillance to the Met in the early hours of 14 July in preparation for his arrest. Fryers was arrested at 9.25 a.m., shortly after he had parked his car in Neasden. He was found in possession of a timer and power unit (TPU) connected to 2 pounds of Semtex explosive and a plastic container with half a gallon of petrol. On arrival at Paddington Green police station, the seriously overweight Fryers initially refused to put on any of the clothing provided for him, on the grounds that it was not big enough, and draped himself in a blanket instead. Soon afterwards Jack, together with a number of his relatives and associates, was arrested by Central Scotland police.[84] A holdall dumped by Jack in local woods was found to contain six blocks of Semtex, six detonators and six TPUs which would have been used to manufacture six car bombs to continue the bombing campaign in the City begun by Fryers.[85]

In the course of the investigation T2 had manned a twenty-four-hour operations room in London and co-ordinated the work in London, Scotland and Belfast of A4 static and mobile surveillance, A1 and A2 operations, the H1 and Scottish Office units which dealt with warrants, advice from the Service's lawyers on evidential and warrantry issues, S (Special Branch surveillance) Squad, B (Special Branch Irish) Squad, SO13 (Met anti-terrorist branch), SO19 (Met firearms), several special branches, especially Central Scotland and Strathclyde, the Central Scotland technical support unit, and surveillance and armed support by the police forces of Greater Manchester, Northumbria, Lothian, Borders and West Yorkshire.[86] Lander saw the operation as proof of the transformation brought about by ASCRIBE:

The operation was an important success for the Service in its new Mainland work against PIRA. As importantly it was a clear demonstration of the ability of police forces and ourselves to work to a common end. Both the Metropolitan Police and the Scottish forces involved performed impressively as did our A and T Branch teams. These arrests will be a serious blow to PIRA's Mainland campaign.[87]

John Major sent personal congratulations to the Service on the arrests.[88]

In December 1993 a report by the Intelligence Co-ordinator, Gerry Warner, concluded that the ASCRIBE changes had 'settled down extraordinarily well'. Since October 1992 there had been over sixty actual or attempted PIRA attacks on the mainland, a few major, most minor. Thanks to good intelligence, the perpetrators of most of the attacks had been identified; forty-nine individuals associated with PIRA had been arrested and seventeen subsequently charged with serious terrorist offences.[89] Despite attempted mortar attacks on Heathrow Airport in March 1994, PIRA mainland operations during the first eight months of 1994 were at a much lower level than in the previous year. The Security Service reported to Whitehall that in the twelve months up to July 1994 eighteen of thirty-four planned PIRA mainland operations 'were frustrated through Service-led intelligence operations'.

On 2 June 1994, however, the UK's Irish operations suffered a serious setback when a Chinook helicopter carrying twenty-five British counter-terrorism personnel, among them the DCI, John Deverell, and three other members of the Security Service, crashed in the Mull of Kintyre, killing all on board. Unlike the army and the RUC, the Service was unaccustomed to facing death in the line of duty. The DDG(O) left for Belfast on the morning after the crash to visit bereaved families and staff, and to see the coffins leave Aldergrove Airport. Stella Rimington, who also visited the families, attended the funerals and went to see the crash site, remembers the tragedy as one 'which I will never truly get over'. Many members of the Security Service still have the Order of Service for the memorial service held in the chapel at Sandhurst. Most also reflected that throughout the Troubles the far more visible RUC had paid a much heavier price than the Security Service. Despite some narrow escapes, PIRA had not succeeded in killing a single Service officer in Northern Ireland. By contrast, over 300 RUC officers were killed and more than 9,000 injured, the great majority by the Provisionals. The price paid by the army was heavier still, with 763 military personnel killed as a direct result of terrorist operations. Members of the Security Service attended many of the RUC and army funerals, sometimes – in the tradition of both Irish communities – walking behind the coffins of their former comrades.

During June and July 1994, there was increasing intelligence and other evidence that the Provisionals were moving slowly towards a ceasefire. When Major returned from his summer holiday on 25 August, the Northern Ireland Office, reflecting the view of the Security Service, confidently forecast that a ceasefire was imminent – though it also predicted accurately that it would fall short of a permanent PIRA renunciation of violence. On 31 August the Provisionals declared a 'complete cessation of military operations': 'We believe that an opportunity to secure a just and lasting settlement has been created . . . A solution will only be found as a result of inclusive negotiations.' The PIRA ceasefire threatened, if it became permanent, to lead to a drastic decline in counter-terrorist operations and further MI5 staff cutbacks. As the Service's Annual Report for 1994–95 acknowledged, 'Pleasure at the ceasefire and the Service's contribution to it was naturally linked with concern about the implications for job security of the possible eventual demise of one of our core areas of work.'[90] Eliza Manningham-Buller, who had succeeded Lander as Director T, was asked by a senior Home Office official 'how small we could be and remain viable'.[91] In September 1994 the Management Board discussed a paper with the gloomy title 'Viability: What is the minimum size at which the Security Service remains viable?', and concluded after a worst-case analysis that the irreducible minimum would be a Service of about one-third its current size – between 600 and 735 staff.[92] Director H, Stephen Lander, argued that, even if cut back drastically, as had happened between the wars, 'History shows that the Service can expand effectively from [a] reduced base to meet new threats.'[93]

A 'reduced base', however, was a highly undesirable option. Lander and Rimington were agreed that, if the PIRA ceasefire held and there was a substantial decline in counter-terrorism, the Service was faced with two stark choices:

(1) Do nothing and accept significant reduction in size of Service; or
(2) Move towards acquisition of new work, e.g. in Organized Crime, by one of
    two routes:
    • 'Big Bang' (immediate and overt bid for an expanded role)
    • Incremental, undisclosed approach

The Board decided in favour of the incremental approach. The Service
should expand its role by 'developing creatively work at existing boundaries, and by lending "packages" of Service skills/techniques to police
and other agencies'. So far as possible, however, this had to remain for the
time being a secret strategy – even so far as most of the Service was
concerned. Lander's speaking notes (agreed with the DG) for briefing
the Senior Management Group (SMG) concluded: 'Service's strategy will
become visible in part through pushing out at edges – but it will fail if
complete intentions are revealed prematurely – therefore essential that
SMG does not disclose this agenda to any other staff at this stage.'[94]

The most dramatic proposal for a changed role considered by the
Security Service management was for amalgamation with SIS. Though
neither the Service nor SIS had any enthusiasm for amalgamation, both
gave it detailed consideration in 1994 chiefly because they anticipated that
the issue might be raised by the newly founded Intelligence and Security
Committee (ISC). Both Services decided against it. In arguing the case
against amalgamation, the Security Service, probably for the first time,
defined its own work culture:

The Security Service's culture is based largely in its traditional role of operating as
a relatively small, politically independent national institution secretly defending
Britain against covert, hostile adversaries. This, perhaps especially the element of
operational secrecy (which mostly remains) and its small size, has given rise to a
familial or club atmosphere and a generally considerate management style. Management operates more commonly by consensus than by edict, historically somewhat
inclined to paternalism. The Service is a compassionate employer. In general, staff
are committed, loyal and enjoy a strong sense of identity as members of an organisation they perceive as special. They identify with the Service's protective/defensive
role. Staff have high standards of honesty and integrity. Core staff are team players.
About half are women. There are strong traditions of intellectual horsepower and
analytical ability. Operational capability against hard targets and close engagement
with Whitehall have more recently become significant factors in the Service's culture.
The Service has tended to undersell itself in Government.

The Security Service review recognized that SIS had traditionally been better at selling itself to government: 'Staff value the respect SIS commands in Whitehall and in the international intelligence community.' SIS also had a different work culture:

SIS has a culture that attaches greatest importance to individual achievement in operational work. Officers are required to be independent self-starters to operate effectively in small overseas stations in potentially, or actually, hostile environments. Whereas Security Service G[eneral] I[ntelligence] D[uties] officers tend to be team players, SIS I[ntelligence] B[ranch] officers are more likely to have a 'fighter pilot' mentality . . . Officers tend to be assertive and self-confident.[95]

To the relief of the Service, the pressure from the ISC for amalgamation with SIS which had prompted the review did not materialize. The remaining MI5–SIS joint sections[96] became victims of the budget cuts and were dissolved.

During 1995 the Management Board continued to plan a cautious expansion of the Service's areas of work as a strategy for protecting it from further cutbacks. Of the four main areas discussed by the Board at intervals over the previous few years, there was no enthusiasm for operations to defend the UK's 'economic well-being' or to counter the threat from animal-rights extremists. The threat to the UK's economic well-being was judged to lack the 'hostile, strategic, intention' which would justify the Service's involvement, while animal-rights activists, despite having 'the potential to cause grave damage to people and property', were 'small in number and lacking in coordination'.[97] The two favoured areas for expansion were counter-proliferation and support for the police against serious organized crime (especially drug-trafficking). A small counter-proliferation unit, K10B, had been set up in 1991, though it did not become self-standing until 1994.[98] SIS and GCHQ, however, had more important counter-proliferation roles and the Service was disinclined to devote major resources to it. The main discussion in 1995 focused on operations against serious organized crime. 'This', Stephen Lander recalls, 'had the support of Ministers, who had been won over by our work against PIRA. We could demonstrate an unusual combination of analytical skills and operational ability, plus high quality of staff.'[99] The 1989 Security Service Act was amended in 1996 to allow the Security Service to act in support of the police in serious crime investigations.

PIRA's sudden and dramatic announcement of the end of its ceasefire on 9 February 1996 largely removed the Service's fears of further cutbacks in its budget. Two months later Director H, Stephen Lander, succeeded

Rimington as DG. Lander had been a pupil at Bishop's Stortford College, which had previously produced both one of the Security Service's most distinguished DGs, Sir Dick White, and its best-known maverick, Peter Wright. Aged forty-eight at the time of his appointment, Lander was the youngest DG since White (who had been forty-six) and the only DG appointed from within the Service who had not previously been DDG. He was also the first (and so far the only) DG with a PhD. After taking a BA in history at Queens' College, Cambridge, he had written a dissertation on the diocese of Chichester during the English Reformation which won him, against stiff competition, a post-doctoral post at the Institute of Historical Research at London University. In 1975, however, having decided against an academic career, Lander joined the Security Service.

When Stella Rimington became DG in 1992, though impressed with Lander's work against PIRA as Director T for the past two years, she did not yet think of him as her likely successor.[100] By 1995 she had changed her mind. It was clear to Sir Richard Wilson, then PUS at the Home Office (later cabinet secretary), that Lander, whom she took with her to meetings at the Home Office 'to bring him along', was now her preferred candidate.[101] Before such meetings, however, she tried to spruce him up: though visibly ambitious, Lander struck Eliza Manningham-Buller as 'a man completely without personal vanity' who paid little attention to his appearance.[102] Rimington saw all the directors individually and asked them their view on the succession. Lander mentioned one of the DDGs – whereupon, he recalls, Rimington 'made a face'. Some weeks later, to his surprise, she told him he was the best candidate and that most of the Board would support him, though he would have to go on 'some bloody course' to learn more about top management.[103] In 1996, unlike 1992, there was a formal selection process with interviews of shortlisted candidates by a panel of senior mandarins, chaired by the cabinet secretary, Sir Robin Butler. Though the other candidates included one of the DDGs and two senior outsiders, Lander was the unanimous choice of the panel. Lander probably owed his reputation chiefly to his record as Director T at a critical time in counter-PIRA operations. He struck Sir Richard Wilson as 'knowing Northern Ireland like the back of his hand'. As both PUS at the Home Office and later as cabinet secretary, Wilson found Lander 'straightforward, with a nice line in slightly witty understatement but not an ounce of show business – very easy to deal with'.[104]

At Rimington's final meeting with the Home Secretary before retirement, on 20 March 1996, she replied, when asked for 'any last thoughts', that 'In her view, the Service was probably quite significantly short of the staff it needed to be able to cover effectively all the tasks it now had.'[105] With more money in the 1996 bargaining round, the Service began to grow slightly once more, but it was not until after 9/11 that it returned to, and then surpassed, its size at the end of the Cold War.[106] Though the Service's work against serious organized crime started only in October 1996, demand for its assistance quickly began to outstrip the resources available. In the financial year 1997/8, the first full year of the Service's anti-crime operations, its intelligence helped in the recovery of over 50 kilos of heroin and in bringing about sixty-five arrests – chief among them that of Paul Ferris,[107] described by BBC Scotland as 'former king of the Glasgow under-world' and on the cover of his own memoirs as 'Glasgow's most feared gangster' with a 'capacity for extreme violence'. Strathclyde police told the Service that they 'had been pursuing Ferris for many years without result'.[108] Investigation by the Service revealed that he was also involved in a London criminal network. On 23 May 1997 Ferris was caught red-handed in London. In the boot of his car police found three MAC-10 sub-machine guns capable of firing 1,200 rounds a minute, two sawn-off shotguns, a Thompson sub-machine gun, handguns, silencers and ammu-nition.[109] Lander wrote to Sir Richard Wilson, then PUS at the Home Office: 'I have been encouraged by the smooth running of this operation, and by its overall success . . . I understand the police are delighted with our contribution. More of the same to come I hope.'[110]

During the trial, A4 surveillance reports were read out in court and were not challenged by the defence.[111] Ferris claims in his memoirs that before his arrest, 'For two years I'd been watched by MI5 in what they called Operation Shillelagh.'[112] In reality, the Service had become involved only in December 1996, five months before his arrest, at the request of the Strathclyde police, who said that Ferris had made himself 'untouch-able'.[113] In January 1998 Ferris, who had no previous convictions, was given a jail term of ten years for trafficking in guns and explosives.[114] Operation SHILLELAGH was the first serious organized crime case in which the Service's involvement became public knowledge. About three-quarters of Service crime investigations were drugs-related, including associated money-laundering, with police and public-service corruption accounting for another 10 per cent. By July 1999 the Service had success-fully completed about half of the sixty investigations requested since October 1996 by law-enforcement bodies and was devoting about 8 per cent of its resources to them. With demand for its assistance increasing, it expected that figure to rise to over 10 per cent[115] – an expectation which was to be undermined by 9/11. Because of the increasing priority of counter-terrorism, the Service's involvement in anti-crime operations was to last less than a decade.[116]

A Security Service Staff Attitude Survey in February 1997, the first since 1993,[117] indicated that the cutbacks and changes of the mid-1990s had taken some toll on morale. The morale of about 25 per cent of the Service was judged to be high (or very high), that of about 50 per cent to be 'moderate', and that of about 25 per cent to be low (or very low). Those who felt morale had declined in recent years were almost twice as numerous as those who felt it had risen.[118] Among reasons given were:

- 'Constant change as we have had over the last five years is not good for morale.'
- 'Recent changes have improved efficiency but at the expense of the camaraderie which used to be the Service's main asset.'[119]

By the spring of 1997, for the first time in its history, the Service had decided to begin advertising openly for recruits – mainly in the belief that this was now the best way of attracting high-quality staff. To minimize political controversy, however, it was decided to delay the advertising campaign until after the general election of 1 May which ended in a landslide victory for Labour under Tony Blair.[120] The first advertisement for jobs in the Security Service was placed in the *Guardian* on 21 May 1997 by the advertising agency Austin Knight, which had earlier devised anonymous recruiting campaigns for the Service.[121] It was headed 'intelligence. Use it to create waves and prevent repercussions' and carried a striking image of the ripples in a pool caused by drops of intelligence.[122] Lander personally amended the copy to correct the grammar.[123] The response to the advertisement exceeded all expectations: 12,000 telephone calls to Austin Knight on the first day, around 20,000 by the end of the week, and a final total of well over 30,000 – more than double the number who had responded to the previous record-breaking campaign of Austin Knight's parent company to recruit two British astronauts.[124] The DG's Newsletter reported that 'The overwhelming majority of the media coverage was positive in tone and generally supportive of the Service (if occasionally frivolous). This would not have been the case a few years ago, when media reports about the Service were almost invariably ill informed and hostile.' On this occasion, despite many applications from 'high quality candidates',[125] only four were recruited.[126] Advertising campaigns, however, quickly became central to Service recruitment. 'Both the ease of recruitment and the motivation and quality of our recruits', wrote Lander five years later, 'have improved greatly as a result.'[127]

The advertising campaign had the additional advantage of extending the

ıntelligence.

The reports had been filtering through for months. But suddenly there seemed to be a slight change of pattern and emphasis. How much credence should be placed on this particular source? Is there any independent corroboration? What could or should you do about it?

We're inviting you to tackle these issues in a career with a very special part of Her Majesty's Government – the Security Service. It's a career like no other but it is one that requires qualities which a lot of people in face already possess.

We're looking for strong candidates at two levels of entry.

Level 1: Your starting point is 3-4 years of work experience and a good honours degree or the intellectual clout with which you could have gained one had you so chosen. You need the analytical ability to cut through a mass of detail to get at the true picture. You'll be working in a team with people who approach the issues from many different angles. You need to be an excellent judge of human nature and someone who communicates well with people both face-to-

face and in writing. On top of all this your sound common sense, integrity and discernment enable you to find the most effective way to get your point across and make firm recommendations for action.

Level 2: In addition to the above you will have greater experience of work and the world. Your involvement would be more in managing the information gathering process and responding to the other operational needs of the Service. You'll need a proven track record of managing people and resources, and juggling conflicting priorities, with a clear understanding of the impact of your decisions. Exceptional powers of communication and persuasion will make you adept at talking your way into situations with the opportunity for gathering useful information, as well as the resourcefulness to extract yourself from less promising circumstances. The ability to deal with ambiguity and make decisions on partial information is essential. Security threats never conform to a neat routine and neither will your work – so flexibility is also essential.

People from a wide range of backgrounds

find this work uniquely satisfying: our list includes marketing executives, teachers, fund raisers, overseas aid workers, academics and journalists. You'd enjoy comprehensive training and development, with full involvement in work of national and international importance. The salary's good rather than lavish: you'll be working in a friendly and supportive environment and able to take advantage of the excellent facilities at our central London headquarters. In terms of its constantly changing mix of challenge and achievement, this is probably the career for you.

The Security Service has a firm equal opportunities policy and we are keen to recruit people from ethnic minorities or with disabilities. However you do need to be a British citizen to apply.

For more information telephone our Recruitment Advisor at Austin Knight Limited, London W1A 1DS on 0181 439 5803 (24 hour answering service). But try and avoid telling your friends about your application, because discretion is a serious part of working for the Security Service.

Please quote reference A1478.

Use it to create waves and prevent repercussions.

M I 5
THE SECURITY SERVICE

Service's openness policy – as did the decision in 1997 to begin releasing its early files to the Public Record Office. Some of the favourable publicity generated by the Service's public recruitment campaign and other aspects of its openness programme was undone as a result of the allegations made by David Shayler, a disaffected officer who left in October 1996 after an undistinguished career lasting less than five years.[128] Sir Richard Wilson found both Lander and Eliza Manningham-Buller, who became DDG in 1997, 'desperately upset' by what they regarded as Shayler's treachery: 'It really got to them.'[129] The dilemma, Lander reported, was that:

While his allegations of Service impropriety and incompetence do not stand up to close scrutiny ... it has not been possible for the Service to put the public record straight for fear of undermining the legal actions in train and also of compounding the damage to sources and methods already caused by his revelations.[130]

Among Shayler's claims taken up by some of the media were that SIS had told him it had been involved in a plot to assassinate Qaddafi; that, but for MI5 incompetence, PIRA's hugely destructive 1994 bomb attack on the NatWest Tower in Bishopsgate[131] could have been prevented; that MI5 was involved in the attempted blackmail of a Libyan student who was secretly filmed having sex and taking drugs; and that Peter Mandelson MP had been suspected of being a Soviet 'sleeper' and his phone had been bugged.[132] In Lander's view, the injunction obtained by the Attorney General against the publication of information derived from Shayler by the *Mail on Sunday* in August 1997[133] 'stopped the media feeding frenzy in its tracks'. After the injunction had stemmed the flow of information, the Service was 'able to put the record straight to ministers privately as new allegations seeped out'.[134] In Sir Richard Wilson's view, the fear of the Service leadership that the Shayler affair might turn ministers against them was exaggerated; neither they nor Whitehall regarded it as more than a minor irritant.[135] After seeking refuge in France for three years (four months of which were spent in jail after the issue of an extradition warrant), Shayler returned to Britain in 2000 and was sentenced to six months' imprisonment on official secrets charges.

During Tony Blair's first term as prime minister (May 1997 to June 2001) the Security Service thought it detected only limited interest in its work at Number Ten, save on issues concerning PIRA and Northern Ireland. As shadow home secretary, Blair had described as 'a matter of grave concern' proposals for the Service to expand its operations into fighting organized crime and other areas.[136] During each public spending round in Blair's first term, the intelligence agencies feared Treasury attempts to make their Whitehall customers pay for the intelligence they received – thus inevitably cutting their budgets. The threat to Security Service funding was exacerbated by a sudden huge increase in the cost of the new GCHQ headquarters in Cheltenham. The Treasury line was that this had to be absorbed within the Single Intelligence Vote (SIV, the successor from 1994 to the Secret Vote) – and thus to be paid for by the whole of the intelligence community.[137] The support of the cabinet secretary in keeping the Treasury at bay was of great, possibly crucial, importance in protecting the Security Service budget.

After the cuts of the mid-1990s, the Service was thus able to grow slightly during the remainder of the decade. In the course of the decade, the proportion of operational staff increased steadily. In Lander's view:

We ended the 1990s as a result far better equipped to handle the demands of our 'new work' than we began it with:

i. larger operational teams for surveillance, interception, eavesdropping and other technical operations;

ii. more officers capable of hard agent running (e.g. against terrorist or drugs targets);

iii. a far smaller clerical and bureaucratic tail facilitated by an excellent new building; and

iv. an SCS [senior civil service] equivalent senior management nearly 40% smaller.

By any measure as a consequence we left the decade a more capable and efficient organisation than we began it.[138]

One of the Service's ablest strategic thinkers at the end of the Cold War, H1/0, had correctly forecast in 1990 that, though the disappearance of the Communist threat might diminish the coherence of its role 'during the next few years', it would recover that coherence if it succeeded in gaining 'responsibility for all internal and external terrorism'.[139]

At 6 p.m. on 9 February 1996, PIRA abruptly announced the end of a seventeen-month ceasefire. Just over an hour later, a huge bomb placed in a car park near South Quay Docklands Light Railway station by Canary Wharf on the Isle of Dogs exploded, killing two men, injuring more than a hundred, laying waste a large area and causing £85 million worth of damage. A close observer of the Provisionals concluded that 'Had the IRA not bombed Docklands, it would have probably split.'[140] The South Quay attack was followed by the planting of two smaller devices; one was successfully defused, the second exploded prematurely on 18 February. An arms cache discovered subsequently indicated that these were probably intended to be the beginning of a prolonged campaign.[141] Though there were three relatively small-scale bomb attacks in London during March and April, T2 reported on 11 June: 'Intelligence suggests that PIRA is disappointed with the performance of its mainland-based ASUs since South Quay, and is anxious to rectify the situation.'[142] On the same day the DDG told the Cabinet Official Committee on Terrorism, 'It seemed that preparations for a major attack in Great Britain were well advanced . . .'[143] Five days later, on the morning of 15 June, a total of five warning telephone calls, using an authenticated PIRA codeword, were received by three television stations, Salford University and North Manchester General Hospital, warning that a bomb would explode at the Arndale Centre in central

Manchester in an hour's time. Though, thanks to a hasty mass evacuation of the city centre, there were no fatalities, more than 200 people were injured in the blast, which also caused damage to buildings estimated at £450 million. Operation SITUATED failed to identify the members of the ASU responsible.[144]

The Security Service leadership remained anxious that the Manchester bombing should not stand in the way of negotiations with the Provisionals. One of the directors recalls being struck by the 'step-change' in the Service's intelligence assessments, which now regularly included political analysis: 'We had helped to formulate similar assessments produced at Stormont for SOSNI, but earlier Box 500 reports issued on the mainland focused on security intelligence, and presumably left political assessments to the Cabinet Office and the JIC.' Though ASCRIBE was partly responsible for the 'step-change', it was also influenced by 'the personalities driving our Irish work, especially Stephen Lander and Eliza Manningham-Buller'. On 17 June, two days after the bomb attack in Manchester, Lander, who had succeeded Rimington as DG two months earlier, recommended to Major that 'the Government should *continue with its current strategy*', which included 'providing reassurance to the Provisional leadership about the nature of the talks process which is on offer'.[145]

While Lander was briefing the Prime Minister, PIRA was launching an audacious attempt to disrupt the whole of Greater London's power supply. Operation AIRLINES, which defeated the PIRA attempt to do so, began with intelligence that a member of an ASU had taken up residence at 58 Woodbury Street, Tooting Broadway. Surveillance on 8 July 1996 observed an individual codenamed PARADISE NEWS (later identified after his arrest as Donal Gannon, a trained electrician and one of PIRA's leading experts in the design and manufacture of explosive devices) arriving at the address. Less than an hour later another individual, codenamed ANOTHER TOMORROW (subsequently identified as the former US marine John Crawley, who had served ten years in jail in the Irish Republic from 1984 to 1994 for his part in shipping arms from America to the Provisionals),[146] emerged from the house. Not long afterwards Gannon and TULIP STEM (later identified as Gerard Hanratty, who had been convicted in 1988 on the continent of relatively minor arms offences) were followed as they travelled in a blue Peugeot 405 to reconnoitre electricity sub-stations. While Gannon returned to Woodbury Street, Hanratty was tailed to a flat in Verona Court, 68 St James's Drive, in Tooting. Next day a fourth member of the ASU, codenamed BREAD BOARD (quickly identified as Eoin Morrow, a PIRA specialist in the manufacture of improvised explosive devices (IEDs) and the use of radio-control systems who had served a prison term in the Republic for armed robbery), was observed at Woodbury Street, and Gannon was followed to a house at 61 Lugard Road in Peckham. In the course of the day Crawley and Gannon were observed making inquiries about self-storage facilities and the transmission of Irish money orders. That evening Gannon was observed meeting a fifth ASU member, RAVE DOWN, at Wimbledon Park Underground station; RAVE DOWN went to stay with Hanratty in the Verona Court flat. On 11 July Gannon was followed to Birmingham where he met an individual codenamed GALLERY PICTURE in the Brewery Tap public house, before the two men went to view a storage unit on the Brownhills industrial estate. Meanwhile two further ASU members were observed entering 61 Lugard Road: CRAFT FAIR and EXCESS MONEY (later identified as, respectively, Patrick Martin, a Belfast Provisional and known associate of Hanratty, and Francis Rafferty, also from Belfast but previously unknown to the Security Service).[147] John Grieve, commander of SO13 at Scotland Yard, later described the ASU as one of the ablest and most experienced in PIRA history.[148]

Over the next few days the members of the ASU were observed purchasing a Ford Sierra for £2,200 in cash, moving around bulky holdalls, reconnoitring further electricity sub-stations and carrying out various anti-surveillance procedures. At 2.35 a.m. on 15 July the police entered all three ASU addresses. Crawley, Gannon, Hanratty, Martin and RAVE DOWN were arrested at Woodbury Street, Rafferty and Morrow at Lugard Road. The timers and power units (though not the detonators and Semtex explosive) for thirty-seven partially assembled IEDs were also discovered during the search of Lugard Road. The flat at Verona Court was empty; it was subsequently discovered that the ASU had abandoned it after compromising its security by using a forged £20 note to pay the rent. Later the same day, GALLERY PICTURE was arrested in Birmingham. With the exception of RAVE DOWN, whose case in court was that he had been a mere messenger, and GALLERY PICTURE, the arrested ASU members were each convicted and sentenced to thirty-five years' imprisonment. Had the ASU achieved its aims, the results would have been devastating.[149] The ASU members claimed improbably during the trial that they had intended only to use hoax devices and not actually to disrupt the London power supply.[150]

But for the arrest of the AIRLINES ASU, its next major target might well have been Birmingham – as had been indicated by a series of intelligence reports in June and July. Gannon's attempt to obtain a storage facility in Birmingham also points clearly in that direction.[151] AIRLINES, possibly the Security Service's most successful anti-PIRA operation, was followed by Operation TINNITUS, which disrupted a Provisional attempt during August and September 1996 to mount a major attack – probably using vehicle-borne IEDs – against central London. On 23 September 1996 four members of an ASU operating in London were arrested; a fifth (Dermot O'Neill) was shot during the arrests and later died from his wounds. Four large boxes each containing a large quantity of HME-ANS (ammonium nitrate/sugar), an additional 3 tonnes of bagged HME-ANS, weapons and under-vehicle devices were recovered from a self-storage unit in Cranford Way, Hornsey.[152]

In the aftermath of AIRLINES and TINNITUS, Lander was in cautiously confident mood. In a private lecture on terrorism, he told the audience: 'Even terrorists regard the UK as a hostile and risky environment. We know this from what intelligence tells us terrorist groups and hostile states think. We also hear it from the terrorists themselves.' 'No one', claimed Lander, 'has a better record.'[153] That record, in the Service's view, contributed to PIRA's renewed willingness to consider a compromise political settlement.

Labour's landslide election victory on 1 May 1997 was quickly followed by a new political initiative. The new SOSNI, Mo Mowlam, whose forcefully frank negotiating style and ability to win Republican trust (at the inevitable cost of provoking Unionist distrust) made her a crucial part of that initiative, greeted the DG at their first meeting with the question: 'Why should I believe a word you say?' She quickly came to do so.[154] On 19 July PIRA announced an 'unequivocal' restoration of the August 1994 ceasefire from noon on the following day. Despite what seemed to be Tony Blair's general lack of interest in the intelligence community on taking office,[155] the Security Service noted that he appeared to pay 'close attention' to its Northern Ireland Intelligence Reports (NIIRs).[156] In 1997–8 the Service's Whitehall and Northern Ireland customers judged 80 per cent of NIIR reporting 'very valuable' or 'exceptionally valuable'.[157] Lander was able to tell the Prime Minister at a meeting on 30 October 1997 that, while he could not rule out the possibility of a further PIRA surprise attack such as that on Canary Wharf, intelligence on the thinking and plans of the Provisional leadership had improved. Though a meeting earlier in the month of the General Army Convention, which represented PIRA rank and file, had led to some resignations by hardliners, the overall outcome had 'boosted the leadership's confidence': 'Some key figures . . . probably see the ceasefire as a genuine opportunity to reach a settlement. Both intelligence and overt reporting indicate that they are prepared to consider a settlement which stops short of a united Ireland.'[158]

By January 1998 it was clear that the only settlement on offer by London and Dublin was one which balanced British and Irish constitutional change: a Northern Ireland assembly, a new Anglo-Irish agreement, a British–Irish Council linking the Assembly to other UK bodies, and North–South structures. Parts of the final Belfast (Good Friday) Agreement were, unsurprisingly and perhaps creatively, ambiguous. The core of the Agreement, however, was unambiguous. Northern Ireland would remain part of the United Kingdom as long as it was supported by a majority of its people. In return Unionists were required to accept power-sharing and cross-border co-operation – and to allow Sinn Fein a 'soft landing' into the political arena. The issues of the release of Republican prisoners and, still more, of decommissioning the large PIRA arsenal inevitably remained contentious. The Security Service reported before the referendum on the Agreement: 'Whilst many members of PIRA were initially sceptical about the Agreement, the long-held assumption by volunteers that PIRA would return to violence in May appears to have diminished.'[159] The referendum on 22 May produced the highest turnout in Northern Ireland since 1921, with a 71.1 per cent majority in favour – substantially higher, according to opinion polls, among the nationalist community than among the Unionists.[160] The large nationalist majority in favour increased its acceptability to Republicans.

President Bill Clinton had declared after the signing of the Belfast (Good Friday) Agreement: 'Peace is no longer a dream, it is a reality.'[161] More than a decade later, despite the manifold travails of the peace process, it remains so.

2

Holy Terror

Like thousands of other foreign Muslims, Usama bin Laden (UBL), son of a Saudi billionaire and the most dangerous religious extremist in the history of contemporary terrorism, travelled to Afghanistan in the 1980s to take part in the victorious jihad* against Soviet occupying forces. 'In our religion,' he later told *Time* magazine, 'there is a special place in the hereafter for those who participate in jihad. One day in Afghanistan was like 1,000 days of praying in an ordinary mosque.'[1] In 1988 he established Al Qaida ('The Base') to continue jihad outside Afghanistan when the war was over.[2] UBL first came to the notice of the Security Service in January 1993 in connection with the attempted assassination a month earlier of a member of the Politburo of the Marxist Yemeni Socialist Party (regarded by UBL as apostates) and bomb attacks aimed at US servicemen in two Aden hotels. The attacks were bungled, killing an Australian tourist and a Yemeni hotel worker but no Americans or Yemeni Marxists. The perpetrators were caught and confessed that the operations had been organized by the Egyptian terrorist group Islamic Jihad led by Ayman al Zawahiri (later UBL's deputy) and financed by Bin Laden.[3] As yet, however, both Bin Laden and the Yemen attacks attracted little attention from intelligence communities on either side of the Atlantic.[4] Though the Security Service was receiving reports on Bin Laden from early in 1993, a permanent file was not opened until two years later.

A wide-ranging internal Security Service study on 'The Origins of Terrorism' commissioned in 1994 still saw no serious threat from the transnational Islamist terrorism which was to preoccupy the Service in the first decade of the twenty-first century. 'Religious terrorism', the study concluded, became a 'potent' force only when allied to national interests.[5] For most of the 1990s the Service believed that the principal non-Irish

---

* Most Muslims saw jihad primarily as non-violent (for example, as a spiritual struggle to lead a better life). UBL was obsessed with the idea of jihad as holy war.

terrorist threat came from Middle Eastern state-sponsored terrorism.[6] The main practitioner of state terrorism in Britain during the 1990s was believed to be the Iranian Ministry of Intelligence and Security (MOIS). Within Europe MOIS's most frequent targets were Iranian Kurdish dissidents, of whom at least seventeen were assassinated between 1989 and 1997. The highest-profile victim of MOIS foreign operations, assassinated in Paris in 1991, was the Shah's last Prime Minister, Shahpur Bakhtiar, an outspoken critic of the Islamic Republic established by the Ayatollah Khomeini twelve years before.[7] The fact that none of the killings took place in the UK[8] probably owed much to successful Security Service and Special Branch surveillance and periodic disruption of MOIS operations against dissidents.

The main target of MOIS UK operations during the 1990s, some of them assisted by its Lebanese Shia ally, Hizballah ('Party of God'),[9] was one of Britain's best-known writers, the Indian-born Salman Rushdie, author of the novel *The Satanic Verses*, whose title referred to the medieval legend (deeply insulting to most Muslims), retold by Rushdie, that some of the Quran's original verses originated with Satan and were later deleted by Muhammad. In February 1989, four months before his death, Ayatollah Khomeini issued a fatwa condemning Rushdie and his publishers to death for blasphemy: 'I call on zealous Muslims to execute them quickly, wherever they find them, so that no one will dare to insult Islam again.' Faced with 'the loudest death-threat in history', Rushdie was forced to go into hiding, protected by the Special Branch. A few days after the issue of the fatwa, he watched on television as he was burned in effigy at a demonstration in Pakistan attended by tens of thousands of chanting protesters.[10] Protests among British Muslims had begun even before the fatwa but increased greatly afterwards. An estimated 20,000 protesters from across Britain took part in an anti-Rushdie demonstration in London on 27 May 1989. There were several arson attacks on bookshops selling *The Satanic Verses*, but the amateurish devices used in the attacks indicated that no established terrorist group was involved.[11] The hate campaign against Rushdie, though its significance was not fully grasped at the time, began the radicalization of a minority of young British Muslims.

The main threat to Rushdie's life, however, came not from extremist British Muslims but from MOIS operations.[12] The deadly seriousness of the threat was demonstrated by the stabbing in 1991 of both the Japanese translator of *The Satanic Verses*, who was killed, and the Italian translator, who survived. In 1993 the Norwegian publisher was injured in a gun attack.[13] The Security Service learned in May 1992 that Mehdi Seyed

Sadighi of the MOIS London station was tasked with collecting operational intelligence on Rushdie. Sadighi was expelled,[14] as was a second MOIS officer who operated under student cover. Over the next few months there was a series of MOIS-inspired operations to target Rushdie.[15] Others continued more intermittently for the rest of the decade.[16] The fact that none succeeded, despite MOIS's success in carrying out assassinations on the continent, was probably due mainly to a combination of expert protection and good intelligence.

Stella Rimington declared during the Dimbleby Lecture in June 1994: 'The threat to British interests from terrorism of international origin is lower than it was in the 1980s.' Among the first terrorist bomb attacks in Britain after the Cold War not mounted by Irish Republicans were the car-bombings of the Israeli embassy and a London Jewish charity in July, only a month after Rimington's lecture.[17] Suspicion initially fell on Hizballah, which had already planned one attack on the Israeli embassy, successfully disrupted by the Security Service.[18] Subsequent intelligence, however, indicated that, though Hizballah had indeed been planning another attack, it had been both surprised and annoyed to be upstaged by a secular Palestinian group which struck first.[19] Two members of the group were later sentenced to twenty years' imprisonment.[20]

While continuing to warn of the threat from Iranian state-sponsored terrorism, the Service told the heads of special branches in December 1995 that transnational Islamist terrorism was much less of a problem:

Suggestions in the press of a world-wide Islamic extremist network poised to launch terrorist attacks against the West are greatly exaggerated ... The contact between Islamic extremists in various countries appears to be largely opportunistic at present and seems unlikely to result in the emergence of a potent trans-national force.[21]

The Security Service saw Usama bin Laden chiefly as a terrorist financier rather than as the emerging leader of 'a potent trans-national force'. Throughout the 1990s it regarded the source of his wealth as a 'mystery': 'He owns construction companies etc. but these do not appear to be sufficiently large to provide the scale of income needed to fund his organisation.' The Service was sceptical of reports that he received money from 'the rest of the Bin Laden clan', noting contrary claims, of which it was also sceptical, 'that the family were planning to assassinate him'.[22] The Service's decision to open a permanent file on UBL in 1995 reflected the increasing number of references to him in intelligence reports. It noted in September: 'No matter where you look in studying Islamic Extremism from Kashmir to Algeria, the name Bin Laden seems to crop up. He is clearly an important figure and we are intensifying our efforts to discover what influence he has over individuals and groups in this country . . .'[23]

Though a new section was created in 1995 to investigate the Islamist threat, its main initial priority was not UBL but Algerian extremists in Britain connected to the Algerian Armed Islamic Group (GIA) which was believed to be responsible for bomb attacks in France which killed seven and wounded 180.[24] A Service investigation, prompted by requests for assistance from the French DST and supported by MPSB and the Met's Anti-Terrorist Branch, led to the arrest in December 1995 of six Algerian militants in London, one of whom was helping to finance a terrorist campaign in France. Another operation, in conjunction with the French and other foreign services, led to the arrest of the UK-based co-ordinator of GIA arms procurement in Europe.[25] Records found in one GIA militant's home showed that he had received funding from UBL's headquarters, then in Khartoum.[26] Bin Laden was also reported to be financing Mujahedin groups in Afghanistan and Pakistan, as well as al Zawahiri's Egyptian Islamic Jihad, but as yet the Service had no intelligence 'that Bin Laden is personally involved in planning or carrying out terrorist attacks':[27] 'Should Bin Laden come to the UK we do not believe he would instigate acts of terrorism here or use Britain as a base for organising terrorism. However, there is little doubt he would take the opportunity to encourage Islamic extremist groups in the UK to continue their activities.'[28]

Late in 1995 there was a probably erroneous (though prophetic) intelligence report that 'Bin Laden is involved in a plot to mount a suicide bomb attack in the UK.'[29] On the recommendation of the Security Service, in January 1996 the Home Secretary signed an exclusion order prohibiting UBL from entering the UK in the interests of national security.[30] The Service was bemused by continuing reports in the media and even from some foreign intelligence agencies that Bin Laden had visited, or was about to visit, Britain.[31] It dismissed as 'risible' reports by the US television channel NBC and the *Evening Standard* that Bin Laden regularly flew in and out of London by private jet.[32] The Director of the US Congressional Task Force on Terrorism and Unconventional Warfare, Yossef Bodansky, later claimed, however, that in the mid-1990s Bin Laden 'settled in the London suburb of Wembley', where 'he purchased property'.[33] Since Bin Laden was then, at an estimated 6 foot 7 inches, probably the world's tallest leading terrorist, had a long beard and dressed in flowing robes, it is unlikely that he would have passed unnoticed in Wembley.

Until 9/11, instead of referring to Al Qaida (a name never used by UBL in public), Security Service intelligence reports used phrases such as 'Bin

Laden and his associates'. Stella Rimington had never heard the name Al Qaida until March 1996, when it cropped up during a farewell visit to the United States a few weeks before her retirement.[34] She and SLO Washington were taken aback by the interest shown in UBL by those they met in the US. During their meeting with the National Security Advisor, Tony Lake, on 4 March, the threat from Bin Laden was the first issue raised by Lake after an initial discussion of PIRA and the Troubles. 'We were', reported SLO, 'unprepared for this, and were able only to acknowledge reporting of his extensive role as a financier of Islamic terrorist groups.' Unusually, the DG had been poorly briefed before the meeting. She and SLO were unaware till after the meeting that, a few days earlier, senior CIA counter-terrorist officers had paid a prearranged visit to Thames House where, wrote a doubtless irritated SLO, UBL 'issues were presumably discussed exhaustively'.[35] Shortly afterwards, however, the Security Service became, it believed, 'the first UK, and perhaps first Western, agency to obtain a sample [recording] of Bin Laden's voice', which it shared with the Americans.[36]

The Security Service's role in helping to contain state-sponsored terrorism enhanced its reputation in Whitehall. The percentage of its reports on this subject rated 'extremely valuable' or 'very valuable' by its Whitehall customers rose from 33 per cent in 1996–7 to 52 per cent in 1997–8.[37] The tone of these reports was increasingly reassuring. The Security Service was cautiously confident by 1998 that, save for the continuing menace to Rushdie, the threat to Britain from state-sponsored terrorism had been successfully contained: 'This may reflect international pressure to desist from terrorism. But it also owes much to HMG's commitment to a tough visa regime towards identified intelligence officers; and the continued deployment of intelligence resources to investigate their intelligence activity.'[38]

The Security Service Annual Report for 1997–8, completed in July 1998, was the first to mention Bin Laden by name and 'important collaboration with the Americans' against him.[39] Soon afterwards, on 7 August 1998, Al Qaida carried out its first major terrorist attack. Huge bombs in trucks driven by suicide bombers almost demolished the US embassy and surrounding buildings in Nairobi and, ten minutes later, badly damaged the embassy in Dar es Salaam. This first use of simultaneous suicide-bomber attacks against different targets was to be repeated on a much larger scale on 9/11. In Nairobi 213 were killed (only twelve of them American) and several thousand injured, of whom 150 were blinded by flying glass. In Dar es Salaam the toll was eleven dead and eighty-five wounded, all

Africans.[40] On 20 August Tomahawk cruise missiles were fired from US navy vessels in the Arabian Ocean at two Al Qaida targets: the Khost training camp in Afghanistan and a Khartoum pharmaceutical plant which, according to US intelligence reports, was manufacturing a precursor agent for nerve gas with financial support from UBL. Though the targets were hit, Bin Laden survived the attack; he was reported to have left Khost with only a few hours to spare. Controversy continues over whether the Sudanese target had really been involved in nerve-gas production.[41]

In the aftermath of the Al Qaida attacks in August 1998, the Security Service recognized for the first time that the main international terrorist threat no longer came from the state sponsors with which it had become well acquainted over the past two decades but from the growth of trans-national Islamist terrorism of which it had far less experience.[42] Seven weeks after the East African embassy bombings, Security Service surveillance of Islamist extremists in London led to the disruption of a plot to bomb the US embassy in Tirana by members of al Zawahiri's Egyptian Islamic Jihad (EIJ). In late July, the Service had received intelligence indicating that the EIJ leader in the UK, Ibrahim Eidarous, had instructed EIJ militants in Albania to reconnoitre the US embassy in preparation for a terrorist attack.[43] He and five other EIJ members were arrested in London on 23 September. There were further arrests in Turin on 2 October and an EIJ militant was killed while resisting arrest in Tirana. The Service reported that:

With the main players in the UK and Albania now neutralised, the planned attack against the Embassy will have been disrupted. Although Eidarous indicated that a separate team would enter Albania to launch the attack itself, we believe that this would be difficult to do without an infrastructure of support already in place and the basic reconnaissance incomplete.[44]

The Service's Annual Report for 1998–9 put the disruption of the attack on the US Tirana embassy at the top of its 'successes against international terrorism' in the course of the year, but warned of worse to come.[45] In the year after the East African embassy bombings, there was increasing intelligence that 'UBL and his allies' were planning widely dispersed attacks on US targets in the Gulf, the Middle East, Central Asia, South-east Asia, the Indian sub-continent, Europe, North America and East, West and Central Africa. According to a Security Service report of 21 July 1999: 'Intelligence has linked UBL to plans for bomb attacks, the use of biological toxins, kidnaps, hijackings, and missile attacks on aircraft. Most intelligence has pointed to attacks against US embassies although reports suggest that UBL now also sees the UK as one of his prime targets.'

On the strength of these reports, in June 1999 the United States closed its embassies in Gambia, Senegal, Liberia, Madagascar and Namibia. Britain followed suit except in Liberia. The Security Service puzzled over why there were so many more reports of threats than actual attacks:

The allied intelligence community does not have a clear view of UBL's terrorist planning process. Even the most reliably sourced intelligence received on this question usually consists of a snapshot of a proposed plan being discussed. Most of the reporting does not make clear how far advanced the plan is. It is rare that intelligence has named those who are to take part in a planned attack.

The fact that there had been no attacks by Bin Laden since the East African embassy bombings, however, did not necessarily mean that the warnings of further attacks were false: 'Intelligence on planned attacks may reflect initial targeting/planning rather than fully formulated attack plans.' It was possible that some of the planned attacks had been disrupted by the arrests of Islamist militants in Albania, Egypt, Ethiopia, Mauretania and Tajikistan. The Security Service also believed that some attack warnings might have derived from deliberate disinformation by UBL. A senior member of Egyptian Islamic Jihad was reported to have said that there had never been any intention to attack the US and UK embassies in Africa which had been closed in the summer of 1998. Bin Laden had simply been conducting psychological warfare 'to instil fear in the minds of Americans and Britons'.[46]

Since 1995, G Branch had had a desk officer responsible for studying the problem of radicalization within the British Muslim community which was to preoccupy the Security Service during the early twenty-first century.[47] The Service's Annual Report for 1998–9 was the first to highlight the problem:

In recent years we have given much thought to how to identify those in the UK who develop extreme Islamic views and to deter them from subsequently becoming involved in terrorism ... The challenge for us is to find ways of predicting the associations and conditioning factors in the UK which convert young Muslims into militant extremists, but to do so in a way which does not exacerbate religious and racial sensitivities. In short, we need to understand how individuals who are attracted by militant Islam at home become terrorists or potential terrorists when overseas, and to find ways of undermining that connection.[48]

The Service still failed to foresee that radicalized Muslim 'militant extremists' might engage in terrorism *inside* as well as outside the United Kingdom.

The growing priority given to the Islamist threat was, however, marked by the appointment of Jonathan Evans, one of the leading high-fliers of his generation, as G9 (Middle Eastern counter-terrorism) in the autumn of 1998. Evans had joined the Service in 1980 immediately after graduating from Bristol University in classical studies. On his first day in Gower Street, he was greeted by an older Service officer from a military background with the words: 'Ah, one of the young intellectuals!' 'The nicest thing anyone ever said about me,' Evans recalls.[49] Nine years after his appointment as G9, he became DG.

Like all other Western security and intelligence agencies, the Security Service had no prior warning of the 9/11 attacks on New York and Washington. A Service report in the summer of 1999 somewhat exaggerated the obstacles in the way of an Al Qaida attack in North America: 'Intelligence suggests that whilst UBL is seeking to launch an attack inside the US, he is aware that the US will provide a tough operating environment for his organisation.'[50] We now know that by the time the Service issued this report, planning for the 9/11 attacks by Khalid Sheikh Mohammed (KSM), with the active personal involvement of UBL, had already begun. Though KSM was still 'off the Service's radar',[51] he had helped his nephew Ramzi Yousef plan and finance the first, failed attempt to bring down one of the twin towers of the New York World Trade Center in 1993 as well as the unsuccessful 'Bojinka' plot to plant bombs in twelve US airliners timed to explode in mid-air over the Pacific in 1994. The failed 1993 attack on the World Trade Center was remembered in the United States chiefly for the bizarre behaviour of Mohammed Salameh, the terrorist who had rented the truck used in the bombing and tried afterwards to get back his $400 deposit by claiming the truck had been stolen. What tended to be forgotten was the technical ingenuity of Ramzi Yousef, who planted a bomb which ripped a hole through seven storeys of the World Trade Center, killing six (a miraculously low figure) and wounding a thousand.[52] The level of protective security at the US airports which were to be used by the suicide hijackers on 9/11 scarcely justified the Security Service claim that Bin Laden was faced with 'a tough operating environment' in the United States. Over the previous few years the Federal Aviation Authority had reported repeated security violations at Logan Airport, Boston, from which two of the hijacked planes took off.[53]

In July 2000 a Security Service operation, codenamed LARGE, uncovered the first Islamist bomb factory to be detected in Britain. A Bangladeshi-born British Muslim in Birmingham, Moinul Abedin, was discovered to be seeking to purchase weapons and explosives. Together with a chemist and fellow Muslim, Dr Faisal Mustafa, who was alleged to have advised him on the production of home-made explosives, he was arrested on 17 November.[54] It was later revealed at their trial that fifteen Service officers and four agents had been involved in the surveillance operation. The A Branch team leader gave evidence in court from behind a screen, revealing that they had codenamed Abedin PIVOTING DANCER. Despite Abedin's claim that he had simply been setting up a fireworks business, he was convicted and sentenced to twenty years' imprisonment. Mustafa was acquitted.[55] At the time of his arrest it was believed that Abedin had no Al Qaida connection – or even, as the DG, Sir Stephen Lander, told Service staff, 'any obvious affiliation to a specific Islamic group or network'. The targets for his explosives remained unknown.[56] That was still the belief at the time of Abedin's conviction in 2002. Opinions within the Service on the likelihood that Abedin had an Al Qaida connection later varied. At one point, as Dame Eliza Manningham-Buller revealed in a public speech, it was believed that Operation LARGE had uncovered an Al Qaida operation 'to detonate a large bomb in the UK'.[57] Further research, however, concluded that, though the operation was *inspired* by Al Qaida's global jihad ideology, there was no intelligence to show that 'Al Qaida tasked or directed the operation.'[58]

Well before 9/11 it was believed that the greatest potential long-term threat from Bin Laden came from his desire to acquire chemical, biological, radiological and even nuclear weapons. The CIA believed that Al Qaida had been deeply impressed by the sarin-gas attack on the Tokyo subway by the fanatical Japanese cult Aum Shinrikyo in March 1995 'and saw the attack as a model for achieving their own ambitions'.[59] Al Qaida's understanding of radiological and nuclear material, however, still remained unsophisticated. According to intelligence received in the autumn of 1999, Bin Laden fell for a nuclear scam which had been current for a quarter of a century, purchasing a substance known as 'red mercury' – physically similar to uranium oxide but chemically quite different.[60]

We now know that a year before 9/11, thanks to its counter-proliferation operations, the Security Service – without realizing it at the time – succeeded in disrupting an attempt by Al Qaida to develop biological weapons (BW). In September 2000 the Pakistani microbiologist Rauf Ahmad attended a conference in Britain on dangerous pathogens, where he sought samples from other delegates as well as help in obtaining a bioreactor and cell counter. The Service was alerted to his activities and a search of his luggage on departure from the UK revealed £13,000, which he claimed was 'to buy equipment', documents detailing his contacts (including UK companies) and a copy of his CV. The CV revealed that Ahmad had a PhD from a university in Pakistan, had attended earlier conferences in Britain in 1997 and 1999 and had published scientific papers on anthrax. Security Service officers visited the UK companies with which Ahmad had made contact and they broke off their dealings with him.[61]

Ahmad's visits to Britain had much greater significance than was apparent at the time. Their purpose only became clear after 9/11, from documents recovered by US forces in Afghanistan in 2001. Among the documents was correspondence between 'Abu Mohamed' and 'Abu Ibrahim' about procurement of equipment, cultures and training for BW production. 'Abu Mohamed' was quickly identified as UBL's deputy, Ayman al Zawahiri. 'Abu Ibrahim' took longer to track down. References in the correspondence to his foreign travels, attendance at conferences in the UK and attempts to procure dangerous pathogens, however, were discovered to match exactly the information on Ahmad in Security Service files.[62] That discovery confirmed existing fears that UBL continued to regard as 'a religious duty' the acquisition of weapons of mass destruction for use against the monstrous conspiracy of 'Jews and Crusaders' who – in his deluded imagination – have threatened Islam for the last thousand years.

Morale in the Security Service at the beginning of the twenty-first century, following the end of the era of cutbacks, was high. In April 2000 a 'Staff Opinion Survey', conducted for the first time by an external consultant, produced 'some of the highest scores we have seen in the ten years we have been involved with staff surveys and this applies to both the public and private sector . . .'[63] In recent years only the romantic publisher Mills and Boon had registered even higher job satisfaction ratings in surveys carried out by the consultant.[64] Collaboration with SIS was closer than at any time since Cumming and Kell sat in the same office in the Drew detective agency in 1909. In the spring of 2001 the Security Service carried out an 'audit' of relations with SIS among its nineteen section heads. All reported that they knew their opposite numbers in SIS and that members of their sections had visited SIS within the last three months. Two-thirds of operational section heads reported that they 'routinely' invited SIS colleagues to planning meetings.[65]

From the early summer of 2001 onwards the Security Service received mounting intelligence which pointed to a major Al Qaida attack on US targets, but gave no indication of the attack plan. An early warning to senior Whitehall officials on 22 June reported specific threats to American interests in Saudi Arabia, Bahrain, Kuwait, Jordan, Turkey, Italy and Kenya.[66] The Service concluded on 6 July:

It is not yet clear to what extent the recent rise in threat reporting reflects increased intelligence coverage. The reporting itself is of varying reliability, and is too recent to expect much corroboration. But the increase in volume is sufficient to indicate that *UBL and those who share his agenda are currently well advanced in operational planning for a number of major attacks on Western interests.* References to vehicle bombs and suicide bombs in some of the intelligence are consistent with UBL's modus operandi, although such details are not usually discussed so openly.

The most likely *location* for an attack on Western interests by UBL and those who share his agenda is in the Gulf States, or the wider Middle East. But the recent references to e.g. Rome and Nairobi are a reminder of UBL's and his associates' readiness to target further afield.[67]

Similar Security Service warnings to Whitehall of imminent attack continued at intervals over the next two months, up to and including the morning of 11 September. The intelligence received during the summer of 2001, however, did not point either to a major attack in the United States or to an operation based on hijacked aircraft.[68]

The terrorist attacks of 11 September 2001 in the United States brought the Security Service more visibly to centre-stage in Whitehall than ever before in its history. Three months into the second term of Blair's government, 9/11 produced an overnight transformation in his attitude to the Service.[69] The news of the attacks on the twin towers and the Pentagon by suicide hijackers who had taken over US passenger jets reached the Prime Minister in a Brighton hotel where he was putting the finishing touches to his speech to the TUC annual conference. Instead of delivering the speech, he made a brief appearance on the conference platform, then took the train to London, leaving the text to be circulated in his absence.[70] By the time Blair reached Downing Street, COBR had already met under the chairmanship of Sir Richard Wilson who had become cabinet secretary in 1998.[71] Before COBR convened again, this time chaired by the Prime Minister, he was briefed by Wilson, Lander and John Scarlett, chairman of the Joint Intelligence Committee.[72] In the light of later intelligence, the briefing paper prepared by G9 for Lander before his meeting with Tony Blair somewhat underestimated Bin Laden's direct control, through Khalid Sheikh Mohammed, of the 9/11 attack plans:

We should not think of Usama Bin Laden as the head of a coherent unified terrorist structure. He is not a terrorist commander in the sense that, for example, Abu Nidhal was.

The group which he nominally commands, Al Qaida, is not hierarchical and does not have formal membership. We should think in terms simply of those who are most inspired by Bin Laden's teachings and most loyal to him.[73]

Alastair Campbell, Blair's adviser and director of communications and strategy, wrote in his diary after the briefings:

Scarlett and Lander were both pretty impressive, didn't mess about, thought about what they said, and said what they thought . . . Lander said this was a logical step-up from the car bomb. Turning a plane into a bomb and destroying one of the great symbols of America takes some doing but they have done it and they have been able to do it because they have any number of terrorists prepared to kill themselves.[74]

Campbell noted after further briefings next day that 'both C [Sir Richard Dearlove] and Lander were very good on big picture and detail.'[75] Lander, in Sir Richard Wilson's view, was 'brilliant'.[76] The DG was struck by 'how unprepared some key Government figures were on 11 September'. He later told Service staff:

None of the key Ministerial team had any direct experience of major terrorism and some key officials were new in post. The Prime Minister picked up the issues very quickly indeed following the intelligence briefings, involving us, on 11 and 12 September. By the evening of the second day it was clear that the Taleban and Al Qa'ida was on his agenda.[77]

Though the great majority of lives lost on 9/11 were American, more British citizens – sixty-seven of them – were also killed than in any other terrorist attack.

The Al Qaida attacks on New York and Washington immediately gave a new intensity to the intelligence Special Relationship. While Lander stayed in London to brief Blair and COBR, the DDG, Eliza Manningham-Buller, flew to Washington on 12 September – at a time when US airspace was still officially closed – with the Chief of SIS, Sir Richard Dearlove, and the Director of GCHQ. Their aircraft was accompanied to Andrews Air Force Base by an escort of eight USAF F-16s, and the British delegation was immediately whisked away to dinner and prolonged crisis talks at the CIA's Langley headquarters with the DCI, George Tenet, the Director of the National Security Agency and the Deputy Director of the FBI. Lander told Security Service staff: 'It was clear that the American side, who were exhausted (few had had any sleep) and angry, deeply appreciated seeing friends from the UK, coming to offer support and help.'[78] It was an emotional moment – in Tenet's view, 'as touching an event as I experienced during my seven years at the CIA'.[79]

9/11 transformed relations between Blair and Lander from distant to warm. Like previous DGs at meetings with ministers, Lander always wore a dark suit. Blair and his advisers were sometimes casually dressed. Campbell wrote after one intelligence briefing, 'The spooks were all in dark suits and carrying their battered briefcases.' Blair told them, 'If I didn't know you were all so young, I'd say there was a generational gap.'[80] He was plainly unaware that, while Rimington was DG, efforts had to be made to spruce up Lander, who had no great liking for dark suits and well-polished black shoes, before he met ministers and senior officials. David Blunkett, who had become home secretary three months before 9/11, was less enthusiastic about Lander than Blair. He was, however, almost certainly in a Whitehall minority in complaining that 'it's almost as though [Lander] talks in riddles, which makes it very difficult to pin him down.'[81]

Not all Security Service staff were happy with President Bush's call for a 'War on Terror' (a phrase later lampooned in a Service revue entitled 'The War on Terry (WOT)'). Lander sought to reassure staff on 27 September: 'This is a war on terrorism in the same sense as we talk of a war on drugs. A military response is obviously under consideration, but you should be reassured that political, humanitarian and intelligence/law enforcement responses are also high on the UK agenda.'[82] The 'military response' began with the bombing of Afghanistan on 7 October by the USAF and the RAF after the ruling Taleban regime had refused to hand over Bin Laden for trial in the United States and close down Al Qaida bases. Alastair Campbell was struck by how quickly War Cabinet meetings at Number Ten became routine, 'with the spooks and defence guys sitting up straight and getting ready to do their stuff, Scarlett, C [Dearlove], Lander, C[hief of the] D[efence] S[taff, Admiral Sir Michael Boyce] all chipping in, very matter-of-fact and straightforward'.[83] By early December, though Bin Laden escaped from his mountain hideout in the Tora Bora caves, the land forces of the US-led coalition had defeated the Taleban. Shortly before Christmas, Blair wrote to Lander:

The Government and the British people are fortunate to be served by security and intelligence organisations whose professionalism is admired and, by our enemies, feared throughout the world. My thanks on behalf of the Government for all you are doing. We all have cause to be grateful for your efforts.

Lander told staff early in the New Year:

For once Government has put its money where its mouth is and has given us extra money this year and next year for additional effort on ICT [international counter-terrorism], so funding should not be a problem. Until recruitment can catch up, however, that will continue to mean lower priority work having to be reduced or put on a care and maintenance basis.[84]

During Blair's remaining years at Number Ten, the Security Service received far more public praise from the Prime Minister and successive Home Secretaries than from any previous government. Reflecting on the period since the end of the Cold War before his retirement in October 2002, Lander noted the major 'change in the relationship between the Service and the rest of Government':

During the Cold War the day to day work of the Service did not engage ministerial attention at all since it concerned the intricacies of security (vetting, visas etc) in the context of a well understood strategic threat. Today with over 60% of our work on terrorism, what we do and what we find out can be of direct relevance to Ministers' day to day concerns and thus to those of their Departments.[85]

3

After 9/11

During the year after 9/11 the Security Service's most visible successes were in counter-espionage rather than in counter-terrorism, which for the past decade had been its main priority. The Service succeeded in catching two employees of British Aerospace who were attempting to sell highly classified defence secrets to Russian intelligence. Both were caught by sting operations. The first was Rafael Bravo, a security guard at the British Aerospace offices in Stanmore, Middlesex, who made a ham-fisted attempt to pass classified documents to the Russians which he was believed to have found in a security cabinet that had been left unlocked.[1] Bravo pleaded guilty at his trial, which opened in December 2001, and revealed that he had tried to telephone the Russian embassy to offer his services, but the number he found in a phone book connected him only to an answering machine: 'So I decided to post a document with a post-[it-]note saying if they were interested in more documents to contact me on my pager number.'[2] Soon afterwards Bravo was telephoned by a Russian-speaking G Branch officer, who introduced himself as 'Volodya', a Russian intelligence officer, and arranged a meeting at the White House Hotel in central London. Despite technical hitches (a concealed microphone malfunctioned and the view of a Service photographer in the hotel was obstructed by a piano),[3] Bravo handed over four further classified documents to 'Volodya' and demanded substantial payment for them, thus enabling the police to make an arrest. The whole operation lasted only eleven days.[4] The Home Office sent its congratulations to Thames House: 'Short, sharp operations like this are always of interest to Ministers and you may like to know that we have briefed the Home Secretary [David Blunkett] about the operation.'[5] It was later discovered that Bravo intended to offer the Russians classified documents on state-of-the-art electronics warfare surveillance, defence systems of British warships, and equipment for Harrier jump-jets and Apache helicopters. He was sentenced to eleven years' imprisonment.[6] When the sting was revealed during Bravo's trial, the Service was surprised to receive a formal protest from the officially declared London representative of the SVR at 'Volodya's' impersonation of a Russian intelligence officer.[7]

On 4 March 2002, just over a month after Bravo's conviction, a disaffected test co-ordinator at BAE Systems Avionics in Basildon, Ian Parr (who appears to have been on holiday during Bravo's trial in January and unaware of it), also attempted to make contact with Russian intelligence, by passing a packet to the Russian embassy containing three floppy discs with a typed note which read: 'Attached are sample documents available. I will telephone Friday 8th March at 3pm to confirm your interest, and discuss a meeting. I will give the code word "Piglet".' Parr had failed to realize, however, that 8 March was International Women's Day, a Russian holiday, and the Russian embassy was closed. On 8 March he received a phone call from the Security Service officer who had earlier contacted Bravo and this time called himself 'Aleksei'. They later arranged to meet at the Tower Bridge Thistle Hotel on 19 March. At a further meeting at the Esplanade pub in Southend-on-Sea on 22 March, Parr handed over fifty-six floppy disks and fourteen sets of classified documents relating to the STORM SHADOW missile system. 'Aleksei' paid him and left. Parr stayed behind and had just ordered a lager when the Essex police moved in and arrested him on suspicion of theft and of committing offences under the Official Secrets Act. He was later sentenced to eight years' imprisonment for passing classified information and two years for theft, to run concurrently.[8]

By the time Parr was jailed, the counter-espionage budget was once again under threat. Though almost 20 per cent of the Service's budget in 2000–2001 was devoted to CE (up from 12 per cent in 1996–7),[9] it was cut back once again after 9/11. As the Annual Report for 2001–2 acknowledged: 'The gearing up of work against international terrorism post 11 September was achieved at a cost to the Service's counter-espionage work. Coverage was reduced effectively to four potentially hostile states and lower priority casework was suspended.'[10] At the time of Sir Stephen Lander's retirement as DG in October 2002, however, the full extent of the threat to Britain from Islamist terrorism was still not grasped. Deputy Assistant Commissioner Peter Clarke, head of Counter-Terrorism Command at Scotland Yard, later acknowledged, 'In 2002 the perception was that if there was a threat to the UK, its origins were overseas. The spectre of a home grown terrorist threat was not yet with us.'[11]

Well before Lander's retirement, the DDG, Eliza Manningham-Buller,[12] then aged fifty-four, was widely regarded as the front-runner to succeed him. Good at managing personal relations with both her colleagues and Whitehall, she succeeded in conveying authority and friendliness at the same time. As the daughter of the first Viscount Dilhorne (born Reginald Manningham-Buller), successively Solicitor General, Attorney General and Lord Chancellor in the Conservative governments of 1951 to 1964, she was the only DDG or DG in Service history who had been used since childhood to the company of ministers. At Lady Margaret Hall, Oxford, where she read English, she had been a prominent member of OUDS (Oxford University Dramatic Society) and was chosen in 1968 to play the Fairy Godmother in *Cinderella*, the first ever OUDS pantomime. The producer, Gyles Brandreth, later a Tory MP, described her performance as 'absolutely superb'. 'It is great fun,' Manningham-Buller was quoted as saying, 'but I am not intending to be a professional actress.'[13] After a few years teaching English following graduation, she was talent-spotted by a Security Service officer who met her at a party; she joined the Service in 1974. Her brief career as an English teacher left its mark on her MI5 career. She later told alumnae of her Oxford college: 'I have a reputation inside the Service for being particular about grammar. A draft letter or note presents the opportunity for me to indulge my struggle for maintaining standards of written English.' Some of her colleagues, she admitted, probably wished she had taught mathematics or geography instead.[14] Her insistence on high standards (not merely of English grammar), which some of her staff found intimidating, was balanced by a sense of fun which made her many friends. Manningham-Buller later became the first DG (perhaps the first head of any intelligence agency anywhere) to give a talk to staff entitled, 'Fun at Work'.[15] She first began to establish herself as a potential DG under Stella Rimington, when her interpersonal as well as intelligence skills as first head of T2, with responsibility for mainland Republican counter-terrorism, played a crucial part in the fraught but successful transfer of the lead role from MPSB to the Service.[16]

In April 2002, six months before Lander's retirement, four senior mandarins, chaired by Sir Richard Wilson, now cabinet secretary, interviewed a shortlist of three applicants (all internal) for the post of DG. As Manningham-Buller later acknowledged, the essence of her letter of application for the post of DG was that, after the Lander era, 'I was going to be Miss Continuity.'[17] The letter had a characteristically engaging conclusion, influenced by memories of the paparazzi pursuit of Stella Rimington a decade earlier and the thought that they might turn up at the farm where she and her husband spent as many of their weekends as possible: 'I am supported by a happy marriage, many friends and lots of other interests, so can keep work in perspective and switch off. I also derive strength from my home life to sustain me in crises. What really frightens me is the prospect of being photographed in my farm overalls by the Sun.'[18] The panel unanimously recommended Manningham-Buller's appointment as DG:

She would be a first-rate choice to lead the Service over the next three years or so. She had immense credibility both in the Service and externally. She had the confidence and understanding of the issues facing the Service to lead it well. The Panel agreed to suggest that a three-year contract would keep open the possibility of appointing someone else with different skills at the end of that period if, for instance, a more strategic view of the Service's role were needed at that stage.[19]

The panel's assessment of Manningham-Buller was well balanced. Her leadership qualities and intelligence judgement are generally regarded by those who know her, inside and outside the Service, as outstanding. She was not, however, an original strategic thinker. Manningham-Buller said of herself at the end of her period as DG: 'I'm not myself a great generator of fantastic ideas, but I'm good at catching the mood of the moment.'[20] When it became clear in 2003 that the threat from Al Qaida had been underestimated and that Britain was directly threatened by home-grown terrorists, Manningham-Buller caught the mood of the moment once again, abandoned any ambition of remaining Miss Continuity and opted decisively for change.[21] At the end of her three-year term as DG, she was renewed for another two years.

The first serious UK-based Islamist plot uncovered by the Security Service and the police during Manningham-Buller's term as DG was a conspiracy by North African extremists to use lethal poisons – chiefly ricin.[22] A trail of petty fraud and false identity documents led to the discovery at Thetford, in the heart of rural Norfolk, of recipes written in Arabic (beginning 'In the Name of God the Merciful, the Compassionate') for ricin and other poisons. That led in turn to the discovery on 5 January 2003 of castor-oil beans, the raw material for ricin, in north London at a house in Wood Green. During arrests in Manchester, Detective Constable Stephen Oake was stabbed to death by Kamel Bourgass, an Algerian Islamist. Bourgass was later sentenced to twenty-two years' imprisonment for Oake's murder and to seventeen years for conspiracy to create a public nuisance by use of poisons and explosives. But the available evidence was insufficient to prove the involvement of any other North African extremist in what became known as the 'ricin plot'.[23]

The first evidence of a major Islamist conspiracy to bomb British targets in the UK was uncovered as a result of Operation CREVICE, which began with the investigation in the spring of 2003 of a group based in London and Luton which was believed to be supplying money and equipment to Al Qaida fighters and affiliates in Pakistan and Afghanistan. Investigation revealed that most members of the network were second-generation British citizens of Pakistani origin. In the summer of 2003 some of the network travelled to Pakistan for weapons and explosives training. Following their return to Britain, intelligence accumulated that some members of the group had begun planning attacks in the UK – the first since 9/11 by British-based extremists linked to Al Qaida.[24] One of the most important intelligence leads, Jonathan Evans recalls, was a tip-off from a member of the public.[25] CREVICE became the largest counter-terrorist operation yet undertaken by either the Security Service or the police. In early February 2004 intelligence indicated that the network had become 'operationally active' and that a bomb attack was being prepared. For the next seven weeks the Security Service Emergency Room operated twenty-four hours a day and 34,000 hours of surveillance were logged.[26] The CREVICE plotters were discovered to be planning attacks against nightclubs, pubs and shopping centres which were intended to cause mass casualties. All the key suspects were arrested at the end of March before they were ready to begin a bombing campaign.[27] On 1 April, for the first time in Security Service history, the DG was invited to a meeting of the full cabinet, at which Tony Blair congratulated the Service on a 'fantastic job'. The cabinet applauded.[28] Though the CREVICE trial was delayed, five British Islamists were later sentenced to life imprisonment for terrorist offences.[29]

The growing threat of Islamist terrorist attacks and the diffuse nature of intelligence on it persuaded Security Service top management during 2003 that continued expansion, though essential, was not sufficient. There must also be a step-change in the way that intelligence was collected and assessed.[30] The decision was taken, for the first time since the RSLOs of the Second World War,[31] to set up regional offices – initially at undisclosed locations in the Midlands, North-east, North-west, South, East and Scotland, later also in Wales and the South-east. As well as bringing the Service closer to the regional centres of extremist activity, the new offices also improved collaboration with local police forces. The Intelligence and Security Committee (ISC) later declared itself 'impressed by the speed at which the regionalisation programme has been carried out and the clear benefits it has brought'.[32] Changes in intelligence assessment were equally radical. In June 2003 the Joint Terrorism Analysis Centre (JTAC) was set up in Thames House as 'the UK's national centre for the assessment of international terrorism', with representatives of around a dozen government departments and agencies concerned with various aspects of counter-terrorism.[33] It was also responsible for issuing threat warnings and assessing the threat level, initially on a seven-point scale (later simplified) going from 'Negligible' to 'Critical' (attack 'expected imminently').[34] In addition to collaborating closely with G Branch, the head of JTAC was accountable to the DG as well as to an oversight board of senior customers across Whitehall. The DG reported on it to the JIC. During its first nine months JTAC processed more than 25,000 items of intelligence and issued over 3,000 reports. Manningham-Buller reported that 'Formal customer feedback shows high levels of satisfaction.'[35] The ISC agreed. JTAC staff, however, sometimes complained that they were in danger of becoming a 'tourist site', with ministers from friendly countries around the world anxious to see for themselves how it functioned.

One aspect of the step-change in counter-terrorism was the reorganization of protective security. In 2001 the Security Service had taken the lead role in founding the interdepartmental National Infrastructure Security Co-ordination Centre (NISCC), designed to give advice on protection against e-threats. Its early successes included timely warnings of the 'I love you' and 'Kournikova' viruses.[36] The NISCC set up its own website and developed contacts among journalists and businesses, who were aware of its connection with the Security Service.[37] The increase in the Islamist terrorist threat against British targets refocused attention on more traditional forms of protective security. In 2004 the Service set up the National Security Advice Centre (NSAC) to give advice on how 'to reduce the risk of a terrorist attack, or to limit the damage terrorism might cause'.[38] With information on the NSAC posted on the new Security Service website, inaugurated in April 2004, the aim was to 'extend the provision of advice to new audiences outside the CNI [Critical National Infrastructure], including local government, small and medium-sized businesses and the general public'.[39] The work of NISCC and NSAC, however, was inadequately co-ordinated. Both developed separate systems to deliver their information electronically to their users – despite the fact that the users were frequently the same.[40] The problem was resolved in 2007 by merging the two organizations to form the interdepartmental Centre for the Protection of the National Infrastructure (CPNI), which used resources and expertise from a number of government departments and agencies. Its website declared: 'Our advice aims to reduce the vulnerability of the national infrastructure to terrorism and other threats, keeping the UK's essential services (delivered by the communications, emergency services, energy, finance, food, government, health, transport and water sectors) safer.'[41]

Despite changes in the Service and mounting pressure of work, a Staff Opinion Survey in May 2003, conducted once again by an outside consultant, found morale even higher than three years earlier – probably due to strong belief in the Service's role and its ability to make a difference.[42] The main source of dissatisfaction was pay. Fifty-four per cent thought their pay compared unfavourably with that of the police and only 44 per cent (up 5 per cent since 2000) believed they received a fair salary. Though not an issue inquired into by staff surveys, there was also minor irritation among some staff at the growing inroads made into the Service's vocabulary by ephemeral jargon invented by Whitehall bureaucrats and management consultants with a tin ear for the English language and a passion for performance indicators. Irritation was reflected in the enthusiastic applause at a Service revue for a sketch on the appraisal interview of a wartime fighter ace, disappointed by his 'overall box marking':

WING-COMMANDER 'TIN-ARSE' FROBISHER: Well, the thing is, Smedley, you've done jolly well on shooting down the Hun. In fact, you've exceeded your target by 953%. Trouble is, you have personal development needs.

FLIGHT LIEUTENANT SMEDLEY: Personal development needs, Sir?

WING-CO: Yes, Smedley. You have personal development needs in the areas of policy formation, project management and resource planning.

SMEDLEY: But Sir, I'm a Spitfire pilot. Surely, my job is to shoot down Nazi bombers before they obliterate London?

WING-CO: That's all very well, Smedley, but we senior managers have to ... consider broader issues.

A similar theme was pursued in another sketch, when pirates of the Caribbean, despite record levels of stolen booty, complain that their careers are being blighted by the lack of 'a skills-based competency audit framework'.[43] Such minor irritants had no significant influence on overall morale. A later report by 'Investors in People' found that 'the Service is in a remarkable state of health, despite the pressures,' 'morale is very positive' and 'staff have a real passion for the work that they do.'[44]

Operation RHYME in 2004 pre-empted an even more dangerous Islamist attack than Operation CREVICE. The chief plotter was a British Hindu convert to Islam, Dhiren Barot, who, the DG told staff, was 'believed to have been personally selected and groomed for operational deployment by Khalid Sheikh Mohammed, the A[l] Q[aida] planner behind 9/11'.[45] Among the plots devised by Barot was the 'Gas Limos Project', which aimed to explode three limousines crammed with gas cylinders, explosives and nails in London underground car parks. He wrote gleefully about another of his projects: to explode a bomb on a tube train travelling in a tunnel beneath the Thames: 'Imagine the chaos that would be caused if a powerful explosion were to rip through here and actually rupture the river itself. This would cause pandemonium, what with the explosions, flooding, drowning, etc that would occur/result.'[46] It was also Barot's ambition to explode a radioactive 'dirty bomb', though he acknowledged that 'for the time being we do not have the contacts that would allow us to purchase such items.'[47] In the summer of 2004 Operation RHYME faced the Security Service and the police with an acute form of a familiar counter-terrorist dilemma. Further surveillance and investigation seemed to be required in order to gather the material for a successful prosecution. Delay in disrupting the plot, however, might give Barot and his accomplices time to mount an attack. It was therefore decided to arrest Barot on 3 August. Peter Clarke wrote later:

> It is no exaggeration to say that at the time of the arrest there was not one shred of admissible evidence against Barot . . . I know that some in the media were sharpening their pencils, and that if we had been unable to bring charges in that case, there would have been a wave of criticism . . .[48]

The massive surveillance before the arrest and the complex hunt for evidence afterwards made RHYME the most labour-intensive CT operation so far in the history of both the Security Service and Scotland Yard. More than 300 computers and 1,800 discs, CDs, zip drives and hard drives, many encrypted, had to be examined and the information on them decrypted. Police officers also found more than 600 sets of keys and spent fourteen months visiting over 4,000 garages and lock-ups, trying to match them up and succeeding in only seventy-seven cases. The hunt continued for so long for fear that one of the premises might contain explosives or even radioactive material.[49] The end-result was to gather so much evidence that Barot became the first Islamist terrorist in Britain to plead guilty to conspiracy to murder. At his trial two years after his arrest, evidence was produced that he had planned attacks against high-profile US as well as UK targets. It included film of the New York World Trade Center taken by Barot before 9/11 with a commentary including a voice imitating an explosion. Though Barot was a protégé of the chief planner of 9/11, Khalid Sheikh Mohammed, he is highly unlikely to have had advance knowledge of the attacks on the twin towers. His film was, as the prosecution put it, more in the nature of a 'macabre prophecy'.[50] Barot was given a life sentence with a minimum term of forty years (reduced to thirty on appeal). At a separate trial seven of his co-conspirators also received lengthy prison terms.

For almost four years after 9/11 the only successful Islamist attacks against British targets took place outside the United Kingdom, notably a car-bomb attack in Istanbul on the British consulate and the HSBC Bank in November 2003. British citizens were also among those killed in the bombing of Bali nightclubs in October 2002 and of Madrid commuter trains in March 2004. The Service knew, however, that sooner or later an attack in the UK was bound to succeed. Manningham-Buller warned in the summer of 2004:

There are worrying developments in the radicalisation of some young British Muslims. Action collectively and internationally has prevented or deterred some [terrorist] attacks. But it can only be a matter of time before something on a serious scale occurs in the UK.

. . . It remains the case that we do not know nearly enough about Islamist extremists in the UK, their whereabouts, networks and activities, to give confidence that terrorist attacks in planning in the UK can usually be disrupted.[51]

The bombings of three Underground trains and one London bus by four suicide bombers on the morning of Thursday 7 July 2005, with the loss of fifty-two other lives, were the first successful Islamist attacks in the UK. Jonathan Evans, who had become DDG in February, recalls that it had been 'a quiet and routine week', memorable only for the unexpected announcement on the Wednesday that London was to host the 2012 Olympics. Though he received the news of the first of the explosions at 9.20 a.m. on 7 July, it was not until after 10 a.m. that the evidence pointed to a series of terrorist attacks. Evans remembers the day as a classic example of 'the fog of war', with senior officers watching television to discover what was going on. By lunchtime, with tube carriages still trapped in Underground tunnels, Evans feared that the casualties might rise as high as the 191 deaths caused by Islamist attacks on crowded commuter trains in Madrid in February 2004. Initially, there was only one possible lead to go on. An email in Arabic received from North Africa a few days earlier, but only just translated, offered to provide information on plans for an attack in London in return for a visa to the UK. The sender of the email later agreed to a meeting in North Africa but failed to turn up. Convincing evidence quickly emerged that he was a fraud.[52]

Though no member of Security Service staff was killed or injured on 7 July, a majority had come to work by Underground or bus, and phoned anxious relatives to say that they were safe. For a time the Thames House phone system was in danger of being swamped. The impact of 7/7, as it came to be called, was thus direct and personal. One member of the Board recalls that even fellow intelligence agencies 'did not understand just how deeply the Service felt about the July attacks, the shock, anxiety, and deep need to ensure it didn't happen again'.[53] In the immediate aftermath of the attacks, the Service was bound to ask itself whether there was more it could have done or whether warning intelligence had been overlooked. In May investigations of several Islamist groups (not including the 7/7 suicide bombers) had concluded that none of them was planning an attack. JTAC had reported, 'We judge at present there is not a group with both the current intent and the capability to attack the UK,' and took the decision to reduce the UK threat level from 'Severe General' to 'Substantial'. Alert levels, however, were not affected.[54]*

The DG told staff meetings in the Thames House restaurant on 8 July: 'What happened on Thursday [7 July] is what we've feared, been warning about and have worked so hard to prevent. We were shocked by the horror but, while we had no intelligence that could have prevented it, not surprised.'[55] The Home Secretary, Charles Clarke, visited Thames House at midday and seemed impressed by the early stages of Operation STEP-FORD, the Service's investigation into the 7/7 attacks. After meetings with ministers, Manningham-Buller told her senior colleagues that evening that Blair and Clarke were 'onside, not keen on knee-jerk responses, not witch-hunting and keen to let the Police and MI5 get on with the job'.[56] During STEPFORD the Service discovered that it had previously encountered two of the suicide bombers, thirty-year-old Mohammed Siddique Khan, the leading plotter, and twenty-two-year-old Shehzad Tanweer, on the periphery of its investigation into Operation CREVICE. Both were British Islamists of Pakistani origin, born and brought up in the UK. The Service also discovered that it had on record a telephone number which, after (but not before) the attacks, it was able to identify as that of a third suicide bomber, Jermaine Lindsay, a nineteen-year-old Jamaican-born British convert to Islam. There was no trace in Service records of the youngest suicide bomber, eighteen-year-old Hasib Hussein, like Khan and Tanweer a British Islamist of Pakistani origin.[57]

The first evidence of Mohammed Siddique Khan's involvement was discovered on 9 July, when credit cards in his name were found at the

---

* Threat levels assess the likelihood of attack; alert levels concern protective-security measures in place.

sites of the two attacks.[58] Subsequent investigation by the Service revealed that Khan had visited Pakistan in 2003 and spent several months there with Shehzad Tanweer in the winter of 2004–5, probably in contact with Al Qaida, planning and training for the 7/7 attacks. However, the Service concluded, and the Intelligence and Security Committee agreed, that 'even with the benefit of hindsight, it would have been impossible from the available intelligence to conclude that either Khan or Tanweer posed a terrorist threat to the British public.' During Operation CREVICE they had figured only as petty fraudsters in peripheral contact with the plotters.[59]

The shock generated within the Security Service by the slaughter of innocents on 7/7 was reinforced by further, this time unsuccessful, Islamist bomb attacks a fortnight later on three Underground trains and a London bus. Once again the Service had no advance warning. The search for the four would-be suicide bombers – Muktah Said Ibrahim, Yassin Hassan Omar, Ramzi Mohammed and Hussein Osman (all East African immigrants in their twenties who had come to Britain during the 1990s) – turned into the UK's largest ever manhunt.[60] Intelligence provided by the Service during Operation HAT contributed to the arrests and the discovery of a bomb factory in Omar's eighth-floor north London flat.[61] Ibrahim and Mohammed were seen live on television emerging in their underpants with their hands up from Mohammed's Dalgarno Gardens flat, forced out by police use of CS gas. Omar was arrested in Birmingham, whither he had fled dressed in a burka. Osman was tracked down in Rome.[62] Subsequent investigation revealed that Ibrahim, the leading plotter, like Siddique Khan and Tanweer had travelled to Pakistan late in 2004 for training in suicide-bomb attacks. Ibrahim, Omar, Mohammed and Osman were later sentenced to life imprisonment with minimum terms of forty years.[63]

Jonathan Evans remembers 21/7 as 'even more of an emotional blow than 7/7': 'We were already feeling under the cosh and wondered, "Have they got wave after wave to throw at us?"' Late summer and autumn 2005 was the period when the Service felt under the greatest pressure since 9/11. Evans recalls: 'With new threat intelligence each week, we asked ourselves: "Can we cope? Are we running out of troops?"'[64] The main lesson learned from the July attacks, Manningham-Buller told the ISC, was the need to penetrate the terrorist 'unknowns'. Hitherto the Service had been fully occupied in following up intelligence leads generated by its own investigations and by SIS, GCHQ and foreign liaison.[65] Among the most successful ways of diminishing the 'unknowns' over the next few years was a closer working relationship with the police at a local level through the MI5 regional offices. The head of Scotland Yard's Counter-Terrorism Command, Deputy Assistant Commissioner Peter Clarke, declared in 2007:

There can be no doubt that the most important change in counter terrorism in the UK in recent years has been the development of the relationship between the police and the security service ... It is no exaggeration to say that the joint working between the police and MI5 has become recognised as a beacon of good practice. Colleagues from across the globe, in law enforcement and intelligence, look to the UK as a model, and many of them are, quite frankly, envious. That is why it is sometimes frustrating to hear and read the same tired old comments about MI5 and the police not working together. That is out of date. It is wrong, and is a lie that deserves to be well and truly nailed.[66]

SIS 'disruption operations' against terrorist groups abroad (almost 50 per cent greater in 2006 than in 2005) also made an increasing contribution to counter-terrorism in the UK.[67] Ten per cent of the members of the Security Service CT teams were SIS officers. By 2007 over a third of GCHQ's effort was devoted to counter-terrorism – much of it in support of MI5. Its Director, Sir David Pepper, acknowledged a year later: 'We don't quite meet the targets they [MI5] set, but, frankly, the targets they set are at a level where it is very unlikely we would be able to meet them ... I think their aspirations would almost always exceed our capability.'[68] By 2009 GCHQ was more optimistic and reported that it was now confident of meeting 'Security Service key requirements.'[69]

The increased range of foreign liaisons and the much greater volume of counter-terrorist intelligence which they generated after 9/11 posed difficult issues. There were media claims that the Security Service condoned the use of torture to extract information by some foreign services. The issue of principle was, and remains, straightforward. The Service has consistently condemned torture,[70] and the 1988 Criminal Justice Act makes it illegal for British officials to acquiesce in acts of torture anywhere in the world.* The Home Office has reaffirmed that members of the Service, like the rest of the intelligence community, 'do not participate in, solicit, encourage or condone the use of torture and inhumane or degrading treatment'. In practice, however, according to Manningham-Buller:

---

* The 1988 Criminal Justice Act makes it an offence for officials of any nationality intentionally to inflict severe pain or suffering on another person in the performance or purported performance of their official duties. It would be an offence for any British official to aid and abet torture by encouraging or assisting it.

It is pretty well impractical always to check whether something has been derived from torture unless you have reason to suspect it at the beginning. Literally thousands of pieces of intelligence are shared daily between the UK, our allies and people who might not so reasonably be described as our allies.[71]

Information obtained by torture is inadmissible in prosecutions in UK courts. The House of Lords, however, ruled in December 2005 that intelligence operations can be taken on the basis of 'tainted evidence'.[72]

Service management accepted that intelligence liaison on counter-terrorism with states 'whose standard of treatment of individuals, especially in custody, may fall below the international norms supported by the UK' raised significant 'ethical issues': 'In conducting these relations we have to pursue our need for CT co-operation with safeguards to ensure that we do not encourage or cause mistreatment.'[73] In April 2006 a circular from Manningham-Buller entitled 'Ethics and the Security Service' urged staff with ethical concerns not to suppress them: 'The Service goes to some length to recruit people with a keen sense of conscience who will raise questions if they are uncomfortable . . . I urge staff to say if they have qualms. The idea that airing concern on the proper channels risks damage to career is a myth.'[74] Staff who preferred not to raise ethical issues with line managers already had the option of taking their concerns to the Staff Counsellor in the Cabinet Office, to whom all members of the intelligence community had direct access. From May 2006 MI5 staff also had the option of consulting a part-time 'ethics counsellor' within the Service, who had the rank of director and guaranteed confidentiality to those who came to see him.[75] Though not many did so (fewer than twenty over the next two years), there is no evidence that staff with ethical concerns felt inhibited from raising them.[76]

The most controversial case involving allegations that the Security Service connived in the use of torture is that of Binyam Mohamed al-Habashi, an Ethiopian and British resident arrested in Pakistan in 2002 who claims he was moved by US 'extraordinary rendition' operations to Morocco and Afghanistan before being interned in Guantánamo in 2004. While in Guantánamo, Mohamed told his British lawyer Clive Stafford Smith that British officials had interrogated him after his arrest in Pakistan and that 'one of them did tell me that I was going to get tortured by the [Arabs].' He also claimed that he was later tortured by the Moroccans, told that 'they were working with the British Security Service' and 'asked questions, containing details about his life that could only have come from UK sources'. In evidence to the Intelligence and Security Committee in 2006, Manningham-Buller denied that the Security Service officer who had questioned Binyam Mohamed in Pakistan had told him he would be tortured or that he had seen any evidence of torture. Since then the Service had had no contact with Mohamed and did not know whether he had been tortured in Morocco. Manningham-Buller acknowledged, however, that, 'with hindsight, we would regret not seeking full assurances at the time' from the Americans about Mohamed's treatment. The ISC also found the Service's failure to seek these assurances 'regrettable'.[77]

The controversy aroused by the Binyam Mohamed case continues. The English High Court ruled in February 2009 that classified American documents in the case of Mohamed 'give rise to an arguable case of torture or cruel, inhuman or degrading treatment'. The evidence, however, could not be disclosed because of the damage that would have been caused were the British to reveal US intelligence without consent.[78] The Attorney General, Baroness Scotland QC, announced on 26 March: 'I have decided that the appropriate course of action is to invite the Commissioner of the Metropolitan Police to commence an investigation into the allegations that have been made in relation to Binyam Mohamed.' Though the announcement carried with it no presumption of guilt, this appears to be the first time in the history of the Security Service that its actions have been the subject of criminal investigation.

The Binyam Mohamed case led in February 2010 to the most severe criticism of MI5 ever made by a British judge. A banner headline in the *Guardian* on 11 February declared, 'Devious, dishonest and complicit in torture – top judge on MI5'. As justification for this headline, the *Guardian* quoted a letter to the Court of Appeal from a barrister acting for the FCO, Jonathan Sumption QC, asking for the removal from a draft judgment in the Binyam Mohamed case by the Master of the Rolls, Lord Neuberger, of what he described as 'an exceptionally damaging criticism of the good faith of the Security Service as a whole':

The Master of the Rolls' observations . . . will be read as statements by the Court (i) that the Security Service does not in fact operate a culture that respects human rights or abjures participation in coercive interrogation techniques: (ii) that this was in particular true of witness B [of MI5] whose conduct was in this respect characteristic of the Service as a whole; (iii) that officials of the Service deliberately misled the Intelligence and Security Committee; (iv) that this reflects a culture of suppression which penetrates the Service to such a degree as to undermine any UK government assurances based on the Service's information and advice.

Though Lord Neuberger's draft judgement and his subsequent final version were not made public for another fortnight,[79] reports of his unprecedented criticism of MI5 inevitably gave rise to a media furore. The Security Service's response was also unprecedented. Jonathan Evans became the first DG to publish a newspaper article defending the Service against attacks made on it. 'Allegations that MI5 has been trying to "cover up" its activities' were, he declared, 'the opposite of the truth': 'The material our critics are drawing on to attack us is taken from our own records, not prised from us by some external process but willingly provided by us to the court, in the normal way. No cover-up there.'[80] MI5's case was promptly supported by the Home Secretary, Alan Johnson, by the Foreign Secretary, David Miliband, and by the chairman of the Intelligence and Security Committee, Dr Kim Howells MP. A substantial section of the media, as well as human rights groups, however, remained on the attack. Richard Norton-Taylor in the *Guardian* dismissed Evans's article as 'MI5's propaganda own-goal: The head of the security service is denouncing the media for simply reporting the judicial truth of its complicity in torture.'[81]

Because much evidence in the Binyam Mohamed case remains *sub judice*, final judgement will have to await the conclusion of the police investigation into the actions of 'Witness B' of MI5 (and any subsequent trial, if the Director of Public Prosecutions concludes that the evidence justifies it and a prosecution is in the public interest). Since September 2008, a series of civil cases have also been winding their way through the English courts, brought by litigants who claim involvement by the British intelligence services in their mistreatment mainly in Afghanistan and Pakistan. Claims that the Service is permeated by 'a culture of suppression' are, however, difficult to square with the fact that since 2006 its members have been 'urged' (not merely permitted) to take ethical concerns in confidence to an ethics counsellor, who addresses every induction course of new recruits.[82]

The main difficulty faced by the Security Service in monitoring the Islamist threat in the aftermath of 7/7 and 21/7 was that, for several years, the threat continued to increase. On 9/11 only about 250 individuals in Britain had been identified as having links with international (mostly Islamist) terrorism. By the end of 2007 their numbers had risen to around 2,000, and thirty 'active plots' were under investigation. Manningham-Buller told the ISC in October 2006, 'My main concern has been, and still is, we do not have enough people to do the job.' The Security Service planned to double in size within a decade: from 2,000 on 9/11 to 4,100 in 2011. Manningham-Buller believed that for the Service to expand even more rapidly would risk compromising the quality of its personnel. Maintaining quality, she argued, was 'incredibly important because people get access to secrets and responsibility and the capacity to make a major [mistake] very early on'.[83] SIS agreed. In the view of its Chief, John Scarlett, 'If you try to bring in more than a certain number of new people each year, you can literally bust the system . . . You can only tolerate a certain number of inexperienced people dealing with very sensitive subjects.'[84]

As it approached its centenary, the Service had no doubt that Islamist terrorism was a serious long-term threat rather than a short-term problem. Islamist 'radicalization' continued to convert a minority of British Muslims and Muslim converts to the Manichean worldview of a cosmic struggle between good and evil (Muslim versus apostate and unbeliever), underpinned by the conspiracy theory of a Western war against Islam which went back at least to the First Crusade. A minority of the Islamist minority posed a continuing terrorist threat. Manningham-Buller forecast in December 2005: 'We will continue to stop most [terrorist attacks] but we will not stop all of them.'[85] In the two and a half years after 7/7 and 21/7, which MI5 had failed to prevent, it successfully disrupted six other Islamist plots.[86]

One of the disrupted plots, to use suicide bombers to bring down in mid-air a series of transatlantic aircraft en route from Heathrow to North American cities, was assessed by the Security Service as the most dangerous terrorist conspiracy in British history. Within Britain the organizer of the plot was an unemployed engineering graduate of London City University, Abdullah Ahmed Ali (formerly Ahmed Ali Khan), who had been born in 1980 into a devout East London Muslim family with close links to Pakistan. Ali said in what he intended to be a martyrdom video to be broadcast after his death as one of the suicide bombers:

. . . I was over the moon that Allah has given me the opportunity to lead this blessed operation. Thanks to God, I swear by Allah I have the desire since the age of fifteen/ sixteen to participate in Jihad in the path of Allah. I had the desire since then to punish the Kuffar [a derogatory term for non-Muslims] for the evil they are doing, I had the desire since then for Jannya [Paradise] for the Koran.[87]

Ali succeeded in recruiting a group of other young Islamist conspiracy theorists who shared his conviction that a glorious martyrdom as suicide bombers in the Holy War against the Kuffar would guarantee them eternal bliss in paradise.

Ali first came to the attention of the Security Service in 2003 during surveillance of an Islamist network which it believed had sent 'significant amounts of funds, goods and trainees' from Britain to Al Qaida in Pakistan.[88] Early investigation of Ali, however, led to the conclusion that he was 'predominantly involved in criminal rather than extremist activity'.[89]

That view of Ali changed in January 2005 when intelligence revealed that he had sent funds to Pakistan extremists. By March 2005, he was known to be in contact with Rashid Rauf,[90] a sinister and influential Al Qaida figure who had fled to Pakistan from his native Birmingham in 2002 after a warrant was issued for his arrest following the fatal stabbing of his uncle. Subsequent intelligence investigations suggested Rauf's involvement in terror plots around the world, including the 7/7 bombings and the attempted 21/7 attacks in London. The Security Service believed that Ali's transition from an Al Qaida support role to attack planning came during a trip to Pakistan in May and June 2006 when he met Rashid Rauf.[91] Once Ali returned to Britain on 24 June, Rauf remained the conduit by which he received instructions from Al Qaida in preparing the suicide-bomb plot to destroy transatlantic aircraft in mid-air.[92]

The British Islamist who became Ali's quartermaster, Assad Ali Sarwar, visited Pakistan from 13 June to 8 July, made contact with Rauf and is believed to have been taught how to reduce hydrogen peroxide, used by hairdressers to bleach hair and easily available in Britain, to the concentration required to turn it into the explosive which was to be used in the aircraft bomb plot.[93] Sarwar's barrister later described him at his trial as 'Mr Bean', a 'plonker' and one of life's losers.[94] MI5 assessed him rather differently as a reliable and competent quartermaster. Since Al Qaida intended Sarwar to play a support role in future terrorist attacks, he was not selected as one of the suicide bombers. Among the targeting information which he collected on memory sticks which were later discovered during a search of his house were details of Canary Wharf, the gas pipeline between Belgium and the UK, British airports and the London electricity grid.[95] Like Ali, Sarwar continued to receive regular guidance from Rashid Rauf.[96]

Soon after Ali returned to Heathrow from Pakistan on 24 June, the Security Service discovered that he had brought with him large quantities of AA batteries and a powdered soft-drink concentrate called Tang, whose purpose did not become clear until MI5 was able to watch Ali and his associates making the bombs they intended to explode on board transatlantic aircraft. The opportunity to do so came on 20 July when a member (or members) of Ali's family purchased for £138,000 in cash a two-bedroom flat at 386a Forest Road, not far from Ali's Walthamstow home, which within a few days was turned by Ali and other plotters into a bomb factory.[97] Despite the fact that the plotters were wary of surveillance, the flat was quickly fitted with listening devices and a miniature camera in what Jonathan Evans remembers as 'a difficult but spectacularly successful operation.' Evans was reminded of the operation which had kept the leading PIRA bomber, 'Rab' Fryers, under surveillance before his arrest in 1994 and stopped the Provisionals' bombing campaign against the City of London: 'We could see what they were doing in some detail, and that's a very reassuring place to be. We could play it long because of the penetrative coverage and be reasonably confident we could control the risk.' The MI5 surveillance team were able to monitor the flat at 386a Forest Road in real time, choosing daily edited highlights to show to senior management.[98]

On 3 August the camera in the flat showed Ali and his chief lieutenant, Tanvir Hussain, drilling a hole in the bottom of a soft-drink bottle in order to replace its contents with concentrated hydrogen peroxide without breaking the seal on the cap. The hydrogen peroxide had been purchased by Sarwar using the alias Jona Lewis from a garden centre in South Wales; he had also been detected buying a probe thermometer and other equipment to produce the correct concentration of hydrogen peroxide. The Tang powder which Ali had brought from Pakistan was to have been used to colour the hydrogen peroxide to give it the appearance of a soft drink and increase its explosive potential. The surveillance camera in the bomb factory showed that the detonators for the explosive soft-drink bottles which Ali, Hussain and their fellow suicide bombers planned to take on board transatlantic flights were to be disguised as AA batteries whose contents had been replaced with HMTD (hexamethylene triperoxide diamine). Placed inside disposable cameras in hand luggage, the batteries were highly unlikely to arouse suspicion. When bomb-making, Ali and Hussain spoke in semi-coded language: 'stock' was hydrogen peroxide, a 'cricket bat' was a detonator.[99] Though they were to be arrested before any of the bombs was ready, in a later BBC TV *Panorama* programme one of the explosive devices they had intended to construct, assembled by the weapons expert Dr Sidney Alford, blew a hole in an aircraft fuselage.

On 3 August, the day when the surveillance camera in the Forest Road flat provided the first evidence of bomb-making, an email sent by Ali to Pakistan (later obtained by the Met) appeared to give a coded indication that the attack plan was almost complete: '. . . I've set up my mobile shop now. Now I only need to sort out an opening time.'[100] Operation OVERT had become the largest surveillance operation in the history of MI5 and the Met. Andy Hayman, the Met's Assistant Commissioner Specialist Operations, wrote later: 'We logged every item they bought, we sifted every piece of rubbish they threw away (at their homes or in litterbins). We filmed and listened to them . . .'[101] Sarwar was tracked as he travelled to South Wales to buy large quantities of hydrogen peroxide, and was videoed buying a suitcase in which he hid some of his purchases in woods near his High Wycombe home.

As well as being used as a bomb factory, the Forest Road flat was also used by six of the plotters to record martyrdom videos to be made public after their deaths and (they believed) entry into paradise.[102] Wearing headscarf and black robe, and jabbing his finger repeatedly at the camera, Ali declared angrily (though not always coherently):

... Sheikh Usama [bin Laden] warned you many times to leave our land or you will be destroyed, and now the time has come for you to be destroyed and you have nothing but to expect that floods of martyr operations, volcanoes and anger and revenge and raping among your capital and yet, taste that what you have made up taste for a long time and now you have bear the fruits that you have sown.[103]

Other martyrdom videos also emphasized that there would be many more such attacks. Tanvir Hussain regretted that he could only be a suicide bomber once:

For many years, you know, I dreamt of doing this, you know, but I didn't have no chance of doing this. I didn't have any means. (Thank God) Allah has accepted my duas [prayers], yeah, and provided a means to do this. You know I only wish I could do this again, you know, come back and do this again and just do it again and again until people come to their senses and realise, realise you know, don't mess with the Muslims.[104]

On 6 August Ali was observed in a Walthamstow internet café noting from airline websites the departure times of transatlantic flights. On the 9th a co-conspirator was overheard asking him in the Forest Road flat, 'What's the timeframe anyway?' 'A couple of weeks,' Ali replied.[105]

During the final stages of the plot both the DG and the Prime Minister were on holiday. Manningham-Buller was at her farm some way from London (though in daily contact with, and returning frequently to, Thames House). Tony Blair was in Barbados. The DG's deputy, Jonathan Evans, briefed the Home Secretary, John Reid, twice a day. Reid in turn briefed Blair in Barbados. Evans found Reid 'very, very interested in the operational detail and very focused, but scrupulous in not interfering in the conduct of the operation'. Delaying the arrest of the plotters until there was enough usable evidence to convict them required political courage by Reid as well as a strong nerve by MI5 and Met senior management. At one critical moment in Operation OVERT Reid told Evans: 'If this goes wrong, I'm out of a job, you're out of a job, and the government will fall.'[106]

US intelligence chiefs were, unsurprisingly, nervous at the prospect of another terrorist attack on the scale of 9/11, this time mounted by British Islamists from Heathrow, and worried that any delay in arresting the plotters might allow them to go ahead. Though unable to influence the timing of the arrests in Britain, the Americans brought pressure to bear on the Pakistanis to arrest Rashid Rauf.[107] When stopped by local police in a taxi in Rawalpindi on 9 August, Rauf initially gave his name as Ghulam Hassan. A search of his bedroom, however, found the UK passport in his real name which he had used to enter Pakistan when fleeing from a murder investigation in Britain in 2002. Police also found two other passports with Rauf's photograph (one British, one South African, each in a different name), two other identity cards, six Visa cashpoint and bank cards in three different names, five mobile phones, a laptop with a USB external drive (which contained targeting information and details of chemical and biological weapons), a stun gun and twenty-nine small bottles of hydrogen peroxide.[108]

The premature arrest of Rauf, which dismayed MI5 and the Met, denied them the two further days they had wanted to complete the pre-arrest phase of Operation OVERT. Peter Clarke said later: 'We were at a critical point in building our case. If word got out that [Rauf] had been arrested, evidence might well be destroyed or scattered to the four winds. More worrying still was the prospect of a desperate attack [by the plotters in Britain].'[109] Arrests of the alleged plotters and their associates began the same evening. In Ali's possession, when he was arrested with Assad Sarwar in a Walthamstow car park, was a computer memory stick containing details of seven transatlantic flights due to take off from Heathrow Terminal 3 within a period of two hours thirty-five minutes. For much of their journeys to cities in the United States and Canada, they would have been airborne simultaneously.[110] The destruction of seven aircraft in mid-air by suicide bombers would have caused loss of life on the scale of 9/11 (even greater if some of the planes had exploded over cities).

At about 10 p.m., John Reid, wearing dark glasses because of a painful eye condition, chaired a first meeting of COBR, which continued until after midnight.[111] At 2 a.m., with most of the suspected plotters under arrest, the news that JTAC had raised the alert level to 'critical' was made public. COBR reconvened at 5 a.m. At the height of the holiday season airports were thrown into chaos as passengers were suddenly forbidden to take on board liquids, gels or cream, as a precaution against the kind of explosive devices being manufactured in the Forest Road bomb factory, and severe restrictions were imposed on hand luggage. At COBR Andy Hayman watched 'politicians' stress levels ... rising as they saw television news pictures of irate holidaymakers waiting for delayed and cancelled flights'.[112]

On the morning of 10 August Reid announced to a Westminster press conference that the 'main players' involved in preparations for a terrorist attack which would have caused deaths on an 'unprecedented scale' were under arrest. In Barbados Blair paid public tribute to MI5 and the police for their 'extraordinary amount of hard work' in tracking the plot over a 'long period of time'.[113] A few days later, with Manningham-Buller back at Thames House, Evans left on a delayed family holiday, substituting a few days in Paris by Eurostar for the longer Mediterranean vacation he had planned. Shortly after the Prime Minister returned from Barbados on 25 August, Manningham-Buller, Evans and the counterterrorist director went to brief him. Blair invited them into his study and watched intently video footage on the counter-terrorist director's encrypted laptop of Ali and Tanvir constructing bombs in the Forest Road flat.[114] A few weeks later there was a series of detailed briefings, this time including dramatic extracts from the martyrdom videos (of which copies had been found in Sarwar's possession), for MI5 staff in the Thames House basement restaurant. It was easy for those present[115] to imagine extracts from the videos being broadcast, as Al Qaida had intended, by TV stations around the world in the aftermath of what would have been the most devastating terrorist attack in aviation history.

Most of those who had seen the intelligence obtained from the Forest Road bomb factory were incredulous that, despite the large amount of evidence which the jury had to consider, it took a six-month trial and a six-month retrial for the three ringleaders – Ali, Sarwar and Hussain – to be found guilty of conspiracy to murder by causing explosions on aircraft. In September 2009, at the end of the retrial, Ali, Sarwar and Hussain were sentenced to life imprisonment with minimum terms of, respectively, forty, thirty-six and thirty-two years. As a result of the first trial, the retrial and a further trial which concluded in December 2009, two other plotters were convicted of conspiracy to commit murder and five others of lesser charges.[116]

Though Islamist terrorism remained by far the greatest threat to national security, the Service allocated 15 per cent of its resources in the financial year 2007–8 to dealing with Irish-related terrorism. In October 2007, for the first time in its history, the Service was given the lead intelligence role in Northern Ireland, with a new Belfast headquarters. In its report for 2007–8, the ISC endorsed the Service's assessment that 'dissident republican groups such as the Real IRA and Continuity IRA ... continue to pose a threat to Great Britain and to Northern Ireland in particular.'[117]

These groups had mounted a number of unsuccessful attacks principally against police officers. On 7 March 2009 the Real IRA claimed responsibility for the deaths of two soldiers of 38 Regiment, Royal Engineers, Sappers Patrick Azimkar and Mark Quinsey, killed by gunmen as they came to the entrance of Massereene Barracks, County Antrim, to collect pizzas. No soldier had been killed in Northern Ireland for the past twelve years. Two other soldiers and the pizza delivery men were seriously wounded. On 9 March PC Stephen Carroll, a member of the Police Service of Northern Ireland (PSNI), was shot dead as he answered a 999 call in Craigavon. This time Continuity IRA claimed responsibility. Carroll was the first member of the PSNI to be killed since it succeeded the RUC in 2001. Though such killings had been sadly commonplace during the Troubles, the response to them in March 2009 was eloquent testimony to the progress made by the peace process over the previous decade. Martin McGuinness of Sinn Fein, Deputy First Minister in the power-sharing government headed by Peter Robinson, leader of the Democratic Unionists, denounced those responsible for the murders as 'traitors to the island of Ireland' and appealed to the public to help the police find the murderers.

There was no sign, however, of a full-scale return to the Troubles. A representative of the Real IRA Army Council declared in April 2009 that it would limit itself to 'tactical use of armed struggle': 'The days of a campaign involving military operations every day or every few days are over. We're looking for high-profile targets, though we'll obviously take advantage when other targets present themselves.'[118] Though there were no more killings by dissident Republicans for the remainder of 2009, two huge bombs which failed to explode came close to causing serious loss of life. In August a 600-pound bomb was discovered in Armagh with a command wire running across the border with the Irish Republic. A robbery near by had been apparently intended to bring PSNI officers to the vicinity where some would have been killed had the bomb been successfully detonated. In November the Independent Monitoring Commission reported that the dissident Republican threat in Northern Ireland was at its highest level for almost six years. Shortly afterwards a car containing a 400-pound bomb was driven through a barrier outside the Policing Board headquarters in Belfast. The men inside ran off and the car burst into flames, but the bomb only partially exploded. There were no casualties.

Dissident Republican violence continued during the early months of 2010. In January a thirty-three-year-old Catholic PSNI officer was seriously injured by an under-car bomb in County Antrim, and the Real IRA opened fire twice on police stations in County Armagh. In February forty families had to be evacuated from their homes after a pipe-bomb attack on a Belfast police station, and a large car bomb exploded outside Newry Courthouse in County Down, while police were evacuating the area. The PSNI said that it was a 'sheer miracle' that no one had been killed or injured. It seemed only a matter of time before one of the dissident attacks ended in tragedy.

By 2008–9 three-quarters of Security Services resources were devoted to countering Islamist terrorism (up from two-thirds in 2007–8).[119] In 2005 the Service had identified five key elements in the radicalization process: attendance at a mosque linked to Islamist extremism; the influence of Islamist friends and associates; the role of an extreme spiritual leader; the influence of Islamist propaganda; and attendance at jihad training camps. Operation OVERT helped to modify the Security Service's view of the problem of Islamist radicalization. By 2007 the Service placed less emphasis on the mosque:

Extremists are moving away from mosques to conduct their activities in private homes and business premises ... We assess that radicalisation increasingly occurs in private meeting places, be they closed prayer groups at mosques, self-defence classes at gyms or training camps in the UK or overseas.

Social networks, MI5 now believed, could sometimes be more important than Islamist preachers: 'In the case of Op OVERT, it is assessed that friendships from school and universities were the initial basis for many of the relationships of those involved.' The most effective Islamist propaganda was increasingly spread in cyberspace rather than by radical mosques:

Recent study has also raised the importance of the internet as a vehicle for extremist propaganda, which may be of particular importance to younger individuals, for whom access to more conventional meeting places (and the radicalising influences therein) may be restricted. Chat rooms, message boards and forums provide opportunities for extremists to establish contacts and radicalise each other.[120]

The Security Service was well aware that its own operations could do no more than contain the threat from Islamist terrorism. The success of a broader government strategy, summarized as Prevent, Pursue, Protect and Prepare, was vital:

- preventing terrorism by tackling the radicalisation of individuals
- pursuing terrorists and those that sponsor them
- protecting the public, key national services and UK interests overseas
- preparing for the consequences

In an address to Security Service staff early in 2009, Jonathan Evans added a fifth 'P': Perseverance to underpin the other four.

In the two years from January 2007 to January 2009 eighty-six people (almost half of whom pleaded guilty) were convicted of Islamist terrorist offences. Among them, in December 2008, was Bilal Abdulla, a twenty-eight-year-old doctor at the Royal Alexandria Hospital, Paisley, described as 'a religious extremist and bigot' by the judge who sentenced him to life imprisonment with a minimum term of thirty-two years. With a fellow Islamist, Kafeel Ahmed, Abdulla had staged unsuccessful attacks on London nightclubs and Glasgow airport, using cars loaded with explosive material. Ahmed died from severe burns sustained in the Glasgow attack before he could be brought to trial. After the arrest of Abdulla, two further vehicles were discovered, together with gas cylinders and petrol cans, which, it appeared, were intended for a further series of attacks designed to cause mass casualties.

The success in bringing Islamist terrorists to court paradoxically made MI5 operations against them more difficult. What they learned from court cases about operational methods also increased their ability to take evasive action. The Security Service believed that the core Al Qaida leadership on Pakistan's north-west frontier continued to plan major attacks in Britain, using British nationals and residents. Seventy-five per cent of the British Islamists investigated by the Security Service in recent years had links with Pakistan.[121] In January 2009, Jonathan Evans publicly acknowledged that, if another attack took place, the Service would probably discover, as after 7/7, that some of the terrorists responsible were already on its books. 'But the fact we know of an individual and the fact that they have had some association with extremists doesn't mean we are going to be indefinitely in a position to be confident about everything that they are doing, because we have to prioritise.' In the summer of 2009 as the Security Service approached its centenary it was engaged in almost 200 major investigations of Islamist terrorism, over 15 per cent of which, it concluded, represented 'a high level of threat'.[122] Almost none of the 2009 investigations were publicly revealed. A rare exception was Operation PATHWAY. Late in 2008 the Security Service began investigating intelligence reports that Al Qaida attack personnel were present in the north of England. By the spring of 2009 its investigations focused on Abid Naseer, a twenty-three-year-old Pakistani living in Manchester and studying for a BSc in computer studies at John Moores University Liverpool, who was believed to be linked to Al Qaida. On 3 April Naseer was seen seated at a keyboard in an internet café in Cheetham Hill, Manchester. An unsigned email (subsequently recovered) sent while he was at the keyboard, and believed to be from him, included what was thought to be a coded reference to attack planning:

My mates are well and yes my affair with Nadia is soon turning to family life. I met with Nadia family and we both parties have agreed to conduct the Nikkah [Muslim marriage ceremony] after 15th and before 20th of this month. I have confirmed the dates from them and you should be ready between these dates. I am delighted that they have strong family values . . .

Surveillance and investigation of Naseer and other students in Manchester and Liverpool with whom he was in contact (all but one of them Pakistani) had found no sign of Nadia (or of Naseer's involvement with any other woman) and no evidence of wedding preparations. In two previous Islamist terrorist cases which had led to convictions similar coded language had been used to indicate attack planning. It thus seemed possible that the reference to 15 to 20 April (in the Islamic calendar the Easter-holiday period) referred to the planned timing of a terrorist attack, and it was decided to go ahead with the arrest of Naseer and ten of his alleged associates in Manchester and Liverpool. All but one of those arrested worked as security guards.[123] At the time of their arrest, two of the Pakistani students were working for a cargo firm with access to secure areas at Manchester airport.[124]

On 8 April Jonathan Evans took part in a Downing Street meeting to brief the Prime Minister, Gordon Brown, and senior ministers. Unlike Security Service staff, senior police officers sometimes entered Number Ten by the front door. Assistant Commissioner Bob Quick, a key counter-terrorist officer, did so when arriving for the briefing meeting. Unhappily, he had in his hand classified documents relating to the pending arrests which should have been concealed inside a briefcase or folder; some were visible in pictures taken by press photographers. The editor of the *Evening Standard*, Geordie Grieg, responded to an appeal from the Security Service not to publish the photographs until the following day. As a result of Quick's indiscretion, for which he resigned the next day, the arrests had to be brought forward and began at 5.30 p.m. rather than taking place at night as had been intended.[125]

Some of the arrests took place in full public view rather than more discreetly at the homes of the suspects, as would have happened during night-time arrests. Though none of those arrested offered any resistance, a number were forced to the ground before being handcuffed. Merseyside police said later that they had to take into account the possibility that those arrested might include a suicide bomber or someone with a mobile telephone capable of detonating explosive devices (as had been attempted in failed terrorist attacks against a London nightclub). Police also had in mind the murder of Detective Constable Stephen Oake during the arrest in Manchester of an Algerian Islamist in 2003. An inquiry by the Independent Reviewer of Terrorism Legislation, Lord Carlile of Berriew QC, later made the curious comment that 'the arrests lacked visual subtlety', but concluded that 'it is probably right that in such circumstances no chances should have been taken by the police'.[126]

Gordon Brown announced on the day after the arrests:

We are dealing with a very big terrorist plot. We have been following it for some time. There were a number of people who were suspected of it who have been arrested . . . We had to act pre-emptively to ensure the safety of the public, and the safety of the public is the paramount and utmost concern of all that we do.

Subsequent investigation, though generating significant intelligence, failed to produce evidence for a successful prosecution. By acting 'pre-emptively to ensure the safety of the public', but proving unable to bring a prosecution, the Security Service and the police inevitably laid themselves open to the charge that, to quote one of those arrested, 'It was all bullshit!' The only British citizen among Naseer's alleged associates was released soon after his arrest. No charges were brought against the other ten. On 22 April all were transferred to immigration custody and served by the Home Office with deportation notices.[127] All maintained their innocence.[128]

The later report by Lord Carlile concluded, however, after reviewing the intelligence available to the Security Service and the police, 'There was no realistic alternative to arresting at least some of the suspects. Arrests were necessary because of public safety concerns.'[129]

Though the total number of those with Islamist terrorist connections investigated by the Security Service in 2009 was little different from the totals over the previous few years, the Service reported a decline in the proportion of those engaged in 'late stage attack planning'. Jonathan Evans told the Intelligence and Security Committee:

We have been giving quite a lot thought as to why that is. It's not because the people aren't here, because they very clearly are and we believe their strategic intent is the same, but I think there are a number of factors in play. One is the very large number of cases that have come through the courts and been successfully prosecuted by the CPS [Crown Prosecution Service], which has had an effect on the willingness of groups to take risks and to do things. Secondly, I think there has been a degree of disruption, particularly in the FATA [Federally Administered Tribal Areas on Pakistan's north-west frontier].[130]

The Security Service believed, as it reached its centenary in 2009, that though a major Islamist terrorist attack would remain a serious danger for the foreseeable future, the observable threat was less acute than it had been in recent years.

Conclusion

The First Hundred Years of the Security Service

When MI5's first and youngest head, the thirty-six-year-old Vernon Kell, began work in October 1909 in the office of a private detective at 64 Victoria Street, his only target was German spies. Today's Security Service, by contrast, is overwhelmingly a counter-terrorist agency; in 2007–8 it spent a mere 3.5 per cent of its budget on counter-espionage.[1] So small were Kell's resources, however, that before the First World War he had less to spend on counter-espionage than the Service does today. It was not until January 1911 that he was able to afford an assistant. Even at the outbreak of war Kell had a total staff of only seventeen (including himself and the caretaker) – fewer in number than the spies whose arrest he ordered in August 1914. The keys to Kell's pre-war counter-espionage strategy – securing the co-operation of the police, using the Home Office Warrant system introduced by Churchill, establishing a state-of-the-art database – are, however, still central to Service operations in the twenty-first century. At the outbreak of war, to the fury of the Kaiser, Kell's Bureau succeeded, with police assistance, in rounding up all the German spies of any significance, thus depriving the enemy of advance warning of the despatch of the British Expeditionary Force to the Western Front. A much expanded MI5 also defeated the wartime German espionage offensive.

Gauging the full extent of MI5's achievements during its first decade, as at most other periods in its history, however, is more difficult than for most government agencies and departments. The success of a security service is better judged by things that do not happen (which are necessarily unquantifiable) than by things that do. MI5's post-war assessment of its First World War counter-espionage operations concluded: 'It is apparently a paradox, but it is none the less true, and a most important truth, that the efficiency of a counter espionage service is not to be measured chiefly by the number of spies caught by it.' Though MI5 caught most German spies in the first half of the war, it was even more effective in the second half when the deterrent effect of its counter-espionage successes left it with few foreign agents to catch. MI5 attributed much of its wartime success to good preventive security (later called protective security) which turned Britain into a hard target for sabotage as well as espionage. The blowing up by German saboteurs in 1916 of a huge ammunition dump at Black Tom Pier, New Jersey, destined for a Russian offensive on the Eastern Front, would undoubtedly have been replicated in Britain had protective security there been as poor as it was in the United States. The fact that there was no successful sabotage at all in mainland Britain is another indication of MI5's wartime success – and a further example of how difficult it is to use the 'performance indicators' (commonly defined as 'numerical measures of achievement') fashionable in twenty-first-century government bureaucracies to measure that success.

The First World War established as one of the enduring characteristics of the Security Service its camaraderie and *esprit de corps*, the main theme of its 1919 victory celebrations and 'Hush-Hush' Revue. It is difficult to imagine members of Lenin's Cheka (still less of its Stalinist successors) celebrating, as the programme for the 'Hush-Hush' Revue did, 'the jokes and laughter and the fun' which had punctuated their intelligence careers. Ever since the First World War MI5's sociable work culture has been singled out by retired staff members as one of their main memories of the Service.[2]

One 1953 recruit recalls being told by a personnel officer, 'One of the best things about working here is that the percentage of bastards is extremely low.' The aloof management style of a number of the director generals selected by ministers and Whitehall committees during the Cold War did little to diminish the sociability of the Service as a whole. Despite the dip in morale produced by the post-Cold War cutbacks, twenty-first-century Staff Opinion Surveys recorded some of the highest job-satisfaction ratings in either the public or the private sector.

During its first century the Security Service had to reorient itself repeatedly to new threats to national security which, in most cases, were difficult, if not impossible, to foresee. For eighty years its changing priorities were largely determined by unprecedented upheavals in the political systems of the two largest continental powers, Germany and Russia. The threat to British national security from Germany, which dominated MI5 operations for most of its first decade, declined dramatically after Germany's defeat in the First World War, the abdication of the Kaiser and the foundation of the Weimar Republic with an army limited by the Treaty of Versailles to only 100,000 men. No one in August 1914 could have predicted that in the course of the war Russia would be transformed from Europe's most authoritarian monarchy into the world's most revolutionary regime with a following in Britain which became and remained a major preoccupation of the Service until the closing years of the Cold War. Only a few weeks before the February 1917 Revolution which overthrew the Tsar, even Lenin declared, 'We the old [he was forty-six at the time] will probably not live to see the decisive battles of the coming revolution.' The interwar rise of Hitler was equally unpredictable. When the former British ambassador to the Weimar Republic, Lord D'Abernon, published his two-volume memoirs in 1929, the only reference to Hitler was a footnote which mentioned that he had spent six months in prison in 1924, 'thereafter fading into oblivion'. 'You will not think it possible, gentlemen,' the German President Field Marshal Paul von Hindenburg told two of his generals in January 1932, 'that I should appoint that Austrian lance-corporal Chancellor.'[3]

Even when the former lance-corporal became chancellor (his first full-time salaried civilian job) a year later at the age of forty-three, almost no one except Hitler himself could have foreseen that he would rapidly transform Germany into the most aggressive power in the history of twentieth-century Europe. In 1936, however, the Security Service became probably the first department of government to issue a warning that the vast territorial ambitions set out by Hitler in *Mein Kampf* should be taken seriously as a guide to his future conduct: 'It is emphatically not a case of irresponsible utterances which have been discarded by a statesman on obtaining power.' In the aftermath of the 1938 Munich crisis Kell personally delivered to Sir Robert Vansittart at the Foreign Office what was in effect a devastating indictment of the policy of appeasement pursued by the Chamberlain government. In the light of reliable intelligence which MI5 had provided over the last few years, there was 'nothing surprising and nothing which could not have been foreseen' about the coming of the Munich crisis. British policy during the crisis had convinced Hitler of 'the weakness of England'. There are few more remarkable examples of an intelligence agency telling truth to power than Kell's decision to inform Chamberlain that Hitler considered him an 'arsehole'.[4]

Before the Second World War, as before the First, MI5 achieved considerably more than would nowadays be expected from an agency with such slender resources. Despite having only twenty-six officers at the beginning of 1938, it had succeeded in penetrating the German embassy, the British Fascist movement and the headquarters of the CPGB. By running Major Christopher Draper as a double agent against Germany, MI5 also discovered the cover address in Hamburg used by the Abwehr agent SNOW, whose later recruitment as a double agent marked the first step in the creation of the Double-Cross System. Both before and during the Second World War, the Security Service was less successful against Soviet than against Nazi intelligence. In particular, it underestimated Soviet success in recruiting bright young British graduates as long-term penetration agents. Lacking the budget for a major staff expansion, MI5 recruited only two recent graduates in the decade before the war (each of whom later became DG) – significantly fewer than the British graduate recruits of Soviet intelligence. Even had the Service possessed greater resources and a better understanding of the NKVD's graduate-recruitment programme, there was not much it could have done to prevent 'Stalin's Englishmen' (as Peter Hennessy later called them) penetrating the corridors of power. The woeful state of interwar protective security in Whitehall made it a soft target. Before the outbreak of war the Foreign Office had no security officer, let alone a security department. At various times during the 1930s, as well as failing to prevent the haemorrhage of classified documents from the Rome embassy, many of which the Centre forwarded to Stalin, the FO employed at least four Soviet agents: two young diplomats (Donald Maclean and John Cairncross) and two FO cipher clerks (Ernest Oldham and Captain John King).

Intelligence agencies, like governments, need, from time to time, a measure of good fortune. So far as its operations against Soviet intelligence in the 1930s were concerned, MI5 did not have it. In the summer of 1934, at the very moment when Kim Philby, who had graduated from Trinity College, Cambridge, in the previous year, was putting the NKVD in touch with his Trinity friend Guy Burgess, MI5 was pursuing an investigation at the College. Its target, however, was not the student body but a Trinity fellow, the Russian physicist and future Nobel laureate Pyotr Kapitsa, who there was good reason to suspect (even though the suspicions were probably unfounded) was engaged in scientific and technological espionage. With limited resources, MI5 was right to concentrate on Kapitsa, who was in contact with the leading Cambridge Communist academic Maurice Dobb, rather than on Dobb's former pupil Philby. Though MI5 did not suspect any of the Cambridge Five until 1951, it came quite close before the war to catching their two leading controllers, Teodor Maly and Arnold Deutsch. During 1937, while Olga Gray was working as an MI5 agent for Percy Glading, the CPGB organizer of the Woolwich Arsenal spy-ring, she met both Maly and Deutsch. Had they remained in England, Deutsch in particular would probably have been tracked down because of his recurrent security lapses. As a result of the paranoia which swept through the Centre during Stalin's Terror, however, first Maly, then Deutsch was abruptly recalled. By January 1939 only one NKVD officer remained in London. Kell drew the understandable but false conclusion that '[Soviet] activity in England is non-existent, in terms of both intelligence and political subversion.'[5] He failed to make allowance for the remarkable motivation and determination of the Five and other agents even after they had been abandoned by their pre-war case officers. All the Cambridge Five went on to get jobs within the intelligence agencies or within other corridors of power, whence they provided so much classified material that the Centre sometimes had difficulty in keeping up with it.

The Second World War began badly for MI5. Kell had stayed on too long as director (longer indeed than the head of any other twentieth-century government agency or department), had forgotten the lessons of the previous war and could not cope with the huge increase in wartime work. His immediate successor, Jasper Harker, was not up to the job. Under Sir David Petrie, however, the Service entered a golden age. In the Second World War the British intelligence community produced better (and better-used) intelligence than that available to any combatant in any previous conflict. It was taken by surprise by the extent of its own success. Though the breaking of the German Enigma machine cipher has since become perhaps the best-known intelligence success in British history, at the outbreak of war the cipher was widely regarded as unbreakable – even in Bletchley Park. Frank Birch, who became head of Bletchley's naval section, was told 'it wasn't *worthwhile*' trying to crack Enigma.[6]

MI5 found similar difficulty in coming to terms with the astonishing fact that, in the words of J. C. Masterman, chairman of the Twenty Committee, '*we actively ran and controlled the German espionage system in this country.*' But for that success, the FORTITUDE operations, the greatest deception in the history of warfare, on which the D-Day landings depended, would have been impossible. Masterman saw the Double-Cross System in the tradition of the Great Game, though – unlike Kipling – the game he had in mind was cricket. His friend, the Yale professor and wartime OSS officer in London Norman Holmes Pearson, called the Double-Cross System 'the greatest test match of the century'. The ingenuity of the deceptions practised by B1a owed much to the sense of fun which was already a distinctive strand of MI5 culture in the First World War. 'Breaking rules is fun,' Masterman had written before the war, 'and the middle-aged and the respectable have in this regard a capacity for innocent enjoyment at least as great as that of the youthful and rebellious.'[7]

GARBO and his case officer, Tomás Harris, made such a successful partnership partly because of their shared sense of the absurd. Like

ULTRA, the Double-Cross System was one of the best-kept secrets in British history. Even Churchill was not told until the spring of 1943. While Bletchley welcomed the Prime Minister's personal interest in its work, the DG, Sir David Petrie, preferred to keep Churchill at arm's length for fear that he might try to interfere. At some point, possibly after the war, King George VI was also told. Masterman was informed that his classified report on the Double-Cross System, written in the summer of 1945, was still in the King's private despatch case at the time of his death seven years later.[8]

Guy Liddell was well aware, as head of counter-espionage during the Second World War, that post-war Soviet intelligence would prove a more difficult target than the wartime Abwehr. He wrote in November 1942: 'There is no doubt that the Russians are far better in the matter of espionage than any country in the world. I am perfectly certain that they are well bedded down here and that we should be making more investigations. They will be a great source of trouble to us when the war is over.'[9] Liddell did not suspect, however, that the areas where Soviet intelligence was 'well bedded down' included the intelligence community. With very few exceptions (of whom Hollis was the most notable), Anthony Blunt was popular with staff at all levels of the Security Service. Liddell was so impressed by Guy Burgess, who was recruited by Blunt as an MI5 agent, that he would have liked him to become an officer. As a wartime SIS officer, Kim Philby too successfully ingratiated himself with MI5 both by the use of his considerable personal charm and by claiming to have told the head of SIS Section V, Felix Cowgill, that he had been 'quite wrong' to withhold some Abwehr decrypts from MI5. When Philby, by then head of Section IX, was posted abroad late in 1946, Liddell was 'profoundly sorry' to see him go.

But if MI5 misjudged the Five, so did the Centre. Though the Soviet Union had an unequalled ability before and during the Second World War to attract to its intelligence services well-educated ideological Western agents seduced by the myth-image of Stalin's Russia as the world's first worker-peasant state, it was not, as Liddell believed, 'far better in the matter of espionage than any country in the world'. Soviet agent-running during and immediately after the Second World War was less sophisticated than it later became. Much of what the Five achieved was in spite, rather than because, of their handling by the Centre. The KGB later concluded that they were the ablest group of foreign agents in its history. During the Second World War, however, the Five increasingly fell victim to the para-noid tendencies of the Stalinist intelligence system. In October 1943 the Centre informed its London residency that it was now clear that all along the Five had been double agents, working on the instructions of SIS and MI5. There were few more farcical moments in the history of Soviet intelligence than the Centre's decision to despatch to London an eight-man surveillance team, none of whom spoke English, to trail the Five and other supposedly bogus agents in the hope of discovering their meetings with their non-existent MI5 case officers. Perhaps to compensate for the failure of this impossible mission the team misidentified some of the visitors to the Soviet embassy in London as suspected MI5 agents provocateurs. The Five were not officially absolved of the charge of being British deception agents until after the D-Day landings. MI5's subsequent failure to recognize the gap between the outstanding achievements of the Five and the some-times dismal quality of the Centre's management of them hampered its investigation of the case, which was not fully resolved until almost half a century after Philby's recruitment.

Many Labour MPs elected in the landslide victory of 1945, who were unaware of the still classified triumphs of the Double-Cross System, viewed MI5 with suspicions dating back to the Zinoviev letter of 1924, which they blamed for the fall of Ramsay MacDonald's first Labour government. Once the former chief constable Sir Percy Sillitoe became DG, however, Clement Attlee placed more confidence in MI5 than in some of his cabinet ministers, whom he excluded from the decision to build a British atomic bomb on the grounds that they 'were not fit to be trusted with secrets of this kind'. It was Attlee who began the tradition that after every general election MI5 informs the incoming prime minister if there is evidence that anyone nominated for ministerial office is a security risk. Unlike subsequent prime ministers, he also asked to be informed of any sign of subversion among ministers' families. Attlee had more frequent personal meetings with Sillitoe than any other prime minister had with the DG during MI5's first hundred years. Sillitoe was instructed to inform Attlee whenever the Service had information that any MP of whatever party was 'a proven member of a subversive organisation'. Though very little record survives of matters discussed when Sillitoe called at Number Ten, in 1947 Attlee told the DG he had no doubt that the Labour MP Stephen Swingler 'was a C.P. member'. Attlee almost certainly also mentioned other 'crypto-Communists' on Labour benches. Morgan Phillips, general secretary of the Labour Party during the Attlee government, kept a 'Lost Sheep' file on pro-Soviet MPs such as Swingler.[10] In 1961, after Labour had been out of power for ten years, Attlee's successor as Party leader, Hugh Gaitskell, following discussion with his closest associates, decided to give MI5 a list of sixteen Labour MPs who, they believed, 'were in effect members of the

CPGB . . . or men under Communist Party direction', as well as the names of nine 'possible' crypto-Communists. The DDG, Graham Mitchell, declined even to discuss the list, on the grounds that MI5 records 'could be used only in the interests of the security of the realm as a whole' – and not to assist any political party.[11] The Service has maintained that position ever since.

The onset of the Cold War began the most dangerous period in the history of the United Kingdom. When the Second World War began, no intelligence community could have foreseen that it would end with the dawn of the nuclear age. 'A single demand of you, comrades!' Stalin told a secret meeting in the Kremlin after the US Army Air Forces dropped an atomic bomb on Hiroshima in August 1945. 'Provide us with atomic weapons in the shortest possible time. You know that Hiroshima has shaken the whole world.'[12]

The discovery in September 1949 that the Soviet Union had successfully tested an atomic bomb, about two years earlier than expected, shocked many British intelligence officers. The chairman of the JIC, William Hayter, was so taken aback that, before announcing the news, he cleared the room of secretaries and, despite the fact that all of the committee had an obligation to keep secrets, asked any member who doubted whether he could keep this particular secret to leave as well. The sense of shock was amplified by the almost simultaneous discovery that the plans of the first US atomic bomb, tested in the New Mexico desert less than a month before Hiroshima, had been betrayed to Soviet intelligence by Klaus Fuchs. The atom spies provided much of the motivation for the Attlee government's introduction of the Purge Procedure, designed to prevent Communists and the few remaining Fascists from gaining access to classified material. The Security Service was well aware of the implications for civil liberties and anxious not to gain a reputation as 'black reactionaries' out to 'victimise unfortunate Civil Servants'. In the event the Purge Procedure seems to have led to few injustices. Between 1947 and 1956, US purges led to the sacking of 2,700 federal employees and the resignation of another 12,000. In Britain from 1948 to 1954 there were 124 dismissals (a total which probably included resignations and transfers to other jobs).

British fears of thermonuclear war were never greater than in the five years before the Cuban Missile Crisis. A government White Paper publicly admitted for the first time in 1957 that there was 'no means of providing adequate protection for the people of this country against the consequences of an attack by nuclear weapons'. A schoolgirl interrupted her diary, which she acknowledged was mainly devoted to 'boys, boys, boys', to ask the question: 'I wonder if World War III is on the way, it certainly seems like it, doesn't it? The future is like a great gloomy cloud looming ahead that will swallow us up.'[13]

Like the schoolgirl, MI5's top management felt forced to peer into the nuclear abyss. It decided, without informing most staff, that in a nuclear war 'it was no good envisaging an organised Head Office existing anywhere; indeed there would be nothing to do.' Once officially informed that 'we were not to plan for any long-term war', the Service abandoned most of the plans it had made for wartime internment of the Soviet Union's leading supporters. For the first time, the Security Service was left with no major role in the preparations for war set out in the government's War Book.[14] As DG at the time of the 1962 missile crisis, Sir Roger Hollis knew that if the Third World War began he was likely to end his days with the Prime Minister, the War Cabinet and senior defence and intelligence staff in the doomsday bunker in the Cotswolds which had been chosen as the wartime seat (and probable grave) of the British government.

Though the prospect of a nuclear Armageddon began to recede after the peaceful settlement of the missile crisis, the 1960s were on the whole a depressing decade for MI5 senior management. Both Mitchell and Hollis suffered the unparalleled humiliation of being investigated on suspicion of being Soviet agents. The Security Service meanwhile found it increasingly difficult to cope with the steady increase in the size of the KGB and GRU residencies which, as it later acknowledged, 'threatened to swamp our then meagre resources'. A long campaign by the Service in Whitehall ended in October 1971 with Operation FOOT: the unprecedented expulsion of 105 Soviet intelligence officers. Over the previous year, the long-drawn-out nightmare of the investigation of Mitchell and Hollis had ended with both being found innocent of charges for which there had never been any serious evidence. FOOT had an extraordinary international impact, enhancing the Service's prestige with foreign friends in several continents. The Ghanaian intelligence liaison officer, for example, was reported to be 'clearly delighted' and 'remarked that this was good ammunition to use to persuade Cabinet Ministers that the threat from Russian espionage and its scale were serious'.[15]

FOOT marked a major turning point in MI5's counter-espionage operations. The expulsions, combined with the ceiling placed on Soviet officials in London and a policy of refusing visas to known hostile intelligence officers, turned the United Kingdom, for the first time, into a hard target for Soviet intelligence: a considerable achievement which, as in the First World War, was too elusive to be adequately identified by 'performance indicators'. For the remainder of the Cold War, Soviet Bloc intelligence agencies diverted a significant amount of their operations against UK targets to third countries, where the local security services were judged to be less effective.

For most of the Cold War, however, there was much about the role of intelligence in the Soviet system which MI5, like the rest of Western intelligence, did not fully understand. Part of the problem was the lack of a reliable account of the long-term development of Soviet intelligence. The founding father of US intelligence analysis, Sherman Kent, had complained in 1955 that intelligence was the only profession which lacked a serious literature: 'From my point of view this is a matter of greatest importance. As long as this discipline lacks a literature, its methods, its vocabulary, its body of doctrine, and even its fundamental theory run the risk of never reaching full maturity.'[16] Practising economists and politicians, among others, are rightly critical of the remoteness of some academic research from the real world in which they operate. But economics without economic history and politics without political history, without, in other words, a dependable record of past experience, would be what Kent forecast intelligence would remain without a serious intelligence literature – immature disciplines.[17]

The lack of a reliable history of Soviet intelligence made it much easier for Peter Wright to weave his vast conspiracy theories of Soviet strategic deception of Western intelligence. Soviet intelligence, he claimed, had already run such a deception a generation earlier in the TRUST operation of the 1920s in which a bogus anti-Bolshevik monarchist underground run by the OGPU had lured the former SIS agent Sidney Reilly across the Russian border to interrogation and execution, as well as deceiving a series of Western intelligence officers. Reilly was no longer (if he ever had been) the 'master spy' portrayed by some of his admirers. One of his secretaries complained that he sometimes became delusional: 'Once he thought he was Jesus Christ.' TRUST was a well-executed operation against less than first-rate opponents.[18]

Wright, however, transformed it into a strategic deception comparable in importance to the Double-Cross System before the Normandy landings. 'The Trust', he claimed, 'persuaded the British not to attack the Soviet Government because it would be done by internal forces,' organized by the supposed monarchist underground.[19] A reliable history of the interwar duel between Soviet and British intelligence would have exposed this claim as nonsense, but at the time no such history was available. Both ULTRA and the Double-Cross System were still classified top secret and it was not difficult for the unscrupulous Wright to assert that he had privileged access to more major secrets and to fend off challenges with the argument, 'If you knew what I know . . .'[20] The TRUST precedent, as falsified by Wright, gave an element of plausibility (albeit inadequate) to his argument that 'in 1963, there was no doubt that the Soviets had the necessary conditions to begin a major disinformation exercise.'[21] In reality, the 'necessary conditions' did not exist.

The lack of a long-term perspective on the relationship between intelligence and policy in the Soviet Union did some damage to even the best-balanced British intelligence assessments during much of the Cold War. The long history of autocratic rulers reveals the almost invariable requirement to tell the ruler what the ruler wishes to hear. Western intelligence analysts who worked to a shorter timescale tended to underestimate the degree to which that requirement degraded the intelligence supplied to the Soviet leadership, and thus to misunderstand the gulf which often separated frequently impressive Soviet intelligence collection from the dismal level of intelligence analysis. Though the gulf was greatest under Stalin, twenty years after his death political correctness remained a key constituent of intelligence reports to Leonid Brezhnev. According to Vadim Kirpichenko, first deputy head of the FCD (KGB foreign intelligence), anything which might 'upset Leonid Ilyich' was removed from the reports. When Soviet policy suffered setbacks, analysts knew they were on safe ground if they blamed them on imperialist conspiracies. Western intelligence analysts underestimated the role of conspiracy theory in Soviet intelligence assessment.[22]

It simply did not occur to MI5 officers (or, so far as is known, to those of any other Western intelligence agency) to suspect at any stage during the investigation of the Cambridge Five that the Five's recurrent failure to report what the Centre wished to hear might have caused them to be classed in the middle of the Second World War as a British deception operation – or that, forty years later, the Centre might believe President Reagan, supported by his British allies, to be planning a nuclear first strike against the Soviet Union. The intelligence provided by Oleg Gordievsky on Operation RYAN in 1982 came as a complete surprise on both sides of the Atlantic.[23]

Lack of a long-term perspective also hampered the Security Service's early response to the Northern Ireland Troubles. No file has been found in Service archives for the 1970s which makes any reference to the experience of British intelligence in Ireland in the period between the Easter Rising of 1916 and the founding of the Free State in 1922. Had the intelligence community and the security forces been aware at the beginning of the

Troubles of the problems caused half a century earlier by the lack of co-ordination between the military, the police and the metropolitan intelligence agencies,[24] similar kinds of confusion would have been less likely to recur. For historical reasons which went back to the Fenian 'Dynamite War' of the 1880s, intelligence confusion during the Troubles extended to the British mainland. The Security Service did not gain the lead intelligence role against Irish Republican terrorism in Britain until 1992 – despite the fact it already had the lead role against PIRA on the continent and the lead role in Britain against all other terrorists, including even Loyalist paramilitaries from Northern Ireland.

The beginning of the Troubles coincided with the end of most Security Service involvement in the Empire and Commonwealth. 'Overseas Service', wrote Anthony Simkins, then B1 (personnel), in 1954, 'brings good young officers on very fast indeed' – so fast, in his view, that there was 'a risk that they become a bit swollen headed in the process'.[25] For a quarter of a century after the Second World War, MI5 officers and many other staff spent, on average, a quarter to a third of their careers on overseas postings. As a result the Service acquired more expertise on, *inter alia*, Anglophone Africa, India, South-East Asia and the West Indies than it yet possessed on Northern Ireland. The only occasion on which the Service ever admitted that it had gone 'a little outside the strict terms' of its Charter (the 1952 Maxwell Fyfe Directive) was in the surveillance of colonial delegations during independence negotiations in the early 1960s. The Home Secretary, Rab Butler, immediately condoned the breach because of the 'great value to the government negotiators' of the intelligence obtained.[26] Following the transfer of most of the Service's Commonwealth responsibilities to SIS, MI5 officers were, for some years, more reluctant to accept postings to Belfast than they had been to Nairobi or Kingston, Jamaica. After the introduction of direct rule in Northern Ireland in 1972, the Service was asked to fill the new post of director and co-ordinator of intelligence in Belfast, but, because no suitable MI5 officer could be found, the first DCI was an outsider. After an urgent request for more intelligence at the beginning of direct rule from the newly created Northern Ireland Office, an Irish Joint Section was established by MI5 and SIS with jointly staffed offices in Belfast and London. Because of MI5's lack of Northern Ireland expertise, SIS was initially the senior partner. By the end of the decade, however, MI5 had come to terms with its new role; the Belfast station was wholly funded and mainly staffed by the Security Service. The IJS was wound up in 1984.[27]

At the beginning of 1989 Security Service staff had no more idea than the rest of the British people that before the end of the year they would see on their television screens the fall of the Berlin Wall and other unforgettable images of the collapse of Communist rule. The end of the Soviet era (finally concluded with the disintegration of the Soviet Union two years later) was almost as unexpected as its beginning almost three-quarters of a century before. Like the Bolshevik Revolution, it transformed MI5 objectives in ways no one had foreseen. It also led to some questioning of past priorities. Looking back on the way the CPGB had dwindled into insignificance well before the end of the Cold War, some – perhaps many – staff wondered if they had devoted too much of their energies to investigating subversion. Among the doubters was the officer who had served as Director F (counter-subversion) from 1985 to 1987 and who concluded in retrospect that 'we had always overstated the threat since Communists at no stage would have filled a football stadium.'[28]

No one in the Security Service had taken such a relaxed view of the CPGB forty years earlier when the Cold War threatened to turn into hot war and the leadership of the Party, like many of its militants, mistook the most brutal despot in Europe, Joseph Stalin, for the hope of the human race. Service transcribers eavesdropping on Party headquarters in 1950 heard the industrial organizer, Peter Kerrigan, describe as 'a bloody let-off' the failure of the media to notice the links of Klaus Fuchs with British Communists. The other most important Soviet agents discovered in the early Cold War were also Communists or inspired by Communist ideology. Though confident that it knew subversion when it discovered it, the Service made no attempt to define it until 1972. Its definition then – 'activities threatening the safety or well-being of the State and intended to undermine or overthrow Parliamentary democracy by political, industrial or violent means' – was adopted by the Heath government and its Labour successors.

The suggestion that an alarmist MI5, prone to see subversives in improb-able places, attempted to transfer its alarmism to the government is wholly mistaken. Though there was never any prospect of a British revolution, all governments during the Cold War were troubled from time to time by subversive attempts to undermine democracy by political or industrial means – often more troubled than the Security Service. The problem of 'crypto-Communists' on Labour benches in the Commons was of more concern to the Party leadership under both Attlee and Gaitskell than to MI5. The Service did not consider any of the sixteen alleged and nine 'possible' crypto-Communists whose names were passed to it on Gaitskell's instructions in 1961 worth further investigation. Despite his later, unfounded suspicions of an MI5 plot against him, during the seamen's strike in 1966 Harold Wilson showed greater enthusiasm for regular MI5 briefings than any previous prime minister during an industrial dispute. His celebrated denunciation of the strike leaders to the Commons as a 'tightly knit group of politically motivated men' was, like other parts of his speech, coined by the Security Service. Director F, the main Service briefer at Number Ten during the strike, was concerned, however, that Wilson might not be making adequate allowance for non-Communist as well as Communist influences on the strike. Under a series of governments, the Service had to resist repeated attempts during industrial disputes to persuade it to go beyond its Charter, which limited it to investigating the 'actions of persons and organizations ... which may be judged to be subversive of the state', and therefore excluded industrial disruption by union officials who were not members of, or sympathizers with, Communist or Trotskyist movements. In December 1971, for example, after power-station workers began a work-to-rule which threatened to disrupt electricity supplies, Heath 'enquired about the possibility' of the Security Service bugging the room at the Electricity Council where the four unions involved were due to meet. The Service replied that it would be a breach of its Charter 'to seek intelligence from a target which could not properly be regarded as subversive'.

John Jones, then DDG, wrote in 1977 that ministers and their senior officials had 'a natural tendency', which the Service must continue to resist, 'to equate subversion with [any] activity which threatens a Government's policies or may threaten its very existence'.[29] Though the Service stuck to its much narrower definition of subversion, the way that it kept track of subversives fell increasingly behind the times. Much of the ritual recording of the activities and membership of the CPGB, however insignificant, struck most new recruits and a growing number of more senior staff as a waste of its resources. By the end of the Cold War the word 'subversion' had become an embarrassment and was omitted from the 1989 Security Service Act, though it remained the responsibility of the Service to defend the realm against 'actions intended to overthrow or undermine parliamentary democracy by political, industrial or violent means'. In 1992 the Service gained government permission to cease recording 'rank-and-file members of subversive organisations', once the first, tedious assignment at MI5 headquarters of most new graduate entrants – among them Stella Rimington, who in that year became the first female DG.

The Security Service found it difficult to come to terms with its role in the post-Cold War world. Most staff were still unused to strategic thinking and horizon scanning. H1/0, who had been asked by the DG to prepare a strategic review, reported to the Management Board at the end of 1990: 'We must recognise the fact, unfortunate though it is, that the need for us to respond to the new situation by devising an articulate and coherent strategy is appreciated by few colleagues in the Service.' PIRA's mainland bombing campaigns, however, gave the Service a renewed sense of direction. The shift in its priorities during the last two decades of the Cold War from counter-espionage and counter-subversion to counter-terrorism (CT) had been very gradual. The Service had no sense during the 1970s, or even for much of the 1980s, that CT was destined to become its main priority. Following the nearly successful PIRA attempt to fire a mortar into a cabinet meeting at Number Ten in 1991, the transfer from the MPSB of the lead intelligence role against Republican terrorism in Britain in the following year completed the Service's emergence, for the first time in its history, as primarily a counter-terrorist agency. Terrorism, declared Stephen Lander, then Director T, 'is here to stay. The circumstances that give rise to it may change, and terrorist organisations and state sponsors may come and go, but the phenomenon is very unlikely to disappear.'[30]

Over the next few years PIRA's bombing campaigns against the City of London threatened to put at risk its survival as Europe's main financial capital. (Sir) Joe Pilling, later PUS at the Northern Irish Office, wrote after the destruction of the Baltic Exchange in April 1992: 'Only a combination of good intelligence, good policing and good luck prevented several more incidents on a similar scale.'[31] The same was true after the PIRA bombing of the NatWest Tower in Bishopsgate in April 1993. The Provisionals warned foreign financial institutions in the City to relocate or face a similar fate. Had the bombings continued, some might well have done so. In July, however, the UK's most intensive counter-terrorist operation so far, co-ordinated by the Security Service, led to the arrest of the senior Belfast Provisional Rab Fryers on his way to plant another large bomb in the City. His arrest was followed by the discovery of the materials for six car bombs which PIRA had intended to use to continue its attacks on the Square Mile. Probably the most audacious of PIRA's plans to attack London was the attempted disruption in July 1996 of the capital's electricity supply. John Grieve, commander of SO13 at Scotland Yard, later described the ASU involved as 'one of the best teams the IRA ever put together. We thought it was the mainland "A Team" . . .' The fact that all were on the lookout for surveillance made the extensive surveillance mounted on them before their arrest in Operation AIRLINES all the more impressive.[32] Lander, who had become DG earlier in the year, felt confident enough to declare in October: 'Even terrorists regard the UK as a hostile and risky environment . . . No one has a better record.'[33] That record, in the Service's view, contributed to PIRA's willingness to consider a compromise political settlement which would postpone for the foreseeable future the achievement of Irish unity.

Though effective against PIRA, the Security Service was slow to see the coming menace of Islamist terrorism. The Service told heads of special branches in December 1995 that, despite Iranian state-sponsored terrorism, with Salman Rushdie as its main British target, 'Suggestions in the press of a world-wide Islamic extremist network poised to launch terrorist attacks against the West are greatly exaggerated.' Bruce Hoffman, the terrorism expert who identified the future threat from Holy Terror most clearly, did so largely because he took a longer-term view than the Service. Of the sixty-four terrorist groups active in 1980, only two, both closely associated with the Islamic Revolution in Iran, had a mainly religious motivation. Over the next fifteen years, however, Hoffman noted a dramatic return to an old tradition of Holy Terror. (Until the French Revolution the only justifications advanced for terror had been religious.) By 1995 almost half the active international terrorist groups were religiously based. All the most lethal attacks that year were carried out by religious terrorists.[34]

While aware of Bin Laden as a terrorist financier, Stella Rimington had never heard the name Al Qaida until March 1996, when it cropped up during talks at the White House and the CIA during her farewell visit as DG to the United States. Even when Al Qaida launched its first suicide bomb attacks against the US embassies in Nairobi and Dar es Salaam in the summer of 1998, there was little sense within the Security Service that similar attacks might take place in the UK.[35] The Service later concluded that by late 2000, before the September 2001 attacks in New York and Washington, the UK had become an Al Qaida target.[36] For over a year after 9/11, however, the Islamist threat to the UK was thought to come from abroad, not from home-grown terrorists. Once the Security Service had identified the home-grown threat in 2003, it responded quickly to it. Operation CREVICE, the largest counter-terrorist operation yet undertaken by either the Security Service or the police, forestalled attacks against nightclubs, pubs and shopping centres which were intended to cause mass casualties. For the first time in Security Service history, the DG was invited to a meeting of the full cabinet in April 2004 to be congratulated by the Prime Minister. The Service knew, however, that, because it lacked the resources to keep track of all potential Islamist terrorists, 'it can only be a matter of time before something on a serious scale occurs in the UK.' The

Great assumptions about a career at MI5

No 1: Application by invitation only

No 2: You'll have to live your life undercover

No 3: You'll get a great company car

No 4: It's like a gentleman's club

Four advertisements from the MI5 2002–3 recruitment campaign, designed to help dispel myths about the Security Service and indicate that a sense of humour was part of Service culture.

suicide bombings of 7 July 2005 and the attempted bombings of 21 July caused much greater shock than surprise.

The Service's strategy for extending regional coverage of Islamist terrorist networks looked back to its earliest days. In the summer of 1910 Kell established personal contact with forty English, Scottish and Welsh chief constables, all of whom 'expressed themselves most willing to assist me in every way'. Almost a century later, one of the Service's most successful strategies for improving its counter-terrorist operations was closer co-operation with the police at a local level through newly established MI5 regional offices. The head of Scotland Yard's Counter-Terrorism Command, Deputy Assistant Commissioner Peter Clarke, declared in 2007: 'There can be no doubt that the most important change in counter terrorism in the UK in recent years has been the development of the relationship between the police and the security service.' MI5's regional offices built on the experience of the regional security liaison officers during the Second World War. Though the main reason for the establishment of the wartime RSLOs had been to prepare for a German invasion which never occurred, they had been successful in bringing the Service 'into closer touch with provincial Police Forces'.[37]

While the terrorist threat to British national security will no doubt fluctuate in intensity, it may well last as long as the Cold War. During the two years from January 2007 to January 2009 eighty-six people were convicted of Islamist terrorist offences. Like the number of spies caught in the First World War, terrorist convictions are an incomplete measure of MI5 success. The best indicator of counter-espionage success in the First World War came when Britain had become such a hard target that there were few spies left to catch. Terrorists willing to sacrifice their lives are far harder to deter than the sometimes weakly motivated German agents of the First World War. Jonathan Evans noted, however, in early 2009 that the success of counter-terrorist operations over the last few years had had 'a chilling effect on the enthusiasm of the plotters' for mounting new attacks. It is too early to tell whether the 'chilling effect' is a short-term fluctuation or a long-term trend.

Save for climate change, the study of long-term trends has had little appeal to early twenty-first-century policy-makers. The shock caused by the sub-prime crisis and credit crunch of 2008–9 derived, at least in part, from what I have termed Historical Attention Span Deficit Disorder (HASDD). To many bankers and financial commentators, the precedent of 1929 and the Wall Street Crash, to which they had previously paid little attention, suddenly seemed surprisingly relevant. Short-termism has been the distinguishing intellectual vice of the late twentieth and early twenty-first centuries. For the first time in recorded history, there has been a widespread assumption that the experience of all previous generations is irrelevant to present policy.[38] Institutions, like individuals, however, diminish their effectiveness if they fail to reflect on past successes and failures. The most senior MI5 officer to write some of its history was Anthony Simkins, who after his retirement collaborated with Sir Harry Hinsley in writing the official history of security and intelligence in the Second World War. 'I would have been a better DDG', Simkins said afterwards, 'if I had written my history first.'[39]

Even the historical profession has suffered from a degree of Historical Attention Span Deficit Disorder so far as the Security Service and the rest of the intelligence community are concerned. The well-publicized successes of British codebreakers against Germany during the First World War should have alerted historians to the possibility that there might have been similar successes in the Second World War. Until the revelation of the ULTRA secret in 1973, however, almost no historian suspected that SIGINT had played a significant role in the defeat of Nazi Germany.[40] In 1984 David Dilks and I described intelligence as the 'missing dimension' of twentieth-century British historiography.[41]

Though intelligence is no longer missing, British historians in a great variety of fields have yet to consider the relevance of Security Service history to their own research. The fact that both the first female financial controller of any British government department and the first female head of any of the world's major intelligence services worked for MI5 has, for example, so far failed to attract the interest of gender historians. Many histories of British decolonization do not mention the role of MI5. Many biographies of British prime ministers have little, if anything, to say about their attitude to intelligence and the intelligence services. As usual, however, lapses by one generation of historians provide some of the main research opportunities for their successors.[42]

The Security Service, like many other institutions, has in the past paid too little attention to the lessons of its own history. Some senior officers have mistakenly seen all but the most recent 'lessons learned' as a barrier to innovation. Sir David Petrie, one of the Service's most successful DGs, believed that 'Too much of a past that is now remote can help but little with useful lessons.' In reality there were a number of 'useful lessons' from the past that senior management had overlooked. Kell had failed to heed the warning in an MI5 report at the end of the First World War that, in the event of another war, the Service would be deluged with 'a flood of paper'. The Service's lack of preparedness to deal with fifth-column scares in 1940 reflected a failure, once again, to learn from the experience of the last war, whose outbreak had provoked 'a virulent epidemic' of spy mania.[43]

During the remainder of the twentieth century, underestimation of the deficiencies of Soviet intelligence analysis, intelligence confusion at the beginning of the Northern Ireland Troubles and delay in identifying the threat from Islamist terrorism provided further evidence of HASDD. In each instance, however, the Security Service learned from its mistakes. Within six months of the near-collapse of MI5 administration in the summer of 1940, the Twenty Committee under an MI5 chairman was running the Double-Cross System. The intelligence provided by Oleg Gordievsky later gave the Security Service, like the rest of the intelligence community, an unprecedented, if belated, insight into the blinkered mindset of the Centre and its misunderstandings of the West. Once the Service had gained the lead intelligence role in Britain against Republican terrorism in 1992, with police help it successfully prevented PIRA's most dangerous mainland campaigns from achieving their objectives. Since MI5 began to focus fully on the threat from home-grown Islamist terrorism in 2003, it has – so far – successfully prevented the majority of planned terrorist attacks.

Seen in long-term perspective, there is greater continuity between past and present threats to national security than is often supposed. Elie Wiesel, Nobel laureate, Holocaust survivor and human rights activist, forecast several years before 9/11: 'The principal challenge of the twenty-first century is going to be exactly the same as the principal challenge of the twentieth century: How do we deal with fanaticism armed with power?'[44] The three men who have posed the greatest threats to British security since the 1930s – Adolf Hitler, Joseph Stalin and Usama bin Laden – have all been 'fanatics armed with power'.

Fanaticism, like other disorders, however, evolves over time. What makes the early twenty-first century a less dangerous place than the twentieth is that fanatics no longer control any of the world's major powers. There is no realistic prospect of another Hitler in Berlin or another Stalin in Moscow. Unlike Hitler and Stalin, today's most dangerous fanatics – terrorist groups (Al Qaida chief among them) and rogue regimes – are on the margins of the international system rather than at its centre. But if the political power of fanaticism has declined, its destructive capacity over the next generation is likely to be increased by the proliferation of weapons of mass destruction.[45] Bin Laden declared in 1998 that acquiring these weapons is a 'religious duty'. A year before 9/11, without realizing it at the time, Security Service counter-proliferation operations disrupted a first attempt by Al Qaida to obtain material in Britain to develop biological weapons. The ambition of Dhiren Barot, the chief Islamist plotter arrested as a result of Operation RHYME in 2004, was to explode a radioactive 'dirty bomb'. Though, as Barot acknowledged, he failed to make the contacts necessary to achieve his ambition, other terrorists will try to succeed where Barot failed.

In the twenty-first century, as in the twentieth, some of the challenges faced by the Security Service will be difficult, if not impossible, to predict. One of the lessons of its first hundred years is that it will respond to these challenges best if it has a long-term perspective. In the words of Winston Churchill, for half a century a committed supporter and occasional critic of the Service, 'The further backwards you look, the further forward you can see.'

Appendix 1

Directors and Director Generals, 1909–2009

1909–1940	Sir Vernon Kell
1940–1941	Brigadier Oswald Allen 'Jasper' Harker
1941–1946	Sir David Petrie
1946–1953	Sir Percy Sillitoe
1953–1956	Sir Dick White
1956–1965	Sir Roger Hollis
1965–1972	Sir Martin Furnival Jones
1972–1978	Sir Michael Hanley
1978–1981	Sir Howard Smith
1981–1985	Sir John Jones
1985–1988	Sir Antony Duff
1988–1992	Sir Patrick Walker
1992–1996	Dame Stella Rimington
1996–2002	Sir Stephen Lander
2002–2007	Baroness Manningham-Buller
2007	Jonathan Evans

Note: The title of director general was first used by Sir David Petrie. Kell and Harker were both designated director.

Appendix 2

Security Service Strength, 1909–2009

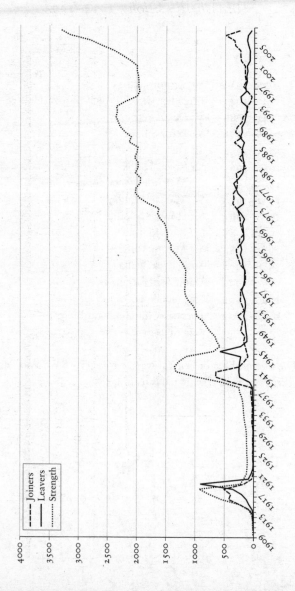

Appendix 3

*Nomenclature and Responsibilities of Security Service
Branches/Divisions, 1914–1994*

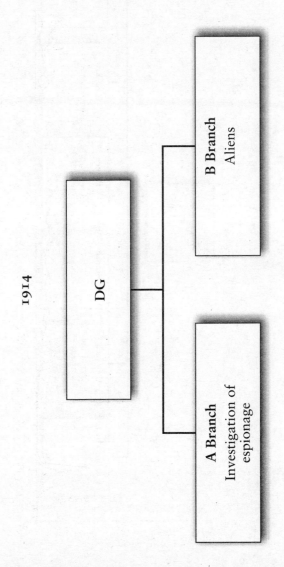

1914

DG

A Branch
Investigation of
espionage

B Branch
Aliens

1916

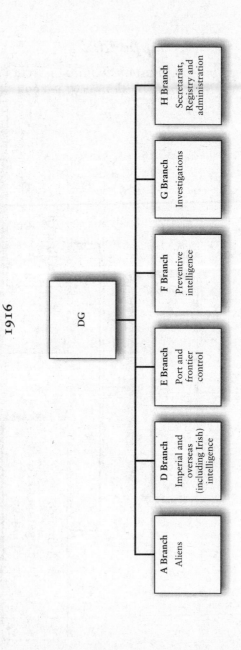

1931

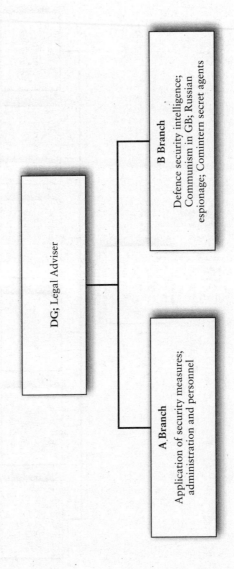

DG; Legal Adviser

A Branch
Application of security measures; administration and personnel

B Branch
Defence security intelligence; Communism in GB; Russian espionage; Comintern secret agents

1941

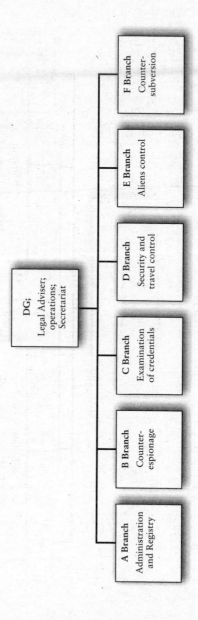

DG;
Legal Adviser;
operations;
Secretariat

A Branch
Administration
and Registry

B Branch
Counter-
espionage

C Branch
Examination
of credentials

D Branch
Security and
travel control

E Branch
Aliens control

F Branch
Counter-
subversion

1953

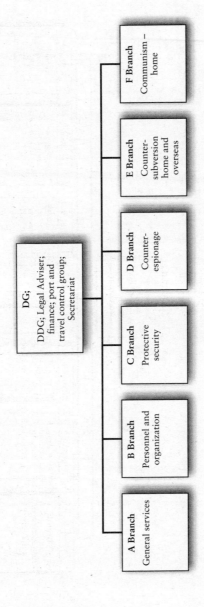

DG;

DDG; Legal Adviser; finance; port and travel control group; Secretariat

A Branch
General services

B Branch
Personnel and organization

C Branch
Protective security

D Branch
Counter-espionage

E Branch
Counter-subversion home and overseas

F Branch
Communism – home

After reorganization by Sir Dick White

1968

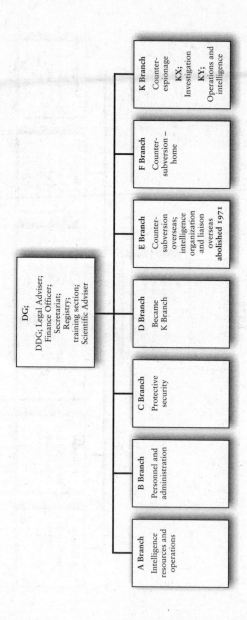

| A Branch
Intelligence resources and operations | B Branch
Personnel and administration | C Branch
Protective security | D Branch
Became K Branch | E Branch
Counter-subversion overseas; intelligence organization and liaison overseas abolished 1971 | F Branch
Counter-subversion – home | K Branch
Counter-espionage
KX; Investigation
KY; Operations and intelligence |

DG;
DDG; Legal Adviser;
Finance Officer;
Secretariat;
Registry;
training section;
Scientific Adviser

1976

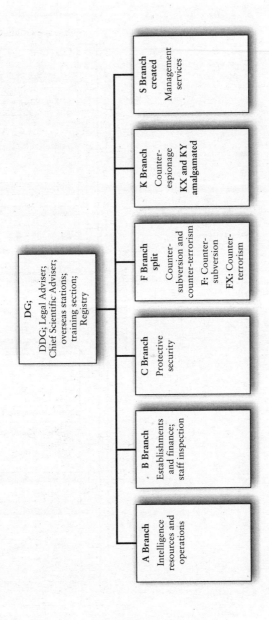

DG;
DDG; Legal Adviser; Chief Scientific Adviser; overseas stations; training section; Registry

A Branch
Intelligence resources and operations

B Branch
Establishments and finance; staff inspection

C Branch
Protective security

F Branch split
Counter-subversion and counter-terrorism
F: Counter-subversion
FX: Counterterrorism

K Branch
Counter-espionage
KX and KY amalgamated

S Branch created
Management services

1988

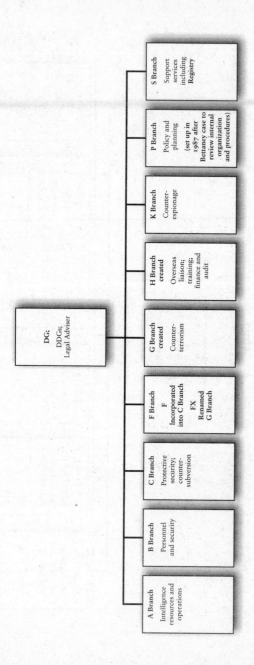

DG;
DDGs;
Legal Adviser

A Branch
Intelligence
resources and
operations

B Branch
Personnel
and security

C Branch
Protective
security;
counter-
subversion

F Branch
F
Incorporated
into C Branch
FX
Renamed
G Branch

**G Branch
created**
Counter-
terrorism

**H Branch
created**
Overseas
liaison;
training;
finance and
audit

K Branch
Counter-
espionage

P Branch
Policy and
planning
(set up in
1987 after
Bettaney case to
review internal
organization
and procedures)

S Branch
Support
services
including
Registry

1991

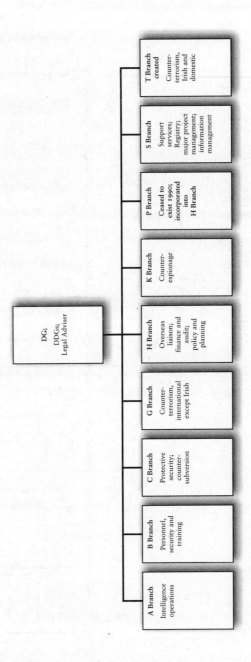

DG;
DDGs;
Legal Adviser

A Branch
Intelligence operations

B Branch
Personnel, security and training

C Branch
Protective security; counter-subversion

G Branch
Counter-terrorism, international except Irish

H Branch
Overseas liaison; finance and audit; policy and planning

K Branch
Counter-espionage

P Branch
Ceased to exist 1990; incorporated into H Branch

S Branch
Support services; Registry; major project management; information management

T Branch created
Counter-terrorism, Irish and domestic

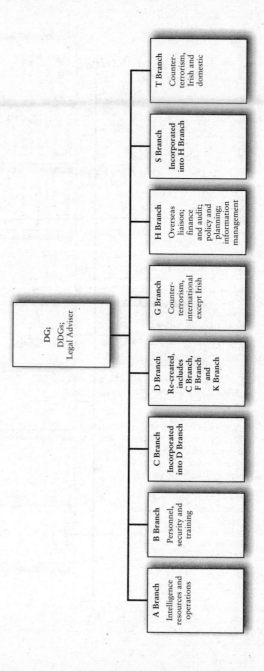

1994

DG;
DDGs;
Legal Adviser

A Branch
Intelligence resources and operations

B Branch
Personnel, security and training

C Branch
Incorporated into D Branch

D Branch
Re-created, includes C Branch, F Branch and K Branch

G Branch
Counter-terrorism, international except Irish

H Branch
Overseas liaison; finance and audit; policy and planning; information management

S Branch
Incorporated into H Branch

T Branch
Counter-terrorism, Irish and domestic

Notes

ABBREVIATIONS

AVIA	Ministry of Aviation
BUL	Birmingham University Library
CAB	Cabinet Office
CCAC	Churchill College Archive Centre, Cambridge
CHAR	Chartwell papers (CACC)
CO	Colonial Office
CUL	Cambridge University Library
CUSS	Cambridge University Socialist Society
DEFE	Ministry of Defence
DNB	*Oxford Dictionary of National Biography*
DO	Dominions Office
FCO	Foreign and Commonwealth Office
FO	Foreign Office
GEN	Cabinet Sub-Committee
HLRO	House of Lords Record Office
HO	Home Office
HW	Papers of the Government Communications Headquarters (GCHQ)
INF	Papers of the Central Office of Information
IWM	Imperial War Museum
KV	Papers of the Security Service
LHC	Liddell Hart Centre for Military Archives, King's College London
MEPO	Papers of the Metropolitan Police
MISC	Cabinet temporary sub-committee
NAW	National Archives, Washington, DC
NMM	National Maritime Museum
PREM	Prime Minister's Office
RG	Record Group (NAW)
SLYU	Sterling Library, Yale University
T	Treasury
TNA	The National Archives
WC	War Cabinet
WO	War Office

SECTION A: THE GERMAN THREAT, 1909–1919

Introduction: The Origins of the Secret Service Bureau

1 Memorandum re Formation of a S.S. Bureau [minutes of meeting on 26 Aug. 1909, approved by Sir Charles Hardinge, PUS at the Foreign Office, on 14 Sept. 1909], TNA WO 106/6292. The date set for the Bureau to open business had been 1 October, but it was not until the 10th that both Cumming and Kell started work in the office and money from the Foreign Office Secret Vote came on stream. Cumming had paid his first visit to the office on the 7th 'and remained all day but saw no-one, nor was there anything to do there.' Judd, *Quest for C*, pp. 86, 100.

2 Mansfield Cumming diary, 4 Oct. 1909, SIS Archives. Kell later told Gilbert Wakefield, subsequently an in-house MI5 historian, that he 'first met "C" in the office of a private detective' (identified by Wakefield as Drew).

3 Evidence by Kell to Secret Service Committee, Secret Service Committee Minutes, 10 March 1925, TNA FO 1093/68. Cumming's diary suggests, however, that Kell and Cumming rarely worked in the room at the same time.

4 'Report and Proceedings of a Sub-Committee of the Committee of Imperial Defence Appointed by the Prime Minister to Consider the Question of Foreign Espionage in the United Kingdom', Oct. 1909, TNA CAB 16/8.

5 Ibid.

6 Le Queux, *England's Peril*, p. 42.

7 Le Queux's name rhymed with Drew's. Like Drew he had an English mother and a French father. On visits to France Drew used his real name, Dreux.

8 Le Queux, *Secrets of the Foreign Office*.

9 'William Tufnell Le Queux', *Oxford DNB*.

10 *Kim* was first published as a magazine serial, beginning in December 1900. It appeared in book form in October 1901.

11 Hinsley et al., *British Intelligence in the Second World War*, vol. 1, p. 16n.

12 Andrew, *Secret Service*, ch. 1.

13 Warwick (ed.), *South African War*, p. 66.

14 *Report of the Royal Commission on the War in South Africa*, Cd 1789 (1903), p. 128. See also Andrew, *Secret Service*, pp. 28–9.

15 Cook, *M: MI5's First Spymaster*, pp. 146–8, 253.

16 Ibid., pp. 248–9. Melville also received Austrian, Danish, French, Italian, Portuguese and Spanish decorations in recognition of his services during the travels of British and foreign royals.

17 Both the alias and the address appeared on Melville's business card, which survives both in his papers (ibid., p. 254) and in Security Service files.

18 On the Nachrichten-Abteilung and Steinhauer's role in it, see Boghardt, *Spies of the Kaiser*, pp. 13–20.

19 Steinhauer, *Steinhauer*, pp. 310–19. Cook, *M: MI5's First Spymaster*, pp. 134–7. Boghardt, *Spies of the Kaiser*, pp. 47–8. On Steinhauer's place in the German naval intelligence hierarchy, see Boghardt, *Spies of the Kaiser*, appendix 1, p. 148. An interwar MI5 assessment of Steinhauer's memoirs concluded: 'Comparison with the records of the Security Service shows this book to be a very fair account of his organisation in this country.' 'Gustav Steinhauer', 'Game Book', vol. 1: 1909–1915, TNA KV 4/112.

20 Report by Melville on Long's mission, 8 April 1904; reproduced in Cook, *M: MI5's First Spymaster*, appendix, p. 256. Long's first name sometimes appears wrongly as 'Henry'.

21 'Historical Papers', TNA KV 6/47.

22 Cohn, *Warrant for Genocide*, pp. 76–86, 113.

23 Untitled memoir by Melville, 31 Dec. 1917, pp. 15–16, TNA KV 1/8.

24 Ibid., p. 2.

25 Ibid., pp. 21–2.

26 Edmonds, 'Origins of MI5', LHC Edmonds MSS VIII/3; Edmonds, Unpublished Memoirs, ch. 20, LHC Edmonds MSS III/5.

27 Untitled memoir by Melville, 31 Dec. 1917, p. 3, TNA KV 1/8. Le Queux claimed inaccurately that the German translation ended with a German victory.

28 The new 'voluntary Secret Service Department', in so far as it existed outside Le Queux's imagination, had its main home in the patriotic Legion of Frontiersmen founded by Roger Pocock at the end of 1904. Pocock inhabited a Walter Mitty world as extravagant as Le Queux's, full of *Boy's Own Paper* villains and heroes.

29 Le Queux, *Invasion of 1910*. Clarke, *Voices Prophesying War*, p. 145. Kennedy, *Rise of the Anglo-German Antagonism*, pp. 362, 371. Andrew, *Secret Service*, pp. 74–6. Patrick and Baister, *William Le Queux*, pp. 57–63.

30 Le Queux, *Things I Know*, p. 237.

31 Standish, *Prince of Storytellers*.

32 Morris, 'And is the Kaiser Coming for Tea?', pp. 58–61. Gooch, *Plans of War*, pp. 284–5.

33 Steiner, *Britain and the Origins of the First World War*, pp. 53, 287 n.23.

34 Marder, *From the Dreadnought to Scapa Flow*, vol. 1, ch. 7.

35 Thwaites to Gleichen, 7 May 1907, TNA WO 32/8873. Hiley, 'Failure of British Espionage', p. 874.

36 Edmonds, Unpublished Memoirs, ch. 20, LHC Edmonds MSS III/5.

37 'Report and Proceedings of a Sub-Committee of the Committee of Imperial Defence Appointed by the Prime Minister to Consider the Question of Foreign Espionage in the United Kingdom', Appendix 1: 'Cases of Alleged German Espionage which have been reported to the Director of Military Operations', Oct. 1909, TNA CAB 16/8.

38 Among them Christopher Andrew in *Secret Service*.

39 'Sir James Edward Edmonds', *Oxford DNB*. Though the War Office Intelligence Division was formally renamed the Intelligence Department only in 1901, it was often called by the latter title in the 1890s.

40 'Report and Proceedings of a Sub-Committee of the Committee of Imperial Defence Appointed by the Prime Minister to Consider the Question of Foreign Espionage in the United Kingdom: First Meeting, Tuesday, 30th March, 1909', Oct. 1909, TNA CAB 16/8.

41 *Security Service*, p. 64; cf. Stieber, *Chancellors' Spy*: a source to be treated with some caution.

42 Edmonds, 'Espionage in the time of peace', Jan. 1909, pp. 22–32, TNA KV 1/2.

43 CID, 'The Question of Foreign Espionage in the United Kingdom', 30 March 1909, p. 2, TNA CAB 16/18.

44 Edmonds, 'Espionage in the time of peace', Jan. 1909, p. 24, TNA KV 1/2. Stieber, *Chancellors' Spy*.

45 'Report and Proceedings of a Sub-Committee of the Committee of Imperial Defence Appointed by the Prime Minister to Consider the Question of Foreign Espionage in the United Kingdom: First Meeting, Tuesday, 30th March, 1909', Oct. 1909, TNA CAB 16/8. In talks to new recruits early in the Cold War, the DDG, Guy Liddell, explained that 'When visiting Berlin and Moscow and after his return, [Edmonds] gathered that the Germans had opened a section of their Intelligence Service to deal with England.' Guy Liddell diary, 1 Nov. 1950. The Liddell diaries for the Second World War are in TNA KV 4/185–194; extensive extracts have been published in West (ed.), *Guy Liddell Diaries*, 2 vols. The post-war diaries are in Security Service Archives.

46 Boghardt, *Spies of the Kaiser*, pp. 13–20.

47 Andrew, *Théophile Delcassé*, pp. 284–5. Hiley, Introduction to Le Queux, *Spies of the Kaiser*, pp. xix–xx.

48 'Sir James Edward Edmonds', *Oxford DNB*.

49 Kell wrote to Holt-Wilson soon after the war: 'Old Edmonds wrote to me asking that we should take him on! I have not replied. I would not have minded, if I could be sure he was not *more* cranky than he was in the old days.' Security Service Archives.

50 J. E. Edmonds, 'Intelligence Systems: Germany', 9 Feb. 1909, IWM Kell MSS.

51 Le Queux, *Spies of the Kaiser*. Le Queux identified closely with the narrator, Jacox, at one point taking over as the narrator himself; Patrick and Baister, *William Le Queux*, p. 66.

52 Edmonds, Unpublished Memoirs, ch. 20, LHC Edmonds MSS III/5.

53 Introduction by Sir Robert Gower MP to Sladen, *The Real Le Queux*, p. xv. Le Queux also persuaded Gower, though he can scarcely have persuaded Edmonds, that his own unpaid

'Secret Service operations' exceeded 'in their daring the most colourful adventures of his bravest fictional heroes'.

54 Edmonds, Unpublished Memoirs, ch. 20, LHC Edmonds MSS III/5.

55 'Report and Proceedings of a Sub-Committee of the Committee of Imperial Defence Appointed by the Prime Minister to Consider the Question of Foreign Espionage in the United Kingdom', Oct. 1909, appendix no. 1, case no. 26, TNA CAB 16/8.

56 Edmonds, Unpublished Memoirs, ch. 20, LHC Edmonds MSS III/5.

57 Lady Kell, 'Secret Well Kept: an account of the work of Sir Vernon Kell', p. 113 (unpublished manuscript, IWM).

58 Its other members were the First Lord of the Admiralty, the Home Secretary, the Postmaster General, Lord Esher, the permanent under secretaries of the Treasury and the Foreign Office, the Commissioner of the Metropolitan Police, the Director of Military Operations, the Director of Naval Intelligence, the Director of Military Training and Rear Admiral Sir C. L. Ottley.

59 'Report and Proceedings of a Sub-Committee of the Committee of Imperial Defence Appointed by the Prime Minister to Consider the Question of Foreign Espionage in the United Kingdom', Oct. 1909, TNA CAB 16/8. Edmonds, Unpublished Memoirs, ch. 20, LHC Edmonds MSS III/5.

60 Col. W. G. Simpson, 'The Duties of Local Authorities in War Time', *Journal of the Royal United Service Institution*, LVIII (Jan. 1914), pp. 5–30; Gilbert Mellor, 'The Status under the Hague Conference of Civilians Who Take up Arms during the Time of War', *Journal of the Royal United Service Institution*, LVIII (May 1914), pp. 559–78; Col. G. H. Ovens, 'Fighting in Enclosed Country', *Journal of the Royal United Service Institution*, XLIX (1905), pp. 524–46.

61 'Report and Proceedings of a Sub-Committee of the Committee of Imperial Defence Appointed by the Prime Minister to Consider the Question of Foreign Espionage in the United Kingdom: First Meeting, Tuesday, 30th March, 1909', Oct. 1909, TNA CAB 16/8.

62 'Report and Proceedings of a Sub-Committee of the Committee of Imperial Defence Appointed by the Prime Minister to Consider the Question of Foreign Espionage in the United Kingdom', Oct. 1909, Appendix 1, case no. 10, TNA CAB 16/8. Untitled memoir by Melville, 31 Dec. 1917, pp. 24–5, TNA KV 1/8.

63 Dr Nicholas Hiley was the first to discover the meaning of 'TR', 'Tariff Reformer' and 'Tiaria'.

64 Mansfield Cumming diary, SIS Archives.

65 Herbert Dale Long to Melville, 23 March 1909, TNA KV 6/47. The 'party' refers to 'Tariff Reform Party' (German intelligence). Only fragmentary records survive of the secret investigations of Herbert Dale Long at home and abroad, often on half-pay. On his early work for Melville, see Cook, *M: MI5's First Spymaster*, pp. 148–9. Dr Nicholas Hiley's research has shown that in 1911 Long was sent to Brussels to run an operation for Cumming (SS Bureau: General Organisation, TNA KV 1/53).

66 'Report and Proceedings of a Sub-Committee of the Committee of Imperial Defence Appointed by the Prime Minister to Consider the Question of Foreign Espionage in the United Kingdom. Appendix 1: Cases of Alleged German Espionage which have been reported to the Director of Military Operations', Oct. 1909, TNA CAB 16/8.

67 Ibid. Boghardt, *Spies of the Kaiser*, p. 32.

68 'Report and Proceedings of a Sub-Committee of the Committee of Imperial Defence Appointed by the Prime Minister to Consider the Question of Foreign Espionage in the United Kingdom. Appendix 1: Cases of Alleged German Espionage which have been reported to the Director of Military Operations', Oct. 1909, TNA CAB 16/8.

69 'Report and Proceedings of a Sub-Committee of the Committee of Imperial Defence Appointed by the Prime Minister to Consider the Question of Foreign Espionage in the United Kingdom: First Meeting, Tuesday, 30th March, 1909', Oct. 1909, TNA CAB 16/8.

70 Brett (ed.), *Journals and Letters of Reginald Viscount Esher*, vol. 2, p. 379.

71 'Report and Proceedings of a Sub-Committee of the Committee of Imperial Defence Appointed by the Prime Minister to Consider the Question of Foreign Espionage in the United Kingdom: First Meeting, Tuesday, 30th March, 1909', Oct. 1909, TNA CAB 16/8.

72 Koss, *Lord Haldane*, pp. 15–16, 65, 69.

73 'Report and Proceedings of a Sub-Committee of the Committee of Imperial Defence

Appointed by the Prime Minister to Consider the Question of Foreign Espionage in the United Kingdom: First Meeting, Tuesday, 30th March, 1909', Oct. 1909, TNA CAB 16/8.

74 'Report and Proceedings of a Sub-Committee of the Committee of Imperial Defence Appointed by the Prime Minister to Consider the Question of Foreign Espionage in the United Kingdom: Second Meeting, Tuesday, 20th April, 1909', Oct. 1909, TNA CAB 16/8.

75 Haldane also reported a meeting with 'a member of the Russian government', who argued that, given the reinforcement of French and German defences, Germany must be tempted 'by the possibility of successfully invading England'. 'Report and Proceedings of a Sub-Committee of the Committee of Imperial Defence Appointed by the Prime Minister to Consider the Question of Foreign Espionage in the United Kingdom: Third Meeting, Monday, 12th July, 1909', Oct. 1909, TNA CAB 16/8.

76 Edmonds, Unpublished Memoirs, ch. 20, LHC Edmonds MSS III/5.

77 'Report and Proceedings of a Sub-Committee of the Committee of Imperial Defence Appointed by the Prime Minister to Consider the Question of Foreign Espionage in the United Kingdom', Oct. 1909, TNA CAB 16/8.

78 Judd, Quest for C, p. 72.

79 Le Queux to the Editor, Manchester Guardian, 4 Jan. 1910 (I am grateful to Dr Nicholas Hiley for this reference). For further evidence that Le Queux was aware of the founding of the Secret Service Bureau, see Hiley, Introduction to Le Queux, Spies of the Kaiser, p. xviii.

80 The case of Lieutenant Siegfried Helm is an example of a private intelligence-gathering initiative by a German army officer (see below, pp. 32–3). The Nachrichten-Abteilung agent Paul Brodtmann, though not working for military intelligence, submitted several reports to the German military attaché in London (see above, p. 18).

81 Memorandum re Formation of a S.S. Bureau [minutes of meeting on 26 Aug. 1909, approved by Sir Charles Hardinge, PUS at the Foreign Office, on 14 Sept. 1909], TNA WO 106/6292.

82 'Conclusions of the Sub-Committee requested to consider how a secret service bureau could be established in Great Britain', 28 April 1909, TNA WO 106/6292.

83 Lady Kell, 'Secret Well Kept', chs 1, 2, IWM.

84 Ibid., p. 110.

85 Kell's record of service notes that he was 'Engaged by Col. Edmonds' as from 1 October 1909. Edmonds confirms his role in his Unpublished Memoirs, ch. 19, p. 7, ch. 20, p. 5; LHC Edmonds MSS III/4–5.

86 Boghardt, Spies of the Kaiser, p. 38.

87 Lady Kell, 'Secret Well Kept', IWM.

88 No such evidence of contact with Kell was discovered by the best and most recent biographers of Le Queux, Patrick and Baister. Nor has any evidence come to light in Security Service files.

89 Lady Kell, 'Secret Well Kept', IWM.

90 Andrew, Secret Service, p. 123.

91 Judd, Quest for C, ch. 1. For further detail on Cumming's appointment see Jeffery, Official History of the Secret Intelligence Service, part I.

92 Mansfield Cumming diary; cited by Judd, Quest for C, pp. 84–7, 110.

93 Judd, Quest for C, p. 87.

94 Mansfield Cumming, diary, 22 Oct. 1909.

95 Kell, [Six-monthly report], April 1910–October 1910 [which begins by summarizing the work of the previous six months], TNA KV 1/9.

96 See below, p. 31.

97 Mansfield Cumming, typed note, 1 Nov. 1909, filed with diary; Judd, Quest for C, p. 115.

98 Mansfield Cumming diary, 1 Nov. 1909; Judd, Quest for C, p. 114.

99 Judd, Quest for C, pp. 114–15.

100 Mansfield Cumming diary, 26, 30 Nov. 1909; Judd, Quest for C, p. 119.

101 Security Service Archives.

102 Judd, Quest for C, pp. 151, 155.

103 Mansfield Cumming diary, 17 March 1910.

104 Ibid., 23 March 1910; Judd, Quest for C, pp. 151–2.

105 Mansfield Cumming diary, 5, 6 April 1910, SIS Archives.

106 Ibid., 28 April 1910.

107 Ibid., 9 May 1910.

Chapter 1: 'Spies of the Kaiser'

1 The title used in some of Kell's progress reports.

2 *Security Service*, pp. 67–9.

3 Their names are identified in the Security Intelligence Service Seniority List and Register of Past and Present Members (December 1919) and some earlier lists. Few records of service survive for early staff.

4 Commander B. J. Ohlson, RNR (who joined in May 1911), Major R. J. Drake (April 1912), Captain E. E. B. Holt-Wilson (December 1912), Captain F. B. Booth (January 1913), Captain M. Brodie (July 1913), Captain J. B. Fetherston (January 1914) and Lieutenant Colonel M. M. Haldane (April 1914). Major J. F. C. Carter joined on 4 August 1914. In addition, Captain Stanley Clarke served in the Bureau from January 1911 to November 1912, and Captain K. E. Lawrence from January 1913 to March 1914. Ohlson's position is somewhat unclear. According to staff lists, he was continuously employed by Kell's Bureau from May 1911 to November 1914. However, according to an interwar MI5 Who's Who, Ohlson returned to his previous employer, P&O, from May 1913 to May 1914. One possible explanation is that the P&O posting provided cover while he was working for Kell's Bureau.

5 J. Regan (June 1911) and H. I. Fitzgerald (November 1912).

6 J. R. Westmacott (March 1910), Miss D. Westmacott (January 1911), Corporal F. S. Strong (September 1911), Miss H. M. Newport (October 1911), Miss S. Holmes (February 1913) and Miss D. Bowie (January 1914).

7 Mrs Sumner.

8 Churchill, *My Early Life*, p. 355.

9 Ewart to Churchill, 27 April 1910, CCAC Churchill MSS, CHAR 13/1/25.

10 E. Marsh (Home Office) to Chief Constables of England and Wales, 28 April 1910, CCAC Churchill MSS CHAR 13/1/25.

11 Kell diary, 8 June 1910, TNA KV 1/10.

12 Kell, [Second Progress Report], April 1910–October 1910, TNA KV 1/9.

13 Security Service Archives.

14 On the *Meldewesen* before 1914, see the first-hand assessment by a US police official in Fosdick, *European Police Systems*, pp. 349–51. On policing in imperial Germany, see Evans, 'Police and Society from Absolutism to Dictatorship'.

15 'Office instructions to preparation of possible suspects list', Holt-Wilson papers, Security Service Archives.

16 See above, p. 3.

17 Kell, First Progress Report, 25 March 1910, TNA KV 1/9. G Branch History, p. 22, TNA KV 1/39.

18 See above, p. 20.

19 Kell diary, 6 June 1910, TNA KV 1/10.

20 Ibid., 28 July, 5 Aug. 1910.

21 Seligmann, *Spies in Uniform*, pp. 61–2, 69–70, 170–71. Copies of despatches from Colonel Trench, 24 June, 15 Dec. 1910, TNA KV 3/1. Kell diary, 29 Aug. 1910, KV 1/10.

22 Andrew, *Secret Service*, pp. 130–31. Judd, *Quest for C*, pp. 178–82.

23 Kell diary, 30 Aug. 1910, TNA KV 1/10.

24 Ibid., 5 Sept. 1910.

25 Andrew, *Secret Service*, pp. 104–5. Boghardt, *Spies of the Kaiser*, pp. 48–9.

26 Kell diary, 6 Sept. 1910, TNA KV 1/10. Since Helm was the second German officer to become her lover, Miss Wodehouse's explanation does not carry complete conviction.

27 Andrew, *Secret Service*, pp. 104–5. Boghardt, *Spies of the Kaiser*, pp. 50–51.

28 *The Times*, 22, 23 Dec. 1910. Brandon and Trench were released in 1913.

29 Correspondence between German Foreign Ministry and Prussian War Ministry, 12 Sept. 1910, 7 Dec. 1910, Politisches Archiv des Auswärtigen Amtes, Berlin; cited by Boghardt, *Spies of the Kaiser*, p. 50.

30 Kell diary, 14 Nov. 1910, TNA KV 1/10. Boghardt, *Spies of the Kaiser*, p. 51.

31 Kell described the appointment of Thwaites as DMI in 1918 as 'a very good choice too – a fortunate one for us, as he knows us all so well and appreciates our work'. Kell to Holt-Wilson, 7 Sept 1918, Holt-Wilson papers, Security Service Archives.

32 Kell diary, 18 Nov. 1910, TNA KV 1/10.

33 The report seems to have been related to the belief by Thwaites's sister that the Germans had 'insulted her'. Kell diary, 24 Nov. 1910, TNA KV 1/10.

34 Kell, [Second Progress Report], April 1910–October 1910, TNA KV 1/9.

35 Kell diary, 15 Nov. 1910, TNA KV 1/10.

36 According to Security Service records, Clarke left MO5, for unexplained reasons, on 30 November 1912. (Within the War Office, the cover name for Kell's Bureau was MO5(g).)

37 Kell, 'Progress during the quarter ending 31st March, 1911', TNA KV 1/9. Kell diary, 17 March 1911, TNA KV 1/10.

38 Kell diary, 3 March 1911, TNA KV 1/10.

39 Recent research shows that Melville was born in 1850 (Cook, M: MI5's First Spymaster, p. 14). Kell's Bureau, however, did not know his birth-date. An interwar career summary in Security Service Archives gives the date as 'about 1847'.

40 'IIIrd Report of the work done by the Counter-espionage Section of the Secret Service Bureau from October 1910 to May 1911', TNA KV 1/9.

41 Security Service staff registers (one of which is reproduced in Cook, M: MI5's First Spymaster, p. 259).

42 On 16 December 1910, Kell noted in his diary: 'Lt J. Ohlson of P & O offered job as marine assistant at £350 per annum with £10 per annum rise to £400. Will try for a year leave of absence in the first instance.' TNA KV 1/10.

43 'IIIrd Report of the work done by the Counter-espionage Section of the Secret Service Bureau from October 1910 to May 1911', TNA KV 1/9.

44 Kell, 'Progress Report for the Quarter ending 30th June, 1911', TNA KV 1/9.

45 'Steinhauer, Gustav', 'Game Book', vol. 1: 1909–1915, TNA KV 4/112. 'Information Obtained by Chance', G Branch History, p. 33, TNA KV 1/39. Holt-Wilson, 'Security Intelligence in War', 1934, IWM Kell MSS. The earliest surviving reference to this episode appears in Kell's 'Progress report for the quarter ending 30th September 1911' (filed with his diary for 1911 in TNA KV 1/10): 'The Leith case investigations are in hand, due to information received from Leith, that have led to the discovery of the name and address of a genuine German agent abroad, and the name and addresses of several of his correspondents in this country. The matter is being very carefully investigated.' Kell's progress reports never mentioned the name of the recipient of the letter (in this case Holstein). None of the surviving accounts explains how Clarke (about whom little is known) found himself in the same railway carriage as Holstein. He had originally joined a Scottish regiment and may have been visiting family and friends. Or, which is perhaps more likely, Clarke had gone to investigate reports of suspicious Germans in Leith, the port for Edinburgh.

46 See below, pp. 37–8.

47 Boghardt, Spies of the Kaiser, p. 71.

48 Ibid., p. 54.

49 Security Service, p. 68.

50 Churchill to Sir Edward Grey, 22 Nov. 1911, CCAC Churchill MSS, CHAR 13/1/25.

51 KV 1/48 'Rough Draft Summary of G-Branch', p. 36.

52 The Times, 6 Aug. 1913, 14 Nov. 1914.

53 'Steinhauer, Gustav', 'Game Book', vol. 1: 1909–1915, TNA KV 4/112. The Times, 6 Aug. 1913, 14 Nov. 1914. Andrew, Secret Service, pp. 116–18.

54 'Steinhauer, Gustav', 'Game Book', vol. 1: 1909–1915, TNA KV 4/112.

55 'G' Report, Part 1, ch. 3, TNA KV 1/39. Andrew, Secret Service, pp. 105–6. Boghardt, Spies of the Kaiser, pp. 54–6.

56 Parl. Deb. (Lords), 25 July 1911, col. 642.

57 Williams, Not in the Public Interest, pp. 24–8.

58 Parl. Deb. (Commons), 18 Aug. 1911, cols. 2252ff.

59 Kell, 'Progress Report for the Quarter ending 30th September 1911', TNA KV 1/9.

60 Kell, 'Report on Counter-Espionage from December 1911 to 31 July 1912', TNA KV 1/9. 'Espionage in Portsmouth', The Times, 10 Feb. 1912. Boghardt, Spies of the Kaiser, pp. 56–9. Andrew, Secret Service, p. 64.

61 Graves, The Secrets of the German War Office, p. 136.

62 Boghardt, Spies of the Kaiser, pp. 60–61.

63 Kell had become a second lieutenant in the South Staffordshire Regiment in 1894; Drake, three years younger than Kell, became a second lieutenant in the North Staffordshire Regiment in 1896.

64 Security Service Archives.

65 Lady Kell, 'Secret Well Kept', IWM.

66 Security Service Archives.

67 Security Service Archives. Information on Clarke's career from Gloucestershire County Archives, GBR/L6/23/B715.

68 Cook, M: MI5's First Spymaster, p. 220.

69 Lady Kell, 'Secret Well Kept', p. 222, IWM. Andrew, Secret Service, p. 102. On Holt-Wilson's resignation, see below, p. 227.

70 Holt-Wilson diary, p. 9, CUL Holt-Wilson papers. I owe this reference to Dr Victor Madeira.

71 Letter to Kell from Holt-Wilson, Security Service Archives.

72 'G' Report, Part 1, ch. 4, TNA KV 1/40.

73 Though Fitzgerald, about whom very little is known, officially joined Kell's Bureau as a detective on 1 November 1912, according to the Staff Register, it is possible that, as in the case of some other early recruits, he had worked informally for the Bureau before that date.

74 'G' Report, Part 1, ch. 4, TNA KV 1/40.

75 'Graves, Armgaard Karl', 'Game Book', vol. 1: 1909–1915, TNA KV 4/112.

76 Boghardt, Spies of the Kaiser, pp. 61–3.

77 'Rough Draft of G-Branch History', p. 7, TNA KV 1/48. Andrew, Secret Service, p. 68. Boghardt, Spies of the Kaiser, pp. 63–7.

78 'Hentschel, Karl Paul Gustav', 'Game Book', vol. 1: 1909–1915, TNA KV 4/112.

79 'Parrott, George Charles', 'Game Book', vol. 1: 1909–1915, TNA KV 4/112.

80 'Hentschel, Karl Paul Gustav', 'Game Book', vol. 1: 1909–1915, TNA KV 4/112.

81 See above, p. 35.

82 Boghardt, Spies of the Kaiser, pp. 64–5.

83 'Parrott, George Charles', 'Game Book', vol. 1: 1909–1915, TNA KV 4/112.

84 On Otto Kruger, see below, p. 874.

85 'Ireland, Frederick James R.N.', 'Game Book', vol. 1: 1909–1915, TNA KV 4/112.

86 'Hattrick, John James @ Devlin, Walter John', 'Game Book', vol. 1: 1909–1915, TNA KV 4/112.

87 'Parrott, George Charles', 'Game Book', vol. 1: 1909–1915, TNA KV 4/112.

88 The Times, 17 Jan. 1913.

89 Boghardt, Spies of the Kaiser, p. 66.

90 The Times, 10, 19 Nov. 1913. Andrew, Secret Service, p. 113.

91 The Times, 7, 14, 21 March 1913. 'Klare, William', 'Game Book', vol. 1: 1909–1915, TNA KV 4/112.

92 Boghardt, Spies of the Kaiser, p. 67.

93 Andrew, Secret Service, p. 115.

94 Boghardt, Spies of the Kaiser, p. 68.

95 'Gould, Frederick Adolphus (real name: Schroeder)', 'Game Book', vol. 1: 1909–1915, TNA KV 4/112.

96 Andrew, Secret Service, p. 115.

97 Kell to Troup (Home Office), 11 Dec. 1913, TNA HO 48/10629/199699.

98 Security Service, p. 69.

99 The list consisted of Austro-Hungarians, Belgians, Danes, Germans, Dutch, Norwegians, Swedes and Swiss. It also included naturalized British formerly citizens of these countries. Although allied to the Central Powers, Italians were excluded, as were the small number of resident Turks. 'General Staff Policy in connection with Enemy Alien Civilians during war'. This document formed part of a wartime 'Summary of the work and duties of Branch F of MO5', Security Service Archives. According to Constance Kell, 'naturalised Englishmen, originally Germans, were especially under suspicion'. Lady Kell 'Secret Well Kept', p. 125, IWM.

100 The British licensee of the US Roneo Company was established in 1909, making Kell one of its earliest customers. One of the founding directors and investors of Roneo was Edmund

Trevor Lloyd Williams, the founding chairman of another equally modern high-tech business, the Gramophone Company Ltd. For additional details see 'General Staff Policy in connection with Enemy Alien Civilians during war' in 'Summary of the work and duties of Branch F of MO5', n.d., Holt-Wilson papers, Security Service Archives, and was evidently added to in the course of the war. The first round of aliens registration was evidently complete by the first anniversary of the Bureau, for on 3 November 1910 Kell noted: 'The Home Secretary approved the Aliens Return. I ordered 1500 copies to be printed by Mr C. Harrison.' Kell diary, TNA KV 1/10.

101 The information contained in this section is derived from a 1929 account by Mrs L. F. Edmonds of the Registry filing system as it then existed, with some additional notes on its beginning. Such was the quality of this account that Vernon Kell described it as 'An extraordinarily interesting report. The most complete we have yet had on the subject, without being in too much detail. I am glad to have seen it. Mrs. Edmonds is to be congratulated.' His deputy Eric Holt-Wilson noted, 'I congratulate Mrs. Edmonds and your staff. I consider this a *monument* of common sense in the practical development into an easy routine system of conflicting elements which might have led to inextricable chaos.' Major Phillips observed, 'I think this note will supply a "long felt" want and the writer has set out the details very clearly.' Security Service Archives.

102 *Security Service*, p. 68.

103 Kell, 'Report on Counter-Espionage from December, 1911 to 31 July, 1912', TNA KV 1/9.

104 'The letters of a spy', *The Times*, 24 July 1912.

105 'Steinhauer, Gustav', 'Game Book', vol. 1: 1909–1915, TNA KV 4/112.

106 Steinhauer also claimed, not very plausibly in view of the arrest of his agents in August 1914, that he used his letters to Britain in order to deceive the British authorities with bogus information. Steinhauer, *Steinhauer*, p. 6.

107 'Steinhauer, Gustav', 'Game Book', vol. 1: 1909–1915, TNA KV 4/112.

108 Steinhauer, *Steinhauer*, pp. 18–24.

109 F Branch Report, vol. 1, pp. 54–6, TNA KV 1/35. Hiley, 'Entering the Lists', p. 49.

110 Lady Kell, 'Secret Well Kept', p. 140, IWM.

111 The names of the seven suspects arrested by local police forces without instructions from Kell appear on a list of twenty-one arrests included in a draft wartime history compiled in 1921 by an MI5 historian, Dr Lucy Farrar (whose PhD was in literary history); G Branch Report, vol. 1, pp. 48–9, TNA KV 1/40. Farrar, however, failed to realize that this list, mainly composed of the first suspects to be arrested, was a mixture of arrests ordered by Kell and others arrested by local police forces. The chronic post-war lack of resources in MI5, which had only thirteen officers at the end of the 1920s, prevented the draft history (prepared for purely internal use) being either checked or, in all probability, much read. But the error was eventually noticed and a correct list of the twenty-two arrests ordered by Kell in August 1914 compiled in 1931 (again for internal use); AR (L. F. M. Edmonds), minute to DCDS, 12 May 1931, TNA KV 4/114. As Edmonds noted, Farrar's list contained 'several names which were not M.I.5. cases'. The fact that all the arrests in the 1931 list actually occurred can be corroborated from other files.

112 Arrests in August 1914 of German agents identified by Kell's Bureau:

1 **Alberto Rosso (aka 'Rodriguez' and other aliases)**
Language teacher in Portsmouth, whose correspondence with German intelligence office in Brussels, which sent 'lengthy questionnaires on naval matters', was first intercepted in March 1914. Arrested on 3 August 1914 and later imprisoned under Aliens Restriction Act.

2 **Frederick Apel**
First detected by letter interception in May 1913 sending information on Vickers Shipyard at Barrow to German intelligence in Antwerp. Arrested on 4 August 1914 and later imprisoned under Aliens Restriction Act.

3 **Commander Friedrich von Diederichs**
Espionage mission to Medway, Sheerness and Chatham on eve of war discovered through intercepted correspondence. Arrested on 4 August 1914 and subsequently imprisoned under Aliens Restriction Act.

4 Johann Engel

German naval veteran who had settled in Falmouth; discovered in December 1911 to be receiving quarterly payments from German naval intelligence; correspondence intercepted. Arrested on 4 August 1914 and later imprisoned under Aliens Restriction Act.

5 Karl Gustav Ernst

Identified by postal intercepts late in 1911 as Steinhauer's most active postman (see above, p. 38), as well as carrying out other intelligence missions. Arrested on 4 August 1914 and discovered to be a British citizen (previously thought to be German); charged under Official Secrets Act and sentenced on 12 September to seven years' penal servitude

6 & 7 Lina Maria Heine and her husband, **Max Power Heinert**

Language teachers in, respectively, Portsmouth and Southsea. Mrs Heine's correspondence with German intelligence was intercepted and in May 1914 she was observed in Ostend meeting 'a known German Secret Service agent'. She was arrested on 4 August in the company of Heinert, not on the original arrest list or previously identified as her husband. Unable to 'give a satisfactory account of himself', he was also arrested. Both were later imprisoned under Aliens Restriction Act.

8 August Wilhelm Julius Klunder

Discovered from letter interception in 1912 to be involved in distributing correspondence to German agents. Arrested on 4 August 1914, later imprisoned under Aliens Restriction Act

9 Frans Heinrich Lozel

Though long suspected of being a German agent, no proof was obtained until he was identified by Hentschel (see above, p. 46) on 18 October 1913. Believed to have been well paid by the Nachrichtendienst for photographing naval installations, he was arrested on 4 August 1914 and later imprisoned under Aliens Restriction Act.

10 Adolf Schneider

Intercepted correspondence revealed that he was used by Steinhauer to forward correspondence to agents in Britain. Arrested on 4 August 1914, later imprisoned under Aliens Restriction Act.

11 Major Enrico Lorenzo Bernstein (various aliases)

Involved in various attempts to traffic in intelligence before First World War (uncertain whether some of these were detected by letter checks). Arrested on 5 August 1914 when he approached Naval Intelligence Department with offer to supply information on German intelligence; later imprisoned under Aliens Restriction Act on 12 August but released in September to work for Cumming. Bernstein's case remains confused. Though Cumming appears to have trusted him, Cumming's biographer concludes that, before the war, Bernstein was 'possibly also in touch with Germans' (Judd, *Quest for C*, p. 230). Kell seems to have shared that suspicion.

12 Frederick William Fowler

Hairdresser at Penarth, married to sister of Otto Kruger (Arrest no. 13); intercepted correspondence with German intelligence in Hamburg through Klunder (Arrest no. 8). Arrested under Official Secrets Act on 5 August 1914; severely cautioned and discharged on 19 August.

13 Otto Moritz Walter Kruger

Hairdresser at Abercynon, Glamorganshire, working for Steinhauer; correspondence with Steinhauer presumably intercepted but no specific reference in the one surviving case summary (of only 100 words). Admitted persuading his British nephew, Frederick Ireland (Arrest no. 14), to enlist in the Royal Navy to collect information for German intelligence. Arrested on 5 August 1914 under Official Secrets Act as 'a known agent of a foreign Secret Service'; imprisoned on 13 August under Aliens Restriction Act.

14 Frederick James Ireland

Arrested in February 1912 for passing information to German naval intelligence while in the Royal Navy but not tried because of 'undesirability' of revealing intercept evidence in court (see above, p. 45); rearrested on 5 August 1914. Released on 19 August; subsequent surveillance revealed 'nothing . . . to suggest that he was in any way working against British interests'.

15 **Heinrich Christian Wilhelm Schutte**
Intercepted correspondence revealed that he was sending information (much 'not of great value') to German intelligence. Arrested on 5 August 1914 and later imprisoned under Aliens Restriction Act.

16 **Heinrich Charles Grosse**
After correspondence intercepted, convicted of espionage under Official Secrets Act in February 1912 (see above, pp. 39–40); believed after his release from prison on licence in May 1914 to have renewed contact with German intelligence. Arrested on 6 August and later interned.

17 **William Francis Brown**
British subject of German origin, discovered through letter intercepts to be in communication with Steinhauer in October 1911; subsequently aroused suspicion by applying for jobs in aircraft factories. Arrested on 7 August 1914 but later discharged when no incriminating evidence was discovered during a search of his house.

18 **Marie Kronauer**
Widow of the German agent Wilhelm Kronauer; intercepted correspondence revealed that she renewed contact with Steinhauer after her husband's death. Arrested on 8 August 1914 and later imprisoned under Aliens Restriction Act.

19 **Hauptmann Kurd von Weller**
Former Prussian officer, reported to Kell by Royal Irish Constabulary in December 1913 after visiting Ireland; arrested on 10 August 1914 in possession of 'information which might be useful to an enemy' and subsequently imprisoned under Aliens Restriction Act. Though he attempted 'to convey information to the enemy' (probably not of much significance) from prison, he was exchanged for a British officer POW in October 1915.

20 **Heinrich Schmidt**
Intercepted correspondence in March 1913 revealed that he was in contact with German intelligence via August Klunder. Arrested on 12 August 1914 and later imprisoned under Aliens Restriction Act.

21 **Harold Dutton**
Former army clerk discovered to have copied classified documents on Portsmouth defences. When arrested at request of Kell's Bureau on 15 August 1914, at first denied, then admitted possessing the documents. Later sentenced to six months' hard labour for breach of the Official Secrets Act.

22 **Robert A. Blackburn**
Nineteen-year-old former merchant seaman discovered through letter check in June 1914 to be in contact with German intelligence via August Klunder. When arrested on 16 August 1914, admitted sending information about the Mersey defences to the Germans. Later sentenced to two years in a Borstal (young offenders' institution) for breach of the Official Secrets Act.

The correct list of arrests in August 1914 on which this reconstruction is based was drawn up in 1931 from files which no longer exist (see note 111 above). Further details of the evidence against each of those arrested are given in the file summaries in 'Game Book', vol. 1: 1909–1915, TNA KV 4/112. Very few original records of pre-First World War counter-espionage were retained after the war.

Several other surviving lists of arrests in August 1914, like Dr Farrar's, also contain a mixture of those arrested on Kell's instructions and suspects arrested on the initiative of local police forces. A 1915 DPP list of twenty-four 'German spies . . . arrested on the outbreak of war under the Official Secrets Act, 1911' contained nine police cases but omitted seven of Kell's. These lists have come to light as a result of the pioneering research of Dr Nicholas Hiley. I do not, however, share Dr Hiley's conclusion, based partly on an examination of these lists, that Kell's claim to have 'masterminded the arrest of 21 out of the 22 German agents working in Britain' on the eve of war was 'a complete fabrication' and a 'remarkable lie', which Kell and Holt-Wilson 'stuck to . . . for the rest of their careers' (Hiley, 'Entering the Lists'). All but one of the twenty-two August 1914 arrests listed above followed pre-war investigation by Kell's Bureau.

113 AR (L. F. M Edmonds), minute to DCDS, 12 May 1931, TNA KV 4/114.

114 See reconstructed arrest list in note 112 above.

115 'Rimann, Walter @ Friese, Gustav @ Germanikus', 'Game Book', vol. 1: 1909–1915, TNA KV 4/112.

116 In several cases local police forces believed that the main credit for a German agent's arrest belonged to them rather than to Kell's Bureau. A 1915 report by the DPP gave the 'instructing authority' in the cases of Marie Kronauer and Frans Lozel as, respectively, the Met and the Kent Police, rather than the War Office (Kell); Hiley, 'Entering the Lists', pp. 60–61. Kronauer's correspondence had, however, been monitored by Kell's Bureau, which had also been centrally involved in the Karl Hentschel case which led to the detection of Lozel. In these and other cases, it is difficult, if not impossible, to estimate the relative contributions of Kell's Bureau and the police. Both were important. When the revised list of August 1914 arrests was being compiled in 1931, Holt-Wilson instructed: 'Do not worry whether they are "M.I.5 Cases" in any narrow sense. Action taken by our colleagues, or agents, or the police counts as bringing them within the above definition [those 'officially penalised for some action prejudicial to Defence Security'] from the national point of view.' Holt-Wilson to AR (L. F. M. Edmonds), Minute 10 [May 1931], TNA KV 4/114.

117 Cases 1–8, 10, 12, 14–18, 20, 22 in the reconstructed arrest list (note 112 above) largely depended on letter checks under HOWs mainly (if not wholly) obtained by Kell. Letter checks were probably involved in case 13 to monitor contacts with Steinhauer, but there is no specific reference in the 100-word case summary (all that survives). Case 11 may well have involved letter checks but direct evidence does not survive. Case 7 (Heinert) did not involve letter checks but his wife's (case 6) did, and it was this which led to his arrest. There is no evidence that case 9 (Lozel) involved letter checks but Lozel was discovered as a result of the Hentschel case, which did. There is no evidence that case 19 (von Weller) involved letter checks but there is no doubt that Kell played a central role in it; the case was referred to him by the Royal Irish Constabulary. Though there is no evidence that case 21 (Dutton) involved letter checks, it was Kell who ordered the arrest.

118 See below, p. 53.

119 Possibly misled by the Home Secretary's statement on 5 August that the arrests had already been carried out, Steinhauer believed they must have taken place before Britain's declaration of war.

120 Steinhauer, Steinhauer, p. 37.

121 Holt-Wilson, 'Security Intelligence in War', 1934, p. 17, IWM Kell MSS.

122 Trumpener, 'War Premeditated? German Intelligence Operations in July 1914', pp. 58–85.

123 Nicolai, Nachrichtendienst, Presse, und Volksstimmung im Weltkrieg; English trans.: Nicolai, German Secret Service, pp. 52–4.

Chapter 2: The First World War:
Part 1 – The Failure of German Espionage

1 According to Thomson, 'Throughout the War the Special Branch was combined with the Criminal Investigation Department'; Thomson, Queer People, p. 47. The size of the Special Branch early in the war is given in a minute of 20 Nov. 1914; TNA MEPO 2/1643/ON 856720. Thomson said later that during the war, 'Special Branch and the Central Branch of the CID were combined,' Morning Post, 24 April 1919.

2 Thomson, Queer People, pp. 36–7. Andrew, Secret Service, pp. 264–7.

3 Parl. Deb. (Commons), 5 Aug. 1914.

4 See below, pp. 871–3.

5 Security Service Archives.

6 Security Service Archives.

7 Bird, 'Control of Enemy Alien Civilians'.

8 Kell's mobilization orders, dated 4 August 1914, 'as an attached officer at the War Office' and his 5 August 1914 appointment as a general staff officer (GSO2) and 'competent military authority' have been preserved in his record of service in Security Service files.

9 'Historical Sketch of the Directorate of Military Intelligence during the Great War of 1914–1919', TNA WO 32/10776.

10 'The Women's Staff', p. 26, TNA KV 1/50.
11 *The Times*, 15 Oct. 1915.
12 Security Service Archives.
13 Le Queux, *German Spies in England*.
14 Hazlehurst, *Politicians at War*, p. 146. Gillman, *Collar the Lot*, p. 10. Over the next thirty years Simon became home secretary (twice), foreign secretary, chancellor of the exchequer and lord chancellor.
15 In 1915, there were also sixty-three departures (twenty-one male, forty-two female). Security Intelligence Service Seniority List and Register of Past and Present Members, December 1919.
16 'Outbursts from Waterloo[se] House', printed for private circulation, 1917.
17 Security Service Archives.
18 Security Service Archives. Hinchley Cooke's alertness to the use of secret inks probably derived from his scientific education in Germany which, Kell believed, was 'of special value in the detection of enemy agents'. Though no details survive of which cases Hinchley Cooke helped to resolve, Sir Archibald Bodkin, the main prosecutor in espionage trials and courts martial (later DPP), paid tribute to the importance of his 'translation and examination of numerous documents in foreign languages and in code and occasionally in "secret inks"'. Security Service Archives.
19 Security Service Archives.
20 Lady Kell, 'Secret Well Kept', pp. 110, 122, IWM. Interwar MI5 Who's Who.
21 'Historical Sketch of the Directorate of Military Intelligence during the Great War of 1914–1919', TNA WO 32/10776.
22 Dansey to Major Van Deman (US military intelligence), 1 May 1917; lecture by Dansey, 4 May 1917, NAW RG 165, 9944–A–4/5.
23 F Branch Report, part II, ch. 5, section XVII, pp. 116–20, TNA KV 1/35.
24 Ibid. The secret MI5 classification handbook added:

> It will be appreciated that an actively hostile person may fall under several of the above special classifications. Such cases are designated thus: e.g. Class: SI/BL. BEFHKJ France. To a Special Intelligence Officer who has memorized the standard classifications this abbreviation conveys the following information:
>
> 'Is considered an enemy (prefixed BL [Black List]); already expelled from allied territory during the war (B); considered an active enemy agent (E); who has been known to carry false papers (F); is suspected of trading with the enemy (H); was formerly a German official (K); and French S.I. is anxious to hear of his present whereabouts and actions (J).'

MI5f, 'Notes on Preventive Intelligence Duties in War', April 1918; copy in NAW RG 165 11013–21.
25 F Branch Report, part II , ch. 5, section XVII, p. 118, TNA KV 1/35.
26 Security Service Archives.
27 'Report on Women's Work', 1920, p. 26, TNA KV 1/50.
28 Ibid.
29 Ibid., p. 13. Three of MO5(g)'s seven clerks at the outbreak of war had been male.
30 Ibid., p. 16.
31 Security Service Archives.
32 Their names and dates of service appear in Security Intelligence Service Seniority List and Register of Past and Present Members, December 1919.
33 Of Miss Lomax and the transformation she wrought in the Registry Constance Kell wrote: 'Miss Lomax was for many years the head of this section and her work was so excellent that Kell could rest assured that whatever she and those working with her, and under her, were asked to do, would be quickly and eagerly carried out.' Lady Kell, 'Secret Well Kept', p. 148, IWM.
34 Security Service Archives.
35 H Branch History, ch. 2, p. 38, TNA KV 1/49.
36 Security Service Archives.
37 'Report on Women's Work', 1920, p. 54, TNA KV 1/50.
38 Security Service Archives.

39 Like most officer recruits, Marsh, who joined MO5(g) in May 1915, was also fond of sports and outdoor pursuits, listing his recreations as polo, shooting, fishing, golf and lawn tennis. Security Service Archives.

40 See p. 62.

41 'Report on Women's Work', 1920, p. 19, TNA KV 1/50.

42 See p. 62.

43 'Historical Sketch of the Directorate of Military Intelligence during the Great War of 1914–1919', TNA WO 32/10776.

44 Unpublished Hall memoirs (ghostwritten by Ralph Strauss), draft Chapter C, CCAC HALL 3/2. Hall claimed he had been responsible for persuading Asquith to found the War Trade Intelligence Department (later subsumed by the Ministry of Blockade) whose first head was Freddie Browning.

45 'Historical Sketch of the Directorate of Military Intelligence during the Great War of 1914–1919', TNA WO 32/10776. For details of wartime censorship, see TNA KV 1/73–4.

46 Boghardt, Spies of the Kaiser, pp. 89–90.

47 'Lody, Carl Hans @ Inglis, Charles A', 'Game Book', vol. 1: 1909–1915, TNA KV 4/112.

48 Boghardt, Spies of the Kaiser, pp. 98, 102.

49 Hiley, 'Counter-Espionage and Security in Great Britain during the First World War', p. 639.

50 See below, pp. 248ff.

51 Lady Kell, 'Secret Well Kept', p. 144, IWM. Thomson, Queer People, pp. 122–6. Felstead, German Spies at Bay, ch. 3.

52 Lady Kell, 'Secret Well Kept', p. 150, IWM.

53 F. B. Booth (MO5(g)), memo for Kell, 27 July 1915, TNA HO 45/10741/263275. Carsten, War against War, p. 56.

54 Boghardt, Spies of the Kaiser, p. 106.

55 Ibid., pp. 81–2.

56 G Branch Report for 1915, pp. 59ff., TNA KV 1/42. Boghardt, Spies of the Kaiser, pp. 106–7.

57 'Kupferle, Anthony', 'Game Book', vol. 1: 1909–1915, TNA KV 4/112.

58 Thomson, Queer People, pp. 126–9. Felstead, German Spies at Bay, ch. 3.

59 See below, pp. 70, 71–2.

60 'Muller, Carl Friedrich Heinrich @ Leidec [and] Hahn, John', 'Game Book', vol. 1: 1909–1915, TNA KV 4/112. Dr Boghardt's researches identify Müller as a Baltic German. Boghardt, Spies of the Kaiser, p. 96.

61 W. E. Hinchley Cooke to DG (Petrie), 'Motor-car purchased by MI5 out of German Secret Service Funds during the 1914–18 War', 29 June 1943, TNA KV 4/200.

62 Though Müller's MI5 file was destroyed after the war, summaries of the bogus reports sent in his name survive in German archives: RW 5/v. 48 – Geheimer Nachrichtendienst und Spionageabwehr des Heeres – von Generalmajor z.V. Gempp (1939), 8. Abschnitt: Die Ergebnisse das Nachrichtendienstes der mobilen Abt Illb in westen vom Fruhjahr 1915 bis Ende 1916, IV: Die Kriegsnachrichtenstelle Antwerpen Anlage 5: Meldungen der Kriegsnachrichtenstelle Antwerpen vom 25.3.15–14.6.15, Bundesarchiv Militärarchiv, Freiburg. I am grateful to Dr Emily Wilson for this reference.

63 Wilson, 'War in the Dark', pp. 118–19.

64 'Muller, Carl Friedrich Heinrich @ Leidec [and] Hahn, John', 'Game Book', vol. 1: 1909–1915, TNA KV 4/112.

65 RW 5/v. 48 – Geheimer Nachrichtendienst und Spionageabwehr des Heeres – von Generalmajor z.V. Gempp (1939), 8. Abschnitt: Die Ergebnisse das Nachrichtendienstes der mobilen Abt Illb in westen vom Fruhjahr 1915 bis Ende 1916, IV: Die Kriegsnachrichtenstelle Antwerpen Anlage 5: Meldungen der Kriegsnachrichtenstelle Antwerpen vom 25.3.15–14.6.15, Bundesarchiv Militärarchiv, Freiburg.

66 W. E. Hinchley Cooke to DG (Petrie), 'Motor-car purchased by MI5 out of German Secret Service Funds during the 1914–18 War', 29 June 1943, TNA KV 4/200.

67 'The Secret Services: Inquiry by the Minister without Portfolio [Lord Hankey]. Second Report dealing with the Security Service (MI5)', Jan.–May 1940, TNA CAB 127/383.

68 W. E. Hinchley Cooke to DG (Petrie), 'Motor-car purchased by MI5 out of German Secret Service Funds during the 1914–18 War', 29 June 1943, TNA KV 4/200.

69 See below, pp. 248-50, 253.

70 'Rosenthal, Robert @ Berger, Harry B.', 'Game Book', vol. 1: 1909-1915, TNA KV 4/112. Draft History of G Branch, vol. 4, pp. 111ff., TNA KV 1/42.

71 Felstead, *German Spies at Bay*, pp. 44-56. Felstead appears to have had access to MI5 as well as Special Branch reports when writing his book. Drake later told Hall, 'B[asil] T[homson] gave him my reports to read, I understand.' Drake to Admiral Hall, 1 Nov. 1932, CCAC HALL 1/3.

72 Boghardt, *Spies of the Kaiser*, p. 115.

73 Felstead, *German Spies at Bay*, p. 56.

74 Security Service Archives.

75 '(i) Janssen, Haicke Marinus Petrus (ii) Roos, Willem Johannes', 'Game Book', vol. 1: 1909-1915, TNA KV 4/112. 'Principal German Espionage Agents captured in the United Kingdom by M.I.5, 1909 to 1919', May 1919, TNA KV 4/114.

76 Commandant Hue, head of the French mission at the Bureau Central Interallié, complained in 1917 that 'Up to now, attempts at establishing [intelligence] liaison with allied armies seem to have produced few results.' Aubin, 'French Counterintelligence and British Secret Intelligence in the Netherlands', p. 19.

77 Major General Sir Walter Kirke diary, 15 June 1915, IWM.

78 Felstead, *German Spies at Bay*, ch. 4. Lady Kell, 'Secret Well Kept', p. 154, IWM.

79 Andrew, *Secret Service*, pp. 133, 221.

80 'Marks, Josef @ Multer, Josef Marks', 'Game Book', vol. 2: 1916[*sic*]-1937, TNA KV 4/113. 'Principal German Espionage Agents captured in the United Kingdom by M.I.5, 1909 to 1919', May 1919, TNA KV 4/114.

81 Albert Meyer, Frank Greite, Mrs Albertine Stanaway, Leopold Vieyra. 'Principal German Espionage Agents captured in the United Kingdom by M.I.5, 1909 to 1919', May 1919, TNA KV 4/114. 'Game Book', vol. 2: 1916-1937, TNA KV 4/113.

82 George Vaux Bacon; see below, pp. 73-5.

83 Felstead, *German Spies at Bay*, p. 109.

84 Boghardt, *Spies of the Kaiser*, p. 106.

85 Felstead, *German Spies at Bay*, pp. 110, 139, 150, 209-15, 284. 'Hurwitz y Zender, Ludovico', 'Game Book', vol. 2: 1916-1937, TNA KV 4/113.

86 Security Service Archives.

87 'Bacon, George Vaux', 'Game Book', vol. 2: 1916-1937, TNA KV 4/113.

88 'Principal German Espionage Agents captured in the United Kingdom by M.I.5, 1909 to 1919', May 1919, TNA KV 4/114.

89 'Bacon, George Vaux', 'Game Book', vol. 2: 1916-1937, TNA KV 4/113.

90 Boghardt, *Spies of the Kaiser*, pp. 136-7.

91 Draft G Branch History, ch. 12, pp. 155ff., TNA KV 1/43. 'Bacon, George Vaux', 'Game Book', vol. 2: 1916-1937, TNA KV 4/113.

92 MI5's first foreign double agent had been the German spy Armgaard Karl Graves, recruited by Kell in 1912. Graves, however, deceived both Kell and German intelligence. See above, pp. 40-41. The first wartime double agents were two Indians recruited in October 1915 to report on German attempts to subvert the British Raj. See below, p. 92.

93 'Wife Sues Editor Whytock', *New York Times*, 9 Sept. 1911.

94 Whytock's identity and role are revealed in 'Bacon, George Vaux', 'Game Book', vol. 2: 1916-1937, TNA KV 4/113. Further details (though not Whytock's identity) are contained in Draft G Branch History, ch. 12, pp. 160ff., TNA KV 1/43.

95 Captain Roslyn Whytock's position in US military intelligence was mentioned by the *New York Times* on 30 Oct. 1918 in a report on an injury suffered by his brother, Lieutenant Norman R. Whytock, while fighting in France.

96 'Bacon, George Vaux', 'Game Book', vol. 2: 1916-1937, TNA KV 4/113.

97 Boghardt, *Spies of the Kaiser*, p. 138.

98 Andrew, *Secret Service*, pp. 169-77.

99 Andrew, *For the President's Eyes Only*, pp. 31-46.

100 'Game Book', vol. 1: 1909-1915, TNA KV 4/112; vol. 2, 1916-1937, TNA KV 4/113. A post-war MI5 count of 'persons convicted of espionage, treason &c' also arrived at a figure of sixty-five; 'Certain Offences against the Defence of the Realm Regulations 1914-1919.

Estimate of Cases leading to conviction or executive action, as dealt with by the Security Service (Approximate figures)', TNA KV 4/114.

101 The names and/or codenames of agents recorded in German archives are listed in Boghardt, *Spies of the Kaiser*, appendix 3.

102 The first three names on Dr Boghardt's list fit this category. In many other cases details of agents' roles have not survived. Ibid.

103 See above, p. 51.

104 Security Service Archives. On COMO's first attempt to track down German spies in Britain who were out of contact, see above, p. 72.

105 After the First World War, numerous authors published accounts of alleged German secret missions to Britain, most of which have since proved to be vastly exaggerated or wholly invented. In a book entitled *The Invisible Weapons*, published in 1932, Jules Crawford Silber claimed he had conveyed a wealth of critical information to Berlin which he had obtained while working as a British censor in Edinburgh. Dr Boghardt, among others, has doubted the truth of Silber's claim, arguing that there is no trace of a 'Silber' in German archives, and pointing out that Silber revealed in his book only information that was already in the public domain. In the wartime censors' office the names of known German agents and their addresses were written on large blackboards, for all the censors to see. Had this information really been passed to German intelligence, it would presumably have lost fewer of its main British agents. As Boghardt notes, however, German records on the 120 wartime agents sent to Britain are far from complete. Boghardt, *Spies of the Kaiser*, pp. 97, 109.

106 E Branch History, ch. 11, pp. 134-5, TNA KV 1/34.

107 Ibid.

108 Simpson, 'Duties of Local Authorities in War Time', pp. 5-30. Mellor, 'Status under the Hague Conference of Civilians who Take up Arms during the Time of War', pp. 559-78. Ovens, 'Fighting in Enclosed Country', pp. 524-46.

109 Boghardt, *Spies of the Kaiser*. Several accidental explosions aboard transatlantic shipping were also wrongly blamed on Sektion P.

110 Boghardt, *Spies of the Kaiser*, pp. 122-3. Andrew, *For the President's Eyes Only*, p. 37.

111 Basil Thomson was surely right to argue, 'The Germans made great use of sabotage in America. Unquestionably, they would have done the same in England if they could...' Thomson, *Queer People*, p. 194.

112 F Branch Report, TNA KV 1/36. By August 1915, F Branch, headed by Holt-Wilson, contained six officers and seven clerks.

113 Branch nomenclature during MO5(g)'s rapid expansion in 1915 was fluid and somewhat confusing. On its foundation in August 1915, E Branch was commonly referred to as MO5(e). As part of a larger War Office reorganization of MO5, the three existing branches were renamed. MO5(g)A (counter-espionage) became MO5(a); MO5(g)B (aliens, DORA and preventive security) became MO5(f); and MO5(g)C (records, personnel, administration) became MO5(h). These four branches became collectively known as MI5 on 3 January 1916. 'Historical Sketch of the Directorate of Military Intelligence during the Great War of 1914-1919', TNA WO 32/10776.

114 Security Service Archives.

115 Security Service Archives.

116 A surviving letter from Major Money to Hinchley Cooke in 1916 begins, 'My dear old Koch'. Security Service Archives.

117 'Boehm, Captain Hans W @ Thrasher, Jelks Leroy', 'Game Book', vol. 2: 1916-1937, TNA KV 4/113.

118 German naval documents captured after the Second World War revealed that plans to set up a shipping agency as cover for intelligence operations which included the contamination and poisoning of cargoes bound for enemy ports had begun before the First World War. Security Service Archives.

119 Boghardt, *Spies of the Kaiser*, pp. 133-4.

120 Major J. F. C. Carter (MI5), 'Alfred Hagn. Alleged German agent', 30 May 1917, CUL Templewood Papers. Boghardt, *Spies of the Kaiser*, p. 130.

121 'F-Branch Report: Preventative Security', p. 9, TNA KV 1/35.

122 General Staff Paper, 'The Organization of the Services of Military Secrecy, Security and Publicity', Oct. 1917, p. 44, TNA INF 4/9.

123 Though offering an implausible analysis of her involvement in wartime espionage, Howe, *Mata Hari*, successfully dismantles the pre-war myths constructed by Zelle about her upbringing and early career.

124 Zelle's two-volume MI5 file is in TNA KV 2/1-2.

125 Thomson, *Queer People*, pp. 182-3.

126 TNA KV 2/2.

127 Howe, *Mata Hari*, pp. 11-12.

128 H. A. Pakenham (Paris) to R. D. Waterhouse, 28 Nov. 1917, TNA KV 2/2.

129 Bird, 'Control of Enemy Alien Civilians'.

130 According to later MI5 statistics, it recommended 354 aliens for deportation, 226 'persons of hostile origin or association' for internment, 650 'suspected persons' for exclusion from certain areas, and 25 'hostile persons' to be made subject to other personal restrictions. 'Certain Offences against the Defence of the Realm Regulations 1914-1919. Estimate of Cases leading to conviction or executive action, as dealt with by the Security Service (Approximate figures)', TNA KV 4/114.

131 After the war Holt-Wilson wrote an enthusiastic reference for Hinchley Cooke. Security Service Archives.

132 Holt-Wilson, 'Memorandum on the Military Inexpediency of permitting persons of German blood to remain at large during the present organization of this country for war', 15 June 1915, TNA KV 1/65, pp. 271-5.

133 See above, p. 38.

134 See above, pp. 71, 72.

135 Thomson, *Scene Changes*, *passim*.

136 Holt-Wilson, 'Security Intelligence in War', 1934, IWM Kell MSS.

137 Drake to Admiral Hall, 1 Nov. 1932, CCAC HALL 1/3. An MI5 summary of espionage cases over the previous decade confirms that 'There is no instance on record of any spy, enemy agent, sub-agent or associate having been discovered, detected or captured as a result of original information obtained or supplied by Scotland Yard or any of the Civil Police of the United Kingdom.' 'Principal German Espionage Agents captured in the United Kingdom by M.I.5, 1909-1919', TNA KV 4/114, s. 8a.

138 Bell to Leland Harrison, 2 May 1919, enclosing memo on British intelligence, Library of Congress, Leland Harrison MSS.

139 Newman, *Speaking from Memory*, p. 93.

Chapter 3: The First World War:
Part 2 – The Rise of Counter-Subversion

1 *Security Service*, p. 72.

2 339 of the departures occurred in 1918. Security Intelligence Service Seniority List and Register of Past and Present Members, December 1919.

3 Security Intelligence Service Seniority List and Register of Past and Present Members, December 1919.

4 Kell was also at work on Christmas Day, 1916; see below, p. 97.

5 H Branch Report, Security Service Archives. Much of the increase in the card index during the later stages of the war was due to the MI5 Ports Police. A memoir of the Registry records that by 1917 the card index filled 748 large boxes; Security Service Archives. A later head of Registry believes that each box was capable of holding up to a thousand cards.

6 Only vol. 24 of the Black List, dated October 1918, survives in MI5 records, containing names numbered from 10914 to 11275; TNA KV 1/61. By this time the suspects were global in range, from as far afield as North and South America, Japan and Polynesia. Some names had been supplied by the French, Belgian and US liaison.

7 Security Service Archives.

8 Security Service Archives.

9 W. E. Hinchley Cooke to DG (Petrie), 'Motor-car purchased by MI5 out of German Secret

Service Funds during the 1914–18 War', 29 June 1943, TNA KV 4/200. By a curious coincidence, which some might interpret as conspiracy, Cumming's official car was also stolen.

10 'Historical Sketch of the Directorate of Military Intelligence during the Great War of 1914–1919', TNA WO 32/10776.

11 *Security Service*, p. 98. There are minor discrepancies between Curry's and other figures.

12 Boghardt, *Spies of the Kaiser*, pp. 117–18.

13 Two telegrams marked 'Private and Secret' from Findlay (Christiania) to FO, 30 Oct. 1914, with minutes by Grey, TNA MEPO 2/10660. Details of several Irish agents who also provided intelligence on Casement to British intelligence agencies still remain classified in order to maintain government policy of neither confirming nor denying the names of former agents.

14 Copies of Casement to MacNeill, 28 Nov. 1914, with covering letter from Casement to Mrs A. S. Green, TNA KV 2/8. The letter to Mrs Green is quoted in Sawyer, *Casement*, p. 119.

15 Sawyer, *Casement*, p. 115.

16 Andrew, *Secret Service*, p. 356. Frank Hall, then a captain, had joined MO5(g) in December 1914; Security Intelligence Service Seniority List and Register of Past and Present Members, December 1919.

17 Dudgeon, *Roger Casement – The Black Diaries*, pp. 481–5.

18 Security Service Archives.

19 Churchill too admired Hall's expertise. Churchill to Lord French, 17 April 1919, CCAC CHAR 16/6.

20 Andrew, *Secret Service*, p. 356.

21 Inspector Edward Parker (Special Branch), 'Interview with Sir E. Blackwell, Home Office', 18 July 1916, TNA MEPO 2/10664.

22 O'Halpin, 'British Intelligence in Ireland', pp. 59–61.

23 TNA KV 2/8.

24 Findlay (Christiania) to FO, 30 Oct. 1914, with minute by Grey, TNA MEPO 2/10660.

25 Findlay (Christiania) to Nicolson (FO), 3 Jan. 1915, 'Most Private and Secret', TNA KV 2/6; Statement by Christensen to Chief Inspector Ward in Philadelphia, 23 May 1916, TNA KV 2/9.

26 Dudgeon, *Roger Casement – The Black Diaries*.

27 Report by Dr Audrey Giles in Daly (ed.), *Roger Casement in Irish and World History*.

28 On the use of forged documents in KGB 'active measures', see Andrew and Mitrokhin, *Mitrokhin Archive*. Though British intelligence did not forge the 'Black Diaries', Captain Hall and others made unscrupulous use of them after Casement's conviction to undermine the campaign to secure clemency. Andrew, 'Casement and British Intelligence'.

29 Andrew, *Secret Service*, ch. 8. O'Halpin, 'British Intelligence in Ireland'.

30 Fussell, *The Great War and Modern Memory*.

31 D Branch Report, p. 63, TNA KV 1/36.

32 Following the assassination in London of Sir William Curzon Wyllie in 1909, a four-man Indian section was added to the MPSB. Popplewell, *Intelligence and Imperial Defence*, p. 132.

33 Ibid., p. 139.

34 Ibid., p. 176.

35 Fraser, 'Germany and Indian Revolution', p. 258.

36 Popplewell, *Intelligence and Imperial Defence*, pp. 178–9.

37 Ibid., pp. 220–21.

38 Ibid., pp. 219–20.

39 Security Intelligence Service Seniority List and Register of Past and Present Members, December 1919.

40 Popplewell, *Intelligence and Imperial Defence*, p. 218. The committee had representatives from the Indian, Colonial, Foreign and War Offices, and the Admiralty.

41 Popplewell, *Intelligence and Imperial Defence*, p. 220.

42 Ibid.

43 Datta, *Madan Lal Dhingra*, p. 77.

44 Popplewell, *Intelligence and Imperial Defence*, pp. 225–6.

45 Ibid., pp. 226–9.

46 Nathan left MI5 on 29 February 1916. Security Intelligence Service Seniority List and

Register of Past and Present Members, December 1919. In August 1919 Nathan joined SIS as head of the Political Section.

47 Popplewell, *Intelligence and Imperial Defence*, pp. 245–51.

48 Thomson, *Queer People*, p. 103.

49 Popplewell, *Intelligence and Imperial Defence*, p. 251.

50 Ibid., p. 219.

51 Ibid., p. 189.

52 D Branch Report, p. 14, TNA KV 1/35. D Branch Report, p. 135, TNA KV 1/36. On 15 January 1917 a new section, MI5(b), was set up to deal with 'questions affecting natives of India and other Oriental races'; this was absorbed by D Branch on 1 September 1917.

53 D Branch Report, p. 13, TNA KV 1/19.

54 See below, p. 138.

55 Thomson, *Queer People*, p. 266.

56 Security Service Archives.

57 Hiley, 'Counter-Espionage and Security in Great Britain during the First World War', p. 651.

58 Major V. Ferguson (MI5) to Sir Ernley Blackwell (Legal Adviser, Home Office), 30 June 1916, TNA HO 45/1081/307402, file 75.

59 Major V. Ferguson, Note for Kell, 14 June 1916, TNA HO 45/10801/307402, file 75. I am very grateful to Dr Nicholas Hiley for providing a photograph of this document. The original is now missing from the file.

60 Holt-Wilson, General Staff paper, 'The organisation of the Services of military secrecy, security and publicity', 1917, TNA INF 4/9.

61 Thomson, *Queer People*, p. 269.

62 Clarke, *Hope and Glory*, p. 79.

63 'Revolutionary Agencies at Work', pp. 62ff., TNA KV 1/43.

64 Debo, 'Georgii Chicherin in England', p. 655.

65 'Memorandum regarding the Russian section of the Communist Club', enclosed with recommendation by Kell for Chicherin's internment, dated 26 Jan. 1917, TNA HO 144/2158.

66 Two other gang members perished in the celebrated 'Siege of Sidney Street' in January 1911. Winston Churchill, then home secretary, could not resist visiting the scene and advising on operations from the front line. Leggett, *Cheka*, pp. 266–7. Cook, *M: MI5's First Spymaster*, pp. 266–7.

67 'Revolutionary Agencies at Work', pp. 62ff., TNA KV 1/43.

68 McLean, *Legend of Red Clydeside*, ch. 7.

69 'Historical Sketch of the Directorate of Military Intelligence during the Great War of 1914–1919', p. 13, TNA WO 32/10776. Biographical details on Labouchere in interwar MI5 Who's Who.

70 McLean, *Legend of Red Clydeside*, p. 83.

71 Ibid., p. 84.

72 CX 491, 16 Sept. 1916, TNA KV 2/1532.

73 Thomson, *Scene Changes*, p. 312. E. F. Wodehouse (New Scotland Yard) to Home Office, 23 April 1917, TNA HO 45/11000/223532. 'Historical Sketch of the Directorate of Military Intelligence during the Great War of 1914–1919', p. 13, TNA WO 32/10776. The most celebrated case investigated by PMS2 was an alleged plot to assassinate Lloyd George by a Derby second-hand-clothes dealer of 'extreme anarchical opinions', Mrs Alice Wheeldon, her daughters Harriet and Winnie, and Winnie's husband Alfred Mason, a chemist who had 'made a special study of poisons'. According to PMS2, the farcical plot finally devised by Mrs Wheeldon to murder Lloyd George was to fire a poisoned dart from an air rifle while he was playing golf on Walton Heath. The plotters were arrested in January 1917 and given jail sentences two months later.

74 Kell to War Office, 'Memorandum concerning a proposed transfer of certain duties from the Ministry of Munitions (P.M.S.2) to M.I.5', 3 March 1917; reproduced in A Branch History, TNA KV 1/13.

75 Security Intelligence Service Seniority List and Register of Past and Present Members, December 1919.

76 'Revolutionary Agencies at Work', pp. 62ff., TNA KV 1/43.

77 'Memorandum regarding the Russian section of the Communist Club' and 'The Russian

Political Prisoners and Exiles Relief Committee in London'; enclosed with recommendation by Kell for Chicherin's internment, dated 26 Jan. 1917, TNA HO 144/2158 (322428/2). In November 1916 Chicherin had publicly announced that his Committee's campaign to persuade Russian exiles not to enlist had been largely successful. Debo, 'Chicherin in England', pp. 656–7.

78 'I don't quite see what he [the liaison officer] would do,' he wrote in his diary. Mansfield Cumming diary, 25 Dec. 1916.

79 Recommendation by Kell for Chicherin's internment, 26 Jan. 1917, TNA HO 144/2158.

80 Kell to Edmonds, 29 March 1917, LHC Edmonds MSS II/2. Lady Kell, 'Secret Well Kept', p. 156, IWM.

81 Security Service Archives. A few months earlier Kell had seemed in good health. On 29 September 1916 he had written to the MCO at Falmouth, Major R. Money, 'I am keeping very fit'. Security Service Archives.

82 Security Service Archives.

83 Security Service Archives.

84 Carsten, War against War, p. 102.

85 Thomson, Queer People, p. 273.

86 Andrew, First World War, p. 46.

87 Swartz, Union of Democratic Control, p. 175. Taylor, English History, p. 128.

88 G1, 'The British Socialist Party', 4 Oct. 1916, TNA KV 2/1655.

89 Undated note by Major Ferguson on information from Victor Fischer [sic], TNA KV 2/1532.

90 'Albert Edward Inkpin', Oxford DNB.

91 Note by Deputy Director of Recruiting (London region), 16 Nov. 1917, TNA KV 2/1532. Minute by Kell to DSI, 23 Nov. 1917, TNA KV 2/585.

92 'Albert Edward Inkpin', Oxford DNB.

93 Report from SW 5 (Berne) of 13 April 1917 forwarded by Cumming, TNA KV 2/585. The Germans also financed Trotsky's return from exile.

94 Figes, People's Tragedy, pp. 385–6.

95 Pipes, Russian Revolution, pp. 392–4.

96 Figes, People's Tragedy, pp. 432–4.

97 Minute by Dansey, 16 Aug. 1917, TNA KV 2/585.

98 TNA HO 144/2158.

99 Debo, 'Chicherin in Britain', p. 659.

100 See above, p. 7.

101 Watson, Clemenceau, pp. 260–64, 286–9.

102 WC 245(20), 4 Oct. 1917, TNA CAB 23/4.

103 WC 253(1), 19 Oct. 1917, TNA CAB 23/4.

104 Thomson, Scene Changes, p. 359.

105 Thomson, 'Pacifist and Revolutionary Organizations in the United Kingdom', included in G 173, 13 Nov. 1917, TNA CAB 24/4.

106 Ullman, Anglo-Soviet Relations, vol. 1, p. 3.

107 G 173, 13 Nov. 1917, TNA CAB 24/4. GT 2809, 24 Nov. 1917, TNA CAB 24/34.

108 GT 2980, 13 Dec. 1917, TNA CAB 24/35.

109 Hiley, 'Counter-Espionage and Security in Great Britain during the First World War', p. 658.

110 Security Service, p. 86.

111 Ullman, Anglo-Soviet Relations, vol. 1, p. 20. Carsten, War against War, pp. 109–11.

112 Draft telegram from Chicherin to Trotsky, 4 Dec. 1917, TNA HO 144/2158 322428/45a. The prison governor sought permission from the Home Office to send the telegram. Had permission been refused, this would probably have been noted on the file. There is, however, no written confirmation that the telegram was sent.

113 Debo, 'Chicherin in England', pp. 660–62. Maksim Litvinov succeeded Chicherin as the representative in London of the Bolshevik regime, and was given diplomatic immunity and semi-official status before being deported in September 1918.

114 Andrew, First World War, p. 44.

115 GT 4624, 23 May 1918, TNA CAB 24/52.

116 Security Intelligence Service Seniority List and Register of Past and Present Members, December 1919.

117 Sixty-six MI5 staff served in Italy between 1 January 1918 and 31 August 1919 (when the station was closed): twenty-eight were officers, thirty-eight clerical and secretarial support staff. Security Intelligence Service Seniority List and Register of Past and Present Members, December 1919.

118 Andrew, *Secret Service*, pp. 299-304.

119 CUL Templewood Papers, Part III, Italy and the Vatican 1917-1918, files 1-5. Hoare's other tasks in Rome included counter-espionage and curtailing the extensive contraband activities (especially flows of specie and other prohibited goods to and from Germany through Switzerland).

120 Security Intelligence Service Seniority List and Register of Past and Present Members, December 1919. The largest postings recorded on this List are those of ten new recruits posted to Washington on 1 March 1918 and seven to New York on 1 August. Not all the final US destinations, however, correspond to those in the List. Thwaites was stationed in New York.

121 Army War College Washington, Lecture by Lieutenant Colonel C. E. Dansey, 4 May 1917, NAW RG 165, 9944-A-4.

122 Since joining MI5 in March 1917, Pakenham had already served as liaison officer in Paris and South Africa. 'Alphabetical list and register of past and present [MI5] members', Nov. 1921. See above, p. 80.

123 Security Service Archives. Typically for MI5 officer recruits, Pakenham listed his recreations as 'fishing, shooting, golf'.

124 Security Service Archives.

125 The first recorded visit to MI5 HQ was on 21 August 1918 by W. Lee Hurley, special attaché at the US embassy; the last on 26 February 1919 by Sergeant M. Y. Hughes, of the US Intelligence Corps. Security Service Archives. There may well have been a series of meetings between US intelligence and MI5 officers for which no record survives.

126 Thwaites left MI5 on 22 July 1918. Security Intelligence Service Seniority List and Register of Past and Present Members, December 1919.

127 Andrew, *For the President's Eyes Only*, pp. 38-9.

128 Ibid., pp. 39-40, 552 n. 39.

129 Memorandum, 28 March 1918, SLYU Wiseman MSS, series 1, box 6, folder 172.

130 See above, pp. 74-5.

131 Wiseman to Cumming, 6 Sept. 1918, in SLYU Wiseman MSS, series 1, box 6, folder 171. Andrew, *For the President's Eyes Only*, p. 90.

132 Thomson, *Scotland Yard*, ch. 20. Jeffery and Hennessy, *States of Emergency*, p. 5.

133 Andrew, *First World War*, p. 48.

134 GT 6079, 21 Oct. 1918, TNA CAB 24/67.

135 Thomson, *Scene Changes*, pp. 358, 377. See above, p. 107.

136 C. E. Russell to Thomson, 14 Oct. 1918, enclosing memo by Long, Wiltshire Public Record Office, Long MSS. I am grateful to Professor Eunan O'Halpin for this reference.

137 Thomson to Long, 15 Oct. 1918, enclosing 'Comments on the Attached Memorandum. Scheme for the Reorganisation and Coordination of Intelligence', Wiltshire Public Record Office, Long MSS.

138 Long to Thomson, 16 Oct. 1918; Long to Lloyd George, n.d., Wiltshire Public Record Office, Long MSS.

139 Long to Lloyd George, 18 Nov. 1918, Wiltshire Public Record Office, Long MSS.

140 Security Service Archives. According to Constance Kell the visit to Dublin was 'to inspect port facilities'. Lady Kell 'Secret Well Kept', p. 167, IWM. She also refers to the trip to Alnwick, her eventual visit to join Kell and her difficulties in mastering the art of fly fishing (p. 172).

141 Report of the Secret Service Committee, Feb. 1919, TNA CAB 127/356. Curzon to Long, 18 Feb. 1919, Wiltshire Record Office, Long MSS. Long to Austen Chamberlain, 2 Nov. 1921, BUL Chamberlain MSS AC 23/2/1.

142 Edward Bell to Leland Harrison, 2 May 1919, Library of Congress, Leland Harrison MSS, box 102. MI5's Washington office had closed on 26 March 1919. 'Alphabetical list and register of past and present [MI5] members', Nov. 1921.

SECTION B: BETWEEN THE WARS

Introduction: MI5 and its Staff –
Survival and Revival

1 Security Service Archives.
2 Lady Kell, 'Secret Well Kept' , pp. 171–2, IWM.
3 Report of the Secret Service Committee, Feb. 1919, TNA CAB 127/356. On the Committee, see above, pp. 108–9.
4 Security Service Archives.
5 Cumming's reaction will be discussed in Jeffery, *Official History of the Secret Intelligence Service.*
6 'Record of a Meeting held at the Admiralty on the 7th April, 1919, to consider the question of Secret Service Expenditure', TNA KV 4/182, s. 2a.
7 *Daily Mail,* 25 April 1919.
8 Churchill, 'Reduction of Estimates for Secret Services', 19 March 1920, HLRO Lloyd George MSS F/9/2/16.
9 'Defence Security Intelligence Service. List of Personnel', May 1920, TNA KV 4/127. The List of Personnel totals 150 but does not include Kell.
10 Security Service Archives.
11 The memo added:

> 4. Any proposal to transfer the present staff and records bodily to Sir Basil Thomson would suffer, not only from the disadvantages attached to civilian control over what is, and must remain, mainly a military organization, but also from the fact that economy would not thereby be secured. The Army Council is satisfied that the proposed expenditure is necessary and can see no advantages and many disadvantages from any change in the existing organization.

Security Service Archives.
12 Obituary, Captain H. M. Miller, *The Times,* 15 June 1934.
13 Security Service Archives.
14 See below, p. 130.
15 Churchill to Lloyd George and other ministers, 19 March 1920, HLRO Lloyd George MSS F/9/2/16.
16 Churchill, 'Reduction of Estimates for Secret Services', 19 March 1920, HLRO Lloyd George MSS F/9/2/16.
17 Andrew, *Secret Service,* pp. 404–6.
18 Hinsley and Simkins, *British Intelligence in the Second World War,* vol. 4, pp. 6–7, 9.
19 Andrew, *Secret Service,* pp. 421–2.
20 Recollections of a Kell family member.
21 Andrew, *Secret Service,* p. 421. Sinclair also had designs on the minuscule Indian Political Intelligence (IPI) which shared offices with MI5.
22 Minutes of Secret Service Committee, 10 March 1925, TNA FO 1093/68.
23 Evidence by Kell to Secret Service Committee, 10 March 1925, TNA FO 1093/68.
24 Security Service Archives. 'Bar Examination', *The Times,* 27 April 1922.
25 Black and Brunt, 'Information Management in MI5'.
26 See below, pp. 227, 228–9.
27 Security Service Archives.
28 Secret Service Committee 1925, minutes of 10 March 1925, TNA FO 1093/68.
29 Security Service Archives.
30 Bennett, *Churchill's Man of Mystery,* pp. 71–4.
31 Information kindly supplied by Gill Bennett; cf. Bennett, *Churchill's Man of Mystery,* pp. 72, 81. On Boddington and 'Finney', see below, p. 152.
32 Security Service Archives.
33 Security Service Archives.
34 Knight, *Pets Usual and Unusual,* pp. 13–14, 78–9. Obituaries in *The Times,* 27, 31 Jan. 1968.

35 Matthews and Knight, *Senses of Animals*, p. 13.

36 Security Service Archives.

37 Recollections of a former Security Service officer.

38 See above, p. 108.

39 Dorril, *Blackshirt*, p. 196.

40 Hope, 'Surveillance or Collusion?', pp. 652–8.

41 Security Service Archives.

42 Knight, 'Policy Re Study and Investigation of Fascism and other Right Wing or Kindred Movements and Activities, 1933–1945', s. 1z, 'Fascism in Great Britain', 22 August 1933, pp. 1–2. TNA KV 4/331.

43 Andrew, *First World War*, p. 67.

44 Bennett, *Churchill's Man of Mystery*, pp. 129, 345 n. 22.

45 'List of names of past staff prepared for mobilisation as necessary', Summary of General Strike, minutes of 1 May 1926, TNA KV 4/246.

46 'The Secret Services: Inquiry by the Minister without Portfolio [Lord Hankey]. Second Report dealing with the Security Service (MI5)', Jan.–May 1940, TNA CAB 127/383. Security Service Archives.

47 P. Report No. 2, 6 May 1926, TNA KV 4/246. 'Communist Effort to Undermine Loyalty and Discipline in H.M. Forces During the General Strike', May 1926, part III, TNA KV4/246. Quinlan, 'Human Intelligence Tradecraft and MI5 Operations in Britain', pp. 104–6.

48 Joint control ended in 1927, when ownership passed to the TUC.

49 Summary of General Strike, 'Report sent to M.I(B) 15 May 1926', 'Strike News and Communist News, May 13th, 1926', TNA KV 4/246. Quinlan, 'Human Intelligence Tradecraft and MI5 Operations in Britain', pp. 108–10.

50 Kell, letter to staff, 16 May 1926, Summary of General Strike, Appendix 4, TNA KV 4/246.

51 Security Service Archives.

52 Security Service Archives.

53 Davidson, *Memoirs of a Conservative*, p. 272.

54 Ramsden, *Making of Conservative Party Policy*, chs 3, 4. Entry on Ball by Lord Blake in *DNB 1961–1970*.

55 *Security Service*, p. 99.

56 Security Service Archives. During the 1970s the scope of protective security was extended to cover protection against terrorist attack.

57 Security Service Archives.

58 Security Service Archives.

59 *Security Service*, p. 99. 'Defence Security Service (Peace Organisation)', 31 May 1929, TNA KV 4/127. Statistics on Registry and secretarial staff do not survive. During the 1920s MI5 sometimes used the name 'Defence Security Service' or 'Defence Security Intelligence Service'.

60 Security Service Archives.

61 *Morning Post*, 25 Oct. 1933.

62 Recollections of former Security Service officers.

63 'Defence Security Service (Peace Organisation)', 31 May 1929, TNA KV 4/127. See above, p. 63.

64 Security Service Archives.

65 Recollections of a former Security Service officer.

66 Recollections of a former Security Service officer.

67 Recollections of a former Security Service officer.

68 Sissmore's duties in 1929 were officially designated as 'Defence Security Intelligence concerning Russia'. 'Defence Security Service (Peace Organisation)', 31 May 1929, TNA KV 4/127.

69 See below, pp. 265ff.

70 *Security Service*, p. 99.

71 Security Service Archives.

72 Bennett, *Churchill's Man of Mystery*, pp. 128–9.

73 Security Service Archives.

74 Bennett, *Churchill's Man of Mystery*, pp. 128–33. Interwar MI5 Who's Who.

75 See below, pp. 158–9.

76 Summary of proceedings of Secret Service Committee, 24 June 1931, TNA FO 1093/74.
77 Security Service Archives.
78 Hinsley and Simkins, *British Intelligence in the Second World War*, vol. 4, p. 8.
79 Ibid.
80 *Security Service*, p. 102.
81 See above, p. 118.
82 Security Service Archives.
83 Obituary, Captain H. M. Miller, *The Times*, 15 June 1934.
84 Obituary, Guy Liddell, *The Times*, 6 Dec. 1958.
85 Recollections of a former Security Service officer.
86 Philby, *My Silent War*, p. 74.
87 Christopher Andrew, interview with Sir Dick White, 1984.
88 Guy Liddell diary, 6 Dec. 1940.
89 Security Service Archives.
90 Recollections of a former Security Service officer. Unlike Sissmore, however, Bagot did not gain officer rank until 1949.
91 Security Service Archives.
92 *Security Service*, p. 107. Andrew, *Secret Service*, p. 521. See below, p. 132.
93 Security Service Archives.
94 Recollections of a former Security Service officer.
95 Security Service Archives.
96 Security Service Archives.
97 Recollections of a former Security Service officer. Born in 1909, Catherine Morgan-Smith changed her name by deed poll in 1938 to Weld-Smith (later Weldsmith). She retired on her marriage in 1963, taking her husband's surname Gibb. After his death she remarried and took the name of her second husband, Shackle.
98 Recollections of a former Security Service officer.
99 See above, pp. 56, 94, 96.
100 Security Service Archives.
101 Holt-Wilson to Audrey Stirling, 10 Sept. 1931, CUL Holt-Wilson papers. I am grateful to Dr Nicholas Hiley for drawing my attention to this correspondence.
102 Holt-Wilson to Audrey Stirling, n.d. ('Sunday–Midnight'), CUL Holt-Wilson papers.
103 Audrey Holt-Wilson to Holt-Wilson, 12 June 1940, CUL Holt-Wilson papers.
104 Hinsley and Simkins, *British Intelligence in the Second World War*, vol. 4, p. 9.
105 Recollections of a former Security Service officer.
106 *Security Service*, p. 142. Security Service Archives. TNA KV 2/2733, 2734, 2735.
107 *Security Service*, p. 373.
108 Security Service Archives.
109 *Security Service*, pp. 69–76.
110 See below, p. 176.
111 Security Service Archives.
112 Security Service Archives.
113 Christopher Andrew, interview with Sir Dick White, 1984. Andrew, *Secret Service*, p. 542.
114 Security Service Archives.
115 Security Service Archives.
116 Security Service Archives.
117 Christopher Andrew, interview with Sir Dick White, 1984. Andrew, *Secret Service*, p. 542.
118 Andrew, 'Secret Intelligence and British Foreign Policy', pp. 22–3.
119 See below, p. 185.
120 TNA KV 2/1021. Petrie, *Communism in India*, pp. 95–6.
121 TNA KV 2/611–15. Petrie, *Communism in India*, pp. 103–5.
122 An HOW was first taken out on Spratt at the request of IPI on the grounds that he was 'suspected of being engaged in revolutionary activities in India and known to be in receipt of instructions from certain persons in this country. It is desired to ascertain who his associates in this country are.' Security Service Archives.
123 H. Burgess to Holt-Wilson, 8 Nov. 1929, Security Service Archives.
124 Itinerary in Security Service Archives. While on the tour, Holt-Wilson suffered a personal

tragedy. One of his two sons by his first marriage, Lieutenant Charles Holt-Wilson of the Royal Artillery, was accidentally killed while serving in Bombay. Holt-Wilson had one other son, a naval lieutenant, and a daughter, from his first marriage.

125 Security Service Archives. CUL, Holt-Wilson papers.
126 Holt-Wilson, 'Security Intelligence in War', 1934, IWM Kell MSS.
127 'Paper on SIME compiled for Hinsley's official history', Security Service Archives; 'Report on the operation of Overseas Control in connection with the establishment of DSO's in the British colonies & liaison with the security authorities in the Dominions during the war of 1939–1945', TNA KV 4/18.
128 Shelley, 'Empire of Shadows'.
129 Security Service Archives.
130 *Security Service*, pp. 396–7.

Chapter 1: The Red Menace in the 1920s

1 Andrew and Gordievsky, *KGB*, p. 83.
2 Andrew, *Secret Service*, pp. 57–8.
3 MacMillan, *Peacemakers*, p. 5.
4 Andrew and Gordievsky, *KGB*, pp. 84–5.
5 Kell, lecture to Scottish chief constables at Edinburgh, 26 Feb. 1925, IWM Kell MSS. This lecture was probably typical of those to other chief constables.
6 Ullman, *Anglo-Soviet Relations*, vol. 2, pp. 130–31. Thomson, 'A Survey of Revolutionary Feeling in the Year 1919', CP 462, TNA CAB 24/96.
7 Report of the Secret Service Committee, 1 Dec. 1925, published as Annex E in Bennett, *'A most extraordinary and mysterious business'*.
8 Andrew, *Secret Service*, p. 380.
9 Kell, memorandum, 24 Nov. 1922, TNA WO 32/3948 5/Bills/1873. 'Seditious Literature etc', Jan. 1932, TNA WO 32/3948 110/Gen/4638. There are further details of MI5 pressure for new legislation in TNA WO 32/3948.
10 B1a (W. A. Alexander), memo, 24 June 1930, TNA KV 4/199, s. 42a. Alexander noted that there were 'no exact detailed figures available prior to 1927'. I am grateful to Dr Victor Madeira for this reference.
11 B3, HOW application for Harry Pollitt, Minute 12, 26 Nov. 1926, TNA KV2/1034.
12 HOW for David Ramsey, 30 June 1929, TNA KV 2/1868, s. 160a.
13 HOW for Robert Robson, 9 May 1923, TNA KV 2/1176, s.2a.
14 Unusually among leading Communists, the HOW on him was first taken out by the Special Branch; HOW, 19 April 1921, TNA KV 2/1186, s. 3a. When Campbell later moved house, however, it was MI5 which took the initiative in applying for the HOW to be updated; HOW, 4 July 1927, TNA KV 2/1186, s. 27a.
15 HOW for Robert Stewart, 30 Jan. 1921, TNA KV 2/1180–83, s. 3a.
16 *Security Service*, p. 93; 'Eva Collet Reckitt', TNA KV 2/1369.
17 Major O. N. Solbert to DMI Washington, 30 Oct. 1920, NAW RG 165 9944–A–165.
18 Major R. F. Hyatt to DMI Washington, 15 Dec. 1920, NAW RG 165 9944–A–166.
19 'War Book 1926. War Book Chapter', p. 70, TNA WO 33/1077. 'Field Security Police', 1923, pp. 2–3, TNA WO 33/1025. Kell, Lecture to Scottish chief constables, 26 Feb. 1925, IWM Kell MSS.
20 See above, p. 56.
21 Security Service Archives.
22 Freeman, 'MI1(b) and the Origins of British Diplomatic Cryptanalysis', p. 216.
23 Andrew, *Secret Service*, pp. 376–7.
24 Ibid., pp. 377–94.
25 Freeman, 'MI1(b) and the Origins of British Diplomatic Cryptanalysis', pp. 217–18. The decrypts are in TNA HW 12/332; copies of many of them are in HLRO Lloyd George MSS.
26 Andrew, *Secret Service*, pp. 377, 384–8, 394.
27 H1 summary of reports on Klishko from 1 September 1915 to 9 September 1918, TNA KV 2/1411.
28 'Nicholas Klyshko' [*sic*], 21 Feb. 1918, TNA KV 2/1410.

29 Report by M. W. Bray (G4), 11 July 1918, TNA KV 2/1411. Bray served in MI5 from May 1917 to January 1919; Security Service Archives.

30 'Clandestine Activities of William Norman Ewer 1919–1929', September 1949, p. 1, TNA KV 2/1016, s. 1101a.

31 On SIS operations against Soviet Russia in the 1920s, see Jeffery, *Official History of the Secret Intelligence Service*, part II.

32 Andrew, *Secret Service*, pp. 398–400.

33 Note by A. G. Denniston (GC&CS Director), 16 April 1921, TNA KV 2/501 SZ/2132.

34 Taylor, *English History*, pp. 269–70.

35 Kell to Troup (Home Office), 2 May 1918, enclosing 'Return no. 2' of cases considered for prosecution with 'remarks by MI5', TNA HO 45/10743/263275.

36 See above, p. 116.

37 Marquand, *Ramsay MacDonald*, pp. 314–15. Andrew, *Secret Service*, pp. 425–7.

38 Andrew, *Secret Service*, p. 426. When Winston Churchill returned to power in November 1924, eager to catch up on the backlog of intercepts from GC&CS, he discovered that 'In MacDonald's time he was himself long kept in ignorance of them by the Foreign Office.' Churchill to Austen Chamberlain, 21 Nov. 1924, BUL Chamberlain MSS AC 51/58.

39 Roskill, *Hankey*, vol. 2, p. 358.

40 Barnes, 'Special Branch and the First Labour Government'.

41 Williams, *Not in the Public Interest*, p. 134.

42 SIS Report CX/9668, 'Counter-Bolshevik report: Soviet Propaganda in the British Colonies', 2 July 1924, TNA KV 2/1183, SZ/2514.

43 Jeffery and Hennessy, *States of Emergency*, pp. 79–86.

44 Industrial Unrest Committee Interim Report (with memorandum by Home Secretary summarizing intelligence on the CPGB), 30 April 1924, CP 273(24), TNA CAB 24/166.

45 Ibid.

46 Cabinet conclusion 32 (24) 5, 15 May 1924, TNA CAB 23/48.

47 The most authoritative study of the Zinoviev letter, and the only one to draw on SIS archives, is Bennett, 'A most extraordinary and mysterious business'.

48 B3 noted during a 1928 inquiry: 'CSI [Kell] asked me to prepare a statement showing that the Zinoviev Letter contained nothing new or different from the intentions and propaganda of the USSR prior to the issue of this particular letter on 15/9/24.' Security Service Archives.

49 *Security Service*, p. 59.

50 On Makgill and Finney, see above, p. 123.

51 Bennett, 'A most extraordinary and mysterious business', p. 36. Bennett, *Churchill's Man of Mystery*, p. 81.

52 Director B (Jasper Harker) later noted that the date of the distribution of the Zinoviev letter to army commands on 22 October 1924 and related contacts with SIS on the two previous days had been 'verified by Colonel Holt Wilson from the files'. Security Service Archives.

53 Statement by Donald Im Thurn read to the Commons by the Prime Minister, Stanley Baldwin, on 19 March 1928; reprinted in the *Morning Post* and other newspapers on 20 March.

54 Bennett, 'A most extraordinary and mysterious business', ch. 2. Further details of the careers of Im Thurn and Alexander from Security Service Archives.

55 See above, p. 126.

56 Andrew, *Secret Service*, pp. 436–8.

57 Bennett, 'A most extraordinary and mysterious business', p. 26.

58 The Labour vote actually went up by more than a million (by 3 per cent of votes cast in a higher turnout). What made the 1924 general election so decisive was what happened to Labour's Liberal coalition partners, whose vote fell to well under 20 per cent. Clarke, *Hope and Glory*, p. 127.

59 Taylor, *Beaverbrook*, pp. 223–41.

60 Andrew, 'Secret Intelligence and British Foreign Policy', p. 20. By permission of the then Foreign Secretary, Christopher Andrew presented a re-enactment of this remarkable episode in the Foreign Secretary's room for BBC2 *Timewatch* in 1987. On 4 November 1924 a committee chaired by MacDonald reported to the final cabinet meeting of the outgoing government that they had 'found it impossible on the evidence before them to come to a conclusion on the subject'.

61 Bennett, *Churchill's Man of Mystery*, pp. 82–3.

62 Security Service Archives.

63 Security Service Archives.

64 See above, p. 123.

65 In 1969 when Milicent Bagot was preparing a report for the Security Service on the Zinoviev letter, about which controversy had revived, she informed Director B that Boddington (then retired) had been 'a particular help to her in her enquiries' and 'had in fact provided her with the key lead on which her report is likely to be based'. Boddington received an official letter of thanks and a Christmas hamper; Security Service Archives. The 'key lead' was the information that 'Finney' had not provided the corroboration of the Zinoviev letter's arrival which Morton said he had and which led Eyre Crowe to assure MacDonald that there was 'absolutely reliable' evidence that the letter had been discussed by the CPGB leadership (information kindly supplied by Gill Bennett).

66 'Re Advertisement in Daily Herald', 1 Jan. 1925, TNA KV 2/1101, s. 19b. For my analysis of the Ewer case I am indebted to the pioneering study by Victor Madeira, 'Moscow's Interwar Infiltration of British Intelligence', and to the Cambridge PhD theses by Dr Madeira, 'British Intelligence in "A New Kind of War" against Soviet "Subversion" 1917–1929' and by Dr Kevin Quinlan, 'Human Intelligence Tradecraft and MI5 Operations in Britain 1919–40'.

67 'From Box 573 Daily Herald in reply to (19a)', 9 Jan. 1925, TNA KV 2/1101, s. 23a; 'Report on interview by "D"(R)', 3 Feb. 1925, TNA KV 2/1101, s. 27a. Quinlan, 'Human Intelligence Tradecraft and MI5 Operations in Britain', pp. 143–5.

68 Minute of 7 Feb. 1925, TNA KV 2/1101. 'History of a Section of the Russian Intelligence Service, operating in this country, under management of William Norman Ewer 1919–1929', 8 Jan. 1930, TNA KV 2/1016, s. 809a; 'Synopsis of Telephone Conversations of the Federated Press of America', n.d., TNA KV 2/1101, s. 46a.

69 Some of the packets also included messages from 'Anne' in Paris to 'C.P.D.' After consultation with IPI, MI5 concluded that the messages were from Evelyn Roy, wife of the leading Indian Communist M. N. Roy (who had recently been expelled from France and was living in Moscow), to Clemens Palme Dutt, brother of CPGB Executive Committee member Rajani Palme Dutt. Minute of 3 Feb. 1925, TNA KV 2/1101; minute of 13 April 1925, TNA KV 2/1099; letter to Morton, 4 March 1925, TNA KV 2/1099, s. 48a. Quinlan, 'Human Intelligence Tradecraft and MI5 Operations in Britain', pp. 146–9.

70 'Memorandum on Slocombe', 29 April 1930, TNA KV 2/485, s. 205a; 'HOW on George Slocombe', minutes of 15 May 1925, KV 2/1099; 'History of a Section of the Russian Intelligence Service . . .', 8 Jan. 1930, TNA KV 2/1016, s. 809a. Callaghan and Morgan ('The Open Conspiracy of the Communist Party and the Case of W. N. Ewer') cast doubt on Ewer's involvement in espionage, largely on the grounds that he was 'an open communist'. The most important espionage trial of the 1930s, however, similarly involved a spy-ring run by a well-known Communist, this time a senior Party official (see below, pp. 167, 182). Though later understandably anxious to underplay the significance of his covert activities in the 1920s, Ewer himself acknowledged that his involvement with Slocombe amounted to espionage. For further comment on the case put forward by Callaghan and Morgan, see the theses by Madeira and Quinlan.

71 Bennett, *Churchill's Man of Mystery*, p. 123.

72 Madeira, 'Moscow's Interwar Infiltration of British Intelligence', p. 923 n. 31; CPGB's annual allocation according to Allen, TNA KV 2/989, s. 77a, 'Mr. Harker's notes on interview of 2.9.28', 11 Sept. 1928; 'History of a Section of the Russian Intelligence Service . . .', 8 Jan. 1930, TNA KV 2/1016, s. 809a.

73 Minute of 18 April 1925, TNA KV 2/1101.

74 Minute of 6 March 1925, TNA KV 2/1101.

75 Kell did, however, show the DPP's ruling to Sir Wyndham Childs. On Sinclair's Whitehall connections, see above, pp. 136–7.

76 The MI5 files on the ARCOS raid are in TNA KV 3/15–16, KV 2/818. Bennett, *Churchill's Man of Mystery*, pp. 94–106. Madeira, 'British Intelligence in "A New Kind of War" against Soviet "Subversion", 1917–1929', ch. 7.

77 Bennett, *Churchill's Man of Mystery*, p. 94. Madeira, 'British Intelligence in "A New Kind of War" against Soviet "Subversion", 1917–1929', ch. 7.

78 Intercepted telegrams from Yakovlev to Moscow of 13 April and 18 May, published in Cmd. 2874 (1927), *Documents Illustrating the Hostile Activities of the Soviet Government and Third International against Great Britain*, p. 31.

79 Security Service Archives.

80 Cab. 23(27), TNA CAB 23/55.

81 *Parl. Deb. (Commons)*, 24 May 1927, cols 1842–54.

82 Ibid., 26 May 1927, cols 2207–22, 2299–306.

83 Chamberlain to Rosengolz, 26 May 1927, *Documents on British Foreign Policy*, series 1A, vol. III, no. 215.

84 Cmd. 2874 (1927), *Documents Illustrating the Hostile Activities of the Soviet Government and Third International against Great Britain*.

85 See below, pp. 175, 368.

86 Denniston, 'Government Code and Cypher School between the Wars', p. 55. Andrew, *Secret Service*, pp. 469–71.

87 Harker to Kell, minute, 21 May 1928, TNA KV 2/989; B.4 report re Allen, 25 June 1928, TNA KV 2/989, s. 1a; B.4 report re Allen, 27 June 1928, TNA KV 2/989, s.54a. Quinlan, 'Human Intelligence Tradecraft and MI5 Operations in Britain', pp. 152–4.

88 Harker to Kell, 24 July 28, TNA KV 2/989, s. 63a.

89 Allen's statement regarding the activities of the FPA, 20 Aug. 1920, TNA KV 2/989, s. 69a; 'History of a Section of the Russian Intelligence Service . . .', 8 Jan. 1930, TNA KV 2/1016, s. 809a; 'Comparative Statement of information obtained from Allen and MI5 records', 29 Aug. 1928, TNA KV 2/989, s. 72a. Quinlan, 'Human Intelligence Tradecraft and MI5 Operations in Britain', pp. 155–8.

90 'History of a Section of the Russian Intelligence Service . . .', 8 Jan. 1930, TNA KV 2/1016, s. 809a. Madeira, 'Moscow's Interwar Infiltration of British Intelligence, 1919–1929', p. 927.

91 'History of a Section of the Russian Intelligence Service . . .', 8 Jan. 1930, TNA KV 2/1016, s. 809a.

92 In 1950 Ewer agreed to be interviewed by Maxwell Knight; TNA KV 2/1099.

93 'Charles Jane', TNA KV 2/1398.

94 See above, p. 127.

95 Bennett, *Churchill's Man of Mystery*, p. 125.

96 Guy Liddell diary, 17 June 1949, Security Service Archives.

97 Ibid., 25 May 1949.

98 'Clandestine Activities of William Norman Ewer 1919–1929', Sept. 1949, TNA KV 2/1016. 'History of a Section of the Russian Intelligence Service . . .', 8 Jan. 1930, TNA KV 2/1016, s. 809a. Bennett, *Churchill's Man of Mystery*, p. 125. No file on Hayes survives.

99 See below, p. 130.

Chapter 2: The Red Menace in the 1930s

1 Carr, *Foundations of a Planned Economy*, vol. 3, pp. 376–99. Carr, *Twilight of Comintern*, pp. 209–14.

2 'Internal Security of H.M. Forces during 1929', 3 Feb. 1930, TNA WO 32/3948 110/Gen/ 4399.

3 Haslam, *Soviet Foreign Policy, 1930–1933*, p. 56.

4 Andrew and Mitrokhin, *Mitrokhin Archive*, pp. 49, 53–4. Andrew and Gordievsky, *KGB*, pp. 165–8.

5 'Internal Security of H.M. Forces during 1929', 3 Feb. 1930, TNA WO 32/3948 110/Gen/ 4399.

6 Roskill, *Naval Policy between the Wars*, vol. 2, ch. 4. Roskill, *Hankey*, vol. 2, p. 556. Ereira, *Invergordon Mutiny*, ch. 10.

7 'Most Secret' cabinet minute, 21 Sept. 1931, TNA CAB 23/90B.

8 'Transcript of shorthand notes at an interview at New Scotland Yard, S.W., 3rd October 1931: statement by Telegraphist Stephen Bousfield, HMS "Warspite"', TNA KV 2/604, s. 7a. Harker took part in questioning Bousfield at Scotland Yard.

9 *The Times*, 17, 26 Oct., 3, 27 Nov. 1931. On Allison's earlier career, see above, p. 164.

10 S8 (Sissmore) to Harker, Minute 53, 8 June 1932, TNA KV 2/604.

11 In February 1933 Hutchings was joined in Moscow by his wife, also a committed Communist. S10, Minute 79, 24 Feb. 1933, TNA KV 2/604.

12 Ereira, *Invergordon Mutiny*, ch. 11. In his authoritative later study of naval policy between the wars Captain Stephen Roskill found no evidence of any Communist activity in the navy save for a few cases of naval ratings attending CPGB meetings in Hyde Park in support of the miners' strike in 1926. Roskill, *Naval Policy between the Wars*, vol. 2, pp. 115n., 116n.

13 V. Baddeley (for Lords Commissioners of the Admiralty) to Under Secretary of State, War Office, 16 Nov. 1931, TNA KV 4/129, s. 42a.

14 Boddington had first joined the CPGB in 1923 (see above, p. 122) but from 1924 to 1926, when working both for MI5 and SIS, he joined instead the British Fascists and the Italian Fascist Party. No details of his operations while posing as a Fascist survive in Security Service files. Boddington left the British and Italian Fascists in 1926 and rejoined the CPGB. In 1932 he 'discreetly faded out' of the Communist Party (Security Service Archives). His reasons for fading out are unknown. It is possible that he feared that his cover was wearing thin and that Harker believed that Knight's agents were henceforth better placed to penetrate the CPGB.

15 *Parl. Deb. (Commons)*, 16 April 1934, cols 740–43. Anderson, *Fascists, Communists and the National Government*, p. 70.

16 Hyde, *I Believed*, pp. 42–3.

17 The Security Service memorandum of October 1932 was cited in an untitled War Office memorandum of 16 March 1933, TNA WO 32/3948 110/Gen/4771.

18 Olga Gray (see below, pp. 179ff.) is one of a number of possible sources of the 'information of the highest importance'; this may help to explain the 'most handsome bonus' given by Kell to Knight later in the year (see above, p. 132). Very few reports from Knight's agents survive.

19 Untitled War Office memorandum, 16 March 1933, TNA WO 32/3948 110/Gen/4771.

20 *Security Service*, p. 107. See above, p. 142.

21 Cab 52(33)6, 18 Oct. 1933, TNA CAB 23/77.

22 Andrew, *Secret Service*, pp. 518–19. The only prosecution under the Act was of a Leeds University student 'of extreme political views' sentenced in 1937 to a year's imprisonment for suggesting to an RAF pilot that he steal an aeroplane and use it to help the Spanish Republicans. His sentence was drastically reduced on appeal.

23 MI5 and Scotland Yard note to DDMO&I, 5 March 1930, TNA KV 5/71, s. 131a. Guy Liddell (then at MPSB), 'Russian Oil Products Limited', 14 Jan. 1931, TNA KV 5/72, s. 191a.

24 G. M. Liddell (then at MPSB), 'The activities of Russian Soviet organizations in Great Britain and Ireland since the ARCOS raid, May 1927–April 1929', 17 April 1929, TNA KV 5/71, s. 64a; 'Russian Oil Products', 5 May 1932, TNA KV 5/72, s. 356z.

25 'Note of discussion at the Home Office on ROP Petrol depots', 13 March 1934, TNA KV 5/74, s. 604a.

26 Holt-Wilson noted in May 1931: 'By arrangement with Scotland House . . . we are, for the most part, concerning ourselves only with the espionage and sabotage side of the Russian Oil Products problem. Scotland House are making themselves responsible for the collations of information with regard to personnel employed at the various depots throughout the country and we are passing to them all material on this subject that comes into our hands.' Holt-Wilson to J. C. MacIver (Home Office), 19 May 1931, TNA KV 5/72, s. 221a. In October, following the transfer of the counter-subversion section of the Special Branch to MI5, the Security Service became responsible for all aspects of the ROP investigation.

27 MI5 and Scotland Yard note to DDMO&I, 5 March 1930, TNA KV 5/71, s. 131a.

28 MPSB report to Security Service, 20 April 1932, TNA KV 5/72, s. 341c.

29 See below, p. 182.

30 Valentine Vivian (SIS) to Liddell, 'The Olsen case', 14 Oct. 1932, TNA KV 2/2880, s. 25a.

31 O. A. Harker (DB), 'Joseph Volkovich Volodarsky and Elisabeth Grigorievna Volodarskaya', 4 Nov. 1932, TNA KV 2/2280, s. 46a.

32 Security Service Archives. On Brandes, see below, p. 181. Volodarsky was interned in Canada during the Second World War, admitted working for the NKVD, co-operated in debriefings and was allowed to settle in Montreal.

33 MI5 report, 'Pyotr Kapitza', 17 Sept. 1930, TNA KV 2/777, s. 42a. Report on Maurice Dobb, 19 Sept. 1930, TNA KV 2/1758, s. 12a.

34 Andrew and Gordievsky, *KGB*, pp. 205, 210.

35 22 June 1934, TNA KV 2/777, s. 81a.

36 TNA KV 2/777, ss. 79a, 80a, 82. Burke, *The Spy Who Came in from the Co-op*, ch. 6.

37 Holloway, *Stalin and the Bomb*, pp. 26–7.

38 The first to identify Philby's potential as a Soviet agent – and probably to draw him to the attention of Arnold Deutsch – was Litzi's friend Edith Suschitsky, who was herself recruited by Deutsch and given the transparent codename EDITH. Andrew and Mitrokhin, *Mitrokhin Archive*, p. 76.

39 Philby, untitled memorandum, Security Service Archives. On Philby's partial confession before his 1963 defection, see below, pp. 435–6.

40 J. C. Brown, 'Interview of Frau Josefine (Fini) Deutsch, 21–22 May 1972', 2 June 1972, PF 48,871, s. 71b.

41 Andrew and Mitrokhin, *Mitrokhin Archive*, pp. 73–4.

42 On SVR attempts to give greater credit to the more senior NKVD officer, Aleksandr Orlov, see ibid., pp. 77–8.

43 Ibid., p. 75.

44 Borovik, *Philby Files*, p. 29.

45 Andrew and Mitrokhin, *Mitrokhin Archive*, p. 74.

46 In October 1936, and subsequently, Oscar Deutsch applied for permission to employ his cousin Arnold as a psychologist with his cinema chain. The Home Office refused permission on the grounds that there was no reason why the job should not be given to a British subject. Security Service Archives. Information on the Odeon acronym from Peter Hennessy.

47 Security Service Archives.

48 After his arrival in England in April 1934, Deutsch spent a term at UCL studying phonetics, probably because it was too late in the academic year to begin work for the Psychology Diploma. Security Service Archives.

49 Security Service Archives.

50 Security Service Archives. Controversy has continued ever since Burt's death in 1971 over whether he fabricated some of the evidence used in his research.

51 Costello and Tsarev, *Deadly Illusions*, p. 146.

52 Andrew and Mitrokhin, *Mitrokhin Archive*, ch. 4.

53 Originally known as the Cambridge University Labour Club and affiliated to the Labour Party, it was taken over by Communists on 29 November 1930, disaffiliated from Labour and renamed itself the Cambridge University Socialist Society (CUSS). CUSS minute book, 29 Nov. 1930.

54 The official title of the CUSS treasurer, as in other Cambridge student societies, was 'Junior Treasurer'. The title 'Senior Treasurer' was reserved for a senior member of the University who was supposed to ensure the orderly functioning of the society.

55 CUSS minute book.

56 Andrew and Mitrokhin, *Mitrokhin Archive*, ch. 4.

57 Ibid., chs 3, 4.

58 Primakov et al. (eds), *Ocherki istorii rossiiskoi vneshnei razvedki*, vol. 3, ch. 13.

59 Andrew and Mitrokhin, *Mitrokhin Archive*, pp. 66, 71–2.

60 Denniston, 'Government Code and Cypher School between the Wars', p. 58.

61 H. C. Kenworthy, 'A Brief History of Events Relating to the Growth of the "Y" Service', TNA HW 3/81. Smith, 'Government Code and Cypher School and the First Cold War'.

62 *Security Service*, pp. 105–6.

63 William Morrison PF, TNA KV 2/606.

64 Jane Sissmore, 'William Morrison', 1 Aug. 1939, TNA KV 2/606. After returning from Spain in April 1938 (Sissmore had 'a very shrewd suspicion that he deserted' from the Republican forces), Morrison broke contact with the CPGB and gave a 'frank' account to MI5 of his previous career. Knight (B5b), 'William Morrison', 30 Oct. 1939, TNA KV 2/606.

65 *Security Service*, p. 106.

66 Denniston, 'Government Code and Cypher School between the Wars', p. 58.

67 All that survives in Security Service files is a brief file summary.

68 CB 16 (22 April 1931–19 May 1932), TNA HW 17/70. I am grateful to Dr Victor Madeira for this reference.

69 Decrypts of Comintern traffic between Moscow and London from February 1934 to January 1937 are published in West, *MASK*, pp. 41–199.

70 Decrypted message from Moscow to Pollitt, 16 Feb. 1934, reporting on Kenyatta's return to London; West, *MASK*, p. 120.

71 Security Service Archives.

72 *Security Service*, p. 106. There are numerous references to the subsidies in the decrypts published in West, *MASK*.

73 Memo by Vansittart (PUS Foreign Office), 28 May 1935; Sir John Simon to Moscow embassy, 30 May 1935, TNA FO 371/19467 N2761. Andrew, 'Secret Intelligence and British Foreign Policy', p. 21.

74 Millar, 'British Intelligence and the Comintern in Shanghai', pp. 136–50. Smith, 'Government Code and Cypher School and the First Cold War', pp. 29–30. Smith, *Foley*, pp. 51–61. *Security Service*, pp. 103–5.

75 Numerous volumes of Comintern messages to various parts of the world were not passed to the Security Service until 1952 when interest in them revived during the VENONA investigation and copies were also forwarded to the FBI and CIA. Security Service Archives.

76 See above, pp. 123, 164.

77 'John Harold Salisbury', 5 Sept. 1935, TNA KV 2/2499, s. 231a.

78 Untitled report by Harker on conference in Admiralty, 8 Jan. 1936, TNA KV 2/2499, s. 276a. Ba, Copy of interrogation of J. H. Salisbury, 13 Jan. 1936, TNA KV 2/2499, s. 278a.

79 Minutes 281a, 282a, 1 Feb. 1936, TNA KV 2/2499.

80 Harker to Rae (Treasury), 9 Oct. 1936, enclosing MI5 reports on Trebilcock and other Communists 'employed in Civil Establishments under the Admiralty'; Secret report by Carter Committee on 'Undesirable Employees in Naval Establishments', 4 Nov. 1936; Macleod (Admiralty) to Rae (Treasury), 7 Jan. 1937; Notes prepared for Baldwin's meeting with Bevin, Feb. 1937, TNA T 162 424/E13264/04. Notes by Sir Horace Wilson on meeting between Baldwin, Bevin and First Sea Lord, 9 Feb. 1937, TNA PREM 1/206.

81 Special Branch report, 29 March 1935, TNA FO 371/19467 N1781. Andrew, 'Secret Intelligence and British Foreign Policy', pp. 21–2. Surviving MASK decrypts include a number of reprimands to the *Daily Worker* when it failed to follow the current Moscow line with the precision demanded of it. West, *MASK*, pp. 102, 181, 182.

82 'M.S. Report', pp. 18, 33–4, TNA KV 4/227. 'The Woolwich Arsenal Case – Summary Report', 13 Feb. 1950, p. 13, TNA KV 2/1023, s. 871a. 'Statement of "X" the informant in this case', 25 Jan. 1938, p. 1, TNA KV 2/1022, s. [illegible]. Quinlan, 'Human Intelligence Tradecraft and MI5 Operations in Britain', pp. 178–9.

83 'Statement of "X" the informant in this case', 25 Jan. 1938, pp. 1–2, TNA KV 2/1022; 'M.S. Report', pp. 35–8, TNA KV 4/227. Quinlan, 'Human Intelligence Tradecraft and MI5 Operations in Britain', pp. 181–90.

84 're 82 Holland Road', 24 April 1937, TNA KV/2008, s. 1a; 're "Mr Peters"', 29 April 1937, ibid., s. 2a; M (Knight), minute, 13 Jan. 1938, ibid., s. 4a. Security Service Archives.

85 'Statement of "X" the informant in this case', 25 Jan. 1938, p. 3, TNA KV 2/1022. The NKVD defector Walter Krivitsky said later that Maly too had described Deutsch as 'bumptious'; 'Note re information from Krivitsky', 23 Jan. 1940, p. 8, TNA KV 2/804, s. 2b.

86 See below, p. 420.

87 'Statement of "X" the informant in this case', 25 Jan. 1938, pp. 3–6, TNA KV 2/1022. 'The Woolwich Arsenal Case – Summary Report', 13 Feb. 1950, pp. 1–3, TNA KV 2/1023, s. 871a. 'M.S. Report', pp. 39–40, TNA KV 4/227. Quinlan, 'Human Intelligence Tradecraft and MI5 Operations in Britain', pp. 189–90.

88 'Willy and Mary Brandes', TNA KV 2/1004.

89 'The Woolwich Arsenal Case – Summary Report', 13 February 1950, p. 4, TNA KV 2/1023, s. 871a; 'Statement of "X" the informant in this case', 25 Jan. 1938, p. 7, TNA KV 2/1022, s. [illegible]. Quinlan, 'Human Intelligence Tradecraft and MI5 Operations in Britain', pp. 191–4.

90 Trial reports in *The Times*, 4, 8 Feb., 15 March 1938. Masters, *The Man Who was M*, ch. 4.

91 Burke, *The Spy Who Came in from the Co-op*, p. 95. Vivian spelt Sirnis 'Sirness'. He also identified an address found on a slip of paper in Glading's diary as her address.

92 Security Service Archives. M2 wrongly assumed that either 'Sirnis' or 'Steadman' was her

married name and the other her maiden name. In fact Melita Norwood at this period seems not to have used her married name in Party circles.

93 Security Service Archives.

94 Security Service Archives.

95 Andrew and Mitrokhin, *Mitrokhin Archive*, p. 153. The suggestion in Dr David Burke's generally impressive pioneering biography of Melita Norwood, *The Spy Who Came in from the Co-op* (p. 103), that 'someone involved with the case must have taken a decision to inform the Russians that her cover had not been blown' is implausible.

96 Security Service Archives.

97 See below, pp. 579–80.

98 Andrew and Mitrokhin, *Mitrokhin Archive*, pp. 102–3. The Centre and perhaps Deutsch may well have misinterpreted a visit he received from the police in September 1937. The visit was prompted not by any suspicion of espionage but solely by the fact that, having given up his diploma course at University College, he was trying to regularize his position in England by employment with his cousin, Oscar Deutsch. Security Service Archives.

99 See below, pp. 426–8.

100 Burke, *The Spy Who Came in from the Co-op*, ch. 6.

101 Security Service Archives.

102 Security Service Archives.

103 Grafpen's file was destroyed some years ago. A record remains, however, that he had first been identified as a Soviet intelligence officer by the Security Service in 1927 and held posts in Soviet trade delegations in London, New York and Milan.

104 Andrew and Mitrokhin, *Mitrokhin Archive*, pp. 107, 109.

105 'Compte-rendu de Mission à Londres les 30 & 31 janvier 1939', 1 Feb. 1939, SHD-DAT, ARR, dr. 250; 'Prévisions britanniques', 19 Feb. 1939, SHD-DAT, ARR, dr. 251. I am grateful to Dr Peter Jackson for this reference.

106 Andrew and Mitrokhin, *Mitrokhin Archive*, pp. 107–9.

Chapter 3: British Fascism and the Nazi Threat

1 Security Service Archives.

2 *Parl. Deb. (Commons)*, 26 May 1927, cols 2257–8.

3 Nicolai, *Nachrichtendienst, Presse, und Volksstimmung im Weltkrieg*. On Nicolai, see above, pp. 52, 77.

4 Nicolai, *Geheime Mächte*; English trans.: Nicolai, *German Secret Service*, pp. 265–7 for quotation.

5 Holt-Wilson, 'Military Administration of occupied territory in time of war', 22 March 1922, TNA KV 4/313, s. 2a. *Security Service*, p. 78.

6 The lack of detailed studies of the intelligence services of imperial Germany and the Weimar Republic, due largely to the scarcity of sources, is in striking contrast to the voluminous literature on policing. On the current state of research on intelligence in the Weimar period, see Richter, 'Military and Civil Intelligence Services in Germany'.

7 'The Deutsche Uberseedienst', 1923, TNA KV 2/1116, s. 139a. *Security Service*, p. 98.

8 SIS to Major Ball, MI5, 11 Oct. 1922, TNA KV 2/1116, s. 10a.

9 SIS report, 'Alleged German espionage activities', 10 March 1923, TNA KV 2/1116, s. 37a. On interwar SIS operations against Germany, see Jeffery, *Official History of the Secret Intelligence Service*, part III.

10 SIS to Harker, MI5, 7 July 1928, TNA KV 2/1116, s. 204a. Major Ball, 'The Deutsche Uberseedienst', 30 March 1929, TNA KV 2/1116, s. 207a.

11 Major Ball, 'The Deutsche Uberseedienst', 30 March 1929, TNA KV 2/1116, s. 207a.

12 Holt-Wilson, 'German espionage in the UK', 12 Aug. 1931, TNA KV 3/93, s. 88a. SIS to Major Alexander, 24 March 1932, TNA KV 3/93, s. 112a.

13 MI5 did, however, identify as German spies some of the Etappe Dienst agents, without realizing what network they belonged to. Security Service Archives.

14 *Security Service*, p. 109.

15 *The Times*, 31 Jan. 1933.

16 Kershaw, *Hitler 1889–1936*, pp. 457–61.

17 *The Times*, 22 March 1933.

18 G. M. Liddell, 'The Liquidation of Communism, Left-Wing Socialism and Pacifism. Visit to Berlin, (30 March 1933–9 April 1933)', TNA KV 4/111, s. 1a.

19 Trenchard to Polizei President Berlin, 24 March 1933, TNA KV 4/111. Unsigned copy of letter of thanks from Kell to Admiral Sinclair (SIS), May 1933, TNA KV 4/111.

20 Diels later lost a struggle for power with the leader of the SS, Heinrich Himmler, who in April 1934 also became head of the Gestapo.

21 G. M. Liddell, 'The Liquidation of Communism, Left-Wing Socialism and Pacifism. Visit to Berlin, (30 March 1933–9 April 1933)', TNA KV 4/111, s. 1a.

22 Ibid.

23 Guy Liddell diary, 21 April 1940.

24 Curry joined the Indian Police in 1907 at the age of twenty, retiring in 1932. The invitation to join B Branch came from its head, Jasper Harker, who had first met him while working for the Indian Police before returning to Britain in 1919. Security Service Archives.

25 Security Service Archives.

26 On Knight's earlier Fascist contacts, see above, pp. 123–4.

27 'M' report, 21 March 1934, TNA KV 3/53, s. 1c.

28 'M' report, 13 April 1934, TNA KV 3/53, s.1e.

29 'The Revival of Fascism in Britain. Memorandum by the Security Service', Dec. 1945, TNA KV 4/331.

30 Kell to Scott (Home Office), 18 June 1934, enclosing Report no. 1 on the BUF, TNA HO 144/21041.

31 Anderson, *Fascists, Communists and the National Government*, chs 6, 7. Dorril, *Blackshirt*, ch. 15.

32 Kell to Scott (Home Office), 1 Aug. 1934, enclosing Report no. 2 on the BUF, TNA HO 144/21041.

33 Dorril, *Blackshirt*, p. 307.

34 Though both the Mosleys and Hitler intended the wedding to be secret, it was quickly known to the Foreign Office. Dorril, *Blackshirt*, pp. 393–4.

35 B7, 'Lady Diana Mosley', 26 June 1940, TNA KV 2/884, s. 48a.

36 Kell to Scott (Home Office), 8 Oct. 1934, enclosing Report no. 3 on the BUF, TNA HO 144/21041.

37 Kell to Scott (Home Office), 11 March 1935, enclosing Report no. 5 on the BUF, TNA HO 144/21041.

38 Kell to Scott (Home Office), 10 July 1936, enclosing Report no. 8 on the BUF, TNA HO 144/21041.

39 Ibid.

40 Kell to Scott (Home Office), 27 Nov. 1936, enclosing Report no. 9 on the BUF, TNA HO 144/21041.

41 Anderson, *Fascists, Communists and the National Government*, chs 10, 11.

42 Kell to Scott (Home Office), 27 Nov. 1936, enclosing Report no. 9 on the BUF; minute by Liddell, 10 Dec. 1936; minute by Harker, 10 July 1937, TNA HO 144/21041.

43 Anderson, *Fascists, Communists and the National Government*, ch. 11.

44 Home Office Notes on DR18b, April 1949, TNA HO 45/26018. Grant, 'Desperate Measures', ch. 1.

45 'Order of priority of foreign countries from SIS point of view', n.d. [1935 or 1936], TNA WO 106/5392.

46 Andrew, *Secret Service*, pp. 532–3, 547–8. Details of Secret Service vote in TNA T 160787/F6139/053.

47 Vansittart, *Mist Procession*, p. 397.

48 See above, p. 136.

49 Security Service Archives.

50 Vansittart, *Mist Procession*, p. 398.

51 Minute, 6 May 1933, CCAC VNST 2/3. 'Robert Gilbert Vansittart', *Oxford DNB*.

52 Rose, *Vansittart*, pp. 104, 164, 182.

53 Curry later·recalled that Kell was initially reluctant for the Security Service to penetrate a foreign embassy for the first time, but was persuaded to do so by Vansittart. Security Service Archives.

54 Putlitz, *Putlitz Dossier*.

55 Security Service Archives.

56 Putlitz, *Putlitz Dossier*, ch. 12.

57 Kell was introduced to Ustinov on 9 August 1934 by Vansittart's private secretary, Clifford Norton (later knighted); Security Service Archives.

58 Rose, *Vansittart*, p. 74.

59 Security Service Archives.

60 Ustinov, *Klop and the Ustinov Family*, p. 66.

61 The portrait appears as the frontispiece to *The Security Service*.

62 Bower, *Perfect English Spy*, p. 29.

63 Security Service Archives.

64 In June, however, HOWs were granted on two addresses in Hamburg with which it was known that the London office of the Auslands Organisation was corresponding. *Security Service*, p. 110.

65 Curry's evidence on Kell's initial reluctance to investigate the Auslands Organisation is made more credible by the fact that he simultaneously put on record 'the highest respect and regard for our chief'. Security Service Archives.

66 [Curry] 'Memorandum on the possibilities of sabotage by the organisations set up in British countries by the totalitarian governments of Germany and Italy', July 1936, p. 11, TNA KV 4/290, s. 2a; see also *Security Service*, p. 111.

67 'Conference held at the Home Office on 26 May, 1936, to consider the position arising from the organisation in Great Britain of Branches of the German Nazi and Italian Fascist Parties', TNA FO 371/19942, s. 128.

68 McKale, *Swastika outside Germany*, p. 157.

69 The Foreign Office argued that banning the Auslands Organisation would merely drive its activities underground. MI5 replied that it would still be able to monitor it, and in fact the 'squeeze' put on the underground organization would probably make it easier to watch. 'Conference held at the Home Office on 26 May, 1936, to consider the position arising from the organisation in Great Britain of Branches of the German Nazi and Italian Fascist Parties', TNA FO 371/19942, s. 128.

70 B2a, Note, 24 March 1939, TNA KV 4/301, s. 88b. J. C. Curry, Unpublished Memoirs, Security Service Archives. *Security Service*, pp. 132–3. McKale, *Swastika outside Germany*, p. 157.

71 Security Service Archives.

72 Kell to Sir Maurice Hankey, CID, 6 July 1936, enclosing [Curry] 'Memorandum', p. 5, TNA KV 4/290, s. 2a.

73 Security Service Archives.

74 'Note on Information Received in Connection with the Crisis of September, 1938', [7 Nov. 1938], TNA KV 4/16.

75 Willans, *Peter Ustinov*, pp. 39–41.

76 'Note on Information Received in Connection with the Crisis of September, 1938', [7 Nov. 1938], TNA KV 4/16. The Security Service had no file on the abdication or on King Edward VIII's lover and future wife Mrs Simpson. The Special Branch, however, had a file on Simpson (declassified in 2003) which revealed that in 1936 she was simultaneously conducting an affair with a married car salesman. 'Mrs Simpson's Secret Lover Revealed', *The Times*, 30 Jan. 2003.

77 See below, p. 209.

78 'Note on Information Received in Connection with the Crisis of September, 1938', [7 Nov. 1938], TNA KV 4/16.

79 Security Service Archives.

80 Security Service Archives.

81 Security Service Archives.

82 Andrew, *Secret Service*, pp. 533–4.

83 See below, pp. 241–2.

84 Security Service Archives.

85 Andrew, *Secret Service*, pp. 553–9.

86 According to an MI5 report to the Foreign Office, on 16 August 1938 'Herr von S.', an important German 'not unconnected with the German General Staff' 'sent us a warning that a sudden invasion of Czechoslovakia was contemplated. Early in the second half of August we established close contact with him.' 'Note on Information Received in Connection with the Crisis of September, 1938', [7 Nov. 1938], TNA KV 4/16. The note refers to, but does not identify, four other German informants.

87 Ustinov, *Dear Me*, pp. 102–3. Klop's recollection of 'Herr von S's' central message agrees with that in surviving MI5 records. On Ribbentrop's bellicose statements on Czechoslovakia in August 1938, see Kershaw, *Hitler, 1936–45*, p. 91. Schweppenburg had been military attaché in London from 1933 to 1937 and later became a well-known panzer commander.

88 'Note on Information Received in Connection with the Crisis of September, 1938', [7 Nov. 1938], TNA KV 4/16. Another MI5 report, which distinguishes less precisely between different German sources, suggests that Putlitz also supplied a copy of this document. Security Service Archives.

89 Dilks (ed.), *Cadogan Diaries*, pp. 94–7. Weinberg, *Foreign Policy of Hitler's Germany*, pp. 394, 396, 421, 428. Vansittart later had doubts about Kordt's motives, believing that 'what he really wanted was a German maximum without war with us. His real game was to get a free hand in expansion east ... Otherwise he was a decent, humane man, and emphatically not a Nazi.' Rose, *Vansittart*, pp. 136–8, 222.

90 Rose, *Vansittart*, p. 228. Dilks (ed.), *Cadogan Diaries*, p. 95.

91 Curry later recalled, possibly with a memory improved by hindsight, that he knew of no one in the Security Service who thought the outcome of Chamberlain's negotiations with Hitler 'a great success'. Security Service Archives.

92 Malcolm Woollcombe, 'What Should We Do?', 18 Sept. 1938; Fisher to Sinclair (copy), 20 Sept. 1939, Woollcombe MSS. A copy of 'What Should We Do?', marked 'Views of SIS', is to be found in TNA FO 371/21659 C14471/42/18. A previous memorandum by Woollcombe, 'Germany and Colonies', 3 Feb. 1938, had been well received by Neville Chamberlain, who at one point added the marginal note: 'What did I say[?]'. Andrew, 'Secret Intelligence and British Foreign Policy', p. 24.

93 'Note on Information Received in Connection with the Crisis of September, 1938', [7 Nov. 1938], TNA KV 4/16.

94 J. C. Curry, 'Note on the aggressive policy of Hitler and Ribbentrop: and consequent instructions to the Abwehr', Security Service Archives (no file ref.). J. C. Curry, 'Information on Hitler's Germany's intentions in 1938 obtained from M.I.5 sources', 5 Sept. 1941, TNA KV 4/16.

95 'Note on Information Received in Connection with the Crisis of September, 1938', [7 Nov. 1938], TNA KV 4/16.

96 Security Service Archives.

97 Andrew, *Secret Service*, pp. 547–50.

98 Whether Hitler really did use the words attributed to him remains doubtful. One of MI5's informants may well have decided to embroider some of Hitler's actual comments in an attempt to stiffen British resolve.

99 'Note on Information Received in Connection with the Crisis of September, 1938', [7 Nov. 1938], TNA KV 4/16.

100 Security Service Archives.

101 'Note on Information Received in Connection with the Crisis of September, 1938', [7 Nov. 1938], TNA KV 4/16.

102 Security Service Archives.

103 *Security Service*, pp. 121–2.

104 Brendon, *Dark Valley*, p. 522.

105 'Note on Information Received in Connection with the Crisis of September, 1938', [7 Nov. 1938], TNA KV 4/16.

106 Cadogan diary, 28, 29 Nov., 1, 6 Dec. 1938, CCAC ACAD 1/7.

107 On Hoare's First World War career in MI5 and MI1c, see above, pp. 104–5. For six months in 1936 Hoare was an unsuccessful foreign secretary.

108 Security Service Archives.

109 Brendon, *Dark Valley*, p. 536.

110 Security Service Archives.

111 Putlitz, *Putlitz Dossier*, ch. 21. Curry corroborates Putlitz's account of Vansittart's offer of asylum; Security Service Archives.

112 *Security Service*, p. 122.

113 Security Service Archives.

114 Dilks (ed.), *Cadogan Diaries*, p. 151.

115 Feiling, *Neville Chamberlain*, p. 396.

116 Vansittart sent his report to Halifax on 20 February. Putlitz later recalled in his memoirs (*Putlitz Dossier*, pp. 164–5) that he had telephoned Ustinov on 21 February 1939 with a warning that Hitler would invade Czechoslovakia on 15 March. It seems likely that Putlitz slightly misremembered the date of his telephone call, that he made it a day or so earlier, and that it prompted Vansittart's warning to Halifax. It is also likely that Putlitz was slightly less specific than he later recalled about the date of the German invasion.

117 Rose, *Vansittart*, pp. 232–3.

118 Dilks (ed.), *Cadogan Diaries*, pp. 153–7, 163. Rose, *Vansittart*, p. 233. Andrew, *Secret Service*, pp. 585–6.

119 Colvin, *Chamberlain Cabinet*, p. 188.

120 See above, p. 198.

121 The precise point at which White succeeded Curry as Ustinov's liaison officer is not recorded in the surviving files. The most probable date is February 1939, when Curry had a serious eye operation. The operation failed and a second was only partly successful. He was on sick leave for seven months. Security Service Archives.

122 Christopher Andrew, interview with Sir Dick White, 1984.

123 Dilks (ed.), *Cadogan Diaries*, p. 170. Andrew, *Secret Service*, p. 590.

124 Douglas, *Advent of War*, pp. 11–12.

125 Hinsley et al., *British Intelligence in the Second World War*, vol. 1, pp. 41, 85.

126 Dilks (ed.), *Cadogan Diaries*, p. 158. Cadogan diary, 21 April 1939, CCAC ACAD 1/8.

127 Hinsley et al., *British Intelligence in the Second World War*, vol. 1, pp. 42–3.

128 Hinsley and Simkins, *British Intelligence in the Second World War*, vol. 4, pp. 11–12.

129 Security Service Archives.

130 Security Service Archives.

131 Heinemann, 'Abwehr', p. 1.

132 For Hitler's 1935 ban on Abwehr espionage in Britain, see Leverkuehn, *German Military Intelligence*, p. 93; Kahn, *Hitler's Spies*, pp. 346–7.

133 Curry's account of pre-war Abwehr espionage in Britain (*Security Service*, pp. 125–6), written in 1945–6, now requires to be revised and updated.

134 'Major Christopher Draper', n.d., TNA KV 2/365. 'Pre-War Espionage on behalf of Germany in Great Britain', March 1942, TNA KV 3/47. Draper, *Mad Major*.

135 Hinchley Cooke, Minute 7, 19 Aug. 1937, TNA KV 2/19. 'Pre-War Espionage on behalf of Germany in Great Britain', March 1942, TNA KV 3/47. *Security Service*, p. 136.

136 Andrew, *For the President's Eyes Only*, p. 90.

137 *Security Service*, pp. 148, 163.

138 Minute 34, 8 Feb. 1938, TNA KV 2/2618.

139 Security Service Archives.

140 See below, p. 248.

141 *Security Service*, pp. 127–8.

142 Ibid.

143 TNA KV 3/205–8.

144 TNA KV 3/206.

145 Masterman, *Double-Cross System*, pp. 36–9. The MI5 SNOW files are in TNA KV 2/444–53; description of SNOW from KV 2/444.

146 Masterman, *Double-Cross System*, pp. 39–40.

147 Security Service Archives. The first public identification of Folkert van Koutrik as an Abwehr-controlled double agent, based on captured Abwehr files, is in Farago, *Game of the Foxes*, ch. 11.

148 See below, pp. 241-2, 244-5.
149 Guy Liddell diary, 30 Aug. 1939.
150 Dilks (ed.), *Cadogan Diaries*, pp. 204-6. Andrew, *Secret Service*, p. 605.

SECTION C: THE SECOND WORLD WAR

Introduction: The Security Service and its Wartime Staff: 'From Prison to Palace'

1 According to a Security Service colleague, the author of the phrase was Major Malcolm Cumming.
2 Security Service Archives.
3 Recollections of a former Security Service officer.
4 Security Service Archives.
5 'It girls' father was Pink Panther thief', *Sunday Times*, 23 Sept. 2007.
6 Memoir by Milicent Bagot, Security Service Archives. On Bagot's early Service career, see above, p. 131.
7 Security Service Archives.
8 Security Service Archives.
9 Security Service Archives.
10 Security Service Archives.
11 Security Service Archives.
12 Security Service Archives.
13 Lady Kell, 'A Secret Well Kept', IWM.
14 Kell to Cadogan, 8 Dec. 1938, Cabinet Office papers.
15 Cadogan to Sir Warren Fisher, 23 Dec. 1938, Cabinet Office papers.
16 Sir James Rae (Treasury) to C. Howard Smith (Foreign Office), 31 Jan. 1939, Cabinet Office papers.
17 Curry later noted: 'For some time previous to his retirement Sir Vernon Kell had felt the onerous nature of his duties weighed heavily on him.' *Security Service*, p. 163.
18 Director General's report on the Security Service, Feb. 1941, TNA KV 4/88.
19 See below, pp. 255-6.
20 Rose, *Elusive Rothschild*. On Blunt, see below, pp. 268ff.
21 Andrew, *Secret Service*, p. 642.
22 Christopher Andrew, interview with Sir Ashton Roskill, 1984.
23 Masterman, *Chariot Wheel*, p. 219.
24 Officer numbers (not including Security Control personnel in ports) declined to 323 in January 1944, to 273 in January 1945 and to 250 in July 1945. Secretarial and Registry staff (not including Security Control personnel in ports) declined to 852 in January 1944, to 748 in January 1945 and to 647 in July 1945. *Security Service*, p. 373.
25 According to official statistics, the numbers of 'other ranks' in Security Control personnel were 328 in September 1939, 825 in May 1943 and 415 (plus 39 ATS) in April 1945. The apparent decline in 'other ranks' during the last two years at a time when officer numbers were rising may be accounted for by increased use of locally recruited support staff who do not figure in central MI5 statistics. *Security Service*, pp. 323-4.
26 Ibid., pp. 396-7.
27 Recollections of a former Security Service officer. Security Service Archives. On Jane Archer's earlier career in the Service, see above, pp. 122, 128, 131.
28 See below, pp. 265ff.
29 Guy Liddell wrote in his diary on 18 Nov. 1940, 'I heard today that Jane had been sacked for insubordination. This is a very serious blow to us all. There is no doubt that she was on completely the wrong leg but somehow I feel that the incident should not have happened. I am trying to think whether there is anything to be done.' If Liddell did intervene, he was clearly unsuccessful.
30 Guy Liddell diary, 5 Nov. 1947.
31 See below, pp. 236, 343.

32 Rothschild wrote in September 1941: 'Before the new arrangements as regards women in the office, it was agreed that Miss Sherer should be an officer.' Security Service Archives.

33 See above, pp. 179ff. Since 1937 Knight's section had been known as B5b. In 1940 it became B5. In August 1941, according to a staff list, it was 'transferred to DG staff and renamed MS'.

34 Miller later revealed her role in *One Girl's War*.

35 See below, pp. 224–5.

36 Security Service Archives.

37 [Maxwell Knight], 'M.S. Report', TNA KV 4/227. In a note of October 1942 Knight said that he 'counted as officers' the two women (one of whom was Joan Miller) on his staff of eleven.

38 See above, pp. 80–81.

39 Guy Liddell diary, 30 Aug. 1939.

40 *Security Service*, pp. 149–50.

41 Further MI5 and police investigations led to a rise in the numbers of those interned to a total of about 2,000 by May 1940. Wilson, 'War in the Dark', pp. 59–60.

42 *Security Service*, pp. 149–50.

43 Guy Liddell, 1943, minute in D. G. White Lecture Notes, TNA KV 4/170.

44 Ibid., 17 Dec. 1939. Wilson, 'War in the Dark', p. 61.

45 *Security Service*, p. 148.

46 Ibid., ch. 4, part 1.

47 Wasserstein, *Britain and the Jews of Europe*, p. 88. Gilbert, *Finest Hour*, p. 342. Cross, *Swinton*, p. 225.

48 McLaine, *Ministry of Morale*, pp. 74, 80–1.

49 'Summary of the work of B3 sections during the war 1939–1945. An investigation of markings on telegraph poles for suspected codes', TNA KV 4/12.

50 'Report on the use of Carrier Pigeons by the German Intelligence Service, 1940–1941'; 'Report on the operations of B3 C in connection with suspected communication with the enemy by the use of carrier pigeons, during 1939–1945', TNA KV 4/10.

51 Wilson, 'War in the Dark'. Minute by Petrie, 13 April 1946; Minute no. 27 on Curry History, TNA KV 4/3.

52 See above, p. 53.

53 Andrew, *Secret Service*, p. 667.

54 Minute by Petrie, 13 April 1946; Minute no. 27 on Curry History, TNA KV 4/3.

55 'Recommendations of the Chiefs of Staff', WP(40)168, TNA CAB 65/7. Wilson, 'War in the Dark', p. 62.

56 Guy Liddell diary, 25 May 1940.

57 Muggeridge, *Chronicles of Wasted Time*, vol. 2, p. 108.

58 The best analysis of the Kent/Wolkoff case is Quinlan, 'Human Intelligence Tradecraft and MI5 Operations in Britain', ch. 5. My own account draws on Dr Quinlan's.

59 'Proofs of statements for the case WOLKOFF', 11 June 1940, Proof 1, statement of M/Y, TNA KV 2/841, s. 140c.

60 Dorril, *Blackshirt*, pp. 450, 492. Thurlow, *Fascism in Modern Britain*, p. 53.

61 'Proofs of statements for the case WOLKOFF', 11 June 1940, Proof 1, statement of M/Y, TNA KV 2/841, s. 140c. Bearse and Read, *Conspirator*, p. 134. Liddell succeeded Harker as head of B Division in June 1940.

62 [Knight], 'M.S. Report', TNA KV 4/227. On Joyce, see above, pp. 193–4.

63 'Proofs of statements for the case WOLKOFF', 11 June 1940, Proof 1, statement of M/Y, TNA KV 2/841, s. 140c.

64 Ibid.

65 'From M/Y re Anna and Kira WOLKOFF', 16 May 1940, TNA KV 2/840, s. 49a.

66 'Proofs of statements for the case WOLKOFF', 11 June 1940, Proof 1, statement of M/Y, TNA KV 2/841, s. 140c.

67 Bearse and Read, *Conspirator*, p. 129.

68 B5b (Knight) report on visit to US embassy, 19 May 1940, TNA KV 2/840, s. 57a. 'Case of Anna Wolkoff, Tyler Kent, and Others', 22 May 1940, TNA KV 2/840, s. 57g. 'From Foreign Office enclosing memorandum on Kent case by the United States Government', 29 Aug. 1944 (report dated 17 Aug. 1944), TNA KV 2/544, s. 86a. 'Tyler Kent', June 1944,

TNA FO 371/38704, s. 2. 'Report by M.K. re interview with KENT', 28 May 1940, TNA KV 2/840, s. 80a. Griffiths, *Patriotism Perverted*, pp. 125–42. Quinlan, 'Human Intelligence Tradecraft and MI5 Operations in Britain', pp. 236–7.

69 'B.5b report on interrogation of Tyler KENT, at the American Embassy', 20 May 1940, TNA KV 2/543, s. 22a.

70 Bearse and Read, *Conspirator*, pp. 6, 164; Leutze, 'Secret of the Churchill–Roosevelt Correspondence', p. 467.

71 Gilbert, *Finest Hour*, pp. 485–6. After Kent and Wolkoff had been tried in camera, the press were allowed into the Old Bailey on 7 November, after Roosevelt's re-election, to see them sentenced to, respectively, seven and ten years' imprisonment.

72 Guy Liddell diary, 21 May 1940.

73 War Cabinet minutes, 22 May 1940, TNA CAB 65/7. Wilson, 'War in the Dark', p. 79.

74 Dorril, *Blackshirt*, p. 500.

75 Wilson, 'War in the Dark', p. 73.

76 TNA KV 2/898.

77 Cross, *Swinton*, pp. 225–9. As deputy chairman Swinton brought in the former MI5 officer Joseph Ball from Conservative Central Office.

78 Wilson, 'War in the Dark', p. 72.

79 Security Service Archives.

80 *Security Service*, p. 163.

81 Sir Horace Wilson, 'Security Service', 11 June 1940, Cabinet Office papers.

82 Kell diary, 10 June 1940, IWM Kell papers.

83 Kell to Cadogan, 8 Dec. 1938, Cabinet Office papers.

84 Holt-Wilson to Lady Holt-Wilson, 11 June 1940; Lady Holt-Wilson to Sir Eric Holt-Wilson, 12 June 1940, CUL Holt-Wilson papers.

85 Kell to Cadogan, 8 Dec. 1938, Cabinet Office papers.

86 Cadogan to Sir Warren Fisher, 23 Dec. 1938, Cabinet Office papers. When Fisher, the chairman of the Secret Service Committee, saw Kell in January 1939, he 'agreed that Harker was the right man to succeed' him. Sir James Rae (Treasury) to C. Howard Smith (Foreign Office), 31 Jan. 1939, Cabinet Office papers.

87 Sir Horace Wilson to Sir James Grigg, 11 June 1940, Cabinet Office papers.

88 More precisely, Harker was to be 'responsible to the Lord President [Chamberlain until October 1940] through [Swinton]'. In practice his dealings seem to have had been exclusively with Swinton. Sir Horace Wilson to Lord Swinton, 11 June 1940, Cabinet Office papers.

89 Eric Holt-Wilson to Audrey Holt-Wilson, 11 June 1940, CUL Holt-Wilson papers. Unwilling to serve under Harker, Holt-Wilson accepted a post in the War Office constabulary on 1 July; Holt-Wilson to Lady Holt-Wilson, 2 July 1940, CUL Holt-Wilson papers (I am grateful to Dr Nicholas Hiley for this reference).

90 Security Service Archives.

91 Christopher Andrew, interview with the late Sir Ashton Roskill, 1984.

92 Hinsley and Simkins, *British Intelligence in the Second World War*, vol. 4, p. 65.

93 *Security Service*, p. 170.

94 Security Service Archives.

95 Director General's report on the Security Service, Feb. 1941, TNA KV 4/88.

96 Hinsley and Simkins, *British Intelligence in the Second World War*, vol. 4, p. 68.

97 *Security Service*, pp. 119–20, 145–50. Guy Liddell diary, 6 Sept. 1940.

98 Hugh Trevor-Roper, 'The man who put intelligence into spying', *Sunday Telegraph* (Review section), 9 April 1995.

99 Guy Liddell diary, 3 July 1940.

100 Wilson, 'War in the Dark', pp. 88–9.

101 Stammers, *Civil Liberties in Britain*, ch. 2. Wasserstein, *Britain and the Jews of Europe*, pp. 102–4. Cross, *Swinton*, pp. 228–30.

102 Wilson, 'War in the Dark', p. 82.

103 Stafford, *Churchill and Secret Service*, pp. 180–1.

104 Wilson, 'War in the Dark', p. 82.

105 Cradock, *Know your Enemy*, pp. 18–19.

106 TNA CAB 93/2. Wilson, 'War in the Dark', p. 92.

107 See above, p. 223.

108 DG (Petrie) to Eden, 26 June 1944, TNA KV 4/87.

109 'History of DR18b detention', May 1945, TNA KV 4/256.

110 *Security Service*, p. 175.

111 Security Service Archives.

112 Work continued afterwards on eliminating unnecessary cards, destroying duplicates and amalgamating other files. The new card index, finally completed in March 1944, consisted of about one and a quarter million cards. Security Service Archives.

113 Recollections of a former Security Service officer.

114 Security Service Archives.

115 Security Service Archives.

116 Security Service Archives.

117 M. B. Heywood (Security Service) to Bursar, Keble College, 18 Oct. 1940. Keble College Archives, KC/BF 8/1/53.

118 Recollections of former Security Service officers.

119 Bursar, Keble College, to M. B. Heywood (Security Service), 3 May 1941. Heywood to Bursar, 5 May 1941, Keble College Archives, KC/BF 8/1/53. I am grateful to the College Archivist, Robert Petre, for copies of this correspondence.

120 Security Service Archives.

121 Most of the flowers were sold by the Duke and Duchess in aid of war charities. Security Service Archives.

122 Security Service Archives.

123 Recollections of a former Security Service officer.

124 Recollections of a former Security Service officer.

125 Recollections of a former Security Service officer.

126 Recollections of a former Security Service officer.

127 See below, p. 250.

128 Wilson, 'War in the Dark', p. 92.

129 Ibid., p. 82.

130 Churchill to Foreign and Home Secretaries, 25 Jan. 1941, TNA PREM 4/39/3. Wilson, 'War in the Dark', p. 93.

131 Baron Croft to Churchill, 25 Nov. 1940, TNA PREM 7/6.

132 Security Service Archives.

133 Before going to Number Ten, Lennox informed Liddell who wondered whether Lennox had been chosen to succeed Harker: 'I . . . told him that in my view neither he nor I were suitable, and if anybody was to come in Valentine Vivian was far the best choice.' Lennox 'entirely agreed'. Guy Liddell diary, 26 Nov. 1940.

134 Ibid.

135 Ibid.

136 Stafford, *Churchill and Secret Service*, pp. 182–3. Hinsley and Simkins, *British Intelligence in the Second World War*, vol. 4, pp. 68–9.

137 Minute by Petrie, 13 April 1946; Minute no. 27 on Curry History, TNA KV 4/3.

138 Petrie Report, 13 Feb. 1941, TNA KV 4/88. Hinsley and Simkins, *British Intelligence in the Second World War*, vol. 4, p. 69.

139 Minute by Petrie, 13 April 1946; Minute no. 27 on Curry History, TNA KV 4/3. Petrie was responsible through the Security Executive to the Lord President of the Council (then Sir John Anderson) for the running of MI5 but free from interference in staff matters and its day-to-day work. Petrie's appointment as DG was agreed at a meeting to discuss his report with Churchill, the Lord President, the Home Secretary and Swinton. Hinsley and Simkins, *British Intelligence in the Second World War*, vol. 4, p. 69.

140 Petrie kept a daily diary during his time as DG. After retiring in 1946, he left it in the safe of Charles Butler, Director of A Division. On Petrie's instructions, it was destroyed in 1951. Security Service Archives.

141 While Harker was director, Butler had also served as his deputy. Sir Horace Wilson, 'Security Service', 11 June 1940, Cabinet Office papers.

142 *Security Service*, pp. 201–2. For a detailed analysis of the responsibilities of MI5's wartime Divisions, see ibid., chs 4, 5.

143 Christopher Andrew, interview with the late Sir Dick White, 1984.

144 Christopher Andrew, interview with the late Sir Ashton Roskill, 1984.

145 Recollections of a former Security Service officer.

146 Recollections of a former Security Service officer.

147 Recollections of a former Security Service officer.

148 *Security Service*, p. 199.

149 See below, p. 256.

150 Masterman, *Chariot Wheel*, p. 212.

151 The medieval historian Christopher Cheney (later professor of medieval history at the University of Cambridge), who served in MI5 from June 1940 to October 1944, later told Christopher Andrew that he found MI5 files less gripping than the medieval manuscripts to which he could not wait to return.

152 That is the sense of many surviving memoirs, taped interviews and correspondence from wartime members of the Service, though the least enthusiastic were less likely to put their views on record.

153 Security Service Archives. See below, p. 808.

154 Security Service Archives.

155 Petrie to Duff Cooper, 13 March 1943, TNA KV 4/83, s. 3a.

156 Hinsley and Simkins, *British Intelligence in the Second World War*, vol. 4, p. 288.

157 See below, p. 287.

158 Rose, *Elusive Rothschild*, pp. 66–9.

159 Security Service Archives.

160 Rose, *Elusive Rothschild*, p. 70.

161 See above, pp. 30, 36–7.

162 Andrew, introduction to *Security Service*, p. 3.

163 Andrew, 'Churchill and Intelligence', p. 182.

164 See below, p. 305.

Chapter 1: Deception

1 See above, pp. 204–5.

2 Bond (ed.), *Chief of Staff*, p. 223n.

3 Dear and Foot (eds), *Oxford Companion to the Second World War*, p. 886.

4 See above, p. 200.

5 Guy Liddell noted in his diary that Putlitz had been shown the list by 'a member of the legation staff' (diary, 15 Sept. 1939). In post-war interrogation the head of The Hague Abwehr station at the time, Traugott Protze, revealed that 'In spite of a specific veto, the German ambassador confronted Putlitz with the facts [list] and Putlitz immediately fled with his servant.' Security Service Archives.

6 Guy Liddell diary, 15 Sept. 1939.

7 Security Service Archives.

8 Security Service Archives.

9 Bland to Sinclair, 27 Oct. 1939, NMM Sinclair MSS 81/091.

10 Hankey to Sinclair, 31 Oct. 1939, NMM Sinclair MSS 81/091.

11 Andrew, 'Secret Intelligence and British Foreign Policy', pp. 25–6. On the Venlo affair, see also Jeffery, *Official History of the Secret Intelligence Service*, part IV.

12 Curry later recalled phoning SIS about the fate of Stevens and 'his assistant'. Though personally acquainted with Stevens, he may not have known Payne Best's name. Unpublished memoirs (unpaginated) of a former Security Service officer; Security Service Archives.

13 See above, p. 242.

14 Guy Liddell diary, 12 Nov. 1939. A later scheme to get the head of the Abwehr station in Brussels, Dr Unterberg, to recruit 'Barton' for operations against Britain, thus allowing her to become a double agent, though getting off to a promising start, came to nothing. Security Service Archives.

15 Dilks (ed.), *Cadogan Diaries*, pp. 230–33.

16 See above, pp. 200–201.

17 See above, pp. 212–13.

18 Though van Koutrik does not appear to have known the name of either Putlitz or Krüger, he was able to provide identifying details. Security Service Archives.

19 Though there is no documentary evidence on the reasons for van Koutrik's flight to England, it is inconceivable that his Abwehr case officer, at one or more of their weekly meetings, had not explained what was expected of him if and when the SIS station returned to London. The Abwehr must have been anxious to retain the services of its only penetration agent in the British intelligence community – especially since, within the past year, van Koutrik had successfully identified the leading German agents of both SIS and MI5.

20 Security Service Archives.

21 The only operation by van Koutrik for E1c of which record survives was to investigate Dutch fishermen at Fleetwood in January 1941. Security Service Archives.

22 Security Service Archives.

23 Security Service Archives.

24 On the recruitment of Blunt, see below, p. 269.

25 Security Service Archives.

26 Security Service Archives.

27 Security Service Archives. In 1943 van Koutrik joined the Dutch navy.

28 Andrew, Secret Service, pp. 533–4.

29 Security Service Archives. On the unmasking of Captain King, the Soviet spy in the Foreign Office Communications Department, see below, pp. 263–4.

30 Security Service Archives.

31 The most important information on Hooper's career as a German agent came from Hermann Giskes, former head of the Abwehr in the Netherlands. Security Service Archives. Giskes, who was interrogated at Camp 020 (see below. p. 250), struck 'Tin-eye' Stephens as one of the ablest German intelligence officers he had encountered; Hoare (ed.), Camp 020, p. 356.

32 Security Service Archives.

33 A year before the outbreak of war the Abwehr had sent to Britain 'a private individual who had very good connections in high British government circles', who was expected to be 'questioned closely by the British about German policy'. With the personal approval of Canaris, he was supplied with a plausible mixture of information and disinformation likely to deceive the British. 'Preliminary note on the use by German Intelligence of Deception as an aid to military operations', Security Service Archives. No similar operation was mounted after the outbreak of war.

34 The continuing ability of German intelligence to run a successful deception operation was demonstrated by the SD Englandspiel in the Netherlands in 1942–3, which completely deceived SOE and cost the lives of fifty-four agents, as well as other Dutch civilians and about fifty RAF personnel. The limitations of German deception policy were shown, however, by the fact that the Englandspiel was not used for strategic deception. Dear and Foot (eds), Oxford Companion to the Second World War, pp. 338–40.

35 With the assistance of the Special Branch, the Security Service rounded up the entire resident German spy network in Britain as it existed in 1939, when it was far smaller than in August 1914. Karl Burger, Eugen Horsfall Ertz, Arthur Owens, P. W. Rapp, Stanley Scott and William Wishart were arrested on the outbreak of war, My Eriksson was interned shortly afterwards. Surviving MI5 files, however, are incomplete; there may have been other arrests. Security Service Archives. On arrests in August 1914, see above, pp. 50–51.

36 See above, p. 212. SNOW's ten-volume file is TNA KV 2/444–53.

37 TNA KV 2/468.

38 Masterman, Double-Cross System, pp. 40–41.

39 Ibid., p. 41. B13, 'Mathilde Caroline Krafft', 2 Dec. 1939, TNA KV 2/701, s. 46a.

40 'Selected papers from the CHARLIE case', TNA KV 2/454. Masterman, Double-Cross System, pp. 40–41.

41 Smith, 'Bletchley Park, Double-Cross and D-Day', pp. 283–4. Security Service, pp. 179, 207n. Holt, Deceivers, p. 127.

42 Masterman, Double-Cross System, pp. 42–3.

43 Guy Liddell diary, 19 May 1940.

44 MI5 was never certain where SNOW's real loyalties lay. See below, p. 258.

45 Masterman, Double-Cross System, pp. 43–4.

46 'Mr Dick White's lecture for new RSLO's', 9 Jan. 1943, p. 5, TNA KV 4/170, s. 1a.

47 Security Service Archives.

48 Obituary, T. A. Robertson, *The Times*, 16 May 1994. On the Invergordon Mutiny, see above, pp. 162–3.

49 Wilson, 'War in the Dark', p. 126.

50 Holt, *Deceivers*, p. 131.

51 Security Service Archives.

52 Security Service Archives.

53 Security Service Archives.

54 *Security Service*, pp. 232–3.

55 Masterman, *Double-Cross System*, p. 49.

56 Hinsley and Simkins, *British Intelligence in the Second World War*, vol. 4, p. 88.

57 Security Service Archives.

58 Hoare (ed.), *Camp 020*, p. 7. Macintyre, *Agent Zigzag*, pp. 113–14.

59 Hoare (ed.), *Camp 020*, pp. 16–17.

60 Ibid., pp. 137–40.

61 Guy Liddell diary, 22 Sept. 1940.

62 Hoare (ed.), *Camp 020*, p. 140n.

63 Guy Liddell diary, 3 Oct. 1943.

64 Hoare (ed.), *Camp 020*, p. 58.

65 *Security Service*, p. 229.

66 Hoare (ed.), *Camp 020*, p. 140. TATE later gave an alternative explanation for becoming a double agent which made no mention of his fury at SUMMER's 'betrayal': 'Nobody ever asked me why I changed my mind,' he said after the war, 'but the reason was really very straightforward. It was simply a matter of survival. Self-preservation must be the strongest instinct in man.' Andrew, *Secret Service*, p. 671.

67 TNA KV 2/61.

68 See below, pp. 300, 304, 309, 316.

69 Masterman, *Double-Cross System*, p. 66. *Security Service*, p. 250. Wilson, 'War in the Dark'.

70 While MUTT's deception campaigns were highly successful, his Norwegian colleague Tör Glad (JEFF), who was despatched with MUTT to Britain by the Abwehr, proved to be unreliable and was interned until 1945. Hoare (ed.), *Camp 020*.

71 Hinsley and Simkins, *British Intelligence in the Second World War*, vol. 4, p. 89.

72 A. G. Denniston (Director GC&CS) to 'C' (Menzies), 10 Dec. 1941, TNA HW 14. Smith, 'Bletchley Park, Double-Cross and D-Day', p. 287. Hinsley and Simkins, *British Intelligence in the Second World War*, vol. 4, p. 108. On the origins of ISOS, see above, p. 248.

73 TNA KV 2/845–66.

74 Howard, *British Intelligence in the Second World War*, vol. 5, pp. 18–19. The fullest accounts of GARBO's extraordinary career are: Pujol and West, *GARBO*; and Seaman (ed.), *GARBO*.

75 Guy Liddell diary, 26 March 1942.

76 Hinsley and Simkins, *British Intelligence in the Second World War*, vol. 4, p. 19.

77 Complaints about Cowgill from Montagu and the War Office, wrote Dick White, 'must prevent it being said that the attack upon Section V is due purely to M.I.5 rivalry'. Security Service Archives.

78 Security Service Archives.

79 Hinsley and Simkins, *British Intelligence in the Second World War*, vol. 4, p. 20.

80 Howard, *British Intelligence in the Second World War*, vol. 5, pp. 7–8. 'Formation of the W. Board in connection with Special [Double] Agents, 1939–1945', TNA KV 4/70.

81 Minutes in TNA KV 4/63.

82 Security Service Archives.

83 Security Service Archives.

84 In the 1920s Masterman was also reputed to be the best squash player in Oxford University. 'Times Portrait Gallery: J. C. Masterman', *The Times*, 10 Oct. 1958.

85 Masterman, *Double-Cross System*, pp. 90, 114.

86 See below, p. 298.

87 Security Service Archives.

88 Masterman, *Chariot Wheel*, ch. 21.

89 Masterman, *Double-Cross System*, pp. 58–9.

90 See above, pp. 245–6.

91 Masterman, *Double-Cross System*, p. 51.

92 Major Dixon (RSLO Cambridge) to Dick White, 14 Jan. 1941, TNA KV 2/60.

93 Captain P. E. S. Finney, 're Mills' Circus', 9 April 1941, TNA KV 4/211, s. 23a. Hotel details (subsequently amended) in 'Accommodation Plan', s. 38a.

94 B2a, 'Suggestions for dealing with Double Agents in case of invasion', 1 Feb. 1941, TNA KV 4/211, s. 1a.

95 Masterman, *Double-Cross System*, pp. 90–92.

96 B2a, 'Suggestions for dealing with Double Agents in case of invasion', 1 Feb. 1941, TNA KV 4/211, s. 1a.

97 TNA KV 2/448.

98 Unsigned letter to G.W., 12 March 1941, marked 'Handed to G.W. on 24.3.41 and memorised by him', TNA KV 4/211, s. 4a.

99 New Scotland Yard to T. A. Robertson, 25 March 1941, TNA KV 4/211, s. 19a.

100 T. A. Robertson to Major Stephens, 12 March 1941, TNA KV 4/211, s. 10a.

101 DG, 'Orders for Mr Atkinson', 3 April 1941, TNA KV 4/211, s. 22a.

102 No legal opinion by the Service Legal Adviser or any other lawyer appears to survive on this controversial subject.

103 Security Service Archives.

104 Alcázar had successfully deceived both the British ambassador in Madrid, Sir Samuel Hoare, who recommended him to the Foreign Office in what seemed to MI5 'the most fulsome terms', and the British press attaché, who described him as 'anti-German to the core'. Security Service Archives.

105 Security Service Archives.

106 West and Tsarev, *Crown Jewels*, p. 140.

107 Ibid., p. 141.

108 Security Service Archives.

109 Guy Liddell diary, 1 Jan. 1942.

110 Churchill was informed about this activity by a Security Service report on 1 June 1943. Security Service Archives.

111 Security Service Archives.

112 Though GW could no longer be used as part of the Double-Cross System, his loss was more than compensated by the expanding recruitment of other double agents.

113 Security Service Archives.

Chapter 2: Soviet Penetration and the Communist Party

1 Cadogan diary, 4 Sept. 1939, CCAC ACAD 1/8. Andrew, *Secret Service*, p. 606.

2 Washington embassy to Foreign Office, telegram, 3 Sept. 1939 (received 4 Sept. 1939), TNA KV 2/802, s. 7a.

3 Cadogan diary, 21, 25 Sept. 1939, CCAC ACAD 1/8. Andrew, *Secret Service*, p. 606.

4 Liddell noted on 20 September, 'It is doubtful if we shall prosecute.' Guy Liddell diary, 20 Sept. 1939.

5 On MI5 opposition to physical brutality in interrogation, see above, pp. 251–2.

6 Andrew, *Secret Service*, pp. 606–7. Cadogan to Treasury, 2 Dec. 1939, TNA T 162 574/ E40411. Cadogan diary, 26 Sept., 30 Nov. 1939, CCAC ACAD 1/8. Dilks (ed.), *Cadogan Diaries*, p. 235.

7 Harker to Gladwyn Jebb (Foreign Office), 8 Nov. 1939, TNA KV 2/802, s. 13ax.

8 On Sissmore's marriage see above, p. 220.

9 Archer to Vivian, 10 Nov. 1939, TNA KV 2/802, s. 13a.

10 Harker to Gladwyn Jebb (FO), 20 Nov. 1939, TNA KV 2/802, s. 16a.

11 Guy Liddell diary, 20 Jan. 1940, TNA KV 4/185.

12 'Information obtained from Krivitsky', TNA KV 2/805, s. 55x. This document is published in West, *MASK*, appendix 2.

13 'Report re interview with Krivitsky', 23 Jan. 1940, TNA KV 2/804, s. 1a. Contrary to the

initial expectation of Harker and Archer, Vivian took part in only the first few sessions of the debriefing.

14 Ibid.

15 Guy Liddell diary, 2 Feb. 1940.

16 Security Service Archives.

17 'Information obtained from Krivitsky', TNA KV 2/805, s. 55x.

18 West and Tsarev, *Crown Jewels*, pp. 88–9.

19 Andrew and Mitrokhin, *Mitrokhin Archive*, p. 119.

20 A point first persuasively made in Quinlan, 'Human Intelligence Tradecraft and MI5 Operations in Britain', pp. 290–97.

21 'Report re interview with Krivitsky', 23 Jan. 1940.TNA KV 2/804, s. 1a. Emphasis in original.

22 'Note to B. re secret document seen in Moscow by K.', 3 Feb. 1940, TNA KV 2/804, s. 29a.

23 The supposedly aristocratic breeding of the Cambridge Five became so deeply embedded in KGB mythology that Yevgeni Primakov, first head of the post-Soviet foreign intelligence service, the SVR, referred to Maclean, whom he knew personally, as a 'Scottish lord', and made the absurd claim that he gave up a family fortune large enough to pay the running costs of Soviet foreign intelligence. Andrew and Mitrokhin, *Mitrokhin Archive II*, p. 484.

24 'Information obtained from Krivitsky', TNA KV 2/805, s. 55x.

25 'B.4 note re F.O. Document', 10 Feb. 1940, TNA KV 2/804, s. 41a.

26 'Mally, Theodore', in 'Information obtained from Krivitsky', TNA KV 2/805, s. 55x.

27 See below, p. 343.

28 Andrew and Mitrokhin, *Mitrokhin Archive*, p. 87.

29 Security Service Archives.

30 Security Service Archives.

31 Security Service Archives. On King's arrest and trial, see above, p. 264.

32 Security Service Archives. Hooper did not admit to having worked for the Russians before the Second World War until 1957; Security Service Archives.

33 See above, p. 246.

34 In February 1941 Krivitsky was found dead from a gunshot wound in a New York hotel room. Despite the suicide note by his side, it is possible that he had been killed by a Soviet assassin.

35 See above, p. 185.

36 Security Service Archives.

37 On Blunt's visit to the Soviet Union, see Carter, *Blunt*, pp. 131–8.

38 Security Service Archives.

39 See above, p. 173.

40 Report by Blunt on his life and work for Soviet intelligence, submitted to the Centre in February 1943; cited by West and Tsarev, *Crown Jewels*, p. 133.

41 West and Tsarev, *Crown Jewels*, p. 134.

42 Security Service Archives.

43 West and Tsarev, *Crown Jewels*, p. 135.

44 The official reason for not keeping him on at Trinity after the expiry of his Research Fellowship was that there was 'nothing for Blunt to teach'; Security Service Archives. It is often supposed that Cambridge University in the 1930s was full of uninhibited homosexual coupling. In reality, much of Cambridge was as prejudiced against gays as the rest of Britain.

45 West and Tsarev, *Crown Jewels*, p. 132.

46 Security Service Archives.

47 Rose, *Elusive Rothschild*, p. 232.

48 Security Service Archives.

49 Penrose and Freeman, *Conspiracy of Silence*, p. 251.

50 Recollections of a former Security Service officer.

51 Recollections of a former Security Service officer.

52 Carter, *Blunt*, pp. 262–3.

53 Security Service Archives.

54 Security Service Archives.

55 Unpublished memoirs of J. C. Curry, who does not refer explicitly to Burgess's homo-

sexuality, noting euphemistically instead that 'there was reason to think that he belonged to a medical category which made him likely to be unstable and unreliable.' Security Service Archives

56 Blunt was also aware of Krivitsky's (correct) claim, excluded from the report, that Jack Hooper was a former Soviet agent. Security Service Archives.

57 West and Tsarev, *Crown Jewels*, pp. 144–6, 161–2, 170. Few of the reports and MI5 documents provided by Blunt to his Soviet case officers still survive in Russian intelligence archives.

58 West and Tsarev, *Crown Jewels*, pp. 159–61.

59 Hinsley and Simkins, *British Intelligence in the Second World War*, vol. 4, pp. 36–7, 81, appendix 2.

60 Recollections of a former Security Service officer and Security Service Archives.

61 Recollections of a former Security Service officer and Security Service Archives.

62 Hinsley and Simkins, *British Intelligence in the Second World War*, vol. 4, pp. 284–5.

63 Recollections of a former Security Service officer and Security Service Archives.

64 MI5 to Colonel Allen (GPO), 19 May 1942, TNA KV 2/1177, s. 142b, F2A to Hunter (B6), 1 July 1942, TNA KV 2/1177, s. 143e. F2A note, 12 June 1942, TNA KV 2/1177, s. 144d.

65 Recollections of a former Security Service officer and Security Service Archives. On Mrs Grist, see below, pp. 336–7.

66 Recollections of a former Security Service officer and Security Service Archives.

67 Security Service Archives.

68 Blunt's report in KGB archives is undated. West and Tsarev, *Crown Jewels*, pp. 154–5.

69 Security Service Archives.

70 Security Service Archives.

71 *Security Service*, p. 350. 'Note of interview with Oliver Charles Green at Brixton Prison on 11 Aug., 1942', TNA KV 2/2203, s. 69a. On the Green case, see Walton, 'British Intelligence and Threats to National Security, 1941–1951'.

72 Chief Constable Birmingham to MI5, 2 Dec. 1935, TNA KV 2/2203, s. 2a.

73 'Oliver Green', 30 Oct. 1942, TNA KV 2/2204, s. 125a. *Security Service*, p. 362.

74 *Security Service*, p. 350. 'Note of interview with Oliver Charles Green at Brixton Prison on 11 Aug., 1942', TNA KV 2/2203, s. 69a. Guy Liddell diary, 11 Aug. 1942, TNA KV 4/190. My analysis of the Green case draws on Walton, 'British Intelligence and Threats to National Security, 1941–1951'.

75 'Oliver Green', 30 Nov. 1942, TNA KV 2/2204, s. 125a.

76 'K.S. [King Street] microphone conversation between Green and Robson', 7 Oct. 1943, TNA KV 2/2206, s. 4a.

77 'The present state of the Green Case', 19 Oct. 1942, TNA KV 2/2203, s. 10a. M. Johnstone to H. J. Cleeve, 29 Nov. 1942, TNA KV 2/2233, s. 17a. W. J. Skardon 'Alan Ernest Osborne', 18 March 1953, TNA KV 2/2235, s. 183a. Home Office Warrant on Alonzo Elliott, 4 Feb. 1942, TNA KV 2/2236, s. 20a. 'Typewritten copy of statement made after caution by Alan Ernest Osborne to C. A. G. Simkins', 15 Dec. 1952, TNA KV 2/2205, s. 265z.

78 David Clarke, 'The case of D. F. Springhall', 25 Aug. 1943, TNA KV 2/1596, s. 300a.

79 *Security Service*, p. 363.

80 'Leakage of information from the Air Ministry', 16 June 1943, TNA KV 2/1596, s. 271bc. 'Court proceedings against Douglas Frank Springhall, 'Preliminary observations by MI5', 21 June 1943, TNA KV 2/1596. Guy Liddell diary, 17 June, 28 July 1943, TNA KV 4/192. 'The Springhall case', March 1950, TNA KV 2/1597, s. 388a.

81 Memo by Edward Cussen (MI5 Legal Adviser), 7 Oct. 1943, TNA KV 2/1598, s. 28a. 'The Springhall case', March 1950, TNA KV 2/1597, s. 388a. Guy Liddell diary, 1 Nov. 1943, TNA KV 4/192.

82 Guy Liddell diary, 7 Sept. 1943, TNA KV 4/192.

83 Ibid., 29 Sept. 1943.

84 *Security Service*, p. 357.

85 David Clarke, 'The case of D. F. Springhall', 25 Aug. 1943, TNA KV 2/1596, s. 300a.

86 Hinsley and Simkins, *British Intelligence in the Second World War*, vol. 4, pp. 286–7.

87 Andrew, *Secret Service*, p. 619.

88 David Clarke, 'Communists engaged on secret work', 21 Oct. 1943, TNA KV 4/251, s. 3a.

89 *Security Service*, pp. 346–8.
90 Hinsley and Simkins, *British Intelligence in the Second World War*, vol. 4, pp. 287–9. See above, p. 239.
91 Guy Liddell diary, 16 March 1943, TNA KV 4/191.
92 West and Tsarev, *Crown Jewels*, pp. 149–60, 168–9.
93 Andrew and Mitrokhin, *Mitrokhin Archive*, pp. 159–60.
94 Remarkably, the suspicions recurred among some in the Centre at the beginning of the Cold War. In 1948 Modrzhinskaya, still head of the British department, wrote a memorandum concluding that all the Cambridge Five were British deception agents. Lyubimov, 'Martyr to Dogma', pp. 278–9. In the middle years of the Cold War, Lyubimov was the KGB's leading British expert. Despite the defection of Philby, Burgess and Maclean to Moscow, he recalls being told even in the Gorbachev era by a former deputy head of KGB counter-intelligence: 'Philby and that whole crew – it was all a fiendishly clever plant by British intelligence.'
95 West and Tsarev, *Crown Jewels*, pp. 168–9.
96 Andrew and Mitrokhin, *Mitrokhin Archive*, pp. 183–4.
97 Duff Cooper to Churchill (copied to Roger Hollis), 26 Oct. 1943, TNA KV 4/251, s. 4a.
98 Security Service Archives.
99 West and Tsarev, *Crown Jewels*, pp. 309–10.
100 Security Service Archives. See above, p. 255.
101 Security Service Archives.
102 Hollis, 'The revolutionary programme of the communists', enclosed with Petrie to Sir Alexander Maxwell (Home Office), 6 July 1942, TNA KV 4/266, s. 7a. Kerr, 'Roger Hollis and the dangers of the Anglo-Soviet treaty of 1942'.
103 Roger Hollis, Minute 145a, 24 Dec. 1942, TNA KV 4/267.
104 Sir David Petrie, Minute 176a, 31 Jan. 1945, TNA KV 4/267. Walton, 'British Intelligence and Threats to National Security, 1941–1951'.
105 Roger Hollis, Minute 52a, 5 Sept. 1945, TNA KV 4/251. Walton, 'British Intelligence and Threats to National Security, 1941–1951'.
106 See below, pp. 341–2.
107 Security Service Archives.
108 Security Service Archives.
109 See below, pp. 510ff.

Chapter 3: Victory

1 Masterman, *Double-Cross System*, pp. 8–9, 58.
2 Howard, *British Intelligence in the Second World War*, vol. 5, pp. 20–1.
3 Shelley, 'Empire of Shadows'. Holt, *Deceivers*.
4 Howard, *British Intelligence in the Second World War*, vol. 5, p. xi.
5 West and Tsarev, *Crown Jewels*, pp. 308–9.
6 Ibid., pp. 317–19.
7 Holt, *Deceivers*, p. 43. An inquiry by Lord Gort concluded that Clarke 'seems in all other respects to be mentally stable'. Wilson, 'War in the Dark', p. 193.
8 Howard, *British Intelligence in the Second World War*, vol. 5, pp. 26–7.
9 Ibid., pp. 55–63.
10 Masterman, *Double-Cross System*, pp. 17, 109.
11 Tomás Harris was in B1G (Spanish counter-espionage), based in Jermyn Street, but worked in close co-operation with B1A, which he visited almost daily. Recollections of a former Security Service officer.
12 Sir Michael Howard calls their collaboration 'one of those rare partnerships between two exceptionally gifted men whose inventive genius inspired and complemented one another'. Howard, *British Intelligence in the Second World War*, vol. 5, p. 231.
13 Security Service Archives.
14 Carter, *Blunt*, pp. 94–5, 257. Harris's file also describes him as a close friend of Blunt's flatmate, Guy Burgess. His friendship with them, and also with Philby, led later to an investigation which uncovered no evidence of his involvement in Soviet espionage. Security Service Archives.

15 Howard, *British Intelligence in the Second World War*, vol. 5, pp. 62–3.

16 Holt, *Deceivers*, p. 268.

17 Security Service Archives.

18 Holt, *Deceivers*, p. 370.

19 Security Service Archives

20 Howard, *British Intelligence in the Second World War*, vol. 5, p. 89. Soon after devising the deception, Cholmondeley returned, for reasons unknown, to the Air Ministry. Security Service Archives.

21 Security Service Archives.

22 Macintyre, *Operation Mincemeat*, chs 9 & 1b. On Ivor Montagu see below, p. 381.

23 Bevan, 'Mincemeat', n.d., TNA CAB 154/67/63; cited by Holt, *Deceivers*, p. 376.

24 Macintyre, *Operation Mincemeat*, ch. 9.

25 Recollections of former Security Service officers.

26 Holt, *Deceivers*, p. 375.

27 Ibid., p. 374.

28 Recollections of former Security Service officers. Montagu, *The Man Who Never Was*.

29 Macintyre, *Operation Mincemeat*, ch. 22.

30 Duff Cooper to Petrie, 9 March 1943, TNA KV 4/83, s. 1a. Duff Cooper was so enthused by MINCEMEAT that in 1950 he published a novel based on it, *Operation Heartbreak*.

31 Guy Liddell diary, 10 March 1943.

32 Duff Cooper to Petrie, 9 March 1943, TNA KV 4/83, s. 1a.

33 *Security Service*, p. 231; Chapman's MI5 file is TNA KV 2/455–63.

34 'The HARLEQUIN case', enclosed with Petrie to Duff Cooper, 16 April 1943, TNA KV 4/83, s. 9a.

35 Ibid.

36 Duff Cooper to Petrie, 9 March 1943, TNA KV 4/83, s. 1a.

37 Guy Liddell diary, 10 March 1943.

38 Petrie to Duff Cooper, 13 March 1943, TNA KV 4/83, s. 3a.

39 Guy Liddell diary, 16 March 1943. ADB1 (White) to DG through DB, 26 March 1943, TNA KV 4/83, s. 5a. The limited number of Soviet espionage cases which came to light were, however, included in the monthly reports.

40 Zec was not in fact a controversial cartoonist, let alone subversive. After the war, Morrison apologized to him. Kellett, 'Philip Zec', pp. 87–95; Zec, *Don't Lose it Again!*, pp. 73–81 (I am grateful to Dr Nicholas Hiley for these references.)

41 ADB1 (White) to DG through DB, 26 March 1943, TNA KV 4/83, s. 5a.

42 This is confirmed by the recollections of former Security Service officers. Cf. Blunt (B1B) to DB, 13 July 1945, TNA KV 4/83, s. 61a.

43 Few details are available of how many classified British documents obtained by Soviet intelligence were passed to Stalin personally. It is known, however, that in 1935 these included over a hundred Foreign Office reports (Andrew and Elkner, 'Stalin and Intelligence', p. 73). The MI5 monthly reports to Churchill would probably have been, on average, of even greater interest to Stalin.

44 Arrangements were made for this and subsequent reports to be returned to the Security Service after Churchill had read them. ADB1 (White) to DG through DB, 26 March 1943, TNA KV 4/83, s. 5a.

45 Duff Cooper to Guy Liddell, 2 April 1943, TNA KV 4/83, s. 8a. Guy Liddell diary, 3 April 1943.

46 'Report on Activities of Security Service', with minute by Churchill of 2 April 1944, TNA KV 4/83, s. 7a. This report, like its successors, was returned to the Security Service after being read by Churchill.

47 Petrie to T. L. Rowan (No. 10), 23 Jan. 1946, Security Service Archives.

48 'Report on Activities of Security Service', n.d. [March 1943], TNA KV 4/83, s. 7a.

49 Duff Cooper to Guy Liddell, 2 April 1943, TNA KV 4/83, s. 8a.

50 'The HARLEQUIN case', enclosed with Petrie to Duff Cooper, 16 April 1943, TNA KV 4/83, s. 10a.

51 Third Report on Activities of Security Service, 1 June 1943, TNA KV 4/83, s. 16a. Since

HARLEQUIN had been captured by the Americans in North Africa, he became a US POW. H. P. Milmo (B1B) to SIS, 6 May 1943, TNA KV 2/268, s. 46a.

52 V. B. Carol (B1H) to ADB1 (through B1B, H. P. Milmo), 22 April 1943, TNA KV 2/268, s. 43b; H. P. Milmo to Major Stopford-Adams, 4 May 1943, TNA KV 2/268, s. 45a.

53 Second Report on Activities of Security Service, 1 May 1943, TNA KV 4/83, s. 13a.

54 Macintyre, *Agent Zigzag*, ch. 20.

55 Duff Cooper to Dick White, 5 May 1943, TNA KV 2/459; Macintyre, *Agent Zigzag*, p. 223.

56 Macintyre, *Agent Zigzag*, pp. 147-8, 176.

57 'Report on the Activities of the Security Service during June, 1944', 3 July 1944, TNA KV 4/83, s. 42a.

58 Apart from HARLEQUIN, GARBO was the only agent to be the subject of a special MI5 report to the Prime Minister in addition to being mentioned in some of the monthly reports. The fact that a copy of ZIGZAG's file was sent for by Duff Cooper suggests that he aroused a roughly comparable level of interest in the Prime Minister.

59 *Security Service*, p. 254.

60 'GARBO' (described in MI5 note of 5 Nov. 1943 as a 'report which Mr Duff Cooper prepared to show to the Prime Minister', based on information from the Security Service), TNA KV 4/83, s. 21a.

61 Guy Liddell diary, 22, 23, 24 June 1943.

62 Howard, *British Intelligence in the Second World War*, vol. 5, pp. 106-7.

63 Stafford, *Ten Days to D-Day*, pp. 48-50.

64 Masterman, *Double-Cross System*, pp. 152-4.

65 Stafford, *Ten Days to D-Day*, pp. 157-8.

66 'Tenth Report on Activities of Security Service', 7 March 1944, TNA KV 4/83, s. 29a.

67 Guy Liddell noted in his diary on 16 April 1944, 'ARTIST has made it clear that he knows all about the GARBO set up and believes it to be a blind.'

68 Reile, *Geheime Westfront*, pp. 194-205.

69 Masterman, *Double-Cross System*, pp. 140-41. Hinsley and Simkins, *British Intelligence in the Second World War*, vol. 4, pp. 117-18.

70 Christopher Harmer to Hugh Astor, 28 Oct. 1992, Security Service Archives.

71 Reile, *Geheime Westfront*, pp. 194-205.

72 Masterman, *Double-Cross System*, p. 142.

73 Hugh Astor to Roger Fleetwood-Hesketh, 10 July 1984, Security Service Archives.

74 Guy Liddell diary, 4 July 1944.

75 Willan, *D-Day to Berlin*, ch. 1.

76 Mary Sherer (B1A), 'Nathalie Sergueiew', 4 July 1944, TNA KV 2/466, s. 377a.

77 Masterman, *Double-Cross System*, pp. 143, 149, 161.

78 Security Service Archives. On the wartime bar on officer rank for female staff, see above, p. 220.

79 Sergueiev, *Secret Service Rendered*.

80 Mary Sherer (B1A), 'Nathalie Sergueiew', 4 July 1944, TNA KV 2/466, s. 377a.

81 Ibid.

82 'Tenth Report on Activities of Security Service', 7 March 1944, TNA KV 4/83, s. 29a. SIS transported the transmitter back to London on TREASURE's behalf; Mary Sherer (B1A), 'Nathalie Sergueiew', 4 July 1944, TNA KV 2/466, s. 377a.

83 Mary Sherer (B1A), 'Nathalie Sergueiew', 4 July 1944, TNA KV 2/466, s. 377a.

84 Masterman, *Double-Cross System*, p. 161.

85 'Report on the Activities of the Security Service during May, 1944', 3 June 1944, TNA KV 4/83, s. 41a.

86 'Report on the Activities of the Security Service during April, 1944', May 1944, TNA KV 4/83, s. 38a.

87 'Report on the Activities of the Security Service during May, 1944', 3 June 1944, TNA KV 4/83, s. 41a.

88 Mary Sherer (B1A), 'Nathalie Sergueiew', 4 July 1944, TNA KV 2/466, s. 377a.

89 Henceforth, however, Robertson considered it 'out of the question' to include disinformation in TREASURE's radio messages to Lisbon which thus made no further contribution to FORTITUDE deceptions. Ibid.

90 'Report on the Activities of the Security Service during May, 1944', 3 June 1944, TNA KV
   4/83, s. 41a. Stafford, *Ten Days to D-Day*, p. 204.

91 See above, pp. 297–8.

92 'Report on the Activities of the Security Service during May, 1944', 3 June 1944, TNA KV
   4/83, s. 41a. Stafford, *Ten Days to D-Day*, p. 204.

93 Masterman, *Double-Cross System*, p. 154. ARTIST is believed to have died in the Oranien-
   burg concentration camp. Hinsley and Simkins, *British Intelligence in the Second World War*,
   vol. 4, pp. 224–5.

94 Holt, *Deceivers*, pp. 565–7.

95 Ibid., p. 577. Stafford, *Ten Days to D-Day*, p. 307.

96 According to the official history of strategic deception (usually the most authoritative
   account), GARBO did not get through to Madrid until 6.08 a.m.; Howard, *British Intelligence
   in the Second World War*, vol. 5, p. 185. Some other accounts claim that GARBO did not
   make contact until 8 a.m.

97 Stafford, *Ten Days to D-Day*, pp. 306–8. Eisenhower's appeal to the French not to rise
   against the German occupiers until 'the proper time' could also have been interpreted as a
   veiled reference to the fact that further landings were planned – and for that reason, GARBO
   told the Abwehr, it was deplored by the PWE Director.

98 See above, p. 293.

99 Stafford, *Ten Days to D-Day*, pp. 308–9.

100 The Abwehr case officer claimed more speciously that, because GARBO's reports had left
    the high command 'completely forewarned and prepared', the arrival of his warning that the
    Allied invasion forces were on their way to the Normandy beaches would have had little
    greater impact 'had it arrived three or four hours earlier'. Howard, *British Intelligence in the
    Second World War*, vol. 5, p. 185.

101 'Report on the Activities of the Security Service during June, 1944', 3 July 1944, TNA KV
    4/83, s. 42a.

102 Holt, *Deceivers*, p. 581.

103 Howard, *British Intelligence in the Second World War*, vol. 5, pp. 189–91.

104 'Report on the Activities of the Security Service during June, 1944', 3 July 1944, TNA KV
    4/83, s. 42a.

105 Holt, *Deceivers*, p. 586.

106 Howard, *British Intelligence in the Second World War*, vol. 5, pp. 193–4.

107 T. E. Bromley (Foreign Office) to DG/Sec, 13 March 1944, TNA KV 4/83, s. 30a. For
    unexplained reasons, the Security Service produced a consolidated report for November 1943,
    December 1943 and January 1944, issued on 1 February 1944. This was the first report to be
    sent to Eden. The PUS, Sir Alexander Cadogan, seems to have read them with greater attention
    than the Foreign Secretary.

108 Eden had been made minister responsible for MI5 (not a responsibility he appears to have
    exercised very actively) at the suggestion of Duff Cooper when he gave up his post as chairman
    of the Security Executive late in 1943. *Security Service*, p. 400.

109 TNA KV 4/87. On D-Day plus 10, 16 June, the Vice Chief of the Imperial General
    Staff, Lieutenant General (Sir) Archibald Nye, informed Petrie that there was clear evi-
    dence that the timing of the Normandy landings had taken the Germans completely by
    surprise, and congratulated the Security Service, 'who contributed so much to the initial
    success of the operation', for its 'remarkable achievement'. Nye to Petrie, 16 June 1944, TNA
    KV 4/130.

110 TNA KV 4/130.

111 'Summary of the Activities of the Security Service up to September, 1944', 5 Oct. 1944,
    TNA KV 4/83, s. 51a. This was the first of the monthly reports to be signed by Petrie. The
    captured German map is reproduced in Holt, *Deceivers*, p. 569.

112 'Summary of the Activities of the Security Service up to September, 1944', 5 Oct. 1944,
    with minute by Churchill of 7 Oct. 1944, TNA KV 4/83, s. 51a.

113 Guy Liddell diary, 21 Dec. 1944.

114 Howard, *British Intelligence in the Second World War*, vol. 5, p. 169.

115 Dear and Foot (eds), *Oxford Companion to the Second World War*, pp. 1249–53.

116 Howard, *British Intelligence in the Second World War*, vol. 5, pp. 171–2.

117 Ibid., p. 174. B1A followed with some amusement subsequent German wrangles over the award of an Iron Cross to a non-combatant foreigner.

118 See above, p. 304.

119 T. A. Robertson, 'TREASURE', 15 June 1944, TNA KV 2/466, s. 367a. Mary Sherer (B1A), 'TREASURE', 17 June 1944, TNA KV 2/466, s. 368a.

120 'Report on the Activities of the Security Service during June, 1944', 3 July 1944, TNA KV 4/83, s. 42a.

121 See above, p. 288.

122 'Report on the Activities of the Security Service during June, 1944', 3 July 1944, TNA KV 4/83, s. 42a. For details of ZIGZAG's return, see Macintyre, *Agent Zigzag*, ch. 25.

123 Report by Michael Ryde, 26 July 1944, TNA KV 2/460. Macintyre, *Agent Zigzag*, p. 282. Most of ZIGZAG's messages to the Abwehr do not survive.

124 Michael Ryde to Tar Robertson, 13 Sept. 1944, TNA KV 2/460; Macintyre, *Agent Zigzag*, p. 282.

125 Macintyre, *Agent Zigzag*, p. 282. Masterman, *Double-Cross System*, p. 179.

126 'Report on the Activities of the Security Service during June, 1944', 3 July 1944, TNA KV 4/83, s. 42a.

127 Howard, *British Intelligence in the Second World War*, vol. 5, pp. 176–7.

128 Ibid., p. 177.

129 Ibid., pp. 180–81.

130 Guy Liddell diary, vol. 10, 25 Aug. 1944, TNA KV 4/194.

131 Ibid., 9, 11 Sept. 1944.

132 Ibid., 15 Sept. 1944.

133 Masterman, *Double-Cross System*, p. 181.

134 Macintyre, *Agent Zigzag*, pp. 295–6.

135 None of the messages transmitted and received by TATE during this period survive. However, later evidence shows that he was central to the V-2 deception. See below, pp. 314–16.

136 Hoare (ed.), *Camp 020*, pp. 217–25.

137 Macintyre, *Agent Zigzag*, chs 26–8.

138 Guy Liddell diary, 31 Oct. 1944. Oddly, this episode does not appear in Macintyre's excellent biography, *Agent Zigzag*.

139 Report by Michael Ryde, 24 Oct. 1944, TNA KV 2/460. Macintyre, *Agent Zigzag*, p. 305.

140 'Report on the Activities of the Security Service, March 1946', 4 April 1946, Security Service Archives. This episode too does not appear in Macintyre's biography.

141 The Security Service later informed Churchill: 'In the second half of 1944 there is no known case of the enemy sending an agent with a mission to the United Kingdom.' 'Report on the Activities of the Security Service during January, 1945', 19 Feb. 1945, TNA KV 4/83, s. 56a.

142 Masterman, *Double-Cross System*, pp. 170–71.

143 'Report on the Activities of the Security Service during January, 1945', 19 Feb. 1945, TNA KV 4/83, s. 56a.

144 Masterman, *Double-Cross System*, p. 181.

145 TATE's German case officer gave him a week's advance warning of a renewed V-1 attack in March when 275 were fired at British targets. 'Report on the Activities of the Security Service during February, 1945', 13 March 1945, TNA KV 4/83, s. 57a.

146 Dear and Foot (eds), *Oxford Companion to the Second World War*, pp. 1249–53.

147 Howard, *British Intelligence in the Second World War*, vol. 5, pp. 182–3.

148 The device was known to the Americans as 'snorkel' and to the British as 'snork'. Dear and Foot (eds), *Oxford Companion to the Second War*, pp. 981, 1080.

149 Howard, *British Intelligence in the Second World War*, vol. 5, p. 228.

150 'Report on the Activities of the Security Service during January, 1945', 19 Feb. 1945, TNA KV 4/83, s. 56a.

151 Howard, *British Intelligence in the Second World War*, vol. 5, pp. 228–30.

152 Masterman, *Double-Cross System*, p. 184.

153 Ibid., pp. 184–5.

154 Because of the decline in the B1A case-load, Astor had been earmarked for the Delhi Intelligence Bureau but instead asked for a transfer to SOE in the hope of being transferred to South-East Asia. Recollections of a former Security Service officer.

155 Guy Liddell diary, 4 May 1945.

156 Recollections of a former Security Service officer.

157 Gilbert, *Road to Victory*, ch. 69.

158 Security Service Archives.

159 Wilson, 'War in the Dark', p. 2.

160 LCS (44) 3, TNA CAB 81/78.

161 'Historical Record of Deception in the War against Germany and Italy', TNA CAB 154/100–101.

162 HC (49) 3, TNA CAB 81/80. The LCS, which had lapsed after the Second World War, was reconstituted early in 1947.

163 TNA CAB 154/104. Wilson, 'War in the Dark', pp. 221–6.

164 See below, p. 426.

SECTION D: THE EARLY COLD WAR

Introduction: The Security Service and its Staff in the Early Cold War

1 See above, pp. 148–52.

2 Recollections of former Security Service officers.

3 Aldrich, *Hidden Hand*, pp. 94–5. From 1932 to 1936 Strong had been seconded to the Security Service as DSO first in Malta, then in Gibraltar.

4 During the 1945 election campaign Churchill had warned, absurdly, of the danger that a Labour victory would result in the introduction of a British Gestapo.

5 Guy Liddell diary, 17 Dec. 1945, Security Service Archives. In transcribing Liddell's dictated diary, his secretary mistakenly called the DG designate 'Shillito'. Possibly in an attempt to spare Guy Liddell's feelings, Petrie told him that the Whitehall committee might have passed him over because it preferred him to have his hands 'free to deal with the intelligence side of things'.

6 Andrew, *Secret Service*, pp. 682–3. Charles Butler, Director A (administration), and Reginald Horrocks, head of Registry (with the rank of assistant director), seem to have sided with Sillitoe. Recollections of a former Security Service officer.

7 Recollections of a former Security Service officer.

8 Recollections of a former Security Service officer.

9 Security Service Archives. Recollections of a former Security Service officer.

10 Security Service Archives.

11 Report of the Committee appointed to inquire into the Interception of Communications, 1957 (Cmnd 283). Williams, *Not in the Public Interest*, pp. 134–5.

12 Security Service Archives.

13 Security Service Archives.

14 Guy Liddell diary, 26 Feb. 1946, Security Service Archives.

15 Security Service Archives.

16 Guy Liddell diary, 19 Nov 1946, Security Service Archives. Though Liddell's comments apply specifically to his meeting with Attlee on 19 November 1946, he noted: 'I had the same impression on the other occasions when I spoke to him, and, from what I can gather from others who have seen him, it is his usual form.'

17 Guy Liddell diary, 4 March 1950, Security Service Archives.

18 Ibid., 27 July 1950. Brook's initial judgement was perceptive. For the first half of the Cold War, the balance was arguably tilted too far in favour of counter-espionage.

19 'Norman Craven Brook', *Oxford DNB*.

20 Security Service Archives.

21 Security Service Archives.

22 The Security Service Act of 1989 did not alter this important distinction between the Security Service and the other intelligence agencies. Security Service Archives.

23 Bower, *Perfect English Spy*, pp. 137–8.

24 Security Service Archives.

25 Sir David Maxwell Fyfe to the Prime Minister, 25 June 1953, Home Office Archives. The other members of the committee were Sir Frank Newsam, Sir William Strang, Sir Norman Brook, Sir Harold Parker, General Sir Nevil Brownjohn and Sir Thomas Padmore.

26 Home Office Archives.

27 Home Office Archives.

28 Bower, *Perfect English Spy*, p. 138.

29 Trevor-Roper, 'The man who put intelligence into spying', *Sunday Telegraph* (Review section), 9 April 1995.

30 J. L. Garbutt to Sir David Maxwell Fyfe, 15 July 1953, Home Office Archives.

31 Security Service Archives. On the D-Notice Committee, see the official history by Nicholas Wilkinson, *Secrecy and the Media*.

32 After leaving Blenheim Palace in the autumn of 1945, a majority of the Service had moved to unsuitable temporary accommodation in Princes Gate. The DG, A and B Divisions remained in St James's Street.

33 Recollections of a former Security Service officer.

34 These figures do not include Security Control personnel at the ports, whose numbers continued to increase throughout the war: from 357 in September 1939 to 942 in May 1943 to 621 (plus 39 ATS) in April 1945. *Security Service*, pp. 323–4, 373.

35 Security Service Archives.

36 Security Service Archives.

37 Security Service Archives.

38 Security Service Archives.

39 Home Office Archives.

40 See above, pp. 281–2.

41 Home Office Archives.

42 Home Office Archives.

43 Home Office Archives.

44 Home Office Archives.

45 Home Office Archives.

46 Home Office Archives.

47 Home Office Archives.

48 Security Service Archives.

49 Recollections of a former Security Service officer.

50 Andrew, *For the President's Eyes Only*, pp. 292–6.

51 Recollections of former Security Service officers.

52 Security Service Archives.

53 Ministry of Defence War Book, Appendix D, Aug. 1963, TNA DEFE 2/225; cited by Hennessy, *Secret State*, pp. 177–80. Christopher Andrew visited the bunker on 10 September 2008.

54 Hennessy, *Secret State*, ch. 5.

55 See below, p. 493.

56 See below, Section D, ch. 10.

57 The Legal Adviser, Bernard Sheldon, among others, considered FJ 'much the clearest brain of the whole lot'. Recollections of former Security Service officers.

58 Home Office Archives.

59 Security Service Archives.

60 Recollections of a former Security Service officer.

61 Recollections of a former Security Service officer.

62 Recollections of a former Security Service officer.

63 See below, pp. 808, 819.

64 Security Service Archives.

65 See above, pp. 61, 85.

66 Recollections of a former Security Service officer.

67 Recollections of a former Security Service officer.

68 Recollections of a former Security Service officer.

69 Recollections of a former Security Service officer.

70 Wright, *Spycatcher*, p. 70.

71 Security Service Archives.

72 Security Service Archives.

73 On the 1931 reorganization, see above, p. 129.

74 Security Service Archives.

75 Even Peter Wright, who regarded Bagot as 'slightly touched', acknowledged her 'extraordinary memory for facts and files'; Wright, *Spycatcher*, pp. 37–8.

76 A former Security Service officer later recalled: 'In E1, under Milicent Bagot, I studied the activities of some international Communist front organisations in the UK. I was less happy here because of the dominant and possessive personality of Milicent, who seemed more concerned with form and detail, rather than content, and could also be rather rude to her officers.' Recollections of a former Security Service officer.

77 Recollections of a former Security Service officer.

78 The letter of appointment of the future DG John Jones appears to have been typical. He was told: 'You may like to know that the employment in question is pensionable, subject to a probationary period of two years, but it involves an obligation to serve anywhere in the Commonwealth for tours of three or four years each, amounting in all to between a quarter and a third of your total service.' Security Service Archives. In fact, Jones spent one year in Hong Kong, four and a half years in Singapore and three years at British Services Security Organization: a total of eight and a half years abroad out of thirty years' service, the predicted quarter to a third of his career.

79 Recollections of a former Security Service officer.

80 On Weldsmith, see above, p. 888 n. 97.

81 Recollections of a former Security Service officer.

82 Recollections of a former Security Service officer.

83 Recollections of a former Security Service officer.

84 Security Service Archives.

85 Security Service Archives.

86 Security Service Archives.

87 Security Service Archives.

88 How large the minority was is disputed. Ms Rimington acknowledges: 'Maybe it was not as bad as I remember. I was very low down in the hierarchy and from low down you often get a very partial view of what is going on.' Rimington, *Open Secret*, pp. 101–2.

89 Personal memoir by his brother.

90 Recollections of former Security Service officers.

91 Recollections of a former Security Service officer.

92 Recollections of former Security Service officers.

93 Recollections of a former Security Service officer.

94 Recollections of a former Security Service officer.

95 Recollections of a former Security Service officer.

96 Recollections of a former Security Service officer.

97 See above, pp. 400–401.

98 Rimington, *Open Secret*, p. 96.

99 Though A4 came in theory under the control of the Senior Officer in charge of A1, in practice it remained largely autonomous.

100 Security Service Archives.

101 Security Service Archives. By the later Cold War the word 'watcher' was regarded as rather demeaning and had passed out of Service vocabulary.

102 Recollections of a former Security Service officer.

103 Security Service Archives.

104 Security Service Archives.

105 See below, pp. 387–8.

106 Security Service Archives. The unconvincing reason given for the refusal to promote Skardon was that he was not equipped to occupy the full range of posts to which Service officers might be appointed.

107 Recollections of a former Security Service officer. Security Service Archives. Wright, *Spycatcher*, p. 45.

108 Wright, *Spycatcher*, p. 44. Security Service Archives.

109 Security Service Archives.
110 Security Service Archives.
111 Guy Liddell diary, 23 Jan. 1950, Security Service Archives.
112 Security Service Archives.
113 Wright, *Spycatcher*, pp. 47–8.
114 Security Service Archives.
115 Recollections of a former Security Service officer. Security Service Archives. Wright, *Spycatcher*, pp. 39–41.
116 Security Service Archives.
117 Cram made this assessment in a detailed discussion with Christopher Andrew after the US publication of *Spycatcher* in 1987.
118 Wright, *Spycatcher*, p. 54.
119 Security Service Archives.
120 See below, pp. 766–7.
121 Security Service Archives.
122 Wright, *Spycatcher*, p. 169.
123 Though A5 advised on and supervised the production of operational equipment, the manufacturing work was undertaken by external suppliers.
124 Security Service Archives.
125 Security Service Archives.
126 Security Service Archives.
127 Recollections of a former Security Service officer.
128 Recollections of a former Security Service officer.
129 Rimington, *Open Secret*, pp. 102–3.
130 Recollections of a former Security Service officer.
131 Security Service Archives. The five-year restriction was removed in 1975 as a result of the Sex Discrimination Act.
132 Recollections of a former Security Service officer.
133 Recollections of a former Security Service officer.
134 'The Report of the Committee on the Civil Service', Cmnd 3638 (1968).
135 Recollections of a former Security Service officer.
136 Security Service Archives.

Chapter 1: Counter-Espionage and Soviet Penetration:
Igor Gouzenko and Kim Philby

1 Andrew and Mitrokhin, *Mitrokhin Archive*, pp. 183–5.
2 See below, Section D, ch. 3.
3 The large literature on the Gouzenko case includes Bothwell and Granatstein (eds), *Gouzenko Transcripts*; Granatstein and Stafford, *Spy Wars*, ch. 3; Hyde, *Atom Bomb Spies*, chs 1, 2; Sawatsky, *Gouzenko: The Untold Story*; Brook-Shepherd, *Storm Birds*, ch. 21; Black and Rudner (eds), *Gouzenko Affair*. Christopher Andrew interviewed Mrs Gouzenko and her daughter (both of whom lived under assumed names) in Toronto in November 1991. The account of the Gouzenko case in this chapter draws on Andrew and Walton, 'The Gouzenko Case and British Secret Intelligence'.
4 See below, pp. 349–50.
5 Security Service Archives.
6 Hyde, *Atom Bomb Spies*, p. 30.
7 The most recent assessment is Black and Rudner (eds), *Gouzenko Affair*.
8 'Miscellaneous notes taken from Grant's safe, telegram from Moscow to Ottawa, 22 Aug. 1945', TNA KV 2/1427, s. 105a.
9 Alan Nunn May had first come to the attention of the Security Service in February 1938 when, as a representative of the British Association of Scientific Workers to the World Boycott Conference in London, he was noticed attending a 'Communist Party fraction meeting' outside the main conference; TNA KV 2/2209. There is no further record of him in Service files until after Gouzenko's revelations in 1945.
10 Andrew and Gordievsky, *KGB*, p. 326.

11 See above, p. 220.

12 Cecil, 'The Cambridge Comintern', p. 179.

13 Philby, *My Silent War*, p. 102.

14 Borovik, *The Philby Files*, p. 239.

15 The most reliable account of Volkov's attempted defection is in Brook-Shepherd, *Storm Birds*, pp. 40–53, which corrects a number of inventions and inaccuracies in Philby's version of events.

16 Andrew and Mitrokhin, *Mitrokhin Archive*, p. 182.

17 Andrew and Gordievsky, *KGB*, p. 379.

18 Guy Liddell diary, 5 Oct. 1945, Security Service Archives.

19 Andrew and Gordievsky, *KGB*, p. 379.

20 Andrew and Mitrokhin, *Mitrokhin Archive*, pp. 182–3.

21 Philby, *My Silent War*, p. 113.

22 West and Tsarev, *The Crown Jewels*, p. 238. Grant to the Director, telegram no. 244, 22 Aug. 1945, TNA KV 2/1427.

23 CXG telegram 273, 11 Sept. 1945, TNA KV 2/1420, s. 5a.

24 West and Tsarev, *Crown Jewels*, p. 238.

25 T. E. Bromley, 'Corby Case', 1 March 1946, TNA KV 2/1422, s. 86a.

26 'Ignacy Samuel Witczak', TNA KV 2/1635.

27 Philby, *My Silent War*, pp. 103–4.

28 Political Affairs Department, Commonwealth Relations Office, to High Commissioner Ottawa, telegram, 4 May 1950; Sir Percy Sillitoe (DG MI5) to S. P. Osmond, Prime Minister's Office, 5 May 1950, TNA PREM 8/1280.

29 Unsigned [Canadian] Memorandum, [25 March 1950], TNA PREM 8/1280. Among the evidence seen by Hollis was a notebook belonging to Israel Halperin (later tried and acquitted), seized in February 1946 by the RCMP, which contained a list of names and addresses, including that of Klaus Fuchs. As the Lord Chancellor, Viscount Jowitt, acknowledged after the trial of Fuchs in 1950, 'Subsequent events here have, of course, attached a significance to that name which it did not then bear,' *Parl. Deb. (Lords)*, 5 April 1950, col. 817. Jowitt and other government ministers made no reference to the role of Hollis, or any other MI5 officer, in the Gouzenko case. A top-secret Commonwealth Relations Office telegram to the Ottawa High Commission of 4 May 1950 noted that Hollis's 'attention was not repeat not specifically drawn to the address book or to . . . names contained in it . . . Security Service have still no copy of the address book.' TNA PREM 8/1280.

30 Hyde, *Atom Spies*, p. 49.

31 Ibid., pp. 37–38.

32 P. C. Gordon Walker, untitled memo to Lord Chancellor, 31 March 1950, TNA PREM 8/1280.

33 Guy Liddell diary, 16 Feb. 1946, Security Service Archives.

34 Ibid., 20 Feb. 1946. Hyde, *Atom Spies*, pp. 55–6. May also declined to identify his recruiter. MI5 later concluded that this was probably Engelbert Broda, a refugee Austrian Communist physicist who worked at the Cambridge Cavendish Laboratory from 1941 to 1947 before returning to Austria. Material from KGB archives revealed in 2009 confirms this conclusion. Against MI5 advice, Broda was employed on the wartime TUBE ALLOYS project; KGB archives show that he became a valued Soviet atom spy. In 1953, after May's release from prison, he married Broda's ex-wife. Gibbs, 'British and American Counter-Intelligence and the Atom Spies', pp. 58, 117–18. Haynes, Klehr and Vassiliev, *Spies*, pp. 64–9.

35 Alan Nunn May's Last Statement – Dictated to his step-granddaughter, Alice Evelegh, 23 Dec. 2002; cited by Gibbs, 'British and American Counter-Intelligence and the Atom Spies', p. 109.

36 Hyde, *Atom Spies*, pp. 44, 46, 55–60.

37 See below, p. 378.

38 Philby to R. Hollis, 19 Feb. 1946, TNA KV 2/1421, s. 64a.

39 Hollis to Philby, 19 Feb. 1946, TNA KV 2/1421, s. 65a.

40 Guy Liddell diary, 18 Sept. 1946, Security Service Archives. Though Philby took pride in deceiving Liddell, like his other intelligence colleagues, his memoirs suggest that he had a degree of affection for him and respect for 'his subtle and reflective mind'. Philby, *My Silent War*, p. 74.

41 Guy Liddell diary, 20 March 1946, Security Service Archives.

42 As late as October 1981, a note on ELLI concluded, 'The ELLI lead was extremely vague and has never been resolved.' Security Service Archives.

43 Wright, *Spycatcher*, pp. 278–86, 290, 293, 381. Chapman Pincher, *Their Trade is Treachery*, pp. 39–41.

44 Andrew and Gordievsky, *KGB*, pp. 26–7. Kerr, 'Roger Hollis and the Dangers of the Anglo-Soviet Treaty of 1942'.

45 Andrew and Gordievsky, *KGB*, pp. 310–12. On one significant point, Gouzenko also confused Blunt with his sub-agent ELLI, wrongly believing that ELLI had the access to the MI5 files on Russians in London enjoyed by Blunt. Like other significant KGB agents, Long's codename also changed over time. At one point he was called RALPH: West and Tsarev, *Crown Jewels*, pp. 130, 133.

46 'A Digest of CORBY's Information on the Organisation of the H.Q. of the Chief Directorate of Intelligence of the Red Army [GRU]', p. 18, enclosed with Philby to J. H. Marriott (MI5), 2 Nov. 1945, TNA KV 2/1421, s. 43a.

47 Memorandum from J. C. Curry to DDG, 1 Oct. 1946, TNA KV 4/158.

48 See below, Section D, ch. 3.

Chapter 2: Zionist Extremists and Counter-Terrorism

1 The Security Service reported to the Colonial Office early in 1946: 'In recent months, the Stern Group is reported to have increased its membership, and its *active* strength is now estimated by the C.I.D. as 500 . . . The strength of the Irgun is estimated between 1200 and 3500. The lower figure probably represents the number of trained fighters, while the higher figure would include auxiliaries and recruits.' Security Service Archives.

2 Walzer, *Just and Unjust Wars*, p. 197. I owe this reference to Dr Calder Walton.

3 On the Security Service's post-war Divisions, see above, p. 327.

4 On the wartime role of SIME and its post-war transition to Security Service control, see the 2007 University of Cambridge PhD thesis by Adam Shelley, 'Empire of Shadows: British Intelligence in the Middle East, 1939–1945'.

5 Recollections of former Security Service officers. Le Carré (David Cornwell) would have known Kellar during his career in the Security Service.

6 Maxine Magan, *In the Service of Empire*, p. 217. William Magan, *Middle Eastern Approaches*, p. 14.

7 William Magan, *Middle Eastern Approaches*, p. 91.

8 B3a (J. C. Robertson), Minute 19a, 29 March 1946, TNA KV 5/4.

9 DG (Petrie), Minute 24a, 30 March 1946, TNA KV 5/4. Walton, 'British Intelligence and the Mandate of Palestine', p. 439.

10 The Security Service reported that Begin, who had a £2,000 price on his head, was 'responsible in the past for the liquidation of members of the police and the military whose activities have been judged especially worthy of Jewish resentment in Palestine'. 'Threatened Jewish Activity in the United Kingdom, Palestine and Elsewhere', Aug. 1946, TNA KV 3/41.

11 Clarke, *By Blood and Fire*.

12 Recollections of a former Security Service officer.

13 Hennessy, *Never Again*, pp. 238–41. Acheson, *Present at the Creation*, pp. 172–3.

14 Security Service Archives.

15 'Threatened Jewish Activity in the United Kingdom, Palestine and Elsewhere', Aug. 1946, TNA KV 3/41. Walton, 'British Intelligence and the Mandate of Palestine'.

16 B3A, 'Present Trends in Zionism', 2 Sept. 1946, TNA KV 3/67.

17 SIS to H. J. Seager, MI5, 13 Feb. 1947, TNA KV 2/2251, s. 38a. Walton, 'British Intelligence and the Mandate of Palestine', p. 447.

18 Begin, *Revolt*, pp. 103, 308–11.

19 'Palestine: Terrorist Outrages. Extension to the United Kingdom', TNA CO 733/457/13.

20 Denniston, 'Government Code and Cypher School between the Wars', pp. 51–2. Cryptographic Reports issued by R Signals, No. 2 Wireless Company, Sarafand, Palestine, TNA HW 41/361–70.

21 Guy Liddell diary, 8 Oct. 1942, TNA KV 4/190, vol. 6.

22 Begin, *Revolt*, p. 148.

23 Security Service Archives.

24 Guy Liddell diary, 19 Nov. 1946, Security Service Archives.

25 'Extract from Report on interview with Kollek, forwarded by DSO Palestine, dated 18.8.45, reference DSO/P/13576', TNA KV 5/34, s. 57c. I am grateful to Jonathan Chavkin of the Cambridge Intelligence Seminar for this reference.

26 T. A. Robertson, Minute 2a, 19 Sept. 1946, TNA KV 4/216. Walton, 'British Intelligence and the Mandate of Palestine', p. 450.

27 A. J. Kellar, (B1B), Minute 86, 30 April 1945, TNA KV 2/1435.

28 J. C. Robertson, (B3A), Minute 19a, 29 March 1946, TNA KV 5/4. Walton, 'British Intelligence and the Mandate of Palestine', pp. 448–50.

29 B3A, 'Present Trends in Zionism', 2 Sept. 1946, TNA KV 3/67, s. 113a; F. C. Derbyshire, 'Report on Betar', 26 July 1946, TNA KV 5/4, s. 57d.

30 Security Service Archives. The names of the agents, originally recorded in the minute, have been obliterated. The file itself exists only in microfilm; the original was destroyed.

31 B3A, 'Present Trends in Zionism', 2 Sept. 1946, TNA KV 3/67, s. 113a.

32 Security Service Archives.

33 Security Service Archives.

34 Guy Liddell diary, 14 June 1947, Security Service Archives.

35 Burt, *Commander Burt of Scotland Yard*, pp. 126–7. Walton, 'British Intelligence and the Mandate of Palestine', p. 440.

36 Security Service Archives.

37 Security Service Archives.

38 H. E. Watts (Chief Inspector of Explosives), 'Outrages 1947–1948: letter bombs', TNA EF 5/12. Walton, 'British Intelligence and Threats to National Security, 1941–1951', p. 137.

39 Security Service Archives. Five alleged members of the Stern Gang had been arrested in Paris on 22 May. In the room of one of them bomb-making equipment and plastic-explosive wrappings were discovered which matched those used in the Colonial Office bomb and material found in Knouth's suitcase. Security Service Archives.

40 'Stern Gang Give Bomb Girl a Party', *Daily Express*, 25 Aug. 1948. Knouth was released after serving eight months of her sentence.

41 Guy Liddell diary, 14 June 1947, Security Service Archives.

42 Security Service Archives.

43 Security Service Archives.

44 'Stern Gang Give Bomb Girl a Party', *Daily Express*, 25 Aug. 1948.

45 'Director-General [Sillitoe]'s Lecture', 16 March 1948, TNA KV 3/41, s. 7a. Walton, 'British Intelligence and Threats to National Security, 1941–1951', p. 168.

46 Security Service Archives.

47 Security Service Archives.

48 Security Service Archives.

49 Security Service Archives.

50 Security Service Archives.

51 Security Service Archives.

52 Security Service Archives.

53 Security Service Archives.

54 Security Service Archives.

55 Hennessy, *Never Again*, p. 239.

56 Brendon, *Decline and Fall of the British Empire*, p. 476.

57 Guy Liddell diary, 4 June 1947, Security Service Archives.

58 For other kidnappings, see TNA FO 371/52530.

59 Aldrich, *Hidden Hand*, pp. 262–3.

60 Security Service Archives.

61 Bethell, *Palestine Triangle*, p. 331.

62 Security Service Archives.

63 Heller, 'Failure of a Mission: Bernadotte and Palestine, 1948'; Marton, *Death in Jerusalem*.

64 Security Service Archives.

65 Security Service Archives. Stanley also claimed to have an influential Zionist friend in the

United States, who he said had '80 Senators working with him'. The Security Service assessed the friend as 'a gifted charlatan claiming a peculiar facility of access to influential political figures in the USA'; Security Service Archives.

66 Security Service Archives.
67 Security Service Archives.
68 Slowe, *Shinwell*, p. 286.
69 Security Service Archives.
70 Sillitoe later told the Chief of SIS, Sir Stewart Menzies, that 'Stanley's connection with Shinwell had . . . come to our notice, that he had spoken to Sir Eric Speed [Shinwell's PUS] about it and that as a result of enquiries made by the latter it was clear that Shinwell had acted perfectly correctly and refused to be drawn on the point.' Security Service Archives.
71 Baron, *Contact Man*, p. 145. There is some doubt about the date of the dinner party.
72 Ibid., pp. 145-6.
73 Security Service Archives.
74 Baron, *Contact Man*, p. 194.
75 Ibid., p. 187.
76 Ibid., pp. 167, 224.
77 Security Service Archives.
78 There is no evidence, however, that Stanley became involved in plans for terrorist attacks in Britain.
79 Security Service Archives.
80 Security Service Archives.
81 DOS (J. V. W. Shaw), Minute no. 131, 5 Aug. 1953, TNA KV 2/2252.
82 Security Service Archives.
83 Security Service Archives. A small number of mostly (if not entirely) female Jews slipped through the general prohibition.
84 Security Service Archives.
85 Security Service Archives.
86 When discussing a Jewish applicant in 1974, Director B and the DDG agreed that:

> There are no grounds for imposing a general bar on the recruitment of Jews of British nationality. An important factor however in determining the suitability of a candidate will be the extent to which he practises his faith. A secondary factor, and one more easy to assess during our formal interviews, will be the representational quality of the candidate.

Security Service Archives. A note records, after the rejection of the candidate at the staff board:

> Director B was invited at this very unusual and difficult case to record that the Board's rejection of the candidate should not prejudice our consideration of future applications from Jews. Were any such applications to be received, recruiting staff should satisfy themselves on two major counts before bringing a candidate to Final Board. First, that the candidate's loyalty to the Crown and the antecedents of his/her parents and grandparents offered no grounds to sustain the fear that the candidate could become subject to pressure; and secondly, that the candidate's physical appearance and demeanour was unlikely to inhibit his relations with other members of the staff and outside contacts of the Service.

87 Hennessy, *Never Again*, p. 239.
88 Comments as prejudiced as Attlee's occur from time to time in post-war Service files. In 1949, for example, B1A speculated that the quarrel between the Communist MP Phil Piratin and another Stepney Communist, Michael Shapiro, might 'simply be the ravings of two Jews jockeying for Party honours'. B1A, 'The Shapiro–Piratin Row', 14 Oct. 1949, TNA KV 2/2033, s. 268c.

Chapter 3: VENONA and the Special Relationships with the United States and Australia

1 Andrew, *For the President's Eyes Only*, pp. 150–56, 161–3.
2 Guy Liddell diary, 5 Feb. 1946, Security Service Archives. It had never occurred to Petrie to pay a liaison visit himself. Because of his failure to attach adequate importance to the Special

Relationship, he thought it sufficient to conduct liaison at a lower level. His poor personal relations with his DDG were probably also partly responsible for the humiliating formula which he proposed. Though Petrie may have suspected that in the course of the trip Liddell intended to see some of his children who were living in the US with his estranged wife, this is unlikely to have been the main reason for his decision.

3 VENONA replaced the previous codename DRUG (which had replaced BRIDE in the late 1950s) on 1 December 1961. Security Service Archives.

4 The method of decryption is summarized in a number of NSA publications, among them the account by Cecil James Phillips of NSA, 'What Made Venona Possible?' Reference to this account does not imply that it is corroborated by HMG or any British intelligence agency.

5 By 1948 GCHQ cryptanalysts were working full time on the VENONA material at the ASA HQ at Arlington Hall. www.nsa.gov/publications/publi00039.cfm.

6 Security Service Archives describe the collaboration as having taken place between GCHQ and the Armed Forces Security Agency (AFSA). The original collaboration, however, was between GCHQ and ASA. AFSA was not founded until July 1949, when it was set up in an attempt to co-ordinate SIGINT operations by the three armed services. It then took over the VENONA programme.

7 Security Service Archives.

8 www.cia.gov/csi/books/venona/preface.htm.

9 Guy Liddell diary, 25 Nov. 1947, Security Service Archives.

10 See below, pp. 375–6.

11 The VENONA decrypts, together with some explanatory material, are accessible on the NSA website: http://www.nsa.gov:8080/. Benson and Warner (eds), *VENONA*, provide a valuable introduction to, and a selection of, the decrypts.

12 See below, pp. 375–6.

13 Security Service Archives. For some details of the Soviet decrypts which revealed the penetration of External Affairs, see Ball and Horner, *Breaking the Codes*, chs 12, 14 .

14 Security Service Archives.

15 Off-the-record account of Chifley's comments given by Shedden during a visit to London to Guy Liddell; Guy Liddell diary, 27 July 1949, Security Service Archives.

16 Security Service Archives.

17 Security Service Archives.

18 Andrew, 'Growth of the Australian Intelligence Community', pp. 226–7; Ball and Horner, *Breaking the Codes*, pp. 174–6, 286.

19 Security Service Archives.

20 Andrew, 'Growth of the Australian Intelligence Community', pp. 223–5. Guy Liddell noted after a meeting with Shedden in London, 'There is clearly no love lost between Shedden and Evatt. Shedden fully realises how much Evatt's pose as a mediator between East and West had done to Australian relations with the United States.' Guy Liddell diary, 27 July 1949, Security Service Archives.

21 Both Evatt and the Secretary of External Affairs, Dr John Burton, had a general distaste for intelligence and had previously declined indoctrination into SIGINT, of which they appear to have had an imperfect understanding. Andrew, 'Growth of the Australian Intelligence Community', pp. 224–5; Ball and Horner, *Breaking the Codes*, pp. 150–53.

22 Ball and Horner, *Breaking the Codes*, pp. 288–90.

23 Andrew, 'Growth of the Australian Intelligence Community', pp. 226–9. The foundation of ASIO was, however, insufficient to restore US confidence in Australian security. The supply of US secret information (save for collaboration with the Australian SIGINT agency) did not resume until the mid-1950s.

24 Ball and Horner, *Breaking the Codes*, p. 290.

25 Security Service Archives.

26 Recollections of a former Security Service officer.

27 Ball and Horner, *Breaking the Codes*, chs 12–14, 17.

28 Security Service Archives.

29 Christopher Andrew, interview with Charles Spry in Melbourne, April 1987.

30 The SLO also arranged for the operational head of the ASIO investigation to study the VENONA material in London. Recollections of a former Security Service officer.

31 Ball and Horner, *Breaking the Codes*, chs 12-14, 17. Nosov was a TASS correspondent in Australia from 1943 to 1950, identified by Petrov after his defection in 1954 as an MGB co-optee. Though appointed head of the London TASS Bureau in 1952, he was refused a British visa. Security Service Archives.

32 Security Service Archives.

33 Guy Liddell diary, 4 May 1950. Security Service Archives.

34 Security Service Archives.

35 Ball and Horner, *Breaking the Codes*, chs 12-14, 17.

36 'At the persuasion of the C[ommunist] P[arty of] A[ustralia] acting, it is believed, on instructions from Moscow, Clayton and his wife were planning to leave Australia at the beginning of [April 1957]. They were booked by K.L.M. via Amsterdam to London but it was believed that their ultimate destination was an Iron Curtain country and that they might change planes for Eastern Europe at an intermediate stop.' Security Service Archives.

37 A. S. Martin (B2B) wrote in April 1949 that 'we guessed the [US VENONA] material existed some six months ago ... as a result of our work on the Australian case.' Security Service Archives.

38 Security Service Archives.

39 Security Service Archives. The USCIB was chaired by the Director of Naval Intelligence, Rear Admiral Inglis, and included the Director of Central Intelligence, Admiral Hillenkoeter (Security Service Archives). ASA was unwilling to share VENONA with either.

40 Security Service Archives.

41 Security Service Archives. Liddell noted that 'The FBI are playing up extremely well, and Thistle is in almost daily contact with Lamphere in the FBI who has been making a detailed study of the whole matter.' Guy Liddell diary, 21 April 1949, Security Service Archives.

42 Security Service Archives.

43 Security Service Archives.

44 Security Service Archives.

45 Security Service Archives. Inglis and USCIB had, however, been informed of the Australian VENONA.

46 H. B. Fletcher to D. M. Ladd, [FBI] Office Memorandum, 18 Oct. 1949. This important memorandum, which reports General Omar Bradley's decision not to inform Truman of the VENONA decrypts, was declassified late in 1997 as the result of a determined campaign by Senator Daniel Patrick Moynihan as chairman of the Commission on Reducing and Enforcing Government Secrecy; Moynihan, *Secrecy*, pp. 69-73. Fletcher's version of events was confirmed by G. T. D. Patterson (SLO Washington); Security Service Archives.

47 Donovan, *Conflict and Crisis*, pp. 338-9.

48 Moynihan, *Secrecy*, pp. 69-73. Benson and Warner (eds), *VENONA*, p. xxiv.

49 Security Service Archives.

50 Andrew, 'The VENONA Secret'. Christopher Andrew, interviews with Dr Cleveland Cram, September 1996. Because CIA employed very much stricter vetting procedures than OSS, it does not appear to have been penetrated by Soviet agents in the early Cold War.

51 See below, pp. 427-8.

52 Andrew, 'The VENONA Secret'.

53 Since the intermittent Soviet reuse of one-time pads, the basis of the VENONA breakthrough, did not begin until several months after the German invasion of the Soviet Union in June 1941, the messages intercepted and recorded up to August 1941 proved of little post-war value to GCHQ.

54 Security Service Archives.

55 Of the twenty-five telegrams sent by the Centre to the London residency in the period 15-21 September 1945, twenty-four were decrypted in whole or part; Security Service Archives.

56 See below, Section D, ch. 6.

57 Security Service Archives.

58 Security Service Archives. Material from KGB archives published in 2009 identifies QUANTUM as Boris Podolsky, a Russian-born US physicist. Haynes, Klehr and Vassiliev, *Spies*, pp. 73-5.

59 Security Service Archives.

60 Security Service Archives.

61 Benson and Warner (eds), *VENONA*, pp. xxviii, 167–70. KGB files show that Weisband had been recruited as a Soviet agent in 1934; Weinstein and Vassiliev, *Haunted Wood*, p. 291.

62 Interviews with Cecil Phillips and Meredith Gardner in the BBC Radio 4 documentary *VENONA*, written and presented by Christopher Andrew (producers: Mark Burman and Helen Weinstein), first broadcast on 18 March 1998.

63 Weinstein and Vassiliev, *Haunted Wood*, p. 291.

64 Security Service Archives.

65 Security Service Archives.

66 Benson and Warner (eds), *VENONA*, pp. xxvii–xxviii.

67 Interview with Meredith Gardner by Christopher Andrew, broadcast in the BBC Radio 4 documentary *VENONA*. Claims that Philby made further visits to AFSA and looked over Gardner's shoulder as he decrypted VENONA are inaccurate. A Security Service report in 1986 concluded that, 'apart from Weisband and Philby there are no known spies who had access [to VENONA].' Security Service Archives.

68 Security Service Archives.

69 Security Service Archives.

70 A CIA study confirms that Philby regularly received translated VENONA decrypts and assessments from AFSA. www.cia.gov/csi/books/venona/preface.htm.

71 Security Service Archives.

72 Because of lack of usable evidence, Weisband was never prosecuted for espionage. After his suspension from AFSA on suspicion of disloyalty, he was convicted of contempt for failing to attend a federal grand jury hearing on Communist Party activity and sentenced to a year's imprisonment (Benson and Warner (eds), *VENONA*, p. xxviii).

73 Some of the decrypts which identified Fuchs, Greenglass and the Rosenbergs are reproduced in ibid. On Fuchs, see below, pp. 386–8.

74 See below, pp. 431–2.

75 Security Service Archives.

76 Security Service Archives.

77 See below, p. 433.

78 Security Service Archives.

79 Security Service Archives.

80 Security Service Archives. The final total of KGB, GRU and naval GRU messages between Moscow and Stockholm decrypted in whole or part was over 450; www.nsa.gov/publications/publi00039.cfm.

81 Security Service Archives. The first published analysis of the X Group by Nigel West mis-identifies NOBILITY as Ivor Montagu and INTELLIGENTSIA as Haldane; West, *Venona*, ch. 3. West was, however, the first historian to pay serious attention to the GRU decrypts.

82 Security Service Archives. Following a Commons question in 1997, an MI5 officer noted, 'As far as I can tell from the VENONA records we have never seriously attempted to identify BARON.' Security Service Archives. Peter Wright (*Spycatcher*, p. 238) identified BARON as 'probably' the Czech intelligence officer Karel Sedlacek, as does West, *Venona*, pp. 67–9. NSA regards BARON as unidentified; www.nsa.gov/publications/publi00039.cfm.

83 Security Service Archives.

84 Security Service Archives.

85 Security Service Archives.

Chapter 4: Vetting, Atom Spies and Protective Security

1 Security Service Archives.

2 A. J. D. Winnifrith, 'The Evolution of the Present Security System in the Civil Service', 5 Dec. 1955, Security Conference of Privy Counsellors, S.C.P.C.(55)4, 6 Dec. 1955, TNA CAB 134/1325. Winnifrith's memorandum does not identify the Communist private secretary.

3 Ibid.

4 See above, p. 348.

5 Cabinet Committee on Subversive Activities, 'The Employment of Civil Servants etc. Exposed to Communist Influence', 29 May 1947, GEN 183/1, TNA CAB 130/20.

6 Minute by Attlee, 21 Dec. 1947, GEN 183/1, TNA CAB 130/20.

7 Security Service Archives.

8 Security Service Archives.

9 Security Service Archives.

10 Security Service Archives.

11 Initially the Treasury had envisaged that the cases of all those purged should be referred to a senior civil servant who would co-ordinate policy in the operation of the procedure. The other founder members of the Tribunal, in addition to Gardiner, were Sir Frederick Leggett and Sir Maurice Holmes, both retired civil servants. Holmes was soon replaced by W. J. Bowen, an ex-trade unionist, but continued to act as a reserve in the absence of any other member of the board. Security Service Archives.

12 Security Service Archives.

13 See below, pp. 400–401.

14 Security Service Archives.

15 It was originally envisaged that those sacked in the 'Industrial Purge' would be given a right of appeal, similar to that enjoyed by government servants. However, this concept was abandoned on the advice of both the TUC and employers as represented on the National Joint Advisory Council. Sackings were rare and handled by the industrial section, C2, in consultation at first with B1D (Communism in industry). Security Service Archives.

16 Hennessy and Brownfeld, 'Britain's Cold War Security Purge', p. 968.

17 Guy Liddell diary, 1 Jan. 1950, Security Service Archives.

18 Andrew, For the President's Eyes Only, p. 177.

19 Guy Liddell diary, 24 Sept. 1949, Security Service Archives.

20 Ibid.

21 Benson and Warner (eds), VENONA, p. xxv.

22 Guy Liddell diary, 20 Sept. 1949, Security Service Archives.

23 Details of the MI5 investigation into Fuchs are in TNA KV 2/1245ff. The most up-to-date secondary accounts include Gibbs, 'British and American Counter-Intelligence and the Atom Spies', ch. 3; Walton, 'British Intelligence and Threats to National Security', pp. 237–48.

24 Andrew and Gordievsky, KGB, p. 322.

25 Guy Liddell diary, 12 Sept. 1949, Security Service Archives.

26 James Robertson, 'Progress report', 16 Sept. 1949, TNA KV 2/1246, s. 124. TNA KV 2/1266–7 include telephone checks and eavesdropping reports on Fuchs.

27 TNA KV 2/1246; Walton, 'British Intelligence and Threats to National Security', p. 243.

28 Guy Liddell diary, 25 Jan. 1950, Security Service Archives.

29 Ibid., 29 Oct. 1949.

30 Ibid., 19 Dec. 1949.

31 Ibid., 21 Dec. 1949.

32 W. J. Skardon, 'Emil Julius Klaus Fuchs. Fourth, Fifth, Sixth and Seventh Interviews', 31 Jan. 1950, TNA KV 2/1250, s. 443ab.

33 James Robertson, Note, 24 Jan. 1950, TNA KV 2/1250, s. 433a.

34 Walton, 'British Intelligence and Threats to National Security', p. 244.

35 Security Service Archives.

36 Security Service Archives.

37 Guy Liddell diary, 27 March 1950, Security Service Archives.

38 Security Service Archives.

39 Security Service Archives. TNA KV 4/242, s. 52b.

40 'Extract from statement made by Dr. Fuchs to the FBI', 26 May 1950, TNA KV 2/1255, s. 689a; Goodman, 'Who is Trying to Keep What Secrets from Whom and Why?'

41 PV(50)11, Committee on Positive Vetting. Report, 27 Oct. 1950, TNA CAB 120/30. Hennessy, Secret State, p. 90.

42 GEN 183, 5th Meeting, 5 April 1950, TNA CAB 130/20.

43 Guy Liddell diary, 1 Jan. 1950, Security Service Archives.

44 JIC (50) 21 (Final), 'Clandestine use of atomic weapons', 12 June 1950, TNA CAB 158/9.

45 Andrew, For the President's Eyes Only, pp. 184–7.

46 Hennessy, Secret State, pp. xvii–xviii; TNA AVIA IR (50) 5 Final, 'Ministry of Defence. Imports Research Committee, report to Chiefs of Staff', 2 Nov. 1950, p. 5.

47 'Review of B Division', July 1950, TNA KV 4/162.

48 Security Service Archives.

49 'Security Service action in the case of Pontecorvo', Ministry of Supply brief drafted with help of Roger Hollis, 6 Nov. 1950, TNA KV 4/242, s. 54d. The best accounts of the Pontecorvo case which draw on declassified MI5 files are Gibbs, 'British and American Counter-Intelligence and the Atom Spies', ch. 5, and Walton, 'British Intelligence and Threats to National Security', pp. 248–52.

50 G. T. D. Patterson (SLO Washington) to London, 13 Nov. 1950, TNA KV 4/242, s. 64a.

51 Guy Liddell diary, 23 Oct. 1950, Security Service Archives.

52 Ibid., 21 Oct. 1950.

53 'Security Service Action in the case of Pontecorvo', TNA KV 4/242. Gibbs, 'British and American Counter-Intelligence and the Atom Spies', ch. 5.

54 Hollis to Geoffrey Patterson (SLO Washington), 23 Nov. 1950, TNA KV 4/252. Gibbs, 'British and American Counter-Intelligence and the Atom Spies', ch. 5.

55 G. T. D. Patterson (SLO Washington) to London, 22 Oct. 1950, TNA KV 4/242, s. 45a.

56 Meeting by DDG [Liddell] and Director B [White] with SIS, 21 Oct. 1950, TNA KV 4/242, s. 13a.

57 Michael Serpell, Account of meeting between Prime Minister and Director General, 2 Nov. 1950, TNA KV 4/242. Gibbs, 'British and American Counter-Intelligence and the Atom Spies', ch. 5.

58 Andrew and Gordievsky, *KGB*, p. 327.

59 Security Service Archives. Boris Davison's PF was declassified in 2007: TNA KV 2/2579–85.

60 A. J. D. Winnifrith, 'The Evolution of the Present Security System in the Civil Service', 5 Dec. 1955, Security Conference of Privy Counsellors, S.C.P.C.(55)4, 6 Dec. 1955, TNA CAB 134/1325.

61 'Boris Davison', April 1952 (paper handed by DG to Home Secretary on 15 May 1952), Security Service Archives.

62 GEN 183, 6th Meeting, 13 Nov. 1950, TNA CAB 130/20.

63 Ibid.

64 A. J. D. Winnifrith, 'The Evolution of the Present Security System in the Civil Service', 5 Dec. 1955, Security Conference of Privy Counsellors, S.C.P.C.(55)4, 6 Dec. 1955, CAB 134/1325.

65 See below, pp. 425–6.

66 GEN 183, 7th Meeting, 17 Aug. 1951, TNA CAB 130/20.

67 A. J. D. Winnifrith, 'The Evolution of the Present Security System in the Civil Service', 5 Dec. 1955, Security Conference of Privy Counsellors, S.C.P.C.(55)4, 6 Dec. 1955, CAB 134/1325.

68 GEN 183, 7th Meeting, 17 Aug. 1951, TNA CAB 130/20.

69 Walton, 'British Intelligence and Threats to National Security', p. 260.

70 Hennessy, *Cabinets and the Bomb*, p. 69.

71 The five ministers were Bevin, Morrison, A. V. Alexander (Minister of Defence), Lord Addison (Dominions Secretary) and John Wilmot (Minister of Supply). GEN 163, 1st Meeting, 8 Jan. 1947, 'Confidential Annex Minute 1. Research in Atomic Weapons', TNA CAB 130/16.

72 Lord Cherwell to Prime Minister, 29 July 1954; minute by Churchill, 4 Aug. 1954, TNA PREM 11/761.

73 Security Service Archives.

74 Two other committees reported to the Official Committee: the Personnel Committee (previously the Positive Vetting Committee), chaired by the Treasury, and the Committee on General Security Procedures, under the chairmanship of the Home Office. A Security Service officer, the Hon. J. L. Vernon, was seconded to the Cabinet Office in December 1953 to serve as secretary of both committees. The Personnel Committee, with Director C as the Service representative, worked comparatively smoothly. The Committee on General Security Procedures did not. In 1957, after the exasperated Security Service representative, Michael Serpell (C1), complained to the Home Office that it had not met for nearly two years, it was replaced by a new and more active Security (Policy and Methods) Committee, which also subsumed the JIC Security Committee. Security Service Archives.

75 SCPC(55)5, 'Role of the Security Service in Personnel Security. Note by the Security Service', 7 Dec. 1955, TNA CAB 134/1325.

76 How poor security remained was demonstrated on 15 September 2004 when five pro-hunt protesters burst into the Commons Chamber during a debate.

77 S (PS) (54), 6th Meeting, 17 Nov. 1954; TNA CAB 134/1165; cited by Schlaepfer, 'British Governance, Intelligence and the Communist Threat', ch. 3.

78 A. J. D. Winnifrith, 'The Evolution of the Present Security System in the Civil Service', 5 Dec. 1955, Security Conference of Privy Counsellors, S.C.P.C.(55)4, 6 Dec. 1955, TNA CAB 134/1325.

79 SCPC(55)5, 2nd Meeting, 9 Dec. 1955, TNA CAB 134/1325.

80 Attlee, 'Britain and America', p. 202; I owe this reference to Christian Schlaepfer of the Cambridge Intelligence Seminar.

81 Caute, Great Fear, p. 275.

82 Aldrich, Hidden Hand, pp. 426–7. These figures do not agree with those from an unattributable source given in Hennessy, Secret State, p. 97.

83 De la Mare, Perverse and Foolish, pp. 99–100. Aldrich, Hidden Hand, p. 547.

84 Security Service Archives.

85 Security Service Archives.

86 Recollections of a former Security Service officer.

87 Security Service Archives.

88 Security Service Archives.

89 See below, pp. 484ff.

90 Recollections of a former Security Service officer.

91 Security Service Archives.

92 Security Service Archives.

93 Aldrich, Hidden Hand, p. 549.

94 The first four volumes of the BBC, by Asa Briggs, make no reference to vetting. This subject will, however, be discussed in some detail in the forthcoming volume five by Professor Jean Seaton.

95 Harker told Kell after a meeting with Colonel Dawnay (BBC controllor of programmes) in 1933: 'I gather that the general [BBC] line is the one which we ourselves try to follow; that is to say that political views which look upon the ballot box as the proper political solution of their problems are reasonable politics; anything that goes outside the ballot box – such as Communism or Fascism – is considered subversive if not seditious.' Security Service Archives. Reith also sought information about Communists from the Met but was asked by Harker in 1935 to channel all his inquiries through MI5. Security Service Archives. When the BBC finally admitted the existence of vetting in 1985, it also acknowledged that it had been introduced almost half a century earlier at the request of the Corporation. 'Unions confront BBC after vetting is admitted', Financial Times, 20 Aug. 1985.

96 The 1937 arrangements were finally admitted by the BBC in 1985. 'Unions at BBC threaten action on BBC vetting', The Times, 20 Aug. 1985.

97 Security Service Archives. The only BBC staff to be positively vetted were a small number to be involved in war planning, whose vetting was carried out initially by the Ministry of Post and Telecommunications (later by the Home Office). Security Service Archives.

98 These statistics on the proportion of 'adverse reports' cover the period (during the Korean War) from 1 January 1952 to 19 July 1952; Security Service Archives. No similar statistics for any other period appear to survive in MI5 files.

99 A statement by the BBC Board of Management in August 1985 declared: 'Only the BBC decides who to appoint to any post within the corporation ...' 'Unions at BBC threaten action on BBC vetting', The Times, 20 Aug. 1985.

100 Security Service Archives.

101 Security Service Archives.

102 Security Service Archives.

103 Chris Hastings, 'Revealed: how the BBC used MI5 to vet thousands of staff', Sunday Telegraph, 2 July 2006.

104 Security Service Archives.

105 Neil Tweedie, 'National Archives: Harold Wilson considered scrapping licence fee due to

BBC spending', *Daily Telegraph,* 29 Dec. 2008. Professor Jean Seaton's research shows that BBC management, which was closely involved in government war planning, was also worried by possible Trotskyist disruption during a national emergency.

106 Security Service Archives.

107 See the forthcoming volume five of the BBC official history by Jane Seaton.

108 See, for example, David Leigh and Paul Lashmar, 'The Blacklist in Room 105', *Observer,* 18 Aug. 1985.

109 A. J. D. Winnifrith, 'The Evolution of the Present Security System in the Civil Service', 5 Dec. 1955, Security Conference of Privy Counsellors, S.C.P.C.(55)4, 6 Dec. 1955, TNA CAB 134/1325.

110 Security Service Archives.

111 Vassall, *Vassall,* p. 67.

112 Security Service Archives.

113 Security Service Archives.

114 Security Service Archives.

115 Security Service Archives.

Chapter 5: The Communist Party of Great Britain, the Trade Unions and the Labour Party

1 Security Service Archives.

2 MI5 report, 'The Communist Party: Its Strengths and Activities: Its Penetration of Government Organisations and the Trade Unions', 1 April 1948, Annex to GEN 226/1, 26 May 1948, TNA CAB 130/37.

3 Security Service Archives.

4 Security Service Archives.

5 Security Service Archives.

6 Security Service Archives.

7 Security Service Archives.

8 Security Service Archives. Such covert entries, though sometimes referred to as 'burglaries', do not meet the legal definition of burglary.

9 Guy Liddell diary, 27 May 1949, Security Service Archives.

10 See above, pp. 179ff.

11 After the war Knight's section was initially B4C; it was renamed B1K in 1952 and B1F in 1952. In the reorganization of 1953 it became F4.

12 Recollections of a former Security Service officer.

13 Security Service Archives.

14 Recollections of a former Security Service officer.

15 Security Service Archives.

16 Security Service Archives.

17 Security Service Archives.

18 Security Service Archives.

19 Security Service Archives.

20 Security Service Archives.

21 Security Service Archives.

22 Security Service Archives.

23 Security Service Archives.

24 Security Service Archives. The eavesdropping equipment at King Street was installed in 1942.

25 In 1948, however, an unidentified technician carried out tests for the CPGB which revealed abnormalities in the King Street telephone circuit. Security Service Archives.

26 'Source TABLE conversation', 22 Jan. 1948, TNA KV 2/1777, s. 474bc.

27 Security Service Archives. Philby's memoirs, published in 1968, revealed the wartime bugging of King Street.

28 Some details are given in the PF for Eileen Palmer, now in TNA KV 2/2508. Most other Communist Parties in the West and the Third World also received secret subsidies, usually delivered by the KGB. For further details, based on Russian sources, see Riva, *Oro da*

Mosca; Andrew and Mitrokhin, *Mitrokhin Archive*; Andrew and Mitrokhin, *Mitrokhin Archive II*.

29 Eaden and Renton, *Communist Party of Great Britain*, p. 114.

30 Security Service Archives.

31 TNA KV 2/2042–7. Obituary, Betty Reid, *Guardian*, 11 Feb. 2004.

32 Beckett, *Enemy Within*, pp. 121–3.

33 Security Service Archives.

34 Beckett, *Enemy Within*, ch. 8.

35 Hennessy, *Secret State*, pp. 78–9.

36 Sir Norman Brook to Attlee, 'Prime Minister's Briefs 1948', 31 Dec. 1947, TNA CAB 21/2244. Sherman, 'Learning from Past Mistakes?', p. 10.

37 Rust, *Story of the Daily Worker*, p. 123.

38 Guy Liddell diary, 9 Aug. 1950, Security Service Archives.

39 The Service's definition of 'full-time employee' included '(a) Part-time district officials of the Party; (b) Members of the Party employed at District headquarters in a clerical or other capacity'. Security Service Archives.

40 JIC(56)41, 'Likely Scale and Nature of Attack on the United Kingdom in a Global War up to 1960', 10 May 1956, TNA CAB 158/24. Sherman, 'Learning from Past Mistakes?', p. 39.

41 Hennessy, *Secret State*, pp. 132–3.

42 Security Service Archives.

43 Security Service Archives.

44 Security Service Archives.

45 Security Service Archives.

46 A memorandum of 14 December 1962 noted, 'The Security Service has no primary responsibility for any of the measures in the existing Government War Book'. Security Service Archives.

47 Security Service Archives.

48 Jeffery and Hennessy, *States of Emergency*, p. 196. Schlaepfer, 'British Governance, Intelligence and the Communist Threat', ch. 5.

49 Guy Liddell diary, 17 Nov. 1947, Security Service Archives.

50 MI5 report, 'The Communist Party: Its Strengths and Activities: Its Penetration of Government Organisations and the Trade Unions', 1 April 1948, Annex to GEN 226/1, 26 May 1948, TNA CAB 130/37.

51 Aldrich, *Hidden Hand*, pp. 443–4. GEN 226, 2nd Meeting, 1 June 1948, TNA CAB 130/37.

52 Aldrich, *Hidden Hand*, p. 454. Security Service Archives.

53 Taylor, *Trade Union Question in British Politics*, p. 43.

54 Security Service Archives.

55 The paper given to the Home Secretary did not identify the intelligence sources. 'Industrial Policy of the British Communist Party', Security Service Archives.

56 Security Service Archives. F1 did not mention exactly when the provision of industrial intelligence to the Ministry of Labour began, but said that it 'certainly antedates my own experience of sixteen years'.

57 Untitled note handed to Home Secretary by Sillitoe 'at Room 16 H[ouse] of C[ommons]', Security Service Archives.

58 Security Service Archives. The Ministry of Labour was initially involved in the working group, but subsequently withdrew.

59 Security Service Archives.

60 Security Service Archives.

61 Security Service Archives.

62 Security Service Archives.

63 Preface by John Freeman to Rolph, *All Those in Favour?*, pp. 9–10. Chapple, *Sparks Fly!*, p. 57.

64 Chapple had no doubt that Woodrow Wyatt was 'our best media friend'. Chapple, *Sparks Fly!*, pp. 63–4. Wyatt also provided financial support for Chapple (and possibly for Cannon) as they prepared for the civil action against the ETU leadership.

65 Ibid., ch. 6.

66 Recollections of a former Security Service officer.

67 Security Service Archives.

68 Security Service Archives.

69 Recollections of a former Security Service officer.

70 Chapple, *Sparks Fly!*, p. 65.

71 Recollections of a former Security Service officer.

72 Rolph, *All Those in Favour?*, ch. 6.

73 Thompson, *Good Old Cause*, p. 127. Eaden and Renton, *Communist Party of Great Britain*, p. 133. Francis Beckett also concludes that, when the CPGB denied any knowledge of ETU ballot rigging, 'The balance of probability seems to be that the Party was telling the truth'; *Enemy Within*, p. 151.

74 Eaden and Renton, *Communist Party of Great Britain*, p. 133.

75 Hyde, *I Believed*, p. 212. In 1951 SIS forwarded notes from Malcolm Muggeridge, a wartime SIS officer, on his discussions with Hyde about crypto-Communists, fellow-travellers and other matters. Graham Mitchell noted: 'I think this is interesting and good. It fits in very well with what is known. It should certainly be followed up.' Security Service Archives.

76 Beckett, *Enemy Within*, p. 104.

77 Security Service Archives.

78 Lilleker, *Against the Cold War*, p. 86.

79 Aldrich, *Hidden Hand*, pp. 456–7.

80 Douglas Hyde believed that Platts-Mills, Hutchinson and Solley were 'crypto-Communists' at the time of the 1945 election, but that Hutchinson left the CPGB soon afterwards. Zilliacus, however, he rated only as a fellow-traveller. Hyde also identified Stephen Swingler, Harold Lever and Geoffrey Bing as 'crypto-Communists' in 1945. All had subsequently left the Party, though Hyde thought Bing had rejoined. Security Service Archives. ' "I Believed" by Douglas Hyde', n.d. [*c*. Feb. 1951], Security Service Archives.

81 Lilleker, *Against the Cold War*, p. 89.

82 The fifteen Lost Sheep, in the order in which Morgan Phillips placed them on the list, were: J. Mack, S. Silverman, B. Stross, W. Warbey, G. Bing, S. Swingler, G. Wigg, H. Austin, G. Cooper, H. Davies, I. Mikardo, J. Silverman, C. G. P. Smith, W. Vernon and R. Chamberlain. Morgan Phillips, 'Lost Sheep' file, n.d., General Secretary's papers, Labour Party Archive, National Museum of Labour History, Manchester.

83 Security Service Archives.

84 Guy Liddell diary, 27 May 1949, Security Service Archives.

85 Lilleker, *Against the Cold War*, p. 100. Zilliacus lost his seat in the 1950 election but returned to the Commons in 1957.

86 Security Service Archives.

87 Chapman Pincher, 'A Communist Spy in the Labour Machine', *Daily Express*, 28 June 1968.

88 The handwritten list, on House of Commons notepaper, read as follows:

CP:–	*Possible*
W. Owen	Zilliacus
Warbey	V. Yates
Leo Abse	A. Lewis
F. Allaun	S. O. Davies
J. Silverman	B. Stross
J. Baird	Emrys Hughes
J. Mendelson	W. Griffiths
T. Driberg	S. Silverman
R. Parker	E. Fernyhough
S. Swingler	
J. Rankin	
H. Davies	
L. Plummer	
R. Kell[e]y	
T. Swain	
J. Hart	

The fact that a seventeenth name has been crossed out suggests that, as indicated by the inaccurate pencilled total on the document, the CP list may originally have contained more names. The list is filed in Security Service Archives.

89 See below, pp. 542–3.

90 Security Service Archives. The Service believed that the twenty-five MPs on Gordon Walker's list posed little threat and had limited influence. 'The ten MPs who appear to be of most significance' were:

Harold Davies (Leek): believed never to have been CP member but 'in contact with leading members of the Party'.

S. O. Davies (Merthyr Tydfil): there was 'evidence from LASCAR to show that if not of the Party, he is at least very close to it indeed'.

Richard Kelley (Don Valley): believed to have been a CPGB member 1932–55. There was some evidence that he left 'on purely tactical grounds' but 'The CPGB have, and quite rightly, a low opinion of his intelligence.'

Julius Silverman (Aston): 'He has, for a long time, had extremely close relations with the Soviet Embassy, and may well be considered a useful source of Parliamentary information, if nothing more.'

Stephen Swingler (Newcastle-under-Lyne): believed to have joined the CPGB c. 1934, left in 1940 and rejoined in 1945. 'According to Douglas Hyde, he was a crypto-Communist when he was first elected to Parliament in 1945, but there is sufficient evidence to suggest that he finally left about 1951. He has, nevertheless, continued to associate with extreme left-wing and Communist-dominated concerns ...'

Frank Allaun (Salford East): believed to have been a CPGB member 1936–44, after which he was variously assessed as a Titoist or Trotskyist and was still believed to have 'Trotskyist sympathies'. There were 'repeated reports that Allaun has been doing undercover work for the CPGB, though LASCAR reports that Peter Zinkin, the Daily Worker parliamentary correspondent, has no very high opinion of his integrity and considers that he usually follows a safe line, even though on the left'.

John Baird (Wolverhampton): 'The CPGB's assessment of him as a Trotskyist is probably correct.'

John Mendelson (Penistone): despite LASCAR evidence that he was a Party member in the 1940s, the CPGB 'appears to think that he may have been working for the Foreign Office, the Security Service or the Police'. It was probably wrong on all counts. In 1956 he was described by Harry Pollitt as a 'fishy' sort of character. He later came under some suspicion of espionage and an HOW was obtained in 1962 – apparently as a result of his meetings with a suspected Russian intelligence officer. In 1960 he had had meetings with a Czechoslovak intelligence officer. Though only part of Mendelson's file survives, no evidence of espionage appears to have been obtained.

Thomas Swain (North East Derbyshire): there were F4 reports alleging donations by him to the East Midlands district of the CPGB and the Daily Worker fighting fund. 'He is also known to have passed Minutes of the Executive Committee of the NUM to the Party.'

Sir Leslie Plummer (Deptford): two LASCAR reports in January 1961 'suggest that the Party thinks well of his activities'.

91 Security Service Archives.
92 Security Service Archives.
93 Chapman Pincher, 'Labour Made Loyalty Probe', Daily Express, 15 Feb. 1967.
94 Daily Mail, 15 Feb. 1967.
95 Security Service Archives.
96 Security Service Archives.
97 Security Service Archives.
98 Chapman Pincher, 'A Communist Spy in the Labour Machine', Daily Express, 28 June 1968. Pincher's article did not identify Bax by name.
99 Security Service Archives.
100 Security Service Archives.
101 Security Service Archives. Wilson became secretary for overseas trade at the Board of Trade in March 1947 before his appointment as president and cabinet minister in October.
102 Security Service Archives.
103 Security Service Archives.
104 Hennessy, Never Again, p. 417.
105 In April 1952 Bernard Buckman, a CPGB member who had been to a Moscow trade

conference, boasted that he had 'five MPs whom he has got together and is educating in progressive theory. The Party are very pleased with him for the work he has done. There is Harold Wilson, Sidney Silverman, Geoffrey Bing and so on.' The claim that Wilson's involvement in trade with the Soviet Union owed anything of significance to Bernard Buckman's influence is deeply improbable. Security Service Archives.

106 Richard West, 'Comments on the Week's News: Moscow', *New Statesman*, 14 June 1963.
107 'Harold Wilson Sees Molotov', *Daily Worker*, 22 May 1953.
108 Security Service Archives.
109 Security Service Archives. A minute on 3 July 1954 noted 'continued contact' between Wilson and Skripov, who had been 'identified almost with certainty as an Intelligence Officer'; Security Service Archives. Wilson's last recorded contact with Skripov was in February 1956; Security Service Archives. Skripov was later expelled from Australia. Security Service Archives.
110 Security Service Archives. Belokhvostikov was stationed as counsellor at the Soviet London embassy from June 1952 to November 1955; Security Service Archives.
111 He made this claim at his first meeting as Prime Minister with the DG, Sir Roger Hollis, in November 1964. Security Service Archives.
112 Andrew and Mitrokhin, *Mitrokhin Archive*, p. 528.
113 Security Service Archives.
114 *Daily Mirror*, 18 Jan. 1956.
115 *Sunday Dispatch*, 20 June 1956.
116 Pimlott, *Wilson*, p. 199.
117 Andrew and Mitrokhin, *Mitrokhin Archive*, p. 528.
118 Ziegler, *Wilson*, p. 94.
119 Andrew and Mitrokhin, *Mitrokhin Archive*, p. 528. Allegations that Wilson was ever a KGB agent derive not from credible evidence but from unfounded conspiracy theories, some of them elaborated by the KGB defector Anatoli Golitsyn, who may have known of the existence of Wilson's 'agent development file' and claimed after his defection in December 1961 that Wilson was a Soviet mole. When Gaitskell died suddenly in 1963, Golitsyn developed the bizarrely improbable theory that he had been poisoned by the KGB to enable Wilson to succeed him as Labour leader. Sadly, a minority of British and American intelligence officers with a penchant for conspiracy theory – among them James Angleton of the CIA and Peter Wright of MI5 – were seduced by Golitsyn's fantasies. Andrew and Mitrokhin, *Mitrokhin Archive*, pp. 528–9. Wise, *Molehunt*, pp. 97–9. Mangold, *Cold Warrior*, pp. 95–7.
120 Security Service Archives.
121 *Daily Worker*, 21 Jan. 1963.
122 Andrew and Mitrokhin, *Mitrokhin Archive*, p. 529.

Chapter 6: The Hunt for the 'Magnificent Five'

1 See below, p. 423.
2 See above, pp. 183–4.
3 See above, pp. 272–3, 280. Lyubimov, 'Martyr to Dogma', pp. 278–9.
4 Andrew and Mitrokhin, *Mitrokhin Archive*, pp. 202–3.
5 Security Service Archives.
6 Security Service Archives.
7 Security Service Archives.
8 Cecil, *Divided Life*, chs 6, 7. On Alger Hiss, see Andrew and Mitrokhin, *Mitrokhin Archive*, pp. 137–41, 176–7, 187, 189; Haynes, Klehr and Vassiliev, *Spies*, ch. 1.
9 Andrew and Mitrokhin, *Mitrokhin Archive*, p. 204.
10 Rees, *Chapter of Accidents*, p. 7.
11 Security Service Archives.
12 Security Service Archives.
13 Hill was a solicitor who had become the Service's legal adviser in 1946.
14 Guy Liddell diary, 23 Jan., 16 Feb. 1950, Security Service Archives.
15 Andrew and Mitrokhin, *Mitrokhin Archive*, pp. 204–6.

16 See above, pp. 345–6, 349.

17 Guy Liddell diary, 11 Sept. 1950, Security Service Archives.

18 Philby, *My Silent War*, pp. 152–4. Cecil, *Divided Life*, p. 118. Andrew and Mitrokhin, *Mitrokhin Archive*, pp. 206–7.

19 This is acknowledged by Maclean's controller, Yuri Modin; Modin, *My Five Cambridge Friends*, p. 199.

20 Philby, *My Silent War*, p. 156. The later KGB claim that the escapades which led to Burgess's recall were pre-planned is deeply implausible and not corroborated by, among other sources, Mitrokhin's notes from KGB files; the escapades were much in line with similar, unpremeditated 'scrapes' by Burgess over the previous few years.

21 Andrew and Mitrokhin, *Mitrokhin Archive*, p. 207.

22 Modin, *My Five Cambridge Friends*, pp. 199–204. Costello and Tsarev, *Deadly Illusions*, pp. 338–9.

23 Aldrich, *Hidden Hand*, p. 436.

24 Security Service Archives.

25 Security Service Archives.

26 Andrew and Mitrokhin, *Mitrokhin Archive*, p. 208. A4 stopped work at Saturday lunchtime until 1956; see above, p. 335.

27 Aldrich, *Hidden Hand*, p. 437.

28 Andrew and Mitrokhin, *Mitrokhin Archive*, p. 208.

29 Security Service Archives.

30 Andrew and Mitrokhin, *Mitrokhin Archive*, p. 208.

31 Ibid., p. 209.

32 Ibid.

33 Ibid., ch. 9.

34 Borovik, *Philby Files*, p. 294.

35 Philby, *My Silent War*, pp. 168–9.

36 Security Service Archives.

37 Security Service Archives.

38 Philby, *My Silent War*, p. 169.

39 Security Service Archives.

40 Security Service Archives. VENONA is not mentioned by name; there is reference only to 'the secret sources which eventually led to the suspicions about Maclean'.

41 See above, p. 376.

42 Security Service Archives.

43 Andrew and Gordievsky, *KGB*, p. 406. Modin, *My Five Cambridge Friends*, pp. 213–18. Modin is apparently unaware that Colville had recorded his 1939 meetings with Cairncross in his diary, and is wrongly sceptical of his ability to identify Cairncross as the author of a note describing one of those meetings, found in Burgess's flat.

44 Security Service Archives.

45 In the course of his eventual confession in 1964, Cairncross admitted that he had taken the initiative in arranging an emergency meeting with Modin on 7 April 1952 by making a chalk mark on a pre-arranged 'signal site'. Security Service Archives.

46 Security Service Archives.

47 Modin, *My Five Cambridge Friends*, pp. 221–4, 229–32. Andrew and Gordievsky, *KGB*, pp. 406–7.

48 Security Service Archives.

49 Security Service Archives.

50 Security Service Archives.

51 Philby, *My Silent War*, pp. 151, 171. Andrew and Gordievsky, *KGB*, pp. 439–40.

52 Recollections of a former Security Service officer.

53 Philby, *My Silent War*, ch. 13.

54 Security Service Archives.

55 Security Service Archives.

56 Security Service Archives.

57 Knightley, *Philby*, pp. 192–4. Philby, *My Silent War*, ch. 13.

58 Security Service Archives.

59 Philby, *My Silent War*, ch. 13.

60 Security Service Archives. 'B% Report' in the intercept indicates that 'Report' was a likely but not certain decryption; C% indicated a lesser likelihood.

61 Security Service Archives. The Gouzenko case was also known to a small number of Security Service and Whitehall officials.

62 Security Service Archives.

63 Security Service Archives.

64 Director D, Graham Mitchell, initialled without comment de Wesselow's note of 13 October commenting on the importance of the newly decrypted message, but there is no clear evidence that he saw the note of 18 October which specifically referred to Philby as one of the few possible candidates for STANLEY. Security Service Archives. Included in the case later mounted against Mitchell as a suspected Soviet agent was the unfounded claim that he had 'suppressed' the VENONA evidence. One paper setting out the case against him claimed that he saw de Wesselow's note of 18 October 1955. However, a marginal annotation to this paper adds, 'These facts are wrong!' Security Service Archives.

65 See above, p. 380.

66 Security Service Archives.

67 Security Service Archives.

68 Security Service Archives.

69 Security Service Archives.

70 Security Service Archives.

71 Seale and McConville, *Philby*, p. 226. Knightley, *Philby*, pp. 191–2, 203.

72 Security Service Archives.

73 It is uncertain whether Philby realized that Burgess had accompanied Maclean to Moscow at the insistence of the KGB. He later gave a rather embarrassed explanation to Phillip Knightley of his failure to see Burgess in Moscow after his defection in 1963: '[The KGB] kept us apart to avoid recriminations. I didn't get to see him before he died. I'm sorry we didn't meet one last time. He'd been a good friend.' (Knightley, *Philby*, p. 223.) The implication that the KGB was in some way to blame for Philby's refusal either to see Burgess or to attend his funeral was a misleading attempt by Philby to excuse his own callous behaviour. Maclean, who had never been a close friend of Burgess, gave the oration at his funeral. Philby later had an affair with Melinda Maclean.

74 Security Service Archives.

75 Security Service Archives.

76 Security Service Archives.

77 See below, pp. 420–21, 426.

78 Wright, *Spycatcher*, p. 144.

79 Furnival Jones noted that 'although we would have much preferred not to produce such a note for the Home Secretary, the [PUS] Charles Cunningham's advice had been that this was inescapable – the Home Secretary would not forget his request . . .' Security Service Archives.

80 Security Service Archives.

81 Rose, *Elusive Rothschild*, p. 230.

82 Borovik, *Philby Files*, pp. 344–5.

83 Security Service Archives.

84 Security Service Archives.

85 Security Service Archives.

86 Security Service Archives.

87 Security Service Archives.

88 Security Service Archives.

89 Security Service Archives.

90 Security Service Archives.

91 Security Service Archives.

92 Security Service Archives. In 1972 the URG was absorbed into K3.

93 A report of 29 August 1974, which shows the continuing influence of Golitsyn's mistaken definition of the Ring of Five, concluded: 'The fourth may have been Blunt although there

remains some doubt as to whether he was an original member of the Ring.' Security Service Archives.

94 See above, p. 380.
95 Security Service Archives.
96 Security Service Archives.
97 See below, p. 707.

Chapter 7: The End of Empire: Part 1

1 Security Service Archives. The files of SLO reports from New Delhi, as from most of the Empire and Commonwealth, were, alas, later destroyed because of shortage of space in the Security Service Archives. Extracts and copies of individual reports, however, sometimes surface in other files.
2 Security Service Archives.
3 Security Service Archives.
4 Security Service Archives.
5 Security Service Archives.
6 See below, p. 481.
7 Security Service Archives.
8 Guy Liddell diary, 31 May, 22 July 1949, Security Service Archives.
9 TNA KV 2/2509.
10 Guy Liddell diary, 22 July 1949, Security Service Archives.
11 Ibid., 6 Oct. 1949.
12 Andrew and Mitrokhin, *Mitrokhin Archive II*, pp. 314–15, 561 n. 20.
13 Security Service Archives.
14 Murphy, 'Creating a Commonwealth Intelligence Culture', p. 142. On the first Commonwealth Security Conference, see above, pp. 371–2.
15 'Sir Percy Sillitoe's Visit to South Africa', 14 Nov. 1949, TNA PREM 8/1283; cited by Chavkin, 'British Intelligence and the Zionist, South African and Australian Communities'.
16 Sillitoe to SLO Central Africa, 20 Dec. 1951, TNA KV 2/2053, s. 148a; cited by Chavkin, 'British Intelligence and the Zionist, South African and Australian Communities'.
17 De Quehen to DG, 31 Dec. 1951, TNA KV 2/2053, s. 152a; cited by Chavkin, 'British Intelligence and the Zionist, South African and Australian Communities'.
18 Security Service Archives.
19 Security Service Archives.
20 Security Service Archives.
21 Security Service Archives.
22 Security Service Archives.
23 Security Service Archives.
24 Security Service Archives.
25 Andrew and Mitrokhin, *Mitrokhin Archive II*, pp. 323, 330.
26 Security Service Archives.
27 Security Service Archives.
28 Security Service Archives.
29 Security Service Archives.
30 On KGB operations in India, see Andrew and Mitrokhin, *Mitrokhin Archive II*, chs 17, 18.
31 DG (Hollis) to Sir Burke Trend (cabinet secretary), 18 Nov. 1965, TNA CO 1035/187, no serial number. Freeman was concerned by news that budget cutbacks, imposed by the Treasury, might put the SLO's post at risk. Freeman was himself one of the targets of KGB active measures in India aimed at discrediting US and British policy. Before the 1967 Indian elections a bogus letter from Freeman forged by the KGB, claiming that the CIA was secretly giving vast sums to right-wing parties and politicians, appeared in the press. On this occasion, however, Service A (the KGB active measures department) slipped up. The latter wrongly identified Mr Freeman as *Sir* John Freeman. Andrew and Mitrokhin, *Mitrokhin Archive II*, pp. 317–18.
32 Rimington, *Open Secret*, pp. 66–7.
33 Louis and Robinson, 'The Imperialism of Decolonisation'.

34 In some posts SLOs/DSOs answered to the heads of SIME and SIFE.

35 A rare exception to the goodwill usually engendered by Sillitoe's imperial tours was a bad-tempered clash in 1948 with the head of the Malayan Security Service from which he eventually emerged victorious. See below, p. 448.

36 Recollections of former Security Service officers.

37 Security Service Archives.

38 Recollections of former Security Service officers.

39 On 28 October 1953 White wrote to Shaw: 'Now that my plans for the reorganisation of the office have come into effect, the Overseas Division of which you were the Director no longer exists. For the time being you have accepted the special responsibility for seeing that the new organisation is properly geared to the requirements of our overseas representatives. I feel, however, that the job of Director of Overseas Service is bound to suffer a gradual run-down as the new organisation finds its feet and, in the circumstances, have suggested, and you have agreed, that the date of your retirement should be fixed for the end of the year, 31 December 1953.' Security Service Archives.

40 Darwin, *Britain and Decolonisation*, p. 167.

41 Chin Peng, *My Side of History*, pp. 171–90. Much about Lai Teck's career remains mysterious; Bayly and Harper, *Forgotten Wars*, p. 350.

42 SIFE, which was responsible for 'the collation and dissemination of security intelligence affecting British territories in the Far East', was established in 1946 at the request of the Chiefs of Staff, prompted by a Mountbatten memo. Soon after its establishment, about twenty-five of its staff of sixty-five came from the Security Service (among them SIFE's head). Information from a former Security Service officer.

43 Security Service Archives. On SIFE see the pioneering MPhil thesis by Samuel Roskams, 'British Intelligence, Imperial Defence and the Early Cold War in the Far East'.

44 Guy Liddell diary, 18 Nov. 1947, Security Service Archives.

45 Bayly and Harper, *Forgotten Wars*, pp. 427–8. Aldrich, *Hidden Hand*, pp. 496–7

46 Chin Peng, *My Side of History*, pp. 212–14. Roskams, 'British Intelligence, Imperial Defence and the Early Cold War in the Far East', pp. 70–71.

47 On his earlier career in the Middle East, see above, pp. 352–3.

48 Security Service Archives.

49 Blake, *View from Within*, p. 89. Roskams, 'British Intelligence, Imperial Defence and the Early Cold War in the Far East', pp. 69–70.

50 This replacement of MSS had also been proposed in a report by Colonel Gray, who had been sent out from London to conduct an inquiry and later became commissioner of police in the Malayan Union. Security Service Archives.

51 Aldrich, *Hidden Hand*, pp. 496–501.

52 Bayly and Harper, *Forgotten Wars*, pp. 523–4. Aldrich, *Hidden Hand*, pp. 502–3.

53 Hennessy, *Having It So Good*, p. 304.

54 Chin Peng, *My Side of History*, pp. 268–9.

55 Bayly and Harper, *Forgotten Wars*, p. 524.

56 Smith, 'General Templer and Counter-Insurgency in Malaya'. Miller, *Jungle War in Malaya*, chs 8, 9. Smith provides a balanced assessment of conflicting accounts of Templer's contribution to victory.

57 Security Service Archives.

58 White's minute to Sillitoe turning down his appointment as director of intelligence in Malaya did not, understandably, mention his ambition to succeed him as DG. He gave three reasons. He considered his present post in MI5 to be more important; he wished to be on the MI5 Board of Directors when the new DG was appointed; and, for domestic reasons, he did not wish to accept a foreign posting. Dick White, Security Service Archives.

59 Security Service Archives.

60 Templer wrote in a letter of thanks on Morton's departure: 'You must . . . know how much I personally shall miss you. I used so very much to enjoy our talks together.' Morton's Indian memoirs in Security Service Archives.

61 Smith, 'General Templer and Counter-Insurgency in Malaya'. Miller, *Jungle War in Malaya*, chs 8, 9.

62 Chin Peng, *My Side of History*, pp. 324–6.

63 Security Service Archives.
64 Security Service Archives. Morton's successor as director of intelligence, Arthur Martin, was less successful and caused such ructions by his attempts to reorganize the Special Branch that Bill Magan had to be sent out to pour oil on troubled waters. Recollections of former Security Service officers.
65 Bayly and Harper, *Forgotten Wars*, pp. 496, 524.
66 See above, pp. 251–2.
67 'Interrogation. Notes on the Administrative, Technical and Physical Problems involved in the running of an Interrogation Centre', March 1961. Earlier, undated lecture notes reach the same conclusion, for example:

> Physical violence or mental torture – apart from moral and legal considerations – opposed to – short-sighted – like wilfully damaging engine of car wanted for long journey – under violence anyone will talk – you may get a confession to prevent torture but it will not be the truth – Intelligence gained usually useless.

68 Security Service Archives.
69 Comber, 'The Malayan Special Branch on the Malayan–Thai Frontier during the Malayan Emergency', pp. 88–94.
70 Recollections of former Security Service officers.
71 Comber, 'The Malayan Special Branch on the Malayan–Thai Frontier during the Malayan Emergency', pp. 88–94. The Emergency continued, informally, until well into the 1960s in the form of the 'Confrontation' in Borneo. At the height of the 'Confrontation', the Security Service had SLOs and supporting staff in Sarawak and North Borneo, as well as in Malaya, Singapore and on the staff of C-in-C Far East.
72 Security Service Archives.
73 Security Service to D. Bates (CO), 31 Oct. 1946; TNA CO 537/3566, s. 2. Security Service to Sir Marston Logan (CO), 3 Dec. 1946, TNA CO 537/3566, s. 6.
74 Nkrumah, *Autobiography*, pp. 45–6. On Nkrumah and WANS, see Walton, 'British Intelligence and Threats to National Security', pp. 291–2. The TNA sources in the remainder of this paragraph were first identified by Dr Walton.
75 B. H. Smith (MI5) to Special Branch, 29 June 1946, TNA KV 2/1847, s. 3a.
76 Telephone check on CPGB headquarters, 5 June 1947, TNA KV 2/1847, s. 11a.
77 C4, 'Note', 1 Nov. 1947, TNA KV 2/1847, s. 28a.
78 Captain R. W. H. Bellantine to Sir Percy Sillitoe, 16 March, 1948, TNA KV 2/1847; Nkrumah, *Autobiography*, p. 65.
79 On Nkrumah's post-imperial vision of sub-Saharan Africa, see, *inter alia*, his books *I Speak of Freedom* and *Africa Must Unite*.
80 G. T. D. Patterson (B3C), Minute 50, 1 April 1948, TNA KV 2/1848. M. J. E. Bagot (B1B), Minute 58, 30 April 1948, TNA KV 2/1848.
81 Andrew and Mitrokhin, *Mitrokhin Archive II*, p. 426.
82 Guy Liddell diary, 20 Dec. 1949, Security Service Archives. There appears to be no surviving written reference to 'nigger' by any other Security Service officer.
83 'Personality Note', June 1948, TNA KV 2/1847, s. 61b.
84 R. Stephens to Director General, 17 June 1949, TNA KV 2/1848, s.100a.
85 Walton, 'British Intelligence and Threats to National Security', pp. 302–4.
86 Guy Liddell diary, 21 Dec. 1950, Security Service Archives.
87 TABLE extract, 11 June 1951, TNA KV 2/1848, s. 160b; TABLE extract, 1 July 1951, TNA KV 2/1848, s. 174c; Sir John Shaw, Minute 209, 1 Jan. 1952, TNA KV 2/1850. Walton, 'British Intelligence and Threats to National Security', pp. 300–310.
88 Walton, 'British Intelligence and Threats to National Security', p. 260.
89 Security Service Archives.
90 Security Service Archives.
91 Security Service Archives.
92 Security Service Archives.
93 Hennessy, *Having It So Good*, p. 302.
94 'Record of the Conference of Colonial Commissioners of Police at the Police College, Ryton-on-Dunsmore', April 1951, p. 24, TNA CO 885/119.

95 Lonsdale, 'Jomo Kenyatta, God, and the Modern World', pp. 31–3.

96 DG (Sillitoe), draft letter to Sir Evelyn Baring (marked 'not despatched'), 9 Jan. 1953, TNA KV 2/2542, s. 374a. A shorter letter making the same point was despatched on 12 January; TNA KV 2/2542, s. 376a.

97 Walton, 'British Intelligence and Threats to National Security', pp. 319–21.

98 'Visit to England of the General Secretary of the Kikuyu Central Association, Johnstone Kenyatta', Jan. 1929–Feb. 1930, TNA CO 533/384/9. 'Johnstone Kenyatta', 11 Nov. 1931, TNA KV 2/1787, s. 2a.

99 Superintendent E. Parker, 'Secret Report on Communist Party Activities in Great Britain Among Colonials', 22 April 1930; cited in Howe, Anticolonialism in British Politics, p. 66.

100 MI6 to Captain Miller, MI5, 9 July 1930, TNA KV 2/1787, s. 1y.

101 Suchkov, 'Dzhomo Keniata v Moskve'. McClellan, 'Africans and Blacks in the Comintern Schools'. Andrew and Mitrokhin, Mitrokhin Archive II, pp. 4, 423–4.

102 MPSB to MI5, 6 Dec. 1933, TNA KV 2/1787, s. 19a.

103 McClellan, 'Africans and Blacks in the Comintern Schools'.

104 Kell to D. C. J. McSweeney (CO), 16 Dec. 1933; Sir Vernon Kell to Commissioner of Police, Kenya, 18 Jan. 1934, TNA KV 2/1787, s. 13a.

105 Home Office Warrant, 3 Jan. 1934, TNA KV 2/1787, s. 23a; Cross-reference, 18 Jan. 1934; Jane Archer, Minute 60, TNA KV 2/1787, ss. 9, 27a. Walton, 'British Intelligence and Threats to National Security', pp. 311–12.

106 Andrew and Mitrokhin, Mitrokhin Archive II, pp. 4, 423–4.

107 O. J. Mason (MI5) to J. D. Bates (CO), 29 Dec. 1945, TNA KV 2/1788, s. 248a.

108 B. M. de Quehen, SLO Central Africa, to DG, 23 July 1951, TNA KV 2/1788, s. 333b; cited by Walton, 'British Intelligence and Threats to National Security', p. 316. For corroboration of this report, see Andrew and Mitrokhin, Mitrokhin Archive II, pp. 504–5 n. 8.

109 DG (Sillitoe), draft letter to Sir Evelyn Baring (marked 'not despatched'), 9 Jan. 1953, TNA KV 2/2542, s. 374a. A shorter letter making the same point was despatched on 12 January; TNA KV 2/2542, s. 376a.

110 Security Service Archives.

111 Berman, 'Nationalism, Ethnicity and Modernity'.

112 Anderson, Histories of the Hanged, pp. 59–60. Lonsdale, 'Authority, Gender and Violence', pp. 59–60.

113 C. R. Major (SLO East Africa), to DG, 17 Nov. 1952, TNA KV 2/1788, s. 357c.

114 SLO East Africa Quarterly Review, 20 Oct. 1952, TNA KV 2/1788, s. 357b; Lonsdale, 'Kenyatta's Trials'.

115 Lonsdale, 'Kenyatta's Trials'. Anderson, Histories of the Hanged, pp. 62–8.

116 Recollections of a former Security Service officer. Broadbent was SLO in Kenya from February 1953 to July 1954, and in East Africa from July 1954 to May 1957.

117 Recollections of a former Security Service officer.

118 Recollections of former Security Service officers. Prendergast went on to become chief of intelligence in Cyprus (1958–60), director of Special Branch in Hong Kong (1960–66), and director of intelligence in Aden (1966–7).

119 Anderson, Histories of the Hanged, ch. 7. Elkins, Britain's Gulag, gives an even bleaker assessment of the horrors of the police state. The accuracy of her account, however, has been challenged by Elstein, 'The End of the Mau Mau'.

120 Sir G. Colby to Colonial Secretary, telegram no. 485, 7 Sept. 1953, TNA CO 0115/457, no. 1; published in Murphy and Ashton (eds), Central Africa, document 98.

121 Murphy and Ashton (eds), Central Africa, p. 247.

122 Security Service Archives.

123 Murphy, 'Creating a Commonwealth Intelligence Culture', p. 140. Aldrich, Hidden Hand, p. 517.

124 Security Service Archives.

125 Security Service Archives.

126 Security Service Archives.

127 Security Service Archives.

128 Security Service Archives. On British Guianan business interests, see Drayton, 'Anglo-American "Liberal" Imperialism', pp. 327–8.

129 Security Service Archives.

130 Security Service Archives.

131 Churchill to Lyttelton, 2 May 1953, TNA PREM 11/827; cited by Gallagher, 'Intelligence and Decolonisation in British Guiana'.

132 Andrew and Mitrokhin, *Mitrokhin Archive II*, pp. 169-70.

133 See below, pp. 478-9.

134 Cabinet papers (3908), Sept. 1953, PREM 11/827; cited by Gallagher, 'Intelligence and Decolonisation in British Guiana'.

135 Security Service Archives.

136 Churchill to Lyttelton, 27 Sept. 1953; Memo for the Prime Minister, 6 Oct. 1953; Savage to Lyttelton, 7 Oct. 1953; Lyttelton to Savage, 7 Oct. 1953, TNA PREM 11/827; cited by Gallagher, 'Intelligence and Decolonisation in British Guiana'.

137 *Annual Register*, 1953, pp. 125-6.

138 See below, p. 480.

139 Security Service Archives.

140 See below, pp. 479-80.

141 See below, pp. 478-9.

Chapter 8: The End of Empire: Part 2

1 Security Service Archives.

2 Security Service Archives.

3 Security Service Archives.

4 Security Service Archives.

5 Aldrich, *Hidden Hand*, pp. 571, 579.

6 Security Service Archives.

7 Aldrich, *Hidden Hand*, pp. 572-3.

8 Ibid., p. 574.

9 Security Service Archives.

10 Aldrich, *Hidden Hand*, p. 575.

11 Security Service Archives.

12 Horne, *Macmillan*, vol. 2, p. 100.

13 Security Service Archives. Magan's terms of reference, approved 16 Oct. 1958, were as follows: 'Brigadier Magan is accredited to the Governor of Cyprus under whose authority he will apply himself, in close association with the Cyprus intelligence authorities, especially to those aspects of intelligence best calculated to assist in the capture of Grivas and his principal assistants. The duration of the appointment will not exceed six months.'

14 Security Service Archives.

15 Security Service Archives.

16 The final version of Bill Magan's 57-page personality profile of Grivas, dated 11 March 1959, was 'written in the last week of EOKA's existence'. Security Service Archives. Sir Hugh Foot wrote after Magan's departure: 'All of us here were tremendously impressed with the way he tackled the job, spending long hours going over all the documents and all the evidence and gradually piecing together a picture of Grivas and his character and abilities and his weaknesses, and then putting in hand several courses of action . . .' Security Service Archives.

17 The Colonial Secretary Lennox Boyd (succeeded in 1959 by Iain Macleod), cited by Brendon, *Decline and Fall of the British Empire*, p. 565.

18 Aldrich, *Hidden Hand*, pp. 577-8.

19 Security Service Archives.

20 Horne, *Macmillan*, vol. 2, p. 103.

21 Security Service Archives.

22 Security Service Archives.

23 Security Service Archives.

24 Security Service Archives.

25 Security Service Archives.

26 Edgerton, *Mau Mau*, ch. 7.

27 Security Service Archives.

28 Security Service Archives.

29 Walter Bell, who had served in Nairobi previously as assistant SLO 1949–50 and as SLO in 1950–51, returned to Nairobi as SLO in June 1961.

30 DG (Hollis), Note, 11 Oct. 1963, enclosed with J. A. Harrison (Security Service) to J. N. A. Armitage-Smith (Colonial Office), 17 Oct. 1963, TNA CO 1035/171, s. 8.

31 Horne, *Macmillan*, vol. 2, pp. 389–90.

32 Security Service Archives.

33 See above, p. 454.

34 Kellar to W. S. Bates (CAO), 5 Sept. 1962, TNA DO 183/480, no. 1; published in Murphy and Ashton (eds), *Central Africa*, document 331.

35 Murphy and Ashton (eds), *Central Africa*, p. 327.

36 Security Service Archives.

37 Security Service Archives.

38 The SLO in New Delhi had written in 1959 that he was 'quite closely integrated in the Political Division of the High Commission. This seems to me a sound development for which we should perhaps strive in the younger commonwealth countries . . .' Security Service Archives.

39 Security Service Archives.

40 Security Service Archives.

41 Security Service Archives.

42 Security Service Archives. DG (Hollis) to Sir Burke Trend (cabinet secretary), 18 Nov. 1965, TNA CO 1035/187, no serial number.

43 Recollections of a former Security Service officer.

44 Security Service Archives.

45 Andrew and Mitrokhin, *Mitrokhin Archive II*, pp. 435, 582 n. 22. Rooney, *Kwame Nkrumah*, p. 226.

46 Security Service Archives.

47 Andrew and Mitrokhin, *Mitrokhin Archive II*, p. 434.

48 Ibid., pp. 434–5. The text of Nkrumah's letter to Johnson, dated 26 February 1964, is published in Rooney, *Kwame Nkrumah*, pp. 243–5.

49 Security Service Archives. Hollis replied that he regretted that he could not extend Thomson's tour of duty. Security Service Archives. Smedley wrote to Hollis after Thomson's departure: 'John Thomson's contribution to this post has gone well beyond his work as Security Liaison Officer. His sincerity of heart and purpose and genuine liking for Ghanaians have brought him a host of friends outside his official contacts, while his knowledge of Ghana going back many years has been of great value to me and my staff here.' Security Service Archives.

50 Security Service Archives.

51 Recollections of a former Security Service officer.

52 Security Service Archives.

53 Security Service Archives.

54 Security Service Archives.

55 Security Service Archives.

56 Security Service Archives.

57 Security Service Archives.

58 Recollections of a former Security Service officer. The SLO later commented that, but for the Civil War, his role would have been much less important.

59 Christopher Andrew, interview with former deputy head of Kenyan Special Branch in Sydney, NSW, 1987.

60 Security Service Archives.

61 Security Service Archives.

62 Percox, *Britain, Kenya and the Cold War*, pp. 171–2. Edgerton, *Mau Mau*, pp. 227–8. KGB active measures sought to portray Kenyatta as in the pay of the CIA. Andrew and Mitrokhin, *Mitrokhin Archive II*, pp. 441, 584 n. 55.

63 The main training courses then run by the Security Service were for police and administrative personnel in colonies on the verge of independence and other parts of the Commonwealth, rather than for its own staff; see above, p. 334.

64 Security Service Archives.

65 Recollections of a former Security Service officer.

66 Security Service Archives.

67 Macmillan memorandum, 28 June 1958, TNA PREM 11/2616/46. Walker, *Aden Emergency*, p. 22.

68 Of the four states of the East Aden Protectorate, consumed by rivalries with each other, only one joined the Federation. Walker, *Aden Emergency*, pp. 21-6, 35-6.

69 Ibid., pp. 25-6, 71-3, 78-9.

70 Ibid., p. 88.

71 Trevaskis to Sandys, 18 Dec. 1963, IOR R/20/D/27; Trevaskis to Sandys, 31 March 1964, Appendix 5, Trevaskis papers, part 1, Rhodes House Library, University of Oxford (documents cited by Mawby, *British Policy in Aden and the Protectorates*, p. 99).

72 Security Service Archives.

73 Security Service Archives.

74 Security Service Archives.

75 Security Service Archives.

76 Security Service Archives.

77 Security Service Archives.

78 Interim Report by Chairman of JIC Working Party, 'Intelligence Organisation in Aden', Annex to JIC/1061/65, TNA CO 1035/184.

79 'Intelligence Organisation in Aden', 17 Dec. 1965, JIC(IAF)(65)3, TNA CO 1035/184.

80 Security Service Archives.

81 Security Service Archives. Service pressure succeeded in 1967 in securing the withdrawal of an Intelligence Corps manual on interrogation which it considered 'ethically untenable'. Security Service Archives.

82 Walker, *Aden Emergency*, p. 278.

83 Recollections of a former Security Service officer.

84 Security Service Archives. It was also suggested that the NLF had kidnapped the mother of the 'houseboy' of a British diplomatic couple in Aden and pressured him into planting the bomb by threatening to kill her if he refused. Walker, *Aden Emergency*, p. 221.

85 Crossman, *Diaries of a Cabinet Minister*, vol. 2, 5 Sept., 30 Oct. 1967.

86 See above, pp. 460-61.

87 Recollections of a former Security Service officer.

88 Security Service Archives.

89 Security Service Archives.

90 Weiner, *Legacy of Ashes*, p. 192. Almost certainly with Kennedy's approval, the CIA was pursuing a number of inept attempts to bring about Castro's assassination. Andrew, *For the President's Eyes Only*, pp. 274-6, 303-6.

91 *Foreign Relations of the United States (FRUS)*, 1961-63, vol. XII, pp. 544-5.

92 Macmillan, minute on Rusk to Home, 19 Feb. 1962, TNA PREM 11/3666; Home to Rusk, 26 Feb. 1962, TNA PREM 11/3666; Drayton, 'Anglo-American "Liberal" Imperialism', pp. 334-5.

93 Drayton, 'Anglo-American "Liberal" Imperialism', p. 338.

94 Weiner, *Legacy of Ashes*, p. 192. *FRUS*, 1964-1968, vol. XXXII, editorial note.

95 Security Service Archives.

96 Security Service Archives.

97 Security Service Archives.

98 Security Service Archives.

99 Daniels and Waters, 'The World's Longest General Strike'.

100 US consul in Georgetown to Dean Rusk, 8 May 1963, John F. Kennedy Presidential Library; cited by Gallagher, 'Intelligence and Decolonisation in British Guiana'.

101 Dean Rusk circular, 10 Oct. 1961, John F. Kennedy Presidential Library; cited by Gallagher, 'Intelligence and Decolonisation in British Guiana'.

102 US consul in Georgetown to Dean Rusk, 1 May 1963, John F. Kennedy Presidential Library; cited by Gallagher, 'Intelligence and Decolonisation in British Guiana'.

103 'Extract from SLO's Trinidad letter of 20.8.63', TNA CO 1036/173, s. 1/1. Cf. 'SLO's visit to British Guiana 11th-15th May, 1964', TNA CO 1036/173, s. 6/6.

104 Security Service Archives.

105 Security Service Archives.

106 Security Service Archives.

107 Drayton, 'Anglo-American "Liberal" Imperialism', p. 337. Jagan, by then an advocate of a mixed economy, returned to power in 1992.

108 'Cheddi Berret Jagan', *Oxford DNB*. On Castro's response to the crushing of the Prague Spring, see Andrew and Mitrokhin, *Mitrokhin Archive II*, pp. 53–5.

109 Director E noted in 1971 that the cabinet secretary, Sir Burke Trend, had made clear there was 'little if any possibility of MI5 representation [SLO positions] being restored whatever the circumstances. The policy henceforth was for MI6, where necessary, to represent both Services overseas, leaving MI5 to concentrate on the security of the home base. Once out of an overseas post, MI5 would not be given the money to get back. The heat was now on MI5 to liquidate its SLO posts in favour of MI6. Financial pressure would continue to be applied to this end.' Security Service Archives.

110 Security Service Archives.

111 The DIB listed among the assistance it had received from the Security Service: training courses; special (i.e. technical) equipment; general security advice (e.g. on counter-sabotage); counter-espionage and intelligence; vetting inquiries and activities of Indians in the UK. Security Service Archives.

112 Security Service Archives.

113 Security Service Archives.

Chapter 9: The Macmillan Government: Spy Scandals and the Profumo Affair

1 Horne, *Macmillan*, vol. 2, p. 467.

2 Security Service Archives.

3 Security Service Archives.

4 This phrase was later quoted with approval by Harold Wilson in his *Governance of Britain*.

5 See above, pp. 433–4.

6 See below, pp. 488–90.

7 Security Service Archives.

8 Security Service Archives.

9 Samolis (ed.), *Veterany Vneshnei Razvedki Rossii*, pp. 103–5.

10 Andrew and Mitrokhin, *Mitrokhin Archive*, pp. 532–3.

11 Recollections of a former Security Service officer. Security Service Archives. Wright, *Spycatcher*, pp. 130–31.

12 Recollections of a former Security Service officer.

13 Security Service Archives. Wright, *Spycatcher*, pp. 130–31.

14 Security Service Archives.

15 Snelling, *Rare Books and Rarer People*, p. 208.

16 Recollections of a former Security Service officer. Security Service Archives. Wright, *Spycatcher*, pp. 136–7.

17 Security Service Archives.

18 Information from Professor Peter Hennessy.

19 Recollections of former Security Service officers.

20 Security Service Archives.

21 Recollections of former Security Service officers. Under the pseudonym 'Elton', Elwell later published much of the painstaking research which established Lonsdale's real identity and his Russian family background in the *Police Journal*, vol. XLIV, no. 2 (April–June 1971).

22 Recollections of a former Security Service officer.

23 Security Service Archives.

24 Security Service Archives.

25 Blake, *No Other Choice*, chs 2–5. Cf. Hyde, *Blake*. Though acknowledging his affection and admiration for his cousin Curiel, Blake unconvincingly downplays his influence on him. According to KGB General Oleg Kalugin, who in the mid-1970s was head of FCD Directorate K (counter-intelligence), Blake 'already held far-leftist views' at the outbreak of the Korean War (Kalugin, *Spymaster*, p. 141). For examples of other distortions in Blake's memoirs,

see Andrew and Gordievsky, *KGB*, pp. 755–6 (n. 117); Murphy, Kondrashev and Bailey, *Battleground Berlin*, pp. 217, 482–3 (n. 36).

26 Murphy, Kondrashev and Bailey, *Battleground Berlin*, pp. 214–15.

27 Security Service Archives.

28 Security Service Archives.

29 'STARFISH [Blake] estimated that on average no more than ten per cent of his production was spoilt by bad photography ... General information gained through gossip and personal contact was passed briefly and verbally at monthly contact with his RIS case officer. This type of information was necessarily brief, limited and not detailed.' Security Service Archives.

30 Security Service Archives.

31 Security Service Archives.

32 Hollis noted on 10 April that 'the Prime Minister had thought it right to make a short statement to the President.' Security Service Archives.

33 Andrew, *For the President's Eyes Only*, pp. 256, 264–5.

34 Andrew and Mitrokhin, *Mitrokhin Archive*, pp. 520–21. The whole of the agent network was not, however, identified in 1953–5. The Stasi reported that in 1958–61 Blake identified about 100 further agents. He is unlikely to have had detailed information on the S&T network. Maddrell, *Spying on Science*, pp. 145–7.

35 Interview with Sir Dick White, cited by Bower, *Perfect English Spy*, p. 268.

36 Cleve Cram, one of the CIA officers present at the meeting, later recalled to Christopher Andrew that he had suggested to Blake that they have lunch afterwards. Blake apologetically refused, pleading pressure of work (very possibly the need to photograph the meeting papers for the KGB).

37 Security Service Archives.

38 There is no credible evidence to support claims that the intelligence generated by Operation GOLD was muddied by significant amounts of KGB disinformation. The best accounts of the Berlin tunnel operation, based both on material made available by the SVR and on declassified CIA files, is Murphy, Kondrashev and Bailey, *Battleground Berlin*, ch. 11 and appendix 5, and Stafford, *Spies beneath Berlin*, which correct numerous errors in earlier accounts.

39 Security Service Archives.

40 Interview with Sir Dick White, cited by Bower, *Perfect English Spy*, p. 268.

41 Security Service Archives.

42 Horne, *Macmillan*, vol. 2, p. 457.

43 William H. Stoneman, 'Red Spy Served British 8 Years', *Washington Post*, 5 May 1961.

44 See below, p. 565.

45 Andrew and Gordievsky, *KGB*, p. 518. West, *Matter of Trust*, pp. 115–19.

46 Security Service Archives.

47 See above, p. 398.

48 Security Service Archives. Recollections of a former Security Service officer.

49 Horne, *Macmillan*, vol. 2, pp. 460–61. The defection of Philby to Moscow in January 1963 and the revelation that, despite being cleared by Macmillan in the Commons eight years earlier, he had been a major Soviet spy caused the Prime Minister further annoyance.

50 Brook was more sympathetic to the Service than the Prime Minister. Largely as a result of the counter-espionage cases of 1961–2, he approved the recruitment by the Service of an additional 50 officers, 150 other ranks and 100 secretarial/clerical grades. Security Service Archives.

51 Schecter and Deriabin, *Spy Who Saved the World*. (The authors were the first to gain access to many of Penkovsky's debriefs.) Bower, *Perfect English Spy*, p. 274.

52 In May 1961 Hollis, the DDG (Mitchell), Director D (Furnival Jones) and three other members of the Security Service were indoctrinated into both YOGA (Penkovsky's identity) and RUPEE (his intelligence product). One further YOGA and RUPEE indoctrination followed in July. In 1961–2 some further staff were given RUPEE indoctrination only. Security Service Archives.

53 Andrew, *For the President's Eyes Only*, pp. 290ff. Andrew and Mitrokhin, *Mitrokhin Archive*, pp. 238–41.

54 Horne, *Macmillan*, vol. 2, p. 466. When published in 1989, Macmillan's description of

Mitchell caused resentment among Service veterans. One recalls Mitchell as a 'civilised, humane man', considerate in his treatment of junior colleagues.

55 See below, p. 509.
56 Security Service Archives.
57 Security Service Archives.
58 Security Service Archives.
59 Security Service Archives.
60 Interview with Ward by Warwick Charlton, *Today*, 11 May 1963.
61 Security Service Archives.
62 Security Service Archives.
63 Security Service Archives.
64 Security Service Archives.
65 Security Service Archives.
66 Security Service Archives.
67 Security Service Archives.
68 Security Service Archives.
69 Security Service Archives.
70 Security Service Archives.
71 Security Service Archives. Ward later gave a similarly inflated account of his role during the Cuban Missile Crisis to the writer Warwick Charlton, who published it in *Today* on 11 May 1963.
72 Scott, *Macmillan, Kennedy and the Cuban Missile Crisis*, pp. 104–7.
73 Security Service Archives.
74 Security Service Archives.
75 Knightley and Kennedy, *Affair of State*, ch. 1.
76 Introduction by Lord Denning to 1992 reissue of *The Denning Report*.
77 Security Service Archives.
78 Security Service Archives.
79 Christopher Andrew, interview with Sir Dick White, 1984.
80 Security Service Archives.
81 Security Service Archives.
82 Security Service Archives.
83 Security Service Archives.
84 Pearson, *Profession of Violence*, pp. 115–16, 120, 122.

Chapter 10: FLUENCY: Paranoid Tendencies

1 Golitsyn did indeed possess intelligence, whose importance he exaggerated, about the Cambridge 'Ring of Five'; though Philby did not realize it, he did not have information which clearly identified Philby as a member of it.
2 Security Service Archives.
3 See above, pp. 350–51, 433–4; below, pp. 488–9.
4 Security Service Archives.
5 Security Service Archives. Recollections of a former Security Service officer.
6 Security Service Archives.
7 Security Service Archives.
8 Wright, *Spycatcher*, p. 170.
9 Security Service Archives.
10 Security Service Archives.
11 Security Service Archives.
12 Security Service Archives.
13 The same D Branch officer recalls taking FJ to task a year or two later about his accusations against Mitchell. FJ conceded that he had been wrong. Recollections of a former Security Service officer.
14 Security Service Archives. Wright later claimed that Hollis secretly seconded him to work with Martin on the Mitchell investigation. There is no evidence in Security Service files to confirm this claim; Security Service Archives.

15 Wright, *Spycatcher*, pp. 315–16.
16 Security Service Archives.
17 Security Service Archives.
18 Security Service Archives.
19 Security Service Archives.
20 Security Service Archives.
21 Horne, *Macmillan*, vol. 2, p. 466. See above, p. 483.
22 When Home became prime minister, his successor as foreign secretary, Rab Butler, was also briefed, on 18 October 1963. Security Service Archives.
23 Security Service Archives.
24 Recollections of a former Security Service officer.
25 Security Service Archives. Cf. Wright, *Spycatcher*, p. 268.
26 Security Service Archives.
27 Wright, *Spycatcher*, pp. 200–201.
28 Security Service Archives.
29 Security Service Archives. On Cumming's early career in MI5, see above, p. 136.
30 Security Service Archives. Reports on the PETERS case in July and shortly before he retired in September both concluded that he was guilty, though – as Trend later noted – the second report reached that conclusion 'perhaps rather less confidently than the first'; Security Service Archives.
31 Security Service Archives. See above, p. 494.
32 Security Service Archives.
33 Security Service Archives.
34 Security Service Archives.
35 Security Service Archives.
36 Security Service Archives.
37 See above, pp. 436–7.
38 Security Service Archives.
39 Security Service Archives.
40 Wright, *Spycatcher*, p. 233.
41 Security Service Archives. Though Martin's suspension was not officially announced within the Service, he gave his account of how it came about to a number of colleagues.
42 Security Service Archives.
43 Security Service Archives.
44 Security Service Archives.
45 Wright, *Spycatcher*, pp. 213, 233–4.
46 Recollections of a former Security Service officer.
47 Security Service Archives.
48 Security Service Archives.
49 Security Service Archives.
50 Security Service Archives.
51 Security Service Archives.
52 Security Service Archives.
53 Security Service Archives.
54 Wright, *Spycatcher*, pp. 295–7, 301–2.
55 See above, p. 510.
56 Wright, *Spycatcher*, pp. 320–23.
57 Recollections of a former Security Service officer.
58 Recollections of a former Security Service officer.
59 Recollections of a former Security Service officer.
60 Wright, *Spycatcher*, p. 324.
61 Security Service Archives.
62 Security Service Archives.
63 Security Service Archives.
64 Security Service Archives.
65 Security Service Archives.

66 Mangold, *Cold Warrior*, p. 155.
67 Personal recollection by the programme presenter, Christopher Andrew.
68 Security Service Archives.
69 Security Service Archives.
70 Wright, *Spycatcher*, p. 316.
71 Security Service Archives.
72 Security Service Archives.
73 Wright, *Spycatcher*, p. 331.
74 Security Service Archives.
75 Security Service Archives.
76 Rimington, *Open Secret*, p. 100.
77 Security Service Archives.
78 FJ wrote to Golitsyn:

> You are invited by the Heads of both Services to visit the UK in order to assist them with problems of penetration of British Intelligence.
>
> ... On the basis of their past research the Security Service intend to provide you with briefs covering the individuals who have fallen within their field of scrutiny in the context of penetration. These briefs will cover a wider area than the limited proposals discussed between yourself and Mr Wright in November last year. Each case will be identified by a serial number but the full names of the individual concerned will be supplied on request ... The briefs which will be supplied initially will be prepared in summary form ...

Memorandum of Understanding [with Golitsyn], May 1970, Security Service Archives. There is no indication that Golitsyn was ever allowed to see the original Records of Service.
79 Recollections of a former Security Service officer. Wright's account of this episode is inaccurate and, characteristically, puts Wright himself at centre-stage. Wright, *Spycatcher*, pp. 316-17.
80 Security Service Archives.
81 Security Service Archives.
82 Security Service Archives.
83 Recollections of a former Security Service officer.
84 Security Service Archives. The worst that emerged from the prolonged investigation of Hollis was some evidence that he had been less than frank about his life immediately before the Second World War.
85 Security Service Archives.
86 Security Service Archives. See above, pp. 280-82.
87 Security Service Archives.
88 Security Service Archives.
89 Security Service Archives.
90 Security Service Archives.
91 Security Service Archives.
92 Security Service Archives.
93 Wright, *Spycatcher*, p. 341.
94 Ibid., p. 243.
95 Rimington, *Open Secret*, p. 118.
96 Security Service Archives.
97 Security Service Archives.
98 Security Service Archives.
99 Elsa Bernaut was the widow of the Soviet illegal Ignace Poretsky (also known as Reiss), who had been assassinated after defecting in 1937. In a bizarre and bullying interview with Bernaut in 1970, Wright perversely suggested that, though she had 'muddled up' the dates, there was a reference in her memoirs to Ignace Reiss using Philby as a penetration agent. 'This', noted Wright with evident self-satisfaction, 'was entirely the right tactic. She blew up and was angry with me.' Security Services Archives.
100 Security Service Archives.
101 Security Service Archives.

Chapter 11: The Wilson Government 1964–1970:
Security, Subversion and 'Wiggery-Pokery'

1 Benn, *Out of the Wilderness*, p. 37.
2 Ian Aitken, 'Sinister backbench MP played key role in downfall', *Guardian*, 11 March 2006.
3 Ziegler, *Wilson*, p. 178.
4 See below, p. 524.
5 See above, p. 930 n. 82.
6 Cunningham and Hollis agreed that 'The proposal would also mean that the Director General would be deprived of the advice which he was able to get from the PUS Home Office, which had been so strongly advocated by Sir Norman Brook, for Colonel Wigg who would be located in No. 10 would have no staff who could give such advice.' Security Service Archives.
7 Wilson considered Trend the best civil servant he had ever known. Castle, *Castle Diaries*, p. 115.
8 Security Service Archives.
9 Ziegler, *Wilson*, p. 178.
10 Security Service Archives.
11 Jenkins, *Life at the Centre*, p. 383.
12 Ziegler, *Wilson*, p. 178.
13 Castle, *Castle Diaries*, p. 172.
14 See below, pp. 532-3.
15 Christopher Andrew, interview with the Rev. Anne Kiggell, July 2006.
16 See below, p. 633.
17 After a kerb-crawling episode in 1976, Wigg (then seventy-six years old) was found not guilty by the magistrate of using insulting behaviour likely to cause a breach of the peace on the grounds that kerb-crawling at that period was not in itself an offence. The police officer who gave evidence against Wigg referred to a previous occasion on which he had found him kerb-crawling and given him a warning. The officer also said that Wigg was known to officers of the Vice Squad covering the Hilton Hotel. 'Kerb-Crawling Lord Wigg Stopped Six Women, Says PC', *Daily Telegraph*, 5 Nov. 1976. 'Lord Wigg is cleared of insulting behaviour', *The Times*, 4 Dec. 1976.
18 Security Service Archives.
19 Security Service Archives.
20 Benn, *Out of the Wilderness*, p. 328.
21 Jenkins, *Life at the Centre*, p. 175.
22 Benn, *Out of the Wilderness*, p. 328.
23 Andrew, *Secret Service*, p. 699.
24 Benn, *Out of the Wilderness*, p. 329.
25 See above, pp. 415-18.
26 Security Service Archives.
27 See above, pp. 412-14.
28 In the Bax case (see above, p. 415), however, Wilson told Hollis that 'he thought it entirely right that we should have warned the Party that one of their employees was receiving money from Communist intelligence services.' Security Service Archives.
29 When Gordon Walker made the proposal late in 1961, he was unaware that Clarke had attracted D2's attention in 1959 as a result of his contacts with officials at the Czechoslovak embassy, one of whom was believed to be an StB officer. When interviewed by D2 in February 1962, however, Clarke 'gave a full account of his contacts with SovBloc officials in London. He was cooperative and made a good impression.' Security Service Archives.
30 Security Service Archives.
31 Security Service Archives.
32 See below, pp. 637-8.
33 Ziegler, *Wilson*, p. 169.
34 Security Service Archives.
35 Security Service Archives. See below, pp. 711-12.
36 Ziegler, *Wilson*, pp. 250-51.

37 Recollections of a former Security Service officer.
38 Security Service Archives.
39 Recollections of a former Security Service officer.
40 Recollections of a former Security Service officer.
41 Security Service Archives.
42 Security Service Archives.
43 Ziegler, *Wilson*, p. 251.
44 Security Service Archives.
45 Security Service Archives.
46 The initial membership consisted of Ramelson, Jack Coward, Jack Dash, Gordon Norris and Harry Watson (President of the Lightermen's Union). All were Communists. Security Service Archives.
47 Security Service Archives.
48 Security Service Archives.
49 Security Service Archives.
50 Security Service Archives.
51 Security Service Archives.
52 Jenkins made no mention of the seamen's strike in his memoirs, *A Life at the Centre*.
53 See above, p. 410.
54 Security Service Archives.
55 Security Service Archives.
56 Recollections of a former Security Service officer.
57 *Parl. Deb. (Commons)*, 28 June 1966, cols 1613–14.
58 Castle, *Castle Diaries*, pp. 135–6.
59 Crossman, *Diaries of a Cabinet Minister*, vol. 1, p. 534. Castle, *Castle Diaries*, p. 136.
60 Ziegler, *Wilson*, p. 252.
61 Chapman Pincher, 'Labour Made Loyalty Probe', *Daily Express*, 15 Feb. 1967.
62 Pincher, *Inside Story*, p. 228.
63 Security Service Archives.
64 Williams, *Inside Number Ten*, pp. 184, 185, 195–6.
65 Pincher, *Inside Story*, p. 233.
66 Palmer, 'History of the D-Notice Committee', pp. 244–5.
67 Wilkinson, *Secrecy and the Media*, section 7.
68 Pincher, *Inside Story*, pp. 22, 232.
69 Security Service Archives.
70 'Obituary: Roy Jenkins', BBC News, 5 Jan. 2003. There is no evidence that Jenkins was abusing his position by trying to find out if his affair with Radziwill had been revealed by phone tapping.
71 Castle, *Castle Diaries*, p. 268.
72 Security Service Archives.
73 Security Service Archives.
74 Thorpe to 'Bruno', gay US lover, 23 April 1961. This letter was among the documents disclosed by the prosecution to the defence at Thorpe's trial in 1979; Freeman and Penrose, *Rinkagate*, p. 355. Security Service Archives.
75 'After reference to the DG through the relevant sections a formal NRA ['Nothing Recorded Against' Thorpe] was sent to the Foreign Office about the subject; but at the DG's request the Director also told Street (FO Security Department) orally [about evidence of homosexuality].' Security Service Archives.
76 Security Service Archives.
77 Security Service Archives.
78 Security Service Archives.
79 Marcia Williams later mistakenly claimed that MI5 had concealed its knowledge of Thorpe's homosexuality: 'MI5 knew about Thorpe but did not tell Harold because they wanted to destabilise us.' Freeman and Penrose, *Rinkagate*, pp. 121–2.
80 Morgan, *Callaghan*, p. 610.
81 No evidence has been found that either 'ploy' went ahead. Security Service Archives.
82 Security Service Archives.

83 Security Service Archives.

84 Security Service Archives.

85 Security Service Archives.

86 Security Service Archives. At FJ's request, Simkins asked Sr Philip Allen 'what points weighed most with the Prime Minister and Home Secretary when they decided not to authorise a H.O.W. on Jack Jones at this juncture'. Allen regretted that he was unable to provide 'any more detail'. Security Service Archives.

87 Security Service Archives.

88 See above, p. 500.

89 Report of the Security Commission, June 1965 (Cmnd 2722).

90 Security Service Archives.

91 Security Service Archives.

92 Security Service Archives.

93 Security Service Archives.

94 Security Service Archives.

95 Report of the Security Commission, November 1968 (Cmnd 3856).

96 Security Service Archives. At his first meeting with Heath in July 1970, FJ informed him that 'I had persuaded Sir William Armstrong to establish a body under Lord Helsby's chairmanship to examine the scope of protective security.' Security Service Archives.

97 Once in Moscow, Blake and Bourke rapidly fell out. Blake writes in his memoirs that 'Arrangements were made for [Bourke] to return to Ireland.' He does not mention, and may not have known, that on the instructions of Sakharovsky, the head of KGB foreign intelligence, Bourke was given before his departure a drug designed to cause brain damage and thus limit his potential usefulness if he fell into the hands of British intelligence. Bourke's premature death in his early forties probably owed as much to KGB drugs as to his own heavy drinking. Blake, *No Other Choice*, chs 11, 12. Andrew and Mitrokhin, *Mitrokhin Archive*, p. 522.

98 Crossman, *Diaries of a Cabinet Minister*, vol. 2, p. 87.

99 Jenkins, *Life at the Centre*, pp. 197–8, 201.

100 Security Service Archives.

101 Security Service Archives.

102 Security Service Archives.

103 Security Service Archives.

104 Security Service Archives.

105 'Hammond' told Floud at the beginning of the interview that he 'expected a colleague to drop in'. Security Service Archives.

106 Security Service Archives.

107 Security Service Archives.

108 Wright commented in his account of the interview with Floud on 17 March 1967, 'We know that Phoebe Pool has told Blunt that she used to act as a courier between Jenifer and the Floud brothers when Jenifer was in the Home Office.' (Bernard Floud's brother, Peter, had also been a Communist at Oxford.) Security Service Archives.

109 Security Service Archives.

110 Security Service Archives.

111 Wright's memoirs contain a garbled account of the questioning of Floud which concludes with the claim that Floud committed suicide the day after the questioning ended (in fact there was a six-month gap), shortly followed by Phoebe Pool (who in reality committed suicide four years later). Wright, *Spycatcher*, pp. 264–6.

112 'Very depressed MP killed himself', *Evening Standard*, 13 Oct. 1967.

113 Andrew, *Secret Service*, p. 643.

114 Material from KGB archives published in the spring of 2009 appears to resolve the question of a hitherto unidentified Soviet agent, codenamed SCOTT, active at Oxford University before the Second World War. According to this material, SCOTT was Arthur Wynn, who graduated from Trinity College, Cambridge in 1932 with first-class honours in natural sciences and later became a postgraduate at Oxford. Wynn was an active talent-spotter as well as a committed Communist. His case officer, Teodor Maly, reported in 1937 that he had provided twenty-five names. Wynn was later criticized, however, for suggesting too many names of known Communists. It remains unclear whether any of those talent-spotted became significant

Soviet agents. (Haynes, Klehr and Vassiliev, 'Spy Mystery Solved'. 'Civil Servant Arthur Wynn revealed as recruiter of Oxford spies', *The Times*, 13 May 2009.) A later MI5 investigation, which included intermittent interviews with Wynn beginning in 1951, concluded that 'he appears to have acted in some capacity for the RIS until at least 1944', but discovered little about his role. At interview Wynn seemed determined not to give 'one bloody inch' about his past activities. By the time he passed the Purge Procedure in 1948 and embarked on a distinguished career in the civil service, however, MI5 concluded that he had ceased to represent a significant security risk. (Security Service Archives.)

115 Frolik, *Frolik Defection*, pp. 58, 96-7.
116 Security Service Archives.
117 See below, p. 707.
118 Frolik, *Frolik Defection*, pp. 58, 96-7.
119 See above, p. 413.
120 Frolik, *Frolik Defection*, pp. 58, 96-7. A Security Service investigation confirmed that 'The records of the House of Commons, though scanty, show that Owen had been in possession of a Secret brief on the British Army of the Rhine,' which he was believed to have passed to the StB. 'William James Owen' [prepared for Home Secretary], Security Service Archives.
121 Security Service Archives.
122 Security Service Archives.
123 Security Service Archives.
124 Security Service Archives.

SECTION E: THE LATER COLD WAR

Introduction: The Security Service and its Staff in the Later Cold War

1 Home Office Archives.
2 See below, p. 587.
3 As well as winning over Maudling, J. H. Waddell also had the support of the cabinet secretary, Sir Burke Trend, and Heath's principal private secretary, Robert Armstrong. Remarkably, Sir Dick White told Allen that he too was in favour of appointing the Home Office candidate rather than an internal candidate as the next DG – although, Allen noted, 'for obvious reasons he would prefer that Furnival Jones did not know this.' Home Office Archives.
4 Home Office Archives.
5 Home Office Archives.
6 Heath was not, however, worried about 'the Americans clamming up if we have confidence in the man we appoint'. Home Office Archives.
7 Home Office Archives. Peter Wright's later claim that, at his instigation, Victor Rothschild had intervened with Heath to secure Hanley's appointment (*Spycatcher*, pp. 348-55) has been shown by Rothschild's biographer to be highly implausible; Rose, *Elusive Rothschild*, pp. 243-5.
8 Security Service Archives.
9 Unattributable interview with eyewitness cited by Baston, *Reggie*, pp. 404-5.
10 Rimington, *Open Secret*, p. 116.
11 Recollections of Sir Michael Hanley.
12 Security Service Archives.
13 Security Service Archives.
14 Security Service Archives.
15 Security Service Archives.
16 Security Service Archives.
17 Security Service Archives.
18 Recollections of a Security Service officer.
19 A4 was responsible for training its own surveillance officers as well as providing training for police forces and overseas agencies. Training courses for new A4 recruits began on a regular basis in 1966 when the first training officer was appointed. By 1976 there was a ten-week induction course.

20 Recollections of a former Security Service officer.
21 Security Service Archives.
22 Recollections of a former Security Service officer.
23 Recollections of a former Security Service officer. I have discovered no corroboration for this claim.
24 Recollections of a former Security Service officer.
25 Recollections of a former Security Service officer.
26 Recollections of a former Security Service officer. Though the remark itself may be apocryphal, it probably reflected the feelings of some of the non-graduates.
27 Recollections of a former Security Service officer.
28 Security Service Archives.
29 Security Service Archives.
30 Rimington, *Open Secret*, p. 124.
31 Ibid., p. 149.
32 Recollections of a former Security Service officer.
33 A female recruit who worked in the Service during the 1970s wrote nostalgically in 2004: 'I can only thank the Office for some interesting and funny times.' Recollections of a former Security Service officer.
34 Walden, *Lucky George*, p. 148. See below, pp. 571-2.
35 Security Service Archives.
36 Recollections of a former Security Service officer.
37 Rimington, *Open Secret*, p. 201.
38 Recollections of Sir Michael Hanley.
39 Security Service Archives.
40 Security Service Archives. (A note on the file records that no copy was kept of Hanley's letter to Jenkins on his departure from the Home Office.)
41 Security Service Archives.
42 Christopher Andrew, interview with Sir David Goodall, 22 July 2005.
43 Recollections of Sir Michael Hanley.
44 Recollections of a former Security Service officer.
45 See below, p. 634.
46 Recollections of Sir Michael Hanley.
47 Morgan, *Callaghan*, pp. 611-12. Security Service Archives.
48 Security Service Archives. Home Office Archives. Callaghan later claimed that it was his idea that Smith should inform Gromyko: 'My personal relations with Andrei Gromyko, the Soviet foreign minister at the time, were quite good and therefore I proposed to Howard Smith that before he left Moscow he should see Gromyko to tell him that he was to become the new head of MI5.' Interview with Callaghan on 9 May 1996, cited by Richard Norton-Taylor, 'Out of the fog of paranoia', *Guardian*, 10 May 1996.
49 Home Office Archives.
50 Christopher Andrew, interview with retired Home Office official, August 2008.
51 Home Office Archives. Sir Patrick Walker later confirmed Hanley's complaint that, as head of the FCO Northern Department, Smith had turned down Security Service requests to refuse visas for Soviet Bloc intelligence officers operating under diplomatic cover: 'He did not want to offend anybody – he was a disaster.' Recollections of Sir Patrick Walker.
52 Home Office Archives.
53 Recollections of Sir Michael Hanley.
54 Security Service Archives. There was, however, a willingness to consider 'near-miss' CSSB candidates, some of whom might turn out to have the qualities required for security and intelligence work.
55 Security Service Archives.
56 Security Service Archives.
57 Morgan, *Callaghan*, pp. 611-12.
58 Security Service Archives.
59 There were some teething problems with the new system. Rather than direct candidates to a specific grade, it was left to the CSSB to determine the level of entry. It was concluded that Grade 5 boards might be pitched too high for the purposes of the Service: 'I think there may

be some grounds for looking at our criteria to see if we have not gone for "superman", while 9b, (where there were more passes) seems like "the poor relation".' Security Service Archives.

60 Recollections of a former Security Service officer.

61 The remark was in fact attributed not to a president but to Henry Stimson when US secretary of state in 1929. Whether or not Stimson actually articulated this celebrated remark, he would almost certainly have endorsed it (though he later changed his mind). Andrew, *For the President's Eyes Only*, pp. 72–3, 106–8.

62 Security Service Archives. On Manningham-Buller, see below, pp. 776, 814–15.

63 See below, p. 776.

64 Recollections of a former Security Service officer. 'DG does not want long briefs'; Security Service Archives.

65 Recollections of Sir Patrick Walker. Walker does, however, give Smith credit for making the attempt – albeit unsuccessful – to communicate with senior staff at the outset of his term of office.

66 Security Service Archives.

67 Christopher Andrew, interview with Sir David Goodall, 22 July 2005. Lady Smith died in 1982.

68 Recollections of a former Security Service officer. An A Branch veteran similarly recalls that Smith 'did not want to dirty his hands with operations . . . He never went to [A Branch] presentations, he left all that to John Jones.'

69 Recollections of a former Security Service officer.

70 Home Office Archives.

71 Home Office Archives.

72 Home Office Archives.

73 Home Office Archives. The lack of MI5 career planning, Sir Brian Cubbon (PUS Home Office) reported, had been discovered at the time of Jones's appointment.

74 Security Service Archives.

75 Security Service Archives. Obituary, Sir John Jones, *Daily Telegraph*, 11 March 1998.

76 Recollections of a former Security Service officer.

77 Security Service Archives.

78 Recollections of a former Security Service officer. 'John Jones had quite a good sense of humour once you got to know him.' Few, however, did.

79 Recollections of a former Security Service officer.

80 Recollections of a former Security Service officer.

81 See below, pp. 714ff.

82 Recollections of a former Security Service officer.

83 Home Office Archives.

84 Security Service Archives. Rimington, *Open Secret*, p. 178.

85 Home Office Archives.

86 Home Office Archives.

87 Home Office Archives.

88 Recollections of a former Security Service officer.

89 Recollections of a former Security Service officer.

90 Ian Black, 'The spy catchers strike a new note', *Guardian*, July 1984; copy (with further handwritten details) attached to recollections of a former Security Service officer.

91 Smith, *New Cloak, Old Dagger*, pp. 66–8.

92 Rimington, *Open Secret*, p. 76.

93 Security Service Archives.

94 Security Service Archives.

95 Security Service Archives.

96 Security Service Archives.

97 Security Service Archives.

98 'Promotion in the 1970s and early 1980s was, in some cases, influenced by length of service. This changed with the reforms of the mid-1980s.' Security Service Archives.

99 Recollections of a former Security Service officer.

100 See below, p. 702.

101 Recollections of Sir Patrick Walker.

102 Rimington, *Open Secret*, pp. 215–16.

103 Security Service Archives.
104 Security Service Archives.
105 Security Service Archives.
106 Home Office Archives.
107 Home Office Archives.
108 Home Office Archives.
109 Home Office Archives.
110 See below, pp. 763–5.
111 Home Office Archives.
112 *Parl. Deb. (Commons)*, 2 Nov. 1987, col. 508; 3 Nov. 1987, col. 781.
113 Home Office Archives.
114 See below, pp. 766–8.

Chapter 1: Operation FOOT and Counter-Espionage in the 1970s

1 Security Service Archives. Recollections of a former Security Service officer.
2 Security Service Archives.
3 Security Service Archives.
4 Security Service Archives.
5 Andrew and Mitrokhin, *Mitrokhin Archive*, pp. 327–38.
6 Security Service Archives.
7 Heath, *Course of my Life*, pp. 474–5. Thorpe, *Douglas-Home*, pp. 415–16.
8 Walden, *Lucky George*, p. 144.
9 Security Service Archives. On KGB Operation PROBA against Courtney, see Andrew and Mitrokhin, *Mitrokhin Archive*, pp. 530–31.
10 Baston, *Reggie*, p. 405. Walden, *Lucky George*, p. 143.
11 Security Service Archives.
12 *Documents on British Policy Overseas*, series III, vol. I, pp. 337–43, 359. Maudling later admitted to cabinet colleagues that his early opposition to proposals for FOOT had been misjudged. Baston, *Reggie*, p. 405.
13 Security Service Archives.
14 Thorpe, *Douglas-Home*, p. 416.
15 Security Service Archives.
16 Security Service Archives.
17 On Department V, founded in 1967, see Andrew and Mitrokhin, *Mitrokhin Archive*, ch. 23. Golitsyn had provided some intelligence on the FCD Thirteenth Department, the predecessor of Department V, after his defection to the CIA late in 1961. However, Lyalin supplied 'the first detailed evidence' of the presence of Department V officers in the London residency as well as of illegals support officers. Security Service Archives. When stationed in residencies these officers were known respectively as Line F and Line N.
18 Security Service Archives. The two Savins were not related.
19 Security Service Archives.
20 Security Service Archives.
21 Security Service Archives.
22 Security Service Archives.
23 Security Service Archives.
24 Security Service Archives.
25 Security Service Archives. When the GLC Licensing Department was transferred to the Department of the Environment in 1970, Abdoolcader became a civil servant, signing the Official Secrets Act in July.
26 On Britten, see above, p. 537.
27 Security Service Archives.
28 *Documents on British Policy Overseas*, series III, vol. I, pp. 388–9. On Ippolitov's status as a KGB agent, see Andrew and Mitrokhin, *Mitrokhin Archive*, p. 547.
29 Walden, *Lucky George*, p. 148.
30 *Documents on British Policy Overseas*, series III, vol. I, p. 389n.
31 Contrary to some predictions, Operation FOOT caused no lasting damage to British–Soviet

relations. In December 1973 Douglas-Home was invited to visit Moscow and Gromyko came to the airport to meet him. During the visit Gromyko toasted Douglas-Home and the British delegation 'at every opportunity'. Thorpe, *Douglas-Home*, pp. 417, 434.

32 Barron, *KGB*, pp. 413–15. Kuzichkin, *Inside the KGB*, p. 81.
33 Andrew and Mitrokhin, *Mitrokhin Archive*, p. 546.
34 Kalugin, *Spymaster*, pp. 131–2.
35 Security Service Archives. Voronin's dismissal is also recalled by Gordievsky, *Next Stop Execution*, p. 184.
36 Obituary, Oleg Lyalin, *The Times*, 24 Feb. 1995.
37 Security Service Archives.
38 Security Service Archives.
39 Security Service Archives.
40 Security Service Archives.
41 Obituary, Antony Lambton, 'Raffish aristocrat caught out in Seventies sex scandal', *The Week*, 13 Jan. 2007. Lambton renounced the earldom of Durham, which he inherited from his father in 1970, in the interests of his political career, but caused controversy by attempting to keep the courtesy title 'Lord Lambton' in the Commons.
42 Security Service Archives.
43 Security Service Archives.
44 Sheldon, however, added that, though the Service had been briefed orally by the Met, it had not yet seen the latest written reports on the case and 'could not therefore be absolutely sure that we had taken full account' of the latest information. Security Service Archives.
45 John Stradling Thomas MP to Francis Pym (Chief Whip), 14 May 1973 (marked 'Immediate copy to PM 2-15 pm 14 May 1973'), TNA PREM 15/190.
46 Record of meeting chaired by Prime Minister, 18 May 1973, TNA PREM 15/1904.
47 TNA PREM 15/1904. 'Obituary: Lord Lambton', *The Times*, 2 Jan. 2007. On 13 June at the Marylebone Magistrates' Court, Lambton was fined £300 for illegal possession of cannabis and amphetamines.
48 Security Service Archives.
49 BBC News (online), 'Sex scandal Tory blamed pressure', 1 Jan. 2004, quoting newly declassified government documents. Obituary, Antony Lambton, 'Raffish aristocrat caught out in Seventies sex scandal', *The Week*, 13 Jan. 2007.
50 BBC News (online), 'Sex scandal Tory blamed pressure', 1 Jan. 2004, quoting newly declassified government documents.
51 Security Service Archives.
52 Andrew and Mitrokhin, *Mitrokhin Archive*, p. 546.
53 Some of the KGB officers who were expelled from, or denied entry to, Britain were redeployed to Commonwealth capitals with substantial British expatriate communities – notably Delhi, Colombo, Dar-es-Salaam, Lagos and Lusaka. The FCD files seen by Vasili Mitrokhin suggest that few significant recruitments resulted. Andrew and Mitrokhin, *Mitrokhin Archive*, pp. 547–8.
54 Security Service Archives. Ramelson was subject to an HOW, occasionally supplemented by A4 surveillance to monitor particular meetings.
55 Security Service Archives.
56 Rosen, *Old Labour to New*, p. 441.
57 Security Service Archives.
58 Security Service Archives.
59 Security Service Archives. Ramelson told Gollan, the CPGB leader, that the TUC had made 'the biggest fucking mess' of the meeting. Security Service Archives.
60 Security Service Archives.
61 Andrew and Mitrokhin, *Mitrokhin Archive*, p. 450.
62 Security Service Archives.
63 Andrew and Mitrokhin, *Mitrokhin Archive*, p. 450. On the KGB's resumption of contact with Prime in 1980 and his arrest in 1982, see below, pp. 712–13.
64 See above, p. 183.
65 Andrew and Mitrokhin, *Mitrokhin Archive*, p. 548.
66 A Home Office briefing (not based on Security Service material) after the publication of *The

Mitrokhin Archive, claimed that Mrs Norwood was not employed by BNFMRA in 1945. This claim is disproved by Burke, *The Spy Who Came in from the Co-op*, p. 9.

67 Security Service Archives.

68 Burke, *The Spy Who Came in from the Co-op*, p. 64.

69 Security Service Archives.

70 Andrew and Mitrokhin, *Mitrokhin Archive*, p. 168.

71 Security Service Archives. On pre-war reports on Norwood, see above, pp. 182–3.

72 Security Service Archives.

73 Andrew and Mitrokhin, *Mitrokhin Archive*, p. 519.

74 Ibid., pp. 152–3. Burke, *The Spy Who Came in from the Co-op*, chs 10–12.

75 Security Service Archives. The claim in a file summary a generation later that, 'though the checks provided no proof and were discontinued after a year', 'the officers investigating her case [in 1965–6] strongly suspected that she was a KGB agent,' is at variance with the conclusion of D1/Inv in 1966. Security Service Archives.

76 Though the BNFRMA currently had no classified contracts, Mrs Norwood's boss was a member of a top-secret Admiralty Committee. D1/Inv noted, 'It is fairly obvious that it would not be too difficult for her to find out something about the work if she was so minded.' But 'She is clearly regarded as reliable and a pillar of the firm, which is not surprising after so many years' service.' Security Service Archives.

77 Security Service Archives.

78 A proposal to interview Letty Norwood in 1968 was rejected on the grounds that there was no prospect of persuading her to admit involvement with the KGB at any stage of her career. Security Service Archives.

79 Andrew and Mitrokhin, *Mitrokhin Archive*, p. 519.

80 Security Service Archives.

81 Security Service Archives.

82 Security Service Archives.

83 Burke, *The Spy Who Came in from the Co-op*, p. 164.

84 Andrew and Mitrokhin, *Mitrokhin Archive*, p. 548.

85 Ibid., pp. xxv–xxvii, 548.

86 Ibid., p. 548.

87 Security Service Archives.

88 Security Service Archives.

89 Security Service Archives. The intelligence on NAGIN later provided by Mitrokhin added little to what the Security Service had already discovered.

90 Security Service Archives. The Attorney General concluded in 1996 that there was no admissible evidence against YUNG and therefore no prospect of successful prosecution.

91 Security Service Archives.

92 Security Service Archives.

93 Security Service Archives.

94 Andrew and Mitrokhin, *Mitrokhin Archive*, p. 549.

95 Security Service Archives.

96 Security Service Archives.

97 John Steele, '25 years for the Spy Who Stayed in the Cold', *Daily Telegraph*, 18 November 1993.

98 Andrew and Mitrokhin, *Mitrokhin Archive*, p. 550.

99 Report of the Security Commission (Cm 2930), July 1995.

100 Security Service Archives.

101 Security Service Archives.

102 Director K wrote in 1994: 'The message from the defector reports – particularly in the mid 1980s – is consistent: exceptions could be made, there was no ban on *former* members etc.' Security Service Archives.

103 Report of the Security Commission (Cm 2930), July 1995, chs 2–4.

104 Andrew and Mitrokhin, *Mitrokhin Archive*, pp. 550–51.

105 Ibid., pp. 551–2.

106 ' "Boring" idealist who spied for Russia gets 25 years', *The Times*, 19 Nov. 1993.

107 Report of the Security Commission, July 1995 (Cm 2930). Andrew and Mitrokhin, *Mitrokhin Archive*, pp. 552–3.

108 Though Smith was tried only on charges relating to his espionage between 1990 and 1992, the Security Commission concluded that 'the most serious of Smith's known espionage activities occurred whilst he was working for EMI.' Report of the Security Commission, July 1995 (Cm 2930).

109 Andrew and Mitrokhin, *Mitrokhin Archive*, p. 550.

110 Ibid., pp. 283–4.

111 Polmar and Allen, *Spy Book*, p. 83.

112 Andrew and Mitrokhin, *Mitrokhin Archive*, p. 724. In 1980, 61.5 per cent of all Soviet S&T came from American sources, 10.5 per cent from West Germany, 8 per cent from France and 7.5 per cent from the UK. These statistics, however, do not tell the full story since they include material obtained from unclassified as well as classified sources. Hanson, *Soviet Industrial Espionage*. Andrew and Mitrokhin, *Mitrokhin Archive*, p. 597.

Chapter 2: The Heath Government and Subversion

1 Heath, *Course of my Life*, pp. 473–4.

2 Ibid., p. 321.

3 Security Service Archives.

4 Security Service Archives.

5 Security Service Archives.

6 Security Service Archives.

7 Security Service Archives.

8 Security Service Archives.

9 Security Service Archives.

10 Heath, *Course of my Life*, p. 334.

11 Security Service Archives.

12 Security Service Archives.

13 Security Service Archives.

14 Security Service Archives.

15 Security Service Archives.

16 Security Service Archives.

17 Security Service Archives.

18 Security Service Archives.

19 Security Service Archives.

20 Heath, *Course of my Life*, p. 350.

21 Campbell, *Heath*, pp. 412–13.

22 Ibid., p. 413.

23 The Service had obtained an HOW on McGahey in October 1970 on the grounds that he was likely 'at least covertly [to] encourage unofficial strike action with the [Communist] Party's support'. The intercept warrant was cancelled in November 1970 when the prospect of strike action diminished, but was reimposed in October 1971 when the likelihood of a major NUM strike increased, beginning with an overtime ban in the following month. Security Service Archives.

24 Security Service Archives.

25 Beckett, *Enemy Within*, pp. 152–3, 158.

26 After membership of the Young Communist League, Daly had joined the CPGB in 1940 at the age of sixteen but resigned in 1956 at the time of the Hungarian Uprising. In 1964 he defeated a Communist candidate to become general secretary of the Scottish Area NUM. Daly's election as NUM general secretary in 1968, however, was believed by the Service to owe much to 'active and comprehensive Communist support' over the previous fifteen months. Security Service Archives.

27 Daly was reported to have said that McGahey was 'on the road to corruption . . . This sort of boozing at union expense and putting him up [in] hotels and so on had been going on for a long time in Scotland but it was wrong.' Security Service Archives.

28 Security Service Archives.
29 Security Service Archives.
30 Security Service Archives.
31 Scargill had first come to Security Service attention as a member of the Barnsley branch of the Young Communist League in 1955, though he later left the Party. Security Service Archives.
32 Campbell, *Heath*, pp. 413–14.
33 Ibid.
34 Hennessy and Jeffery, *States of Emergency*, p. 235.
35 See above, pp. 139–40.
36 Security Service Archives.
37 Security Service Archives.
38 Security Service Archives.
39 Security Service Archives.
40 Security Service Archives.
41 See above, pp. 548, 587.
42 Security Service Archives.
43 Security Service Archives.
44 See above, p. 547.
45 Security Service Archives.
46 Security Service Archives.
47 Security Service Archives.
48 Security Service Archives.
49 Security Service Archives.
50 Security Service Archives.
51 Security Service Archives.
52 Security Service Archives.
53 Security Service Archives.
54 Heath, *Course of my Life*, p. 505.
55 Security Service Archives.
56 Security Service Archives.
57 See above, p. 530.
58 Security Service Archives.
59 Recollections of a recently retired Security Service officer.
60 Morgan, *People's Peace*, p. 351.

Chapter 3: Counter-Terrorism and Protective Security in the Early 1970s

1 Security Service Archives.
2 See below, pp. 606–7, 654–5. Until the 1970s peacetime 'protective security' had been mainly concerned with 'the protection of classified information'. Security Service Archives. Thereafter its scope was extended to cover protection against terrorist attack.
3 See below, p. 619.
4 See above, pp. 353–61.
5 Follain, *Jackal*, pp. 20–1.
6 Security Service Archives.
7 Security Service Archives.
8 Security Service Archives.
9 Security Service Archives.
10 Boyce, *Irish Question and British Politics*, p. 106.
11 Taylor, *Provos*, p. 32.
12 Security Service Archives.
13 Security Service Archives.
14 Security Service Archives.
15 Security Service Archives.
16 Security Service Archives.
17 Security Service Archives.

18 Rimington, *Open Secret*, p. 105.

19 The 1967 JIC working group on intelligence priorities made no mention of Irish affairs. 'Confidential Annexe to Item 1 of JIC (67) 27th meeting (held on 29th June 1967)', TNA CAB 159/47; I owe this reference to Professor Eunan O'Halpin.

20 JIC (A) (69) 27 (Final) (16 June 1969), TNA CAB 186/3.

21 Crossman, *Diaries of a Cabinet Minister*, vol. 3, p. 636. Bew and Gillespie, *Northern Ireland*, p. 19.

22 O'Halpin, *Defending Ireland*, p. 307.

23 Andrew and Mitrokhin, *Mitrokhin Archive II*, pp. 246–50.

24 On Lyalin, see above, pp. 567–74.

25 Security Service Archives.

26 The Security Service does not appear to have discovered details of the appeal by Goulding and Costello to Andropov or of the arms deliveries to the Official IRA until Vasili Mitrokhin defected in 1992, bringing with him intelligence on them from KGB files. Andrew and Mitrokhin, *Mitrokhin Archive*, pp. 492–3, 501–3.

27 After a dispute with Goulding in 1974, Costello was expelled from the Official IRA and founded a new Trotskyist movement, the Irish Republican Socialist Party (IRSP). He was murdered by the Officials in 1977.

28 Security Service Archives.

29 Unpublished memoir of a former Security Service officer.

30 Security Service Archives.

31 Security Service Archives.

32 There is no record of any communication between FJ and Heath on the hijacks in the Security Service Archives. On Heath's low opinion of FJ, see Heath, *Course of my Life*, p. 474.

33 Interview with Lord Wilson of Dinton, Jan. 2007.

34 Security Service Archives.

35 Security Service Archives.

36 Security Service Archives.

37 *Evening Standard*, 15 Dec. 1971.

38 Security Service Archives. The Service played only a peripheral part in the investigation, which it left mainly to the police.

39 Security Service Archives.

40 de la Billière, *Looking for Trouble*, pp. 280–81.

41 Christie, *Christie File*, p. 227.

42 Security Service Archives. The hitherto unknown Angry Brigade had previously claimed responsibility for shots fired at the Spanish embassy on 3 December 1970 and for an explosive device left at the Department of Employment on 9 December. Both attacks, however, caused so little damage that they attracted almost no media attention.

43 Security Service Archives.

44 Security Service Archives.

45 Christie, *Christie File*, p. 239. Christie acknowledged his 'sympathy with what the Angry Brigade did' (p. 335), but denied any involvement with it and in 1972 was found not guilty of conspiring to cause explosions at the trial of the 'Stoke Newington Eight'.

46 Security Service Archives.

47 Security Service Archives.

48 Security Service Archives.

49 Christie, *Christie File*, p. 248.

50 Security Service Archives.

51 Security Service Archives.

52 Security Service Archives.

53 Security Service Archives.

54 F1B believed that, rather than investigating terrorist attacks after they had occurred, 'The role of the Security Service should surely be to foresee future anarchist acts of violence. To this end we need to foster as much as possible our liaison with security authorities all over the world.' Security Service Archives.

55 Security Service Archives.

56 See above, p. 476.

57 Recollections of a former Security Service officer.

58 Security Service Archives.

59 Hoffman, *Inside Terrorism*, pp. 74–5.

60 de la Billière, *Looking for Trouble*, pp. 281–2.

61 Security Service Archives.

62 Security Service Archives.

63 The investigation of the letter bombs was carried out mainly by the MPSB, assisted by the Forensic Explosives Laboratory of the Royal Arsenal'. EM2 Branch, R.A.R.D.E., Security Service Archives. The report notes (p. 3) that 'Many similar devices have been examined by this laboratory commencing with the murder of Dr Ami Shachori at the Israeli Embassy in London on 19th September 1972.'

64 Recollections of a former Security Service officer.

65 Security Service Archives.

66 Security Service Archives.

67 Security Service Archives.

68 Security Service Archives. COBR was used for all kinds of emergencies, not simply those involving terrorists.

69 Security Service Archives.

70 Security Service Archives.

71 Security Service Archives.

72 Security Service Archives.

73 Security Service Archives.

74 Security Service Archives.

75 Security Service Archives.

76 Security Service Archives.

77 Security Service Archives.

78 Security Service Archives.

79 Security Service Archives.

80 Security Service Archives.

81 Security Service Archives.

82 Security Service Archives.

83 Security Service Archives.

84 Dobson and Payne, *War without End*, p. 174. Follain, *Jackal*, pp. 39–41.

85 Security Service Archives.

86 Laqueur, *Age of Terrorism*, p. 299. I owe this quotation to Eoin Jennings of the Cambridge Intelligence Seminar.

87 Andrew, *Secret Service*, ch. 8.

88 Recollections of a former Security Service officer.

89 Security Service Archives.

90 Security Service Archives.

91 Security Service Archives.

92 Moloney, *Secret History of the IRA*, p. 103.

93 Heath, *Course of my Life*, pp. 427–8.

94 Bew and Gillespie, *Northern Ireland*, pp. 36–7.

95 Recollections of a former Security Service officer.

96 Unpublished memoir of former Security Service officer.

97 In April 1971 the DG informed the Home Secretary that 'there is a possible threat of sabotage to Concorde from the IRA and . . . with the agreement of the Ministry of Aviation Supply and BAC we have recently reviewed security measures at the aerodrome from which the prototype flies.' Security Service Archives. This appears to be the first example of Security Service involvement in protective security against Republican terrorism on the mainland drawn to government attention after the beginning of the Troubles.

98 Security Service Archives.

99 Security Service Archives.

100 An EKP is defined as 'any installation, the products or services of which are of such importance that total loss or severe damage would critically impair Defence or Security, or the Functioning of Government, or the Economy'. Security Service Archives. The concept of

the EKP, though not the term, went back at least to the Second World War, when the Service was responsible for advising on the security of munitions and aircraft factories, arsenals, dockyards, railways and public utilities.

101 Security Service Archives.

102 Security Service Archives.

103 Bew and Gillespie, *Northern Ireland*, pp. 44–6.

104 Security Service Archives.

105 Security Service Archives. Recollections of former Security Service officers.

106 Recollections of a former Security Service officer.

107 Recollections of a former Security Service officer. Security Service Archives.

108 Recollections of former Security Service officers.

109 Recollections of former Security Service officers.

110 Security Service Archives.

111 Security Service Archives.

112 Anderson, *Cahill*, p. 270.

113 Security Service Archives. Cahill's authorized biography confirms his involvement in the shipment; Anderson, *Cahill*, pp. 13–14, ch. 11.

114 Security Service Archives.

115 Security Service Archives.

116 Security Service Archives.

117 Security Service Archives. Claims that the *Claudia* realized it was being watched and had begun throwing arms overboard appear to be unfounded.

118 Anderson, *Cahill*, p. 272 (quoting Cahill).

119 Security Service Archives.

120 See below, pp. 737–8.

121 Recollections of a former Security Service officer.

122 Taylor, *Provos*, pp. 164–5.

123 Security Service Archives.

124 Recollections of a former Security Service officer.

125 In evidence to the Bloody Sunday Inquiry in June 2004 (Week 118, ADO 199.0001), Duddy said that he knew Ruairí Ó Brádaigh.

126 Brian Rowan, 'Derry man breaks silence in "McGuinness plea" ', *Belfast Telegraph*, 21 June 2007.

127 Security Service Archives.

128 Security Service Archives.

129 Security Service Archives.

130 Security Service Archives.

131 Recollections of a former Security Service officer.

132 Security Service Archives.

133 See below, pp. 637–8.

134 Security Service Archives. The fact that the DCI's meeting with Wilson is not recorded in Security Service Archives is further evidence of the clandestine nature of the DCI's visit to Chequers.

Chapter 4: The 'Wilson Plot'

1 Ziegler, *Wilson*, p. 184.

2 Security Service Archives.

3 Security Service Archives.

4 See above, pp. 567–74.

5 Security Service Archives.

6 Security Service Archives.

7 Security Service Archives.

8 Security Service Archives.

9 Security Service Archives.

10 Security Service Archives.

11 Security Service Archives.

12 Ziegler, *Wilson*, p. 366.

13 Donoughue, *Downing Street Diary*, pp. 608–9. Donoughue believed that 'a number of H[arold] W[ilson]'s "personal list" were much closer to Marcia.'

14 Security Service Archives.

15 Security Service Archives.

16 According to the *Evening Standard* in 1961: 'In the cut-throat worlds of commerce and politics [Rudy Sternberg] is regarded as one of the most controversial business men in Britain.' A decade later a Security Service source described him as 'utterly unscrupulous and not to be trusted in any business capacity'. Security Service Archives.

17 *Dictionary of National Biography 1971–1980*, p. 808.

18 Security Service Archives.

19 Security Service Archives.

20 Security Service Archives.

21 Security Service Archives.

22 Donoughue noted in his diary on 6 November 1974 after a discussion with Armstrong about the New Year's Honours List: 'H[arold] W[ilson] even put in Rudi Sternberg, who is connected with a Swiss bank which went broke with an account of HW's, but Robert Armstrong made him take it out.' Donoughue, *Downing Street Diary*, p. 238.

23 Ziegler, *Wilson*, p. 494.

24 Donoughue, *Downing Street Diary*, pp. 608–9, 710.

25 Haines, *Glimmers of Twilight*, p. 161.

26 Donoughue, *Downing Street Diary*, p. 172.

27 Ibid., pp. 66, 86, 114, 132, 172, 194, 343, 347, 385, 391.

28 Security Service Archives.

29 Security Service Archives.

30 Security Service Archives.

31 Security Service Archives.

32 Security Service Archives.

33 Donoughue noted on 26 April 1974 that Kissin was worried because 'His peerage has been delayed.' Donoughue, *Downing Street Diary*, p. 108.

34 Security Service Archives.

35 However, the brothel later complained that Kissin had not yet come round with the champagne. Security Service Archives.

36 Security Service Archives.

37 Security Service Archives.

38 Donoughue, *Downing Street Diary*, pp. 66, 86, 114, 132, 172, 194, 343, 347, 385, 391.

39 Pimlott, *Wilson*, p. 719.

40 Security Service Archives. See above, pp. 415–18.

41 Security Service Archives.

42 Security Service Archives.

43 Haines, Donoughue, *Downing Street Diary*, p. 128. Wilson clearly did not believe Wigg's claim that the Labour MP Harold Davies was behind the press attacks on Marcia Williams; Donoughue, *Downing Street Diary*, p. 122.

44 Donoughue, *Downing Street Diary*, p. 87.

45 See above, pp. 531–2.

46 Security Service Archives.

47 Security Service Archives.

48 Security Service Archives.

49 Security Service Archives.

50 Donoughue, *Downing Street Diary*, p. 207. Donoughue added acerbically, 'In the Labour Party that is quite an achievement.'

51 Security Service Archives. At the CPGB's bugged HQ, Ramelson had been overheard saying 'that he was convinced Hayward was a genuine militant left-winger who recognised the role of the Communist Party inside the Trade Union Movement and who, basically, was for unity with the CPGB, although conscious of the problems involved in pursuing this aim.' Security Service Archives.

52 See above, p. 516.

53 Security Service Archives.

54 Security Service Archives.

55 Donoughue, *Downing Street Diary*, p. 224.

56 Ziegler, *Wilson*, pp. 477–8.

57 Recollections of Sir Michael Hanley.

58 Donoughue, *Downing Street Diary*, pp. 11, 13. Cf. Ziegler, *Wilson*, p. 473.

59 Ziegler, *Wilson*, p. 475.

60 Andrew, *For the President's Eyes Only*, ch. 10.

61 Donoughue, *Downing Street Diary*, p. 669. On another occasion Wilson claimed on what Donoughue described as 'no evidence' that the former Labour MP Maurice Foley was 'paid by the CIA'; ibid., p. 640.

62 Thorpe and his former friend John Holmes were found not guilty of involvement in the assassination at their trial in 1979.

63 Freeman and Penrose, *Rinkagate*, chs 12, 13.

64 Ibid., p. 377.

65 See above, p. 633.

66 Donoughue, *Downing Street Diary*, p. 677.

67 Winter's own accounts of his activities are unreliable. Freeman and Penrose describe him as 'an unscrupulous man who would do and say anything for money', 'a fool as well as a crook'. Freeman and Penrose, *Rinkagate*, pp. 178–84, 203–4.

68 Security Service Archives.

69 Hooper passed on Wilson's comments to the Security Service. Security Service Archives.

70 Freeman and Penrose, *Rinkagate*, p. 182.

71 JIC (A) (72) (Sec) 179 (preserved within TNA CAB 187/19). Donoughue noted on 10 March 1976: 'H[arold] W[ilson] saw Hooper – a senior intelligence man who has been looking into the South African connection.' Donoughue, *Downing Street Diary*, p. 689.

72 Donoughue, *Downing Street Diary*, p. 678.

73 Ibid., p. 688.

74 Ziegler, *Wilson*, p. 479. The Intelligence Co-ordinator seems to have been unimpressed by Wilson's evidence of South African involvement. Security Service Archives.

75 Ziegler, *Wilson*, pp. 486–7.

76 Ibid., pp. 477–8.

77 Morgan, *Callaghan*, p. 610.

78 Donoughue, *Downing Street Diary*, p. 670.

79 Ibid., pp. 656–7.

80 Ziegler, *Wilson*, p. 500.

81 Ibid., pp. 477–8.

82 Wilson's words were quoted in the *Observer* on 28 August 1977.

83 Security Service Archives. The DG privately acknowledged that the submission on which Wilson's briefing was based was 'inadequate'.

84 Ziegler, *Wilson*, p. 490.

85 Ibid., p. 494.

86 Penrose and Courtiour, *Pencourt File*, p. 13. Freeman and Penrose, *Rinkagate*, pp. 242–5. On another occasion Wilson startled a Northern Ireland official by inviting him to 'ring the number of a callbox in the Mile End Road at a certain time when a certain person would be waiting to give him information he might need to hear'. Hennessy, *Prime Minister*, p. 572.

87 Freeman and Penrose, *Rinkagate*, pp. 274–5.

88 Ibid., pp. 273–81.

89 Security Service Archives.

90 Security Service Archives.

91 Security Service Archives.

92 Morgan, *Callaghan*, pp. 610–11.

93 Security Service Archives.

94 Security Service Archives. Wallace also alleged that there had been a deliberate campaign to discredit Wilson; Ziegler, *Wilson*, p. 477. The pro-Wallace case is put in Foot, *Who Framed Colin Wallace?*

95 Holroyd makes his allegations in Holroyd and Burbridge, *War without Honour*.

96 Security Service Archives. Hain suspected South African intelligence of plotting against him: 'If so, were they working with a section of MI5 as part of a much wider project to destabilize Harold Wilson's Labour Government and restructure British politics?' Hain, *Putney Plot?*, pp. 137–54.

97 Peter Wright, interviewed by John Ware on *Panorama*, BBC1, 13 Oct. 1988. See above, p. 518.

98 Ziegler, *Wilson*, pp. 476–7.

99 Security Service Archives.

100 Rimington, *Open Secret*, p. 190.

Chapter 5: Counter-Terrorism and Protective Security in the Later 1970s

1 Security Service Archives.

2 McGladdery, *Provisional IRA in England*, pp. 102–4. The Security Service file on the Balcombe Street siege contains no indication that the Security Service provided significant support to the Met in bringing the siege to an end.

3 Security Service Archives.

4 Security Service Archives.

5 *Parl. Deb. (Commons)*, 25 March 1976, col. 647.

6 Security Service Archives.

7 Security Service Archives.

8 Security Service Archives.

9 Security Service Archives.

10 See above, pp. 604–5.

11 Security Service Archives.

12 Security Service Archives.

13 Security Service Archives.

14 Security Service Archives.

15 Donoughue wrote on 17 February 1977: 'How "responsible" is it not to have a long-term policy?' Donoughue, *Downing Street Diary*, vol. 2, p. 149.

16 Security Service Archives. It was noted in 1978 that, for earlier entrants, 'We have to rely on volunteers and cannot order a staff officer to serve there [Northern Ireland]. At the moment we have only five volunteers, two of whom are unwilling to go until the latter part of this year.' Security Service Archives.

17 Security Service Archives. See above, p. 603.

18 Security Service Archives. FX Branch was originally to be called FZ. Its name was changed because of the fear that, in handwritten form, FZ might be confused with F2.

19 Initially F Branch included Sections F1, F2 and F3, while Sections F4, F5 and F6 belonged to FX Branch. Security Service Archives.

20 Security Service Archives.

21 Security Service Archives.

22 Security Service Archives.

23 Security Service Archives. The main exceptions were Iraqis, Libyans and the staff of Middle Eastern embassies in London.

24 Donoughue, *Downing Street Diary*, vol. 2, p. 248.

25 Security Service Archives.

26 Security Service Archives.

27 Andrew and Mitrokhin, *Mitrokhin Archive*, pp. 506–8. Andrew and Mitrokhin, *Mitrokhin Archive II*, p. 255.

28 Security Service Archives.

29 The last PIRA mainland killing of the 1970s was of a passer-by killed by a bomb placed outside the London home of the Conservative MP Hugh Fraser on 22 October 1975.

30 Statistics in Bew and Gillespie, *Northern Ireland*. 'Deaths arising from the Troubles' were as follows: 1974 – 220; 1975 – 275; 1976 – 297; 1977 – 112; 1978 – 81; 1979 – 113.

31 Anderson, *Cahill*, pp. 314–15.

32 Security Service Archives.

33 Taylor, *Provos*, p. 210.

34 Security Service Archives.
35 Security Service Archives.
36 Security Service Archives.
37 Security Service Archives.
38 Security Service Archives.
39 Security Service Archives.
40 Security Service Archives.
41 The British Minister to NATO, Paul Holmer, had been selected as a PIRA target after plans to assassinate the ambassador to NATO, Sir John Killick, fell through. Security Service Archives.
42 Security Service Archives.
43 Security Service Archives.
44 Coogan, *IRA*, pp. 467–8.
45 Security Service Archives.
46 The Service discounted later press reports that Lord Mountbatten had been warned not to go to Ireland earlier in the summer by Sir Maurice Oldfield, former Chief of SIS. Security Service Archives.
47 English, *Armed Struggle*, pp. 219–21, 224.
48 Security Service Archives.
49 Security Service Archives.
50 Security Service Archives.
51 Security Service Archives.
52 Security Service Archives.
53 Security Service Archives.
54 Wood, *Crimes of Loyalty*, pp. 330–31.
55 Security Service Archives.
56 Security Service Archives. Wood, *Crimes of Loyalty*, p. 329.
57 McMahon, *British Spies and Irish Rebels*, pp. 265–7.
58 Security Service Archives.
59 Security Service Archives.
60 Security Service Archives.
61 Security Service Archives.
62 Security Service Archives.

Chapter 6: The Callaghan Government and Subversion

1 Beckett, *Enemy Within*, p. 182.
2 Security Service Archives.
3 See above, pp. 527–31, 535; below, pp. 659, 664–5.
4 Clarke, *Hope and Glory*, pp. 352–4.
5 Security Service Archives.
6 See below, p. 711.
7 Security Service Archives.
8 Security Service Archives.
9 Security Service Archives.
10 Clarke, *Hope and Glory*, pp. 349–50.
11 Security Service Archives.
12 Security Service Archives.
13 Security Service Archives.
14 Security Service Archives.
15 Security Service Archives.
16 Security Service Archives.
17 Beckett, *Enemy Within*, pp. 182–3.
18 Security Service Archives.
19 JIC (A) (71) 16, 'The Security of the United Kingdom Base in a situation leading to a threat of general war', 23 March 1971, TNA CAB 186/8. I am grateful to Professor Peter Hennessy for this reference.

20 Security Service Archives.

21 See above, pp. 412–14.

22 McSmith, *Faces of Labour*, pp. 89–90.

23 Benn, *Against the Tide*, pp. 20–21.

24 Seyd, *Rise and Fall of the Labour Left*, pp. 50–53. McSmith, *Faces of Labour*, pp. 101–5.

25 Security Service Archives.

26 Security Service Archives.

27 Security Service Archives.

28 Morgan, *Callaghan*, pp. 702–3. While Callaghan was foreign secretary in 1975, the Security Service had been informed that he had been 'most interested' in a Service report on 'Trotskyist activities' in his constituency but had minuted that the Trotskyists were 'all running for cover at present' rather than attacking him. Security Service Archives.

29 Security Service Archives.

30 Security Service Archives. Early work in F1A had included investigating constituencies where 'there are grounds for suspecting that left-wing militants are attempting to remove right-wing Labour MPs'; Security Service Archives.

31 Security Service Archives.

32 Security Service Archives.

33 Security Service Archives.

34 Security Service Archives.

35 Beckett, *Enemy Within*, pp. 185–6.

36 McSmith, *Faces of Labour*, p. 106.

37 Seyd, *Rise and Fall of the Labour Left*, pp. 50–51.

38 McSmith, *Faces of Labour*, pp. 107–8.

39 Security Service Archives.

40 Security Service Archives.

41 Security Service Archives.

42 Security Service Archives.

43 Security Service Archives.

44 Security Service Archives.

45 Security Service Archives.

46 Security Service Archives.

47 Westlake, *Kinnock*, p. 316.

48 Security Service Archives.

49 McSmith, *Faces of Labour*, p. 107.

50 Westlake, *Kinnock*, p. 318n.

51 Security Service Archives.

52 Note of a meeting at Chequers, 26 June 1977, TNA PREM 15/1491, s. B12.

53 Note by Callaghan on memo sent to him on Grunwick dispute, TNA PREM 16/1491.

54 Security Service Archives.

55 Security Service Archives.

56 'August 8 Day of Action Called Off', *Daily Telegraph*, 1 Aug. 1977.

57 Security Service Archives.

58 'Unions ready for defeat at Grunwick', *Sunday Telegraph*, 11 Sept. 1977.

59 Security Service Archives.

60 Security Service Archives.

61 'Up to 104% pay rise needed, police tell Home Office', *The Times*, 27 Aug. 1977.

62 Denis Healey (Chancellor) to Callaghan, 21 Oct. 1977 (reporting what Rees had told him Police Commissioners said about reaction to a 10 per cent pay rise); Note of a telephone conversation between Prime Minister and Home Secretary, 23 Oct. 1977. TNA PREM 16/1406.

63 Comments by Callaghan of 'Final version' of Home Secretary's speech sent to 10 Downing Street on 25 Oct. 1977, TNA PREM 16/1406.

64 Police Supplement, 4 Nov. 1977; copy in TNA PREM 16/1406.

65 Security Service Archives.

66 Security Service Archives.

67 Security Service Archives.

68 Security Service Archives.
69 Security Service Archives.
70 Security Service Archives.
71 Morgan, *Callaghan*, p. 674.
72 Security Service Archives.
73 See below, p. 681.
74 See above, pp. 579–81, 583–4.
75 Rimington, *Open Secret*, p. 95.
76 Recollections of a former Security Service officer.
77 Security Service Archives.
78 Security Service Archives.
79 Recollections of a former Security Service officer.
80 See below, pp. 670–72.

Chapter 7: The Thatcher Government and Subversion

1 Security Service Archives.
2 Security Service Archives.
3 Security Service Archives.
4 Security Service Archives.
5 Rothschild was at the time scheming unsuccessfully to become Thatcher's security adviser. He also hoped, in vain, to become the next 'C'. Rose, *Elusive Rothschild*, pp. 250–51.
6 Security Service Archives. When Director F briefed the PUS at the Department of Employment about the work of the unit, both were concerned about its ability to live up to ministerial expectations. Security Service Archives.
7 Security Service Archives.
8 Security Service Archives.
9 Thatcher, *Downing Street Years*, pp. 116–20.
10 ' "I'm not to blame for Rover" – Red Robbo', BBC Online, 28 March 2000.
11 Security Service Archives.
12 Security Service Archives.
13 Security Service Archives. In March 1980 Deverell sought help in identifying open-source evidence of union militants' membership of subversive organizations, particularly in the civil service unions and the NUM, above all in South Wales where the leadership appeared to be pushing for industrial action for political reasons in the face of clear opposition from the rank and file.
14 Security Service Archives.
15 Thatcher, *Downing Street Years*, p. 267.
16 Security Service Archives.
17 Security Service Archives.
18 Security Service Archives.
19 Security Service Archives.
20 Security Service Archives.
21 Security Service Archives.
22 For examples, see Andrew and Gordievsky (eds), *Instructions from the Centre*.
23 Security Service Archives.
24 Security Service Archives.
25 Security Service Archives.
26 Security Service Archives.
27 Gordievsky, *Next Stop Execution*, pp. 277–8.
28 Security Service Archives.
29 Security Service Archives. Kent was not, however, always even-handed. In 1983 he praised the *Morning Star* for its 'steady, honest and generous coverage of the whole disarmament case'. Julian Lewis, 'When is a Smear Not a Smear?', *Salisbury Review*, Oct. 1984.
30 Security Service Archives.
31 Security Service Archives.
32 Security Service Archives.

33 Security Service Archives.
34 Security Service Archives.
35 Recollections of a former Security Service officer.
36 Security Service Archives.
37 Recollections of a former Security Service officer.
38 Security Service Archives.
39 Security Service Archives.
40 Security Service Archives. Director F noted on 26 June that, though the NUM and Coal Board were due to hold talks in the following week, 'there was still little room for optimism about the outcome.' Security Service Archives.
41 See above, p. 598. Security Service Archives.
42 Security Service Archives.
43 Milne, *Enemy Within*, pp. 341–2. 'MI5's Official Secrets', *Observer*, 3 Jan. 1988.
44 Milne, *Enemy Within*, p. 342.
45 Recollections of Dame Stella Rimington. 'Unaffiliated subversive' was a 'special category' which required the approval of an officer with the rank of assistant director or above, defined as 'UK citizen or foreigner who is not a member of, or sympathetic to, one subversive organisation, but who threatens parliamentary democracy'; Security Service Archives.
46 Security Service Archives.
47 Security Service Archives.
48 Recollections of Dame Stella Rimington.
49 Milne, *Enemy Within*, ch. 4; a summary of Windsor's libel action appears on the website of his lawyers, Carter-Ruck; *Parl. Deb. (Commons)*, 12 June 1991.
50 Recollections of Dame Stella Rimington. Security Service Archives.
51 Security Service Archives.
52 Thatcher, *Downing Street Years*, p. 363.
53 Ibid., pp. 365–8.
54 Security Service Archives.
55 Security Service Archives.
56 Security Service Archives.
57 Security Service Archives.
58 See above, p. 599.
59 Security Service Archives.
60 Milne, *Enemy Within*, p. 268.
61 Gordievsky, *Next Stop Execution*, p. 308.
62 Security Service Archives.
63 Security Service Archives.
64 Security Service Archives. Director FX had reported to the Directors' Meeting on 24 July that Ramelson had a low opinion of the current CPGB industrial organizer and was trying to persuade the Party to 'extend their influence in the miners' strike'. Security Service Archives.
65 Security Service Archives.
66 Thatcher, *Downing Street Years*, p. 369 and n.
67 Duff said later that the decision to seek an HOW on Cox was 'a matter of judgement', and implied that his judgement would have been different. Security Service Archives. He also commented that a paper on the CND file on subversive influence in CND may have concentrated 'rather too much on CND activities as such'.
68 Security Service Archives.
69 Security Service Archives.
70 Security Service Archives.
71 Security Service Archives.
72 Security Service Archives.
73 Security Service Archives.
74 *Scotsman*, 2 July 1986. Security Service Archives.
75 Security Service Archives.
76 Security Service Archives.
77 Security Service Archives.

78 Security Service Archives.
79 Security Service Archives.

Chapter 8: Counter-Terrorism and Protective Security in the Early 1980s

1   Security Service Archives.
2   See above, p. 647.
3   Security Service Archives.
4   Recollections of a former Security Service officer.
5   See above, pp. 653–4.
6   Security Service Archives.
7   See above, p. 600.
8   Security Service Archives.
9   Security Service Archives.
10 Security Service Archives.
11 See above, pp. 620–21.
12 Security Service Archives.
13 Security Service Archives.
14 Thatcher, *Downing Street Years*, p. 90. According to Peter de la Billière, that strategy was subsequently slightly modified: 'After extensive discussions in the COBR, Whitelaw decided that an assault on the Embassy would be justified if two or more of the hostages were killed. One death, he ruled, could occur as the result of an accident, and negotiations might carry on after it; but if a second hostage were murdered, and more were threatened, that would be sufficient cause for an attack.' de la Billière, *Looking for Trouble*, p. 322.
15 See above, pp. 613, 655.
16 Thatcher, *Downing Street Years*, p. 89. On the origins of Service involvement in COBR, see above, p. 614.
17 Security Service Archives.
18 Security Service Archives.
19 Security Service Archives.
20 Security Service Archives.
21 Security Service Archives.
22 Security Service Archives.
23 Thatcher, *Downing Street Years*, p. 90.
24 Security Service Archives.
25 de la Billière, *Looking for Trouble*, p. 326.
26 Ibid., pp. 333–5.
27 Security Service Archives.
28 *Parl. Deb. (Commons)*, 6 May 1980, cols 28–35.
29 Security Service Archives.
30 Security Service Archives.
31 See above, pp. 555–6.
32 The first full-scale British counter-terrorist exercise in 1973 had been devised to deal with the threat of aircraft hijacking. See above, p. 615.
33 Security Service Archives.
34 Thatcher, *Downing Street Years*, p. 89.
35 Security Service Archives.
36 In December 1980 the DG (Sir Howard Smith) told the Home Secretary (Willie Whitelaw) that 'At the present time the Libyans were the biggest threat and I hoped that everything possible would be done in Tripoli to see that undesirables do not get visas. At the same time we must recognise that some would get through the net and if they did I hoped that the Home Secretary would be prepared to follow up a vigorous policy towards undesirables who turned up here.' Security Service Archives.
37 Security Service Archives.
38 Security Service Archives.
39 Security Service Archives.

40 Security Service Archives.
41 Security Service Archives.
42 Security Service Archives.
43 Security Service Archives.
44 Security Service Archives.
45 Security Service Archives. The Hampshire Special Branch found 3 grams of thallium hidden in a Portsmouth building. Security Service Archives.
46 'Shared-out peanuts foiled poison plot, QC says', *The Times*, 23 June 1981. Malcolm Stuart, 'Poisoner who got it all wrong', *Guardian*, 3 July 1981.
47 Security Service Archives.
48 Security Service Archives.
49 Security Service Archives.
50 Security Service Archives.
51 Security Service Archives.
52 Security Service Archives.
53 Follain, *Jackal*, pp. 160–61.
54 Security Service Archives.
55 On ASALA and the rival Justice Commandos of the Armenian Genocide (JCAG), see Hoffman, *Inside Terrorism*, pp. 76–7.
56 Security Service Archives.
57 Security Service Archives.
58 Security Service Archives.
59 An alleged accomplice was found not guilty.
60 *The Times*, 25 July 1983.
61 Hoffman, *Inside Terrorism*, p. 77.
62 English, *Armed Struggle*, ch. 5.
63 Security Service Archives.
64 Moloney, *Secret History of the IRA*, pp. 206–7.
65 Security Service Archives.
66 Security Service Archives.
67 Thatcher, *Downing Street Years*, p. 392.
68 Moloney, *Secret History of the IRA*, p. 206. English, *Armed Struggle*, ch. 5.
69 Security Service Archives.
70 Thatcher, *Downing Street Years*, p. 391.
71 See above, p. 651.
72 Recollections of a former Security Service officer.
73 Security Service Archives.
74 Recollections of a former Security Service officer.
75 Security Service Archives.
76 Security Service Archives.
77 Security Service Archives. The Working Party thought that the absence of public funds, other inducements and sanctions made many EKP owners (the majority in the private sector) reluctant to incur the sometimes heavy expenditure required to achieve a satisfactory level of protective security. It was also believed that the criteria used to identify EKPs were too inflexible and that the list (later simplified) was too large.
78 Recollections of a former Security Service officer.
79 Security Service Archives.
80 The main committees on which the Service argued the case for improved protective security within Whitehall were the EKP sub-committees of the Official Committee on Terrorism (TO) and the Official Committee on Home Defence (HDO); the HDO sub-committee dealt with measures to protect EKPs in time of war and major international crises.
81 Security Service Archives.
82 Security Service Archives.
83 Bew and Gallagher, *Northern Ireland*, pp. 159–60.
84 Security Service Archives.
85 Security Service Archives.
86 Recollections of Sir Stephen Lander.

87 Security Service Archives.
88 Security Service Archives.
89 Security Service Archives.
90 Security Service Archives.
91 Security Service Archives.
92 Moloney, *Secret History of the IRA*, p. 209.
93 Security Service Archives.
94 David Pallister, 'US court clears five of IRA gunrunning plot', *Guardian*, 6 Nov. 1982.
95 Security Service Archives.
96 Security Service Archives.
97 Security Service Archives.
98 Security Service Archives.
99 Security Service Archives.
100 It was later concluded that the driver had made two previous, undetected arms deliveries. Security Service Archives.
101 A second Provisional who was unloading the container with McVeigh escaped. Security Service Archives.
102 Security Service Archives.
103 Security Service Archives.
104 Security Service Archives.
105 Security Service Archives.
106 Security Service Archives.
107 Security Service Archives.
108 F became once again a counter-subversion branch.
109 Security Service Archives.
110 Security Service Archives.
111 Information from MPSB.
112 Security Service Archives.
113 Recollections of an MPSB officer.
114 Recollections of an MPSB officer.
115 Security Service Archives.
116 Recollections of MPSB officer. On US intelligence on Libyan terrorism in the mid-1980s, see Andrew, *For the President's Eyes Only*, pp. 483–4.
117 See above, p. 689.
118 Andrew and Gordievsky, *KGB*, p. 632.
119 Security Service Archives.
120 Recollections of Sir Patrick Walker.
121 Security Service Archives.
122 Security Service Archives.
123 Security Service Archives.
124 Al Jahour's assassin has yet to be identified. Security Service Archives.
125 Dobson and Payne, *War without End*, pp. 190–91. Security Service Archives.
126 Security Service Archives.
127 Security Service Archives.
128 Security Service Archives.
129 Dobson and Payne, *War without End*, pp. 191–2.
130 Ibid., p. 187.
131 See below, pp. 637–8.
132 Security Service Archives.
133 'Terrorists Jailed for Marita Ann Cache', *The Times*, 12 Dec. 1984. Two other crew members, who were said to be unaware of the trawler's mission when it sailed from Co. Kerry, were given five-year suspended sentences.
134 Security Service Archives.
135 Recollections of Sir Stephen Lander.
136 Recollections of Sir Stephen Lander.
137 Security Service Archives.
138 Security Service Archives.

Chapter 9: Counter-Espionage in the Last Decade of the Cold War

1 Media interest was provoked by the publication of Andrew Boyle's book *Climate of Treason*, which told part of the Blunt story but, for fear of libel proceedings, referred to him as 'Maurice' and concealed his identity. On the media and Blunt's exposure, see Carter, *Blunt*, pp. 468–82.

2 Security Service Archives.

3 I am grateful to Nicholas Wilkinson, one of the Cabinet Office official historians, for passing on this information from Blunt's confidant, who does not wish his identify to be published.

4 Beves had first been wrongly identified as a likely Soviet mole in 1977.

5 Security Service Archives. While stationed at the Centre in the FCD Third Department (whose responsibilities included Britain), Gordievsky had learned, after the exposure in London of Blunt as the 'Fourth Man', that Cairncross had been the fifth. In 1981, while editing a history of the Third Department, he discovered that Cairncross's achievements as a Soviet agent had been comparable to those of Philby, Burgess and Maclean.

6 Cairncross, who had already been named as a Soviet spy, was first publicly identified as the Fifth Man in Andrew and Gordievsky, *KGB*, published in 1990.

7 See above, p. 542.

8 Security Service Archives.

9 Stonehouse, *Ralph*. Andrew and Gordievsky, *KGB*, pp. 522–3.

10 Security Service Archives.

11 Security Service Archives.

12 Chapman Pincher, 'Minister Sold our Concorde Secrets to KGB', *Daily Express*, 16 Jan. 2006.

13 Christopher Andrew, interview with Dame Stella Rimington, Sept. 2001.

14 Security Service Archives.

15 Andrew and Gordievsky (eds), *Instructions from the Centre*, ch. 4.

16 Security Service Archives. Francis Pym, then Foreign Secretary, was also indoctrinated on 23 December 1982.

17 Howe, *Conflict of Loyalty*, pp. 349–50.

18 Security Service Archives.

19 Recollections of a former Security Service officer.

20 Security Service Archives.

21 Security Service Archives.

22 Security Service Archives. See above, pp. 536, 657.

23 Gordievsky, *Next Stop Execution*, pp. 285–6.

24 Security Service Archives.

25 Security Service Archives.

26 Security Service Archives.

27 Gordievsky, *Next Stop Execution*, pp. 286–7.

28 Security Service Archives.

29 Security Service Archives.

30 Pincher, *Their Trade is Treachery*.

31 See above, pp. 518–19.

32 Andrew and Gordievsky, *KGB*, p. 27.

33 Security Service Archives.

34 Security Service Archives.

35 Security Service Archives.

36 Security Service Archives. See above, p. 578.

37 On Prime's own assessment of the ideological element in his motivation, see above, p. 578.

38 By beginning its analysis in 1952, the brief omitted Burgess, Maclean and the main atom spies – all of whose motives were primarily ideological.

39 Security Service Archives.

40 Gordievsky originally supposed that KOBA was a codename applied by the Centre to the anonymous author of the letter; Security Service Archives. When he became resident-designate in the spring of 1985 and gained access to Bettaney's letters to Guk, however, he discovered that Bettaney had signed himself 'Koba'.

41 Andrew and Gordievsky, *KGB*, pp. 585–7. Gordievsky, *Next Stop Execution*, pp. 249–52.
42 Security Service Archives.
43 Security Service Archives. Recollections of a former Security Service officer.
44 Security Service Archives.
45 Security Service Archives.
46 Security Service Archives. The use of ELMEN meant that the reports did not go into the files used for other Gordievsky reports and thus restricted knowledge of the lead even further.
47 Security Service Archives.
48 Recollections of a former Security Service officer.
49 Security Service Archives.
50 Security Service Archives.
51 Recollections of a former Security Service officer. Security Service Archives.
52 Recollections of a former Security Service officer.
53 Security Service Archives.
54 Security Service Archives.
55 Security Service Archives.
56 Security Service Archives.
57 Recollections of a former Security Service officer.
58 Security Service Archives.
59 On 27 July DG and Director K discussed the ELMEN case with Sir Robert Armstrong and the PUS at the Home Office, and reported that, though the case had been solved, there was still no evidence on which to base a prosecution. Security Service Archives.
60 Security Service Archives.
61 Security Service Archives.
62 Security Service Archives.
63 After returning from leave on 10 August, Gordievsky reported that G. F. Titov, head of the FCD Third Department (whose responsibilities included the UK), shared Guk's view that Bettaney's letters were a British provocation. Security Service Archives.
64 Security Service Archives.
65 Security Service Archives.
66 Security Service Archives.
67 Security Service Archives.
68 Security Service Archives.
69 Security Service Archives.
70 Security Service Archives.
71 Security Service Archives.
72 Security Service Archives. DDG made clear that Bettaney's assumption was correct: there could be no offer of immunity from prosecution in return for a full confession.
73 Recollection of a former Security Service officer. Security Service Archives.
74 Security Service Archives.
75 Security Service Archives.
76 Security Service Archives.
77 Security Service Archives.
78 Security Service Archives.
79 Security Service Archives.
80 Security Service Archives.
81 Security Service Archives.
82 Security Service Archives.
83 Recollections of a former Security Service officer.
84 Andrew and Gordievsky (eds), *Instructions from the Centre*, pp. 69–73.
85 Ibid., pp. 95–8.
86 Howe, *Conflict of Loyalty*, pp. 349–50. At the time CIA analysts were more sceptical. Andrew, *For the President's Eyes Only*, pp. 476–7.
87 Andrew and Gordievsky, *KGB*, pp. 582–605. Andrew and Gordievsky (eds), *Instructions from the Centre*, ch. 4. On US response to Gordievsky's intelligence, see Andrew, *For the President's Eyes Only*, pp. 476–7.

88 'Russian Ignored Bettaney "Letter Boxes", Jury Told', *The Times*, 11 April 1984. Report of the Security Commission, May 1985, Cmnd 9514.

89 Security Service Archives. As a Line KR officer, Guk was not really au fait with Line PR work.

90 Security Service Archives.

91 Security Service Archives.

92 Security Service Archives.

93 Security Service Archives.

94 Gordievsky, *Next Stop Execution*, p. 270.

95 Security Service Archives.

96 Security Service Archives.

97 Security Service Archives.

98 Gordievsky, *Next Stop Execution*, pp. 310–11.

99 Thatcher, *Downing Street Years*, p. 461.

100 Gordievsky, *Next Stop Execution*, pp. 310–11, 317–18. Gordievsky's appointment as resident-designate was complicated by premature announcement of it at an FCD conference in January 1985.

101 Security Service Archives.

102 Gordievsky, *Next Stop Execution*, pp. 318–19.

103 The instructions from the Centre to the London residency on the £8,000 payment to DARIO are published in Andrew and Gordievsky (eds), *Instructions from the Centre*, pp. 61–3.

104 Gordievsky, *Next Stop Execution*, p. 315. Andrew and Gordievsky, *KGB*, p. 34. Gordievsky was informed about the recall of the illegals after his return to Moscow by an FCD colleague who was unaware that he was under suspicion.

105 Gordievsky, *Next Stop Execution*, ch. 1. Andrew and Gordievsky, *KGB*, pp. 28–35.

106 Gordievsky, *Next Stop Execution*, p. 346.

107 Security Service Archives.

108 Security Service Archives.

109 Gordievsky, *Next Stop Execution*, pp. 350–52. Leila Gordievsky and their two daughters, Anna and Maria, were finally allowed to leave Russia after the failure of the hardline coup of August 1991.

110 Security Service Archives.

111 Security Service Archives.

112 Security Service Archives.

113 Security Service Archives.

114 Security Service Archives.

115 Security Service Archives.

116 Security Service Archives.

117 Security Service Archives.

118 Security Service Archives.

119 Rimington, *Open Secret*, p. 186.

120 Security Service Archives.

121 Security Service Archives.

122 Security Service Archives. On 19 November 2005 the Czech newspaper *Dnes* reported that Jelínek was to publish his memoirs.

123 Security Service Archives.

124 Howe, *Conflict of Loyalty*, pp. 349–50. On Gordievsky's meetings with Margaret Thatcher, see Gordievsky, *Next Stop Execution*, pp. 368–72.

125 Security Service Archives.

126 Andrew and Mitrokhin, *Mitrokhin Archive*, pp. 548–53.

127 See above, pp. 583–5.

128 Security Service Archives.

129 During the early 1980s statistics on Soviet S&T were obtained by a French agent in FCD Directorate T, Vladimir Vetrov (codenamed FAREWELL). Hanson, *Soviet Industrial Espionage*. Andrew and Mitrokhin, *Mitrokhin Archive*, pp. 618–20.

130 Security Service Archives.
131 Security Service Archives.
132 Security Service Archives.
133 Security Service Archives.
134 Security Service Archives.
135 Security Service Archives.
136 Recollections of a former Security Service officer.
137 See above, pp. 583-5.
138 Recollections of a former Security Service officer.

Chapter 10: Counter-Terrorism and Protective Security in the Later 1980s

1 Rimington, *Open Secret*, pp. 219-20.
2 Security Service Archives.
3 Security Service Archives.
4 Security Service Archives. On the attempted assassination of Argov, see above, pp. 690-91.
5 Security Service Archives.
6 *Der Spiegel*, 14 Oct. 1985. 'Abu Nidal, a hired gun who turned on himself', *The Times*, 20 Aug. 2002.
7 Security Service Archives.
8 The Service acknowledged in 1988 that it had still not discovered whether Abu Nidal had established 'a structure' in Britain. Security Service Archives.
9 Andrew and Mitrokhin, *Mitrokhin Archive II*, pp. 144, 259. The JIC reported in October 1989 that there had been no report of ANO involvement in 'any international terrorist attacks' since an attack on a Greek cruise ship fifteen months earlier. Security Service Archives.
10 See above, p. 730.
11 Security Service Archives.
12 Security Service Archives.
13 See above, pp. 648, 691.
14 Frank, *Indira*, pp. 480-83, 492-4, 498-9.
15 Security Service Archives.
16 Security Service Archives.
17 Security Service Archives.
18 Security Service Archives.
19 Moloney, *Secret History of the IRA*, pp. 3-6.
20 Security Service Archives.
21 Taylor, *Provos*, pp. 277-8.
22 Security Service Archives.
23 Information from Sir Stephen Lander.
24 Security Service Archives.
25 Recollections of Sir Patrick Walker.
26 Taylor, *Brits*, pp. 251-3. Taylor concludes, 'If there had been a "Brit" conspiracy to get rid of Stalker (which I do not believe), then appointing Colin Sampson as his successor, in the expectation that he would collude in a cover-up, was a major mistake. This is one of the main reasons why the conspiracy theory does not hold water.'
27 Bolton, *Death on the Rock*, pp. 189-91.
28 Security Service Archives.
29 Eckert, *Fatal Encounter*, pp. 13-14.
30 Ibid., p. 11.
31 Security Service Archives.
32 Security Service Archives.
33 Eckert, *Fatal Encounter*, pp. 14, 19, 21.
34 *The Windlesham/Rampton Report*, pp. 103-7. Unsurprisingly, given the sudden, confusing and shocking nature of the shootings, there were differences in witness accounts.
35 See above, p. 000.
36 *The Windlesham/Rampton Report*, pp. 45-7, 81-2, 86-8. The *World in Action* team,

reliance on a mistaken version of Spanish surveillance given them by some of the Spanish authorities.

37 Transcript of 'Death on the Rock', 28 April 1988; *The Windlesham/Rampton Report*, pp. 47–8.

38 See, e.g., Taylor, *Brits*, p. 282. Among other errors of fact in 'Death on the Rock' was the assertion (for which no evidence was given) that 'Mary Parkin' (Siobhan O'Hanlon), wrongly described as the 'fourth member' of a three-person ASU, returned to the Rock on 1 March, only five days before the shootings and several days after she had in fact returned to Ireland. Transcript of 'Death on the Rock', 28 April 1988; *The Windlesham/Rampton Report*, p. 41.

39 Security Service Archives.

40 Security Service Archives.

41 Bolton, *Death on the Rock*, p. 300.

42 Security Service Archives.

43 Security Service Archives.

44 Security Service Archives.

45 See below, pp. 772, 773–4.

46 Security Service Archives.

47 Security Service Archives.

48 Security Service Archives.

49 Security Service Archives; additional information from Dame Eliza Manningham-Buller.

50 Security Service Archives.

51 Security Service Archives. The Scottish Lord Advocate, Lord Fraser of Carmyllie, who had ultimate responsibility for the Lockerbie investigation, recalls that evidence that the clothing had been bought in Malta by Al Megrahi laid the foundation of the Crown case: 'For me that was the most significant breakthrough.' Interview with Lord Fraser, *The Times*, 19 Dec. 2008.

52 Recollections of a former Security Service officer.

53 Naftali, *Blind Spot*, p. 220.

54 A first appeal by Al Megrahi was unsuccessful. He later abandoned a second appeal. In August 2009 he was freed from prison in Scotland on compassionate grounds and returned to Libya.

55 Security Service Archives.

56 Security Service Archives.

57 Rimington, *Open Secret*, p. 216.

58 Bew and Gillespie, *Northern Ireland*, p. 236.

59 Security Service Archives.

60 On the less successful operations of the early 1980s, see above, pp. 697–8.

61 Security Service Archives. Peter Eamon Maguire, a senior, long-standing member of PIRA's Engineering Department based in Dublin who worked as a technician for Aer Lingus, escaped arrest and went on the run before being extradited to the USA five years later. Maguire was convicted in 1995.

62 Security Service Archives. This retrospective 1989 report wrongly gives 1985 as the date when the attempt began to trace the order for the fifty switches. The FBI's bid to question Johnson about them in 1984 demonstrates that the attempt began a year earlier.

63 Security Service Archives.

64 Security Service Archives.

65 Security Service Archives. The main reason for the arrest may have been more prosaic. Since Johnson had discovered he was under close surveillance, failure to arrest him at once would have allowed him to warn his PIRA associates. Arrest warrants were rapidly issued for his associates.

66 Security Service Archives.

67 Security Service Archives.

68 Security Service Archives.

69 Security Service Archives.

70 Thatcher, *Downing Street Years*, pp. 414–15.

71 Security Service Archives.

72 Security Service Archives.
73 Security Service Archives.
74 Security Service Archives.
75 Security Service Archives.
76 Security Service Archives.
77 Security Service Archives.
78 Security Service Archives.
79 Security Service Archives.
80 Security Service Archives.

Chapter 11: The Origins of the Security Service Act

1 *Parl. Deb. (Commons)*, 15 Dec. 1924, col. 674.
2 Andrew, 'British View of Security and Intelligence', p. 11.
3 See above, pp. 634–41.
4 Wilson, *Governance of Britain*, ch. 9.
5 On Callaghan's dissatisfaction with Service management, see above, pp. 552, 554.
6 *Parl. Deb. (Commons)*, 28 July 1977, col. 1223.
7 Andrew, 'British View of Security and Intelligence'.
8 Security Service Archives.
9 Andrew, 'British View of Security and Intelligence'. In January 1983 Philip Aldridge was sentenced to three years' imprisonment. He admitted at his trial that as a twenty-year-old lance corporal in military intelligence he had tried to contact the Soviet embassy in the previous year.
10 Lustgarten and Leigh, *In from the Cold*, p. 69.
11 *Parl. Deb. (Commons)*, 12 March 1985, col. 170.
12 Ibid., col. 151. Wood, 'Construction of Parliamentary Accountability for the British Intelligence Community'.
13 Hooper, *Official Secrets*, pp. 174–9.
14 Ibid., pp. 179–81.
15 See above, p. 675.
16 *Parl. Deb. (Commons)*, 12 March 1985, cols 168, 169, 203, 227; cited by Wood, 'Construction of Parliamentary Accountability for the British Intelligence Community'.
17 Security Service Archives.
18 Rimington, *Open Secret*, pp. 194–5.
19 Recollections of former and current members of the Security Service.
20 European Court of Human Rights, Leander Case (10/1985/96/144), 26 March 1987, para. 50. Wood, 'Construction of Parliamentary Accountability for the British Intelligence Community'.
21 European Court of Human Rights, Leander Case (10/1985/96/144), 26 March 1987, para. 51.
22 Ibid., para. 60.
23 Rose, *Elusive Rothschild*, pp. 241–58.
24 Security Service Archives.
25 Security Service Archives. The Legal Adviser reported that the Service was 'reasonably satisfied' that Wright was Pincher's 'main and possibly sole source'.
26 Security Service Archives.
27 Security Service Archives.
28 Security Service Archives.
29 Press reports, 2 Aug. 1984; Security Service Archives.
30 Security Service Archives.
31 Security Service Archives.
32 Security Service Archives. *Commonwealth of Australia* v *John Fairfax & Sons Ltd* (1980) 147 CLR 39.
33 Rimington, *Open Secret*, p. 188.
34 Hooper, *Official Secrets*, pp. 305–7, 314–15. On Hollis's role in the founding of ASIO, see above, pp. 370–71.

35 Hooper, *Official Secrets*, pp. 305–8.
36 Turnbull, *Spycatcher Trial*.
37 A former Security Service officer, who said that he had taken part in training Wright, gave evidence on affidavit. The government's only other witness was the Australian cabinet secretary, Michael Codd. Hooper, *Official Secrets*, pp. 323–4.
38 Rimington, *Open Secret*, pp. 188–9.
39 Turnbull, *Spycatcher Trial*. Rose, *Elusive Rothschild*, pp. 260–61.
40 Hooper, *Official Secrets*, pp. 320–23.
41 *Parl. Deb. (Commons)*, 9 November 1987, cols 13–14.
42 Lustgarten and Leigh, *In from the Cold*, pp. 280–82.
43 Rimington, *Open Secret*, p. 188.
44 See above, p. 642.
45 Rose, *Elusive Rothschild*, p. 268.
46 *Parl. Deb. (Commons)*, 3, 6, 17 Dec. 1989. Smith, *New Cloak, Old Dagger*, p. 69.
47 See above, pp. 589–91.
48 Security Service Archives.
49 Hurd, *Memoirs*, pp. 323–4.
50 Lustgarten and Leigh, *In from the Cold*, pp. 151–2.
51 Security Service Archives.
52 *Parl. Deb. (Commons)*, 22 Nov. 1988, col. 4.
53 Security Service Archives.
54 Lustgarten and Leigh, *In from the Cold*, pp. 77, 438. The first four annual reports of the Commissioner were published as Cm 1480 (1991), Cm 1946 (1992), Cm 2174 (1993) and Cm 2523 (1994). During the first three years of the Act's operation, 102 people complained. The Commissioner concluded that in ninety-nine cases no such inquiries were made and that in three cases, where inquiries were made, the Security Service had 'reasonable grounds' for doing so.
55 Andrew, 'British View of Security and Intelligence'.
56 Recollections of Sir Stephen Lander.
57 Andrew, 'British View of Security and Intelligence'. Christopher Andrew took part in the Ditchley Conference.

SECTION F: AFTER THE COLD WAR

Chapter 1: The Transformation of the Security Service

1 Security Service Archives.
2 Major, *Autobiography*, p. 432.
3 'Lord Butler, the man who will investigate', *Guardian*, 4 Feb. 2004.
4 Security Service Archives.
5 Recollections of a former Security Service officer.
6 Rimington, *Open Secret*, p. 220.
7 Security Service Archives.
8 Security Service Archives.
9 Security Service Archives.
10 Security Service Archives.
11 Rimington, *Open Secret*, p. 223.
12 Security Service Archives.
13 Recollections of Sir Stephen Lander. Security Service Archives.
14 Security Service Archives.
15 Security Service Archives.
16 Recollections of Sir Stephen Lander.
17 Security Service Archives.
18 Security Service Archives.
19 Security Service Archives.

20 Security Service Archives.

21 From 1985 to 1996 the Service had two DDGs: for Administration (DDG(A)) and for Operations (DDG(O)).

22 Rimington, *Open Secret*, p. 241. Rimington remembers Walker telling her she was to be DG 'shortly before Christmas' 1991. However, Walker must have passed on the news a few weeks earlier since in late November he informed the Home Office PUS, Sir Clive Whitmore, that he had discussed with Rimington who was to replace her as DDG(A). On 3 December Walker told Whitmore that he had told the DDG(O) of Rimington's appointment as DG and 'he had taken it well'. Security Service Archives; Home Office Archives.

23 Home Office Archives.

24 Recollections of Dame Stella Rimington.

25 See below, p. 776.

26 Rimington, *Open Secret*, pp. 222-3.

27 Recollections of Sir Stephen Lander.

28 Recollections of Dame Stella Rimington.

29 Rimington, *Open Secret*, pp. 241-3.

30 Christopher Andrew, interview with Dame Stella Rimington, *The Times*, 17 Sept. 2001.

31 Ibid. Rimington, *Open Secret*, pp. 245-6.

32 Lowri Turner, 'Success and the Dowdy Englishwoman', *Evening Standard*, 6 Jan. 1993.

33 Christopher Andrew, interview with Dame Stella Rimington, *The Times*, 17 Sept. 2001.

34 Undated cutting from the *Sun*. Home Office Archives.

35 Security Service Archives.

36 Security Service Archives.

37 Recollections of Sir Stephen Lander.

38 Security Service Archives.

39 Security Service Archives.

40 Home Office Archives.

41 Security Service Archives.

42 In her Annual Report a year later, Rimington claimed that 'The launch of the booklet about the Security Service in July 1993 marked a substantial, and I believe successful, development in our strategy to gain greater public understanding of and support for the Service and its work.' Security Service Archives.

43 Rimington, *Open Secret*, pp. 254-5.

44 Security Service Annual Report 1993-94. See below, p. 777.

45 Rimington, *Open Secret*, p. 256.

46 Security Service Archives. By agreement with the Home Office, however, Rimington did not set up a public press department.

47 Rimington, *Open Secret*, p. 257 and illustrations.

48 Richard Norton-Taylor, 'The Slick Spymaster', *Guardian*, 20 June 1994.

49 Interview with Lord Wilson of Dinton, Jan. 2007. On the origins of the ISC, see above, pp. 755, 768.

50 Security Service Archives.

51 Security Service Archives.

52 Interview by Christopher Andrew with Dame Eliza Manningham-Buller, 3 April 2007.

53 See above, p. 483.

54 Security Service Archives.

55 Security Service Archives.

56 Security Service Archives.

57 Recollections of Jonathan Evans.

58 Security Service Archives.

59 Security Service Archives.

60 Security Service Archives.

61 When William Waldegrave became chief secretary of the Treasury in 1995 (a post he continued to hold until the Labour election victory two years later), budget negotiation became less confrontational. Rimington found him interested and well informed about the intelligence community. Rimington, *Open Secret*, pp. 226-7.

62 H Branch in 1994 took over the former responsibilities of the Registry and information management of S Branch, which was wound up. See Appendix 3. It was abolished in 1997, a year after Lander became DG.
63 Recollections of Sir Stephen Lander.
64 Security Service Archives.
65 Interview with Dame Eliza Manningham-Buller, 3 April 2007.
66 Recollections of Sir Stephen Lander.
67 Security Service Archives.
68 Security Service Archives.
69 The 68 per cent response rate was rated 'unusually high for a staff survey of this kind'; 40 per cent, it reported, was 'common for organisational surveys'. Security Service Archives.
70 Security Service Archives.
71 Security Service Archives.
72 Security Service Archives.
73 Security Service Archives.
74 Anderson, *Cahill*, p. 379.
75 Taylor, *Provos*, p. 331.
76 Security Service Archives.
77 Taylor, *Brits*, pp. 178–9. See above, pp. 625, 646.
78 Major, *Autobiography*, pp. 444–7.
79 Recollections of Sir Stephen Lander.
80 Security Service Archives.
81 Security Service Archives.
82 Security Service Archives.
83 Security Service Archives.
84 Security Service Archives.
85 Security Service Archives.
86 Security Service Archives.
87 Security Service Archives.
88 Security Service Archives.
89 Security Service Archives.
90 Security Service Archives.
91 Security Service Archives.
92 Security Service Archives.
93 Security Service Archives.
94 Security Service Archives.
95 Security Service Archives.
96 See above, pp. 684, 700, 708.
97 Security Service Archives.
98 Security Service Archives.
99 Recollections of Sir Stephen Lander. On 13 July 1995 Director D noted that the Home Secretary had accepted that the Service has 'a significant role ... in working with the law enforcement agencies on organised crime: drugs are the key issue and the Service's role must include this subject.' Security Service Archives.
100 Security Service Archives.
101 Interview by Christopher Andrew with Lord Wilson of Dinton, Jan. 2007.
102 Interview with Dame Eliza Manningham-Buller, 3 April 2007.
103 Recollections of Sir Stephen Lander.
104 Interview with Lord Wilson of Dinton, Jan. 2007.
105 Security Service Archives.
106 Recollections of Sir Stephen Lander.
107 Security Service Archives.
108 Security Service Archives.
109 Ferris, *Ferris Conspiracy*, p. 234.
110 Security Service Archives.
111 Security Service Archives.
112 Ferris, *Ferris Conspiracy*, p. 234.

113 Security Service Archives.

114 Ferris was released on parole in January 2002 after serving four years of his jail term. He was sent back to jail four months later for breaching the terms of his parole. 'From crime fact to crime fiction', BBC News, 18 April 2002. 'Ferris heads back to jail', BBC News, 3 May 2002.

115 Security Service Archives.

116 Security Service Archives.

117 See above, p. 784.

118 Security Service Archives.

119 Security Service Archives. What most shocked management was that 12 per cent of respondents reported incidents of harassment and bullying. Though informed that the average figure in staff surveys was of the order of 15 per cent, management regarded 12 per cent as unacceptable. (Security Service Archives. Recollections of a former Security Service officer.) A series of initiatives followed to address the complaints made by staff. The next survey three years later showed both a significant improvement in morale and a drop of over 50 per cent in reports of harassment and bullying. (See below, p. 808.)

120 Security Service Archives.

121 See above, p. 562.

122 Security Service Archives.

123 Security Service Archives.

124 Security Service Archives.

125 Security Service Archives.

126 Security Service Archives.

127 Security Service Archives. In 1994–5, admittedly a period of low recruitment, because of budget cutbacks, of eighty-one new entrants almost half (thirty-nine) were personally recommended by existing staff members. Security Service Archives.

128 Security Service Archives.

129 Interview with Lord Wilson of Dinton, Jan. 2007.

130 Security Service Annual Report 1997–8.

131 On this attack, see above, p. 783.

132 Security Service Archives.

133 Campbell, Blair Years, pp. 230–31.

134 Memo by Sir Stephen Lander, 30 Aug. 2007.

135 Interview with Lord Wilson of Dinton, Jan. 2007.

136 Security Service Archives.

137 Recollections of a senior civil servant.

138 Security Service Archives.

139 Security Service Archives.

140 Taylor, Provos, p. 352.

141 Security Service Archives.

142 Security Service Archives. In her final meeting with the Home Secretary on 20 March 1996, Rimington reported that 'we thought that there were about 20 Active Service Unit (ASU) members on the mainland at present; that we had identified 10 of these and knew broadly where they were. We were working on the others.' Security Service Archives.

143 Security Service Archives.

144 Security Service Archives.

145 Security Service Archives.

146 On Crawley, see above, p. 704.

147 Security Service Archives.

148 McGladdery, Provisional IRA in England, p. 205.

149 Security Service Archives.

150 Security Service Archives.

151 Security Service Archives.

152 Security Service Archives.

153 Stephen Lander, 'Terrorism: The Genie out of the Bottle', closed lecture to Strategic and Combat Studies Institute, Staff College, Camberley, October 1996.

154 Recollections of Sir Stephen Lander.

155 Interview by Christopher Andrew with Sir Stephen Lander.
156 Security Service Archives.
157 Security Service Archives.
158 Security Service Archives.
159 Security Service Archives.
160 Bew and Gallagher, *Northern Ireland*, pp. 359–65.
161 Ibid., p. 365.

Chapter 2: Holy Terror

1 'The Paladin of Jihad', *Time*, 6 May 1996.
2 *The 9/11 Commission Report*, p. 56.
3 Security Service Archives.
4 The 9/11 Commission in the United States later reported that the Yemen attacks remained 'unknown' to the US intelligence community until 1996–7. *The 9/11 Commission Report*, p. 341.
5 Security Service Archives.
6 Security Service Archives.
7 Hoffman, *Inside Terrorism*, p. 262.
8 Security Service Archives. During the Khomeini era only one of the attacks against Iranian dissidents (in 1987) had taken place in the UK.
9 Security Service Archives.
10 'Salman Rushdie: His life, his work and his religion', *Independent*, 13 Oct. 2006.
11 Security Service Archives.
12 Security Service Archives.
13 Hoffman, *Inside Terrorism*, p. 262.
14 Security Service Archives.
15 Security Service Archives.
16 The Security Service concluded in December 1998: 'Despite the assurances given by [President] Khatami and Foreign Minister Kharrazi, there are indications that elements of the Iranian regime, not under their control, remain committed to carrying out the *fatwa* . . .' Security Service Archives. Over the next few years, however, no specific intelligence emerged of a plot to assassinate Rushdie in the UK.
17 David Shayler's various allegations against the Security Service later included the claim that it had possessed intelligence which would have enabled it to prevent the attack on the embassy, but had failed to act on it. After investigation by the Service, the Home Secretary wrote to the editor of the *Mail on Sunday* on 30 October 1997: 'It is not the case that such information as the Security Service had in their possession would have enabled it to prevent the Israeli Embassy bombing from happening. I can, however, see how Mr Shayler, as a junior member of the Service who was not involved in the relevant area of work at the time, could have gained this mistaken impression.' Security Service Archives.
18 Recollections of Sir Stephen Lander.
19 Security Service Archives.
20 Security Service Archives. Appeals by the two convicted Palestinians, Jawad Botmeh, an electronics expert, and Samar Alami, were dismissed by the Court of Appeal in November 2001. Their later application to the European Court of Human Rights was dismissed in June 2007.
21 Security Service Archives.
22 Security Service Archives.
23 Security Service Archives.
24 Security Service Archives.
25 Security Service Archives.
26 'The Paladin of Jihad', *Time*, 6 May 1996.
27 Security Service Archives.
28 Security Service Archives.
29 Security Service Archives.
30 Security Service Archives.
31 Security Service Archives.

32 'Britain accused of harbouring New York bomber', *Evening Standard*, 17 Jan. 1997. Security Service Archives.

33 Bodansky, *Bin Laden*, p. 101. Bodansky's biography, published in 1999, contained a glowing tribute from Professor Jeane Kirkpatrick of Georgetown University, formerly US representative at the United Nations. A new edition, repeating the claims about Bin Laden's residence in Dollis Hill, was published two years later, after 9/11.

34 Recollections of Dame Stella Rimington.

35 Security Service Archives.

36 Security Service Archives.

37 Security Service Archives.

38 Security Service Archives.

39 Security Service Archives.

40 Wright, *Looming Tower*, pp. 270-72.

41 *The 9/11 Commission Report*, pp. 116-17. Tenet, *At the Center of the Storm*, p. 117.

42 Security Service Archives.

43 Security Service Archives.

44 Security Service Archives.

45 Next on the list of 'successes against international terrorism' in 1998-9 came the 'disruption of UBL-instigated attack in the Gulf through the passage of pre-emptive intelligence; winding up of Algerian Islamic extremist cell in London through the arrest of eight Algerians and 2 Tunisians'. Security Service Archives.

46 The Security Service believed that other possible reasons which Bin Laden might have for planting false reports of impending terrorist attacks were:

   (i) to test for leaks. UBL believes that his organisation is penetrated by hostile intelligence services. Thus, he may spread a rumour about an attack plan to a select number of people and then see if there is a response by the security authorities.

   (ii) to maintain morale. It is possible that UBL activists may become disillusioned with the lack of attacks against western interests. UBL may spread rumours to buoy up morale among his cadres.

   Security Service Archives.

47 Security Service Archives.

48 Security Service Archives.

49 Interview by Christopher Andrew with Jonathan Evans, 3 Feb. 2009.

50 Security Service Archives.

51 Recollections of a Security Service officer.

52 *The 9/11 Commission Report*, pp. 71-3.

53 'Crashes in NYC had grim origins at Logan', *Boston Globe*, 12 Sept. 2001.

54 Security Service Archives.

55 'Men "Planned Fireworks Business" ', BBC News [online], 8 Feb. 2002. 'Bomb Maker Jailed for Twenty Years', BBC News [online], 27 Feb. 2002. 'Abedin Team May Go Abroad', BBC News [online], 27 Feb. 2002.

56 Security Service Archives.

57 Speech by DG, Dame Eliza Manningham-Buller, 9 Nov. 2006; the full text appears on the Security Service website.

58 This was the conclusion of the Joint Terrorism Assessment Centre (JTAC). Security Service Archives.

59 Tenet, *At the Center of the Storm*, p. 260.

60 Security Service Archives. Claims that UBL had also fallen for a 'red mercury' scam in 1993 are disputed. Wright, *Looming Tower*, pp. 190-91, 411-12.

61 Security Service Archives.

62 Security Service Archives.

63 Security Service Archives.

64 Security Service Archives.

65 Security Service Archives.

66 Security Service Archives.

67 Security Service Archives.

68 Security Service Archives.

69 Interview with Lord Wilson of Dinton, Jan. 2007. Recollections of Sir Stephen Lander. Significantly, Alastair Campbell's published diaries, which begin in 1994, contain no reference to the Security Service (save for a reference to the government injunction against Shayler) until 9/11 – at which point they begin to acknowledge that Lander was 'pretty impressive' and 'very good on big picture and detail'.

70 Campbell, *Blair Years*, p. 560.

71 Interview by Christopher Andrew with Lord Wilson of Dinton, Jan. 2007.

72 Campbell, *Blair Years*, pp. 560–61.

73 Security Service Archives.

74 Campbell, *Blair Years*, p. 561.

75 Ibid., p. 563.

76 Interview with Lord Wilson of Dinton, Jan. 2007.

77 Security Service Archives.

78 At Langley they were joined by Blair's chief foreign policy adviser, Sir David Manning, who happened to be in Washington. Recollections of Baroness Manningham-Buller.

79 Tenet, *At the Center of the Storm*, p. 174.

80 Campbell, *Blair Years*, pp. 567–8.

81 Blunkett, *Blunkett Tapes*, p. 333.

82 Security Service Archives.

83 Campbell, *Blair Years*, p. 578.

84 Security Service Archives.

85 Security Service Annual Review 2001–2.

Chapter 3: After 9/11

1 Security Service Archives.

2 'Guard admits stealing secrets', BBC News, 17 Dec. 2001. 'Guard jailed for stealing secrets', BBC News, 1 Feb. 2002.

3 Security Service Archives.

4 It would have been shorter still but for Bravo's decision to take a brief holiday abroad. Security Service Archives.

5 Security Service Archives. 'Guard admits stealing secrets', BBC News, 17 Dec. 2001. 'Guard jailed for stealing secrets',

6 BBC News, 1 Feb. 2002.

7 Security Service Archives.

8 Security Service Archives. 'Plane engineer admits spying', BBC News, 29 Nov. 2002. 'Southend sting halts a spy called Hazard', *Guardian*, 30 Nov. 2002. 'Spy engineer jailed for 10 years', BBC News, 4 April 2003.

9 Security Service Archives.

10 Security Service Archives.

11 Deputy Assistant Commissioner Peter Clarke, 'Learning from Experience – Counter Terrorism in the UK since 9/11', the Colin Cramphorn Memorial Lecture, 24 April 2007. On 30 October 2003, Manningham-Buller told the Sub-Committee on International Terrorism of the Ministerial Committee on Defence and Overseas Policy:

At that stage [9/11] the intelligence suggested that the United Kingdom was seen as a comparatively safe haven and secure operating base for A[l] Q[aida], with little indication that they were intent on carrying out attacks here. Since then our understanding of the threat had evolved significantly. As a result of our investigations here and intelligence from overseas, it had become clear that the United Kingdom itself and our interests overseas were a prime target for attack by AQ and its allies.

Security Service Archives.

12 In 1997, with ministerial approval, Lander had appointed Manningham-Buller as the only DDG, discontinuing the practice since 1985 of having both a DDG(A) and a DDG(O).

13 'Fairy Godmother of the security service', *Daily Mail*, 11 August 1997.

14 DG talk to Lady Margaret Hall London dinner, 21 May 2003.

15 Security Service Archives.

16 See above, p. 815. The PUS at the Home Office, Sir Clive Whitmore, wrote to Rimington in October 1992: 'I welcome the news that Eliza Manningham-Buller is to be promoted to Director [in 1993] and that as Director A she will be in a position where she can build on the links that she is at present making with the police on intelligence against the PIRA on the mainland.' Security Service Archives, Home Office Archives.

17 Interview with Dame Eliza Manningham-Buller, 3 April 2007. The first paragraph of her application, despite a reference to 'step-change', embodied the 'Miss Continuity' approach:

> I see plenty for the Service to do: developing our work on International Terrorism and the proliferation of Weapons of Mass Destruction in response to the threat to the UK, including the provision of security advice to a significantly wider range of customers; shaping a changed role for the Service in countering Irish terrorism with the devolution of policing to the Northern Irish Assembly; evolving the National Infrastructure Security Co-ordination Centre and the Service's work on electronic attack; helping to strengthen law enforcement intelligence and assessment skills to improve the UK's approach to serious crime; delivering an IM [information management] programme so that there is a step-change in the Service's efficiency and effectiveness; and making best use of the extra resources allocated to the Service to generate more intelligence, action and advice to reduce the threat to the UK's national security.

Home Office Archives.

18 Home Office Archives.

19 Home Office Archives.

20 Interview by Christopher Andrew with Dame Eliza Manningham-Buller, 3 April 2007.

21 See below, p. 817.

22 Ricin had been used to murder the Bulgarian dissident Georgi Markov almost a quarter of a century previously; see above, p. 648.

23 Clarke, 'Learning from Experience: Counter-Terrorism in the UK since 9/11'. Security Service Archives.

24 The initiative for an earlier Al Qaida-linked plan, to attack Heathrow, was believed to have originated outside the UK.

25 Interview by Christopher Andrew with Jonathan Evans, 3 Feb. 2009.

26 Security Service Archives.

27 One of the plotters, Salahuddin Amin, then in Pakistan, handed himself in to the Pakistani authorities, who arrested him on 2 April. He was repatriated and arrested in the UK in February 2005.

28 Security Service Archives. On 14 April the DG circulated to staff written congratulations from the Prime Minister. Together with other intelligence chiefs, Lander had attended meetings of the Afghan War Cabinet in the winter of 2001/2. Recollections of Sir Stephen Lander.

29 On 30 April 2007, Omar Khyam, Anthony Garcia and Waheed Mahmood were sentenced to a minimum of twenty years' imprisonment, Jawad Akbar and Salahuddin Amin to a minimum of seventeen and a half years'. Two other defendants were cleared of all charges. In June 2004 Mohammed Junaid Babar had pleaded guilty in the USA to a range of terrorist-related offences, including 'providing material support to terrorist activity, specifically, the British bomb plot'. He subsequently acted as a witness for the prosecution during the CREVICE trial.

30 Security Service Archives.

31 See above, pp. 229–30.

32 Intelligence and Security Committee, *Annual Report 2006–2007* (Cm 7299), Jan. 2008.

33 MI5 website. Security Service Archives.

34 The threat levels were listed in Intelligence and Security Committee, *Report into the London Terrorist Attacks on 7 July 2005* (Cm 6785), May 2006.

35 Security Service Archives. JTAC's record as a multi-agency organization was praised in the 2004 Butler report.

36 Security Service Archives.

37 Interview with a former Security Service officer.

38 MI5 website.

39 Security Service Archives.

40 Interview with a former Security Service officer.

41 CPNI website.

42 The response rate of 60 per cent was 6 per cent down on the 2000 survey but was considered still good enough by BDI to give confidence in the findings. The overall satisfaction rate was up 4 per cent on the last survey in 2000. Ninety-nine per cent of respondents believed the Service's work was important. Ninety-five per cent were 'proud to work for the Service' and understood how they as individuals contributed towards its aims.

43 Security Service 'War on Terry (WOT)' revue in June 2007; the pirates drew some inspiration from a sketch by the broadcaster and scriptwriter Andy Hamilton.

44 December 2006 report by 'Investors in People'.

45 Security Service Archives. The US 9/11 Commission Report identified Barot, under his alias Issa al-Britani, as an associate of Khalid Sheikh Mohammed.

46 Metropolitan Police website.

47 Robert Wesley, 'British Terrorist Dhiren Bharot's Research on Radiological Weapons', *Terrorism Focus*, 14 Nov. 2006.

48 Clarke, 'Learning from Experience: Counter-Terrorism in the UK since 9/11'.

49 Press Association, 'Barot operation posed complex challenge', 7 Nov. 2006.

50 CBS News, 'British Terror Plotter Gets Life in Prison', 7 Nov. 2006.

51 Security Service Archives.

52 Such bogus leads were not uncommon. Interview with Jonathan Evans, 3 Feb. 2009.

53 Interview with a former Security Service officer.

54 Intelligence and Security Committee, *Report into the London Terrorist Attacks on 7 July 2005* (Cm 6785), May 2006.

55 Security Service Archives.

56 Interview with Jonathan Evans, 3 Feb. 2009.

57 The Security Service had other reports on an unidentified extremist whom it discovered only after 7/7 to be Siddique Khan. Intelligence and Security Committee, *Report into the London Terrorist Attacks on 7 July 2005* (Cm 6785), May 2006.

58 Interview with Jonathan Evans, 3 Feb. 2009.

59 Intelligence and Security Committee, *Report into the London Terrorist Attacks on 7 July 2005* (Cm 6785), May 2006. 'Links between the 7 July bombers and the fertiliser plotters', MI5 website. On 30 April 2007 *Panorama* ('Real Spooks', BBC 1) made the sensational (but, in the author's view, unconvincing) claim that 'the ISC was either never given all the precise details by the Security Service or was fully informed but chose to omit [information] that would have fuelled demands for an independent or public inquiry.'

60 A Ghanaian, Manfo Kwaku Asiedu, who was carrying a fifth bomb, changed his mind and dumped it in a London park.

61 Security Service Archives.

62 The Service had no involvement in the tragic shooting during the man-hunt of the Brazilian electrician, Jean Charles de Menezes, who was mistaken by police for Osman.

63 Asiedu was sentenced to thirty-three years' imprisonment.

64 Interview with Jonathan Evans, 3 Feb. 2009.

65 Intelligence and Security Committee, *Report into the London Terrorist Attacks on 7 July 2005* (Cm 6785), May 2006, p. 36.

66 Clarke, 'Learning from Experience: Counter-Terrorism in the UK since 9/11'.

67 Intelligence and Security Committee, *Annual Report 2006–2007* (Cm 7299), Jan. 2008, p. 12.

68 Intelligence and Security Committee, *Annual Report 2007–2008* (Cm 7542), March 2009, pp. 12 22

69 Intelligence and Security Committee, *Annual Report 2008–2009* (Cm 7807), p. 8

70 See above, pp. 251–2, 450–51, 476.

71 Baroness Manningham-Buller, *Parl. Deb. (Lords)*, 5 Feb, 2009.

72 House of Lords judgment in case of *A and Others* v *Secretary of State for the Home Department*, 8 Dec. 2005.

73 Security Service Archives.

74 Security Service Archives.

75 Security Service Archives.

76 Security Service Archives.

77 Intelligence and Security Committee, *Rendition* (Cm 7171), July 2007, pp. 33–4.

78 Richard Norton-Taylor, 'MI5 criticised for role in case of torture, rendition and secrecy', *Guardian*, 22 Aug. 2008. Richard Norton-Taylor, 'Evidence of torture "buried by ministers" ', *Guardian*, 5 Feb. 2009. Richard Ford and Francis Elliott, 'US threatens to stop sharing intelligence if "torture" of British detainee is revealed', *The Times*, 5 Feb. 2009.

79 Lord Neuberger's final judgment, made public on 26 February, though somewhat less sweeping and more clearly focused on the Binyam Mohamed case than his first draft, was still the most devastating judicial judgment on MI5 in its history. Neuberger concluded in his first draft: 'Not only is there an obvious reason for distrusting any UK Government assurance, based on S[ecurit]y S[ervice] advice and information because of previous "form", but the Foreign Office and the S[ecurit]y S[ervice] have an interest in the suppression of such information.' In the final judgment this became: 'Not only is there some reason for distrusting such a statement ['concerning the mistreatment of Mr Mohamed'], given that it is based on Security Services' advice and information, because of previous, albeit general, assurances in 2005, but also the Security Services have an interest in the suppression of such information.' EWCA Civ 158. Case No: T1/2009/2331. 26 February 2009.

80 Jonathan Evans, 'Conspiracy theories aid Britain's enemies', *Daily Telegraph*, 12 Feb. 2010.

81 Richard Norton-Taylor. 'MI5's propaganda own-goal:', *Guardian*, 12 Feb. 2010.

82 I find it difficult to believe, on the basis of my own experience in talking to induction courses, that recruits would feel inhibited from taking ethical concerns to the counsellor.

83 Intelligence and Security Committee, *Annual Report 2006–2007* (Cm 7299), Jan. 2008.

84 Intelligence and Security Committee, *Report into the London Terrorist Attacks on 7 July 2005* (Cm 6785), May 2006, p. 38

85 Ibid., p. 39.

86 Security Service Archives.

87 Transcript of Ali's suicide video.

88 Security Service Archives.

89 Security Service Archives.

90 Security Service Archives.

91 Security Service Archives.

92 Security Service Archives.

93 A conversation on 9 August about 'HP' (hydrogen peroxide) between Ali and his chief lieutenant, Tanveer Hussain, recorded by MI5, said of Sarwar: 'he's got to boil it down'. Security Service Archives.

94 Press reports of Sarwar's trial.

95 Security Service Archives.

96 Security Service Archives.

97 Security Service Archives.

98 Interview by Christopher Andrew with Jonathan Evans, 26 Jan. 2010. On the surveillance and arrest of Fryers, see above, p. 784.

99 Security Service Archives.

100 Press reports of trial evidence.

101 Andy Hayman. 'Why I suspect jittery Americans nearly ruined efforts to foil plot', *The Times*, 8 Sept. 2009.

102 MI5 listening devices picked up the recording of only one of the martyrdom videos. Security Service Archives.

103 Transcript of Ali's martyrdom video. Before being broadcast, editing of the video by those Ali called Al Qaida's 'media brothers' would probably have made it more coherent.

104 Transcript of Tanvir Hussain's martyrdom video.

105 Press reports of trial evidence.

106 Interview by Christopher Andrew with Jonathan Evans, 26 Jan. 2010.

107 Ibid.

108 Security Service Archives.

109 'Hunt for Rashid Rauf that ended with hellfire', *Sunday Times*, 23 Nov. 2008.

110 Security Service Archives.

111 'A terror plot, 24 arrests and the day when chaos reigned', *Independent*, 11 Aug. 2006. Interview by Christopher Andrew with Jonathan Evans, 26 Jan. 2010.

112 'A terror plot, 24 arrests and the day when chaos reigned', *Independent*, 11 Aug. 2006. Andy Hayman, 'Why I suspect jittery Americans nearly ruined efforts to foil plot', *The Times*, 8 Sept. 2009. On 14 August, as a result of the arrests, JTAC lowered the threat level to severe – indicating that a terrorist threat was still highly likely but was no longer thought to be imminent.

113 ' "Airlines terror plot" disrupted', *BBC News*, 10 Aug. 2009.

114 Interview by Christopher Andrew with Jonathan Evans, 26 Jan. 2010.

115 Among them Christopher Andrew.

116 At the end of the first OVERT trial, which concluded in September 2008, the three ring-leaders – Ali, Sarwar and Hussein – were found guilty of conspiracy to murder persons known and conspiracy to cause explosions. The jury, however, failed to agree a verdict on charges that they and four other defendants – Ibrahim Svant, Umar Islam, Waheed Zaman and Arafat Khan – had conspired to commit murder by detonating bombs aboard transatlantic airliners. All seven pleaded guilty to conspiracy to commit a public nuisance. The eighth defendant, Mohammed Yasar Gulzar, was acquitted on all charges.

At a retrial which concluded a year later in September 2009 Ali, Sarwar and Hussein were found guilty of conspiracy to murder by causing explosions on aircraft. The jury failed to agree a verdict on the same charge against Umar Islam but found him guilty of conspiracy to murder. The jury found Savant, Zaman and Arafat Khan not guilty of conspiracy to murder by causing explosions on aircraft and failed to reach a verdict on the charge of conspiracy to murder. Donald Stewart-White, who had not featured in the first trial, was acquitted on all charges.

At a further trial which ended in December 2009 Adam Khatib was convicted of conspiracy to murder persons unknown, Nabeel Hussain of engaging in preparation of terrorist acts and Shamin Uddin of possessing documents/information which might be useful to terrorists. In March 2010 Ali's wife, Cossor Ali, was found not guilty of failing to pass on information to prevent terrorism.

117 Intelligence and Security Committee, *Annual Report 2007–2008* (Cm 7542), March 2009, p. 39.

118 Suzanne Breen, 'Exclusive – Real IRA: We will take campaign to Britain', *Sunday Tribune*, 12 April 2009.

119 The services also expected to devote 75 per cent of its resources to countering Islamist terrorism in 2009–10. Intelligence and Security Commitee, *Annual Report 2008–2009* (Cm 7807), p. 13, Intelligence and Security Commitee *Annual Report 2009–2010* (Cm 7844), p. 11.

120 Security Service Archives.

121 MI5 also reported an increasing number of British-based Islamist Extremists visiting Somalia 'for training purposes'. By 2009 15 per cent of its investigations involved Islamist extremist links with East Africa, especially Somalia. Intelligence and Security Committee, Annual Report 2008–2009 (Cm 7807), p. 13.

122 Intelligence and Security Committee, *Annual Report 2008–2009* (Cm 7807), p. 13.

123 'Operation Pathway Report following Review' by Lord Carlile of Berriew QC, Independent Reviewer of Terrorism Legislation, Oct. 2009.

124 'Manchester terror suspects cleared to work as guards, *Sunday Times*, 13 Dec. 2009.

125 Interview by Christopher Andrew with Jonathan Evans, 26 Jan. 2010. Close-up images of the documents also appeared in the following day's *Daily Telegraph*. Evans ordered his own office to get rid of all folders with transparent covers.

126 'Operation Pathway Report following Review' by Lord Carlile of Berriew QC, Independent Reviewer of Terrorism Legislation, Oct. 2009. On Oake's murder, see above, p. 816.

127 All initially appealed against deportation. By the end of 2009, however, all but two had returned to Pakistan.

128 Declan Walsh, 'Interviews with Pakistani students: "I'd figured this was all a big mistake" ', *Guardian*, 3 Dec. 2009.

129 'Operation Pathway Report following Review' by Lord Carlile of Berriew QC, Independent Reviewer of Terrorism Legislation, Oct. 2009.

130 Early in 2010 the Service was investigating around 200 Islamist terrorist cases, about the same number as in the previous year. Intelligence and Security Committee, *Annual Report 2008–2009* (Cm 7807), March 2010, p. 13. Intelligence and Security Committee, *Annual Report 2009–2010* (Cm 7844), March 2010, p. 11.

CONCLUSION

1 Intelligence and Security Committee, *Annual Report 2007–2008* (Cm 7542), March 2009, p. 18. Most espionage investigated by the Security Service in 2007–8 was conducted by China and Russia.

2 The memories of the minority without happy memories of the Service are, of course, less likely to be recorded than those of the majority. Even the disaffected Peter Wright, however, recalls in his memoirs 'years of fun' and 'infectious laughter' before he became obsessed by his hunt for imaginary traitors.

3 Andrew, *First World War*, pp. 42, 106–7.

4 See above, pp. 198–205.

5 See above, p. 185.

6 Andrew, *Secret Service*, p. 631.

7 Norman Holmes Pearson, foreword to Masterman, *Double-Cross System*.

8 Security Service Archives.

9 Guy Liddell diary, 1 Nov. 1942.

10 See above, pp. 394, 411–12.

11 See above, pp. 412–15.

12 Andrew and Gordievsky, *KGB*, p. 383.

13 Sandbrook, *Never Had It So Good*, pp. 218, 261.

14 A memorandum of 14 December 1962 noted, 'The Security Service has no primary responsibility for any of the measures in the existing Government War Book'. Security Service Archives.

15 Security Service Archives.

16 Kent, 'Need for an Intelligence Literature'.

17 Andrew, 'Reflections on Intelligence Historiography'. MI5 staff had, however, some awareness of their own history. Curry wrote a history (since declassified) of the period 1909 to 1945; another MI5 officer later wrote a still classified history of the next quarter-century. Anthony Simkins collaborated with Sir Harry Hinsley on the official history of security and intelligence in the Second World War published in 1990. A historical pamphlet was produced in 1959 to mark the Service's fiftieth anniversary.

18 Andrew and Mitrokhin, *Mitrokhin Archive*, pp. 45–6. The best biography of Reilly is Cook, *On His Majesty's Secret Service*.

19 Wright, *Spycatcher*, p. 206.

20 See above, p. 520.

21 Wright, *Spycatcher*, p. 206.

22 Andrew and Mitrokhin, *Mitrokhin Archive II*, pp. 21–3. On improvements in Soviet intelligence collection during the Gorbachev era, see Andrew and Mitrokhin, *Mitrokhin Archive*, p. 722.

23 The surprise would have been somewhat less had British and US intelligence analysts realized that in the early 1960s the KGB had also reported to the Politburo – with horrendous inaccuracy – that the United States was planning a nuclear first strike against the Soviet Union. Andrew and Mitrokhin, *Mitrokhin Archive*, pp. 235–8.

24 Andrew, *Secret Service*, ch. 8.

25 Security Service Archives.

26 See above, p. 466.

27 See above, pp. 621, 684–5.

28 Security Service Archives. Though British Communists could not have provided a capacity crowd at Wembley or Old Trafford, the CPGB at its peak could have filled many smaller stadiums.

29 See above, p. 659.

30 Security Service Archives.

31 See above, p. 845.

32 Taylor, *Brits*, p. 351.

33 Stephen Lander, 'Terrorism: The Genie out of the Bottle', closed lecture to Strategic and Combat Studies Institute, Staff College, Camberley, October 1996.

34 Hoffman, ' "Holy Terror" '. Hoffman, *Inside Terrorism* (first published in 1998), ch. 4.

35 Early in 1998 I argued in a talk at Thames House that the long-term threat to UK security came from Holy Terror. I claim no credit for my foresight, which was based on long-term trends identified not by me but by Bruce Hoffman.

36 *The United Kingdom's Strategy for Countering International Terrorism* (Cm 7547), March 2009, pp. 26–7.

37 *Security Service*, pp. 174–5, 328–31. When setting up the new regional offices, the Service was mindful of the Second World War precedent. The History team were asked to prepare a report on the RSLOs.

38 Andrew, 'Historical Attention Span Deficit Disorder'.

39 Security Service Archives.

40 Andrew, 'Reflections on Intelligence Historiography'.

41 Andrew and Dilks (eds), *Missing Dimension*.

42 The importance of these research opportunities is well illustrated by Dr Calder Walton's forthcoming history of intelligence and decolonization.

43 Andrew, introduction to *Security Service*, pp. 3, 10–11.

44 Andrew, 'Historical Attention Span Deficit Disorder'.

45 Andrew, 'Future of European Security and the Role of Intelligence'.

Bibliography

Acheson, Dean, *Present at the Creation* (New York: W. W. Norton, 1969)

Adams, Gerry, *Before the Dawn: An Autobiography*, paperback edn (Dingle, Co. Kerry: Brandon, 2001)

Agrell, Wilhelm, *Venona: Spåren från ett underrättelsekrig* (Lund: Historiska Media, 2003)

Aldrich, Richard, *The Hidden Hand: Britain, America and Cold War Secret Intelligence* (London: John Murray, 2001)

Anderson, Brendan, *Joe Cahill: A Life in the IRA* (Dublin: O'Brien Press, 2002)

Anderson, David, *Histories of the Hanged: Britain's Dirty War in Kenya and the End of Empire* (London: Weidenfeld & Nicolson, 2005)

Anderson G. D., *Fascists, Communists and the National Government: Civil Liberties in Great Britain 1931–1937* (Columbia: University of Missouri Press, 1983)

Andrew, Christopher, *Théophile Delcassé and the Making of the Entente Cordiale* (London: Macmillan, 1968)

Andrew, Christopher, *The First World War: Causes and Consequences*, vol. 19 of *The Hamlyn History of the World* (London/New York: Hamlyn, 1970)

Andrew, Christopher (ed.), *Codebreaking and Signals Intelligence* (London: Frank Cass, 1986)

Andrew, Christopher, 'Secret Intelligence and British Foreign Policy 1900–1939', in Christopher Andrew and Jeremy Noakes (eds), *Intelligence and International Relations 1900–1945* (Exeter: Exeter University Press, 1987)

Andrew, Christopher, 'Churchill and Intelligence', *Intelligence and National Security*, vol. 3, no. 3 (1988)

Andrew, Christopher, 'The Growth of the Australian Intelligence Community and the Anglo-American Connection', *Intelligence and National Security*, vol. 4, no. 2 (1989)

Andrew, Christopher, 'The British View of Security and Intelligence', in A. Stuart Farson, David Stafford and Wesley K. Wark (eds), *Security and Intelligence in a Changing World: New Perspectives for the 1990s* (London: Frank Cass, 1991)

Andrew, Christopher, *Secret Service: The Making of the British Intelligence Community*, 3rd paperback edn (London: Sceptre, 1991)

Andrew, Christopher, *For the President's Eyes Only: Secret Intelligence and the American Presidency from Washington to Bush* (London: HarperCollins, 1995)

Andrew, Christopher, 'The Future of European Security and the Role of Intelligence', *Irish Studies in International Affairs*, vol. 7 (1997)

Andrew, Christopher, 'Historical Attention Span Deficit Disorder: Why Intelligence Analysis Needs to Look Back before Looking Forward', in *New Frontiers of Intelligence Analysis: Papers Presented at the Conference on New Frontiers of Intelligence Analysis: Shared Threats, Diverse Perspectives, New Communities* (Rome, 2005)

Andrew, Christopher, 'Casement and British Intelligence', in Mary E. Daly (ed.), *Roger Casement in Irish and World History* (Dublin: Royal Irish Academy, 2005)

Andrew, Christopher, 'Intelligence and the Cold War', in Melvyn Leffler and Odd Arne Westad (eds), *The Cambridge History of the Cold War* (Cambridge: Cambridge University Press, 2009), vol. 2

Andrew, Christopher, 'Reflections on Intelligence Historiography since 1939', in Gregory A.

Treverton, and Wilhelm Agrell, *National Intelligence Systems: Current Research and Future Prospects* (Cambridge: Cambridge University Press, 2009)

Andrew, Christopher and Elkner, Julie, 'Stalin and Intelligence', in Harold Shukman (ed.), *Redefining Stalinism* (London: Frank Cass, 2003)

Andrew, Christopher and Dilks, David (eds), *The Missing Dimension: Governments and Intelligence Communities in the Twentieth Century* (London: Macmillan, 1984)

Andrew, Christopher and Gordievsky, Oleg (eds), *Instructions from the Centre: Top Secret Files on KGB Foreign Operations 1975–1985* (London: Hodder & Stoughton, 1990); slightly revised US edn published as *Comrade Kryuchkov's Instructions: Top Secret Files on KGB Foreign Operations 1975–1985* (Stanford: Stanford University Press, 1993)

Andrew, Christopher and Gordievsky, Oleg, *KGB: The Inside Story of its Foreign Operations from Lenin to Gorbachev*, paperback edn (London: Sceptre, 1991)

Andrew, Christopher and Gordievsky, Oleg (eds), *More Instructions from the Centre: Top Secret Files on KGB Global Operations 1975–1985* (London: Frank Cass, 1991)

Andrew, Christopher and Mitrokhin, Vasili, *The Mitrokhin Archive: The KGB in Europe and the West* (London: Penguin, 1999)

Andrew, Christopher and Mitrokhin, Vasili, *The Mitrokhin Archive II: The KGB and the World* (London: Penguin, 2005)

Andrew, Christopher and Walton, Calder, 'The Gouzenko Case and British Secret Intelligence', in J. L. Black and Martin Rudner (eds), *The Gouzenko Affair: Canada and the Beginnings of Cold War Counter-Espionage* (Manotick, Ontario: Penumbra Press, 2006)

Ansari, Ali M., *Iran, Islam and Democracy: The Politics of Managing Change*, 2nd edn (London: Royal Institute of International Affairs, 2006)

Attlee, Clement R., 'Britain and America: Common Aims, Different Opinions', *Foreign Affairs* 32 (1953–4)

Aubin, Chantal, 'French Counterintelligence and British Secret Intelligence in the Netherlands 1920–40', in Beatrice de Graaf, Ben de Jong and Wies Platje (eds), *Battleground Western Europe: Intelligence Operations in Germany and the Netherlands in the Twentieth Century* (Amsterdam: Het Spinhuis, 2007)

Ball, Desmond and Horner, David, *Breaking the Codes: Australia's KGB Network 1944–1950* (St Leonards, NSW: Allen & Unwin, 1998)

Barnes, Trevor, 'Special Branch and the First Labour Government', *Historical Journal*, vol. XXII (1979)

Baron, Stanley Wade, *The Contact Man: The Story of Sidney Stanley and the Lynskey Tribunal* (London: Secker & Warburg, 1966)

Barron, John, *KGB: The Secret Work of Soviet Secret Agents*, paperback edn (New York: Bantam Books, 1974)

Baston, Lewis, *Reggie: The Life of Reginald Maudling* (Stroud: Sutton Publishing, 2004)

Bayly, Christopher and Harper, Tim, *Forgotten Wars: The End of Britain's Asian Empire* (London: Allen Lane, 2007)

Beach, Jim, 'Origins of the Special Intelligence Relationship? Anglo-American Intelligence Co-operation on the Western Front 1917–18', *Intelligence and National Security*, vol. 22, no. 2 (2007)

Bearse, Ray and Read, Anthony, *Conspirator: The Untold Story of Churchill, Roosevelt and Tyler Kent, Spy* (London: Macmillan, 1991)

Beckett, Francis, *Enemy Within: The Rise and Fall of the British Communist Party* (London: John Murray, 1995)

Begin, Menachem, *The Revolt*, revised edn (London: W. H. Allen, 1979)

Bell, J. Bowyer, *The Secret Army: The IRA 1916–1979* (Dublin: Poolberg Press, 1990)

Bell, J. Bowyer, *The Irish Troubles: A Generation of Violence 1976–1992* (New York: St Martin's Press, 1993)

Benn, Tony, *Out of the Wilderness: Diaries 1963–67* (London: Hutchinson, 1987)

Benn, Tony, *Against the Tide: Diaries 1973–76* (London: Hutchinson, 1989)

Benn, Tony, *Conflicts of Interest: Diaries 1977–80* (London: Hutchinson, 1990)

Bennett, Gill, '*A most extraordinary and mysterious business*': The Zinoviev Letter of 1924, FCO History Note no. 14 (London: FCO, 1999)

Bennett, Gill, 'The Secret Service Committee 1919–1931', in *The Records of the Permanent*

Undersecretary's Department: Liaison between the Foreign Office and British Secret Intelligence 1873–1939 (London: FCO, 2005)

Bennett, Gill, *Churchill's Man of Mystery: Desmond Morton and the World of Intelligence* (London: Routledge, 2007)

Benson, Robert Louis and Warner, Michael (eds), *VENONA: Soviet Espionage and the American Response 1939–1957* (Washington, DC: National Security Agency/Central Intelligence Agency, 1996)

Bentsur, Eytan and Kolokolov, Boris L. (eds), *Documents on Israeli–Soviet Relations 1941–1953*, part I: *1941–1949* (London: Frank Cass, 2000)

Berger, Peter L., *Holy War Inc.: Inside the Secret World of Osama bin Laden* (London: Weidenfeld & Nicolson, 2001)

Berman, Bruce J., 'Nationalism, Ethnicity and Modernity: The Paradox of Mau Mau', *Canadian Journal of African Studies*, vol. 25, no. 2 (1991)

Bethell, Nicholas, *The Palestine Triangle: The Struggle between the British, the Jews and the Arabs 1935–1948* (London: André Deutsch, 1979)

Bew, Paul and Gillespie, Gordon, *Northern Ireland: A Chronology of the Troubles 1968–1999* (Dublin: Gill & Macmillan, 1999)

Bird, J. C., 'Control of Enemy Alien Civilians in Great Britain 1914–1918' (PhD dissertation, London University, 1981)

Bishop, Patrick and Mallie, Eamonn, *The Provisional IRA* (London: Heinemann, 1987)

Black, Alistair and Brunt, Rodney, 'Information Management in MI5: Before the Age of the Computer', *Intelligence and National Security*, vol. 16, no. 2 (2001)

Black, J. L. and Rudner, Martin (eds), *The Gouzenko Affair: Canada and the Beginnings of Cold War Counter-Espionage* (Ottawa: Penumbra Press, 2006)

Blake, Christopher, *A View from Within: The Last Years of British Rule in South-East Asia* (Somerset: Mendip Publishing, 1990)

Blake, George, *No Other Choice: An Autobiography* (London: Jonathan Cape, 1990)

Blunkett, David, *The Blunkett Tapes: My Life in the Bearpit* (London: Bloomsbury, 2006)

Bodansky, Yossef, *Bin Laden: The Man Who Declared War on America*, revised edn (Roseville, Calif.: Prima Publishing, 2001)

Boghardt, Thomas, *Spies of the Kaiser: German Covert Operations in Britain during the First World War Era* (Basingstoke: Palgrave Macmillan, 2004)

Bolton, Roger, *Death on the Rock* (London: W. H. Allen, 1990)

Bond, Brian (ed.), *Chief of Staff: The Diaries of Lieutenant General Sir Henry Pownall*, 2 vols (London: Leo Cooper, 1972–4)

Borovik, Genrikh, *The Philby Files* (London: Little, Brown, 1994)

Bothwell, Robert and Granatstein, J. L. (eds), *The Gouzenko Transcripts: The Evidence Presented to the Kellock–Taschereau Royal Commission of 1946* (Ottawa: Deneau, 1982)

Bower, Tom, *A Perfect English Spy: Sir Dick White and the Secret War 1935–90* (London: Heinemann, 1995)

Boyce, D. G., *The Irish Question and British Politics 1868–1996*, 2nd edn (London: Palgrave Macmillan, 1996)

Boyle, Andrew, *The Climate of Treason*, revised edn (Sevenoaks: Coronet, 1980)

Brendon, Piers, *Dark Valley: A Panorama of the 1930s* (London: Jonathan Cape, 2000)

Brendon, Piers, *The Decline and Fall of the British Empire 1781–1997* (London: Jonathan Cape, 2007)

Brent, Jonathan and Naumov, Vladimir P., *Stalin's Last Crime: The Plot against the Jewish Doctors 1948–53* (London: HarperCollins, 2003)

Brett, M. V. (ed.), *Journals and Letters of Reginald Viscount Esher*, 4 vols (London: Nicholson & Watson, 1934–8)

Brook-Shepherd, Gordon, *The Storm Birds: Soviet Post-War Defectors* (London: Weidenfeld & Nicolson, 1988)

Burke, David, 'Theodore Rothstein, Russian Emigré and British Socialist', *Immigrants and Minorities*, vol. 2 (1983)

Burke, David, *The Spy Who Came in from the Co-op: Melita Norwood and the Ending of Cold War Espionage* (Woodbridge: Boydell Press, 2009)

Burke, Jason, *Al Qaeda: Casting a Shadow* (London: I. B. Tauris, 2003)

Burt, Leonard, *Commander Burt of Scotland Yard* (London: Heinemann, 1959)

Callaghan, John and Morgan, Kevin, 'The Open Conspiracy of the Communist Party and the Case of W. N. Ewer, Communist and Anti-Communist', *Historical Journal*, vol. 49 (2006)

Campbell, Alastair, *The Blair Years: Extracts from the Alastair Campbell Diaries* (London: Hutchinson, 2007)

Campbell, John, *Edward Heath: A Biography*, paperback edn (London: Pimlico, 1994)

Carr, E. H., *Foundations of a Planned Economy 1926–1929*, 3 vols (London: Macmillan, 1982)

Carr, E. H., *The Twilight of Comintern 1930–1935* (London: Macmillan, 1982)

Carsten, F. L., *War against War* (London: Batsford Academic, 1982)

Carter, Miranda, *Anthony Blunt: His Lives* (London: Macmillan, 2001)

Castle, Barbara, *The Castle Diaries 1964–70* (London: Weidenfeld & Nicolson, 1984)

Catterall, Peter (ed.), *The Macmillan Diaries: The Cabinet Years 1950–57* (London: Macmillan, 2003)

Caute, David, *The Great Fear: The Anti-Communist Purge under Truman and Eisenhower* (London: Secker & Warburg, 1978)

Cecil, Robert, 'The Cambridge Comintern', in Christopher Andrew and David Dilks (eds), *The Missing Dimension: Governments and Intelligence Communities in the Twentieth Century* (London: Macmillan, 1984)

Cecil, Robert, *A Divided Life: Donald Maclean* (London: Bodley Head, 1988)

Cesarani, David, *Major Farran's Hat: Murder, Scandal and Britain's War against Jewish Terrorism 1945–1948* (London: Heinemann, 2009)

Chamberlain, Phil, 'Mr Mills' Circus', *History Today*, vol. 54 (2004)

Chapple, Frank, *Sparks Fly! A Trade Union Life*, updated edn (London: Michael Joseph, 1985)

Chavkin, Jonathan, 'British Intelligence and the Zionist, South African and Australian Communities during and after the Second World War' (PhD dissertation, Cambridge University, 2009)

Chenevix Trench, Charles, *Men Who Ruled Kenya: The Kenya Administration 1892–1963* (London and New York: Radcliffe Press, 1993)

Chin Peng, *My Side of History* (Singapore: Media Masters, 2003)

Christie, Stuart, *The Christie File* (Sanday, Orkney Islands: Cienfuegos Press, 1980)

Churchill, Winston S., *My Early Life 1874–1908*, paperback edn (London: Fontana, 1959)

Clarke, I. F., *Voices Prophesying War 1763–1984* (Oxford: Oxford University Press, 1966)

Clarke, Peter, *Hope and Glory: Britain 1900–1990*, paperback edn (London: Penguin Books, 1997)

Clarke, Peter, 'Learning from Experience: Counter-Terrorism in the UK since 9/11' (London: Policy Exchange, 2007)

Clarke, Thurston, *By Blood and Fire: The Attack on the King David Hotel* (London: Hutchinson, 1981)

Cline, C. A., *E. D. Morel 1873–1914: The Strategies of Protest* (Belfast: Blackstaff, 1980)

Clinton, Bill, *My Life*, paperback edn (London: Arrow Books, 2005)

Cohen, Paul, 'The Police, the Home Office and Surveillance of the British Union of Fascists', *Intelligence and National Security*, 1 (1986)

Cohn, Norman, *Warrant for Genocide* (London: Eyre & Spottiswoode, 1967)

Colvin, Ian, *The Chamberlain Cabinet* (London: Victor Gollancz, 1971)

Comber, Leon, 'The Malayan Special Branch on the Malayan–Thai Frontier during the Malayan Emergency (1948–1960)', *Intelligence and National Security*, vol. 21, no. 1 (2006)

Coogan, Tim Pat, *The IRA*, revised edn (London: HarperCollins, 1995)

Coogan, Tim Pat, *The Troubles: Ireland's Ordeal 1966–1995 and the Search for Peace* (London: Hutchinson, 1995)

Cook, Andrew, *On His Majesty's Secret Service: Sidney Reilly Codename ST1* (Stroud: Tempus Publishing, 2002)

Cook, Andrew, *M: MI5's First Spymaster* (Stroud: Tempus, 2004)

Corera, Gordon, *Shopping for Bombs: Nuclear Proliferation, Global Insecurity and the Rise and Fall of the A. Q. Khan Network* (London: Hurst, 2006)

Costello, John and Tsarev, Oleg, *Deadly Illusions* (London: Century, 1993)

Coughlin, Con, *Saddam: The Secret Life*, paperback edn (London: Pan Macmillan, 2003)

Cradock, Sir Percy, *Know your Enemy: How the Joint Intelligence Committee Saw the World* (London: John Murray, 2002)

Cragin, R. Kim, 'The Early History of Al-Qa'ida', *Historical Journal*, vol. 51, no. 4 (2008)

Craig, Anthony, 'Anglo-Irish Relations 1966–1974: Interdependence from Economics to Security' (MPhil thesis, University of Cambridge, 2006)

Cross, J. A., *Lord Swinton* (Oxford: Clarendon Press, 1982)

Crossman, Richard, *The Diaries of a Cabinet Minister*, vol. 1: *Minister of Housing 1964–1966*, ed. Janet Morgan (London: Hamish Hamilton and Jonathan Cape, 1975)

Crossman, Richard, *The Diaries of a Cabinet Minister*, vol. 2: *Lord President of the Council and Leader of the House of Commons 1966–1968*, ed. Janet Morgan (London: Hamish Hamilton and Jonathan Cape, 1976)

Crossman, Richard, *The Diaries of a Cabinet Minister*, vol. 3: *Secretary of State for Social Services 1968–70*, ed. Janet Morgan (London: Hamish Hamilton and Jonathan Cape, 1977)

Daly, Mary E. (ed.), *Roger Casement in Irish and World History* (Dublin: Royal Irish Academy, 2005)

Daniels, Gordon and Waters, Robert, 'The World's Longest General Strike: The AFL-CIO, the CIA and British Guiana', *Diplomatic History*, vol. 29, no. 2 (2005)

Darwin, John, *Britain and Decolonisation: The Retreat from Empire in the Post-War World* (London: Macmillan, 1998)

Datta, V. N., *Madan Lal Dhingra and the Revolutionary Movement* (New Delhi: Vikas, 1978)

Davidson, John C. C., Viscount, *Memoirs of a Conservative*, ed. Robert Rhodes James (London: Weidenfeld & Nicolson, 1969)

Dear, I. C. B. and Foot, M. R. D. (eds), *The Oxford Companion to the Second World War* (Oxford: Oxford University Press, 1995)

Debo, Richard, 'The Making of a Bolshevik: Georgii Chicherin in England 1914–1918', *Slavic Review*, vol. XXV, no. 4 (1966)

Debo, Richard, *Revolution and Survival: The Foreign Policy of Soviet Russia 1917–1918* (Liverpool: Liverpool University Press, 1979)

Deedes, W. F., *Dear Bill: W. F. Deedes Reports* (London: Macmillan, 1997)

de la Billière, General Sir Peter, *Storm Command: A Personal Account of the Gulf War* (London: HarperCollins, 1992)

de la Billière, General Sir Peter, *Looking for Trouble: An Autobiography – from the SAS to the Gulf* (London: HarperCollins, 1994)

Denning, Lord, *The Denning Report: The Profumo Affair*, reprint of 1962 report (Cmnd 2512) with new introduction by Denning (London: Pimlico, 1992)

Denniston, A. G., 'The Government Code and Cypher School between the Wars', in Christopher Andrew (ed.), *Codebreaking and Signals Intelligence* (London: Frank Cass, 1986)

Devji, Faisal, *Landscapes of the Jihad: Militancy, Morality, Modernity* (London: Hurst, 2005)

The Dictionary of National Biography 1971–1980, ed. Lord Blake and C. S. Nicholls (Oxford: Oxford University Press, 1986)

Dilks, David (ed.), *The Diaries of Sir Alexander Cadogan, O.M., 1938–1945* (London: Cassell, 1971)

Dobson, Christopher and Payne, Ronald, *War without End. The Terrorists: An Intelligence Dossier* (London: Harrap, 1986)

Documents on British Foreign Policy, series III, vol. I: *Britain and the Soviet Union 1968–1972*, ed. G. Bennett and K. A. Hamilton (London: The Stationery Office, 1998)

Donoughue, Bernard, *Downing Street Diary: With Harold Wilson in No. 10* (London: Jonathan Cape, 2005)

Donoughue, Bernard, *Downing Street Diary*, vol. 2: *With James Callaghan in No. 10* (London: Jonathan Cape, 2008)

Donovan, Robert J., *Conflict and Crisis* (New York: W. W. Norton, 1977)

Dorril, Stephen, *Blackshirt: Sir Oswald Mosley and British Fascism* (London: Penguin Viking, 2006)

Douglas, Roy, *The Advent of War 1939–40* (London: Macmillan, 1980)

Draper, Christopher, *The Mad Major* (Dunstable and London: Waterlow & Sons, 1962)

Drayton, Richard, 'Anglo-American "Liberal" Imperialism, British Guiana, 1953–64, and the World since September 11', in Wm. Roger Louis (ed.), *Yet More Adventures with Britannia: Personalities, Politics and Culture in Britain* (London: I. B. Tauris, 2005)

Dudgeon, Jeffrey, *Roger Casement – The Black Diaries: With a Study of his Background, Sexuality and Irish Political Life* (Belfast: Belfast Press, 2002)

Eaden, James and Renton, David, *The Communist Party of Great Britain since 1920* (London: Palgrave, 2002)

Eckert, Nicholas, *Fatal Encounter: The Story of the Gibraltar Killings* (Dublin: Poolbeg Press, 1998)

Edgerton, Robert B., *Mau Mau: An African Crucible* (London: I. B. Tauris, 1990)

Elkins, Caroline, *Britain's Gulag: The Brutal End of Empire in Kenya* (London: Jonathan Cape, 2005)

Elstein, David, 'The End of the Mau Mau', *New York Review of Books*, 52 (June 2005)

English, Richard, *Armed Struggle: The History of the IRA*, paperback edn (London: Pan Books, 2004)

Ereira, Alan, *The Invergordon Mutiny* (London: Routledge & Kegan Paul, 1981)

Evans, Richard, 'Police and Society from Absolutism to Dictatorship', in Richard Evans, *Rereading German History 1800–1996* (London: Routledge, 1997)

Farago, Ladislav, *The Game of the Foxes* (London: Hodder & Stoughton, 1972)

Feiling, Keith, *The Life of Neville Chamberlain* (London: Macmillan, 1946)

Felstead, Sidney T., *German Spies at Bay* (London: Hutchinson, 1920)

Ferris, Paul (with McKay, Reg), *The Ferris Conspiracy* (Edinburgh and London: Mainstream Publishing, 2001)

Figes, Orlando, *A People's Tragedy: The Russian Revolution 1891–1924* (London: Jonathan Cape, 1996)

Firmin, Stanley, *They Came to Spy* (London: Hutchinson, 1946)

Fitch, Herbert T., *Traitors Within: The Adventurers of Detective Inspector Herbert T. Fitch* (London: Hurst & Blackett, 1933)

Follain, John, *Jackal: The Secret Wars of Carlos the Jackal* (London: Weidenfeld & Nicolson, 1998)

Foot, Paul, *Who Framed Colin Wallace?* (London: Pan, 1990)

Fosdick, R. B., *European Police Systems* (Montclair, NJ: Patterson Smith, 1969 [New York: Century, 1915])

Fouda, Yosri, 'The Masterminds', *Sunday Times*, 8 Sept. 2002

Frank, Katherine, *Indira: The Life of Indira Nehru Gandhi* (London: HarperCollins, 2001)

Fraser, T. G., 'Germany and Indian Revolution 1914–18', *Journal of Contemporary History*, vol. 12, no. 2 (1977)

Freeman, Peter, 'MI1(b) and the Origins of British Diplomatic Cryptanalysis', *Intelligence and National Security*, vol. 22, no. 2 (2007)

Freeman, Simon and Penrose, Barrie, *Rinkagate: The Rise and Fall of Jeremy Thorpe*, paperback edn (London: Bloomsbury, 1997)

Frolik, Josef, *The Frolik Defection* (London: Leo Cooper, 1975)

Fussell, Paul, *The Great War and Modern Memory* (Oxford: Oxford University Press, 1975)

Gallagher, Pete, 'Intelligence and Decolonisation in British Guiana' (History Part II dissertation, University of Cambridge, 2009)

Gibbs, Tim, 'British and American Counter-Intelligence and the Atom Spies 1941–1950' (PhD dissertation, University of Cambridge, 2008)

Gilbert, Martin, *Finest Hour: Winston S. Churchill 1939–1941* (London: Heinemann, 1983)

Gilbert, Martin, *Road to Victory: Winston S. Churchill 1941–1945* (London: Heinemann, 1986)

Gill, Peter, *Policing Politics: Security Intelligence and the Liberal Democratic State* (London: Frank Cass, 1994)

Gillman, Peter and Leni, *Collar the Lot: How Britain Interned and Expelled its Wartime Refugees* (London: Quartet Books, 1980)

Gilmour, Raymond, *Dead Ground* (London: Little, Brown, 1998)

Gooch, John, *The Plans of War: The General Staff and British Military Strategy 1900–1916* (London: Routledge & Kegan Paul, 1974)

Goodman, Michael S., 'Who is Trying to Keep What Secrets from Whom and Why? MI5–FBI Relations on the Klaus Fuchs Case', *Journal of Cold War Studies*, vol. 7, no. 3 (2005)

Goodman, Michael S., *Spying on the Nuclear Bear: Anglo-American Intelligence and the Atomic Bomb* (Stanford: Stanford University Press, 2007)

Gordievsky, Oleg, *Next Stop Execution* (London: Macmillan, 1995)

Granatstein, J. L. and Stafford, David, *Spy Wars: Espionage and Canada from Gouzenko to Glasnost* (Toronto: Key Porter Books, 1990)

Grant, Jennifer, 'Desperate Measures: Britain's Internment of British Fascists during the Second World War' (PhD dissertation, University of Cambridge, 2009)

Graves, A. K., *The Secrets of the German War Office* (New York: McBride Nast, 1914)

Griffiths, Richard, *Patriotism Perverted: Captain Ramsay, the Right Club and English Anti-Semitism 1939–40* (London: Constable, 1998)

Gromyko, Andrei, *Memories* (London: Hutchinson, 1989)

Gunaratna, Rohan, *Inside Al Qaeda: Global Network of Terror* (New York: Columbia University Press, 2002)

Hain, Peter, *A Putney Plot?* (London: Spokesman Books, 1987)

Haines, Joe, *Glimmers of Twilight: Harold Wilson in Decline* (London: Politico's, 2003)

Hamza, Khidir, *Saddam's Bombmaker* (New York: Scribner, 2000)

Hanson, Philip, *Soviet Industrial Espionage: Some New Information* (London: Royal Institute of International Affairs, 1987)

Harris, Ralph and Sewill, Brendon, *British Economic Policy 1970–74: Two Views* (London: Institute of Economic Affairs, 1975)

Harris, Tomás, *GARBO: The Spy Who Saved D-Day* (London: Public Record Office, 2000)

Haslam, Jonathan, *Soviet Foreign Policy 1930–1933: The Impact of the Depression* (London: Macmillan, 1983)

Haynes, John Earl, Klehr, Harvey and Vassiliev, Alexander, *Spies: The Rise and Fall of the KGB in America* (New Haven and London: Yale University Press, 2009)

Haynes, John Earl, Klehr, Harvey and Vassiliev, Alexander, 'Spy Mystery Solved', *Weekly Standard*, 5 April 2009

Hazlehurst, Cameron, *Politicians at War, July 1914–May 1915* (London: Jonathan Cape, 1971)

Heath, Edward, *The Course of my Life: My Autobiography* (London: Hodder & Stoughton, 1998)

Heinemann, Winfried, 'Abwehr', in I. C. B. Dear and M. R. D. Foot (eds), *The Oxford Companion to the Second World War* (Oxford: Oxford University Press, 1995)

Heller, Joseph, 'Failure of a Mission: Bernadotte and Palestine, 1948', *Journal of Contemporary History*, vol. 14, no. 3 (1979)

Hennessy, Peter, *Never Again: Britain 1945–1951*, paperback edn (London: Vintage, 1993)

Hennessy, Peter, *The Prime Minister: The Office and its Holders since 1945*, revised paperback edn (London: Penguin Books, 2001)

Hennessy, Peter, *The Secret State: Whitehall and the Cold War* (London: Allen Lane, The Penguin Press, 2002)

Hennessy, Peter, *Having It So Good: Britain in the Fifties* (London: Allen Lane, The Penguin Press, 2006)

Hennessy, Peter, *Cabinets and the Bomb* (London: British Academy, 2007)

Hennessy, Peter (ed.), *The New Protective State: Government, Intelligence and Terrorism* (London: Continuum, 2007)

Hennessy, Peter and Brownfeld, Gail, 'Britain's Cold War Security Purge: The Origins of Positive Vetting', *Historical Journal*, vol. 25, no. 4 (1982)

Hennessy, Peter and Jeffery, Keith, *States of Emergency: British Governments and Strikebreaking* (London: Routledge & Kegan Paul, 1983)

Heussler, Robert, *Completing a Stewardship: The Malayan Civil Service* (London: Greenwood, 1983)

Hewitt, Steve, *Spying 101: The RCMP's Secret Activities at Canadian Universities* (Toronto: University of Toronto Press, 2002)

Hiley, Nicholas, 'The Failure of British Counter-Espionage against Germany 1907–1914', *Historical Journal*, vol. 28, no. 4 (1985)

Hiley, Nicholas, 'British Internal Security in Wartime: The Rise and Fall of P.M.S.2, 1915–17', *Intelligence and National Security*, vol. 1, no. 3 (1986)

Hiley, Nicholas, 'Counter-Espionage and Security in Great Britain during the First World War', *English Historical Review*, vol. 101 (1986)

Hiley, Nicholas, Introduction to William Le Queux, *Spies of the Kaiser: Plotting the Downfall of England* (London: Frank Cass, 1996)

Hiley, Nicholas, 'Entering the Lists: MI5's Great Spy Round-up of August 1914', *Intelligence and National Security*, vol. 21, no. 1 (2006)

Hinsley, F. H. et al., *British Intelligence in the Second World War*, vol. 1: *Its Influence on Strategy and Operations* (London: HMSO, 1979)

Hinsley, F. H. and Simkins, C. A. G., *British Intelligence in the Second World War*, vol. 4: *Security and Counter-Intelligence* (London: HMSO, 1990)

Hoare, Oliver (ed.), *Camp 020: MI5 and the Nazi Spies: The Official History of MI5's Wartime Interrogation Centre* (London: PRO Publications, 2001)

Hoffman, Bruce, '"Holy Terror": The Implications of Terrorism Motivated by a Religious Imperative', *Studies in Conflict and Terrorism*, vol. 18, no. 4 (1995)

Hoffman, Bruce, *Inside Terrorism*, 2nd edn (New York: Columbia University Press, 2006)

Holloway, David, *Stalin and the Bomb: The Soviet Union and Atomic Energy 1939–1956* (New Haven: Yale University Press, 1994)

Holroyd, Fred and Burbridge, Nick, *War without Honour* (Hull: Medium, 1989)

Holt, Thaddeus, *The Deceivers: Allied Military Deception in the Second World War* (London: Weidenfeld & Nicolson, 2004)

Hooper, David, *Official Secrets: The Use and Abuse of the Act* (London: Secker & Warburg, 1987)

Hope, John G., 'Surveillance or Collusion? Maxwell Knight, MI5 and the British Fascisti', *Intelligence and National Security*, vol. 9, no. 4 (1994)

Horne, Alistair, *Macmillan*, vol. 2: *1957–1986* (London: Macmillan, 1989)

Howard, Sir Michael, *British Intelligence in the Second World War*, vol. 5 (London: HMSO, 1990)

Howe, Sir Geoffrey, *Conflict of Loyalty* (London: Macmillan, 1994)

Howe, Russell Warren, *Mata Hari: The True Story* (New York: Dodd, Mead & Co., 1986)

Howe, Stephen, *Anticolonialism in British Politics: The Left and the End of Empire* (Oxford: Clarendon Press, 1993)

Hull, Mark M., 'German Military Intelligence Operations in Ireland 1939–45' (PhD dissertation, University College Cork 2000)

Hull, Mark M., *Irish Secrets: German Espionage in Wartime Ireland 1939–1945* (Dublin: Irish Academic Press, 2002)

Hurd, Douglas, *Memoirs* (London: Little, Brown, 2003)

Hyde, Douglas, *I Believed: The Autobiography of a Former British Communist* (London: Heinemann, 1950)

Hyde, H. Montgomery, *The Atom Bomb Spies* (London: Hamish Hamilton, 1980)

Jeffery, Keith, *The Official History of the Secret Intelligence Service 1909–1949* (London: Bloomsbury: forthcoming in 2010)

Jeffery, Keith and Hennessy, Peter, *States of Emergency* (London: Routledge & Kegan Paul, 1983)

Jenkins, Roy, *A Life at the Centre* (London: Macmillan, 1991)

Johnston, Roy H. W., *Century of Endeavour. A Biographical and Autobiographical View of the Twentieth Century in Ireland*, revised edn (Carlow: Tyndall Publications/Dublin: Lilliput Press, 2006)

Judd, Alan, *The Quest for C: Sir Mansfield Cumming and the Founding of the British Secret Service* (London: HarperCollins, 1999)

Kahn, David, *Hitler's Spies: German Military Intelligence in World War II* (London: Hodder & Stoughton, 1978)

Kalugin, Oleg, *Spymaster: My 32 Years in Intelligence and Espionage against the West* (London: Smith Gryphon, 1994)

Kellett, David, 'Philip Zec: Cartoonist in a Propaganda War' (MA thesis, University of Kent, 1999)

Kennedy, Paul, *The Rise of the Anglo-German Antagonism 1860–1914* (London: Allen & Unwin, 1980)

Kent, Sherman, 'The Need for an Intelligence Literature', in Donald P. Steury (ed.), *Sherman Kent and the Board of National Estimates: Collected Essays* (Washington, DC: CIA Center for the Study of Intelligence, 1994)

Kerr, Sheila, 'Roger Hollis and the Dangers of the Anglo-Soviet Treaty of 1942', *Intelligence and National Security*, vol. 5, no. 3 (1990)

Kershaw, Ian, *Hitler 1889–1936: Hubris* (London: Allen Lane, 1998)

Kershaw, Ian, *Hitler 1936–1945: Nemesis* (London: Allen Lane, 2000)

Kluiters, F. A. C., *De Nederlandse inlichtingen-en veiligheidsdiensten* (The Hague: Sdu Uitgeverij Koninginnengracht, 1993)

Knight, Maxwell, *Pets Usual and Unusual* (London: Routledge, 1951)

Knightley, Phillip, *Philby: KGB Masterspy* (London: André Deutsch, 1988)

Knightley, Phillip and Kennedy, Caroline, *An Affair of State: The Profumo Case and the Framing of Stephen Ward* (London: Jonathan Cape, 1987)

Koss, S. E., *Lord Haldane: Scapegoat for Liberalism* (New York: Columbia University Press, 1969)

Kuzichkin, Vladimir, *Inside the KGB: Myth and Reality* (London: André Deutsch, 1990)

Laqueur, Walter, *The Age of Terrorism* (London: Weidenfeld & Nicolson, 1987)

Lawrence, Bruce (ed.), *Messages to the World: The Statements of Osama bin Laden* (London: Verso, 2005)

Leggett, George, *The Cheka: Lenin's Political Police* (Oxford: Oxford University Press, 1981)

Le Queux, William, *England's Peril: A Story of the Secret Service* (London: George Newnes, 1903)

Le Queux, William, *Secrets of the Foreign Office* (London: Hurst & Blackett, 1903)

Le Queux, William, *The Invasion of 1910* (London: E. Nash, 1906)

Le Queux, William, *Spies of the Kaiser: Plotting the Downfall of England* (London: Hurst & Blackett, 1909); reissued with introduction by Nicholas Hiley (London: Frank Cass, 1996)

Le Queux, William, *Things I Know* (London: E. Nash & Grayson, 1923)

Leutze, James, 'The Secret of the Churchill–Roosevelt Correspondence: September 1939–May 1940', *Journal of Contemporary History*, vol. 10 (1975)

Leverkuehn, Paul, *German Military Intelligence* (London: Weidenfeld & Nicolson, 1954)

Levy, Adrian and Scott-Clark, Catherine, *Deception: Pakistan, the United States and the Secret Trade in Nuclear Weapons* (London: Atlantic Books, 2007)

Lilleker, Darren G., *Against the Cold War: The History and Traditions of Pro-Sovietism in the British Labour Party* (London: I. B. Tauris, 2004)

Lonsdale, John, 'Kenyatta's Trials: Breaking and Making of an African Nationalist', in Peter Cross (ed.), *The Moral World of the Law* (Cambridge: Cambridge University Press, 2000)

Lonsdale, John, 'Jomo Kenyatta, God and the Modern World', in J.-G. Deutsch, P. Probst and H. Schmidt (eds), *African Modernities* (Oxford: James Currey, 2002)

Lonsdale, John, 'Authority, Gender and Violence: The War within Mau Mau's Fight for Land and Freedom', in E. S. Atieno Odhiambo and John Lonsdale (eds), *Mau Mau and Nationhood: Arms, Authority and Narration* (Oxford: James Currey, 2003)

Louis, W. Roger and Robinson, Ronald, 'The Imperialism of Decolonisation', *Journal of Imperial and Commonwealth History*, vol. 22, no. 3 (1994)

Lustgarten, Laurence and Leigh, Ian, *In from the Cold: National Security and Parliamentary Democracy* (Oxford: Oxford University Press, 1994)

Lyubimov, Mikhail, 'A Martyr to Dogma', in Rufina Philby (with Hayden Peake and Mikhail Lyubimov), *The Private Life of Kim Philby: The Moscow Years* (London: St Ermin's Press, 1999)

McClellan, 'Africans and Blacks in the Comintern Schools', *International Journal of African Historical Studies*, vol. 26, no. 2 (1993)

McGladdery, Gary, *The Provisional IRA in England: The Bombing Campaign in England* (Dublin: Irish Academic Press, 2006)

Macintyre, Ben, *Agent Zigzag: The True Wartime Story of Eddie Chapman, Lover, Betrayer, Hero, Spy* (London: Bloomsbury, 2007)

Macintyre, Ben, *Operation Mincemeat: The True Spy Story that Changed the Course of World War Two* (London: Bloomsbury, 2010)

McIvor, Arthur, ' "A Crusade for Capitalism": The Economic League 1919–39', *Journal of Contemporary History*, vol. 23 (1988)

McKale, Donald M., *The Swastika outside Germany* (Kent, Ohio: Kent State University Press, 1979)

McLaine, Ian, *Ministry of Morale* (London: Allen & Unwin, 1978)

McLean, Ian, *The Legend of Red Clydeside* (Edinburgh: J. Donald, 1983),

McMahon, Paul, 'Covert Operations and Official Collaboration: British Intelligence's Dual Approach to Ireland during the Second World War', *Intelligence and National Security*, vol. 18, no. 1 (2003)

McMahon, Paul, *British Spies and Irish Rebels: British Intelligence and Ireland 1916–1945* (Woodbridge, Suffolk: Boydell Press, 2008)

MacMillan, Margaret, *Peacemakers: The Paris Conference of 1919 and its Attempt to End War* (London: John Murray, 2001)

McSmith, Andy, *Faces of Labour: The Inside Story* (London: Verso, 1996)

Maddrell, Paul, *Spying on Science: Western Intelligence in Divided Germany 1945–1961* (Oxford: Oxford University Press, 2006)

Madeira, Victor, 'Moscow's Interwar Infiltration of British Intelligence 1919–1929', *Historical Journal*, vol. 46 (2003)

Madeira, Victor, ' "No Wishful Thinking Allowed": Secret Service Committee and Intelligence Reform in Great Britain 1919–23', *Intelligence and National Security*, vol. 18 (2003)

Madeira, Victor, ' "Because I Don't Trust Him, We Are Friends": Signals Intelligence and the Reluctant Anglo-Soviet Embrace 1917–24', *Intelligence and National Security*, vol. 19 (2004)

Madeira, Victor, 'British Intelligence in "A New Kind of War" against Soviet "Subversion" ' (PhD dissertation, University of Cambridge, 2008)

Magan, Maxine, *In the Service of Empire* (privately published, 2002)

Magan, William, *Middle Eastern Approaches: Experiences and Travels of an Intelligence Officer* (Wilby, Norfolk: Michael Russell, 2001)

Major, John, *The Autobiography* (London: HarperCollins, 1999)

Mangold, Tom, *Cold Warrior: James Jesus Angleton: The CIA's Master Spy Hunter* (New York/London: Simon & Schuster, 1991)

Marder, A. J., *From the Dreadnought to Scapa Flow*, 5 vols (London: Oxford University Press, 1961–70)

de la Mare, Arthur, *Perverse and Foolish: A Jersey Farmer's Son in the British Diplomatic Service* (Jersey: La Haule Books, 1994)

Marquand, David, *Ramsay MacDonald* (London: Jonathan Cape, 1977)

Martland, Peter, *Lord Haw Haw: The English Voice of Nazi Germany* (Kew: The National Archives, 2003)

Marton, Kati, *A Death in Jerusalem* (New York: Pantheon Books, 1994)

Masterman, J. C., *The Double-Cross System in the War of 1939 to 1945*, paperback edn (London: Sphere Books, 1973)

Masterman, J. C., *On the Chariot Wheel* (London: Oxford University Press, 1975)

Masters, Anthony, *The Man Who Was M: The Life of Maxwell Knight* (Oxford: Basil Blackwell, 1984)

Matthews, L. Harrison and Knight, Maxwell, *The Senses of Animals* (London: Methuen, 1963)

Mawby, Spencer, *British Policy in Aden and the Protectorates 1955–67: Last Outposts of a Middle East Empire* (London: Routledge, Taylor & Francis Group, 2005)

May, Ernest R., *Strange Victory: Hitler's Conquest of France* (New York: Hill & Wang, 2000)

May, Ernest R., 'Die Nachrichtendienste und die Niederlage Frankreichs', in Wolfgang Krieger (ed.), *Geheimdienste in der Weltgeschichte* (Munich: C. H. Beck, 2003)

Mellor, Gilbert, 'The Status under the Hague Conference of Civilians Who Take up Arms during the Time of War', *Journal of the Royal United Service Institution*, vol. LVIII (1914)

Menashri, David, *Post-Revolutionary Politics in Iran: Religion, Society and Power* (London: Frank Cass, 2001)

Millar, Alexander, 'British Intelligence and the Comintern in Shanghai 1927–37' (PhD thesis University of Cambridge, 2009)

Miller, Harry, *Jungle War in Malaya: The Campaign against Communism 1948–60* (London: Arthur Barker, 1972)

Miller, Joan, *One Girl's War: Personal Exploits in MI5's Most Secret Station* (Dingle, Co. Kerry: Brandon, 1986)

Milne, Seumas, *The Enemy Within: The Secret War against the Miners*, revised edn (London: Verso, 2004)

Modin, Yuri, *My Five Cambridge Friends* (London: Headline, 1994)

Moloney, Ed, *A Secret History of the IRA*, paperback edn (London: Penguin, 2003)

Montagu, Ewen, *The Man Who Never Was*, revised paperback edn (Oxford: Oxford University Press, 1996)

Morgan, Kenneth O., *The People's Peace: British History 1945–1990*, paperback edn (Oxford: Oxford University Press, 1992)

Morgan, Kenneth O., *Callaghan: A Life* (Oxford: Oxford University Press, 1997)

Morris, A. J., 'And is the Kaiser Coming for Tea?', *Moirae*, vol. 5 (1980)

Moynihan, Daniel Patrick, *Secrecy: The American Experience* (New Haven/London: Yale University Press, 1998)

Muggeridge, Malcolm, *Chronicles of Wasted Time*, vol. 2: *The Infernal Grove* (London: Collins, 1973)

Mullik, B. N., *The Chinese Betrayal* (Bombay: Allied Publishers, 1971)

Mullik, B. N., *My Years with Nehru 1948–1964* (Bombay: Allied Publishers, 1972)

Murphy, David E., Kondrashev, Sergei A. and Bailey, George, *Battleground Berlin: CIA vs KGB in the Cold War* (New Haven: Yale University Press, 1997)

Murphy, Philip, 'Creating a Commonwealth Intelligence Culture: The View from Central Africa 1945–65', *Intelligence and National Security*, vol. 17, no. 2 (2002)

Murphy, Philip and Ashton, S. R. (eds), *Central Africa: Closer Association 1945–1958* (London: Stationery Office, 2005)

Murphy, Philip and Ashton, S. R. (eds), *Central Africa: Crisis and Dissolution 1959–1965* (London: Stationery Office, 2005)

Musharraf, Pervez, *In the Line of Fire: A Memoir* (London: Simon & Schuster, 2006)

Naftali, Timothy, *Blind Spot: The Secret History of American Counterterrorism* (New York: Basic Books, 2005)

Newman, Bernard, *Speaking from Memory* (London: H. Jenkins, 1960)

Nicolai, Walter, *Nachrichtendienst, Presse, und Volksstimmung im Weltkrieg* (Berlin: E. S. Mittler, 1920)

Nicolai, Walter, *Geheime Mächte. Internationale Spionage und ihre Bekämpfung im Weltkrieg und heute* (Leipzig: K. F. Koehler, 1923)

Nicolai, Walter, *The German Secret Service* (London: S. Paul, 1924)

The 9/11 Commission Report: Final Report of the National Commission on Terrorist Attacks upon the United States (New York: W. W. Norton, 2004)

Nkrumah, Kwame, *The Autobiography of Kwame Nkrumah* (Edinburgh: Nelson, 1959)

Nkrumah, Kwame, *I Speak of Freedom: A Statement of African Ideology* (London: Heinemann, 1961)

Nkrumah, Kwame, *Africa Must Unite* (London: Heinemann, 1963)

Odhiambo, E. S. Atieno and Lonsdale, John (eds), *Mau Mau and Nationhood: Arms, Authority and Narration* (Oxford: James Currey, 2003)

O'Halpin, Eunan, *Defending Ireland: The Irish State and its Enemies* (Oxford: Oxford University Press, 1999)

O'Halpin, Eunan (ed.), *MI5 and Ireland 1939–1945: The Secret History* (Dublin: Irish Academic Press, 2002)

O'Halpin, Eunan, 'Intelligence and Anglo-Irish Relations 1922–1973', in E. O'Halpin, R. Armstrong and J. Ohlmeyer (eds), *Intelligence, Statecraft and International Power* (Dublin: Irish Academic Press, 2006), 132–50

O'Halpin, Eunan, 'British Intelligence in Ireland 1914–21', in Christopher Andrew and David Dilks (eds), *The Missing Dimension: Governments and Intelligence Communities in the Twentieth Century* (London: Macmillan, 1984)

O'Halpin, Eunan, ' "A poor thing but our own": The Joint Intelligence Committee and Ireland 1965–72', *Intelligence and National Security*, vol. 23, no. 5 (2008), 658–80

Ovens, Colonel G. H., 'Fighting in Enclosed Country', *Journal of the Royal United Service Institution*, vol. XLIX (1905)

Palmer, Alasdair, 'The History of the D-Notice Committee', in Christopher Andrew and David Dilks (eds), *The Missing Dimension: Governments and Intelligence Communities in the Twentieth Century* (London: Macmillan, 1984)

Patrick, Chris and Baister, Stephen, *William Le Queux: Master of Mystery* (privately published by the authors, 2007)

Pearson, John, *Profession of Violence: The Rise and Fall of the Kray Twins* (London: Harper-Collins, 1995)

Penrose, Barrie and Courtiour, Roger, *The Pencourt File* (London: Harper & Row, 1978)

Penrose, Barrie and Freeman, Simon, *Conspiracy of Silence* (London: Grafton Books, 1986)

Percox, David, *Britain, Kenya and the Cold War: Imperial Defence, Colonial Security and Decolonisation* (London: I. B. Tauris, 2004)

Perkins, Anne, *A Very British Strike: 3 May–12 May 1926* (London: Macmillan, 2006)

Petrie, Sir David, *Communism in India 1924–1927*, ed. M. Saha, 2nd edn (Calcutta: Government of India Press, 1972)

Philby, Kim, *My Silent War*, paperback edn (London: Panther Books, 1969)

Philby, Rufina (with Peake, Hayden and Lyubimov, Mikhail), *The Private Life of Kim Philby: The Moscow Years* (London: St Ermin's Press, 1999)

Phillips, Cecil James, 'What Made Venona Possible?', in Robert Louis Benson and Michael Warner (eds), *VENONA: Soviet Espionage and the American Response 1939–1957* (Washington, DC: National Security Agency/Central Intelligence Agency, 1996)

Pillar, Paul R., 'Good Literature and Bad History: The 9/11 Commission's Tale of Strategic Intelligence', *Intelligence and National Security*, vol. 21, no. 6 (2006)

Pimlott, Ben, 'The Labour Left', in Chris Cook and Ian Taylor (eds), *The Labour Party: An Introduction to its History, Structure and Politics* (London: Longman, 1980)

Pimlott, Ben, *Harold Wilson* (London: HarperCollins, 1992)

Pincher, Chapman, *Inside Story: A Documentary of the Pursuit of Power* (London: Sidgwick & Jackson, 1978)

Pincher, Chapman, *Their Trade is Treachery* (London: Sidgwick & Jackson, 1981)

Pinkus, Benjamin and Frankel, Jonathan, *The Soviet Government and the Jews 1948–1967: A Documentary Study* (Cambridge: Cambridge University Press, 1984)

Pipes, Richard, *The Russian Revolution 1899–1919* (London: Collins Harvill, 1990)

Polmar, Norman and Allen, Thomas B., *Spy Book: The Encyclopedia of Espionage* (London: Greenhill Books, 1997)

Popplewell, Richard J., *Intelligence and Imperial Defence: British Intelligence and the Defence of the Indian Empire 1904–1924* (London: Frank Cass, 1995)

Porter, Bernard, *Plots and Paranoia: A History of Political Espionage in Britain 1790–1988* (London: Unwin Hyman, 1989)

Primakov, Evgenii et al. (eds), *Ocherki istorii rossiiskoi vneshnei razvedki* (Moscow: Mezhdunarodnoye otnosheniya, 1995–2007)

Prince, Simon, 'The Global Revolt of 1968 and Northern Ireland', *Historical Journal*, vol. 49, no. 2 (2006)

Pujol, Juan (with Nigel West), *GARBO* (London: Weidenfeld & Nicolson, 1985)

Putlitz, Wolfgang zu, *The Putlitz Dossier* (London: Allan Wingate, 1957)

Quinlan, Kevin, 'Human Intelligence Tradecraft and MI5 Operations in Britain 1919–40' (PhD dissertation, University of Cambridge, 2007)

Ramsden, John, *Making of Conservative Party Policy* (London: Longman, 1980)

Ranelagh, John, *The Agency: The Rise and Decline of the CIA* (London: Weidenfeld & Nicolson, 1986)

Ranstorp, Magnus, *Hizb'allah in Lebanon: The Politics of the Western Hostage Crisis* (London, Macmillan, 1997)

Ranstorp, Magnus, 'The Virtual Sanctuary of Al-Qaeda and Terrorism in an Age of Globalisation', in Johan Eriksson and Giampiero Giacomello (eds), *International Relations and Security in the Digital Age* (London: Routledge, 2007)

Ray, Philip, *Jesus through the Spyglass* (Darlington: Serendipity, 2007)

Rees, Goronwy, *A Chapter of Accidents* (London: Chatto & Windus, 1971)

Reile, Oscar, *Geheime Westfront. Die Abwehr 1935 bis 1945* (Munich/Wels: Welsermühl, 1962)

Richelson, Jeffrey T. and Ball, Desmond, *The Ties that Bind* (Boston: Unwin Hyman, 1990)

Richter, Ludwig, 'Military and Civil Intelligence Services in Germany from World War I to the End of the Weimar Republic', in Heike Bungert, Jan G. Heitmann and Michael Wala (eds), *Secret Intelligence in the Twentieth Century* (London: Routledge, 2003)

Rimington, Stella, *Open Secret: The Autobiography of the Former Director-General of MI5* (London: Hutchinson, 2001)

Riva, Valerio, *Oro da Mosca* (Milan: Mondadori, 1999)

Rolph, C. H., *All Those in Favour? An Account of the High Court Action against the Electrical Trades Union and its Officers for Ballot-Rigging in the Election of Union Officials (Byrne & Chapple v. Foulkes & Others, 1961)*, with a preface by John Freeman (London: André Deutsch, 1962)

Rooney, David, *Kwame Nkrumah: The Political Kingdom in the Third World* (London: I. B. Tauris, 1988)

Rose, Kenneth, *Elusive Rothschild: The Life of Victor, Third Baron* (London: Weidenfeld & Nicolson, 2003)

Rose, Norman, *Vansittart* (London: Heinemann, 1978)

Rosen, Greg, *Old Labour to New: The Dreams that Inspired, the Battles that Divided* (London: Politico's, 2005)

Roskams, Samuel, 'British Intelligence, Imperial Defence and the Early Cold War in the Far East' (MPhil thesis, University of Cambridge, 2007)

Roskill, Stephen, *Hankey: Man of Secrets*, 3 vols (London: Collins, 1970–74)

Roskill, Stephen, *Naval Policy between the Wars* (London: Collins, 1976)

Rust, William, *The Story of the Daily Worker* (London: People's Press Printing Society, 1949)

Saidabadi, Mohammad R., 'Iran's European Relations since 1979', in Ali Mohammadi and Anoushiravan Ehteshami (eds), *Iran and Eurasia* (Reading: Ithaca Press, 2000)

Samolis, T. V. (ed.), *Veterany Vneshnei Razvedki Rossii: Kratkiy Biografichesky Spravochnik* (Moscow: SVR Press, 1995)

Sandbrook, Dominic, *Never Had It So Good: A History of Britain from Suez to the Beatles* (London: Little, Brown, 2005)

Sandbrook, Dominic, *White Heat: A History of Britain in the Swinging Sixties* (London: Little, Brown, 2006)

Sawatsky, John, *Gouzenko: The Untold Story* (Toronto: Macmillan of Canada, 1984)

Sawyer, Roger, *Casement: The Flawed Hero* (London: Routledge & Kegan Paul, 1984)

Schecter, Jerrold L. and Deriabin, Peter S., *The Spy Who Saved the World* (New York: Scribner's, 1992)

Schlaepfer, Christian, 'British Governance, Intelligence and the Communist Threat *c.*1945–1962' (MPhil thesis, University of Cambridge, 2009)

Schoenberg, David, 'Kapitza: Fact and Fiction', *Intelligence and National Security*, vol. 3, no. 4 (1988)

Scott, L. V., *Macmillan, Kennedy and the Cuban Missile Crisis: Political, Military and Intelligence Aspects* (London: Macmillan, 1999)

Seale, Patrick and McConville, Maureen, *Philby: The Long Road to Moscow* (London: Hamish Hamilton, 1968)

Seaman, Mark (ed.), *GARBO: The Spy Who Saved D-Day* (London: PRO Publications, 2004)

The Security Service 1908–1945, with introduction by Christopher Andrew (Kew: Public Record Office, 1999)

Seligmann, Matthew S., *Spies in Uniform: British Military and Naval Intelligence on the Eve of the First World War* (Oxford: Oxford University Press, 2006)

Sellers, Leonard, *Shot in the Tower* (London: Leo Cooper, 1997)

Sergueiev, Lily, *Secret Service Rendered* (London: Kimber, 1968)

Setting the Record Straight: A Record of Communications between Sinn Fein and the British Government, October 1990–November 2003 (Sinn Fein, 2 December 2003)

Seyd, Patrick, *The Rise and Fall of the Labour Left* (London: Macmillan, 1987)

Shelley, Adam, 'Empire of Shadows: British Intelligence in the Middle East 1939–1945' (PhD dissertation, University of Cambridge, 2007)

Sherman, Daniel, 'Learning from Past Mistakes? Planning for Internment of Subversives during a Transition to War 1948–1964' (MA thesis, Queen Mary and Westfield College, University of London, 2005)

Sillitoe, Sir Percy, *Cloak without Dagger* (London: Cassell, 1955)

Simpson, Colonel W. G., 'The Duties of Local Authorities in War Time', *Journal of the Royal United Service Institution*, vol. LVIII (1914)

Sladen, N. St Barbe, *The Real Le Queux: The Official Biography of William Le Queux* (London: Nicholson & Watson, 1938)

Slowe, Peter, *Manny Shinwell: An Authorised Biography* (London: Pluto Press, 1993)

Smith, Cyril, *Big Cyril: The Autobiography of Cyril Smith* (London: W. H. Allen, 1977)

Smith, Michael, *New Cloak, Old Dagger* (London: Victor Gollancz, 1996)

Smith, Michael, *Foley: The Spy Who Saved 10,000 Jews* (London: Hodder, 1999)

Smith, Michael, 'Bletchley Park, Double Cross and D-Day', in Michael Smith and Ralph Erskine (eds), *Action This Day: Bletchley Park from the Breaking of the Enigma Code to the Birth of the Modern Computer* (London: Bantam Press, 2001)

Smith, Michael, 'The Government Code and Cypher School and the First Cold War', in Michael Smith and Ralph Erskine (eds), *Action This Day: Bletchley Park from the Breaking of the Enigma Code to the Birth of the Modern Computer* (London: Bantam Press, 2001)

Smith, Michael and Erskine, Ralph (eds), *Action This Day: Bletchley Park from the Breaking of the Enigma Code to the Birth of the Modern Computer* (London: Bantam Press, 2001)

Smith, Simon, 'General Templer and Counter-Insurgency in Malaya: Hearts and Minds, Intelligence and Propaganda', *Intelligence and National Security*, vol. 16, no. 3 (2001)

Snelling, O. F., *Rare Books and Rarer People: Some Personal Reminiscences of 'The Trade'* (London: Werner Shaw, 1982)

Stafford, David, *Churchill and Secret Service* (London: John Murray, 1997)

Stafford, David, *Spies beneath Berlin* (London: John Murray, 2002)

Stafford, David, *Ten Days to D-Day: Countdown to the Liberation of Europe* (London: Little, Brown, 2004)

Stalker, John, *Stalker* (London: Harrap, 1988)

Stammers, Neil, *Civil Liberties in Britain during the Second World War* (London: Croom Helm, 1983)

Standish, Robert (pseud.), *The Prince of Storytellers: The Life of E. Phillips Oppenheim* (London: P. Davies, 1957)

Steiner, Zara, *Britain and the Origins of the First World War* (London: Macmillan, 1977)

Steinhauer, Gustav, *Steinhauer: The Kaiser's Masterspy as Told by Himself*, ed. Sidney Felstead (London: The Bodley Head, 1930)

Stieber, Wilhelm, *The Chancellor's Spy: The Revelations of the Chief of Bismarck's Secret Service* (New York: Grove Press, 1980)

Stonehouse, John, *Ralph* (London: Jonathan Cape, 1982)

Suchkov, D. I., 'Dzhomo Keniata v Moskve', *Vostok*, no. 4 (1993)

Summers, Anthony and Dorril, Stephen, *Honeytrap: The Secret Worlds of Stephen Ward* (London: Weidenfeld & Nicolson, 1987)

Swartz, M., *The Union of Democratic Control in British Politics during the First World War* (Oxford: Oxford University Press, 1971)

Taylor A. J. P., *Beaverbrook* (London: Hamish Hamilton, 1972)

Taylor A. J. P., *English History 1914–1945*, Pelican revised edn (London, 1975)

Taylor, Peter, *Provos: The IRA and Sinn Fein* (London: Bloomsbury, 1997)

Taylor, Peter, *Brits: The War against the IRA*, paperback edn (London: Bloomsbury, 2002)

Taylor, Robert, *The Trade Union Question in British Politics: Government and Unions since 1954* (Oxford: Basil Blackwell, 1993)

Tenet, George, *At the Center of the Storm: My Years at the CIA* (New York: HarperCollins, 2007)

Thatcher, Margaret, *The Downing Street Years* (London: HarperCollins, 1993)

Thompson, Willie, *The Good Old Cause: British Communism 1920–1991* (London: Pluto, 1992)

Thomson, Sir Basil, *Queer People* (London: Hodder & Stoughton, 1922)

Thomson, Sir Basil, *The Story of Scotland Yard* (London: Grayson & Grayson, 1935)

Thomson, Sir Basil, *The Scene Changes* (London: Collins, 1939)

Thorpe, D. R., *Alec Douglas-Home* (London: Sinclair-Stevenson, 1996)

Thurlow, Richard, *The Secret State: British Internal Security in the Twentieth Century* (Oxford: Basil Blackwell, 1995)

Thurlow, Richard, *Fascism in Modern Britain* (Stroud: Sutton Publishing, 2000)

Thwaites, Norman G., *Violet and Vinegar* (London: Grayson, 1932)

Trumpener, Ulrich, 'War Premeditated? German Intelligence Operations in July 1914', *Central European History*, vol. 9, no. 1 (1976)

Turnbull, Malcolm, *The Spycatcher Trial* (London: Heinemann, 1988)

Turrou, Leon G., *The Nazi Spy Conspiracy in America* (London: G. G. Harrap, 1939)

Ullman, R. H., *Anglo-Soviet Relations 1917–21*, 3 vols (London: Princeton University Press, 1961–72)

Ustinov, Nadia Benois, *Klop and the Ustinov Family* (London: Sidgwick & Jackson, 1973)

Ustinov, Peter, *Dear Me* (London: Heinemann, 1977)

Vansittart, Lord, *The Mist Procession: The Autobiography of Lord Vansittart* (London: Hutchinson, 1958)

Vassall, John, *Vassall* (London: Sidgwick & Jackson, 1975)

Walden, George, *Lucky George: Memoirs of an Anti-Politician* (London: Allen Lane, 1999)

Walker, Jonathan, *Aden Emergency: The Savage War in South Arabia 1962–67* (Staplehurst: Spellmount, 2005)

Walton, Calder, 'British Intelligence and Threats to National Security 1941–1951' (PhD dissertation, University of Cambridge, 2006)

Walton, Calder, 'British Intelligence and the Mandate of Palestine: Threats to British National Security Immediately after the Second World War', *Intelligence and National Security*, vol. 23, no. 4 (2008)

Walzer, Michael, *Just and Unjust Wars: A Moral Argument with Historical Illustrations*, 3rd edn (London and New York, 2000)

Warwick, Peter (ed.), *South African War: The Anglo-Boer War 1899–1902* (Harlow: Longman, 1980)

Wasserstein, Bernard, *Britain and the Jews of Europe 1939–1945* (Oxford: Clarendon Press, 1979)

Watson, David Robin, *Georges Clemenceau: A Political Biography* (London: Eyre Methuen, 1974)

Weinberg, Gerhard, *The Foreign Policy of Hitler's Germany: Starting World War II 1937–1939* (Chicago/London: University of Chicago Press, 1980)

Weiner, Tim, *Legacy of Ashes: The History of the CIA* (London: Allen Lane, 2007)

Weinstein, Allen and Vassiliev, Alexander, *The Haunted Wood: Soviet Espionage in America – The Stalin Era* (New York: Random House, 1999)

Werner, Ruth, *Sonya's Report* (London: Chatto & Windus, 1991)

West, Nigel, *A Matter of Trust: MI5 1945–72* (London: Weidenfeld & Nicolson, 1982)

West, Nigel, *Venona: The Greatest Secret of the Cold War* (London: HarperCollins, 1999)

West, Nigel (ed.), *The Guy Liddell Diaries*, vol. 1: *1939–1942*; vol. 2: *1942–1945* (London: Routledge, 2005)

West, Nigel, *MASK: MI5's Penetration of the Communist Party of Great Britain* (London: Routledge, 2005)

West, Nigel and Tsarev, Oleg, *The Crown Jewels: The British Secrets at the Heart of the KGB Archives* (London: HarperCollins, 1998)

Westlake, Martin (with St John, Ian), *Kinnock: The Biography* (London: Little, Brown, 2001)

Wheen, Francis, *Tom Driberg: His Life and Indiscretions* (London: Chatto & Windus, 1990)

Whitelaw, William, *The Whitelaw Memoirs* (London: Aurum Press, 1989)

Wigg, Lord, *George Wigg* (London: Michael Joseph, 1972)

Wilkinson, Nicholas, *Secrecy and the Media: The Official History of the UK's D-Notice System* (London: Routledge, 2009)

Willan, Andrew, *D-Day to Berlin* (London: Hodder & Stoughton, 2004)

Willans, Geoffrey, *Peter Ustinov* (London: Peter Owen, 1957)

Williams, David G. T., *Not in the Public Interest: The Problem of Security within Democracy* (London: Hutchinson, 1965)

Williams, Marcia, *Inside Number Ten* (London: Weidenfeld & Nicolson, 1972)

Wilson, Emily, 'The War in the Dark: The Security Service and the Abwehr 1939–1944' (PhD dissertation, University of Cambridge, 2003)

Wilson of Rievaulx, Baron, *The Governance of Britain* (London: Weidenfeld & Nicolson, 1976)

Wincott, Len, *Invergordon Mutineer* (London: Weidenfeld & Nicolson, 1974)

Windlesham, Lord and Rampton, Richard, *The Windlesham/Rampton Report on 'Death on the Rock'* (London: Faber & Faber, 1989.

Wise, David, *Molehunt: The Secret Search for Traitors that Shattered the CIA* (New York: Random House, 1992)

Wolf, Markus (with McElvoy, Anne), *Man without a Face: The Autobiography of Communism's Greatest Spymaster* (London: Jonathan Cape, 1997)

Wood, Angus, 'The Construction of Parliamentary Accountability for the British Intelligence Community 1979–2002' (MPhil thesis, University of Cambridge, 2003)

Wood, Ian S., *Crimes of Loyalty: A History of the UDA* (Edinburgh: Edinburgh University Press, 2006)

Wright, Lawrence, *The Looming Tower: Al-Qaeda's Road to 9/11* (London: Allen Lane, 2006)

Wright, Peter, *Spycatcher* (New York: Viking, 1987)

Yong, C. F., *The Origins of Malayan Communism* (Singapore: South Seas Society, 1997)

Zec, Donald, *Don't Lose it Again! The Life and Wartime Cartoons of Philip Zec* (London: Political Cartoon Society, 2005)

Ziegler, Philip, *Wilson: The Authorised Life of Lord Wilson of Rievaulx* (London: Weidenfeld & Nicolson, 1993)

Index

A Branch/Division 84, 127, 134, 236, 325, 335–6, 551; AI 335, 738–9;A2 335–6; A2A 334–5, 527; A4 333–4, 337–8, 394, 425, 571–2, 741; A5 336; *see also* Appendix 3

Abbu Nafa, Mahmoud 689, 690

Abedin, Moinul 806–8

Abu Nidal Organization (ANO) 648, 691, 734–6

Abwehr (German intelligence agency): foundation 186; pre-war espionage 186, 209–11, 212–13; British pre-war view of 209, 210; despatches agents to Britain to prepare for invasion 235, 248, 250, 259; double agents' penetration of SIS and MI5 244–7, 256–7; Abwehr agents converted to double agents 248–55, 259; GC&CS's decrypts of ciphers 248, 249–50, 253, 254–5, 262, 278, 281; disinformation supplied to 285, 287, 288, 292, 294, 297, 299, 300–301, 304, 305, 308, 311, 314–16

Aden 473–7, 605, 801; DSOs/SLOs 138, 220, 480, 612

Afghanistan 92, 799, 802, 804, 808, 811, 817, 825, 827

AIRLINES, Operation 795–7, 855

Ali, Abdullah Ahmed 828–33

Al Megrahi, Abdelbaset Ali Mohmed 747, 748

Al Qaida 607, 799, 802–4, 806–11, 816–17, 823, 828, 829, 836, 856, 860–51

al Zawahiri, Ayman 799, 802, 804, 808

Alca´zar de Velasco, Angel 260–62

alcoholism 331, 415, 421–2, 433, 439, 592, 599, 714, 723

Allen, Albert 156–9

Allen, John 445, 446, 519, 629, 761

Allen, Sir Philip 492, 517–18, 531, 535, 536, 547, 574, 588, 590, 596, 597, 602, 603–4, 620, 629

Allison, George 137, 164, 402

Alverstone, Richard Webster, 1st Viscount 38–9, 40

Ames, Aldrich 713, 726

Anderson, Sir John 129, 226, 235, 236

Andropov, Yuri 565–6, 585, 605, 606, 709, 722, 723

Angleton, James 'Jim' 511, 512–15, 520

Angry Brigade 610–12

anti-Semitism 7, 125, 189–90, 193–4, 224–5, 362, 364

appeasement 195, 198, 202, 203, 205–6, 853

Arafat, Yasir 608, 648, 736

Archer, Kathleen 'Jane' (*née* Sissmore): background and character 122, 131; recruitment of 122, 128; head of Registry 122; interrogation skills 128, 220; MBE 128; responsibility for Soviet intelligence 128, 220, 341; and Invergordon Mutiny 164; and Krivitsky case 220, 264,

265, 267–8, 341; marriage 220; sacked 220, 235; moves to SIS 220, 341; and Philby 341–2

ARCOS (All-Russian Cooperative Society) 153, 154–6, 157–8, 167

Arden-Clarke, Sir Charles 451, 453

Argov, Shlomo 690–91, 734

Arkell, John 396

Armed Forces Security Agency (United States; AFSA) 372, 373, 375–6

Armstrong, Sir Robert: and appointment of Smith as DG 553; and appointment of Duff as DG 557; and 'Oberon Singers' 558; and industrial subversion and unrest 594, 671, 672; and Wilson's business friends 630, 631; and Wilson's suspicions of Security Service 634; chairs Interdepartmental Working Group on Subversion in Public Life 658; and Bettaney case 720; and expulsion of Guk 724; and Gordievsky case 726–7; and review of vetting procedures 751; and *Spycatcher* affair 761, 762, 763–4; and Security Service Act 766

Armstrong, Sir William 533, 537

Army Security Agency (United States; ASA) 366, 372–3, 374

Arnold, Henry 385, 389, 390
Asquith, Herbert 3, 9, 20, 66, 81, 86
Astor, Hugh 249, 299, 316
atom spies 340–41, 345–6, 349, 375, 377, 383–8, 389–91, 420, 858
Atomic Energy Authority 323, 491
Atomic Energy Cabinet Committee (GEN 163) 392
atomic and nuclear weapons: British atomic bomb project (TUBE ALLOYS) 183, 279, 313, 384, 392, 579–80, 584–5, 847; bombing of Hiroshima 340, 341, 858; Los Alamos 346, 366, 377, 384, 385, 550, 858; Soviet atomic weapons 366, 383–4, 386, 388, 405, 858; thermonuclear warfare threat 405, 722–3, 781, 858–9; anti-nuclear movement 559, 673–6; KGB/GRU Operation RYAN 709, 722–3, 861; and Islamist terrorism 807; 'dirty bombs' 820, 861; see also atom spies
Attlee, Clement: appointment of Sillitoe as DG 319, 321, 847; relations with Sillitoe 321–2, 682, 847; character 322; and Zionist extremism 352, 353, 355, 360, 361–2; and appointment of Jews 364; and VENONA project 367; vetting procedures 380–81, 382, 383, 387, 391, 392, 393, 858; and atom spies 384, 387, 390, 391; and CPGB 401, 402, 853; Communist influence in trade unions 406, 407; and pro-Soviet Labour MPs 411, 412; on operations in Commonwealth countries 443; and British Guiana 461
Auslands Organisation 197
Australia 106, 366, 367–73, 430, 517, 520, 762–5, 768–9

B Branch/Division 126, 127–8, 130, 134, 150, 197, 229–30, 254, 255, 268; reorganization of 236, 325, 388, 549; B1a 248–50, 252–3, 256, 258, 284, 285–6, 287–8, 293–4, 297–300, 310, 855; B1b 249–50, 286; B1c 219; B1d 250; B1E 382, 388; B1F 134; B1G 261; B2 322; B2b 369; B3a 350–51, 353, 360, 362; B4 128, 152, 184, 385, 394, 427; see also Appendix 3
Bacon, George Vaux 73–4, 75
Bagot, Milicent 131, 217, 232, 330, 550
Baldwin, Stanley 146, 151, 154, 155–6, 178, 199
Balfour, Arthur 75, 108
Ball, Sir Joseph 126, 150
Baltic Exchange bombing (1992) 782, 784, 855
Baring, Sir Evelyn 454, 456, 467
'barium meal' operations 507, 508
Barot, Dhiren 819–21, 861
BBC: Burgess at 173, 270; coverage of Cuban Missile Crisis 327; programmes on union ballot-rigging 409, 410, 529, 530; news presentation 663; Dimbleby Lecture 777, 801
'Beavers' (B1b decrypt analysers) 249–50
Beckett, Francis 411, 592
Bedell Smith, Walter 426, 428
Begin, Menachem 351, 352–3, 354, 363
Belfast: SLO 602, 604, 618; British troops posted to 604–5, 618–19; terrorist attacks in 620, 646; unpopular posting 621, 646–7, 852; IJS station 684, 692, 693, 696, 700, 852; Long Kesh 692–3
Belgium: First World War 66; Second World War 205, 222, 223, 230, 241; Zionist extremists operating in 355; reaction to FOOT 574; PIRA terrorist attacks in 651,

652, 696; PIRA bases in 699, 748, 772; Sûreté 772
Bell, Eddie 82, 109
Bell, Walter 444–5, 468
Bella, Leo 357–8, 359
Benn, Tony 522, 525–6, 638, 660
Berger, Roland 400–401, 404, 417
Berlin Wall 419, 771, 853
Bernstorff, Count Johann Heinrich von 86, 87, 105
Bethell, Sir Alexander Edward 25, 26, 27, 32
Bethmann-Hollweg, Theobald von 86, 91
Bettaney, Michael 557, 558, 564, 714–22, 723–4, 732, 754, 756
Bevan, J. H. 284, 286, 296, 310, 318
Bevin, Ernest 177, 178, 351–2, 355, 358, 359, 360, 361, 412, 424
Bin Laden, Usama (UBL) 799, 801–11, 856, 860
Birmingham pub bombings (1974) 624
Bishopsgate bombing (1993) 783–4, 793, 855
Black List 58–9, 84, 143
Black September (Palestinian terrorist organization) 608, 612, 613
Blair, Tony 766, 791, 793, 797, 809, 811–12, 817, 822, 831, 833, 856
Blake, George 488, 489–91, 492, 503, 509, 537–8, 587, 716, 718, 720
Bland, Sir Nevile 223, 242
Blenheim Palace 217, 231–5, 317
Blunkett, David 811, 813
Blunt, (Sir) Anthony: early academic career 173, 232, 269; recruited by Deutsch 173, 268–9, 420, 438; and Cairncross 173; sexuality 174, 269, 429; and Rothschild 219, 269, 270; joins MI5 245, 268–70; wartime intelligence work and supply of information to Soviets 261, 272, 280–81, 289–90; prewar Communist associations 268, 269; recruitment of subagents 269, 436–7, 509; appearance and

character 270; recruitment of Burgess 270–72, 856; codename TONY 272, 349; and VIPER investigation 275; Hollis's suspicions of 282, 517, 856; interrogation by Wright 282, 439, 520; recommends Harris to MI5 284–5; leaves Security Service 281, 339, 429, 439, 540, 706; post-war intelligence supplied to Soviets 339, 402; and VENONA decrypts 374; suspicions of following Burgess and Maclean's defection 424, 428, 429; liaison between Philby and Modin 430; confession 435, 437–8, 509, 517; identification as Fourth Man 438–40, 564; alcoholism 439; publicly exposed as Fourth Man 706, 754; stripped of knighthood 761

Boddington, Herbert 'Con' 122, 123, 152, 164, 177

Bolshevik Revolution (1917) 95, 99, 100–101, 102, 103–4, 139–40, 435, 853

Box 500 reports 659, 666, 677, 679, 680, 795

Bradley, Omar-Nelson 373–4, 377

Brandes, Willy 167, 181, 184

Brandon, Vivien 32, 33–4

Brandreth, Gyles 815

Bravo, Rafael 813–14

Brezhnev, Leonid 573, 605, 709, 861

Brighton bombing (1984) 704–5, 734, 735, 737, 772

British Guiana (later Guyana) 459–61, 473, 477–80

British National Party 738

British Non-Ferrous Metals Research Association (BNFMRA) 182, 183, 579–81

British Socialist Party (BSP) 99, 102, 103

British Union of Fascists (BUF) 124, 190–94, 226–7, 228, 853

Brittan, Leon 557, 677, 681, 701–2, 757

Brockway, Fenner, Baron 674–5, 676

Brook, Sir Norman 322, 392, 404, 493, 496

Brooke, Henry 492, 498, 501, 502, 507

Brown, George 412, 413, 415, 476, 532

Brown, Gordon 837, 838

Browning, Freddie 64, 150

budgets: MO5(g) 29, 31, 35, 36, 41, 64; MI5 117, 118–19, 134, 222–3, 779–80, 788, 790, 811–12, 814, 861; see also Secret Vote

bugging: legislation for 336, 758–9; Wilson's obsession with 526, 637–8

Burgess, Guy: background and character 172; at Cambridge 172, 420, 854; recruitment 172, 420, 854; BBC radio producer 173; sexuality 174, 272, 422, 429; defection (1951) 184, 272, 318, 344, 391, 424–6, 433, 438–9; joins SIS (1938) 185; recruited as MI5 agent by Blunt 270–72, 856; Foreign Office information supplied to Soviets 339, 342, 426; identified in VENONA decrypts 374, 429; heavy drinking 422, 423; outrageous behaviour 422, 424, 425; Washington posting 422–3, 424; and Philby and Makayev 423; White Paper on defection 431; death 433

Burt, Leonard 345–6, 355

Butler, R. A. 'Rab' 462, 466, 483, 492, 779, 852

Butler, Sir Robin 751, 771, 773, 774, 789

Byrne, Jock 409, 410

C Branch/Division 63, 134, 236, 325, 384, 399, 536–7, 551, 584, 600, 606–7, 612, 614, 615, 654–5, 695, 731, 772; C2 584; C3 275; C4 609; see also Appendix 3

Cabinet Committee on Subversive Activities (GEN 183) 380–81, 387–8, 391

Cabinet Office 126–7, 552–3, 614, 671–3, 695, 731–2, 751–2, 782

Caccia, Sir Harold 496, 497

Cadogan, Sir Alexander 201–2, 204, 206, 207, 208–9, 213, 218, 244, 263–4, 319

Cahill, Joe 622–3, 649

Cairncross, John: background and character 173, 707, 854; recruitment 173, 420, 438; sexuality 174; Treasury career 174, 339, 428; codename MOLIÉRE 349; former Communist Party member 428; suspicions of following defection of Burgess and Maclean 428–9; confession 435, 436, 437, 438; identification as Fifth Man 438, 440–41, 707

Callaghan, James: and identification of Fifth Man 440; and allegations against Hollis 519; Home Secretary 534–8, 602–3, 604–5; interest in industrial subversion 534–5; and Communist influence in trade unions 534–6; dislike of Hanley 552; appointment of Smith as DG 552; and Northern Ireland 602–3, 604–5, 644–6, 653; and alleged plot against Wilson 640–41, 642; becomes prime minister (1976) 644–5, 656; and counter-terrorism 647–8; economic crises 655, 657; and labour unrest 656, 664–5, 667; and subversive penetration of Labour Party 661, 663, 664; on secrecy 754

Calvo, Luis 261, 262

Cambridge Five: recruitment of 168–73; Soviets' suspicions and mishandling of 169, 173, 339, 420–21, 426, 433, 434, 856–7; successes of 169, 173, 339, 420, 434, 855, 856; sexuality of 173–4; ego as motive 713; see also Blunt, Anthony; Burgess,

Cambridge – *cont.*
Guy; Cairncross, John;
Maclean, Donald; Philby,
Kim
Cambridge University 170–71,
329–2, 420, 440, 854;
Cavendish Laboratory
167, 168; *see also* Trinity
College; Trinity Hall
Camp 020 (Second World War
interrogation centre) 250,
251–3, 288, 295, 450
Campbell, Alastair 810, 811
Canada: wartime deportation
of aliens to 230; Soviet
spy-ring in 339–41,
344–49, 380, 431–2;
Anglo-Canadian nuclear
research 340–41, 389–90;
Commonwealth Security
Conferences 369, 398–9,
516; ban on employment
of homosexuals in
sensitive work 398–9;
reaction to FOOT 574;
see also Royal Canadian
Mounted Police
Canaris, Wilhelm 209, 293
Canary Wharf bombing
(1996) 794, 797
Cannon, Les 409, 410
CARDOON, Operation
703–4
'Carlos the Jackal' (Ilich
Ramírez Sánchez) 617–18
Carr, Robert 592, 596, 597,
613; bombing of home
610, 611
Carter, J. F. C. 73, 128–9
Casement, Sir Roger 86–90
Castle, Barbara 524, 530–31,
532
Castro, Fidel 477, 480, 490,
635
CAZAB (secret collaborative
counter-intelligence
association) 514–16, 518
Chamberlain, Sir Austen 124,
151, 155, 156, 753
Chamberlain, Neville: and
Viscount Davidson 126;
succeeds Baldwin as
prime minister 199;
Munich agreement
202–3, 205, 206, 207,
208, 853; Hitler's
insulting references to
205–6, 853; introduction
of conscription 207; and
outbreak of war 241;
predicts short war 244

Chapman, Eddie (double agent
ZIGZAG) 253, 287–8,
293–4, 312–13, 314
Chapple, Frank 409, 410
Cheka (Soviet intelligence
agency) 95, 174, 852
Chernenko, Konstantin 723,
725
Chicherin, Georgi 95, 97, 100,
103–4, 151
CHIFFON, Operation 783
Chifley, J. B. 'Ben' 367–9, 370
Chin Peng 447, 449, 450, 451
China, People's Republic of
384, 467, 472, 512–13,
514, 731–2
Cholmondeley, Charles 285–6,
287
Christensen, Adler 86, 89
Christie, Stuart 610, 611
Churchill, Sir Winston: in
Asquith cabinet 10, 20,
37; enthusiasm for
intelligence 20, 29,
118–19, 239–40, 670,
856; and Secret Service
Bureau 20, 29–30; Home
Secretary 29; and Kell
29–30, 37, 88, 239; and
registration of aliens 30;
expansion of HOW 36–7,
49–50, 52, 239, 861;
facilitates interception of
correspondence 36–7,
49–50, 63; First Lord of
the Admiralty 37, 63, 86,
225; and Indian
nationalism 92; on Lenin
99; and security services
budget cuts 118–19;on
Mussolini 124; supports
backbench campaign
against Soviet subversion
155; on Auslands
Organisation 197;
becomes prime minister
217, 225, 241, 248; and
'fifth column' fears 223,
224, 225, 227, 228, 229,
230; founding of Security
Executive 227; appoints
Harker 228; visits
Blenheim 234; unease at
state of Security Service
235–6; relations with
Petrie 238–9, 288–9, 292,
308, 856; briefed on
operations 239, 286, 287,
288–94, 296, 300–301,
305; and secret work
279; and D-Day landings

305–10; VE Day 316–17;
peacetime government
322, 407; Zionist letter
bomb sent to 355;
expansion of positive-
vetting 391–2; and atomic
bomb 392; and British
Guiana 460–61; on
history 861
CIA (US Central Intelligence
Agency): London station
335; and VENONA
project 366, 373–4, 428;
suspected of being
penetrated 374, 428; and
defection of Burgess and
Maclean 427–8; and
British Guiana 460, 461,
477–8, 479; alleged
clandestine operations in
Africa 470–71; and
Castro 477, 490, 635;
recruitment of
Goleniewski 484–5, 487,
488, 511; and alleged
Soviet penetration of
security services 509,
511, 514–16, 518;
Wilson's suspicions of
632, 635, 638; scrutinized
in 'Year of Intelligence'
(1975) 635; daily brief to
President 682; and Irish
Republican terrorism 698;
and Islamist terrorism
803, 807, 810; *see also*
OSS
Clan na Gael 698–9
Clarke, Carter W. 372, 373–4,
377
Clarke, David 278, 279
Clarke, Peter 814, 820, 824,
832, 858
Clarke, Stanley 34, 35, 36, 42
CND (Campaign for Nuclear
Disarmament) 559, 673,
674, 675–6, 758
COBR (emergency Cabinet
Office briefing room)
614, 685–6, 687–8, 702,
809, 810
Cockcroft, Sir John 389–90
COE, Operation 717–20
Cohen, Morris and Lona
('Peter and Alice Kroger')
376, 487–8, 520
Comintern (Communist
International): presidents
99; British Communists'
links with 128, 135,
141–2, 147–8, 161–2,

176, 178–9; founding 139; Second Congress (1920) 141–2; and subversion in Western armed forces 161–2, 165, 176; interception of messages 175–7, 178; Lenin School 176, 455, 456; SIS agents in 177; Popular Front 178–9; Nazi capture of material 189–90; and wartime Soviet espionage 281–2

Committee of Imperial Defence 3, 9, 15, 17, 30, 31, 39, 81, 166, 194, 266

Commonwealth Security Conferences 469, 516; (1948) 369;(1951) 444; (1953) 445;(1957) 445; (1963) 398–9

Communist Party of Great Britain (CPGB): Inkpin as first general secretary 88, 152; undercover agents in 122, 123, 124, 132, 149, 152, 165, 179–83, 220–21, 401–2, 853; Soviet funding 135, 144, 148, 176, 400, 403; couriers to India 137, 179–80; formation 142; Soviet imposed discipline 142, 148, 160, 176, 273, 404; and labour unrest 147–8, 406–11, 592–3, 594–5, 598–9, 665–6; membership numbers 148, 160, 402, 404, 594; Politburo 148; Central Committee 149; and Zinoviev letter 149; electoral performance 160–61, 404; relations with Comintern 160–62, 178–9; and subversion in armed forces 161, 164–6; and industrial sabotage 166, 177–8; attacks on Royal Family 178–9; clashes with BUF 192;MI5's wartime penetration of 273–7; and wartime Soviet espionage 277–9, 282; changes name to British Communist Party 278; identification of members 332–3, 400–403; and Purge Procedure 381, 382, 383, 400, 402; and

Fuchs case 386, 853; bugging and phone tapping of HQ 402–3, 409, 410, 416, 451–2, 577, 592, 672–7; International Department 403, 466; *British Road to Socialism* manifesto (1951) 404; penetration of trade union movement 406–11, 534–5, 594–5, 598–9, 656–7, 666–7, 670, 672; and ballot rigging in trade union movement 409–11; hopes of influencing Wilson 418; and Africa 451–2, 453, 466–7; and seamen's strike (1966) 527–9, 530–31; and supply of TUC documents to Soviets 577–8; attempts to penetrate Labour NEC 577–8; influence on Labour left wing 656, 657, 668–9; Trotskyists in 659–60; Security Service's disproportionate use of resources in monitoring 667–9, 853; and peace movement 673, 675–6; and miners' strike (1984–5) 676–7, 680

Conservative Party: agents in Labour Party HQ 126; Research Department 126; and Zinoviev letter 150–51; 1924 election 151; 1951 election 392, 416; 1979 election 555; 1970 election 566, 587; Brighton conference bombing (1984) 704–5, 734, 735, 737, 772

Continuity IRA 833, 834

Cooke, William Hinchley 56, 57, 68–9, 78, 81, 143

Cooper, Duff 238, 239, 281, 287–8, 289, 293, 321

Courtauld Institute 339, 429, 430, 437, 439, 540

Courtiour, Roger 639, 640, 641

Cowgill, Felix 254–5, 268, 278, 281, 856

Crabb, Lionel 'Buster' 326, 409

Crawley, John 704, 795–6

CREVICE, Operation 816–17, 819, 822, 823, 856

Crocker, William 229, 236

Crossman, Richard 'Dick' 476–7, 522, 531, 532, 538, 604

Crowe, Sir Eyre 149, 151

Cuba: Bay of Pigs landing 477, 490; Missile Crisis 326–7, 494, 497, 499, 565, 721, 858; intelligence service 576

Cubbon, Sir Brian 557, 561, 563

Cumming, Malcolm 135, 136, 427, 508

Cumming, Sir Mansfield: recruitment 3, 21, 22, 25–8; and Kell 3, 25–6, 27–8, 96, 97; First World War espionage investigations 17, 32, 104; background and character 25; First World War subversion investigations 96, 99; and proposed merger of MI5 and SIS 116; death 120

Cunningham, Sir Charles 328, 406, 435, 507, 522–3, 539

Curran, Sir Charles 397

Curry, John 'Jack': and BUf 190–91; in Indian police 190, 206; diplomatic connections 196; and Ustinov 196, 200–201; and Auslands Organisation 197; and Stevens 200–201; and Munich agreement 203, 205, 206; and wartime aliens investigations 222, 223; on organizational improvements 227, 228, 237; made deputy director 237; and Venlo affair 244; refuses to recruit Burgess 272; and wartime Soviet espionage 278; memorandum on Soviet counter-espionage (1946) 349

Curwen, Sir Christopher 724, 726

Curzon, George, 108, 144–5, 155

Cussen, Edward 219, 275–7, 296, 344

Cyprus 459, 462–6, 474, 735

Czechoslovakia 200, 201, 202, 203, 207–8, 379, 728–30; see also Prague Spring; StB

D Branch/Division 84, 93–4,
134, 236, 237, 325, 518;
DI 429, 495, 509; DI/ Inv
432, 509–10, 515, 580;
D2 484; D3 539; D4 415,
501; *see also* Appendix 3
D-Day landings (1944) 212,
280–81, 296–7, 300,
304–10, 855; *see also*
FORTITUDE, Operation
D-Notice affair (1967)
531–2
Dale, Walter 152, 153, 158
Dale Long, Herbert 6, 17, 25,
26, 31
Dalton, H. E. 201, 246
Dansey, Sir Claude 58,
100, 105
Dar es Salaam, bombing of US
embassy (1998) 803–4,
856
Darling, Charles, 1st Baron
40, 45
Day, John 512, 516–17, 518
de la Billiére, Sir Peter 610,
612–13, 685, 687
de Quehen, B. M. 'Bob' 444,
456, 458
de Wesselow, Peter 378, 431,
432
dead letter-boxes (DLB) 426,
571, 578, 712, 715
Dearlove, Sir Richard 810, 811
'Death on the Rock' (television
programme) 743, 744–5
Dedman, John 367, 368
Defence, Ministry of (MoD)
336, 388, 475, 536, 570,
610, 613, 673, 676, 732,
752
Defence of the Realm Act
(DORA; 1914) 53–4, 58,
80, 94, 119, 142
del Pozzo, Miguel Piernavieja
259–61
Delhi Intelligence Bureau
(DIB) 137, 138, 236,
442–6, 481
Denning, Alfred, Baron 499,
500
Denniston, Alastair 156, 175,
353
Deutsch, Arnold: academic
career 169–70, 171, 184;
appearance and character
169, 171; photograph in
MI5 files 169; recruitment
of Cambridge Five
169–73, 180–81; security
lapses 169, 184, 854;
Jewish origins 170, 184;

and Olga Gray 180; and
Woolwich Arsenal
spy-ring 181; recalled to
Moscow 184, 420,
854–5; Krivitsky's
information on 265;
Jenifer Fischer Williams
538, 540
Deverell, John 557, 671–3,
715–16, 717, 718,
720–21, 726, 785
Dicker, Mary 127, 132, 133,
218
Directorate of Intelligence
109, 116, 117–18,
119–20, 140
Dobb, Maurice 167–8, 844
Donoughue, Bernard
630–31, 633, 635, 636,
638, 646
Double-Cross System:
development of 65,
69–70, 73, 211–12,
248–53, 283, 854, 860;
importance in Second
World War 69, 70, 248,
317–18, 855–6; German
intelligence use of 247;
role of SIS 253–4; and
Twenty Committee
255–7, 860; planned
relocation of agents to
North Wales 257–9; main
aims 283; Masterman's
history of 317–18, 855;
classified top secret
860–51
Douglas-Home, Sir Alec 478,
496, 497, 501, 507, 566,
567, 573, 622
Drake, Reginald 'Duck' 41–2,
65, 68, 82, 98
Draper, Christopher 209–10,
211–12, 853
Drew, Edward 'Tricky'
3, 808
DSE (Spanish security service)
741, 742, 744
DST (French security service)
574–5, 772, 802
Dublin 605, 699; British
embassy 620, 623; Special
Criminal Court 704
Duddy, Brendan 625, 646,
783
Duff, Sir Antony 'Tony':
appointment as DG
(1985) 557, 559, 561;
background and character
557, 559; reforms of
Security Service 336, 557,

559–60, 561, 564, 779;
relations with Thatcher
559; and appointment of
successor 562, 563; and
alleged plot against Wilson
642; on dirty-tricks
allegations 642; reduces
emphasis on counter-
subversion 681, 682;
review of counterterrorism
operations 702; on Jack
Jones's links with KGB
711; and Gordievsky case
726; and international
terrorism 736; review of
vetting procedures 751–2;
on oversight and
accountability of Security
Service 755; promotes
case for Security Service
Act 758–9, 766; and
Spycatcher affair 762
Duff, Hugh 38, 40, 42

E Branch/Division 77–8, 79,
84, 220, 236, 325,
481–2; E1 611; EIC 245,
246; *see also* Appendix 3
East Germany (German
Democratic Republic)
385, 419, 490, 630, 730;
Stasi 470
Easter Rising (1916) 87, 88,
618, 861
Economic Key Points (EKPs)
620, 654–5, 695
Eden, Sir Anthony 175, 199,
309–10, 321, 325–6, 327,
355, 408–9, 431
Edmonds, Sir James 7–8,
10–21, 23, 25
Edwards, Robert 'Bob' 527,
538, 711, 711–12
Egyptian Islamic Jihad
(EIJ) 799, 802,
804, 805
Eisenhower, Dwight D. 286,
287, 297, 309, 319, 373
elections, general: (1924) 148,
149, 150, 151; (1929)
158–9, 160; (1935) 193;
(1945) 319, 404, 411,
847; (1950) 391, 404,
412; (1951) 391, 392,
404, 407, 412,
416; (1959) 484; (1964)
480, 520; (1966) 527;
1970 547, 566, 587;
(February 1974) 578,
599, 623–4, 625, 627;
(October 1974) 633;

1979 667, 669, 670; (1987) 681; (1992) 775; (1997) 791, 797

Elias, Jacob (Yaacov Levstein) 355-6

Elizabeth II, Queen 406, 555, 694, 706, 767

ELLI (Soviet agents) 282, 348-9, 503; see also Long, Leo Elliott, Nicholas 427, 435-6

ELMEN (Bettaney case investigations) 715-17, 720-21

Elwell, Charles 486-7, 488, 492, 576, 668-9

EMBASE, Operation 727

Enigma (German cipher) 248, 253, 374, 855-6, 859

Ernst, Karl 38, 49, 81

Etappe Dienst (German naval intelligence network) 187-8, 210-11

European Convention on Human Rights 756, 759, 765

European Court of Human Rights 756, 759-60, 765, 766-7

Evans, Jonathan 779-80, 806, 817, 821, 823, 829-30, 831, 837, 838, 858

Evatt, H. V. 'Bert' 367, 368

Ewart, Sir John Spencer 10-11, 19, 20, 24, 29-30

Ewer, William Norman 145, 152-4, 156, 157-9

F Branch/Division 84, 236, 268, 281, 325, 551, 558, 561, 600, 622-3, 647, 648-9, 681, 683, 745; F1 408, 611, 664; F1A 332, 527-8, 529, 530, 660, 664, 673; F1B 604; F1C 332, 668; F2 561, 656; F2A 274, 278; F2C 277, 332, 561; F3 611, 615, 684; F4 402, 408, 498; F5 619, 622, 684, 700, 740-41; F8 700; see also Appendix 3

Falber, Reuben 386, 418

Falklands conflict (1982) 697, 755, 757

'false flag' technique 167, 583

Farrell, Maire'ad 739, 740, 741-3, 744-5

Fascism: Italy 105, 124, 191, 193, 197; internment of British Fascists 192, 194,

227, 230-31, 235; Spain 259, 260; and labour unrest 595; see also British Union of Fascists

Faux, Julian 607, 613, 619, 751

FBI (US Federal Bureau of Investigation): pre-war 210; and VENONA project 366, 372-3, 377; and atom spies 386-7, 389, 390; involvement in investigations into alleged Soviet penetration of security services 509, 514; Irish Republican investigations 697, 749-50; categorization of double agents' motives 713

Ferguson, Victor 94, 96, 99

'fifth column' fears: wartime 223-4, 225, 227, 228, 229-30, 859-50; Cold War 400, 405

Findlay, Mansfeldt de Carbonnel 86, 89

'Finney, Jim' (IIB agent) 123, 149, 152

First United States Army Group (FUSAG) 284, 299, 305, 309

First World War: outbreak 50, 53-4; spy mania 53-5, 81, 223; Western Front 55, 73, 91, 96, 98-9, 104, 105, 106, 108, 861; opposition to 66, 94-5, 99, 101-4, 106; battle of Jutland 72; naval operations 72, 463; sabotage operations 75, 77, 78-9, 852; Eastern Front 77, 98; conscription 94-5; Caporetto 104; Amiens 106; Armistice 106; demobilization 140; Holt-Wilson on 187

Fischer Williams, Jenifer (later Hart) 375, 538-9, 540

Fisher, Sir Warren 119, 120, 136-7, 203, 218-19, 227

FLAVIUS, Operation 739-45

Fletcher, Yvonne 701, 702

Floud, Bernard 538-41

FLUENCY (joint Security Service-SIS working party) 510-12, 515-18, 521, 634

Foot, Sir Hugh 464, 465

Foot, Michael 166, 418, 464, 578, 638, 663

FOOT, Operation (1971 expulsion of Soviet intelligence personnel) 565-7, 571-3, 574-5, 576, 579, 586, 732, 859

Foreign and Commonwealth Office (FCO) 481, 552-3, 566, 701, 724

Foreign Office 25, 35, 119, 174-5, 207, 208-9, 244, 246, 263-5, 268, 279, 393-4, 407, 410, 421, 425, 495, 496-7, 533, 854

FORTITUDE, Operation 296-8, 299-300, 310, 855

Foulkes, Frank 410, 411, 529, 530

FOXHUNTER, Operation 463

France: Triple Entente 8; Franco-Prussian War (1870-71) 11, 12; pre-First World War German intelligence in 52, 66; liaison with British intelligence 71, 137, 185; First World War 80, 98-9, 101; post-First World War threat 117; French Communist Party (PCF) 161; Nazi occupation 205, 222, 223, 230, 298; Allied invasion 284, 296-7, 304-10; decolonization 442; Suez crisis 445, 473; reaction to FOOT 574-5; terrorist attacks in 691, 692; PIRA bases in 699, 772; Islamist terrorism 802; see also DST

Franco, Francisco 260, 267

Frazer, John 409, 410

Freeman, John 410, 446, 529, 530

Frolik, Josef 535, 541-3, 707

Fryers, Robert 'Rab' 777, 784-5, 855

Fuchs, Klaus: investigation, interrogation and confession 334, 371, 385-6, 858, 853; conviction and imprisonment 345, 377, 386-7; and Gouzenko defection 346; identified

Fuchs – *cont.*
through VENONA decrypts 375, 376, 377, 384–5; case causes crisis in Special Relationship 386–7, 390; run by female GRU controller 550, 580; links with Melita Norwood 580
Fulton Report (1968) 338
Furnival Jones, Sir Martin ('FJ'): recruited to MI5 219; on Masterman 317–18; appointed DG (1965) 328; background and character 328, 332; introduction of new career structure 332; management style 338, 547; and Philby case 432, 435; stationing of SLOs in Africa 469, 471; and phasing out of SLOs 481; and Portland spy-ring 485, 486; and Blake case 489; and investigations of Mitchell and Hollis 506–7, 515, 516, 517–18, 520; and FLUENCY working party 511–12, 515; and Golitsyn and Angleton's conspiracy theories 513, 515, 516; and Wigg 524–5; industrial subversion investigations 528, 529, 588, 590–91, 594–6; and D-Notice affair 531; advises Marcia Williams's removal 533; and Callaghan 534–6; and Thorpe affair 534; review of protective security 537, 607; and Blake escape and defection 538; and Floud and Owen cases 539, 542; Heath's dislike of 547, 587; retirement (1972) 547; appointment of successor 547–8; and FOOT 567, 574; and Arab terrorism 601–2; and Northern Ireland 602–3, 604, 607, 618 FX Branch 560, 647, 683, 700, 702, 734, 745–6

G Branch 84, 93, 94, 745–6, 772, 805, 818; G1; 95–6, 97; G4 145; *see also* Appendix 3

Gaitskell, Hugh 412, 416, 418–19, 526, 847–8, 853
Gallacher, Willie 148, 166, 278, 381, 404
Gandhi, Indira 446, 736–7
Gannon, Donal 795–7
Garby-Czerniawski, Roman (double agent BRUTUS) 298–9, 300, 309, 312, 316
Gardiner, Gerald, Baron 410, 525
Gardner, Meredith 366, 376, 423, 431, 433–4
GCHQ (Government Communications Headquarters): collaboration with American A(F)SA 366, 372–3; VENONA project 366, 372, 378, 434; at Eastcote 428; Prime case 578–9, 712–13, 754, 756; counter-proliferation role 788
Gee, Ethel 'Bunty' 485, 487
General Strike (1926) 125–6
George V, King 146, 179
George VI, King 297, 310, 416, 856
German Communist Party (KPD) 188, 189–90
German embassy (London) 195–7, 199, 853
Germany, Imperial: pre-war espionage and invasion threat 3, 7–21, 30–52, 861; navy 8, 55, 64, 162; *Meldewesen* system 30; wartime espionage and sabotage attempts 66–80, 861–2; wartime subversion 86–7, 90–92, 94, 99–100, 101–3, 106–7, 852; Treaty of Brest-Litovsk (1918) 104; Treaty of Versailles (1919) 186, 195, 198, 852
Germany, Weimar 117, 186–8, 198, 852
Germany, Nazi: anti-Semitism 7, 189–90; Hitler's rise 188–9; violence and repression 188–9, 190; concentration camps 189, 352, 364; rearmament 195; and Rhineland 198; annexation of Austria 200; threat to Czechoslovakia 200, 202,

207–8; pre-war espionage 210–11, 212–13; invasion of Poland 213; invasion of France and Low Countries 222, 223; planned invasion of Britain 230–31, 235, 250, 257–9, 858; invasion of Soviet Union 273, 292
Germany, post-war *see* East Germany; West Germany
Ghana (*formerly* Gold Coast) 451–4, 468, 470–71, 859
Gibraltar: DSO 138, 220; Burgess goes wild in 422; attempted PIRA terrorist attack (1988) 739–45, 748
Glad, Tör (double agent JEFF) 292
Glading, Percy 137, 167, 179, 180–82, 183, 854
Gladstone, Hugh 62, 63, 64, 84
Glasgow 41, 139, 246, 254, 448, 653, 654; pub bombings (1979) 654; organized crime 790; terrorist attack on airport (2007) 836
GOLD, Operation 490
Goleniewski, Michal 484–5, 487, 488, 511
Golitsyn, Anatoli: intelligence on Cambridge Five 378, 435, 438, 439; defection 435, 503, 504; paranoia and exaggeration 439, 503, 504, 516; Vassall case 492; and Hollis and Mitchell 503–4, 507, 511, 512–13, 516, 518, 519; limitations of his evidence 503, 504; temporary move to Britain 504, 505, 506; and Sino-Soviet split 512–14; and CAZAB investigations 514–15
Gollan, John 402–3, 404, 410, 528, 592
Good Friday Agreement (1998) 782, 798
Gorbachev, Mikhail 680, 723, 725
Gordievsky, Oleg: posting to London 348, 708–12; identification of ELLI 348–9; on Pontecorvo 390; and identification of Fifth Man 440–41,

707–6; identification of Bob Edwards as KGB agent 527, 710–11, 711–12; on Jack Jones 536, 589, 657, 710–11; on KGB contacts with anti-nuclear movement 674–5; on funding of NUM 679; on Libyan terrorism 701; on Soviet fear of nuclear attack 709, 722–3, 861, 860; and Thatcher 709, 720, 725, 727, 730; succeeds Titov 710–11; and Hollis investigations 712; and Bettaney 714–18, 721; and Guk's expulsion from London 724–5; appointed London resident designate 724–6; exposure and defection 726–7, 730; on Mikardo 758

Gordon Walker, Patrick 345, 412–13, 415, 416, 480, 526

Gorsky, Anatoli 184, 269, 272, 280

Gouzenko, Igor 282, 339–2, 343–49, 380, 431–2, 434

Government Code and Cypher School (GC&CS): SIS control of 120; decrypts of Soviet ciphers 143–4, 146, 147, 154–5, 175–7, 178, 261; and ARCOS affair 156; surveillance of employees 158; decrypts of German ciphers 248, 253, 254, 300, 305, 855; relocation to Bletchley Park 248; Churchill's interest in 287, 856; and Palestine intercept station 353; see also GCHQ; ISOS; ULTRA

Government War Book 194, 404, 406, 859

Grant, Ted 660, 661, 682

Graves, Karl 40–41, 42–4, 50, 70

Gray, Olga 179–82, 183, 220–21, 401, 854

Green, Oliver 277, 281

Greene, Sir Hugh 396

Greenhill, Sir Denis, 565, 571, 572

Gregory, Ivor (Soviet agent ACE) 579, 582–3, 585

Grey, Sir Edward 37, 86, 89

Grieve, John 796, 855

Grist, Evelyn 274, 334–5

Grivas, George 462–5

Gromyko, Andrei 553, 566, 567, 573

Grosse, Heinrich 39–40, 42

GRU (Soviet military intelligence): pre-war anti-Western imperialist operations 161; wartime espionage 280, 374, 378–9; Canadian spy-ring 339–41, 344–49; messages decrypted by VENONA 378; growth of London residency in 1960s 491, 565–7; mass expulsion of London personnel (Operation FOOT) 565, 567, 571–3, 574–5, 732, 859; Operation RYAN 709, 722–3, 861; expulsion of agents following Gordievsky defection 727, 730, 736; policy on visas for 732–3

Guantánamo Bay 825

Guk, Arkadi 710, 714–17, 718, 719, 723–5, 732

H Branch 84, 779–80; H2 section see Registry; see also Appendix 3

Haddad, Wadi 60, 601, 605, 607

Hague, The 80, 651; SIS mission 200–201, 212–13, 241–2, 244–5, 246

Hahn, John 67, 68

Hain, Peter 641–2, 942

Haines, Joe 629, 631, 633, 634

Haldane, Maldwyn Makgill 59, 60, 63

Haldane, Richard Burdon, 1st Viscount 14–15, 19–20, 39, 54, 59

Halifax, E. F. L. Wood, 1st Earl of 199, 202, 204, 205, 206, 207–8, 223, 264, 345

Hall, Frank 87–8, 89, 90, 93

Hall, Sir Reginald 'Blinker' 63–4, 75, 87, 88, 90, 106–7, 115, 150

Hankey, Sir Maurice 69, 136, 147, 162, 163, 242, 244

Hanley, Sir Michael: identification of Fifth Man 440; questioned as possible grade spy 512; head of C Branch 536; appointment as DG 548; management style 548, 552; character 552; relations with ministers 552, 553, 559, 596; and Smith as successor 553, 555; and Lambton affair 575; and Communists' attempts to penetrate Labour Party 577–8; and committee on Subversion in Public Life 596–7; industrial subversion and unrest investigations 597–8; and Northern Ireland 626, 645–6, 647; and Wilson's business friends 629, 630; and Wilson's Security Service file 632; and alleged plot against Wilson 632, 633–4, 634–5, 639–41, 765; and Thorpe affair 641; and Arab terrorism 647–8; establishment of FX Branch 647; and subversive penetration of Labour Party 660–61

Hanratty, Gerard 795–6

Hardinge, Charles 19, 116

Harker, Oswald A. 'Jasper': background and character 127–8, 130, 855; head of B Branch 127–8, 255; on Dick White 135; Soviet espionage investigations 152, 154, 156–8, 263–6; Communist subversion investigations 177; and sacking of Jane Archer 220, 235; succeeds Kell 220, 228, 237; on internment of aliens 230; decline in confidence in his leadership 235–6; replaced by Petrie and made deputy director general 236, 855; and recruitment 540

Harley, J. W. K. 470, 471

Harman, Harriet 559, 766–7

Harmer, Christopher 249, 298–9

Harris, Tomás 'Tommy' 284–5, 294–6, 297, 305, 308, 310, 312, 855

Harrods bombing (1983) 699–700

Hart, Herbert 250, 255, 375, 538

Hart, Jenifer (née Fischer Williams) 375, 538–9, 540

Hart, Judith 634, 640

HAT, Operation 823

Havers, Sir Michael 723–4, 757, 762–3, 765

Haxell, Frank 409, 410, 411

Hayman, Andy 830, 832

Hayter, Sir William 383–4, 858

Healey, Denis 407, 659

Heath, Sir Edward: and investigation of Hollis 518, 519; becomes prime minister 547, 566; dislike of Furnival Jones 547, 587; appointment of Hanley as DG 548, 552; and Lambton affair 575–6; interest in industrial subversion intelligence 587–8, 595–6, 854; Industrial Relations Act (1971) 589; and work-to-rule 589–90, 854; and miners' strikes 591, 593–4, 598–9; 1974 election 599; and counter-terrorism 612, 614; and Northern Ireland 618–19; and identification of Blunt as Fourth Man 706; criticism of Security Service after Spycatcher 765–6

Heathrow airport 538, 608, 609, 613, 614, 617, 726, 746–7, 785, 828, 829, 831, 832

Helm, Siegfried 32–3, 34, 35, 39, 44

Helms, Richard 513, 518, 574

Helsby, Sir Laurence 523, 532–3, 537

Hemblys-Scales, Robert 368, 369, 370

Henderson, Arthur 66, 147

Henderson, Sir Nevile 195, 207

Hennessy, Peter 755, 854

Hentschel, Karl 44, 45–6

Herbert, Christopher 335, 469

Hewitt, Patricia 559, 766–7

hijacking 601, 606, 607–9, 615–16, 647–8, 688; see also September 11, 2001 terrorist attacks Hill, Bernard 422, 487, 490

Himsworth, Norman 237, 273–5, 276, 320, 401, 406

Hinsley, Sir Harry 209, 859

Hitler, Adolf: talks with Eden 175; rise to power 188, 853; territorial ambitions 189, 198, 853; and BUF 191, 192, 193; appointment of Ribbentrop 198; remilitarization of Rhineland 198; and espionage in Britain 199–200, 209; and Czechoslovakia 201, 202; Munich agreement 202, 205; views on Chamberlain 205–6, 853; invasion of France and Low Countries 222; invasion of Soviet Union 273; plan to assassinate 293–4; and D-Day landings deceptions 296–7, 305, 308–9, 310; fanaticism 860; Mein Kampf 7, 189, 198, 853

Hizballah 800, 801

Hoare, Sir Samuel 104–5, 206

Hollis, Sir Roger: background and character 135, 136, 320, 325, 483; recruited by MI5 (1938) 135, 136; wartime intelligence work 278, 280, 281–2, 289, 517; Soviet double-agent allegations 282, 327–28, 348, 503, 504–5, 510–11, 512, 515, 516–19, 520–21, 634, 706, 712, 754, 760–61, 763, 859; suspicions of Blunt 282, 517, 856; appointed DDG 325; appointed DG 326–7, 483; and Cuban Missile Crisis 326–7, 859; management style 326, 547; retirement as DG 328, 510, 511, 518; and Gouzenko case 342, 344–5, 347; role in founding of ASIO 367, 368–70, 763; and vetting procedures 380, 383, 394, 395–6; and atom

spies 384, 389; and protective security 392; and Communists 406, 409–10, 412; and Wright 434–5; and Philby 436; imperial tours 445–6, 462; posts Magan to Cyprus 464; and surveillance of colonial delegations 466, 467–8; and operations in Commonwealth countries 468, 469, 471, 478; policy on Special Political Action 478; Macmillan 483, 494, 500; and Blake 489; and Vassall 493; and Profumo affair 496, 498; and Boothby and Kray scandal 501, 502; and investigation of Mitchell 505–6, 507, 508–9; suspension of Martin 510; death 518; and Wilson 523, 524, 526–7

Holt-Wilson, Audrey, Lady (née Stirling) 133, 227–8

Holt-Wilson, Sir Eric: and pre-First World War German espionage 33, 52; background and character 42; nickname 42; recruited 42; and Defence of the Realm Act 53–4; First World War security measures 77, 81; on Metropolitan Police's role 82; heads A, D, E and F Branches 84; Christmas/New Year card design 103; case for post-war existence of MI5 117–18; Thomson 117–18; and General Strike 125; memorandum on reorganization 130; knighthood 133; marriages and family 133; and Meerut Conspiracy 137–8; on imperial aspirations of Security Service 138, 458; international tours 138; industrial sabotage investigations 166; report on First World War 187; and internment 194; resignation 227–8; on Harker's succession 228

Home Office 7, 48, 53, 98, 101, 166, 191, 192, 193, 547–8, 552–3, 620, 752

Home Office Warrant (HOW) system 37, 49–50, 52, 122, 147, 239, 320–21, 523

homosexuality 86, 89, 172, 174, 196, 269, 396–7, 429, 500, 533–4, 564, 633, 635–6, 641, 706

Hooper, William John 'Jack' 246–7, 249, 257, 268

Hoover, J. Edgar: and prewar espionage investigations 210; and Kent–Wolkoff case 225; and British–American counter-intelligence collaboration 131; suspicions of CIA 374, 428; and VENONA project 374, 377, 428; and Fuchs case 386, 387, 390; and defection of Burgess and Maclean 427–8, 431; and Philby case 431, 436, 509; and Blake case 489, 491; and Profumo affair 500; reaction to FOOT 574

Horrocks, Reginald 228–9, 275

Horwood, Sir William 119, 120, 121

Houghton, Harry 484–5, 487–8

Howard, Sir Michael 249, 283–4, 783

Howe, Sir Geoffrey 709, 723, 725, 730, 740, 743, 766

Howells, Dr Kim 827

Human Rights Convention 756, 759, 765

Hungarian Uprising (1956) 404, 409, 418, 445

Hunt, Sir John 519, 552, 553, 631, 633–4, 658, 670–71

Hurd, Douglas 681, 766

Hussain, Tanvir 830, 831

Hyde, Douglas 164–5, 411

Hyde Park bombing (1982) 697, 699

ICON (counter-terrorism exercise) 615–16

Independent Labour Party (ILP) 66, 98, 99, 102, 103, 580

India: North-West Frontier 4, 108; German subversion in 86, 90–92; First World War 91; Ghadr ('Revolt') Party 92–3; CPGB couriers to 137, 179–80; Delhi Intelligence Bureau (DIB) 137, 138, 236, 442–6, 481; liaison with British intelligence 137–8, 442, 443–4, 444–6; Meerut Conspiracy trial 137–8; Comintern links with Indian Communists 190; recruitment of officers from 331; independence 442, 443, 447; influence of Communists at Indian high commission 443; Communist Party 445; Indo-Soviet relations 445, 446, 447; assassination of Indira Gandhi 736–7

Industrial Intelligence Bureau (IIB) 122–3, 124, 149

Inkpin, Albert 99, 152

INLA (Irish National Liberation Army) 651, 698

Intelligence and Security Committee (ISC) 755, 778, 787, 788, 817, 823, 825, 828

interception: of postal correspondence 36–7, 52, 63–5, 71, 86–7, 334, 549, 554, 758, 767; of cables 63, 71; of telephone calls 134–5, 147, 320–21, 334, 526–7, 542, 756–7, 758, 767

Interception of Communications Act (1985) 756–7, 758, 767, 768

internment: of aliens during First World War 80–81, 97, 221–2; of Communists 97, 100; of Fascists 192, 194, 227, 230–31, 235; Government War Book regulations 194, 404; of aliens during Second World War 222, 223, 224, 227, 229, 230–31; Advisory Committee on Internment 230, 235; proposed internment of Communists in event of war with Soviet Union 404–6, 417; in Northern Ireland 619

interrogation techniques 251–2, 539

Invergordon Mutiny (1931) 162–4, 249

invisible ink 67, 70–71, 74

Ippolitov, Ivan Ivanovich 571–2, 577

IRA (Irish Republican Army) 122–3, 600, 602–4, 605–6, 618–20, 654; see also Continuity IRA; Official IRA; Provisional IRA; Real IRA

Iran 460, 685, 800–802, 803, 856

Iranian embassy siege (1980) 685–8

Iraq 284, 536, 648, 686, 691

Ireland: Fenians 5, 600, 852; German funding of Republicans 86–7; Easter Rising (1916) 87, 88, 618, 861; development of nationalism 90, 618, 861; Soviet aid to Sinn Fein 'germ cells' 145–6; status as dominion 369; emigration 602; constitution 605; Communist Party 606; navy's interception of arms supplies to PIRA 623, 704; see also Northern Ireland

Irgun Zvai Leumi 350, 351–5, 358–60, 362

Irish Joint Section (IJS) 621, 624, 645, 646, 649, 652, 683, 684–5, 692, 693–4, 696, 697, 700, 852

Irish National Liberation Army (INLA) 651, 698

ISK (Second World War decrypts) 253, 254–5

Islamism 7, 91, 800–801, 828

Islamist terrorism: emergence of 799–809, 856; threat to Britain 814, 816–18, 819–29, 828–35, 836, 837–8, 856, 858, 860–51; see also jihad; July 2005 terrorist attacks; September 11, 2001 terrorist attacks

Ismay, Sir Hastings 'Pug' 239, 319

ISOS (Second World War decrypts) 248, 249–50, 253, 254–5, 262, 278, 281

Israel 351–2, 358, 359, 362, 547, 601, 613, 648, 691

Israeli embassy (London) 613, 801

Italy 104–5, 124, 191, 193, 197, 208, 225, 808

Ivanov, Evgeni 'Eugene' 494–5, 496–7, 498, 499–500

Japan 6, 23, 117, 807

Jebb, Gladwyn 196, 207

Jebsen, Johann (double agent ARTIST) 297–8, 304–5

Jelínek, Václav ('Erwin Van Haarlem') 727–30, 731

Jellicoe, George, 2nd Earl 575, 576

Jenkins, Roy: on Wigg 523–4; on Soskice 525; Home Secretary 529, 532, 533–4, 552, 578, 626; and seamen's strike 529, 530; love affairs 532; and Thorpe affair 533–4; and Blake 538; and Floud case 539;on Kagan 627; and alleged plot against Wilson 642; on Bridge inquiry 758

Jerusalem 352, 353–5, 363; King David Hotel bomb (1946) 351, 352, 354, 355, 363

Jewish Agency 351, 353–4, 358

Jews: refugees in Palestine 352, 359; immigrants to Palestine 358, 359; Security Service's recruitment of 363–4; terrorist attacks on Britain 601–2, 801; demonstrations against trials of Russian Jews 628; 'refuseniks' 727–8; see also anti-Semitism; Zionism

Joint Intelligence Committee (JIC): establishment of 208–9; and atom spies 383–4, 388, 858; and planned internment of Communists in event of war 405; and influence of Communists at Indian high commission 443; and Communist links in Africa 452; and Aden

Emergency 475; Hanley's view of 552, 596; Current Intelligence Group on Northern Ireland 603, 615, 621; and Arab terrorism 608; establishes Security Services lead intelligence role in counter-terrorism 614–15

Joint Terrorism Analysis Centre (JTAC) 817–18, 822

Johnson, Alan 827

Jones, E. M. 378, 428

Jones, Sir Elwyn 525, 530, 543

Jones, Jack 379, 535–6, 587, 588–9, 657, 711

Jones, Sir John: Deputy Director General 552, 555; appointment as DG (1981) 555–6; background and character 556, 696; management style 556–7, 688, 696, 721; reputation as DG 556; and Massiter case 559; on industrial subversion 591, 658–9, 854; and counter-terrorism 613, 616–17, 621, 696, 701–2, 734; and alleged plot against Wilson 640; and peace movement 674, 676; and Bettaney case 720; and Spycatcher affair 761, 762

Jordan 607–8, 609, 808

Joseph, Sir Keith 671, 672

Joyce, William 193–4, 225

Joynson-Hicks, Sir William 154, 155–6

July 2005 terrorist attacks (London) 821–3, 858

K Branch 548, 584, 713, 745; KIoB 788; K3 708; K4 714, 715, 716; K6 441, 710, 718, 731; K7 571; K8 731, 732; see also Appendix 3

Kagan, Sir Joseph 627–30, 631, 639

Kapitsa, Pyotr 167–8, 172, 854

Kaufman, Sir Gerald 756–7, 758

Keeler, Christine 494–5, 496, 497–8, 499, 500

Kell, Constance, Lady 23, 108; 'Secret Well Kept' 41, 42, 50, 56, 66, 71–2, 98, 113–14, 218

Kell, Sir Vernon: recruitment 3, 21, 22, 24, 25–8; and Cumming 3, 25–6, 27–8, 96, 97; and Haldane 15; background and character 21–3, 29, 82, 120; development of MO5(g) 28, 29–30, 31, 48–9, 52, 58; and Churchill 29–30, 37, 88, 239; contacts with chief constables 29–30, 31, 35, 48, 50–51, 191, 239; 861, 858; pre-First World War German espionage investigations 30–52, 861; and Defence of the Realm Act 53, 142; division of MO5(g) 56–8; and counter-subversion 65–6, 95, 96–7, 103, 129, 140, 142, 185, 268; and opposition to First World War 66; and First World War German espionage and sabotage attempts 67, 70–72, 77, 861; and forensic science 70–71; and censorship 71; rivalry with Thomson 81–3, 106–7, 108, 115; domestic life 97–8, 108, 132–3; health problems 97–8, 108, 219; quarrel with Drake 98; knighthood 109; fights for survival of MI5 114–16, 117, 121–2; and Makgill 122–3; founds Intelligence and Police dining club 125; and General Strike 125–6; management style 133; and recruitment of staff 133, 135; relations with Whitehall officials 136–7, 154; and classification of subjects by race 143; and Labour Party 146; and Zinoviev letter 149, 154; and ARCOS raid 154; and dockyard sabotage 177–8; reports on Fascist movement 191, 192, 193; and Ustinov 196; and investigation of Auslands Organisation 197; on Hitler 198; memorandum on Nazi Germany (1936) 198; and Munich crisis 203, 206, 853; and outbreak of Second World War 207; wartime economy measures 217–18; question of succession as head 218–19, 228, 237; wartime shortcomings 219, 222–3, 227, 855, 859; dismissal as director (1940) 227, 237; on Kenyatta's time in Moscow 455; views on recruitment 549

Kellar, Alex 350–51, 448–9, 450, 456, 468–9, 478–9

Kennedy, John F. 477, 478, 490, 493, 494, 497, 500, 504, 509, 532

Kennedy, Joseph 225, 226

Kennedy, Robert 500, 509 Kent, Bruce 673, 675 Kent, Tyler 224–5, 226, 230 Kenya 454, 456–8, 466–8, 472–3, 474, 475, 803, 808, 809, 856

Kenyatta, Jomo 176, 454–7, 466, 467–8

Kerrigan, Peter 386, 410, 853

KGB (Soviet intelligence agency): disinformation department 90; use of forgery 90; Second World War codenames 349; and American Communist Party 366; Wilson and 417, 418–19; mishandling of Cambridge Five 420–21, 426, 433, 434, 856–7; African operations 452, 470; growth of London residency 491, 565–7; contacts with British trade union movement 536, 589, 657; mass expulsion of London personnel (Operation FOOT) 565–7, 571–3, 574–5, 576, 579, 585–6, 732, 859; Department V (sabotage and covert attack) 567–9, 573–4, 605; resumes operations

after expulsions 579–86; 'psycho-physiological' testing of agents 585; supply of arms to PFLP and IRA 605–6, 622; and Middle Eastern terrorism 648; and peace movement 673, 674–5, 675–6; and Libyan terrorism 701; Operation RYAN 709, 722–3, 861; Lines in KGB residencies 710; First Chief Directorate 713; Third Directorate 713; recall of illegals from Britain 726, 727; expulsion of agents following Gordievsky defection 727, 730, 736; return of illegals to Britain 727–8; monitoring of Jewish dissidents 728; effect of British visa-refusal policy 732, 733

Khan, Mohammed Siddique 822–3

Khomeini, Ayatollah Ruhollah 685, 800

Khrushchev, Nikita 326, 327, 404, 417, 445, 497

King, John 174, 263–6, 268, 854

Kinnock, Neil 642, 663, 664, 667, 681, 766

Kipling, Rudyard 855; *Kim* 4, 401

Kirby Greene, Philip 463, 464

Kirke, Sir Walter 25, 71

Klugmann, James 404, 438, 538–9

Knight, (Charles Henry) Maxwell: background and character 123, 132; eccentricities 123; exotic pets 123; infiltration of Fascist movement 123–4, 132, 191, 193; member of IIB 123–4; penetration of Right Club 124, 221, 224–7; political views 124; Communist subversion investigations 128–9, 132, 165, 179–80, 221, 401; recruited by SIS 128–9; Special Branch surveillance of 129; transferred to MI5 131–2; working methods 132, 179; women agents 221, 401; recruitment of Himsworth 273

Knightsbridge bombing (1982) 697, 699

Knouth, Betty (Gilberte/Elizabeth Lazarus) 355–7

Kollek, Teddy 353, 354

Korean War 388, 407, 488, 489

Korovin (Nikolai Rodin; KGB resident) 520

Kriegsnachrichtenstelle (German war intelligence centre) 66–8, 72–3, 76

Krivitsky, Walter 180, 220, 263–8, 272, 341

Kroger, Peter and Helen *see* Cohen, Morris and Lona

Krüger, Otto 245, 246

Labouchere, Frank 96, 97

Labour Party: suspicions about Security Service 116, 146, 522, 525–6, 531, 758, 793, 847; control of *Daily Herald* 125; Conservative agents in Labour HQ 126; first Labour government (1924) 146–9, 159, 186, 319, 847; 1924 election 150, 151; 1929 election 160; 1945 election landslide 319, 411, 847; and extension of vetting system 380, 381–2, 392, 393; 1950 and 1951 elections 391, 412; International Department 407; NEC 411, 536, 577–8, 660–61, 663–4; search for crypto-Communist MPs 411–15, 522, 526, 531, 660, 847–8, 84; 1964 election 480, 520; 1966 election 527; Communists' attempts to penetrate NEC 577–8; 1974 elections 578, 627, 633; Communists' influence on left wing 656, 657, 668–9; Militant Tendency 660–64, 667, 680, 681–2; 1979 election 667; 1987 election 681; policy for establishment of intelligence and security committee 755; and Interception of Communications Act (1985) 756–7; 1997 election landslide 791, 797

Labour Party Young Socialists (LPYS) 661–2, 664
labour unrest 65–6, 95–7, 107, 122–3, 125–6, 147–8, 588–99, 594, 656, 664–7, 670–73; see also strikes; trade unions
Lakey, Arthur see Allen, Albert
Lamphere, Robert 372, 387
Lander, Sir Stephen: background and character 561, 789–90, 811; training reforms 561; on John Jones 696; on European security and intelligence collaboration 748; and Irish Republican terrorism investigations 751, 773, 775–6;on Rimington 774;on budget and staffing cuts 781, 786–7; installation of new computer systems 781; and Northern Ireland peace process 783, 795, 797; and acquisition of new work 787, 788, 794; apppointed DG 788–9; and recruitment advertising 791; and Shayler affair 792–3;on counter-terrorism and terrorism threat 797, 855–6; and Islamist terrorism 807, 809–12, 814; relations with Blair 811–12; retirement (2002) 814
Landman, Samuel 359–61
LARGE, Operation 806–7
Lazarus, Gilberte/Elizabeth (Betty Knouth) 355–7
le Carré, John (David Cornwell) 131, 350
Le Queux, William 4, 8–9, 13–14, 18, 20–21, 23, 47, 54–5
Leander, Torsten 759–60, 766, 767
Lenin, Vladimir 99–100, 139, 141, 144, 147, 853
Libya: support for PIRA 622–3, 649, 699, 703, 737–8; funding for NUM 679, 680; Qaddafi's assassination campaigns against émigrés 688–90, 700–702; sponsorship of Abu Nidal 691, 734, 735;

Britain breaks off diplomatic relations with 701; US air-raid on (1986) 735; Lockerbie (PanAm 103 bombing) 746–8
Libyan embassy/People's Bureau (London) 689; siege (1984) 700–701, 702
Liddell, Guy: early career 118, 130; joins MI5 118, 120, 130; background and character 130–31, 190, 229; private life 131; management style 133, 323; and Zinoviev letter 158;and Kapitsa investigation 168; visits Berlin (1933) 189–90; recruitment of agents 190, 219, 329; and Munich crisis 206; and outbreak of war 213; and wartime aliens' investigations 222; on 'fifth column' fears 224, 229–30; and Kent–Wolkoff case 225, 226; establishment of RSLOs 230; made head of B Division 236–7, 255; wins respect of wartime recruits 238;on Putlitz 242;on interrogation of TATE 251–2; and GARBO 254, 310; member of Twenty Committee 255, 256; on Krivitsky's interrogation 264, 265; offers job to Blunt 269; and recruitment of Burgess 270, 272, 856; and wartime Soviet espionage 277, 278, 280, 856; and Churchill 287, 289, 308; on threat of V-weapons 313–14;on VE Day 316–17; and postwar double agents 317–18; on Sillitoe's appointment as DG 319–2; on Attlee 321–2; and Sir Norman Brook 322; retirement from Security Service 323; and Gouzenko defection 340, 345–6, 347–8; and Volkov attempted defection 343; and Zionist extremists 353–4, 358; and Special Relationship 365–6; and

VENONA 366, 371, 372; and vetting system 381–2; and atom spies 383–4, 385, 387, 389; and investigations into CPGB 401; and crypto-Communists on Labour's backbenches 411;on Burgess's behaviour 422; refuses Philby's approach to become Washington SLO 423; establishment of SLO in India 442, 443; and Malayan Emergency 448;on African nationalist movements 452, 453; double-agent allegations 706
Lines (departments) of Soviet residencies 710; Line F 569, 574; Line KR 714–15; Line PR 675, 679, 709, 710–12, 730; Line X 579–86, 710, 730, 732
Litvinov, Maksim 95, 145, 175, 281
Lloyd George, David 37, 96, 98, 99, 101, 106, 139, 144, 145, 147
Lockerbie (PanAm 103 bombing) (1988) 746–8
Lod Airport massacre (1972) 609–10, 613, 614
Lody, Carl 64–5, 67, 68, 89
London Controlling Section (LCS) 284, 318
London Reception Centre (LRC) 250–51
Long, Leo 269, 280, 348–9
Long, Walter 107, 109
Lonsdale, Gordon (Konon Trofimovich Molody) 485–8, 520, 728
LORELEI, Operation 553
'Lost Sheep' 411–15, 522, 847–8
Loyalist paramilitaries 600, 619, 624, 653–4, 683–4, 738, 852
LUCKY ALPHONSE, Operation 463
Lyalin, Oleg 567–71 573–4, 584, 605, 627, 710
Lynskey Tribunal (1948–9) 361–2
Lyttelton, Oliver 449, 454, 460

M Section 131–2, 134; *see also* Appendix 3

Macassey, Sir Lynden 9, 96

McCann, Danny 739, 740, 741, 742–3, 744–5

McCarthy, Joseph 393, 440, 460

MacDonald, A. M. 432, 456–7, 458–9, 463, 513–14

MacDonald, Ramsay: opposition to First World War 66; correspondence with Mussolini 124; changes to MI5's role 129–30; National Government (1931–5) 132, 160; background 146; first government (1924) 146–9, 159, 186, 319, 847; and labour unrest 147–8; relations with intelligence agencies 147, 151; and Zinoviev letter 149, 319; second government (1929–31) 159, 160

Macdonogh, Sir George 25–6, 26–7, 28

McGahey, Mick 592–3, 598–9, 659, 677, 679, 680

McGuinness, Martin 783, 834

McKenna, Reginald 10, 32–3, 53, 54, 64, 81

Mackenzie King, William 340, 345, 346

Maclean, Donald: background and character 172, 266–7; at Cambridge 172, 340, 420, 438; recruitment by Deutsch 172, 420; early career 174, 185, 854; sexuality 174; defection (1951) 184, 272, 318, 344, 391, 424–6, 438–9; Krivitsky's information on 266–7; Foreign Office information supplied to Soviets 339, 342, 420, 426; identified by VENONA decrypts 375, 420, 423–4; Cairo posting 420–21, 434; mishandling by Soviets 420–21, 434; psychological problems 421–2; in Moscow 430;

White Paper on defection 431

Macmillan, Harold: and Cuban Missile Crisis (1962) 327; reluctant clearing of Philby in Parliament 431, 484, 491; and CIA involvement in British Guiana 460, 478; and Cypriot independence 464, 465–6; and African independence 466, 468, 473; Middle East policy 473; relations with White and Hollis 483, 493, 494; irritation at Blake, Vassall and Philby cases 490, 491, 492, 493; July 1962 cabinet reshuffle 492; and Profumo affair 494, 497, 499, 500; and allegations against Mitchell and Hollis 507, 509, 518, 519; on secrecy 754

Macnamara, John 'Jack' 172

Magan, William 'Bill' 320, 351, 398, 464–5, 475

Magee, Patrick 704–5

Maisky, Ivan 168, 176

Major, Sir John 678, 771, 773, 774, 775, 778, 781, 782, 783, 785, 795

Makarios III, Archbishop 463, 464, 465

Makayev, Valeri (illegal agent HARRY) 423, 426

Makgill, Sir George 122–3, 124, 149

Malaya: Security Service recruits from 331; Communist Party 447–8, 449, 450; Malayan Emergency (1948–60) 448–51, 454, 458, 459, 462, 474; Malayan Security Service 448–9; Malayan Criminal Investigation Department 449, 450

Malone, James 756–7, 759

Maly, Teodor 180–81, 183–4, 265–6, 267, 420, 854–5

Manchester bombing (1996) 794–5

MANHATTAN (Los Alamos atomic bomb project) 346, 366, 377, 384, 385, 550, 858

Manningham-Buller, Dame Eliza: early Security

Service career 554, 776, 786; and Northern Ireland 776, 786, 795; on Rimington 778, 781; on possibility of 'reduced base' for Security Service 786; on Lander 789; appointed DDG 792; and Shayler affair 792, 793; and Islamist terrorism 807, 810, 817, 818, 821, 822, 823, 824–6, 831, 833; succeeds Lander as DG 814, 815–16; background and character 815–16 and ethical issues 825

Manningham-Buller, Sir Reginald 487, 815

Marriott, John H. 285, 318, 331, 332, 337, 363, 394, 504, 580 Marsh, Percy 61, 62, 63

Martin, Arthur: claims against Hollis 282, 504–5, 510; investigation of Blunt 282, 437; recruitment and Security Service career 372, 428, 503–4; reports on Philby's presumed treachery 428; and Profumo affair 496; conspiracy theories encouraged by Golitsyn defection 503, 504; character 504, 509, 519; collaboration with Wright 504, 507, 510; investigation of Mitchell 505–7, 508–9; suspension and transfer 509–10; leaves Security Service 510

MASK, Operation 175–7, 178

Mason, Roy 634, 649, 650, 651

Massiter, Cathy 558–9, 675–6, 677–8, 757, 758, 766, 768

Masterman, Sir John 219, 220, 238, 255–7, 283, 298–9, 300, 304, 305, 314–15, 316, 317–18, 855–6

Masterton, Miss A. W. 63, 127

Mata Hari (Margaretha Geertruida Zelle) 79–80, 221

Maudling, Reginald 518, 547–8, 567, 588–9, 589–91, 595–6, 613, 654

Maxwell, Sir Alexander 222, 540

Maxwell Fyfe, Sir David 322, 323–4, 408

Maxwell Fyfe Directive (1952) 323, 443, 615, 626, 670–71, 767, 852

May, Alan Nunn 340–41, 343–4, 345–6, 380, 384

Melville, William: background and character 5, 6; recruited by Secret Service Bureau 5–6; and Rachkovsky 6–7, 100–101; and German espionage and invasion threat 7–8, 10–11, 17, 26, 30, 31, 34, 35, 44–5, 46; and MO5(g) 25, 28, 30, 31, 35, 36; retirement and death 5 101

Menzies, Sir Robert 370, 373

Menzies, Sir Stewart 238, 255, 313, 342, 347, 362

Metropolitan Police: Criminal Investigation Department (CID) 53, 97, 450, 462, 611; and Indian nationalism 90–91; strikes (1918 and 1919) 106, 107, 159; Anti-Terrorist Branch (SO13) 644, 692, 751, 785, 796, 802; Balcombe Street siege 644; Diplomatic Protection Group 685; Iranian embassy siege 685, 686; see also Special Branch

MI1C 104, 105–6

'MI5's Official Secrets' (television documentary) 757–8

MI9 64, 251

MI(B) 125

Michael, Glyndwr 286, 287

Mikardo, Ian 364, 758

Militant Tendency (MT) 660–64, 667, 680, 681–2

Miller, Hugh M. 118, 120, 130, 131

Milmo, Sir Helenus 'Buster' 219, 250, 427, 432

MINCEMEAT, Operation 286–7

miners' strikes: (1972) 591–4;(1974) 598–9; (1984–5) 676–81

Mitchell, Graham: investigated as alleged double agent 327, 494, 503, 504, 505–9, 510, 512, 515, 516, 518, 519, 520–21, 634, 706, 859; and VENONA project 378, 433–4; and vetting procedures 382–3, 399; and atom spies 384; and identification of crypto-Communists in Labour Party 412–15, 858;on Wilson 416; operations against Polish UB 484; and Portland spy-ring 486; and Henry Brooke 492; and Golitsyn 504; retirement 507, 509

Mitrokhin, Vasili 434, 574, 579, 580, 581–3, 586

MO25, 6 MO35, 6

MO56–8, 11–12

MO5(g): development of 29–31, 52; resourcing of 29, 31, 35, 36, 41, 64; Registry 48–9, 58; integration into War Office 54; expansion of 55–6, 58, 77–8; divided into three branches 56–8, 84; renamed as MI5 72, 84

MO964

Modin, Yuri 424, 428, 429, 430, 432

Modrzhinskaya, Elena 272–3, 280

Moe, Helge John Niel (double agent MUTT) 253, 292

Mohamed, Binyam al-Habashi 825, 826–7

Mohammed, Khalid Sheikh 806, 809, 819, 820

Mohammed, Ramzi 823

Molody, Konon Trofimovich see Lonsdale, Gordon

Montagu, Ewen 254–5, 286, 287

Montagu, Ivor 286, 379

Montague L. Meyer Ltd 416, 417, 418

Montgomery, Bernard 297, 309

morale, staff 218, 228–9, 236, 338, 551, 555, 556–7, 558, 559, 781–2, 791, 808, 819, 852

Morgan, Kenneth O. 534, 641

Morgan-Smith, Catherine (later Weldsmith, then Shackle) 132–3, 237, 331

Morrison, Herbert 289, 381, 424–5

Morton, Sir Desmond 124–5, 128–9, 149, 151–2, 154, 236, 239, 279

Mosley, Sir Oswald 191–4, 226

Mountbatten, Louis, 1st Earl Mountbatten of Burma 286, 287, 319, 442; killing of 652

'Mr Mills' Circus' (planned relocation of double agents) 257–9

Müller, Karl 67–9, 70, 85

Mullik, B. N. 443–4, 444–6

Munich crisis (1938) 202–7, 541, 853

Munich Olympic Games (1972) 612, 613, 614

Murdoch, Rupert 575–6

Murray, Sir George 19, 20

Muslims: in Britain 91, 800, 805, 817, 821, 833–4; and jihad 799; see also Islamism

Mussolini, Benito 105, 124, 175, 191, 192, 193, 208

Nachrichten-Abteilung (German naval intelligence) 6, 12, 12, 18, 21, 36–52, 64–5, 66, 187

Nachrichtendienst (German military intelligence) 186, 187

'Nadgers' (Bettaney case investigators) 715–17, 720–21

Nairobi, bombing of US embassy (1998) 803, 809, 856

Nasser, Gamal Abdel 454, 473–4

National Front 738

National Liberation Front (Aden; NLF) 474, 475, 476

National Minority Movement 142, 149, 160, 164

Nationalist Party (South African) 444

NATO 542, 586, 709; ABLE ARCHER exercise 722, 723

NatWest tower bombing (1993) 783–4, 793, 855

Naval Intelligence Department 4–5, 17, 163
negative vetting 383, 389, 390, 681
Nehru, Jawaharlal 442, 443, 445, 446
Netherlands: First World War 66, 71, 72, 73, 87; Second World War 205, 212–13, 222, 223, 230, 241, 247; reaction to FOOT 575; arrest of Patrick Magee 704; PIRA terrorist attacks in 748; see also Amsterdam; Hague, The
Neuberger, Lord 826
New Delhi 351, 445; SLOs 442, 444, 446–7, 469, 481, 774; Soviet embassy 446; see also Delhi Intelligence Bureau
New York 43, 73, 74, 75, 105–6, 389, 423, 426, 693, 697, 806; see also September 11, 2001 terrorist attacks
New Zealand Security Service (NZSS) 514, 516, 774
Newman, Sir Kenneth 645, 696
Newton, Andrew 635, 641
Nicolai, Walter 52, 77, 186
Nikitenko, Leonid 715, 724, 725
Njonjo, Charles 468, 472
NKGB (Soviet intelligence agency) 174, 342, 348, 374, 420
Nkrumah, Kwame 451–4, 468, 470–71
NKVD (Soviet intelligence agency) 174, 183–4, 854, 265–6, 374
No-Conscription Fellowship 94, 102–3
NORAID (Northern Aid Committee) 697, 698
Northern Ireland: Troubles 600, 602–6, 618–26, 644–7, 649–55, 683–5, 692–700, 703–5, 737–45, 748–51, 771–3, 782–6, 794–7, 861–2, 855–6; peace process 625, 646, 782–3, 795, 797–8, 834, 856; alleged Security Service dirty tricks in 641; Security Service given lead intelligence role 833–4; see also IRA; Irish Joint

Section; Loyalist paramilitaries; Provisional IRA; Royal Ulster Constabulary Northern Ireland Office (NIO) 621, 625, 645, 700, 704, 786, 852
Norton-Taylor, Richard 827
Norwood, Melita 'Letty' (née Sirnis) 182–3, 579–82
Nyasaland (later Malawi) 458, 468, 469
Nye, Sir Archibald 287, 442–3
Nyerere, Julius 469, 688
Ó Conaill, Dáithí (David O'Connell) 622, 625

Odinga, Oginga 466–7, 468, 472–3
Office of Strategic Services (US; OSS) 366, 374, 520
Official Committee on Terrorism 614, 615, 654, 695, 794; Key Points Sub-Committee 620, 654
Official IRA 606, 619, 620, 622
Official Secrets Act (1889) 31, 39
Official Secrets Act (1911) 39, 49, 271, 757
Official Unionist Party (Northern Ireland) 623
OGPU (Soviet intelligence agency) 161–2, 170, 171, 174, 265, 267, 456, 860
O'Hanlon, Siobhan 740, 741, 742
Okhrana (Russian intelligence and security service) 6–7, 100–101
Oldham, Ernest 174, 854
one-time pad (encryption system) 156, 366, 376, 378, 486, 487, 491, 712, 728
Oshchenko, Viktor Alekseyevich 583, 584, 732
Ottaway, John 128, 152–3, 156–7, 158
OVERT, Operation 830, 831, 832, 835
OVERTHROW, Operation 284
Owen, David 640, 755
Owen, Will 413, 541–3, 640
Oxford University 59–60, 139, 170, 219, 232, 233, 255, 329–2, 440, 538, 540, 541

P Branch 559–60, 779; see also Appendix 3
Pakenham, Hercules 80, 105
Pakistan 369, 442, 444, 445, 800, 802, 817, 823, 825, 827, 828, 839
Palestine: DSO 138; British mandate 350, 358, 359, 362; Zionist extremists in 350–51, 353–4; Jewish refugees admitted 352, 358, 359; Sarafand intercept station 353; partition 358, 360; and Aden Emergency 476; see also Black September; Popular Front for the Liberation of Palestine
Palestine Liberation Organization (PLO) 608, 648, 691, 736
PanAm 103 bombing (Lockerbie; 1988) 746–8
Paris, terrorist attacks in 691, 692, 800
Parker, Hubert, Baron Parker of Waddington 487, 491
Parrott, George 44–5, 46, 52
PARTY PIECE, Operation 400–401
PATHWAY, Operation 836
Patterson, Geoffrey 372, 373, 374, 377, 386, 387, 390, 426
Payne Best, Sigismund 242, 244
Penrose, Barrie 639, 640, 641
Petrie, Sir David: head of Delhi Intelligence Bureau 137, 331; on outbreak of war 219; and promotion of women 220; onspy mania 224; on Registry efficiency measures 229; on British Fascists 231; appointed DG 236–8, 855; background and character 236, 237, 559; management style 236, 237, 238; report on organizational breakdown 236–7, 779; relations with Churchill 238–40, 288–9, 292, 308, 856; on Jack Hooper 247; execution of double agents 258–9; and wartime Soviet espionage 276, 282, 517; and D-Day landings deceptions 308, 309, 310;

Petrie – cont.
　retirement as DG 319,
　351; and Gouzenko
　defection 343, 345;on
　Zionist threat 351; and
　Special Relationship 365;
　reputation as DG
　559; on lessons of history
　859
Petrov, Vladimir and Evdokia
　430, 517, 520
Philby, Kim: views on Liddell
　131, 341; at Cambridge
　167–8, 172, 420, 438,
　854; early career 168,
　341; marriages 168, 433,
　503; recruitment 169,
　170–71, 171–2, 420;
　background and character
　171, 856; head of SIS
　Section IX 241, 341–2,
　344, 856; on circulation
　of ISOS and ISK decrypts
　255; Krivitsky's
　information on 266, 267;
　on Cowgill 281; heavy
　drinking 284, 433, 503;
　retailing of personal
　scandals 284; and
　Gouzenko and Volkov
　cases 341–7, 349, 431–2,
　434; views on Hollis 344;
　transferred to Istanbul
　347, 856; welcomes
　Zionist terror campaign
　362; and VENONA
　decrypts 374, 376–7,
　378, 420, 429; SIS liaison
　officer in Washington
　376–7, 422–4; and atom
　spies 387, 390;
　mishandling by Soviets
　420, 422, 426, 434;
　identification of Maclean
　as HOMER 423–4;
　learns of Burgess and
　Maclean's defection 426,
　433; recalled from
　Washington and retired
　from SIS 426–7;
　presumed treachery
　427–8, 429–31, 509, 517;
　cleared through lack of
　evidence 431, 484, 491;
　new evidence against
　431–5; in Beirut 433,
　435; confession 435–6,
　503; defection 436,
　438, 503, 754;
　recommendation of
　Martin as MI5 recruit

　504; Bettaney's
　sympathies with 716,
　718, 720
Phillips, Morgan 411, 412,
　522, 847
Phillips, William A. 127,
　128–9, 143
Pilling, Sir Joe 782, 855
Pincher, Chapman: on Fuchs
　case 386; and search for
　crypto-Communists in
　Labour Party 412, 414,
　415, 531; D-Notice affair
　531–2; Wilson's
　suspicions of 633–4, 638;
　allegations against Hollis
　712, 754, 761;
　collaboration with Wright
　712, 761; Their Trade is
　Treachery 754, 761, 764
Poland 119, 139, 213,
　298, 354, 587; Polish
　agents in Britain
　484–5
police: Kell's contacts with
　chief constables 29–30,
　31, 35, 48, 50–51, 191,
　239, 861, 858; training of
　colonial and
　Commonwealth police
　462, 468; pay dispute
　(1977) 665; Security
　Service's collaboration
　with organized crime
　investigations 780, 787,
　788, 790, 793;
　collaboration in
　antiterrorism operations
　785, 817, 820, 824, 830,
　858, 860; corruption 790;
　see also Metropolitan
　Police; Royal Ulster
　Constabulary
Pollitt, Harry 142, 148, 160,
　176, 179, 180, 278, 404
Pontecorvo, Bruno 375,
　389–90, 391
Ponting, Clive 757
Popov, Dusˇan 'Dusˇko'
　(double agent
　TRICYCLE) 253, 297,
　301, 304–5
Popov, Viktor 723, 724
Popular Front for the
　Liberation of Palestine
　(PFLP) 601–2, 605, 606,
　607–9, 613, 617, 618,
　648, 747
Port Control section (E
　Branch) 77–8, 79, 84,
　220

Portland spy-ring 485–8, 492,
　493, 537
positive vetting (PV) 387–8,
　391–7, 493
Post Office 37, 63, 134–5,
　334, 455; Investigation
　Department 549
Powell, Philip 763, 765
Prague 208, 371, 426
Prague Spring (1968) 480,
　536, 541, 566, 583, 588
Precautionary 143
premises: Adelphi Court 56,
　85; Babcock House,
　Gower Street 551, 555–6,
　677, 710, 717, 719, 780;
　Blenheim Palace 217,
　231–5, 317; Cork Street
　85; Curzon Street House
　551; Great Marlborough
　Street 328, 551; Greener
　House, Adelphi 85;
　Grosvenor Street 549;
　Leconfield House, Curzon
　Street 324–5, 334, 483,
　551, 611; Oliver House,
　Cromwell Road 117,
　134; Queen's Gate 117; St
　James's Street 231, 235,
　311, 316; St Martin's Le
　Grand 334; Thames
　House, Millbank 134,
　217, 778–9, 822; Union
　House 334; Victoria
　Street 3, 6, 35, 861;
　Watergate House,
　Adelphi 42, 50, 56, 85;
　Waterloo House, Charles
　Street 85, 113, 117;
　Wormwood Scrubs
　217–18, 219, 231; see
　also the maps
Prendergast, Sir John 458, 476
Prime, Geoffrey 578–9,
　712–13, 716, 754, 756
PROBA, Operation 567
Profumo, John 494, 495, 496,
　497–8, 499, 500, 522
Profumo affair 323, 494–500,
　576
protective security: and
　First World War
　counterespionage and
　sabotage 76–7, 79, 80;
　and Port Control 77, 78;
　and internment 80–81; of
　MI5 HQ 85, 127;
　definition 126; first
　interdepartmental
　committee 126–7;
　inadequacies in Whitehall

174–5, 393, 854;
American pressure to
strengthen 392–3;
reviewed following
Portland spy-ring and
Blake and Vassall cases
492, 493; Helsby
Committee review 537;
and counter-terrorism
600, 606–7, 612–14,
654–5, 695; Economic
Key Points (EKPs) 620,
654–5, 695

Provisional IRA (PIRA):
foundation 606, 618;
upsurge in recruitment
619; arms procurement
622–3, 649, 684, 697–9,
703–4, 737–8, 749;
bombing on mainland
624–5, 655; 1975
ceasefire 625–6, 644;
Security Service's secret
back-channel 625, 644–5,
646, 783; resumes
mainland bombing 644,
645; Balcombe Street
siege 644; terrorist
attacks on the continent
649–50, 651–2, 684, 696,
748; 1978 bombing
campaign in Britain
650–51; Army Council
650, 699, 700; informers
650–51; killing of Earl
Mountbatten and
Warrenpoint bombings
652; hunger strikers
692–4, 696, 697, 699;
Overseas Department
694, 700; Sullom Voe
bombing 694–5; launches
new bombing campaign
in London (1981–2) 697;
England Department 697,
699, 704; Harrods
bombing 699–700;
Brighton Conservative
Party conference bombing
704–5, 734, 735, 737,
772; attempted attack on
Gibraltar garrison
739–45, 748; renewed
mainland campaign
(1990) 750–51; attack on
Downing Street 771–2,
782, 855; bombing
campaign against City of
London 782–5, 793, 855;
1994 ceasefire 786, 788,
794, 797; London

Docklands and
Manchester city centre
bombings 794–5, 797;
attempt to disrupt
Greater London power
supply 795–7, 855;
decommissioning of
arms 798

Pujol Garcia, Juan (double
agent GARBO):
background and character
253–4, 256; recruited by
SIS 254; transferred to
MI5 254; inventive
supplier of disinformation
284–5, 294, 855;
partnership with Harris
284; German payments to
292; deception of his wife
294–6; and D-Day
landings deceptions
297–8, 299, 305, 308–9;
awarded Iron Cross and
MBE 309, 310, 312;
and V-weapons 310–12;
reported arrest 311–12,
314

Purge Procedure 381–3, 393,
395, 400, 402, 858

Putlitz, Wolfgang zu:
background and character
195–6; friendship with
Klop Ustinov 196, 200;
intelligence provided by
196–7, 197–8, 201, 203,
204, 206, 207, 208;
sexuality 196; and
Ribbentrop 198,
199–200; transferred to
SIS 200; and Munich
crisis 203, 204, 206–7;
and Hague SIS station
213, 241–2, 244; seeks
asylum 213, 241–2;
betrayed by van Koutrik
244–5, 247

Qaddafi, Muammar 793; see
also Libya

Rachkovsky, Pyotr 6–7, 101
Radcliffe inquiry (1962)
394–5, 492, 493
Ramadan, Muhammad 689,
690
Ramelson, Bert: and seamen's
strike (1966) 527–30;
contacts in trade union
movement 535, 592–3,
595, 599, 657, 659,
664–5; supplies TUC

documents to Soviets
577–8; background and
character 592; on the
Angry Brigade 611;
succeeded by Costello as
CPGB industrial
organizer 665–6; and
miners' strike (1984–5)
680
Ramsay, Archibald 225,
226
Rauf, Rashid 829, 832
Reagan, Ronald 682, 709,
722, 861
Real IRA 833, 834
recruitment and staffing:
numbers of recruits 52,
84, 85, 117, 122, 134,
220, 320, 549, 702,
793–4, 836, 854;
recruitment from
universities 59–60,
170–71, 329–2, 548–9,
550, 554, 854; women
staff 59–63, 122, 127,
133, 220–21, 325, 320,
549–51, 554, 774;
attributes sought in
officers 61, 328–29, 331,
551, 553; staff cuts 117,
122, 325, 781, 786–7,
789–90, 791; security and
vetting 127, 394–5;
recruitment interviews
133, 320, 549, 554;
wartime expansion
219–20, 236, 238;
recruitment from colonies
331; recruitment of Jews
363–4; testing for recruits
549; reliance on personal
recommendation for
recruitment 553–4; Civil
Service Selection Board
(CSSB) 553–4; Croham
reforms (1978) 554; Duff
era reforms (mid-1980s)
559–60; recruitment
advertising 562, 791–2,
847; see also morale;
staff; salaries; staff
surveys; training;
Appendix 2
RED KNIGHT, Operation
400
Reed, Ronnie 287, 293, 430
Rees, Merlyn: relations with
Hanley 552; and
appointment of Smith as
DG 553; Secretary of
State for Northern Ireland

Rees – *cont.*
  624, 625–6, 644–5, 646;
  and alleged plot against
  Wilson 640; and Thorpe
  affair 641; Home
  Secretary 647–8, 665;
  concern with subversive
  penetration of Labour
  Party 659–60, 660–61,
  663, 664
Regan, John 36, 47–8
Regent's Park bombing (1982)
  697
Registry (H2 section): MO5(g)
  origins 48–9, 58; data
  management 49, 52, 58,
  122, 228–9, 231, 551,
  781; classification of
  suspects 58–9, 143; size
  58, 85, 122, 134, 220,
  237; women staff 59–63,
  336–7; staff turnover 84,
  337; working practices
  84, 228–9; Examiners
  333; computerization of
  record-keeping 551, 781;
  premises 551
Reid, Betty 403, 418
Reid, John 831, 832, 833
Rhodesia 444, 456, 469, 636,
  652; *see also* Zambia;
  Southern Rhodesia
RHYME, Operation 819–20,
  861
Rice-Davies, Mandy 498
Right Club 124, 221, 224–7
Riley, Patricia (*later* Hentschel)
  44, 45–6
Rimann, Walter 51, 76
Rimington, Dame Stella:
  recruitment and Security
  Service career 331, 333,
  337, 446–7, 550–51,
  560–61, 604, 667–8, 746,
  772; on Wright 515, 518;
  and Massiter case 559;
  and alleged plot against
  Wilson 642; publication
  of memoirs 642; on
  miners' strike 677–8; and
  Van Haarlem case 728;
  on aftermath of Brighton
  bombing 734; as first
  woman branch Director
  and DG 746, 774; on
  PIRA's continental
  campaigns 748; on
  suspension of
  eavesdropping operations
  759; on *Spycatcher* affair
  762, 763; appointment as

DG (1992) 773–5;
  public visibility 774–5,
  776, 777–8; and
  transfer of lead role
  in Irish Republican
  counterterrorism to
  Security Service 773 775;
  openness programme
  776–7, 778–9; amateur
  dramatics 777; Dimbleby
  Lecture 777, 801;on end
  of Cold War 'peace
  dividend' 781; and
  Chinook helicopter crash
  (1994) 785–6;
  incremental approach to
  acquisition of new work
  786–7; retirement (1996)
  788, 789–90, 803; on
  Lander as successor 789;
  and Islamist terrorism
  801, 803, 856
Ritter, Nikolaus 212, 248,
  249, 258
ROAST POTATO, Operation
  539
Robertson, J. C. 429, 432
Robertson, Norman 325, 345
Robertson, Thomas Argyll
  'Tar' 133, 249, 253, 258,
  283, 285, 289, 293, 295,
  304, 308
Robinson, Derek 'Red Robbo'
  672
Robson, Robert 'Robby' 142,
  274–6, 277
Rommel, Erwin 240, 310
Roosevelt, Franklin Delano
  224, 225, 226, 365, 366,
  367, 520
Rosenberg, Julius and Ethel
  377–8, 387
Roskill, Sir Ashton 219, 228,
  237
Rothermere, Harold
  Harmsworth, 1st
  Viscount 151, 193
Rothschild, Victor, 3rd Baron:
  recruitment by Liddell
  190, 219; background
  and character 219,
  234–5, 239; and Blunt
  219, 269, 270; and
  microfilming of Registry
  card 231; emotion on
  leaving Security Service
  238; wartime successes
  239; Jewishness 363;
  double-agent allegations
  375, 706; and
  Philby case 435; and

Thatcher 670; encourages
  Wright's publication of
  Spycatcher 760–61
Rotterdam 66, 67, 69, 72, 73,
  86, 248, 699
Royal Air Force (RAF):
  prewar 195; size 195,
  230; tracking of Soviet
  atomic tests 383; signals
  units' information passed
  to KGB 537; Dawson's
  Field airbase, Jordan
  607–8; Northwood
  Command Centre 704;
  Akrotiri airbase, Cyprus
  735; Chinook helicopter
  crash (1994) 785–6;
  bombing of
  Afghanistan 811
Royal Canadian Mounted
  Police (RCMP) 344, 345,
  348, 400, 509, 514
Royal Navy 8, 38, 44–5, 47,
  52, 64, 70, 176;
  Invergordon Mutiny
  162–4, 249
Royal Ulster Constabulary
  (RUC): lead role in
  anti-terrorism in
  Northern Ireland 600,
  603–4, 645, 684; Special
  Branch 600, 604, 618;
  bomb attacks on HQ
  624; Security Section 655;
  AI assistance to 738–9;
  alleged shoot-to-kill
  policy 739, 743, 744;
  casualties 785, 786;
  succeeded by Police
  Service of Northern
  Ireland 834
Ruddock, Joan 675, 758
Rushdie, Salman 801–2, 803,
  856
Russia (Tsarist) 6–7, 8, 23, 52,
  66, 100–101, 143, 162
Russia (post-Soviet) 813–14;
  SVR (foreign intelligence
  service) 161, 707, 81
Russian Revolution (1917) 95,
  98, 99, 100–101, 102,
  103–4, 139–40, 435, 853
RYAN, Operation 709,
  722–3, 861

S Branch 549; *see also*
  Appendix 3
Saddam Hussein 648, 686
salaries 5, 26, 35, 43, 47, 76,
  126, 132, 329, 331–2,
  560, 819

Salter, William 40, 42
Sander, Albert 73, 74, 75
Sandhurst (Royal Military
    Academy) 11, 23, 135,
    249, 786
Sands, Bobby 693–4, 697
Sandys, Duncan 467, 468,
    472, 474, 478
Sarwar, Assad Ali 829, 830,
    831. 832, 833
SAS (Special Air Service) 610,
    613, 647, 685, 686–7
Savage, Seán 739, 740, 742–3,
    744–5
Savin, Aleksandr 568,
    570–71
Savin, Vladislav 568, 569
Scanlon, Hugh 534–5
Scargill, Arthur 593, 598, 599,
    664–5, 676–80
Scarlett, Sir John 809, 810,
    811, 828
Scarman, Leslie, Baron 664–5
Schneider, Willy 196, 242
Schroeder, Frederick
    Adolphus ('Gould')
    47–8, 50, 52, 81
Schultz, Max 38–9, 40, 42, 50
Schweppenburg, Baron Geyr
    von ('Herr von S') 201,
    202, 204–5
Scotland, Alexander 251, 252
Scott, Norman 534, 635–6,
    639, 641
SDLP (Northern Ireland
    Social Democratic and
    Labour Party) 623
SEALION, Operation (Nazis'
    planned invasion of
    Britain) 230–31, 235,
    250, 257–9
seamen's strike (1966)
    527–31, 588, 598, 853–4
Second World War: outbreak
    205, 213, 219, 241, 855;
    German invasion of
    France and Low
    Countries 205, 222, 223,
    230, 241; 'fifth column'
    fears 223–4, 225, 227,
    228, 229–30, 859–50;
    Germans' planned
    invasion of Britain
    230–31, 235, 250, 257–9;
    air-raids 231, 241; North
    African campaign 240,
    284, 285; German
    invasion of Soviet Union
    273; battle of Kursk 280;
    Middle East campaigns
    283–4; D-Day landings

212, 280–81, 296–7, 300,
    304–10; V-weapons
    310–16; VE Day 316–17
Secret Intelligence Service (SIS;
    MI6): origins 3, 28;
    separation from MI5 28,
    129, 135; proposed
    mergers with MI5 116,
    118, 120–22, 787–8;
    Communist subversion
    investigations in Britain
    128–9, 135, 176;
    reorganization (1931)
    129, 135; Section V 135,
    174, 176, 177, 254;
    surveillance of employees
    by Dale and others 158;
    and embassy security 174;
    agents in Comintern 177;
    Section D 185; secrecy
    surrounding 186, 753–4,
    763; and Weimar
    Republic espionage 187;
    and Munich crisis 203;
    and Double-Cross System
    253–4; wartime
    collaboration with MI5
    253, 254–6; Section IX
    341–2, 856; and
    VENONA project 372;
    and hunt for Cambridge
    Five 427, 428, 430, 432;
    activities in India 442–3;
    precluded from
    clandestine operations
    in Commonwealth
    countries 443; SLOs
    phased out in favour of
    sole representation by SIS
    481–2; FLUENCY joint
    working party 510–12,
    515–18, 521, 634; and
    Gordievsky case 708–9,
    710; and Gordievsky
    defection 726; counter-
    proliferation role 788;
    'audit' of relations with
    (2001) 808;
    counterterrorist
    'disruption operations'
    824; see also Irish Joint
    Section
Secret Service Bureau 3,
    20–27, 28, 861; see also
    MO5(g)
Secret Service Committee:
    establishment of 108–9;
    members of 108, 136;
    first report 109, 115–16;
    recommends Thomson
    109; and proposed

merger of security services
    115–16, 120–21; and
    Thomson's dismissal
    119–20; transfers SSI to
    MI5 129–30; and
    overseeing intelligence
    services 136; and
    counter-subversion
    141; and leadership of
    MI5 237
Secret Vote 116, 134, 195,
    763, 793
Section IX (SIS) 341–2, 856
Section D (SIS) 185
Section V (SIS) 135, 174, 176,
    177, 254
Security Commission 500,
    536–7, 557, 713–14, 718,
    723–4, 755–6, 758
Security Executive (Home
    Defence (Security)
    Executive) 227, 229–30,
    235, 236, 238, 311, 314,
    320
Security Intelligence Far East
    (SIFE) 448, 450
Security Intelligence Middle
    East (SIME) 138, 342,
    350–51, 353, 362–3, 462,
    463, 464
Security Service Act (1989)
    564, 766–8, 788, 854
September 11, 2001 terrorist
    attacks 607, 790, 806,
    809–11, 820, 856
Serebryansky, Yakov 'Yasha'
    161–2, 267
Sergueiev, Nathalie 'Lily'
    (double agent
    TREASURE)
    299–300, 301, 304, 305,
    312
Shackle, Catherine see
    Morgan-Smith, Catherine
Shaw, Sir John 355, 363, 447,
    453, 456, 458
Shayler, David 792–3
Shedden, Sir Frederick 325,
    367, 368, 369 Sheldon,
    Bernard 543, 575, 632,
    717, 718, 760, 762
Sherer, Mary 300, 304
SHILLELAGH, Operation
    790
Shinwell, Emmanuel 'Manny'
    ·360–61
Shipp, Cecil 556, 574,
    608–9, 674, 702, 715,
    716, 762
'shoot-to-kill policy' 739, 743,
    744

Sicherheitdienst (SS security
    service; SD) 242, 244
Sidney Street, siege of (1911)
    95
Sikh extremism 736–7
Sillitoe, Sir Percy: appointed
    DG 238, 319–20, 321,
    324, 328, 847;
    background and character
    319, 320, 323, 324, 444,
    448; relations with Attlee
    321–2, 682, 847; retires
    as DG 323; and Zionist
    extremism 350, 362–3;
    tours of Empire and
    Commonwealth 367,
    444, 447, 448–9, 456;
    and VENONA project
    367, 372, 373; and atom
    spies 385, 387, 390; and
    vetting procedures 387–8,
    388–9; and investigations
    into CPGB 401; and
    Communist influence in
    labour unrest 408; and
    pro-Soviet Labour MPs
    412; and Burgess and
    Maclean's defection 427;
    on Kenyatta and Mau
    Mau 454, 456; reputation
    547, 548
Simkins, Anthony: official
    history of Second World
    War security and
    intelligence 209, 859; on
    Dick White 324; on
    attributes of Security
    Service officers 328–29;
    background and character
    328; and Philby case 432;
    questioned by Roy
    Jenkins over HOWs 532;
    and industrial subversion
    intelligence 589–90; and
    Northern Ireland 602,
    603–4; and letter bombs
    613; on overseas postings
    852
Simon, Sir John 55, 175, 176,
    192, 194, 195, 202
Sinclair, Sir Hugh 'Quex': and
    Secret Service Committee
    116, 120, 121, 128,
    136–7; background and
    character 120, 136–7;
    private life 120, 136; ·
    proposes merger of
    security services 120–21;
    and Communist
    subversion investigations
    in Britain 128; relations

with Whitehall officials
    136–7, 154; and Zinoviev
    letter 150, 151; and Ewer
    network 153;
ARCOS raid 154; and
    Munich crisis 203; and
    The Hague mission 242,
    244
Sinclair, Sir John 'Sinbad' 326,
    430
Singapore 138, 220, 469
Single Intelligence Vote 793
Sinn Fein 90, 145–6, 618,
    623, 626, 645, 692–3,
    697, 798, 834
Sissmore, Kathleen 'Jane' see
    Archer, Kathleen 'Jane'
SITUATED, Operation 795
Skardon, William 'Jim' 275–6,
    334, 371, 385–7, 427,
    428–9
Smith, Clive Stafford 825
Smith, Sir Howard 552–3,
    553–5; 561, 670, 671,
    683, 687–8
Smith, Michael John 583–6,
    586, 730, 732
Snelling, Sir Arthur 471, 552,
    553
SNOW (Second World War
    double agent) 212,
    248–9, 250, 256, 258–9,
    853–4
Socialist Workers Party 660,
    666
SOE (Special Operations
    Executive) 251, 278, 287,
    655
SOLO I, Operation 284
Soskice, Sir Frank 523, 524,
    525, 526–7, 533
South Africa 5, 8, 29, 93, 444,
    456; intelligence service
    (BOSS)
    536, 632, 635, 636–7,
    639, 641
South Quay bombing (1996)
    794, 797
Southern Rhodesia 468
Soviet embassy (London) 185,
    280, 333–4, 374, 483,
    496, 566, 572, 605
Soviet Trade Delegation
    (London) 144–6, 154–6,
    157, 280, 483–4, 566,
    567, 569, 629, 727, 733
Soviet Union: Treaty of
    Brest-Litovsk (1918) 104;
    Anglo-Soviet Trade
    Agreement (1921) 144–6;
    Labour government

recognizes Soviet regime
    146–7; Great Terror 161,
    183–4, 266, 404, 456,
    854; Nazi invasion 273,
    292; British–Soviet Treaty
    (1942) 282; limitations of
    intelligence assessment
    349, 420; support for
    Israel 362; atomic
    weapons 366, 383–4,
    386, 388, 405, 858; 1956
    Party Congress 404;
    crushing of Hungarian
    Uprising 404, 409, 418,
    445; relations with India
    445, 446, 447; backing of
    Nasser 454; presence in
    Commonwealth countries
    470, 473; crushing of
    Prague Spring 480, 536,
    541, 566, 583, 588, 711;
    Sino-Soviet split 512–13,
    514; and PFLP and IRA
    605–6, 622; funding of
    NUM 679, 680; fear of
    nuclear attack 709,
    722–3, 861; 'refuseniks'
    727–8; disintegration
    730–31, 771, 853;
    Afghan war 799; see also
    Administration for
    Special Tasks; Cheka;
    GRU; KGB; NKGB;
    NKVD
SPA (Special Political Action)
    460, 474, 477–9, 480
Spain; Fascist 259, 260;
    wartime espionage
    network 259–62; First of
    May Group 610, 611;
    security service (DSE)
    741, 742, 744
Spanish Civil War 174, 176,
    241, 253–4, 263, 277,
    341
Special Branch (Metropolitan
    Police; MPSB):
    foundation 5, 600; size
    53; and First World War
    79, 82, 102; counter-
    subversion responsibilities
    transferred to MI5 128–9,
    130, 131, 159; penetrated
    by Soviet intelligence 129,
    158–9; and Woolwich
    Arsenal spy-ring 181–2;
    and Fascist movement
    193, 194; wartime
    espionage investigations
    277; and Zionist
    extremists 355, 358; and

Profumo affair 495; and Lyalin defection 567, 571; responsibility for Irish Republican terrorism on mainland 600, 603, 615, 619–20, 622, 653, 684, 696, 734, 751; and Arab terrorism 601, 609; Angry Brigade investigation 611–12; and Libyan terrorism 700–701, 703; Van Haarlem case 728; transfer of lead role in Irish Republican terrorism to Security Service 772–3, 775–6, 852; and Islamist terrorism 800, 802

Special Intelligence Bureau see MO5(g)

Special Intelligence Missions 93–4

Special Political Action (SPA) 460, 474, 477–80

Special Relationship (US–UK) 365–6, 372–3, 490, 494, 509, 514, 810; crises in 386–7, 427

Springhall, Douglas Frank 278–9, 281

Spycatcher (Wright) 329, 336, 507, 512, 519, 642, 759; fabrications and distortions of evidence 520; failed attempt to prevent publication 563–4, 760–65; damage to Security Service's public image 563–4, 765–6, 767, 768

Sri Lanka (formerly Ceylon) 294, 369, 444

SSI (Special Branch counter-subversion section) 128–9; transferred to MI5 129–30, 131 staff surveys 782, 791, 808, 819, 852 staffing see recruitment and staffing

Stalin, Joseph: conspiratorial worldview 161, 175; Great Terror 161, 183–4, 266, 404, 456, 854; Eden's view of 175; wartime intelligence revealed to 175, 289; and mission to assassinate Franco 267; Nazi–Soviet Non-Aggression Pact (1939) 273; anti-Semitism

362; atomic weapons project 858; fanaticism 860

Stanley, Sidney 360–2

StB (Czechoslovak State Security) 413, 415, 535, 541–2, 543, 640, 707–8, 728, 729

Steinhauer, Gustav 6, 12, 36, 37–8, 40, 41, 44–5, 47–8, 49–52, 81

STEPFORD, Operation 822–3

Stephens, Donald 462–3, 463–4

Stephens, Robin 'Tin-eye' 250, 251, 252, 255, 258, 288, 314, 451, 453

Stephenson, Sir John 219, 227

Stern Gang 350, 351–60

Sternberg, Sir Rudy 630–31

Stevens, Richard 200–201, 242, 244

Stewart, Robert 'Bob' 142, 147, 403

STILL LIFE, Operation 400–402

'Stoke Newington Eight' 611

Stonehouse, John 541, 632, 707–8

Stop-the-War Committee 66

Straight, Michael 436–7, 509

strikes: Metropolitan Police (1918 and 1919) 106, 107; General Strike (1926) 125–6; dockers and tramway workers (1924) 147, 148; seamen (1966) 527–31, 588, 598, 853–4; dockers (1970) 587; miners (1972 and 1974) 591–4, 598–9, 664; Ulster Workers Council (1974) 624, 641; miners (1984–5) 676–81; see also labour unrest

Strong, Sir Kenneth 319, 32

Stuart, Judi 476, 612

Stuart, Sandy 475–6, 612, 613–14

Subversion at Home Committee (SH) 658, 659

Subversion in Public Life, Interdepartmental Working Group on (SPL) 596–7, 658, 780

Sudan 331, 556, 802, 804, 856

Suez crisis (1956) 445, 473, 499

Sullum Voe oil terminal 694–5

Sumption, Jonathan 826

SUNSHINE, Operation 465

Sutherland, David 613, 655, 685

Swann, Sir Michael 397

Swingler, Stephen 412, 847

Swinton, Philip Cunliffe-Lister, Viscount (later 1st Earl of Swinton) 227, 228–30, 235, 236, 238, 321

Switzerland 92, 99, 426, 608, 680

Syria 284, 648, 747

T Branch 772–3, 783; T2 776, 785; see also Appendix 3

Taaffe, Peter 661, 663, 680

Taleban 809, 810, 811

Tanweer, Shehzad 822–3

Tanzania (formerly Tanganyika and Zanzibar) 469, 470, 688

Tel Aviv: Lod Airport massacre (1972) 609, 610, 613, 614

Templer, Sir Gerald 449–50, 459, 463

Terry, Walter 415, 533

Thatcher, Margaret (later Baroness Thatcher): Leader of the Opposition 553, 670; appointment of Jones as DG 556; appointment of Duff as DG 557 support for intelligence community 559, 670, 682, 725; Security Service reforms 564; becomes PM 651, 669, 670; target of Irish terrorism 651, 694, 704–5; and 'wreckers' in industry 670–73; and peace movement 673, 674, 675; and miners' strike 676–81; meeting with Gorbachev (1984) 680, 725; and Iranian embassy siege 685, 686; exposure of Blunt as Fourth Man 706, 754; and Gordievsky case 709, 720, 725, 727, 730; and Bettaney case 720–21; attends Andropov's funeral 723; and expulsion of Guk 724; international threat to assassinate 735; and PIRA's attempted terrorist attack in Gibraltar 741, 745;

Thatcher – *cont.*
  dissatisfaction with response to PIRA's mainland campaign 750–51; and allegations against Hollis 754;on secrecy 754; and Franks Committee 755; and *Spycatcher* affair 762; and Security Service Act 766, 768
Thistlethwaite, Dick 372, 373
Thomson, Sir Basil: head of CID 53, 56; on spy mania 53, 223; and First World War German espionage and subversion 67, 80, 87, 90, 91, 92–3; rivalry with Kell 81–3, 106–7, 108–9, 115; background and character 82, 116; and pacificism 94, 101–3, 104; and labour unrest 96–7, 98; and post-war intelligence service 106–7, 108–9; and Metropolitan Police strike 106; head of Directorate of Intelligence 109, 116, 117–20; knighthood 109; Holt-Wilson's attack on 117–18; dismissal 119–20; late career 119–20; responsibility for civilian subversion 140, 142, 143; and Soviet Trade Delegation 144–5
Thomson, R. J. S. 'John' 454, 468, 470–71
Thorpe, Jeremy 533–4, 633, 635–7, 639, 641
Thwaites, Sir William 10–11, 34, 115–16
Tiltman, John 175, 176
TINNITUS, Operation 797
Tinsley, Richard 72, 73–4
Titov, Igor 710, 712
TORCH, Operation 284, 285
torture 824–5
Trade and Industry, Department of (DTI) 566, 582, 606, 608
trade unions: vetting of civil service union officials 395; Communist influence 406–11, 534–5, 594–5, 598–9, 656–7, 666–7, 670, 672; Trotskyist penetration 408, 592, 595, 596, 666,

670, 681–2; ballot-rigging scandals 409–11, 529–30, 681
Trades Union Congress (TUC): industrial truce during First World War 66; control of *Daily Herald* 125; General Strike 125; Communist influence in 406–7, 593, 595, 657, 659, 711; General Council 406, 407, 410, 577, 593, 659, 681, 711; expulsion of ETU 411; confidential documents supplied to Soviets 577–8; and Labour's wage-restraint policy 656, 657, 659; Alternative Economic Policy 659 training (of Security Service staff) 332–3, 549, 549–50, 554–5, 557, 561
Travis, Sir Edward 372, 373
Treasury: and intelligence services' budgets 69, 116, 119, 321, 332, 793; Cairncross's career at 174, 339, 428; and vetting procedures 382, 387, 399, 421
Trebilcock, Edward 178
Trench, R. M. 32, 33–4
Trend, Sir Burke 95, 337, 338, 510, 517, 523, 526, 528–9, 588, 590, 594–6, 601, 603, 607, 634
Trevor-Roper, Hugh 229, 324
Trinity College, Cambridge 167, 168, 172, 173, 269, 428, 437, 706, 707, 854
Trinity Hall, Cambridge 172, 340
Trotsky, Leon 99, 103, 162
Trotskyists: NKVD pursuit of 183; penetration of union movement 408, 592, 595, 596, 666, 670; infiltration of civil rights movement 604; infiltration of Labour Party 659–60, 661; penetration of universities and the media 662–3; influence in peace movement 673, 675; *see also* Militant Tendency
Truman, Harry S. 345, 352, 365, 367, 373–4, 377, 384

TRUST, Operation 860–51
TUBE ALLOYS *see under* atomic weapons
Tudor-Hart, Edith 184, 640
Turkey 342–3, 648, 691–2, 736, 821
Turnbull, Malcolm 763–5
Twenty Committee 254–7, 283, 284, 286, 297–8, 311, 860

UB (Polish intelligence) 484–5
Uganda 459, 469, 470, 708
Ulster Defence Association (UDA) 653–4, 683–4, 738
Ulster Volunteer Force (UVF) 87, 653, 654, 683–4, 738
ULTRA (Second World War decrypts) 248, 253, 280, 287, 299, 308, 365, 366–7, 374, 856, 860–51, 859
United Force (British Guiana; UF) 478, 480
United Nations 358, 360, 474, 533, 573
United States of America: First World War 73, 74–5, 77, 78, 92–3, 98, 104, 105–6, 861; isolationism 225; Second World War 292; atomic bomb project 346, 366, 377, 384, 385, 550; support for Israel 362, 547; Special Relationship with Britain 365–6, 372–3, 386, 427, 490, 494, 514, 810; American Communist Party 366; Soviet agents working in 366, 374, 586; purges 393, 440, 460, 858; Irish Republican arms supply and fundraising 697–8, 699, 703–4, 749; air-raid on Libya (1986) 735; *see also* Armed Forces Security Agency; Army Security Agency; CIA; FBI; September 11, 2001 terrorist attacks; US embassies
United States Communications Intelligence Board (USCIB) 372, 373
U'ren, Bill 442, 443
US embassies 805; London 82, 224, 225–6, 611; Helsinki 747; Dar es Salaam

803–4, 856; Nairobi 803, 856; Tirana 804

Ustinov, Jona 'Klop' 196, 198, 200–201, 204, 206, 213, 242

Ustinov, Peter 198–9, 201

V-1 and V-2 weapons 310–16

'Van Haarlem, Erwin' (Václav Jelínek) 727–30, 731

van Koutrik, Folkert 213, 244–7, 256–7

Vansittart, Sir Robert: on Dick White 136; background and character 195, 196; early career 195; opposition to appeasement policy 195, 202, 207, 853; support for security services 195; and investigation of Auslands Organisation 197; and Munich crisis 202, 203–4, 206–7, 853; and German invasion of Czechoslovakia 207–8

Vassall, John 400, 492–3

Vaygauskas, Richardas 627–9

Venlo affair (1939) 244, 247, 248

VENONA project (intercepted Soviet telegrams) 366–79; secrecy about 366–7, 372–3, 373–5, 377, 378; identification of atom spies 375, 376, 377, 384–5; and Cambridge Five 375 378, 420, 423, 428, 429, 431–2, 433–4, 440, 517

vetting: introduction of 380–2; Purge Procedure 381–3, 393, 395, 400, 402, 858; 'Industrial Purge' 383, 389; negative vetting 383, 389, 390, 681; positive vetting 387–8, 391–7, 493; of homosexuals 398–9; numbers of inquiries 607, 681, 752; review of procedures 751–2; decline in proportion of subversives detected 780

VIPER investigation (1942) 275

Vivian, Valentine 135, 174, 182, 254, 263–5, 267–8, 281

Volkov, Konstantin Dmitrievich 341, 342–3, 517

Voronin, Yuri Nikolayevich 571, 574

VOSTOK, Operation 605

W Board (Wireless Board) 255, 283

Waddell, J. H. 547, 552

Walden, George 551, 566, 572

Walker, Sir Patrick: appointment as DG (1987) 56, 561, 563, 682; on Howard Smith 555; background 560; early Security Service career 560, 561; and Northern Irish counterterrorist operations 699, 700, 734, 739, 751, 772; and interational terrorism 702, 734, 736, 745, 773; selection of Stella Rimington as successor 774; retirement 774; appearance on Desert Island Discs vetoed 778; strategic review 779–80

Wallace, Colin 641

War Book, Government 194, 404, 406, 859

War Office: and establishment of Secret Service Bureau 4–6, 21, 23, 25–6, 28; Intelligence Department (ID) 5, 11, 56, 82; MO2 5, 6; MO3 5, 6; MO5 6–8, 11–12; and pre-First World War German espionage 10–12, 13, 15, 19–20, 23, 30–31, 41; MO964; and Double-Cross System 73; MI(B) 125; Security Service ceases to be section of 130; economy measures 217–18; see also MO5(g)

Ward, Stephen 495–7, 498–9

Warner, Sir Gerry 773, 785

Washington DC 93, 105, 376–7, 422–4; see also

September 11, 2001 terrorist attacks

Weimar Republic 186–90, 198, 852–3

Weisband, William 375–6, 377

Weldsmith, Catherine see Morgan-Smith, Catherine

West Germany (German Federal Republic) 490, 575, 608, 612, 747; PIRA attacks on British army bases 650, 651, 696, 748

White, Sir Dick: on Liddell 131; background and character 135, 136, 320, 324, 483, 547, 789; recruited by MI5 (1934) 135–6, 508; and Ustinov 196; and Italian invasion of Albania 208; wartime recruitment 219–20, 238, 255; on Petrie 237; and The Hague SIS mission 242, 243, 244; on penetration of Abwehr 249;on screening of refugees 251; on Blunt 269–70; and Churchill 289, 293; on Sillitoe 321, 323; appointed DG 323–4, 325, 447, 779; moved to SIS 325–6, 483, 763–4; and Cuban Missile Crisis 327; on ASIO 370; and VENONA project 378, 433–4; and atom spies 384; and Burgess and Maclean's defection 426–7; and Philby case 430, 433–4, 436; disbanding of Overseas Service 447; refuses post in Malaya 449; relations with Macmillan and Heath 483, 493, 500, 547; and Blake case 489, 491; and Profumo affair 500; Hollis and Mitchell 505, 509, 511; and Sino-Soviet split deception theory 513; and Wilson government 523

Whitelaw, William 'Willie': and appointment of Jones as DG 555; Secretary of State for Northern Ireland 620, 621, 623;

Whitelaw – *cont.*
   Home Secretary 670,
      677, 709; and industrial
      unrest 598 670, 671, 672;
      and Iranian embassy siege
      685, 686, 687
Whitmore, Sir Clive 773, 774
Whytock, Roslyn 74–5, 106
Wigg, George 522–5, 526,
   528–31, 532, 534, 536,
   633
Wilhelm II, Kaiser 5, 6, 32,
   51–2, 162, 861
Williams, Marcia 528, 531,
   533, 534, 632–3,
   634, 636, 637,
   639, 642
Wilson, Harold: early political
   career 412, 416; Security
   Service file on 416, 526,
   632; contacts with Soviet
   Union 416–19; and KGB
   417, 418–19; becomes
   PM 419, 522–3; and
   Aden Emergency 475;
   policy in British Guiana
   480; and Hollis and
   Mitchell 518, 519, 634;
   and Wigg 522–4, 536,
   633; paranoia about plots
   and bugging 524, 526,
   532, 552, 632–3, 635–6,
   637–8, 642, 754; and
   tapping of MPs'
   telephones 526–7, 542;
   and intelligence on
   industrial subversion 527,
   534, 535, 854; and
   seamen's strike 527–31,
   588, 598, 854; D-Notice
   affair 531–2; and Thorpe
   affair 533, 534, 535–7,
   539, 541–2; and Blake
   escape and defection 538;
   and Floud case 539; and
   Owen case 542–3; and
   Northern Ireland 625,
   626, 644, 654; returned
   to power in 1974 625,
   627; disreputable business
   friends 627–32, 638–9;
   growing suspicions of
   Security Service 632–5;
   alleged conspiracy to
   overthrow 635–43, 765;
   mental and physical
   decline 637; resignation

638–9, 640; Governance
   of Britain 754
Wilson, Sir Horace 202, 206,
   227
Wilson, Sir Richard 608, 778,
   789, 790, 792, 793, 809,
   810, 815
Wilson, Woodrow 75, 139
WINDSOR, Operation
   460–61
Windsor, Roger 677–8
Winn, Sir Rodger 410, 500
Winnick, David 758, 765
Winnifrith, Sir John 387, 391,
   393
Winterborn, Hugh 486, 508–9
Wireless Board (W Board)
   255, 283
Wiseman, Sir William
   105, 106
Wolfenden Committee (1957)
   398, 399
Wolkoff, Anna 224–6, 230
women: recruitment of 59–60,
   122, 127, 133, 220–21,
   336–7, 774; Registry staff
   60–62, 336–7; secretaries
   61–3; clothing regulations
   218; promotion of
   220–21, 325, 332,
   549–51; advice to women
   on overseas postings 331;
   surveillance roles
   337–8; guidelines on
   interrogation of 451;as
   agent-runners 550–51,
   708; women peace
   protesters 673–4; Stella
   Rimington as first
   woman branch director
   and DG 746, 774
Woollcombe, Malcolm
   'Woolly' 151, 203
Woolwich Arsenal spy-ring
   167, 181–2, 183, 854
World in Action (television
   programme) 663, 761;
   'Death on the Rock'
   documentary 743, 744–5
World Disarmament
   Campaign 674
Wright, Peter: allegations
   against Hollis 282, 348,
   349, 434–5, 510–12, 518,
   519, 760, 761, 763;
   damage caused by his
   conspiracy theories 282,

348, 439, 507, 511,
   519; interrogation of
   Blunt 282, 439, 520;
   on Denman 334;
   background, recruitment
   and Security Service
   career 335–6, 507, 760,
   789; on Philby case 432;
   imagined view of KGB
   sophistication 434–5;
   860–51; and Portland
   spy-ring 486;
   collaboration with Martin
   504, 507, 510; and
   Golitsyn 504, 507, 511;
   and investigation of
   Mitchell 507, 508–9,
   519; chair of FLUENCY
   working party 510–12,
   513; damaged reputation
   within Security Service
   512, 515; and Angleton
   513–14; retirement
   (1976) 518, 520, 760;
   questioning of Floud
   539–40; and alleged plot
   against Wilson 642–3;
   collaboration with
   Pincher 712, 761; pension
   760, 761; and Rothschild
   760–61; CBE 761–2;
   conspiracy theory on
   Operation TRUST
   860–51; *see also*
   Spycatcher
Wünnenberg, Karl 73, 75

Young, Courtenay 270, 370
Young, George 633, 638
Young Communist League
   405

Zambia (*formerly* Northern
   Rhodesia) 444, 468, 469,
   470
Zelle, Margaretha Geertruida
   (Mata Hari) 79–80, 221
Ziegler, Philip 418, 629, 630,
   637
Zilliacus, Konni 411, 412
Zinoviev, Grigori: president
   of Comintern 139,
   147; Zinoviev letter
   148–52, 155, 158–9,
   319, 847
Zionism 350–63, 600–601,
   617

PENGUIN HISTORY

THE STORM OF WAR:
A NEW HISTORY OF THE SECOND WORLD WAR
ANDREW ROBERTS

Why did the Axis lose the Second World War? Andrew Roberts's previous book, *Masters and Commanders*, studied the creation of Allied grand strategy; the central theme of *The Storm of War* is how Axis strategy evolved. Examining the Second World War on every front, Roberts asks whether, with a different decision-making process and a different strategy, the Axis might even have won. Were those German generals who blamed everything on Hitler after the war correct, or were they merely scapegoating their former Führer once they could criticism him with impunity?

In researching this uniquely vivid history, Roberts has walked many of the key battlefield and wartime sites of Russia, France, Italy, Germany and the Far East. The book also employs a number of important yet hitherto unpublished documents, such as the letter from Hitler's director of military operations explaining what the Führer was hoping for when he gave the order to halt the Panzers outside Dunkirk. It is full of illuminating sidelights on the principal actors on both sides that bring their characters and the ways in which they reached decisions into fresh focus, and it presents the tales of many little-known individuals whose experiences make up the panoply of extraordinary courage, self-sacrifice but also terrible depravity and cruelty that was the Second World War.

'Britain's finest contemporary military historian' *Economist*

'Andrew Roberts is a superb historian' Jonathan Dimbleby, *Mail on Sunday*

PENGUIN POLITICS

THE LOOMING TOWER
LAWRENCE WRIGHT

'One of the best and most important books of recent years. A masterful combination of reporting and writing' Dan Rather

Brilliantly written, compelling and highly original, *The Looming Tower* is the first book to tell the full story of al-Qaeda from its roots up to 9/11. Drawing on astonishing interviews and first-hand sources, it investigates the extraordinary group of idealogues behind this organization – and those who tried to stop them.

Interweaving this story with events including the Israel–Palestine conflict, the Soviet invasion of Afghanistan and the first attack on the World Trade Center, Lawrence Wright takes us into training camps, mountain hideouts and top-secret meetings to explore how it all fed into the planning and execution of 9/11 – and reveals the real, complex origins of al-Qaeda's hatred of the West.